THE LAW of
THELEMA

THE LAW of THELEMA

Aleister Crowley's Philosophy of True Will

Antti P. Balk

THELEMA PUBLICATIONS
Helsinki • Washington D.C. • London

Published by
Thelema Publications, LLC
UK: BCM Agape, London WC1N 3XX
US: PO Box 10102, Washington, DC 20018-0102

First published 2018

Original material, revisions, and edits
Copyright © Antti Pekka Balk, 2018

The author asserts the moral right to be
identified as the author of this work in accordance
with the UK Copyright, Designs and Patents Act 1988

Works of Aleister Crowley not in public domain
Copyright © Ordo Templi Orientis
Used with kind permission

Notice: Product or corporate names may be trademarks or
registered trademarks, and are used only for identification
and explanation without intent to infringe.

All rights reserved. No part of this publication, in part or in whole, may be reproduced, transmitted or utilized, in any form or by any means, electronic or mechanical, or other means, now known or hereafter invented, including photocopying, recording, or by any information storage and retrieval system, without permission in writing from the copyright holder, except as permitted by the UK Copyright, Designs and Patents Act 1988 or under the terms of a licence issued by the Copyright Licensing Agency Ltd, Barnard's Inn, 86 Fetter Lane, London, England EC4A 1EN. Applications for the copyright holder's written permission to reproduce any part of this publication should be addressed to the publisher.

British Library Cataloguing-in-Publication Data
A catalogue record for this book is available from the British Library

Library of Congress Control Number: 2017916505

ISBN-13: 978 952 5700 66 4 (Pbk)
ISBN-10: 952 5700 66 6 (Pbk)

*For my
fellow-soldiers*

Contents

Preface	ix
Introduction	1
PART I: THEORY	
1 Axioms, or First Principles	7
2 Philosophy of History	34
3 Thelemic Morality	67
4 Ontology	93
5 Epistemology	126
6 Soteriology	171
PART II: PRAXIS	
7 Thelemic Pedagogy	215
8 The Secret Self	250
9 Transcending Duality	282
10 Scientific Illuminism	329
PART III: POLEMIC	
11 Religious Aspects (Part I)	379
12 — — (Part II)	422
13 Political Implications	483
APPENDICES	
A The Book of the Law	537
B Rights of Man	548
C Duty	549
D The Book of the Balance	555
E Diagrams and Tables	558
Bibliography	563
Index	587

Preface

Do what thou wilt shall be the whole of the Law.

I never thought I would write this book, or any other book, on Thelema, because I thought all the necessary books on the subject had already been written—by Aleister Crowley. Yes, I am well aware that there's a veritable cottage industry of dumbing down the Law for the ADHD Generation, while the bulk of Crowley's corpus remains out of print—and I want no part of that.

The first proper, grown-up English-language book I read from cover to cover in the original was Bram Stoker's *Dracula*. My mother, the scientist, grudgingly bought me a copy from the Atlantis Bookshop across the street from the British Museum on my first and still fondest visit to Crowley's native England. I was 13, and I loved the classic Gothic adventure novel. On my first trip to the United States a couple of years later, I saw a trailer to the movie *Bram Stoker's Dracula* and eagerly awaited for its theatrical release back home in Finland. It is a kitschy and entertaining movie that doubtlessly appeals to a certain audience, but it is Francis Ford Coppola's Dracula, not Stoker's. It left me cold, irritated, and confused. And this is more or less how I feel about most books with the name Aleister Crowley (or the word Thelema) on the cover that were not written by him.

I read Crowley's works, nearly all of them, in my teens, before the advent of the World Wide Web. I also devoured my father's extensive library on yoga, body culture, and spirituality, my mother's on science, history, and philosophy, my grandfather's on fine art, nature, and technology, along with my grandmother's novels, word puzzles, and dictionaries. I read Blavatsky, Steiner, and Ervast; Goethe, Nietzsche, and Russell; Hume, Gibbon, and Tocqueville; Mallory, Scott, and Dumas. I had never even heard of Rodney Orpheus or Lon DuQuette before I joined the O.T.O. at the age of twenty. I knew of Frater Achad and Gerald Gardner, but not of Soror Meral or Michael Aquino.

By the time I was 35, I had written two thick books of my own, one on the secular and religious history of Western civilization and the other on every contemporary aspect of moral philosophy. Yet when my Swedish friend, Calle Abrahamsson, asked me to contribute an essay on the Law of Thelema to the upcoming issue of *The Fenris Wolf*, I was stumped. I could barely produce three pages on the subject—a subject that had been my daily thought and practice for all my adult life. Everything changed when I finally received my copy of the anthology and read the essay following my own. In it, another old friend, Kjetil Fjell, laments the state of Thelemic scholarship and the fact that our community hasn't even managed to publish a first principles on our beloved philosophy. I wrote the Norwegian neuropsychologist and asked him did he not consider the *Commentaries on AL* a first principles—his blunt reply was that no, he did not, but that they could certainly be used as a starting point.

Stunned by the answer, I re-read the Commentaries, probably for the dozenth time in the last twenty years, and was shocked to discover that while they *do* contain all the first principles, they're not all in one place, or in a logical order, or necessarily accessible to someone not intimately familiar with not only Crowley and Thelema, but the whole Western Mystery Tradition and much of Eastern philosophy as well. As clear as they were in my own mind, in the Commentaries they're obscured by the constant sidetracking, name-dropping, and needless verbosity I think most Thelemites both love and hate in Crowley's writing.

Despite all that, it took me just three days to parse together the *axiomatibus* printed in this volume. I followed it by erecting an academic framework divided into sections according to the pertinent branches of philosophy: theory of history for Crowley's model of "Æons," moral philosophy for Thelemic ethics, ontology for the Crowleyan "theogony," epistemology for the New Æon theory of knowledge, and so forth. I even included two long and carefully researched chapters on the religious aspects of the Law (three, if you count the chapter on Thelemic soteriology), although I'm a staunch atheist and pretty much despise *all* organized religion, finishing with a chapter on politics—which, like it or not, is also a branch of philosophy and part of Thelema. What you won't find is pop psychology, LARP fantasies, ridiculous anecdotes, or personal interpretations passed off as received truth.

Though my obvious aim is to make this treatise accessible to people who have no prior knowledge of Thelema, I try to avoid delving too deeply into things that have already been done to death by other post-Crowley writers. For ease of reference, I cite the title and chapter of each Crowley book, instead of the usual author and year of a particular edition. Books and articles by other authors are cited the regular way, with the exception of works where Crowley is the translator and/or editor. (This is thus also useful in distinguishing between primary and secondary sources.) Since most of Crowley's unedited works are now in the public domain, I have avoided paraphrasing as much as possible. As for works published and edited posthumously, the quotations have been adjusted to reflect the original manuscripts, typescripts, and/or revisions thereof, where available. Footnotes appearing in quoted text are enclosed in curly "{}" brackets and *italicized*. The abbreviations used are given in the back.

Love is the law, love under will.

Antti P. Balk
Costa del Silencio
December 2017 e.v.

Introduction

As every self-described Thelemite undoubtedly knows, *thelēma* is the Koine Greek word for will. The Classical Latin word for will, however, is *voluntas*, and voluntarism is the school of thought that regards the will as superior to both the intellect and emotion.[1] At different points of history, the view has been applied in every academic field from metaphysics and theology to psychology and sociology. In his *magnum opus*, *The Story of Philosophy*, the celebrated, self-taught historian Will Durant defines voluntarism as the "doctrine that will is the basic factor, both in the universe and in human conduct."[2]

But what exactly is the "will"? The concept of the will itself only evolved gradually, and its proposed originators include Plato, Aristotle, the Stoics, the Epicureans, St. Augustine, and Maximus the Confessor. The term developed somewhat independently of the concept, and Plato's Academy used the word *boulēsis* to describe rational desire for the good, *thumos* to describe the desire for honour, and *epithumia* to describe the desire for pleasure. *Boulēsis* is commonly translated as "will."[3]

In the Christian era, another Greek word for willing, *thelein*, became more prominent, and the term *thelēma* is frequently used in the New Testament, along with *thelēsis* in the Septuagint version of the Old Testament. When Jesus asks for the cup to pass from him, but nevertheless for his Father's will, not his, to be done, the verb most often used is *thelein*, the noun being *thelēma*. The contemporary pagans used the verb often enough, but not the corresponding noun, with the exception of the Neoplatonist Plotinus, who has *thelēma* for the will of the One. Not until the seventh century CE did Maximus the Confessor make *thelēsis* the standard word for will.[4]

However, the most important terminological developments were in Latin, the expression *libera voluntas*, "free will," first appearing in the Epicurean Lucretius. He bases its possibility on the unpredictable swerve of atoms, but what seems to do the work in his explanation of freedom is the swerve rather than the will.[5] Epicurus himself made a very early use of the metaphor of freedom, saying of the wise man: "He laughs down that fate which is introduced by some as mistress of all, and says instead that some things happen of necessity, some by chance, and some things are due to us.

---

[1] Not to be confused with "voluntaryism," which is the political philosophy that holds all forms of human association should be voluntary.
[2] Durant 1953, 534.
[3] R. Sorabji, "The Concept of the Will from Plato to Maximus the Confessor," in Pink & Stone 2004.
[4] *Ibid.*
[5] *Ibid.*

For he sees that necessity is unaccountable, and chance unstable, but what is up to us (*eph' hēmin*) has no master and it is to this last that blameworthiness and the reverse naturally belong."[6]

The Stoic Epictetus connects Aristotle's concept of *proairesis* (deliberate choice) not only with freedom, but with what is up to us (*eph' hēmin*). Aristotle himself did not, however, associate *proairesis* very closely with freedom and even dissociates it from moral responsibility. He emphasizes that voluntariness, which he links with moral responsibility, extends much more widely to the actions of animals and children, who to him are incapable of anything as rational as *proairesis*. Epictetus, on the other hand, holds that nothing is up to us except what falls under our *proairesis* and all that falls under *proairesis* is up to us. He is also the first to make clear that physical activity is never up to us, on the grounds that it could always be frustrated.[7]

St. Augustine finally makes willing ubiquitous in all action: "Yet, if we attend more subtly, even what anyone is compelled to do unwillingly (*invitus*) he does by his will, if he does it. It is because he would prefer something else that he is said to do it unwillingly (*invitus*), that is, wanting not to (*nolens*). . . .But because the effect follows his will, we cannot say control over his act was missing."[8] Augustine also expanded enormously the functions of the will. In Augustine, will performs some of the functions of directing action, it unites perception with the perceptible, memory with internal vision, and intellect with objects taken from memory. To Augustine, will is responsible for imagination. Faith, according to Augustine, is also due to will. Emotions are acts of will, and the will forms the centrepiece of Augustine's objections to lust.[9]

However, it has never been easy for the Church to admit that people have the ability to make their own free decisions. Predestination, perhaps the most significant theological doctrine of Augustine, got polished when it clashed with the opinion of Pelagius, an Irish monk who defended a heretical degree of free will.[10] In opposition to the Pelagians, who believed that man was created by God in His image and is, by nature, good, but can fall into sin through misuse of his free will (*liberum arbitrium*), Augustine argued that since the Fall of Adam, all humanity is inescapably predisposed to evil and cannot respond to the will of God without Divine Grace.[11] The Church has always held baptism to be "for the remission of sins," and the Augustinian doctrines of Original Sin and Total Depravity offered the first comprehensive theological explanation for the practice of baptizing infants, guilty of no actual personal sin. However, if man does not have the power to choose the good and refuse the evil, he cannot be morally accountable for his actions, which is why the Catholic Church never fully accepted

---

[6] *Letter to Menoeceus*, in Diogenes Laertius 10.133, as translated in Pink & Stone, *op. cit.*, 17.
[7] Sorabji, *loc. cit.*
[8] *On the Spirit and the Letter*, 31.53, as translated in Pink & Stone, *op. cit.*, 19.
[9] Sorabji, *loc. cit.*
[10] Balk 2008.
[11] J. Lössl, "Intellect with a (Divine) Purpose: Augustine on the Will," in Pink & Stone, *op. cit.*

Augustine's doctrines, and only out of respect for him, never publicly banned them.[12]

The centuries-long controversy between free will and determinism was finally solved by the Edwardian magus Aleister Crowley, when he posited a True Will.[13] "He who seeks the origin of evil," Crowley wrote, "seeks the source of what is not. Evil is the disordered appetite for good, the unfruitful attempt of an unskilful will."[14] Those who think they have free will reckon they can freely will this or that and just as easily will the contrary, being masters of their resolution, whereas the advocates of determinism would have us believe that the power of decision lay with God, who in his infinite wisdom has made all the decisions for all the ages. The third option, of course, is following your True Will in every situation.[15] "Then, and then only, art thou in harmony with the Movement of Things, thy will part of, and therefore equal to, the Will of God. And since the will is but the dynamic aspect of the self, and since two different selves could not possess identical wills; then, if thy will be God's will, *Thou art That*."[16]

A version of this introduction was originally published as "Thelema: Aleister Crowley's Philosophy of True Will—A Preliminary Sketch" in *The Fenris Wolf*, No. 7, ed. by Carl Abrahamsson (Stockholm: Edda Publishing, 2014).

---

[12] Balk, *op. cit.*

[13] *Idem.* 2012. Note that there is no mention of "true will" anywhere in *The Book of the Law*, upon which work his philosophy is ostensibly based.

[14] In his translation of *The Key of the Mysteries*, published in *The Equinox*, Vol. I, No. 10. In his Introduction, Crowley deems it "the high-water mark of the thought of Eliphas Levi," that "may be regarded as written by him as his Thesis for the Grade of Exempt Adept, just as his *Ritual and Dogma* was his Thesis for the grade of a Major Adept." In *Liber Aleph*, Crowley further specifies the latter work as "the second part of my Thesis for the Grade of Major Adept, when I was clothed about with the Body called Alphonse Louis Constant"—i.e. he considered Lévi one of his many past incarnations. According to Crowley's *One Star in Sight*, an Exempt Adept of the A∴A∴ "will have attained all but the supreme summits of meditation" and "must prepare and publish a thesis setting forth His knowledge of the Universe, and his proposals for its welfare and progress." It cites the works of Emmanuel Swedenborg, Karl von Eckartshausen, Robert Fludd, Paracelsus, Sir Isaac Newton, János Bolyai, Charles Howard Hinton, Bishop Berkeley, and St. Ignatius of Loyola as other examples.

[15] The dialectic of thesis, antithesis, and synthesis. Although often named after G. W. F. Hegel, he never used that specific formulation, ascribing that terminology to Immanuel Kant. According to Walter Kaufmann, it was Johann Fichte who greatly elaborated the Kantian model and popularized it. Hegel "never once used these three terms together to designate three stages in an argument or account in any of his books. And they do not help us understand his *Phenomenology*, his *Logic*, or his philosophy of history; they impede any open-minded comprehension of what he does by forcing it into a scheme which was available to him and which he deliberately spurned." (Kaufmann 1965, 154.) The present author considers the dialectic method absolutely central to Crowley's philosophy.

[16] *Liber II: The Message of the Master Therion.* Emphasis in original.

PART I
Theory

CHAPTER 1
Axioms, or First Principles

AXIOM I.
Do what thou wilt shall be the whole of the Law.[1]
From these considerations it should be clear that "Do what thou wilt" does not mean "Do what you like." It is the apotheosis of Freedom; but it is also the strictest possible bond.[2]

Again "Do what thou wilt...", the most sublimely austere ethical precept ever uttered, despite its apparent licence, is seen on analysis to be indeed "...the whole of the Law.", the sole and sufficient warrant for human action, the self-evident Code of Righteousness, the identification of Fate with Freewill, and the end of the Civil War in Man's nature by appointing the Canon of Truth, the conformity of things with themselves, to determine his every act. "Do what thou wilt..." is to bid Stars to shine, Vines to bear grapes, Water to seek its level; man is the only being in Nature that has striven to set himself at odds with himself.[3]

Whoso denies "Do what thou wilt shall be the whole of the Law" confesses that he still clings to the conflict in his own nature; he is not, and does not want to be, true to himself.[4]

AXIOM II.
Love is the law, love under will.[5]
"Love is the law, love under will", is an interpretation of the general law of Will. It is dealt with fully in the Book *Aleph*.[6]

"This is the evident and final Solvent of the Knot Philosophical concerning Fate and Freewill, that it is thine own Self, omniscient and omnipotent, sublime in Eternity, that first didst order the Course of thine own Orbit, so that that which befalleth thee by Fate is indeed the necessary Effect of thine own Will. These two, then, that like Gladiators have made War in Philosophy through these many Centuries, art made One by the Love under Will which is the Law of Thelema."[7]

This is to be taken as meaning that while Will is the Law, the nature of that Will is Love. But this Love is as it were a by-product of that Will; it does not contradict or supersede that Will; and if apparent contradiction should arise in any crisis, it is the Will that can guide us aright.[8]

---

[1] AL I.40.
[2] *Liber II*, as quoted in NC on AL I.40.
[3] "Notes for an Astral Atlas," *MITAP*, Appendix III.
[4] *MITAP*, Ch. XXI, Sec. II, fn.
[5] AL I.57.
[6] NC on AL I.57.
[7] *Liber Aleph*, "De harmonia voluntatis cum destinia," as quoted in NC on AL I.57.
[8] *Liber II*, as quoted in NC on AL I.40.

The method of Magick: Love the mode in which Will operates. The method of Magick in this—and in all—Work is: "love under will." The word love (Αγαπη in Greek) has the value of 93, like that of Θελημα, will.[9] This implies that love and will are in truth one and the same, two phases of one theme. Love is thus shown as the means by which will may be brought to success.[10]

COROLLARY I.

The word of the Law is Θελημα.[11]

That is, this word is defined in minute detail by the secret value of the letters, numbers, sounds, virtues in Nature, and all other functions of this Greek name for Will.[12]

Compare Rabelais. Also it may be translated, "Let Will and Action be in harmony."

But Θελημα also means Will in the Higher sense of Magical One-pointedness, and in the sense used by Schopenhauer and Fichte.[13]

By "the word" one means the magical formula, symbol, or expression.[14]

There are many other mysteries in this Word, so that it is impossible to write a full commentary. The Book *Aleph* (*Wisdom or Folly*) is almost wholly devoted to its explanation.

Let every Star see to it that its own life is a wise comment on this word![15]

COROLLARY II.

There is no law beyond Do what thou wilt.[16]

There are of course lesser laws than this, details, particular cases, of the Law. But the whole of the Law is Do what thou wilt, and there is no law beyond it. This subject is treated fully in *Liber CXI Aleph*, and the student should refer thereto.

Far better, let him assume this Law to be the Universal Key to every problem of Life, and then apply it to one particular case after another. As he comes by degrees to understand it, he will be astounded at the simplification of the most obscure questions which it furnishes. Thus he will assimilate the Law, and make it the norm of his conscious being; this by itself will suffice to initiate him, to dissolve his complexes, to unveil himself to himself; and so shall he attain the Knowledge and Conversation of his Holy Guardian Angel.

I have myself practiced constantly to prove the Law by many and divers modes in many and divers spheres of thought, until it has become

---

[9] "Numbers are the network of the structure of the Universe, and their relations the form of expression of our Understanding of it. In Greek and Hebrew there is no other way of writing numbers; our 1, 2, 3 etc. comes from the Phoenicians through the Arabs." *MWT*, Introduction.
[10] DC on AL I.55–6.
[11] AL I.39.
[12] DC on AL I.39.
[13] OC on AL I.39.
[14] NC on AL I.39.
[15] NC on AL I.40.
[16] AL III.60.

absolutely fixed in me, so much so that it appears an "identical equation," axiomatic indeed, and yet not a platitude, but a very sword of Truth to sunder every knot at a touch.[17]

COROLLARY III.

Every man and every woman is a star.[18]

Take this carefully; it seems to imply a theory that if every man and every woman did his and her will—the true Will—there would be no clashing. "Every man and every woman is a star", and each star moves in an appointed path without interference. There is plenty of room for all; it is only disorder that creates confusion.[19]

This thesis is fully treated in *The Book of Wisdom or Folly*. Its main statement is that each human being is an Element of the Cosmos, self-determined and supreme, co-equal with all other Gods.

From this the Law "Do what thou wilt" follows logically. One star influences another by attraction, of course; but these are incidents of self-predestined orbits. There is, however, a mystery of the planets, revolving about a star of whom they are parts; but I shall not discuss it fully in this place.

Man is the Middle Kingdom. The Great Kingdom is Heaven, with each star as an unit; the Little Kingdom is the Molecule, with each Electron as an unit. (The Ratio of these three is regularly geometrical, each being 10 to the 22nd times greater in size than its neighbour.)

See *The Book of the Great Auk* for the demonstration that each "star" is the Centre of the Universe to itself, and that a "star" simple, original, absolute, can add to its omnipotence, omniscience and omnipresence without ceasing to be itself; that its one way to do this is to gain experience, and that therefore it enters into combinations in which its true Nature is for awhile disguised, even from itself. Analogously, an atom of carbon may pass through myriad Proteus-phases, appearing in Chalk, Chloroform, Sugar, Sap, Brain and Blood, not recognizable as "itself" the black amorphous solid, but recoverable as such, unchanged by its adventures.

This theory is the only one which explains *why* the Absolute limited itself, and why It does not recognize Itself during its cycle of incarnations. It disposes of "Evil" and the Origin of Evil; without denying Reality to "Evil", or insulting our daily observation and our common sense.[20]

All elements must at one time have been separate—that would be the case with great heat. Now when atoms get to the sun, when we get to the sun, we get that immense, extreme heat, and all the elements are themselves again. Imagine that each atom of each element possesses the memory of all his adventures in combination. By the way, that atom, fortified with that memory, would not be the same atom; yet it is, because it has gained nothing from anywhere except this memory. Therefore, by the lapse of time and by virtue of memory, a thing (although originally an

---

[17] NC on AL III.60.
[18] AL I.3.
[19] *Liber II*, as quoted in NC on AL I.40.
[20] NC on AL I.3. Emphasis in original.

Infinite Perfection) could become something more than itself; and thus a real development is possible. One can then see a reason for any element deciding to go through this series of incarnations (god, that was a magnificent conception!) because so, and only so, can he go; and he suffers the lapse of memory of His own Reality of Perfection which he has during these incarnations, because he knows he will come through unchanged.

Therefore you have an infinite number of gods, individual and equal though diverse, each one supreme and utterly indestructible. This is also the only explanation of how a being could create a world in which war, evil, *etc.* exist. Evil is only an appearance because, like "good", it cannot affect the substance itself, but only multiply its combinations. This is something the same as mystic monism, but the objection to that theory is that God has to create things which are all parts of himself, so that their interplay is false. If we presuppose many elements, their interplay is natural. It is no objection to this theory to ask who made the elements—the elements are at least there; and God, when you look for him, is not there. Theism is *obscurum per obscurius.*[21]

COROLLARY IV.

I am divided for love's sake, for the chance of union.[22]

In order to have Motion one must have Change. In fact, one must have this in order to have anything at all. Now this Change is what we call Love, thus "love under will" is the Law of Motion. The re-entrant character of this Motion is difficult to conceive; but the Aspirant is urged to try to assimilate the idea. A Hindu might compare the Cosmic process to a churn which out of milk made butter to feed a milk-producing woman, every step in the cycle being a Progress of Joy.

Time is necessarily created by us in order to make room for the apparent existence of the duality which we devise for the presentation of unity, or nihility.

"Two things" must evidently exist either in two places, or at two times, or both; else they would be indistinguishable.

Two phenomena which differ in time would be considered simultaneous if separated in space so that our observation of the former were delayed, for several reasons; and it is fairly easy to realize the possibility. But it seems as if separation in space were somehow more intractable. I can see no *priori* reason for this distinction; I think it arises from the fact that space is directly presented to our senses, while time is proper to the mental apprehension of impressions.

Our universe is (after all) in one place, so far as we are concerned, *i.e.*, in our sensoria, so that any two impressions can only be registered by us as consecutive. Even when we are aware of their simultaneity, we are compelled to place them in sequence. Our sensorium makes no distinction between concrete and abstract ideas in this respect. Sensory impressions and general ideas are equally grist for the mill. But we make a distinction

---

[21] Diary entry, 14 May 1919, 6.30 p.m., as quoted in NC on AL I.3.
[22] AL I.29.

between our record of events whose sequence is a necessary part of our comprehension of them, and those which are independent of our history. We insist on the sequence of school and college, but our general judgments are recognized as independent of time. This is peculiarly the case with our idea of the Ego, which we instinctively regard as if it were eternal and unchanging, though in fact it grows and decays continually. Yet we think of the incidents of boyhood as having occurred to the Ego, forming part of its character.

Now since this Ego is only conscious by virtue of having formulated itself, or the Universe (as it happens to view the case), in the form of Duality, and since all the experiences of the Ego are necessary to it, as all phenomena soever are necessary, it is permissible to regard the totality of the experience of the Ego as the presentation in duality of a single simultaneous fact.

In other words, life is an attempt to realize one's own nature in one's own soul.

The man who fails to recognize it as such is hopelessly bewildered by the irrational character of the universe, which he takes to be real; and he cannot but regard it as aimless and absurd. The adventures of his body and mind, with their desires for material and moral well-being, are obviously as foredoomed to disaster as Don Quixote's. He must be a fool if he struggles on (against inexorable fate) to obtain results which he knows can only end in catastrophe, a climax the more bitter as he clings the more closely to his impossible ideals.

But once he acquiesces in the necessity of the course of events, and considers his body and mind as no more than the instruments which interpret himself to himself by means of dualistic presentation, he should soon acquire a complete indifference to the nature of the incidents which occur to him.[23]

The experiences of each angle of a triangle are common to all, for one can express any relation as a function of any angle, at will. Each may be taken as the starting-point of the study of the properties to the triangle. But each angle is necessary to the triangle, and each is equally important to its existence. Each is bound to the others, and moreover each is in a sense illusory in respect of the triangle, which is an idea, simple and ideal, whose unity is compelled to express itself and manifest its properties by extension as a plane figure. For no triangle can express the idea of a triangle. Any triangle must be either equilateral, isosceles or scalene, either acute, right-angled, or obtuse; and no one triangle can be all these at once; while the idea of a triangle includes all these, and infinite other, possibilities.

In a similar way, Nuith and Hadith include all possible forms of existence; they can only realize Themselves by creating an infinite variety of forms of Themselves, each one real as it is Their image, illusory as it is a partial and divided aspect of Them.

Each such Star is intelligible to Them, as a poem is to its author as a part of this soul mirrored by his mind. But it is not intelligible to itself, because it

---

[23] NC on I.29.

has no relation with any other ideas; it only knows itself as the babe of its mother Nuith, to whom it yearns, being stirred by its father Hadith to express that instinctive attachment by inarticulate cries.

To know itself, each such Star, or Soul, must eat of the Fruit of the Tree of Knowledge of Good and Evil, by accepting labour and pain as its portion, and death as its doom. That is, it must reveal its nature to itself by formulating that nature as duality. It must express itself by a series of symbolic gestures ostensibly external to it, just as a painter reveals one facet of his Delight-Diamond by covering a canvas with colours in such a way that the picture seems at first sight to represent something outside himself. It must, in fact, repeat for itself the original Magick of Nuith and Hadith which created it.

As They made Themselves visible piecemeal by fashioning particular Souls, expressing the Impersonal and Absolute Homogeneity by means of Personal Relative Heterogeneity, so, not forgetting their true nature as forms of the Infinite, whereby they are one with all, must the stars devise methods of studying themselves.

They must make images of themselves, apparently external, and they must represent their highly complex qualities in a duality involving space and time. For each Star is of necessity related to every other star, so that no influence is alien to its individuality; it must therefore observer its reaction to every other star.

Just so are most chemical elements possessed of but few qualities directly appreciable by our senses; we must learn their natures by putting them into relation with the other Elements in turn. (Note well that this knowledge were impossible unless there were a variety of elements; so also the fact of our self-consciousness proves the existence of individual souls; all related, all parts of the One Soul, in one sense, but none the less independent in themselves, eternal entities expressing particular elements of existence.)[24]

We invent Space, Time, Sense-Impression, *etc.* to enable us to distinguish between "experiences" to express our conception of the multiplicity of the possibilities contained in the Idea of Zero. Each human consciousness being a case of one particular way of grouping elements, its conception of the Cosmos is limited by the necessary relations of that group to other groups. It grows by "union" with such groups, and is glad, partly because it satisfied its Oedipus-complex by thus approaching Nuit, partly because it fulfils its natural function of Creation.[25]

COROLLARY V.

The word of Sin is Restriction.[26]

The Key to this Message is this word—Will. The first obvious meaning of this Law is confirmed by antithesis; "The Word of Sin is Restriction."[27]

---

[24] *Ibid.*
[25] *Ibid.*
[26] AL I.41.
[27] *Liber II*, as quoted in NC on I.40.

Sin is defined as Restriction: that is; the setting of limits, or the desire to set limits, to any thing that is, seeing that as above set forth the true Nature of all things is to fulfil themselves in all Ways. Yet though all things be thus lawful in themselves, it is often Restriction to act, and Freedom to refrain. For that Freedom is worth the other, and each case must be judged by its own Nature.[28]

Anything soever that binds the will, hinders it, or diverts it, is Sin. That is, Sin is the appearance of the Dyad.[29]

Interference with the will of another is the great sin, for it predicates the existence of another.[30]

Sin is restriction, that is, it is "being" as opposed to "becoming". The fundamental idea of wrong is the static as opposed to the dynamic conception of the Universe.[31]

COROLLARY VI.

There is no bond that can unite the divided but love: all else is a curse.[32]

Duty of a Thelemite towards others. Seek not to control the will of any other in the matter of Love, setting Limits either to the Will to Love or the Will to seek elsewhere the Goal of Will. For Love itself is the sole bond; all others set up strains against the Nature of Things: whereby cometh at last the ruin of all.[33]

There shall be no property in human flesh. The sex-instinct is one of the most deeply-seated expressions of the will; and it must not be restricted, either negatively by preventing its free function, or positively by insisting on its false function.

What is more brutal than to stunt natural growth or to deform it?

What is more absurd than to seek to interpret this holy instinct as a gross animal act, to separate it from the spiritual enthusiasm without which it is so stupid as not even to be satisfactory to the persons concerned?

The sexual act is a sacrament of Will. To profane it is the great offence. All true expression of it is lawful; all suppression or distortion is contrary to the Law of Liberty. To use legal or financial constraint to compel either abstention or submission, is entirely horrible, unnatural and absurd.[34]

Sex is the main expression of the Nature of a person; great Natures are sexually strong; and the health of any person will depend upon the freedom of that function.[35]

---

[28] DC on AL I.41.
[29] NC on AL I.41.
[30] OC on AL I.41.
[31] NC on AL I.41.
[32] AL I.41.
[33] DC on AL I.41.
[34] NC on AL I.41.
[35] *Ibid.*

COROLLARY VII.

Let it be that state of manyhood bound and loathing. So with thy all; thou hast no right but to do thy will.[36]

Do what thou wilt—then do nothing else. Let nothing deflect thee from that austere and holy task. Liberty is absolute to do thy will; but seek to do any other thing whatever, and instantly obstacles must arise. Every act that is not in definite course of that one orbit is erratic, an hindrance. Will must not be two, but one.[37]

The Right of Man. This case may be taken as a guide to other problems of ethics. The rule is in truth single, the same in essence for all matters of conduct. Each has the perfect right to do his Will, that for which he is fit; all other use of power is an abuse.[38]

Remember, also, that, unless you know what your true will is, you may be devoting the most laudable energies to destroying yourself. Remember that every word and deed is a witness to thought, that therefore your mind must be perfectly organized, its sole duty to interpret circumstances in terms of the Will so that speech and action may be rightly directed to express the Will appropriately to the occasion. Remember that every word and deed which is not a definite expression of your Will counts against it, indifference worse than hostility. Your enemy is at least interested in you: you may make him your friend as you never can do with a neutral.[39]

A man who is not doing his will is like a man with cancer, an independent growth in him, yet one from which he cannot get free. The idea of self-sacrifice is a moral cancer in exactly this sense.

Similarly, one may say that not to do one's will is evidence of mental or moral insanity. When "duty points one way, and inclination the other", it is proof that you are not one, but two. You have not centralized your control. This dichotomy is the beginning of conflict, which may result in a Jekyll-Hyde effect. Stevenson suggests that man may be discovered to be a "mere polity" of many individuals. The sages knew it long since. But the name of this polity is Choronzon, mob rule, unless every individual is absolutely disciplined to serve his own, and the common, purpose without friction.

It is of course better to expel or destroy an irreconcilable. "If thine eye offend thee, cut it out." The error in the interpretation of this doctrine has been that it has not been taken as it stands. It has been read: If thine eye offend some artificial standard of right, cut it out. The curse of society has been Procrustean morality, the ethics of the herd-men. One would have thought that a mere glance at Nature would have sufficed to disclose Her scheme of Individuality made possible by Order.[40]

---

[36] AL I.42.
[37] *Liber II*, as quoted in NC on AL I.40.
[38] DC on AL I.42–3.
[39] NC on AL I.37.
[40] NC on AL I.42.

COROLLARY VIII.

Do that, and no other shall say nay. For pure will, unassuaged of purpose, delivered from the lust of result, is every way perfect.[41]

Will: its possible defects. Purpose takes the edge off pure will; for it implies conscious thought, which should not replace what Nature intends. Work is done best when the mind does not know of it, either to urge or check its course. The lust of result also spoils work; one must not distract one's forces from their task by thoughts of the profit of success.[42]

Recommends "non-attachment." Students will understand how in meditation the mind which attaches itself to hope of success is just as bound as if it were to attach itself to some base material idea. It is a bond and the aim is freedom.[43]

This verse is best interpreted by defining "pure will" as the true expression of the Nature, the proper or inherent motion of the matter, concerned. It is unnatural to aim at any goal. The student is referred to *Liber LXV*, Cap. II, v. 24, and to the *Tao Teh King*. This becomes particularly important in high grades. One is not to do Yoga, *etc.*, in order to get Samadhi, like a schoolboy or a shopkeeper; but for its own sake, like an artist.

"Unassuaged" means "its edge taken off by" or "dulled by". The pure student does not think of the result of the examination.[44]

But the phrase may also be interpreted as if it read "with purpose unassuaged"—*i.e.* with tireless energy. The conception is, therefore, of an eternal motion, infinite and unalterable. It is Nirvana, only dynamic instead of static—and this comes to the same thing in the end.[45]

COROLLARY IX.

Also, take your fill and will of love as ye will, when, where and with whom ye will! But always unto me.[46]

We are to enjoy life thoroughly in an absolutely normal way, exactly as all the free and great have always done. The only point to remember is that one is a "Member of the Body of God", a Star in the Body of Nuith. This being sure, we are urged to the fullest expansion of our several Natures, with special attention to those pleasures which not only express the soul, but aid it to reach the higher developments of that expression.

The act of Love is to the bourgeois (as the "Christian" is called now-a-days) a gross animal gesture which shames his boasted humanity. The appetite drags him at its hoofs; it tires him, disgusts him, diseases him, makes him ridiculous even in his own eyes. It is the source of nearly all his neuroses.

Against this monster he has devised two protections. Firstly, he pretends that it is a Fairy Prince disguised, and hangs it with the rags and

---

[41] AL I.43–4.
[42] DC on AL I.44.
[43] OC on AL I.44.
[44] NC on AL I.44.
[45] *Liber II*, as quoted in NC on AL I.40.
[46] AL I.51.

tinsel of romance, sentiment, and religion. He calls it Love, denies its strength and truth, and worships this wax figure of him with all sorts of amiable lyrics and leers.

Secondly, he is so certain, despite all his theatrical-wardrobe-work, that it is a devouring monster, that he resents with insane ferocity the existence of people who laugh at his fears, and tell him that the monster he fears is in reality not a fire-breathing worm, but a spirited horse, well trained to the task of the bridle. They tell him not to be a gibbering coward, but to learn to ride. Knowing well how abject he is, the kindly manhood of the advice is, to him, the bitterest insult he can imagine, and he calls on the mob to stone the blasphemer. He is therefore particularly anxious to keep intact the bogey he so dreads; the demonstration that Love is a general passion, pure in itself, and the redeemer of all them that put their trust in Him, is to tear open the raw ulcer of his soul.

We of Thelema are not the slaves of Love. "Love under will" is the Law. We refuse to regard love as shameful and degrading, as a peril to body and soul. We refuse to accept it as the surrender of the divine to the animal; to us it is the means by which the animal may be made the Winged Sphinx which shall bear man aloft to the House of the Gods.

We are then particularly careful to deny that the object of love is the gross physiological object which happens to be Nature's excuse for it. Generation is a sacrament of the physical Rite, by which we create ourselves anew in our own image, weave in a new flesh-tapestry the Romance of our own Soul's History. But also Love is a sacrament of trans-substantiation whereby we initiate our own souls; it is the Wine of Intoxication as well as the Bread of Nourishment. "Nor is he for priest designed Who partakes only in one kind."[47]

We therefore heartily cherish those forms of Love in which no question of generation arises; we use the stimulating effects of physical enthusiasm to inspire us morally and spiritually. Experience teaches that passions thus employed do serve to refine and to exalt the whole being of man or woman. Nuith indicates the sole condition: "But always unto me."

The epicure is not a Monster of gluttony, nor the amateur of Beethoven a "degenerate" from the "normal" man whose only music is the tom-tom. So also the poisons which shook the bourgeois are not indulgences, but purifications; the brute whose furtive lust demands that he be drunk and in darkness that he may surrender to his shame, and that he lie about it with idiot mumblings ever after, is hardly the best judge even of Phryne. How much less should he venture to criticize such men and women whose imaginations are so free from grossness that the element of attraction which serves to electrify their magnetic coil is independent of physical form? To us the essence of Love is that it is a sacrament unto Nuith, a gate of grace and a road of righteousness to Her High Palace, the abode of peerless purity whose lamps are the Stars.

"As ye will." It should be abundantly clear from the foregoing remarks that each individual has an absolute and indefeasible right to use his sexual

---

[47] *The Sevenfold Sacrament*, Sec. V, as quoted in NC on AL I.51.

vehicle in accordance with its own proper character, and that he is responsible only to himself. But he should not injure himself and his right aforesaid; acts invasive of another individual's equal rights are implicitly self-aggressions. A thief can hardly complain on theoretical grounds if he is himself robbed. Such acts as rape, and the assault or seduction of infants, may therefore be justly regarded as offences against the Law of Liberty, and repressed in the interests of that Law.

It is also excluded from "as ye will" to compromise the liberty of another person indirectly, as by taking advantage of the ignorance or good faith of another person to expose that person to the constraint of sickness, poverty, social detriment, or childbearing, unless with the well-informed and uninfluenced free will of that person.

One must moreover avoid doing another injury by deforming his nature; for instance, to flog children at or near puberty may distort the sensitive nascent sexual character, and impress it with the stamp of masochism. Again, homosexual practices between boys may in certain cases actually rob them of their virility, psychically or even physically.

Trying to frighten adolescents about sex by the bogeys of Hell, Disease, and Insanity, may warp the moral nature permanently, and produce hypochondria or other mental maladies, with perversions of the enervated and thwarted instinct.

Repression of the natural satisfaction may result in addition to secret and dangerous vices which destroy their victim because they are artificial and unnatural aberrations. Such moral cripples resemble those manufactured by beggars by compressing one part of the body so that it is compensated by a monstrous exaggeration in another part.

But on the other hand we have no right to interfere with any type of manifestation of the sexual impulse on *a priori* grounds. We must recognize that the Lesbian leanings of idle and voluptuous women whose refinement finds the grossness of the average male repugnant, are as inexpugnably entrenched in Righteousness as the parallel pleasures of the English Aristocracy and Clergy whose aesthetics find women disgusting, and whose self-respect demands that love should transcend animal impulse, excite intellectual intimacy, and inspire spirituality by directing it towards an object whose attainment cannot inflict the degradation of domesticity, and the bestiality of gestation.

Every one should discover, by experience of every kind, the extent and intention of his own sexual Universe. He must be taught that all roads are equally royal, and that the only question for him is "Which road is mine?" All details are equally likely to be of the essence of his personal plan, all equally "right" in themselves, his own choice of the one as correct as, and independent of, his neighbour's preference for the other.

He must not be ashamed or afraid of being homosexual if he happens to be so at heart; he must not attempt to violate his own true nature because public opinion, or mediaeval morality, or religious prejudice would wish he were otherwise.[48]

---

[48] NC on AL I.51.

It is better for a person of heterosexual nature to suffer every possible calamity as the indirect environment-evoked result of his doing his true will in that respect than to enjoy health, wealth and happiness by means either of suppressing sex altogether, of debauching it to the service of Sodom or Gomorrah.

Equally it is better for the androgyne, the urning, or their feminine counterparts to endure blackmailers private and public, the terrors of police persecution, the disgust, contempt and loathing of the vulgar, and the self-torture of suspecting the peculiarity to be a symptom of a degenerate nature, than to wrong the soul by damning it to the hell of abstinence, or by defiling it with the abhorred embraces of antipathetic arms.

Every star must calculate its own orbit. All is Will, and yet all is Necessity. To swerve is ultimately impossible; to seek to swerve is to suffer.

The Beast 666 ordains by His authority that every man, and every woman, and every intermediately-sexed individual, shall be absolutely free to interpret and communicate Self by means of any sexual practices soever, whether direct or indirect, rational or symbolic, physiologically, legally, ethically, or religiously approved or no, provided only that all parties to any act are fully aware of all implications and responsibilities thereof, and heartily agree thereto.

Moreover, the Beast 666 adviseth that all children shall be accustomed from infancy to witness every type of sexual act, as also the process of birth, lest falsehood fog, and mystery stupefy, their minds, whose error else might thwart and misdirect the growth of their subconscious system of soul-symbolism.

"when, where, and with whom ye will!"

The phrase "with whom" has been practically covered by the comment on "as ye will". One need no more than distinguish that the earlier phrase permits all manner of acts, the latter all possible partners. There would have been no Furies for Oedipus, no disaster for Othello, Romeo, Pericles of Tyre, Laon and Cythna, if it were only agreed to let sleeping dogs lie, and mind one's own business. In real life, we have seen in our own times Oscar Wilde, Sir Charles Dilke, Parnell, Canon Aitken and countless others, many of them engaged in first-rate work for the world, all wasted because the mob must make believe to be "moral". This phrase abolishes the Eleventh Commandment, Not to be Found Out, by authorizing Incest, Adultery, and Paederasty, which every one now practices with humiliating precautions, which perpetuate the schoolboy's enjoyment of an escapade, and make shame, slyness, cowardice and hypocrisy the conditions of success in life.

It is also the fact that the tendency of any individual to sexual irregularity is emphasised by the preoccupation with the subject which follows its factitious importance in modern society.

It is to be observed that Politeness has forbidden any direct reference to the subject of sex to secure no happier result than to allow Sigmund Freud and others to prove that our every thought, speech, and gesture, conscious or unconscious, is an indirect reference!

Unless one wants to wreck the neighbourhood, it is best to explode one's gunpowder in an unconfined space.

There are very few cases of "perverted hunger-instinct" in moderately healthy communities. War restrictions on food created dishonest devices to procure dainties, and artificial attempts to appease the ache of appetite by chemical counterfeits.

The South-Sea Islanders, pagan, amoral and naked, are temperate lovers, free from hysterical "crimes of passion", sex obsessions, and puritan persecution-mania; perversion is practically unknown, and monogamy is the general custom.

Even the civilized psychopaths of cities, forced into every kind of excess by the omnipresence of erotic suggestions and the contact of crazed crowds seething with suppressed sexuality, are not wholly past physic. They are no sooner released from the persistent pressure by escaping to some place where the inhabitants treat the reproductive and the respiratory organs as equally innocent than they begin insensibly to forget their "fixed idea" forced on them by the fog-horn of Morality, so that their perversions perish, just as a coiled spring straightens itself when the external compulsion is removed. They revert to their natural sex-characters, which only in rare cases are other than simple, pure, and refined. More, sex itself ceases to play Principal Boy in the Pantomime of Life. Other interests resume their proper proportions.

We may now inquire why the Book is at pains to admit as to love "when" and "where" we will. Few people, surely, have been seriously worried by restrictions of time and place. One can only think of lovers who live with fearsome families or in inhospitable lodgings, on a rainy night, buffeted from one police-bullied hotel to another.

Perhaps this permission is intended to indicate the propriety of performing the sexual act without shame or fear, not waiting for darkness or seeking secrecy, but by daylight in public places, as serenely as if it were a natural incident in a morning stroll.

Custom would soon surfeit curiosity, and copulation attract less attention than a new fashion in frocks. For the existing interest in sexual matters is chiefly because, common as the act is, it is closely concealed. Nobody is excited by seeing others eat. A "naughty" book is as dull as a volume of sermons; only genius can vitalize either.

Beyond this, once love is taken for granted, the morbid fascination of its mystery will vanish.

The pander, the prostitute, the parasite will find their occupation gone.

Disease will go straight to the doctor instead of to the quack, as it does; the altars of Mrs. Grundy run red with the blood of her faithful!

The ignorance or carelessness of a raw youth will no longer hound him to hell. A blighted career or a ruined constitution will no more be the penalty of a moment's exuberance.

Above all, the world will begin to appreciate the true nature of the sexual process, its physical insignificance as one among many parts of the body, its transcendent importance as the vehicle of the True Will and the first of the sheaths of the Self.

Hitherto our sexual tabus have kept far ahead of Gilbert and Sullivan. We have made love the lackey to property, as who should pay his rent by sneezing. We have swaddled it in politeness, as who should warn God off the grass.

We have muddled it up with morality, as who should frown at the Himalayas on the one hand, and, on the other, regulate his behaviour by that of an ant-heap.[49]

Love: its law is complete Freedom. Also as to Love: be wholly free to make the best of your gifts in all respects, fearless and shameless.

All acts to be understood as Acts of Worship of Nuit. Yet all these acts must not be done for their results in success or pleasure, and the like; for they are holy and to be performed strictly as acts of Love under Will in worship of Nuit; that is, to fulfil all that may be and your own whole Nature by so doing.[50]

Remember that every act of "love under will" is lawful as such; but that when any act is not directed unto Nuith, who is here the inevitable result of the whole Work, that act is waste, and breeds conflict within you, so that "the kingdom of God which is within you" is torn by civil war.[51]

COROLLARY X.

The rituals of the old time are black. Let the evil ones be cast away: let the good ones be purged by the prophet![52]

Now, "the rituals of the old time," are no longer valid vehicles; Knowledge cannot "go aright" until they are adapted to the Formula of the New Æon. Their defects are due principally to two radical errors. (1.) The Universe was conceived as possessing a fixed centre, or summit; an absolute standard to which all things might be referred; an Unity, or God. (Mystics were angry and bewildered, often enough, when attaining to "union with God" they found him equally in all). This led to making a difference between one thing and another, and so to the ideas of superiority, of sin, *etc.*, ending by absurdities of all kinds, alike in theology, ethics, and science. (2) The absolute antithesis between the pairs of opposites. This is really a corollary of (1). There was an imaginary "absolute evil" which made Manichaeanism necessary—despite the cloaks of the Casuists—and meant "That which leads one away from God." But each man, while postulating an absolute "God" defined Him unconsciously in terms of a Freudian Phantasm created by his own wish-fulfilment machinery. Thus "Good" and "Evil" were really expressions of personal prejudice. A man who "bowed humbly to the Authority of" the Pope, or the Bible, or the Sanhedrim, or the Oracle of Apollo, or the tribal Medicine-Man, none the less expressed truly his own Wish to abdicate responsibility. In the light of this Book, we know that the centre is everywhere, the circumference nowhere; that "Every man and every woman is a star," a "Khabs," the name of the house of Hadit; that "The word of Sin is Restriction." To us, then, "evil" is a relative term; it is "that which hinders

---

[49] *Ibid.*
[50] DC on AL I.51.
[51] NC on AL I.37.
[52] AL II.5.

one from fulfilling his true Will." (*E.g.*, rain is "good" or "bad" for the farmer according to the requirements of his crops).

The Osirian Rituals inculcating self-sacrifice to an abstract ideal, mutilation to appease an *ex cathedra* morality, fidelity to *a priori* formulæ, *etc.* teach false and futile methods of acquiring false Knowledge; they must be "cast away" or "purged". The Schools of Initiation must be reformed.[53]

COROLLARY XI.

Remember all ye that existence is pure joy: that all the sorrows are but as shadows; they pass & are done: but there is that which remains.[54]

Hadit now sayeth to all that they should be mindful of the Nature of that which exists; it is pure joy, since all Events are Acts of Love under Will. The Shadow called Sorrow is caused by the error of thinking of any two Events as opposed or even distinct; which fault was in the first chapter of this Book thus condemned: "for thereby cometh hurt." (Hurt, in French, *heurter*, to jostle.) Sorrows, being thus errors of vision, not real in themselves, pass and are done as soon as the mind ceases to dwell on them; yet, being false thoughts about True Events, the Event endures, and the Point-of-View endures; so that Hadit hath attained His Will no less than in all other cases.[55]

This verse is very thoroughly explained in *Liber Aleph*. "All in this kind are but shadows" says Shakespeare, referring to actors.[56] The Universe is a Puppet-Play for the amusement of Nuit and Hadit in their Nuptials; a very Midsummer Night's Dream. So then we laugh at the mock woes of Pyramus and Thisbe, the clumsy gambols of Bottom; for we understand the Truth of Things, how all is a Dance of Ecstasy. "Were the world understood, Ye would know it was good, a Dance to a lyrical measure!"[57] The nature of events must be "pure joy"; for obviously, whatever occurs is the fulfilment of the Will of its master. Sorrow thus appears as the result of any unsuccessful—therefore, ill-judged—struggle. Acquiescence in the order of Nature is the ultimate Wisdom.

One must understand the Universe perfectly, and be utterly indifferent to its pressure. These are the virtues which constitute a Master of the Temple. Yet each man must act What he will; for he is energized by his own nature. So long as he works "without lust of result" and does his duty for its own sake, he will know that "the sorrows are but shadows." And he himself is "that which remains"; for he can no more be destroyed, or his true Will be thwarted, than Matter diminish or Energy disappear. He is a necessary Unit of the Universe, equal and opposite to the sum total of all the others; and his Will is similarly the final factor which completes the equilibrium of the dynamical equation. He cannot fail if he would; thus, his sorrows are but

---

[53] NC on AL II.5.
[54] AL II.9.
[55] DC on AL II.9.
[56] "The best in this kind are but shadows: and the worst are no worse if imagination amend them." *A Midsummer Night's Dream*, Act 5, Scene 1.
[57] "Were the world understood / Ye would see it was good, / A dance to a delicate measure." *Orpheus*, Liber Quartus vel Mortis, "Finale: Nuith."

shadows—he could not see them if he kept his gaze fixed on his goal, the Sun.[58]

COROLLARY XII.

These are dead, these fellows; they feel not. We are not for the poor and sad: the lords of the earth are our kinsfolk. Is a God to live in a dog? No! but the highest are of us. They shall rejoice, our chosen: who sorroweth is not of us. Beauty and strength, leaping laughter and delicious languor, force and fire, are of us.[59]

Those who sorrow are not real people at all, not "stars"—for the time being. The fact of their being "poor and sad" proves them to be "shadows," who "pass and are done."[60]

Such folk "feel not", even though they suppose themselves to feel more keenly than those who enjoy life and death—those whom they call callous. But the truth is that since Events compose Life, and each Event is an act of Love under Will, all feelings except those of joy, conquest, triumph and rapture are not Events at all and so do not belong to Life.

The poor and sad are not of Hadit; for to know that one is He confers full wealth and complete joy: it is the title to Lordship of the Earth. All leaders of men are active, finding pleasure even in toil, hardship, and defeat: they accept every Event as proper to their chosen course of action, and conquer even when they are beaten down for the moment. They die at the crisis of the battle, with failure certain; yet they rejoice, having lived and loved and fought and done their will; those for whose cause they fought will reap at last where they have sowed.[61]

The "lords of the earth" are those who are doing their Will. It does not necessarily mean people with coronets and automobiles; there are plenty of such people who are the most sorrowful slaves in the world. The sole test of one's lordship is to know what one's true Will is, and to do it.[62]

The highest are those who have mastered and transcended accidental environment. They rejoice, because they do their Will; and if any man sorrow, it is clear evidence of something wrong with him. When machinery creaks and growls, the engineer knows that it is not fulfilling its function, doing its Will, with ease and joy.[63]

A God cannot live in a dog; the token of Godship is to be free to act, to dwell in an abode, and work with tools, suited to the nature of their Will. The Highest only are of Hadit; all failure to attain the perfect marks some lack of knowledge of one's nature as a Symbol of Him in one or other Form. Aiwass repeats his doctrine about joy and sorrow in more solemn terms, thus leading up to the full Force of His thought.[64]

---

[58] NC on AL II.9.
[59] AL II.18–20.
[60] NC on AL II.18.
[61] DC on AL II.18.
[62] NC on AL II.18.
[63] NC on AL II.19.
[64] DC on AL II.19.

Beauty and strength, the sense of the fitness of the object perceived as a symbol of the success of one's will, and the power of that will itself; leaping laughter and delicious languor, the rapture of joyous uprush in full freedom of spirit and the delight that follows the success of one's efforts, luring the victor to enjoy the pleasure of knowing himself worthy; force and fire, the ardour of motion, achieving one's will, and the light and heat evolved by the love under will of the Self and its desires: these are the marks of those who know their True Self to be Hadit. (Note that all these statements are hidden in the basic complex of thought which defines Hadit.)[65]

COROLLARY XIII.

We have nothing with the outcast and the unfit: let them die in their misery. For they feel not. Compassion is the vice of kings: stamp down the wretched & the weak: this is the law of the strong: this is our law and the joy of the world.[66]

The outcast: these are passive; they do not seek and conquer all that may be but are the sport of Events not of their own making, which hustle against them and thrust them from the path. The unfit: these fail to adjust themselves to what is about them; they cannot love (which implies a fitness of the one to the other) under will (which implies fitness of the agent to the patient).

They had better "die in their misery"; that is, cease once and for all to react so feebly and wrongly as they do: for such a Point-of-View as they shew forth is not to be endured. It is not truly Hadit at all; not any one Point, but a shifting fulcrum: let it be no more counted among True Things. Again Aiwass repeats that "they feel not."

Compassion, the noblest virtue of the Buddhist, is damned outright by Aiwass. To "suffer with" some other being is clearly to cease to be oneself, to wander from one's Way. It always implies error, no Point-of-View being the same as any other: and in Kings—leaders and rulers of men—such error is a vice. For it leads straight to the most foolish Rule ever laid down, "Do unto others as you would that they should do unto you." True men know their own needs and find ways to supply them. To judge the sick by the healthy is pregnant with error. The wretched and the weak are simply not real beings; they cannot be helped or mended. They must be expunged as falsehoods likely to infect the truth. This is the law of Nature, and it is the Law of the Lords of the Æon. Put into force it will fill the world with joy.[67]

There is a good deal of the Nietzschean standpoint in this verse. It is the evolutionary and natural view. Of what use is it to perpetuate the misery of Tuberculosis, and such diseases, as we now do? Nature's way is to weed out the weak. This is the most merciful way, too. At present all the strong are being damaged, and their progress hindered by the dead weight of the weak limbs and the missing limbs, the diseased limbs and the atrophied limbs. The Christians to the Lions!

---

[65] DC on AL II.20.
[66] AL II.21.
[67] DC on AL II.21.

Our humanitarianism, which is the syphilis of the mind, acts on the basis of the lie that the King must die. The King is beyond death; it is merely a pool where he dips for refreshment. We must therefore go back to Spartan ideas of education; and the worst enemies of humanity are those who wish, under the pretext of compassion, to continue its ills through the generations. The Christians to the Lions!

Let weak and wry productions go back into the melting-pot, as is done with flawed steel castings. Death will purge, reincarnation make whole, these errors and abortions. Nature herself may be trusted to do this, if only we will leave her alone. But what of those who, physically fitted to live, are tainted with rottenness of soul, cancerous with the sin-complex? For the third time I answer: The Christians to the Lions![68]

COROLLARY XIV.

If Will stops and cries Why, invoking Because, then Will stops & does nought. If Power asks why, then is Power weakness.[69]

We now come to a challenge which is in some ways even more daring than any yet made. Before, the moral sense of men was outraged. He now turns to attack the Reason itself. He looks on reason as a soulless machine. Its proper function is to express the Will in terms of conscious thought, the will being the need of the inmost self to express itself by causing some Event. This will (as such) is not conscious. We can only become aware of it, and thus enjoy and learn from the Event, by making an Image of it. Reason is the machine whose function it is to do this. When reason usurps the higher functions of the mind, when it presumes to dictate to the Will what its desires ought to be, it wrecks the entire structure of the star. The Self should set the Will in motion, that is, the Will should only take its orders from within and above. It should not be conscious at all. But even worse may come to it. Once it is conscious, it becomes able to doubt; and, having no means of getting rid of this by appeal to the Self, it seeks a reason for its action. The reason, knowing nothing of the matter, promptly replies, basing its judgement, not on the needs of the self, but on facts outside and alien to the star. It is, in fact, guided by strangers of whose very language it knows little and that mostly wrong. The Will having stopped in doubt, goes on again in error. The Will must never ask why. It ought to be as sure of itself as the Law of Gravity.[70]

There is no "reason" why a Star should continue in its orbit. Let her rip! Every time the conscious acts, it interferes with the Subconscious, which is Hadit. It is the voice of Man, and not of a God. Any man who "listens to reason" ceases to be a revolutionary. The newspapers are Past Masters in the Lodge of Sophistry Number 333. They can always prove to you that it is necessary, and patriotic, and all the rest of it, that you should suffer intolerable wrongs.

---

[68] NC on AL II.21.
[69] AL II.30–31.
[70] DC on AL II.28–31.

The Qabalists represent the mind as a complex of six elements, whereas the Will is single, the direct expression as "The Word" of the Self. The mind must inform the Understanding, which then presents a simple idea to the Will. This issues its orders accordingly for unquestioning execution. If the Will should appeal to the mind, it must confuse itself with incomplete and uncoordinated ideas. The clamour of these cries crowns Anarchy, and action becomes impossible.[71]

It is ridiculous to ask a dog why it barks. One must fulfil one's true Nature, one must do one's Will. To question this is to destroy confidence, and so to create an inhibition. If a woman asks a man who wishes to kiss her why he wants to do so, and he tries to explain, he becomes impotent. His proper course is to choke her into compliance, which is what she wants, anyhow.

Power acts: the nature of the action depends on the information received by the Will; but once the decision is taken, reflection is out of place. Power should indeed be absolutely unconscious. Every athlete is aware that his skill, strength, and endurance depend on forbidding mind to meddle with muscle. Here is a simple experiment. Hold out a weight at arm's length. If you fix your attention firmly on other matters, you can support the strain many times longer than if you allow yourself to think of what your body is doing.[72]

COROLLARY XV.

Also reason is a lie: for there is a factor infinite & unknown; & all their words are skew-wise.[73]

Aiwass now leaps to the supreme stroke. Reason itself is a lie. He explains that this must be the case in the nature of things. The Reason may be in perfect order and never make a mistake, that is, within the limits of its powers. But it can never be certain of being right unless its knowledge is complete, which of course can never happen. In fact, being bound by its own laws, it has no means of finding out whether in any one case there may not be some factor vital to the problem of whose very nature it has no knowledge at all. Its axioms themselves merely state its limits. It is as if a bishop on a chess board were to assert that it could never move except in an oblique straight line, which is only true in respect of the laws of the game, and takes no account of the laws of motion as such. Aiwass asserts that some such factor always lurks in every problem which may be put to reason. He calls it "a factor infinite and unknown"—unknown since no mind can ever contain the whole of the facts of nature which may apply. It must therefore be content to work within narrow limits and state its results under the reserve that they are only correct if we assume that its data suffices. The factor is also infinite in the same way as an atom in the world of solid bodies is greater than the greatest surface. More, the plane is not real at all to the solid; it is no more than a way which the real being has

---

[71] NC on AL II.30.
[72] NC on AL II.31.
[73] AL II.32.

chosen to express one item of his knowledge of nature. The reason of man should never allow itself to forget that it is only real in the hardly likely case of the world ending with itself. It is wiser to keep in mind that all Events, however true and real they seem (and are, as measured by the laws of the game) are after all signs of a code which Hadit has designed in order to express his nature in terms of its acts of love under will with one or other part of Nuit.

The Angel concludes by saying that the statements of the reason are "skew-wise." The fact that the reason employs a set of symbols to work with distorts the whole work. It is as when a painter obtains the effect of solid form on a plane surface by adroit use of the laws of optics. No matter, therefore, how truly the reason works, and how well it brings back to the mind the events it describes, its thoughts are never the same as the things thought of. It follows from this that we should be fools to trust reason to guide us to answer Because.[74]

COROLLARY XVI.

Yea! deem not of change: ye shall be as ye are, & not other. Therefore the kings of the earth shall be Kings for ever: the slaves shall serve. There is none that shall be cast down or lifted up: all is ever as it was.[75]

It has naturally been objected by economists that our Law, in declaring every man and every woman to be a star, reduces society to its elements, and makes hierarchy or even democracy impossible. The view is superficial. Each star has a function in its galaxy proper to its own nature. Much mischief has come from our ignorance in insisting, on the contrary, that each citizen is fit for any and every social duty. But also our Law teaches that a star often veils itself from its nature. Thus the vast bulk of humanity is obsessed by an abject fear of freedom; the principal objections hitherto urged against my Law have been those of people who cannot bear to imagine the horrors which would result if they were free to do their own wills. The sense of sin, shame, self-distrust, this is what makes folk cling to Christianity-slavery. People believe in a medicine just in so far as it is nasty; the metaphysical root of this idea is in sexual degeneracy of the masochistic type. Now "the Law is for all"; but such defectives will refuse it, and serve us who are free with a fidelity the more dog-like as the simplicity of our freedom denotes their abjection.[76]

No one is better aware than I am that the Labour Problem has to be settled by practical and not ideal considerations, but in this case the ideal considerations happen to be extremely practical. The mistake has been in trying to produce a standard article to supply the labour market; it is an error from the point of view of capital and labour alike. Men should not be taught to read and write unless they exhibit capacity or inclination. Compulsory education has aided nobody. It has imposed an unwarrantable constraint on the people it was intended to benefit; it has been asinine

---

[74] DC on AL II.32.
[75] AL II.58.
[76] NC on AL II.58.

presumption on the part of the intellectuals to consider a smattering of mental acquirements of universal benefit. It is a form of sectarian bigotry. We should recognize the fact that the vast majority of human beings have no ambition in life beyond mere ease and animal happiness. We should allow these people to fulfil their destinies without interference. We should give every opportunity to the ambitious, and thereby establish a class of morally and intellectually superior men and women. We should have no compunction in utilizing the natural qualities of the bulk of mankind. We do not insist on trying to train sheep to hunt foxes or lecture on history; we look after their physical well being, and enjoy their wool and mutton. I this way we shall have a contented class of slaves who will accept the conditions of existence as they really are, and enjoy life with the quiet wisdom of cattle. It is our duty to see to it that this class of people lack for nothing. The patriarchal system is better for all classes than any other; the objections to it come from the abuses of it. But bad masters have been artificially created by exactly the same blunder as was responsible for the bad servants. It is essential to teach the masters that each one must discover his own will, and do it. There is no reason in nature for cut-throat competition. All this has been explained previously in other connections; here it is only necessary to emphasize the point. It must be cleanly understood that every man must find his own happiness in a purely personal way. Our troubles have been caused by the assumption that everybody wanted the same things, and thereby the supply of those things has become artificially limited; even those benefits of which there is an inexhaustible store have been cornered. For example, fresh air and beautiful scenery. In a world where everyone did his own will none would lack these things. In our present society, they have become the luxuries of wealth and leisure, yet they are still accessible to any one who possesses sufficient sense to emancipate himself from the alleged advantages of city life. We have deliberately trained people to wish for things that they do not really want.[77]

"Consider, my Son, that word in the Call or Key of the Thirty Æthyrs: Behold the Face of your God, the Beginning of Comfort, whose eyes are the Brightness of the Heavens, which provided you for the Government of the Earth, and the Unspeakable Variety! And Again: let there be no Creature upon her or within her the same. All her Members let them differ in their Qualities, and let there be no Creature equal with another. Here also is the voice of true Science, crying aloud that Variation is the Key of Evolution. Thereunto Art cometh the third, perceiving Beauty in the Harmony of the Diverse. Know then, o my Son, that all Laws, all Systems, all Customs, all Ideals and Standards which tend to produce uniformity, are in direct opposition to Nature's Will to change and to develop through Variety, and are accursed. Do thou with all thy Might of Manhood strive against these Forces, for they resist Change, which is Life; and thus they are of Death."[78]

---

[77] *Ibid.*
[78] *Liber Aleph*, "De lege motus," as quoted in NC on AL II.58.

COROLLARY XVII.

Wisdom says: be strong! Then canst thou bear more joy. Be not animal: refine thy rapture! If thou drink, drink by the eight and ninety rules of art: if thou love, exceed by delicacy; and if thou do aught joyous, let there be subtlety therein![79]

It is absurd to suppose that "to indulge the passions" is necessarily a reversion or degeneration. On the contrary, all human progress has depended on such indulgence. Every art and science is intended to gratify some fundamental need of nature. What is the ultimate use of the telephone and all the other inventions on which we pride ourselves? Only to sustain life, or to protect or reproduce it; or to subserve Knowledge and other forms of pleasure.

On the other hand, the passions must be understood properly as what they are, nothing in themselves, but the diverse forms of expression employed by the Will. One must preserve discipline. A passion cannot be good or bad, too weak or too strong, *etc.* by an arbitrary standard. Its virtue consists solely in its conformity with the plan of the Commander-in-Chief. Its initiative and elan are limited by the requirements of his strategy. For instance, modesty may well cooperate with ambition; but also it may thwart it. This verse counsels us to train our passions to the highest degree of efficiency. Each is to acquire the utmost strength and intelligence; but all are equally to contribute their quota towards the success of the campaign.

It is nonsense to bring a verdict of "Guilty" or "Not Guilty" against a prisoner without reference to the law under which he is living. The end justifies the means: if the Jesuits do not assert this, I do. There is obviously a limit, where "the means" in any case are such that their use blasphemes "the end": *e.g.* to murder one's rich aunt affirms the right of one's poor nephew to repeat the trick, and so to go against one's own Will-to-live, which lies deeper in one's being than the mere Will-to-inherit. The judge in each case is not ideal morality, but inherent logic.

This then being understood, that we cannot call any given passion good or bad absolutely, any more than we can call Knight to King's Fifth a good or bad move in chess without study of the position, we may see more clearly what this verse implies. There is here a general instruction to refine Pleasure, not by excluding its gross elements, but by emphasizing all elements in equilibrated development. Thus one is to combine the joys of Messalina with those of Saint Theresa and Isolde in one single act. One's rapture is to include those of Blake, Petrarch, Shelley, and Catullus. *Liber Aleph* has detailed instruction on numerous points involved in these questions.[80]

"Exceed by delicacy": this does not mean, by refraining from so-called animalism. One should make every act a sacrament, full of divinest ecstasy and nourishment. There is no act which true delicacy cannot consecrate. It is one thing to be like a sow, unconscious of the mire, and unable to discriminate between sweet food and sour; another to take the filth firmly

---

[79] AL II.70.
[80] NC on AL II.70.

and force oneself to discover the purity therein, initiating even the body to overcome its natural repulsion and partake with the soul at this Eucharist. We "believe in the Miracle of the Mass" not only because meat and drink are actually "transmuted in us daily into Spiritual Substance", but because we can make the "Body and Blood of God" from any materials soever by Virtue of our royal and Pontifical Art of Magick.[81]

We therefore train our adepts to make the Gold Philosophical from the dung of witches, and the Elixir of Life from Hippomanes; but we do not advocate ostentatious addiction to these operations. It is good to know that one is man enough to spend a month or so at a height of twenty thousand feet or more above the sea-level; but it would be unpardonably foolish to live there permanently.

This illustrates on case of a general principle. We consider the Attainment of various Illuminations, incomparably glorious as that is, of chief value for its witness to our possession of the faculty which made success possible. To have climbed alone to the summit of Iztaccihuatl is great and grand; but the essence of one's joy is that one possesses the courage, knowledge, agility, endurance, and self-mastery necessary to have done it.

The Goal is ineffably worth all our pains, as we say to ourselves at first; but in a little while are aware that even that Goal is less intoxicating than the Way itself.[82]

"Be strong!" We need healthy robust bodies as the mechanical instruments of our souls. Could Paganini have expressed himself on the "fiddle for eighteen pence" that some one once bought when he was "young and had no sense"? Each of us is Hadit, the core of our Khabs, our Star, one of the Company of Heaven; but this Khabs needs a Khu or Magical Image, in order to play its part in the Great Drama. This Khu, again, needs the proper costume, a suitable "body of flesh", and this costume must be worthy of the Play.

We therefore employ various magical means to increase the vigour of our bodies and the energy of our minds, to fortify and sublime them.

The result is that we of Thelema are capable of enormously more achievement than others, even in terrestrial matters, from sexual orgia to creative Art. Even if we had only this one earth-life to consider, we exceed our fellows some thirtyfold, some sixtyfold, some an hundredfold.

One most important point, in conclusion. We must doubtless admit that each one of us is lacking in one capacity or another. There must always be some among the infinite possibilities of Nuith which possesses no correlative points of contact in any given Khu. For example, the Khu of a male body cannot fulfil itself in the quality of motherhood. Any such lacuna must be accepted as a necessary limit, without regret or vain yearnings for the impossible. But we should beware lest prejudice or other personal passion exclude any type of self-realization which is properly ours. In our initiation the tests must be thorough and exhaustive. The neglect to develop

---

[81] *Ibid.*
[82] *Ibid.*

even a single power can only result in deformity. However slight this might seem, it might lead to fatal consequences; the ancient adepts taught that by the parable of the heel of Achilles. It is essential for the Aspirant to make a systematic study of every possible passion, icily aloof from all alike, and setting their armies in array beneath the banner of his Will after he has perfectly gauged the capacity of each unit, and assured himself of its loyalty, discipline, courage, and efficiency. But woe unto him who leaves a gap in his line, or one arm unprepared to do its whole duty in the position proper to its peculiar potentialities![83]

COROLLARY XVIII.

But exceed! exceed! Strive ever to more![84]

"The Road of Excess leads to the Palace of Wisdom".[85]

Progress, as its very etymology declares, means A Step Ahead. It is the Genius, the Eccentric, the Man Who Goes One Better than his fellows, that is the Saviour of the Race. And while it is unwise possibly (in some senses) to exceed in certain respects, we may be sure that he who exceeds in no respect is a mediocrity.

The key of Evolution is Right Variation.

Excess is evidence at least of capacity in the quality at issue. The golf teacher growls tirelessly: "Putt for the back of the hole! Never up, never in!" The application is universal. Far from me be it to deny that excess is too often disastrous. The athlete who dies in his early prime is the skeleton at every Boat Supper. But in such cases the excess is almost always due to the desire to excel other men, instead of referring the matter to the only competent judge, the true Will of the body. I myself used to "go all out" on mountains; I hold more World's Records of various kinds than I can reckon—for pace, skill, daring, and endurance. But I never worried about whether other people could beat me. For this reason my excesses, instead of causing damage to health and danger to life, turned me from a delicate boy, too frail for football, doomed by my doctors to die in my teens, into a robust ruffian who throve on every kind of hardship and exposure.

On the contrary, every department of life in which, from distaste or laziness, I did not "exceed", is constantly crippling me in one way or another—and I recognize with savage remorse that the weakness which I could have corrected so easily in my twenties is in my forties an incurably chronic complaint.[86]

This striving is to be strenuous. We are not to set our lives at a pin's fee. "Unhand me, gentlemen! I'll make a ghost of him that lets me!" Death is the End that crowns the Work.

Evolution works by variation. When an animal develops one part of itself beyond the others, it infringes the norm of its type. At first this effort is made at the expense of other efforts, and it seems as if, the general balance being upset, the Nature were in danger. (It must obviously appear

---

[83] *Ibid.*
[84] AL II.71–2.
[85] William Blake, *Proverbs of Hell*, as quoted in NC on II.71.
[86] NC on AL II.71.

so to the casual observer—who probably reproaches and persecutes the experimenter). But when this variation is intended to meet some new, or even foreseen, change in environment, and is paid for by some surplus part, or some part now superfluous, although once useful to meet a quality of the environment which no longer menaces the individual, the adaptation is biologically profitable.

Obviously, the whole idea of exercise, mental or bodily, is to develop the involved organs in manner physiologically and psychologically proper.

It is deleterious to force any faculty to live by an alien law. When parents insist on a boy adopting a profession which he loathes, because they themselves fancy it; when Florence Nightingale fought to open hospital windows in India at night; then the Ideal mutilates and murders.

Every organ has "no law beyond Do what thou wilt". Its law is determined by the history of its development, and by its present relations with its fellow-citizens. We do not fortify our lungs and our limbs by identical methods, or aim at the same tokens of success in training the throat of the tenor and the fingers of the fiddler. But all laws are alike in this: they agree that power and tone come from persistently practising the proper exercise without overstraining. When a faculty is freely fulfilling its function, it will grow; the test is its willingness to "strive ever to more"; it justifies itself by being "ever joyous". It follows that "death is the crown of all". For a life which has fulfilled all its possibilities ceases to have a purpose; death is its diploma, so to speak; it is ready to apply itself to the new conditions of a larger life. Just so a schoolboy who has mastered his work, dies to school, reincarnates in cap & gown, triumphs in the trips, dies to the cloisters, and is reborn to the world.[87]

COROLLARY XIX.
Despise also all cowards: professional soldiers who dare not fight, but play; all fools despise![88]

To fight is the right and duty of every male, as of every woman to rejoice in his strength and to honour and perpetuate it by her love. My primary objection to Christianity is "gentle Jesus, meek and mild," the pacifist, the conscientious objector, the Tolstoyan, the "passive resister."[89]

The Book of the Law flings forth no theological fulminations; but we have quarrels enough on our hands. We have to fight for Freedom against oppressors, religious, social, or industrial; and we are utterly opposed to compromise. Every fight is to be a fight to the finish; each one of us for himself, to do his own will; and all of us for all, to establish the Law of Liberty.

We do not want "professional soldiers," hired bravos sworn to have no souls of their own. They "dare not fight"; for how should a man dare to fight unless his cause be a love mightier than his love of life? Therefore they "play"; they have sold themselves; their Will is no more theirs; life is no

---
[87] NC on AL II.72.
[88] AL III.57.
[89] NC on AL III.57.

longer a serious thing to them; therefore they wander wastrel in clubs and boudoirs and greenrooms; bridge, billiards, polo, pettie coats puff out their emptiness; scratched for the Great Race of Life, they watch the Derby instead.

Brave such may be; they may well be (in a sense) classed with the rat; but brainless and idle they must be, who have no goal beyond the grave, where, at the best, chance flings fast-withering flowers of false and garish glory. They serve to defend things vital to their country; they are the skull that keeps the brain from harm? Oh foolish brain! Wert thou not wiser to defend thyself, rather than trust to brittle bone that hinders thee from growth?

Let every man bear arms, swift to resent oppression, generous and ardent to draw sword in any cause, if justice or freedom summon him!

"All fools despise." In this last phrase the word "fools" is evidently not to be taken in its deeper mystical sense, the context plainly bearing reference to ordinary life.

But the "fool" is still as described in the Tarot Trump. He is an epicene creature, soft and sottish, with an imbecile laugh and a pretty taste in fancy waistcoats. He lacks virility, like the ox which is the meaning of the letter Aleph which describes the Trump, and his value is Zero, its number. He is air, formless and incapable of resistance, carrier of sounds which mean nothing to it, swept up into destructive rages of senseless violence from its idleness, incalculably moved by every pressure or pull. One-fifth is the fuel of fire, the corruption of rust; the rest is inert, the soul of explosives, with a trace of that stifling and suffocating gas which is yet food for vegetable, as it is poison to animal, life.

We have here a picture of the average man, of a fool; he has no will of his own, is all things to all men, is void, a repeater of words of whose sense he knows nought, a drifter, both idle and violent, compact partly of fierce passions that burn up both himself and the other, but mostly of inert and characterless nonentity, with a little heaviness, dullness, and stupefaction for his only positive qualities.

Such are the "fools" whom we despise. The man of Thelema is vertebrate, organized, purposeful, steady, self-controlled, virile; he uses the air as the food of his blood; so also, were he deprived of fools he could no live. We need our atmosphere, after all; it is only when the fools become violent madmen that we need our cloak of silence to wrap us, and our staff to stay us as we ascend our mountain-ridge; and it is only if we go down into the darkness of mines to dig us treasure of earth that we need fear to choke on their poisonous breath.[90]

COROLLARY XX.

But the keen and the proud, the royal and the lofty; ye are brothers! As brothers fight ye![91]

---

[90] *Ibid.*
[91] AL III.58–9.

Lo, while in the Book of the Law is much Love, there is no word of Sentimentality. Hate itself is almost like Love! Fighting most certainly is Love! "As brothers fight ye!" All the many races of the world understand this. The Love of Liber Legis is always bold, Virile, even orgiastic. There is delicacy, but it is the delicacy of strength. Mighty and terrible and glorious as it is, however, it is but the pennon upon the sacred lance of Will, the damascened inscription upon the swords of the Knight-Monks of Thelema.[92]

"The keen": these are the men whose Will is as a sword sharp and straight, tempered and ground and polished its flawless steel; with a Wrist and an Eye behind it.

"The proud": these are the men who know themselves to be stars, and bend the knee to none. True pride prevents a man from doing aught unworthy of himself.

"The royal": these are the men whose nature is kingly, the men who "can." They know themselves born rulers, whether their halidom be Art, or Science, or aught else soever.

"The lofty": these are the men who, being themselves high-hearted, endure not any baseness.[93]

Fight! Fight like gentlemen, without malice, because fighting is the best game in the world, and love the second best! Don't slander your enemy, as the newspapers would have you do; just kill him, and then bury him with honour. Don't keep crying "Foul" like a fifth-rate pugilist. Don't boast! Don't squeal! If you're down, get up and hit him again! Fights of that sort make fast friends.

There is perhaps a magical second-meaning in this verse, a reference to the Ritual of which we find hints in the legend of Cain and Abel, Esau and Jacob, Set and Osiris, *et cetera*. The "Elder Brother" within us, the Silent Self, must slay the younger brother, the conscious self, and he must be raised again incorruptible.[94]

SCHOLIUM.

The above is merely a crude editing together of all the entries dealing with the first principles of the Law of Thelema in Crowley's "Old Comment," "New Comment," and "Djeridensis Comment," supplemented with some additional material from *Magick in Theory and Practice* and *Magick Without Tears*.[95] (A first principle is one that cannot be deduced from any other: e.g. in physics, a calculation is considered *ab initio*, or from first principles, if it starts directly at the level of established laws; in philosophy, first principles are also commonly referred to as *a priori* terms and arguments, in contradistinction to *a posteriori* terms, reasoning, and arguments—the latter being "posterior" i.e. deduced or inferred during the reasoning process, while the former are assumed and exist prior to that process.)

---

[92] *Liber II*, as quoted in NC on AL I.40.
[93] NC on AL III.58.
[94] NC on AL III.59.
[95] Cited in footnotes where applicable, and abbreviated throughout the present work as OC, NC, DC, *MITAP*, and *MWT* respectively.

CHAPTER 2
Philosophy of History

The Hierarchy of the Egyptians gives us this genealogy: Isis, Osiris, Horus.

Now the 'pagan' period is that of Isis; a pastoral, natural period of simple magic. Next with Buddha, Christ, and others there came in the Equinox of Osiris; when sorrow and death were the principal objects of man's thought, and his magical formula is that of sacrifice.

Now, with Mohammed perhaps as its forerunner, comes in the Equinox of Horus, the young child who rises strong and conquering (with his twin Harpocrates) to avenge Osiris, and bring on the age of strength and splendour.

His formula is not yet fully understood.

Following him will arise the Equinox of Ma, the Goddess of Justice, it may be a hundred or ten thousand years from now; for the Computation of Time is not here as There.

—The Old Comment on AL III.34

It may be presumptuous to predict any details concerning the next Æon after this.

—The New Comment on AL III.34

Simplistic attempts have been made by latter-day Thelemites to identify this Crowleyan "Precession of the Æons" with the astronomical Precession of the Equinoxes (also known as axial precession, lunisolar precession, or the precession of the equator), but Crowley himself never unequivocally did so.[1] Though the discovery of the latter phenomenon is commonly attributed to Hipparchus of Rhodes, a Greek astronomer of the 2nd century BCE, there is evidence that Aristarchus of Samos possessed distinct values for the sidereal and tropical years as early as c. 280 BCE.[2] Other evidence suggests

---

[1] The closest he comes is in the description of Atu XI in *The Book of Thoth:* "The main subject of the card refers to the most ancient collection of legends or fables. It is necessary here to go a little into the magical doctrine of the succession of the Æons, which is connected with the procession of the Zodiac. Thus, the last Æon, that of Osiris, is referred to Aries and Libra, as the previous Æon, that of Isis, was especially connected with the signs of Pisces and Virgo, while the present, that of Horus, is linked with Aquarius and Leo." However, in the section on Atu 0, Crowley writes: "The precession of the Equinoxes has made Spring begin with the entry of the Sun into Aries the Ram, instead of Pisces the Fishes as was the case in the earliest times recorded." No allusion is ever made to Aquarius at any point having yet supplanted Aries (or more correctly Pisces, as Crowley peculiarly has the two reversed)—either in that book or perhaps more significantly in *The General Principles of Astrology*, which Crowley co-wrote with (or ghost-wrote for) the famous American astrologer Evangeline Adams.

[2] D. Rawlins, "Continued Fraction Decipherment: the Aristarchan Ancestry of Hipparchos' Year-length & Precession," *DIO* 9(1), June 1999, 30–42.

that this phenomenon, which is observed as the stars moving retrograde across the sky at about 50 arc seconds per year, was known in ancient Egypt even prior to the time of Aristarchus; e.g. certain buildings in the Karnak temple complex seem to have been oriented toward the point on the horizon where specific stars rose or set at key times of the year.[3]

Whether or not the ancient Egyptians knew of the mechanics of the precession before its definition by Hipparchus, as avid stargazers, they could not fail to note its effects. From the precision with which the Pyramids at Giza are aligned to the cardinal points, it is clear that sophisticated astronomical observation was practised in Egypt by the 3rd millennium BCE—and possibly even before that date. In fact, the Precession of the Equinoxes appears fundamental to understanding what powered the development of Egypt, for the land as a nation-state and the king of Egypt as a living god were the products of the realization by the Egyptians of the astronomical changes brought on by the immense apparent movement of the heavenly bodies which the precession implies. The Egyptians would alter the orientation of a temple when the star on whose position it had originally been set moved as a consequence of the precession, an event that took place several times during the New Kingdom.[4]

Variously called the Grand Cycle or the Yuga Cycle, the most common name for one complete cycle of axial precession found in use from ancient Europe to ancient China was simply the "Great Year." This precession was known to Plato, who defined the "Perfect Year" in the 5th century BCE as the return of the celestial bodies and the diurnal rotation of the fixed stars to their original position.[5] The Roman Cicero followed Plato in defining the "Platonic Year" as a combination of solar, lunar, and planetary cycle. In *De Natura Deorum* (45 BCE), he writes: "From these unequal motions of the planets, mathematicians have called that the 'great year' in which the sun, moon, and five wandering stars, having finished their revolutions, are found in their original situation. In how long a time this is effected is much disputed, but it must be a certain and definite period."[6]

Some time around the middle of the 2nd century BCE, the Greek astronomer Hipparchus first recognized and assessed the Precession of the Equinoxes at about one degree per century, which is close enough to the actual value of 1.38°. However, it has even been argued that Hipparchus believed 36,000 years to be the maximum figure for a full rotation, while computing the true rate of one complete precession cycle at just under

---

[3] Rice 1997.
[4] *Ibid.* Notably, one of Crowley's Masonic associates writes: "The religious symbols of Egypt, according to Mr. William Oxley's work on Egypt, changed with the progress of the sun through the signs of the zodiac, an assertion confirmed by much evidence. The era of Osiris and Isis is mythical, yet they are represented as parents of the twins Horus and Harmachis. In the year 4,565 B.C. the sun entered Taurus, and the Bull became the emblem of Osiris. It entered Aries 2,410 B.C., and the Ram becomes the emblem of Amen at Thebes. It entered Pisces 255 B.C., and we have crocodile-shaped gods, and the fish is a Christian symbol." (Yarker 1909, 58.)
[5] Plat. *Tim.* 39d.
[6] Cic. *N.D.* ii.51–52.

26,000 years.⁷ The confusion apparently originates with the great classical astronomer Ptolemy of Alexandria, who adopted the larger, erroneous figure in his authoritative work, the *Almagest* (c. 150 CE). The precession of Earth's axis was finally explained by Newtonian physics: as an oblate spheroid, our planet has a non-spherical shape, bulging outward at the equator; the gravitational forces of the Moon and Sun apply torque to the equator, seeking to pull the equatorial bulge into the plane of the ecliptic, but cause it to precess instead. The torque exerted by the planets, Jupiter in particular, also plays a role.⁸

Due to its ambiguity, the term "Great Year" may be applied to any concept of Eternal Return in the world's mythologies and philosophies. The period of 36,000 years was Babylonian and Heraclitus' 18,000 years is exactly half that period, a fact which could be connected with his way of dividing all cycles into an "upward and downward path." The Stoics held that the Great Year was a period between one world-conflagration and the next, but were careful to make it a great deal longer than Heraclitus did.⁹ In Hinduism, a *yuga* is an epoch or era within a four-age cycle, and according to the *Laws of Manu* (or *Mānava-Dharmaśāstra*), one of the earliest known texts to describe the yugas, their length is 4,800 + 3,600 + 2,400 + 1,200 years, for a total of 12,000 years for one arc, or 24,000 years to complete the cycle.¹⁰ The four yugas thus follow a timeline ratio of 4:3:2:1. However, according to the *Śrīmad-Bhāgavatam*, which is dated between the 8th and 10th century CE, the yugas are quite a bit longer, that is, 1,728,000, 1,296,000, 864,000, and 432,000 years respectively.¹¹

The long yuga count is more popular, but it unlike the short count, it does not correlate to any celestial motion found in the astronomical almanac. The value of 24,000 years, on the other hand, fits closely with the modern astronomical calculation of one full Precession of the Equinox, i.e. 25,772 years. The *Śrīmad-Bhāgavatam* describes the time spans of the demigods, in which a year of a yuga corresponds to a year of a demigod. Indian astrologers were certainly aware of axial precession since before the Common Era, *ayanāṃśa* (from *ayana* "movement" + *aṃśa* "component") being the Sanskrit term in Indian astronomy for the amount of precession. In fact, some orthodox schools of Vedic astrology reject modern astronomy and still base their computations on traditional texts such as the *Sūrya-Siddhānta* or treatises based on it.

Although many of the classic astronomical texts stored in Taxila were destroyed during the Muslim invasion of India, the 6th-century *Sūrya-Siddhānta* survived.¹² According to a 12th-century Hindu commentary, "The retrograde revolutions of that point in a *Kalpa* amount to 30,000 according to the author of the *Súrya-Siddhánta*. The motion of the solstitial points

---

⁷ Neugebauer 1975.
⁸ Bradt 2004.
⁹ Burnet 1920.
¹⁰ *Manusmṛti*, i.63–73; also *Mahābhārata*, xii.231.11–32.
¹¹ *Bhāgavata Purāṇa*, 3.11.19.
¹² Burgess 1860.

spoken of by Munjála and others is the same with this motion of the equinox: according to these authors its revolutions are 199,669 in a *Kalpa*. The place of the *Kránti-Páta*, or the amount of the precession of the equinox determined through the revolutions of the *Kránti-Páta* must be added to the place of a planet; and the declination then ascertained."[13] The Wilkinson translation of the last of these three verses is too concise to convey the full meaning, but the final value of period of precession can be obtained by combining +199,669 revolutions of *ayana* with -30,000 revolutions of *sampāt*, yielding +169,669 per Kalpa, i.e. one revolution in 25,461 years, a close approximation of the modern value of 25,772 years.

Platonism and, in particular, Plato's statement in *Timaeus* that great periods of history correspond to the complete cycles of the planets bequeathed Western culture a view of history as purposeful and directional, a view that was reinforced by Christian cosmology. Eventually, in the 18th century, this led to the formulation of the theory of progress, and Sir Isaac Newton used precession to date historical events in his *Chronology of Ancient Kingdoms Amended* (1728).[14] By the 1790s, this idea has led to the formulation of the notion of astrological ages, such as the now famous "Aquarian Age." In fact, New Age culture can by and large be considered a modern manifestation of Western millenarianism, a concept built around the expectation of an imminent historical crisis followed by the advent of a golden age—a notion which holds a key place in the history of Western ideas and continues to drive revolutionary change.[15]

The around 2,150 years for each astrological age correspond to the average time it takes for the Vernal Equinox to move from one constellation of the Zodiac into the next. This figure is obtained by dividing the Earth's 25,800-year gyroscopic precession period by twelve, the number of constellations used in astrology. When the International Astronomical Union defined the edges of all the 88 official constellations in 1929, the edge established between Pisces and Aquarius put the beginning of the Aquarian Age around the year 2600. Astrologers, however, generally dispute this approach due to the varying sizes and overlap between the zodiacal constellations.[16] According to different astrologers' calculations, approximate dates for the dawning of the Age of Aquarius range from 1447 to 3597. Rudolf Steiner, for example, thought the New Age would dawn as late as 3573.[17]

---

[13] *Siddhānta Śiromani*, vi.17–19.
[14] As Dobbs (1991, 7) points out, "one result of the restricted interests of modernity has been to look askance at Newton's biblical, chronological, and alchemical studies: to consider his pursuit of the *prisca sapientia* as irrelevant. None of those was irrelevant to Newton, for his goal was considerably more ambitious than a knowledge of nature. His goal was Truth, and for that he utilized every possible resource." That being said, Newton's original commentaries on the *Principia Mathematica* (1687), which attempt to show that the Ancients had known the phenomena and laws of gravitational astronomy, were not published until 1984 as "Newton: The Classical Scholia," in *History of Science*, Vol. 22, pp. 1–58. The present author would also hazard a guess that Crowley was much more influenced by Newton's scientific work than his Scriptural exegeses.
[15] Campion 2005.
[16] Grasse 2002.
[17] Campion 1999.

In his autobiography, *The Confessions*,[18] a title borrowed from St. Augustine, Crowley claims that his *Book of the Law* "reconciles cosmological conceptions which transcend time and space with a conventional, historical point of view. In the first place it announces unconditional truth, but in the second is careful to state that the 'Magical Formula' (or system of principles) on which the practical part of the book is based is not an absolute truth by one relative to the terrestrial time of the revelation. (It is a strong point in favour of the Book that it make no pretence to settle the practical problems of humanity once and for all. It contents itself with indicating a stage in evolution.)"[19] Éliphas Lévi explains the theory of progress in *The Key of the Mysteries*, which Crowley translated[20] and published in *The Equinox*, Vol. I, No. 10:[21]

"Progress is movement, and movement is life. To deny progress is to affirm nothingness, and to deify death. Progress is the only reply that reason can give to the objections which the existence of evil raises. All is not well, but all will be well one day. God begins His work, and He will finish it. Without progress, evil would be immutable like God. Progress explains ruins, and consoles the weeping of Jeremiah. Nations succeed each other like men; and nothing is stable, because everything is marching towards perfection. The great man who dies bequeaths to his country the fruit of his works; the great nation which becomes extinguished upon earth transforms itself into a star to enlighten the obscurities of History. . . . Civilization transforms men of good will into angels of light, and lowers the selfish man beneath the brute; it is the corruption of bodies and the emancipation of souls. The impious world of the giants raised to Heaven the soul of Enoch; above the Bacchanals of primitive Greece rises the harmonious spirit of Orpheus. . . . Christianity is the fruit of the meditations of all the sages of the East, who live again in Jesus Christ. Thus the light of the spirits has risen where the sun of the world rises; Christ conquered the West, and the soft rays of the sun of Asia have touched the icicles of the North."[22]

In *The Gospel According to St. Bernard Shaw*—which Crowley originally wrote as a criticism of the Preface to *Androcles and the Lion*,[23] as he felt the eminent playwright's "ignorance of the Asiatic life and thought had led him in to the most grotesque misapprehensions"[24]—we read: "There is nothing

---

[18] Or "autohagiography" as Crowley himself termed it, no doubt because many of the stories related therein are at least partly apocryphal.
[19] Ch. 49.
[20] *Cf. MITAP*, Ch. VII, Sec. VI.I: "When Aleister Crowley became Frater OY MH and had to write his thesis for the grade of Adeptus Exemptus, he had already collected his ideas when Lévi's *La Clef des Grands Mystères* fell into his hands. It was remarkable that he, having admired Lévi for many years, and even begun to suspect the identity, had not troubled (although an extravagant buyer of books) to get this particular work. He found, to his astonishment, that almost everything that he had himself intended to say was there written. The result of this was that he abandoned writing his original work, and instead translated the masterpiece in question."
[21] *The Equinox*, Vol. I, was "the official organ of the A∴A∴" issued between Spring 1909 and Autumn 1913 in 10 numbers.
[22] *The Key of the Mysteries*, Part I, "Sketch of the Prophetic Theology of Numbers."
[23] "Preface on the Prospects of Christianity."
[24] *Confessions*, Ch. 82.

whatever in the sayings of Jesus to show that he saw his way through any mass of popular passion and illusion. Everything that he said was perfectly commonplace to those people of his time who knew any mysticism. But esoteric doctrine having more or less slept in the west, despite such people as Boehme and William O'Neill (in whom persons not genealogically inclined may be pleased to recognize William Blake) until the Great Revival, initiated by certain persons whom I will not specify, through the medium of Eliphaz Levi, Anna Kingsford, and H. P. Blavatsky, the whole world into which Mr. Shaw was born was undoubtedly in the material bondage of which he complains."[25] The section entitled "Jesus as the typical god of Asia (with contributions from Egypt, Greece, and Rome)" goes into further detail:

> Let us therefore take a cursory survey of various Asiatic religions; we shall find many essential features practically universal, with no graver differences than unimportant local variations.
> I trust that I shall not go too far astray from the teaching of Dr. J. G. Frazer—I am proud to be the humblest member of the college of which he is so honourable a boast—if I try to summarize corn-worships, wine-worships, sun-worships, moon-worships, phallic-worships, and the rest, by indicating one point in which all agree; namely in possessing a periodic cycle.
> Nature repeats herself, like history. Whatever in Nature we most cherish, whatever we regard as most necessary to our life and joy, we celebrate; thus, all celebration being lyrical or dramatic, we choose the moment of the triumph of our 'hero' over death, whether that be the renewal of the earth in spring, or the renewal of the sun at dawn.
> In all such dramas, then, the central point is the death and resurrection of whatever it is that saves us (from starvation or what not), in a word, of "Our Savior". *{I do not here wish to imply adherence to any particular doctrine of the original reason for such celebration; on any basis the facts stand.}*
> It is also to be remembered that these celebrations were not originally merely such; the early peoples of the earth, with their history and geography limited to a few years and a few miles, had not our present certainty that nature would repeat herself, and the approach of winter may have seemed too such as a catastrophe. At first the savage sowed no seed; he simply noticed that things grew again. When some genius grasped the idea of cause and effect deeply enough to induce him to till the earth, it was a sort of magic, a direct conspiracy of man to conquer nature—and so it was. He therefore sowed his seed with all kinds of formalities intended to propitiate the unknown powers that presided over the destinies of the earth. When, therefore, we find the rising of the Nile attributed to the tears of Isis, and when we know that Isis, the great Mother of Nature, wept on the death of Osiris, the reaping of the corn, we can understand that corn would be thrown into the Nile,

---

[25] *Liber 888*, "The Alternative to Barabbas."

as it were to give her something to weep for! But Osiris being personified later as a man or man-god, the rite would soon develop into the hewing asunder of a man as the representative of Osiris, and casting his limbs into the Nile, instead of the actual corn. And the King of the country being responsible for the prosperity of the people, what more natural than to sacrifice the King himself? In hundreds of tribes this was actually done; the King had to suffer in person. This was true even of daily sacrifice in some cases. But the savage more often tried to fool Nature by dressing up a common man as the King, rendering him worship, and then slaying him.

"The above is not an actual example in all details, but it will suffice to show part of the general reasoning which led to the custom of a periodic sacrifice of a man dressed as a King. The reader may study the subject in elaborate (and even rather overwhelming) detail in *The Golden Bough*. Associate with this main idea of ritual a few obvious points of ceremonial like preliminary dedication to the powers of Nature by purification by water and consecration by fire, and we are ready to study the magical life of Jesus the typical Asiatic god."[26] In "The Death of Jesus," Crowley proposes that "the whole story of the Crucifixion is not a record of fact, but the scenario of a sacred drama or ritual of initiation":

The entire symbolism of the Jesus who died and rose again is astrological and mystic in its minutest points. The incident of the anointing, which is a regular part of any ritual, like the ceremonial purification elsewhere recorded; the "man bearing a pitcher of water" (Luke xxii. 10) which suggests the Zodiacal sign of Aquarius; the command of Jesus (Luke xxii. 36–38); to furnish swords which were not to be used, however (Luke xxii. 50, 51); the ceremonial robings and crownings and scourgings; all these things suggest a drama and not a history; a symbolic representation of John Barleycorn; not at all the record of what happened to any one man, but of what happens to all men.

The mere facts of the Nativity at the Winter Solstice, and the Crucifixion at the Equinox of Spring, suggest the birth of the year and the elevation of the Sun above the equator, which was pictorially represented exactly in this way long before the time of Pilate.

"There are dozens of variations upon this theme, but the symbols are always equivalent. The subject of the picture or the story is always the same; it is the eternal miracle of abounding life, ever self-restored, triumphant over death, the return of the Sun and the resurrection of the Seed, which makes even George Bernard Shaw, professional sceptic, iconoclast of romance, scourge of poets, break out into lyrical prose 'he will not resist you nor reproach you, but will rise again in golden beauty amidst

---

[25] *Ibid.*, "Jesus as the typical god of Asia (with contributions from Egypt, Greece, and Rome)."

a great burst of sunshine and bird music, and save you and renew your life.'[27] It is indeed a triumph for Solar-Phallic worship to add to the names of General Forlong, Sir Richard Burton, Sir R. Payne Knight, Messrs. Hargrave Jennings, Godfrey Higgins, Gerald Massey and Theodor Reuss the name of Bernard Shaw! It has been impossible in so few brief words even to glance at the evidence for this view that the Story of the Death of Jesus is merely a variation intended to epitomize many older variations of a ritual of commemoration of the mysterious activities of the Father of All in Macrocosm and in Microcosm."[28]

According to Crowley, "all ancient religions were symbolic celebrations, either of the forces of nature in the macrocosm, and so primarily of the Sun, or of the forces of nature in the microcosm and so primarily of generation. In other words, all religious ideas are related either to the life of the Earth, or to the life of man. Owing to the numerous accidents which occurred in the gradual development of civilization—and in particular we would refer to the growth of the Roman Empire—these ideas became, to some extent, confused. Political considerations entered into theology; adaptations and compromises were made by priests who had become ignorant or careless of the true traditions, and we accordingly find that these two lines of thought are interlocked to such an extent that not all the acumen of scholars, even of initiated scholars, can satisfactorily dissociate them. To take one striking example, it is very strange that the spring festival which we now call Easter should be connected with suffering and death, as in the case of Attis, Dionysus and some others. The solution is given by considering what death is—we will not say a euphemism or a blind, but a mystic truth, which only initiates of the highest class are likely in any way to understand. But the obvious meanings given by the fact that the birth of the Sun and of the year occurs nine months later at the winter solstice when Sol enters Capricornus."[29]

A whole set of traditions originating in the East continue to insist that the transcendent and the immanent are inseparable, that the body and mind, sexuality and spirituality, the divine and the human, are really the same things on a deeper level. In fact, Crowley insists that the "demonstration of anthropologists that all religious rites are celebrations of the reproductive energy of nature is irrefutable; but I, accepting this, can still maintain that these rites are wholly spiritual. Their form is only sexual because the phenomena of reproduction are the most universally understood and pungently appreciated of all. I believe that when this position is generally accepted, mankind will be able to go back with a good

---

[27] Shaw 1916, xxviii.
[28] *Liber 888*, "The Death of Jesus." Shaw was actually good friends with Professor Gilbert Murray of Oxford, one of the leading scholars associated with Frazer's "Myth and Ritual" school of interpretation; the character of Adolphus Cusins in Shaw's play *Major Barbara* (1905) was based on Murray, with the Professor's wife and mother-in-law serving as inspiration for Barbara and Lady Britomart Undershaft respectively—Murray is himself best known for his verse translations of Greek drama, with the controversial English rendering of *Œdipus Rex* (1911) being famously commissioned by Crowley's old nemesis, W. B. Yeats.
[29] *Liber DXXXVI*, Ch. V, Sec. II.

conscience to ceremonial worship. I have myself constructed numerous ceremonies where it is frankly admitted that religious enthusiasm is primarily sexual in character."[30]

From time immemorial, powerful social taboos have surrounded menstruating women. The word "menstruation" comes from the Greek μένος, which means both "moon" and "power." In pre-patriarchal times, and in many "primitive" cultures to this day, the purpose of menstrual taboos was to safeguard the woman at a receptive time, during which she might go inwards and produce prophetic information or a dream which could be useful to the community. In particular, the *menarche*, or first menstruation, was regarded as a point of both mental and physical opening, during which a girl would have dreams or other experiences that would guide her later in life, and if she were to become a shamaness or a witch doctor, this was the time when she came into a special relationship with the potent spirits of the menses.[31]

With the patriarchal takeover, however, menstrual taboos became a protection *against* women and against their powerful magic. Since men obviously cannot menstruate, they needed to come up with other ways of producing blood for magical purposes. Even St. Paul contends that, "without shedding of blood is no remission" (Hebrews 9:22 KJV). The menstruating shamaness was dangerous, so the patriarchate needed to render her powerless with taboos, and kill something—or someone—instead. *Hoc est corpus*. In his 1938 Introduction to *The Book of the Law*, Crowley writes:

> The third chapter of the Book is difficult to understand, and may be very repugnant to many people born before the date of the book (April, 1904).
>
> It tells us the characteristics of the Period on which we are now entered. Superficially, they appear appalling. We see some of them already with terrifying clarity. But fear not!
>
> It explains that certain vast "stars" (or aggregates of experience) may be described as Gods. One of these is in charge of the destinies of this planet for periods of 2,000 years. *{The moment of change from one period to another is technically called The Equinox of the Gods.}* In the history of the world, as far as we know accurately, are three such Gods: Isis, the mother, when the Universe was conceived as simple nourishment drawn directly from her; this period is marked by matriarchal government.
>
> Next, beginning 500 B.C., Osiris, the father, when the Universe was imagined as catastrophic, love, death, resurrection, as the method by which experience was built up; this corresponds to patriarchal systems.
>
> Now, Horus, the child, in which we come to perceive events as a continual growth partaking in its elements of both these methods, and not to be overcome by circumstance. This present period involves the recognition of the individual as the unit of society.

---

[30] *Confessions*, Ch. 61.
[31] Shuttle & Redgrove 1978.

In *Magick Without Tears*, Crowley explains that, in one sense, "it might be asserted that the final formula of Nature is Inertia; in other words, that the dyad of manifested existence is an arbitrary and artificial development of the Zero to which everything must always cancel out. Now by saying that, we have to all intents and purposes, answered the question which it poses; all positive development must be a conflict with that Inertia. It is the opposition between the magical Path and the Mystical; we may therefore say fearlessly that all forms of progress, although they make use of the formulae of nature which have brought them to their present situation, are attempts to proceed further on the way of the True Will."[32]

We realize ourselves as explained in the first paragraphs of this essay. Every event, including death, is only one more accretion to our experience, freely willed by ourselves from the beginning and therefore also predestined.

This "God," Horus, has a technical title: Heru-Ra-Ha, a combination of twin gods, Ra-Hoor-Khuit and Hoor-Paar-Kraat. The meaning of this doctrine must be studied in *Magick*. (He is symbolized as a Hawk-Headed God enthroned.)

He rules the present period of 2,000 years, beginning in 1904. Everywhere his government is taking root. Observe for yourselves the decay of the sense of sin, the growth of innocence and irresponsibility, the strange modifications of the reproductive instinct with a tendency to become bisexual or epicene, the childlike confidence in progress combined with nightmare fear of catastrophe, against which we are yet half unwilling to take precautions.[33]

According to Crowley, "the Æon of Isis, that of the Mother, appears to have regarded the whole of Nature as a spontaneous growth of universal scope. In the Æon of Osiris, the restriction of Family appears for the first time":[34]

The world of sentient beings is separated into clusters, each family, clan, gens, or nation, acting as a unit and standing upon armed neutrality with respect to similar groups. But in the Æon of Horus this system has broken down. That such is the case is already abundantly manifest.

Totalitarianism in any of its forms tends to break down the family structure. It considers only the Individual, and him, merely as a unit in the welter of the state.

Experience will doubtless prove that this idea simply will not work. The Individual will come to his own, but it will be impossible to reconstruct the Family System.

---

[32] *MWT*, Ch. LIII.
[33] *Liber AL*, Introduction.
[34] *MWT, loc. cit.*

It will in particular be impossible to maintain the intimate relation between Mother and Child, which has been so dominant a feature of past civilizations.

The very social and economic causes which in the old time tended to cement the relationship, have become centrifugal in their effect.[35]

Crowley asks us to consider "the outcrop of dictatorships, only possible when moral growth is in its earliest stages, and the prevalence of infantile cults like Communism, Fascism, Pacifism, Health Crazes, Occultism in nearly all its forms, religions sentimentalised to the point of practical extinction."[36]

Consider the popularity of the cinema, the wireless, the football pools and guessing competitions, all devices for soothing fractious infants, no seed of purpose in them.

Consider sport, the babyish enthusiasms and rages which it excites, whole nations disturbed by disputes between boys.

Consider war, the atrocities which occur daily and leave us unmoved and hardly worried.

We are children.

How this new Æon of Horus will develop, how the Child will grow up, these are for us to determine, growing up ourselves in the way of the Law of Thelema under the enlightened guidance of the Master Therion.[37]

During many historical periods, no difference was made between an adult and a child. In fact, the child did not enter the annals of Western history until after the European Middle Ages. The Christ Child depicted in the mediaeval Madonnas is a strange, often unpleasant-looking creature, something between an adult and an infant. It was not that the old masters did not know how to paint a child—they just did not see the child as a child. Eighteenth-century Britons were the first Westerners to dress children differently from adults, and it would appear that as life-expectancy grew, so did the length of childhood, or rather, childishness. In pre-industrial society, which did not even have a word for "adolescence," post-pubescent teens were considered adults; by imposing all the restrictions it does on teenagers, modern society infantilizes them as a part of its grand scheme to extend childhood.[38]

The only logical solution to teenage angst and irresponsibility is to go to the opposite direction and treat adolescents as grown-ups, yet today we actually have laws to protect grown people from themselves. Until quite recently, people who had reached the age of thirteen—the traditional age of both the Jewish *Bar Mitzvah* and the Christian Confirmation—were not considered children at all. And once you had been Bar Mitzvahed or Confirmed, you could marry. We are, as humans, in fact designed to breed in

---

[35] *Ibid.*
[36] *Liber AL, loc. cit.*
[37] *Ibid.*
[38] Balk 2012.

our youth. Not only is high maternal age universally recognized as the main risk factor for birth defects, but mid-teens is physiologically the best time to give birth. As a species, our reasoning abilities peak at twelve and our brain size at fourteen; at sixteen, the brain and intelligence are fully developed, yet whereas mediaeval king's minority lasted only until puberty, the voting age in most democracies is eighteen.[39]

In the U.S., the number of first babies born to mothers over thirty is currently more than double what it was just a generation ago. Many of these mothers have built up a bank account before they got married, and a half of them continue working after the children are born. And partly because the mothers are older, the families are smaller. The toy industry was once a largely Christmas-time business; until the late 1970s, two-thirds of all toys were sold in the six weeks before the winter holidays, now that industry brings in about $30 billion, and kids are getting showered with toys all year round. What is more, parents today think it is a good thing for their children to have more say over money. They want them to be "empowered," to "make their own decisions," to choose their own clothes. Younger parents, in particular, are letting their children control even the household purchases. They want decisions about the next car or house to be a family affair.[40] One might perhaps call this "filiarchy?"

To recapitulate the historical basis of *The Book of the Law*, let me say that evolution (within human memory) shows three great steps: 1. the worship of the Mother, when the universe was conceived as simple nourishment drawn directly from her; 2. the worship of the Father, when the universe was imagined as catastrophic; 3. the worship of the Child, in which we come to perceive events as a continual growth partaking in its elements of both these methods.

Egyptian theology foresaw this progress of humanity and symbolized it in the triad of Isis, Osiris, Horus. The neophyte ceremony of the Golden Dawn prepared me for the New Æon; for, at the Equinox, the officer who represented Horus in the West took the throne of Osiris in the East.

The Book of the Law is careful to indicate the nature of the formula implied by the assertion that the residing officer of the temple (the earth) is Horus, the Crowned and Conquering Child. And again, Egyptology and psychology help us to understand what is implied, and what effect to expect, in the world of thought and action.

Horus avenged his father Osiris. We know that the sun (indeed, every element of nature) does not suffer death.

The child is not merely a symbol of growth, but of complete moral independence and innocence. We may then expect the New Æon to release mankind from its pretence of altruism, its obsession of fear and its consciousness of sin. It will possess no consciousness of the purpose of its own existence. It will not be possible to persuade it that it should

---

[39] *Ibid.*
[40] *Ibid.*

submit to incomprehensible standards; it will suffer from spasms of transitory passion; it will be absurdly sensitive to pain and suffer from meaningless terror; it will be utterly conscienceless, cruel, helpless, affectionate and ambitious, without knowing why; it will be incapable of reason, yet at the same time intuitively aware of truth. I might go on indefinitely to enumerate the stigmata of child psychology, but the reader can do it equally for himself, and every idea that comes to him as characteristic of children will strike him as applicable to the events of history since 1904, from the Great War to Prohibition. And if he possess any capacity for understanding the language of symbolism, he will be staggered by the adequacy and accuracy of the summary of the spirit of the New Æon given in *The Book of the Law*.[41]

The German word *Zeitgeist*, literally translated as "time ghost" is usually attributed to Hegel, but he never actually used that word. In his *Lectures on the Philosophy of History*, he uses the phrase *der Geist seiner Zeit*, "the spirit of his time," for example, when he says that, "no man can surpass his own time, for the spirit of his time is also his own spirit."[42] This concept contrasts with the Great Man theory, which was popularized by the British proto-fascist philosopher Thomas Carlyle, who saw history as the result of the actions of great heroes and geniuses. Hegel, on the contrary, believed that art by its very nature reflected the culture of the time in which it was created. Culture and art are thus inextricable, an individual artist being a product of their time, and thereby bringing that culture to any given work of art. According to Hegel, philosophy did not stand between religion and poetry but towered above both: philosophy was its Age comprehended in thought, and the task of the philosopher was to actually comprehend what the religious person and the poet only felt.[43]

In 1818, Hegel took over Fichte's chair at the University of Berlin, and remained professor of philosophy there until his death. Encouraged by his father to become a clergyman, Hegel had initially studied not philosophy, but theology, and in a sense, all his philosophy is essentially theology, exploration of the workings of the "Universal Spirit."[44] Thanks to Hegel, the history of philosophy was established as a central academic discipline and the core of any philosophical education. It was also Hegel who established the view that the different systems of philosophy that we find in history are to be understood in the terms of development and are generally one-sided because they owe their origins to a reaction against what has gone before. Moreover, most of the significant philosophical movements since his death have been reactions against his own idealism and cannot be fully comprehended without first understanding his philosophy. The first two

---

[41] *Confessions*, Ch. 49.
[42] As quoted in Magee 2010.
[43] Hendrix 2005.
[44] Balk 2008.

great revolts involved Kierkegaard and Marx, both of whom swallowed easily as much of his thought as they rejected, most notably, his dialectic.[45]

Among Hegel's earliest writings were *The Life of Jesus* and *The Positivity of the Christian Religion*, but his sphere of interests soon encompassed all conceivable fields of study, from metaphysics to political science, and from the interpretation of ancient history to the creation of new.[46] Hegel gave the ancient concept of dialectics new life by making his dialectically dynamic model of nature and history a fundamental aspect of the nature of reality—instead of regarding the contradictions into which dialectics leads as a sign of the sterility of the dialectical method, as Immanuel Kant did in his *Critique of Pure Reason*.[47] It is not that Hegel believed that such propositions as "two plus two equals four" were true at one time but not at another, but that he thought that the truth comes to light gradually and this is what he tried to show in his pioneering lectures on the history of philosophy. Rather than emphasizing how utterly wrong his predecessors had been, he focused on how much truth they had seen; however, as opposed to being the "whole of the truth," Plato's and Spinoza's truths required subsequent qualification and amendment.[48]

Included in the Curriculum of A∴A∴ (Course I, Section 1: Books for Serious Study) is Erdmann's *History of Philosophy*, a "compendious account of philosophy from the earliest times," which Crowley found "most valuable as a general education of the mind." Johann Erdmann was a German pastor, historian of philosophy, and philosopher of religion. He studied theology at Berlin, where he fell under the influence of Hegel, and was known never to miss any of his lectures. He obtained a doctorate from the University of Kiel with his 1830 treatise, *What Is the Distinction between Philosophy and Theology?*, in which he argued that philosophy and religions converge in a common truth, even though they differ in approach. In 1834, he started writing his habilitation thesis in order to qualify in Berlin, and this would eventually become the first volume of his *Attempt at a Scientific Presentation of the History of Modern Philosophy*.[49]

As John Dewey, father of American education, wrote in the *Andover Review*: "The combination of qualities necessary to produce a work of the scope and grade of Erdmann's is rare....Erdmann wrote his book, not as a reference book . . . but as a genuine history of philosophy, tracing in a genetic way the development of thought in its treatment of philosophic problems. Its purpose is to develop philosophic intelligence rather than to furnish information.... Erdmann unites a minute and exhaustive knowledge of philosophic sources at first hand, equalled over the entire field of philosophy probably by no other one man... To the student who wishes . . . a somewhat detailed knowledge of the evolution of thought, and of what

---

[45] Kaufmann 1959.
[46] Balk, *op. cit.*
[47] Nicholson 1950.
[48] Kaufmann, *op. cit.*
[49] S. Bitter, "Erdmann: Appropriation and Criticism, Error and Understanding," in Stewart 2007.

this and the other writers have contributed to it, Erdmann is indispensable; there is no substitute."[50]

Søren Kierkegaard studied and was inspired by Erdmann's work, but although he integrated much it into his own, the only work in which Erdmann was actually cited by him was his doctoral dissertation, *On the Concept of Irony with Continual Reference to Socrates* (1841).[51] In the mid-19th century, the concept of "dialectic" was appropriated by Karl Marx and Friedrich Engels, who retooled it in what they claimed to be a non-idealist manner, and it would form a crucial element in later representations of Marxism as a philosophy of "dialectical materialism." These representations often contrasted dramatically, Henri Lefebvre's "humanist" *Dialectical Materialism* (1940), for instance, being written to directly challenge Stalin's dogmatic epistle on the same. The vigorous debate among different Marxist groups led some prominent Marxists, e.g. Louis Althusser in France and Galvono Della Volpe in Italy, to completely abandon the idea of dialectics. Either way, the concept played a long and prominent role on the world stage, and according to Hegel, dialectic is the method by which all human history unfolds, i.e. history progresses as a dialectical process.[52]

Just as in the Socratic dialectic, Hegel purported to proceed by making implicit contradictions explicit: each stage of the process is the product of contradictions inherent in the preceding stage. Only Hegel saw the whole of history as one great dialectic, major stages of which chart a progression from self-alienation as slavery to self-unification and self-realization as the rational, constitutional state of free and equal citizens. However, the Hegelian dialectic cannot be mechanistically applied just to any chosen thesis, since the selection of any antithesis, other than the logical negation of the thesis, is subjective; and if the logical negation is used as the antithesis, there is no rigorous way to derive a synthesis. Thus, when an antithesis is selected to suit the user's subjective purpose, the resulting contradictions are rhetorical, not logical, and the resulting synthesis is not rigorously defensible against any number of other possible syntheses. The problem with this Fichtean model of thesis–antithesis–synthesis is that it implied that contradictions or negations come from outside of things—Hegel's point was that they are internal to and inherent in things. This dynamic view of dialectics derives from Heraclitus.[53]

In the 19th century, the hypothesis of matriarchy representing an early, mostly prehistoric stage of human development gained popularity in Western scholarship, and this hypothesis survived into the 20th century, notably in the context of second-wave feminism. While most modern anthropologists believe that there are no known societies that are unambiguously matriarchal, the reluctance to accept the existence of matriarchies might be predicated on a culturally biased notion of how matriarchy is defined: since in a patriarchy, men rule over women, a

---

[50] As quoted in "Notices of the Press," Erdmann 1893.
[51] Bitter, *op. cit.*
[52] Williams 1989.
[53] *Ibid.*

matriarchy has frequently been envisioned as women ruling over men, excluding egalitarian non-patriarchal systems from the definition. The historical record contain no primary sources on any society in which women dominated, and the controversy surrounding prehistoric or "primal" matriarchy began in reaction to a three-volume work by law professor J. J. Bachofen, *Myth, Religion, and Mother Right: An Investigation of the Religious and Juridical Character of Matriarchy in the Ancient World* (1861).[54]

Following Bachofen and the Cambridge Ritualist Jane Harrison, several generations of scholars argued from known myths and examination of Neolithic female cult-figures not only that many ancient societies might have been matriarchal, but that there existed a wide-ranging matriarchal society prior to the ancient cultures with which we are familiar. Countless researchers studied the phenomenon, but the basis was laid by the classics of sociology. Bachofen's notion of a "woman-centered" society impacted the way classicists such as Harrison, Sir Arthur Evans, and James Mellaart looked at the evidence of matriarchal religion in pre-Hellenic societies.[55] Friedrich Engels, for his part, claimed in 1884 that the earliest stages of human social development were marked by group marriage, which made paternity disputable, whereas maternity never was, meaning that a family could only be traced through the female line. Following Bachofen, Engels argued that this was connected with a *Mutterrecht*, or the dominance of women over men, but further speculated that the domestication of animals increased the wealth claimed by men, who wished to have control over women for use as labour and to pass on their wealth to their children, necessitating monogamy. According to Engels, the status of women declined until they became mere objects in the exchange trade between men and patriarchy was established.[56]

In relating a tale about the rivalry between Athene and Poseidon, St. Augustine writes that the victor was determined by the vote of the Athenian citizens, both men and women, since it was customary those days for women to participate in public affairs. The men voted for the god, the women for the goddess, and since the latter exceeded the former by one, Athene prevailed. However, to appease Poseidon's wrath, the menfolk inflicted a threefold punishment on the womenfolk—"they would no longer have any vote, none of their children would be named after their mothers; and no one was to call them Athenians," after their goddess.[57] The citizens

---

[54] Ruether 2005.
[55] Ibid.
[56] Eller 1995. Once Engels had endorsed it, the theory was destined to become a casualty of the central ideological conflict of the era—except in the Soviet Union, where it became incorporated into state dogma. "As a result," Marxist anthropologist Chris Knight laments, "Darwinians became cut off from specialist knowledge about cross-cultural variability in human kinship arrangements and from processes driving historical change. Forced to draw narrowly on their own cultural assumptions, would-be Darwinian scientists recurrently mistook monogamy, paternal inheritance and other contemporary instantiations of Judaeo-Christian morality for core features of human nature." (Allen et al. 2008, 74.) Unlike socialists and some modern neo-pagans, however, Crowley never wished to restore the matriarchal system.
[57] *De Civitate Dei*, xviii.9.

were summoned by Cecrops, whose name tradition associates with the introduction of the patriarchal form of marriage. Athenaeus, quoting Aristotle's far-travelled student and colleague, Clearchus of Soli, says that "before his time unions had been loose and promiscuity was general. ...earlier men did not know who was their own father, there were so many [possible ones]." According to tradition, Cecrops was the first to call Zeus the Highest, and with the worship of the Father were introduced the social conditions of patriarchy.[58]

"Within the memory of man," Crowley writes in *The Equinox of the Gods*, "we have had the Pagan period, the worship of Nature, of Isis, of the Mother, of the Past; the Christian period, the worship of Man, of Osiris, of the Present. The first period is simple, quiet, easy, and pleasant; the material ignores the spiritual; the second is of suffering and death: the spiritual strives to ignore the material. Christianity and all cognate religions worship death, glorify suffering, deify corpses. The new Æon is the worship of the spiritual made one with the material, of Horus, of the Child, of the Future."[59] In *Magick in Theory and Practice*, Crowley further elaborates on the "Æon of Isis" or the "Matriarchal Age"—"The Great Work [is] conceived as a straightforward simple affair. We find the theory reflected in the customs of Matriarchy. Parthenogenesis is supposed to be true. The Virgin ... contains in herself the Principle of Growth—the epicene Hermetic seed. It becomes the Babe in the Egg ... by virtue of the Spirit ... and this becomes the Sun or Son."[60]

According to the classical anthropologists, sexuality was perceived as a divine, regenerative force to be channelled through women until ascetic patriarchy relegated such notions to the realm of heresy and witchcraft. Aphrodite, for example, was not only the goddess of love, but the goddess of eroticism; her power to remain virgin no matter how many lovers she took on terrified men more than all the lightning bolts of Zeus ever could. It was natural enough in day when man was mainly concerned with hunting and fighting that agriculture and the ritual attendant on it should fall to the woman. To this social necessity was added, and still is among many primitive communities, a deep-seated superstition. The theory goes that primitive man refuses to interfere with agriculture, assuming it to be magically dependent for success on woman, and connected with childbearing. Common to all primitive tribes are ceremonies of sympathetic magic, the gist of which is the mimicking of nature's processes. The women of ancient Attica fasted seated on the ground because the earth was desolate; they rose and revelled, they stirred the *megara* to mimic the impulse of spring—when they no longer knew why they did these things they made a goddess their prototype.[61]

Modern neo-pagans differ from the ancient pagans precisely in their nature worship; man has not had any kind of mastery over nature until very

---

[58] Harrison 1921.
[59] "Genesis Libri AL," Ch. VIII.
[60] *MITAP*, Ch. V.
[61] Harrison, *op. cit.*

recently—people of old approached her with fear. Their "nature rites" were to propitiate the caprice of the gods, not necessarily to honour them, and the first pagan revivalists like Nietzsche, Crowley, and even Gerald Gardner, well understood this. Matriarchy bestowed upon women a false, since a superstitious, prestige. The shift from matriarchy to patriarchy was a necessary stage in the evolution of man, and came with the inevitable facing of the fact that man had something to do with conception.[62] When man outgrew his belief in the magical potency of woman, he proceeded by an excusable practical logic to treat women as second-rate citizens, weaker, and not as intelligent as men. He was to no longer live in harmony with nature, he was to have dominion over her: "And God said, Let us make man in our image, after our likeness: and let them have dominion over the fish of the sea, and over the fowl of the air, and over the cattle, and over all the earth, and over every creeping thing that creepeth upon the earth."[63]

The present author further contends that the matriarchal period was dominated by the belief that events were predetermined, while the patriarchal age brought to fore the concept of free will. The fundamental difference between the Shakespearean and the Greek forms of tragedy is that, in the former, the source of causal initiative is always a flaw in the protagonist's character, while in the latter, the source of causal initiative is circumstantial. Shakespeare paints his characters larger than life: they usually have political or social power, but are shown to be flawed and secretly weak despite their great power. In Shakespeare's plays, the characters always know what they "should" do, they just refuse to do it—in fact, they often do stupid things to make their problems even worse. In contrast, the characters in the Theban plays are sincerely doing what they think is right: they don't wind up in the situations they do because of some inner moral flaw; they go about their business, do their best, one thing leads to another, and they find themselves downhill from some σκατά—which we all know rolls downhill. As simple as that.[64]

The modern novel was conceived only two centuries ago—prior to then the writer was expected to impress upon the reader the difference between right and wrong. During his internship at the Supreme Court of the Holy Roman Empire in Wetzlar, Goethe, the German poet, playwright, scientist, and statesman, befriended many intelligent young men and women, who provided the theme for his first great literary success, *Die Leiden des jungen Werthers* (1774). The now world-famous novel met with vehement opposition at first, for the author depicted the events and people as they were, leaving moral judgement to the reader. To the displeasure of the author, it also caused a mild wave of suicides, and still affects minds, albeit in a less grave manner. Romanticism was set in motion by young writers, and it is the young people who have always been the most captivated by it. In "The Sorrows of Young Werther" everyone recognized their own image,

---

[62] *Ibid.*
[63] Genesis 1:26 KJV.
[64] For an account of the gradual shift from the Homeric "shame-culture" to the Archaic "guilt-culture," *see* Dodds 1951.

and it became the symbol for and the conclusion to that oscillation between defiance and boredom, which embodied the *Sturm und Drang* period.⁶⁵

There are fundamental differences between men and women that have been shaped over millennia of evolution. For one, men and women think differently—brain scans prove this, as does plenty of other research. On average, women gather more data, consider the context, sympathize with others, and think more long-term. Men, on the other hand, are more focused, think linearly, focus on rules and the short term. In the ages past, men tended to be the hunters and needed to focus; women, in contrast, had a much broader field of responsibilities, which included bringing up children and picking the plants. Double-income families are not a modern invention: in prehistoric times, double incomes were the norm, with women putting 60–80% of the food on the table. However, following the invention of the plough and the resulting need for hard manual labour, the balance of power shifted. A situation where a woman had to take care of herself came to be considered dishonourable: the women of prosperous, respectable families were always looked after by someone else—a lone woman was a failure. Only since the World Wars have women re-entered the Western workforce and begun to regain their status in our society.⁶⁶

Crowley outlines some of the more elusive yet no less important differences between the sexes in *Liber Aleph: The Book of Wisdom or Folly*, which he addressed to Charles Stansfeld Jones, his magical son by Jeanne Robert Foster:

> Mark then, o my Son, how in the Antient Books of Magick it is Man that selleth his Soul unto the Devil, but Woman that maketh Pact with him. For she hath constantly the Wit and Power to arrange Things at his Bidding, and she payeth this Price of his Alliance. But a Man hath one Jewel, and, bartering this, he becometh the Mockery of Satanas. Let then his tutor thee in thine own Art of Magick, that thou employ Women in all Practical Matters, to order them with Cunning, but Men in thy Need of Transfiguration or Transmutation. In a Trope, let the Woman direct the Chess-Play of Life, but the Man alter the Rules, if he so will. Lo! in ill Play is Mischief and Disorder, but in a New Law is Earthquake, and Destruction of the Root of Things. Therefore is Fear of any Man that is in Commerce with his Genius, for none knoweth if his Law shall amend the Game or do it Hurt; and of this the Proof is in Experience, won after the

---

⁶⁵ Balk 2008. *Cf.* e.g. "England Speaks," *The International*, January 1918, 2: "For some curious reason, perhaps because I like to collect lunatics as George Windsor likes to collect postage stamps, I find myself regarded by superficial thinkers as a radical and revolutionary. I am in truth the most crusted of Tories, bred in the bone, and dyed in the wool. I believe, for example, that if we abandon the Catholic ideal of marriage, one may as well not have marriage at all. So, if we abandon the hierarchical system in religion or politics, one cannot stop short of anarchy, as soon as some occasion of stress forces people to make decisions.... Men are fit to hunt, fight, and create; women to cook, to labor in the fields, and to bear children. Abandon this conception with all its obvious demerits, and you merely arrive at a Bottomless Pit of vague argument, ending in the query 'What is a man? What is a woman?' A very nauseating mess!"
⁶⁶ *Idem.* 2012.

Victory of his Will, when there is no Way of Return; even thus saith the Poet, *Vestigia Nulla Retrorsum*. Nor do thou fear to create: for even as I have written in *The Book of Lies* (falsely so-called), thou canst create nothing that is not God. But beware of false Creations wrought by Women in whom is no Function thereof, for they are Phantoms, poisonous Vapours, bred of the Moon in her Witchcraft of Blood.[67]

My son, my Delight, Honey of the Comb of my Life, I will say also this concerning the Odds of the Formulæ of Male and Female, that mine Initiation was ordered as followeth. First, unto the Middle of the Way, the Attainment of the Knowledge and Conversation of the Holy Guardian Angel, were these Men appointed to mine Aid, Jerome Politt of Kendal, Cecil Jones of Basingstoke, Allan Bennett of the Border, and Oscar Eckenstein of the Mountain with no Woman. But after that Attainment hath Word come to me only through Women, Ouarda the Seer, and Virakam, and in mine Initiation into the Degree of Magus, the Cat ἹΛΑΡΙΩΝ thy Mother, Helen the Play-Actress the Serpent, with Myriamne the Drunkard, and Rita the Harlot to bear Dagger and Poison; then these others Alice the Singing Woman for an Owl; then Catherine the Dog of Anubis, and Ahitha the Camel that renewed the Work of Virakam, with Olun the Dragon and—but here I do restrict myself in Speech, for the End is wrapped about with a Veil, as the Face of a Virgin. But do thou meditate strictly upon these Things, distinguishing the right Property, Order, and Use of the Other and the other in the Relative, even as thou makest them All-One, that is None, in the Absolute.[68]

In the "Patriarchal age" or "Æon of Osiris", "the Babe is pursued by the Dragon, who casts a flood from his mouth to swallow it."[69] (See Revelation, Chapter VII.)

The Dragon is also the Mother—the "Evil Mother" of Freud. It is Harpocrates, threatened by the crocodile in the Nile. We find the symbolism of the Ark, the Coffin of Osiris, etc. The Lotus is the Yoni; the Water the Amniotic Fluid. In order to live his own life, the child must leave the Mother, and overcome the temptation to return to her for refuge. Kundry, Armida, Jocasta, Circe, etc., are symbols of this force which tempts the Hero. He may take her as his servant *{Her sole speech in the last Act is "Dienen: Dienen".}* when he has mastered her, so as to heal his father (Amfortas), avenge him (Osiris), or pacify him (Jehovah). But in order to grow to manhood, he must cease to depend on her, earning the Lance (Parzival), claiming his arms (Achilles), or making his club (Hercules) *{Note that all these three remain for a time as neuters among woman, prevented from living the male life.}*, and wander in the waterless wilderness like Krishna, Jesus, Œdipus, κ.τ.λ.—until the hour

---

[67] "De hac re altera intelligenda."
[68] "De sua initiatione."
[69] *MITAP, loc. cit.*

when, as the "King's Son" or knight-errant, he must win the Princess, and set himself upon a strange throne. Almost all the legends of heroes imply this formula in strikingly similar symbols. . . .the Sun—Son. He is supposed to be mortal; but how is this shewn? It seems an absolute perversion of truth: the sacred symbols have no hint of it. This lie is the essence of the Great Sorcery. Osirian religion is a Freudian phantasy fashioned of man's dread of death and ignorance of nature. The parthenogenesis-idea persists, but is now the formula for incarnating demi-gods, or divine kings; these must be slain and raised from the dead in one way or another. *{All these ideas may be explained by reference to anthropology. But this is not their condemnation, but their justification; for the customs and legends of mankind reflect the true nature of the species.}*[70]

"The central mystery in that past Æon was that of Incarnation; all the legends of god-men were founded upon some symbolic story of that kind. The essential of all such stories was to deny human fatherhood to the hero or god-man. In most cases, the father is stated to be a god in some animal form, the animal being chosen in accordance with the qualities that the authors of the cult wished to see reproduced in the child. Thus, Romulus and Remus were twins begotten upon a virgin by the god Mars, and they were suckled by a wolf. On this the whole magical formula of the city Rome was founded."[71] Indeed, it is "the great idea of magicians in all time" to "obtain a Messiah by some adaptation of the sexual process. In Assyria they tried incest; also in Egypt; the Egyptians tried brothers and sisters, the Assyrians mothers and sons. Phoenicians tried fathers and daughters; Greeks and Syrians mostly bestiality. This idea came from India. The Jews sought to do this by invocation methods. A.C.—also by *pædicatis feminarum* [Lat. 'buggery of women']—The Mohammedans tried homosexuality; mediæval philosophers tried to produce homunculi by making chemical experiments with semen. But the root idea is that any form of procreation other than the normal is likely to produce results of a magical character. Either the father of the child should be a symbol of the sun, or the mother a symbol of the moon."[72]

But to return to the Magical Formula of I.A.O., the "principal and most characteristic formula of Osiris," or the Dying God, formed by the "three vowel-consonants of the Hebrew alphabet, Aleph, Yod, 'Ayin," where "*I* is Isis, Nature, ruined by *A*, Apophis the Destroyer, and restored to life by the Redeemer Osiris"—"in the Seventeenth year of the Æon" (or 1921 CE), the "Master Therion," that is, Crowley, "reconstructed the Word . . . to satisfy the new conditions of Magick imposed by progress. The Word of the Law being Thelema, whose number is 93, this number should be the canon of a corresponding Mass. Accordingly, He has expanded I.A.O. by . . . adding *vau* as prefix and affix. The full word is then ויאעו whose number is 93. We may

---

[70] *Ibid. Cf.* e.g. Malinowski 1927.
[71] *The Book of Thoth*, Part II, Atu XI.
[72] *The Paris Working*, Opus XIII.

analyse this new Word in detail and demonstrate that it is a proper hieroglyph of the Ritual of Self-Initiation in this Æon of Horus."[73]

> Thus "The Devil" is Capricornus, the Goat who leaps upon the loftiest mountains, the Godhead which, if it become manifest in man, makes him Ægipan, the All.
> ...he is Man made God, exalted, eager; he has come consciously to his full stature, and so is ready to set out on his journey to redeem the world. But he may not appear in this true form; the Vision of Pan would drive men mad with fear. He must conceal Himself in his original guise.
> He therefore becomes apparently the man that he was at the beginning; he lives the life of a man; indeed, he is wholly man. But his initiation has made him master of the Event by giving him the understanding that whatever happens to him is the execution of this true will. Thus the last stage of his initiation is expressed in our formula as the final:
> F. The series of transformations has not affected his identity; but it has explained him to himself. Similarly, Copper is still Copper after $Cu + O = CuO: + H_2SO_4 = CuSO_4 (H_2O): + K_2S = CuS (K_2SO_4):$ + blowpipe and reducing agent $= Cu(S)$.
> It is the same copper; but we have learnt some of its properties. We observe especially that it is indestructible, inviolably itself throughout all its adventures, and in all its disguises. We see moreover that it can only make use of its powers, fulfill the possibilities of its nature, and satisfy its equations, by thus combining with its counterparts. Its existence as a separate substance is evidence of its subjection to stress; and this is felt as the ache of an incomprehensible yearning until it realises that every experience is a relief, an expression of itself; and that it cannot be injured by aught that may befall it. In the Æon of Osiris it was indeed realised that Man must die in order to live. But now in the Æon of Horus we know that every event is a death; subject and object slay each other in "love under will"; each such death is itself life, the means by which one realises oneself in a series of episodes.[74]

As the Roman poet Lucretius put it in the 1st century BCE, "every change that involves a thing outstepping its own limits means the instantaneous death of what previously existed."[75] However, "The seers in the early days of the Æon of Osiris foresaw the Manifestation of this coming Æon in which we now live, and they regarded it with intense horror and fear, not understanding the precession of the Æons, and regarding every change as catastrophe. This is the real interpretation of, and the reason for, the diatribes against the Beast and the Scarlet Woman in the XIII, XVII and XVIII-th chapters of the Apocalypse; but on the Tree of Life, that path of Gimel, the Moon, descending from the highest, cuts the path of Teth, Leo, the

---

[73] *MITAP, loc. cit.*
[74] *Ibid.*
[75] Lucr. 1.670–1; repeated at 1.792–3, 2.753–4, and 3.519–20.

house of the Sun, so that the Woman in the card may be regarded as a form of the Moon, very fully illuminated by the Sun, and intimately united with him in such wise as to produce, incarnate in human form, the representative or representatives of the Lord of the Æon."[76]

Crowley describes the Æonic dialectic thus: "Isis was Liberty; Osiris, bondage; but the new Liberty is that of Horus. Osiris conquered her because she did not understand him. Horus avenges both his Father and his Mother. This child Horus is a twin, two in one. Horus and Harpocrates are one, and they are also one with Set or Apophis, the destroyer of Osiris. It is by the destruction of the principle of death that they are born."[77] Dualism regards opposites as mutually exclusive entities, while monism finds each to be an epiphenomenon of the other—dialectical thought rejects both of these views. In the Æon of Horus, there are "two sexes in one person throughout; so that each individual is self-procreative sexually, whereas Isis knew of only one sex, and Osiris thought the two sexes opposed. Also the formula is now Love in all cases; and the end is the beginning, on a higher plane."[78]

The dialectical method looks for a transcendence of the opposites entailing a leap of the imagination to a higher level, which, firstly, provides justification for rejecting both alternatives as false and, secondly, helps elucidate an integral but previously concealed relationship between the apparent opposites that have been kept apart and regarded as distinct. The superposition principle of quantum physics can thus be explained using the dialectical method, as can even the evolution of the species and the planet: Darwinian theory posits the competition of a variety of species, each with heterogeneous members, within a given environment, which leads to changing species and to new species arising. A dialectical biologist accepts this picture, but looks for ways in which the competing creatures—serving as the internal conflicts in the environment—cause changes that manifest in both the creatures themselves and their environment. The creatures embrace biological adaptations that provide them with advantages, while the action of microbes, for example, encourages the erosion of rocks. What is more, each species forms a part of the environment of all the others.[79]

The above examples show the relationship of the dialectical method to the scientific method and thus largely negate the famous claim by Karl Popper that the two are mutually exclusive. In Chapter 12 of Volume II of his widely discussed book, *The Open Society and Its Enemies* (1944), Popper viciously and unjustly attacked Hegelian dialectics as being to some degree responsible for the rise of fascism in Europe by encouraging and justifying irrationalism. Hegel is now, as then, largely known though secondary sources and a few incriminating slogans and generalizations, but until that time, the resulting myth lacked a comprehensive, documented statement. According to its critics, Popper's treatment contained more misconceptions about Hegel than any other single essay, yet in his 1961 "addenda" to *The*

---

[76] *The Book of Thoth*, loc. cit.
[77] *The Equinox of the Gods*, "Genesis Libri AL," loc. cit.
[78] *MITAP*, loc. cit.
[79] Levins & Lewontin 1987.

Open Society, entitled "Facts, Standards and Truth: A Further Criticism of Relativism," Popper refused to tone down his anti-Hegelian rhetoric.[80]

Popper argued that the Hegelian dialectic "played a major role in the downfall of the liberal movement in Germany . . . by contributing to historicism and to an identification of might and right, encouraged totalitarian modes of thought . . . [and] undermined and eventually lowered the traditional standards of intellectual responsibility and honesty."[81] Whether Hegel did or did not influence the Nazis is not particularly relevant to Popper's central theses in his book, but then, according to Walter Kaufmann, most of his book is not: "The Nazi did find some support for their racism in Schopenhauer, with whom Popper constantly makes common cause against Hegel, and in Richard Wagner, who Popper eccentrically insinuates was something of a Hegelian (p. 228) though he was, of course, a devoted disciple of Schopenhauer."[82] Amusingly, "if one agrees with Popper that 'intellectual honestly is fundamental for everything we cherish' (p. 253), one should protest against his methods; for although his hatred of totalitarianism is the inspiration and central motif of his book, his methods are unfortunately similar to those of totalitarian 'scholars'—and they are spreading in the free world, too."[83]

Kaufmann laments the fact that "familiarity with Hegel has waned to the point where reviewers of the original edition of *The Open Society and Its Enemies*, while expressing reservations about the treatment of Plato and Aristotle, have not generally seen fit to protest against the treatment of Hegel; and on the jacket of the English edition Bertrand Russell actually hails the attack on Hegel as 'deadly'—for Hegel."[84] After the first American edition was published in 1950, both John Wild and R. B. Levinson wrote books to defend Plato against Popper and his followers, which go a long way towards exposing their methods. As Eric Voegelin wrote to Leo Strauss the same year, "Popper is philosophically so uncultured, so fully a primitive ideological brawler, that he is not able even approximately to reproduce correctly the contents of one page of Plato. Reading is of no use to him; he is too lacking in knowledge to understand what the author says."[85] The expressions "closed" and "open society" were taken from Henri Bergson's *Deux Sources* merely because they sounded good to Popper. He does not bother explaining the difficulties that induced Bergson to create the concepts, and "if Bergson's theory of open society is philosophically and historically tenable . . . then Popper's idea of the open society is ideologically rubbish."[86]

---

[80] Kaufmann, *op. cit.*
[81] Popper 1966, 395.
[82] Kaufmann, *op cit.*, 126.
[83] *Ibid.*, 97.
[84] *Ibid.*, 127.
[85] As quoted in Emberley & Cooper 2004, 68.
[86] *Ibid.* Incidentally, Popper's main claim to fame, the Paradox of Tolerance, was formulated years earlier by Crowley as "We are infinitely tolerant, save of intolerance" (NC on AL II.57). Both men owe a less-than-straightforward debt to Bergson, who also happened to be the brother-in-law of Crowley's erstwhile mentor, S. L. Mathers.

This "Devil" is called Satan or Shaitan, and regarded with horror by people who are ignorant of his formula, and, imagining themselves to be evil, accuse Nature herself of their own phantasmal crime. Satan is Saturn, Set, Abrasax, Adad, Adonis, Attis, Adam, Adonai, etc. The most serious charge against him is that he is the Sun in the South. The Ancient Initiates, dwelling as they did in lands whose blood was the water of the Nile or the Euphrates, connected the South with life-withering heat, and cursed that quarter where the solar darts were deadliest. Even in the legend of Hiram, it is at high noon that he is stricken down and slain. Capricornus is moreover the sign which the sun enters when he reaches his extreme Southern declination at the Winter Solstice, the season of the death of vegetation, for the folk of the Northern hemisphere. This gave them a second cause for cursing the south. A third; the tyranny of hot, dry, poisonous winds; the menace of deserts or oceans dreadful because mysterious and impassable; these also were connected in their minds with the South. But to us, aware of astronomical facts, this antagonism to the South is a silly superstition which the accidents of their local conditions suggested to our animistic ancestors. We see no enmity between Right and Left, Up and Down, and similar pairs of opposites. These antitheses are real only as a statement of relation; they are the conventions of an arbitrary device for representing our ideas in a pluralistic symbolism based on duality. "Good" must be defined in terms of human ideals and instincts. "East" has no meaning except with reference to the earth's internal affairs; as an absolute direction in space it changes a degree every four minutes. "Up" is the same for no two men, unless one chance to be in the line joining the other with the centre of the earth. "Hard" is the private opinion of our muscles. "True" is an utterly unintelligible epithet which has proved refractory to the analysis of our ablest philosophers.[87]

The case is summed up nicely in *The Heart of the Master*, where Crowley describes "how in the first period of recorded history men thought that life came from Woman alone, and worked by the Formula of Isis, worshipping Nature chaste and kindly, not understanding Death, or the Arcanum of Love. So, when the time was ripe, appeared the Brethren of the Formula of Osiris, whose word is I A O; so that men worshipped Man, thinking him subject to Death, and his victory dependent upon Resurrection. Even so conceived they of the Sun as slain and reborn with every day, and every year. Now, this great Formula being fulfilled, and turned into abomination, this Lion came forth to proclaim the Æon of Horus, the crowned and conquering child, who dieth not, nor is reborn, but goeth radiant ever upon His Way. Even so goeth the Sun: for as it is now known that night is but the shadow of the Earth, so Death is but the shadow of the Body, that veileth his Light from its bearer. Of this Prophet the Word is Θελημα."[88]

---

[87] *MITAP, loc. cit.; cf.* Fabre d'Olivet 1915.
[88] Part III, "The Initiation."

Every creed in the world that has destroyed people has been based on love. All Old Æon traditions have a version of the "Golden Rule," itself but basic human empathy.[89] Christians will tell you that the Golden Rule is their invention, for Jesus said: "Do unto others as thou wouldst have others do unto thee."[90] He may have said it, but he was not the only one, and definitely not the first. Epictetus, too, declared in the first century that, "What you would avoid suffering yourself, seek not to impose on others."[91] The Talmud says: "What is hateful to you, do not to your fellow man. This is the law: all the rest is commentary."[92] The *Mahābhārata* (c. 150 BCE) sums up duty as: "Do naught unto others which would cause you pain if done to you."[93] Five centuries before Christ, Confucius proclaimed that "What you do not want done to yourself, do not do to others."[94] And these are just a few examples. As we read in Crowley's *New Comment* on AL I.31:

> All this talk about "suffering humanity" is principally drivel based on the error of transferring one's own psychology to one's neighbour. The Golden Rule is silly. If Lord Alfred Douglas (for example) did to others what he would like them to do to him, many would resent his action.
>
> The development of the Adept is by Expansion—out to Nuit—in all directions equally. The small man has little experience, little capacity for either pain or pleasure. The bourgeois is a clod. I know better (at least) than to suppose that to torture him is either beneficial or amusing to myself.
>
> This thesis concerning compassion is of the most palmary importance in the ethics of Thelema. It is necessary that we stop, once for all, this ignorant meddling with other people's business. Each individual must be left free to follow his own path. America is peculiarly insane on these points. Her people are desperately anxious to make the Cingalese wear furs, and the Tibetans vote, and the whole world chew gum, utterly dense to the fact that most other nations, especially the French and British, regard "American institutions" as the lowest savagery, and forgetful or ignorant of the circumstance that the original brand of American freedom—which really was Freedom—contained the precept to leave other people severely alone, and thus assured the possibility of expansion on his own lines to every man.

As far as Nietzsche could see, the struggle for survival is not the rule of nature, but the exception in life. By far, it is the richness of resources that prevails in the world, not the want of them. And most importantly, where

---

[89] Though now in daily use, the concept of empathy was not introduced until the mid-19th century, originally in aesthetics, where the German word *Einfühlung* was used to describe the emotional knowing of a work of art from within; the English version of the term (from the Greek *en* "in" + *pathos* "suffering") was coined as late as 1903.
[90] Luke 6:31.
[91] *Fragments*, xxxviii. As quoted in Balk, *op. cit.*, 35.
[92] *Shabbat*, 31a. As quoted in *ibid.*
[93] 5:1517. As quoted in *ibid.*
[94] *Analects*, 15:23. As quoted in *ibid.*

there is a struggle for life, it is the strong, not the weak, who always seem to come up short. The term is not the "survival of the strongest," but the survival of the fittest. It is usually the smartest who survive—not the best, but the best adapted.[95] The whole of the formula of the dying god "depends upon ignorance of the laws of nature; there is in fact no catastrophe. *Natura non facit saltum*; all change proceeds with perfect order, ease and harmony. It is the great task set before mankind at the present moment to realize, and therefore to adjust, means of action to the facts of the case, thus preventing the illusion of catastrophe by eliminating the element of surprise."[96] The number of people who truly are helpless is minuscule, perhaps even non-existent. When the "strong" are allowed to thrive and create, those who are not as strong also benefit. When the "strong" create and innovate, work and succeed, those not willing to take the same risks benefit with employment and entertainment, knowledge and innovation. Competition may not be perfect, but it creates room for improvement while its antithesis suffocates growth and stifles freedom. Humans are hardwired by biology to want to improve and if we are not allowed to truly fail, many people will not take the necessary steps to better themselves.

As the father of economics, Adam Smith, said in 1755, "Little else is requisite to carry a state to the highest degree of opulence from the lowest barbarism, but peace, easy taxes, and a tolerable administration of justice; all the rest being brought about by the natural course of things. All governments which thwart this natural course, which force things into another channel, or which endeavour to arrest the progress of society at a particular point, are unnatural, and to support themselves are obliged to be oppressive and tyrannical."[97] Spontaneous order, also known as "self-organization," is the spontaneous emergence of order out of apparent chaos. It is a process found in biological, physical, and social networks alike, though the term "spontaneous order" is typically used to describe the emergence of various kinds of social orders from a combination of self-interested individuals who have not intentionally set out to create order through planning.[98]

Not only the evolution of life on Earth, but language, crystal structure, free market economy, and even the Internet are all examples of systems which can be said to have evolved through spontaneous order. The Scottish Enlightenment thinkers were the first to advance and inquire into the idea of the market as a spontaneous order. In *An Essay on the History of Civil Society* (1767), the philosopher and historian Adam Ferguson describes the phenomenon of spontaneous order in society as the "result of human action, but not the execution of any human design."[99] However, probably the most famous theorist of social spontaneous orders is Nobel laureate Friedrich Hayek. In *The Constitution of Liberty: Law, Legislation and Liberty* (1960)

---

[95] Balk, *op. cit.*
[96] *The Book of Thoth*, Appendix B, Diagram 5.
[97] Lecture to the Royal Society of Edinburgh, as quoted in Stewart 1858, 68.
[98] Barry 1982.
[99] Ferguson 1767, 205.

and *The Sensory Order* (1952), the Austrian-born economist and political philosopher argued that common law and the brain, respectively, are also types of spontaneous orders. The Hungarian-British polymath Michael Polanyi, for his part, made the argument in *The Republic of Science: Its Political and Economic Theory* (1962) that science itself is a spontaneous order.

"To the mind of the early Philosopher," however, "any variation in type must appear as a disaster; yea, intelligence itself must perforce prove its value to the brute, or he distrusteth it and destroyeth it. Yet as thou knowest, that variation which is fitted to the environment is the salvation of the species. Only among men, his fellows turn ever upon the Saviour, and rend him, until those who follow him in secret, and it may be unconsciously, prove their virtue and his wisdom by their survival when his persecutors perish in their folly. But we, being secure against all primary enemies of the individual, or the common weal, may, nay, we must, if we would attain the summit for our race, devote all spare leisure, wealth, and energy to the creation of variation from the Norm, and thus by clear knowledge bought of experiment and of experience, move with eyes well open upon our true path. So therefore Our Law of Thelema is justified also of biology and of social science. It is the true Way of Nature, the right strategy in the way of man with his environment, and the life of his soul."[100]

There is no need to develop the ethics of Thelema in detail, for everything springs with absolute logic from the singular principle, "Do what thou wilt shall be the whole of the Law." Or, to put it another way, "There is no law beyond Do what thou wilt." And, "thou hast no right but to do thy will." This formula itself springs ineluctably from the conception of the individual outlined in the preceding section. "The word of Sin is Restriction." "It is a lie, this folly against self." The theory is that every man and every woman has each definite attributes whose tendency, considered in due relation to environment, indicate a proper course of action in each case. To pursue this course of action is to do one's true will. "Do that, and no other shall say nay."

The physical parallel still holds. In a galaxy each star has its own magnitude, characteristics and direction and the celestial harmony is best maintained by its attending to its own business. Nothing could be more subversive of that harmony than if a number of stars set up in a uniform standard of conduct insisted on everyone aiming at the same goal, going at the same pace, and so on. Even a single star, by refusing to do its own will, by restricting itself in any way, would immediately produce disorder.

We have a sentimental idea of self-sacrifice, the kind which is most esteemed by the vulgar and is the essence of popular Christianity. It is the sacrifice of the strong to the weak. This is wholly against the principles of evolution. Any nation which does this systematically on a

---

[100] *Liber Aleph*, "De scientiæ modo."

sufficiently large scale, simply destroys itself. The sacrifice is in vain; the weak are not even saved. Consider the action of Zanoni in going to the scaffold in order to save his silly wife. The gesture was magnificent; it was evidence of his own supreme courage and moral strength; but if everyone acted on that principle the race would deteriorate and disappear.

There is here a conflict between private and public morality. We should not protect the weak and the vicious from the results of their inferiority. By doing so, we perpetuate the elements of dissolution in our own social body. We should rather aid nature by subjecting every newcomer to the most rigorous tests of his fitness to deal with his environment. The human race grew in stature and intelligence as long as the individual prowess achieved security, so that the strongest and cleverest people were able to reproduce their kind in the best conditions. But when security became general through the operation of altruism the most degenerate of the people were often the offspring of the strongest.

The Book of the Law regards pity as despicable. The reason is partly indicated in the above paragraph. But further, to pity another man is to insult him. He also is a star, "one, individual and eternal." The Book does not condemn fighting—"If he be a King, thou canst not hurt him."

There are many ethical injunctions of a revolutionary character in the Book, but they are all particular cases of the general precept to realize one's own absolute God-head and to act with the nobility which springs from that knowledge. Practically all vices spring from failure to do this. For example: falsehood is invariably the child of fear in one form or another.[101]

Aristotle begins his ten-volume *Nichomachean Ethics* by declaring that every human pursuit is geared towards some good. What he meant is that we all try to do everything as skilfully as we can; it is philosophically a self-contradictory notion for us to seek to do something badly. As Crowley points out, it "is absolutely sophistical to pretend that Christianity is not Manichaean in essence. The Vedanta theory of Advaitism in the Upanishads makes evil—and indeed all manifested existence—Maya, pure illusion. But even at this, there is no satisfactory explanation of the appearance of the illusion. In Christianity evil is just as real as good; and so long as two opposites exist they must either be equal or there must be a third component to balance them. Now this is in itself sophistical, for the third component only exists as a makeweight; and it is pure fiction to discriminate between two things whose only function is to counterbalance a third thing. In respect of the universe of discourse involved, a proposition cannot have two contradictories. If the opposite of good exists at all, as it must, if 'good' is to have any meaning, it must be exactly equal in quantity and quality to that good. On the Christian hypothesis, the reality of evil

---

[101] *Confessions, loc. cit.*

makes the devil equal to God. This is the heresy of Manes, no doubt. But those who condemn Manes must, despite themselves, implicitly affirm his theorem."[102]

> He who seeks the origin of evil, seeks the source of what is not.
> Evil is the disordered appetite of good, the unfruitful attempt of an unskilful will.
> Every one possesses the fruit of his work, and poverty is only the spur to toil.
> For the flock of men, suffering is like the shepherd dog, who bites the wool of the sheep to put them back in the right way.
> It is because of shadow that we are able to see light; because of cold that we feel heat; because of pain that we are sensible to pleasure.
> Evil is then for us the occasion and the beginning of good.
> But, in the dreams of our imperfect intelligence, we accuse the work of Providence, through failing to understand it.
> We resemble the ignorant person who judges the picture by the beginning of the sketch, and says, when the head is done, "What! Has this figure no body?"
> Nature remains calm, and accomplishes its work.
> The ploughshare is not cruel when it tears the bosom of the earth, and the great revolutions of the world are the husbandry of God.[103]

As the Victorian polymath and classical liberal political theorist Herbert Spencer famously put it in his *Essays: Scientific, Political, and Speculative* (1858), "The ultimate result of shielding men from the effects of folly, is to fill the world with fools."[104] According to Crowley, "We of Thelema encourage every possible variation; we welcome every new 'sport'; its success or failure is our sole test of its value. We let the hen's queer hatching take to water, and laugh at her alarms; and we protect the 'ugly duckling', knowing that Time will tell us whether it be a cygnet. Herbert Spencer, inexorably condemning the Unfit to the gallows, only echoed the High-Priest who protected Paul from the Pharisees. Sound biology and sound theology are for once at one! The question of the limits of individual Liberty is fully discussed in *Liber CXI* (*Aleph*), to which we refer the student."[105] Crowley

---

[102] *Ibid.*, Ch. 14.
[103] *The Key of the Mysteries*, loc. cit.; cf. e.g. *Liber CL*, Ch. IV: "Now here is the Mystery of the Origin of Evil. Firstly, by Evil we mean that which is in opposition to our own wills: it is therefore a relative, and not an absolute, term. For everything which is the greatest evil of some one is the greatest good of some other, just as the hardness of the wood which wearieth the axeman is the safety of him that ventureth himself upon the sea in a ship built of that wood. And this is a truth easy to apprehend, being superficial, and intelligible to the common mind. All evil is thus relative, or apparent, or illusory: but, returning to philosophy, I will repeat that its root is always in duality. Therefore the escape from this apparent evil is to seek the Unity, which you shall do as I have already shewn you."
[104] Spencer 1868, 349.
[105] NC on AL II.72.

proceeds to quote four chapters of which it is here prudent to include the first two:

> Consider the Bond of a cold Climate, how it maketh man a Slave; he must have Shelter and Food with fierce Toil. Yet thereby he becometh strong against the Elements, and his moral Force waxeth, so that he is Master of such Men as live in Lands of Sun where bodily Needs are satisfied without Struggle.
>
> Consider also him that willeth to excel in Speed or in Battle, how he denieth himself the Food he craveth, and all Pleasures natural to him, putting himself under the harsh Order of a Trainer. So by this Bondage he hath, at the last, his Will.
>
> Now then the one by natural, and the other by voluntary, Restriction have come each to a greater Liberty. This is also a general law of Biology, for all Development is Structuralization; that is, Limitation and Specialization of an originally indeterminate Protoplasm, which latter may therefore be called free, in the definition of a Pendant.[106]

> In the Body every Cell is subordinated to the general physiological Control, and we who will that Control do not ask whether each individual Unit of that Structure be consciously happy. But we do care that each shall fulfil its Function, and the Failure of even a few Cells, or their Revolt, may involve the Death of the whole Organism. Yet even here the Complaint of a few, which we call Pain, is a Warning of general Danger. Many Cells fulfil their Destiny by swift Death, and this being their Function, they in no wise resent it. Should Hæmoglobin resist the Attack of Oxygen, the Body would perish, and the Hæmoglobin would not thereby save itself. Now, o my Son, do then consider deeply of these Things in thine Ordering of the World under the Law of Thelema. For every Individual in the State must be perfect in his own Function, with Contentment, respecting his own Task as necessary and holy, not envious of another's. For so only mayest thou build up a Free State, whose directing Will shall be singly directed to the Welfare of all.[107]

In *The Heart of the Master*, under the subheading "The Mystery of Sin," Crowley writes: "Know therefore that this Law of Thelema 'Do what thou wilt' is the first Law ever given to man which is a true Law for all men in every place and time. All earlier Laws have been partial, according to the faith of the hearer, or the customs of a people, or the philosophy of their sages. Nor is there need, with this Law of Thelema, of threats or promises: for the Law fulfilleth itself, so that the one reward is Freedom for him who doeth his will, and the one punishment is Restriction for him that goeth astray." This is not too dissimilar to the statement of Schopenhauer *On the Freedom of the Will* (1839)—"Man can do what he wills but he cannot will

---

[106] "De vi per disciplinam colenda."
[107] "De ordine rerum."

what he wills."[108] In other words, "I then, though I were perfect in Magick, might not work in Metals as a Smith, or become rich by Commerce as a Merchant; for I have not in my Nature the Engines proper to these Capacities, and therefore it is not of my will to seek to exercise them. Here then is my Case, that I can not because I will not, and it were Conflict, should I turn thither. But let every man become perfect in his own Work, not heeding the Rebuke of another, that some Way not his own is more Noble, or Profitable, but being constant in mindfulness concerning his Business."[109]

There is a key concept in the sacred traditions of India called *Dharma*, which has no single-word translation in Western languages. In fact, it has multiple meanings in Hinduism, Buddhism, Sikhism, and Jainism. In Buddhism, for example, Dharma means "cosmic law and order," but can also be applied to the teachings of the Buddha. In Hinduism, Dharma refers to behaviors that are considered to be in accord with *Ṛta*, the order that makes life and universe possible, and thus encompasses duties, rights, laws, conduct, virtues, and "right way of living." The precise meaning depends on the context, and the general meaning evolved as ideas of Hinduism developed over its incredibly long history. In the earliest texts and the ancient myths, Dharma signified cosmic law, the rules that created the universe out of chaos, as well as cultic rituals; its meaning became richer and more complex in the later Vedas, Upanishads, Puranas, and the Epics, where the word would be used in diverse contexts.[110]

The antonym of Dharma is *Adharma*, "that which is not Dharma," and as with Dharma, the word embodies and implies many different ideas. In common parlance, however, Adharma means that which is against nature, immoral, unethical, or unlawful: "Do what thou wilt shall be the whole of the Law! Refuse this, and fall under the curse of destiny. Divide will against itself, the result is impotence and strife, strife-in-vain. The Law condemns no man. Accept the Law, and everything is lawful. Refuse the Law, you put yourself beyond its pale."[111] In his translation of Éliphas Lévi's *La clef des grands mystères* (1861), Crowley phrases it thus: "Liberty is not licence, for licence is tyranny. Liberty is the guardian of duty, because it reclaims right." He is careful to note that "Right—'droit'—a word much in evidence at the time, [is] with no true English equivalent, save in such phrases as 'the right to work.'" Lucifer—literally the "Light-Bringer"—"of whom the dark ages have made the genius of evil, will be truly the angel of light when, having conquered liberty at the price of infamy, he will make use of it to submit himself to eternal order, inaugurating thus the glories of voluntary obedience."[112]

It is strangely convincing proof of the true care of Nature for Her instruments, despite the superficial evidence to the contrary on which

---

[108] As translated in Zucker 1945, 531.
[109] *Liber Aleph*, "De eadem re altera verba."
[110] Bowker 1997.
[111] *The Equinox of the Gods, loc. cit.*
[112] *The Key of the Mysteries, loc. cit.*

the doctrines of pessimism are based, that the most precious, the one ultimately essential Grace that can possibly be bestowed on mankind is, of all Magical benefit, that which may be attained with more ease and certainty than any other. For Energy is itself all that is: and we vary with the quantity and quality thereof, which we can call "ourselves."

The price which She demands is without doubt heavy enough for a certain class; but it is equally to be paid, in varying degree, for every type of Mystical and Magical Adventure.

This price is in essence the full Understanding of the Mind of Nature Herself, and complete sympathy with Her Way of Work. All the moral codes of mankind, for all their absurd diversities, have one common factor: they pretend to have found motives and methods which are superior to Hers.[113]

---

[113] *Little Essays Toward Truth*, "Energy." *Cf.* also *Confessions*, Ch. 81: "My own word, Thelema, supplies a new and scientifically sound basis for ethics. Self-sacrifice is a romantic folly; death does not end life; it is a temporary phase of life as night and winter are of terrestrial activity. Many other conceptions are implied in this word, Thelema. In particular, each individual is conceived as the centre of his own universe, his essential nature determining his relations with similar beings and his proper course of action. It is obvious that these ideas are revolutionary. Yet to oppose them is to blaspheme science. Already, in a thousand ways, the principles involved have replaced those of the Dying God. Little remains but to accept Thelema consciously as a statement of law, so that any given problem may be solved by applying it to each case."

CHAPTER 3
Thelemic Morality

By reconciling the most opposite points of view, the Law of Thelema has supplied a Master Key to every strong room in the Safe Deposit of the human soul. The evils which afflict humanity have not an independent cause for each; the only possible form of error is the violation of the law of one's own nature. This is no more and no less true of a cripple who wants to be a wrestler, or a miser who wants to be loved for himself alone, as of a cranberry bush that should want to live in the Sahara, or an atom of gold whose dream was to combine with argon.
—The Method of Thelema

The unveiling is the Proclamation of the Truth previously explained, that the Body of Nuith occupies Infinite Space, so that every Star thereof is Whole in itself, an independent and absolute Unit. They differ as Carbon and Calcium differ, but each is a simple immortal Substance, or at least a form of some simpler Substance. Each soul is thus absolute, and "good" or "evil" are merely terms descriptive of relations between destructible combinations. Thus Quinine is "good" for a malarial patient, but "evil" for the germ of the disease. Heat is "bad" for ice-cream and "good" for coffee. The indivisible essence of things, their "souls", are indifferent to all conditions soever, for none can in any way affect them.
—The New Comment on AL I.5

A footnote in Chapter XVIII, Section II, of *Magick in Theory and Practice* quotes Crowley's "Magical Diary" on the topic: "All elements must at one time have been separate—that would be the case with great heat. Now when atoms get to the sun, when we get to the sun, we get that immense, extreme heat, and all the elements are themselves again. Imagine that each atom of each element possesses the memory of all his adventures in combination. By the way, that atom (fortified with that memory) would not be the same atom; yet it is, because it has gained nothing from anywhere except this memory. Therefore, by the lapse of time, and by virtue of memory, a thing could become something more than itself; and thus a real development is possible. One can then see a reason for any element deciding to go through this series of incarnations; because so, and only so, can he go; and he suffers the lapse of memory which he has during these incarnations, because he knows he will come through unchanged. Therefore you can have an infinite number of gods, individual and equal though diverse, each one supreme and utterly indestructible. This is also the only explanation of how a 'Perfect Being' could create a world in which war, evil, etc., exist. God is only an appearance, because (like 'good') it cannot affect the substance itself, but only multiply its combinations. This is something the same as mystic monotheism; but all parts of himself, so that their interplay is false. If we presuppose many elements, their interplay is natural."

Theorem 28 in his Introduction to the same book reads: "Every man has a right to fulfill his own will without being afraid that it may interfere with that of others; for if he is in his proper place, it is the fault of others if they interfere with him." Crowley appends this illustration: "If a man like Napoleon were actually appointed by destiny to control Europe, he should not be blamed for exercising his rights. To oppose him would be an error. Any one so doing would have made a mistake as to his own destiny, except insofar as it might be necessary for him to learn the lessons of defeat. The sun moves in space without interference. The order of Nature provides an orbit for each star. A clash proves that one or the other has strayed from its course. But as to each man that keeps his true course, the more firmly he acts, the less likely others are to get in his way. His example will help them to find their own paths and pursue them. Every man that becomes a Magician helps others to do likewise. The more firmly and surely men move, and the more such action is accepted as the standard of morality, the less will conflict and confusion hamper humanity."

There are, thus, "no 'standards of Right.' Ethics is balderdash. Each Star must go on its orbit. To hell with 'moral Principle'; there is no such thing; that is a herd-delusion, and makes men cattle. Do not listen to the rational explanation of How Right It All Is, in the newspapers."[1] Chapter XLVI of *Magick Without Tears*, entitled "Selfishness," makes the point very clear: "*The Book of the Law* is at pains to indicate the proper attitude of one 'King' to another. When you fight him, 'As brothers fight ye!' Here we have the old chivalrous type of warfare, which the introduction of reason into the business has made at the moment impossible. **Reason and Emotion; these are the two great enemies of the Ethic of Thelema. They are the traditional obstacles to success in Yoga as well as in Magick.**"[2] In other words, reason and emotion do not help, but rather hinder the discovery of one's will:

> This Property of thy Mind, my Son, is verily of sublime Virtue; for the Vulgar are befogged, and their Judgment made null, by their emotional Reaction. They are swayed by the Eloquence of a Numscull, or overpowered by a Name or an Office, or the Magic of a Tailor; else, it may be, they, being made Fools too often, reject without Reflection even as at first they accepted. Again, they are wont to believe the best of the worst, as Hope or Fear predominateth in them at the Moment. Thus, they lose Touch of the Blade of Reality, and it pierceth them. Then they in Delirium of their Wounds increase Delusion fortifying themselves in Belief of those Phantasies created by their Emotions or impressed upon their Silliness, so that their Minds have no Unity, or Stability, or

---

[1] NC on AL II.28.
[2] Emphasis added.

Discrimination, but become Hotchpot, and the Garbage-Heap of Choronzon. O my Son, against this the Law of Thelema is a Sure Fortress, for through the Quest of thy True Will the Mind is balanced about it, and confirmeth its Flight, as the Feathers upon an Arrow, so that thou hast a Touchstone of Truth, Experience holding thee to Reality, and to Proportion. Now therefore see from yet another Art of Heaven the Absolute Virtue of Our Law.[3]

Crowley marvels at the Puritan who "has even succeeded in attaching a foul connotation to a colourless word like 'certain'—'In a section of the city with a certain reputation women of a certain class suffering from certain diseases are charged with performing certain acts' is a common enough item in the newspapers. It allows the fullest play to the dirtiest imaginations—which appears to be the aim of the societies for the Suppression of Vice, and their like."[4] Nietzsche points out that morality, as such, "is merely an interpretations of certain phenomena—more precisely, a misinterpretation" and moral judgements, "like religious ones, belong to a stage of ignorance at which the very concept of the real and the distinction between what is real and imaginary, are still lacking... Moral judgments are therefore never to be taken literally; so understood, they always contain mere absurdity. Semiotically, however, they remain invaluable; they reveal, at least for those who know, the most valuable realities of cultures and inwardnesses that did not know how to 'understand' themselves. Morality is mere sign-language, mere symptomology; one must know what it is all about to be able to profit from it."[5]

"The Method of Equilibrium," as outlined in the "Postcards to Probationers" in *The Equinox*, Vol I, No. 2, makes these three points about moral philosophy: "I. Since the ultimate truth of teleology is unknown, all codes of morality are arbitrary. II. Therefore the student has no concern with ethics as such. III. He is consequently free 'to do his duty in that state of life to which it has pleased God to call him.'" As Éliphas Lévi contends in *The Key of the Mysteries*, man "has the right to do his duty, and he has no other right. O man! thou hast the right to resist even unto death any who prevents thee from doing thy duty."[6] *The Method of Thelema* further expounds the formula of this law: "Do what thou wilt. Its moral aspect is simple enough in theory. Do what thou wilt does not mean Do as you please, although it implies this degree of emancipation, that it is no longer possible to say *à priori* that a given action is 'wrong.' Each man has the right—and an absolute right—to accomplish his True Will."

It makes no difference whether it is the divine or legal law which is to decide upon good and evil as far as its justification is concerned: both are inherently arbitrary and unable to justify their universal aspirations. As Samuel Huntington points out in *The Clash of Civilizations and the Remaking of World Order*: "Hypocrisy, double standards, and 'but nots' are the price of

---

[3] *Liber Aleph*, "Laus Legis Thelema."
[4] NC on AL III.27.
[5] *Twilight of the Idols*, "The 'Improvers' of Mankind."
[6] Part I, "Sketch of the Prophetic Theology of Numbers."

universalist pretensions."[7] Can anyone really be true to themselves until and unless they break free from the shackles of morality and convention? "Every Star has its own Nature, which is 'Right' for it. We are not to be missionaries, with ideal standards of dress and morals, and such herd-ideas. We are to do what we will, and leave others to do what they will. We are infinitely tolerant, save of intolerance."[8] Crowley uses this illustration: "To insist that any one else should comply with one's own standards is to outrage, not only him, but oneself, since both parties are equally born of necessity."[9] Those who respect themselves as individuals, by definition also respect individuality in others—without this mutual respect there can be no manners.

"In the question of ethics it again becomes vital, for to many people it seems impossible to consider the merits of any act without dragging in a number of subjects which have no real connection with it."[10] As Crowley explains, the word "morality" derives "from *Mos*, Latin for custom, manner. Similarly, ethics: from Greek ΕΘΟΣ, custom. 'It isn't done' may be modern slang, but it's correct. Interesting to study the usage of '*mœurs*' and '*manières*' in French. 'Manner' from '*manus*'—hand: it is 'the way to handle things.'"[11] Trouble is, today's "morality and manners suppress all natural instincts, keep people ignorant of the facts of nature and make them fighting drunk on bogey tales. They consequently seize upon every incident of this kind to let off steam. Knowing nothing and fearing everything, they rant and rave and riot like so many maniacs. The subject does not matter. Any idea which gives them an excuse of getting excited will serve. They look for a victim to chivy, and howl him down, and finally lynch him in a sheer storm of sexual frenzy which they honestly imagine to be moral indignation, patriotic passion or some equally avowable emotion."[12]

"At the present moment," Nietzsche writes in *The Will to Power*, "we are face to face with the necessity of testing the assumption that moral values are the highest values. Method in research is attained only when all moral prejudices have been overcome: it represents a conquest over morality."[13] The present author reckons Oscar Wilde had it right: "It is absurd to divide people into good and bad. People are either charming or tedious."[14] Just as a happy and fulfilled individual is pleasant and refreshing to be around, a repressed and self-loathing person makes for tiring and irritating company. From the smallest acts of petty insult to criminal acts of physical violence, the ill will that builds up between people comes from this frustration—"ill will" and not "conflict," because happy people will still come into conflict with each other due to competing desires; they will still verbally fight with each other over conflicting values; and they will still physically attack each

---

[7] Huntington 1996, 184.
[8] NC on AL II.57.
[9] *MITAP*, Introduction, Theorem 24.
[10] *Book 4*, Part II, Ch. VIII.
[11] *MWT*, Ch. LXX.
[12] *Confessions*, Ch. 57.
[13] §583.C.
[14] *Lady Windemere's Fan*. Wilde 1997, 490.

other at times. Now, these conflicts can be viewed in a sporting sense if one diminishes the sense of threat. We are accustomed to identifying with our bodies, but we also identify with numerous ideas, images, and representations, and we react to attacks on those abstract things in the same way we would to personal attacks on ourselves.[15]

"Every individual is essentially sufficient to himself. But he is unsatisfactory to himself until he has established himself in his right relation with the universe. (Illustration: A microscope, however perfect, is useless in the hands of savages. A poet, however sublime, must impose himself upon his generation if he is to enjoy (and even to understand) himself, as theoretically should be the case.)"[16] According to Crowley, the Rosicrucian injunction to "wear the costume of the country in which you are travelling" is just another way of saying "When in Rome, do as the Romans do." However, the "object of this is not merely to avoid interference or annoyance, but to teach the mind to think down to the roots of the local customs. You learn also the great lesson of Thelema, that nothing is right or wrong in itself: as we say 'Circumstances alter cases.' One trains oneself to adapt one's life to the impinging facts: to 'cut one's coat according to one's cloth.' . . . But always behind all these must be Will, the restraining and controlling purposefulness which prevents one getting flabby, as worn rubber does. . . Remember that the slightest sign of inelasticity means that the rubber has already 'perished'; and that the test of perfection is that one can 'Snap back' to the original condition, with no trace of the stress to which it has been subjected."[17]

"Beyond all, be armed against the 'doctrinaire' type of mind, in yourself or in another. One very soon falls into the habit of repeating ones pet ideas; as the French say, *'C'est enfoncer une porte ouverte'*; and, probably before you know it yourself, you have become that most obscene, abhorred and incurable of human monsters, a BORE."[18] Obviously, one cannot follow both one's will and an artificial code of morality—even when the two don't conflict. "A Man who is doing his True Will has the inertia of the Universe to assist him. (Illustration: The first principle of success in evolution is that the individual should be true to his own nature, and at the same time adapt himself to his environment.)"[19] Moral codes that stipulate a fixed set of rules for every individual to follow equally lower the capacity of each person for their own development in their unique ways. To evolve is, by definition, to become different from what has gone before. All living things have to change and develop, and a fixed code of ethics cannot grow with them. Only the individual himself can judge what action is right for him at any one time—if he becomes rigid and unbending, he stops growing and begins to die.[20]

---

[15] Balk 2012.
[16] *MITAP, loc. cit.*, Theorem 22.
[17] *MWT*, Ch. LXII.
[18] *Ibid.*
[19] *MITAP, loc. cit.*, Theorem 9.
[20] Balk, *op. cit.*

Of course, "there are no rules until one finds them: a man leaving Ireland for the Sahara does well to discard such 'indispensable' and 'proper' things as a waterproof and a blackthorn for a turban and a dagger. The 'moral' man is living by the no-reason of Laws, and that is stupid and inadequate even when the Laws still hold good; for he is a mere mechanism, resourceless should any danger that is not already provided for in his original design chance to arise. Respect for routine is the mark of the second-rate man. The 'immoral' man, defying convention by shouting aloud in church, may indeed be 'brawling'; but equally he may be a sensitive who has felt the first tremor of an earthquake."[21] Thus, "there is for every one of us an instinct, at least, of what is 'right' and what is wrong... And it is plain enough that you understand the validity of this sense in itself, in its own right, wholly independent of any Codes or systems whatsoever. Of what, then, is this instinct the hieroglyph? Our destructive criticism is perfect as regards teleology; nobody knows what to do in order to act 'for the best.' Even the greatest Chess Master cannot be sure how his new pet variation will turn out in practice; and the chessboard is surely an admirable type of a limited 'universe of discourse' and 'field of action.'"[22]

"The Law of Thelema helps us deal with the question [Does the end justify the means?] very simply and succinctly. First, it obviates the need of defining the proper 'End'; for with us this becomes identical with the 'True Will'; and we are bound to assume that the man himself is the sole arbiter; we postulate that his 'End' is self-justified. Then as to his 'Means': as he cannot possibly know for certain whether they are suitable or not, he can only rely on his inherited instincts, his learning, his traditions, and his experience. Of these all but the first lie wholly in the intellectual Sphere... and can accordingly be knocked into any desired shape at will, by dint of a little manipulation: and if Thelema has freed him morally, as it should have done, from all the nonsense of Plato, Manu, Draco, Solon, Paul (with his harpy brood), John Stuart Mill and Kant, he can make his decision with purely objective judgment. (Where would mathematics be if certain solutions were *a priori* inadmissible?) ... What I really mean is that these two terms are unconnected. One decides about the 'End' in one way: about the 'Means' in another. But every proposition in your sorites has got to justify itself; and, having done so, to estimate its exact weight in relation to all the other terms of your problem."[23]

> Shameful confession, one of my own Chelas (or so it is rather incredibly reported to me) said recently: "Self-discipline is a form of Restriction." (That, you remember, is "The word of Sin...".) Of all the utter rubbish! (Anyhow, he was a "centre of pestilence" for discussing the Book at all.) About 90% of Thelema, at a guess, is nothing but self-discipline. One is only allowed to do anything and everything so as to have more scope for exercising that virtue.

---

[21] NC on AL II.72.
[22] *MWT*, Ch. XLIX.
[23] *Ibid.*

Concentrate on "...thou hast no right but to do thy will." The point is that any possible act is to be performed if it is a necessary factor in that Equation of your Will. Any act that is not such a factor, however harmless, noble, virtuous or what not, is at the best a waste of energy. But there are no artificial barriers on any type of act in general. The standard of conduct has one single touchstone. There may be—there will be—every kind of difficulty in determining whether, by this standard, any given act is "right" or "wrong": but there should be no confusion. No act is righteous in itself, but only in reference to the True Will of the person who proposes to perform it. This is the Doctrine of Relativity applied to the moral sphere.[24]

Thus: "It is a virtue in a diabetic not to eat sugar, but only in reference to his own condition. It is not a virtue of universal import. Elijah said on one occasion: 'I do well to be angry;' but such occasions are rare. Moreover, one man's meat is another man's poison. An oath of poverty might be very useful for a man who was unable intelligently to use his wealth for the single end proposed; to another it would be simply stripping himself of energy, causing him to waste his time over trifles."[25] Keep in mind, "the opposition of two movements is not always evidence of conflict or error. For two opposite points upon the rim of a wheel move one North, the other South; yet are they harmonious parts of the same system. And the rowlock which resisteth the oar hindereth not but aideth the True Will of that oar. So then self-control is nowise the enemy of Freedom, but that which maketh it possible. And he who would deliver a muscle from its bondage to its bone by severing it rendereth that muscle impotent."[26]

"There is no such thing as self-denial. Self-denial is merely the self-indulgence of self-denying people."[27] In *The Gospel According to St. Bernard Shaw*, Crowley relates "an old, old story of an old-old woman, very benighted, who had not heard of Christianity till the Scripture reader came and read her the story of the Crucifixion, at which she wept copiously; but she soon dried her tears, remarking: 'after all, it was 'is 'obby'. Do what thou wilt shall be the whole of the Law; or, as Mr. Shaw himself once said, 'The golden rule is that there is no golden rule.'"[28]

Again, it is almost impossible for the well-mannered Christian to realize that Jesus Christ ate with his fingers. The temperance advocate makes believe that the wine at the marriage feast of Cana was non-alcoholic.
It is a sort of mad syllogism.
"Nobody whom I respect does this."
"I respect So-and-so."
"Therefore, So-and-so did not do this."

---

[24] *Ibid.*, Ch. LXX.
[25] *Book 4*, Part II, Ch. VI.
[26] *The Heart of the Master*, Part III, "The Mystery of Sin."
[27] *Liber 888*, "The Case for Marriage."
[28] *Ibid.*

The moralist of today is furious when one points to the fact that practically every great man in history was grossly and notoriously immoral.

Enough of this painful subject!

As long as we try to fit facts to theories instead of adopting the scientific attitude of altering the theories (when necessary) to fit the facts, we shall remain mired in falsehood.

The religious taunt the scientific man with this open-mindedness, with this adaptability. "Tell a lie and stick to it!" is *their* golden rule.[29]

According to Crowley, the sexual morality of *The Book of the Law* "is not very different from that maintained secretly by aristocrats since the world began. It is the system natural to any one who has psycho-analysed away all his complexes, repressions, fixations and phobias."[30] Regardless of what "your sexual predilections may be, you are free, by the Law of Thelema, to be the star you are, to go your own way rejoicing. It is not indicated here in this text, though it is elsewhere implied, that only one symptom warns that you have mistaken your true Will, and this, if you should imagine that in pursuing your way you interfere with that of another star. It may, therefore, be considered improper, as a general rule, for your sexual gratification to destroy, deform, or displease any other star. Mutual consent to the act is the condition thereof. It must, of course, be understood that such consent is not always explicit. There are cases when seduction or rape may be emancipation or initiation to another. Such acts can only be judged by their results."[31]

"Any man who is Abnormal sexually, if he should combine with this defect a powerful intellect and some degree of personality, is a far more dangerous wild beast than any dragon of fable. Paul was evidently a monster of this type. . . .It is Paul who is obsessed by sex, and to such an extent that he makes 'sin' of it; instead of regarding it as a perfectly natural human appetite like eating or drinking. A celibate *is* a sort of monster. The sexual process is connected so closely with consciousness (or, if you prefer it, subconsciousness *{The psycho-analysts now call this 'unconsciousness', an awkwardly ambiguous word.}*) that any departure from the normal colours not only the mind but the character in the most fantastic ways. We have only to think of the notorious cruelty of eunuchs, the peculiar modifications of character noticeable in old maids, and the actual changes in physical appearance determined by these limitations. One may think of the extremely common insanities associated with puberty on the one hand, and on the other the occurrence of the menopause in women, and of impotence in men. . . The average man, if deprived of proper care in this matter, may become a dangerous lunatic for the time being."[32]

"It is possible for people engaged in violent athletic exercise involving real hardship and bodily emaciation, such as explorers, to be perfectly

---

[29] *Book 4*, Part II, Ch. VIII. Emphasis in original.
[30] *MWT*, Ch. XLVIII.
[31] NC on AL I.52.
[32] *Liber 888*, "Paul." Emphasis in original.

undisturbed by long privation. But any one with any knowledge of schools and universities is acquainted with the lack of mental balance caused by this kind of disturbance. Religious hysteria at the age of puberty is an almost universal phenomenon. We do not find the average man of the world is in any way obsessed by sex. It is the abnormal people who talk, and talk, and talk about it in a way which is nauseating even though it be so pitiful!"[33] Once again, Éliphas Lévi concurs:

> Magnetic maladies are the road to madness; they are always born from the hypertrophy or atrophy of the nervous system.
> They resemble hysteria, which is one of their varieties, and are often produced either by excesses of celibacy, or those or exactly the opposite kind.
> One knows how closely connected with the brain are the organs charged by Nature with the accomplishment of her noblest work: those whose object is the reproduction of being.
> One does not violate with impunity the sanctuary of Nature.
> Without risking his own life, no one lifts the veil of the great Isis.
> Nature is chaste, and it is to chastity that she gives the key of life.
> To give oneself up to impure loves is to plight one's troth to death.
> Liberty, which is the life of the soul, is only preserved in the order of Nature. Every voluntary disorder wounds it, prolonged excess murders it.[34]

Crowley's *New Comment* on AL III.20 reads: "There is here a perception of the profound law which opposes thought to action. We act, when we act aright, upon the instructive wisdom inherited from the ages. Our ancestors survived because they were able to adapt themselves to their environment; their rivals failed to breed, and so 'good' qualities are transmitted, while 'bad' are sterile. Thus the race-thought, subconscious, tells a man that he must have a son, cost what it may. Rome was founded on the rape of the Sabine women. Would a reasoner have advocated that rape? Was it 'justice' or 'mercy' or 'morality' or 'Christianity'." If there is no God or anyone else who can without invocation of blind faith in paradoxes due to absence of both reason and logic set a universal good and evil, then we have only one place to look for right and wrong: the amoral reality of nature itself. There is no good or evil in biology, chemistry, or physics, any more than there is in the mathematics of the multiplication of two times two. But there is a right and a wrong, and it is nature—and only nature—which unilaterally, unconsciously, amorally, and through the economics of its variables, establishes it.

"There is much on the ethics of this point in Chapter II of this Book. Thomas Henry Huxley in his essay 'Ethics and Evolution' pointed out the antithesis between these two ideas; and concluded that Evolution was bound to beat Ethics in the long run. He was apparently unable to see, or

---

[33] *Ibid.*
[34] *The Key of the Mysteries*, Part III, Book I, Ch. III.

unwilling to admit, that his argument proved Ethics (as understood by Victorians) to be false. The Ethics of *Liber Legis* are those of Evolution itself. We are only fools if we interfere. Do what thou wilt shall be the whole of the Law, biologically as well as in every other way."[35] A "selfless" deed usually interferes with the will of another; as Arthur Koestler observes, "wars are not fought for personal gain, but out of loyalty and devotion to king, country or cause. . . . Homicide for unselfish reasons, at the risk of one's own life, is the dominant phenomenon in history."[36] Conversely, as long as we do not interfere, selfishness has no adverse consequences: in fact, the only way we can really better society is by bettering ourselves. This is, of course, also consonant with the Buddhist belief that there is no such thing as a truly selfless act: if someone strives to be totally altruistic, he only does so from the egotistical need to achieve an altruistic state of being.[37]

People who think they're making the world a better place violently dislike having this belief challenged, because their motivator is feeling good about themselves. Even mother's love has been proven selfish by modern science; after all, it is the protection of what one definitely knows to be one's own DNA. And is a person who gives his life for another because it's "not worth living without them" really sacrificing anything? As Eric Hoffer remarked in his famous investigation of mass movements, self-sacrifice is easier than self-realization: "The burning conviction that we have a holy duty toward others is often a way of attaching our drowning selves to a passing raft. What looks like giving a hand is often a holding on for dear life. Take away our holy duties and you leave our lives puny and meaningless. There is no doubt that in exchanging a self-centered for a selfless life we gain enormously in self-esteem. The vanity of the selfless, even those who practice utmost humility, is boundless."[38] The fanatic is always more interested in other people than he is in himself, and the kind of person who cares nothing of himself will never have anything of worth to offer others.

"'But the A∴A∴ oath; aren't you—we—all out to improve the race, not counting the cost to ourselves!' Pure selfishness, child, with foresight! I want a decent place to live in next time I come back. And a longer choice of first-rate vehicles for my Work."[39] Nietzsche's answer to the question "For what does one have to atone most?" is "For one's modesty; for having failed to listen to one's most personal requirements; for having mistaken oneself; for having underestimated oneself; for having lost a good ear for one's instincts: this lack of reverence for oneself revenges itself through every kind of deprivation: health, friendship, well-being, pride, cheerfulness, freedom, firmness, courage. One never afterward forgives oneself for this lack of genuine egoism: one takes it for an objection, for a doubt about a

---

[35] NC on AL III.20. *Cf.* also *Liber 888*, "For Better, for Worse"—"It appears to lead to the conclusion that kindness and conscientiousness and altruism are really drawbacks to the progress of humanity. As Nietzsche said this, and I too agree with him, there is little more to be said."
[36] Koestler 1981, 130.
[37] Balk, *op. cit.*
[38] Hoffer 1951, 14–15.
[39] *MWT*, Ch. XLVI.

real ego."[40] Self-interested and self-responsible individuals selfishly pursuing their dreams tend to contribute as much to the well-being of others as to their own, and at the very least, leave others free to pursue their own dreams.

Even Mahatma Gandhi, perhaps the world's most renowned pacifist, declared that: "A 'No' uttered from deepest conviction is better and greater than a 'Yes' merely uttered to please, or what is worse, to avoid trouble."[41] A man at odds with himself is at odds with the whole universe, and "a city divided against itself cannot stand."[42] We never really make enemies, we just run into them: "Having crushed all volitions in ourselves, and if necessary in others, which we find opposing our real Will, that Will itself will grow naturally with greater freedom. But it is not only necessary to purify the temple itself and consecrate it; invocations must be made. Hence it is necessary to be constantly doing things of a positive, not merely of a negative nature, to affirm that Will. Renunciation and sacrifice are necessary, but they are comparatively easy. There are a hundred ways of missing, and only one of hitting. To avoid eating beef is easy; to eat nothing but pork is very difficult."[43]

"Ultimately the Magical Will so identifies itself with the man's whole being that it becomes unconscious, and is as constant a force as gravitation. One may even be surprised at one's own acts, and have to reason out their connection. But let it be understood that when the Will has thus really raised itself to the height of Destiny, the man is no more likely to do wrong than he is to float off into the air."[44] Crowley answers the question "Is there not a conflict between this development of the Will and Ethics?" in the affirmative: "With many people custom and habit—of which ethics is but the social expression—are the things most difficult to give up: and it is a useful practice to break any habit just to get into the way of being free from that form of slavery. Hence we have practices for breaking up sleep, for putting our bodies into strained and unnatural positions, for doing difficult exercises of breathing—all these, apart from any special merit they may have in themselves for any particular purpose, have the main merit that the man forces himself to do them despite any conditions that may exist. Having conquered internal resistance one may conquer external resistance more easily. In a steam boat the engine must first overcome its own inertia before it can attack the resistance of the water."[45]

> Yet this I charge thee with my Might: Live Dangerously. Was not this the Word of thine Uncle Friedrich Nietzsche? Thy meanest Foe is the Inertia of the Mind. Men do hate most those things which touch them closely, and they fear Light, and persecute the Torchbearers. Do thou therefore analyse most fully all those Ideas which Men avoid; for the

---

[40] *The Will to Power*, §918.
[41] Gandhi 1935, 119.
[42] Matthew 12:25.
[43] *Book 4*, Part II, Ch. VI.
[44] *Ibid.*
[45] *Ibid.*

Truth shall dissolve Fear. Rightly indeed Men say that the Unknown is terrible; but wrongly do they fear lest it become the Known. Moreover, do thou all Acts of which the common Sort beware, save where thou hast already full knowledge, that thou mayest learn Use and Control, not falling into Abuse and Slavery. For the Coward and the Foolhardy shall not live out their Days. Every Thing has its right Use; and thou art great as thou hast Use of Things. This is the Mystery of all Art Magick, and thine Hold upon the Universe. Yet if thou must err, being human, err by excess of courage rather than of Caution, for it is the Foundation of the Honour of Man that he dareth greatly. What sayth Quintus Horatius Flaccus in the third Ode of his First Book? Die thou standing![46]

As Crowley attests in his *Eight Lectures on Yoga*: "It is much more difficult to comply with the Law of Thelema than to follow out slavishly a set of dead regulations. Almost the only point of emancipation, in the sense of relief from a burden, is just the difference between Life and Death."[47] It is the 21st Axiom of Lévi's Theory of the Will that a "chain of iron is easier to break than a chain of flowers."[48] Most people tend to go on "from day to day with a little of this and a little of that, a few kind thoughts and a few unkind thoughts; nothing really gets done. Body and mind are changed, changed beyond recall by nightfall. But what *meaning* has any of this change? How few there are who can look back through the years and say that they have made advance in any definite direction? And in how few is that change, such as it is, a variable with intelligence and conscious volition! The dead weight of the original conditions under which we were born has counted for far more than all our striving. The unconscious forces are incomparably greater than those of which we have any knowledge."[49]

As the 7th Theorem from *Magick in Theory and Practice* puts it: "Every man and every woman has a course, depending partly on the self, and partly on the environment which is natural and necessary for each. Anyone who is forced from his own course, either through not understanding himself, or through external opposition, comes into conflict with the order of the Universe, and suffers accordingly." Crowley illustrates this thus: "A man may think it is his duty to act in a certain way, through having made a fancy picture of himself, instead of investigating his actual nature. For example, a woman may make herself miserable for life by thinking that she prefers love to social consideration, or vice versa. One woman may stay with an unsympathetic husband when she would really be happy in an attic with a lover, while another may fool herself into a romantic elopement when her only pleasures are those of presiding over fashionable functions. Again, a boy's instinct may tell him to go to sea, while his parents insist on his becoming a doctor. In such a case he will be both unsuccessful and unhappy in medicine."

---

[46] *Liber Aleph*, "De virtute audendi."
[47] Ch. 2, Sec. 10.
[48] *The Key of the Mysteries*, Part III, Book II, Ch. I.
[49] *Book 4*, Part II, Ch. IX. Emphasis in original.

My Son, there are afflictions many and woes many, that come of the errors of men in respect of the will; but there is none greater than this, the interference of the busy-body. For they make pretence to know a man's thought better than he doth himself, and to direct his will with more wisdom than he, and to make plans for his happiness. And of all these the worst is he that sacrificeth himself for the weal of his fellows. He that is so foolish as not to follow his own will, how shall be so wise as to pursue that of another? If mine horse balk at a fence, should some varlet come behind him, and strike at his hoofs? Nay, Son, pursue thy path in peace, that thy brother beholding thee may take courage from thy bearing, and comfort from his confidence that thou wilt not hinder him by thy superfluity of compassion. Let me not begin to tell thee of the mischiefs that I have seen, whose root was in kindness, whose flower was in self-sacrifice, and whose fruit in catastrophe. Verily I think there should be no end hereof. Strike, rob, slay thy neighbour, but comfort him not unless he ask it of thee, and if he ask it, be wary.[50]

The idea of enduring political peace is a relatively new concept. For the first time since a furless biped grabbed a stone in anger, the Charter of the United Nations seeks to eliminate war and to help the nations of the world to "live together in peace with one another as good neighbours," despite the abysmal failure of millennia of philosophical and religious teaching to accomplish anything of the sort. Talking as a means of resolving conflict actually goes against every biological instinct that we have; we feel threatened, so we fight, or if we don't have the stomach for that, we run. People go out of their way to get along, because they've been trained to "go along to get along" since they were in kindergarten; at some point, a person has to have personal principles, because otherwise he can get talked into anything. Accepting an external code of behaviour is likely to cause internal conflict, and is it not the inner peace that matters?[51] "All life is conflict. Every breath that you draw represents a victory in the struggle of the whole Universe. You can't have peace without perfect mastery of circumstance."[52]

Conflict is a natural state at every level of human existence. Outward peace involves structures, organizations, and laws which exist to manage that conflict over many years. Far from being a natural condition, peace is something that always develops only over long periods of time with a great deal of hard work and much backsliding. It is no more a natural state of society than war is. Conflicts are perpetual, and during peacetime, boil up until they explode into open warfare.[53] "To allow oneself to be carried away by a multitude of conflicting concerns, to surrender to too many projects, to want to help everyone in everything is to succumb to violence. More than that, it is cooperation in violence," wrote Thomas Merton. "The frenzy of the activist neutralizes his work for peace. It destroys his own inner capacity

---

[50] *Liber Aleph*, "De stultis malignis."
[51] Balk, *op. cit.*
[52] *MWT*, Introduction.
[53] Balk, *op. cit.*

for peace."⁵⁴ Crowley offered this blunt advice to the young yogi: "If the barking of a dog disturbs your meditation, it is simplest to shoot the dog, and think no more about it."⁵⁵

The fact is, "we are plagued with Meddlesome Matties, male and female, whose one overmastering passion is to mind other peoples' business. They can think of nothing but 'control.' They aim at an Ethic like that of the convict Prison; at a civilization like that of the Bees or the Termites. But neither history nor biology acquaint us with any form of progress achieved by any of these communities. Penal settlements and Pall Mall Clubs have not even made provision for the perpetuation of their species; and all such 'well-ordered' establishments are quite evidently defenceless against any serious change in their environment. They have failed to comply with the first requirements of biology; at best, they stagnate, they achieve nothing, they never 'get anywhere.' A settled society is useful at certain periods; when, for instance, it is advisable to consolidate the gains gotten by pioneer adventurers; but history shows with appalling clarity that the very qualities which serve to protect must inevitably destroy the very conditions which they aim to preserve."⁵⁶

So how is humanity able to progress? "Not by the tinkering of the meliorist; not by the crushing of initiative; not by laws and regulations which hamstring the racehorse, and handcuff the boxer; but by the innovations of the eccentric, by the phantasies of the hashish-dreamer of philosophy, by the aspirations of the idealist to the impossible, by the imagination of the revolutionary, by the perilous adventure of the pioneer. Progress is by leaps and bounds, but breaking from custom, by working on untried experiments; in short, by the follies and crimes of men of genius, only recognizable as wisdom and virtue after they have been tortured to death, and their murderers reap gloatingly the harvest of the seeds they sowed at midnight."⁵⁷ As Lévi observes, the "abysses of grace correspond to the abysses of perversity. God has often made saints of scoundrels; but He has never done anything with the half-hearted and the cowardly. Under penalty of reprobation, one must work, one must act. Nature, moreover, sees to this, and if we will not march on with all our courage towards life, she flings us with all her forces towards death. She drags those who will not walk."⁵⁸

> The most fatal enemy of our souls is idleness. Inertia intoxicates us and sends us to sleep; but the sleep of inertia is corruption and death. The faculties of the human soul are like the waves of the ocean. To keep them sweet, they need the salt and bitterness of tears: they need the whirlwinds of Heaven: they need to be shaken by the storm.
>
> When, instead of marching upon the path of progress, we wish to have ourselves carried, we are sleeping in the arms of death. It is to us

---

⁵⁴ Merton 1966, 73.
⁵⁵ *Book 4*, Part I, Ch. III.
⁵⁶ *MWT*, Ch. LXIX.
⁵⁷ *Ibid.*
⁵⁸ *The Key of the Mysteries, loc. cit.*, Ch. IV.

that it is spoken, as to the paralytic man in the Gospel, "Take up thy bed and walk!" It is for us to carry death away, to plunge it into life.

Consider the magnificent and terrible metaphor of St. John; Hell is a sleeping fire. It is a life without activity and without progress; it is sulphur in stagnation: *stagnum ignis et sulphuris*.

The sleeping life is like the idle word, and it is of that that men will have to give an account in the Day of Judgment.[59]

"There is no harm in man's experimenting with opium-smoking or feeding on nuts," Crowley insists, "but the moment he ceases to examine, to act from habit and without reflection, he is in trouble. We all of us eat too much, because people, liveried and obsequious, have always bustled up five times daily with six months' provisions, and it was less trouble to feed and be done with it, than to examine the question whether we were hungry. If you cook your own food, you soon find that you don't cook more or less than you want; and health returns. If, however, you go to the other extreme and think of nothing but diet, you are almost sure to acquire that typical form of melancholia, in which the patient is convinced that all the world is in league to poison him. Professor Schweinhund has shown that beef causes gout; Professor Naschtikoff proves that milk causes consumption. Sir Ruffon Wratts tells us that old age is brought on by eating cabbage. By and by you reach the state of which Mr. Hereward Carrington make his proud boast: your sole food is chocolate, which you chew unceasingly, even in your dreams. Yet no sooner have you taken it into you than you awake to the terrible truth demonstrated by Guterbock Q. Hosenscheisser, Fourth Avenue, Grand Rapids, that chocolate is the cause of constipation, and constipation of cancer, and proceed to get it out of you by means of an enema which would frighten a camel into convulsions."[60]

But the worst of all phantasms are the moral ideas and the religious ideas. Sanity consists in the faculty of adjusting ideas in proper proportion. Any one who accepts a moral or religious truth without understanding it is only kept out of the asylum because he does not follow it out logically. If one really believed in Christianity, *{"One would go mad if one took the Bible seriously; but to take it seriously one must be already mad."—Crowley.}* if one really thought that the majority of mankind was doomed to eternal punishment, one would go raving about the world trying to "save" people. Sleep would not be possible until the horror of the mind left the body exhausted. Otherwise, one must be morally insane. Which of us can sleep if one we love is in danger of mere death? We cannot even see a dog drown without at least interrupting all our business to look on. Who then can live in London

---

[59] *Ibid.*, Ch. II; *cf.* also *Liber CL*, Ch. IV: "The first step being Will, Evil appears as by this definition, 'all that hinders the execution of the Will.' Therefore is it written: 'The word of Sin is Restriction.' It should also be noted that in *The Book of the Thirty Æthyrs* Evil appears as Choronzon whose number is 333, which in Greek importeth Impotence and Idleness: and the nature of Choronzon is Dispersion and Incoherence."

[60] *Book 4*, Part II, Ch. XVI.

and reflect upon the fact that of its seven million souls, all but about a thousand Plymouth Brethren will be damned? Yet the thousand Plymouth Brethren (who are the loudest in proclaiming that they will be the only ones saved) seem to get on very well, thank you. Whether they are hypocrites or morally insane is a matter which we can leave to their own consideration.[61]

But what if one were to discard all definitions and just attempt to do good? Well, it is not that easy: one might for example invent the theory of relativity and later discover one has laid the foundation for the atomic bomb. "The road to Hell is paved with good intentions." All human actions have unforeseen consequences. Even if we wanted only good and had thoroughly thought out what we needed to do to accomplish this, unpredictable factors could thwart our goals. "We need not fear those who do evil in the name of evil, but Heaven protect us from those who do evil in the name of good," as Arthur C. Adams put it.[62] *Karma*, literally Sanskrit for "action," is a concept first recorded in the Upanishads. Every action has a reaction, and one theory goes that this force determines one's next incarnation. Some schools of Hinduism consider Karma and rebirth linked and simultaneously essential, others consider Karma but not rebirth essential, and few even conclude them both to be flawed fiction.[63] The Buddha's detailed conception of the connections between Karma, rebirth, and causality is set out in the Twelve Nidānas (or links) of dependent origination (*pratītyasamutpāda*).

In the *Ṛgveda*, a central concept is that created beings fulfill their true natures when they follow the path set for them by the ordinances of Ṛta, and it was the failure to follow those divine ordinances that led to the appearance of various forms of calamity and suffering. The concept of Dharma itself was originally understood as a subordinate component of the essentially metaphysical Ṛta, but eventually "became so useful for framing religious, moral and social regulations, that interest in it and discussion of its applications to social and moral order eclipsed all discussions of metaphysical and theological ideas."[64] This shift of emphasis from Ṛta—a metaphysical principle governing action in the universe—to Dharma, the codex of social and ritual precepts believed to uphold Ṛta, had an immense impact on the subsequent development of Hinduism under the direction of the Brahmin priesthood. The inherent goodness of Ṛta and its absolute power over the operation of the universe made the presence of glaring injustice and inequality in the world a serious religious, philosophical, and ethical dilemma, which the notion of Karma helped to overcome. Karma was perceived as a law of moral causation, which effectively excused the

---

[61] *Ibid.*
[62] As quoted in Balk 2012, 27.
[63] W. R. P. Kaufman, "Karma, rebirth, and the problem of evil," *Philosophy East and West* 55(1), January 2005, 15–32.
[64] Day 1982, 42.

deities and Ṛta from the appearance of evil in the world, placing all responsibility squarely on the individual.[65]

This idea of *karma* has been confused by many who ought to have known better, including the Buddha, with the ideas of poetic justice and of retribution.

We have the story of one of the Buddha's *arahats*, who being blind, in walking up and down unwittingly killed a number of insects. [The Buddhist regards the destruction of life as the most shocking crime.] His brother *arahats* inquired as to how this was, and Buddha spun them a long yarn as to how, in a previous incarnation, he had maliciously deprived a woman of her sight. This is only a fairy tale, a bogey to frighten the children, and probably the worst way of influencing the young yet devised by human stupidity.

Karma does not work in this way at all.

In any case moral fables have to be very carefully constructed, or they may prove dangerous to those who use them.

You will remember Bunyan's Passion and Patience: naughty Passion played with all this toys and broke them, good little Patience put them carefully aside. Bunyan forgets to mention that by the time Passion had broken all his toys, he had outgrown them.

Karma does not act in this tit-for-tat-way. An eye for an eye is a sort of savage justice, and the idea of justice in our human sense is quite foreign to the constitution of the Universe.

Karma is the Law of Cause and Effect. There is no proportion in its operations. Once an accident occurs it is impossible to say what may happen; and the Universe is a stupendous accident.

We go out to tea a thousand times without mishap, and the thousand-and-first time we meet some one who changes radically the course of our lives for ever.

There is a sort of sense in which every impression that is made upon our minds is the resultant of all the forces of the past; no incident is so trifling that it has not in some way shaped one's disposition. But there is none of this crude retribution about it. One may kill a hundred thousand lice in one brief hour at the foot of the Baltoro Glacier, as Frater P. once did. It would be stupid to suppose, as the Theosophist inclines to suppose, that this action involves one in the doom of being killed by a louse a hundred thousand times.

This ledger of *karma* is kept separate from the petty cash account; and in respect of bulk this petty cash account is very much bigger than the ledger.

If we eat too much salmon we get indigestion and perhaps nightmare. It is silly to suppose that a time will come when a salmon will eat us, and find us disagree.

---

[65] *Ibid.*

On the other hand we are always being terribly punished for actions that are not faults at all. Even our virtues rouse insulted nature to revenge.

Karma only grows by what it fees on: and if *karma* is to be properly brought up, it requires a very careful diet.

With the majority of people their actions cancel each other out; no sooner is effort made than it is counterbalanced by idleness. Eros gives place to Anteros.

Not one man in a thousand makes even an apparent escape from the commonplace of animal life.[66]

"People with diets and breathing exercises and the like are usually walking sepulchres—some of them whited! The animal who thinks about his health is already sick. Absence of noise and friction is the witness of free mechanical function. Fear actually creates disease, for the mind begins to explore and so interferes with, the unconscious rhythm of the body, as the *Edinburgh Review* killed John Keats."[67] Crowley noted that, "nine vegetarians in ten have to give up their revolting habit sooner or later; and there is this argument for the inherence of some metaphysical quality in living protoplasm which does not depart immediately on the occurrence of death, that fresh meat is found by the experience of explorers to be much more revivifying than canned meat; and the canned meat itself degenerates noticeably with time, though there is no apparent change in the food. In the extreme case of eating living food, it is within the experience of everybody that raw oysters pick one up quicker than anything else. It is not a question of nutriment alone, the replacing of the tissues to repair their expenditure. It is the actual entrance into the body of some subtle substance, or, as the ancients would have said, divine substance, which manifests itself in the eater as abundance of life and joy. It is also impossible to doubt that Catholics obtain real spiritual sustenance from the Host."[68]

"The man with the best chance of prolonged youth is he who eats and drinks heartily, not much caring what; who does things vigorously in the open air, with the minimum of common-sense precautions; and who keeps his mind at the same time thoroughly active, free from worry, and his heart high. He has come, with William Blake, to the Palace of Wisdom by the Road of Excess. He is on friendly terms with Nature, and though he does not fear her he heeds her, and does not provoke her. It is better says he, to wear out than to rust out. True, but is there need to wear out? He tires himself improperly, and he digs his grave with his teeth."[69] As Crowley declares in his *New Comment* on AL II.60, "our Law does not indulge in the frothings of impotent fury, like the priestly frauds of Moses, the Rishis, and Buddha, in the weeping and wailing and gnashing of teeth of the Galilean fishwife. Our

---

[66] *Book 4*, Part II, Ch. IX.
[67] *The Elixir of Life: Our Magical Medicine.*
[68] *Liber 888*, "John Barleycorn."
[69] *The Elixir of Life.*

Law knows nothing of punishment beyond that imposed by ignorance and awkwardness on their possessor."[70]

In Section V of *Science and Buddhism*, which Crowley wrote while he still considered himself an "intellectual Buddhist," he gives Karma this definition: "Karma means 'that which is made,' and I think it should be consider with strict etymological accuracy. If I place a stone on the roof of a house, it is sure to fall sooner or later, *i.e.*, as soon as the conditions permit. Also, in its ultimation, the doctrine of Karma is identical with determinism. On this subject much wisdom, with an infinite amount of rubbish, has been written. I therefore dismiss it in these few words, confident that the established identity can never be shaken." To sum up, the "*karma* of a man is his *ledger*. The balance has not been struck and he does not know what it is; he does not even fully know what debts he may have to pay, or what is owed him; nor does he know on what dates even those payments which he anticipates may fall due. A business conducted on such lines would be in a terrible mess; and we find in fact that man is in just such a mess. While he is working day and night at some unimportant detail of his affairs, some giant force may be advancing *pede claudo* to overtake him. Many of the entries in this 'ledger' are for the ordinary man necessarily illegible; the method of reading them is given in that important instruction of the A∴A∴ called 'Thisharb,' *Liber CMXIII*."[71]

> And though a man may have a tremendous Will in one direction it need not always be sufficient to help him in another; it may even be stupid.
>
> There is the story of the man who practised for forty years to walk across the Ganges; and, having succeeded, was reproached by his holy *guru*, who said: "You are a great fool. All your neighbours have been crossing every day on a raft for two *pice*."
>
> This occurs to most, perhaps to all, of us in our careers. We spend infinite pains to learn something, to achieve something, which when gained does not seem worth even the utterance of the wish.
>
> But this is a wrong view to take. The discipline necessary in order to learn Latin will stand us in good stead when we wish to do something quite different.
>
> At school our masters punished us; when we leave school, if we have not learned to punish ourselves, we have learned nothing.
>
> In fact the only danger is that we may value the achievement in itself. The boy who prides himself on his school knowledge is in danger of becoming a college professor.
>
> So the *guru* of the water-walking Hindu only meant that it was now time to be dissatisfied with what he had done—and to employ his powers to some better end.

---

[70] NC on AL II.60.
[71] *Book 4*, Part II, *loc. cit.*

And, incidentally, since the Divine Will is One, it will be found that there is no capacity which is not necessarily subservient to the Destiny of the man who possesses it.[72]

As the 9th Axiom of Lévi's Theory of the Will states: "The will of the just man is the will of God himself, and the law of Nature." In his *Little Essays Toward Truth*, Crowley lays things bare: "In the idea of Laughter is inherent that of Cruelty, as has been shewn by many philosophers; and this is doubtless why it has been excluded by the Mystic Schools of Pitymongers from their dull curricula. The only answer is to shrug the shoulders in humorous contempt. For on this rock and no other have all their brave barks foundered one by one amid the [GRK WRDS (countless smiles)] of Ocean. Nature is full of cruelty; its highest points of joy and victory are marked by laughter. It is the true physiological explosion and relaxation which produces it. Notably, such drugs as *Cannabis Indica* and *Anhalonium Lewinii*, which do actually 'loosen the girders of the soul which give her breathing,' cause immediate laughter as one of their most characteristic effects."[73]

Crowley recalls coming upon "a copy of Graham Greene's *The Ministry of Fear*—after a long search. He points out that pity is a mature emotion; adolescents do not feel it. Exactly; one step further, and he would have reached my own position as set forth above. It is the twin of 'moral responsibility,' of the sense of guilt or sin. The Hebrew fable of Eden and the 'Fall' is clearly constructed. But remember that the serpent *Nechesh* נחש is equivalent to *Messiach*, משיח, the Messiah. The M is the 'Hanged Man,' the sinner; and is redeemed by the insertion of the Phallic Yod."[74] There is, indeed, "another solution to the problem of human sorrow, and that is indeed one which the wandering ascetics of the world have known. Whoever said 'The kingdom of heaven is within you' certainly knew it. Man is only a very little lower than the angels. He is far more independent of circumstance than most people are aware. Happiness is not so utterly beyond his reach as those who do not climb mountains are sometimes apt to suppose."[75]

> The only drawback to the use of drugs is that toleration is so soon set up, and the effect diminished; while for weaklings there is always the danger of the formation of a habit, when the treacherous servant becomes master, and takes toll for the boon of his ephemeral heavens by the bane of an abiding hell. These remarks have only been introduced to emphasize that happiness is an interior state; for every one of these drugs gives happiness supreme and unalloyed, entirely irrespective of the external circumstances of the individual. It would be folly to fill the apartment of an opium-smoker with the masterpieces of Rembrandt or Sōtatsu, when a dirty tower or a broken chair suffices to flood his soul

---

[72] *Ibid.*, Ch. VI.
[73] "Laughter."
[74] *MWT*, Ch. XLVI.
[75] *Liber 888*, "Vital Distribution."

with more glories than it can bear, when he realizes that light itself is beautiful, no matter on what it may fall, and when, if you asked him what he would do if he were blind, he would condescend from heaven to reply that darkness was more lovely still, that light was but a disturbance of the serenity of the soul, a siren to seduce it from the bliss of the contemplation of its own ineffable holiness."[76]

"Primitive Peoples," on the other hand, "by which I mean those in whom the sense of causality is not assimilated into the very structure of the mind, have a certain dread of happiness. There is a kind of feeling that luck will not last. We therefore find sacrifices offered in the moment of success. The vow of Jephthah to sacrifice the first living thing that met him, should he return victorious, is a case in point. So also the Romans and Greeks enjoined that at the pinnacle of prosperity the thing which was dearest to the man should be sacrificed to the infernal gods. Greek drama is full of stories of the punishment of 'hybris', the state of mind which declared that everything was going well and would always do so, that the man was a fine fellow much too big to fall. We still 'touch wood', or, in Scotland, 'cauld airn'."[77] It is thus "not so much the idea of escaping punishment as of escaping bad luck. There is little trace of the idea of sin in our modern sense of the word before Paul, except in the religions of the effeminate and cowardly inhabitants of some parts of the Indian Peninsula. Sacrifice is in Egypt simply a magical ritual to ensure the due rising of the Nile."[78]

"The 'conviction of sin' is a modern invention due principally to the tyranny of a Pauline priestcraft. In the dark ages every calamity was attributed by the priests to sin; and, as calamities were frequent, the spirit of the people was broken. Today we have even a form of melancholia whose principal delusion is that the victim has committed the 'sin against the Holy Ghost'. Such ravings are only possible to slave-peoples, just as the melancholia which persuades the sufferer that he has lost all his money only occurs in a commercialized civilization. The Jews themselves had the sense of sin derived from their four hundred years of bondage in Egypt, but nothing of the sort is found among virile peoples such as the Arabs and Afghans, who do not permit the domination of the priests. It does not appear even in India until the Brahmins had supplanted the Kshatriya or warrior caste. The sense of justice is very one-sided in the strong man armed. All he means by justice is the execution of his will upon the weaker man. The whole idea of sin and redemption is a direct metaphysical creation of the slave spirit."[79]

The task of the Buddhist recluse is roughly as follows. He must plunge every particle of his being into one idea: right views, aspirations, word, deed, life, will-power, meditation, rapture, such are the stages of his liberation, which resolves itself into a struggle against the law of

---

[76] *Ibid.*
[77] *Ibid.*, "The Difference between Atonement and Punishment."
[78] *Ibid.*, "Salvation at first a Class Privilege; and the Remedy."
[79] *Ibid.*

causality. He cannot prevent past causes taking effect, but he can prevent present causes from having any future results. The exoteric Christian and Hindu rather rely on another person to do this for them, and are further blinded by the thirst for life and individual existence, the most formidable obstacle of all, in fact a negation of the very object of all religion. Schopenhauer shows that life is assured to the will-to-live, and unless Christ (or Krishna, as the case may be) destroys these folk by superior power—a task from which almightiness might well recoil baffled!—I much fear that eternal life, and consequently eternal suffering, joy, and change of all kinds, will be their melancholy fate. Such persons are in truth their own real enemies.[80]

Knowledge of good and evil is unattainable for a non-omniscient being. The fact is that Hitler based his Final Solution on a prediction of the future. He believed that Jews had betrayed Germany in World War I, and were now plotting to take over the world and destroy the Aryan people. For Hitler, the Holocaust was basically a chance to "kill baby Hitler." He knew the future and the atrocities that the bad guys were going to commit, so he took steps to kill them first—perfectly logical, if you think you are omniscient. Even though the present author places Hinduism and Buddhism miles above Christianity and Islam, each of them is, at bottom, nonetheless just another "religion of suffering": you are going to suffer for the evil deeds you committed in your previous lives, even though you have no idea what you have done. This is a pretty bad motivator for cleaning up your act in anticipation of your next life, especially considering the fact that you can never know if one of your good deeds ultimately ends up harming someone else.

A priori moral knowledge is impossible—we can perhaps see a couple of steps ahead, but our perspective is never any more extensive than that. Which is exactly why man has reasoned that it is up to some power external to himself to decide what is good and what is evil; however, it is hardly logical for an omniscient and omnipotent divinity to create an imperfect world and then blame humanity for his mistakes. "The Christian ideas of humility and weakness as 'virtues' are natural to slaves, cowards, and defectives. The type of tailless simian who finds himself a mere forked radish in a universe of giants clamouring for *hors d'œuvres* must take refuge from Reality in Freudian phantasies of 'God'. He winces at the touch of Truth; and shivers at his nakedness in Nature."[81] As Nietzsche put it, faith "means not wanting to know what is true. The pietist, the priest of both sexes, is false because he is sick: his instinct demands that truth shall not come into its own at any point. 'What makes sick is good; what proceeds from abundance, from superfluity, from power, is evil': that is what the believer feels."[82]

---

[80] *Berashith*.
[81] NC on AL II.77.
[82] *The Antichrist*, §52.

Herein the twisted ingenuity of slave morality lay exposed: by glorifying slave morality, the slaves are actually seeking to glorify themselves. The virtues which slave morality demands are those of which slaves are capable, indeed, the only virtues of which they are capable.[83] The weakness of sickness is turned into the "virtue" of sacrifice and suffering, ugliness becomes not an inability to acquire a mate but virtuous chastity, and poverty transforms into the virtue of the holy ascetic who boasts indifference to earthly wealth. "He therefore invents a cult of fear and shame, and makes it presumption and blasphemy to possess courage and self-respect. He burrows in the slime of 'Reverence, and godly fear' and makes himself houses of his own excrement, like the earthworm he is. He shams dead, like other vile insects, at the approach of danger; he tries to escape notice by assuming the colour and form of his surroundings, using 'protective mimicry' like certain other invertebrates. He exudes stink or ink like the skunk or the cuttle-fish, calling the one Morality and the other Decency. He is slippery with Hypocrisy, like a slug; and, labelling the totality of his defects Perfection, defines God as Faeces so that he may flatter himself with the epithet divine. The whole manoeuvre is described as Religion."[84]

And it is thus through religion that the slave tries to become master—not by heightening his own potency, but by bringing down his superiors under the guise of "improving" them in accord with his slave morality. "In all ages ... this above all is what morality has meant. But one word can conceal the most divergent tendencies. Both the taming of the beast man and the breeding of a certain species of man has been called 'improvement': only these zoological termini express realities—realities, to be sure, of which the typical 'improver', the priest, knows nothing—wants to know nothing. To call the taming of an animal its 'improvement' is in our ears almost a joke. Whoever knows what goes on in menageries is doubtful whether the beasts in them are 'improved'. They are weakened, they are made less harmful, they become sickly beasts through the depressive emotion of fear, through pain, through injuries, through hunger.—It is no different with the tamed human being whom the priest has 'improved'.... Like a caricature of a human being, like an abortion: he had become a 'sinner', he was in a cage, one had imprisoned him behind nothing but sheer terrifying concepts. There he lay now, sick, miserable, filled with ill-will towards himself; full of hatred for the impulses towards life, full of suspicion of all that was still strong and happy."[85]

The Bible, the anthology of writings upon which Christianity is supposed to be founded, does not say what Christianity is, what a Christian is, or even what one must do in order to be a Christian. Nowhere in the Gospels is there a precept for confessions, oaths, dogmas, or any of the other nonsense that make up Christianity. "Jesus was all virtue, and acted from impulse, not from rules," observed William Blake in *The Marriage of*

---

[83] We have all but forgotten that *virtue* originally meant "strength," "worth," or "excellence," and was thus thought to be rare.
[84] NC on AL II.77.
[85] *Twilight of the Idols, loc. cit.*

Heaven and Hell. "If thine eye offend thee" has been interpreted not as it stands, but as if it read: "If thine eye offend some artificial standard of morality, cut it out." Ethics, moral standards and principles were all invented by sociopaths to catch the conscience of people who actually have one to control them with. "This is the code of the 'Slave-Gods,' very thoroughly analysed, pulverized, and de-loused by Nietzsche in *Antichrist*. It consists of all the meanest vices, especially envy, cowardice, cruelty and greed: all based on over-mastering Fear."[86]

"I condemn Christianity," fumes *The Antichrist*. "Let anyone dare to speak to me of its 'humanitarian' blessing! To *abolish* any distress ran counter to its deepest advantages: it lived on distress, it *created* distress to externalise *itself.*"[87] Christianity is the fix—grace—to the problem—guilt—that would not exist without it; the sole *raison d'être* for Christian clergy is to administer penance, or to grant absolution, the one sacrament that is neither a ritual nor a part of the original six "borrowed" from the ancient mystery cults, i.e. to make people feel so guilty that they just have to confess, and the only person they can confess to safely, in confidence, is the parish priest (or, in the case of a mediaeval monarch, his personal confessor).[88] "It has been often said that power corrupts," writes Hoffer in *The Passionate State of Mind*. "But it is perhaps equally important to realize that weakness, too, corrupts. Power corrupts the few, while weakness corrupts the many. Hatred, malice, rudeness, intolerance, and suspicion are the fruits of weakness. The resentment of the weak does not spring from any injustice done to them but from the sense of their inadequacy and impotence. They hate not wickedness but weakness. When it is in their power to do so, the weak destroy weakness wherever they see it. Woe to the weak when they are preyed upon by the weak. The self-hatred of the weak is likewise an instance of their hatred of weakness."[89]

"The 'bringer of glad tidings'," says Nietzsche of Jesus, "died as he had lived, as he had taught—*not* to 'redeem men' but to show how one must live."[90] The life that Christ led was obviously not the life led by the ordinary Christian, nor was his practice that followed by the Church named after him. People often conceive being good as simply not doing anyone any harm personally; however, to change the world in some manner, be it for better or for worse, entails direct involvement in some activity, and whatever one does is inevitably going to offend someone else's notion of what is right or wrong. The Church's lack of courage and will to profess the acts Jesus demanded resulted in the corruption of his teachings: Paul, unable to fulfill even the Jewish life, substituted faith as the path to redemption.[91] "It is useless to multiply examples. All I wish to do is to justify

---

[86] *MWT*, Ch. LXX.
[87] *The Antichrist*, §62. Emphasis in original.
[88] Balk 2008. *Cf.* e.g. *The Book of Lies*, Ch. 44.
[89] Hoffer 1955, 28.
[90] *The Antichrist*, §35. Emphasis in original.
[91] Balk, *op. cit.*

my agreement with Shelley and Nietzsche in defining Christianity as the religious expression of the slave-spirit in man."[92]

"I take it that Christianity is not only the cause but the symptom of slavery. There were slaves in Rome, of course, even under the republic. But it was only through Paul that the slime found tongue, and uttered its agony and blasphemy."[93] Not only did Paul invent a way for himself and his fellow believers to be redeemed, but this "bringer of ill tidings" also fostered the idea of a place of final judgement in the afterlife, where the unbelievers would be punished. The passion, death, and resurrection of Christ were supposed to give us hope; instead, they gave us only despair. They served as a promise of more pain and suffering to come before the end of times, leaving Christians in panic about whether or not they will gain admittance to Heaven. By sanctioning the ideas of punishment and revenge, Paul betrayed Jesus' basic message of love and forgiveness. In fact, Nietzsche was thoroughly convinced that no Christian ever held true to Jesus' teachings—"In reality, there has been only one Christian, and he died on the Cross."[94]

For Nietzsche, Jesus was not a meek and mild son of God, but a rebel and a human teacher with absolutely no divine purpose. When he vandalized the Temple stalls at Jerusalem in protest against the way a holy shrine had been turned into a marketplace, he was committing a criminal felony as an act of civil disobedience. He was a "political criminal," fighting against "caste, privilege, order, and formula... He died for his guilt. All evidence is lacking... that he died for the guilt of others."[95] As Lévi writes in *The Key of the Mysteries*: "The divine ideal of the ancient world made the civilization which came to an end, and one must not despair of seeing the god of our barbarous fathers become the devil of our more enlightened children. One makes devils with cast-off gods." The translator appends a note here, saying "Christianity has fallen, and so Christ has already become the 'devil' to such thinkers as Nietzsche and Crowley."[96] Lévi continues: "Satan is only so incoherent and so formless because he is made up of all the rags of ancient theogonies. He is the sphinx without a secret, the riddle without an answer, the mystery without truth, the absolute without reality and without light."[97]

> O thou that hast beheld the City of the Pyramids, how shouldst thou behold the House of the Juggler? For he is wisdom, and by wisdom hath he made the Worlds, and from that wisdom issue judgements 70 by 4, that are the 4 eyes of the double-headed one; that are the 4 devils, Satan, Lucifer, Leviathan, Belial, that are the great princes of the evil of the world.

---

[92] *The World's Tragedy*, Preface.
[93] *Ibid.*
[94] *The Antichrist*, §39.
[95] *Ibid.*, §27.
[96] *Cf.* also *The World's Tragedy, loc. cit.*: "I therefore hold the legendary Jesus in no wise responsible for the trouble: it began with Luther, perhaps, and went on with Wesley: but no matter!—what I am trying to get at is the religion which makes England to-day a hell for any man who cares for freedom. That religion they call Christianity; the devil they honour they call God."
[97] *The Key of the Mysteries*, Part I, "Sketch of the Prophetic Theology of Numbers."

And Satan is worshipped by men under the name of Jesus; and Lucifer is worshipped by men under the name of Brahma; and Leviathan is worshipped by men under the name of Allah; and Belial is worshipped by men under the name of Buddha.

(This is the meaning of the passage in *Liber Legis*, Chap. III.)[98]

---

[98] *Liber 418*, 3rd Æthyr.

CHAPTER 4
Ontology

This Book explains the Universe.

The elements are Nuit—Space—that is, the total of possibilities of every kind—and Hadit, any point which has experience of these possibilities. (This idea is for literary convenience symbolized by the Egyptian Goddess Nuit, a woman bending over like the Arch of the Night Sky. Hadit is symbolized as a Winged Globe at the heart of Nuit.)

Every event is a uniting of some one monad with one of the experiences possible to it.

"Every man and every woman is a star," that is, an aggregate of such experiences, constantly changing with each fresh event, which affects him or her either consciously or subconsciously.

Each one of us has thus an universe of his own, but it is the same universe for each one as soon as it includes all possible experience. This implies the extension of consciousness to include all other consciousness.

In our present stage, the object that you see is never the same as the one that I see; we infer that it is the same because your experience tallies with mine on so many points that the actual differences of our observation are negligible. For instance, if a friend is walking between us, you see only his left side, I his right; but we agree that it is the same man, although we may differ not only as to what we may see of his body but as to what we know of his qualities. This conviction of identity grows stronger as we see him more often and get to know him better. Yet all the time neither of us can know anything of him at all beyond the total impression made on our respective minds.

The above is an extremely crude attempt to explain a system which reconciles all existing schools of philosophy.

—Introduction to THE BOOK OF THE LAW

As Crowley writes in *The Temple of Solomon the King*, "the root-thought of all philosophy and religion, both Eastern and Western, is that the universe is only an appearance, and not a reality."[1] He quotes the distinguished Indologist Paul Deussen, who edited Schopenhauer's works and was friends with both Nietzsche and Vivekananda: "The entire external universe, with its infinite ramifications in space and time, as also the involved and intricate sum of our inner perceptions, is all merely the form under which the essential reality presents itself to a consciousness such as ours, but is not the form in which it may subsist outside of our consciousness and

---

[1] "Vedanta."

independent of it; that, in other words, the sum total of external and internal experience always and only tells us how things are constituted for us, and for our intellectual capacities, not how they are in themselves and apart from intelligences such as ours."[2]

It must here be noted that atomism is itself a reductive argument: it says that not only is everything composed of atoms and void, but that nothing they compose really exists; the only things that really exists are atoms mechanistically ricocheting off each other in an otherwise empty void. However, the Epicurean Lucretius tried to allow for "free will which living things throughout the world have" by postulating an indeterministic tendency for atoms to swerve randomly in this physicalistic universe.[3] The idea that matter is made up of discrete units is quite an old one and appears in many ancient cultures from Greece to India, but these ideas were founded on philosophical and theological reasoning, not on evidence or experimentation, so they failed to convince everyone. The Indian Jain, Ājīvika, and Cārvāka schools of atomism date back at least to the 4th century BCE, and the Nyāya and Vaiśeṣika schools would later develop theories on how atoms combined to form more complex objects. In the West, atomism first emerged in the 5th century BCE with the pre-Socratic Leucippus and Democritus, but whether Greek culture influenced India or vice versa or whether both evolved independently is a matter of dispute.[4]

Leucippus of Miletus and his pupil, Democritus, proposed that all matter was composed of small invisible particles known as atoms, in order to reconcile the two conflicting schools of thought on the nature of reality: on one side stood Heraclitus, who believed the nature of all existence to be ever-present change; on the other side was Parmenides, who thought instead that all change is illusion. Parmenides not only denied the existence of change, but the existence of motion and void itself. The founder of the Eleatic school of philosophy believed all existence to be a single, all-encompassing and unchanging mass, a concept known as "monism." While this conclusion, as well as the reasoning behind it, may seem baffling to the modern empirical mind, Parmenides explicitly rejected sensory experience as a path to understanding the universe, and utilized purely abstract reasoning in its stead.[5] Heraclitus, on the other hand, was famous for insisting that, as Plato puts his doctrine, "you cannot step twice into the same stream."[6] Subsequently dubbed "the Obscure," Heraclitus characterized all existing entities by pairs of contrary properties, whereby no entity may ever occupy a single state at a single time, which—along with his cryptic statement that "all things come to pass in accordance with this *Logos*"[7]—has been the subject of countless different interpretations.

---

[2] Deussen 1906, 40.
[3] Lucr. 2.251–260.
[4] Teresi 2002.
[5] Melsen 1952.
[6] Plat. *Crat.* 402a.
[7] DK B1.

"There are"—thus—"three main theories of the Universe; Dualism, Monism and Nihilism. . . .All are reconciled and unified in the theory which we shall now set forth. The basis of this Harmony is given in Crowley's *Berashith*—to which reference should be made."[8] Crowley wrote *Berashith: An Essay in Ontology—With Some Remarks On Ceremonial Magic* in Delhi, April 1901, that is, three years before the reception of *The Book of the Law*. בראשית is, of course, Hebrew for "in the beginning," the first word and original title of the Biblical book of Genesis. In his *New Comment* on AL I.28—"None, breathed the light, faint & faery, of the stars, and two."—Crowley quotes "the essential passages" from *Berashith* at length in order to expound "the plain statement of the Perfect Metaphysick":

I ASSERT THE ABSOLUTENESS OF THE QABALISTIC ZERO.

When we say that the Cosmos sprang from 0, what kind of 0 do we mean? By 0 in the ordinary sense of the term we mean "absence of extension in any of the categories."

When I say "No cat has two tails," I do not mean, as the old fallacy runs, that "Absense-of-cat possesses two tails"; but that "In the category of two-tailed things, there is no extension of cat."

Nothingness is that about which no positive proposition is valid. We cannot truly affirm: "Nothingness is green, or heavy, or sweet."

Let us call time, space, being, heaviness, hunger, the categories. If a man be heavy and hungry, he is extended in all these, besides, of course, many more. But let us suppose these five are all. Call the man X; his formula is then $X^{t+s+b+h+h}$. If he now eat he will cease to be extended in hunger; if he be cut off from time and gravitation as well, he will now be represented by the formula X^{s+b}. Should he cease to occupy space and to exist, his formula would then be X^0. This expansion is equal to 1; whatever X may represent, if it be raised to the power of 0 (this meaning mathematically "If it be extended in no dimension or category"), the result is Unity, and the unknown factor X is eliminated.

Now if there was in truth 0, "before the beginning of years," THAT 0 WAS EXTENDED IN NONE OF THE CATEGORIES, FOR THERE COULD HAVE BEEN NO CATEGORIES IN WHICH IT COULD EXTEND! If our 0 was the ordinary 0 of mathematics, there was not truly absolute 0, for 0 is, as I have shown, dependent on the idea of categories. If these existed, then the whole question is merely thrown back; we must reach a state in which 0 is absolute. Not only must we get rid of all subjects, but of all predicates. By 0 (in mathematics) we really mean 0^n, where *n* is the final term of a natural scale of dimensions, categories, or predicates. Our Cosmic Egg, then, from which the present universe arose, was Nothingness, extended in no categories, or, graphically, 0^0. This expression is in its present form meaningless. Let us discover its value by a simple mathematical process!

---

[8] *MITAP*, Ch. 0.

$$0^0 = 0^{1-1} = 0^1 \div 0^1 \text{ [Multiply by } 1 = n \div n \text{]}$$
Then $0^1 \div n \times n \div 0^1 = 0 \times \infty$.

Now the multiplying of the infinitely great by the infinitely small results in SOME UNKNOWN FINITE NUMBER EXTENDED IN AN UNKNOWN NUMBER OF CATEGORIES. It happened, when this our Great Inversion took place, from the essence of all nothingness to finity extended in innumerable categories, that an incalculably vast system was produced. Merely by chance, chance in the truest sense of the term, we are found with gods, men, stars, planets, devils, colours, forces, and all the materials of the cosmos; and with time, space, and causality, the conditions limiting and involving them all.

Remember that it is not true to say that our 0^0 existed; nor that it did not exist. The idea of existence was just as much unformulated as that of toasted cheese.

But 0^0 is a finite expression, or has a finite phase, and our universe is a finite universe; its categories are themselves finite, and the expression "infinite space" is a contradiction it terms. The idea of an absolute and of an infinite God is relegated to the limbo of all similar idle and pernicious perversions of truth. Infinity remains; but only as a mathematical conception as impossible in nature as the square root of -1.

"It remains true that 'infinite space is a contradiction in terms', and so on; but this is no argument against the Cosmogeny of this Book. For above the Abyss every idea soever is necessarily a contradiction in terms."[9] Referring to his poem *Tannhäuser*, which he wrote in Mexico City, August 1900, Crowley further boasts that "four years before the appearance of Einstein's world-shaking paper, I described space as 'finite yet boundless,' which is exactly the description in general terms that he gave in more mathematical detail. You will see at once that these three words do describe a curved geometry; a sphere, for instance, is a finite object, yet you can go over the surface in any direction without ever coming to an end."[10]

The *New Comment* on AL I.27 describes the "attempt to resolve All into One" as a "philosophical blunder"—"It explains nothing; neither how One came to be, nor how Two came to be. The only sound conception is that of 'Zero not extended' with a phase of 'Something' ('$0^0 = X$') which makes the answer to both questions self-evident. The idea 'One' is intelligible enough as the result of the resolutions of Two. But in itself it is meaningless because of the absence of any co-ordinates. A point can heave no qualities except as it is related to a second point. It is only 'high' if there be another which is 'low'. It cannot even be said to exist unless there be something which does not exist."

In *Berashith*, Crowley shows, "and metaphysicians practically admit, the falsity alike of Dvaitism and Advaitism. The third, the only remaining theory, this theory, must, however antecedently improbable, however

---

[9] NC on AL I.28.
[10] *Eight Lectures on Yoga*, Ch. 6, Sec. 25.

difficult to assimilate, be true." The note reads: "I may remark that the distinction between this theory and the normal one of the Immanence of the Universe, is trivial, perhaps even verbal only. Its advantage, however, is that, by hypostatising nothing, we avoid the necessity of any explanation. How did nothing come to be? is a question which requires no answer." The passage concludes: "Let there be hereafter no discussion of the classical problems of philosophy and religion! In the light of this exposition the antitheses of noumenon and phenomenon, unity and multiplicity, and their kind, are all reconciled."

"Immanence" generally refers to those metaphysical theories of divine presence in which the divine encompasses or is manifested in the material world. The word is usually applied in monotheistic and pantheistic religions to suggest that the spiritual world permeates the mundane, and is often contrasted with theories of "transcendence," in which the divine is seen to lay outside the material reality. While every major faith expounds and has recourse to both of these divine aspects in some way, Jewish mysticism, particularly the Qabalah, gives explanations of greater depth to the interconnectedness of the two. The Qabalah only began to be taught openly in Europe in the 12th century, but offers the full, traditional system of Jewish metaphysics. It describes the ten Sephiroth, or divine emanations, of the Tree of Life, through which the infinite, unknowable divine essence reveals, emanates, and continuously creates existence.[11]

> The Qabalists explain the "First Cause" *{An expression they carefully avoid using.}* by the phrase: "From 0 to 1, as the circle opening out into the line." The Christian dogma is really identical, for both conceive of a previous and eternally existing God, though the Qabalists hedge by describing this latent Deity as "Not." Later commentators, notably the illustrious *{I retain this sly joke from the first edition.}* MacGregor Mathers have explained this Not as "negatively-existing." Profound as is my respect for the intellectual and spiritual attainments of him whom I am proud to have been permitted to call my master, *{See [previous note].}* I am bound to express my view that when the Qabalists said Not, they meant Not, and nothing else. In fact, I really do claim to have re-discovered the long-lost and central Arcanum of those divine philosophers.[12]

But, "how do we get over this difficulty of something coming from Nothing? Only by enquiring what we mean by Nothing. We shall find that this idea is totally inconceivable to the normal mind. For if Nothing is to be Nothing, it must be Nothing in every possible way. (Of course, each of these

---

[11] Scholem 1954. The same paradox of the ultimate reality in terms of dialectical unity between the opposites of transcendence and immanence is also expressed e.g. in the *T'ai Chi T'u*. (See Appendix E.)
[12] *Berashith*.

ways is itself an imaginary something, and there are Aleph-Null—a transfinite number—of them.)"[13]

So then, if Nothing is to be really the absolute Nothing, we mean that Nothing does not enter into the category of existence. To say that absolute Nothing exists is equivalent to saying that everything exists which exists, and the great Hebrew sages of old time noted this fact by giving it the title of the supreme idea of reality (behind their tribal God, Jehovah, who, as we have previously shown, is merely the Yoga of the 4 Elements, even at his highest,—the Demiourgos) Eheieh-Asher-Eheieh,—I am that I am.

If there is any sense in any of this at all, we may expect to find an almost identical system of thought all over the world. There is nothing exclusively Hebrew about this theogony. We find, for example, in the teachings of Zoroaster and the neo-Platonists very similar ideas. We have a Pleroma, the void, a background of all possibilities, and this is filled by a supreme Light-God, from whom drive in turn the seven Archons, who correspond closely to the seven planetary deities, Aratron, Bethor, Phaleg and the rest. These in their turn constitute a Demiurge in order to create matter; and this Demiurge is Jehovah. Not far different are the ideas both of the classical Greeks and the neo-Platonists. The differences in the terminology, when examined, appear as not much more than the differences of local convenience in thinking. But all these go back to the still older cosmogony of the ancient Egyptians, where we have Nuit, Space, Hadit, the point of view; these experience congress, and so produce Heru-Ra-Ha, who combines the ideas of Ra-Hoor-Khuit and Hoor-paar-Kraat. These are the same twin Vau and Hé final which we know. Here is evidently the origin of the system of the Tree of Life.[14]

"The basis of this theology is given in *Liber CCXX, AL vel Legis*" and "it would require a separate treatise to discuss even the true meaning of the terms employed, and to show how *The Book of the Law* anticipates the recent discoveries of Frege, Cantor, Poincaré, Russell, Whitehead, Einstein and others."[15] *The Spirit of Solitude: An Autohagiography; Subsequently re-Antichristened—The Confessions of Aleister Crowley* is dedicated "To Three Friends," J. W. N. Sullivan, "who suggested this booklet," Augustus John, "who first gave practical assistance," and P. R. Stephensen, "who saw the point." John William Navin Sullivan (1886–1937) was a popular science writer, who penned some of the earliest non-technical accounts of Einstein's theory of relativity. As Tobias Churton put it, "Sullivan popularized the idea of a universe fit for metaphysicians, and the train he started still runs, often to the chagrin of numerous anti-mystical physicists."[16]

---

[13] *Eight Lectures, loc. cit.*, Sec. 15.
[14] *Ibid.*, Secs. 16–17.
[15] *MITAP*, Ch. 0, fn.
[16] Churton 2014, 169.

Crowley and Sullivan first met when both men were visiting Paris in 1921. As Crowley recalls in his *Confessions*, "I astounded his science by setting forth the facts of its origin, and the evidence of its contents that the author possessed the key to several problems insoluble by any intellect hitherto incarnate. We talked day and night for a fortnight. On his part, he showed me a great many mysteries in *The Book of the Law* that I had not suspected till then. I may indeed say that more than once he asked me some questions on a subject of which I was quite ignorant, and that on searching *The Book of the Law* I discovered a satisfactory reply in a text whose meaning had escaped me through my ignorance of the subject in question."[17]

Sullivan also became friends with Aldous Huxley in Florence in 1924. Huxley was apparently attracted to Sullivan's idea that "at the back of the mystery of the scientific universe is the mystery of man's mind."[18] In 1930, the two eminent authors came together again to compile a series of "Interviews with Great Scientists" to be published by *The Observer* in February 1931—and reprinted in Sullivan's *Contemporary Mind: Some Modern Answers* (1934). On 2 October 1930, Crowley received a letter in Berlin informing him Sullivan and Huxley would be in town that night. The next day, Crowley was unable to locate Sullivan, so he wired Einstein—then director of Berlin's Kaiser Wilhelm Institute for Physics—and eventually found Sullivan with the help of Erwin Schrödinger, Max Planck's successor at Berlin's Friedrich Wilhelm University and creator of the famous quantum mechanical wave function equation. Crowley was ultimately not included as one of the great men of science in the newspaper series, though he was interviews as one, but that he "could wire Einstein and use Schrödinger as a useful contact says something about the character of Berlin at the time, and Crowley's real place in it."[19]

"The theogony of our Law is entirely scientific, Nuit is Matter, Hadit is Motion, in their full physical sense. They are the Tao and Teh of Chinese Philosophy; or, to put it very simply, the Noun and Verb in grammar. Our central Truth—beyond other philosophies—is that these two infinities cannot exist apart."[20] In his *Science of Logic*, Hegel describes a dialectic of existence: first existence must be posited as pure Being; but pure Being, upon examination, is found to be indistinguishable from Nothing—when it is realized that what is coming into being is, at the same time, also returning to nothing, both Being and Nothing are united as Becoming.[21] Or as Chuang-tzŭ has it: "Birth is not beginning; death is not an end. There is existence without limitation; there is continuity without a starting-point. Existence without limitation is Space. Continuity without a starting point is

---

[17] Ch. 90.
[18] D. Bradshaw, "The best of companions: J. W. N. Sullivan, Aldous Huxley, and the New Physics (Concluded)," *Review of English Studies*, XLVII(187), September 1996, 352-68.
[19] Churton, *op. cit.*, 171.
[20] NC on AL I.1.
[21] §§132-4.

Time. There is birth, there is death, there is issuing forth, there is entering in."[22]

"Nuit is All that which exists, and the condition of that existence. Hadit is the Principle which causes modifications in this Being. This explains how one may call Nuit Matter, and Hadit Motion, in the highest physico-philosophical sense of those terms."[23] As Crowley explains in a lecture delivered before the National Psychological Institute, "The grossest qualities of any substance, not less than the most subtle, are nowadays conceived as being various modes of its motion. All the ultimate terms employed by modern thinkers to attempt to define the real nature of a thing have become infinitely subtle in conception, appreciable only by the noblest intelligences; and (even so) they are found to be indefinable, so much so that certain modern writers have been able to form a daisy-chain of the ten principal conceptions, a chain in which no link exists except in relation to the others. This fundamental revolution in our whole habit of thought has become familiar to all of us; even the merest readers of newspapers in little paragraphs know that an element is not, as was supposed fifty years ago, an ultimate substance *sui generis*."[24]

Atomism is usually contrasted with a substance theory wherein a prime material continuum remains qualitatively invariant under division, e.g. the ratio of the four classical elements would be the same in any portion of a homogenous material. Aristotle, for instance, considered the existence of a void, which was required by atomic theories, to violate physical principles, and asserted that the elements were not made of atoms, but were continuous.[25] The concept of *prima materia*, commonly described as everywhere found, but nowhere seen, is sometimes erroneously attributed to him, but the earliest roots of the idea can be found in the philosophy of Anaxagoras, who described the *nous* in relation to chaos.[26] In the Aristotelian scheme, the very simplest substances which lay at the very edge of nonentity, clinging to the last remnant of form, are the four elements of Earth, Air, Fire, and Water. Beyond them, once their forms are stripped away, lay only the prima materia, characterless, intangible, doomed to remain, by definition, eternally potential.[27] When alchemy developed in Ptolemaic Egypt on the foundations of Hellenistic philosophy, it included the concept of prima materia, which has been one of its central tenets ever since.

Before Empedocles formulated his cosmogony, Greek philosophers had debated which substance was the primordial element from which everything else was made: Heraclitus was in favour of Fire, Thales supported Water, and Anaximenes voted for Air, while Anaximander

---

[22] Giles 1889, 304.
[23] NC on AL I.22.
[24] *The Elixir of Life.*
[25] Lloyd 1970.
[26] Jung 1953.
[27] H. R. King, "Aristotle without prima materia," *Journal of the History of Ideas* 17(3), June 1956, 370–89.

argued that the primordial substance was not any of the known substances, but could be transformed into any of them.[28] In *Book 4*, Part 2, Crowley writes: "Fire is not matter at all; water is a combination of elements; air almost entirely a mixture of elements; earth contains all both in admixture and in combination."[29] However, in *The Book of Thoth*, he is careful to point out that, "the terms used by ancient and medieval philosophers do not mean at all what they mean nowadays. 'Water' does not mean to them the chemical compound H_2O; it is an intensely abstract idea, and exists everywhere. The ductility of iron is a watery quality. [Its magnetic virtue (similarly) is fiery, its conductivity airy, and its weight and hardness earthy. Yet, weight is but a function of the curvature of the 'space-time Continuum' ['Earth is the Throne of Spirit.'] The word 'element' does not mean a chemical element; it means a set of ideas; it summarizes certain qualities or properties."[30]

Empedocles' cosmogenic theory calls for powers known as Love and Strife, which would act as the forces that bring about the mixture and separation of the elements. However, he never actually used the term "element," which appears to have been first utilized by Plato in *Timaeus*.[31] According to the late Roman Neoplatonist Simplicius, the four elements are both eternally brought into union and separated from one another by the two divine powers, Love and Strife. If those elements make up the universe, then these powers explain their variation and harmony. As the optimal, original state, the pure elements and the two powers once co-existed in a condition of rest and inertness in the form of a sphere. The elements abided together in their purity, without mixture or separation, but with the uniting power of Love prevailing in the sphere, while the separating power of Strife guarded its extreme edges.[32]

Babylonian mythology also involves four gods that might be seen as personified cosmic elements: sea, earth, sky, and wind. The cosmogony called *Enûma Eliš* was written down between the 18th and 16th centuries BCE, and was recognized as being related to the Biblical story of creation from its first publication in 1876 as "The Chaldean Account of Genesis"—leading to the recognition of the common roots of ancient Near Eastern myths. Aristotle added a fifth element, or "quintessence," reasoning that whereas fire, earth, air, and water were temporal and corruptible, since no changes can be observed in the heavenly regions, the stars cannot be composed of any of the four elements; they must be made of a different, unchangeable, heavenly substance, which was known as *aither* in ancient Greece[33] and *Akasha* in India. This concept of the five elements forms a

---

[28] Russell 1945.
[29] Ch. IX.
[30] *The Book of Thoth*, Part I, Sec. II.
[31] Plat. *Tim.* 48b–c.
[32] Russell, *op. cit.*
[33] Lloyd, *op. cit.* Against Aristotle, Proclus argued for a fourfold "Chaldaean" arrangement that points to this cosmic order: light; heavenly Fire; sublunary Fire, Air, Water and Earth—"as light is the simplest of all these (among the elements fire is the most incorporeal, but light more so than fire), it is manifest that place is light, the purest among bodies" (Simpl. *In Phys.* 615.26, as

basis of analysis in both Hinduism and Buddhism. In Hinduism, the four states-of-matter describe matter and a fifth element describes that which is beyond the material world. In Buddhism, the elements are not viewed as substances, but as categories of sensory experience.[34] Similar concepts also existed in ancient China and Japan.

Both in the Vedic literature and the Sāṃkhya philosophy, the "great" or "gross" elements (*mahābhūta*) are associated with the five senses, and act as the gross medium for the experience of sensations. The basest element, earth, has been created using all the other elements, and can be perceived by all five senses, hearing, touch, sight, taste, and smell. The next higher element, water, has no odour, but can be heard, felt, seen, and tasted. Then comes fire, which can be heard, felt, and seen. Next is air, which can be heard and felt. And finally, Akasha, or ether, which acts as a medium for sound, but is inaccessible to all other senses.[35] The Sanskrit word derives from the root *kāś*, "to be visible." It first appears as a masculine noun in Vedic Sanskrit with a generic meaning of "open space" or "vacuity." In Classical Sanskrit, however, the noun acquires the neuter gender and expresses the concept of "sky" or "atmosphere," and in many modern Indo-Aryan languages, the corresponding word retains a generic meaning of "sky." In Vedantic philosophy, the term refers to "an ethereal fluid imagined as pervading the cosmos,"[36] and in Buddhism, *Ākāśa* is identified as the first *arūpajhāna*, but usually translated as "infinite space."[37]

The *Taittirīya Upaniṣad* describes the five "sheaths" (*puruṣa*) of a person, starting with the grossest level of the five great elements: "From this very self (*ātman*) did space come into being; from space, air; from air, fire; from fire, the waters, from the waters, the earth; from the earth, plants; from plants, food; and from food, man. . . . Different from and lying within this man formed from the essence of food is the self (*ātman*) consisting of lifebreath. . . . Different from and lying within this self consisting of breath is the self (*ātman*) consisting of mind. . . . Different from and lying within this self consisting of mind is the self (*ātman*) consisting of perception. . . . Different from and lying within this self consisting of perception is the self (*ātman*) consisting of bliss."[38] The *Śvetāśvatara Upaniṣad* says that, "When earth, water, fire, air and akasa arise, when the five attributes of the elements, mentioned in the books on yoga, become manifest then the yogi's body becomes purified by the fire of yoga and he is free from illness, old age and death."[39]

In early Buddhism, the four great elements (*catudhātu*)—earth, water, fire, and air—were a basis for understanding that leads one through unbinding of *rūpa*, or materiality, to the supreme state of pure "Emptiness"

---

translated in Sambursky 1982, 67). *See* Siorvanes 1996.
[34] Raju 1985.
[35] *Ibid.*
[36] Iannone 2001.
[37] Vetter 1988.
[38] 2.1–5.
[39] 6.1–2.

or *Nirvāṇa*. They are used in Buddhist texts to both elucidate the concept of *dukkha*, or suffering, and as an object of mediation. The earliest texts explain that the four primary material elements are the sensory qualities of solidity, fluidity, temperature, and mobility, while their characterization as earth, water, fire, and air, respectively, is seen as an abstraction. Rather than concentrating on the fact of material existence, the Buddhist observes how a physical thing is sensed, felt, and perceived.[40] Similarly, when Hindu Tāntrikas contemplate the five elements, they see it as cleansing and healing their senses, the doorways to their soul, and it forms one of the most important Tantric rituals.

In the West, the Aristotelian tradition and mediaeval alchemy eventually gave rise to modern scientific theories, and by the time of Lavoisier, a list of elements would no longer refer to classical elements, which correspond more closely to the four state of matter: solid, liquid, gas, and plasma.[41] As Crowley writes, "All advance in understanding demands the acquisition of a new point-of-view. Modern conceptions of Mathematics, Chemistry, and Physics are sheer paradox to the 'plain man' who thinks of Matter as something that one can knock up against."[42] Einstein made the universe once more a playground for mystics: gone was the Victorian "nightmare universe of infinitesimal billiard balls"[43]; the Einsteinian universe appeared to have—or perhaps even be—a mind of its own, which human language could only access through symbolism on a par with poetry or music.[44]

> For general reading there is no better introduction than *The Bases of Modern Science*, by my old and valued friend the late J. W. N. Sullivan. I do not want to detain you too long with quotations from this admirable book. I would much rather you got it and read it yourself; you could hardly make better use of your time. But let us spend a few moments on his remarks about the question of geometry.
>
> Our conceptions of space as a subjective entity has been completely upset by the discovery that the equations of Newton based on Euclidean Geometry are inadequate to explain the phenomena of gravitation. It is instinctive to us to think of a straight line; it is somehow axiomatic. But we learn that this does not exist in the objective universe. We have to use another geometry, Riemann's Geometry, which is one of the curved geometries. (There are, of course, as many systems of geometry as there are absurd axioms to build them on. Three lines make one ellipse: any nonsense you like: you can proceed to construct a geometry which is correct so long as it is coherent. And there is nothing right or wrong about the result: the only question is: which is the most convenient

---

[40] Lusthaus 2002.
[41] Kikuchi 2011.
[42] *MITAP, loc. cit.*
[43] Huxley 1945, 86.
[44] Sullivan 1926.

system for the purpose of describing phenomena? We found the idea of Gravitation awkward: we went to Riemann.)[45]

"The essence of Science to-day is far more mysterious than the cloudiest speculations of Leibnitz, Spinoza or Hegel; the modern definition of Matter reminds one irresistibly of the definition of Spirit given by such mystics as Ruysbroeck, Boehme and Molinos. The idea of the Universe in the mind of a modern mathematician is singularly reminiscent of the ravings of William Blake."[46] Almost daily, we hear highly educated people say that we don't know what consciousness is. The nature of consciousness is apparently a great unsolved mystery, the ultimate hard problem. Which is strange, since we know exactly what consciousness is—if by "consciousness" we mean what most people do in this debate: experience of any kind whatsoever. It is, in fact, the most familiar thing there is, whether it be experience of emotion, pain, joy, understanding what someone is saying, seeing, hearing, touching, tasting, or feeling. It is the only thing in the universe the ultimate intrinsic nature of which we can really claim to know. The nature of our physical reality, by contrast, is deeply mysterious, and the science of physics only grows stranger by the day.

The nature of matter is mysterious except insofar as consciousness is itself a state of matter. In his essay *Mind and Matter*, Bertrand Russell puts it thus: "Since we know nothing about the intrinsic quality of physical events except when these are mental events that we directly experience, we cannot say either that the physical world outside our heads is different from the mental world or that it is not. The supposed problem of the relations of mind and matter arises only through mistakenly treating both as 'things' and not as groups of events."[47] From a physics standpoint, Crowley argues, "the original Inertia expresses itself as two complementary forms of Energy—the small active Negative Electron (Hadit) and the large passive Positive Proton (Nuit). (It has recently been shown that the mass of Matter is zero). When these satisfy each other, two phenomena occur: (1) their opposed equalities cancel out to Zero. (Perhaps even to $0°$, thus restoring the original Indeterminate Nothing.) (2) a 'child' is born of the union; i.e., a positive phenomenon is produced, whose nature is entirely different from that of either of its 'parents'; for it is finite, and possesses limitations and qualities of its own. Groups of such primaeval units form the various kinds of 'atom', according to the number and geometric disposition thereof."[48]

As the *Djeridensis Comment* has it, "Nuit is all that may be, and is shewn by means of any one that is.... *The Book of the Law* shows forth all things as God....All things are able to know all; all are alike in this, at the end of all."[49] Or as the *New Comment* phrases it: "Every man and every woman is not

---

[45] *Eight Lectures, loc. cit.,* Sec. 24.
[46] *The Book of Thoth, loc. cit.,* Sec. III.
[47] Russell 1997, 292.
[48] NC on AL I.29.
[49] DC on AL I.1–4.

only a part of God, but the Ultimate God. 'The Centre is everywhere and the circumference nowhere'. The old definition of God takes new meaning for us. Each one of us is the One God."[50] Crowley then goes on to describe the trance called by him the "Star-Sponge," which "began as 'Nothingness with Sparkles' in 1916 E.V. by Lake Pasquaney in New Hampshire, U.S.A. and developed into fullness on various subsequent occasions. Each 'Star' is connected directly with every other star, and the Space being Without Limit (Ain Soph) the Body of Nuith, any one star is as much the Centre as any other. Each man instinctively feels that he is the Centre of the Cosmos, and philosophers have jeered at his presumption. But it was he that was precisely right. The yokel is no more 'petty' than the King, nor the earth than the Sun. Each simple elemental Self is supreme, Very God of Very God. Ay, in this Book is Truth almost insufferably splendid, for Man has veiled himself too long from his own glory: he fears the abyss, the ageless Absolute. But Truth shall make him free!"[51]

We know what conscious experience is, because having conscious experience *is* knowing what it is. People can make all sorts of mistakes about what is going on, but none of that threatens the fundamental sense in which we know exactly what experience is just in having it. "The essence of a Man and Woman—each being a Star or sovereign God poised in Space by its own act—is clothed in thoughts and deeds as is its Nature, hidden by them. This essence is all-worthy; adore it, and the light of all that may be shall be shed upon you."[52]

> It is important to understand the necessity of our present Universe. Perfection could do not otherwise than create Imperfection. But was there not original Imperfection? No; for Perfection is hardly more than that original state, since we cannot conceive the total as susceptible of addition. *{Note that ∞, the sum of the series of natural numbers, is not increased in value by the addition, or diminished by the subtraction of any finite number. Yet 2 is greater than ... ! The fact illustrates our "Naught and Two" theory in a most instructive manner.}* This is another view of the God going through the combinations, on a larger scale, and shows not only why He does it, but why He must do it. But is not all this based on the accident that I personally am bored by omniscience on any given matter? Yes, but Imperfection is a fact, and a God whom Perfection did not bore would not have created Imperfection. But why not suppose a wicked God, or a foolish God? Things which seem to me wrong, or stupid, are so because I am the sole judge. But these things are not my creations, but those of other Gods. True, but those Gods are all part of me, so far as I know them. So then, in my own nature are these contrary Gods, which (as above said) I have created in myself to give variety. You see that you cannot conceive these divers Gods without conceiving also a Whole, in which the entire equation cancels out to Naught. One cannot

---

[50] NC on AL I.4.
[51] *Ibid.*
[52] DC on AL I.8–9.

conceive it as a Unity, because 1^0 like 1^1, 1^2, etc., is only one, 1, and cannot become 2 by reflection, as I thought 75 years ago, because there is nothing else to reflect it, or it could not be both All and One. (A heterogeneous One, with a mirror in its All, would be two). Now Evil is only minus to anyone's Plus; you cannot have an Evil to destroy the Whole (or we have Two again.) Therefore no Evil can possibly do any harm; it can only be part of the Play. The Whole is destroyed as soon as understood; that is, it is conceived as 0^0 again; this then bursts forth in some new combination, with no gain or loss except (perhaps ? ?) the gain due to Time, as explained elsewhere. But in this case what is Time? It is a fundamental condition of experience, to say nothing of memory, so is necessary to the Finity Phase of 0^0, that is, to any Universe where change occurs. Is there any possible connexion between two successive such Phases? No; they must be alike in one respect that they each cancel out, so Balance is a necessary principle. More so than time; for one could have a Samadhi Phase which developed Nirvikalpa instantly. But if no Time, then a Unity, which could never become Naught; no such Phase is possible. Duality is therefore the nature of any manifested Universe.[53]

"1 exists, true; but only by a fiction; for there is always a -1 to cancel it. But we get the illusion of 1 when we add 1/2 to 1/2 or 1/3 to 2/3, etc., things—each conscious of its fractional character—seeking to be Whole. Now the bigger any 'One' gets, the more conscious it is of its 'Minus One' wife, the more clearly it sees that 'One' is illusion, and had better cancel out. The general process of Initiation is therefore the same for all possible universes."[54] Crowley defines *samādhi* as "the trance in which Subject and Object become one. In this orgiastic ecstasy is experienced at first; later, the character of the consciousness changes to continuously calm delight, and later still, the delight deepens in a manner wholly indescribable. The technical terms used by Oriental Initiates to denote these conditions are untranslatable; in any case, they serve rather to darken counsel."[55] According to Crowley, the "sun and moon, in their occult sense, are secondary representatives of this original duality which is a phase of the Qabalistic Zero."[56] Other correspondence include Yin and Yang, Yod and He, Shiva and Shakti, etc. "But most such dualities have been conceived in very gross and unphilosophical forms."[57]

The Chinese, like ourselves, begin with the idea of "Absolute Nothing." They "make an effort, and call it the Tao"; but that is exactly what the Tao comes to mean, when we examine it. They see quite well,

---

[53] NC on AL I.29.
[54] *Ibid. Cf.* also *Liber CL*, Preface: "Know that the Universe is not at rest, but in extreme motion whose sum is Rest. And this understanding that Stability is Change, and Change Stability, that Being is Becoming, and Becoming Being, is the Key to the Golden Palace of this Law."
[55] NC on AL I.30.
[56] NC on AL I.16.
[57] *Ibid.*

as we have done above, that merely to assert Nothing is not to explain the Universe; and they proceed to do so by means of a mathematical equation even simpler than ours, involving as it does no operations beyond simple addition and subtraction. They say "Nothing obviously means Nothing; it has no qualities nor quantities." (The Advaitists said the same, and then stultified themselves completely by calling it One!) "But," continue the sages of the Middle Kingdom, "it is always possible to reduce any expression to Nothing by taking any two equal and opposite terms." (Thus $n + (-n) = 0$.) "We ought therefore to be able to get any expression that we want *from* Nothing; we merely have to be careful that the terms shall be precisely opposite and equal." ($0 = n + (-n)$). This then they did, and began to diagrammatize the Universe as the Yi—a pair of opposites, the Yang or active male, and the Yin or passive Female, principles. They represented the Yang by an unbroken (———), the Yin by a broken (— —), line. (The first manifestation in Nature of these two is Tai Yang, the Sun, and the Tai Yin, the Moon.) This being a little large and loose, they doubled these lines, and obtained the four Hsiang. They then took them three at a time, and got the eight Kwa. These represent the development from the original Yi to the Natural Order of the Elements.[58]

The *Yî King*, or *I Ching*, is probably the best-known Chinese book in the world. In East Asia, it is a foundational text for both the Taoist and Confucian philosophical traditions, while in the West, it has attracted the attention of prominent intellectuals and cultural figures since the Enlightenment. Leibniz, for instance, was in correspondence with Jesuits in China and wrote the first European commentary on the *I Ching* as early as 1703. He argued that it proved the universality of both theism and binary numbers, on the basis that the broken lines, the "0" or "nothingness," cannot become solid lines, the "1" or "oneness," without the intervention of God. After the Xinhai Revolution, the *I Ching* was no longer part of Chinese political philosophy, but it maintained cultural influence as China's most ancient text. Taking cue from Leibniz, "Red Chinese" writers drew parallels between the *I Ching* and subjects such as linear algebra and computational logic, seeking to demonstrate that modern Western discoveries had been anticipated by ancient Chinese cosmology.[59]

Secret teachings on the *I Ching* were spread in mediaeval Japan by both the Rinzai Zen patriarch Kokan Shiren and the Shinto priest Yoshida Kanetomo. Kokan studied under the eminent Chinese monk Yishan Yining and their relationship is regarded as inaugurating the golden age of the Literature of the Five Mountains in Japan, while Kanetomo was seminal in the evolution of a coherent descriptive and interpretive schema of Shinto ritual and mythology. The Japanese *I Ching* studies gained a renewed importance in the Edo period, during which over a thousand books were

---

[58] *MWT*, Ch. V. Emphasis in original.
[59] Smith 2008.

published on the subject by several hundred authors. Many of them tried to use the *I Ching* to explain Western science in a Japanese framework, with one writer, Shizuki Tadao, even attempting to employ Newtonian mechanics and the Copernican principle within an *I Ching* cosmology—a line of argument later revived in China by the famous Qing scholar and politician Zhang Zhidong.[60]

Zeno of Citium, the founder of the Stoic school of philosophy, also taught that there are "two principles in the universe, the active principle and the passive. The passive principle, then, is a substance without quality, *i.e.* matter, whereas the active is the reason inherent in this substance, that is God."[61] According to the Stoics, there is a difference "between principles and elements; the former being without generation or destruction, whereas the elements are destroyed when all things are resolved into fire. Moreover, the principles are incorporeal and destitute of form, while the elements have been endowed with form."[62] Similarly, the theologies of Nuit and Hadit "reflect mystic experiences of Infinite Contraction and Expansion, while philosophically they are two opposing Infinities whose interplay gives Finity."[63] Nuit is "one extreme without limit," Hadit the other. "He hath no Nature of His own, for He is that to which all Events occur. His House, that is, the sphere of his action, is called Khabs, a Star. This is the Light which He conceals about Him through His Deeds of Love for Her, so that there may appear in glory the Record of those Works which pertain to any Point in Space."[64]

On surface (pun intended) this is similar to Pascal's "an infinite sphere, the center of which is everywhere, the circumference nowhere," variously attributed to Empedocles, Nicholas of Cusa, and even Hermes Trismegistos himself. However:—

> Why is Nuit restricted to two dimensions? We usually think of space as a sphere. "None—and two": extension and potentiality are Her only projections of Naught. It is strange, by the way to find that modern mathematics says "Spherical space is not very easy to imagine" (Eddington, [*Space, Time and Gravitation: An Outline of the General Relativity Theory*] p. 158) and prefers to attribute a geometrical form whose resemblance to the Kteis is most striking. For Nuit is, philosophically speaking, the archetype of the Kteis, giving appropriate Form to all Being, and offering every possibility of fulfilment of every several point that it envelops. But Nuit cannot be symbolized as three-dimensional, in our system; each unit has position by three spatial, and one temporal, coordinates. It cannot exist, in our consciousness, with less, as a reality. Each "individual" must be a "point-interval"; he must be the product of some part of the Matter of Nuit (with special energies)

---

[60] *Ibid.*
[61] D. L. 7.134.
[62] *Ibid.*
[63] OC on AL II.2.
[64] DC on AL II.2.

determined in space by his relations with his neighbours, and in time by his relations with himself.[65]

"The real philosophical difficulty about this cosmogony is not concerned with any particular equation, or even with the Original Equation. We can understand $x = ab$, $x = a, b,$ & c; and also $0^0 = pa + qb$, whether $pa - qb = 0$ or not. But we ask how the homogeneity of both Nuit and Hadit can ever lead to even the illusion of 'difference.' The answer appears to be that this difference appears naturally with the self-realization of Nuit as the totality of possibilities; each of these, singly and in combination, is satisfied or set in motion by Hadit, to compose a particular manifestation. 0^0 could possess no signification at all, unless there were diverse dimensions wherein it had no extension. 'Nothing' means nothing save from the point of view of 'Two,' just as 'Two' is monstrous unless it is seen as a mode of 'Nothing.'"[66] Crowley concedes that this explanation "appears somewhat disingenuous, since there is no means whatever of distinguishing any Union $H + N = R$ from another. We must postulate a further stage. R (Ra-Hoor-Khuit) Kether, Unity, is always itself; but we may suppose that a number of such homogeneous positive manifestations may form groups differing from each other as to size and structure so as to create the illusion of diversity."[67]

Remarking on the opening verses of each of the three chapters of *The Book of the Law*, Crowley writes in his diary: "I.1. & II.1. N[u] hides the individual in infinity. N[u] is manifested in the individual. III.1. are the ABRAs the 2 which are 0."[68] The *Djeridensis Comment* on AL I.28–29 reads: "Nuit is that which is equally 0 & 2. This Equation 0 = 2 is the Master-Key of the Understanding of Nature of the Universe.[69] She answered: None and Two. This also is a marvel of number, and is the Truth of the Essence of Nature of all Things, the Root of the Tree of Thought, as I shall the shew elsewhere. Nuit shews the object of creating the Illusion of Duality. She said: The world exists as two, for only so can there be known the Joy of Love, whereby are Two made One. Aught that is One is alone, and has little pain in making itself two, that it may know itself, and love itself, and rejoice therein." Or as the *New Comment* puts it: "The Soul interprets the Universe; and the Universe veils the Soul. Nature understands Herself by becoming self-conscious in Her units; and the Consciousness loses its sense of separateness by dissolution in Her."[70]

One may be unable to tell when a thread of a particular colour will be woven into the carpet of Destiny. It is only when the carpet is finished and seen from a proper distance that the position of that particular

---

[65] NC on AL II.7.
[66] NC on AL II.2.
[66] *Ibid.*
[68] 30 September 1923, 1.26 a.m.
[69] Spelled out as "None is Two" in the *New Comment*; as "Zero is Two" in *The Heart of the Master*; and as "Zero equals Two" in *The Book of Thoth*.
[70] NC on AL II.1.

strand is seen to be necessary. From this one is tempted to break a lance on that most ancient battlefield, Free Will and Destiny.

But even though every man is "determined" so that every action is merely the passive resultant of the sum-total of the forces which have acted upon him from eternity, so that his own Will is only the echo of the Will of the Universe, yet that consciousness of "Free Will" is valuable; and if he really understands it as being the partial and individual expression of that internal motion in a Universe whose sum is rest, by so much will he feel that harmony, that totality. And though the happiness which he experiences may be criticised as only one scale of a balance in whose other scale is an equal misery, there are those who hold that misery consists only in the feeling of separation from the Universe, and that consequently all may cancel out among the lesser feelings, leaving only that infinite bliss which is one phase of the infinite consciousness of that ALL.[71]

"Mysticism," Crowley argues, "unless it be a mere barren intellectual doctrine, always involves some personal religious experience of this kind; and the real strength of every religion is consequently in its mystics. The conviction of truth given by any important spiritual experience is so great that although it may have lasted for a few seconds only, it does not hesitate to pit itself against the experience of the lifetime in respect of reality. The mystic doubts whether he the man exists at all, because he is so certain of the existence of him the God; and the two are difficult to conceive intellectually as coexistent! Now the extreme state of Being, Knowledge, and Bliss which characterizes the intermediate stages of mystic experience, is a thousandfold more intense than any other kind of happiness. It is totally independent of circumstance."[72] Nuit "is known," as Hadit "goeth on His Way, and doth His Will; each Event adds to His Knowledge of Her Nature. He cannot be known, for He hath no parts whereby to define Him."[73] Hadit "is thus Any Point-of-View, any Centre to which all Events may be measured. He is life itself in its Essence, and He causes Life to appear to itself. For this reason is the knowledge of Him the knowledge of Death, since the meaning of Life implies death. Hadit saith 'the knowledge of me': this is not against His former word that He shall be known never. It means only that death is one of the Events that must needs be known as soon as the nature of Life is known."[74]

"Professor Eddington, in the masterly exposition of modern thought already quoted, presents, clearly enough, the case against supposing that any phenomenon soever is a 'fact' in any absolute sense. Each account of it must be incomplete, symbolic, and variable with the position and faculties of the observer."[75] Sir Arthur Stanley Eddington (1882–1944) was the

---

[71] *Book 4*, Part II, Ch. VI. Emphasis in original.
[72] *Liber 888*, "Vital Distribution."
[73] DC on AL II.4.
[74] DC on AL II.6.
[75] NC on AL I.27.

Plumian Professor of Astronomy and Experimental Philosophy at Cambridge, Crowley's *alma mater*. He was also a populariser of science and famous for the countless articles that announced and explained Einstein's theory of general relativity to the English-speaking public between the world wars. The Eddington limit, the natural limit to the luminosity of stars, is named after him. In *The Nature of the Physical World* (1928), he famously remarked that "If an army of monkeys were strumming on typewriters, they *might* write all the books in the British Museum,"[76] which is often misunderstood as promoting the infinite monkey theorem. It is clear from the context, however, that rather than suggesting that the probability of this happening is worthy of serious consideration, Eddington is, on the contrary, inferring that below certain levels of probability, the term improbable is functionally equivalent to impossible.

> And here we come upon what is apparently a paradox of the most disconcerting order. For *The Book of the Law*, anticipating the most subtle of recent mathematical conceptions, that of the greatest genius of this generation, makes the unit of existence consist in an Event, an Act of Marriage between Nuit and Hadit; that is, the fulfillment of a certain Point-of-View. And is not the procession of events the very conditions of Sorrow as opposed to the perfection of "Pure Existence?" That is the old philosophy, a tangle of false words: we see more clearly. Thus:
>
> Each Event is an Act of Love, and so generates Joy: all existence is composed solely of such Events. But how comes it then that there should be even an illusion of Sorrow?
>
> Simply enough; by taking a partial and imperfect Vision. An example: in the human body each cell is perfect, and the man is in good health; but should we choose to regard almost any portion of the machine which sustains him, there will appear various decompositions and the like, which might well be taken to imply the most tragic Events. And this would inevitably be the case had we never at any time seen the man as a whole, and understood the necessity of the divers processes of nature which combine to make life.[77]

The following is the "comparatively full account" of Crowley's aforementioned "Star-Sponge Vision" as given in *The New Comment*:

> There is a vision of a peculiar character which has been of cardinal importance in my interior life, and to which constant reference is made in my magical diaries. So far as I know, there is no extant description of this vision anywhere, and I was surprised on looking through my records to find that I had given no clear account of it myself. The reason apparently is that it is so necessary a part of myself that I unconsciously assume it to be a matter of common knowledge, just as one assumes that

---

[76] Eddington 2014, 82. Emphasis in original.
[77] *Little Essays Toward Truth*, "Sorrow."

everybody knows that one possesses a pair of lungs, and therefore abstains from mentioning the fact directly, although perhaps alluding to the matter often enough.

It appears very essential to describe this vision as well as is possible, considering the difficulty of language, and the fact that the phenomena involve logical contradictions, the conditions of consciousness being other than those obtaining normally.

The vision developed gradually. It was repeated on so many occasions that I am unable to say at what period it may be called complete. The beginning, however, is clear enough in my memory.

I was on a retirement in a cottage overlooking Lake Pasquaney in New Hampshire. I lost consciousness of everything but an universal space in which were innumerable bright points, and I realized this as a physical representation of the Universe, in what I may call its essential structure. I exclaimed: "Nothingness, with twinkles!" I concentrated upon this vision, with the result that the void space which had been the principal element of it diminished in importance; space appeared to be ablaze, yet the radiant points were not confused, and I thereupon completed my sentence with the exclamation "But what Twinkles!"

The next stage of this vision led to an identification of the blazing points with the stars of the firmament, with ideas, souls, etc. I perceived also that each star was connected by a ray of light with each other star. In the world of ideas, each thought possessed a necessary relation with each other thought; each such relation is of course a thought in itself; each such ray is itself a star. It is here that logical difficulty first presents itself. The seer has a direct perception of infinite series. Logically, therefore, it would appear as if the entire space must be filled up with a homogeneous blaze of light. This however is not the case. The space is completely full; yet the monads which fill it are perfectly distinct. The ordinary reader might well exclaim that such statements exhibit symptoms of mental confusion. The subject demands more than cursory examination. I can do no more than refer the critic to the Hon. Bertrand Russell's *Introduction to Mathematical Philosophy*, where the above position is thoroughly justified, as also certain positions which follow. At the time I had not read this book; and I regard it as a striking proof of the value of mystical attainment, that its results should have led a mind such as mine, whose mathematical training was of the most elementary character, to the immediate consciousness of some of the most profound and important mathematical truths; to the acquisition of the power to think in a manner totally foreign to the normal mind, the rare possession of the greatest thinkers in the world.

A further development of the vision brought the consciousness that the structure of the universe was highly organized, that certain stars were of greater magnitude and brilliancy than the rest. I began to seek similes to help me to explain myself. Several such attempts are mentioned later in this note. Here again are certain analogies with some of the properties of infinite series. The reader must not be shocked at the idea of a number which is not increased by addition or multiplication, a series of infinite series, each one of which may be twice as long as its predecessor, and so on. There is no "mystical humbug" about this. As Mr. Russell shows, truths of this order are more certain than the most universally accepted axioms; in fact, many axioms accepted by the intellect of the average man are not true at all. But in order to appreciate these truths, it is necessary to educate the mind to thought of an order which is at first sight incompatible with rationality.

...

Further developments of this vision emphasized the identity between the Universe and the mind. The search for similes deepened. I had a curious impression that the thing I was looking for was somehow obvious and familiar. Ultimately it burst upon me with fulminating conviction that the simile for which I was seeking was the nervous system. I exclaimed: "The mind is the nervous system," with all the enthusiasm of Archimedes, and it only dawned on me later, with a curious burst of laughter at my naïveté, that my great discovery amounted to a platitude.

From this I came to another discovery: I perceived why platitudes were stupid. The reason was that they represented the summing up of trains of thought, each of which was superb in every detail at one time. A platitude was like a wife after a few years; she has lost none of her charms, and yet one prefers some perfectly worthless woman.

I now found myself able to retrace the paths of thought which ultimately come together in a platitude. I would start with some few simple ideas and develop them. Each stage in the process was like the joy of a young eagle soaring from height to height in ever increasing sunlight as dawn breaks, foaming, over the purple hem of the garment of ocean, and, when the many coloured rays of rose and gold and green gathered themselves together and melted into the orbed glory of the sun, with a rapture that shook the soul with unimaginable ecstasy, that sphere of rushing light was recognized as a common-place idea, accepted unquestioningly and treated with drab indifference because it had so long been assimilated as a natural and necessary part of the order of Nature. At first I was shocked and disgusted to discover that a series of brilliant researches should culminate in a commonplace. But I soon understood that what I had done was to live over again the triumphant career of conquering humanity; that I had experienced in my own person the succession of winged victories that had been sealed by a treaty of peace whose clauses might be summed up in some such trite expression as "Beauty depends upon form".

It would be quite impracticable to go fully into the subject of this vision of the Star-Sponge, if only because its ramifications are omniform. It must suffice to reiterate that it has been the basis of most of my work for the last five years, and to remind the reader that the essential form of it is "Nothingness with twinkles".[78]

---

[78] NC on AL I.59.

Like the pioneering quantum physicists of his day, Crowley had fully grasped the ambiguity of the mind-matter distinction, arriving at the same basic conclusion as the Hermetic philosophers of late antiquity had: just as the mind could be seen as a manifestation of the brain, the brain could equally be seen as a manifestation of mind. Perceived this way, the world would be material through and through, but equally, there would be no perfectly solid matter. Things then appear to exist only insofar as a force is applied to the universe of the smallest particle that makes "it" vibrate for a fleeting moment and appear on limiting sense organs or equipment.[79] Ironically, the people most likely to doubt or deny the existence of consciousness on the ground that everything is physical, are also the ones most insistent on the primacy of science. It is precisely science that highlights the key point that, in a fundamental respect, the ultimate intrinsic nature of the stuff of the universe is unknown to us—except insofar as it is consciousness.

As Crowley writes in his *Eight Lectures on Yoga*, "Immanuel Kant, who founded an epoch-making system of subjective idealism, is perhaps the first philosopher to demonstrate clearly that space, time, causality (in short, all conditions of existence) are really no more than conditions of thought. I have tried to put it more simply by defining all possible predicates as so many dimensions. To describe an object properly it is not sufficient to determine its position in the space-time continuum of four dimensions, but we must enquire how it stands in all the categories and scales, its values in all 'kinds' of possibility. What do we know about it in respect of its greenness, its hardness, its mobility, and so on? And then we find out that what we imagine to be the description of the object is in reality nothing of the sort. All that we recorded is the behaviour of our instruments."[80]

> What did our telescopes, spectroscopes, and balances tell us? And these again are dependent upon the behaviour of our senses; for the reality of our instruments, of our organs of sense, is just as much in need of description and demonstration as are the most remote phenomena. And we find ourselves forced to the conclusion that anything we perceive is only perceived by us as such "because of our tendency so to perceive it." And we shall find that in the fourth stage of the great Buddhist practice, Mahāsatipaṭṭhāna, we become directly and immediately aware of this fact instead of digging it out of the holts of these interminable sorites which badger us! Kant himself put it, after his fashion: "The laws of nature are the laws of our own minds." Why? It is not the contents of the mind itself that we can cognise, but only its structure. But Kant has not gone to this length. He would have been extremely shocked if it had ever struck him that the final term in his sorites was "Reason itself is the only reality." On further examination, even this ultimate truth turns out to be meaningless. It is like the well-

---

[79] Churton, *op. cit.*
[80] *Eight Lectures, loc. cit.*, Sec. 21.

known circular definition of an obscene book, which is: one that arouses certain ideas in the mind of the kind of person in whom such ideas are excited by that kind of book.[81]

Crowley finishes the chapter with "One last quotation from Mr. Sullivan. 'The universe may ultimately prove to be irrational. The scientific adventure may have to be given up.' But that is all he knows about science, bless his little heart! We do not give up. 'You lied, d'Ormea, I do not repent!' The results of experiment are still valid for experience, and the fact that the universe turns out on enquiry to be unintelligible only serves to fortify our ingrained conviction that experience itself is reality. We may then ask ourselves whether it is not possible to obtain experience of a higher order, to discover and develop the faculty of mind which can transcend analysis, stable against all thought by virtue of its own self-evident assurance. In the language of the Great White Brotherhood (whom I am here to represent) you cross the abyss. 'Leave the poor old stranded wreck'—Ruach—'and pull for the shore' of Neschamah. For above the abyss, it is said, as you will see if you study [*Liber 418*, or "The Vision and the Voice," first published as] the Supplement of the fifth number of the First Volume of *The Equinox*, an idea is only true in so far as it contains its contradictory in itself."[82]

In *The Temple of Solomon the King*, Crowley points out "how that in the West symbols has been added to symbol, and how that in the East symbol has been subtracted from symbol. How in the West the Magician has said: 'As all came from God so must all proceed to God,' the motion being a forward one, and acceleration of the one already existing. Now let us analyze what is meant by the words of the Yogi when he says: 'As all came from God so must all return to God,' the motion being, as it will be at once seen, a backward one, a slowing down of the one which already exists, until finally is reached that goal from which we originally set out by a cessation of thinking, a weakening of the vibrations of illusion until they cease to exist in Equilibrium."[83] The footnote quotes the controversial French academic and amateur physicist Dr. Gustave Le Bon's popular work, *The Evolution of Matter* (1905): "The forces of the universe are only known to us, in reality, by disturbances of equilibrium. The state of equilibrium constitutes the limit beyond which we can no longer follow them."[84]

---

[81] *Ibid.*, Sec. 22.
[82] *Ibid.*, Secs. 31–32.
[83] Part IV, "The Agnostic Position."
[84] Le Bon 1905, 94. *Cf.* also Spencer 1867, 517: "Thus from the persistence of force follow, not only the various direct and indirect equilibrations going on around, together with that cosmical equilibration which brings Evolution under all its forms to a close; but also those less manifest equilibrations shown in the re-adjustments of moving equilibria that have been disturbed. By this ultimate principle is proveable the tendency of every organism, disordered by some unusual influence, to return to a balanced state. To it also may be traced the capacity, possessed in a slight degree by individuals, and in a greater degree by species, of becoming adapted to new circumstances. And not less does it afford a basis for the inference, that there is a gradual advance towards harmony between man's mental nature and the conditions of his existence. After finding that from it are deducible the various characteristics of Evolution, we finally draw from it a warrant for the belief, that Evolution can end only in the establishment of the greatest perfection

The false alternatives presented by formal dualism—materialism vs. idealism, rationalism vs. empiricism, mind vs. body—can also examined using the dialectic method, which looks for ways to transcend the opposites and form a synthesis. Both sides have something in common, and understanding of the parts requires understanding their relationship with the whole system. The dialectic method thus sees the whole of reality as an evolving process. In *Liber Aleph*, "The Book of Wisdom or Folly," which the Curriculum of the A∴A∴ describes as an "extended and elaborate commentary on the *Book of the Law*," Crowley outlines the concept from a Thelemic perspective:

> I believe generally, on Ground both of Theory and Experience, so little as I have, that a Man must first be Initiate, and established in Our Law, before he may use this Method. For in it is an Implication of our Secret Enlightenment, concerning the Universe, how its Nature is utterly Perfection. Now every Thought is a Separation, and the Medicine of that is to marry Each one with its Contradiction, as I have showed formerly in many Writings. And thou shalt clasp the one to the other with Vehemence of Spirit, swiftly as Light itself, that the Ecstasy be Spontaneous. So therefore it is expedient that thou have travelled already in this Path of Antithesis, knowing perfectly the Answer to every Glyph or Problem, and thy Mind ready therewith. For by the Property of the Grass all passeth with Speed incalculable of Wit, and an Hesitation should confound thee, breaking down thy Ladder, and throwing back thy Mind to receive Impression from Environment, as at thy first Beginning. Verily, the Nature of this Method is Solution, and the Destruction of every Complexity by Explosion of Ecstasy, as every Element thereof is fulfilled by its Correlative, and is annihilated (since it loseth Separate Existence) in the Orgasm that is consummated within the Bed of thy Mind.[85]

"It is therefore unnecessary to fret over social problems and the rest of it; the root of the cause is duality, the antithesis of the Ego and the Non-Ego; and the cure is Realization of the Unity. Why treat symptoms, when we can eradicate the disease, especially as in this case the symptoms are sheer hullucinations [sic] on the part of the patient? It is the old story of the man in the railroad car with a basket, and the importunate stranger. 'Say, stranger, 'scuse me, but may I ask what you have in that basket?' 'Mongoose.' 'What'n Hades is a mongoose?' 'Mongoose eats snakes.' 'But what do you want with a mongoose?' 'My brother sees snakes.' (A pause) 'But, say, stranger, them ain't no real snakes.' 'This ain't a real mongoose.' Socialism, and religion, and love, and art, are all phantastic things, good to

---

and the most complete happiness."
[85] *Liber Aleph*, "Sequitur de hac re."

lull the ills of life, dreams pitted against dreams. But the only cure is to attack the cause of all the trouble, the illusion of duality."[86]

According to Crowley, the whole secret of Yoga is given in Matthew 6:22, "The light of the body is the eye: if therefore thine eye be single, thy whole body shall be full of light."—"This is a perfectly simple statement of the virtue of what the Hindus call 'Ekāgratā', 'one-pointedness'. The gospel of John, too, is full of dithyrambs expressing the results of mystic practice. 'I and my Father are one'; 'I am the Way, the Truth, and the Life'; 'I am in my Father, and ye in me, and I in you.' κτλ."[87] However, "Hadit is 'unique'. Every point that exists is Hadit. Each one is without limit, and thus all are in the end alike in every respect. At the same time no two are in any way alike, if compared at any given point-moment. This is one of the statements of this book which involves a new view of nature—a view far beyond any yet set forth and one with the virtue to resolve every problem which the cosmos presents to our minds. I may explain the matter simply in this way. No two points on a line are the same. Their distance from all other points differs. Each line, AB, AC, etc., is unique, even though $AB = A'B'$, they differ in respect of C'. AC' cannot be equal to $A'C'$. Lines drawn in two ways from a point are equal only in length; each point in each differs only in respect of any other point. At the same time, the line being supposed endless, the sum of what can be said about all points is the same. No point can claim that it is an unique distance from some other point."[88]

In his description of Atu XVII, "The Star," in *The Book of Thoth*, Crowley writes: "In this may be discovered the doctrine which asserts that the blindness of humanity to all the beauty and wonder of the Universe is due to this illusion of straightness. It is significant that Riemann, Bolyai and Lobatchewsky seem to have been the mathematical prophets of the New Revelation. For the Euclidian geometry depends upon the conception of straight lines, and it was only because the Parallel Postulate was found to be incapable of proof that mathematicians began to conceive that the straight line had no true correspondence with reality. *{The straight line is no more than the limit of any curve. For instance, it is an ellipse whose foci are an 'infinite' distance apart. In fact, such use of the Calculus is the one certain way of ensuring 'straightness'.}*" Hadit is, then, "both the Maker of Illusion and its destroyer. For though His interplay with Nuit results in the production of the Finite, yet His withdrawing into Himself is the destruction thereof."[89] Crowley repeatedly tells us that *yoga* means union, and that this union is "the cause of all phenomena. Consciousness results from the conjunction of a mysterious stimulus with a mysterious sensorium. The kind of Yoga which is the subject of these remarks is merely an expansion of this, the union of self-consciousness with the universe."[90]

---

[86] *Liber 888, loc. cit.*
[87] *Ibid.*
[88] DC on AL II.49.
[89] OC on AL II.7.
[90] *Eight Lectures*, Ch. 5, Sec. 1.

The *Śvetāśvatara Upaniṣad* (6.1-2) identifies God as the source of the great elements: "Some wise men say it is inherent nature, while others say it is time—all totally deluded. It is rather the greatness of God present in the world by means of which this wheel of brahman goes around. Who always encompasses this whole world—the knower, the architect of time, the one without qualities, and the all-knowing one—it is at his command that the work of creation, to be conceived of as earth, water, fire, air, and space, unfolds itself." Crowley disagrees: "It is no objection to this theory to ask who made the elements—the elements are at least there, and God, when you look for him, is not there. Theism is *obscurum per obscurius*. A male star is built up from the centre outwards; a female from the circumference inwards. This is what is meant when we say that woman has no soul. It explains fully the difference between the sexes."[91]

There is a point, which Stephen Hawking phrases dramatically in *A Brief History of Time*, that was commonplace a hundred years ago, but has gotten lost in the recent public debate. Physics, he says, is "just a set of rules and equations." The question is what "breathes fire into the equations and makes a universe for them to describe?"[92] The answer, once again, is that we simply don't know, except insofar as whatever it is takes the form of conscious experience. "What was the first mental process?" Crowley asks. "Obliged to describe Nothing, the only way to do so without destroying its integrity was to represent it as the union of a Plus Something with an equivalent Minus Something. One may call these two ideas, the Active and Passive, the Father and Mother. But although the Father and Mother can make a perfect union, thereby returning to Zero, which is a retrogression, they can also go forward into Matter, so that their union produces a Son and a Daughter. The idea works out in practice as a method of describing how the union of any two things produces a third thing which is neither of them."[93]

"The more advanced Yogis of the East, like the Nonconformists at home, have practically abandoned ceremonial as idle. I have yet to learn, however, by what dissenters have replaced it! I take this to be an error, except in the case of the very advanced Yogi. For there exists a true magical ceremonial, vital and direct, whose purpose has, however, at any rate of recent times, been hopelessly misunderstood."[94] Theorem 14 from *Magick in Theory and Practice* reads: "Man is capable of being, and using, anything which he perceives, for everything which he perceives is in a certain sense a part of his being. He may thus subjugate the whole of the Universe of which he is conscious to his individual Will." The illustration runs thus: "Man has used the idea of God to dictate his personal conduct, to obtain power over his fellows, to excuse his crimes, and for innumerable other purposes, including that of realizing himself as God. He has used the irrational and

---

[91] *MITAP*, Ch. XVIII, Sec. II, fn.; *cf.* also *MWT*, Ch. V; and NC on AL I.3. The passage, dated 14 May 1919, is believed to originate in the work entitled *The Book of the Great Auk*, no longer extant.
[92] Hawking 1998, 190.
[93] *The Book of Thoth*, loc. cit., Sec. II.
[94] *Berashith*.

unreal conceptions of mathematics to help him in the construction of mechanical devices. He has used his moral force to influence the actions even of wild animals. He has employed poetic genius for political purposes."

Theorem 19 states that, "Man's sense of himself as separate from, and opposed to, the Universe is a bar to his conducting its currents. It insulates him." This is illustrated by the following examples: "A popular leader is most successful when he forgets himself and remembers only 'The Cause'. Self-seeking engenders jealousies and schism. When the organs of the body assert their presence other by silent satisfaction, it is a sign they are diseased. The single exception is the organ of reproduction. Yet even in this case its self-assertion bears witness to its dissatisfaction with itself, since it cannot fulfil its function until completed by its counterpart in another organism." In *Eight Lectures on Yoga*, Crowley contends that "all true religion has been the artistic, the dramatic, representation of the sexual process, not merely because of the usefulness of this cult in tribal life, but as the veil of this truer meaning which I am explaining to you tonight."[95]

"Every 'act of love under will' has the dual result (1) the creation of a child combining the qualities of its parents, (2) the withdrawal by ecstasy into Nothingness. Please consult what I have elsewhere written on 'The Formula of Tetragrammaton'; the importance of this at the moment is to show how 0 and 2 appear constantly in Nature as the common Order of Events."[96] The *Eight Lectures* give an example from biology: "The spermatozoon and the ovum are biologically the separation of an unmanifested single cell, which is in its function simple, though it contains in itself, in a latent form, all the possibilities of the original single cell. Their union results in the manifestation of these qualities in the child. Their potentialities are expressed and developed in terms of time and space, while also, accompanying the act of union, is the ecstasy which is the natural result of the consciousness of their annihilation, the necessary condition of the production of their offspring."[97]

"The formula of Tetragrammaton is the most important for the practical magician."[98] It is a formula that "covers the entire universe of magical operations. The word usually pronounced Jehovah is called the Ineffable Name; it is alleged that when pronounced accurately its vibrations would destroy the universe; and this is indeed quite true, when we take the deeper interpretation."[99] This name "is in Hebrew a name of four letters, יהוה; and the true pronunciation of it is known to very few. I myself know some score of different mystical pronunciations of it. The true pronunciation of it is a most secret arcanum, and is a secret of secrets. 'He who can rightly pronounce it, causeth heaven and earth to tremble, for it is the name which rusheth through the universe.'"[100] This formula "is the

---

[95] *Eight Lectures*, loc. cit., Sec. 5.
[96] *MWT*, Ch. V.
[97] *Eight Lectures*, loc. cit., Sec. 4.
[98] *MITAP*, Ch. 0.
[99] *Eight Lectures*, loc. cit., Sec. 2.
[100] *The Temple of Solomon the King*, Part V.

complete mathematical expression of Love. Its essence is this: any two things unite, with a double effect; firstly, the destruction of both, accompanied by the ecstasy due to the relief of the strain of separateness; secondly, the creation of a third thing, accompanied by the ecstasy of the realisation of existence, which is Joy until with development it becomes aware of its imperfection, and loves."[101]

"This formula of Love is universal; all the laws of Nature are its servitors. Thus, gravitation, chemical affinity, electrical potential, and the rest—and these are alike mere aspects of the general law—are so many differently-observed statements of the unique tendency. The Universe is conserved by the duplex action involved in the formula. The disappearance of Father and Mother is precisely compensated by the emergence of Son and Daughter. It may therefore be considered as a perpetual-motion-engine which continually develops rapture in each of its phases.... The process of Love under Will is evidently progressive. The Father who has slain himself in the womb of the Mother finds himself again, with her, and transfigured, in the Son. This Son acts as a new Father; and it is thus that the Self is constantly aggrandized, and able to counterpoise an ever greater Not-Self, until the final act of Love under Will which comprehends the Universe in Sammasamadhi."[102]

The formula of the invocation of Thoth—the Egyptian Hermes or Mercury—"may also be classed under Tetragrammaton. The first part is fire, the eager prayer of the magician, the second water, in which the magician listens to, or catches the reflection of, the god. The third part is air, the marriage of fire and water; the god and the man have become one; while the fourth part corresponds to earth, the condensation or materialization of those three higher principles."[103] A footnote in *Magick* explains that the whole subject is "an example of Mythopœia in that particular form called Disease of Language. Thoth, God of Magick, was merely a man who invented writing, as his monuments declare clearly enough. 'Grammarye', Magick, is only the Greek 'Gramma'. So also the old name of a Magical Ritual, 'Grimoire', is merely a Grammar. It appeared marvellous to the vulgar that men should be able to communicate at a distance, and they began to attribute other powers, merely invented, to the people who were able to write. The Wand is then nothing but the pen; the Cup, the Inkpot; the Dagger, the knife for sharpening the pen; and the disk (Pantacle) is either the papyrus roll itself; or the weight which kept it in position, or the sandbox for soaking up the ink."[104]

> This formula is of most universal aspect, as all things are necessarily comprehended in it; but its use in a magical ceremony is little understood.

---

[101] *Little Essays Toward Truth*, "Love."
[102] *Ibid.*
[103] *MITAP*, Ch. II.
[104] *Ibid.*, Ch. VIII, Sec. III, fn.

The climax of the formula is in one sense before even the formulation of the *yod*. For the *yod* is the most divine aspect of the force—the remaining letters are but a solidification of the same thing. It must be understood that we are here speaking of the whole ceremony considered as a unity, not merely of that formula in which *yod* is the God invoked, *hé* the Archangel, and so on. In order to understand the ceremony under this formula, we must take a more extended view of the functions of the four weapons than we have hitherto done.

The formation of the *yod* is the formulation of the first creative force, of that Father who is called "self-begotten," and unto whom it is said: "Thou has formulated thy Father, and made fertile thy Mother." The adding of the *hé* to the *yod* is the marriage of that Father to the great co-equal Mother, who is a reflection of Nuit as he is of Hadit. Their union brings forth the Son *vau* who is the heir. Finally the Daughter *hé* is produced. She is both the twin sister and the Daughter of *vau*. *{There is a further mystery herein, far deeper, for initiates.}*

His mission is to redeem her by making her his bride; the result of this is to set her upon the throne of her Mother, and it is only she whose youthful embrace can reawaken the eld of the All-Father. In this complex family relationship *{The formula of Tetragrammaton, as ordinarily understood, ending with the appearance of the daughter, is indeed a degradation.}* is symbolised the whole course of the Universe. It will be seen that (after all) the Climax is at the end. It is the second half of the formula which symbolises the Great Work which we are pledged to accomplish. The first step of this is the attainment of the Knowledge and Conversation of the Holy Guardian Angel, which constitutes the Adept of the Inner Order.

The re-entry of these twin spouses into the womb of the mother is that initiation described in *Liber 418*, which gives admission to the Inmost Order of the A∴A∴.

Of the last step we cannot speak.[105]

It is "a Woman whose Cup must be filled. It is rather the sacrifice of the Man, who transfers life to his descendants. For a woman does not carry in herself the principle of new life, except temporarily, when it is given her. But here the formula implies much more even than this. For it is his whole life that the Magus offers to OUR LADY. The Cross is both Death and Generation, and it is on the Cross that the Rose blooms. . . . Of the preservation of this blood which OUR LADY offers to the ANCIENT ONE, CHAOS"—the footnote defines CHAOS as "a general name for the totality of the Units of Existence; it is thus a name feminine in form" and each of its units "is itself All-Father"—"the All-Father, to revive him, and of how his divine Essence fills the Daughter (the soul of Man) and places her upon the Throne of the Mother, fulfilling the Economy of the Universe, and thus ultimately rewarding the Magician (the Son) ten thousandfold, it would be

---

[105] *Ibid.*, Ch. III.

still more improper to speak in this place. So holy a mystery is the Arcanum of the Masters of the Temple, that it is here hinted at in order to blind the presumptuous who may, unworthy, seek to lift the veil, and at the same time to lighten the darkness of such as may be requiring only one ray of the Sun in order to spring into life and light."[106] It is "at once the Formula of the Feminine Trinity and of the All-Father."[107]

According to Plato, the four elements derive from a common source, or *prima materia*, associated with chaos.[108] "Prima materia" is also the name alchemists gave to the starting ingredient in making the philosopher's stone. We can say that it is energy that "breathes fire into the equation," using the word "energy" as Heisenberg does, when he says that "all particles are made of the same substance: energy."[109] However, the same fundamental question arises again: What is the intrinsic nature of this energy? And the answer still is that we just don't know, or that physics cannot tell us. This point about the limits of physics arises every time we consider any of the deep problems of the science, e.g. problems with "dark matter" or "dark energy," or with reconciling quantum mechanics and general relativity. In *An Essay upon Number*, Crowley writes that four is the "terrible number of Tetragrammaton, the great enemy. The number of the weapons of the Evil Magician. The Dyad made Law," whereas the number five, the "Pentagram, symbol of the squaring of the circle by virtue of אלהים = 3.1415, symbol of man's will, of the evil 4 dominated by man's spirit. Also Pentagrammaton, Jeheshua, the Saviour. Hence the Beginning of the Great Work."

"יהשוה, *Yeheshuah* or Jesus; but how do I know that this word and not another has power to make man triumphant over matter, to harmonize and sanctify the blind forces of the universe? Thus: I know that יהוה represents the four elements; that 4 is a number symbolizing limitation. It is the square of 2, the only number which cannot be formed harmoniously into a 'Magic Square'. (Two represents the Dyad, the original Error.) I know also that the letter Shin represents a triune essence, the fire of the Spirit, and in particular *Ruach Elohim*, the Spirit of the Gods, because these two words have the numerical value of 300, which is also that of Shin itself. I thus interpret the word Yeheshuah as the descent of the Holy Spirit into the balanced forces of matter, and the name Yeheshuah is therefore that of a man made divine by the descent of the Holy Spirit into his heart, exactly as the name George means a farmer."[110] The common Hebrew name Yeshua is a verbal derivative from "to deliver" or "to rescue," and thus often translated as "He saves." (*Cf.* Matthew 1:21.) Similarly, the English name George derives from the Latin *Georgius*, "farmer" (*ge* "earth" + *ergon* "work"), the *Georgics* being a famous bucolic by the Roman epic poet Virgil.

---

[106] *Ibid.*, Ch. VII, Sec. I. Emphasis in original.
[107] *Liber 418*, 3rd Æthyr, fn.
[108] Plat. *Tim.* 48b.
[109] Heisenberg 1958, 71.
[110] *Confessions*, Ch. 72.

"In *Liber A. vel Armorum*, the official instruction of the A∴A∴ for the preparation of the elemental weapons, it is said that each symbolic representation of the Universe is to be approved by the Superior of the Magician. To this rule the Lamp is an exception; it is said: 'A Magical Lamp that shall burn without wick or oil, being fed by the Æthyr. This shall he accomplish secretly and apart, without asking the advice or approval of his Adeptus Minor.' This Lamp is the light of the pure soul; it hath no need of fuel, it is the Burning Bush inconsumable that Moses saw, the image of the Most High."[111] In *Liber Aleph*, Crowley reminds Achad how he has "already written unto thee, my Son, of the Paradox of Liberty, how the Freedom of thy Will dependeth upon the Bending of all thy forces to that one End. But now also learn how great is the Œconomy of our Magick, and this will I declare unto thee in a Figure of the Holy Qabalah, to wit, the Formula of the Tetragrammaton. Firstly, the Operation of Yod and He is not Vau only, but with Vau appeareth also a new He, as a By-Product, and She is mysterious, being at once the Flower of the three others, and their Poison. Now by the Operation of Vau upon that He is no new Creation, but the Daughter is set upon the Throne of Her Mother, and by this is rekindled the Fire of Yod, which, consuming that Virgin, doth not add a Fifth Person, but balanceth and perfecteth all. For his Shin, that is the Holy Spirit, pervadeth these, and is immanent. Thus in three Operations is the Pentagram formulated."[112]

"The element of Fire is very close kin to the idea of Spirit; so the letter Shin, belonging to Fire, may be taken to mean Spirit as well. There is a special reason why this should be so, although it only applies in later ages, since the introduction of the dogma that Spirit rules the four elements, and the formation of the 'Pentagram of Salvation' connected with the Hebrew word IHShVH, Yeheshuah."[113] A Jewish Qabalist will be the first to point out that Yeshua is actually spelled ישוע. However, the variant spelling, also known as the Pentagrammaton, did not originate with Crowley but with Christian Qabalists of the Renaissance; one is a mythical character in a Gentile legend, the other a universal magical formula.

> The cleansed and consecrated Magician takes his cleansed and consecrated instruments into that cleansed and consecrated place, and there proceeds to repeat that double ceremony in the ceremony itself, which has these same two main parts. The first part of every ceremony is the banishing; the second, the invoking. The same formula is repeated even in the ceremony of banishing itself, for in the Banishing Ritual of the Pentagram we not only command the demons to depart, but invoke the Archangels and their hosts to act as guardians of the Circle during our preoccupation with the ceremony proper.
>
> In more elaborate ceremonies it is usual to banish everything by name. Each element, each planet, and each sign, perhaps even the

---

[111] *Book 4*, Part II, Ch. X.
[112] "De operibus stellæ microcosmi. Quorum sunt quattour minores."
[113] *The Book of Thoth*, loc. cit., Sec. III.

Sephiroth themselves—all are removed, including the very one which we wished to invoke, for that forces as existing in Nature is always impure. But this process, being long and wearisome, is not altogether advisable in actual working. It is usually sufficient to perform a general banishing, and to rely upon the aid of the guardians invoked. Let the banishing therefore be short, but in no wise slurred—for it is useful, as it tends to produce the proper attitude of mind for the invocations. "The Banishing Ritual of the Pentagram" (as now rewritten {Liber 333, Cap. XXV}) is the best to use. {See also the ritual called "The Mark of the Beast" given in an Appendix. But this is pantomorphous.}[114]

"Only the Four Elements are specifically mentioned, but these Four Elements contain the Planets and the Signs—the Four Elements are Tetragrammaton; and Tetragrammaton is the Universe."[115] The footnote points out that the sign and the planets also "of course" contain the elements: "It is important to remember this fact, as it helps one to grasp what all these terms really mean. None of the 'Thirty-two Paths' [on the Qabalistic Tree of Life] is a simple idea; each one is a combination, differentiated from the others by its structure and proportions. The chemical elements are similarly constituted, as the critics of Magick have at last been compelled to admit." Another footnote, this time to *The Palace of the World*, says of the Lesser Ritual of the Pentagram, that people who regard it "as a mere device to invoke or banish spirits, are unworthy to possess it. Properly understood, it is the Medicine of Metals and the Stone of the Wise."

"The Circle of the Magician will have been perfected by his habit of Magical work. In the truest sense of that word, he will never step outside the Circle during his whole life. But the consecration, being the application of a positive force, can always be raised to a closer approximation to perfection. Complete success in banishing is soon attained; but there can be no completeness in the advance to holiness."[116] Crowley asks his magical son, "is it not a marvel, this Light whereof we are the Quintessence and the Seed? By it are we made Whole, dissolved in the Body and in the Soul of Our Lady Nuit even as Her Lord Hadit, so that the Gnostic Sacrament of the Cosmos is perpetually Elevated before us. We behold all that is and comprehend its Mystery, and its Order in this High Mass eternally celebrated among us, acknowledging the Perfection of the Rite, neither confusing the Parts thereof, nor discriminating in Worship between them. So unto us is every Phenomenon a Shew of Godliness, proceeding continually in a Pageant that returneth unto itself, identical in the Phase of Naught as of Many, but whirling in the Orgia of Ineffable Holiness as it were a Dance that weaveth Figures of Beauty in Variety inexhaustible."[117]

---

[114] *MITAP*, Ch. XIII.
[115] *Ibid.*
[116] *MITAP*, Ch. XIV, Sec. I.
[117] *Liber Aleph*, "De pace perfecta."

It is impossible to alter the ultimate Nature of any Being, however completely we may succeed in transfiguring its external signs as displayed in any of its combinations. Thus, the sweetness, whiteness, and crystalline structure of sugar depend partly on the presence of Carbon; so do the bitterness, greenness, and resinous composition of hashish. But the Carbon is inviolably Carbon. And even when we transmute what seem to be elements, as Radium to Lead, we merely go a step further; there is still an immutable substance—or essence of Energy—which is inevitably Itself, the basis of the diversity.

This holds good even should we arrive at demonstrating Material Monism. It may well be—I have believed so ever since I was fourteen years old—that the elements are all isomers, differentiated by geometrical structure, electrical charge, or otherwise in precisely the same way as ozone from oxygen, red from yellow phosphorous, dextrose from laevulose, and a paraffin from a benzene of identical empirical formula. Indeed, every "star" is necessarily derived from the uniform continuity of Nuit, and resolvable back into Her Body by the proper analytical methods, as the experience of mysticism testifies. But each such complex is none the less uniquely itself; for the scheme of its construction is part of its existence, so that this peculiar scheme constitutes the essence of its individuality. It is impossible to change a shilling into two sixpences, though the value and the material may be identical; for part of the essence of the shilling is the intention to have a single coin.

The above considerations must be thoroughly assimilated by any mind which wishes to gain a firm intellectual grasp of the truth which lies behind the paradox of existence.[118]

---

[118] NC on AL II.57.

CHAPTER 5
Epistemology

The Æon of Horus is here: and its first flower may well be this: that, freed of the obsession of the doom of the Ego in Death, and of the limitation of the Mind by Reason, the best men again set out with eager eyes upon the Path of the Wise, the mountain track of the goat, and then the untrodden Ridge, that leads to the ice-gleaming pinnacles of Mastery!
— Little Essays Toward Truth

In the *New Comment*, Crowley explains at length "that 'reason is a lie' by nature. We may here add certain confirmations suggested by the 'factor.' A and a (not-A) together make up the Universe. As a is evidently 'infinite and unknown,' its equal and opposite A must be so no less. Again, from any proposition S is P, reason deduces 'S is not p'; thus the apparent finitude and knowability of S is deceptive, since it is in direct relation with p."[1]

No matter what n may be, $n + \infty$, the number of the inductive numbers, is unaltered by adding or subtracting it. There are just as many odd numbers as there are numbers altogether. Our knowledge is confined to statements of the relations between certain sets of our own sensory impressions; and we are convinced by our limitations that "a factor infinite and unknown" must be concealed within the sphere of which we see but one minute part of the surface. As to reason itself, what is more certain than that its laws are only the conscious expression of the limits imposed upon us by our animal nature, and that to attribute universal validity, or even significance, to them is a logical folly, the raving of our megalomania? Experiment proves nothing; it is surely obvious that we are obliged to correlate all observations with the physical and mental structure whose truth we are trying to test. Indeed, we can assume an "unreasonable" axiom, and translate the whole of our knowledge into its terms, without fear of stumbling over any obstacle. Reason is no more than a set of rules developed by the race; it takes no account of anything beyond sensory impressions and their reactions to various parts of our being. There is no possible escape from the vicious circle that we can register only the behaviour of our own instrument. We conclude from the fact that it behaves at all, that there must be "a factor infinite and unknown" at work upon it. This being the case, we may be sure that our apparatus is inherently incapable of discovering the truth about anything, even in part.

---

[1] NC on AL II.32.

Let me illustrate. I see a drop of water. Distrusting my eyes, I put it under the microscope. Still in doubt, I photograph and enlarge the slide. I compare my results with those of others. I check them by cultivating the germs in the water, and injecting them into paupers. But I have learnt nothing at all about "the infinite and unknown," merely producing all sorts of different impressions according to the conditions in which one observes it!

More yet, all the instruments used have been tested and declared "true" on the evidence of those very eyes distrust of which drove me to the research.

Modern Science has at last grown out of the very-young-man cocksureness of the 19th century. It is now admitted that axioms themselves depend on definitions, and that Intuitive Certainty is simply one trait of *homo sapiens*, like the ears of the ass or the slime of the slug. That we reason as we do merely proves that we cannot reason otherwise. We cannot move the upper jaw; it does not follow that the idea of motion is ridiculous. The limitation hints rather that there may be an infinite variety of structures which the jaw cannot imagine. The metric system is not the necessary mode of measurement. It is the mark of a mind untrained to take its own processes as valid for all men, and its own judgments for absolute truth. Our two eyes see an object in two aspects, and present to our consciousness a third which agrees with neither, is indeed, strictly speaking, not sensible to sight, but to touch! Our senses declare some things at rest and others in motion; our reason corrects the error, firstly by denying that anything can exist unless it is in motion, secondly by denying that absolute motion possesses any meaning at all.[2]

"Since truth is supra-rational, it is incommunicable in the language of reason."[3] Therefore, "any rational statement is false. . . . Let the student then contradict every proposition that presents itself to him. . . . Rational ideas being thus expelled from the mind, there is room for the apprehension of spiritual truth." However, "It should be remarked that this does not destroy the validity of reasonings on their own plane."[4] From the standpoint of philosophy, "'Because is absurd.' There is no answer to the question 'Why.' The greatest thinkers have been sceptics or agnostics: *omnia exeunt in mysterium*,[5] and *summa scientia nihil scire*[6] are old commonplaces. In my essays 'Truth' (in *Konx Om Pax*), 'The Soldier and the Hunchback,' 'Eleusis' and others, I have offered a detailed demonstration of the self-contradictory nature of Reason. The crux of the whole proof may be summarized by saying that any possible proposition must be equally true with its contradictory, as, if not, the universe would no longer be in equilibrium. It is no objection that to accept this is to destroy conventional Logic, for that

---

[2] *Ibid.*
[3] *Postcards to Probationers*, "Mistakes of Mystics."
[4] *Ibid.*, "The Method of Equilibrium."
[5] "All things pass into mystery." A Scholastic maxim.
[6] "The height of knowledge is knowing nothing." *The Chemical Wedding of Christian Rosenkreutz*.

is exactly what it is intended to do. I may also mention briefly one line of analysis."[7]

I ask "What is (*e.g.*) a tree?" The dictionary defines this simple idea by means of many complex ideas; obviously one gets in deeper with every stroke one takes. The same applies to any "Why" that may be posed. The one existing mystery disappears as a consequence of innumerable antecedents, each equally mysterious.

To ask questions is thus evidently worse than a waste of time, so far as one is looking for an answer.

There is also the point that any proposition S is P merely includes P in the connotation of S, and is therefore not really a statement of relation between two things, but an amendment of the definition of one of them. "Some cats are black" only means that our idea of a cat involves the liability to appear black, and that blackness is consistent with those sets of impressions which we recognize as characteristic of cats. All ratiocination may be reduced to syllogistic form; hence, the sole effect of the process is to make each term more complex. Reason does not add to our knowledge; a filing system does not increase one's correspondence directly, though by arranging it one gets a better grasp of one's business. Thus coordination of our impressions should help us to control them; but to allow reason to rule us is as abject as to expect the exactitude of our ledgers to enable us to dispense with initiative on the one hand and actual transactions on the other.[8]

"Let me set out by restating our original problem; what we want is Truth; we want an even closer approach to Reality; and we want to discover and discuss the proper means of achieving this object. Very good; let us start by the simplest of all possible enquiries—and the most difficult—'What is anything?' 'What do we know?' and other questions that spring naturally from these. I see a tree. I hear it—rustling or creaking in the wind. I touch it—hard. I smell it—acrid. I taste it—bitter. Now all the information given by these five senses has to be put together, although no two agree in any sort of way. The logic by which we build up our complex idea of a tree has more holes than a sponge."[9]

But this is to jump far ahead: we must first analyze the single, simple impression. "I see a tree." This phenomenon is what is called a "point-event." It is the coming together of the two, the seer and the seen. It is single and simple; yet we cannot conceive of either of them as anything but complex. And the Point-Event tells us nothing whatever about either; both, as Herbert Spencer and God knows how many others have shown, unknowable; it stands by itself, alone and aloof. It has happened; it is undeniably Reality. Yet we cannot confirm it; for it can never

---

[7] NC on AL II.33.
[8] *Ibid.*
[9] *MWT*, Ch. III.

happen again precisely the same. What is even more bewildering is that since it takes time for the eye to convey an impression to the consciousness (it may alter in 1,000 ways in the process!) all that really exists is a memory of the Point-Event. not the Point-Event itself. What then *is* this Reality of which we are so sure? Obviously, it has not got a name, since it never happened before, or can happen again! To discuss it at all we must *invent* a name, and this name (like all names) cannot possibly be anything more than a symbol.

Even so, as so often pointed out, all we do is to "record the behaviour of our instruments." Nor are we much better off when we've done it; for our symbol, referring as it does to a phenomenon unique in itself, and not to be apprehended by another, can mean nothing to one's neighbors. What happens, of course, is that similar, though not identical, Point-Events happen to many of us, and so we are able to construct a symbolic language. My memory of the mysterious Reality resembles yours sufficiently to induce us to agree that both belong to the same class.

But let me furthermore ask you to reflect on the formation of language itself. Except in the case of onomatopoeic words and a few others, there is no logical connection between a thing and the sound of our name for it. "Bow-wow" is a more rational name than "dog", which is a mere convention agreed on by the English, while other nations prefer *chien, hund, cane, kalb, kutta* and so on. All symbols, you see, my dear child, and it's no good your kicking!

But it doesn't stop there. When we try to convey thought by writing, we are bound to sit down solidly, and construct a holy Qabalah out of nothing. Why would a curve open to the right, sound like the ocean, open at the top, like you? And all these arbitrary symbolic letters are combined by just as symbolic and arbitrary devices to take on conventional meanings, these words again combined into phrases by no less high-handed a procedure.

And then folk wonder how it is that there should be error and misunderstanding in the transmission of thought from one person to another! Rather regard it as a miraculous intervention of Providence when even one of even the simplest ideas "gets across." Now then, this being so, it is evidently good sense to construct one's own alphabet, with one's own very precise definitions, in order to handle an abstruse and technical subject like Magick. The "ordinary" words such as God, self, soul, spirit and the rest have been used so many thousand times in so many thousand ways, usually by writers who knew not, or cared not for the necessity of definition that to use them to-day in any scientific essay is almost ludicrous.

That is all, just now, sister; no more of your cavilling, please; sit down quietly with your *777*, and get it by heart![10]

Liber 777, subtitled *Prolegomena Symbolica Ad Systemam Sceptico-Mysticæ Viæ Explicandæ, Fundamentum Hieroglyphicum Sanctissimorum*

---

[10] *Ibid*. Emphasis in original.

Scientiæ Summæ, is a "complete Dictionary of the Correspondences of all magical elements, re-printed with extensive additions, making it the only standard comprehensive book of reference ever published." Indeed, according to Crowley, it "is to the language of Occultism what Webster or Murray is to the English language."[11] In his opinion, none of what we learned above "shakes, or even threatens, the Philosophy of Thelema. On the contrary, it may be called the Rock of its foundation. For the issue of all is evidently that all conceptions are necessarily unique because there can never be two identical points-of-view; and this corresponds with the facts; for there are points-of-view close kin, and thus there may be a superficial general agreement, as there is, which is found to be false on analysis, as has been shewn."[12]

What do we do when we "think?"
There are two operations, and only two, possible to thought. However complex a statement may appear, it can always be reduced to a series of one or other of these. If not, it is a sham statement; nonsense masquerading as sense in the cloak of verbiage and verbosity.
Analysis, and Synthesis; or,
Subtraction, and Addition.
1. You can examine A, and find that it is composed of B and C. $A = B + C$.
2. You can find out what happens to B when you add C to it. $B + C = A$.
As you notice, the two are identical, after all; but the process is different.
Example: Raise Copper Oxide to a very high temperature; you obtain metallic copper and oxygen gas. Heat copper in a stream of oxygen; you obtain copper oxide.
You can complicate such experiments indefinitely, as when one analyzes coal-tar, or synthesizes complex products like quinine from its elements; but one can always describe what happens as a series of simple operations, either of the analytical or the synthetic type.[13]

Now, "the first stumbling-block to study is that one never has any certainty as to what the author means, or thinks he means, or is trying to persuade one that he means. Try something simple: 'The soul is part of God.' Now then, when he writes 'soul' does he mean *Atma*, or *Buddhi*, or the *Higher Manas*, or *Purusha*, or *Yechidah*, or *Neschamah*, or *Nephesh*, or *Nous*, or *Psyche*, or *Phren*, or *Ba*, or *Khu*, or *Ka*, or *Animus*, or *Anima*, or *Seele*, or what? As everybody, will he nill he, creates 'God' in his own image, it is perfectly useless to inquire what he may happen to mean by that. But even this very plain word 'part.' Does he mean to imply a quantitative assertion, as when one says sixpence is part of a pound, or a factor indispensable, as when one says 'A wheel is part of a motor-car', or . . . (Part actually means 'a

---

[11] A∴A∴ *Curriculum*.
[12] *Little Essays Toward Truth*, "Knowledge."
[13] *MWT*, Ch. XXVI.

share, that which is provided,' according to Skeat; and I am closer to the place where Moses was when the candle went out than I was before!)"[14]

"The fact is that very few of us know what words mean; fewer still take the trouble to enquire. We calmly, we carelessly assume that our minds are identical with that of the writer, at least on that point; and then we wonder that there should be misunderstandings!"[15] Crowley cautions us to "Never forget the abiding temptation of men of science, the hidden rocks on which so many have been wrecked, to generalize on insufficient data. May the gods keep us from that! I dread it more than all the other snags put together."[16] The motto of *The Equinox* notwithstanding, Crowley was actually an early critic of "scientism," the belief in the universal applicability of the scientific method and approach, and the view that the categories and things recognized in natural science form the only proper elements in any philosophical or other inquiry.

> The knowledge of exoteric science is comically limited by the fact that we have no access, except in the most indirect way, to any other celestial body than our own. In the last few years, the semi-educated have got an idea that they know a great deal about the universe, and the principal ground for their fine opinion of themselves is usually the telephone or the airship. It is pitiful to read the bombastic twaddle about progress, which journalists and others, who wish to prevent men from thinking, put out for consumption. We know infinitesimally little of the material universe. Our detailed knowledge is so contemptibly minute, that it is hardly worth reference, save that our shame may spur us to increased endeavour. Such knowledge as we have got is of a very general and abstruse, of a philosophical and almost magical character. This consists principally of the conceptions of pure mathematics. It is, therefore, almost legitimate to say that pure mathematics is our link with the rest of the universe and with "God".
>
> Now the conceptions of Magick are themselves profoundly mathematical. The whole basis of our theory is the Qabalah, which corresponds to mathematics and geometry. The method of operation in Magick is based on this, in very much the same way as the laws of mechanics are based on mathematics. So far, therefore as we can be said to possess a magical theory of the universe, it must be a matter solely of fundamental law, with a few simple and comprehensive propositions stated in very general terms.[17]

Crowley's Introduction to *Magick in Theory and Practice* quotes *The Golden Bough* by Sir James George Frazer: "The magician does not doubt that the same causes will always produce the same effects, that the performance of the proper ceremony accompanied by the appropriate spell, will inevitably be attended by the desired results, unless, indeed, his

---

[14] *Ibid.*
[15] *Ibid.*
[16] *Ibid.*, Ch. LXVIII.
[17] *MITAP*, Ch. 0.

incantations should chance to be thwarted and foiled by the more potent charms of another sorcerer. He supplicates no higher power: he sues the favour of no fickle and wayward being: he abases himself before no awful deity. Yet his power, great as he believes it to be, is by no means arbitrary and unlimited. He can wield it only so long as he strictly conforms to the rules of his art, or to what may be called the laws of nature as conceived by him. To neglect these rules, to break these laws in the smallest particular is to incur failure, and may even expose the unskilful practitioner himself to the utmost peril. If he claims a sovereignty over nature, it is a constitutional sovereignty rigorously limited in its scope and exercised in exact conformity with ancient usage. Thus the analogy between the magical and the scientific conceptions of the world is close."[18]

Magick is less liable to lead to error than any other Science, because its terms are interchangeable, by definition, so that it is based on relativity from the start. We run no risk of asserting absolute propositions. Furthermore we make our measurements in terms of the object measured, thus avoiding the absurdity of defining metaphysical ideas by mutable standards (cf. Eddington, *Space, Time, and Gravitation*, Prologue), of being forced to attribute the qualities of human consciousness to inanimate things (Poincaré, "La mesure du temps"[19]), and of asserting that we know anything of the universe in itself, though the nature of our senses and our minds necessarily determines our observations, so that the limit of our knowledge is subjective, just as a thermometer can record nothing but its own reaction to one particular type of Energy.

Magick recognizes frankly (1) that Truth is relative, subjective, and apparent; (2) that Truth implies Omniscience, which is unattainable by mind, being transfinite; just as if one tried to make an exact map of England in England, that map must contain a map of the map, and so on, *ad infinitum*; (3) that logical contradiction is inherent in reason (Russell, *Introduction to Mathematical Philosophy*, p. 136; Crowley, "Eleusis," and elsewhere); (4) that a Continuum requires a Continuum to be commensurable with it: (5) that Empiricism is ineluctable, and therefore that adjustment is the only possible method of action; and (6) that error may be avoided by opposing no resistance to change, and registering observed phenomena in their own language.[20]

"Gnana Yoga," Crowley tells us, "is that Yoga which commences with a study of the impermanent wisdom of this world and ends with the knowledge of the permanent wisdom of the Âtman. Its first stage is Viveka, the discernment of the real from the unreal. Its second Vairâgya, indifference to the knowledge of the world, its sorrows and joys. Its third Mukti, release, and unity with the Âtman. . . . Very closely allied to Gnana

---

[18] Frazer 1911–15, i.220–221.
[19] *La valeur de la science*, Ch. 2.
[20] *MITAP*, Ch. IX, fn.

Yoga is Karma Yoga, Yoga through work, which may seem only a means towards the former. But this is not so, for not only must the aspirant commune with the Âtman through the knowledge or wisdom he attains, but also through the work which aids him to attain it." And the Gnana Yoga[21] Crowley, "as the student, had already long practised in his study of the Holy Qabalah; so also had he Karma Yoga by his acts of service whilst a Neophyte in the Order of the Golden Dawn." And at the suggestion of his teacher, Allan Bennett, "he betook himself to practice of Hatha and Raja Yoga."[22]

> The invention of electric machines has in no way interfered with Matter or Motion; it has only helped us to get rid of certain aspects of the Illusion of Time and Space, and so brought the most intelligent minds to the threshold of the Magical and Mystical Doctrine: they have been forced to imagine the possibility of the perception of the Universe as it is, freed of conditions. That is, they have been given a glimpse of the nature of the Attainment of Mastery. And it is surely but a little step to take for the leaders of natural Science, Mathematics their guiding Star, that they should understand the compelling necessity of the Great Work, and apply themselves to its achievement.
>
> Here the great obstacles are these; firstly, the misunderstanding of Self; and secondly, the resistance of the rational mind against its own conclusions. Men must cast off these two restrictions; they must begin to realise that Self is hidden behind, and independent of, the mental and material instrument in which they apprehend their Point-of-View; and they must seek an instrument other than that which insists (with every single observation) on impressing on them what is merely its own most hateful flaw and error, the idea of duality.[23]

"The formula of a mystery," in the words of Éliphas Lévi, "excludes necessarily the very intelligence of that formula, so far as it is borrowed from the world of known things; for, if one understood it, it would express the known and not the unknown. It would then belong to science, and no longer to religion, that is to say, to faith. The object of faith is a mathematical problem, whose x escapes the procedures of our algebra. Absolute mathematics prove only the necessity, and, in consequence, the existence of this unknown which we represent by the untranslatable x. Now science progresses in vain; its progress is indefinite, but always relatively finite; it will never find in the language of the finite the complete expression of the infinite. Mystery is therefore eternal. . . . The hierarchy is the guardian of dogma, for whose letter and spirit she alike demands respect. The sectarians who, in the name of their reason or, rather, of their

---

[21] Also spelled "Jñāna Yoga." The Sanskrit root *jñā-* is cognate to English *know* and to the Greek γνώ- (as in γνῶσις, *gnōsis*).
[22] *The Temple of Solomon the King*, Part IV, "The Yogas."
[23] *Little Essays Toward Truth*, "Mastery."

individual unreason, have laid hands on dogma, have, in the very act, lost the spirit of charity; they have excommunicated themselves."[24]

As Crowley observes, "The reality of that universe, which is the universe of science, is only an abstraction; it is, no doubt, *nearly* true for everybody, roughly speaking; but it is *quite* true for nobody."[25] It is the "failure of philosophers to transcend their own mental limitations" that "has reduced all their systems to circular arguments, and all their ontologies to Solipsism, however elaborately they have endeavoured to cloak the fact with sophistries. You cannot tie a true knot in a cord with a closed circuit. All knowledge is relative to the mind which contains it. . . . It will no doubt be objected that these speculations, even if correct, are sterile; or, even worse, discouraging to that study of the relations between phenomena which has been the basis of all advance in knowledge."[26]

> I might deny the reality of the progress, since it has only exposed the self-contradictions, and emphasized the mysteries, which beset us. But I prefer to take my stand on the ground that we have been totally wrong, hitherto, in our fundamental attitude to the Universe. The only possible issue from the vicious circle wherein we are penned is to refuse resolutely to allow ourselves to accept (1) the evidence of our senses, (2) the pleadings of our minds, (3) the reactions between phenomena as tokens of Truth. All objects are equally capable of conveying any given impression to us; it is merely a question of arranging the conditions of the experiments. We can add or subtract any conceivable quality at will. Thus, "there is no difference"; and each existence is inscrutably itself. We are only the more deceived as it multiplies its Protean projections.
>
> Our proper course is to destroy the instruments of perception which we at present possess, recognizing that they are no more than personal prejudices which limit and delude us in every way. Our senses assure us that the earth is flat, and that the Sun moves across it, until we amend their assertions by the aid of instruments, and of reason. Yet the astronomer with his telescope is no less arbitrary than the cave-man with his eye. We are like the Snark in the Barrister's dream, witnesses, lawyers, and judge in one. We have no standard independent or ourselves; and we know only too well that our witnesses, the senses, are neither competent, clear, trustworthy, intelligent, or even capable of giving evidence on the actual issues.
>
> The mind is in even worse plight. Obviously, its judgments must be based on its own laws, and we have no shadow of reason for supposing that these possess any authority beyond their own jurisdiction. We know that the Structure of the brain has been determined by the animal struggle to survive: it is adapted to the conditions of environment. It is the serf of brute passions, the ape of atavism, the dupe of sense, and the

---

[24] *The Key of the Mysteries*, Part I, Article III. Indeed, the Kuhnian model of scientific revolutions suggests that the paradigms of science are never really more than consensus opinions, whose popularity is transitory and far from conclusive; *cf.* e.g. Cohen 2015.
[25] *The Method of Thelema*. Emphasis in original.
[26] NC on AL I.27.

EPISTEMOLOGY 135

automaton of accident. We have no right to assert that its internal reactions correspond to the external world in any way whatever. Officially recognized thinkers are only just beginning to realize what mystics have known since the Morning Star glimmered through the haze on the horizon of History, that the Laws of Thought are only expressions of the bondage of the thinker. Apart from the dependence of mind upon the unreliable, symbolically communicated, and fragmentary affidavits of sense, apart from the imperfections inseparable from its origin, our judgments are necessarily no more than representations of the consistency of one part of our internal structure with another. We cannot lift ourselves by pulling at our toes. We now know that our most fixed axioms are as arbitrary as a madman's delusions. There is nothing to prevent a man from asserting that "Things which are both equal to the same thing are both greater than each other" and constructing a geometry conformable thereto: neither by reasoning nor by experience could it be proved that his system was not the "truth" of Nature. More, the word "truth" itself has proved on analysis to contain no intelligible significance, but to be an empirical symbol of what can only be described as symptoms of cerebral inadequacy.[27]

"Still worse, even so far as the conclusions of reason express the relations of an animal with itself, they disclose not the consistency which is the test of the fulfilment of this limited function, but an inherent self-contradiction which shatters the validity of the entire process." We must, therefore, "eliminate as far as possible very obvious source of error, such as personality (in particular) involves. But further, we must regulate the motion of the mind, control it, bring it to a standstill. It may be—I know that it is—that as soon as thought is prevented from bewildering us with its torrential turmoil, we may become aware that we possess a subtler and steadier organ of apprehension. This is in fact one of the principal points of initiation."[28]

> Mind is a disease of semen.
> All that a man is or may be is hidden therein.
> Bodily functions are parts of the machine; silent, unless in dis-ease.
> This I persisteth not, posteth not through generations, changeth momently, finally is dead.
> Therefore is man only himself when lost to himself in The Charioting.[29]

"Once the Unknown becomes known it becomes untrue, it loses its Virginity, that mysterious power of attraction the Unknown always possesses; it no longer represents our ideal, though it may form an excellent foundation for the next ideal; and so on until Knowledge and

---

[27] *Ibid.*
[28] *Ibid.*
[29] *The Book of Lies*, Ch. 8.

Nescience are out-stepped. General and popular Knowledge is like a common prostitute, the toy of any man. To maintain this purity, this virginity, are the mysteries kept secret from the multitude."[30] Crowley further cautions us that, "Metaphysics, too, is intellectual bondage; avoid it! Otherwise on falls back to the Law of Hoor from the perfect emancipation of Nuit. This is a great mystery, only to be understood by those who have fully attained Nuit and her secret Initiation."[31]

One reason why Siddhārtha refused to engage in metaphysical speculation is that he saw ultimate reality and *Nirvāṇa* as devoid of sensory mediation and conception, and therefore language itself as *a priori* inadequate to explain it. Gautama's silence thus does not indicate disdain for reason or philosophy, but rather a view that the answers to these questions are not comprehensible by the unenlightened. The Buddha of the earliest Buddhist texts describes *Dharma* as "beyond reasoning" or "transcending logic," and *Pratītyasamutpāda* (commonly translated as "dependent origination") provides a framework for analysis of reality that is not based on metaphysical assumptions regarding existence or non-existence, but instead on imagining direct cognition of phenomena as they present themselves to the mind in yogic meditation.[32]

"What are phenomena?" Crowley asked. "Of noumena I know and can know nothing. All I know is, as far as I know, a mere modification of the mind, a phase of consciousness. And thought is a secretion of the brain. Consciousness is a function of the brain. If this thought was contradicted by the obvious, 'And what is the brain? A phenomenon in mind!' it weighed less with him. It seemed to his mind as yet unbalanced (as all minds are unbalanced until they have crossed the Abyss), that it was more important to insist on matter than on mind. Idealism wrought such misery, was the father of all illusion, never led to research. And yet what odds? Every act or thought is determined by an infinity of causes, is the resultant of an infinity of forces."[33] In other words, "Everything that happens, no matter what, is an inconceivably improbable coincidence. . . . Chance blindly rules the Universe. But what is Chance? And where does purpose intervene? To what extent? . . . *A fortiori*, Coincidence is destroyed by Purpose, if, wishing to enlighten you on the subject, I write this letter and post it to your address, your receipt of it is no longer Coincidence. So then coincidence must be entirely both unforeseen and unintentional; in other words, absolutely senseless. But we have just proved that the Universe is nothing but Coincidence; it therefore is senseless."[34]

As Nietzsche has it, "the 'Will to Truth' would have to be examined psychologically: it is not a moral power, but a form of the Will to Power. This would have to be proved by the fact that it avails itself of every immoral means there is; above all, those of the metaphysicians."[35] His

---

[30] *The Temple of Solomon the King, loc. cit.,* "The Vedanta," fn.
[31] OC on AL I.52.
[32] Hamilton 2000.
[33] *The Temple of Solomon the King*, Part VI, "The Priest."
[34] *MWT*, Ch. XL.
[35] *The Will to Power*, §583.C.

Overman is able to actualize his will-to-power himself and create a "master-morality" that reflects the strength and independence of someone who is liberated from all values, except for those which he himself deems valid.[36] However, "Until the Great Work has been performed, it is presumptuous for the magician to pretend to understand the universe, and dictate its policy. Only the Master of the Temple can say whether any given act is a crime. 'Slay that innocent child?' (I hear the ignorant say) 'What a horror!' 'Ah!' replies the Knower, with foresight of history, 'but that child will become Nero. Hasten to strangle him!' There is a third, above these, who understands that Nero was as necessary as Julius Caesar. The Master of the Temple accordingly interferes not with the scheme of things except just so far as he is doing the Work which he is sent to do. Why should he struggle against imprisonment, banishment, death? It is all part of the game in which he is a pawn. 'It was necessary for the Son of Man to suffer these things, and to enter into His glory.'"[37]

This lack of Understanding with which we all begin is so terrible, so pitiful. In this world there is so much cruelty, so much waste, so much stupidity.

The contemplation of the Universe must be at first almost pure anguish. It is this fact which is responsible for most of the speculations of philosophy.

Mediæval philosophers when hopelessly astray because their theology necessitated the reference of all things to the standard of men's welfare.

They even became stupid: Bernardin de St. Pierre (was it not?) said that the goodness of God was such that wherever men had built a great city, He had placed a river to assist them in conveying merchandise. But the truth is that in no way can we imagine the Universe as devised. If horses were made for men to ride, were not men made for worms to eat?

And so we find once more that the Ego-idea must be ruthlessly rooted out before Understanding can be attained.

There is an apparent contradiction between this attitude and that of the Master of the Temple. What can possibly be more selfish than this interpretation of everything as the dealing of God with the soul?

---

[36] *Beyond Good and Evil*, aphorism sixty-four, declares "Knowledge for its own sake" to be "the last snare of morality; with that one becomes completely entangled in it once more."

[37] *MITAP*, Ch. XXI. Similarly, Sri Aurobindo, for example, tells a disciple (4 Dec 1925): "So long as you need to be virtuous you have not attained the pure spiritual height where you have not to think whether the action is moral or not....By morality you become more human, but you do not go beyond humanity. Morality has done much good to man, maybe; it has also done much harm. The question is whether you can rise to something above man by morality. That sort of mental limitation is not conductive to the growth into the Spirit. . . .Indian culture knew the value of morality, and also its limitations. The Upanishads and the *Gita* are loud with and full of the idea of going beyond morality. For instance, when the Upanishad says: 'he does not need to think whether what he is doing is good or bad'—*Sadhu, Asadhu*. Such a man attains a consciousness in which there is no need to think about morality because the action proceeds from the Truth."

But it is God who is all and not any part; and every "dealing" must thus be an expansion of the soul, a destruction of its separateness.[38]

"The mind is the great enemy," Crowley writes, "so, by invoking enthusiastically a person whom we know not to exist, we are rebuking that mind. Yet we should not refrain altogether from philosophising in the light of the Holy Qabalah. We should accept the Magical Hierarchy as a more or less convenient classification of the facts of the Universe as they are known to us; and as our knowledge and understanding of those facts increase, so should we endeavour to adjust our idea of what we mean by any symbol."[39] Now, "the system of what we may call numerical hieroglyphics, which is about to come under our consideration, dates very much further back than what we call the Middle Ages. Its origin is in fact lost in antiquity. The Book of Revelation is full of numerical symbolism. Witness the problem of 'the number of the beast', over which so many people have gone mad. Note also the four beasts, and the seven seals, and four and twenty elders, and the seven heads, and the ten horns, and foursquare city of God with its twelve gates, and twelve foundations, its length and breadth, and height of twelve thousand furlongs, and its wall of cubits twelve by twelve. Any one who supposes that John meant these numbers as numbers knows nothing of numbers."[40]

Much of Revelation comes from ancient sources, and not exclusively the Old Testament. One such source is the apocryphal Book of Enoch, which has no close parallel in the Hebrew scriptures. And although Revelation contains more allusions to older scriptures than any other New Testament book, it does not record a single direct quotation. Significantly, it chooses different sources than other NT books, with more than half of the references stemming from Daniel, Ezekiel, Psalms, and Isaiah, while neglecting the books of the Pentateuch that are the dominant sources for other NT writers.[41] The Hekhalot literature, from the Hebrew word for "Palaces," relates to visions of ascents into heavenly palaces, and overlaps with Merkabah or "Chariot" literature, concerning Ezekiel's chariot. The two are sometimes referred to together as "Books of the Palaces and the Chariot" and form a genre of Jewish esoteric and revelatory texts produced from late antiquity onwards. Many motifs of later Qabalah are based on the ancient Hekhalot texts, and the Hekhalot literature itself is based on earlier sources, including traditions about heavenly ascents of Enoch and Old Testament pseudepigrapha.[42]

The earliest rabbinic Merkabah homilies were exegetical commentaries on the prophetic visions of God in the heavens, and of the divine retinue of angels and other heavenly creatures surrounding Him. The visionary exegeses of Jewish apocalyptics concerning the divine realm and the divine creatures are remarkably similar to the rabbinical material. Eventually, the

---

[38] *Book 4*, Part II, Ch. VII.
[39] *MITAP*, Ch. II.
[40] *Liber 888*, "Fashion of Belief."
[41] Moyise 1995.
[42] Scholem 1965.

Merkabah commentaries would contain detailed descriptions of multiple layered heavens, usually seven in number, often guarded by angels, and encircled by flames and lightning. The Hekhalot visions were accounts of mystical ascents into heaven, and the summoning and control of angels, often for the purpose of gaining insight into Torah. In their visions, the Hekhalot mystics would enter into the celestial realms and journey through the seven stages of mystical ascent, the Seven Heavens and seven throne rooms. Since such a journey was fraught with danger, the adepts had to undergo elaborate purification in preparation, and not only know the proper incantations, seals, and secret names of God required to clear the fearsome angelic guards, but how to navigate the various forces at work inside and outside the palaces.[43]

While the mystery of creation was not of utmost importance during the era of Merkabah mysticism, the later *Sepher Yetzirah*, or "Book of Formation," attempts to form a cosmogony from within a Merkabah milieu. One of the founding texts of the Qabalah, this treatise was probably composed between the 2nd and 3rd centuries CE, and exhibits Neoplatonic, Pythagorean, and Gnostic influences. It is this work that introduces the linguistic theory of creation, in which God creates the universe by combining the 22 letters of the Hebrew alphabet, along with divine emanations represented by the ten numerals. While most of the speculation concerning the Beast of Revelation has dealt with things like the seven hills of Rome, and Christian theology concerning the Devil, Antichrist, etc., in Diagrams 33 and 51 in *The Equinox*, Vol. I, No. 2, the Beast is associated with the seven palaces. This Beast is a relic of pre-Christian mysticism of unknown antiquity, and with his 7 heads and 10 horns an alternative to the diagram of the seven palaces and a variant of the serpent on the 32 Paths of the Wisdom.[44]

> It seems probable that the Qabalists who invented the Tree of Life were inspired by Pythagoras, or that both he and they derived their knowledge from a common source in higher antiquity. In any case, both schools agree upon one fundamental postulate, which is as follows: Ultimate Reality is best described by Numbers and their interplay. It is interesting to note that modern Mathematical Physics has been finally driven to some similar assumption. Further, the attempt to describe Reality by a single definite term has been abandoned. Modern thought conceives Reality under the image of a ring of ten ideas, such as Potential, Matter, and so on. Each term has no meaning in itself; it can only be understood in terms of the others. This is exactly the conclusion which appears earlier in this essay, with regard to the way in which the planets, elements and signs were all dependent on each other, and composed of each other.

---

[43] *Ibid.*
[44] B. Heidrick, "The Star Sponge and the Fifty Gates: Two Passages to Attainment," *Thelema Lodge Calendar*, May 1990.

But the further attempt to reach Reality led the Qabalists to sum up the qualities of these rather vague and literary ideas by referring them all to the numbers of the decimal scale.[45]

In *Liber O vel Manus Sagittæ*, Crowley admonishes the would-be magician: "In this book it is spoken of the Sephiroth, and the Paths, of Spirits and Conjurations; of Gods, Spheres, Planes, and many other things which may or may not exist. It is immaterial whether they exist or not. By doing certain things certain results follow; students are most earnestly warned against attributing objective reality or philosophic validity to any of them. The advantages to be gained from them are chiefly these: (*a*) A widening of the horizon of the mind. (*b*) An improvement of the control of the mind."[46]

Yet this is true also, that, once the language is mastered, one can divine the unknown by study of the known, just as one's knowledge of Latin and Greek enables one to understand some unfamiliar English word derived from those sources. Also, there is the similar case of the Periodic Law in Chemistry, which enables Science to prophesy, and so in the end to discover, the existence of certain previously unsuspected elements in nature. All discussions upon philosophy are necessarily sterile, since truth is beyond language. They are, however, useful if carried far enough—if carried to the point when it becomes apparent that all arguments are arguments in a circle. *{See "The Soldier and the Hunchback," Equinox I, I. The apparatus of human reason is simply one particular system of coordinating impressions; its structure is determined by the course of the evolution of the species. It is no more absolute than the evolution of the species. It is no more absolute than the mechanism of our muscles is a complete type wherewith all other systems of transmitting Force must conform.}* But discussions of the details of purely imaginary qualities are frivolous and may be deadly. For the great danger of this magical theory is that the student may mistake the alphabet for the things which the words represent.[47]

In his essay *Qabalistic Dogma*, Crowley uses the number 777 as an example to illustrate "the legitimate and illegitimate deductions to be drawn. It represents the sentence אחת רוה אלהים חיים, 'One is the Spirit of the Living God,' and also עלאהם הקלפות, 'The world of the Shells (excrements—the demon-world).' Now it is wrong to say that this idea of the unity of the divine spirit is identical with this idea of the muddle of chaos—unless in that exalted grade in which 'The One is the Many.' But the compiler of Liber 777 was a great Qabalist when he thus entitled his book; for he meant to imply, 'One is the Spirit of the Living God,' *i.e.* I have in this book unified all the diverse symbols of the world; and also, 'the world of

---

[45] *The Book of Thoth*, Part I, Sec. III.
[46] I.2–3.
[47] *MITAP*, Ch. 0.

shells,' *i.e.* this book is full of mere dead symbols; do not mistake them for the living Truth. Further, he had an academic reason for his choice of a number; for the tabulation of the book is from Kether to Malkuth, the course of the Flaming Sword; and if this sword be drawn upon the Tree of Life, the numeration of the Paths over which it passes (taking ג, 3, as the non-existent path from Binah to Chesed, since it connects Macroprosopus and Microprosopus) is 777."

In *An Essay upon Number*, Crowley further describes 777 as useful "as affirming that the Unity is the Qliphoth," but "a dangerous tool, especially as it represents the flaming sword that drove Man out of Eden. A burnt child dreads the fire. 'The devils also believe, and tremble.' Worse than useless unless you have it by the hilt. Also 777 is the grand scale of 7, and this is useless to anyone who has not yet awakened the Kundalini, the female magical soul. Note 7 as the meeting-place of 3, the Mother, and 10, the Daughter; whence Netzach is the Woman, married but no more." Knowledge is "an impossible conception. All propositions come ultimately back to '*A* is *A*'." Daäth, "Knowledge, the Sephira that is not a Sephira" is in "one aspect the child of Chokmah and Binah; in another the Eighth Head of the Stooping Dragon, raised up when the Tree of Life was shattered, and Macroprosopus set cherubim against Microprosopus."

Note that Knowledge is Daath, Child of Chokmah by Binah, and crown of Microprosopus; yet he is not one of the Sephiroth, and his place is in the Abyss. By this symbolism we draw attention to the fact that Knowledge is by nature impossible; for it implies Duality and is therefore relative. Any proposition of Knowledge may be written "*aRb*": "*a* has the relation *R* to *b*." Now if *a* and *b* are identical, the proposition conveys no knowledge at all. If *a* is not identical with *b*, *aRb* implies "*a* is identical with *bc*"; this assumes that not less than three distinct ideas exist. In every case, we must proceed either to the identity which means ultimately "Nothing," or to divergent diversities which only seem to mean something so long as we refrain from pushing the analysis of any term to its logical elements. For example, "Sugar is sugar" is obviously not knowledge. But no more is this: "Sugar is a sweet white crystalline carbohydrate." For each of these four terms describes a sensory impression on ourselves; and we define our impressions only in terms of such things as sugar. Thus "sweet" means "the quality ascribed by our taste to honey, sugar, *etc.*"; "white" is "what champaks, zinc oxide, sugar, etc. report to our eyesight"; and so on. The proposition is ultimately an identity, for all our attempts to evade the issue by creating complications. "Knowledge" is therefore not a "thing-in-itself"; it is rightly denied a place upon the Tree of Life; it pertains to the Abyss.

Besides the above considerations, it may be observed that Knowledge, so far as it exists at all, even as a statement of relation, is no more than a momentary phenomenon of consciousness. It is annihilated in the instant of its creation. For no sooner do we assent to *aRb* than *aRb* is absorbed in our conception of *a*. After the nine-days' wonder of "The earth revolves round the sun," we modify our former idea of Earth.

"Earth" is intuitively classed with other solar satellites. The proposition vanishes automatically as it is assimilated. Knowledge, while it exists as such is consequently *sub judice*, at the best.

What then may we understand by this verse, with its capital K for "Knowledge?" What is it, and how shall it "go aright?" The key is in the word "go." It cannot "be," as we have seen above; it is the fundamental error of the "Black Brothers" in their policy of resisting all Change, to try to maintain it as fixed and absolute. But (as the Tree of Life indicates) Knowledge is the means by which the conscious mind, Microprosopus, reaches to Understanding and to Wisdom, its mother and father, which reflect respectively Nuit and Hadit from the Ain and Kether. The process is to use each new item of knowledge to correct and increase one's comprehension of the Subject of the Proposition. Thus aRb should tell us: a is (not a_1 as we supposed) but a. This facilitates the discovery a_1Rc_1 leading to a_1 is a_2; and so on. In practice, every thing that we learn about (*e.g.*) "horse" helps us to understand—to enjoy—the idea. The difference between the scholar and the schoolboy is that the former glows and exults when he is reminded of some word like "Thalassa." Ourselves: What a pageant of passion empurples our minds whenever we think of the number 93! Most of all, each new thing that we know about ourselves helps us to realize what we mean by our "Star."[48]

The Method of Thelema cites *The Book of the Law*: "Every man and every woman is a star."—"The image is nobly suggestive: no other could show more clearly the essence of the application of the Thelemite formula. Each human being should consider himself the centre of an infinite circle; his universe is, in fact, for him different from that of every other person, and he simply leaves reality for phantasm when he tries to calculate in terms of what he has been stupidly taught to consider as the 'real' universe—that objective universe, which consists merely of phenomena apparently common to all observers. . . . A thousand men looking at a clock see a thousand different clocks, although we assume the unity of the object. But the man who sees the front of the clock is a great pedant if he refuses to tell the time by it, on the ground that somebody else can only see the back. Yet this stupidity is the foundation of the old morality in general, and altruism in particular."

"Each man is therefore absolutely justified in regarding himself as the centre of the universe, and acting accordingly. To displace this centre, to break the harmony of a human system (which corresponds with strange precision, on the one hand, to the Sidereal Universe, and, on the other, to that of electrons) is to break the Law of Thelema, to blaspheme oneself. And, so far as anyone can tell, there is no other self. His fellow-percipients, whether God or his neighbour, are—so far as he knows them—only ideas created by the chemical and mechanical changes in his brain; and he does not really know that! But assuming he knows anything at all, he knows

---

[48] NC on AL II.5.

himself. Therefore to sin against himself is his only possible sin."[49] The only worthy knowledge is self-knowledge: we cannot know all the consequences of our actions in advance, but we can know if it is our will to take them.[50]

Understanding is the structuralization of knowledge.

All impressions are disconnected, as the Babe of the Abyss is so terribly aware; and the Master of the Temple must sit for 106 seasons in the City of the Pyramids because this coordination is a tremendous task.

There is nothing particularly occult in this doctrine concerning knowledge and understanding.

A looking-glass receives all impressions but coordinates none.

The savage has none but the most simple associations of ideas.

Even the ordinary civilized man goes very little further.

All advance in thought is made by collecting the greatest possible number of facts, classifying them, and grouping them.

The philologist, though perhaps he only speaks one language, has a much higher type of mind than the linguist who speaks twenty.

This Tree of Thought is exactly paralleled by the tree of nervous structure.

Very many people go about nowadays who are exceedingly "well-informed," but who have not the slightest idea of the meaning of the facts they know. They have not developed the necessary higher part of the brain. Induction is impossible to them.

This capacity for storing away facts is compatible with actual imbecility. Some imbeciles have been able to store their memories with more knowledge than perhaps any sane man could hope to acquire.

This is the great fault of modern education—a child is stuffed with facts, and no attempt is made to explain their connection and bearing. The result is that even the facts themselves are soon forgotten.

Any first-rate mind is insulted and irritated by such treatment, and any first-rate memory is in danger of being spoilt by it.

No two ideas have any real meaning until they are harmonized in a third, and the operation is only perfect when these ideas are contradictory. This is the essence of the Hegelian logic.[51]

While Western philosophy traces dialectics to ancient Greek thought of Plato and Heraclitus, the idea of tension between two opposing forces leading to synthesis is much older and found also in early Hindu

---

[49] *The Method of Thelema*.
[50] "All relations are meaningless in themselves; but one relation may be contrasted with another. The Ego grows by establishing relations with other points of view, and absorbing them: hence, the bigger the Ego, the less the sense of Egoity. The Universe is a set of Events; they do not *exist*, they occur. It is a dynamic, not a static phenomenon. Any stasis is a mere temporary resolution. Logic describes the process of Thought, which is the essence of Action. Mathematics is the language of Logic. A man must think of himself as a LOGOS, as going, not as a fixed idea. 'Do what thou wilt' is thus necessarily his formula. He only becomes Himself when he attains the loss of Egoity, of the sense of separateness. He becomes All, PAN, when he becomes Zero." *The Antecedents of Thelema*, Sec. VI. Emphasis in original.
[51] *Book 4*, Part II, Ch. VII.

philosophy. Indian philosophy, largely subsumed within the Indian religions, has an ancient tradition of dialectic polemics. The two complements, *Puruṣa*, the active cause, and *Prakṛti*, the passive nature, bring everything into existence. They follow *Ṛta*, the ultimate foundation of everything. The Ṛta is not to be understood in a static sense, but as the expression of the primordial dynamism inherent in all things.[52] It derives from the Sanskrit verb root *ṛ*- "to go, move, rise, tend upwards," while the derivative noun *ṛtam* signifies "fixed or settled order, rule, divine law or truth."[53] The term can equally be translated literally as "that which has moved in a fitting manner," abstractly as "universal law" or "cosmic order," or simply as "truth." The latter meaning is dominant in its Avestan cognate, *Aša*.[54]

Both Avestan *Aša* and Vedic *Ṛta* derive from Proto-Indo-Iranian *ṛtá- "truth," which in turn continues Proto-Indo-European *h_2r-to- "properly joined, right, true," from the root *$h_2$ar. The Old Persian equivalent is *arta*. In all likelihood, the concept originally arose in the Indo-Aryan period from a consideration of the natural order of the world and of the occurrences taking place within it as doing so with a causal necessity of sorts. Both in the Vedas and the Avesta, the concept is seen as having a tripartite function that manifests itself in the physical, ethical, and ritual domains. In the Vedic context, those features of nature which either remain constant or occur on a regular basis were seen as manifestations of the power of Ṛta in the physical universe. In the sphere of human activity, Ṛta was considered to manifest itself as the imperative force behind both the moral order of society and the correct performance of Vedic rituals.[55] Of course, the notion of a universal principle of natural order is nowise unique to the Vedas, and Ṛta has been variously compared to such notions as the Egyptian *Maat*, the Greek *Logos*, the Chinese *Tao*.

Due to the polysemous nature of Vedic Sanskrit, terms like *Ṛta* can be used in reference to numerous different things, and neither European nor Indian scholars have easily found fitting interpretations for the term in all its various usages—only the underlying sense of "ordered action" is universally evident. The word *Ṛta* appears in the *Ṛgveda* as many as 390 times, and has been characterized as "the one concept which pervades the whole of Ṛgvedic thought."[56] The noted American philologist and Sanskrit scholar Maurice Bloomfield described Ṛta as "one of the most important religious conceptions of the Rig Veda." He went so far as to say that, "from the point of view of the history of religious ideas we may, in fact we must, begin the history of Hindu religion at least with the history of this conception."[57]

---

[52] Panikkar 1983.
[53] Monier-Williams 1872.
[54] Oldenberg 1988.
[55] *Ibid.*
[56] G. Ramakrishna, "Origin and Growth of the Concept of *Ṛta* in Vedic Literature," doctoral dissertation, University of Mysore.
[57] Bloomfield 1908, 12–13.

Scholars and philologists have long debated the feasibility of translating between different European languages, let alone between languages from entirely different language families. Words in the modern Indo-European languages often have the same Greek or Latin roots, and there is also a common ancestor between the wisdom traditions of East and West, which is the Sanskrit language. In the 17th and 18th centuries, European scholars began to suspect that the sacred language of ancient India might be related to Greek and Latin. Their suspicions have long since been confirmed, and decades of Indo-European studies have revealed a plethora of similarities between not only Indo-European languages, but Indo-European religions as well. The revelation that Europe had an organic connection to India fuelled an explosion of interest in Indian religion and philosophy in the 19th century.[58] In his essay *On Ethics*, Schopenhauer wrote: "We may therefore hope that one day even Europe will be purified of all Jewish mythology. Perhaps the century has come in which the peoples of the Japhetic group of languages coming from Asia will again receive the sacred religions of their native country; for they have again become ripe for these after having long gone astray."[59]

It follows that all phenomena, internal and external, may be classified for the purpose of discussing their observed relations, in any manner which experience may show to be the most convenient. (Examples: the elaborate classifications of science, chemical, physical, *etc., etc.* There is no essential truth in any of these aids to thinking: convenience is the sole measure.) Now for the purposes of analysing the spiritual nature of man, of recording and measuring his experiences in this kind, of planning his progress to loftier heights of attainment, several systems have been devised. That of the *Abhidhamma* is on the surface alike the most practical, the most scientific, and the most real; but for European students it is certainly far too unwieldly, to say nothing of other lines of criticism.

Therefore, despite the danger of vagueness involved in the use of a system whose terms are largely symbolic, I have, for many reasons, preferred to present to the world as an international basis for classification, the classico-mathematical system which is vulgarly and erroneously (though conveniently) called the Qabalah.

The Qabalah, that is, the Jewish Tradition concerning the initiated interpretation of their Scriptures, is mostly either unintelligible or nonsense. But it contains as it ground-plan the most precious jewel of human thought, that geometrical arrangement of names and numbers which is called the Tree of Life. I call it the most precious, because I have found it the most convenient method hitherto discovered of classifying the phenomena of the Universe, and recording their relations. Whereof the proof is the amazing fertility of thought which has followed my adoption of this scheme.

---

[58] Balk 2008.
[59] §115. Schopenhauer 1974, ii.226.

Since all phenomena soever may be referred to the Tree of Life (which may be multiplied or subdivided at will for convenience' sake) it is evidently useless to attempt any complete account of it. The correspondences of each unit—the Ten Sephiroth and the Two-and-Twenty Paths—are infinite. The art of using it consists principally in referring all our ideas to it, discovering thus the common nature of certain things and the essential differences between others, so that ultimately one obtains a simple view of the incalculably vast complexity of the Universe.[60]

"In the middle of the nineteenth century, there arose a very great Qabalist and scholar, who still annoys dull people by his habit of diverting himself at their expense by making fools of them posthumously. His name was Alphonse Louis Constant, and he was an Abbé of the Roman Church. For his 'nom-de-guerre' he translated his name into Hebrew—Eliphas Levi Zahed, and he is very generally known as Eliphas Levi." As "an artist and a profound symbolist, he was immensely attracted by the Tarot" and in "his works are new presentations by him of the trumps called *The Chariot* and *The Devil*. He seems to have understood that the Tarot was actually a pictorial form of the Qabalistic Tree of Life, which is the basis of the whole Qabalah, so much so that he composed his works on this basis. He wished to write a complete treatise on Magick. He divided his subject into two parts—*Theory and Practice* which he called *Dogma* and *Ritual*. Each part has twenty-two chapters, one for each of the twenty-two trumps; and each chapter deals with the subject represented by the picture displayed by the trump." However, the chapters "correspond wrongly," which according to Crowley, "is only to be explained by the fact that Levi felt himself bound by his original oath of secrecy to the Order of Initiates which had given him the secrets of the Tarot."[61]

"By the aid of this key," Lévi wrote of the Tarot, "one can understand the universal symbolism of the ancient world, and note its striking analogies with our dogmas. One will thus recognize that the divine revelation is permanent in nature and humanity."[62] Crowley further says: "The Tarot should be learnt as early in life as possible; a fulcrum for memory and a schema for mind. It should be studied constantly, a daily exercise; for it is universally elastic and grows in proportion to the use intelligently made of it. Thus it becomes a most ingenious and excellent method of appreciating the whole of Existence."[63]

> The Great Wheel of Samsara.
> The Wheel of the Law [Dhamma].
> The Wheel of the Taro.
> The Wheel of the Heavens.
> The Wheel of Life.

---

[60] *Little Essays Toward Truth*, "Man."
[61] *The Book of Thoth*, loc. cit., Sec. I.
[62] *The Key of the Mysteries*, Part IV, Ch. IV.
[63] *The Book of Thoth*, loc. cit., Sec. III.

All these Wheels be one; yet of all these the Wheel of the TARO alone avails thee consciously.

Meditate long and broad and deep, O man, upon this Wheel, revolving it in thy mind!

Be this thy task, to see how each card springs necessarily from each other card, even in due order from The Fool unto The Ten of Coins.

Then, when thou know'st the Wheel of Destiny complete, mayst thou perceive THAT Will which moved it first. [There is no first or last.]

And lo! thou art past through the Abyss.[64]

"Five wheels are mentioned," Crowley explains, and "all but the third refer to the universe as it is; but the wheel of the Tarot is not only this, but represents equally the Magical Path." He therefore gives this practice to his pupils, "to treat the sequence of the cards as cause and effect. Thence, to discover the cause behind all causes. Success in this practice qualifies for the grade of Master of the Temple."[65]

It is not known why, when, or by whom the Tarot was originally created, nor do we have any facts regarding the cards prior to their surface during the early Renaissance. Rabelais gives *tarau* as the name of one of the games played by the characters in *Gargantua and Pantagruel*, and this is likely the earliest literary appearance of the French form of the name. Divination using playing cards can be traced back to at least as early as 1540, when Marcolino da Forlì published *The Oracles of Francesco*, which gives a simple method of cartomancy. The notion of the ancient Egyptian lineage of the Tarot appears almost simultaneously in the works of three French writers of the mid-18th century: Jean-Baptiste Alliette, or "Etteilla" (his name spelled backwards), Antoine Court de Gébelin, and Louis-Raphaël-Lucrèce de Fayolle, Comte de Mellet. These early writers do not cite any sources in their work or make references to any previous authors.[66] However, considering the general literacy rate in Europe before that period, a much longer oral tradition cannot be ruled out.

In *Le Monde primitif* (1781), Court de Gébelin, a former Protestant pastor and pre-Rosetta Stone linguist, claimed that the Tarot was actually what remains of "The Book of Thoth," saved from one of the temples of ancient Egypt, when all other writings were destroyed by fire. It was he who first placed the Fool at the head of the trumps, rather than at their end, its previous traditional location. Etteilla, a Parisian wigmaker and fortune-teller, claimed that he had been introduced to the art of cartomancy in 1751, long before the appearance of Court de Gébelin's massive tome. Etteilla's *Cour théorique et pratique du Livre du Thot* (1790), for its part, incorporated a reworking of what would later be called the Major and Minor Arcana, as well as the introduction of the four elements and astrology. Lastly, the Comte de Mellet, in his essay *Recherches sur les Tarots, et sur la Divination par les Cartes des Tarots*, not only said Thoth painted the

---

[64] *The Book of Lies*, Ch. 78.
[65] *Ibid.*, Commentary.
[66] Huson 2004.

gods on 22 plates or cards, but explicitly linked the individual trumps with individual Hebrew letters.[67]

The least abject asset in the intellectual bankruptcy of European thought is the Hebrew Qabalah. Properly understood, it is a system of symbolism indefinitely elastic, assuming no axioms, postulating no principles, asserting no theorems, and therefore adaptable, if managed adroitly, to describe any conceivable doctrine. It has been my continual study since 1898, and I have found it of infinite value in the study of the *Tao Teh King*. By its aid I was able to attribute the ideas of Lao Tze to an order with which I was exceedingly familiar, and whose practical worth I had repeatedly proved by using it as the basis of the analysis and classification of all Aryan and Semitic religions and philosophies. Despite the essential difficulty of correlating the ideas of Lao Tze with any others, the persistent application of the Qabalistic keys eventually unlocked his treasure-house. I was able to explain to myself his teachings in terms of familiar systems.[68]

The Curriculum of A∴A∴, Course I, Section 1, "Books for Serious Study," describes the *Tao Teh King* as giving "the initiated Chinese system of Mysticism" and the *Yî King* as giving "the initiated Chinese system of Magick." The ancient divination text *Chou I*, or the "Changes of Chou," was named "the first among the classics" by the Han Emperor Wu, who re-dubbed it the "Classic of Changes," or *I Ching*. While the *Chou I* does not contain any cosmological analogies, the *I Ching* was read as a microcosm of the universe, offering complex, symbolic correspondences, and the official edition of the text was literally set in stone.[69] As Crowley puts it, "The oldest book in the world, *The Yî King*, is based entirely upon what is really a numerical foundation, the combination of two things taken first three and then six at a time."[70] He boasts that his "personal researches have been of the greatest value and importance to the study of the subject of Magick and Mysticism in general," but especially his "integration of the various thought-systems of the world, notably the identification of the system of the *Yî King* with that of the Qabalah."[71]

---

[67] *Ibid.* Interestingly, Court de Gébelin correctly traces playing cards to China, where they first appeared as early as the Tang Dynasty (618–907). They first entered southern Europe in the 14th century, probably from Mamlûk Egypt, since the traditional Latin decks still retain the Mamlûk suits of cups, coins, swords, and polo sticks

[68] *MWT*, Ch. XXXV; *cf.* e.g. M. Zwick, "Symbolic Structures as Systems: On the Near Isomorphism of Two Religious Symbols," in Locker 2011.

[69] Smith 2008.

[70] *Liber 888, loc. cit.*

[71] *MWT*, Introduction. Course V of the A∴A∴ Curriculum also includes Crowley's own *Liber XXVII*, or *Liber Trigrammaton*, "being a book of Trigrams of the Mutations of the Tao with the Yin and the Yang. An account of the cosmic process: corresponding to the Stanzas of Dzyan in another system." These elusive *Stanzas* appear to have been based mainly on the Ṛgvedic "Hymn of Creation" (though they also show Taoist and Qabalistic influences) and formed the basis for *The Secret Doctrine* of H. P. Blavatsky. *Cf.* also OC on AL II.55.

The imagination of the earliest philosophers was exercised by the question, What are Numbers? Simple numerical relations excited them tremendously. 'Magic squares' were considered really magical. It struck them as enormously significant that the number nine should always remain the result of adding together the digits of any number which was divisible by nine. In one of the "Oracles of Zoroaster" it says, "The number nine is sacred, and attains the summit of perfection." and again, "The mind of the Father said 'Into three'; and immediately all things were so divided."

Now then let us try to discover what the ancients meant by the number four. They noticed that you could not make a magic square of any four numbers, though you can of one, or nine, or sixteen, or twenty-five, up the series as far as you care to carry it. They also noticed the four quarters, and of course a hundred other things. From all these consideration [sic], they got the idea of four as expressing principally dominion and limitation and resistance and so on, until ultimately the number four became an extremely complex concept, of which its definition as one more than three and one less than five was the smallest part; Consequently 'four beasts about the throne of God' means that his power extended in every direction. It does not mean that there were four of them.[72]

"It is therefore to be understood that when a medieval philosopher spoke of seven anything or twelve anything, he did not mean that if you counted them there would be seven or twelve. He was characterizing them in an extremely elaborate and subtle manner, which no other words could have expressed. He was conveying an idea beyond words, just as every great poet does. So also the criticisms levelled by Freethinkers at the Doctrine of the Trinity have been merely examples of *ignoratio elenchi*; and Christians were unable to defend it because they too had no idea of what the Fathers of the Church meant by it. Criticisms by Christians of other worships, with their strange rites, have been equally foolish for the most part. The founders wisely shrouded their truth in hieratic symbol."[73] In the Epilogue to *The Key of the Mysteries*, Lévi gives thanks to "God, that thou hast called me to this admirable light! Thou, the Supreme Intelligence and the Absolute Life of those numbers and those forces which obey thee in order to people the infinite with inexhaustible creation! Mathematics proves thee, the harmonies of Nature proclaim thee, all forms as they pass by salute thee and adore thee! Abraham knew thee, Hermes divined thee, Pythagoras calculated thee, Plato, in every dream of his genius, aspired to thee; but only one initiate, only one sage has revealed thee to the children of earth, one alone could say of thee: 'I and my Father are one.' Glory then be his, since all his glory is thine!"

---

[72] *Liber 888, loc. cit.*
[73] *Ibid.*

We have just said that alchemy is the daughter of the Qabalah; to convince oneself of the truth of this it is sufficient to look at the symbols of Flamel, of Basil Valentine, the pages of the Jew Abraham, and the more or less apocryphal oracles of the Emerald Table of Hermes. Everywhere one finds the traces of that decade of Pythagoras, which is so magnificently applied in the *Sepher Yetzirah* to the complete and absolute notion of divine things, that decade composed of unity and a triple ternary which the Rabbis have called the Berashith, and the Mercavah, the luminous tree of the Sephiroth, and the key of the Shemhamphorash.

We have spoken at some length in our book entitled *Dogme et rituel de la haute magie* of a hieroglyphic monument (preserved up to our own time under a futile pretext) which alone explains all the mysterious writings of high initiation. This monument is that Tarot of the Bohemians which gave rise to our games of cards. It is composed of twenty-two allegorical letters, and of four series of ten hieroglyphs each, referring to the four letters of the name of Jehovah. The diverse combinations of those signs, and the numbers which correspond to them, form so many qabalistic oracles, so that the whole science is contained in this mysterious book. This perfectly simple philosophical machine astonishes by the depth of its results.[74]

"This operation of the qabalistic sages, originally intended to discover the rigorous development of absolute ideas, degenerated into superstition when it fell into the hands of the ignorant priests and the nomadic ancestors of the Bohemians who possessed the Tarot in the Middle Ages; they did not know how to employ it properly, and used it solely for fortune-telling." According to Lévi, "The conception of the primitive alphabet was, as one may easily see, the idea of a universal language which should enclose in its combinations, and even in its signs themselves, the recapitulation and the evolutionary law of all sciences, divine and human. In our own opinion, nothing finer or greater has ever been dreamt by the genius of man; and we are convinced that the discovery of this secret of the ancient world has fully repaid us for so many years of sterile research and thankless toil in the crypts of lost sciences and the cemeteries of the past."[75]

But our Magical Alphabet is primarily not letters, but figures, not sounds but mathematical ideas. Sir Humphry Davy, coming out of his famous illumination (with some help from Nitrous Oxide he got in) exclaimed: The Universe is composed solely of ideas. We, analyzing this a little, say: The Universe is a mathematical expression.

Sir James Jeans might have said this, only his banker advised him to cash in on God. The simplest form of this expression is $0 = 2$, elsewhere expounded at great length. This 2 might itself be expressed in an indefinitely great number of ways. Every prime number, including some

---

[74] *The Key of the Mysteries*, Part III, Book I, Ch. III.
[75] *Ibid.*

not in the series of "natural numbers", is an individual. The other numbers with perhaps a few exceptions (*e.g.* 418) are composed of their primes.

Each of these ideas may be explained, investigated, understood, by means very various. Firstly, the Hebrew, Greek and Arabic numbers are also letters. Then, each of these letters is further described by one of the (arbitrarily composed) "elements" of Nature; the Four (or Five) Elements, the Seven (or Ten) Planets, and the Twelve Signs of the Zodiac.

All these are arranged in a geometrical design composed of ten "Sephiroth" (numbers) and twenty-two "paths" joining them; this is called the Tree of Life.

Every idea soever can be, and should be, attributed to one or more of these primary symbols; thus green, in different shades, is a quality or function of Venus, the Earth, the Sea, Libra, and others. So also abstract ideas; dishonesty means "an afflicted Mercury," generosity a good, though not always strong, Jupiter; and so on.

The Tree of Life has got to be learnt by heart; you must know it backwards, forwards, sideways, and upside down; it must become the automatic background of all your thinking. You must keep on hanging everything that comes your way upon its proper bough.[76]

"Unimportant to the present purpose are tradition and authority," Crowley writes in *The Book of Thoth*. "Einstein's Theory of Relativity does not rest on the fact that, when his theory was put to the test, it was confirmed.... One important interpretation of Tarot is that it is a Notariqon of the Hebrew Torah, the Law; also of ThROA, the Gate. Now, by the Yetziratic attributions ... this word may be read The Universe—the new-born Sun—Zero. This is the true Magical Doctrine of Thelema: Zero equals Two. Also, by Gematria, the numerical value of ThROA is 671 = 61 × 11. Now 61 is AIN, Nothing or Zero; and 11 is the number of Magical Expansion; in this way also, therefore, ThROA announces that same dogma, the only satisfactory philosophical explanation of the Cosmos, its origin, mode, and object. Complete mystery surrounds the question of the origin of this system; any theory which satisfies the facts demands assumptions which are completely absurd. To explain it at all, one has to postulate in the obscure past a fantastic assembly of learned rabbins, who solemnly calculated all sorts of combinations of letters and numbers, and created the Hebrew language on this series of manipulations. This theory is plainly contrary, not only to common sense, but to the facts of history, and to all that we know about the formation of language. Nevertheless, the evidence is equally strong that there is something, not a little of something but a great deal of something, a something which excludes all reasonable theories of coincidence, in the correspondence between words and numbers."[77]

---

[76] *MWT*, Ch. IV.
[77] *The Book of Thoth, loc. cit.*, Sec. III.

Crowley "had made a very profound study of the Tarot since his initiation to the Order [of the Golden Dawn] on 18th November, 1898; for, three months later, he had attained the grade of Practicus; as such, he became entitled to know the Secret Attribution. He constantly studied this and the accompanying explanatory manuscripts. He checked up on all these attributes of the numbers to the forms of nature, and found nothing incongruous. But when (8th April, 1904 e.v.) he was writing down the *Book of the Law* from the dictation of the messenger of the Secret Chiefs, he seems to have put a mental question, suggested by the words in Chapter I, verse 57: 'the law of the Fortress, and the great mystery of the House of God' ('The House of God' is one name of the Tarot Trump numbered XVI) to this effect: 'Have I got these attributions right?' For there came an interpolated answer, 'All these old letters of my book are aright; but צ is not the Star. This also is secret; my prophet shall reveal it to the wise'. . . . It was many years later that the solution came to him. Tzaddi is 'The Emperor'; and therefore the positions of XVII and IV must be counterchanged. This attribution is very satisfactory."[78]

Yes, but it is something a great deal more than satisfactory; it is, to clear thought, the most convincing evidence possible that the *Book of the Law* is a genuine message from the Secret Chiefs.

For "The Star" is referred to Aquarius in the Zodiac, and "The Emperor" to Aries. Now Aries and Aquarius are on each side of Pisces, just as Leo and Libra are on each side of Virgo; that is to say, the correction in the *Book of the Law* gives a perfect symmetry in the zodiacal attribution, just as if a loop were formed at one end of the ellipse to correspond exactly with the existing loop at the other end.

These matters sound rather technical; in fact, they are; but the more one studies the Tarot, the more one perceives the admirable symmetry and perfection of the symbolism. Yet, even to the layman, it ought to be evident that balance and fitness are essential to any perfection, and the elucidation of these two tangles in the last 150 years is undoubtedly a very remarkable phenomenon.[79]

Crowley also changed the names of some of the cards in his new deck. Atu VIII, or "Adjustment," was called Justice in the old pack. "This word has none but a purely human and therefore relative sense; so it is not to be considered as one of the facts of Nature. Nature is not just, according to any theological or ethical idea; but Nature is exact."[80] Atu XI, or "Lust," was formerly known as Strength. "But it implies far more than strength in the ordinary sense of the word. Technical analysis shows that the Path corresponding to the card is not the Strength of Geburah, but the influence from Chesed upon Geburah, the Path balanced both vertically and horizontally on the Tree of Life. . . For this reason it has been thought better

---

[78] *Ibid.*, Sec. I.
[79] *Ibid.*
[80] *Ibid.*, Part II, Atu VIII.

to change the traditional title. Lust implies not only strength, but the joy of strength exercised. It is vigour, and the rapture of vigour."[81]

Crowley further cites the Precession of the Æons and contends that Atu XII, or "The Hanged Man," was "an invention of the Adepts of the I.N.R.I.-I.A.O. formula; in the Æon previous to the Osirian, that of Isis (Water), he is 'The Drowned Man'. The two uprights of the gallows shewn in the Mediaeval packs were, in the parthenogenetic system of explaining and ruling Nature, the bottom of the Sea and the keel of the Ark. In this Æon all birth was considered an emanation, without male intervention, of the Mother or Star-Goddess, Nuit; all death a return to Her. This explains the original attribution of the Atu to Water, and the sound M the return to Eternal Silence, as in the word AUM. This card is therefore specially sacred to the Mystic) and the attitude of the figure is a ritual posture in the Practice called 'The Sleep of Shiloam'."[82]

And when it comes to Atu XX, or "The Æon," Crowley finds it "necessary to depart completely from the tradition of the cards, in order to carry on that tradition. The old card was called The Angel: or, The Last Judgment. It represented an Angel or Messenger blowing a trumpet, attached to which was a flag, bearing the symbol of the Æon of Osiris. Below him the graves were opening, the dead rising up. There were three of them. The central one had his hands raised with right angles at the elbows and shoulders, so as to form the letter Shin, which refers to Fire. The card therefore represented the destruction of the world by Fire. This was accomplished in the year of the vulgar era 1904, when the fiery god Horus took the place of the airy god Osiris in the East as Hierophant (see Atu V). At the beginning, then, of this new Æon, it is fit to exhibit the message of that angel who brought the news of the new Æon to earth. . . . It should, by the way, be noted that the name Heru is identical with Hru, who is the great Angel set over the Tarot. This new Tarot may therefore be regarded as a series of illustrations to the *Book of the Law*; the doctrine of that Book is everywhere implicit."[83]

And now an Angel cometh and seeketh to open the door by trying many keys. And they are none of any avail. And the same voice saith: "The five and the six are balanced in the word Abrahadabra, and therein is the mystery disclosed. But the key unto this gate is the balance of the seven and the four; and of this thou hast not even the first letter. Now there is a word of four letters that containeth in itself all the mystery of the Tetragrammaton *{TARO: it conceals all the mysteries of Tetragrammaton through the cards which declare him.}*, and there is a word of seven letters which it concealeth *{This may be Babalon, for Malkuth concealeth Binah. Also 156 = 2 × 78.}*, and that again concealeth the holy word that is the key of the abyss *{This word is N.O.X. = , Babalon conceals this word because She is the Lady of the City of the Pyramids*

---

[81] *Ibid.*, Atu XI.
[82] *Ibid.*, Atu XII.
[83] *Ibid.*, Atu XX.

beneath the Night of Pan. These words are probably BABALON, ChAOS, TARO.}. And this thou shalt find, revolving it in thy mind.[84]

"TARO has 78 symbols and 78 = מזלא, the influence that descends from the Most Holy Ancient One, Kether, and therefore referred to ג. The equation 78 = Aiwass; at this time, the Seer thought that Aiwass was spelled איואס = 78[85], Whereas, as he found later, עיוז = 93 and Αιϝασς = 418. But 78 is actually the number of Aiwass in another way."[86] As we learn in the *Qabalistic Dogma*, "111 is Aleph, the Unity, but also אפל, thick Darkness, and אסן, Sudden Death. This can only be interpreted as meaning the annihilation of the individual in the Unity, and the Darkness which is the Threshold of the Unity; in other words, one must be an expert in Samadhi before this simple Gematria has any proper meaning. How, then, can it serve the student in his research? The uninitiated would expect Life and Light in the One; only by experience can he know that to man the Godhead must be expressed by those things which most he fears."

Crowley purposely avoids "dwelling on the mere silliness of many Gematria correspondences, *e.g.*, the equality of the Qliphoth of one sign with the Intelligence of another. Such misses are more frequent than such hits as אחד, Unity, 13 = אהבה, Love, 13. The argument is an argument in a circle. 'Only an adept can understand the Qabalah,' just as (in Buddhism) Sakyamuni said, 'Only an Arahat can understand the Dhamma.' In this light, indeed, the Qabalah seems little more than a convenient language for recording experience."[87] As Lévi puts it, "Faith begins where science ends. To enlarge the scope of science is apparently to diminish that of faith; but in reality, it is to enlarge it in equal proportion, for it is to amplify its base. One can only define the unknown by its supposed and supposable relations with the known. Analogy was the sole dogma of the ancient magi. This dogma may indeed be called 'mediator,' for it is half scientific, half hypothetical; half reason, and half poetry. This dogma has been, and will always be, the father of all others."[88]

> On the other hand, you must be careful to avoid taking the correspondences given in the books of reference without thinking out why they are so given. Thus, you find a camel in the number which refers to the Moon, but the Tarot card "the Moon" refers not to the letter Gimel which means camel, but to the letter Qoph, and the sign Pisces which means fish, while the letter itself refers to the back of the head; and you also find fish has the meaning of the letter Nun. You must not go on from this, and say that the back of your head is like a camel—the connection between them is simply that they all refer to the same thing.
>
> In studying the Qabalah you mention six months; I think after that time you should be able to realize that, after six incarnations of

---

[84] *Liber 418*, 7th Æthyr.
[85] TS has "418."
[86] *Liber 418*, 17th Æthyr, fn.
[87] *Qabalistic Dogma*.
[88] *The Key of the Mysteries*, Part I, "Sketch of the Prophetic Theology of Numbers."

uninterrupted study, you may realize that you can never know it; as Confucius said about the *Yî King*. "If a few more years were added to my life, I would devote a hundred of them to the study of the *Yî*."

If, however, you work at the Qabalah in the same way as I did myself, in season and out of season, you ought to get a very fair grasp of it in six months. I will now tell you what this method is: as I walked about, I made a point of attributing everything I saw to its appropriate idea. I would walk out of the door of my house and reflect that door is Daleth, and house Beth; now the word "dob" is Hebrew for bear, and has the number 6, which refers to the Sun. Then you come to the fence of your property and that is Cheth—number 8, number of Tarot Trump 7, which is the Chariot: so you begin to look about for your car. Then you come to the street and the first house you see is number 86, and that is Elohim, and it is built of red brick which reminds you of Mars and the Blasted Tower, and so on. As soon as this sort of work, which can be done in a quite lighthearted spirit, becomes habitual, you will find your mind running naturally in this direction, and will be surprised at your progress. Never let your mind wander from the fact that your Qabalah is not my Qabalah; a good many of the things which I have noted may be useful to you, but you must construct your own system so that it is a living weapon in your hand.[89]

"When you are a real adept at all these well-known calculations 'prepare to enter the Immeasurable Region' and dig out the Unknown. *You must construct your own Qabalah!* Nobody can do it for you. What is your own true Number? You must find it and prove it to be correct. In the course of a few years, you should have built yourself a Palace of Ineffable Glory, a Garden of Indescribable Delight. Nor Time nor Fate can tame those tranquil towers, those Minarets of Music, or fade one blossom in those avenues of Perfume!"[90] Indeed, "there is no end to this wondrous science; and when the sceptic sneers, 'With all these methods one ought to be able to make everything out of nothing,' the Qabalist smiles back the sublime retort, 'With these methods One did make everything out of nothing.'"[91] Thus the atheist rises from "a Knight of the Royal Mystery... to understand with the members of the Sovereign Sanctuary that all is symbolic; all, if you will, the Jugglery of the Magician. He is tired of theories and systems of theology and all such toys; and being weary and anhungred and athirst seeks a seat at the Table of Adepts, and a portion of the Bread of Spiritual Experience, and a draught of the wine of Ecstasy."[92]

We tend to forget that many major Western philosophers can be, at times, interpreted as speaking therapeutically, including Plato, Nietzsche, and Wittgenstein. Before mediaeval Schoolmen repurposed philosophical discourse as a conceptual basis for theology, philosophy was a therapeutic practice aiming at peace of mind, inner freedom, and cosmic consciousness.

---

[89] *MWT*, Introduction.
[90] *Ibid.*, Ch. IV. Emphasis in original.
[91] *The Temple of Solomon the King*, Part V.
[92] *An Essay upon Number*, Part II.

Even Descartes, father of modernist rationalism, explicitly wrote the *Meditations* as therapy. He does not offer sceptical arguments to convince his readers of sceptical conclusions, he offers sceptical arguments to make his readers feel the need for an indubitable foundation for knowledge. It was not Freud, but Socrates, who said that "the unexamined life is not worth living."[93] In Plato's *Phaedrus*, Socrates uses the archaic Greek maxim, *gnōthi seauton*, "know thyself," to explain why he has no time for attempts to rationally explain mythology or other far-flung topics. He says, "I have no leisure for them at all; and the reason, my friend, is this: I am not yet able, as the Delphic inscription has it, to know myself; so it seems to me ridiculous, when I do not yet know that, to investigate irrelevant things."[94] In the *Philebus*, Socrates refers back to the earlier dialogue and points out that people make themselves appear ridiculous when they are trying to know obscure things before they know themselves.[95]

"The Atu of Tahuti, who is the Lord of Wisdom," says Crowley in reference to the Tarot trumps, "are also called Keys. They are guides to conduct. They give you the map of the Kingdom of Heaven, and also the best way to take it by force. A complete understanding of any magical problem is necessary before it can be solved. Study from outside, and action from outside, are ways abortive."[96]

> *Sume lege.* Open the Book of THYSELF, take and read. Eat, for this is thy body; drink, for this is the blood of thy redemption. The sun thou seest by day, and the moon thou beholdest by night, and all the stars of heaven that burn above thee, are part of thyself—are thyself. And so is the bowl of Space which contains them, and the wine of Time in which they float; for these two are part of thyself—are Thyself. And God also who casteth them forth from the coffers of his treasury. He, too, though thou knowest it not, is part of thyself—is THYSELF. All is in thee, and thou art in all, and separate existence is not, being but a net of dreams wherein the dreamers of night are ensnared. Read, and thou becomest; eat and drink, and thou art.
>
> Though weak, thou art thine own master; listen not to the babblers of vain words, and thou shalt become strong. There is no revelation except thine own. There is no understanding except thine own. There is no consciousness apart from thee, but that it is held feodal to thee in the kingdom of thy Divinity. When thou knowest thou knowest, and there is none other beside thee, for all becometh as an armour around thee, and thou thyself as an invulnerable, invincible warrior of Light.[97]

---

[93] Plat. *Apol.* 38a.
[94] 229e–230a.
[95] Plat. *Phileb.* 48c. In ancient times, the common aim of all philosophical exercises was to achieve both a concentration of the self, or its separation from anything foreign to it, and an expansion of the self to encompass the infinite totality of all that is. Thus, the study of nature and the origin of things was seen as a spiritual exercise with a moral aim; *cf.* e.g. Hadot 1995.
[96] *The Book of Thoth*, Part I, Sec. III.
[97] *The Temple of Solomon the King*, Part I, "The Child." Emphasis in original.

In the *New Comment* on the third chapter of *Liber AL*, Crowley emphasizes that "Heru-Ra-Ha is not merely a particular form of Ra, but the God enthroned in Ra's seat. That is, His Kingdom on earth is temporary, as explained in verse 34. And he is here conceived as the Hierophant, 'lightening the girders of the soul,' that is, bringing man to initiation."[98] This is a reference to the *Chaldæan Oracles*, attributed to Zoroaster, where one Oracle assures us that, "The girders of the Soul, which give her breathing, are easy to be unloosened."[99] According to Crowley, "These 'girders' imply the skeletal structure on which the soul is supported, the conditions of its incarnation. Man is the heir of ages of evolutionary experience, on certain lines, so that he is organized on formulæ which have determined the type of his development. Of some such formulæ we are conscious, but not of all. Thus it is true for all men—empirically—that a straight line is the shortest distance between two points; some savages may not know this consciously, but they base their actions on that knowledge."[100]

> Now we cannot doubt that consciousness has developed elsewhere than in man; only a blind megalomaniac or a Christian divine could suppose our infinitesimal mote of a planet the sole habitat of Mind, especially as our minds are, at best, totally incompetent to comprehend Nature. It is also unlikely that our Earth's physical conditions of temperature, atmosphere, density and so on, which some still regard as essential to Life, are found frequently; we are only one of nine planets ourselves, and it is absurd to deny that life exists on the others, or in the Sun himself, just because the conditions of our own life are absent elsewhere.
>
> Such Life and Mind may therefore be utterly different to anything we know of; the "girders" of their souls in other spheres may be other than ours.
>
> The above argument is a case of a "girder"; we are bound mentally by our race-experience of the environment in which our own lives flourish. A pioneer choosing a camp must look for wood, water, perhaps shelter, perhaps game. In another planet he might not need any of these.
>
> The "girders" which determine the "form" of our souls are therefore limitations to our thought, as well as supports. In the same way, rails help a train to run easily, but confine it to a definite direction.
>
> The "laws" of Nature and Thought, Mathematics, Logic, and so on, are "girders" of this sort.
>
> Our race-inherited conceptions of space prevented men, until quite recent years, from conceiving a non-Euclidean geometry, or the existence of a fourth Dimension.
>
> The initiate soon becomes aware of the un-truth of many of these limiting laws of his mind; he has to identify Being with not-Being, to perceive Matter as continuous and homogeneous, and so for many

---

[98] NC on AL III.61.
[99] §88.
[100] NC on AL III.61.

another Truth, apprehended directly by pure perception, and consequently not to be refuted by syllogistic methods. The Laws of Logic are thus discovered to be superficial, and their scope only partial.

(It is significant in this connexion that such advanced thinkers as the Hon. Bertrand Russell have found themselves obliged to refer mathematical laws to Logic; it seems to have escaped them that the Laws of Logic are no more than the statement of the limitations of their own intelligence. I quote *The Book of Lies*, ΚΕΦΑΛΗ ΜΕ.)

CHINESE MUSIC
"Explain this happening!"
"It must have a 'natural' cause." ⎫ Let these two asses
"It must have a 'supernatural' cause." ⎭ be set to grind corn.
May, might, must, should, probably, may be, we may safely assume, ought, it is hardly questionable, almost certainly—poor hacks! let them be turned out to grass!

Proof is only possible in mathematics, and mathematics is only a matter of arbitrary conventions.

And yet doubt is a good servant but a bad master; a perfect mistress, but a nagging wife.

"White is white" is the lash of the overseer; "white is black" is the watchword of the slave. The Master takes no heed.

The Chinese cannot help thinking that the octave has 5 notes.

The more necessary anything appears to my mind, the more certain it is that I only assert a limitation.

I slept with Faith, and found a corpse in my arms on awaking; I drank and danced all night with Doubt, and found her a virgin in the morning.

Now then consider the man whose soul has thoroughly explored its structure, is actively conscious of its "girders" of axiom. He must find that they confine him like prison bars, when he would gain the freedom of the initiate.

In this verse therefore doth the God "enthroned in Ra's seat" declare that his Word lightens (or removes) the oppression of these "girders of the soul."

The study of this chapter is accordingly a sound preparatory course for whosoever will become Initiate.

See also the six verses following this; the word increases in value as the reader advances on the Path, just as a Rembrandt is a "pretty picture" to the peasant, a "fine work of art" to the educated man, but to the lover of Beauty a sublime masterpiece, the greater as he grows himself in greatness.[101]

"Let me put it that the body is formed by the super-position of layers, each representing a stage in the history of the evolution of the species. The foetus displays essential characteristics of insect, reptile, mammal (or

---

[101] *Ibid.*

whatever they are) in the order in which these classes of animal appeared in the world's history.[102] Now I want to put forward a thesis—and as far as I know it is personal to myself, based on my work at Cefalù—to the effect that the mind is constructed on precisely the same lines." According to Crowley's theory, "The structure of the mind reveals its history as does the structure of the body. (Capitals, please, or bang on something; that has got to sink in.) Just as your body was at one stage the body of an ape, a fish, a frog (and all the rest of it) so did that animal at that stage possess a mind correlative. Now then! In the course of that kind of initiation conferred by Sammasati, the layers are stripped off very much as happens in elementary meditation (Dharana) to the conscious mind."[103]

"Accordingly, one finds oneself experiencing the thoughts, the feelings, the desires of a gorilla, a crocodile, a rat, a devil-fish, or what have you! One is no longer capable of human thoughts in the ordinary sense of the word; such would be wholly unintelligible. I leave the rest to your imagination; doesn't it sound to you a little like some of the accounts of 'The Dweller on the Threshold?'"[104] In any case, as Crowley writes in his diary, "The only things worth learning are moral qualities and these depend entirely on the results of Sammasati in each case."[105] The *New Comment* continues: "We have seen that Ra-Hoor-Khuit is in one sense the Silent Self in a man, a Name of his Khabs, not so impersonal as Hadit, but the first and least untrue formulation of the Ego. We are to reverse this self in us, then, not to suppress it and subordinate it. Nor are we to evade it, but to come to it. This is done 'through tribulation of ordeal'. This tribulation is that experienced in the process called Psychoanalysis, now that official science has adopted—so far as its inferior intelligence permits—the methods of the magus. But the 'ordeal' is 'bliss'; the solution of each complex by 'tribulation'—note the etymological significance of the word!—is the spasm of joy which is the physiological and psychological accompaniment of any relief from strain and congestion."[106]

---

[102] Though Crowley attributes the recapitulation theory solely to the genius of the eminent German biologist Ernst Haeckel, this "tremendously important doctrine" can actually be traced all the way back to the Egyptian Pharaoh Psammetichus (7th century BCE) who used it as a hypothesis on the origin of language (*Hdt.* 2.2). In an attempt to synthesize the ideas of Lamarckism and the *Naturphilosophie* of German Romanticism with Darwinian concepts of evolution, Haeckel formulated his theory as "ontogeny recapitulates phylogeny." Even if this specific formulation of recapitulation is no longer generally embraced by biologists, its influence is still felt in social sciences today. Indeed, Herbert Spencer articulated the basis for a cultural recapitulation theory five years before Haeckel first published on the subject, writing: "If there be an order in which the human race has mastered its various kinds of knowledge, there will arise in every child an aptitude to acquire these kinds of knowledge in the same order.... Education is a repetition of civilization in little." (Spencer 1860, 5.) Sigmund Freud, who was trained as a biologist during an era when Haeckel's doctrine was the dominant one, retained a Lamarckian outlook while distinguishing between physical and mental recapitulation, with their differences becoming an essential argument in his theory of neuroses. See Gould 1977.
[103] *MWT*, Ch. XXVII.
[104] *Ibid.*
[105] Diary entry, 10 June 1923, 7:06 p.m.
[106] NC on AL III.62.

But in any case any man who is sane at all does make a distinction between the experience of daily life and the experience of dream. It is true that sometimes dreams are so vivid, and their character so persistently uniform that men are actually deceived into believing that places they have seen in dreams repeatedly are places that they have known in a waking life. But they are quite capable of criticising this illusion by memory, and they admit the deception. Well, in the same way the phenomena of high Magick and Samadhi have an authenticity, and confer an interior certainty, which is to the experience of waking life as that is to a dream.

But, apart from all this, experience is experience; and the real guarantee that we have of the attainment of reality is its rank in the hierarchy of the mind.

Let us ask ourselves for a moment what is the characteristic of dream impressions as judged by the waking mind. Some dreams are so powerful that they convince us, even when awake, of their reality. Why then do we criticise and dismiss them? Because their contents are incoherent, because the order of nature to which they belong does not properly conform with the kind of experience which does hang together-after a fashion. Why do we criticise the reality of waking experience? On precisely similar grounds. Because in certain respects it fails to conform with our deep instinctive consciousness of the structure of the mind. *Tendency!* We *happen* to be that kind of animal.[107]

Another chapter of *The Book of Lies* goes on to describe dreams as "imperfections of sleep." And "even so is consciousness the imperfection of waking. Dreams are impurities in the circulation of the blood; even so is consciousness a disorder of life. Dreams are without proportion, without good sense, without truth; so also is consciousness. Awake from dream, the truth is known"—"I.e. the truth that he hath slept"—"awake from waking, the Truth is—The Unknown."[108] Or as the *New Comment* puts it, "For so long as any answer remains, there is no thing known. Knowledge is the loss of the Knower in the Known."[109] In "The Vedanta" section of *The Temple of Solomon the King*, Crowley writes that, "Knowledge is identification, not with the inner or outer of a thing, but with that which cannot be explained by either, and which is the essence of the thing in itself,"—"And yet again this is a sheer deceit, as every conceit must be"—"and which the Upanishads name the Âtman. Identification with this Âtman (Emerson's 'Oversoul') is therefore the end of Religion and Philosophy alike."

I. Man being a finite being, he is incapable of apprehending the infinite. Nor does his communion with infinite being (true or false) alter this fact.

---

[107] *Eight Lectures*, Ch. 8, Secs. 12–13. Emphasis in original.
[108] *The Book of Lies*, Ch. 30.
[109] NC on AL II.13.

EPISTEMOLOGY 161

II. Let then the student contradict every vision and refuse to enjoy it; first, because there is certainly another vision possible of precisely contradictory nature; secondly, because though he is God, he is also a man upon an insignificant planet.

III. Being thus equilibrated laterally and vertically, it may be that, either by affirmation or denial of all these things together, he may attain the supreme trance.[110]

"Direct experience is the key to Yoga; direct experience of that Soul (Âtman) or Essence (Purusha) which acting upon Energy (Prâna), and Substance (Âkâsa) differentiates a plant from a stone, an animal from a plant, a man from an animal, a man from a man, and man from God, yet which ultimately is the underlying Equilibrium of all things; for as the Bhagavad-Gîta says: 'Equilibrium is called Yoga.'"[111] Lévi concurs: "Unity demonstrates the analogy of contraries; it is the foundation, the equilibrium, and the end of numbers. The act of faith starts from unity, and returns to unity."[112] As was pointed out in the previous chapter, "an idea is only true in so far as it contains its contradictory in itself,"[113] and such states of mind "constitute the really important results of Samyama, and these results are not to be destroyed by philosophical speculation, because they are not susceptible of analysis, because they have no component parts, because they exist by virtue of their very Unreason—*certum est quia ineptum!* They cannot be expressed, for they are above knowledge. To some extent we can convey our experience to others familiar with that experience to a less degree by the aesthetic method. And this explains why all the good work on Yoga—alchemy, magick and the rest—not doctrinal but symbolic—the word of God to man, is given in Poetry and Art."[114]

As Lévi writes, "We have said that there is no religion without mysteries; let us add that there are no mysteries without symbols. The symbol, being the formula or the expression of the mystery, only expresses its unknown depth by paradoxical images borrowed from the known. The symbolic form, having for its object to characterize what is above scientific reason, should necessarily find itself without that reason: hence the celebrated and perfectly just remark of a Father of the Church: 'I believe because it is absurd. *Credo quia absurdum.*'"[115] Or as Crowley points out, "A conscious man, according, cannot possibly know anything of these three principles, although they constitute his essence. It is the work of Initiation to journey inwards to them. See, in the Oath of a Probationer of A∴A∴ 'I pledge myself to discover the nature and powers of my own Being.'"[116]

"To know, To dare, To will, To keep silent, are, as we have said elsewhere, the four qabalistic words which correspond to the four letters of

---

[110] *Postcards to Probationers*, loc. cit.
[111] *The Temple of Solomon the King*, Part IV, "The Agnostic Position."
[112] *The Key of the Mysteries*, Part I, Article I.
[113] *Eight Lectures*, Ch. 6, Sec. 32.
[114] Ibid., Sec. 33.
[115] *The Key of the Mysteries*, loc. cit., "Preliminary Considerations."
[116] *Little Essays Toward Truth*, loc. cit.

the tetragram and to the four hieroglyphic forms of the Sphinx. To know, is the human head; to dare, the claws of the lion; to will, the mighty flanks of the bull; to keep silent, the mystical wings of the eagle. He only maintains his position above other men who does not prostitute the secrets of his intelligence to their commentary and their laughter."[117] The creatures associated with the Sphinx originate in the Babylonian symbols of the four fixed signs of the Zodiac: the man, representing Aquarius; the lion, representing Leo; the ox, representing Taurus; and the eagle, representing Scorpio. This symbolism was also common in Greek, Egyptian, and Assyrian mythology, and the early Christians adapted it for the four Evangelists as the tetramorph.[118]

The elements of the Christian tetramorph also appear in the vision of Ezekiel, who describes the four creatures as they appear to him in his book: "As for the likeness of their faces, they four had the face of a man, and the face of a lion, on the right side: and they four had the face of an ox on the left side; they four also had the face of an eagle."[119] The Hebraic mysticism of the Merkabah vision of Ezekiel and the Christian mysticism of the Apocalyptic vision of St. John share the same mystical vision of the Divine Immanence riding an incandescent chariot of flames, drawn by the same four angelic beasts: "And the first beast was like a lion, and the second beast like a calf, and the third beast had a face as a man, and the fourth beast was like a flying eagle."[120] These emblems of the Patriarchal Blessing were borne on the standards of the four leading tribes who ruled respectively over the East, West, South, and North columns in marching, camping, or fighting order, during the mythical Exodus from Egypt.[121] In her *Isis Unveiled*, Madame Blavatsky considers it a fact that, "no less than the *Book of Job*, the whole *Revelation*, is simply an allegorical narrative of the Mysteries and initiation therein of a candidate, who is John himself. No high Mason, well versed in the different degrees, can fail to see it."[122]

However, according to Crowley, "this most arcane of the Mysteries of Antiquity was never at any Period the Tool of the Slave-Gods, but a Witness of Horus through the dark Æon of Osiris to His Light and Truth, His Force and Fire. Thou canst by no means interpret the Sphinx in Terms of the Formula of the Slain God. This did I comprehend even when as Eliphaz Levi Zahed I walked up and down the Earth, seeking a Reconciliation of these Antagonists, which was a Task impossible, for in that Plane they have Antipathy. (Even so may no Man form a Square Magical of Four Units.) But the Light of the New Æon revealeth this Sphinx as the True Symbol of this our Holy Art of Magick under the Law of Thelema. In Her is the equal Development and Disposition of the Forces of Nature, each in its Balanced Strength; also Her True Name is Soul of NU, having the Digamma for Phi, and endeth in Upsilon, not in Xi, so that her Orthography is ΣFINY whose

---

[117] *The Key of the Mysteries*, Part III, Book I, Ch. III.
[118] Whittick 1971.
[119] Ezekiel 1:10.
[120] Revelation 4:7.
[121] Numbers 2.
[122] Blavatsky 1877, ii.351. Emphasis in original.

Numeration is Six Hundred and Three Score and Six. For the Root thereof is *SF*, which signifieth the Incarnation of the Spirit; and of Kin are not only the Sun, Our Father, but Sumer, where Man knew himself Man, and Soma, the Divine Potion that giveth Men Enlightenment, and Scin, Light Astral, and Scire also, by a far Travelling. But especially is this Root hidden in Sus, that is of Sow, Swine, because the Most Holy must needs take its Delight under the Omphalos of the Unclean. But this was hidden by Wisdom, in Order that the Arcanum should not be profaned during the Æon of the Slain God. But now it has been given unto me to understand the Heart of Her Mystery."[123]

"To will and to dare are closely linked Powers of the Sphinx, and they are based on—to know. If one have a right apprehension of the Universe, if he know himself free, immortal, boundless, infinite force and fire, then may he will and dare. Fear, sorrow and failure are but phantoms."[124] The task of a Probationer is to "everywhere proclaim openly his connection with the A∴A∴ and speak of It and Its principles (even so little as he understandeth) for that mystery is the enemy of Truth."[125] Thus, "Silence in the vulgar sense is not the answer to the Riddle of the Sphinx; it is that which is created by that answer. For Silence is the Equilibrium of Perfection; so that Harpocrates is the omniform, the universal Key to every Mystery soever. The Sphinx is the 'Puzzel or Pucelle,' the Feminine Idea to which there is only one complement, always different in form, and always identical in essence. This is the signification of the Gesture of the God; it is shewn more clearly in His adult form as the Fool of the Tarot and as Bacchus Diphues, and without equivocation when He appears as Baphomet."[126]

> When we inquire more closely into His symbolism, the first quality which engages our attention is doubtless His innocence. Not without deep wisdom is He called the twin of Horus; and this is the Æon of Horus: it is He who sent forth Aiwass His minister to proclaim its advent. The Fourth Power of the Sphinx is Silence; to us then who aspire to this power as the crown of our Work, it will be of utmost value to attain His innocence in all its fullness. We must understand first of all that the root of Moral Responsibility, on which Man stupidly prides himself as distinguishing him from the other animals, is Restriction, which is the Word of Sin. Indeed, there is truth in the Hebrew fable, that the knowledge of Good and Evil brings forth Death. To regain Innocence is to regain Eden. We must learn to live without the murderous consciousness that every breath we draw swells the sails which bear our frail vessels to the Port of the Grave. We must cast our Fear by Love; seeing that Every Act is an Orgasm, their total issue cannot be but Birth. Also, Love is the law: thus every act must be Righteousness and Truth. By certain Meditations this may be understood and established; and this ought to be done so thoroughly that we become unconscious of our

---

[123] *Liber Aleph*, "De Sphinge Ægyptiorum."
[124] NC on AL II.46.
[125] *Liber Collegii Sancti*, Sec. A.8.
[126] *Little Essays Toward Truth*, "Silence."

Sanctification, for only then is Innocence made perfect. This state is, in fact, a necessary condition of any proper contemplation of what we are accustomed to consider the first task of the Aspirant, the solution of the question, "What is my True Will?" For until we become innocent, we are certain to try to judge our Will by some Canon of what seems 'right' or 'wrong'; in other words, we are apt to criticise our Will from the outside, whereas True Will should spring, a fountain of Light, from within, and flow unchecked, seething with Love, into the Ocean of Life.[127]

"If any one cause be unknowable, be it first or last, then all causes are unknowable. The will to create is denied, the will to annihilate is denied, and finally the will to act is denied. Propositions perhaps true to the Master, but certainly not so to the disciple. Because Titian was a great artist and Rodin is a great sculptor, that is no reason why we should abolish art schools and set an embargo on clay. If the will to act is but a mirage of the mind, then equally so is the will to differentiate or select. If this be true, and the chain of Cause and Effect is eternal, how is it then that Cause A produces effect B, and Cause B effect C, and Cause A + B + C effect X. Where originates this power of production? It is said there is no change, the medium remaining alike throughout. But we say there is a change—a change of form,"—"Form here is synonymous with the Hindu Mâyâ, it is also the chief power of the Buddhist devil, Mara, and even of that mighty devil, Choronzon"—"and not only a change, but a distinct birth and a distinct death of form. What creates this form? Sense perception. what will destroy this form, and reveal to us that which lies behind it? Presumably cessation of sense perception. How can we prove our theory? By cutting away every perception, every thought-form as it is born, until nothing thinkable is left, not even the thought of the unknowable."[128]

"But now concerning Silence," Crowley writes in *Liber Aleph*, "I will have a further Word with thee. For thereby we mean not the Muteness of him that hath a Dumb Devil. This Silence is the Dragon of thine Unconscious Nature, not only the Ecstasy or Death of thine Ego in the Operation of its Organ, but also, in its Unity with thy Lion, the Truth of thy Self. Thus is thy Silence the Way of the Tao, and all Speech a Deviation therefrom."[129] In the chapter entitled "De herbo sanctissimo Arabico," Crowley further identified the Ox with the Letter Aleph and "that Atu of Thoth whose Number is Zero, and whose name is Maat, Truth, or Maut, the Vulture, the All-Mother, being an Image of Our Lady Nuit, but also it is called the Fool, who is Parsifal, 'der reine Thor,' and so referreth to him that walketh in the Way of the Tao. Also, he is Harpocrates, the Child Horus, walking (as saith Daood, the Badawi that became King, in his Psalms), upon the Lion and the Dragon; that is, he is in Unity with his own Secret Nature, as I have shewn thee in my Word concerning the Sphinx."

---

[127] *Ibid.*
[128] *The Temple of Solomon the King, loc. cit.*
[129] *Liber Aleph*, "Prolegomena de silentio."

Why is the Tao translated "Reason"? Because by "Reason" is here meant the structure of the mind itself; a Buddhist who had succeeded with Mahāsatipaṭṭhāna might call it the Consciousness of the Tendency to Perceive the Sensation of Anything. For in the last resort, and through the pursuit of one line of analysis, this structure is all that we can call our consciousness. Everything of which we can in any way be aware may be interpreted as being some function of this structure.[130]

Note! Function. For now we see why Tao may also be translated "The Way"; for it is the motion of the structure that we observe. There is no Being apart from Going.

You are familiar with the Four Powers of the Sphinx, attributed by the Adepts of old time to their Four Elements. Air is to Know, *Scire;* Fire is to Will, *Velle;* Water is to Dare, *Audere;* and Earth is to Keep Silence, *Tacere.* But now that a fifth Element, spirit, is generally recognized in the Qabalah, I have deemed it proper to add a Fifth Power corresponding: to Go, *Ire.* (*Book of Thoth,* p. 275)

Then, as Spirit is the Origin, the Essence, and the Sum of the other four, so is to Go in relation to those powers. And to Go is the very meaning of the name God, as elsewhere shewn in these letters; hence the Egyptian Gods were signalized as such by their bearing the Ankh, which is a Sandal-strap, and in its form the Crux Ansata, the Rosy Cross, the means whereby we demonstrate the Godhead of our Nature. See then how sweetly each idea slides into the next! How right this is, that the Quintessence should be dynamic and not static! For if there were some form of Being separate from Going, it would necessarily be subject to decay; and, in any case, a thing impossible to apprehend, since apprehension is itself an Act, not an idea immobile which would be bound to change in the very moment of grasping it.

As I have tried to shew in another letter, the "Point-Event" (or whatever it is) of which we are aware is a change, or, less inaccurately, the memory of one; the things that change remain relentlessly unknown.[131]

Crowley found that Lao Tze's "very simplest ideas, the primitive elements of his thought, had no true correspondences in any European terminology. The very first word 'Tao' presented a completely insoluble problem. It had been translated 'Reason', 'The Way', 'To Ov.' None of these convey any true conception of the Tao."[132] The word has a variety of meanings in both ancient and modern Chinese language; for example, the *Hànyǔ Dà Zìdiǎn* dictionary gives 39 different meanings for *dào* and six more for *dǎo*. Some scholars draw sharp distinctions between the moral-philosophical usage of the word in Confucianism and religious Taoism, and

---

[130] *Cf.* also *The Antecedents of Thelema, loc. cit.*: "Note that Events may be considered for convenience in any or all of three modes of projection: (*a*) as extended in space; (*b*) as extended in time; (*c*) as causally connected. These are forms of (*a*) sensation; (*b*) consciousness of going; (*c*) reason."
[131] *MWT*, Ch. XXXIV.
[132] *Ibid.*, Ch. XXXV.

the more metaphysical use of the term in philosophical Taoism and Han Buddhism; others, however, maintain that these are not really separate usages or meanings, but mutually inclusive and compatible views of an intricate concept.[133] In Taoism, Chan and Zen Buddhism, and Confucianism, the object of spiritual practice is to "become one with the Tao," or harmonize one's will with Nature in order to achieve *Wu-wei*, or "effortless action." Similarly, "Faithful to the spirit of truth, the members of the interior Order live in silence, but in real activity."[134]

> The Tao is reason in this sense, that the substance of things may be in part apprehended as being that necessary relation between the elements of thought which determines the laws of reason. In other words, the only reality is that which compels us to connect the various forms of illusion as we do. It is thus evidently unknowable, and expressible neither by speech nor by silence. All that we can know about it is that there is inherent in it a power (which however is not itself) by virtue whereof all beings appear in forms congruous with the nature of necessity.
>
> The Tao is also "the Way"—in the following sense. Nothing exists except as a relation with other similarly postulated ideas. Nothing can be known in itself, but only as one of the participants in a series of events. Reality is therefore in the motion, not in the thing moved. We cannot apprehend anything except as one postulated element of an observed impression of change.
>
> We may express this in other terms as follows. Our knowledge of anything is in reality the sum of our observations of its successive movements, that is to say, of its path from event to event. In this sense the Tao may be translated as "the Way." It is not a thing in itself in the sense of being an object susceptible of apprehension by sense or mind. It is not the cause of any thing; it is rather the category underlying all existence or event, and therefore true and real as they are illusory, being merely landmarks invented for convenience in describing our experiences. The Tao possesses no power to cause anything to exist or to take place. Yet our experience when analyzed tells us that the only reality of which we may be sure is this path or Way which resumes the whole of our knowledge.[135]

"This then is a very great difficulty for the Magician," Crowley writes in *Book 4*, Part II. "He cannot possibly have all experience, and though he may console himself philosophically with the reflection that the Universe is conterminous with such experience as he has, he will find it grow at such a pace during the early years of his life that he may almost be tempted to believe in the possibility of experiences beyond his own, and from a

---

[133] Hansen 1992.
[134] *Liber XXXIII*.
[135] *MWT, loc. cit.*

practical standpoint he will seem to be confronted with so many avenues of knowledge that he will be bewildered which to choose."[136]

> The ass hesitated between two thistles; how much more that greater ass, that incomparably greater ass, between two thousand!
> Fortunately it does not matter very much; but he should at least choose those branches of knowledge which abut directly upon universal problems.
> He should choose not one but several, and these should be as diverse as possible in nature.
> It is important that he should strive to excel in some sport, and that that sport should be the one best calculated to keep this body in health.
> He should have a thorough grounding in classics, mathematics and science; also enough general knowledge of modern languages and of the shifts of life to enable him to travel in any part of the world with ease and security.
> History and geography he can pick up as he wants them; and what should interest him most in any subject is its links with some other subject, so that his Pantacle may not lack what painters call "composition."
> He will find that, however good his memory may be, ten thousand impressions enter his mind for every one that it is able to retain even for a day. And the excellence of a memory lies in the wisdom of its selection.
> The best memories so select and judge that practically nothing is retained which has not some coherence with the general plan of the mind.[137]

"Memory," writes Crowley in the eponymous chapter of his *Little Essays Toward Truth*, "as such is practically worthless; it is like an abandoned library. Its data must be coordinated by judgment, and played upon by skill; it resembles a great Organ which requires an organist. By classifying simple impressions, one obtains ideas of a higher order; the repetition of this process gives a structure to the mind which makes it a worthy instrument of thought. And this means enables one to retain, and to bring at will from their quiet resting-place, a thousandfold the number of facts which would overwhelm the untrained memory. One must model one's mind upon the arrangement of the ends of the nerve-fibres and the brain. At will! Here is the great key to proper selection, that one should resolutely remember all facts that may be useful, and as resolutely forget all those impertinent, to the True Way of one's Star in Space. For so only can one economise the mnemonic faculty; and this is to say: no man can begin to train his memory duly until he is aware of his True Will."

The old-fashioned pedagogues were not all so stupid as some modern educators would have us think. The principle of the system was

---

[136] *Book 4*, Part II, Ch. IX.
[137] *Ibid.*

to strike the brain a series of constantly repeated blows until the proper reaction became normal to the organism.

It is not desirable to use ideas which excite interest, or may come in handy later as weapons, in this fundamental training of the mind. It is much better to compel the mind to busy itself with root ideas which do not mean very much to the child, because you are not trying to excite the brain, but to drill it. For this reason, all the best minds have been trained by preliminary study of classics and mathematics.

The same principle applies to the training of the body. The original exercises should be of a character to train the muscles generally to perform any kind of work, rather than to train them for some special kind of work, concentration of which will unfit them for other tasks by depriving them of the elasticity which is the proper condition of life. *{Some few forms of exercise are exempt from these strictures. Rock-climbing, in particular, trains every muscle in an endless variety of ways. It moreover compels the learner to use his own judgment, to rely on himself, to develop resource, and to depend upon his own originality to attack each new problem that presents itself. This principle may be extended to all departments of the education of children. They should be put into contact with all kinds of truth, and allowed to make their own reflections thereon and reactions thereto, without the least attempt to bias their judgment. Magical pupils should be trained on similar lines. They should be made to work alone from the first, to cover the whole ground impartially, to devise their own experiments and draw their own conclusions.}*

In Magick and meditation this principle applies with tremendous force. It is quite useless to teach people how to perform magical operations, when it may be that such operations, when they have learned to do them, are not in accordance with their wills. What must be done is to drill the Aspirant in the hard routine of the elements of the Royal Art.

So far as mysticism is concerned, the technique is extremely simple, and has been very simply described in Part I of this *Book 4*. It cannot be said too strongly that any amount of mystical success whatever is no compensation for slackness with regard to the technique. There may come a time when Samadhi itself is no part of the business of the mystic. But the character developed by the original training remains an asset. In other words, the person who has made himself a first-class brain capable of elasticity is competent to attack any problem soever, when he who has merely specialized has got into a groove, and can no longer adapt and adjust himself to new conditions.[138]

"Books are not the only medium even of learning; more, what they teach is partial, prejudiced, meagre, sterile, uncertain, and alien to reality. It follows that all the best books are those which make no pretence to accuracy: poetry, theatre, fiction. All others date. Another point is that Truth abides above and aloof from intellectual expression, and

---

[138] *MITAP*, Ch. XXI, Sec. V.

consequently those books which bear the Magic Keys of the Portal of the Intelligible by dint of inspiration and suggestion come more nearly to grips with Reality than those whose appeal is only to the Intellect. 'Didactic' poetry, 'realistic' plays and novels, are contradictions in terms."[139] At the conclusion of *Magick in Theory and Practice*, Crowley sums up "the whole matter in these words: There is no object whatever worthy of attainment but the regular development of the being of the Aspirant by steady scientific work; he should not attempt to run before he can walk; he should not wish to go somewhere until he knows for certain whither he wills to go."[140]

Theorem 23 in the Introduction to the same work defines Magick as "the Science of understanding oneself and one's conditions," and "the Art of applying that understanding in action." By contrast, "It is, and the fact is still more important, utterly fatal and demoralizing to acquire the habit of reliance on others. The Magician must know every detail of his work, and be able and willing to roll up his shirtsleeves and do it, no matter how trivial or menial it may seem. Abramelin (it is true) forbids the Aspirant to perform any tasks of an humiliating type; but he will never be able to command perfect service unless he has experience of such necessary work, mastered during his early training."[141]

> We may therefore admit quite cheerfully that Magick is as mysterious as mathematics, as empirical as poetry, as uncertain as golf, and as dependent on the personal equation as Love.
>
> That is no reason why we should not study, practice and enjoy it; for it is a Science in exactly the same sense as biology; it is no less an Art that Sculpture; and it is a Sport as much as Mountaineering.
>
> Indeed, there seems to be no undue presumption in urging that no Science possesses equal possibilities of deep and important Knowledge; that no Art offers such opportunities to the ambition of the Soul to express its Truth, in Ecstasy, through Beauty; and that no Sport rivals its fascinations of danger and delight, so excites, exercises, and tests its devotees to the uttermost, or so rewards them by well-being, pride, and the passionate pleasures of personal triumph.

---

[139] *MWT*, Ch. LXXII. *Cf.* Plat. *Phaedrus* 274e–275b: "The story goes that Thamus said many things to Theuth in praise or blame of the various arts, which it would take too long to repeat; but when they came to the letters, 'This invention, O king,' said Theuth, 'will make the Egyptians wiser and will improve their memories; for it is an elixir of memory and wisdom that I have discovered.' But Thamus replied, 'Most ingenious Theuth, one man has the ability to beget arts, but the ability to judge of their usefulness or harmfulness to their users belongs to another; and now you, who are the father of letters, have been led by your affection to ascribe to them a power the opposite of that which they really possess. For this invention will produce forgetfulness in the minds of those who learn to use it, because they will not practice their memory. Their trust in writing, produced by external characters which are no part of themselves, will discourage the use of their own memory within them. You have invented an elixir not of memory, but of reminding; and you offer your pupils the appearance of wisdom, not true wisdom, for they will read many things without instruction and will therefore seem to know many things, when they are for the most part ignorant and hard to get along with, since they are not wise, but only appear wise."
[140] *MITAP, loc. cit.*
[141] *Ibid.*, Ch. VIII, Sec. II.

Magick takes every thought and act for its apparatus; it has the Universe for its Library and its Laboratory; all Nature is its Subject; and its Game, free from close seasons and protective restrictions, always abounds in infinite variety, being all that exists.[142]

"The Quest of the Holy Grail, the Search for the Stone of the Philosophers—by whatever name we choose to call the Great Work—is therefore endless. Success only opens up new avenues of brilliant possibility. Yea, verily, and Amen! the task is tireless and its joys without bounds; for the whole Universe, and all that in it is, what is it but the infinite playground of the Crowned and Conquering Child, of the insatiable, the innocent, the ever-rejoicing Heir of Space and Eternity, whose name is MAN?"[143]

Now Initiation is, by etymology, the journeying inwards; it is the Voyage of Discovery (oh Wonder-World!) of one's own Soul. And this is Truth that stands upon the prow, eternally alert; this is Truth that sits with one strong hand gripping the helm!

Truth is our Path, and Truth is our Goal; ay! there shall came to all a moment of great Light when the Path is seen to be itself the Goal; and in that hour every one of us shall exclaim:

"I am the Way, the Truth, and the Life!"[144]

---

[142] Diary entry, as quoted in *MITAP*, Ch. IX.
[143] *Little Essays Toward Truth*, "Man." Emphasis in original.
[144] *Ibid.*, "Truth." John 14:6.

CHAPTER 6
Soteriology

Just as The Book of the Law *reconciles an impersonal and infinite interpretation of the cosmos with an egocentric and practical viewpoint, so it makes "infinite space" speak in the language of a goddess and deals with the details of eating and drinking:*

Be goodly therefore: dress ye all in fine apparel; eat rich foods and drink sweet wines and wines that foam! Also, take your fill and will of love as ye will, when, where and with whom ye will! But always unto me.

The emancipation of mankind from all limitations whatever is one of the main precepts of the Book.

Bind nothing! Let there be no difference made among you between any one thing & any other thing; for thereby there cometh hurt.

—The Confessions of Aleister Crowley

We are not to worship the Khu, to fall in love with our Magical Image. To do this—we have all done it—is to forget our Truth. If we adore Form, it becomes opaque to Being, and may soon prove false to itself. The Khu in each of us includes the Cosmos as he knows it. To me, even another Khabs is only part of my Khu. Our own Khabs is our one sole Truth.

—The New Comment on AL I.9

"We see, then," writes Crowley in *Magick in Theory and Practice*, "that we can never affect anything outside ourselves save only as it is also within us. Whatever I do to another, I do also to myself. If I kill a man, I destroy my own life at the same time. That is the magical meaning of the so-called 'Golden Rule', which should not be in the imperative but in the indicative mood. Every vibration awakens all others of its particular pitch."[1] According to him, *The Book of the Law* issues "a curse against the cringing altruism of Christianity the yielding of the self to external impressions, the smothering of the Babe of Bliss beneath the flabby old nurse Convention."[2] His *New Comment* on "The exposure of innocence" (AL II.22) says: "Exposure means 'putting out' as in a shop-window. The pretence of altruism and so-called virtue 'is a lie'; it is the hypocrisy of the Puritan, which is hideously corrupting both to the hypocrite and to his victim."

To "lust" is to grasp continually at fresh aspects of Nuit. It is the mistake of the vulgar to expect to find satisfaction in the objects of

---

[1] *MITAP*, Ch. XIV.
[2] OC on AL II.22.

sense. Disillusion is inevitable; when it comes, it leads only too often to an error which is in reality more fatal than the former, the denial of "materiality" and of "animalism." There is a correspondence between these two attitudes and those of the "once-born" and "twice-born" of William James (*Varieties of Religious Experience*). Thelemites are "thrice-born"; we accept everything for what it is, without "lust of result," without insisting upon things conforming with *a priori* ideals, or regretting their failure to do so. We can therefore "enjoy" all things of sense and rapture' according to their true nature. For example, the average man dreads tuberculosis. The "Christian Scientist" flees this fear by pretending that the disease is an illusion in "mortal mind." But the Thelemite accepts it for what it is, and finds interest in it for its own sake. For him it is a necessary part of the Universe; he makes "no difference" between it and any other thing. The artist's position is analogous. Rubens, for instance, takes a gross pleasure in female flesh, rendering it truthfully from lack of imagination and analysis. Idealist painters like Bouguereau awake to the divergence between Nature and their academic standards of Beauty, falsify the facts in order to delude themselves. The greatest, like Rembrandt, paint a gallant, a hag, and a carcass with equal passion and rapture; they love the truth as it is. They do not admit that anything can be ugly or evil; its existence justifies itself. This is because they know themselves to be part of an harmonious unity; to disdain any item of it would be to blaspheme the whole. The Thelemite is able to revel in any experience soever; in each he recognizes the tokens of ultimate Truth. It is surely obvious, even intellectually, that all phenomena are interdependent, and therefore involve each other. Suppose $a + b + c = d$, $a = d - b - c$ just as much as $b = d - c - a$. It is senseless to pick out one equation as "nice," and another as "nasty." Personal predilections are evidence of imperfect vision. But it is even worse to deny reality to such facts as refuse to humour them. In the charter of spiritual sovereignty it is written that the charcoal-burner is no less a subject than the duke. The structure of the state includes all elements; it were stupid and suicidal to aim at homogeneity, or to assert it. Spiritual experience soon enables the aspirant to assimilate these ideas, and he can enjoy life to the full, finding his True Self alike in the contemplation of every element of existence.[3]

Indeed, "in practice, there is nothing more certain than that one ought to confirm one's will by all possible acts on all possible planes. The ceremony must not be confined to the formally magical rites. We must neglect no means to our end, neither despising our common sense, nor doubting our secret wisdom."[4] Theorem 27 from *MITAP* states that "Every man should make Magick the keystone of his life. He should learn its laws and live by them." Crowley uses this prosaic illustration: "The Banker should discover the real meaning of his existence, the real motive which led him to choose

---

[3] NC on AL II.22.
[4] *MITAP, loc. cit.*

that profession. He should understand banking as a necessary factor in the economic existence of mankind instead of merely a business whose objects are independent of the general welfare. He should learn to distinguish false values from real, and to act not on accidental fluctuations but on considerations of essential importance. Such a banker will prove himself superior to others; because he will not be an individual limited by transitory things, but a force of Nature, as impersonal, impartial and eternal as gravitation, as patient and irresistible as the tides. His system will not be subject to panic, any more than the law of Inverse Squares is disturbed by elections. He will not be anxious about his affairs because they will not be his; and for that reason he will be able to direct them with the calm, clear-headed confidence of an onlooker, with intelligence unclouded by self-interest, and power unimpaired by passion.)"

The trick is that "one should do one's Will 'without lust of result'. If one is working in accordance with the laws of one's own nature, one is doing 'right'; and no such work can be criticised as 'useless', even in cases of the character here discussed. So long as one's Will prevails, there is no cause for complaint." Crowley quotes his diary in this conjuncture: "To abandon one's Magick would shew lack of self-confidence in one's powers, and doubt as to one's inmost faith in Self and in Nature." The footnote reads: "I.e. on the ground that one cannot understand how Magick can produce the desired effects. For if one possesses the inclination to do Magick, it is evidence of a tendency in one's Nature. Nobody understands fully how the mind moves the muscles; but we know that lack of confidence on this point means paralysis. 'If the Sun & Moon should doubt, They'd immediately Go out,' as Blake said.[5] Also, as I said myself. 'Who hath the How is careless of the Why.'[6]" And, as the diary continues, "Of course one changes one's methods as experience indicates; but there is no need to change them on any such ground as the above."[7]

> That verse (AL. I, 44) condenses the whole magical technique. It makes clear when you have understood it—the secret of success in the Great Work. Of course at first it appears a paradox. You must have an aim, and one aim only: yet on no account must you want to achieve it!!!
>
> Those chapters of *The Book of Lies* quoted in my last letter do throw some light onto this Abyss of self-contradiction; and there is meaning much deeper than the contrast between the Will with a capital W, and desire, want, or velleity. The main point seems to be that in aspiring to Power one is limited by the True Will. If you use force, violating your own nature either from lack of understanding or from petulant whim, one is merely wasting energy; things go back to normal as soon as the stress is removed. This is one small case of the big Equation "Free Will = Necessity" (Fate, Destiny, or Karma: it's all much the same idea). One is

---

[5] *Auguries of Innocence.*
[6] *The Scented Garden of Abdullah the Satirist of Shiraz*, "The Vanity of Metaphysics."
[7] *MITAP*, Ch. IX.

most rigidly bound by the causal chain that has dragged one to where one is; but it is one's own self that has forged the links.

Please refrain from the obvious retort: "Then, in the long run, you can't possibly go wrong: so it doesn't matter what you do." Perfectly true, of course! ("There is no single grain of dust that shall not attain to Buddhahood": with some such words did the debauched old reprobate seek to console himself when Time began to take its revenge.) But the answer is simple enough: you happen to be the kind of being that thinks it does matter what course you steer; or, still more haughtily, you enjoy the pleasure of sailing.[8]

Another footnote in *MITAP* clarifies the point further: "One's True Will is necessarily fitted to the whole Universe with the utmost exactitude, because each term in the equation $a + b + c = 0$ must be equal and opposite to the sum of all the other terms. No individual can ever be aught than himself, or do aught else than his Will, which is his necessary relation with his environment, dynamically considered. All error is no more than an illusion proper to him to dissipate the mirage, and it is a general law that the method of accomplishing this operation is to realize, and to acquiesce in, the order of the Universe, and to refrain from attempting the impossible task of overcoming the inertia of the forces which oppose, and therefore are identical with, one's self. Error in thought is therefore failure to understand, and in action to perform, one's own True Will."[9]

"It is a fact of meditation that everything which becomes manifest is instantly recognized as unreal. All perfect unveiling solves, wholly or in part, the equation 'Something equals 0/0.' ... Adeptship is little more than ability to perceive this 0/0 phase of 'Something' in respect of larger and larger 'Somethings'."[10] In his *Eight Lectures*, Crowley attests that, "All this Yoga that we know and practice, this Yoga that produced these ecstatic results that we call phenomena, includes among its spiritual emanations a good deal of unpleasantness. The more we study this universe produced by our Yoga, the more we collect and synthesize our experience, the nearer we get to a perception of what the Buddha declared to be characteristic of all component things: Sorrow, Change, and Absence of any permanent principle. We constantly approach his enunciation of the first two 'Noble Truths,' as he called them. 'Everything is Sorrow'; and 'The cause of Sorrow is Desire.' By the word 'Desire' he meant exactly what is meant by 'Love' in *The Book of the Law* which I quoted a few moments ago. 'Desire' is the need of every unit to extend its experience by combining with its opposite."[11]

In the *New Comment*, Crowley emphasizes the fact that "Space is omnipresent. The cause of 'sorrow' is the 'imaginary' solutions of continuity in this substance. Ecstasy is produced by the resolution of these illusions. Observe well that to beings in a state of strain or sorrow the 'Great Work' is bound to appear in the guise of a relief or joy. But this is not to assert

---

[8] *MWT*, Introduction.
[9] *MITAP, loc. cit.*
[10] NC on AL I.11.
[11] *Eight Lectures*, Ch. 1, Sec. 13.

Samadhi, that unity with the universe which brings relief and joy by 'love', as an 'absolute good'. It is only good relatively to our present condition as beings divided by Illusion from Nuit. When one returns to the 'simple' state, one soon begins to think out a new route through the Universe, and devise new combinations in the Great Game called Seeing Life." To Crowley, it is "evident that Nuith obtains the satisfaction of Her Nature when the parts of Her Body fulfil their own Nature. The sacrament of live is not only so from the point of view of the celebrants, but from that of the divinity invoked." Thus, "the task of the Initiate" is "to adapt himself to the Totality of Existence, and to develop in himself the means of apprehending it wholly and fully."[12]

Crowley paraphrases AL II.9, "Existence is pure joy. Sorrow is caused by failure to perceive this fact; but this is not a misfortune. We have invented sorrow, which does not matter so much after all, in order to have the exuberant satisfaction of getting rid of it. Existence is thus a sacrament."[13] The *Djeridensis Comment* stresses that "She, the Sum and Essence of All Things that may be, fulfils Herself as these are all fulfilled by each Star in any Event. Indeed, she is not whole while aught remain latent, a phantom of desire; thus doth each act of Love under Will not only perfect him that doeth it, but also Her of whom it is one jewel."[14] According to the *New Comment*, "We are asked to acquiesce in this Law of Nature. That is, we are not to oppose resistance to the perfect fluidity of the 'Becoming' of Nature. Similarly, we are not to attach more importance to any one momentary appearance than to any other. For, the moment we do so, we confirm illusion of Duality. We assert Imperfection as absolute instead of as a device of Perfection for self-appreciation."[15]

If sorrow is caused by clinging to impermanent things, there can be no sensible basis for compassion. "To sympathize with the illusion is not only absurd, but tends to perpetuate the false idea."[16] In his essay *On Thelema*, Crowley attacks pity as implying "two very grave errors—errors which are utterly incompatible with the views of the universe above briefly indicated. The first error therein is an implicit assumption that something is wrong with the Universe, and that moreover one is so insidiously obsessed by the Trance of Sorrow as to have completely failed in the task of solving the riddle of Sorrow, and gone through life with the groan of a hurt animal—'All is Sorrow.' The second error is still greater since it involves the complex of the Ego. To pity another person implies that you are superior to him, and you fail to recognize his absolute right to exist as he is. You assert yourself superior to him, a concept utterly opposed to the ethics of Thelema—'Every man and every woman is a star' and each being is a Sovereign Soul. A moment's thought therefore will suffice to show how completely absurd any such attitude is, in reference to the underlying metaphysical facts."

---

[12] NC on AL I.13.
[13] *MWT*, Ch. VII.
[14] DC on AL I.61.
[15] NC on AL I.22.
[16] NC on AL II.48.

What then determines Tiphareth, the Human Will, to aspire to comprehend Neschamah, to submit itself to the divine Will of Chiah?

Nothing but the realisation, born sooner or later of agonising experience, that its whole relation through Ruach and Nephesch with Matter, *i.e.*, with the Universe, is, and must be, only painful. The senselessness of the whole procedure sickens it. It begins to seek for some menstruum in which the Universe may become intelligible, useful and enjoyable. In Qabalistic language, it aspires to Neschamah.

This is what we mean in saying that the Trance of Sorrow is the motive of the Great Work.

This "Trance of Sorrow" (which must be well-distinguished from any petty personal despair, and "conviction of sin," or other black magical imitations) being cosmic in scope, comprehending all phenomena actual or potential, is then already an Opening of the Sphere of Neschamah. The awareness of one's misfortune is itself an indication of the remedy. It sets the seeker on the right road, and as he develops his Neschamah he soon attains other Experiences of this high order. He learns the meaning of his own true Will, to pronounce his own Word, to identify himself with Chiah.

Finally, realising Chiah as the dynamic aspect of Jechidah, he becomes that pure Being, at once universal and individual, equally nothing, One, and All.[17]

The *New Comment* defines altruism as "This folly against self" (AL II.22), "a direct assertion of duality, which is division, restriction, sin, in its vilest form. I love my neighbour because love makes him part of me; not because hate divides him from me. Our law is so simple that it constantly approximates to truism." As Crowley puts it in *Magick Without Tears*, "The English is very un-English, and the context hardly helpful. But the meaning is clear enough; the idea is to dismiss, curtly and rudely, the entire body of doctrine which insists on altruism as a condition of spiritual progress."[18]

What is to us a huge and dreadful doctrine is to him the simple well-known truth. He tells us now that "this folly against self" "is a lie". By this he means that we must not be ashamed of our own point of view, of pretend that we ought to respect and be tender towards some other. Every true point is well able to take care of itself; if only let alone as it ought to be. Every time we try to put ourselves in the place of some other person we give up truth for fancy. We do not, and we never can, see the world except with our own eyes. The world of one's neighbour is not even the same world as one's own—even if we could assume his point of view. It is a deadly mischief to practise this form of falsehood; and to acclaim it as a virtue in the Christian fashion, both a crime and a blunder. Another lie is the "exposure of innocence." Most people pretend earnestly to be harmless. This not only blasphemes the Godhead of the

---

[17] *Little Essays Toward Truth*, "Man."
[18] *MWT*, Ch. XLII.

self but attempts to create falsehood. Deceit is always danger. The kindest, as the noblest, course is to nail one's colours to the mast, so that others can shelter beneath them or avoid the conflict, as their judgement counsels them. The social and moral code of shallow sham is the tactics of the pirate.[19]

"So '...It is a lie, this folly against self. ...' only means, 'To hell with sentimental altruism, with false modesty, with all those most insidious fiends, the sense of guilt, of shame—in a word, the 'inferiority complex' or something very like it.' The whole tenor of *The Book of the Law*, is to this effect. The very test of worth is that one should be aware of it and not afraid to sock the next man on the jaw if he disputes it!"[20] As *The Heart of the Master* has it, "to deny the Law of Thelema is a restriction in oneself, affirming conflict in the Universe as necessary. It is a blasphemy against the Self, assuming that its Will is not a necessary (and therefore a noble) part of the Whole. In a word he who accepts not the Law of Thelema is divided against himself: that is, he is insane, and the upshot shall be the ruin of the Unity of his Godhead."[21]

"We are not to regard ourselves as base beings, without whose sphere is Light or 'God'. Our minds and bodies are veils of the Light within. The uninitiate is a 'Dark Star', and the Great Work for him is to make his veils transparent by 'purifying' them. This 'purification' is really 'simplification'; it is not that the veil is dirty, but that the complexity of its folds makes it opaque. The Great Work therefore consists principally in the solution of complexes. Everything in itself is perfect, but when things are muddled, they become 'evil'." In other words, "we are warned against the idea of a Pleroma, a flame of which we are Sparks, and to which we return when we 'attain'. That would indeed be to make the whole curse of separate existence ridiculous, a senseless and inexcusable folly. It would throw us back on the dilemma of Manichaeism. The idea of incarnations 'perfecting' a thing originally perfect by definition is imbecile. The only sane solution is as given previously, to suppose that the Perfect enjoys experience of (apparent) Imperfection."[22]

As Crowley explains in *Berashith*, "The Hindus enumerate Brahm, infinite in all dimensions and directions—indistinguishable from the Pleroma of the Gnostics—and Maya, illusion. This is in a sense the antithesis of noumenon and phenomenon, noumenon being negated of all predicates until it becomes almost extinguished in the Nichts under the title of Alles. (*Cf.* Max Muller on the metaphysical Nirvana, in his *Dhammapada, Introductory Essay.*) The Buddhists express no opinion." Hindus believe that the Ātman (self) is intrinsically pure, but because of the layers of I-ness and My-ness, the self goes through transmigration in the cycle of births and deaths. Death destroys the physical body, but not the true self, which is eternal. "Worn-out garments are shed by the body," says the *Bhagavad-Gītā*.

---

[19] DC on AL II.22.
[20] *MWT, loc. cit.*
[21] Part III, "The Mystery of Sin."
[22] NC on AL I.8.

"Worn-out bodies are shed by the dweller within the body. New bodies are donned by the dweller, like garments."[23] According to the Hindu sage Shankara, the world as we ordinarily understand it is like a dream, fleeting and illusory; and as long as the self is enveloped in ignorance (*avidyā*) of the true nature of existence, it remains attached to material desire and subject to a perpetual chain of reincarnation, or *Saṃsāra*.[24]

> What is the sum total of the Vedantist position? "'I' am an illusion, externally. In reality the true 'I' am the Infinite, and if the illusionary 'I' could only realize Who 'I' really am, how very happy we should all be!" And here we have Karma, rebirth, all the mighty laws of nature operating nowhere in nothing!
>
> There is no room for worship or morality in the Advaitist system. All the specious pleas of the *Bhagavad-Gita*, and the ethical works of Western Advaitist philosophers, are more or less consciously confusion of thought. But no subtlety can turn the practical argument; the grinning mouths of the Dvaitist guns keep the fort of Ethics, and warn metaphysics to keep off the rather green grass of religion.
>
> That its apologists should have devoted so much time, thought, scholarship, and ingenuity to this question is the best proof of the fatuity of the Advaitist position.[25]

"The Hindus cannot account intelligibly, though they try hard, for Maya, the cause of all suffering. Their position is radically weak, but at least we may say for them that they have tried to square their religion with their common sense. The Christians, on the other hand, though they saw whither, the Manichean Heresy"—by which Crowley refers to "The conception of Satan as a positive evil force; the lower triangle of the Hexagram"—"must lead, and crushed it, have not officially admitted the precisely similar conclusion with regard to man, and denied the existence of the human soul as distinct from the divine soul. Trismegistus, Iamblichus, Porphyry, Boehme, and the mystics generally have of course substantially done so, though occasionally with rather inexplicable reservations, similar to those made in some cases by the Vedantists themselves."[26]

As the chapter of *Isis Unveiled* entitled "The Fall into Generation" phrases it, "While the ancient Neo-platonists held that the Augoeides never descends hypostatically into the living man, but only sheds more or less its radiance on the inner man—the astral soul—the kabalists of the middle ages maintained that the spirit, detaching itself from the ocean of light and spirit, entered into man's soul, where it remained through life imprisoned in the astral capsule. This difference was the result of the belief of Christian kabalists, more or less, in the dead letter of the allegory of the fall of man."[27]

---

[23] 2.22.
[24] Deussen 1912.
[25] *Berashith*.
[26] *Ibid.*
[27] Blavastky 1877, i.315.

Man is the God of the world, and God is the man of heaven.
Before saying "God wills," man has willed.
In order to understand and honour Almighty God, man must first be free.
Had he obeyed and abstained from the fruit of the tree of knowledge through fear, man would have been innocent and stupid as the lamb, sceptical and rebellious as the angel of light. He himself cut the umbilical cord of his simplicity, and, falling free upon the earth, dragged God with him in his fall.
And therefore, from this sublime fall, he rises again glorious, with the great convict of Calvary, and enters with Him into the kingdom of heaven.[28]

According the *Old Comment* on AL I.27–31, "The dyad (or universe) is created with little pain in order to make the bliss of dissolution possible. Thus the pain of life may be atoned for by the bliss of death. This delight is, however, only for the chosen servants of Nu. Outsiders may be looked on much as the Cartesians looked on animals. Yet, of course, this is only on the plane of Illusion. One must not discriminate between the space marks." The same comment defines the "Christian" as "one who has acquiesced in his own dishonour; a renegade from manhood." The *Djeridensis Comment* on AL I.31 goes further: "Mankind in general not worthy of attention. Heed not the petty woes of men, trifles, with petty joys to square the account. These are but dreams within dreams, and those to whom I speak the Word of Nuit are chosen of Her to pass beyond these phantoms into the world of real Joy and Sorrow—which also is Joy, and the Key and Force thereof."

Hadit is everywhere; fear, sorrow, and failure are only "shadows." It is for this reason that compassion is absurd.
It may be objected that "shadows" exist after all; the "pink rats" of an alcoholic are not to be exorcised by "Christian Science" methods. Very true—they are, in fact, necessary functions of our idea of the Universe in its dualistic "shadow-show." But they do not form any part of Hadit, who is beneath all conditions. And they are in a sense less real than their logical contradictories, because they are patently incompatible with the Changeless and Impersonal. They have their roots in conceptions involving change and personality. Strictly speaking, "joy" is no less absurd than sorrow, with reference to Hadit; but from the standpoint of the individual, this is not the case. One's fear of death is removed by the knowledge that there is no such thing in reality; but one's joy in life is not affected.[29]

According to Lévi, "Human equilibrium is composed of two attractions, one towards death, the other towards life. Fatality is the vertigo which drags us to the abyss; liberty is the reasonable effort which lifts us above

---

[28] *The Key of the Mysteries*, Part I, "Sketch of the Prophetic Theology of Numbers."
[29] NC on AL II.47.

the fatal attractions of death. What is mortal sin? It is apostasy from our own liberty; it is to abandon ourselves to the law of inertia. An unjust act is a compact with injustice; now, every injustice is an abdication of intelligence. We fall from that moment under the empire of force whose reactions always crush everything which is unbalanced."[30] However, Crowley says, "We are not to pity the fallen. The first fact about a 'point-of-view' is that it keeps its place. It goes, true, but never can fall. To fall is to yield to a strain outside oneself; and that is to cease to maintain the 'point-of-view' which is of the essence of Hadit. Hadit never knew the fallen. A real point-of-view cannot be shaken. Should we console such wretches? Useless. He is no better for one extra lie; and who tells that lie is false to his own Godhead."[31]

"Hadit has never defiled His purity with the Illusion of Sorrow, etc. Even love and pity for the fallen is an identification with it (sympathy from συν Παθειν), and therefore a contamination."[32] The *Djeridensis Comment* gives the essence of His doctrine as follows: "That 'existence is pure joy' is His first direct challenge to the whole body of the best and deepest thought of the best and wisest men of this Earth, from the dawn of man's Records even unto this hour of His speaking. It cuts clean across the whole trend of men's minds with sheer sweep of steel; no truce, nor quarter. Now the Second Challenge: a Bugle Call shriller and clearer than the First. Sorrow, pain, regret, are symptoms of diseased thought; those only who have ceased to be able to adjust themselves rightly and gladly to all Change, and to grow thereby, or those who still react, but only feebly and vainly, take Sorrow, pain, and regret to be Real. Those (also) who do not yet know Hadit (that is, know their True Selves to be Hadit) are likewise deceived."[33]

According to Lévi, "The ancient fathers of Christianity counted an eighth deadly sin: it was Sorrow. In fact, to the true Christian even repentance is not a sorrow; it is a consolation, a joy, and a triumph. 'I wished evil, and I wish it no more; I was dead and I am alive.' The father of the Prodigal son has killed the fatted calf because his son has returned. What can he do? Tears and embarrassment, no doubt! but above all joy! . . . Suffering is always a warning. So much the worse for him who does not understand it! When Nature tightens the rein, it is that we are swerving; when she plies the whip, it is that danger is imminent. Woe, then, to him who does not reflect!"[34] As *Liber Aleph* has it, "this doctrine (be it accursed!) that pain and repression are wholesome and profitable in themselves is a lie born of sin and of ignorance, the false vision of the Universe and of its laws that is the basis of the averse formula of the Slain God. It is true that on occasion one limb must be sacrificed to save the whole body, as when one cutteth away one hand that is bitten by a viper, or as when a man giveth his life to save his city. But this is a right and natural subordination of the superficial and particular to the fundamental and general will, and moreover it is a case

---

[30] *The Key of the Mysteries*, Part III, Book II, Ch. IV.
[31] DC on AL II.48.
[32] OC on AL II.48.
[33] DC on AL II.17.
[34] *The Key of the Mysteries*, Part IV, Ch. II.

extraordinary, relating to accident or extremity, not in any wise a rule of life, or a virtue in its absolute nature."[35]

"The dead and the dying, who know not Hadit, are in the Illusion of Sorrow. Not being Hadit, they are shadows, puppets, and what happens to them does not matter. If you insist upon identifying yourself with Hecuba, your tears are natural enough."[36] Indeed, "People who shift their point of view . . . are not truly themselves."—"Though each event is change, these changes form a closed curve so that their sum is zero. I have dealt with this subject fully in other writings. The essence of the doctrine is that things are stable only by virtue of their constant change, which is life. To cease to change is to die, which is the one real change that can occur. When it occurs, it proves that true life was never there. This doctrine is at once applied to the question of the Kings and the slaves." *The Book of the Law* posits "two types of men—the slave can never rise, the king can never fall. Should such things seem to take place, it is a sign of some disguise; the essence of the man, if he be in truth a man, is always the same. It is a point of view which never alters really, though each fresh fact brings it more fully into light. I am told of one case which must not deceive me. I must not assume that a man who seems a beggar is one. He may be a King whose pleasure is to disguise himself. He can, of course, resume his crown and sceptre when he tires of his sport, whereas a beggar has not the means to pretend to be a king."[37]

"Must I therefore be careful how I strike out, lest, thinking to slay a knave, I kill one of my peers? There is no danger of this. One of the tests of kingship is that he should be able to defend himself against the world. I am therefore bidden to strike hard with all my might, and strike to kill."[38] In fact, *The Book of the Law* "insists that we shall use all our functions as fully as we can. We are to enjoy all things, to make them serve our Will and thrill us with rapture. We must dismiss that bogey of those who wish to treat mankind as children without spirit or wit, to frighten us into slavish service to codes of conduct which suit their own servile nature, allay their fears, or procure easy preys for their greed by the threat of some God who will make trouble for those who dare to be themselves and do their own True Wills."[39]

When Epicurus delivered the ancient world from fear of the gods, he did not leave the Greeks adrift with no guidance, no motive, and no mechanism to discern their proper path in nature. The hatred the Osirian religions have always had towards pleasure—a hatred shared by the Stoic philosophers who suppressed emotions along with all joy in life—is motivated by the reverse of Epicurus' insight. The enemies of pleasure are not quite stupid enough to think that sex or drugs are the tools of the Devil or the path to insanity, but they are content with having those not smart enough to see through their argument to think so. The enemies of pleasure are well aware of the fact that pleasure is the most important faculty given to man, more

---

[35] "De formula deorum occisorum."
[36] NC on AL II.17.
[37] DC on AL II.57–58.
[38] DC on AL II.59–60.
[39] DC on AL II.22.

important than sight, hearing, or the sense of smell, because it is only by pleasure that man receives the ultimate guidance of nature on how to live. And it is this ultimate guidance that these ascetic religions and philosophies seek to replace with "holiness" or "virtue," the common theme being their attempt to convince us that nature has left us adrift and helpless, dependent on their own exclusive wisdom of life.

> Know that in the Mind of Man is much Wisdom that is hidden, being the Treasure of his Sire that he inheriteth. Thus, nigh all of his Moral Nature is unknown to him until his Puberty; that is, this Nature pertaineth not unto the Recording and Judging Apparatus of his Brain until it is put therein by the Stirring of that deeper Nature within him. Thou wilt mark also that great Men are commonly great Lovers; and this is in Part also because (consciously or not) they are ware of this Secret following, that every Act of Love communicateth somewhat of the Wisdom stored within him to his Percipient Mind. Yet must such Act be done rightly, according to Art; and unless such Act is of Profit alike to Mind and Body, it is an Error. This then is true Doctrine; which if it be understated aright of thee, shall make diamond-clear thy Path in Love, which (to them that know not this) is so obscure and perilous that I believe there is not one Man in Ten Thousand that cometh not to Misadventure therein.[40]

Crowley contends that, "Two-thirds of modern misery springs from Woman's sexual dissatisfaction. A dissatisfied woman is a curse to herself and to everybody in her neighbourhood. Women must learn to let themselves enjoy without fear or shame, and both men and woman must be trained in the technique of sex. Sex-repression leads to neurosis, and is the cause of social unrest. Ignorance of sexual technique leads to disappointment, even where passion is free and unrestrained. Sex is not everything in life, any more than food is: but until people have got satisfaction of these natural hungers, it is useless to expect them to think of other things. This truth is vital to the statesman, now that women have some direct political power; they will certainly overthrow the Republic unless they obtain full sexual satisfaction. Also, women outnumber men; and one man cannot satisfy a woman unless he be skilful and diligent. The New Aeon will have a foundation of Happy Women: A Woman under Tabu is loathsome to Life, detested by her fellows, and wretched in herself." Crowley exhorts the student to "study in *Liber Aleph* and *Liber 418*, the connection between 'modesty' and the attitude of the 'Black Brothers'."[41]

"Now, if there is any difference at all between the White and the Black Adept in similar case, it is that the one, working by 'love under will' achieves a marriage with the new idea, while the other, merely grabbing, adds a concubine to his harem of slaves. The about-to-be-Black Brother constantly restricts himself; he is satisfied with a very limited ideal; he is

---

[40] *Liber Aleph*, "De viris magnanimis, amore præclarissimis."
[41] NC on AL II.52.

afraid of losing his individuality—reminds one of the 'Nordic' twaddle about 'race-pollution.'"[42] Similarly, for Lévi, "The impious man is he who absorbs others. The pious man is he who loses himself in humanity. If the heart of man concentrate in himself the fire with which God animates it, it is a hell which devours all, and fills itself only with ashes; if he radiates it without, it becomes a tender sun of love."[43] For Lévi, "The fallen angel is then he who, from the beginning, refused to love; he does not love, and that is his whole torture; he does not give, and that is his poverty; he does not suffer, and that is his nothingness; he does not die, and that is his exile. The fallen angel is not Lucifer the light-bearer; it is Satan, who calumniated love. To be rich is to give; to give nothing is to be poor; to live is to love; to love nothing is to be dead; to be happy is to devote oneself; to exist only for oneself is to cast away oneself, and to exile oneself in hell. Heaven is the harmony of generous thoughts; hell is the conflict of cowardly instincts."[44]

The doctrine is that Hadit is the nucleolus (to borrow a term from biology) of any star-organism. To mock at Hadit is therefore evidently very much what is meant by the mysterious phrase in the "New Testament" with regard to the Unpardonable Sin, the "blasphemy against the Holy Ghost." A star forsaken by Hadit would thus be in the condition of real death it is this state which is characteristic of the "Black Brothers," as they are described in other parts of this Comment, and elsewhere in the Holy Books of the A∴A∴.

I may here quote *Liber Aleph*, "De Inferno Servorum" and "De Fratribus Nigris."

"Now, o my Son, having understood the Heaven that is within thee, according to thy Will, learn this concerning the Hell of the Slaves of the Slave-Gods, that it is true Place of Torment. For they, restricting themselves, and being divided in Will, are indeed the Servants of Sin, and they suffer, because, not being united in Love with the whole Universe, they perceive not Beauty, but Ugliness and Deformity; and, not being united in Understanding thereof, conceive only of Darkness and Confusion, beholding Evil therein. Thus at last they come, as did the Manichæans, to find, to their Terror, a Division even in the One, not that Division which we know for the Craft of Love, but a Division of Hate. And this, multiplying itself, Conflict upon Conflict, endeth in Hotchpot, and in the Impotence and Envy of Choronzon, and in the Abominations of the Abyss. And of such the Lords are the Black Brothers, who seek by their Sorceries to confirm themselves in Division. Yet in this even is no true Evil, for Love conquereth All, and their Corruption and Disintegration is also the Victory of BABALON."

"O my Son, know this concerning the Black Brothers, that cry: I am I. This is Falsity and Delusion, for the Law endureth not Exception. So then these Brethren are not Apart, as they Think; but are peculiar

---

[42] *MWT*, Ch. XII.
[43] *The Key of the Mysteries*, Part I, "Sketch of the Prophetic Theology of Numbers."
[44] *Ibid*.

Combinations of Nature in Her Variety. Rejoice then even in the Contemplation of these, for they are proper to Perfection, and Adornments of Beauty, like a Mole upon the Cheek of a Woman. Shall I then say that were it of thine own Nature, even thine, to compose so sinister a complex, thou shouldst not strive therewith, destroying it by Love, but continue in that Way? I deny not this hastily, nor affirm; for it is in mine won Nature to think that in this Matter the Sum of Wisdom is Silence. But this I say, and that boldly, that thou shalt not look upon this Horror with Fear, or with Hate, but accept this as thou dost all else, as a Phenomenon of Change, that is, of Love. For in a swift Stream thou mayst behold a Twig held steady for a while by the Play of the Water, and by this Analogue thou mayst understand the Nature of this Mystery of the Path of Perfection."[45]

"Learn then that it is in the contemplation of Division that Sorrow is, for Division is the Formula of Choronzon. It is therefore discreet for thee to unite each Element of Sorrow with its Opposite; in whose Triumph of Hymen is Ecstasy, until by the Apprehension of the new great Opposite the Idea is again seen as Sorrow. This then is the Issue from Sorrow; and thou mayst understand that I now also am confident in the Necessity of this my Fall to prepare the Formula of Mine Exaltation. Therefore, my Son, thus hail Me: Blessing and Worship to the Beast, the Prophet of the Lovely Star."[46] In the Introduction to *Magick Without Tears*, Crowley defines the Great Work as "the uniting of opposites. It may mean the uniting of the soul with God, of the microcosm with the macrocosm, of the female with the male, of the ego with the non-ego—or what not. By 'love under will' one refers to the fact that the method in every case is love, by which is meant the uniting of opposites as above stated, such as hydrogen and chlorine, sodium and oxygen, and so on. Any reaction whatever, any phenomenon, is a phenomenon of 'love'.... But love has to be 'under will,' if it is to be properly directed. You must find your True Will, and make all your actions subservient to the one great purpose."

The *Djeridensis Comment* gives the "Nature of an Act: its virtue" thus: "All acts are in truth acts of Love. Fulfil all Loves that may be, to the full. Be this in Light, before all Stars, that all may see and rejoice. . . . All events are children of Nuit. Every event doth fulfil some Love, and each is thenceforth of the Body of Nuit, which is event as Her Soul is Lust to bring forth, and the chance so to do."[47] There is, hence, "only one proper reaction to event; that is, to adjust oneself with perfect elasticity to whatever happens."[48] *The Book of the Law* further defines the relation of Nuit "to Gods, Men, Heaven, Earth, to Her Lord Hadit. Nuit is not beheld of any God or Man; for they are fixed Event, they are Facts, and while She is the ever-to-be. She therefore is to be

---

[45] NC on AL II.56.
[46] *Liber Aleph*, "De sua victoria per nomen Babalon."
[47] DC on AL I.12,14.
[48] *MWT*, Ch. XXXII.

held worthy, she and that Self which may enjoy her Love; seek not those joys which, being actual, cease to exhale rapture."[49]

> For, children! when ye halt at one thing, ye cease to open yourselves to all things. For to come to the All, ye must give up the All, and likewise possess the All. Verily ye must destroy all things and out of No-thing found and build the Temple of God as set up by Solomon the King, which is placed between Time and Space; the pillars thereof are Eternity, and the walls Infinity, and the floor Immortality, and the Roof—but ye shall know of this hereafter! Spoil thyself if so thou readest thyself; but if it is written adorn thyself, then spare not the uttermost farthing, but deck thyself with all the jewels and gems of earth; and from a child playing with the sands on the sea-shore shalt thou become God, whose footstool is the Abyss, and from whose mouth goeth forth the sword of the salvation and destruction of the worlds, and in whose hand rest the seven stars of heaven.[50]

The Book of the Law identifies "Reality and illusion: the None, the One, Many & the All" through Nuit. She is "Space beyond the idea of Limit or Measure; She is also All Points of the View no less than All Vistas seen therefrom. Bind nothing, for all things alike pertain to her, and her Nature is to compose All in One and Naught. One thing is in the end like all the rest; the seeming not alike comes as a dream from choosing images after one's own heart to worship them; thus each, though true as one of the All, is false if thought of as one apart from the rest."[51] Crowley insists on "putting forth the immediately useful point of view: 'devotion to Nuit' must mean the eager pursuit of the fulfillment of all possibilities, however unpleasant."[52] According to him, "Understanding of this Mystery the Key to Chieftainship. He is the chief of all who is not tricked into this trap of setting limits to things, by which he blasphemes each, and makes all false."[53]

In reference to the "Black Brothers," Crowley says their "policy is of course to break off all relations with the Supernal Triad, and to replace it by inventing a false crown, Daäth. To them Knowledge will be everything, and what is Knowledge but the very soul of Illusion? Refusing thus the true nourishment of all his faculties, they lose their structural unity, and must be fortified by continuous doses of dope in anguished self-preservation. Thus all its chemical equations become endothermic. . . . To describe the alternative attitude should clarify, by dint of contrast; at least the contemplation should be a pleasant change. Every accretion must modify me. I want it to do so. I want to assimilate it absolutely. I want to make it a permanent feature of my Temple. I am not afraid of losing myself to it, if only because it also is modified by myself in the act of union. I am not afraid of its being the 'wrong' thing, because every experience is a 'play of Nuit,'

---

[49] DC on AL I.21.
[50] *The Temple of Solomon the King*, Part I, "The Child."
[51] DC on AL I.22.
[52] *MWT*, Ch. XXXVII.
[53] DC on AL I.23.

and the worst that can happen is a temporary loss of balance, which is instantly adjusted, as soon as it is noticed, by recalling and putting into action the formula of contradiction."[54] Compare this to Axiom VI in Lévi's Theory of the Will, which states that, "To pass one's life in willing that it is impossible to possess always, is to abdicate life and accept the eternity of death."[55]

As Crowley points out in his *New Comment*, "We are permitted to take our fill and will of love as we will, when, where and with whom we will, but there is nothing said about why we will. On the contrary, despite the infinite variety of lawful means, there is one end held lawful, and no more than one. The act has only one legitimate object; it must be performed unto Nuit." No significance of the sexual gesture is forbidden, "for 'There is no law beyond Do what thou wilt.' But this may and shall be said, that a significance with indicates ignorance or forgetfulness of the central truth of the Universe, is an acquiescence in that opacity caused by the confusion of the veils which conceal the soul from the consciousness, and thus create the illusion which the aspirant calls Sorrow, and the uninitiate, Evil. The sexual act, even to the grossest of mankind, is the agent which dissipates the fog of self for one ecstatic moment. It is the instinctive feeling that the physical spasm is symbolic of that miracle of the Mass, by which the material wafer, composed of the passive elements, earth and water, is transmuted into the substance of the Body of God, that makes the wise man dread lest so sublime a sacrament suffer profanation. It is this that has caused him, in half-instinctive, half-intellectual half-comprehension of the nature of the truth, which has driven him to fence the act about with taboos. But a little knowledge is a dangerous thing. His fear has created phantoms, and his malobservation suggested precautions scarce worthy to be called empirical. We see him combat analogous difficulties in a precisely similar manner."[56]

> Many means of Grace. Thelemites to live beautifully and joyously. The answer is that there are many means of safety. I warn you against fear. Being once free, refuse to admit that any course of conduct can destroy you. I urge you to beware of the pride of the spirit, of the thought of anything as evil or unclean. Make all things serve you in your Magick as weapons. Therefore, be goodly, not humble, base, timid, or frail. Dress like a dandy: eat like a gourmet: drink port and champagne as do the hunting squires and young men about Town.
>
> Love: its law is complete Freedom. Also as to Love: be wholly free to make the best of your gifts in all respects, fearless and shameless.
>
> All acts to be understood as Acts of Worship of Nuit. Yet all these acts must not be done for their results in success or pleasure, and the like; for they are holy and to be performed strictly as acts of Love under Will in worship of Nuit; that is, to fulfil all that may be and your own whole Nature by so doing.[57]

---

[54] *MWT*, Ch. XII.
[55] *The Key of the Mysteries*, Part III, Book II, Ch. I.
[56] NC on AL I.52.
[57] DC on AL I.51.

"Now he who would become as a king unto himself must not renounce the kingdoms of this world, but must conquer the lands and estates of others and usurp their thrones. Should he be poor he must aim at riches without forfeiting his poverty; should he be rich he must aim at possessing poverty as well, without taking one farthing from the coffers of his treasury. The man of much estate must aim at possessing all the land, until there is no kingdom left for him to conquer. The Unobtainable must be obtained, and in the obtaining of it is to be found the Golden Key of the Kingdom of Light. The virgin must become as the wanton, yet though filled with all the itchings of lust, she must in no wise forfeit the purity of her virginity; for the foundations of the Temple are indeed set between Day and Night, and the Scaffolding thereof is as an arch flung between Heaven and Hell."[58] *The Book of the Law* warns of "Danger of error in this matter. This command is enforced, like that as to Restriction above, with a great Curse. The only thing that can do harm is to set limits to That which is by Nature Free and without Bounds. Thus, to find in any special love a distinct joy apart from other loves, or to think that the event of any love, a fixed dead ash of the past, is a living joy, is to fall into the Power of the Lords of Matter, to have to obey the Laws of Death, to lose all Freedom, and so suffer the Burden of Bondage."[59]

"The misunderstanding of sex, the ignorant fear like a fog, the ignorant lust like a miasma, these things have done more to keep back humanity from realization of itself, and from intelligent cooperation with its destiny, than any other dozen things put together. The vileness and falseness or religion itself have been the monsters aborted from the dark womb of its infernal mystery. There is nothing unclean or degrading in any manifestation soever of the sexual instinct, because, without exception, every act is an impulsively projected image of the Will of the individual who, whether man or woman, is a star; the Pennsylvanian with his pig no less than the Spirit with Mary; Sappho with Atthis and Apollo with Hyacinth as perfect as Daphnis with Chloe or as Galahad vowed to the Graal. The one thing needful, the all-perfect means of purification, consecration, and sanctification, is independent of the physical and moral accidents circumstantial of the particular incident, is the realization of love as a sacrament. The use of the physical means as a Magical Operation whose formula is that of uniting two opposites, by dissolving both, annihilating both, to create a third thing which transcends that opposition, the phase of duality which constitutes the consciousness of imperfection, is perceived as the absolute negative whose apprehension is identical with that duality, is the accomplishment of the Great Work."[60]

> From light we turn to the absence of light. Yet this is not real. It is a veil. This veil is not in the order of nature. It has been made by shame and fear, by trying to shut off all that is true and real from the soul. To

---

[58] *The Temple of Solomon the King*, Part I, "The King."
[59] DC on AL I.52.
[60] NC on AL I.52.

resist change and to defy nature, this is the key of the evil Magic of the Black Brotherhood, whose idol is the modest woman. Her veil is sorrow and death. We of Thelema worship Nuit: "all that may be" adored by "all that is." Her forms are without number; and in each she bestows herself freely upon any and every soul that desires Her. Thus Her priestess on earth is the Scarlet Woman, the Whore of the Beast who gives all she can to all that will. Her every act invokes change which is life. On the other hand, the "modest woman" conceals herself and denies herself. She is afraid and ashamed of herself—afraid and ashamed of all men. She dreams that something may happen to her, and thus lies stiff and stark in death even at the height of her youth. This verse of the *Book of the Law* is the final challenge to the past. The Angel strikes his spear with the sharp end upon the craven shield of the coward and slave who lurks behind the mask of a Master, of a phantom, a scarecrow, set up by him to frighten the winged songsters of freedom from the fertile fields which are their own by right. Until this verse, it might perhaps have been within the power of some subtle sophist to explain away the verses of this book. Here Aiwass leaves no shadow of doubt. He says with utmost clearness "Tear down that lying spectre of the centuries: veil not your vices in virtuous words: these vices are my service; ye do well, & I will reward you here and hereafter."

The Angel does not even deign to show that what pious people call vices are in fact virtues: that is, tokens of manhood; or that vices means "flaws." He uses these two words in their vulgar sense. To dare the world to a duel to the death. He does not merely tempt mankind to do what Christians call evil, he says that these vices are of the priesthood of Hadit, means to invoke Him, ways of coming to truth, ladders to climb to Godhead. We shall not be punished for doing wrong, as they call it. Both here and hereafter our reward is sure.

Yet more. The veil is vile. We must not, as the master class of men do now, enjoy ourselves in every way, and pretend with utmost care that we do nothing of the sort. We must take pride in our pleasure. We must be shameless and frank. Since all that is, is God, the only error is to hinder God from being himself or doing his will, or unveiling his truth.[61]

According to the *New Comment*, "The most important condition of the act, humanly speaking, is that the attraction should be spontaneous and irresistible; a leaping up of the will to create with lyrical frenzy. This first condition once recognized, it should be surrounded with every circumstance of worship. Study and experience should furnish a technique of love. All science, all art, every elaboration should emphasize and adorn the expression of the enthusiasm. All strength and all skill should be summoned to fulfil the frenzy, and life itself should be flung with a spendthrift gesture on the counter of the Merchant of Madness. On the steel of your helmet let there be gold inlaid with the motto 'Excess.'"[62]

---

[61] DC on AL II.52.
[62] NC on AL I.52.

I ought to have mentioned the sexual instinct or impulse in itself, careless of magical or any other considerations soever: the thing that picks you up by the scruff of the neck, slits your weasand with a cavalry sabre, and chucks the remains over the nearest precipice.

What is the damn thing, anyway?

That's just the trouble; for it is the first of the masks upon the face of the True Will; and that mask is the Poker-Face!

As all true Art is spontaneous, is genius, is utterly beyond all conscious knowledge or control, so also is sex. Indeed, one might class it as deeper still than Art; for Art does at least endeavour to find an intelligible means of expression. That is much nearer to sanity than the blind lust of the sex-impulse. The maddest genius does look from Chokmah not only to Binah, but to the fruit of that union in Da'ath and the Ruach; the sex-impulse has no use for Binah to understand, to interpret, to transmit. It wants no more than an instrument which will destroy it.

"Here, I say, Master, have a heart!"

Nonsense! (I continue) What I say is the plain fact, and well you know it! More, damned up, hemmed in, twisted and tortured as it has been by religion and morality and all the rest of it, it has learnt to disguise itself, to appear in a myriad forms of psychosis, neurosis, actual insanity of the most dangerous types. You don't have to look beyond Hitler! Its power and its peril derive directly from the fatal fact that in itself it is the True Will in its purest form.

What then is the magical remedy? Obvious enough to the Qabalist. "Love is the law, love under will." It must be fitted at its earliest manifestations with its proper Binah, so as to flow freely along the Path of Daleth, and restore the lost Balance. Attempts to suppress it are fatal, to sublime it are false and futile. But guided wisely from the start, by the time it becomes strong it has learnt how to use its virtues to the best advantage.[63]

"It is obvious to the physiologist that beauty (that is, the fitness of proportion) and love (that is, natural attraction between things whose union satisfies both) need for fulfilment absolute spontaneity and freedom from restriction. A tree grows deformed if it be crowded by other trees or by masonry; and gunpowder will not explode it its particles are separated by much sand. If we are to have Beauty and Love, whether in begetting children or works of art, or what not, we must have perfect freedom to act, without fear or shame or any falsity. Spontaneity, the most important factor in creation, because it is evidence of the magnetic intensity and propriety of the will to create, depends almost wholly on the absolute freedom of the agent. Gulliver must have no bonds of packthread. These conditions have been so rare in the past, especially with regard to love, that their occurrence has usually marked something like an epoch. Practically all men

---

[63] *MWT*, Ch. XV.

work with fear of result or lust of result, and the 'child' is a dwarf or still-born."[64]

According to Crowley, "one must be a flaming harlot—one must let oneself go, whether one's star be twin with that of Shelley, or of Blake, or of Titian, or of Beethoven. Beauty and strength come from doing one's Will; you have only to look at any one who is doing it to recognize the glory of it."[65] The *New Comment* goes so far as to claim that "almost the only love-affairs which breed no annoyance, and leave no scar, are those between people who have accepted the Law of Thelema, and broken for good with the tabus of the slave-gods. The true artist, loving his art and nothing else, can enjoy a series of spontaneous liaisons, all his life long, yet never suffer himself, or cause any other to suffer."[66]

> Moreover, say not thou in thy Syllogism that, since every Change soever, be it the Creation of a Symphony, or a Poem, or the Putrefaction of a Carcass, is an act of Love, and since we are to make no Difference between any Thing and any other Thing, therefore all Changes are equal in respect of our Praise. For though this be a right Conclusion in the term of thy Comprehension as a Master of the Temple, yet it is false in the Eyes of the Mind that hath not attained this Understanding. So therefore any Change (or Phenomenon) appeareth noble or base to the imperfect Mind, according to its Consonance and Harmony with the Will that governeth the Mind. Thus if it be thy Will to delight in Rhythm and Œconomy of Words, the Advertisement of a Commodity may offend thee; but if thou art in Need of that Merchandise, thou wilt rejoice therein. Praise then or blame aught, as seemeth good unto thee; but with this Reflection, that thy Judgment is relative to thine own Condition, and not absolute. This also is a Point of Tolerance, whereby thou shalt avoid indeed those Things that are hateful or noxious to thee, unless thou canst (in our Mode) win them by Love, by withdrawing thine Attention from them; but thou shalt not destroy them, for that they are without Doubt the Desire of another.[67]

> Understand then heartily, o my Son, that in the Light of this my Wisdom all Things are One, being of the Body or Our Lady Nuit, proper, necessary and perfect. There is then none superfluous or harmful, and there is none honourable or dishonourable more than another. Lo! in thine own Body, the vile Intestine is of more Worth to thee than the noble Hand or the proud Eye, for thou canst lose these and live, but not that. Esteem therefore a Thing in Relation to thine own Will, preferring the Ear if thou love Musick, and the Palate if thou love Wine, but the essential Organs of Life above these. Have Respect also to the Will of thy Fellow, not hindering him in his Way save as he may overly jostle thee in thine. For by the Practice of this Tolerance thou shalt come sooner to the

---

[64] NC on AL III.56.
[65] NC on AL II.20.
[66] NC on AL III.56.
[67] *Liber Aleph*, "De mysterio mall."

Understanding of this Equality of all Things in our Lady Nuit, and so the high Attainment of Universal Love. Yet in thy partial and particular Action, as thou art a Creature of Illusion, do thou maintain the right Relation of one Thing to another; fighting if thou be a Soldier, or building if thou be a Mason. For if thou hold not fast this Discipline and Proportion, which alloweth its True Will to every Part of thy Being, the Error of one shall draw all after it into Ruin and Dispersion.[68]

The supreme and absolute injunction, the crux of your knightly oath, is that you lay your lance in rest to the glory of your Lady, the Queen of the Stars, Nuit. Your knighthood depends upon your refusal to fight in any lesser cause. That is what distinguishes you from the brigand and the bully. You give your life on Her altar. You make yourself worthy of Her by your readiness to fight at any time, in any place, with any weapon, and at any odds. For her, from Whom you come, of Whom you are, to Whom you go, your life is no more and no less than one continuous sacrament. You have no word but Her praise, no thought but love of Her. You have only one cry, of inarticulate ecstasy, the intense spasm, possession of Her, and Death, to Her. You have no act but the priest's gesture that makes your body Hers. The wafer is the disk of the Sun, the star in Her body. Your blood is split from your heart with every beat of your pulse into her cup. It is the wine of Her life crushed from the grapes of your sun-ripened vine. On this wine you are drunk. It washes your corpse that is as the fragment of the Host, broken by you, the Priest, into Her golden chalice. You, Knight and Priest of the Order of the Temple, saying Her mass, become god in Her, by love and death. This act of love, thought in its form it be with a horse like Caligula, with a mob like Messalina, with a giant like Heliogabalus, with a pollard like Nero, with a monster like Baudelaire, though with de Sade it gloat on blood, with Sacher-Masoch crave for whips and furs, with Yvette Guilbert crave the glove, or dote on babes like E. T. Reed of *Punch*; whether one love oneself, disdaining every other like Narcissus, offer oneself loveless to every love like Catherine, or find the body so vain as to enclose one's lust in the soul and make one lifelong spinthria unassuaged in the imagination like Aubrey Beardsley, the means matter no whit. Bach takes one way, Keats one, Goya one. The end is everything: that by the act, whatever it is, one worships, loves, possesses, and becomes Nuit.[69]

"*The Book of the Law* emphasizes the importance of these considerations. The act of love must be spontaneous, in absolute freedom. The man must be true to himself. Romeo must not be thrust on Rosaline for family, social, or financial reasons. Desdemona must not be barred from Othello for reasons of race or religion. The homosexual must not blaspheme his nature and commit spiritual suicide by suppressing love or attempting

---

[68] *Ibid.*, "De virtute tolerantia."
[69] NC on AL I.52.

to pervert it, as ignorance and fear, shame and weakness, so often induce him to do. Whatever the act which expresses the soul, that act and no other is right. But, on the other hand, whatever the act may be it is always a sacrament; and, however profaned, it is always efficient. To profane it is only to turn food into poison. The act must be pure and passionate. It must be held as the union with God in the heart of the Holy of Holies."[70]

"Love is an Expression of the Will of the Body; yea, and more also, of That which created the Body; and its Operation is commonly between One and One, so that the Interference of a Third Person is Impurity, and not to be endured. Nay, even the Thought of a Third Person hath by Ordinary not part in Love; so that, as thou seest constantly in thy Life, Love, being strong, taketh no heed of others, and some after-Interference bringeth Misfortune. Now then shall we therefore cast out Love, or accept Impurity therein? God forbid. And for this Cause see thou well to it that in thy Kingdom there be no Interference therewith, nor Hindrance from any. For it is perfect in itself."[71] As we read in *The Temple of Solomon the King*, "when thou hast discovered Beauty and Wisdom and Truth in the swollen veins, in the distended bellies, in the bubbling lips, in the lewd gambollings, in the furious greed, the wanton whisperings, the sly winkings, and all the shameless nonsense of the Outer Court, then indeed shalt thou find that the Key of gold is only to be found in the marriage of wantonness and chastity."[72]

> The act of Love, to the bourgeois, is a physical relief like defaecation, and a moral relief from the strain of the drill of decency; a joyous relapse into the brute he has to pretend he despises. It is a drunkenness which drugs his shame of himself, yet leaves him deeper in disgust. It is an unclean gesture, hideous and grotesque. It is not his own act, but forced on him by a giant who holds him helpless; he is half madman, half automaton when he performs it. It is a gawky stumbling across a black foul bog, oozing a thousand dangers. It threatens him with death, disease, disaster in all manner of forms. He pays the coward's price of fear and loathing when pedlar Sex holds out his Rat-Poison in the lead-paper wrapping he takes for silver; he pays again with vomiting and with colic when he has gulped it in his greed.[73]

"But by 'Love' we mean a thing which the eye of the bourgeois hath not seen, nor his ear heard; neither hath his heart conceived it. We have accepted Love as the meaning of Change, Change being the Life of all Matter soever in the Universe. And we have accepted Love as the mode of Motion of the Will to Change. To us every act, as implying Change, is an act of Love. Life is a dance of delight, its rhythm an infinite rapture that never can weary or stale. Our personal pleasure in it is derived not only from our own part in it, but from our conscious apprehension of its total perfections. We

---

[70] *Ibid.*
[71] *Liber Aleph*, "De castitate."
[72] *The Temple of Solomon the King, loc. cit.*
[73] NC on AL I.52.

study its structure, we expand ourselves as we lose ourselves in understanding it, and so becoming one with it. With the Egyptian initiate we exclaim 'There is no part of us that is not of the Gods'; and add the antistrophe: 'There is no part of the Gods that is not also of us.' Therefore, the Love that is Law is no less Love in the petty personal sense; for Love that makes two One is the engine whereby even the final Two, Self and Not-Self, may become One, in the mystic marriage of the Bride, the Soul, with Him appointed from eternity to espouse her; yea, even the Most High, God All-in-All, the Truth."[74]

> Then I caught up her song and cried: "Yea! O Queen of the Night, O arrow of brightness drawn from the quiver of the moon! O Thou who hast ensnared me in the meshes of thine hair, and caught me up on the kisses of thy mouth; O thou who hast laid aside thy divinity to take refuge in mine arms, listen!
>
> "I have drunk deep of the flagons of passion with the white-veiled virgins of Vesta, and the crimson-girdled daughters of Circe, and the drowsy-eyed maidens of Ind. I have woven love with the lithe girls of Hellas, and the subtle-limbed women of Egypt whose fingers are created to caress; all the virgins of Assyria, and the veiled beauties of Arabia, have been mine; yet amongst them all have I not found one to compare to a lash on the lid of thine eye. O Thou art as the wine of ecstasy, a thousand times more delicious than all these. Ah! but what is this languor which cleaves to me? My strength has left me; my soul has mingled with thine; I am not, and yet I am. Is it Thy weakness that I feel?"
>
> "Nay, O lover, for it is only at the price of the illusion of my strength that thou hast given me the pleasure of unity which I have tasted in thine arms. Beauty has conquered me and drunk up the strength of my might; I am alone, and all things are mine in the mystery of my loneliness.
>
> "*Evoe!* life burns in the brasier of love as a ruby flame in a sapphire bowl. I am dead, yet I live for ever!"[75]

"We [of Thelema] do not deny the existence of the body, or despise it; but we refuse to regard it in any other light than this: it is the organ of the Self. It must nevertheless be ordered according to its own laws; those of the mental or moral Self do not apply to it. We love; that is, we will to unite: then the one must study the other, divine every butterfly thought as it flits, and offer the flower it most fancies. The vocabulary of Love is small, and its terms are hackneyed; to seek new words and phrases is to be affected, stilted. It chills. But the language of the body is never exhausted; one may talk for an hour by means of an eye-lash. There art intimate, delicate things, shadows of the leaves of the Tree of the Soul that dance in the breeze of Love, so subtle that neither Keats nor Heine in words, neither Brahms nor

---

[74] *Ibid.*
[75] *The Temple of Solomon the King, loc. cit.*, "The White Watch-Tower."

Debussy in music, could give them body. It is the agony of every artist, the greater he the more fierce his despair, that he cannot compass expression. And what they cannot do, not once in a life of ardour, is done in all fulness by the body that, loving, hath learnt the lesson of how to love."[76]

As Crowley tells us in his *Eight Lectures on Yoga*, "all those who really know and love art are well aware that classical painting and sculpture are rarely capable of producing these transcendent orgasms of ecstasy, as in the case of the higher arts. One is bound to the impressions of the eye; one is drawn back to the contemplation of a static object. And this fact has been so well understood in modern times by painters that they have endeavoured to create an art within an art; and this is the true explanation of such movements as *surréalisme*. I want to impress upon you that the artist is in truth a very much superior being to the Yogi or the Magician. He can reply as St. Paul replied to the centurion who boasted of his Roman citizenship 'With a great sum obtained I this freedom'; and Paul, fingering the Old School Tie, sneered: 'But I was free born.'"[77]

"It is manifestly a contradiction of the laws of the Conservation of matter and energy, that a substance should lose by being transformed. It is contrary to Nature that a man, with potentialities which can transform the face of the earth, should become nothing but inert carrion when he happens to die. Everything that he was must inevitably persist; and if the manifestation be not to one set of senses, why then, to another! The idea of creation from nothing of something and the destruction of something to nothing, exploded with the theory of Phlogiston."[78] However, "It is not that utterly worthless part of man, his individual consciousness as John Smith, which defies death—that consciousness which dies and is reborn in every thought. That which persists (if anything persist) is his real John Smithiness, a quality of which he was probably never conscious in his life. Even that does not persist unchanged. It is always growing. The Cross is a barren stick, and the petals of the Rose fall and decay; but in the union of the Cross and the Rose is a constant succession of new lives. Without this union, and without this death of the individual, the cycle would be broken."[79]

"And of course the distinction between Ego and Ego is illusion. Hence Hadit, who is the life of all that is, if known, becomes the death of that individuality."[80] Yet since "Hadit can never be known, there is no death. The death of the individual is his awakening to the impersonal immortality

---

[76] NC on AL I.52.

[77] *Eight Lectures*, Ch. 8, Sec. 17; Acts 22:28.

[78] NC on AL I.52.

[79] *MITAP*, Ch. I. *Cf.* also *Liber CL*, Ch. III: "Life then is indestructible as all else is. All destruction and construction are changes in the nature of Love, as I have written to you in the former chapter proximate. Yet even as the blood in one pulse-throb of the wrist is not the same blood as that in the next, so individuality is in part destroyed as each life passeth; nay, even with each thought. What then maketh man, if he dieth and is reborn a changeling with each breath? This: the consciousness of continuity given by memory, the conception of his Self as something whose existence, far from being threatened by these changes, is in verity assured by them."

[80] OC on AL II.6.

of Hadit. This applies less to physical death than to the Crossing of the Abyss... One may attain to be aware that one is but a particular 'child' of the Play of Hadit and Nuit; one's personality is then perceived as being a disguise. It is not only not a living thing, as one had thought; but a mere symbol without substance, incapable of life. It is the conventional form of a certain cluster of thoughts, themselves the partial and hieroglyphic symbols of an 'ego.' The conscious and sensible 'man' is to his Self just what the printed letters on this page are to me who have caused them to manifest in colour and form. They are arbitrary devices for conveying my thought; I could use French or Greek just as well. Nor is this thought, here conveyed, more than one ray of my Orb; and even that whole Orb is but the garment of Me. The analogy is precise; therefore when one becomes 'the knower,' it involves the 'death' of all sense of the Ego. One perceives one's personality precisely as I now do these printed letters; and they are forgotten, just as, absorbed in my thought, the trained automatism of my mind and body expresses that thought in writing, without attention on my part, still less with identification of the extremes involved in the process."[81]

"Yet, O divine Youth who has created thyself! What art thou? Thou art the birthless and the deathless one, without beginning and without end! Thou paintest the heavens bright with rays of pure emerald light, for thou art Lord of the beams of Light. Thou illuminest the two lands with rays of turquoise and beryl, and sapphire, and amethyst; for Lord of Love, Lord of Life, Lord of Immensity, Lord of Everlastingness is thy name. Thou hast become as a tower of Effulgence, whose foundations are set in the hearts of me, yea! as a mountain of chrysoleth slumbering in the Crown of Glory! whose summit is God!"[82] Thus, "death itself is an ecstasy like love, but more intense, the reunion of the soul with its true self. And what are the conditions of this joy, and peace, and glory? Is ours the gloomy asceticism of the Christian, and the Buddhist, and the Hindu? Are we walking in eternal fear lest some 'sin' should cut us off from 'grace'? By no means."[83]

> "Be goodly therefore: dress ye all in fine apparel; eat rich foods and drink sweet wines and wines that foam! Also, take your fill and will of love as ye will, when, where, and with whom ye will! But always unto me."
>
> This is the only point to bear in mind, that every act must be a ritual, an act of worship, a sacrament. Live as the kings and princes, crowned and uncrowned, of this world, have always lived, as masters always live; but let it not be self-indulgence; make your self-indulgence your religion.
>
> When you drink and dance and take delight, you are not being "immoral," you are not "risking your immortal soul"; you are fulfilling the precepts of our holy religion—provided only that you remember to regard your actions in this light. Do not lower yourself and destroy and

---

[81] NC on AL II.6.
[82] *The Temple of Solomon the King*, loc. cit.
[83] *Liber DCCCXXXVII*, Sec. II.

cheapen your pleasure by leaving out the supreme joy, the consciousness of the Peace that passeth understanding. Do not embrace mere Marian or Melusine; she is Nuit Herself, specially concentrated and incarnated in a human form to give you infinite love, to bid you taste even on earth the Elixir of Immortality. "But ecstasy be thine and joy of earth: ever To me! To me!"[84]

"In a deeper sense, the word 'Death' is meaningless apart from the presentation of the Universe as conditioned by 'Time.' But what is the meaning of Time? There is great confusion of thought in the use of the word 'eternal,' and the phrase 'for ever.' People who want 'eternal happiness' mean by that a cycle of varying events all effective in stimulating pleasant sensations; *i.e.*, they want time to continue exactly as it does with themselves released from the contingencies of accidents such as poverty, sickness and death. An eternal state is however a possible experience, if one interprets the term sensibly. One can kindle *flammam æternæ caritatis*, for instance; one can experience a love which is in truth eternal.[85] Such love must have no relation with phenomena whose condition is time. Similarly, one's 'immortal soul' is a different kind of thing altogether from one's mortal vesture. This Soul is a particular Star, with its own peculiar qualities, of course; but these qualities are all 'eternal,' and part of the nature of the Soul. This Soul being a monistic consciousness, it is unable to appreciate itself and its qualities, as explained in a previous entry; so it realizes itself by the device of duality, with the limitations of time, space and causality. The 'Happiness' of Wedded Love or eating Marrons Glacés is a concrete external non-eternal expression of the corresponding abstract internal eternal idea, just as any triangle is one partial and imperfect picture of the idea of a triangle."[86]

"Wedded Love though licensed for a lifetime, is usually intolerable after a month; and Marrons Glacés pall after the first five or six kilogrammes have been consumed. But the 'Happiness,' eternal and formless, is not less enjoyable because these forms of it cease to give pleasure. What happens is that the Idea ceases to find its image in those particular images; it begins to notice the limitations, which are not itself and indeed deny itself, as soon as its original joy in its success at having become conscious of itself wears off. It becomes aware of the external imperfection of Marrons Glacés; they no longer represent its infinitely varied nature. It therefore rejects them, and creates a new form of itself, such as Nightgowns with pale yellow ribbons or Amber Cigarettes."[87]

---

[84] *Ibid.*; AL I.51, 53.
[85] *Accendat in nobis Dominus ignem sui amoris et flammam æternæ caritatis. Amen.* "May the Lord enkindle within us the fire of His love, and the flame of everlasting charity. Amen." The concluding words of the blessing by the priest at the incensing of the offerings in the traditional Roman Catholic High Mass. However, according to *MITAP*, Ch. XIV, Sec. I, the words of consecration are: *Accendat in nobis* Therion *ignem sui amoris et flammam æternæ caritatis*. (Emphasis added.)
[86] NC on AL II.21.
[87] *Ibid.*

"These suffer from the same defects as the other forms; ultimately, 'Happiness' wearies itself in the effort to invent fresh images, and becomes disheartened and doubtful of itself. Only a few people have wit enough to proceed to generalization from the failure of a few familiar figures of itself, and recognize that all 'actual' forms are imperfect; but such people are apt to turn with disgust from the whole procedure, and to long for the 'eternal' state. This state is however incapable of realization, as we know; and the Soul understanding this, can find no good but in 'Cessation' of all things, its creations no more than its own tendencies to create. It therefore sighs for Nibbana."[88]

But there is one other solution, as I have endeavoured to shew. We may accept (what after all it is absurd to accuse and oppose) the essential character of existence. We cannot extirpate or even alter in the minutest degree either the matter or manner of any element of the Universe, here each item is equally inherent and important, each aequipollent, independent, and interdependent.

We may thus acquiesce in the fact that it is apodeictically implicit in the Absolute to apprehend itself by self-expression as Positive and Negative in the first place, and to combine these primary opposites in an infinite variety of finite forms.

We may thus cease either (1) to seek the Absolute in any of its images, knowing that we must abstract every one of their qualities from every one of these equally if we would unveil it; or (2) to reject all images of the Absolute, knowing that attainment thereof would be the signal for the manifestation of that part of its nature which necessarily formulates itself in a new universe of images.

Realizing that these two courses (the materialist's and the mystic's) are equally fatuous, we may engage in either or both of two other plans of action, based on assent to actuality.

We may (1) ascertain our own particular properties as partial projections of the Absolute; we may allow every image presented to us to be of equally intrinsic and essential entity with ourselves, and its presentation to us a phenomenon necessary in Nature; and we may adjust our apprehension to the actuality that every event is an item in the account which we render to ourselves of our own estate. We dare not desire to omit any single entry, lest the balance be upset. We may react with elasticity and indifference to each occurrence, intent only on the idea that the total, intelligently appreciated, constitutes a perfect knowledge not indeed of the Absolute but of that part thereof which is ourselves. We thus adjust one imperfection accurately to another, and remain contented in the appreciation of the righteousness of the relation.[89]

---

[88] *Ibid.*
[89] *Ibid.*

"This path, the 'Way of the Tao,' is perfectly proper to all men. It does not attempt either to transcend or to tamper with Truth; it is loyal to its own laws, and therefore no less perfect than any other Truth. The Equation Five plus Six is Eleven is of the same order of perfection as Ten Million times Ten times Ten Thousand Million is One Billion. In the Universe formulated by the Absolute, every point is equally the Centre; every point is equally the focus of the forces of the whole. . . . There is another Way that we may take, if we will; I say 'another,' though it seems perhaps to some no more than development of the other which happens to be proper to some people. . . . Thus then must every Artist work. First, he must find himself. Next, he must find the form that is fitted to express himself. Next, he must love that form, as a form, adoring it, understanding it, and mastering it, with most minute attention, until it (as it seems) adapts itself to him with eager elasticity, and answers accurately and aptly, with the unconscious automatism of an organ perfected by evolution, to his most subtlest suggestion, to his most giant gesture."[90]

"Next, he must give himself utterly up to that Form; he must annihilate himself absolutely in every act of love, labouring day and night to lose himself in lust for it, so that he leave no atom unconsumed in the furnace of their frenzy, as did of old his Father that begat him. He must realize himself wholly in the integration of the infinite Pantheon of images; for if he fail to formulate one facet of himself, by lack thereof will he know himself falsely. There is of course no ultimate difference between the Artist as here delineated and him who follows the 'Way of the Tao,' though the latter finds perfection in his existing relation with his environment, and the former creates a private perfection of a peculiar and secondary character. We might call one the son, the other the daughter, of the Absolute."[91]

In the second chapter of *The Book of the Law* "is given the word of Hadit, who is the complement of Nuit. He is eternal energy, the Infinite Motion of Things, the central core of all being. The manifested Universe comes from the marriage of Nuit and Hadit; without this could no thing be. This eternal, this perpetual marriage-feast is then the nature of things themselves; and therefore everything that is, is a crystallization of divine ecstasy."[92] Hadit is "described as the snake whose virtue is to give knowledge, for all knowledge consists in the art to perceive events as each new marriage with a new part of Nuit takes place. He gives delight which is a function of such knowledge. He also gives bright glory, that is, he causes men to send forth rays of light. Man is in fact, as it were, a prism. In his dual machine the formless light is split into many colours which mingle in this way and that as the nature of each event requires. Hadit is the flame in every heart of man, and when he stirs that heart is shaken. We call this being inspired, or, in its most sacred sense, being drunken."[93]

The author "denies flatly the truth of all the teaching of the past. He tells us that to worship Hadit, that is, to cause him to stir, we should make

---

[90] *Ibid.*
[91] *Ibid.*
[92] *Liber DCCCXXXVII*, Sec. III.
[93] DC on AL II.22.

ourselves drunk by the use of wine and certain strange drugs. So much is common knowledge. But he adds the startling statement 'They shall not harm ye at all.' One can but gasp; to argue in support of his statement would be beyond the power of any man. The proof must lie with time. Lest there be folly, let me say that this passage does not license reckless debauch. The use of drugs and drink is to be strictly an act of Magick. Compare what is said in the First Chapter with regard to the use of the functions of sex."[94] According to the scribe, "The essence of the idea of Trance is indeed contained in that of Magick, which is pre-eminently the transcendental Science and Art. Its method is, in one chief sense, Love, the very key of Trance; and, in another, the passing beyond normal conditions. The verbs to transcend, to transmit, to transcribe, and their like, are all of cardinal virtue in Magick. Hence 'Love is the law, love under will' is the supreme epitome of Magical doctrine, and its universal Formula."[95] Or as Schopenhauer puts it in his *Essay on the Freedom of the Will*, "by means of wine or opium we can intensify and considerably heighten our mental powers, but as soon as the right measure of stimulus is exceeded, the effect will be exactly the opposite."[96]

> But why should we talk of drugs? They are only counterfeit notes, or at best the Fiat notes of a discredited government, and we are seeking gold.
> This pure gold is ours for the asking; its name is mysticism.
> We may begin by reassuring ourselves. The gold is really in the vaults of the Treasury. The mystic quest is not a chimaera. The drugs assure us of that. They have not put anything supernatural into us; they have found nothing in us that was not already there. They have merely stimulated us. All the peace, the joy, the love, the beauty, the comprehension, they gave us; all these things were in us, bone of our bones, and flesh of our flesh, and soul of our soul. They are in our treasury, safe enough; and the chief reason why we should not burglariously use such skeleton keys as morphia is that by so doing we are likely to hamper the lock.
> We see then that we are but so very little lower than angels that the most trifling stimulus raises us to a plane where we enjoy without consideration even of what it is that we enjoy. Raise humanity by a matter of five per cent, and the problem is solved! Our trouble is due entirely to the law that action and reaction are equal and opposite. We have to pay for the pleasure with pain. We sat up all last night, and now we must go to bed early; we drank too much Champagne, and now it is the turn of Vichy.
> The question then has always been whether we can overcome this law of duality, whether we can reach—one step—to that higher plane where all is ours. Mysticism supplies the answer.

---

[94] *Ibid.*
[95] *Little Essays Toward Truth*, "Trance."
[96] "Will and Consciousness of Other Things." Schopenhauer 1960, 31.

The mystic attainment may be defined as the Union of the Soul with God, or as the realization of itself, or—there are fifty phrases for the same experience. The same, for whether you are a Christian or a Buddhist, a Theist or (as I am myself, thank God!) an Atheist, the attainment of this one state is as open to you as is nightmare, or madness, or intoxication. Religious folk have buried this fact under mountains of dogma; but the study of comparative religion has made it clear. One has merely to print parallel passages from the mystics of all ages and religions to see that they were talking of the same thing: one gets even verbal identities, such as the "That Tao which is Tao is not Tao"[97] of the Chinese, the "Not That, Not That"[98] of the Hindu, the "Head which is above all Heads, the Head which is not a Head"[99] of the Qabalist, the "God is Nothing"[100] of the Christian, and the "That is not which is"[101] of a modern atheistic or pantheistic mystic.[102]

"Through the ages we found this one constant story," writes Crowley in *The Psychology of Hashish*. "Stripped of its local and chronological accidents, it usually came to this—the writer would tell of a young man, a seeker after the Hidden Wisdom, who, in one circumstance or another, meets an adept; who, after sundry ordeals, obtains from the said adept, for good or ill, a certain mysterious drug or potion, with the result (at least) of opening the gate of the Other-world. This potion was identified with the Elixir Vitæ of the physical Alchemists, or one of their 'Tinctures,' most likely the 'White Tincture' which transforms the base metal (normal perception of life) to silver (poetic conception)."[103] The ritual consumption of hallucinogenic drugs was part and parcel of nearly every ancient religious tradition, but an hierarchical Church has no interest in granting its rank-and-file members genuine spiritual experiences, much less the means to independently reach them. The nature and content of the experiences that these substances induce are not artificial products of their pharmacological interaction with the brain, but authentic expressions of the human psyche revealing its functioning on levels ordinarily unavailable for observation and study; that is, a person who has "dropped acid" does not have an "acid trip," but a journey into deep recesses of his own mind.[104]

"There is no better rough test of a soul than its attitude to drugs. If a man is simple, fearless, eager, he is all right; he will not become a slave. If he is afraid, he is already a slave. Let the whole world take opium, hashish, and the rest; those who are liable to abuse them were better dead. For it is in the power of all so-called intoxicating drugs to reveal a man to himself. If

---

[97] Lao-tzŭ, *Tao Te Ching*, 1.1.1.
[98] In Sanskrit, *neti, neti*. (Yājñavalkya, in *Bṛhadāraṇyaka Upaniṣad*, 3.9.26; 4.2.4; 4.4.22; 4.5.15.)
[99] *Zohar*, Part III, fol. 288b. (Attributed to Shimon bar Yochai.)
[100] Jacob Boehme, *Mysterium Magnum*, i.2, i.3, i.8, xxix.1; *De electione gratiae*, i.2–3; *Sex puncta theosophica*, i.1.2, i.1.4, i.1.7; *De signatura rerum*, ii.8–9.
[101] *The Book of Lies*, Ch. 5.
[102] *Liber 888*, "Vital Distribution."
[103] Sec. II.
[104] Balk 2012.

this revelation declare a Star, then it shines brighter ever after. If it declare a Christian—a thing not man nor beast, but a muddle of mind—he craves the drug, no more for its analytical but for its numbing effect. Lytton has a great story of this in *Zanoni*. Glyndon, an uninitiate, takes an Elixir, and beholds not Adonai the glorious, but the Dweller on the Threshold; cast out from the Sanctuary, he becomes a vulgar drunkard."[105] Curriculum of A∴A∴, Course I, Section 2, lists two books by Sir Edward Bulwer Lytton, the above-mentioned *Zanoni*, "Valuable for its facts and suggestions about Mysticism," and *A Strange Story*, "Valuable for its facts and suggestions about Magick."

In the opinion of Blavatsky, *Zanoni* describes the "invocation of his own Augoeides, by the purified adept, . . . in words of unparalleled beauty" and Lord Lytton "gives us to understand that the slightest touch of mortal passion unfits the hierophant to hold communion with his spotless soul."[106] According to Crowley, "The aim of him who would be Master is single; men call it Personal Ambition. That is, he wants his Universe to be as vast, and his control of it as perfect, as possible. Few fail to understand this aim; but many fail in the formulation of their campaign to attain it. Some, for instance, fill their purse with fairy gold, which, when they try to use it, is found to be dead leaves. Others attempt to rule the universe of another, not seeing that they cannot even take true cognizance thereof. The proper method of extending one's universe, besides the conventional apparatus of material Science, is tripartite: evocation, invocation, and vision. Control is a matter of theoretical and practical acquaintance with Magical Formulæ, but notably also of Self-Discipline. The ground is to be consolidated, and all contradictions resolved in higher harmonies, by various Trances."[107]

"To *invoke* is to *call in*, just as to *evoke* is to *call forth*. This is the essential difference between the two branches of Magick. In invocation, the Macrocosm floods the consciousness. In evocation, the magician, having become the Macrocosm, creates a Microcosm. You *in*voke a God into the Circle. You *e*voke a Spirit into the Triangle."[108] And as Crowley points out, "Almost any duffer can 'pull himself together', devote himself to study, break off a bad habit, or conquer a cowardice. This class of work, although the easiest, is yet the most important; for it includes initiation itself in its highest sense. It extends to the Absolute in every dimension; it involves the most intimate analysis, and the most comprehensive synthesis. In a sense, it is the sole type of Magick either necessary or proper to the Adept; for it includes both the attainment of the Knowledge and Conversation of the Holy Guardian Angel, and the Adventure of the Abyss."[109]

"Make thyself puissant, wise, radiant in every System, and balance thyself well in thine Universe. Then with a pure Will tempered in the thousand Furnaces of thy Trials, burn up thyself within thy Self. In the

---

[105] NC on AL II.22.
[106] *Isis Unveiled*, "The Veil of Isis." Blavatsky 1877, i.358.
[107] *Little Essays Toward Truth*, "Mastery."
[108] *MITAP, loc. cit.* Emphasis in original.
[109] *Ibid.*, Ch. XIV.

Preparation thou shalt have learned how thou mayst still all Thoughts, and reach Ecstasy of Trance in many Modes. But in these Marriages thy conscious Self is Bridegroom, and the not-Self Bride, while in this Great Work thou givest up that conscious Self as Bride to thy True Self. This Operation is then radically alien from all others. And it is hard, because it is a total Reversal of the Current of the Will, and a Transmutation of its Formula and Nature. Here, o my Son, is the One Secret of Success in this Great Work: Invoke Often."[110] To quote Lévi, "High magic, as we have proved, leads man back to the laws of the purest morality. Either he finds a thing holy or makes it holy, says an adept—*Vel sanctum invenit, vel sanctum facit*; because it makes us understand that in order to be happy, even in this world, one must be holy."[111]

"All these phantoms, of whatever nature, must be evoked, examined, and mastered; otherwise we may find that just when we want it there is some idea with which we have never dealt; and perhaps that idea, springing on us by surprise, and as it were from behind, may strangle us. This is the legend of the sorcerer strangled by the Devil!"[112] Again, Lévi concurs: "It is that all those who suffer from luminous congestion or contagious somnambulism, perish by a violent or, at least, a sudden death. It is for this reason that one used to attribute to the devil the power of strangling sorcerers. The excellent and worthy Lavater habitually evoked the alleged spirit of Gablidone. He was assassinated. A lemonade-seller of Leipzig, Schroepfer, evoked the animated images of the dead. He blew out his brains with a pistol. One knows what was the unhappy end of Cagliostro. A misfortune greater than death itself is the only thing that can save the life of these imprudent experimenters. They may become idiots or madmen, and then they do not die, if one watches over them with care to prevent them from committing suicide."[113]

"A corollary of this Theorem is that the Magician soon discards evocation almost altogether—only rare circumstances demand any action what ever on the material plane. The Magician devotes himself entirely to the invocation of a god; and as soon as his balance approaches perfection he ceases to invoke any partial god; only that god vertically above him is in his path. And so a man who perhaps took up Magick merely with the idea of acquiring knowledge, love, or wealth, finds himself irrevocably committed to the performance of The Great Work."[114] Conversely, according to Lévi, "Perversity, by modifying the organism whose equilibrium it destroys, creates at the same time a fatality of needs which urges it to its own destruction, to its death. The less the perverse man enjoys, the more thirsty of enjoyment he is. Wine is like water for the drunkard, gold melts in the hands of the gambler; Messalina tires herself out without being satiated. The pleasure which escapes them changes itself for them into a long irritation and desire. The more murderous are their excesses, the more it

---

[110] *Liber Aleph*, "De gradibus ad magnum opus."
[111] *The Key of the Mysteries*, Part IV, Ch. II.
[112] *Book 4*, Part II, Ch. XVI.
[113] *The Key of the Mysteries*, Part III, Book I, Ch. III.
[114] *MITAP*, Ch. XV, Sec. I.

seems to them that supreme happiness is at hand. . . . One more bumper of strong drink, one more spasm, one more violence done to Nature. . . Ah! at last, here is pleasure; here is life . . . and their desire, in the paroxysm of its insatiable hunger, extinguishes itself for ever in death."[115]

"Be thou well aware, O thou who seekest to attain to Mastery, of doing aught 'miraculous': the surest sign of the Master is this, that he is a man of like passions with his fellows. He does indeed transcend them all, and turn them all to perfections: but he does this without suppression (for 'Everything that lives is holy') or distortion (for 'Every Form is a true symbol of Substance') or confusion (for 'Admixture is hatred as Union is love'). Initiation means the Journey Inwards: nothing is changed or can be changed; but all is trulier understood with every step. The Magus of the Gods, with His one Word that seems to overturn the chariot of Mankind in ruin, does not in fact destroy or even alter anything; He simply furnishes a new mode of applying existing Energy to established Forms."[116] As we read in the *Djeridensis Comment*, "Hadit is 'conqueror.' It is his function to make himself master of all that may be and every event that he causes is a victory. He denies kinship with 'slaves that perish.' These are wholly foreign to his nature. Unless one is active, one is damned and dead: and this is the curse on all slaves, on all those who yield to what they meet, that they are condemned to suffer the constraint of their Wills. The world becomes a prison for the self instead of a playground; and in a little the prison gates become the seal of the tomb."[117]

One may compare this to Lévi's description of the "unquiet and tormented creatures whose influence is disturbing and whose conversation is fatal. In their presence one feels one's self irritated, and one leaves their presence angry; yet, by a secret perversity, one looks for them, in order to experience the disturbance and enjoy the malevolent emotions which they give us. Such persons suffer from the contagious maladies of the spirit of perversity. . . .to aspire ceaselessly to suicide, to calumniate life and nature, to invoke death every day without being able to die. This is eternal Hell, it is the punishment of Satan, that mythological incarnation of the spirit of perversity; the true translation into French of the Greek word *Diabolos*, or devil, is *le pervers—the perverse.*"[118] The *Djeridensis Comment* continues: "It must be born in mind that all such beings are not real in any proper sense of the word. They are not stars at all. So far as they think of themselves as 'I' they may be said to possess a point-of-view, but unless this is strong enough to persist through all Events, it is not truly a self but a phantom of Self thrown on a screen by the light of the events about it. The slave souls are in fact details of our device for looking at nature. They help us observe how a given set of events affects this or that conscious mind. They save our time by telling us what they feel and think. We may learn from them how to guide our own course."[119]

---

[115] *The Key of the Mysteries*, Part III, Book II, Ch. IV.
[116] *Little Essays Toward Truth, loc. cit.*
[117] DC on AL II.49.
[118] *The Key of the Mysteries, loc. cit.*
[119] DC on AL II.49.

Here is a mystery which debauchees do not suspect. It is this: one cannot enjoy even the material pleasures of life but by virtue of the moral sense. Pleasure is the music of the interior harmonies; the senses are only its instruments, instruments which sound false in contact with a degraded soul. The wicked can feel nothing, because they can love nothing: in order to love one must be good. Consequently for them everything is empty, and it seems to them that Nature is impotent, because they are so themselves; they doubt everything because they know nothing; they blaspheme everything because they taste nothing; they caress in order to degrade; they drink in order to get drunk; they sleep in order to forget; they wake in order to endure mortal boredom: thus will live, or rather thus will die, every day he who frees himself from every law and every duty in order to make himself the slave of his passions. The world, and eternity itself, become useless to him who makes himself useless to the world and to eternity.[120]

"For until thou love, the Play of Love is but Emptiness; and its cruelty is Cruelty indeed, except thou know it to be but a Sauce to whet Appetite, and to give Emphasis of Contrast, as a Painter dimmeth the Light by Cunning of his Shadows. But all this Delight that thou mayst have of the Universe both in its Veils and in its Nakedness is a Reward of thine Attainment of Truth, and followeth after it. Nor canst thou comprehend this Doctrine by Mind, for the Division in thee crieth aloud in its Agony, denying it, unless thou be wholly Initiate."[121]

A hermit is one who dwells isolated in the desert, exactly as a soul, a star, or an electron in the wilderness of space-time. The doctrine here put forth is that the initiate cannot be polluted by any particular environment. He accepts and enjoys everything that is proper to his nature. Thus, a man's sexual character is one form of his self-expression; he unites Hadit with Nuit sacramentally when he satisfied his instinct of physical love. Of course, this is only one partial projection; to govern, to fight, and so on, must fulfil other needs. We must not imagine that any form of activity is *ipso facto* incapable of supplying the elements of an Eucharist: *suum cuique.* Observe, however, the constant factor in this enumeration of the practices proper to "hermits": it is ecstatic delight. Let us borrow an analogy from Chemistry. Oxygen has two hands (so to speak) to offer to other elements. But contrast the cordial clasp of hydrogen or phosphorus with the weak reluctant greeting of chlorine! Yet hydrogen and chlorine rush passionately to embrace each other in monogamic madness! There is no "good" or "bad" in the matter; it is the enthusiastic energy of union, as betokened by the disengagement of heat, light, electricity, or music, and the stability of the resulting compound, that sanctifies the act. Note also that the utmost external joy in any phenomenon is surpassed a millionfold by the internal joy of the

---
[120] *The Key of the Mysteries, loc. cit.*
[121] *Liber Aleph,* "De ludo amoris."

realization that self-fulfilment in the sensible world is but a symbol of the universal sublimity of the formula "love under will."[122]

In the chapter of *Magick Without Tears* on "Bad Astral Vision," Crowley describes some of the challenges every aspirant faces: "Something one wants to do, perhaps a trifle, and one can't. Then one looks for the obstacle, and then the enemy behind that again; maybe one gets into one of those 'ladder-meditations' (as described in *Liber Aleph* [Chapters 177-182], quoted in *The Book of Thoth*, when discussing 'The Fool' and Hashish, only the wrong way up!) which end by the conception of the Universe itself as the very climax, asymptote, quintessence of frustration—the perfect symbol of all uselessness. This is, of course, the absolute contradictory of Thelema; but it is the sorites on which both Hindu and Buddhist conclusions are based."[123]

> This kind of rage is, accordingly, most noxious; it is direct attack from within upon the virgin citadel of Self. It is high treason to existence. Its results are immediately harmful; it begets depression, melancholy, despair. In fact, one does wisely to take the bear by the ring in his snout; accept his conclusions, agree that it is all abject and futile and silly—and turn the hose-pipe of the Trance of Laughter on him until he dances to your pleasure.
>
> But—is this any answer to your problem? It disturbs me little that you should try to palm off "Peace" upon my sentries as the password. Too often peace is merely the result of war-weariness, and the very negation of victory. It is (or may be) the formula of sloth and the gateway of stagnation.
>
> Life is to be a continuous vibration of ecstasy; and so it is for the Adept, whenever his work allows him time to consider the matter, consciously; and even when his work pre-empts his attention, is an eternal fountain of pure joy springing, a crystal fragrance of reverberation light from the most inmost caverns of the Heart. It secretly informs one's dullest thought with sparkling wine, radiant in the Æthyr—see well! the least excuse, since it is always there, and champing at its bit, to turn the dreary cart-horse drudge into proud Pegasus himself![124]

"We tracked the cause: it was frustration. Good: then we must counter it. How? Only (in the last event) by getting the mind firmly fixed in the complete philosophy of Thelema. There is no such thing as frustration. Every step is a step on the Path. It is simply not true that you were being baulked. The height of your irritation is a direct measure of the intensity of your Energy. Again, you soon come to laugh at yourself for your impatience. Probably (you surmise) your trouble is exactly that: you are pushing too

---

[122] NC on AL II.24.
[123] *MWT*, Ch. LXIII.
[124] *Ibid*.

hard. Your mind runs back to AL I, 44; you realize (again!) that any result actually spoils the Truth and Beauty of the Act of Will; it is almost a burden; even an insult. Rather as if I risked my life to save yours, and you tipped me half-a-crown! Here's that *Book of Lies* popping out its ugly mug again: 'Thou has become the Way.' This is why the Ankh or 'Key of Life' is a sandal-strap, borne in the hand of every God as a mark of his Godhead: a God is one who goes. (If I remember rightly, Plato derives 'Θεως' from a verb meaning 'to run,' and is heartily abused by scholars for so doing. But perhaps the dreary old sophist was not far wrong, for once.) What you need to do, then, is to knit all these ideas into a very close pattern; to make of them a consecrated Talisman. Then, when rage takes you, it can be thrown upon the fire to stifle it: to thrust against the Demon, to disintegrate him. The great point is to have this weapon very firmly constructed, very complete. Your rage will pass in one of those two ways, which are one: Rapture and Laughter."[125]

"But who then are the 'low men,' since 'Every man and every woman is a star?' The *casus belli* is this: there are people who are veiled from themselves so deeply that they resent the bared faces of us others. We are fighting to free them, to make them masters like ourselves. Note verse 60, 'to hell with them': that is, let us drive them to the 'hell' or secret sanctuary within their consciousness. There dwells 'the worm that dieth not and the fire that is not quenched'; that is, 'the secret serpent coiled about to spring' and 'the flame that burns in every heart of man'—Hadit. In other words, we take up arms against falsehood; we cannot help it if that falsehood forces the King it has imprisoned to assent to its edicts, even to believe that his interests are those of his oppressor, and to fear Truth as once Jehovah did the Serpent."[126] As Lévi attests, "True light rests and satisfies the soul; hallucination, on the contrary, tires it and worries it. The satisfactions of madness are like those gastronomic dreams of hungry men which sharpen their hunger without ever satisfying it. Thence are born irritations and troubles, discouragements and despairs.—Life is always a lie to us, say the disciples of Werther, and therefore we wish to die! Poor children, it is not death that you need, it is life. Since you have been in the world you have died every day; is it from the cruel pleasure of annihilation that you would demand a remedy for the annihilation of your pleasure? No, life has never deceived you, you have not yet lived. What you have been taking for life is but the hallucinations and the dreams of the first slumber of death!"[127]

---

[125] *Ibid.*

[126] NC on AL II.24.

[127] *The Key of the Mysteries*, loc. cit. Cf. also *Liber CL*, Ch. III: "There be moreover many other modes of attaining the apprehension of true Life, and these two following are of much value in breaking up the ice of your mortal error in the vision of your being. And of these the first is the constant contemplation of the Identity of Love and Death, and the understanding of the dissolution of the body as an Act of Love done upon the Body of the Universe, as also it is written at length in our Holy Books. And with this goeth, as it were sister with twin brother, the practice of mortal love as a sacrament symbolical of that great Death: as it is written 'Kill thyself': and again 'Die daily.' And the second of these lesser modes is the practice of the mental apprehension and analysis of ideas, mainly as I have already taught you, but with especial emphasis in choice of things naturally repulsive, in particular, death itself, and its phenomena ancillary. Thus the Buddha bade his disciples to meditate upon Ten Impurities, that is, upon ten cases of death of decomposition, so that the Aspirant, identifying himself with his own corpse in all these imagined forms, might lose

All life's true pleasures "are free from any taint of hidden poison. We are to make the present perfect, without the least fear that we are making trouble for ourselves in the future. True, our bodies are dissolved; but this brings us into full timeless rapture. We enjoy all that may be, as we could not even at the best while forced to measure our Magick in terms of the body and mind. It may be that events cease to occur, that they become one single event, a constant state of joy."[128] In *The Book of the Law*, "Nuith cries: 'I love you,' like a lover; when even John reached only to the cold impersonal proposition 'God is love.' She woos like a mistress; whispers 'To me!' in every ear; Jesus, with needless verb, appeals vehemently to them 'that labour and are heavy laden.' Yet he can promise in the present, says: 'I give unimaginable joys on earth,' making life worth while; 'certainty, not faith, while in life, upon death,' the electric light Knowledge for the churchyard corpsecandle Faith, making life fear-free, and death itself worth while: 'peach unutterable, rest, ecstasy,' making mind and body at ease that soul may be free to transcend them when It will."[129]

"Scorpio, the Zodiacal Sign of Death, is really the Sexual or Reproductive function of Nature. It is the Earth-transcending Eagle, the self-restoring Serpent, and the self-immolating Scorpion.[130] In alchemy it is the principle of Putrefaction, the 'Black Dragon', whose state of apparent corruption is but a prelude to the Rainbow-coloured Spring-tide of the Man in Motley.[131] The nymph of Spring, Syrinx, the trembling hollow reed which needs but Breath to fill the world with Music, attracts Pan, the Goat-God of Ecstatic Lust, by whose Work the glory of Summer is established anew."[132] As Crowley instructs his magical son, "herein lieth the Danger and the Treason of thy Scorpion. For his Nature is against himself, being the deepest Ego, that is, a Being separate from the Universe; and this is the Root of the whole Mystery of Evil. For he hath in him the Magick Power, which if he use not, he is self-poisoned, even as any Organ of the Body that refuseth its Function. So then his Cure is in his Ally the Lion, that feareth not the Crocodiles, nor hideth himself, but leapeth eagerly forward."[133]

---

the natural horror, loathing, fear or disgust which he might have had for them. Know this, that every idea of every sort becomes unreal, phantastic, and most manifest illusion, if it be subjected to persistent investigation, with concentration."

[128] DC on AL II.34-44.

[129] *The Equinox of the Gods*, "Genesis Libri AL," Ch. VII, Sec. VII.

[130] Scorpio, one of the four fixed signs, is the only astrological sign with three symbols—the scorpion, the snake, and the eagle—three traditionally being the number of balance, resurrection, and divine perfection. The sign is generally associated with the sexual organs, with its glyph often being said to represent a male member. Scorpio's eagle is sometimes also taken to represent the phoenix, the praeternaturally long-lived giant bird that dies only to be reborn from its own ashes.

[131] *Cf.* also *Liber DXXXVI*, Ch. V, Sec. II.8: "When the Sun enters Scorpio it is the death of the year. The leaves fall, nature putrifies. Scorpio, the balanced form of water, is under the rule of Mars, and its meaning in alchemy is always corruption and putrefaction. This process is necessary to rebirth, and that such is the office of death is shown by the fact that the handle of the scythe is in the shape of a cross, the sacred emblem of salvation in which the true light exists, but in a concealed form. For the letters of the Latin word LVX are formed by the arms of a cross."

[132] NC on AL II.74.

[133] *Liber Aleph*, "De formula recta draconis." *Cf.* also *Liber CL*, Ch. III-IV: "The life of man is but one segment of a serpentine curve which reaches out to infinity, and its zeros but mark the changes from the plus to minus, and minus to plus, coefficients of its equation. It is for this cause, among

Threefold is the Nature of Love, Eagle, Serpent, and Scorpion. And of these the Scorpion is he that, having no Lion of Light and of Courage within him, seemeth to himself encircled by Fire, and, driving his Sting into himself, he dieth. Such are the Black Brothers, that cry: I am I, they that deny Love, restricting it to their own Nature. But the Serpent is the secret Nature of Man, that is Life and Death, and maketh his Way through the Generations in Silence. And the Eagle is that Might of Love which is the Key of Magick, uplifting the Body and its Appurtenance unto high Ecstasy upon his Wings. It is by Virtue thereof that the Sphinx beholdeth the Sun unwinking, and confronteth the Pyramid without Shame. Our Dragon, therefore, combining the Natures of the Eagle and the Serpent, is our Love, the Organ of our Will, by whose Virtue we perform the Work and Miracle of the One Substance, as saith thine Ancestor Hermes Trismegistus, in his Tablet of Smaragda. And this Dragon, is called thy Silence, because in the Hour of his Operation that within thee which saith "I" is abolished in its Conjunction with the Beloved. For this Cause also is its Letter Nun, which in our Rota is the Trump Death; and Nun hath the value of Fifty, the Number of the Gates of Understanding.[134]

"In general, the tens are 'solidifications' of the ideas of the units which they multiply. Thus 50 is Death, the Force of Change in its final and most earthy aspect."[135] There is a list of the Fifty Gates of Binah or Understanding in the back of W. W. Westcott's translation of the *Sepher Yetzirah*, which former the Golden Dawn co-founder borrowed from Athanasius Kircher's *Œdipus Ægyptiacus*. It is a scheme of Qabalistic classification of knowledge emanating from the third Sephira, Binah, and descending by stages through the angels, heavens, humanity, animal, vegetable, and mineral kingdoms to hyle and chaos. According to the Jewish Qabalists, one must enter and pass up through the Gates to attain to the Thirty-Two Paths of Wisdom, but even Moses only passed through the 49th Gate. However, Kircher further asserted that only Jesus Christ penetrated the 50th gate, and Westcott retained this Christian interpolation. The essential idea behind the Fifty Gates appears in many of Crowley's writing, e.g. "Wakeworld" in *Konx Om Pax*, and *The Vision and the Voice*. Diagram 27 in *The Equinox*, Vol. I, No. 2,

---

many others, that wise men in old time chose the Serpent as the Hieroglyph of Life. . . . All those ideas which bred sorrow and fear are known in their truth, and thus become the seed of joy: for you are certain beyond all proof that you can never die; that, though you change, change is part of your own nature: the Great Enemy is become the Great Ally. And now, rooted in this perfection, your Self become the very Tree of Life, you have a fulcrum for your lever: you are ready to understand that this pulsation of Unity is itself Duality, and therefore, in the highest and most sacred sense, still Sorrow and Illusion; which having comprehended, aspire yet again, even unto the Fourth of the Gifts of the Law, unto the End of the Path, even unto Light. . . . The greatest gift of the Law, [Light,] then, cometh forth by the most perfect practice of the Three Lesser Gifts [of Life, Love, and Liberty]. And so thoroughly must you travail in this Work that you are able to pass from one side of the equation to the other at will: nay, to comprehend the whole at once, and for ever. This then your time-and-space-bound soul shall travel according to its nature in its orbit, revealing the Law to them that walk in chains, for that this is your particular function."

[134] *Ibid.*, "De dracone, quæ est aquila, serpens, scorpio."

[135] *An Essay upon Number*, Part I, Sec. IV.

shows the distribution of the ten Sephiroth into seven Palaces, and is a representation of the exact moment of the opening of the 50th gate—the crossing of the Abyss. At that moment, Malkuth and Yesod merge and the upper three Sephiroth appear as one, as Binah. Crowley noted seeing the Supernals as one Sephira on first crossing the Abyss, but unlike his experience with the "Star-Sponge Vision," he apparently never identified this with the pre-existing tradition. This oversight can almost definitely be blamed on the old Golden Dawn representation of these Seven Palaces and the Beast of Revelation in a negative, Christian light.[136]

> Note that the Atu "Death" in the Tarot refers to Scorpio. This sign is threefold: the Scorpion that kills itself with its own poison, when its environment (the ring of fire) becomes intolerable; the Serpent that renews itself by shedding its skin, that is crowned and hooded, that moves by undulations like Light, and gives man Wisdom at the price of Toil, Suffering and Mortality; and the Eagle that soars, its lidless eyes bent boldly upon the Sun. "Death" is, to the initiate, as inn by the wayside; its marks a stage accomplished; it offers refreshment, repose, and advice as to his plans for the morrow.
>
> But in this verse the main point is that death is the "crown" of all. The crown is Kether, the Unity; "Love under will" having been applied to all Nuith-possibilities of all Khu-energies of any Hadit-central-Star, that Star has exhausted itself perfectly, completed one stage of its course. It is therefore crowned by death; and, being wholly itself, lives again by attracting its equal and opposite Counterpart, with whom "love under will" is the fulfilment of the Law, in a sublimer sphere.[137]

"We must not confuse such passing beyond earthly life with death; death is for the dogs. They restrict themselves more and more; fears, greeds, falsehoods gather like vultures to feast on their flesh; until at least they find no way to turn which is not barred by one or another of their sins, their self-made bars to free action. They can no longer cause any event beyond the narrow routine into which they have been forced by their failures, to grapple with Nature, to love, to woo, and to master the beauty of Nuit. Little by little the machine fails to carry on. Its prudence, more than aught else, has helped to destroy its power to meet fresh facts. The least surprises may upset it; and, sooner or later, it either meets some problem which breaks it up, or wears itself out and runs down. It is dead."[138]

In *Liber Aleph*, we learn of the "three Modes of the Path of Nun"—"the Scorpion destroyeth himself, as if it were a Type of Animal Pleasure. Next, the Serpent is proper to Works of Change, or Magick; yet is he poisonous also unless thou hast Wit to enchant him. Lastly, the Eagle is subtlest in this Sort, so that this Path is proper to a Transcendental Labour. Yet all these are in the Way of Death, so that thy Wand is dissolved and corroded in the

---

[136] Heidrick, *op. cit.*
[137] NC on AL II.72.
[138] DC on AL II.45.

Waters of the Cup, and must be renewed by Virtue of thy Nature in Her Course. For Fire is extinguished by Water; but upon Earth it burneth freely, and is inflamed by the Wind. Understand also that which is written concerning the Vesica, that it is the Mother, giving Ease, Sleep, and Death, which Consolations are eschewed by the True Man or Hero."[139]

"There is one Oath more important than all the rest put together, from the point of view of the A∴A∴. You swear to refuse all the 'rewards,' to acquire your new vehicle without a moment's delay, so that you may carry on your work of helping Mankind with the minimum of interruption. Like all true Magical Oaths, it is certain of success. So then we have a man not only very well prepared to reincarnate at once—this means about six months after his death, for his vehicle will be a foetus about three months old, but to extirpate more deliberately all impressions that may assail its integrity."[140] Therefore, "if his Star be of those that are bound by the Great Oath, incarnating without Remission because of Delight in the Cosmic Sacrament, it seeketh a new Vehicle in the appointed Way, and indwelleth the Foetus of a Child, and quickeneth it. And if at this Time the mind of its Former Tabernacle yet cling to it, then is there Continuity Character, and it may be Memory between the two Vehicles. This is, briefly and without Elaboration, the Way of Asar in Amennti, according to mine Opinion, of which I say not: This is the Truth."[141]

In Hinduism, a person is said to have attained liberation, or *Moksha*, when the cycle of rebirth comes to an end. All schools of Vedanta agree that this implies the cessation of worldly desires and freedom from the cycle of birth and death, though the exact definition varies. Followers of Advaita Vedanta believe they will spend eternity absorbed in the perfect peace and happiness of the realization that all existence is One Brahman of which the Ātman is part. Dvaita Vedantists perform ritual worship with the goal of spending eternity in a spiritual plane or heaven (*loka*) in the blessed company of the Supreme Being. Different Buddhist traditions also vary in precise views of rebirth. The Tibetan schools subscribe to the notion of an intermediate state, or *Bardo*, that can last up to 49 days.[142] An accomplished or realized practitioner can choose to return to *Saṃsāra* by maintaining conscious awareness during the death process. The Tibetans believe many Lamas choose to reincarnate again and again as humans, and they refer to them to as Tülkus, or living Buddhas.

"Briefly, the orthodox theory as put forth by H. P. B. is that one works off one's Karma after death in Devachan, or Kama Loka, or some such place; when the balance is exhausted, one may come back to earth, or in some other way carry on the Great Work."[143] In Mahāyāna Buddhism, you are expressly encouraged to forgo *Nirvāṇa* and Arhatship, and to take the Bodhisattva vows to work for the liberation of all sentient beings instead.

---

[139] *Liber Aleph*, "De viis mortis et diaboli, arcanis tou tarot Fraternitatis R∴ C∴."
[140] *MWT*, Ch. XXXVII.
[141] *Liber Aleph*, "De adeptis R.C. eschatologia."
[142] Coleman & Jinpa 2005.
[143] *MWT*, Ch. XLVII.

Similarly, "One who is vowed to the A∴A∴'s Mission for Mankind, who takes it dead seriously, and who will be neither frightened nor bored from Its majestic purpose, may at any time bind himself by an Oath to reject the rewards of Devachan, and reincarnate immediately again and again. By 'immediately' is meant about 6 months before the birth of the new Adept, about 3 months after his last death. It depends to some extent, no doubt, on whether he can find a suitable vehicle. Presumably he will make some sort of a preparation while still alive. It seems that I personally must have taken this Oath quite a long while ago; for the Incarnations which I actually remember leave very few gaps to be filled in the last dozen centuries or so."[144]

"The Adepts have always known how to prolong life and, what is infinitely more important, the activity and enjoyment of life; but as they happen to be men of sense they have refrained from publishing such dangerous information to the world, and they have refrained from applying it even to themselves unless some serious cosmic purpose is to be served by doing so in any set case. In the ordinary way we are liable to say: 'Let us not interfere with natural processes, let us die when the time comes, and start afresh!'"[145] The Adepts "have the secret of the Elixir of Life, and could carry on in the same body indefinitely; yet at least some masters prefer to reincarnate in the regular way, only taking care to waste no time in Amennti, but to get back to the Old Bench and pick up the New Tools with the minimum of delay. By having attained the Freedom of 'Elysian, windless, fortunate abodes Beyond Heaven's constellated wilderness'[146] 'we are blessed; and bless'[147] by refusing to linger therein, but shouldering once more 'Atlantean the load of the too vast orb of'[148] the Karma of Mankind."[149]

---

[144] *Ibid.*
[145] *The Elixir of Life.*
[146] Percy Bysshe Shelley, *Prometheus Unbound*, Act IV, Scene I.
[147] *Ibid.*
[148] Matthew Arnold, *Heine's Grave.*
[149] *MWT*, Ch. LXXV.

PART II
Praxis

CHAPTER 7
Thelemic Pedagogy

This Book lays down a simple Code of Conduct.
  "Do what thou wilt shall be the whole of the Law."
  "Love is the law, love under will."
  "There is no law beyond Do what thou wilt."
  This means that each of us stars is to move on our true orbit, as marked out by the nature of our position, the law of our growth, the impulse of our past experiences. All events are equally lawful—and every one necessary, in the long run—for all of us, in theory; but in practice, only one act is lawful for each one of us at any given moment. Therefore Duty consists in determining to experience the right event from one moment of consciousness to another.
  Each action or motion is an act of love, the uniting with one or another part of "Nuit"; each such act must be "under will," chosen so as to fulfil and not to thwart the true nature of the being concerned.
  The technical methods of achieving this are to be studied in Magick, *or acquired by personal instruction from the Master Therion and his appointed assistants.*
  —Introduction to THE BOOK OF THE LAW

It is not for right that we should dare all, it is for duty.
  Duty is the expansion and the enjoyment of liberty; isolated right is the father of slavery.
  Duty is devotion; right is selfishness.
  Duty is sacrifice; right is theft and rapine.
  Duty is love, and right is hate.
  Duty is infinite life; right is eternal death.
  If one must fight to conquer right, it is only to acquire the power of duty: what use have we for freedom, unless to love and to devote ourselves to God?
  —Éliphas Lévi, THE KEY OF THE MYSTERIES

"What we call liberty is nothing but the all-mightiness of divine compulsion. The martyrs said: 'It is better to obey God than man'. The least perfect act of love is worth more than the best act of piety. Judge not; speak hardly at all; love and act."[1] The *New Comment* seems to make much the same point as Lévi: "It is not true to say either that we are separate Stars, or One Star. Each Star is individual, yet each is bound to the others by Law. This Freedom under Law is one of the most difficult yet important doctrines of

---

[1] *The Key of the Mysteries*, Part I, "Sketch of the Prophetic Theology of Numbers."

this Book. So too the ritual—our lives—must be unto Nuith; for She is the Ultimate to which we tend, the asymptote of our curve. Failure in this one-pointedness sets up the illusion of duality, which leads to excision and destruction."[2]

"In any case what the Eastern calls 'one-pointedness' is an essential preliminary to even early stages of true meditation. And iron will-power is a still earlier qualification. By meditation I do not mean merely 'think about' anything, however profoundly, but the absolute restraint of the mind to the contemplation of a single object, whether gross, fine, or altogether spiritual."[3] Crowley asks, "What is the use then of doing anything if we are but as drops of water which are splashed between the wanton hands of the Sun, the Wind, and the Ocean?—indeed the ways of God are inscrutable and past finding out. Thus the Unobtainable tempts us, and the little segments of God that we see become to us the fiercest and most terrible of the Dog-faced Demons which seduce us from the path. He is always at our elbow, whispering, tempting, jeering, advising and helping us; He it is that casts despair upon us when we have done nothing wrong, and elation when we have done nothing right; He it is who is ever rising before us like a mist to obscure our path or to magnify our goal; yet nevertheless He is not only the cloud but that ultimate fire—if we could only understand Him as He IS; Ah! my brothers, this is THE GREAT WORK."[4]

> Each stage above him is his Ultimate goal for the time being. Possessing one little sphere, his one and only object is to unite it to another, or another to it; not two others, not to the whole, but only to that *One Other*. For the time being (let it appear as if it were for all time to the initiate), that *One Other* is God and Very God—the Omega of his quest, and that *all others* are Devils that would tempt and seduce him. Thus it happens that until you become God, God Himself is in Reality The Tempter, Satan, and the Prince of Darkness, who, assuming the glittering robes of Time and Space, whispers in our ears: "Millions and millions and millions of eternities are as nothingness to me; then how canst thou, thou little mote dancing in the beam of mine eye, hope to span me?" Thus God at the outset comes to us and like the old witch in "Cinderella" strews innumerable lentils before us to count—but begin! and soon you will find that you have left the kitchen of the world behind you and have entered the enchanted Palace "Beyond."[5]

"There is only one thing for anybody to do on a path, and that is to make sure of the next step. And the fact which we all have to comfort us is this: that all human beings have capacities for attainment, each according to his or her present position. . . . The question for each one of us is then: first of all, to ascertain our present positions; secondly, to determine our proper directions; and, thirdly, to govern ourselves accordingly. The question for

---

[2] NC on AL I.52.
[3] *Berashith*.
[4] *The Temple of Solomon the King*, Part II, "The Pillar of Cloud." Emphasis in original.
[5] *Ibid.* Emphasis in original.

me is also to describe a method of procedure which will be sufficiently elastic to be useful to every human being. I have tried to do this by combining the two paths of Magick and Yoga. If we perform the preliminary practices, each according to his capacity, the result will surely be the acquisition of a certain technique. And this will become much easier as we advance, especially if we bear it well in mind not to attempt to discriminate between the two methods as if they were opposing schools, but to use the one to help out the other in an emergency."[6]

According to *The Temple of Solomon the King*, the method of attainment is "also twofold, or twofold in one: I. Exaltation by madness. II. Exaltation by wisdom. In the first we awake from the dream of illusion by a blinding light being flashed across our eyes; in the second, gradually, by the breaking of the dawn. In the first the light of knowledge, though but comparable to the whole of Knowledge as a candle-flame to the sun, may be so sudden that blindness follows the first illumination." The footnote reads: "The greater our ignorance the more intense appears the illumination."[7] The *New Comment* explains the essential difference between the two Arts of Magick and Mysticism thus: "This Finite will evidently be an expression of the particular mood of its Father and Mother at the moment of its conception. Obviously, this 'Child' cannot add to the Universe; it is therefore inevitably twin (Horus and Harpocrates, Osiris and Typhon, Jesus and Barabbas) in Nature, formed of equal and opposite elements. When the Operation is mystical in character, the 'Child' does not appear at all in this manifested form as Two, but as Naught. In the consciousness of the Adept, this is called Samadhi. He has united himself with, and lost himself in, Nuit. When the 'Child' appears as Two, it is Magick, as the other is Mysticism."[8]

According to the *Djeridensis Comment*, Hadit "is the Secret spring of Magick (Compare the Hindu Kundalini). He takes joy when he withdraws into himself which he does in order to prepare a new Event. These Events are of two kinds. One is the act of worship of Nuit, the other is the putting forth of his spirit into matter. We may call one the Mystic, the other the Magical Path."[9] Indeed, as the *New Comment* points out, "The doctrine of the dual character of the God is very important to a proper understanding of Him. 'The Sign of the Enterer is always to be followed immediately by the Sign of Silence': such is the imperative injunction to the Neophyte. In *Book 4* the necessity for this is explained fully."[10] Again, *Magick Without Tears* describes "our Method" as "two-fold"—"(1) Yoga, introversion, (2) Magick, extroversion. (These are rough but useful connotations.) The two seem, at first glance, to be opposed; but, when you have advanced a little in both, you find that the concentration learnt in Yoga is of immense use in attaining the mental powers necessary in Magick; on the other hand, the discipline of Magick is of the greatest service in Yoga."[11]

---

[6] *Eight Lectures*, Ch. 8, Secs. 21–22.
[7] *The Temple of Solomon the King*, Part III, "The Sorcerer."
[8] NC on AL I.14.
[9] DC on AL II.26.
[10] NC on AL III.35.
[11] *MWT*, Ch. LXXXI.

"Let me remark, by the way, that to my mind one of the greatest beauties, and most encouraging confirmations of the validity of our system, is the matchless harmony of its elements. Always, when we pursue any one path to its end, we find that it has become one with some other path which at the outset appeared utterly irreconcilable with it. ('Write down that the tearing apart is the crushing together' comes from an actual experience. See *Liber 418, The Vision and the Voice*, which teems with similar passages, and is itself an outstanding example of the unity of the Yogic and the Magical methods.)"[12] The *New Comment* further says of Heru-Ra-Ha that, "It is important to observe that He claims to be both Horus and Harpocrates; and this two-in-one is a Unity combining Tao and Teh, Matter & Motion, Being & Form. This is natural, for in Him must exist the Root of the Dyad."[13]

"The principles of Yoga, and the spiritual results of Yoga, are demonstrated in every conscious and unconscious happening. This is that which is written in *The Book of the Law*—Love is the law, love under will—for Love is the instinct to unite, and the act of uniting. But this cannot be done indiscriminately, it must be done 'under will,' that is, in accordance with the nature of the particular units concerned. Hydrogen has no love for Hydrogen; it is not the nature, or the 'true Will' of Hydrogen to seek to unite with a molecule of its own kind. Add Hydrogen to Hydrogen: nothing happens to its quality: it is only its quantity that changes. It rather seeks to enlarge its experience of its possibilities by union with atoms of opposite character, such as Oxygen; with this it combines (with an explosion of light, heat, and sound) to form water. The result is entirely different from either of the component elements, and has another kind of 'true Will,' such as to unite (with similar disengagement of light and heat) with Potassium, while the resulting 'caustic Potash' has in its turn a totally new series of qualities, with still another 'true Will' of its own; that is, to unite explosively with acids. And so on."[14] However, "This question of making 'no difference' as ordained is to regard the whole of the non-Ego or universe apparently external to the Self as a single phenomenon; Samadhi on any one thing becomes therefore Samadhi on The Whole. The mystic who 'availeth in this' can then perform his Great Work of 'love under will' in a single operation instead of being obliged to unite himself with the non-Ego piecemeal."[15]

> It will be said that nobody can realize himself so long as the presentation is imperfect, that is, so long as he is incarnated. This is no doubt true in all rigour; but one can obtain an approximation to the intended self-knowledge by withdrawing for a time to the monistic form of self-consciousness, which does not distinguish between the Ego and the Non-Ego; in other words, by attaining Samadhi. But the first experience of Samadhi will then naturally be an ecstasy devoid of name or form, and containing no elements distinguishable as such; and we

---

[12] *Ibid. Cf.* e.g. *Liber 418*, 24th Æthyr, fn.: "The Beast and the Scarlet Woman are attributed to ♌ and Water ♏. They are the two-in-one Chief Officers of the Temple of the New Æon of Heru-Ra-Ha."
[13] NC on AL III.70.
[14] *Eight Lectures*, Ch. 1, Sec. 10.
[15] NC on AL I.22.

know this to be the case. One has simply deprived oneself of the means of expression, and all dual consciousness disappears, together with its forms, time and space. One concludes from this that the Universe is identical with the Ego, and all things dissolve into a formless essence characterized by knowledge and bliss. But this early stage of Samadhi is an illusion, a sort of drunken dizziness. (So in sexual love, the ecstasy abolishes the Ego, apparently; it forgets that duality was its cause, and must be equally real with itself, in one sense or another). But subsequent Samadhi teaches the adept that his universal instantaneous Unity exists as "None and Two"; and he learns that his Samadhi is peculiar to himself as well as common to all.

He becomes able to experience the truth of the statements in the *Book of the Law*, the nature of Nuith and Hadith, and of himself as a Star, unique, individual, and eternal, but yet a part of the Body of Nuith, and therefore identical with all other stars in that respect.

He realizes himself as the "bed in working" of Nuith and Hadit, as a particular form assumed by the latter for the sake of Variety in his "play" with the former; and he partakes in this play by his self-realization, which he synthesizes from the "events of his life."

He understands that these events are the resultant of the Universe as applied to him, so that his experience is equally unique and universal, each star being the centre of the cosmos, and the Cosmos applicable as a whole to each star.[16]

"Undoubtedly, if a boy worried long enough over a text-book on trigonometry he would eventually appreciate the theory and practice of logarithms; but why should he waste his time? why not instead seek a master? Certainly, when he has learnt all the text-books can teach and all the master can tell him, he must strike out for himself, but up to this point he must place his faith in some one. To the ordinary Aspirant a 'Guru'"—or an "Instructor," as the footnote translates it—"is necessary; and the only danger to the uninitiate is that he may place his trust in a charlatan instead of in an adept. This indeed is a danger, but surely after a little while the most ignorant will be able to discriminate, as a blind man can between day and night. And, if the pupil be a true Seeker, it matters little in the end. For as the sacrament is efficacious, though administered by an unworthy priest, so will his love of Truth enable him to turn even the evil counsels of a knave to his advantage."[17]

Each star is in itself immune and innocent; its proper consciousness is monistic; it must therefore employ a body and mind as the instruments for interpreting its relations with other souls, and comparing its nature with theirs. For the mind perceives the contrast of the Self and the not-Self, and presents its experiences, classified and judged, to the soul as documents for the dossier; and the body reports to

---

[16] NC on AL I.29.
[17] *The Temple of Solomon the King*, loc. cit.

the mind the impressions received from its contact with alien forms as the senses receive them.

It must naturally require many incarnations for the soul to begin to know itself with any degree of perfection; and one may recognize advanced souls by their minds, which understand the a nature of their work, are indifferent to the body's preference for any special forms of experience, and seek eagerly after novel adventures (like a philatelist after rare stamps) to complete the collection. They are also as a rule both very careful and very careless about their bodily welfare, taking pains to preserve their powers for the purpose of gaining new experiences, but utterly indifferent to them as valuable in themselves. They rule them with a rod of iron, and train them like pugilists; but they risk them recklessly whenever the Work demands it.[18]

"The Hindus, understanding these difficulties, have taken the God-Almighty attitude about the matter. If you go to a Hindu teacher, he treats you as less than an earthworm. You have to do this, and you have to do that, and you are not allowed to know why you are doing it." Again, the footnote explains, "This does not conflict with the 'go-as-you-please' plan put forward in the previous note. An autocratic Adept is indeed a blessing to the disciple, not because he is able to guide the pupil 'aright' in the particular path which happens to suit his personality, but because he can compel the beginner to grind away at the weariest work and thus acquire all-round ability, and prevent him from picking out the plums which please him from the Pie of Knowledge, and making himself sick of a surfeit of sweets to the neglect of a balanced diet of wholesome nourishment." Apparently, even after "years of experience in teaching," Crowley was "not altogether convinced that this is not the right attitude. When people begin to argue about things instead of doing them, they become absolutely impossible. Their minds begin to work about it and about, and they come out by the same door as in they went. They remain brutish, voluble, and uncomprehending."[19]

But, "how can these multiform desires be silenced, and the one desire be realised so that it engulf the rest? To this question we must answer as we have answered elsewhere—'only by a one-pointedness of the senses'—until the five-sided polygon become pyramidal and vanish in a point. The base must be well established, regular, and of even surface; for as the base so the summit. In other words, the five senses must be strong and healthy and without disease. An unhealthy man is unfitted to perform a magical operation, and an hysterical man will probably end in the Qliphoth or Bedlam. A blind man will not be able to equilibrate the sense of sight, or a deaf man the sense of hearing, like a man who can both see and hear; however, the complete loss of one sense, if this is ever actually the case, is far better than a mental weakness in that sense."[20]

---

[18] NC on AL I.29.
[19] *MITAP*, Ch. XXI, Sec. V.
[20] *The Temple of Solomon the King*, loc. cit.

It may seem that in this verse the word "Death" is used in a sense somewhat other than that explained in the previous note. It is forbidden, observe, to "man". That is, then, the formula must not be used by one who is still an imperfect being. Our definition is surely confirmed by this phrase rather than denied, or even modified. To long for death is to aspire to the complete fulfilment of all one's potentialities. And it would evidently be an error to insist upon passing on to one's next life while there were hawsers unhitched from this one. The mere inexplicability of the various jerks would make for bewilderment, irritation, and clumsiness.

For this reason, alone, it is all-important to ascertain one's true Will, and to work out every detail of the work of doing it, as early in life as one can. One is apt (at the best) to define one's will dogmatically, and to devote one's life almost puritanically to the task, sternly suppressing all side-issues, and calling this course Concentration. This is error, and perilous. For one cannot be sure that a faculty which seems (on the surface) useless, even hostile, to one's work, may not in course of time become one of vital value. If it be atrophied—alas! Its suppression may moreover have poisoned one's whole system, as a breast debarred from its natural use is prone to cancer. At best, it may be too late to repair the mischief; the lost opportunity may be a life-long remorse.

The one way of safety lies in applying the Law of Thelema with the utmost rigour. Every impulse, however feeble, is necessary to the stability of the whole structure; the tiniest flaw may cause the cannon to burst. Every impulse however opposite to the main motive, is part of the plan; the rifling does not thwart the purpose of the barrel. One should therefore acquiesce in every element of one's nature, and develop it as its own laws demand, with absolute impartiality. One need not fear; there is a natural limit to the growth of any species; it either finds food fail, or is choked by its neighbours, or overgrows itself, and is transformed. Nor need one fret about the harmony and proportion of one's various faculties; the fit will survive, and the perfection of the whole will be understood as soon as the parts have found themselves, and settled down after fighting the matter out in the balanced stability which represents their right reaction to each other, and to their environment. It is thus policy for an Aspirant to initiation to analyse himself with indefatigable energy, shrewd skill, and accurate subtlety; but then to content himself with indefatigable energy, shrewd skill, and accurate subtlety; but then to content himself with observing the interplay of his instincts, instead of guiding them. Not until he is familiar with them all should he perform the practices which enable him to read the Word of his Will. And, then having assumed conscious control of himself, that he may do his Will, he should make a point of using every faculty in a detached way (just as one inspects one's pistols and fires a few rounds) without expecting ever to need them again, but on the general principle that if they were wanted, one might as well feel confident of the issue.[21]

Liber Aleph cites "one Affliction" that "shall touch nigh all that come to thee, and that is this great Pox of Sin, that is our Bane inherited of the Æon of Slain Gods. Look the first of all, when any Postulant boweth before thee, whether there be not Conflict and Restriction in his Mind, and in his Will. If he deem Good and Evil to be absolute, instead of as relative to the Health of this Body, or the Weal of the Society of which he is a Member, or what not, as it may be, instruct him. Or, if he will say that he will sacrifice all for Initiation, correct him, as it is written: 'but whoso gives one Particle of Dust shall lose all in that Hour.' For it is Conflict if he weigh one Thing with another; and Renunciation, being sorrowful, is not worthy of Acceptance. But he must with Joy unite all he is and hath, heaping the Whole into one Billow of Love, under Will. Yea, o my son, until thou hast brought the Postulant into our Freedom from Sin, and the Sense and Conviction thereof, he is not ready for the Path of our Magick and Illumination; because every Way soever is a Going, and this Sin is an obstacle and a Fetter and an Hoodwink on every one of them, for it is Restriction, whether he set out by the Meditations of the Dhamma, or by Our Qabalah, or by Vision or Theurgy, or how else soever."[22]

"One must find out for oneself, and make sure beyond doubt, *who* one is, *what* one is, *why* one is. This done, one may put the Will which is implicit in the 'why' into words, or rather into One Word. Being thus conscious of the proper course to pursue, the next thing is to understand the conditions necessary to following it out. After that, one must eliminate from oneself every element alien or hostile to success, and develop those parts of oneself which are specially needed to control the aforesaid conditions. . . . Having discovered his identity, he will soon perceive his purpose. Another process will show him how to make that purpose pure and powerful. He may then learn how to estimate his environment, learn how to make allies, how to make himself prevail against all powers whose error has caused them to wander across his path."[23]

This theory of initiation is so important to every aspirant that I shall illustrate how my own ignorance bred error, and error injury. My Will was, I now know, to be The Beast, 666, a Magus, the Word of the Æon, Thelema; to proclaim this new Law to mankind.

My passion for personal freedom, my superiority to sexual impulses, my resolve to master physical fear and weakness, my contempt for other people's opinions, my poetic genius: I indulged all these to the full. None of them carried me too far, ousted the other, or injured my general well-being. On the contrary, each automatically reached its natural limit, and each has been incalculably useful to me in doing my Will when I

---

[21] NC on AL II.73.
[22] "De prudentia artis docendi."
[23] *MITAP*, Introduction. Emphasis in original.

became aware of it, able to organize its armies, and to direct them intelligently against the inertia of ignorance.

But I suppressed certain impulses in myself. I abandoned my ambitions to be a diplomatist. I checked my ardour for Science. I trampled upon my prudence in financial matters. I mortified my fastidiousness about caste. I masked my shyness in bravado, and tried to kill it by ostentatious eccentricity. This last mistake came from sheer panic; but all the rest were quite deliberate sacrifices on the altar of my God Magick.

They were all accepted, as it then seemed. I attained all my ambitions; yea, and more also. But I know now that I should not have forced my growth, and deformed my destiny. To nail geese to boards and stuff them makes foie gras, very true; but it does not improve the geese. It may be said that I strengthened my moral character by these sacrifices, and that I was indeed compelled to act as I did. The mad elephant Wantobemagus pulled over the team of oxen? We may put it like that, certainly; but still I feel that it might have been better had he not been mad. For, today, if I were an Ambassador, versed profoundly in Science, financially armed and socially stainless, I should be able to execute my Will by pressure upon all classes of powerful people, to make this comment carry conviction to thinkers, and to publish the *Book of the Law* in every part of the world. Instead, I am exiled and suspected, despised by men of science, ostracised by my class, and a beggar. If I were in my teens again! I cannot change my mind about which ridge I'll climb the mountain by, now when I see, above these ice-glazed pinnacles storm-swept, through gashes torn from whirling wreaths of arrowy sleet, the cloud-surpassing summit, not far, not very far.

I regret nothing, be sure! I may be even in error to argue that an evident distortion of nature, and its issue in disaster, are proof of imprudence. Perhaps the other road would not have taken me to Cairo, to the climax of my life, to my true Will fulfilled in Aiwaz and made Word in this Book. Perhaps it is lingering "lust of result" that whispers hideous lies to daunt me, that urges these plausible arguments to accuse me. It may be that my present extremity is the very condition required for the fulfilment of my Work. Who shall say what is power, what impotence? Who shall be bold to measure the Morrow, or declare what causes conjoin to bring forth an Effect that no man knoweth?

Was not Lao-Tze thrust forth from his city? Did not Buddha go begging in rags? Did not Mohammed flee for his life into exile? Was not Bacchus the scandal and the scorn of men? Than Joseph Smith had any man less learning? Yet each of these attained to do his Will; each cried his Word, that all the Earth yet echoes it! And each was able to accomplish this by virtue of that very circumstance which seems so cruel. Shall I, who am armed with all their weapons at once, complain that I must go into the fight unfurnished?[24]

---

[24] NC on AL II.73.

Crowley offers the beginner the following six-point programme: (1) "Furnish your mind as completely as possible with the knowledge of how to inspect and to control it." (2) "Train your body to obey your mind, and not to distract its attention." (3) "Control your mind to devote itself wholly to discover your true Will." (4) "Explore the course of that Will till you reach its source, your Silent Self." (5) "Unite the conscious will with the true Will, and the conscious Ego with the Silent Self. You must be utterly ruthless in discarding any atom of consciousness which is hostile or neutral." (6) "Let this work freely from within, but heed not your environment, lest you make difference between one thing and another. Whatever it be, it is to be made one with you by Love."[25]

> The process of analysing, developing and controlling the mind is the essence of all Yoga practices.
>
> Magick explores and learns to control those regions of Nature which lie beyond the objects of sense. Reaching the highest parts of these regions, called the divine, one proceeds by the exaltation (? = intoxication? Yes, of a sublime sort) of the consciousness to identify oneself with those "celestial" Beings.
>
> In Yoga, various practices prevent the body and its functions from interrupting the mental process. Then, one inhibits that process itself: the stilling of "thoughts" allows one to become aware of mental functions beyond the intellectual; these functions have their own peculiar properties and powers. Each sheath, as one goes deeper, is discarded as "unreal"; finally one apprehends that nothing which is the only true and real form of existence. (But then it does *not* exist: in these regions of thought words always become nightmares of self-contradiction. This is as it should be.)
>
> In Magick, on the contrary, one passes through the veil of the exterior world (which, as in Yoga, but in another sense, becomes "unreal" by comparison as one passes beyond) one creates a subtle body (instrument is a better term) called the body of Light; this one develops and controls; it gains new powers as one progresses, usually by means of what is called "initiation": finally, one carries on almost one's whole life in this Body of Light, and achieves in its own way the mastery of the Universe.
>
> The first step in Yoga is "Keep still."
> The first step in Magick is "Travel beyond the world of the senses."[26]

The "Postcards to Probationers" in *The Equinox*, Vol. I, No. 2, give this simple comparison of the two arts:

> I. Yoga is the art of uniting the mind to a single idea. It has four methods.
> Gnana-Yoga.   Union by Knowledge.
> Raja-Yoga.   Union by Will.

---

[25] NC on AL I.37.
[26] *MWT, loc. cit.* Emphasis in original.

Bhakta-Yoga.	Union by Love.
Hatha-Yoga.	Union by Courage.
add Mantra-Yoga.	Union through Speech.
Karma-Yoga.	Union through Work.

These are united by the supreme method of Silence.

II. Ceremonial Magic is the art of uniting the mind to a single idea. It has four Methods.

The Holy Qabalah.	Union by Knowledge.
The Sacred Magic.	Union by Will.
The Acts of Worship.	Union by Love.
The Ordeals.	Union by Courage.
add The Invocations.	Union by Speech.
The Acts of Service.	Union through Work.

These are united by the supreme method of Silence.[27]

"By Gñana Yoga cometh thy Man to Knowledge; by Karma Yoga thy Bull to Will; by Raja Yoga is thy Lion brought to his Light; and to make perfect thy Dragon, thou hast Bhakta Yoga for the Eagle therein, and Hatha Yoga for the Serpent. Yet mark thou well how all these interfuse, so that thou mayst accomplish no one of the Works separately."[28] However, "The technique of Magick is just as important as that of mysticism, but here we have a very much more difficult problem, because the original unit of Magick, the Body of Light, is already something unfamiliar to the ordinary person. Nevertheless, this body must be developed and trained with exactly the same rigid discipline as the brain in the case of mysticism. The essence of the technique of Magick is the development of the body of Light, which must be extended to include all members of the organism, and indeed of the cosmos."[29]

The most important drill practices are:

1. The fortification of the Body of Light by the constant use of rituals, by the assumption of god-forms, and by the right use of the Eucharist.

2. The purification and consecration and exaltation of that Body by the use of rituals of invocation.

3. The education of that Body by experience. It must learn to travel on every plane; to break down every obstacle which may confront it. This experience must be as systematic and regular as possible; for it is of no use merely to travel to the spheres of Jupiter and Venus, or even to explore the 30 Æthyrs, neglecting unattractive meridians. *{The Aspirant should remember that he is a Microcosm.* "Universus sum et Nihil universi a me alienum puto" *should be his motto. He should make it his daily practice to travel on the Astral Plane, taking in turn each of the most synthetic sections, the Sephiroth and the Paths. These being thoroughly*

---

[27] "Yoga and Magic."
[28] *Liber Aleph*, "De libra, in qua guattuor virtutes æquipollent."
[29] *MITAP*, Ch. XXI, Sec. V.

> *understood, and an Angel in each pledged to guard or to guide him at need, he should start on a new series of expeditions to explore the subordinate sections of each. He may then practice Rising on the Planes from these spheres, one after the other in rotation. When he is thoroughly conversant with the various methods of meeting unexpected emergencies, he may proceed to investigate the regions of the Qliphoth and the Demonic Forces. It should be his aim to obtain a comprehensive knowledge of the entire Astral Plane, with impartial love of truth for its own sake; just as a child learns the geography of the whole planet, though he may have no intention of ever leaving his native land.}*
> The object is to possess a Body which is capable of doing easily any particular task that may lie before it. There must be no selection of special experience which appeals to one's immediate desire. One must go steadily through all possible pylons.[30]

Out-of-body experiences were recorded as long ago as the time of the ancient Egyptians, and the consistency of the descriptions from various sources in itself suggests that it is a real phenomenon. Modern psychologists contend that an "OOBE" begins when a person loses contact with sensory input from the body while remaining conscious. The person retains the illusion of having a body, but this perception is no longer derived from the senses. The perceived world may resemble the world the person inhabits while awake, but that perception does not come from the senses either. The "astral" body and "plane" is made by the ability of the human brain to create fully convincing realms even in the absence of sensory information, as witnessed by each of us every night in our dreams.

"The practice of Rising on the Planes is of such importance that special attention must be paid to it. It is part of the essential technique of Magick. Instruction in this practice has been given with such conciseness in *Liber O*, that one cannot do better than quote verbatim (the 'previous experiment' referred to in the first sentence is the ordinary astral journey.)"—"The previous experiment has little value, and leads to few results of importance. But it is susceptible of a development which merges into a form of Dharana —concentration—and as such may lead to the very highest ends. The principal use of the practice in the last chapter is to familiarise the student with every kind of obstacle and every kind of delusion, so that he may be perfect master of every idea that may arise in his brain, to dismiss it, to transmute it, to cause it instantly to obey his will."[31]

> It is of the utmost importance to the "Clairvoyant" or "traveller in the fine body" to be able to find his way to any desired plane, and operate therein as its ruler.
> The Neophyte of A∴A∴ is examined most strictly in this practice before he is passed to the degree of Zelator.

---

[30] *Ibid.*
[31] *Ibid.*, Ch. XVIII, Sec. III.

In "Rising on the Planes" one must usually pass clear through the Astral to the Spiritual. Some will be unable to do this. The "fine body" which is good enough to subsist on lower planes, a shadow among shadows, will fail to penetrate the higher strata. It requires a great development of this body, and an intense infusion of the highest spiritual constituents of man, before he can pierce the veils. The constant practice of Magick is the best preparation possible. Even though the human consciousness fail to reach the goal, the consciousness of the fine body itself may do so, wherefore whoso travels in that body on a subsequent occasion may be found worthy; and its success will react favourably on the human consciousness, and increase its likelihood of success in its next magical operation.

Similarly, the powers gained in this way will strengthen the magician in his mediation-practices. His Will becomes better able to assist the concentration, to destroy the mental images which disturb it, and to reject the lesser rewards of that practice which tempt, and too often stop the progress of, the mystic.[32]

"The task of consciously classifying and interpreting the phenomena in the Spirit Vision (in contradistinction to optical vision) is one of the chief duties undertaken by the Adeptus Minor, that is to say, of an individual who has passed through the grade of $5°=6^{\square}$. . . . And in another part of the [Golden Dawn cipher] manuscript already referred to it is entitled 'The Task undertaken by the Adeptus Minor,' and is lucidly summarized as follows"[33]—

> This then is the task undertaken by the Adeptus Minor:
> To expel from the Sephiroth of the Nephesch the usurpation of the Evil Sephiroth.
> To equally balance the action of the Sephiroth of the Ruach and those of the Nephesch.
> To prevent the Lower Will and Human Consciousness from falling into and usurping the place of the Automatic Consciousness.
> To render the King of the Body (the Lower Will) obedient and anxious to execute the commands of the Higher Will; so that he be neither a usurper of the faculties of the Higher, nor a Sensual Despot, but an initiated ruler and an anointed King, the Vice-Roy and representative of the Higher Will (because inspired thereby in his Kingdom which is the Man).
> Then shall it happen that the Higher Will, *i.e.*, the Lower Genius, shall descend into the Royal Habitation, so that the Higher Will and the Lower Will shall be as one, and the Higher Genius shall descend into the Kether of the Man, bringing with him the tremendous illumination of his Angelic Nature; and the man shall become what was said of Enoch: "And Chanokh made himself to walk for ever close with the essence of the

---

[32] *Ibid.*, Sec. II.
[33] *The Temple of Solomon the King*, Part II, "The Seer."

Elohim, and he existed not apart, seeing that the Elohim took possession of his being."[34]

"The obvious practical task of the magician is then to discover what his will really is, so that he may do it in this manner, and he can best accomplish this by the practices of *Liber Thisharb* (see *Equinox* I, VII, 105) or such others as may from one time to another be appointed. It should not be perfectly simple for everybody to understand the Message of the Master Therion. Thou must (1) Find out what is thy Will, (2) Do that Will with (*a*) one-pointedness, (*b*) detachment, (*c*) peace. Then, and then only, art thou in harmony with the Movement of Things, thy will part of, and therefore equal to, the Will of God. And since the will is but the dynamic aspect of the self, and since two different selves could not possess identical wills; then, if thy will be God's will, *Thou art That*."[35]

We found that both Ontology and Science, approaching the question of reality from entirely different standpoints, and pursuing their researches by entirely different methods, had yet arrived at an identical "impasse." And the general conclusion was that there could be no reality in any intellectual concept of any kind, that the only reality must lie in direct experience of such a kind that it is beyond the scope of the critical apparatus of our minds. It cannot be subject to the laws of Reason; it cannot be found in the fetters of elementary mathematics; only transfinite and irrational conceptions in that subject can possibly shadow forth the truth in some such paradox as the identity of contradictories. We found further that those states of mind which result from the practice of Yoga are properly called trances, because they actually transcend the conditions of normal thought.

At this point we begin to see an almost insensible drawing together of the path of Yoga which is straight (and in a sense arid) with that of Magick, which may be compared with the Bacchic dance or the orgies of Pan. It suggests that Yoga is ultimately a sublimation of philosophy, even as Magick is a sublimation of science. The way is open for a reconciliation between these lower elements of thought by virtue of their tendency to flower into these higher states beyond thought, in which the two have become one. And that, of course, is Magick; and that, of course, is Yoga.[36]

"Consciousness is a symptom of disease. All that moves well moves without will. All skilfulness, all strain, all intention is contrary to ease. Practice a thousand times, and it becomes difficult; a thousand thousand, and it becomes easy; a thousand thousand times a thousand thousand, and it is no longer Thou that doeth it, but It that doeth itself through thee. Not until then is that which is done well done."[37] As we learn in *Little Essays*

---

[34] *Ibid.*
[35] *Liber II*, as quoted in NC on AL I.40. Emphasis in original.
[36] *Eight Lectures*, Ch. 8, Secs. 2–3.
[37] *The Book of Lies*, Ch. 32.

Toward Truth, "all Magick is useful to produce Trance; for (α) it trains the mind in the discipline necessary to Yoga; (β) it exalts the spirit to the impersonal and divine sublimity which is the first condition of success; (γ) it enlarges the scope of the mind, assuring it full mastery of every subtler plane of Nature, thus affording it adequate material for ecstatic consummation of the Eucharist of Existence."[38]

"At first the victory often comes by trick of mind; extending subject or object, as the case may be, by an effort to escape reality, one seems for a moment to have defeated the Equation; but the clouds regather as the mind recovers its equilibrium. Thus, one invents some 'Heaven,' defining it arbitrarily as free from sorrow: only to find, on exact examination, that its conditions are the same as those of 'Earth.' Nor is there any rational issue from this hell of thought. The transcending of the Trance of Sorrow is to be made by means of such other trances as the Higher Beatific Vision, the Trance of Wonder, and others, even the Trance called the Universal Joke, though this last is thereunto strangely akin! . . . to the normal or dualistic consciousness it is precisely the shadows 'which pass and are done' which constitute perceptibly. . . . The Whole is Infinite Perfection, and so is each Unit thereof. To transcend the Trance of Sorrow it is thus sufficient to cancel the subject of the contemplation by marrying it to its equal and opposite in imagination."[39]

"We may also pursue the analytical method, and resolve the complex which appears Sorrow into its atoms. Each event of it is a sublime and joyous act of Love; or the synthetical method, proceeding from the part to the Whole, with a similar result. And any one of the movements of the mind is (with assiduity and enthusiasm) capable of transforming the Trance of Sorrow itself into the cognate Trance attributed to Understanding, the Trance of Wonder."[40] The "Trance of Wonder, which pertains to the Grade of a Master of the Temple, and is a sort of complete understanding of the organism of the universe, and an ecstatic adoration of its marvel. This Trance is very much higher than the Beatific Vision, for always in the latter it is the heart—the Phren—which is involved; in the former it is the Nous, the divine intelligence of man, whereas the heart is only the centre of the intellectual and moral faculties."[41]

The *New Comment* on AL I.58 explicates the "unimaginable joys" given by Nuit as "principally (1) the Beatific Vision, in which Beauty is constantly present to the recipient of Her grace, together with a calm and unutterable joy; (2) the Vision of Wonder, in which the whole Mystery of the Universe is constantly understood and admired for its Ingenium and Wisdom. (1) is referred to Tiphereth, the Grade of Adept; (2) to Binah, the grade of Master of the Temple. The certainty concerning death is conferred by the Magical Memory, and various Experiences without which Life is unintelligible. 'Peace unutterable' is given by the Trance in which Matter is destroyed; 'rest' by that which finally equilibrates Motion. 'Ecstasy' refers to a Trance

---

[38] *Little Essays Toward Truth*, "Trance."
[39] *Ibid.*, "Sorrow."
[40] *Ibid.*
[41] *Eight Lectures*, Ch. 7, Sec. 16.

which combines these. 'Nor do I demand aught in sacrifice'—the ritual of worship is Samadhi. But see later, verse 61."

In Buddhism, recollection of previous lives—a power possessed by a Buddha—gives direct knowledge of the doctrine of "no-self," or *Anattā*. By casting his mind back over innumerable, previous lifetimes, a Buddha is able to verify in his own experience that there is no unchanging self, constantly reincarnating into different bodies, but rather a constant process of change and chain of causation.[42] According to Crowley, "Whom Men call Gautama, or Siddartha, or The Buddha, was a Magus of Our Holy Order. And His Word was ANATTA; for the Root of His whole Doctrine was that there is no Atman, or Soul, as Men ill translate it, meaning a Substance incapable of Change. Thus, He, like Lao-tze, based all upon a Movement, instead of a fixed Point. And His Way of Truth was Analysis, made possible by great Intention of the Mind toward itself, and that well fortified by certain tempered Rigour of Life. And He most thoroughly explored and Mapped out the Fastnesses of the Mind, and gave the Keys of its Fortresses into the Hand of Man. But of all this the Quintessence is in this one Word Anatta, because this is not only the foundation and the Result of his whole Doctrine, but the Way of its Work."[43]

"We may now consider whether, in view of the final identification of these two elements [of Magick and Yoga] in their highest, there may not be something more practical than sympathy in their lower elements—I mean mutual assistance. I am glad to think that the Path of the Wise has become much smoother and shorter than it was when I first trod it; for this very reason that the old antinomies of Magick and Yoga have been completely resolved. . . . The practices of Yoga are almost essential to success in Magick—at least I may say from my own experience that it made all the difference in the world to my magical success, when I had been thoroughly grounded in the hard drill of Yoga. But I feel absolutely certain that I should never have obtained success in Yoga in so short a time as I did had I not spent the previous three years in the daily practice of magical methods. . . . Of course, nobody understands better than I do that, although nobody can do your work for you, it is possible to make use—to a certain very limited extent—of other people's experience, and the Great Order which I have the honour to serve has appointed what I think you will agree is a very satisfactory and practical curriculum."[44]

"It is explained in *Liber 418* that: 'The man of earth is the adherent. The lover giveth his life unto the work among men. The hermit goeth solitary, and giveth only of his light unto men.' Thus we have in the Order, the Mystic, the Magician, and the Devotee. These correspond closely to the Nuit–Hadit–Ra-Hoor-Khuit Triad."[45] In both Hinduism and Buddhism, uniting the Tāntrika with his chosen deity uses mediation and ritual practices. In Hindu Tantra, these practices are graded into three types, corresponding to the three classes of practitioners: the animal, the heroic,

---

[42] Flood 2004.
[43] *Liber Aleph*, "De Gautama."
[44] *Eight Lectures*, Ch. 8, Secs. 4, 8, 23.
[45] NC on AL I.40.

and the divine. In the animal, the *guna*, or quality, of *tamas*, or "inertia," predominates; in the heroic, the quality of *rajas*, or "activity"; in the divine, *sattva*, or "harmony." In the divine practitioner, the rituals are internal, and it is the Sattvic Tāntrika alone who can attain the object of the rituals and merge with the Godhead.[46]

"Our system of initiation is to be triune. For the outer, tests of labour, pain, etc. For the inner, intellectual tests. For the elect of the A∴A∴, spiritual tests. Further the Order is not to hold Lodges, but to have a chain-system."[47] Now, Crowley may have written this before joining the quasi-Masonic Ordo Templi Orientis, but he was already a long-time regular Freemason, and as late as 1943, two decades after taking over the O.T.O., he contends that, "the idea that you should meet other members first is quite impossible. Even after affiliation, you would not meet anyone unless it were necessary for you to work in cooperation with them. I am afraid you have still got the idea that the Great Work is a tea-party. Contact with other students only means that you criticize their hats, and then their morals; and I am not going to encourage this. Your work is not anybody else's; and undirected chatter is the worst poisonous element in human society."[48]

Freemasonry was a very significant influence on occultism in the modern era, essentially transforming it from a largely solitary to a group activity, complete with graded initiations. Many Western occultists think they are part of a chain going back to Jesus and his disciples or even to pre-Christian mystery religions, but their rituals, degree structures, and so on, have been directly or indirectly influenced by Freemasonry. This transformation was brought on by the fact that Freemasons incorporated Hermetic, Rosicrucian, and related ideas and symbols into their initiation rituals, giving them a more ceremonial, hierarchical structure, and by the fact that Freemasons founded other, more explicitly esoteric fraternities, such as the 18th-century Order of the Golden Rosicrucians. In the following century, the Societas Rosicruciana was founded, and although its primary mission was to study Masonic symbolism and its esoteric nature, it also focussed on the esoteric traditions of the world in general. Like the Golden Rosicrucians, membership of the Societas Rosicruciana was only open to Master Masons, by invitation, but it gave birth to the Hermetic Order of the Golden Dawn and its various offshoots.[49]

Already in the early oral tradition of the Upanishads, the *guru-chela* or teacher-student relationship had evolved into a fundamental component of Hinduism. The term *Upaniṣad* itself derives from the Sanskrit words *upa*,

---

[46] Flood 2006. Similarly, in the Neoplatonic Academy of late antiquity, the students would first be required to master texts in which the subject matter was primarily ethical (e.g. Plato's *Republic* or *Phaedo*), to promote their souls' initial purification; they would then progress to texts that were cosmological (e.g. *Timaeus*), pointing to a transcendent cause of the world's order, to learn to transcend the physical world; and finally, they would proceed to texts that were theological (e.g. the *Parmenides* or *Philebus*), to ascend to the contemplation of "the One." This threefold gradation is also the organizing principle of Plotinus' *Enneads*, as edited by his student Porphyry.
[47] OC on AL I.50.
[48] *MWT*, Introduction. (Letter No. C, April 30, 1943.)
[49] Millar 2013.

"near," ni, "down," and ṣad, "to sit"—thus meaning "sitting down near" a teacher to receive instruction. The relationship between Krishna and Arjuna in the *Bhagavad-Gītā* portion of the *Mahābhārata*, and between Rāma and Hanumān in the *Rāmāyaṇa*, are a couple of examples. In the Upanishads, gurus and disciples appear in a variety of guises and settings, for instance, we have a teenage boy being taught by Yama, Lord of Death, and a husband answering his wife's questions about immortality. Other times, the sages are female, and the instruction may be sought by kings. As Crowley writes, "Before commencing any Yoga practice, according to every Hindu book upon this subject, it is first necessary to find a Guru, a teacher, to whom the disciple (Chela) must entirely devote himself."[50]

"A Guru is as necessary in Yoga as a Music master is in Music."[51] Crowley quotes Chapter III of the *Shiva Samhita*: "11. Only the knowledge imparted by a Guru is powerful and useful; otherwise it becomes fruitless, weak and very painful. 12. He who attains knowledge by pleasing his Guru with every attention, readily obtains success therein. 13. There is not the least doubt that Guru is father, Guru is mother, and Guru is God even: and as such, he should be served by all, with their thought, word and deed."[52] Throughout his youth, Crowley was mostly taught by private tutors—in both mystical and mundane subjects—and even at Cambridge, "he felt himself to be his own master, refused to attend Chapel, Lectures or Hall, and was wisely left alone to work out his own salvation by his tutor, the late Dr. A. W. Verrall."[53] In the Introduction to *Magick Without Tears*, Crowley writes: "It is of the first importance that you should understand my personal position. It is not actually wrong to regard me as a teacher, but it is certainly liable to mislead; fellow-student, or, if you like, fellow-sufferer, seems a more appropriate definition."

> Nuit instructs 666 in his duties as Hierophant. Nuit instructs me now in my Work of training men to become Masters and Adepts by putting them through ordeals. I am to purge their brute souls by fire—to burn out their grossness by kindling the Lust of the Spirit within them. Their minds are to be tested by trials of mind; and those rare souls marked from the hour of birth to attain the lofty summits to the Mountain of Magick must be made perfect by ordeals suited to their natures. Yet by my wit I am bidden to devise such means as may attain all three objects in a single Test, in the manner explained elsewhere.
>
> Three types of Ordeal for three parts of the Soul. Regulations of the Order of A∴A∴. Stars—that is, men whose souls shed Light—must not be grouped at random in the Order, but each must have his own proper place and orbit. Sometimes it may be wise to form a system of stars as are by Nature fit to work in groups: but even so, keep each unit intent on its own proper Going, let it not know, more than needs must, the Way of

---

[50] *The Temple of Solomon the King*, Part IV, "The Yogas."
[51] *Ibid.*, fn.
[52] As quoted in *ibid.*
[53] *The Equinox of the Gods*, "Genesis Libri AL," Ch. I.

other Stars and Systems, lest falling from its own Way, it follow after others, or jostle them, and confuse thus the Order of Heaven.[54]

"There is also a rule that the Members of the A∴A∴ shall not know each other officially, save only each Member his superior who introduced him and his inferior whom he has himself introduced. This rule has been relaxed, and a 'Grand Neophyte' appointed to superintend all Members of the Order of the G.D. The real object of the rule was to prevent Members of the same Grade working together and so blurring each other's individuality; also to prevent work developing into social intercourse."[55]— "For every One hath his own Path and his own Law, and there is no Art in Magick but to seek out that Path, and that Law, that he may pursue the one by the Right Use of the other. It shall be that one cometh unto thee, desiring Amen-Ra (I speak in a Figure or Exemplar), another Asi, a third Hoor-Pa-Kraat; or again, one seeketh Instruction in Obeah, and his Fellow in Wanga; and of all these not one in Ten Thousand shall be aware of his True Way. For albeit our Last Step is One for all, yet his Next Step is particular to each. Therefore is the Preparation of a Student that seeketh Our Holy Order of A∴A∴ most general, informing his Mind of all known Methods, so that his Will may select among these by Instinct: then after, as a Probationer, he practiseth those which he hath preferred, and by the Examination of his Record after the Period appointed thou mayst have Wisdom concerning him, to confirm him in those Ways which are shewed thereby to be germane to his True Nature."[56]

The plain English still discusses the technique of initiation. The "fool", is one such as described in my note on verse 57. The vain, soft, frivolous, idle, mutable sot will make nothing either of this Book, or of my comment thereon. But this fool is the child Harpocrates, the "Babe in the Egg", the innocent not yet born, in silence awaiting his hour to come forth into light. He is then the uninitiated man, and he has four ordeals to pass before he is made perfect. These ordeals are now to be described.

The "Tree of Life" in the Qabalah represents ten spheres arranged in three pillars, the central one of these containing four, and the others three each. These spheres are attributed to certain numbers, planets, metals, and many other groups of things; indeed all things may be referred to one or other of them. (See *Book 4* Part III and *Liber 777*). The four ordeals now to be described represent the ascent of the aspirant from the tenth and lowest of these spheres, which refers to the Earth, unregenerate and confused, in which the aspirant is born. He riseth in the first ordeal to the sphere called the Foundation, numbered 9, and containing, among other ideas, those of the generative organs, Air, the

---

[54] DC on AL I.50.
[55] *One Star in Sight*, Sec. 10.
[56] *Liber Aleph*, "De prudentia ordinis A∴A∴."

Moon, and Silver. Its secret Truth is that Stability is identical with Change; of this we are reminded by the fact that any multiple of 9 has 9 for the sum of its digits.

The initiate will now perceive that the sum of the motions of his mind is zero, while, below their moon-like phases and their Air-like divinations, the sex-consciousness abides untouched, the true Foundation of the Temple of his body, the Root of the Tree of Life that grows from Earth to Heaven. This Book is now to him "as silver." He sees it pure, white and shining, the mirror of his own being that this ordeal has purged of its complexes. To reach this sphere he has had to pass through a path of darkness where the Four Elements seem to him to be the Universe entire. For how should he know that they are no more that the last of the 22 segments of the Snake that is twined on the Tree?

Assailed by gross phantoms of matter, unreal and unintelligible, his ordeal is of terror and darkness. He may pass only by favour of his own silent God, extended and exalted within him by virtue of his conscious act in affronting the ordeal.

The next sphere reached by the aspirant is named Beauty, numbered 6, and referred to the heart, to the Sun, and to Gold. Here he is called an "Adept". The secret Truth in this place is that God is Man, symbolized by the Hexagram, in which two triangles are interlaced.

In the last sphere he learnt that his Body was the Temple of the Rosy Cross, that is, that it was given him as a place wherein to perform the Magical Work of uniting the oppositions in his Nature. Here he is taught that his Heart is the Centre of Light. It is not dark, mysterious, hollow, obscure even to himself, but his soul is to dwell there, radiating Light on the six spheres which surround it; these represent the various powers of his mind. This Book now appears to him as Gold; it is the perfect metal, the symbol of the Sun itself. He sees God everywhere therein.

To this sphere hath the aspirant come by the Path called Temperance, shot as an arrow from a Rainbow. He hath beheld the Light, but only in division. Nor had he won to this sphere except by Temperance, under which name we mask the art of pouring freely forth the whole of our Life, to the last spilth of our blood, yet losing never the least drop thereof.

Now once again the adept aspires and comes to the sphere called the Crown numbered 1, referred to the God Ra-Hoor-Khuit himself in man, to the Beginning of Whirling Motions, and the First Mode of Matter. (See *Liber 777*, the *Equinox*, and *Book 4* for these attributions.) Its secret Truth is that Earth is Heaven as Heaven is Earth, and shows the aspirant to himself as being a star. All that seemed to him reality is not even to be deemed illusion, but all one light infusing star and star. The Many, each of them, are the One; each individual, no twain alike, yet all identical; this he knows and is, for now the Word hath lightened his soul's girders. (The logic of the Ruach—the normal intellect—is transcended in Spiritual Experience. It is, evidently, impossible to "explain" how this can be.)

In the Number 6 he saw God interlocked with man, two trinities made one; but here he knows that there was never but one.

Thus now this Book is "stones of precious water"; its Light is not the borrowed light of gold, but is shed through the Book itself, clear-sparkling, flashed from its facets. Each phrase is a diamond; each is diverse, yet all identical. In each the one Light laughs!

Now to this sphere came he by the Path called the High Priestess; She is his Silent Self, virgin beyond all veils, made free to teach him, by virtue of this third ordeal wherein, passing through the abyss, he has stripped from him every rag of falsehood, his last complexes, even his phantasy that he called "I". And so he knows at last now the soiled harlot's dress was mere disguise; naked in Moonlight shines the maiden Body!

Beyond the one, how shall he pass on? What is this One, which is in every place the Centre of All? Indeed the logic-girders of our souls need lightening, if we would win to freedom of such Truth as this!

Now in the "stones of precious water" the Light leapt clear indeed, but they were not themselves that Light. This sphere of the One is indeed Ra-Hoor-Khuit; is not our Crowned and Conquering Child the source of Light? Nay, he is finite form of Unity, child of two married infinities; and in this last ordeal the aspirant must go beyond even his Star, finding therein the core thereof Hadit, and losing it also in the Body of Nuith.

Here is no Path that he may tread, for all is equally everywhere; nor is there any sphere to attain, for measure is now no more.

There are no words to make known the Way; this only is said, that to him that hath passed through this fourth ordeal this Book is as "ultimate sparks". No more do they reflect or transmit the Light; they themselves are the original, the not-to-be-analysed Light, of the "intimate fire" of Hadit! He shall see the Book as it is, as a shower of the Seed of the Stars![57]

Commenting on AL I.51, Crowley writes: "It seems to me as if this refers to the ascetic life, commonly considered as an essential condition of participation in these mysteries. The answer is that 'there are means and means', implying that no one rule is essential. This is in harmony with our general interpretation of the Law; it has as many rules as there are individuals."[58] Crowley felt he had "proved that the strict letter of the law of Chastity had no more to do with the ultimate success of attainment than refusing to work on a Sabbath had to do with a free pass to the Celestial regions, unless every act of chastity was computed and performed in a magical manner, each act becoming as it were a link in one great chain, a formula in one great operation, an operation not leading to Chastity, the symbol, but beyond Chastity to the essence itself—namely the Âtman, —Adonai. Further he proved to his own satisfaction that, though absolute

---

[57] NC on AL III.63–67.
[58] NC on AL I.51.

Chastity might mean salvation to one man, inducing in the lecherous a speedy concentration, it might be the greatest hindrance to another, who was by nature chaste."[59]

> The reason for this is very simple. Take for example a glutton who lives for his palate and his stomach; he is always longing for tasty foods and spends his whole life seeking them. Let us now substitute the symbol of the Augœides or Âtman for that of food and drink, let him every time he thinks of food and drink push the thought aside and in its place contemplate his Higher Self, and the result is a natural invocation of the Âtman, Augœides, or Higher Self. If the aspirant be an artist let him do the same with his art; if a musician, with his music; if a poet, with his verses and rhymes. For the best foundation to build upon is always to be found upon that which a man *loves best.* It is no good asking a glutton who does not care a row of brass pins for music, to turn music into a magical formula, neither is it of the slightest use to impress upon a clean-minded individual the necessity of living a chaste life. It is like tapping Samson on the shoulder, just after he has carried the pates of Gaza on to the top of the hill before Hebron, and saying: "My good boy, if you ever intend becoming strong, the first thing you must do is to buy a pair of my four pound dumb-bells and my sixpenny book on physical culture."[60]

In his own words, Crowley "realized that there were in this world she-mules as well as she-asses, and that though the former would never foal in spite of all the stallions of Moultan, the latter seldom failed to do so after having been for a few minutes in the presence of a Margate jackass. Discarding Chastity (Brahmachârya)—a good purgative for the prurient—he wrote in its place the word 'Health.' Do not worry about this code and that law, about the jibber of this crank or the jabber of that faddist. To hell with ethical pigs and prigs alike. *Do what you like*; but in the name of your own Higher Self wilfully *do no injury to your own body or mind* by over indulgence or under indulgence. Discover your normal appetite; satisfy it. Do not become a glutton, and do not become a nut-cracking skindlewig."[61]

> Also, asceticism is all right when it is the proper means of attaining some special end. It is when it produces eructations of spiritual pride, and satisfied vanity, that it is poisonous. The Greek word means an athlete; and the training of an athlete is not mortification of the body. Nor is there any rule which covers all circumstances. When men go "stale" a few days before the race, they are "taken off training," and fed with champagne. But that is part of the training. Observe, too, that all men go "stale" sooner or later; training is abnormal, and must be stopped as soon as its object is attained. Even so, it too often strains vital

---

[59] *The Temple of Solomon the King*, op. cit., "The Writings of Truth."
[60] *Ibid.*, fn. Emphasis in original.
[61] *Ibid.* Emphasis in original.

organs, especially the heart and lungs, so that few rowing "Blues" live to be 50. But worst of all is the effect on the temper!

When it is permanent, and mistaken for a "Virtue," it poisons the very soil of the soul. The vilest weeds spring up; cruelty, narrow-mindedness, arrogance—everything mean and horrible flowers in those who "Mortify the flesh." Incidentally, such ideas spawn the "Black Brother." The complete lack of humour, the egomaniac conceit, self-satisfaction, absence of all sympathy for others, the craving to pass their miseries on to more sensible people by persecuting them: these traits are symptomatic.[62]

In Book I, Chapter V of *The Key of the Mysteries*, Éliphas Lévi describes the "Fluidic Phantoms and Their Mysteries" thus: "Theurgy evoked them, and the Qabalah recognized them under the name of elementary spirits. They were not spirits, however, for they were mortal. They were fluidic coagulations which one could destroy by dividing them. There were a sort of animated mirages, imperfect emanations of human life. The traditions of Black Magic say that they were born owing to the celibacy of Adam. Paracelsus says that the vapours of the blood of hysterical women people the air with phantoms; and these ideas are so ancient, that we find traces of them in Hesiod, who expressly forbids that linen, stained by a pollution of any sort, should be dried before a fire. Persons who are obsessed by phantoms are usually exalted by too rigorous celibacy, or weakened by excesses. Fluidic phantoms are the abortions of the vital light; they are plastic media without body and without spirit, born from the excesses of the spirit and the disorders of the body."[63]

According to Crowley, "Lilith is etymologically 'The Woman of Night'; but is diversely described by different authorities. To one she is, 'from the head to the navel, a woman—from the navel to the feet of her, a man'. To another, 'lovely shape that concealeth a black monkey, even as a figure that draweth with her hands small images of men down into hell' (*Liber Ararita* II, 10). She is also the 'first wife of Adam' i.e. the succubus who visits in their sleep those boys and men who have not previously purified themselves by Right Coitus. The whole world of demons was in fact created (according to Rabbinical tradition) by the nocturnal pollutions of Adam. This is a true parable. For every sexual act produces its natural effect on all planes. All forms of spiritual experience may be obtained in this manner, according to the Magical Knowledge and Skill of the Operator. And there is always a Child begotten on some plane or other, as the conditions of the experiment decide."[64]

---

[62] *MWT*, Ch. L.
[63] *Cf.* also *Liber DCCCXI*, Sec. II: "That some form of this doctrine has been generally accepted is shown in the prohibitions of all religions. Sanctity has been assumed to depend on chastity, and chastity has nearly always been interpreted as abstinence. But I doubt whether the relation is so simple as this would imply; for example, I find in myself that manifestations of mental creative force always concur with some abnormal condition of the physical powers of generation. But it is not the case that long periods of chastity, on the one hand, or excess of orgies, on the other, are favourable to its manifestation or even to its formation."
[64] *Liber 418*, 3rd Aethyr, fn.

The fourth is the Assiatic world, עולם העשיה, Olahm ha-Assiah, the world of action, called also the world of shells, עולם הקליפות, Olahm ha-Qliphoth, which is this world of matter, made up of the grosser elements of the other three. In it is also the abode of the evil spirits, which are called "the shells" by the Qabalah, קליפות, Qliphoth, material shells. The devils are also divided into ten classes, and have suitable habitations. (See Tables in *777*).

The demons are the grossest and most deficient of all forms. Their ten degrees answer to the decad of the Sephiroth, but in inverse ratio, as darkness and impurity increase with the descent of each degree. The two first are nothing but absence of visible form and organisation. The third is the abode of darkness. Next follow seven Hells occupied by those demons which represent incarnate human vices, and torture those who have given themselves up to those vices in earth-life. Their prince is סמאל, Samael, the angel of poison and death. His wife is the harlot, or woman of whoredom, אשת זנונים, Isheth Zanunim; and united they are called the beast, חיוא, Chioa. Thus the infernal trinity is completed which is, so to speak, the averse and caricature of the supernal Creative One. Samael is considered to be identical with Satan.[65]

"סמאל, Satan so-called, but really only Samael, the accuser of the brethren, unpopular with the Rabbis because their consciences were not clear. Samael fulfils a most useful function; he is scepticism, which accuses intellectually; conscience, which accuses morally; and even that spiritual accuser upon the Threshold, without whom the Sanctuary might be profaned. We must defeat him, it is true; but how should we abuse and blame him, without abuse and blame of Him that set him there?"[66] The "immense class of devotional apparitions" from Vishnu, Christ, and Jehovah to the Virgin Mary "are nearly always tainted with sexuality, and are excessively dangerous from this cause. 'Dirt is matter in the wrong place,' and to mix, consciously or unconsciously, either morality or immorality with religion is dirty; and dirt makes disease. The victim becomes a fanatic at the best, at the worst and most frequent a driveller. Of a lower type are the loves of Magi and invoked elementals. As Lévi says, 'the love of the Magus for such beings is insensate, and may destroy him.' It surely will, if he beware not in time. Higher again because more purely formless and for this reason truer to the Vedana type are the ecstasies of joy and agony experienced by such men as Luther, Fox, Molinos, and others. Professor William James treats most adequately of this matter in his 'Varieties of Religious Experience.'"[67]

"A man who is normally an 'all-round good sort' often becomes intolerable when he gets rid of his collection of vices; he is swept into monomania by the spiritual pride which had been previously restrained by countervailing passions. Again, there is a worse draught when an ill-fitting

---

[65] *The Temple of Solomon the King*, Part V.
[66] *Ibid.*
[67] *The Psychology of Hashish*, Sec. XIV.

door is closed than when it stands open. It is not as necessary to protect his mother and his cattle from Don Juan as it was from the Hermits of the Thebaid."—"The Magician must therefore take the utmost care in the matter of purification, *firstly*, of himself, *secondly*, of his instruments, *thirdly*, of the place of working. Ancient Magicians recommended a preliminary purification of from three days to many months. During this period of training they took the utmost pains with diet. They avoided animal food, lest the elemental spirit of the animal should get into their atmosphere. They practised sexual abstinence, lest they should be influenced in any way by the spirit of the wife. Even in regard to the excrements of the body they were equally careful; in trimming the hair and nails, they ceremonially destroyed the severed portion."[68]

The footnote reads: "Such destruction should be by burning or other means which produces a complete chemical change. In so doing care should be taken to bless and liberate the native elemental of the thing burnt. This maxim is of universal application." The description continues: "They fasted, so that the body itself might destroy anything extraneous to the bare necessity of its existence. They purified the mind by special prayers and conservations. They avoided the contamination of social intercourse, especially the conjugal kind; and their servitors were disciples specially chosen and consecrated for the work. In modern times our superior understanding of the essentials of this process enables us to dispense to some extent with its external rigours; but the internal purification must be even more carefully performed. We may eat meat, provided that in doing so we affirm that we eat it in order to strengthen us for the special purpose of our proposed invocation."[69]

"In an Abbey of Thelema we 'say Will' before a meal. The formula is as follows. 'Do what thou wilt shall be the whole of the Law.' 'What is thy Will?' 'It is my will to eat and drink.' 'To what end?' 'That my body may be fortified thereby.' 'To what end?' 'That I may accomplish the Great Work.' 'Love is the law, love under will.' 'Fall to!' This may be adapted as a monologue. One may also add the inquiry 'What is the Great Work?' and answer appropriately, when it seems useful to specify the nature of the Operation in progress at the time. The point is to seize every occasion of bringing every available force to bear upon the objective of the assault. It does not matter what the force is (by any standard of judgment) so long as it plays its proper part in securing the success of the general purpose. Thus, even laziness may be used to increase our indifference to interfering impulses, or envy to counteract carelessness. See *Liber CLXXV, Equinox* I, VII, p. 37. This is especially true, since the forces are destroyed by the process. That is, one destroys a complex which in itself is 'evil' and puts its elements to the one right use."[70]

"By thus avoiding those actions which might excite the comment of our neighbours we avoid the graver dangers of falling into spiritual pride."[71] As

---

[68] *MITAP*, Ch. XIII. Emphasis in original.
[69] *Ibid.*
[70] *Ibid.*, fn.
[71] *Ibid.*

always, "Equilibrium is above all things necessary, and even in these early stages, the mind of the aspirant should be entirely free from the obsession of either ungratified or over-gratified appetites. Neither Lust nor Chastity should solely occupy him; for as Krishna says: 'Verily Yoga is not for him who eateth too much, nor who abstaineth to excess, nor who is too much addicted to sleep, nor even to wakefulness, O Arjuna. Yoga killeth out all pain for him who is regulated in eating and amusement, regulated in performing actions, regulated in sleeping and waking.'[72] This balancing of what is vulgarly known as Virtue and Vice,"—"Or more correctly as the Buddhist puts its—skilfulness and unskilfulness."—"and which the Yogi Philosophy does not always appreciate, is illustrated still more forcibly in that illuminating work,"[73] *Konx Om Pax*:

> As above so beneath! said Hermes the thrice greatest. *The laws of the physical world are precisely paralleled by those of the moral and intellectual sphere.* To the prostitute I prescribe a course of training by which she shall comprehend the holiness of sex. Chastity forms part of that training, and I should hope to see her one day a happy wife and mother. To the prude equally I prescribe a course of training by which she shall comprehend the holiness of sex. Unchastity forms part of that training, and I should hope to see her one day a happy wife and mother.
>
> To the bigot I commend a course of Thomas Henry Huxley; to the infidel a practical study of ceremonial magic. Then, when the bigot has knowledge of the infidel faith, each may follow without prejudice his natural inclination; for he will no longer plunge into his former excesses.
>
> So also she who was a prostitute from native passion may indulge with safety in the pleasure of love; and she who was by nature cold may enjoy a virginity in no wise marred by her disciplinary course of unchastity. But the one will understand and love the other.[74]

"Once and for all do not forget that nothing in this world is permanently good or evil; and, so long as it appears to be so, then remember that the fault is the seer's and not in the thing seen, and that the seer is still in an unbalanced state."[75] Crowley bids us never to forget the words of William Blake from *The Marriage of Heaven and Hell*, "Those who restrain desire do so because theirs is weak enough to be restrained; and the restrainer or reason usurps its place and governs the unwilling." We are to not restrain our desires, "but equilibrate them," for "He who desires but acts not, breeds pestilence." Crowley finishes with a quote from Blake's *Visions of the Daughters of Albion*: "Arise, and drink your bliss, for everything that lives is holy."

"That quality in ourselves which we call zeal for virtue," observes Lévi, "is often nothing but a masterful secret self-love, a jealousy in disguise, and a proud instinct of contradiction. 'When we see manifest disorders and

---

[72] *Bhagavad-Gītā*, vi.16, 17.
[73] *The Temple of Solomon the King*, Part IV, "The Yogas."
[74] "Thien Tao," as quoted in *ibid*. Emphasis added.
[75] *The Temple of Solomon the King*, loc. cit.

scandalous sinners,' say mystical theologians, 'let us believe that God is submitting them to greater tests than those with which He tries us, that certainly, or at least very probably, we are not as good as they are, and should do much worse in their place.'"[76] As Crowley puts it in *Liber Aleph*, "watch heedfully the Fault of another, that thou mayst correct it in thyself. For if it were not in thee, thou couldst not perceive it or understand it."[77] In Lévi's estimation, "It is not the hashish intoxication which was useful to the knavery of the Old Man of the Mountain"—a reference to the Ismaili sect of the Assassins and its fabled leader—"it is a dream without sleep, an hallucination without madness, a reasoned and willed vision, a real creation of intelligence and faith."[78]

True Religion is intoxication, in a sense. We are told elsewhere to intoxicate the innermost, not the outermost; but I think that the word "wine" should be taken in its widest sense as meaning that which brings out the soul. Climate, soil, and race change conditions; each man or woman must find and choose the fit intoxicant. Thus hashish in one or the other of its forms seems to suit the Moslem, to go with dry heat; opium is right for the Mongol; whiskey for the dour temperament and damp cold climate of the Scot.

Sex-expression, too, depends on climate and so on, so that we must interpret the Law to suit a Socrates, a Jesus, and a Burton, or a Marie Antoinette and a de Lamballe, as well as our own Don Juans and Faustines.

With this expansion, to the honour and glory of Them, of Their Natures, we acclaim therefore our helpers, Dionysus, Aphrodite, Apollo, Wine, Woman, and Song.

Intoxication, that is, ecstasy, is the key to Reality. It is explained in "Energized Enthusiasm" (*Equinox* I, IX) that there are three Gods whose function is to bring the Soul to the Realization of its own glory: Dionysus, Aphrodite, Apollo; Wine, Woman, and Song.

The ancients, both in the highest civilizations, as in Greece and Egypt, and in the most primitive savagery, as among the Buriats and the Papuans, were well aware of this, and made their religious ceremonies *orgia*, "Works". Puritan foulness, failing to understand what was happening, degraded the word "orgies" to mean debauches. It is the old story of the Fox who lost his tail. If you cannot do anything, call it impossible; or, if that be evidently absurd, call it wicked![79]

"But the crisis in which fear becomes phobia is the unreasoning aversion, the shuddering of panic, above all, the passionate refusal to learn anything about 'drugs,' to analyse the conditions, still less to face them; and the spasmodic invention of imaginary terrors, as if the real dangers were not enough to serve as a warning. Now why? Surely because in the

---

[76] *The Key of the Mysteries*, Part IV, Ch. II.
[77] "De culpis domi petendis."
[78] *The Key of the Mysteries*, loc. cit., Ch. I.
[79] NC on AL I.63.

subconscious lies an instinct that in these obscure medicines indeed lies the key of some forbidden sanctuary. There is a fascination as irrational and therefore as strong, as the fear. Here is the point at which they link up with sex and religion. Oh, how well nigh almighty is the urgency to him who reads those few great writers who understood the subject from experience: de Quincey, Ludlow, Poe and Baudelaire: into whom burn the pointed parallels between their adventures and those of all the mystics, East and West!"[80]

> Concerning the Use of chemical Agents, and be mindful that thou abuse them not, learn that the Sacrament itself relateth to Spirit, and the Four Elements balanced thereunder in its Perfection. So also thy Lion himself hath a fourfold Menstruum for his Serpents. Now to Fire belong Cocaine, which fortifieth the Will, loosing him from bodily Fatigue, Morphine, which purifieth the Mind, making the Thought safe, and slow, and single, Heroin which partaketh as it seemeth, of the Nature of these twain aforesaid albeit in Degree less notable than either of them, and Alcohol, which is Food, that is, Fuel, for the whole Man. To Water, attribute Hashish and Mescal, for they make Images, and they open the hidden Springs of Pleasure and of Beauty. Morphine, for its Ease, hath also part in Water. Air ruleth Ethyl Oxide, for it is as a Sword, dividing asunder every Part of thee, making easy the Way of Analysis, so that thou comest to learn thyself of what Elements thou art compact. Lastly, of the Nature of Earth are the direct Hypnotics, which operate by Repose, and restore thy Strength by laying thee as a Child in the Arms of the Great Mother, I say rather of Her material and physiological Vicegerent.[81]

"To prepare oneself for such work one should strengthen oneself in every way, so as to be able to 'bear more joy.' This does not imply brute vigour. The nature of rapture is such that the finer it is, the stronger it is. Thus, in making oneself drunk to worship Hadit, one should observe the 'eight and ninety rules of art'. . . . Likewise, in love, excess is not to be attained by violent lust. The artist is the model. One must learn to enjoy every least detail; yet blend them all into one single sublime concept. The same tactics apply to all joyous deeds. The key to success is subtlety."[82] Crowley reminds us, "how all our faults love to disguise themselves as virtues; very often, as what our neighbours call virtues, not what we ourselves think them. We are all ashamed to be ourselves; and this is sheer, stark stultification. For we are ourselves; we cannot get away from it; all our hypocrisies and shams are just as much part of ourselves as what we like to think is the real man. All that we do when we make these pretenses

---

[80] MWT, Ch. LXXVIII.
[81] Liber Aleph, "De medicinis secudum quattuor elementa." Cf., however, Liber DCCCXI, Sec. XIII: "One essential difficulty is dosage. One needs exactly enough; and, as Blake points out, one can only tell what is enough by taking too much. For each man the dose varies enormously; so does it for the same man at different times."
[82] DC on AL II.69–70.

is to set up internal strain and conflict; there is nothing objective in it. Instead of adding to our experience, which is the Great Work, we shut ourselves up in this citadel of civil turmoil; it is the Formula of the Black Brothers."[83]

The Golden Mean is more valuable as the extremes which it summarizes are distant from each other; that is the plain mechanics of the lever. So don't pay too much attention to these remarks; they are no more than the quiet fireside reflections of a man who has spent all his life breaking records. The Golden Mean at its best can only keep you from extravagant blunders; it will never get you anywhere.

The Book of the Law constantly implies a very different policy; listen to its climax-exhortation:

"But exceed! exceed!" (AL II, 71)

Remember that which is written: "Moderate strength rings the bell: great strength returns the penny." It is always the little bit extra that brings home the bacon. It is the last attack that breaks through the enemy position. Water will never boil, however long you keep it at 99°C. You may find that a Pranayama cycle of 10–20–30 brings no result in months; put it up to 10–20–40, and Dhyana comes instantly. When in doubt, push just a little bit harder. You have no means of finding out what are exactly the right conditions for success in any practice; but all practices are alike in one respect; the desired result is in the nature of orgasm.[84]

Indeed, *The Book of the Laws* warns us "not take these words to mean that we should dilute our pleasures. We should not be genteel and dainty. Never forget that all the tricks of art are worse than worthless, unless they spring from strength and passion. The essence of success is the intense desire to beat one's own record as well as the world's in every thing one does. The most fatal fault is to become tired of the task, through having chosen one in which one may become perfect, and sigh for more worlds to conquer."[85] According to the *New Comment*, "It is only necessary to kill out the sense of 'sin', with its false shame and its fear of nature." The postscript asserts that Crowley's "Gnostic Mass is intended to supply this need."[86] It is not men, but "her own sisters who are to punish" a woman "for the crime of denying Her nature, not men who are to redeem her, since . . . it is man's own false sense of guilt, his selfishness, and his cowardice, which originally forced her to blaspheme against herself, and so degraded her in her own eyes, and in his. Let him attend to his own particular business, to redeem himself—he has surely his hands full! Woman will save herself if she be but left alone to do it."[87]

---

[83] *MWT*, Ch. XXXIII.
[84] *Ibid.*
[85] DC on AL II.71.
[86] NC on AL I.62.
[87] NC on AL III.52.

In the past man has bludgeoned Woman into gratifying the lust of her loathed tyrant, and trampled the flower of her own love into the mire; making her rape more beastly by calling her antipathy Chastity, and proving her an unclean thing on the evidence of the torn soiled blossom.

She has had no chance to Love unless she first renounced the respect of society, and found a way to drive the wolf of hunger from her door.

Her chance is come! In any Abbey of Thelema any woman is welcome; there she is free to do her will, and held in honour for the doing. The child of love is a star, even as all are stars; but such an one we specially cherish; it is a trophy of battle fought and won![88]

"She is Śakti, the Teh, the Magical Door between the Tao and the Manifested World. The great Obstacle than is if that Door be locked up. Therefore Our Lady must be symbolized as an Whore. (Note Daleth, the Door = Venus. The Dove; free flowing; all this is linked up in the symbol). Clearly, at last, the Enemy is this Shutting up of things. Shutting the Door is preventing the Operation of Change, i.e., of Love. The objection to Calypso, Circe, Armida, Kundry, and Co. is that one is liable to be shut up in their Gardens. The whole of the [Egyptian] Book of the Dead is a device for opening the closed vehicles, and enabling the Osiris to go in and out at his pleasure. On the other hand, there seems to be a Sealing Up, for a definite period, in order to allow the Change to proceed undisturbed. Thus Earth lies fallow; the womb is closed during gestation; the Osiris is plugged with talismans. But it is vital to consider this as a strictly temporary device; and *to cut out the idea of Eternal Rest*. This Nibbana-idea is the coward—'Mother's Boy' idea; one ought to take a refreshing dip in the Tao, no more. I think this must be brought forward as the Cardinal Point of Our Holy Law. Thus though Nuit cries 'To me!' that is balanced by the Formula of Hadit. 'Come unto me' is a foolish word; for it is I that go."[89]

Crowley cautions his magical son, "Thou knowest how great is the Fame of Witch-Women (old and without Man) to cause Events, although they create nothing. It is this Straitness of the Channel which giveth Force to the Stream. Beware, o my Son, lest thou cling overmuch to this Mode of Magick; for it is lesser than that Other, and if thou neglect That Other, then is thy Danger fearful and imminent, for it is the Edge of the Abyss of Choronzon, where are the lonely Towers of the Black Brothers. Also the Formulation of the Object in the Eagle is by a Species of Intoxication, so that His Nature is of Dream or Delirium, and thus there may be Illusion. For this Cause I deem it not wholly unwise if thou use this Way of Magick chiefly as a Cordial; that is for the Fortifying of thine own Nature."[90] Lévi explains that, "The wand of Circe is the power of fascination which woman possesses; and the changing of the companions of Ulysses into hogs is not a story peculiar to that time. But no metamorphosis may be worked without destruction. To change a

---

[88] NC on AL III.56.
[89] NC on AL III.55. Emphasis in original.
[90] *Liber Aleph*, "De aquilæ Sumenda."

hawk into a dove, one must first kill it, then cut it to pierces, so as to destroy even the least trace of its first form, and then boil it in the magic bath of Medea. Observe how modern hierophants proceed in order to accomplish human regeneration; how, for example, in the Catholic religion, they go to work in order to change a man more or less weak and passionate into a stoical missionary of the Society of Jesus."[91]

The Egyptian Book of the Dead "contains many chapters intended to enable the magical entity of a man who is dead, and so deprived (according to the theory of death then current) of the material vehicle for executing his will, to take on the form of certain animals, such as a golden hawk or a crocodile, and in such form to go about the earth 'taking his pleasure among the living.'"[92] The footnote points to *The Book of Lies*, Chapter 44, or "The Mass of the Phœnix," which is explained in Chapter 62 of the same work: "The Phœnix hath a Bell for Sound; Fire for Sight; a Knife for Touch; two cakes, one for taste, the other for smell. He standeth before the Altar of the Universe at Sunset, when Earth-life fades. He summons the Universe, and crowns it with MAGICK Light to replace the sun of natural light. He prays unto, and gives homage to, Ra-Hoor-Khuit; to Him he then sacrifices. The first cake, burnt, illustrates the profit drawn from the scheme of incarnation. The second, mixt with his life's blood and eaten, illustrates the use of the lower life to feed the higher life. He then takes the Oath and becomes free—unconditioned—the Absolute. Burning up in the Flame of his Prayer, and born again—the Phœnix!"

The Book of the Law "describes the hermits of Thelema. We must define a Hermit as one who goes alone. Observe the word 'alone' with regard to Hadit, just above. But these Hermits are to be found taking their pleasure with women and in all other ways, acting like the Masters of Rome in the days of the Empire and of the Renaissance. Great kings and queens of Thebes and Babylon. We are to learn from this to enjoy all things without losing control of ourselves or ceasing to suffice for ourselves or becoming the slaves of our desire or losing our sense of selfhood."[93] As Crowley tells Achad, "Concerning the Love of women, o my Son, it is written in *The Book of the Law* that all is Freedom, if it be done unto our Lady Nuit. Yet also there is this Consideration, that for every Parsifal there is a Kundry. Thou mayst eat a thousand Fruits of the Garden; but there is one Tree whose name for thee is Poison. In every great Initiation is an Ordeal, wherein appeareth a Siren or Vampire appointed to destroy the Candidate. I have myself witnessed the Blasting of not less than ten of my own Flowers, that I tended when I was NEMO, and that although I saw the Cankerworm, and knew it, and gave urgent Warning."[94]

"The whole and sole object of all true Magical and Mystical training is to become free from every kind of limitation. Thus, body and mind, in the widest sense, are the obstacles in the Path of the Wise: the paradox, tragic enough as it seems, is that they are also the means of progress. How to get

---

[91] *The Key of the Mysteries, loc. cit.*
[92] *MITAP*, Ch. XI.
[93] DC on AL II.24.
[94] *Liber Aleph*, "De sirenis."

rid of them, to pass beyond or to transcend them, is the problem, and this is as strictly practical and scientific as that of eliminating impurities from a gas, or of adroitly using mechanical laws. Here is the inevitable logical flaw in the sorites of the Adept, that he is bound by the very principles which it is his object to overcome: and on him who seeks to discard them arbitrarily they haste to take a terrible revenge!"[95] The *New Comment* makes plain that, "One does not need to be constantly popping in and out of Trance. One ought to do both actions with ever increasing length and strength of swing. Hence one's life-periods, where this counts, become gradually larger and more vivid, and one's death-periods though very short, perhaps, may be unfathomably intense."[96]

Crowley is careful to point out that, "The 'mystic path' itself is packed with dangers. Unless the strongest counter-irritants are exhibited, the process is almost certain to become morbid. It is only one step from the Invocation of Zeus, or Apollo, or Dionysus, which does demand identification of oneself with the object of one's worship, to a form of self-worship which soon develops into a maniacal exacerbation of the Ego; and if one persists in this involuted curve, one becomes a 'Black Brother,' or departs for the local loony-bin. Invocations of even the most positive Gods are dangerous, unless care can be taken to keep the personality of the god distinct from one's own. Athene is a superb deity; but one does not want to be nothing but Athene, except in that supreme moment of Samadhi with Her which is the climax of the invocation."[97] According to the *New Comment*, the instructions in AL II.67–68 are "actual indications as to how to behave, so as to get the full effect of the Trance. This too is a general Magical Formula, convenient even in the Work of the physical image of the Godhead. It is of the utmost importance to resist the temptation to let oneself be carried away into trance. One should summon one's reserve forces to react against the tendency to lose normal consciousness. More and more of one's being is gradually drawn into the struggle, and one only yields at the last moment. (It needs practice and courage to get the best results.)"

The aspirant must not "content himself with the mere attainment of spiritual enlightenment, however sublime. All such achievements are barren unless they be regarded as the means rather than the end of spiritual progress; allowed to infiltrate every detail of the life, not only of the spirit, but of the senses. The Tao can never be known until it interprets the most trivial actions of every day routine. It is a fatal mistake to discriminate between the spiritual importance of meditation and playing golf. To do so is to create an internal conflict. 'Let there be no difference made among you between any one thing & any other thing; for thereby there cometh hurt.' He who knows the Tao knows it to be the source of all things soever; the most exalted spiritual ecstasy and the most trivial internal impression are from our point of view equally illusions, worthless

---

[95] *Little Essays Toward Truth, loc. cit.*
[96] NC on AL II.74.
[97] *MWT*, Ch. XLII.

masks, which hide, with grotesque painted pasteboard false and lifeless, the living face of truth. Yet, from another point of view, they are equally expressions of the ecstatic genius of truth—natural images of the reaction between the essence of one's self and one's particular environment at the moment of their occurrence. They are equally tokens of the Tao by whom, in whom, and of whom, they are. To value them for themselves is to deny the Tao and to be lost in delusion. To despise them is to deny the omnipresence of the Tao, and to suffer the illusion of sorrow. To discriminate between them is to set up the accursed dyad, to surrender to the insanity of intellect, to overwhelm the intuition of truth, and to create civil war in the consciousness."[98]

There is a connection between Death, Sleep and Our Lady Nuit. (This is worked out, on profane lines, by Dr. Sigmund Freud, and his school, especially by Jung, *Psychology of the Unconscious*, which the reader should consult). The fatigue of the day's toil creates the toxins whose accumulation is the 'Will to Die'. All mystic attainment is of this type, as all Magick is of the 'Will to Live'. At times we all want Nibbana, to withdraw into the Silence, and so on. The Art of it is to dip deeply into 'Death', but to emerge immediately, a giant refreshed. This plan is also possible on the larger scale, all Life being Magick, all Death Mysticism.

Then why is Death 'forbidden'? All things are surely lawful. But we must work "without lust of result", taking everything as it comes without desire indeed, but with all manner of delight! Let thy Love-Madrigal to Death, thy Mother-Mistress, ripple and swell throughout the years, with all the Starry Heaven for thine Orchestra; but do not imagine that to attain Her is the sole satisfaction. It is the yearning itself that is Beatitude.[99]

"There is a doctrine with regard to death, stranger perhaps than all the others. It is a mark of success in Magick to get one's work done fully in one's prime, so that life has nothing left to offer, and one begins to long for the great journey into the unknown—the Call of the Old Long Trail. It is not lawful to hasten the start. The measure of the splendour of death is the strength and courage needed while waiting for it. The longer one lives and the more one wills to die, the more royal is one's nature."[100] Ultimately, according to *Magick in Theory and Practice*, "there is no distinction between magick and meditation except of the most arbitrary and accidental kind." Or, as the footnote has it, "There is the general metaphysical antithesis that Magick is the Art of the Will-to-Live, Mysticism of the Will-to-Die; but—'Truth comes bubbling to my brim; Life and Death are one to Him!'"[101]

---

[98] *Ibid.*, Ch. XXXV.
[99] NC on AL II.73.
[100] DC on AL II.73–74.
[101] *MITAP*, Ch. XV, Sec. I. *Cf.* also *The Book of Thoth*, Part II, Atu XVI: "There is a direct reference to this card in the *Book of the Law*. In Chapter I, verse 57, the goddess Nuith speaks: 'Invoke me under my stars! Love is the law, love under will. Nor let the fools mistake love; for there are love and love. There is the dove, and there is the serpent. Choose ye well! He, my prophet, hath chosen, knowing the law of the fortress, and the great mystery of the House of God'. The dominating

In *Magick Without Tears*, Crowley says that, "Hindus may maintain that Atmadarshana, or at any rate Shivadarshana, is the equivalent of crossing the Abyss. Beware of any such conclusions! The Trances are simply isolated experiences, sharply cut off from normal thought-life. To cross the Abyss is a permanent and fundamental revolution in the whole of one's being."[102] Elsewhere, he describes the mystic states of a Magister Templi as "the final and perfect identity of the Self with the Holy Guardian Angel, the Vision of Pan, the Four Formless States of Buddhism, namely, Samadhi upon consciousness, Space, Nothing, and that which is neither P nor p', in logical phraseology. Here, too, we should place Shivadarshana, the Vision of the Destruction of the Universe, the Opening of the Eye of Shiva."[103]

"It is absolutely futile to discuss this: it has been tried and failed again and again. Even those with experience of the earlier part of the 'vision' in its fullness must find it totally impossible to imagine anything so subversive of the whole base, not only of the Ego, but of the Absolute behind the Ego. There are, however, many suggestive poetical descriptions which we advise our readers to study. Notable are 'Aha!' (passage quoted below) and many portions of *Liber LXV*, *Liber VII*, and *Liber CCXX*. It must be clearly understood that the *Bhagavad-Gita*, Anna Kingsford, St. John, and all other writers with the possible exception of Lao Tze, describe nothing higher than Atmadarshana. For the first time in the known history of the world there had arisen the combination of the utmost attainment with the intelligence and literary ability to make it comparatively articulate. It is no wonder, then, that we hail Fra. P."—i.e. Crowley—"as the greatest of all Teachers."[104]

"In all previous grades the nature of the Initiation has been light through darkness. In this it is darkness through light. The word of the Adept was L V X, Light. The word of the Master of the Temple is N O X, Night. This is the Night of Pan. The direction of the Path is definitely changed. The Master of the Temple cannot go to the Magus unless bringing the Neophyte himself in his hand, and in this task there is no consolation, as there has always been before. The visions are no more. Silence and stillness and darkness rule the grade. The Adept has throughout his progress been unifying himself. As it is written in *Liber CCCXXXIII*, Chapter III, the Brothers of

---

feature of this card is the Eye of Horus. This is also the Eye of Shiva, on the opening of which, according to the legend of this [Shaivite] cult, the Universe is destroyed. . . . Bathed in the effulgence of this Eye (which now assumes even a third sense, that indicated in Atu XV) are the Dove bearing an olive branch and the Serpent: as in the above quotation. The Serpent is portrayed as the Lion-Serpent Xnoubis or Abraxas. These represent the two forms of desire; what Schopenhauer would have called the Will to Live and the Will to Die. They represent the feminine and masculine impulses; the nobility of the latter is possibly based upon recognition of the futility of the former. This is perhaps why the renunciation of love in all the ordinary senses of the word has been so constantly announced as the first step towards initiation. This is an unnecessarily rigid view. This Trump is not the only card in the Pack, nor are the "will to live" and the "will to die" incompatible. This becomes clear as soon as life and death are understood (See Atu XIII) as phases of a single manifestation of energy."

[102] *MWT*, Ch. XII.
[103] *The Psychology of Hashish*, Sec. XVIII.
[104] *The Temple of Solomon the King*, Part VII, "The Babe."

A∴A∴ are women; the Aspirants to A∴A∴ are men. The Master of the Temple has given birth to a child, which child appears as an Adept among men. But that which was the Adept is but a little pile of dust. Samadhi has been attained once and for all. The process is complete and permanent. The Great Work is accomplished. The new Great Work is proclaimed. He has finished with Solve. He must begin Coagula."[105]

"The Master becomes a Holy Guardian Angel unto another, the Bridegroom of his Bride.... The Holy Guardian Angel presents his Bride to the Mother, who presents her to the Father. One may remark that it is necessary to be a Master of the Temple before anything like a full understanding of these mysteries can be attained. . . . For that which is requisite for every man is *the next step*, and Frater P. has concentrated his message into this one phrase, 'ATTAIN TO THE KNOWLEDGE AND CONVERSATION OF THE HOLY GUARDIAN ANGEL.' All beyond that is useless till that has been done."[106] The above chapter of *The Book of Lies* also states that, "The Brothers of the A∴A∴ are one with the Mother of the Child," and "The Man delights in uniting with the Woman; the Woman in parting from the Child." The commentary notes that, "Masters of the Temple, or Brothers of A∴A∴ have changed the formula of their progress. These two formulæ, *Solve et Coagula*, are now explained, and the universe is exhibited as the interplay between these two. This also explains the statement in *Liber Legis* I, 28-30."[107]

---

[105] *Ibid.*, Part IX, "Nemo."
[106] *Ibid.* Emphasis in original. *Cf.* also *Liber XIII*, Sec. 6, fn.: "This is in truth the sole task; the others are useful only as adjuvants to and preparations for the One Work. Moreover, once this task has been accomplished, there is no more need of human help or instruction; for by this alone may the highest attainment be reached."
[107] *The Book of Lies*, Ch. 3.

CHAPTER 8
The Silent Self

Man is a microcosm: that is, an image (concentrated around the point of consciousness) of the macrocosm, or Universe. This Theorem is guaranteed by the hylo-idealistic demonstration that the perceptible Universe is an extension, or phantasm, of the nervous system.
—Little Essays Toward Truth

None and Two are identical; they are distinct in our minds only because those minds are conscious, and therefore think of "two" as their own state. But the unconscious mind thinks Nothing, and is Nothing. Yet it is the same mind.
—The New Comment on AL I.6

Both the Upanishads, the "Classical Basis of Vedantism, the best-known form of Hindu Mysticism," and the *Bhagavad-Gītā*, a "dialogue in which Krishna, the Hindu 'Christ' expounds a system of Attainment," are included in the Curriculum of A∴A∴, Course I, Section 1, "Books for Serious Study." Numerous commentaries have been written on the *Gītā*, literally "Song of the Lord," with widely differing interpretations of even the essentials. Different Vedanta commentators read varying relations between Ātman and Brahman in the text: Advaita Vedanta sees non-dualism of Ātman and Brahman as its essence, whereas Bhedabheda and Vishishtadvaita see them both different and non-different, while Dvaita just sees them as plain different. As Sivananda puts it: "Madhva said: 'Man is the servant of God,' and established his Dvaita philosophy. Ramanuja said: 'Man is a ray or spark of God,' and established his Vishishtadvaita philosophy. Sankara said: 'Man is identical with Brahman or the Eternal Soul,' and established his Kevala Advaita philosophy."[1]

Crowley's take is this: "Brahman—don't confuse with the Brahma of the Trimurti, as so many Nippies and Clippies are but too liable to do—is the macrocosmic Negative Absolute, when cross-examined; its microcosm is Purusha or Atma. Very near our own Qabalistic Zero—Nought in no dimensions—equals Infinity (*air connu*). Then comes Buddhi, which curates, bookmakers' clerks, miners and Privy Councillors so often mistake for Buddha (Ha! Ha!), the faculty of discrimination. Pretty much like the 0 = 2 equation in our system."[2] The *Old Comment* on the first verse of *The Book of the Law* states that, "In Nu is Had concealed; by Had is Nu

---

[1] Sivananda 2003, 217.
[2] *MWT*, Ch. XLII.

manifested. Nu being 56 and Had 9, their conjunction results in 65, Adonai, the Holy Guardian Angel." The *New Comment* on AL III.63 reads: "The Fool is also the Great Fool, Bacchus Diphues, Harpocrates, the Dwarf-Self, the Holy Guardian Angel, and so forth. 'He understandeth it not', that is, he understandeth that it is NOT, LA, 31."

Now the philosophical fall of the Âtman produces the Macrocosm and the Microcosm, God and not-God—the Universe, or the power which asserts a separateness, an individuality, a self-consciousness—I am! This is explained in Brihadâranyaka, 1. 4. 1. as follows:
"In the beginning the Âtman alone in the form of a man {*"There are two persons of the Deity, one in heaven, and one which descended upon earth in the form of man (*i.e. Adam Qadmon), *and the Holy One, praised be It! unites them (in the union of Samâdhi, that is, of Sam (Greek* σὺν, *together with), and Adhi, Hebrew Adonai, the Lord). There are three Lights in the Upper Holy Divine united in One, and this is the foundation of the doctrine of Every-Thing, this is the beginning of the Faith, and Every-Thing is concentrated therein" ("Zohar III," beginning of paragraph. She'meneeh, fol. 36a.)*} was this universe. He gazed around; he saw nothing there but himself. Thereupon he cried out at the beginning: 'It is I.' Thence originated the name I. Therefore to-day, when anyone is summoned, he answers first 'It is I'; and then only he names the other name which he bears." {*It is fully realized that outside the vastness of the symbol this "Fall of God" is as impertinent as it is unthinkable.*}
This Consciousness of "I" is the second veil which man meets on his upward journey, and, unless he avoid it and escape from its hidden meshes, which are a thousandfold more dangerous than the entanglements of the veil of words, he will never arrive at that higher consciousness, that superconsciousness (Samâdhi), which will consume him back into the Âtman from which he came.
As the fall of the Âtman arises from the cry "It is I," so does the fall of the Self-consciousness of the universe-man arise through that Self-consciousness crying "I am it," thereby identifying the shadow with the substance; from this fall arises the first veil we had occasion to mention, the veil of duality, of words, of belief.[3]

As H. P. Blavatsky writes in *Isis Unveiled*, "Reason being a faculty of our physical brain, one which is justly defined as that of deducing inferences from premises, and being wholly dependent on the evidence of other senses, cannot be a quality pertaining directly to our divine spirit. The latter knows—hence, all reasoning which implies discussion and argument would be useless. So an entity, which, if it must be considered as a direct emanation from the eternal Spirit of wisdom, has to be viewed as possessed of the same attributes as the essence or the whole of which it is a part. Therefore, it is with a certain degree of logic that the ancient theurgists maintained that the rational part of man's soul (spirit) never entered

---

[3] *The Temple of Solomon the King*, Part IV, "The Vedanta."

wholly into the man's body, but only overshadowed him more or less through the irrational or astral soul, which serves as an intermediatory agent, or a medium between spirit and body. The man who has conquered matter sufficiently to receive the direct light from his shining Augoeides, feels truth intuitionally; he could not err in his judgment, notwithstanding all the sophisms suggested by cold reason, for he is ILLUMINATED. Hence, prophecy, vaticination, and the so-called Divine inspiration are simply the effects of this illumination from above by our own immortal spirit."[4]

According to Crowley's *Magick Without Tears*, to begin with our magical experiments, "we must build up an apparatus of examination, and this we do by discovering and developing qualities in our own structure which are suitable for the purpose. The first step is the separation of (what we call, for convenience) the astral body from the physical body. As our experiments proceed, we find that our astral body itself can be divided into grosser and subtler components. In this way we become aware of the existence of what we call, for convenience, the Holy Guardian Angel, and the more we realise the implications of the theory of the existence of such a being, the clearer it becomes that our supreme task is to put ourselves into intimate communication with him. For one thing, we shall find that in the object of sense which we examine there are elements which resist our examination. We must raise ourselves to a plane in which we obtain complete control of such."[5]

"Within the human body is another body of approximately the same size and shape; but made of a subtler and less illusory material. It is of course not 'real'; but then no more is the other body! Before treating of clairvoyance one must discuss briefly this question of reality, for misapprehension on the subject has given rise to endless trouble.... There is no such thing as truth in the perceptible universe; every idea when analysed is found to contain a contradiction. It is quite useless (except as a temporary expedient) to set up one class of ideas against another as being 'more real'. The advance of man towards God is not necessarily an advance towards truth. All philosophical systems have crumbled. But each class of ideas possesses true relations within itself. It is possible ... to deny the existence of water and of wood; but, for all that, wood floats on water. The Magician becomes identical with the immortal Osiris, yet the Magician dies. In this dilemma the facts must be restated. One should preferably say that the Magician becomes conscious of that part of himself which he calls the immortal Osiris; and that Part does not 'die'."[6]

"Now this interior body of the Magician ... does exist, and can exert certain powers which his natural body cannot do. It can, for example, pass through 'matter', and it can move freely in every direction through space. But this is because 'matter', in the sense in which we commonly use the word, is on another plane.... This body, which is called by various authors the Astral double, body of Light, body of fire, body of desire, fine body, scin-

---

[4] Blavatsky 1877, i.305–6. Emphasis in original.
[5] *MWT*, Ch. LXXXIII.
[6] *MITAP*, Ch. XVIII, Sec. I.

laeca and numberless other names is naturally fitted to perceive objects of its own class ... in particular, the phantoms of the astral plane."[7] This plane "lies between the material and the spiritual," and again, according to Crowley, "a great deal of nonsense has been written" about it.[8]

> When a man shuts his eyes and begins to look about him, at first there is nothing but darkness. If he continues trying to penetrate the gloom, a new pair of eyes gradually opens.
> Some people think that these are the "eyes of imagination." Those with more experience understand that this truly represents things seen, although those things are themselves totally false.
> As first the seer will perceive gray gloom; in subsequent experiments perhaps figures may appear with whom the seer may converse, and under whose guidance he may travel about. This "plane" being quite as large and varied as the material Universe, one cannot describe it effectively; we must refer the reader to "Liber O" and to *Equinox* I(2), pages 295 to 334.
> This "Astral Plane" has been described by Homer in the *Odyssey*. Here are Polyphemus and the Læstrygons, here Calypso and the Sirens. Here, too, are those things which many have imagined to be the "spirits" of the dead. If the student once take any of these things for truth, he must worship it, since all truth is worshipful. In such a case he is lost; the phantom will have power over him; it will obsess him.[9]

However, "As long as an idea is being examined you are free from it."[10] Thus, the "testing of the spirits is the most important branch of the whole tree of Magick. Without it, one is lost in the jungle of delusion. Every spirit, up to God himself, is ready to deceive you if possible, to make himself out more important than he is; in short, to lay in wait for your soul in 333 separate ways. Remember that after all the highest of all the Gods is only the Magus, Mayan, the greatest of all the devils."[11] Crowley says that, "You will then perceive all sorts of forms, varying as you travel about. Their nature will depend almost entirely on your power of control. Some people may even perceive the phantoms of delirium and madness, and truly go mad from fear and horror."[12]

"It is not just to suppose that a vision of a Divine being of ineffable splendour is necessarily of higher type than this shadowy form-world. Mistake on this point has led many a student astray. Highest among these things are the three visual and seven auditory phenomena of Yoga. (We omit consideration of the other senses; the subject requires a volume.) These are referred to the Sun, the Moon, and Fire; and their appearance marks the attainment of Dhyana. They are dazzling, and accompanied with

---

[7] *Ibid.*
[8] *Book 4*, Part II, Ch. XVI.
[9] *Ibid.*
[10] *Ibid.*
[11] *MITAP, loc. cit.*
[12] *The Psychology of Hashish*, Sec. XII.

such intense though passionless bliss that they partake of the nature of Vedana and may under certain conditions even rise to touch Sañña. Of the auditory are sounds heard like bells, elephants, thunder, trumpets, sea-shells, 'the sweet-souled Vina,' and so on; they are of less importance and are much more common. As one would expect, such forms leave little impress upon the memory. Yet they are seductive enough, and I am afraid that the very great majority of mystics live all their lives wandering about in this vain world of shadows and of shells."[13]

"All this, too, is the pleasant aspect of the affair. Here belong the awful shapes of delirium and madness, which obsess and destroy the soul that fails to control and dismiss them. Here lives the Dweller of the Threshold, that concentration into a single symbol of the Despair and Terror of the Universe and of the Self. Yet on all the paths is He, ready to smite whoso falters or swerves, though he have attained almost the last height."[14] Indeed, "Some great mystics have laid down the law, 'Accept no messenger of God,' banish all, until at last the Father himself comes forth. A counsel of perfection. The Father does send messengers, as we learn in St Mark xii.; and if we stone them, we may perhaps in our blindness stone the son himself when he is sent. So that is no vain counsel of 'St John' (1 John iv. 1), 'Try the spirits, whether they be of God,' no mistake when 'St Paul' claims the discernment of Spirits to be a principal point of the armour of salvation (1 Cor. xii. 10)."[15]

> Now how should Frater P. or another test the truth of any message purporting to come from the Most High? On the astral plane, its phantoms are easily governed by the Pentagram, the Elemental Weapons, the Robes, the God-forms, and such childish toys. We set phantoms to chase phantoms. We make our Scin-Laeca pure and hard and glittering, all glorious within, like the veritable daughter of the King; yet she is but the King's daughter, the Nephesch adorned: she is not the King himself, the Holy Ruach or mind of man. And as we have seen in our chapter on Yoga, this mind is a very aspen; and as we may see in the last chapter of Captain Fuller's "Star in the West," this mind is a very cockpit of contradiction.
>
> What then is the standard of truth? What tests shall we apply to revelation, when our tests of experience are found wanting? If I must doubt my eyes that have served me (well, on the whole) for so many years, must I not much more doubt my spiritual vision, my vision just open like a babe's, my vision untested by comparison and uncriticized by reason?
>
> Fortunately, there is one science that can aid us, a science that, properly understood by the initiated mind, is as absolute as mathematics, more self-supporting than philosophy, a science of the spirit itself, whose teacher is God, whose method is simple as the divine

---

[13] *Ibid.*
[14] *Ibid.*
[15] *The Temple of Solomon the King*, Part V.

Light, and subtle as the divine Fire, Whose results are limpid as the divine Water, all-embracing as the divine Air, and solid as the divine Earth. Truth is the source, and Economy the course, of that marvellous stream that pours its living waters into the Ocean of apodeictic certainty, the Truth that is infinite in its infinity as the primal Truth with which it is identical is infinite in its Unity.[16]

"Need we say that we speak of the Holy Qabalah?" Crowley asks.[17] "When you are better equipped, you will see that the Qabalah is the best (and almost the only) means by which an intelligence can identify himself. And Gematria methods serve to discover spiritual truths. . . . You need no more of Greek and Hebrew than these values, some sacred words—knowledge grows by use—and books of reference."[18] In *An Essay upon Number*, Crowley gives this example: "Suppose now that a vision purporting to proceed from God is granted to me. The Angel declares his name. I add it up. It comes to 65. An excellent number! a blessed angel! Not necessarily. Suppose he is of a Mercurial appearance? 65 is a number of Mars. Then I conclude that, however beautiful and eloquent he may be, he is a false spirit. The Devil does not understand the Qabalah well enough to clothe his symbols in harmony."

But suppose an angel, even lowly in aspect, not only knows the Qabalah—your own researches in the Qabalah—as well as you do, but is able to show you truths, qabalistic truths, which you had sought for long and vainly! Then you receive him with honour and his message with obedience.

It is as if a beggar sought audience of a general, and showed beneath his rags the signet of the King. When an Indian servant shows me "chits" signed by Colonel This and Captain That written in ill-spelt Babu English, one knows what to do. On the contrary the Man Who Was Lost rose and broke the stem of his wineglass at the regimental toast, and all knew him for one of their own.

In spiritual dealings, the Qabalah, with those secrets discovered by yourself that are only known to yourself and God, forms the grip, sign, token and password that assure you that the Lodge is properly tiled.[19]

Bear in mind, "The spirit is merely a recalcitrant part of one's own organism. To evoke him is therefore to become conscious of some part of one's own character; to command and constrain him is to being that part into subjection. This is best understood by the analogy of teaching oneself some mental-physical accomplishment (e.g. billiards), by persistent and patient study and practice, which often involves considerable pain as well as trouble."[20] Kant's rigorous and systematic separation of noumena and

---

[16] *Ibid.*
[17] *Ibid.*
[18] *MWT*, Introduction.
[19] *An Essay upon Number*, Part II.
[20] *MITAP*, Ch. XVI, Pt. II, Sec. III, fn.

phenomena was an invitation to scepticism, but rather than invite such scepticism, the great German philosopher Johann Fichte made the radical suggestion that we should discard the notion of a noumenal world and accept the fact that consciousness does not have a grounding in any "real world." According to Fichte, consciousness is not grounded in anything outside of itself, and the phenomenal world as such arises from self-consciousness, the activity of the ego, and moral awareness.

"What is the cause of my illusion of seeing a spirit in the triangle of Art?" Crowley asks. "Every smatterer, every expert in psychology, will answer: 'That cause lies in your brain.' English children (*pace* the Education Act) are taught that the Universe lies in infinite Space; Hindu children, in the Akasa, which is the same thing. Those Europeans who go a little deeper learn from Fichte, that the phenomenal Universe is the creation of the Ego; Hindus, or Europeans studying under Hindu Gurus, are told, that by Akasa is meant the Chitakasa. The Chitakasa is situated in the 'Third Eye,' *i.e.*, in the brain. By assuming higher dimensions of space, we can assimilate this fact to Realism; but we have no need to take so much trouble. This being true for the ordinary Universe, that all sense-impressions are dependent on changes in the brain, *{Thought is a secretion of the brain (Weismann). Consciousness is a function of the brain (Huxley).}* we must include illusions, which are after all sense-impressions as much as 'realities' are, in the class of 'phenomena dependent on brain-changes.' Magical phenomena, however, come under a special sub-class, since they are willed, and their cause is the series of 'real' phenomena, called the operations of ceremonial Magic."[21]

> The spirits of the Goetia are portions of the human brain.
> Their seals therefore represent (Mr. Spencer's projected cube) methods of stimulating or regulating those particular spots (through the eye).
> The names of God are vibrations calculated to establish:
> (*a*) General control of the brain. (Establishment of functions relative to the subtle world.)
> (*b*) Control over the brain in detail. (Rank or type of the Spirit.)
> (*c*) Control of one special portion. (Name of the Spirit.)
> The perfumes aid this through smell. Usually the perfume will only tend to control a large area; but there is an attribution of perfumes to letters of the alphabet enabling one, by a Qabalistic formula, to spell out the Spirit's name.
> I need not enter into more particular discussion of these points; the intelligent reader can easily fill in what is lacking.[22]

"To sum up, the first task is to separate the astral form from the physical body, the second to develop the powers of the astral body, in particular those of sight, travel, and interpretation; third, to unify the two bodies

---

[21] *The Book of Goetia of Solomon the King*, "The Initiated Interpretation of Ceremonial Magic."
[22] *Ibid. Cf.* also *Liber DCCCXI*, Sec. III: "Easier I find it to say 'subconsciousness' and 'secretion' than to postulate an external reservoir, to extend my connotation of 'man' than to invent 'God.'"

without muddling them. This being accomplished, the magician is fitted to deal with the invisible."²³ After all, "The most elementary consideration of the nature of Gods, angels, demons, and the rest, as shown by their peculiar faculties, stamps them all instantly as Beings pertaining to more than three dimensions! Just as no number of lines is enough to produce the smallest plane, as a cube is capable of containing an infinite number of squares, so, far from there being no room for heaven, there is absolutely nothing but room! Yet of course the nature of that space is for ever incomprehensible, nay inconceivable, by any being of a lower dimension. Only when we have succeeded in uniting our Conscious (three-dimensional) with our Unconscious (four-dimensional) Self can we expect even a symbolic conception of how things go on 'in them furrin parts.'"²⁴

"The Hebrew word for 'Lord' is Adon or Adonai. Adonai, my Lord, is constantly used in the Bible to replace the name Jehovah where that was too sacred to be mentioned, or for other reasons improper to write down. Adonai has also come to mean, through the Rosicrucian tradition, the Holy Guardian Angel, and thus the object of worship or concentration."²⁵ According to Crowley, "Theosophists call him the Higher Self, Silent Watcher, or Great Master. The Golden Dawn calls him the Genius. Gnostics say the Logos. Zoroaster talks about uniting all these symbols into the form of a Lion—see Chaldean Oracles. Anna Kingsford calls him Adonai (Clothed with the Sun). Buddhists call him Adi-Buddha—(says H. P. B.) The Bhagavad-Gita calls him Vishnu (chapter xi.). The Yi King calls him 'The Great Person.' The Qabalah calls him Jechidah."²⁶

> We also get metaphysical analysis of His nature, deeper and deeper according to the subtlety of the writer; for this vision—it is all one same phenomenon, variously coloured by our varying Ruachs—is, I believe, the first and the last of all Spiritual Experience. For though He is attributed to Malkuth, and the Door of the Path of His overshadowing, He is also in Kether (Kether is in Malkuth and Malkuth in Kether—"as above, so beneath"), and the End of the "Path of the Wise" is identity with Him.
>
> So that while he is the Holy Guardian Angel, He is also Hua *{The supreme and secret title of Kether.}* and the Tao. *{The great extreme of the Yi King.}*
>
> For since Intra Nobis Regnum deI *{I.N.R.I.}* all things are in Ourself, and all Spiritual Experience is a more or less complete Revelation of Him.
>
> Yet it is only in the Middle Pillar that His manifestation is in any way perfect.
>
> The Augoeides invocation is the whole thing. Only it is so difficult; one goes along through all the fifty gates of Binah at once, more or less

---

²³ *MITAP*, Ch. XVIII, Sec. I.
²⁴ *MWT*, Ch. XXXVI.
²⁵ *Eight Lectures*, Ch. 5, Sec. 13.
²⁶ *The Temple of Solomon the King*, Preface.

illuminated, more or less deluded. But the First and the Last is this Augoeides Invocation.[27]

According to Blavatsky, "Socrates entertained opinions identical with those of Pythagoras; and both, as the penalty of their divine philosophy, were put to a violent death. The rabble has been the same in all ages. Materialism has been, and will ever be blind to spiritual truths. These philosophers held, with the Hindus, that God had infused into matter a portion of his own Divine Spirit, which animates and moves every particle. They taught that men have two souls, of separate and quite different natures: the one perishable—the Astral Soul, or the inner, fluidic body—the other incorruptible and immortal—the Augoeides, or portion of the Divine Spirit; that the mortal or Astral Soul perishes at each gradual change at the threshold of every new sphere, becoming with every transmigration more purified. The astral man, intangible and invisible as he might be to our mortal earthly senses, is still constituted of matter, though sublimated. Aristotle, notwithstanding that for political reasons of his own he maintained a prudent silence as to certain esoteric matters, expressed very clearly his opinion on the subject. It was his belief that human souls are emanations of God, that are finally re-absorbed into Divinity."[28]

Commenting on "Adonai, the Holy Guardian Angel," Crowley writes that, "It seems then that He is Hadit. I have never liked the term 'Higher Self'; True Self is more the idea. For each Star is the husk of Hadit, unique and conqueror, sublime in His own virtue, independent of Hierarchy. There is an external hierarchy, of course, but that is only a matter of convenience."[29] He also states that, "We may readily concur that the Augoeides, the 'Genius' of Socrates, and the 'Holy Guardian Angel' of Abramelin the Mage, are identical. But we cannot include this 'Higher Self'; for the Angel is an actual Individual with his own Universe, exactly as man is; or, for the matter of that, a bluebottle. He is not a mere abstraction, a selection from, and exaltation of, one's own favorite qualities, as the 'Higher Self' seems to be. The trouble is (I think) that the Hindu passion for analysis makes them philosophize any limited being out of existence."[30]

According to the Neoplatonist Iamblichus, there is "one personal guardian demon for every one of us.[31] It is not right to assume that it is

---

[27] *Ibid.* Apuleius concludes his treatise *On the God of Socrates* thus: "Nor does Homer teach you any thing else in the same Ulysses, by always giving him Wisdom as a companion, whom he poetically calls Minerva. Hence, attended by this, he encounters all horrible dangers, and vanquishes all adverse circumstances. For, assisted by her, he entered the cavern of the Cyclops, but escaped from it; saw the oxen of the Sun, but abstained from them; and descended to the realms beneath, but emerged from them. With the same Wisdom also for his companion, he passed by Scylla, and was not seized by her; was enclosed by Charybdis, yet was not retained by it; drank the cup of Circe, and was not transformed; came to the Lotophagi, yet did not remain with them; and heard the Sirens, yet did not approach to them" (1822, 318).
[28] Blavatsky, *op. cit.*, i.12.
[29] NC on AL II.65.
[30] *MWT*, Ch. XLII.
[31] This type of daemon makes his first appearance in Archaic Greece, and represents the individual *moira* or "portion" of which Homer speaks, but in a personal form. We meet him first in Hesiod and Phocylides, and while he often appears to be no more than a person's "luck" or fortune, this

common to everybody, or that it is common at all, but only that it is present with every individual as his own. For a distribution to every species, and the diversity existing in the realm of matter, do not admit of the union and identity of things essentially incorporeal. Why is it, then, that the demon 'is invoked by all with a common form of invocation'? It is because their invocation is made through one divinity; the Lord of the demons who from the beginning assigned to every one his personal demon. Even now also at the sacred rites he makes known to all and each their personal demons, according to his own purpose. For always in the theurgic arrangement, the secondary are invoked through the superior divinities. In respect to the demons, therefore, one common leader of the cosmocrators"—i.e. rulers of the cosmic world, the demons allotted to the several regions of the universe (*see* Ephesians 6:12)—"in respect to the nativity, sends down to each and all, his personal demon. Hence when the personal demon is present he makes known his own proper worship and teaches the proper mode by which he is to be invoked."[32]

There is also the question of alliances with various Powers. These again are hardly ever allowable. *{Notwithstanding, there exist certain bodies of spiritual beings, in whose ranks are not only angelic forces, but elementals, and even dæmons, who have attained to such Right Understanding of the Universe that they have banded themselves together with the object of becoming Microcosms, and realize that their best means to this end is devotion to the service of the true interests of Mankind. Societies of spiritual forces, organized on these lines, dispose of enormous resources. The Magician who is himself sworn to the service of humanity may count upon the heartiest help of these Orders. Their sincerity may always be assured by putting them to the test of the acceptance of the Law of Thelema. Whoso denies "Do what thou wilt shall be the whole of the Law" confesses that he still clings to the conflict in his own nature; he is not, and does not want to be, true to himself. À fortiori, he will prove false to you.}* No Power which is not a Microcosm in itself—and even Archangels reach rarely to this centre of balance—is fit to treat on an equality with Man. The proper study of mankind is God; with Him is his business; and with Him alone. Some Magicians have hired legions of spirits for some special purpose; but it has always proved a serious mistake. The whole idea of exchange is foreign to Magick. The dignity of the Magician forbids compacts. "The Earth is the Lord's and the fulness thereof."[33]

---

luck is not conceived as extraneous or accidental, but seen as much part of their natal endowment as beauty or talent. Thus, Herodotus attributes the fate of great kings and generals to neither external accident nor the consequence of character, but to "what had to be." Pindar piously reconciles this popular fatalism with the will of God, asserting that "the great purpose of Zeus *directs* the daemon of the men he loves." (*Pyth.* 5.122 f., as translated in Dodds 1951, 42.)

[32] *De mysteriis*, ix.9.
[33] *MITAP*, Ch. XXI, Sec. II. Psalms 24:1.

On the other hand, "It is sometimes better to act on the advice of a [familiar] spirit even when one knows it to be wrong, though in such a case one must take the proper precautions against an undesirable result. The reason for this is that spirits of this type are very sensitive. They suffer agonies of remorse on realising that they have injured their Master; for he is their God; they know themselves to be part of him, their aim is to attain to absorption in him. They understand therefore that his interests are theirs. Care must be taken to employ none but spirits who are fit for the purpose, not only by reason of their capacity to supply information, but for their sympathy with the personality of the Magician. Any attempt to coerce unwilling spirits is dangerous. They obey from fear; their fear makes them flatter, and tell amiable falsehoods. It also creates phantasmal projections of themselves to personate them; and these phantasms, besides being worthless, become the prey of malicious dæmons who use them to attack the Magician in various ways whose prospect of success is enhanced by the fact that he has himself created a link with them."[34]

In this conjunction, Crowley feels it prudent to warn that, "Divination of any kind is improper in matters directly concerning the Great Work itself. In the Knowledge and Conversation of his Holy Guardian Angel, the adept is possessed of all he can possibly need. To consult any other is to insult one's Angel. Moreover, it is to abandon the only person who really knows, and really cares, in favour of one who by the nature of the case, must be ignorant of the essence of the matter—one whose interest in it is no more (at the best) than that of a well-meaning stranger." The footnote goes into more detail: "No intelligence of the type that operates divination is a complete Microcosm as Man is. He knows in perfection what lies within his own Sphere, and little or nothing beyond it. Graphiel knows all that is knowable about Martial matters, as no Man can possibly do. For even the most Martial man is limited as to Madim by the fact that Mars is only one element in his molecule; the other elements both inhibit concentration on their colleague, and veil him by insisting on his being interpreted in reference to themselves. No entity whose structure does not include the entire Tree of Life is capable of the Formulæ of Initiation. Graphiel, consulted by the aspirant to Adeptship, would be bound to regard the Great Work as purely a question of combat, and ignore all other considerations. His advice would be absolute on technical points of this kind; but its very perfection would persuade the aspirant to an unbalanced course of action which would entail failure and destruction."[35]

"It is pertinent to mention in this connection that one must not expect absolute information as to what is going to happen. 'Fortune-telling' is an abuse of divination. At the utmost one can only ascertain what may reasonably be expected. The proper function of the process is to guide one's judgment. Diagnosis is fairly reliable; advice may be trusted, generally speaking; but prognosis should always be cautious. The essence of the

---

[34] *MITAP*, Ch. XVIII, Sec. IV.
[35] *Ibid.*

business is the consultation of specialists."[36] According to Crowley, "It should go without saying that until the Magician has attained to the Knowledge and Conversation of his Holy Guardian Angel he is liable to endless deceptions. He does not know Himself; how can he explain his business to others? How can those others, though they do their best for him, aid in anything but trifles? One must therefore be prepared for disappointment at every stage until one attains to Adeptship."[37]

"There is no personal identity as a link between the man who is on the brink of 'attainment' and the Being who arises in him, annihilating him, and Whom he subsequently remembers as his 'Genius.'"[38] This Being is, thus, "a Person, a macrocosmic Individual. (We do not know about his birth and so on; but that is because he is, so to speak, a *private* God; he only appears to the world at all through some reference to him by his client; for instance, the genius or Augoeides of Socrates)."[39] Iamblichus tries "to straighten the complicated problem in respect to the personal demon, which is likewise made the theme for various objections. . . .to speak plainly, the treatment of the subject in respect to the personal demon is twofold, theurgic and technic: the one evoking him from the categories above, and the other from the visible periods in the world of generated existence. The former makes no use of the art of casting nativities, but the latter is devoted to such pursuits. The former pays honor to the demon more generally as superior to the province of nature, but the latter specifically as pertaining to the realm of nature altogether. Hence thou seemest to have brought down strangely the most perfect sacred performance to regard as a mere human affair, and to have put thy questions upon this subject as in a gymnastic exercise."[40]

As Crowley puts it, when one applies the term "higher" to the "self," "it becomes a sort of trade name; nobody tells me if he means Khu, or Ba, or Khabs, or Ut of the Upanishads or Augoeides of the Neo-Platonists, or Adonai of Bulwer-Lytton, or—here we are with all those thrice-accurs't alternatives. There is not, cannot be, any specific meaning unless we start with a sound skeleton of ontogenic theory, a well-mapped hierarchy of the Cosmos, and define the term anew." The obvious question is: "Then why use it? To do so can only cause confusion, unless the context helps us to clarify the image. And that is surely rather a defeatist attitude, isn't it?" Crowley explains his somewhat peculiar choice of terminology thus: "When I first set myself to put a name to my 'mission'—the contemplation carried

---

[36] *Ibid.*
[37] *Ibid.* To Hegel, "Socrates is the hero who established in the place of the Delphic oracle, the principle that man must look within himself to know what is Truth" (1892-6, i.435), and who, "in assigning to insight, to conviction, the determination of men's actions—posited the Individual as capable of a moral decision, in contraposition to Country and to Customary Morality, and thus made himself an Oracle, in the Greek sense. He said he had a δαιμόνιον within him, which counselled him what to do, and revealed to him what was advantageous to his friends" (1899, 269-70).
[38] *The Psychology of Hashish*, Sec. XVII.
[39] *MWT*, Ch. LXXVI. Emphasis in original. (Plutarch's dialogue "On the Daimonion of Socrates" is commonly known by its Latin title, *De genio Socratis*.)
[40] *De mysteriis*, ix.1.

me half-way across South-West China—I considered these alternatives. I thought to cut the Gordian Knot, and call it by Abramelin's title the 'Holy Guardian Angel' because (I mused) that will be as intelligible to the villagers of Pu Peng as to the most learned Pundits; moreover, the implied theory was so crude that no one need be bound by it."[41] He draws no parallels to the popular Christian use of the term, and neither did the Egyptian mage Abramelin.

> Now, how did this come about? Not from the meditation on the Reason, which ended once for all in the Destruction of that Reason, but by the "Sammasati" meditation on his Kamma. Baffled again and again, the fall with his horse supplied the one factor missing in his calculations. He had repeatedly escaped from death in manners almost miraculous. "Then I am some use after all!" was his conclusion. "I am indeed SENT to do something." For whom? For the Universe; no partial good could possibly satisfy his equation. "I am, then, the 'chosen Priest and Apostle of Infinite Space.' Very good: and what is the message? What shall I teach men?" And like the lightning from heaven fell upon him these words: "THE KNOWLEDGE AND CONVERSATION OF THE HOLY GUARDIAN ANGEL."
>
> Just that. No metaphysical stuff about the "higher self"; a thing that the very villagers of Pu Peng could understand. Avoid refinements; leave dialectic to the slaves of reason.
>
> His work must, then, be to preach that one method and result. And first must he achieve that for himself; for if the blind lead the blind——[42]

In summary, Crowley adopted Abramelin's—or to be precise, Mathers', since it was his liberal translation—nomenclature of Holy Guardian Angel, because: (1) "Abramelin's system is so simple and effective"; (2) "since all theories of the universe are absurd it is better to talk in the language of one which is patently absurd, so as to mortify the metaphysical man"; (3) "a child can understand it."[43] Crowley "sought a simple statement of his object. His will was sufficiently informed by common sense to decide him to teach man *The Next Step*, the thing which was immediately above him. He might have called this 'God,' or 'the Higher Self,' or 'the *augœides*,' or '*ādi-buddha*,' or 61 other things—but He had discovered that these were all one, yet that each one represented some theory of the Universe which would ultimately be shattered by criticism—for He had already passed through the realm of Reason, and knew that every statement contained an absurdity. He therefore said: 'Let me declare this Work under this title: 'The obtaining of the Knowledge and Conversation of the Holy Guardian Angel,'" because the theory implied in these words is so patently absurd that only simpletons would waste much time in analyzing it. It would be accepted as a

---

[41] *MWT*, Ch. XXVIII.
[42] *The Temple of Solomon the King*, Part VII, "The Babe." Emphasis in original.
[43] *Ibid.*, Preface.

convention, and *no one would incur the grave danger of building a philosophical system upon it.*"[44]

In reference to the Augoeides, Blavatsky quotes no less authority than Max Müller: "In the hymns of the 'Veda' we see man left to himself to solve the riddle of this world.... He invokes the gods around him, he praises, he worships them. But still with all these gods ... beneath him, and above him, the early poet seems ill at rest within himself. There, too, in his own breast, he has discovered a power that is never mute when he prays, never absent when he fears and trembles. It seems to inspire his prayers, and yet to listen to them; it seems to live in him, and yet to support him and all around him. The only name he can find for this mysterious power is 'Brahman'; for *brahman* meant originally force, will, wish, and the propulsive power of creation. But this impersonal brahman, too, as soon as it is named, grows into something strange and divine. It ends by being one of many gods, one of the great triad, worshipped to the present day. And still the thought within him has no real name; that power which is nothing but itself, which supports the gods, the heavens, and every living being, floats before his mind, conceived but not expressed. At last he calls it 'Âtman,' for âtman, originally breath or spirit, comes to mean Self, and Self alone; *Self*, whether Divine or human; Self, whether creating or suffering; Self, whether one or all; but always Self, independent and free. 'Who has seen the first-born,' says the poet, when he who had no bones (*i.e.*, form) bore him that had bones? Where was the life, the blood, the Self of the world? Who went to ask this from any one who knew it?"[45]

"This idea of a divine Self, once expressed, everything else must acknowledge its supremacy; *Self* is the Lord of all things, Self is the King of all things. As all the spokes of a wheel are contained in the nave and the circumference, all things are contained in this Self; all Selves are contained in this Self. Brahman itself is but Self."[46] Crowley asks, "This Ut, of Udgitha, who looms so large in the Upanishads; the God peculiar to yourself, who appears in one of the *Darshanas*; some Individual constructed from the material listed above; are these all one? If not, is the difference between them more than a quibble?"[47] As the *New Comment* states, "Hoor-paar-Kraat or Harpocrates, the 'Babe in the Egg of Blue', is not merely the God of Silence in a conventional sense. He represents the Higher Self, the Holy Guardian Angel. The connexion is with the symbolism of the Dwarf in Mythology. He contains everything in Himself, but is unmanifested.... But the 'Small Person' of Hindu mysticism, the Dwarf insane yet crafty of many legends in many lands, is also this same 'Holy Ghost', or Silent Self of a man, or his Holy Guardian Angel."[48]

"He is almost the 'Unconscious' of Freud, unknown, unaccountable, the silent Spirit, blowing 'whither it listeth, but thou canst not tell whence it cometh or whither it goeth'. It commands with absolute authority when it

---

[44] *MITAP*, Ch. II. Emphasis added.
[45] Blavatsky, *op. cit.*, ii.317-8 fn. Emphasis in original.
[46] *Ibid.*
[47] *MWT*, Ch. XLII.
[48] NC on AL I.7.

appears at all, despite conscious reason and judgment. . . . But on His appearing, He assumes the active form twin to Harpocrates, that of Ra-Hoor-Khuit. The Concealed Child becomes the Conquering Child, the armed Horus avenging his father Osiris. So also our own Silent Self, helpless and witless, hidden within us, will spring forth, if we have craft to loose him to the Light, spring lustily forward with his cry of Battle, the Word of our True Wills. This is the Task of the Adept, to have the Knowledge and Conversation of His Holy Guardian Angel, to become aware of his nature and his purpose, fulfilling them."[49]

The German exile writer and Nobel laureate Thomas Mann pointed out that, "Schopenhauer, as psychologist of the will, is the father of all modern psychology. From him the line runs, by way of the psychological radicalism of Nietzsche, straight to Freud and the men who built up his psychology... Freud's description of the id and the ego—is it not to a hair to Schopenhauer's description of the Will and the Intellect, a translation of the latter's metaphysics into psychology?"[50] Both Freud and Jung were fascinated by Nietzsche's theories, and Freud went so far as to claim that Nietzsche possessed "a more penetrating knowledge of himself than any man who ever lived or was likely to live."[51] A phrase often attributed to Jung sums up his position: "Until you make the unconscious conscious, it will direct your life and you will call it fate."[52]

> The Grade of Adeptus Minor is the main theme of the instructions of the A∴A∴. It is characterized by the Attainment of the Knowledge and Conversation of the Holy Guardian Angel. {See The Equinox, The Temple of Solomon the King; The Vision and the Voice, 8th Æthyr; also "Liber Samekh," etc., etc.} This is the essential Work of every man; none other ranks with it either for personal progress or for power to help one's fellows. This unachieved, man is no more than the unhappiest and blindest of animals. He is conscious of his own incomprehensible calamity, and clumsily incapable of repairing it. Achieved, he is no less than the co-heir of Gods, a Lord of Light. He is conscious of his own consecrated course, and confidently ready to run it. The Adeptus Minor needs little help or guidance even from his superiors in our Order.
>
> His work is to manifest the Beauty of the Order to the world, in the way that his superiors enjoin, and his genius dictates.[53]

According to *The Secret Doctrine: The Synthesis of Science, Religion, and Philosophy*, "The star under which a human Entity is born, says the Occult Teaching, will remain for ever its star, throughout the whole cycle of its incarnations in one Manvantara. But this *is not his astrological star*. The

---

[49] *Ibid.*
[50] Mann 1947, 408.
[51] As quoted in Jones 1955-7, ii.344.
[52] Nietzsche came to hear Dionysos, like Socrates had heard his dæmon, and eventually became Dionysos, signing his letters with that name.
[53] *One Star in Sight*, Sec. 10.

latter is concerned and connected with the *personality*, the former with the INDIVIDUALITY. The 'Angel' of that Star, or the Dhyani-Buddha will be either the guiding or simply the presiding 'Angel,' so to say, in every new rebirth of the Monad, *which is part of his own essence*, through his vehicle, man, may remain for ever ignorant of this fact. The adepts have each their Dhyani-Buddha, their elder 'Twin Soul,' and they know it, calling it 'Father-Soul,' and 'Father-Fire.' It is only at the last and supreme initiation, however, that they learn it when placed face to face with the bright 'Image.' How much has Bulwer-Lytton known of this mystic fact, when describing, in one of his highest inspirational moods, Zanoni face to face with his *Augoeides*?"[54]

According to Crowley, "His Angel shall lead him anon to the summit of the Order of the R.C. and make him ready to face the unspeakable terror of the Abyss which lies between Manhood and Godhead; teach him to Know that agony, to Dare that destiny, to Will that catastrophe, and to keep Silence for ever as he accomplishes the act of annihilation. From the Abyss comes No Man forth, but a Star startles the Earth, and our Order rejoices above that Abyss that the Beast hath begotten one more Babe in the Womb of Our Lady, His concubine, the Scarlet Woman, BABALON."[55] Indeed, every active member of the Order of the A∴A∴ "has destroyed all that He is and all that He has on crossing the Abyss; but a star is cast forth in the Heavens to enlighten the Earth, so that He may possess a vehicle wherein He may communicate with mankind. The quality and position of this star, and its functions, are determined by the nature of the incarnations transcended by Him."[56]

The Angel "is something more than a man, possibly a being who has already passed through the stage of humanity, and his peculiarly intimate relationship with his client is that of friendship, of community, of brotherhood, or Fatherhood. He is not, let me say with emphasis, a mere abstraction from yourself; and that is why I have insisted rather heavily that the term 'Higher Self' implies 'a damnable heresy and a dangerous delusion.' If it were not so, there would be no point in *The Sacred Magic of Abramelin the Mage*. Apart from any theoretical speculation, my Sammasiti and analytical work has never led to so much as a hint of the existence of the Guardian Angel. He is not to be found by any exploration of oneself. It is true that the process of analysis leads finally to the realization of oneself as no more than a point of view indistinguishable in itself from any other point of view; but the Holy Guardian Angel is in precisely the same position. However close may be the identities in millions of ways, no complete identification is ever obtainable."[57]

As Crowley writes in *The Book of Thoth*, "the ancient theory of the Universe included the thesis that every object in Nature possessed a spiritual guardian. Roughly speaking, this did not apply so much to

---

[54] Blavatsky 1888, i.572–3. Emphasis in original.
[55] *One Star in Sight, loc. cit.* Emphasis in original.
[56] *Ibid.*, Sec. 3.
[57] *MWT*, Ch. XLIII.

manufactured objects, though there are exceptions to this, as in the case of the Gods of the Hearth, the Lintel, and the like; or of angels or spirits as supposed to be interested in one's sword or one's spear. A particularly powerful weapon was likely to get the reputation of not having been manufactured at all by human hands, but forged in volcanoes or in fairyland, and thus imbued with preternatural powers. Some famous swords had names, and were regarded as living beings; they were liable to fly out of the window if the owner played about too much, instead of killing people as is proper."[58] At this point, it may again be prudent to quote the classic work of Iamblichus on the subject:

> Thou also declarest that "the person who has learned the scheme of his nativity, and so knowing his own demon, is liberated from fate, is truly favored by divinity." Thou dost not seem to me, however, to be saying these things altogether in harmony, either with themselves or with the truth. For if the demon has been assigned to us from the scheme of nativity, and we may find him from that, how are we released from fate through the knowledge that the demon was given to us according to fate? But if, as thou dost declare, we are really set free from necessity through the demon, how was it allotted to us by Fate?
>
> Hence the things now uttered by thee not only conflict with themselves, but they are also at variance with the truth; seeing that the personal demon does not by any means come to every one by the scheme of his peculiar nativity. On the other hand, its origin, which we will hereafter set forth, was older than this. If, therefore, the demon that comes down should be contemplated alone from that source, the individual who attained a knowledge of the demon of his nativity, would by no means be happy or fortunate. Who, indeed, if in this case it were permitted to him, in order that he might accomplish the allotments from fate, would consent to receive the demon as a guide to liberation from fate? Yet this appears to me as a part of the theory respecting the demon, and to be the last of the kind, but that the whole of his essence is passed over in silence by such a mode of investigation. Yet these things, although they are incorrectly stated, are, nevertheless, not utterly foreign to the subject.[59]

Iamblichus' *De Mysteriis* continues with the "True Account of the Guardian Demon":

> If, however, it is necessary to reveal to thee the true doctrine in relation to the personal demon let me say this: It is not from one part in the sky, nor from any individual element of the objects that are visible, that he is assigned to us. But there is from the whole world and the various kinds of life in it, and the various kinds of body by which the soul comes down into the realm of generated existence, an allotted

---

[58] Part I, Sec. III.

[59] *De mysteriis*, ix.3.

portion, all our own, divided among us to each of the distinctive qualities in us, which distribution is made according to the ruling disposition of each individual.

This demon, therefore, is present as exemplar before the souls descend into the realm of generated existence. As soon as the soul chooses him for leader the demon immediately comes into charge of the completing of its vital endowments, and when it descends into the body, unites it with the body, and becomes the guardian of its common living principle. He likewise himself directs the private life of the soul, and whatever the conclusions we may arrive at by inference and reasoning, he himself imparts to us the principles. We think and do just such things as he brings to us by way of thought. He guides human beings thus continually till through the sacred theurgic discipline we shall obtain a god to be guardian and leader of the soul. For then he gives place to the superior, or delivers over the superintendence, or becomes subject, as a tributary, to him, or in some other way is servant to him as to an Overlord.[60]

Crowley puts it thus: "Imagine for a moment that you are an orphan in charge of a guardian, inconceivably learned from your point of view. Suppose therefore that you are puzzled by some problem suitable to your childish nature, your obvious and most simple way is to approach your guardian and ask him to enlighten you. It is clearly part of his function as guardian to do his best to help you. Very good, that is the first method, and close parallel with what we understand by the word Magick. We are bothered by some difficulty about one of the elements—say Fire—it is therefore natural to evoke a Salamander to instruct you on the difficult point. But you must remember that your Holy Guardian Angel is not only far more fully instructed than yourself on every point that you can conceive, but you may go so far as to say that it is definitely his work, or part of his work; remembering always that he inhabits a sphere or plane which is entirely different from anything of which you are normally aware."[61]

To attain to the Knowledge and Conversation of the Holy Guardian Angel is consequently without doubt by far the simplest way by which you can yourself approach that higher order of being.

That, then, is a clearly intelligible method of procedure. We call it Magick.

It is of course possible to strengthen the link between him and yourself so that in course of time you became capable of moving and, generally speaking, operating on that plane which is his natural habitat.

There is however one other way, and one only, as far as I can see, of reaching this state. It is at least theoretically possible to exalt the whole of your own consciousness until it becomes as free to move on that

---

[60] *Ibid.*, ix.6.
[61] *MWT*, Ch. LXXXII.

exalted plane as it is for him. You should note, by the way, that in this case the postulation of another being is not necessary. There is no way of refuting the solipsism if you feel like that. Personally I cannot accede to its axiom. The evidence for an external universe appears to me perfectly adequate.

Still there is no extra charge for thinking on those lines if you so wish.

I have paid a great deal of attention in the course of my life to the method of exalting the human consciousness in this way; and it is really quite legitimate to identify my teaching with that of the Yogis.

I must however point out that in the course of my instruction I have given continual warnings as to the dangers of this line of research. For one thing there is no means of checking your results in the ordinary scientific sense. It is always perfectly easy to find a subjective explanation of any phenomenon; and when one considers that the greatest of all the dangers in any line of research arise from egocentric vanity, I do not think I have exceeded my duty in anything that I have said to deter students from undertaking so dangerous a course as Yoga.[62]

Iamblichus makes it clear that there is "One Guardian Demon Only to an Individual" and that "The Guardian Demon [is] Not a 'Part of the Soul'":

> From these facts I may easily reply to your next question. For the personal demon does not "preside over specific regions in us," but simply over all at once. He pervades every principle about us, in the same manner as it was assigned from all the orders of intelligence in the universe. For it also seems proper to thee to remark as follows: "That there are demons placed over specific departments of the body, one over health, one over the figure, and another over the bodily habits, forming a bond of union among them, and that one is placed as superior over all of them in common." This very thing thou shouldst consider as proof that the authority over everything in us is vested in one demon alone. Accordingly it is not right to define "one demon as guardian of the body, another of the soul, and another of the mind." For if the living person is one individual and the demon manifold that is placed over him, the notion is absurd. Certainly the ruling powers everywhere are single rather than those that are ruled. But it is still more absurd if the many demons ruling over special departments are not akin, but are to be classified apart from one another.
>
> Thou also declarest that there are contradictory characters among them, saying that "some demons are good and others bad." Evil demons have no allotment whatever as guardians, and they are never classified in opposition to the good, like one party against another, as though having equal importance.[63]

---

[62] *Ibid.*
[63] *De mysteriis*, ix.7.

Having in succession abandoned these points, thou goest quickly over to the conjecture of the (Grecian) philosophy; yet in relation to the personal demon thou overturnest the entire hypothesis. For if the demon is "a part of the soul," as, for instance, the spiritual or intellectible, and "he who has a mind imbued with good sense is the truly favored one," there will be no other order of beings, divine or demonian, assuming authority over the human soul as being superior to it. Instead, there will be special parts of the soul, or some power existing separately supreme over the many forms of the life within us; and these, not as allied by nature, but as having been set apart as superior in their nature to our entire substance.[64]

"It is impossible to lay down precise rules by which a man may attain to the knowledge and conversation of His Holy Guardian Angel; for that is the particular secret of each one of us; as secret not to be told or even divined by any other, whatever his grade. It is the Holy of Holies, whereof each man is his own High Priest, and none knoweth the Name of his brother's God, or the Rite that invokes Him."[65] As Crowley writes in *Book 4*, Part II, "In the Jewish system we read that the High Priest was to wear a plate with twelve stones, for the twelve tribes of Israel (with all their correspondences), and in this plate were kept the Urim and Thummin. . . . In the system of Abramelin the Lamen is a plate of silver upon which the Holy Guardian Angel writes in dew. This is another way of expressing the same thing, for it is He who confers the secrets of that power which should be herein expressed. St. Paul expresses the same thing when he says that the breastplate is faith, and can withstand the fiery darts of the wicked. This 'faith' is not blind self-confidence and credulity; it is that self-confidence which only comes when self is forgotten. It is the 'Knowledge and Conversation of the Holy Guardian Angel' which confers this faith."[66]

"The task of attaining to this Knowledge and Conversation is the sole task of him who would be called Adept. An absolute method for achieving this is given in the Eighth Æthyr"[67]—"The instruction in the 8th Æthyr pertains to Class D, *i.e.* it is an Official Ritual, and the same remarks apply to the account of the proper method of invoking Æthyrs given in the 18th Æthyr."[68] There is no "regular ritual for this central Work of Their Order, save the generalised instructions in *Liber 418* (the 8th Æthyr), and the detailed Canon and Rubric of the Mass actually used with success by Frater Perdurabo in His attainment. This has been written down by Himself in 'Liber Samekh.' But They have published such accounts as those in *The Temple of Solomon the King* and in 'John St. John.' They have taken the only proper course; to train aspirants to this Attainment in the theory and practice of the whole of Magick and Mysticism, so that each man may be expert in the handling of all known weapons, and free to choose and to use

---

[64] *Ibid.*, ix.8.
[65] *One Star in Sight*, Sec. 10.
[66] *Book 4*, Part II, Ch. XV.
[67] *Ibid.*
[68] A∴A∴ *Curriculum*.

those which his own experience and instinct dictate as proper when he essays the Great Experiment."⁶⁹

Now then thou seest that this Hell, or concealed Place within thee, is no more a Fear or Hindrance to Men of a Free Race, But the Treasure-House of the Assimilated Wisdom of the Ages, and the Knowledge of the True Way. Thus are we Just and Wise to discover this Secret in Ourselves, and to conform the conscious Mind therewith. For that Mind is compact solely (until it be illuminated) of Impressions and Judgments, so that its Will is but directed by the sum of the Shallow Reactions of a most limited Experience. But thy True Will is the Wisdom of the Ages of thy Generations, the Expression of that which hath fitted thee exactly to thine Environment. Thus thy conscious Mind is oftentimes foolish, as when thou admirest an Ideal, and wouldst attain it, but thy true Will letteth thee, so that there is Conflict, and the Humiliation of that Mind. Here will I call to Witness the common Event of "Good Resolutions" that defy the Lightning of Destiny, being puffed up by the Wind of an Indigestible Ideal putrefying within thee Thence cometh colic, and presently the Poison is expelled, or else thou diest. But Resolutions of True Will are mighty against Circumstance.⁷⁰

Learn moreover concerning this Hell, or Hidden Wisdom, that is within thee, that it is modified, little by little, in respect of its Khu, through the Experience of the Conscious Mind, which feedeth it. For that Wisdom is the Expression, or rather Symbol and Hieroglyph, of the True Adjustment of thy Being to its Environment. Now then, that Environment being eroded by Time, this Wisdom is no more perfect, for it is not absolute, but standeth in Relation to the Universe. So then a Part thereof may become useless, and atrophy, as (I will instance) Man's Wit of Smell; and the bodily Organ corresponding degenerateth therewith. But this is an Effect of much Time, so that in thy Hell thou art like to find Elements vain, or foolish, or contrary to thy present Weal. Yet, o my Son, this Hidden Wisdom is not thy true Will, but only the Levers (I may say so) thereof. Notwithstanding, there lieth therein a Faculty of Balance, whereby it is able to judge whether any Element in itself is presently useful and benign, or idle and malignant. Here then is a Root of Conflict between the Conscious and the Unconscious, and a Debate concerning the right Order of Conduct, how the Will may be accomplished.⁷¹

The Greek term *eudaimonia*, which was employed by Plato and Aristotle to denote true and complete happiness, derives from *eu*, "well," and *daimōn*, a "divinity."⁷² Its literal significance, then, is the condition favoured by the

---

[69] *One Star in Sight*, loc. cit.
[70] *Liber Aleph*, "De inferno palatio sapientiæ." As quoted in NC on AL II.60.
[71] *Ibid.*, "De vitiis voluntatis secretæ." As quoted in NC on AL II.60.
[72] According to Dodds, *op. cit.*, the words κακοδαίμων and δυσδαίμων are actually 5th-century coinages, whereas εὐδαίμων is as old as Hesiod.

good genius, or success as the state of being in favour with God.[73] Crowley's outline of "The Noble Eightfold Path" in *The Temple of Solomon the King* describes the first four steps as follows: "In Tiphareth the aspirant attains to no less a state than that of conversation with his Holy Guardian Angel, his Jechidah, 'The permanent principle behind the conflicting opinions.' Once Right Comprehension has been attained to, he has discovered a Master who will never desert him until he become one with him. . . . Right Speech is a furthering of Right Aspirations. It consists of a discipline wherein a man not only converses with his Holy Guardian Angel, but outwardly and inwardly lives up to His holy conversation, turning his whole life into one stupendous magical exercise to enter that Silence which is beyond all thought. . . . Having become obedient to his Holy Guardian Angel (the aspirant's Spiritual Guru) or to the Universal Law as the Buddhist prefers to call it, man naturally enters the state of Right Conduct, which brings with it supernormal or magical powers. Self is now put aside from action as well as from speech, and the striver only progresses by a stupendous courage and endurance."

"The canonical Buddhists however strenuously deny the value of these magical powers, Iddhis or Siddhis, and attribute the purification of the striver, the attainment of the state of 'stainless deeds,' to the great love wherein he must now enshrine all things."[74] In his pre-1904 essay, *Science and Buddhism*, Crowley ruminates on the Hindu theory: "They classify the phenomena (whether well or ill matters nothing), but represent them all as pictured in, but not affecting, a certain changeless, omniscient, blissful existence called Atman. Holding to Theism, the existence of evil forces them to the Fichtean position that 'the Ego posits the Non-Ego,' and we learn that nothing really exists after all but Brahm. They then distinguish between Jivatma, the soul-conditioned, and Paramatma, the soul free; the former being the basis of our normal consciousness; the latter of the Nirvikalpa-Samadhi consciousness; this being the sole condition on which morals, religion, and fees to priests can continue."

As the first of the *Letters from the Masters of the Wisdom* issued by the Theosophical Publishing House puts it, "total emancipation from authority of the one all-pervading power or law called God by the priests—Buddha, Divine Wisdom and enlightenment or Theosophy, by the philosophers of all ages—means also the emancipation from that of human law. Once

---

[73] Wilder 1911. As Plato explains in his *Symposium* (201-3), e.g. Love (Eros) is not a deity but a *daimōn*, an intermediate between gods and men, immortals and mortals. Not only does the *daimōn* occupy a position between two opposing orders of reality, it is in the situation of a mediator: "Interpreting and transporting human things to the gods and divine things to men; entreaties and sacrifices from below, and ordinances and requitals from above: being midway between, it makes each to supplement the other, so that the whole is combined in one. Through it are conveyed all divination and priestcraft concerning sacrifice and ritual and incantations, and all soothsaying and sorcery. God with man does not mingle: but the spiritual [*daimonios*] is the means of all society and converse of men with gods and of gods with men, whether waking or asleep. Whosoever has skill in these affairs is a spiritual man [*daimonios aner*] to have it in other matters, as in common arts and crafts, is for the mechanical. Many and multifarious are these spirits, and one of them is Love."

[74] *The Temple of Solomon the King*, Part IV, "The Noble Eightfold Path."

unfettered and delivered from their dead weight of dogmatic interpretations, personal names, anthropomorphic conceptions and salaried priests, the fundamental doctrines of all religions will be proved identical in their esoteric meaning. Osiris, Krishna, Buddha, Christ, will be shown as different names for one and the same royal highway to final bliss, NIRVANA. Mystical Christianity, that is to say that Christianity which teaches self-redemption through our own seventh principle—this liberated Para-Atma (Augoeides) called by some Christ, by others Buddha, and equivalent to regeneration or rebirth in spirit—will be found just the same truth as the Nirvana of Buddhism. All of us have to get rid of our own Ego, the illusory apparent self, to recognize our true self in a transcendental divine life."[75] To Crowley, "Yoga consists in withdrawing the organs of sense from the objects of sense, and by concentrating them on the Inner Self, Higher Self, Augoeides, Âtman, or Adonai, shake itself free from the illusions of Mâyâ—the world of plurality, and secure union with this Inner Self or Âtman."[76]

> Frater P. by now was well acquainted with the Yoga Philosophy, further he was beginning to feel that the crude Animism employed by many of its expounders scarcely tallied with his attainments. The nearer he approached the Âtman the less did it appear to him to resemble what he had been taught to expect. Indeed its translation into worldly comments was a matter of education, so it came about that he discovered that the Great Attainment *per se* was identical in all systems irrespective of the symbol may sought it under. Thus Yahweh as a clay phallus in a band-box was as much a reality to the Jews of Genesis as Brahman in Brahma-loka was to the Aryas of Vedic India; that the vision of Moses when he beheld God as a burning bush is similar to the vision of the fire-flashing Courser of the Chaldean Oracles; and that Nibbâna the Non-existent is little removed, if at all, from the Christian heaven with its harps, halos, and hovering angels. And the reason is, that the man who does attain to any of these states, on his return to consciousness, at once attributes his attainment to his particular business partner—Christ, Buddha, Mrs. Besant, etc., etc., and attempts to rationalize about the suprarational, and describe what is beyond description in the language of his country.
>
> P., under the gentle guidance of Ânanda Metteya, at first found the outward simplicity most refreshing; but soon he discovered that like all other religious systems Buddhism was entangled in a veritable network of words. Realizing this, he went a step further than Gotama, and said: "Why bother about Sorrow at all, or about Transmigration? for these are not 'wrong viewyness,' as Mr. Rhys Davids would so poetically put it, but matters of the Kindergarten and not of the Temple; matters for police regulation, and for underpaid curates to chatter about, and matters that have nothing to do with true progress." He then divided life into two

---

[75] Jinarājadāsa 1948, 5–6.
[76] *The Temple of Solomon the King*, loc. cit., "The Vedanta."

compartments; into the first he threw science, learning, philosophy, and all things built of words—the toys of life; and into the second The Invocations of Adonai—the work of attainment.

Then he took another step forward. "Do as [sic] thou wilt!" Not only is Animism absurd, but so also is Morality; not only is Reincarnation absurd, but so also is Transmigration; not only is the Ego absurd, but so also is the Non-Ego; not only is Karma absurd, but so also is Nibbâna. For, all things and no-things are absurd save "I," who am Soul and Body, Good and Evil, Sorrow and Joy, Change and Equilibrium; who in the temple of Adonai, am beyond all these, and by the fire side in my study—Mr. X, one with each and all.[77]

"We have to thank Freud—and especially Jung—for stating this part of the Magical Doctrine so plainly, as also for their development of the connexion of the Will of this 'child' with the True or Unconscious Will, and so for clarifying our doctrine of the 'Silent Self' or 'Holy Guardian Angel'. They are of course totally ignorant of magical phenomena, and could hardly explain even such terms as 'Augoeides'; and they are seriously to blame for not stating more openly that this True Will is not to be daunted or suppressed; but within their limits they have done excellent work."[78] As Jung puts it, "Our psyche is set up in accord with the structure of the universe, and what happens in the macrocosm likewise happens in the infinitesimal and most subjective reaches of the psyche. For that reason the God-image is always a projection of the inner experience of a powerful *vis-à-vis*. This is symbolized by objects from which the inner experience has taken its initial impulse, and which from then on preserve numinous significance, or else it is characterized by its numinosity and overwhelming force of that numinosity. In this way the imagination liberates itself from the concretism of the object and attempts to sketch the image of the invisible as something which stands behind the phenomenon. I'm thinking here of the simplest basic form of the mandala, the circle, and the simplest (mental) division of the circle, the quadrant or, as the case may be, the cross."[79]

Such experiences have a helpful or, it may be, annihilating effect upon man. He cannot grasp, comprehend, dominate them; nor can he free himself or escape from them, and therefore feels them as overpowering. Recognizing that they do not spring from his conscious personality, he calls them mana, daimon, or God. Science employs the term "the unconscious," thus admitting that it knows nothing about it, for it can know nothing about the substance of the psyche when the sole means of knowing anything is the psyche. Therefore the validity of such terms as mana, daimon, or God can be neither disproved nor affirmed. We can, however, establish that the sense of strangeness connected with

---

[77] *Ibid.*, "The Doctrines of Buddhism."
[78] NC on AL III.22.
[79] Jung 1989, 335–6.

the experience of something objective, apparently, outside the psyche, is indeed authentic.

We know that something unknown, alien, does come our way, just as we know that we do not ourselves *make* a dream or an inspiration, but that it somehow arises of its own accord. What does happen to us in this manner can be said to emanate from mana, from a daimon, a god, or the unconscious. The first three terms have the great merit of including and evoking the emotional quality of numinosity, whereas the latter—the unconscious—is banal and therefore closer to reality. The latter concept includes the empirical realm—that is, the commonplace reality we know so well. The unconscious is too neutral and rational a term to give much impetus to the imagination. The term, after all, was coined for scientific purposes, and is far better suited to dispassionate observation which makes no metaphysical claims that are the transcendental concepts, which are controversial and therefore tend to breed fanaticism.[80]

Writing in the first person, Jung says, "I prefer the term 'unconscious,' knowing that I might equally well speak of 'God' or 'daimon' if I wished to express myself in mythic language. When I do use such mythic language, I am aware that 'mana,' 'daimon,' and 'God' are synonyms for the unconscious."[81] Is it any surprise, then, that modern secular humanists have, in turn, "encounters" with extra-terrestrials, or that these experiences are often sexual in nature, involving "anal probes," "alien embryos," and what not?[82] Crowley's *Liber LXV*, or *Liber Cordis Cincti Serpente*, is an "account of the relations of the Aspirant with his Holy Guardian Angel. This book is given to Probationers, as the attainment of the Knowledge and Conversation of the Holy Guardian Angel is the Crown of the Outer College."[83]

> It is also spoken, "Liber LXV," V:14, of the Sword of Adonai, "that hath four blades, the blade of the thunderbolt, the blade of the Pylon, the blade of the serpent, the blade of the Phallus."
>
> But this Sword is not for the ordinary Magician. For this is the Sword flaming every way that keeps Eden, and in this Sword the Wand and the Cup are concealed—so that although the being of the Magician is blasted by the Thunderbolt, and poisoned by the Serpent, at the same time the organs whose union is the supreme sacrament are left in him.
>
> At the coming of Adonai the individual is destroyed in both senses. He is shattered into a thousand pieces, yet at the same time united with the simple. *{Compare the first set of verses in "Liber XVI." (XVI in the Taro is pe, Mars, the Sword.)}*
>
> Of this it is also spoken by St. Paul in his Epistle to the Church in Thessalonica: "For the Lord shall descend from Heaven, with a shout, with the voice of the Archangel, and with the trump of God; and the dead

---

[80] *Ibid.*, 336. Emphasis in original.
[81] *Ibid.*, 336–7.
[82] *Cf.* Vallée 1969.
[83] A∴A∴ *Curriculum.*

in Christ shall rise first. Then we which are alive and remain shall be caught up together with them into the clouds to meet the Lord in the air; and so shall we be for ever with the Lord."

The stupid interpretation of this verse as prophetic of a "second advent" need not concern us; every word of it is, however, worthy of profound consideration.

"The Lord" is Adonai—which is the Hebrew for "my Lord"; and He descends from heaven, the supernal Eden, the *sahasrāra cakra* in man, with a "shout," a "voice," and a "trump," again airy symbols, for it is air that carries sound. These sounds refer to those heard by the Adept at the moment of rapture.

This is most accurately pictured in the Tarot Trump called "The Angel," which corresponds to the letter *shin*, the letter of Spirit and of Breath.

The whole mind of man is rent by the advent of Adonai, and is at once caught up into union with Him. "In the air," the Ruach.

Note that etymologically the word συν, "together with," is the Sanskrit *sam*; and the Hebrew ADNI is the Sanskrit *adhi*.

The phrase "together with the Lord," is then literally identical with the word *samādhi*, which is the Sanskrit name of the phenomenon described by Saint Paul—this union of the ego and the non-ego, subject and object, this chymical marriage—and thus identical with the symbolism of the Rosy Cross, under a slightly different aspect.[84]

The entry on number 65 in *An Essay upon Number* tells us that, "In Roman characters LXV = LVX, the redeeming light. See the $5°=6^\square$ ritual and 'Konx om Pax.' Note 65 = 13 × 5, the most spiritual form of force, just as 10 × 5 was its most material form. Note הס, 'Keep silence!' and היכל, the palace; as if it were said 'Silence is the House of Adonai.'" *Lux* is Latin for "light," whence derives e.g. *Lucifer*, "light-bringer."[85] The entry on number 300 as also relevant here, and it describes: "The letter ש, meaning 'tooth,' and suggesting by its shape a triple flame. Refers Yetziratically to fire, and is symbolic of the Holy Spirit, רוה אלהים = 300. Hence the letter of the Spirit. Descending into the midst of יהוה, the four inferior elements, we get יהשוה Jeheshua, the Saviour, symbolised by the Pentagram."

---

[84] *Book 4*, Part II, Ch. VIII.
[85] Before contributing to the Satanic ritual abuse panic of the 1990s, Carl Raschke argued that, "the 'meaning' of the unconscious is the strategy of self-concealment. The language of the unconscious is the language of feints, diversions, and masks. It is the vocabulary of the magus. . . .The 'lost word,' the *logos* that does not speak, is the supreme magical cipher, because its power seeps from its very inarticulation. The great work, the *magnum opus*, the transformation of the inchoate into a vast, intelligible content, turns upon the saying of the aboriginal unsaid, the presyntactic. 'An idea is perpetuated because it must never be mentioned.' The refusal to speak, the veiling of what remains so difficult to utter, defines the magician's hegemony within the court of symbols. The magician controls the energy of god because he 'knows' it as the mystery of the cleft, as the message of the vestige, as the manifestation of the trace." ("Jacques Lacan and the Magic of Desire: A Post-Structuralist Subscript," in Wyschogrod, Crownfield & Raschke 1989, 63.)

But Sigma in Hebrew is Shin, 300, the letter of Fire and of the "Spirit of the Gods" which broods upon the Formless Void in the Beginning, being by shape a triple tongue of flame, and by meaning a tooth, which is the only part of the secret and solid foundation of Man that is manifested normally. Teeth serve him to fight, to crush, to cut, to rend, to bite and grip his prey; they witness that he is a fierce, dangerous, and carnivorous animal. But they are also the best witness to the mastery of Spirit over Matter, the extreme hardness of their substance being chiselled and polished and covered with a glistening film by Life no less easily and beautifully than is does with more naturally plastic types of substance.

Teeth are displayed when our Secret Self—our Subconscious Ego, whose Magical Image is our individuality expressed in mental and bodily form—our Holy Guardian Angel—comes forth and declares our True Will to our fellows, whether to snarl or to sneer, to smile or to laugh.

Teeth serve us to pronounce the dental letters which in their deepest nature express decision, fortitude, endurance, just as gutturals suggest the breath of Life itself free-flowing, and labials the duplex vibrations of action and reaction. Pronounce T, D, S or N, and you will find them all continuously forcible exhalations whose difference is determined solely by the position of the tongue, the teeth being bared as when a wild beast turns to bay. The sibilant sound of S or Sh is our English word, and also the Hebrew word, Hush, a strongly aspirated S, and suggests the hiss of a snake. Now this hiss is the common sign of recognition between men when one wants to call another's attention without disturbing the silence more than necessary. (Also we have Hist, our Double letter.) This hiss means: "Attention! A man!" For in all Semitic and some Aryan languages, ISh or a closely similar word means "a man." Say it: you must bare your clenched teeth as in defiance, and breathe harshly out as in excitement.

Hiss! Sh! means "Keep silent! there's danger if you are heard. Attention! There's a man somewhere, deadly as a snake. Breathe hard; there's a fight coming."

This Sh is then the forcible subtle creative Spirit of Life, fiery and triplex, continuous, Silence of pure Breath modified into sound by two and thirty obstacles, as the Zero of Empty Space, though it contain all Life, only takes form according (as the Qabalists say) to the two and thirty "Paths" of Number and Letter which obstruct it.[86]

"Now in the Tarot the Trump illustrating this letter Sh is an old form of the Stele of Revealing, Nuith with Shu and Seb, the pantacle or magical picture of the old Æon, as Nuit with Hadit and Ra Hoor Khuit is of the new. The number of this Trump is XX. It is called the Angel, the messenger from Heaven of the new Word."[87] Or as the *New Comment* phrases it, "S has in the

---

[86] *The Equinox of the Gods*, "Genesis Libri AL," Ch. VII, Sec. III.
[87] *Ibid.*

Tarot the card numbered XX, which represents the Stele of Revealing, and is called the Judgment; i.e., the ending of an Æon."[88] The Stele of Revealing is the funeral tablet of Ankh-af-na-Khonsu, a priest of Montu who lived in Thebes during the late 25th Dynasty, commonly known as the Nubian Dynasty or the Kushite Empire, the last dynasty of the Third Intermediate Period of ancient Egypt. According to Crowley's mythic story, "Across the Gulf," Ankh-af-na-Khonsu (fl. c. 725 BCE) was responsible for ushering in the previous Æon. Also referred to as *Liber LIX*, Crowley describes it as a "fantastic account of a previous incarnation," the principal interest of which "is that its story of the overthrowing of Isis by Osiris may help the reader to understand the meaning of the overthrowing of Osiris by Horus in the present Æon."[89]

According to *The Book of Thoth*, "The card originally called 'The Hierophant', representing Osiris (as is shown by the shape of the tiara) became, in the Renaissance period, the Pope. The High Priestess came to be called 'Pope Joan', representing a certain symbolic legend which circulated among initiates, and became vulgarised in the fable of a Female Pope. More important still, 'The Angel', or 'The Last Judgment', represented the destruction of the world by fire. Its hieroglyph is, in a way, prophetic, for when the world *was* destroyed by fire on 21st March, 1904, one's attention was inevitably called to the similarity of this card to the Stélé of Revealing. This being the beginning of the New Æon, it has seemed more fitting to show the beginning of the Æon; for all that is known about the next Æon, due in 2,000 years' time, is that its symbol is the double-wanded one." As the footnote affirms, "The reference is to Maat, Themis, Lady of the Balance."[90]

Magick in Theory and Practice says of the Holy Guardian Angel that, "It is His constant and eternal Will to become one with the Aspirant, and the moment the conditions of the latter make it possible, That Bridal is consummated." The footnote point out that, "Since this Knowledge and Conversation is not universal, it seems at first as if an omnipotent Will were being baulked. But His Will and your Will together make up that One Will, because you and He are one. That One Will is therefore divided against itself, so long as your Will fails to aspire steadfastly. Also, His Will cannot constrain yours. He is so much one with you that even your Will to separate is His Will. He is so certain of you that He delights in your perturbation and coquetry no less than in your surrender. These relations are fully explained in 'Liber LXV.'"[91] The section on "How Human Spirits Can Be Conferred with" in *Isis Unveiled* reminds us that "we read in the Persian *Desatir*, of the 'Resplendent one'; in the Greek philosopher-initiates, of the Augoeides—the self-shining 'blessed vision resident in the pure light'; in Porphyry, that Plotinus was united to his 'god' six times during his lifetime; and so on."

---

[88] NC on AL I.15.
[89] A∴A∴ *Curriculum*.
[90] *The Book of Thoth, loc. cit.*, Sec. II. Emphasis in original.
[91] *MITAP*, Ch. XVI, Pt. II, Sec. II.

As Crowley's review of *Heavenly Bridegrooms* by Theodore Schroeder and Ida Craddock in *The Equinox*, Vol. III, No. 1, states, "The authoress of the MS. claims that she was the wife of an angel. She expounds at the greatest length the philosophy connected with this thesis. Her learning is enormous. She finds traces of similar beliefs in every country in the world, and (having a similar experience of her own) she can hardly be blamed for arguing that one thing confirms the other. Mr. Schroeder is quite logical in calling her paper An Unintentional Contribution to the Erotogenetic Interpretation of Religion, but commits the errors of *petitio principii* and *non distributio medii* with the most exquisite nonchalance. Only a lawyer could be so shameless. He begs the question with regard to this particular case, assuming that her relation with the angel was pure hallucination, of which he has no evidence whatever. He argues that, since one person both loves and is religious, religion is nothing but a morbid manifestation of the sexual instinct. One does not have even to disagree with him to see how worthless is his reasoning. As a matter of fact, I do half agree with him in my calmer moments in a general way, but the conclusion can be carried a step further. When you have proved that God is merely a name for the sex instinct, it appears to me not far to the perception that the sex instinct is God."[92]

"It is said among Men that the Word Hell deriveth from the Verb *helan*, to hele or conceal, in the Tongue of the Anglo-Saxons. That is, it is the concealed Place, which, since all things are in thine own Self, is the Unconscious. How then? Because Men were already aware how this Unconscious, or Libido, is opposed, for the most Part, to the conscious Will."[93] Mencius, the most famous Confucian after Confucius himself, writes: "There is not a part of the body that a man does not love. And because there is not a part that he does not love, there is not a part of it that he does not nourish. Because there is not an inch of his skin that he does not love, there is not an inch of his skin that he does not take care of. The thing that determines whether a thing is good or bad depends only on his regard for it, or the value he places upon it. Now in our constitution there is a higher and a lower nature, a smaller and a greater self. One should not develop the lower nature at the expense of the higher nature, or develop the smaller self at the expense of the greater self. He who attends to his smaller self becomes a small man, and he who attends to his greater self becomes a great man."[94]

> One of the principal points about the sin stupidity is that it flatters the sinner. All insanity depends upon the exacerbation of the ego. The melancholic hugs the delusion that he has committed the unpardonable

---

[92] *Cf.* also *The Book of Thoth*, Part III, "Prince of Disks"—"The error of Christian Mystics on this point has been responsible for more cruelty, misery, and collective insanity than all others put together; its poison can be traced even in the teaching of Freud, who assumed that the Unconscious was 'the devil', whereas in fact it is the instinct which expresses, beneath a veil, the inherent Point-of-View of each, and, properly understood, is the key to Initiation, and a hint of what seed may blossom and fructify as the 'Knowledge and Conversation of the Holy Guardian Angel'."
[93] *Liber Aleph*, "De libidine secreta."
[94] 6A:14. Chan 1963, 58–59.

sin. Sins grow by repression and by brooding upon their enormity. Few people would go to excess if they were not unwholesomely over-excited about their trivial apishness.

Most people, especially Freud, misunderstand the Freudian position. "The libido of the unconscious" is really "the true will of the inmost self". The sexual characteristics of the individual are, it is true, symbolic indications of its nature, and when those are "abnormal", we may suspect that the self is divided against itself in some way. Experience teaches the adepts who initiate mankind that when any complex (duality) in the self is resolved (unity) the initiate becomes whole. The morbid sexual symptoms (which are merely the complaints of the sick animal) disappear, while the moral and mental consciousness is relieved from its civil war of doubt and self-obsession. The complete man, harmonized, flows freely towards his natural goal.[95]

In the Introduction to *Magick in Theory and Practice*, Crowley interprets "Every man and every woman is a star" (AL I.3) as simply meaning that "every human being is intrinsically an independent individual with his own proper character and proper motion." It is his hope that, "The sincere student will discover, behind the symbolic technicalities of his book, a practical method of making himself a Magician. The processes described will enable him to discriminate between what he actually is, and what he has fondly imagined himself to be." The footnote goes on to explain that, "Professor Sigmund Freud and his school have, in recent years, discovered a part of this body of Truth, which has been taught for many centuries in the Sanctuaries of Initiation. But failure to grasp the fullness of Truth, especially that implied in my Sixth Theorem (above) and its corollaries, has led him and his followers into the error of admitting that the avowedly suicidal 'Censor' is the proper arbiter of conduct. Official psycho-analysis is therefore committed to upholding a fraud, although the foundation of the science was the observation of the disastrous effects on the individual of being false to his Unconscious Self, whose 'writing on the wall' in dream language is the record of the sum of the essential tendencies of the true

---

[95] *Confessions*, Ch. 6. *Cf.* e.g. Freud 1918, 147–8: "In this intermediary stage, the importance of which increases the more we investigate it, the sexual impulses which formerly were seperate, have already formed into a unit and have also found an object; but this object is not external and foreign to the individual, but his own ego, which is formed at this period. This new stage is called *narcism*, in view of the pathological fixation of this condition which may be observed later on. The individual acts as if he were in love with himself; for the purposes of our analysis the ego impulses and the libidinous wishes cannot yet be separated from each other. Although this narcistic stage, in which hitherto dissociated sexual impulses combine into a unity and take the ego as their object, cannot as yet be sharply differentiated, we can already surmise that the narcistic organization is never altogether given up again. To a certain extent man remains narcistic, even after he had found outer subjects for his libido, and the objects on which he bestows it represent, as it were, emanations of the libido which remain with his ego and which can be withdrawn into it. The state of being in love, so remarkable psychologically, and the normal prototype of the psychoses, corresponds to the highest stage of these emanations, in contrast to the state of self-love. This high estimation of psychic acts found among primitives and neurotics, which we feel to be an over-estimation, may now appropriately be brought into relation to narcism, and interpreted as an essential part of it."

nature of the individual. The result has been that psycho-analysts have misinterpreted life, and announced the absurdity that every human being is essentially an anti-social, criminal, and insane animal. It is evident that the errors of the Unconscious of which the psycho-analysts complain are neither more nor less than the 'original sin' of the theologians whom they despise so heartily."[96]

The student of magick "must behold his soul in all its awful nakedness, he must not fear to look on that appalling actuality. He must discard the gaudy garments with which his shame has screened him; he must accept the fact that nothing can make him anything but what he is. He may lie to himself, drug himself, hide himself; but he is always there. Magick will teach him that his mind is playing him traitor. It is as if a man were told that tailors' fashion-plates were the canon of human beauty, so that he tried to make himself formless and featureless like them, and shuddered with horror at the idea of Holbein making a portrait of him. Magick will show him the beauty and majesty of the self which he has tried to suppress and disguise."[97] According to psychoanalytic theory, the deepest layer of the subconscious mind is formed by the disavowed and constricted stream of vital and powerful genital impulses. This is the feared "libido," the buttress of everything that lives, the suppression of which all "worldliness" is about.

Freud and his daughter Anna led corporate psychologists to think they could tame the irrational "secret self" by giving people symbols of power in the form of private houses, personal territory, and consumer goods. His former student, Wilhelm Reich, on the contrary, believed that the irrational inner self was not dangerous unless it was repressed, and that is exactly what Freud's techniques did. Such people will start to hate both themselves and life itself. Life begins to, at least subconsciously, revolt them, because they see how other people are still able to enjoy it. Their efforts to return to life manifest in an exaggerated, nearly hysterical sexual urge. But rather than being liberating, their sexual activities lead to ever worsening bottling up of energy. Anna Freud, herself a virgin analyzed by her father for her excessive masturbation, was committed to her father's legacy, and determined to take Reich down. She discredited his work and got him kicked out of the International Psychoanalytical Association. Reich was ultimately thrown in prison and the FDA ordered all his books and records to be burned.[98]

As Crowley says, "When the organs of the body assert their presence other by silent satisfaction, it is a sign they are diseased. The single exception is the organ of reproduction. Yet even in this case its self-assertion bears witness to its dissatisfaction with itself, since it cannot fulfil its function until completed by its counterpart in another organism."[99] In fact, according to *Liber CDXV*, or *The Paris Working*, "Respectability is the greatest of all blinds. The general key in reading ancient documents of a

---

[96] *MITAP*, Introduction.
[97] *Ibid*.
[98] Balk 2012.
[99] *MITAP*, loc. cit.

magical nature, is to suspect the worst."[100] For Thelemites, "Sex is the first unconscious manifestation of Chiah, the Creative Energy; and although (like everything else) it is shown both on the spiritual and the physical planes, its most important forth-showing is on the 'Magical' plane, because it actually produces phenomena which partake of all these. It is the True Will on the creative plane: 'By Wisdom formed He the worlds.' So soon as its thaumaturgy is accomplished, it is, through Binah, understood as the Logos. Thus in Sex we find every one of the primary Correspondences of Chokmah. Being thus ineffable and sacrosanct, it is (plainly enough) peculiarly liable to profanation. Being profaned, it is naturally more unspeakably nasty than any other of the 'Mysteries.' You will find a good deal on this subject implied in *Artemis Iota*."[101]

"To every man and woman that has not seen Sex as it is, faced it, mastered it . . . it is his secret guilt. Imagine, then, how at any reference however remote, the 'sinner' quails, his inmost mystery laid bare, his evil conscience holding up a tarnished mirror to his deformed and hideous face! Often enough, he does not mind gross jests which admit complicity on the part of the other; but any allusion to the Truth, and his soul shrieks: 'I am found out!' Then apoplectic Fear puts on the mask of Indignation and Disgust. . . . Corresponding to, and the poison bacillus of, that centre of infection, is a Trinity of pure Evil, the total abnegation of Thelema. Well known to the psycho-analyst: the name thereof Shame—Guilt—Fear. The Anglo-Saxon or bourgeois mentality is soaked therein; and his remedy so far from our exploratory-disinfection method, is to hide the gangrened mass with dirty poultices. He has always a text of Scripture or some other authority to paint his foulest acts in glowing colours; and if he wants a glass of beer, he hates the stuff, but—doctor's orders, my boy, doctor's orders. —There is really nothing new to be said about hypocrisy; it has been analysed, exposed, lashed by every great Artist; quite without effect. It gets worse as the socialistic idea thrives, as the individual leans ever harder on the moral support of the herd."[102]

Isis Unveiled, originally entitled *The Veil of Isis*, purports to quote Vrihaspati: "In ancient India, the mystery of the triad, known but to the initiates, could not, under the penalty of death, be revealed to the vulgar." According to Blavatsky, "Neither could it in the ancient Grecian and Samothracian Mysteries. *Nor can it be now.* It is in the hands of the adepts, and must remain a mystery to the world so long as the materialistic savant regards it as an undemonstrated fallacy, an insane hallucination, and the dogmatic theologian, a snare of the Evil One."[103]

---

[100] Opus VIII.
[101] *MWT*, Ch. LXXVIII.
[102] *Ibid.*
[103] Blavatsky 1877, ii.115. Emphasis in original.

CHAPTER 9
Transcending Duality

I must conclude with a warning. So many of these branches of magick are so fascinating that any one of them is liable to take hold of the Magician by the short hair and upset his balance completely. It should never be forgotten for a single moment that the central and essential work of the Magicians is the attainment of the Knowledge and Conversation of the Holy Guardian Angel. Once he has achieved this he must of course be left entirely in the hands of that Angel, who can be invariably and inevitably relied upon to lead him to the further great step—crossing of the abyss and the attainment of the grade of Master of the Temple.

Anything apart from this course is a side issue and unless so regarded may lead to the complete ruin of the whole work of the Magician.

—Magick Without Tears

"The Universe is one, omnipotent, omniscient, omnipresent. Its substance is homogenous, and this substance cannot be said to possess the qualities of Being, Consciousness and Bliss, for these are rather the shadows of it, which are apprehended by the highly illuminated mind when it comes near thereto. Time and space themselves are but illusions which condition under veils. This substance has received many names among many peoples. . . . In later times, it has been called God, or the Absolute, or Spirit, and even, by certain philosophers, Matter. All, however, agree in its attributes, and these are naturally mostly of a negative character, but the Greeks called it the One, and it is because of its essential one-ness that we here so consider it, for One is the first positive manifestation in computation. Since, therefore, this substance is one, homogenous and self-conscious, it cannot be manifest in any way while it is in that state. It would be absurd to enquire into the reasons for its manifestation in any other state because reason is not a quality appertaining to that unity. It is sufficient to know that it did divide itself into two equal and opposite courses, which have been variously described by different schools of philosophy as male and female, or active and passive, or fire and water, or being and form, or matter and motion, or the Yin and the Yang, or again personification such as Shiva and Shakti, and in fact any other pair of deities of the first order. This dual principle, exalted as it is, comes a little nearer to the limits of the human mind, for that mind is itself dualistic, our consciousness being composed of subjective and objective, the ego and the non-ego."[1]

"It is possible to dissolve this duality back again into the unity by a mystic process, but the natural course taken by its own combination is to

---
[1] *Liber DXXXVI*, Ch. V, Sec. I.

form a third entity, partaking of the qualities of both, yet possessing an independent existence. Thus is formed the descending triangle of father, mother, son, the Yod, He, Vau of the Qabalistic Trigrammaton and the pre-Christian trinity of such Gods as Isis, Horus, Osiris, or many others whose names will readily occur to the reader. In the ancient Greek philosophy, of Parmenides, Empedocles, Heraclitus, the Eleatic Zeno, and even in the philosophy of Pythagoras and the Stagyrite, these three principles are recognised under the names of fire, air and water. They are connected with the three possible states in which one can conceive the Universe—Being, Not-Being, and Becoming. The more carefully Plato and Aristotle are studied, the clearer these points become. It must, however, be understood that these principles are all active and causative; they still pertain to the divine hierarchy—in a word, to the Yetziratic world of Rabbi ben Simeon.[2] However, from this trinity of actives is consolidated a passive which, to continue the termination of the Physicist school of philosophy, is called earth. These four form a stable and harmonious combination, the Tetragrammaton, which is the ineffable word, and we say that all things are composed of this fourfold material. The whole of this doctrine is admirably resumed, although amplified, in the Sephirotic system."[3]

"In one, the best, system of Magick, the Absolute is called the Crown, God is called the Father, the Pure Soul is called the Mother, the Holy Guardian Angel is called the Son, and the Natural Soul is called the Daughter. The Son purifies the Daughter by wedding her; she thus becomes the Mother, the uniting of whom with the Father absorbs all into the Crown." The "Magical Will is the wand in your hand by which the Great Work is accomplished, by which the Daughter is not merely set upon the throne of the Mother, but assumed into the Highest."[4] In "the so-called Jetziratic attribution of Pentagrammaton, that followed by Dr. Dee, and by the Hindus, Tibetans, Chinese and Japanese. Fire is the Foundation, the central core, of things."[5] Heraclitus held that change is the only persisting condition of things and that the Supreme Being is Fire—not merely physical heat, but an ethereal principle that acts upon matter producing motion and creative activity.[6]

---

[2] *Cf.* also *The Book of Thoth*, Part II, Atu XXI: "The original three elements, Fire, Air, Water, sufficed for primitive thought; Earth and Spirit represent a later accretion. Neither is to be found in the original twenty-two Paths of the Sepher Yetzirah. The world of Assiah, the material world, does not appear except as a pendant to the Tree of Life."
[3] *Liber DXXXVI, loc. cit.*
[4] *Book 4*, Part II, Ch. VI.
[5] *The Book of Lies*, Ch. 86, Commentary. *Cf.* also *The Book of Thoth*, Appendix B, Diagram 6: "The Elements are four in number; although they are harmonized and balanced and made to revolve, there is an irreconcilable difficulty in their perfection. It is impossible to arrange four numbers into a 'magic square', so that all the sides and all diagonals add up to the same number. Two is the only number of which this is true. Such is the mathematical formula of expressing the doctrine of what was called the Accurséd Dyad. The problem of the Adept was therefore to attack this irreconcilable duality, whose limit is fortified and entrenched by being squared. As therefore the original duality of Fire and Water was overcome by the introduction of a third Element partaking equally of both natures, Air, so a fifth Element was introduced, and the Pentagram instituted as a symbol of salvation."
[6] *Cf.* also *The Book of Thoth*, Part II, Atu 0: "The ultimate sense seems to be that the original god is both male and female, which is, of course, the essential doctrine of the Qabalah; and the thing most difficult to understand about the later debased Old Testament tradition, is that it represents

Iamblichus cautions us that, "these things about which certain mountebank priests and fortune-tellers calumniate those who minister at the worship of the gods, and thou hast spoken in the same way—are none of them at all connected with genuine theology and theurgy. Yet if, in some way, certain things of such a character shoot out as excrescences beside the knowledges of the things that are good, as evil arts sprout up with other arts, these very knowledges are actually more opposed by them than anything else. For that which is evil is more hostile to the good than to that which is not good. . . . Now then it is necessary to consider how he may be unloosed and set free from his bonds. There is no other way except the knowing of the gods. For the ideal or success is the apperceiving of the Good, just as the ideal of badness happens to be forgetting of what is good and deceit in relation to what is bad. The former, therefore, joins with the Divine nature: but the latter, an inferior destiny, is inseparable from the mortal."[7]

"The former seeks the intellectible essences by the sacred paths: but the latter, having swerved from the first principles, yields itself to the measuring out of the ideals of the corporeal environment. The former is the knowing of the Father: but the latter is the going aside from him and a forgetting of God, the Father, first in Essence and sufficient for himself. The former preserves the genuine life and brings it back to its Father, but the latter brings the man ruling in the realm of generated existence down to the world which is never permanent but always changing. Let, then, this superior path to true success, which is the spiritual completing of the union of souls to the divine nature, be cognized by thee. But the sacerdotal and theurgic gift of true success is called the Door to the Creator of the Universe, or Supreme Goodness. In the first place it possesses the power of chastity of soul which is far more perfect than chastity of the body: afterward, the preparing of the understanding for the participation and vision of the Good and its release from everything of a contrary character: and after these, oneness with the gods the givers of all things good."[8]

> After the theurgic discipline has conjoined the soul individually with the several departments of the universe, and with all the divine powers that pervade it, then it leads the soul to the Creator of the world, places it in his charge, and frees it of everything pertaining to the realm of matter, uniting it with the Sole Eternal Reason (Logos).
>
> What I am saying is this: That it unites the soul individually to the One, Father of himself, self-moving. He who sustains the universe,

---

Tetragrammaton as masculine, in spite of the two feminine components. Zeus became too popular, and, in consequence, too many legends gathered around him; but the important fact for this present purpose is that Zeus was peculiarly the Lord of Air. Men who sought the origin of Nature in the earliest days tried to find this origin in one of the Elements. (The history of philosophy describes the controversy between Anaximander and Zenocrates; later, Empedocles.) It may be that the original authors of the Tarot were trying to promulgate the doctrine that the origin of everything was Air. Yet if this were so, it would upset the whole Tarot as we know it, since the order of origin makes Fire the first father. It is Air as Zero that reconciles the antinomy."
[7] *De mysteriis*, x.2.
[8] *Ibid.*, x.5.

spiritual, who arranges all things in order, who leads it to the supreme truth, to the absolute, the efficient, and other creative powers of God: thus establishing the theurgic soul in the energies, the conceptions and creative qualities of those powers. Then it inserts the soul in the entire Demiurgic God.

This, with the Egyptian Sages, is the end of the "Return" as taught in the Sacred Records.[9]

As the *New Comment* on AL I.41 puts it, "One cannot say that it was 'Sin' for Naught to restrict itself within the form of Two; on the contrary. But sin is to resist the operation of the reversion to Naught. 'The wages of Sin is Death'; for Life is a continual harmonious and natural Change." Crowley tells us that, "'The creative Force of the Universe' is quite ready-made. Πυραμις, a pyramid, is that Force in its geometrical form; in its biological form it is Φαλλος, the Yang or Lingam. Both words have the same numerical value, 831. These two words can therefore serve you as the secret object of your Work. How than can you construct the number 831? The Letter Kaph, Jupiter (Jehovah), the Wheel of Fortune in the Tarot—the Atu X is a picture of the Universe built up and revolving by virtue of those Three Principles: Sulphur, Mercury, Salt; or Gunas: Sattvas, Rajas, Tamas—has the value 20. So also has the letter Yod spelt in full."[10]

The Scourge, the Dagger, and the Chain, represent the three alchemical principles of Sulphur, Mercury, and Salt. These are not the substances which we now call by these names; they represent "principles," whose operations chemists have found it more convenient to explain in other ways. But Sulphur represents the energy of things, Mercury their fluidity, Salt their fixity. They are analogous to Fire, Air and Water; but they mean rather more, for they represent something deeper and subtler, and yet more truly active. An almost exact analogy is given by the three Gunas of the Hindus; Sattvas, Rajas, and Tamas. Sattvas is Mercury, equable, calm, clear; Rajas is Sulphur, active, excitable, even fierce; Tamas is Salt, thick, sluggish, heavy, dark.

But Hindu philosophy is so occupied with the main idea that only the Absolute is worth anything, that it tends to consider these Gunas (even Sattvas) as evil. This is a correct view, but only from above; and we prefer, if we are truly wise, to avoid this everlasting wail which characterizes the thought of the Indian peninsula: "Everything is sorrow," etc. Accepting their doctrine of the two phases of the Absolute, we must, if we are to be consistent, class the two phases together, either as good or as bad; if one is good and the other bad we are back again in that duality, to avoid which we invented the Absolute.[11]

---

[9] *Ibid.*, x.6.
[10] *MWT*, Introduction.
[11] *Book 4*, Part II, Ch. VI.

"The word 'Guna' is untranslatable. It is not quite an element, a quality, a form of energy, a phase, or a potential; all of these ideas enter into it. All the qualities that can be predicated of anything may be ascribed to one or more of these Gunas: Tamas is darkness, inertia, sloth, ignorance, death and the like; Rajas is energy, excitement, fire, brilliance, restlessness; Sattvas is calm, intelligence, lucidity and balance. They correspond to the three principal Hindu castes. One of the most important aphorisms of Hindu philosophy is: 'the Gunas revolve'. This means that, according to the doctrine of continual change, nothing can remain in any phase where one of these Gunas is predominant; however dense and dull that thing may be, a time will come when it begins to stir. The end and reward of the effort is a state of lucid quietude, which, however, tends ultimately to sink into the original inertia."[12] In Hinduism, spirit or consciousness likewise has three aspects: the reality of being (*sat*), awareness of others (*chit*), and joyful activity (*ānanda*). These terms often run together as *sat-chit-ānanda* to symbolize the unity of these three aspects.

"You will have noticed that the grade of Master of the Temple is itself intimately associated with Yoga. It is when one reaches this plane that the apparently contradictory forms of the Great Work, Magick and Yoga, begin to converge, though even earlier in the course of the work it must have been noticed that achievements in Yoga have been of great assistance to magical operations, and that many of the mental states necessary to the development of the Magician are identical with those attained in the course of the strictly technical Yogic operations.... Magick is the journey from 0 to 2, Yoga from 2 to 0. It is a very good rule for the Yogi to keep this mind constantly fixed on the fact that any idea soever is false. There is actually a Hindu proverb 'That which can be thought is not true.' Consequently the existence of any idea in the mind is an immediate refutation of it, but equally the contraries as well as contradictory of that idea are false, and the result of this is to knock the second law of formal logic to pieces."[13]

> One puts up a sort of sorites—*A* is *B*, therefore *A* is not *B*; therefore not *A* is not *B*; and all these contrary statements are equally false, but in order to realise this fact they must themselves be announced by the mind as ecstatic discoveries of truth.
>
> The result of all this naturally is that the mind very rapidly becomes a discredited instrument, and one attains to a totally different and much more exalted type of mind, and the same destructive criticism which one applied to the original consciousness applies equally to this higher consciousness, and one gets to one higher still which is again destroyed. In *The Equinox*, Vol. I there is an essay called "The Soldier and the Hunchback: ! and ?" In *Liber Aleph* too there are several chapters about attainment by what is called the Method of Ladders.
>
> All these operations are equally valid and equally invalid, and the result of this is that the whole subject of Yoga leads to constantly

---

[12] *The Book of Thoth*, Part II, Atu X.
[13] *MWT*, Ch. LXXXIII.

increasing confusion. The fineness of the analytical instrument seems to defeat its own purpose and it is perhaps because of that confession that I have always felt in my deepest consciousness that the method of Magick is on the whole less dangerous than that of Yoga. This is particularly the case when discussing these matters with a Western mind.[14]

"Every operation of Love is the satisfaction of a bitter hunger, but the appetite only grows fiercer by satisfaction; so that we can say with the Preacher: 'He that increaseth knowledge increaseth Sorrow.'[15] The root of all this sorrow is in the sense of insufficiency; the need to unite, to lose oneself in the beloved object, is the manifest proof of this fact, and it is clear also that the satisfaction produces only a temporary relief, because the process expands indefinitely. The thirst increases with drinking. The only complete satisfaction conceivable would be the Yoga of the atom with the entire universe. This fact is easily perceived, and has been constantly expressed in the mystical philosophies of the West; the only goal is 'Union with God.' Of course, we only use the word 'God' because we have been brought up in superstition, and the higher philosophers both in the East and in the West have preferred to speak of union with the All or with the Absolute. More superstitions!"[16]

In *An Essay upon Number*, Crowley describes an atheist who is "not really an atheist at all. He is but a traveller in the Land of No God, and knows that it is but a stage on his journey—and a stage, moreover, no far from the goal. Daath is not on the Tree of Life; and in Daath there is no God as there is in the Sephiroth, for Daath cannot understand unity at all. If he thinks of it, it is only to hate it, as the one thing which he is most certainly not (see *Liber 418*, 10th Æthyr. I may remark in passing that this book is the best known to me on Advanced Qabalah, and of course it is only intelligible to Advanced Students). This atheist, not in-being but in-passing, is a very apt subject for initiation. He has done with the illusions of dogma." The entry on number 73 reads: "The two ways to Kether, Gimel and Chokmah. Hence venerable, but not much good to the beginner."

The Paris Working notes the role of "Christ as the mediator: 'No man cometh unto the Father but by me' [John 14:6], and Mercury as Chokmah through whom alone we can approach Kether. The Caduceus contains a complete symbol of the Gnosis; the winged sun or phallus represents the joy of life on all planes from the lowest to the highest. The serpents, besides being active and passive, Horus and Osiris, and all their other well known attributions, are those qualities of Eagle and Lion respectively, of which we know but do not speak. It is the symbol which unites the Microcosm and the Macrocosm, the symbol of the Magical operation which accomplishes this. The Caduceus is life itself, and of universal application. It is the universal solvent. It is quite easy to turn quicksilver into gold on the physical plane,

---

[14] *Ibid.*
[15] Ecclesiastes 1:18.
[16] *Eight Lectures*, Ch. 1, Sec. 14.

and this will soon be done. New life will flow through the world in consequence."[17]

The last four steps on the Noble Eightfold Path are described in *The Temple of Solomon the King* thus, beginning with the "The Right Livelihood":

> Up to this stage man has been but a disciple to his Holy Guardian Angel, but now he grows to be his equal, and in the flesh becomes a flame-shod Adept whose white feet are not soiled by the dust and mud of earth. He has gained perfect control over his body and his mind; and not only are his speech and actions right, but his very life is right, in fact his actions have become a Temple wherein he can at will withdraw himself to pray. He has become a priest unto himself his own Guardian, he may administer to himself the holy sacrament of God in Truth and in Right, he has become Exempt from the shackles of Earth. He is the Supreme Man, one step more he enters the Sanctuary of God and becomes one with the Brotherhood of Light.
>
> Up to this stage progress has meant Work, work terrible and Titanic, one great striving after union which roughly may be compared to the five methods of Yoga.
>
> From this fifth stage work gives place to knowledge, Qabalistically the aspirant enters Daäth.

"Man is now Master of Virtue and Vice and no longer their slave, servant, enemy or friend. The LVX has descended upon him, and just as the dew of the moon within the Sahasâra Chakkra falling upon the two-petaled Ajna-lotus causes the leaves to open out, so now does this celestial light lift him out and beyond the world, as wings lift a bird from the fields of earth, encompassing him, extending to his right hand and to his left like the wings of the Solar Globe which shut out from the ruby ball the twin serpents which twine beneath it." The footnote reads: "The two serpents and central rod of the Caduceus are in Yoga represented by the Ida, Pingala and Sushumnâ. The wings closed, to the Ajna-lotus; open and displaying the solar disk, to the Sahasâra Chakkra."[18]

"So filled with Understanding is he now that he becomes, as it were, the actual mind of the universe, nothing remains uncomprehended; he comes face to face with his goal, he sees HIMSELF as one who gazes into a mirror." Finally, when the adept has reached the Right State of a Peaceful Mind, "The glass vanishes and with it the reflection, the illusion of Mara or of Mâyâ. He is Reality! He is Truth! He is Âtman! He is God. Then Reality vanishes. Truth vanishes. Âtman vanishes. God vanishes. He himself vanishes. He is past; he is present; he is future. He is here, he is there. He is everything. He is nowhere. He is nothing. He is blessed, he has attained to the Great Deliverance. He IS; he IS NOT. He is one with Nibbâna."[19]

---

[17] Opus II.
[18] *The Temple of Solomon the King*, Part IV, "The Noble Eightfold Path."
[19] *Ibid.* Emphasis in original.

Thou knowest right well, o my Son, how a Thought is imperfect in two Dimensions, being separate from its Contradiction, but also constrained in its Scope, because by that Contradiction we do not (commonly) complete the Universe, save only that of its Discourse. Thus if we contrast Health with Sickness, we include in their Sphere of Union no more than one Quality that may be predicted of all Things. Furthermore, it is for the most Part not easy to find or to formulate the true Contradiction of any Thought as a positive Idea, but only as a Formal Negation in vague Terms, so that the ready Answer is but Antithesis. Thus to "White" one putteth not the Phrase "All that which is not White," for this is void, formless; it is neither clear, simple, nor positive in Conception; but one answereth "Black," for this hath an Image of his Significance. So then the Cohesion of Antitheticals destroyeth them only in Part, and one becometh instantly conscious of the Residue that is unsatisfied or unbalanced, whose Eidolon leapeth in thy Mind with Splendour and Joy unspeakable. Let not this deceive thee, for its Existence proveth its Imperfection, and thou must call forth its Mate, and destroy them by Love, as with the former. This Method is continuous, and proceedeth ever from the Gross to the Fine, and from the Particular to the General, dissolving all Things into the One Substance of Light.[20]

Learn now that Impressions of Sense have Opposites readily conceived, as long to short, or light to dark; and so with Emotions and Perceptions, as love to hate, or false to true; but the more Violent is the Antagonism, the more is it bound in Illusion, determined by Relation. Thus, the Word "Long" hath no Meaning save it be referred to a Standard; but Love is not thus obscure, because Hate is its twin, partaking bountifully of a Common Nature therewith. Now, hear this: it was given unto me in my Visions of the Æthyrs, when I was in the Desert of Sahara, by Tolga, that above the Abyss, Contradiction is Unity, and that nothing could be true save by Virtue of the Contradiction that is contained in itself. Behold therefore, in this Method thou shalt come presently to Ideas of this Order, that include in themselves their own Contradiction, and have no Antithesis. Here then is thy Lever of Antinomy broken in thine Hand; yet, being in true Balance, thou mayst soar, passionate and eager, from Heaven to Heaven, by the Expansion of thine Idea, and its Exaltation, or Concentration as thou understandest by thy Studies in the *Book of the Law*, the Word thereof concerning Our Lady Nuit, and Hadit that is the Core of every Star. And this last Going upon thy Ladder is easy, if thou be truly Initiate, for the Momentum of thy Force in Transcendental Antithesis serveth to propel thee, and the Emancipation from the Fetters of Thought that thou hast won in that

---

[20] *Liber Aleph*, "Sequitur de hac re," as quoted in NC on AL I.59. (*Cf.* also *The Book of Thoth*, Part II, Atu 0: "It is characteristic of all high spiritual vision that the formulation of any idea is immediately destroyed or cancelled out by the arising of the contradictory. Hegel and Nietzsche had glimmerings of the idea, but it is described very fully and simply in the Book of Wisdom or Folly.")

Praxis of Art maketh the Whirlpool and Gravitation of Truth of Competence to draw thee unto itself.[21]

"From the above it will be understood how it comes that there are no Trances of Knowledge; and this bids us enquire into the tradition of the Grimoires that all knowledge is miraculously attainable. The answer is that, while all Trances are Destroyers of Knowledge—since, for one thing, they all destroy the sense of Duality—they yet put into their Adept the means of knowledge. We may regard rational apprehension as a projection of Truth in dualistic form; so that he who possesses any given Truth has only to symbolise its image in the form of Knowledge."[22] As the *New Comment* on AL II.4 says, "Hadit possesses the power to know, Nuit that of being known. Nuit is not unconnected with the idea of Nibbana, the 'Shoreless Sea,' in which Knowledge is Not. Hadit is hidden in Nuit, and knows Her, She being an object of knowledge; but He is not knowable, for He is merely that part of Her which She formulates in order that She may be known."

"The Trance of Wonder arises naturally—it is the first movement of the mind—from the final phrase of the Oath of a Master of the Temple. 'I will interpret every phenomenon as a particular dealing of God with my soul.' For, immediately the Understanding illuminates the darkness of knowledge, every fact appears in its true guise miraculous. . . . Let it be known each such step in Meditation is itself a motive Energy capable of inducing the Trance of Wonder; and this Trance (like all others) grows in sublimity and splendour with the quantity and quality of the material which is furnished to the mind by the Adept. . . .this Trance is of its nature not only passive and intuitive. Its occurrence floods the mind with Creative Energy; it fills the Adept with Power, and excites in him the Will to work."[23]

"The Universe is Change: every Change is the effect of an Act of Love; all Acts of Love contain Pure Joy."[24] *The Heart of the Master* quotes St. Paul: "Die daily!"[25] Indeed, "All phenomena are sacraments. Every fact, and even every falsehood, must enter into the Pantacle; it is the great storehouse from which the Magician draws. 'In the brown cakes of corn we shall taste the food of the world and be strong.'[26] When speaking of the Cup, it was shown how every fact must be made significant, how every stone must have its proper place in the mosaic. Woe were it were one stone misplaced! But that mosaic cannot be wrought at all, well or ill, unless every stone be there. These stones are the simple impressions or experiences; not one may be foregone."[27] Verily, "In all the active moods of Nature—her activity is Worship! there is an element of rejoicing; even when she is at her wildest and most destructive. (You know Gilbert's song 'When the tiger is a-lashing

---

[21] *Ibid.*, "Conclusio de hoc Modo Sanctitatis," as quoted in NC on AL I.59.
[22] *Little Essays Toward Truth*, "Knowledge."
[23] *Ibid.*, "Wonder."
[24] *The Heart of the Master*, II.XIII.
[25] I Corinthians 15:31.
[26] *Liber Liberi vel Lapidis Lazuli*, IV.20.
[27] *Book 4*, Part II, Ch. IX.

of his tail'?[28]) Her sadness always goes with the implied threat of cessation—and that we know to be illusion."[29]

"There is no power which cannot be pressed in to the service of the Magical Will: it is only the temptation to value that power for itself which offends."[30] Crowley is careful to note that, "moral obstruction to the right use of this Energy cause at once the most hideous deformations of character, and determine the gravest lesions of the nervous system. Let therefore the Magician divest himself of all preconceptions as to the nature of his True Will, but apply himself eagerly to increasing his Potential. In this discipline (moreover) he is beginning to fit himself for that very abdication of all that he has and all that he is which is the essence of the Oath of the Abyss! Thus then do we find one more of those paradoxes which are the images of the Truth of the Supernals: by destroying our own highest morality, and relying upon our natural instinct as the sole guide, we come unaware upon the most simple, and the most sublime, of all ethical and spiritual conceptions."[31]

"Now Hadit knows Nuit by virtue of his 'Going' or 'Love.' It is therefore wrong to worship Hadit; one is to be Hadit, and worship Her. This is clear even from His instruction 'To worship me' in verse 22 of this chapter. Confer Cap. I, verse 9. We are exhorted to offer ourselves unto Nuit, pilgrims to all her temples. It is bad Magick to admit that one is other than One's inmost self. One should plunge passionately into every possible experience; by doing so one is purged of those personal prejudices which we took so stupidly for ourselves, though they prevented us from realizing our true Wills and from knowing our Names and Natures. The Aspirant must well understand that it is no paradox to say that the Annihilation of the Ego in the Abyss is the condition of emancipating the true Self, and exalting it to unimaginable heights. So long as one remains 'one's self,' one is overwhelmed by the Universe; destroy the sense of self, and every event is equally an expression of one's Will, since its occurrence is the resultant of the concourse of the forces which one recognizes as one's own."[32]

> In this preliminary task of collecting materials, the idea of the Ego is not of such great moment; all impressions are phases of the non-ego, and the Ego serves merely as a receptacle. In fact, to the well regulated mind, there is no question but that the impressions are real, and that the mind, if not a *tabula rasa*, is only not so because of the "tendencies" or "innate ideas" which prevent some ideas from being received as readily as others. *{It does not occur to a newly-hatched chicken to behave in the same way as a new-born child.}*
>
> These "tendencies" must be combated: distasteful facts should be insisted upon until the Ego is perfectly indifferent to the nature of its food.

---

[28] *The Mikado*, Act II, No 12.
[29] *MWT*, Ch. XLIV.
[30] *Book 4*, Part II, Ch. VI.
[31] *Little Essays Toward Truth*, "Energy."
[32] NC on AL II.8.

"Even as the diamond shall glow red for the rose, and green for the rose-leaf, so shalt thou abide apart from the Impressions."

This great task of separating the self from the impressions or *vrittis* is one of the may meanings of the aphorism *solve*, corresponding to the *coagula* implied in Samadhi, and this Pantacle therefore represents all that we are, the resultant of all that we had a tendency to be.[33]

"Death implies change and individuality; if thou be THAT which hath no person, which is beyond the changing, even beyond changelessness, what hast thou to do with death? The birth of individuality is ecstasy; so also is its death. In love the individuality is slain; who loves not love? Love death therefore, and long eagerly for it. Die Daily."[34] Nevertheless, "Those who hold Silence worthy, and seek it, do err if they think to find therein the Truth of their Selves; for Hadit holdeth worthy, and seeketh, Nuit: and though He be Silence, is not be sought. The True Self is Silence, and seeketh Truth in all Ways of Event."[35]

There is, however, a universal solvent and harmonizer, a certain dew which is so pure that a single drop of it cast into the water of the Cup will for the time being bring all to perfection.

This dew is called Love. Even as in the case of human love, the whole Universe appears perfect to the man who is under its control, so is it, and much more, with the Divine Love of which it is now spoken.

For human love is an excitement, and not a stilling, of the mind; and as it is bound to the individual, only leads to greater trouble in the end.

This Divine Love, on the contrary, is attached to no symbol.

It abhors limitation, either in its intensity or its scope. And this is the dew of the stars of which it is spoken in the Holy Books, for NUIT the Lady of the Stars is called "the Continuous One of Heaven," and it is that Dew which bathes the body of the Adept "in a sweet-smelling perfume of sweat."

In this Cup, therefore, though all things are placed, by virtue of this dew all lose their identity. And therefore this Cup is in the hand of BABALON, the Lady of the City of the Pyramids, wherein no one can be distinguished from any other, wherein no one may sit until he has lost his name.[36]

"באבאלען. This most holy and precious name is fully dealt with in *Liber 418*. Notice 12 × 13 = 156. This was a name given and ratified by Qabalah; 156 is not one of the *à priori* helpful numbers. It is rather a case of the Qabalah illuminating St. John's intentional obscurity."[37] According to Crowley, "It is of no account in the orthodox dogmatic Qabalah. Yet it is 12 × 13, the most spiritual form, 13, of the most perfect number, 12, הוא."—"It is

---

[33] *Book 4*, Part II, Ch. IX.
[34] *The Book of Lies*, Ch. 16. Emphasis in original.
[35] DC on AL II.8.
[36] *Book 4*, Part II, Ch. VII.
[37] *An Essay upon Number*, Part II.

ציון, Zion, the City of the Pyramids."³⁸ As he puts it, "'Unity' transcends 'consciousness'. It is above all division. The Father of thought—the Word—is called CHAOS—the dyad. The number Three, the Mother, is called BABALON.... This first triad is essentially unity, in a manner transcending reason. The comprehension of this Trinity is a matter of spiritual experience. All true gods are attributed to this Trinity."³⁹ However, "This triune principle being wholly spiritual, all that can be said about it is really negative. And it is complete in itself. Beyond it stretches what is called The Abyss. This doctrine is extremely difficult to explain; but it corresponds more or less to the gap in thought between the Real, which is ideal, and the Unreal, which is actual. In the Abyss all things exist, indeed, at least *in posse*, but are without any possible meaning; for they lack the substratum of spiritual Reality. They are appearances without Law. They are thus Insane Delusions. Now the Abyss being thus the great storehouse of Phenomena, it is the source of all impressions."⁴⁰

Twenty-two is the "number of letters in the Hebrew Alphabet; and of the paths on the Tree. Hence suggests completion of imperfection. Finality, the fatal finality. Note 2 × 11 = 22, the accursed Dyad at play with the Shells." Thirty-two are the "Sephiroth and Paths, 10 + 22. Hence is completion of perfection. Finality: things as they are in their totality. אהיהוה, the combined אהיה and יהוה, Macroprosopus, and Microprosopus, is here. If we suppose the 3 female letters ה to conceal the 3 mothers א, מ, ש, we obtain the number 358, Messiach, *q.v.* Note 32 = 2^5, the divine Will extended through motion. 64 = 2^6, will be the perfect number of matter, for it is 8, the first cube, squared. So we find it a Mercurial number, as if the solidity of matter was in truth eternal change."⁴¹

It is important to explain the Position of Daath or Knowledge upon the Tree. It is called the Child of Chokmah and Binah, but it hath no Place. But it is really the Apex of a Pyramid of which the three first Numbers for the Base.

Now the Tree, or Minutum Mundum, is a Figure in a Plane of a solid Universe. Daath, being above the Plane, is therefore a Figure of a Force in four Dimensions, and thus it is the Object of the Magnum Opus. The three Paths which connect it with the First Trinity are the three lost Letters or Fathers of the Hebrew Alphabet.

In Daath is said to be the Head of the great Serpent Nechesh or Leviathan, called Evil to conceal its Holiness. (נחש = 358 = משיה, the Messiah or Redeemer, and לויתן = 496 = מלכות, the Bride.) It is identical with the Kundalini of the Hindu Philosophy, the Kwan-se-on of the Mongolian Peoples, and means the magical Force in Man, which is the sexual Force applied to the Brain, Heart, and other Organs, and redeemeth him.⁴²

---

³⁸ *Ibid.*, Part I, Sec. IV.
³⁹ *MITAP*, Ch. 0.
⁴⁰ *Little Essays Toward Truth*, "Man."
⁴¹ *An Essay upon Number, loc. cit.*
⁴² *Qabalistic Dogma.*

"משיה, Messiah, and נחש, the serpent of Genesis. The dogma is that the head of the serpent (נ) is 'bruised,' being replaced by מ, the letter of Sacrifice, and Yod, the letter alike of virginity (י = ♍) and of original deity (י = the foundation or type of all the letters). Thus the word may be read: 'The Sacrifice of the Virgin-born Divine One triumphant (ה, the Chariot) through the Spirit,' while נחש reads 'Death entering the (realm of the) Spirit.' But the conception of the Serpent as the Redeemer is truer."[43] Here Crowley refers to his "explanation of 5=6 ritual" in *The Equinox*, Vol. I, No. 3: "The Higher Self now speaks for Postulant, and they are admitted by the Aspiration of Postulant (Serpent) and the Divine Light descending in answer (Flaming Sword), as it is written 'While he was yet a great way off, his father saw him and ran——.' He hath returned, showing the value of persistent Will. The Serpent and Flaming Sword are Wisdom and Strength, the slow but subtle movement of the Serpent, the rush of the Lightning flash, caring naught for obstacles. These conjoint are 32, that is, the joining of Arikh and Zauir Anpin in AHIHVH (32). And 32= ChZIZ (lightnings) ZKH (was pure) and LB (heart); also LB= ♎ ♀ —the Equilibration of Creation."

O my Son, how wonderful is the Wisdom of this Law of Love! How vast are the Oceans of uncharted Joy that lie before the Keel of thy Ship! Yet know this, that every Opposition is in its Nature named Sorrow, and the Joy lieth in the Destruction of the Dyad. Therefore must thou seek ever those Things which are to thee poisonous, and that in the highest Degree, and make them thine by Love. That which repels, that which disgusts, must thou assimilate in this Way of Wholeness. Yet rest not in the Joy of Destruction of every Complex in thy Nature, but press on to that ultimate Marriage with the Universe whose Consummation shall destroy thee utterly, leaving only that Nothingness which was before the Beginning.

So then the Life of Non-action is not for thee; the Withdrawal from Activity is not the Way of the Tao; but rather the Intensification and making universal of every Unity of thine Energy on every Plane.[44]

Of the Black Brothers, o my Son, will I write these Things following. I have told thee already concerning Change, how it is the Law, because every Change is an Act of Love under will. So then He that is Adept Exempt, whether in our Holy Order or another, may not remain in the Pillar of Mercy, because it is not balanced, but is unstable. Therefore is the Choice given unto him, whether he will destroy his Temple, and give up his Life, extending it to Universal Life, or whether he will make a Fortress about that Temple, and abide therein, in the false Sphere of Daäth, which is in the Abyss. And to the Adepts of our Holy Order this Choice is terrible; by Cause that they must abandon even Him whose Knowledge and Conversation they have attained. Yet, o my Son, they have much Help of our Order in this Æon, because the general Formula

---

[43] *The Temple of Solomon the King*, Part V.
[44] *Liber Aleph*, "De Nuptiis Mysticis," as quoted in NC on AL II.60.

is Love, so that their habit itself urges them to the Bed of our Lady BABALON. Know then the Black Brothers by this true Sign of their Initiation of iniquity, that that they resist Change, restrict and deny Love, fear Death. *Percutiantur*.[45]

In Crowley's opinion, "the principal mark of the Master of the Temple was . . . that he could exercise these powers at will; that he could enter Samadhi at will. He now saw that these words 'At will' really meant at the will of the Universe, and he could only obtain this freedom through the coincidence of his will with the Universal Will. The active and the passive must be perfectly harmonious before free-will became intelligible. Only Destiny could exercise free-will. In order to exercise free-will he must, therefore, become Destiny."[46] According to Crowley, "The Order of the Star called S.S. is, in respect of its existence upon the Earth, an organized body of men and women distinguished among their fellows by the qualities here enumerated. They exist in their own Truth, which is both universal and unique. They move in accordance with their own Wills, which are each unique, yet coherent with the universal will. They perceive (that is, understand, know, and feel) in love, which is both unique and universal. . . . The Order of the S.S. is composed of those who have crossed the Abyss; the implications of this expression may be studied in *Liber 418*, the 14th, 13th, 12th, 11th, 10th, and 9th Æthyrs in particular."[47]

The Hieroglyph shewn in the Seventh Key of the Tarot (described in the 12th Æthyr, *Liber 418*, *Equinox* I, V) is the Charioteer of OUR LADY BABALON, whose Cup or Graal he bears.

Now this is an important formula. It is the First of the Formulae, in a sense, for it is the formula of Renunciation. *{There is no moral implication here. But to choose A implies to refuse not-A: at least, that is so, below the Abyss.}* It is also the Last!

This Cup is said to be full of the Blood of the Saints; that is, every "saint" or magician must give the last drop of his life's blood to that cup. It is the original price paid for magick power. And if by magick power we mean the true power, the assimilation of all force with the Ultimate Light, the true Bridal of the Rosy Cross, then is that blood the offering of Virginity, the sole sacrifice well-pleasing to the Master, the sacrifice whose only reward is the pain of child-bearing unto him.

But "to sell one's soul to the devil", to renounce no matter what for an equivalent in personal gain, *{"Supposed" personal gain. There is really no person to gain; so the whole transaction is a swindle on both sides.}* is black magic. You are no longer a noble giver of your all, but a mean huckster.[48]

---

[45] *Ibid.*, "De fratribus nigris filiis iniquitatis."
[46] *The Temple of Solomon the King*, Part VIII, "The Poet."
[47] *One Star in Sight*, Secs. 1, 3.
[48] *MITAP*, Ch. VII, Sec. I.

As *Book 4*, Part II, puts it, "the real Magical Will must be toward the highest attainment, and this can never be until the flowering of the Magical Understanding. The Wand must be made to grow in length as well as in strength; it need not do so of its own nature. The ambition of every boy is to be an engine-driver. Some attain it, and remain there all their lives. But in the majority of cases the Understanding grows faster than the Will, and long before the boy is in a position to attain his wish he has already forgotten it. In other cases the Understanding never grows beyond a certain point, and the Will persists without intelligence. The business man (for example) has wished for ease and comfort, and to this end goes daily to his office and slaves under a more cruel taskmaster than the meanest of the workmen in his pay; he decides to retire, and finds that life in empty. The end has been swallowed up in the means.[49]

"Only those are happy who have desired the unattainable. All possessions, the material and the spiritual alike, are but dust. Love, sorrow, and compassion are three sisters who, if they seem freed from this curse, are only so because of their relation to The Unsatisfied. Beauty is itself so unattainable that it escapes altogether; and the true artist, like the true mystic, can never rest. To him the Magician is but a servant. His wand is of infinite length; it is the creative Mahalingam. The difficulty with such an one is naturally that his wand being very thin in proportion to its length is liable to wobble. Very few artists are conscious of their real purpose, and in very many cases we have this infinite yearning supported by so frail a constitution that nothing is achieved.[50]

"The Magician must build all that he has into his pyramid; and if that pyramid is to touch the stars, how broad must be the base! There is no knowledge and no power which is useless to the Magician. One might almost say there is no scrap of material in the whole Universe with which he can dispense. His ultimate enemy is the great Magician, the Magician who created the whole illusion of the Universe; and to meet him in battle, so that nothing is left either of him or of yourself, you must be exactly equal to him. At the same time let the Magician never forget that every brick must tend to the summit of the pyramid—the sides must be perfectly smooth; there must be no false summits, even in the lowest layers. This is the practical and active form of that obligation of a Master of the Temple in which it is said: 'I will interpret every phenomenon as a particular dealing of God with my soul.'[51]

"In *Liber CLXXV* many practical devices for attaining this one-pointedness are given, and though the subject of that book is devotion to a particular Deity, its instructions may be easily generalized to suit the development of any form of will. This will is then the active form of understanding. The Master of the Temple asks, on seeing a slug: 'What is the purpose of this message from the Unseen? How shall I interpret this Word of God Most High?' The Magus thinks: 'How shall I use this slug?' And

---

[49] *Book 4*, Part II, Ch. VI.
[50] *Ibid.*
[51] *Ibid.*

in this course he must persist. Though many things useless, so far as he can see, are sent to him, one day he will find the one thing he needs, while his Understanding will appreciate the fact that none of those other things were useless."[52]

As Crowley instructs Achad, "Learn well to apprehend this Mystery, for it is the Great Gate of the College of Understanding, whereby each and all of thy Senses become constant and perpetual Witnesses of the One Eucharist, whereunto also they are Ministers. So then to thee every Phenomenon soever is the Body of Nuith in her Passion; for it is an Event; that is, the Marriage of some one Point of view with some One Possibility. And this State of Mind is notably an Appurtenance of thy Grade of Master of the Temple, and the Unveiling of the Arcanum of Sorrow, which is thy Work, as it is written in *Liber Magi*. Moreover, this State, assimilated in the very Marrow of thy Mind, is the first Stop toward the comprehension of the Arcanum of Change, which is the Root of the Work of a Magus of Our Holy Order. O my Son, bind this within thine Heart, for its Name is the Beatific Vision."[53]

However, he gives this warning: "Confuse thou not this beatific vision with the Trances called Samadhi; yet is Samadhi the Pylon of the Temple hereof. For Samadhi is the orgasm of the coition of the Unlike, and is commonly violent, even as the lightning cometh of the discharge between two vehicles of extreme difference of potentials. But as I shewed formerly concerning love, how each such discharge bringeth either component more nigh to equilibrium, so is it in this other matter, and by experience thou comest constantly to integration of love (or what not) within thyself, just as all effort becometh harmonious and easy by virtue of practice."[54]

There is a Qabalistic saying that, "Knowledge without understanding is static, understanding without wisdom is dangerous stupidity." As Crowley writes in *Magick Without Tears*, "Of course, there must be certain courses of action which, generally speaking, will be right for pretty well everybody. Some, *per contra*, will be generally barred, as interfering with another's equal right. Some cases will be so difficult that only a Magister Templi can judge them, and a Magus carry them wisely into effect."[55] According to *Liber XXXIII*, or *An Account of the A∴A∴*, "In this interior society man finds wisdom and with her All—not the wisdom of this world, which is but scientific knowledge, which revolves round the outside but never touches the centre (in which is contained all strength), but true wisdom, understanding and knowledge, reflections of the supreme illumination. All disputes, all controversies, all the things belonging to the false cares of this world, fruitless discussions, useless germs of opinions which spread the seeds of disunion, all error, schisms, and systems are banished. Neither calumny nor scandal is known. Every man is honoured. Love alone reigns."

"For the pure essence of Magick is a function of ultimate atomic consciousness, and its operations must be refined from all confusion and

---

[52] *Ibid.*
[53] *Liber Aleph*, "De mysterio eucharistico universali."
[54] *Ibid.*, "De ecstasia samadhi, quo illis differit."
[55] *MWT*, Ch. LXX.

contamination. The truly magical operations of Love are therefore the Trances, more especially those of Understanding; as will readily have been appreciated by those who have made a careful Qabalistic study of the nature of Binah. For she is omniform as Love and as Death, the Great Sea whence all Life springs, and whose black womb reabsorbs all. She thus resumes in herself the duplex process of the Formula of Love under Will; for is not Pan the All-Begetter in the heart of the Groves at high noon, and is not Her 'hair the trees of Eternity' the filaments of All-Devouring Godhead 'under the Night of Pan?'[56]

"Yet let it not be forgotten that though She be love, her function is but passive; she is the vehicle of the Word, of Chokmah, Wisdom, the All-Father, who is the Will of the All-One. And thus they err with grievous error and dire who prate of Love as the Formula of Magick; Love is unbalanced, void, vague, undirected, sterile, nay, more, a very Shell, the prey of abject orts demonic: Love must be 'under will.'"[57] According to the Cry of the 3rd Æthyr, Virgin Mary is "a blasphemy against BABALON, for she hath shut herself up"—"She seeks to resist Change, which is Life, she refuses the Formula, 'love under will.' Yet MAPIE (Greek) = 156." She is therefore "the Queen of all those wicked devils that walk upon the earth, those that thou sawest even as little black specks that stained the Heaven of Urania. And all these are the excrement of Choronzon."

"The Master of the Temple is so far from the man in whom He manifests that all these matters are of no importance to Him. It may be of importance to His Work that man shall sit upon a throne, or be hanged. In such a case He informs his Magus, who exerts the power intrusted to Him, and it happens accordingly. Yet all happens naturally, and of necessity, and to all appearance without a word from Him. Nor will the mere Master of the Temple, as a rule, presume to act upon the Universe, save as the servant of his own destiny. It is only the Magus, He of the grade above, who has attained to Chokhmah, Wisdom, and so dare act. He must dare act, although it like Him not. But He must assume the Curse of His grade, as it is written in the Book of the Magus."[58]

> Understanding is the attribute of the Master of the Temple, who has crossed the Abyss (or "Pit") that divides the true Self from its conscious instrument. (See *Liber 418*, "Aha!", and *Book 4*, Part III). We must meditate the meaning of this attack upon the idea of "Because." I quote from my diary the demonstration that Reason is the Absolute, whereof all Truths soever art merely particular cases. The theorem may be stated roughly as follows.
>
> The universe must be expressible either as +/− n, or as Zero. That is, it is either unbalanced or balanced. The former theory (Theism) is unthinkable; but Zero, when examined, proves to contain the possibility

---

[56] *Little Essays Toward Truth*, "Love."
[57] *Ibid.*
[58] *MITAP*, Ch. XXI.

of being expressed as $n - n$, and this possibility must in its turn be considered as $+/- p$.

This thesis appears to me a *reductio ad absurdum* of the very basis of our mathematical thinking.

We knew before, of course, that all reasoning is bound to end in some mystery or some absurdity; the above is only one more antimony, a little deeper than Kant's, perhaps, but of the same character. Mathematicians would doubtless agree that all signs are arbitrary, elaboration of an abacus, and that all "truth" is merely our name for statements that content our reason; so that it is lower than reason, and within it; not higher and beyond, as transcendentalists argue. I seem never to have seen this point before, though "men of sense" instinctively affirm it, I suppose. The pragmatists are mere tradesmen with their definition of Truth as "the useful to be thought"; but why not "the necessary to be thought?" There is a sort of Berkeleyan subjectivity in this view; we might put it: "All that we can know of Truth is 'that which we are bound to think.'" The search for Truth amounts, then, to the result of the analysis of the Mind; and here let us remember my fear of the result of that analysis as I expressed them a month ago.

This analysis is the right method after all.

Now, are we justified in assuming, as we always do, that our reason is either correct or incorrect? That if any proposition can be shown to be congruous with "A is A" it is "true," and so on? Does the "reason" of the oyster comply with the same canon as man's? We assume it. We make the necessity in our thought the standard of the laws of Nature; and thus implicitly declare Reason to be the Absolute. This has nothing to do with the weakness of error in any one mind, or in all minds; all that we rely on is the existence of some purely mental standard by which we could always correct our thinking, if we knew how. It is then this power which constrains our thought, to which our minds owe fealty, that we call "Truth"; and this "Truth" is not a proposition at all, but a "Law!" We cannot think what it is, obviously, as it is a final condition of philosophical thought in the same way as Space and Time are conditions of phenomenal thought. But, can there be some third type of thought which can escape the bonds of that as that can of this? "Samadhic realization," one is tempted to rush in and answer—while angels hesitate. All my "philosophic" thought, as above, is direct reflection upon the meaning of Samadhic experience. Is it simply that the reflections are distorted and dim? I have shown the impossibility of any true Zero, and thus destroyed every axiom, blown up the foundations of my mind. In failing to distinguish between None and Two, I cannot even cling to the straw of "phrases," since Time and Space are long since perished. None *is* Two, without conditions; and therefore it is a positive idea, and we are just as right to enquire how it came to be as in the case of Haeckel's monad, or one's aunt's umbrella. We are, however, this one small step advanced by our initiations, that we can be quite sure this "None-Two" is, since all possible theories of Ontology simplify out to it.[59]

"Nevertheless, with whatever we try to identify this Absolute, we cannot escape from the fact that it is in reality merely the formula of our own Reason. The idea of Space arises from reflection upon the relations of our bodily gestures with the various objects of our senses. (Poincaré—I note after reading him, months later, as I revise this note—explains this fully). So that a 'yard' is not a thing in itself, but a term in the equations which express the Laws according to which we move our muscles. My knowledge consists exclusively of the mechanics of my own mind. All that I know is the nature of its norm. The judgments of the Reason are arbitrary, and can never be verified. Truth and Reality are simply the Substance of the Reason itself."[60] In Qabalistic terms, "An immeasurable abyss divides it from all manifestations of Reason or the lower qualities of man. In the ultimate analysis of Reason, we find all reason identified with this abyss. Yet this abyss is the crown of the mind. Purely intellectual faculties all obtain here. This abyss has no number, for in it all is confusion."[61]

"The Grade of Master of the Temple is described in *Liber 418* as above indicated. There are full accounts in the Magical Diaries of the Beast 666, who was cast forth into the Heaven of Jupiter, and of Omnia in Vno, Vnus in Omnibus, who was cast forth into the sphere of the Elements. The essential Attainment is the perfect annihilation of that personality which limits and oppresses his true self. The Magister Templi is pre-eminently the Master of Mysticism, that is, His Understanding is entirely free from internal contradiction or external obscurity; His word is to comprehend the existing Universe in accordance with His own Mind. He is the Master of the Law of Sorrow (Dukkha)."[62] In Buddhism, *aniccā*, *anattā*, and *dukkhā* together make up the *tilakkhaṇa*, the three "marks" or characteristics of all phenomenal existence.

"The Magus is pre-eminently the Master of Magick, that is, his will is entirely free from internal diversion or external opposition; His work is to create a new Universe in accordance with His Will. He is the Master of the Law of Change (Anicca)."[63] *Ipsissimus* is difficult to translate directly from Latin to English, but it is basically the superlative of "Self," like Generalissimo is the superlative of the military rank of General, thus meaning something like "His Most Selfness," or "Self-est." According to *One Star in Sight*, he who has attained the grade of "Ipsissimus is pre-eminently the Master of all modes of existence; that is, his being is entirely free from internal or external necessity. His work is to destroy all tendencies to construct or to cancel such necessities. He is the Master of the Law of Unsubstantiality (Anatta)."[64]

---

[59] NC on AL II.27. Emphasis in original.
[60] *Ibid.*
[61] *MITAP*, Ch. 0.
[62] *One Star in Sight*, Sec. 6.
[63] *Ibid.*, Sec. 5.
[64] *Ibid.*, Sec. 4.

In the first part we have seen all numbers as Veils of the One, emanations of and therefore corruptions of the One. It is the Universe as we know it, the static Universe.

Now the Aspirant to Magic is displeased with this state of things. He finds himself but a creature, the farthest removed from the Creator, a number so complex and involved that he can scarcely imagine, must less dare to hope for, its reduction to the One.

The numbers useful to him, therefore, will be those which are subversive of this state of sorrow. So the number 2 represents to him the Magus (the great Magician Mayan who has created the illusion of Maya) as seen in the 2nd Æthyr. And considering himself as the Ego who posits the Non-Ego (Fichte) he hates this Magus. It is only the beginner who regards this Magus as the Wonder-worker—as the thing he wants to be. For the adept such little consolation as he may win is rather to be found by regarding the Magus as B = Mercury = 8 = Ch = 418 = ABRAHADABRA, the great Word, the "Word of Double Power in the voice of the Master" which unites the 5 and the 6, the Rose and the Cross, the Circle and the Square. And also B is the Path from Binah to Kether; but that is only important for him who is already in Binah, the "Master of the Temple."

He finds no satisfaction in contemplating the Tree of Life, and the orderly arrangement of the numbers; rather does he enjoy the Qabalah as a means of juggling with these numbers. He can leave nothing undisturbed; he is the Anarchist of Philosophy. He refuses to acquiesce in merely formal proofs of the Excellence of things, "He doeth all things well," "Were the World understood Ye would see it was good," "Whatever is, is right," and so on. To him, on the contrary, whatever is, is wrong. It is part of the painful duty of a Master of the Temple to understand everything. Only he can excuse the apparent cruelty and fatuity of things. He is of the supernals; he sees things from above; yet, having come from below, he can sympathise with all. And he does not expect the Neophyte to share his views. Indeed, they are not true to a Neophyte. The silliness of the New-Thought zanies in passionately affirming "I am healthy! I am opulent! I am well-dressed! I am happy," when in truth they are "poor and miserable and blind and naked," is not a philosophical but a practical silliness. Nothing exists, says the Magister Templi, but perfection. True; yet their consciousness is imperfect. Ergo, it does not exist. For the M.T. this is so: he has "cancelled out" the complexities of the mathematical expression called existence, and the answer is zero. But for the beginner his pain and another's joy do not balance; his pain hurts him, and his brother may go hang. The Magister Templi, too, understands why Zero must plunge through all finite numbers to express itself; why it must write itself as "n – n" instead of 0; what gain there is in such writing. And this understanding will be found expressed in Liber 418 (Episode of Chaos and His Daughter) and Liber Legis (i. 28–30).[65]

---

[65] *An Essay upon Number*, Part II.

"The nature of Knowledge, the culmination and stasis of the Intellectual faculties, . . . implies a contradiction in terms. Understanding is the resolution of this antinomy. It is the chief quality of Neschamah, the Intelligence—an idea insusceptible of true definition because suprarational, and only appreciable by direct experience. One can say, at most, that it is independent of any of the normal modes of motion of the mind.... Samadhi, at first onset productive of bewildering Ecstasy, ultimates in this Understanding; one may say, therefore, that Understanding implies a certain Samadhic quality of apprehension. Duality is (perhaps) not absolutely abolished save in the superstructure of the state; but it assumes a form which it would be absurd to call dualistic.... The only correct and adequate mode of the Attainment of Understanding is to shut off and to inhibit the rational mind altogether, thus leaving a Tabula rasa upon which the entirely alien faculty—*de novo* and *sui generis*—can write its first word. ...Ananda must be mastered manfully, not indulged as a vice in the manner of the Mystic! Samadhi must be clarified by Sila, by the stern virtue of constraint: and then appears the paradox that the new Law of the Mind has 'come not to destroy but to fulfil' the old. The Understanding takes full cognizance of all that vast material which the Reason was unable to build into any coherent structure. The contradictions have disappeared by absorption; they have been accepted as essential factors in the nature of Truth, which without them were a mere congeries of Facts."[66]

> Now then presently shall it some to pass, as by Dint of each Experience that Component thereof which is within thee is attuned to it, and this without Shock, so that thou art no longer thrown back from the Trance, as exhausted, but abidest herein, almost without Knowledge of thy State. So then at last this Samadhi shall become normal to thy Common Consciousness, as it were a Point of View. Thus all Things shall appear to thee very continually as to one in his first Love, by the Vision of Beauty, and by the Vision of Science thou shalt marvel constantly with Joy unfathomable at the Mystery of the Laws whereby the Universe is upheld. This is that which is written: True Wisdom and Perfect Happiness, o my son, it is in this Contemplation that one hath the Reward of the Oath; it is by this that the Tribulations are rolled away as a Stone from thy Tomb; it is with this that thou art wholly freed from the Illusions of Distinctions, being absorbed into the Body of our Lady Nuith. May she grant thee this beatitude; yea, not to thee only, but to all that are.[67]

In *The Temple of Solomon the King*, Crowley tells us that there had been a bar to his progress, "a dualism in his conception of the Cosmos. He had not fully understood that the Universe was One, that one might in very truth eat and drink to the glory of God. He knew that by eating and drinking one did not necessarily detract from the glory of God, but had not fully

---

[66] *Little Essays Toward Truth*, "Understanding."
[67] *Liber Aleph*, "De præmio summo, vera sapientia et beatitudine perfecta."

understood the sacramentalism of the simplest actions. Now he knew that the huddling together of unhewn stones might build a better Temple than that of Luxor or of Karnak. He had still the old illusion that to succeed on one plane you must fail on another; still thought the mind more than the body, the soul more than the mind; did not see that these three must be one in exactly the same sense as the Christian Trinity (as understood by the truest Christians) is One. It was in the course of this illumination that the Truth was ceremonially conveyed to him on the Magical plane, although it was not for three years later that it fully illuminated his mind."[68]

> This illusion, of which it is here spoken, is a most necessary step for the beginner, because to the beginner his ordinary life is not a sacrament. To him things are really common and unclean. He must, therefore, cut them out of his life, and hence to him the name of the Path is Renunciation. But to him who would be a Master of the Temple, the reverse applies. He wishes to remain perpetually in Samadhi, and it is therefore his renunciation to descend further and further into matter. He has volatilized the fixed: now he must fix the volatile. He has ascended from his particular body to the Universal Soul. That Universal Soul must now incarnate itself ever more completely in that body, and in the bodies and minds of all men. He has made his darkness light; that light must illuminate the darkness of all.
> Having then received this last Initiation, this destruction of the opposition, between One and the Many, he descended from the mountain, and awaited nightfall.[69]

"So with these early practices of renunciation it will now be clearly understood that they were but of temporary use. They were only of value as training. The adept will laugh over his early absurdities—the disproportions will have been harmonized; and the structure of his soul will be seen as perfectly organic, with no one thing out of its place. He will see himself as the positive Tau with its ten complete squares within the triangle of the negatives; and this figure will become one, as soon as from the equilibrium of opposites he has attained to the identity of opposites."[70] As *Liber Aleph* phrases it, "This is the evident and final solvent of the Knot Philosophical concerning fate and free will, that it is thine own self, omniscient and omnipotent, sublime in eternity, that first didst order the course of thine orbit, so that the which befalleth thee by fate is indeed the necessary effect of thine own will. These two, then, that like Gladiators have

---

[68] *The Temple of Solomon the King*, Part IX, "Nemo." *Cf.* also *The Book of Thoth*, Part III, "Prince of Disks"—"The fundamental heresy of the Black Lodge is contempt for 'the world, the flesh, and the devil', all which are essential to the plan of the Universe; it is cardinal to the Great Work for the Adept so to order affairs that 'even the evil germs of Matter shall alike become useful and good' [*Chaldæan Oracles*, §191]."
[69] *Ibid.*
[70] *Book 4*, Part II, *loc. cit.*

made war in philosophy through these many centuries, are one by the love under will which is the Law of Thelema."[71]

To attain the Grade of Magister Templi, he must perform Two Tasks—the emancipation from Thought by putting each idea against its opposite, and refusing to prefer either; and the consecration of himself as a pure vehicle for the influence of the Order to which he aspires.

He must then decide upon the critical adventure of our Order; the absolute abandonment of himself and his attainments. He cannot remain indefinitely an Exempt Adept; he is pushed onward by the irresistible momentum that he has generated.

Should he fail, by Will or weakness, to make his self-annihilation absolute, he is none the less thrust forth into the Abyss; but instead of being received and reconstructed in the Third Order, as a Babe in the womb of our Lady BABALON, under the Night of Pan, to grow up to be Himself wholly and truly as He was not previously, he remains in the Abyss, secreting his elements round his Ego as if isolated from the Universe, and becomes what is termed a "Black Brother." Such a being is gradually disintegrated from lack of nourishment and the slow but certain action of the attraction of the rest of the Universe, despite efforts to insulate and protect himself, and to aggrandise himself by predatory practices. He may indeed prosper for a while, but in the end he must perish, especially when with a new Æon a new word is proclaimed which he cannot and will not hear, so that he is handicapped by trying to use an obsolete method of Magick, like a man with a boomerang in a battle where every one else has a rifle.[72]

"The idea of 'Because' makes everything dependent on everything else, contrary to the conception of the Universe which this Book has formulated. It is true that the concatenation exists; but the chain does not fetter our limbs. The actions and reactions of illusion are only appearances; we are not affected. No series of images matters to the mirror. What then is the danger of making 'a great miss?' We are immune—that is the very essence of the doctrine....we must become aware of our True Selves; if we abdicate our authority as absolute individuals, we are liable to submit to Law, to feel ourselves the puppets of Determinism, and to suffer the agonies of impotence which have afflicted the thinker, from Gautama to James Thomson."[73] Now, while "the highest occult attainments are possible even to people who have no intellectual knowledge whatever," according to Crowley, "this has been in the past a source of great iniquity, as it represents an overdevelopment of one organ of the Nature at the expense of others."[74]

"The common Mystic affects to despise Science as 'illusion': this is the most fatal of all errors. For the instruments with which he works are all of

---

[71] "De harmonia voluntatis cum destina."
[72] *One Star in Sight*, Sec. 8.
[73] NC on AL II.27.
[74] A∴A∴ *Curriculum*.

this very order of 'illusory things.' We know that lenses distort images; but for all that, we can acquire information about distant objects which proves correct when the lens is constructed according to certain 'illusory' principles and not by arbitrary caprice. The Mystic of this kind is generally recognized by men as a proud fool; he knows the fact, and is hardened in his presumption and arrogance. One finds him goaded by his subconscious shame to active attacks on Science; he gloats upon the apparent errors of calculation which constantly occur, not at all understanding the self-imposed limitations of validity of statement which are always implied; in short, he comes at last to abandon his own postulates, and takes refuge in the hermit-crab-carapace of the theologian."[75]

"'Don't you think,' says the Scientific Illuminist, 'that instead of dreaming all your lives it would be a good thing to wake up and do a little work? There are four of you, and the Kerubim of Ezekiel might perhaps engage your individual attention.' The truth is, it does not matter one rap by what name you christen the illusions of this life, call them substance, or ideas, or hallucinations, it makes not the slightest difference, for you are in them and they in you whatever you like to call them, and you must get out of them and they out of you, and the less you consider their names the better; for name-changing only creates unnecessary confusion and is a waste of time."[76] Crowley prompts Achad to "Study Logic, which is the Code of the Laws of Thought. Study the Method of Science, which is the Application of Logic to the Facts of the Universe. Think not that thou canst ever abrogate these Laws, for though they be Limitations, they are the rules of thy Game which thou dost play. For in thy Trances though thou becomest That which is not subject to those Laws, they are still final in respect of these Things which thou hast set them to govern. Nay, o my son, I like not this Word, govern, for a Law is but a Statement of the nature of the Thing to which it applieth. Nor nothing is compelled save only by Nature of its own true Will. So therefore human Law is a Statement of the Will and of the Nature of Man, or else it is a Falsity contrary thereunto, and becometh null and of no Effect."[77]

Indeed, in Crowley's view, "the mystics were all wrong when they were pious, and held that their mysteries were too sacred to analyse. They ought to have brought in the idea of Measure. This is exactly what was done by the magicians and Qabalists. The difficulty has been that the units of measurement have themselves been somewhat elastic; they even tend to be literary. Their definitions were as circular as, but not more fugitive than, the definitions of the physicists of to-day. Their methods were empirical, though they strove to make them accurate, as well as lack of precise measures and standard apparatus permitted, because they had not yet formulated any true scientific theory. But their successes were numerous. All depended on individual skill. One would rather trust oneself in illness to the born physician than to the laboratory experts of Battle Creek."[78]

---

[75] *Little Essays Toward Truth*, "Knowledge."
[76] *The Temple of Solomon the King*, Part II, "The Seer."
[77] *Liber Aleph*, "De ratione magi vitæ."
[78] *The Book of Thoth*, Part I, Sec. III.

However, "the intellectual knight must not behave like a Christian footpad; he must trap Voltaire in his own arguments by absorbing the whole of Voltaire—eighty volumes and more—until there is no Voltaire left, and as he does so, apply to each link of Voltaire's armour the fangs of the Pyrrhonic Serpent; and where that serpent bites through the links, those links must be discarded; and where its teeth are turned aside, those links must be kept. Similarly must he apply the serpent to St. Ignatius, and out of the combination of the strongest links of both their armours fashion for himself so invulnerable a coat of mail that none can pierce it. Thus, instead of burying one's reason in the sands of faith, like an ostrich, one should rise like a phoenix of enlightenment out of the ashes of both Freethought and Dogma. This is the whole of Philosophic Scientific Illuminism."[79]

"Those, therefore, who effect to despise 'profane' Science are themselves despicable. It is their own incapacity for true Thought of any serious kind, their vanity and pertness; nay more also! their own subconsciousness sense of their own shame and idleness, that induces them to build these flimsy fortification of pretentious ignorance."[80] In fact, "On the Path of the Wise there is probably no danger more deadly, no poison more pernicious, no seduction more subtle than Spiritual Pride; it strikes, being solar, at the very heart of the Aspirant; more, it is an inflation and exacerbation of the Ego, so that its victim runs the peril of straying into a Black Lodge, and finding himself at home there."[81]

> Against this risk we look to our insurance; there are two infallible: Common Sense and the Sense of Humour. When you are lying exhausted and exenterate after the attainment of Vishvarupadarshana it is all wrong to think: "Well, now I'm the holiest man in the world, of course with the exception of John M. Watkins[82]"; better recall the words of the weary sceptical judge in A. P. Herbert's *Holy Deadlock*; he makes a Mantram of it! "I put it to you—I put it to you—I put it to you—that you *have* got a boil on your bottom."[83]
>
> To this rule there is, as usual with rules, an exception. Some states of mind are of the same structure as poetry, where the "one step from the sublime to the ridiculous" is an easy and fatal step. But even so, pedantry is as bad as ribaldry. Personally, I have tried to avoid the dilemma by the use of poetic language and form; for instance, in *AHA!*
>
> It is all difficult, dammed difficult; but if it must be that one's most sacred shrine be profaned, let it be the clean assault of laughter rather than the slimy smear of sactimoniousness![84]

The common defect of all mystical systems previous to that of the Æon whose Law is Thelema is that there has been no place for Laughter.

---

[79] *The Temple of Solomon the King*, Part III, "The Sorcerer."
[80] *Little Essays Toward Truth*, "Wonder."
[81] *MWT*, Ch. XLIV.
[82] The founder of Watkins Books (est. 1893), London's oldest esoteric bookshop.
[83] Herbert 1934, 343–4.
[84] *MWT, loc. cit.*

But the sadness of the mournful Mother and the melancholy of the dying Man are swept in the limbo of the past by the confident smile of the immortal Child.

And there is no Vision more critical in the career of the Adept of Horus than the Universal Joke.

In this Trance he accepts fully the Formula of Osiris, and in the act transcends it; the spear of the Centurion passes harmlessly through his heart, and the sword of the Executioner strikes idly on his neck. He discovers that the Tragedy of which so many centuries have made such a case is but a farce for children's pleasure. Punch is knocked down only to get up grinning with his gay "Root-too-too-tit! Here we are again!" Judy, the Beadle, the Hangman and the Devil are merely the companions of his playtime.

So, since (after all) the facts which he thought tragic are real enough, the essence of his solution is that they are not true, as he thought, of himself; they are just one set of phenomena, as interesting and as fatuously impotent to affect him as any other set. His personal grief was due to his passionate insistence on contemplating one insignificant congeries of Events as if it were the sole reality and importance in the infinite mass of Manifestation.

It is thus that the Perception of the Universal Joke leads directly to the Understanding of the Idea of Self as conterminous with the Universe, and at the same time one with it, creator of it, and aloof from it; which Triune State is, as is well known, one of the most necessary stages of Samadhi. (It is the culmination of one of the two most important chapters of the *Bhagavadgita*.)[85]

"Beyond all this for practical value—since the signpost at every turn of the Path of the Wise reads DANGER—yet springing directly from it by virtue of this very slaying of the Ego, is the use of Laughter as a safeguard of sanity. How easy for the charlatans of oratory to seduce the simple enthusiasm of the soul! What help have we unless we have the wit to know them as ridiculous? There is no limit to the abyss of Idiocy wherein the quacks would plunge us—our only saving reflex is the automatic joke of the Sense of Humour! ... No, the Universal Joke, though it be not a true Trance, is most assuredly a means of Grace, and often proves the chief ingredient of the Universal Solvent."[86]

"The nineteenth Key contains the text of the original curse on creation. Each phrase formulates some calamity." As Crowley recalls in his *Confessions*, "I had always shuddered at its horror as I recited it. But now, the Abyss being crossed, and all its horror faced and mastered, the words of the Key suddenly thrilled with a meaning that I had never suspected. Each curse concealed a blessing. I understood that sorrow had no substance; that only my ignorance and lack of intelligence had made me imagine the existence of evil. As soon as I had destroyed my personality, as soon as I

---

[85] *Little Essays Toward Truth*, "Laughter."
[86] *Ibid.*

had expelled my ego, the universe which to it was indeed a frightful and fatal force, fraught with every form of fear, was so only in relation to this idea 'I'; so long as 'I am I', all else must seem hostile. Now that there was no longer any 'I' to suffer, all these ideas which had inflicted suffering became innocent. I could praise the perfection of every part; I could wonder and worship the whole.[87]

"This attainment absolutely altered my outlook. Of course, I did not at once enter into full enjoyment. The habit of misunderstanding everything had to be broken, bit by bit. I had to explore every possibility and transmute each base metal in turn into gold. It was years before I got into the habit of falling in love at first sight with everything that came my way. The ninth Æthyr shows this transformation symbolically. The universe is represented as a maiden, all innocence, adorned with all perfection."[88] Crowley quotes Blake: "Everything that lives is holy"[89]—"and hence the creation of life is the most sacred of tasks. It does not matter very much to the creator what it is that he creates; there is room in the universe for both the spider and the fly. It is from the rubbish-heap of Choronzon that one selects the material for a god! This is the ultimate analysis of the Mystery of Redemption, and is possibly the real reason of the existence (if existence it can be called) of form, or, if you like, of the Ego. It is astonishing that this typical cry—'I am I'—is the cry of that which above all is not I."[90]

"Unless our aspiration took form it could not influence form. This also is the mystery of incarnation."[91] As *Liber Aleph* puts it, "Here is thy Light, the Lion, the Necessity of thy Nature, fortified by thy Life, the Bull, the Power of Works, and guided by thy Liberty, the Man, the Wit to adapt Action to Environment. These are three Virtues in One, necessary to all proper Motion, as I may say in a Figure, the Lust of the Archer, the propulsive Force of his Arm, and the equilibrating and directing Control of his Eye. Of these three if one fail, the Mark is not hit. But hold! Is not a Fourth Element essential in the Work? Yea, soothly, all were vain without the Engine, Arrow and Bow. This Engine is thy Body, possessed by thee and used by thee for thy Work, yet not Part of thee, even as are his Weapons to this Archer in my Similitude."[92]

"Now consider that this Karma is all that a man has or is. His ultimate object is to get rid of it completely—when it comes to the point of surrendering the Self to the Beloved." But "To surrender all, one must give up not only the bad but the good; not only weakness but strength. How can the mystic surrender all, while he clings to his virtues?" However, "in the beginning the Magician is not that Self, he is only the heap of refuse from which that Self is to be built up. The Magical instruments must be made before they are destroyed."[93] There must first be "the Adept, who doth Will

---

[87] *Confessions*, Ch. 66.
[88] *Ibid.*
[89] *Visions of the Daughters of Albion.*
[90] *Book 4*, Part II, *loc. cit.*
[91] *Ibid.*, Ch. XVI.
[92] "De quattuor virtutis."
[93] *Book 4*, Part II, Ch. IX.

with solid Energy as the Bull, doth dare with fierce Courage as the Lion, doth know with swift Intelligence as the Man, and doth Keep Silence with soaring Subtlety as the Eagle or Dragon. Moreover, this Sphinx is an Eidolon of the Law, for the Bull is Life, the Lion is Light, the Man is Liberty, the Serpent is Love.[94] Now then his Sphinx, being perfect in true Balance, yet taketh the Aspect of the Feminine Principle, that so She may be Partner of the Pyramid, that is the Phallus, pure Image of our Father the Sun, the Unity creative. The Signification of this Mystery is that the Adept must be whole, Himself, containing all Things in true Proportion, before He maketh Himself Bride of the One Universal Transcendental, in its most Secret Virtue."[95]

Now then at last art thou made ready to confront the Pyramid, if thou art established as a Sphinx. For It also hath the foursquare Base of Law, and the Four Triangles of Light, Life, Love and Liberty for its Sides, that meet in a Point of Perfection that is Hadith, poised to the Kiss of Nuith. But in this Pyramid there is no Difference of Form between the Sides, as it is in thy Sphinx, for these are wholly One, save in Direction. Thou art then an Harmony of the Four by Right of thy Attainment of Adeptship, the Crown of thy Manhood, but not an Identity, as in Godhead. Therefore may it be said from one Point of Sight that thine Achievement is but a Preparation, an Adornment of the Bride for the Temple of Hymen, and his Rite. Verily, o my Son, I deem in my Wisdom that this whole Work of thy Development to Sphinxhood cometh before the Work of Theurgy, for the Lord descendeth not upon a Temple ill-conceived, and builded wry, nor abideth in a Shrine unworthy. Accomplish then this Task in Patience, with Assiduity, not hasting furiously after Godliness. For this is most sure, that to the Beauty of a Maiden answereth the Lust of her Lord, spontaneous and without Effort or Appeal of her Contriving.[96]

There is an indifference which overleaps satisfaction; there is a surrender which overthrows victory, there is a resignation which shatters the fetters of anxiety, a relaxation which casts to the winds the manacles of despair. This is the hour of the second birth, when from the womb of the excess of misery is born the child of the nothingness of joy. *Solve!* For all must be melted in the crucible of affliction, all must be refined in the furnace of woe, and then on the anvil of strength must it be beaten out into a blade of gleaming joy. *Coagula!*

Weep and gnash your teeth, and sorrow sits crowned and exultant; therefore rise and gird on the armour of utter desolation! Slay anger, strangle sorrow, and drown despair; then a joy shall be born which is beyond love or hope, endurable, incorruptible. Come heaven, come hell!

---

[94] *Cf.* e.g. *Liber CL*, Ch. IV: "Yet also the Book *Ararita* is right worthy in the Work of the Light, as *Trigrammaton* in that of Will, *Cordis Cincti Serpente* in the Way of Love, and *Liberi* in that of Life. All these Books also concern all these Four Gifts, for in the end you will see that every one is inseparable from every other."

[95] *Liber Aleph*, "De Natura ΣFINΥ."

[96] *Ibid.*, "De pyramide."

Once the Balances are adjusted, then shall the night pass away, and desire and sorrow vanish as a dream with the breath of the morning.[97]

The "Triune Principle has intended a machine for investigating the Universe; and this machine is the fourth Principle of Man," or *Ruach*. "The Ruach is a closely-knitted group of Five Moral and Intellectual principles, concentrated on their core, Tiphareth, the Principle of Harmony, the Human Consciousness and Will of which the four other Sephiroth are (so to speak) the feelers. And these five principles culminate in a sixth, Daäth, Knowledge. But this is not really a principle; it contains in itself the germ of self-contradiction and so of self-destruction. It is a false principle: for, as soon as Knowledge is analysed, it breaks up into the irrational dust of the Abyss. Man's aspiration to Knowledge is thus simply a false road: it is to spin ropes of sand. We cannot here enter into the doctrine of the 'Fall of Adam,' invented to explain in parable how it is that the Universe is so unfortunately constituted. We are concerned only with the observed facts."[98]

We may moreover consider "Because" as involving the idea of causality, and therefore of duality. If cause and effect are really inseparable, as they must be by definition, it is mere clumsiness to regard them as separate; they are two aspects of one single idea, conceived as consecutive for the sake of (apparent) convenience, or for the general purpose previously indicated of understanding and expressing ourselves in finite terms.

Shallow indeed is the obvious objection to this passage that the *Book of the Law* itself is full of phrases which imply causality. Nobody denies that causality is a category of the mind, a form of condition of thought which, if not quite a theoretical necessity, is yet inevitable in practice. The very idea of any relation between any two things appears as causal. Even should we declare it to be causal, our minds would still insist that causality itself was the effect of some cause. Our daily experience hammers home this conviction; and a man's mental excellence seems to be measurable almost entirely in terms of the strength and depth of his appreciation thereof as the soul of the structure of the Universe. It is the spine of Science which has vertebrated human Knowledge above the slimy mollusc whose principle was Faith.

We must not suppose for an instant that the *Book of the Law* is opposed to reason. On the contrary, its own claim to authority rests upon reason, and nothing else. It disdains the arts of the orator. It makes reason the autocrat of the mind. But that very fact emphasizes that the mind should attend to its own business. It should not transgress its limits. It should be a perfect machine, an apparatus for representing the universe accurately and impartially to its master. The Self, its Will, and its Apprehension, should be utterly beyond it. Its individual peculiarities

---

[97] *The Temple of Solomon the King*, Part I, "The Warrior."
[98] *Little Essays Toward Truth*, "Man."

are its imperfections. If we identify ourselves with our thoughts or our bodily instincts, we are evidently pledged to partake of their partiality. We make ourselves items of the interaction of our own illusions.[99]

"One may now go on to consider the use of the Sword in purifying emotions into perceptions. It was the function of the Cup to interpret the perceptions by the tendencies; the Sword frees the perceptions from the Web of emotion. The perceptions are meaningless in themselves; but the emotions are worse, for they delude their victim into supposing them significant and true. Every emotion is an obsession; the most horrible of blasphemies is to attribute any emotion to God in the macrocosm, or to the pure soul in the microcosm." In a word, "The Magick Sword is the analytical faculty; directed against any demon it attacks his complexity. Only the simple can withstand the sword. As we are below the Abyss, this weapon is then entirely destructive: it divides Satan against Satan. It is only in the lower forms of Magick, the purely human forms, that the Sword has become so important a weapon. A dagger should be sufficient. But the mind of man is normally so important to him that the sword is actually the largest of his weapons; happy is he who can make the dagger suffice!"[100]

The Sword, necessary as it is to the Beginner, is but a crude weapon. Its function is to keep off the enemy or to force a passage through them—and though it must be wielded to gain admission to the palace, it cannot be worn at the marriage feast.

One might say that the Pantacle is the bread of life, and the Sword the knife which cuts it up. One must have ideas, but one must criticize them.

The Sword, too, is that weapon with which one strikes terror into the demons and dominates them. One must keep the Ego Lord of the impressions. One must not allow the circle to be broken by the demon; one must not allow any one idea to carry one away.

It will readily be seen how very elementary and false all this is—but for the beginner it is necessary.

In all dealings with demons the point of the Sword is kept downwards, and it should not be used for invocation, as is taught in certain schools of magick.

If the Sword is raised towards the Crown, it is no longer really a sword. The Crown cannot be divided. Certainly the Sword should not be lifted.

The Sword may, however, be clasped in both hands, and kept steady and erect, symbolizing that thought has become one with the single aspiration, and burnt up like a flame. This flame is the Shin, the Ruach Alhim, not the mere Ruach Adam. The divine and not the human consciousness.

---

[99] NC on AL II.28.
[100] *Book 4*, Part II, Ch. VIII.

The Magician cannot wield the Sword unless the Crown is on his head.

Those Magicians, who have attempted to make the Sword the sole or even the principal weapon, have only destroyed themselves, not by the destruction of combination, but by the destruction of division. *{It should be noted that this ambiguity in the word "destruction" has been the cause of much misunderstanding.* Solve *is destruction, but so is* coagula. *The aim of the Magus is to destroy his partial thought by uniting it with the Universal Thought, not to make a further breach and division in the Whole.}*[101]

As the entry on 214 in *An Essay upon Number* tells us, "רוח is one of the most seductive numbers to the beginner. Yet its crown is Daath, and later one learns to regard it as the great obstacle. Look at its promise 21, ending in the fearful curse of 4! Calamity!" Likewise, to the beginner, even "Daath seems very helpful. He is glad that the Stooping Dragon attacks the Sanctuary. He is doing it himself. Hence Buddhists make Ignorance the greatest fetter of all the ten fetters. But in truth Knowledge implies a Knower and a Thing Known, the accursed Dyad which is the prime cause of misery." Yet, "it must never be forgotten that everyone must begin at the beginning. And in the beginning the Aspirant is a rebel, even though he feel himself to be that most dangerous type of rebel, a King Dethroned." Indeed, "if his revolt succeeds, he will acquiesce in order. The first condition of gaining a grade is to be dissatisfied with the one that you have. And so when you reach the end you find order as at first; but also that the law is that you must rebel to conquer."[102]

"The *via mystica* leading to this pre-eminence may aptly be compared to a circle. Wherever the Aspirant strikes it, there he will find a path leading to the right and another leading to the left. To the right the goal is all things, to the left the goal is nothing. Yet the paths are not two paths, but one path; and the goals are not two goals, but one goal. The Aspirant upon entering the circle must travel by the one or the other, and must not look back; lest he be turned into a pillar of salt, and become the habitation of the spirits of Earth. 'For thy vessel the Beasts of the Earth shall inhabit,' as sayeth Zoroaster.[103] The Magus travels by both simultaneously, if he travels at all; for he has learnt what is meant by the mystery: 'A straight line is the circumference of a circle whose radius in infinity'; a line of infinite length in the mind of the Neophyte, but which in truth is also a line of infinite shortness in that of the Magus, if finite or infinite at all."[104] The Poet "does not allow the Planes to interfere with each other. He perceives that each Plane must work out its own salvation; that it is fatally wrong to appeal to the higher. He has identified himself with the will of the higher, and that will must extend downwards, radiating upon the lower. The lower may aspire to the higher, but not in order to get help from its troubles. It may

---

[101] *Ibid.*
[102] *An Essay upon Number*, Part II.
[103] *Chaldæan Oracles*, §95.
[104] *The Temple of Solomon the King*, Part III, "The Sorcerer."

wish as a whole to unite itself with the higher, to lose itself in the higher, but it should be very wary about asking the higher to rearrange its parts."[105]

In *Magick in Theory and Practice*, Crowley relates a story about an adept who "once found it necessary to slay a Circe who was bewitching brethren. He merely walked to the door of her room, and drew an astral T (*traditore*, and the symbol of Saturn) with an astral Dagger. Within 48 hours she shot herself." The footnote explains that, "he who 'destroys' any being must accept it, with all the responsibilities attached, as part of himself. The Adept here in question was therefore obliged to incorporate the elemental spirit of the girl—she was not human, the sheath of a Star, but an advanced planetary dæmon, whose rash ambition had captured a body beyond its capacity to conduct—in his own magical vehicle. He thereby pledged himself to subordinate all the sudden accession of qualities—passionate, capricious, impulsive, irrational, selfish, short-sightedness, sensual, fickle, crazy, and desperate—to his True Will; to discipline, coordinate and employ them in the Great Work, under the penalty of being torn asunder by the wild horses which he had bound fast to his own body by the act of 'destroying' their independent consciousness and control of their chosen vehicle."[106]

> There are, of course, entirely black forms of magic. To him who has not given every drop of his blood for the cup of BABALON all magic power is dangerous. There are even more debased and evil forms, things in themselves black. Such is the use of spiritual force to material ends. Christian Scientists, Mental Healers, Professional Diviners, Psychics and the like, are all *ipso facto* Black Magicians.
>
> They exchange gold for dross. They sell their higher powers for gross and temporary benefit.
>
> That the most crass ignorance of Magick is their principal characteristic is no excuse, even if Nature accepted excuses, which she does not. If you drink poison in mistake for wine, your "mistake" will not save your life.
>
> Below these in one sense, yet far above them in another, are the Brothers of the Left Hand Path. These are they who "shut themselves up", who refuse their blood to the Cup, who have trampled Love in the Race for self-aggrandisement.
>
> As far as the grade of Exempt Adept, they are on the same Path as the White Brotherhood; for until that grade is attained, the goal is not disclosed. Then only are the goats, the lonely leaping mountain-masters, separated from the gregarious huddling valley-bound sheep. Then those who have well learned the lessons of the Path are ready to be torn asunder, to give up their own life to the Babe of the Abyss which is—and is not—they.
>
> The others, proud in their purple, refuse. They make themselves a false crown of the Horror of the Abyss; they set the Dispersion of

---

[105] *Ibid.*, Part VIII, "The Poet."
[106] *MITAP*, Ch. XXI, Sec. III.

Choronzon upon their brows; they clothe themselves in the poisoned robes of Form; they shut themselves up; and when the force that made them what they are is exhausted, their strong towers fall, they become the Eaters of Dung in the Day of Be-with-us, and their shreds, strewn in the Abyss, are lost.

Not so the Masters of the Temple, that sit as piles of dust in the City of the Pyramids, awaiting the Great Flame that shall consume that dust to ashes. For the blood that they have surrendered is treasured in the Cup of OUR LADY BABALON, a mighty medicine to awake the Eld of the All-Father, and redeem the Virgin of the World from her virginity.[107]

As it is written in the Book of the Magus, "With the Wand createth He. With the Cup preserveth He. With the Dagger destroyeth He. With the Coin redeemeth He. His weapons fulfil the wheel; and on What Axle that turneth is not known unto Him. From all these actions must He cease before the curse of His Grade is uplifted from Him. Before He attain to That which existeth without Form."[108] For "יהוה, the Tetragrammaton, as we shall presently see, contains all the Sephiroth with the exception of Kether, and specially signifies the Lesser Countenance, Microprosopus, the King of the qabalistical Sephirotic greatest Trinity, and the Son in His human incarnation, in the Christian acceptation of the Trinity. Therefore, as the Son reveals the Father, so does יהוה, Jehovah, reveal אהיה, Eheieh. And אדני is the Queen, 'by whom alone Tetragrammaton can be grasped,' whose exaltation into Binah is found in the Christian Assumption of the Virgin."[109]

According to Lévi, "The qabalists say that the occult name of the devil, his true name, is that of Jehovah written backwards. This, for the initiate, is a complete revelation of the mysteries of the tetragram. In fact, the order of the letters of that great name indicates the predominance of the idea over form, of the active over the passive, of cause over effect. By reversion that order one obtains the contrary. Jehovah is he who tames Nature as it were a superb horse and makes it go where he will; Chavajoh (the demon) is the horse without a bridle who, like those of the Egyptians of the song of Moses, falls upon its rider, and hurls him beneath it, into the abyss. The devil, then, exists really enough for the qabalists; but it is neither a person nor a distinguished power of even the forces of Nature. The devil is dispersion, or

---

[107] *Ibid.*, Sec. I; *cf.* also *Confessions*, Ch. 81: "In *The Vision and the Voice*, the attainment of the grade of Master of the Temple was symbolized by the adept pouring every drop of his blood, that is his whole individual life, into the Cup of the Scarlet Woman, who represents Universal Impersonal Life. There remains therefore (to pursue the imagery) of the adept 'nothing but a little pile of dust'. In a subsequent vision the Grade of Magus is foreshadowed; and the figure is that this dust is burnt into 'a white ash', which ash is preserved in an Urn. It is difficult to convey the appropriateness of this symbolism, but the general idea is that the earthly or receptive part of the Master is destroyed. That which remains has passed through fire; and is therefore, in a sense, of the nature of fire. The Urn is engraved with a word or symbol expressive of the nature of the being whose ash is therein. The Magus is thus, of course, not a person in any ordinary sense; he represents a certain nature or idea. To put it otherwise, we may say, the Magus is a word. He is the Logos of the Æon which he brings to pass."

[108] *Liber B vel Magi*, Secs. 7–12.

[109] *The Temple of Solomon the King*, Part V.

the slumber of the intelligence. It is madness and falsehood."[110] Similarly, "Choronzon is described by Sir Edward Kelly as 'that mighty devil', as the first and deadliest of all the powers of evil. Rightly so, for although he is not a person, he is the metaphysical contrary of the whole Process of Magick."[111]

As recorded in *A True & Faithful Relation of what Passed for Many Yeers between Dr. John Dee and Some Spirits*, Kelly put this question to Gabriel: "Whether is this [Angelic or Enochian] Language known in any part of the World or no? if it be, where and by whom?"[112] The Angel answered as follows:

> Gab. ...... Man in his Creation, being made an Innocent, was also authorised and made partaker of the Power and Spirit of God: whereby he not onely did know all things under his Creation and spoke of them properly, naming them as they were: but also was partaker of our presence and society, yea a speaker of the mysteries of God; yea, with God himself: so that in innocency the power of his partakers with God, and us his good Angles, was exalted, and so became holy in the sight of God until that Coronzon (for so is the true name of that mighty Devil) envying his felicity, and perceiving that the substance of his lesser part was frail and unperfect in respect of his pure Esse, began to assail him, and so prevailed: that offending so became accursed in the sight of God; and so lost the Garden of felicity, the judgement of his understanding: but not utterly the favour of God, and was driven forth (as your Scriptures record) unto the Earth which was covered with brambles: where being as dumb, and not able to speak, he began to learn of necessity the Language with thou, E.K. callest [1 Hebrew:] and yet not that [2 Hebrew] amongst you: in the which he uttered and delivered to his posterity, the nearest knowledge he had of God his Creatures: and from his own self divided his speech into three parts, twelve, three, and seven: the number whereof remaineth, but the true form and pronuntiations want; and therefore is not of that force that it was in his own dignity, much lesse to be compared with this that we deliver, which Adam verily spake in innocency, and was never uttered nor disclosed to man since till now, wherein the power of God must work, and wisdom in her true kind be delivered: which are not to be spoken of in any other thing, neither to be talked of with mans imaginations; for as this Work and Gift is of God, which is all power, so doth he open it in a tongue of power, to the intent that the proportions may agree in themselves: for it is written, Wisdom fitteh upon an Hill, and beholdeth the four Winds, and girdeth her self together as the brightnesse of the morning, which is visited with a few, and dwelleth alone as though she were a Widow.
>
> Thus you see there, the Necessity of this Tongue: The Excellency of it, And the Cause why it is preferred before that which you call Hebrew:

---

[110] *The Key of the Mysteries*, Part III, Book I, "Chapter III: The Simple Letters."
[111] *Liber 418*, 10th Æthyr, fn.
[112] Casaubon 1659, 92.

For it is written, Every lesse, consenteth to his greater. I trust this is sufficient.[113]

Crowley, of course, considered both Lévi and Kelley his previous incarnations. The Cotton Manuscript gives a third (or fourth) variant spelling of name of the Demon of Dispersion as "Coronzom."[114] To Lévi, "The great arcanum—that is to say, the unutterable and inexplicable secret—is the absolute knowledge of good and of evil.... Good personified is God. Evil personified is the Devil. To know the secret or the formula of God is to be God. To know the secret or the formula of the Devil is to be the Devil. To wish to be at the same time God and Devil is to absorb in one's self the most absolute antinomy, the two most strained contrary forces; it is the wish to shut up in one's self an infinite antagonism. It is to drink a poison which would extinguish the suns and consume the worlds.... It is to devote one's self to the promptest and most terrible of all deaths. Woe to him who wishes to know too much! For if excessive and rash knowledge does not kill him it will make him mad. To eat the fruit of the Tree of Knowledge of Good and Evil, is to associate evil with good, and assimilate the one to the other. It is to cover the radiant countenance of Osiris with the mask of Typhon. It is to raise the sacred veil of Isis; it is to profane the sanctuary. The rash man who dares to look at the sun without protection becomes blind, and from that moment for him the sun is black."[115]

"Any neophyte of the Order (or, as some say, any person soever) possesses the right to claim the Grade of Master of the Temple by taking the Oath of the Grade. It is hardly necessary to observe that to do so is the most sublime and awful responsibility which it is possible to assume, and an unworthy person who does so incurs the most terrific penalties by his presumption."[116] As *Liber Aleph* exhorts, "Thou must be free in the Law of Thelema, perfectly one with thy true Self, singly and wholly bound in thy true Will, before thou durst (in Prudence) invoke the Name of Choronzon, even for thy good Sport and Phantasy."[117] For "To call forth Choronzon, unless one be wholly above the Abyss, is to ensure the most appalling and immediate catastrophe."[118]

> Very little experience on the mystic path will show him that of all the impressions he receives none is true. Either they are false in themselves, or they are wrongly interpreted in his mind.
>
> There is one truth, and only one. All other thoughts are false.
>
> And as he advances in the knowledge of his mind he will come to understand that its whole structure is so faulty that it is quite incapable, even in its most exalted moods, of truth.

---

[113] *Ibid.*, 92–93.
[114] XLVI Pt. I, fol. 91a.
[115] *The Key of the Mysteries*, Part IV, Ch. IV.
[116] *One Star in Sight*, Sec. 6.
[117] "De periculo jucorum amoris."
[118] *Liber 418*, 10th Æthyr, fn.

He will recognize that any thought merely establishes a relation between the Ego and the non-Ego.

Kant has shown that even the laws of nature are but the conditions of thought. And as the current of thought is the blood of the mind, it is said that the Magick Cup is filled with the blood of the Saints. All thought must be offered up as a sacrifice.[119]

"Heed not the shrieking of women, or the crying of little children; for all must die, and not a stone must be left standing in the city of the World, lest darkness depart not. Haste! bring flint and steel, light the match, fire the thatch of the hovel and the cedar rafters of the palace; for all must be destroyed, and no man must delay, or falter, or turn back, or repent. Then from the ashes of Destruction will rise the King, the birthless and the deathless one, the great monarch who shall shake from his tangled beard the blood of strife, and who shall cast from his weary hand the sword of desolation."[120] You see, the "Magical Will is in its essence twofold, for it presupposes a beginning and an end; to Will to be a thing is to admit that you are not that thing. Hence to Will anything but the supreme thing, is to wander still further from it—any Will but that to give up the self to the Beloved is Black Magic—yet this surrender is so simple an act that to our complex minds it is the most difficult of all acts; and hence training is necessary. Further, the Self surrendered must not be less than the All-Self; one must not come before the altar of the Most High with an impure or an imperfect offering. As it is written in 'Liber LXV,' 'To await Thee is the end, not the beginning.'"[121]

This training may lead through all sorts of complications, varying according to the nature of the student, and hence it may be necessary for him at any moment to Will all sorts of things which to others might seem unconnected with the goal. Thus it is not *à priori* obvious why a billiard player should need a file.

Since, then, we may want *anything*, let us see to it that our Will is strong enough to obtain anything we want without loss of time.

It is therefore necessary to develop the Will to its highest point, even though the last task but one is the total surrender of this Will. Partial surrender of an imperfect Will is of no account in Magick.

The Will being a lever, a fulcrum is necessary; this fulcrum is the main aspiration of the student to attain. All Wills which are not dependent upon this principal will are so many leakages; they are like fat to the athlete.

The majority of the people in this world are ataxic; they cannot coordinate their mental muscles to make a purposed movement. They have no real Will, only a set of wishes, many of which contradict others. The victim wobbles from one to the other (and it is no less wobbling

---

[119] *Book 4*, Part II, Ch. VII.
[120] *The Temple of Solomon the King*, Part I, "The Warrior."
[121] *Book 4*, Part II, Ch. VI.

because the movements may occasionally be very violent) and at the end of life the movements cancel each other out. Nothing has been achieved; except the one thing of which the victim is not conscious: the destruction of his own character, the confirming of indecision. Such an one is torn limb from limb by Choronzon.[122]

How shall a Man attain to the Trance where All is One, if he yet debate within his Mind concerning Virtue as a Thing Absolute? Thus, o my Son, there be those that are fuddled with Doubt whether Meat is to be eaten (I choose this as a Reference with Habit is proper to the Lion, as Grass to the Horse, so that his right Problem is solely thus, what is fitting to his own Nature). Or again, I suppose that he is in Vision, and an Angel, visiting him, imparteth a Truth contrary to his Prejudice, as it fell out in mine own Case, when I inhabited the Body of Sir Edward Kelly, or so do I in Part remember, as it seemeth dimly. This nevertheless is sure (or the learned Casaubon, publishing the Record of that Word with the Magician Dee, sayeth falsely) that an Angel did declare unto Kelly the Very Axiomata of our Law of Thelema, in good Measure, and plainly; but Dee, afflicted by the Fixity of his Tenets that were of the Slave-Gods, was wroth, and by his Authority prevailed upon the other, who was indeed not wholly perfected as an Instrument, or the World ready for that Sowing. Consider also how in this very Life I was the Enemy of mine own Law, and wrote down *The Book of the Law* contrary to my conscious Will by the Virtue of Obedience as a Scribe, and strove constantly to escape mine own Work, and the Utterance of my Word, until by Initiation I was made All-One.[123]

"Every idea, considered as an idea, is lumber, dead weight, poison; but it is all wrong to represent these acts as acts of sacrifice. There is no question of depriving oneself of anything one wants. The process is rather that of learning to discard what one thought one wanted in the darkness before the dawn of the discovery of the real object of one's passion. Hence, note well! Concentration has reduced our moral obligations to their simplest terms: there is a single standard to which everything is to be referred."[124] Indeed, "Everyone has the material, one man's pretty well as good as his brothers; but for that Pantacle to be in any way fashioned to a willed end, or even to an intelligible end, or even to a known end: '*Hoc opus, Hic labor est.*'[125] It is indeed the toil of ascending from Avernus, and escaping to the upper air. In order to do it, it is most necessary to understand our tendencies, and to will the development of one, the destruction of another. And though all elements in the Pantacle must ultimately be destroyed, yet some will help us directly to reach a position from which this task of

---

[122] *Ibid.* Emphasis in original.
[123] *Liber Aleph*, "De mente inimica animo."
[124] *Eight Lectures*, Ch. 5, Sec. 7.
[125] Verg. *A.* 6.129.

destruction becomes possible; and there is no element therein which may not be occasionally helpful."[126]

"The whole Universe is an illusion, but it is an illusion difficult to get rid of. It is true compared with most things. But ninety-nine out of every hundred impressions are false even in relation to the things on their own plane. Such distinctions must be graven deeply upon the surface of the Pantacle by the Holy Dagger."[127] Knowledge "is the demon that purely intellectual or rational religions take as their God. The special danger of Hinayana Buddhism."[128] In fact, "The Sword has been the great weapon of the last century. Every idea has been attacked by thinkers, and none has withstood attack. Hence civilization crumbles. No settled principles remain. To-day all constructive statesmanship is empiricism or opportunism. It has been doubted whether there is any real relation between Mother and Child, any real distinction between Male and Female. The human mind, in despair, seeing insanity imminent in the breaking up of these coherent images, has tried to replace them by ideals which are only saved from destruction, at the very moment of their birth, by their vagueness. The Will of the King was at least ascertainable at any moment; nobody has yet devised a means for ascertaining the will of the people. All conscious willed action is impeded; the march of events is now nothing but inertia."[129]

"This is the only way to deal with reason. Reason is like a woman; if you listen, you are lost; with a thick stick, you have some sort of sporting chance. Reason leads the philosopher to self-contradiction, the statesman to doctrinaire follies; it makes the warrior lay down his arms, and the lover cease to rave. What is so unreasonable as man? The only Because in the lover's litany is Because I love you. We want no skeleton syllogisms at our symposium of souls."[130] There are many "methods of destroying various deep-rooted ideas"—"The best is perhaps the method of equilibrium. Get the mind into the habit of calling up the opposite to every thought that may arise. In conversation always disagree. See the other man's arguments; but, however much your judgment approves them, find the answer."[131]

> Let this be done dispassionately; the more convinced you are that a certain point of view is right, the more determined you should be to find proofs that it is wrong.
> If you have done this thoroughly, these points of view will cease to trouble you; you can then assert your own point of view with the calm of a master, which is more convincing than the enthusiasm of a learner.

---

[126] *Book 4*, Part II, Ch. IX.
[127] *Ibid.*
[128] *The Temple of Solomon the King*, Part V.
[129] *Book 4*, Part II, Ch. VIII.
[130] NC on AL II.33. *Cf.* also *The Book of Thoth*, Part II, Atu XII: "In the former Æon, that of Osiris, the element of Air, which is the nature of that Æon, is not unsympathetic either to Water or to Fire; compromise was a mark of that period. But now, under a Fiery lord of the Æon, the watery element, so far as water is below the Abyss, is definitely hostile, unless the opposition is the right opposition implied in marriage."
[131] *Book 4*, Part II, Ch. VI.

You will cease to be interested in controversies; politics, ethics, religion will seem so many toys, and your Magical Will will be free from these inhibitions.

In Burma there is only one animal which the people will kill, Russell's Viper; because, as they say, "either you must kill it or it will kill you"; and it is a question of which sees the other first.

Now any one idea which is not The Idea must be treated in this fashion. When you have killed the snake you can use its skin, but as long as it is alive and free, you are in danger.

And unfortunately the Ego-idea, which is the real snake, can throw itself into a multitude of forms, each clothed in the most brilliant dress. Thus the Devil is said to be able to disguise himself as an Angel of Light.

Under the strain of a magical vow this is too terribly the case. No normal human being understands or can understand the temptations of the saints.

An ordinary person with ideas like those which obsessed St. Patrick and St. Anthony would be only fit for an asylum.[132]

This dialectical method of truth-seeking is also evident in the traditions of Madhyamaka, Yogācāra, and Tantric Buddhism. Buddhist doctrine was rigorously critiqued, though not ultimately refuted, as early as the 2nd century CE by the Indian monk Nāgārjuna, who is widely considered as the most important Buddhist philosopher after Gautama himself, and often even referred to as "the Second Buddha" by the East Asian Mahāyāna traditions. His dialectical approach to Buddhism became known as the Perfection of Wisdom (or *Prajñāpāramitā*) and was later developed by other notable Indian thinkers, such as Dignāga and Dharmakīrti. Trisong Detsän—one of the three "Dharma Kings" who established Buddhism in Tibet—and later Je Tsongkhapa—the founder of the Gelugpa sect that ruled the country until the Chinese takeover in 1951—championed the value of dialectic and of formalized training in debate in the mountain kingdom.

"In this way let every idea go forth as a triangle on the base of two opposites, making an apex transcending their contradiction in a higher harmony," says *Magick in Theory and Practice*. "It is not safe to use any thought in Magick, unless that thought has been thus equilibrated and destroyed. Thus again with the instruments themselves; the Wand must be ready to change into a Serpent, the Pantacle into the whirling Svastika or Disk of Jove, as if to fulfil the functions of the Sword. The Cross is both the death of the 'Saviour' and the Phallic symbol of Resurrection."[133] The footnote reads: "It is the extension in matter of the Individual Self, the Indivisible Point determined by reference to the Four Quarters. This is the formula which enables it to express its Secret Self; its dew falling upon the

---

[132] *Ibid.*

[133] *Cf.* also *The Book of Thoth*, Part II, Atu 0: "One must constantly keep in mind the bivalence of every symbol. Insistence upon either one or other of the contradictory attributions inherent in a symbol is simply a mark of spiritual incapacity; and it is constantly happening, because of prejudice. It is the simplest test of initiation that every symbol is understood instinctively to contain this contradictory meaning in itself."

Rose is developed into an Eidolon of Itself, in due season." Indeed, "Will itself must be ready to culminate in the surrender of that Will:"—"See *Liber LXV* and *Liber VII*."—"the aspiration's arrow that is shot against the Holy Dove must transmute itself into the wondering Virgin that receives in her womb the quickening of that same Spirit of God.[134]

"Any idea that is thus in itself positive and negative, active and passive, male and female, is fit to exist above the Abyss; any idea not so equilibrated is below the Abyss, contains in itself an unmitigated duality or falsehood, and is to that extent qliphotic—and dangerous. Even an idea like 'truth' is unsafe unless it is realized that all Truth is in one sense falsehood. For all Truth is relative; and if it be supposed absolute, will mislead." Here Crowley again cites the French polymath Henri Poincaré "for the mathematical proof of this thesis." Poincaré's short paper on relativity was published three months before Einstein's first paper on the subject, followed later by a longer version. According to Crowley, "Spiritual Experience goes yet deeper, and destroys the Canon of the Law of Contradiction. There is an immense amount of work by the MASTER THERION on this subject; it pertains especially to His grade of $9°=2^\square$. Such profundities are unsuited to the Student, and may unsettle him seriously. It will be best for him to consider (provisionally) Truth in the sense in which it is taken by Physical Science."[135]

"*The Book of Lies* falsely so called (*Liber 333*) is worthy of close and careful study in this respect. The reader should also consult *Konx Om Pax*, 'Introduction,' and 'Thien Tao' in the same volume. All this is to be expressed in the words of the ritual itself, and symbolised in every act performed."[136] *Liber CCCXXXIII* "deals with many matters on all planes of the very highest importance. It is an official publication for Babes of the Abyss, but is recommended even to beginners as highly suggestive. Its Chapters XXV, XXXVI, and XLIV are in Class D," i.e. official rituals or instructions of the A∴A∴ "Thien Tao," a morality tale in reverse, where a Taoist sage recommends that individuals adopt attitudes and behaviours antithetical to their conscious selves, is described as "An Essay on Attainment by the Way of Equilibrium," and part of the curriculum for a Major Adept.[137]

With the Hindu, *samādhi* is "a result, the result of results indeed. There are higher and lower forms. That called Nirvikalpa-Samadhi, when the trance results from banishing thought altogether, instead of concentrating on one thought, is the highest kind. But, with the Buddhist, Samadhi, though the state of mind meant is the same, is not an end, but a means. The holy-man-of-the-East must keep this state of mind unimpaired during his whole life, using it as a weapon to attack the Three Characteristics (the antithesis of Nibbana) even as one uses one's normal dualistic consciousness to attack that dualism. . . . The Hindu, too, asks this question. 'I,' he says, 'define

---

[134] *MITAP*, Ch. VIII, Sec. I.
[135] *Ibid.*
[136] *Ibid.*
[137] A∴A∴ *Curriculum.*

Phenomena as changeful and Atman the Noumenon as without change. When challenged, I merely retort by distinguishing between Atman and Paramatman. You say the same, but for Atman you say 'Nibbana." The Buddhist can only retort, rudely enough: There is no Atman; and there is Nibbana. The Hindu probably mutters something about criticism of Nibbana having forced some Buddhists to a conception of Parinibbana, simply but neatly defined as That to which none of the criticisms apply! Yet Atman and Nibbana are defined in almost identical terms."[138]

"The Vedanta" portion of *The Temple of Solomon the King* quotes the *Bṛhadāraṇyaka Upaniṣad*, one of the oldest and most important of the 108 Upanishads: "After death there is no consciousness. For where there is as it were a duality, there one sees the other, smells, hears, addresses, comprehends, and knows the other; but when everything has become to him his own self, how should he smell, see, hear, address, understand, or know anyone at all? How should he know him, through whom he knows all this, how should he know the knower?"[139]

> Thus does the Supreme Âtman become unknowable, on account of the individual Âtman *{The illusion of thinking ourselves similar to the Unity and yet separated from It.}* remaining unknown; and further, will remain unknowable as long as consciousness of a separate Supremacy exists in the heart of the individual.
> Directly the seeker realizes this, a new reality is born, and the clouds of night roll back and melt away before the light of a breaking dawn, brilliant beyond all that have preceded it. Destroy this consciousness, and the Unknowable may become the Known, or at least the Unknown, in the sense of the undiscovered. Thus we find the old Vedantist presupposing an Âtman and a σύμβολον of it, so that he might better transmute the unknown individual soul into the known, and the unknowable Supreme Soul into the unknown, and then, from the knowable through the known to the knower, get back to the Âtman and Equilibrium—Zero.
> All knowledge he asserts to be Mâyâ, and only by paradoxes is the Truth revealed.[140]

The section finishes with a quote from the *Kena Upanishad* (also known as the *Talavakāra Upaniṣad*, forming as it does a part of the *Talavakāra Brahmaṇa*), another one of the ancient texts that make up the thirteen Principal or Mukhya Upanishads:

> Only he who knows it not knows it,
> Who knows it, he knows it not;
> Unknown is it by the wise,
> But by the ignorant known.[141]

---

[138] *The Psychology of Hashish*, Sec. XVII.
[139] 2.4.12.
[140] *The Temple of Solomon the King*, Part IV, "The Vedanta."
[141] Kena 11.

The Book of Thoth, describing Atu VI, following a quotation from the 2nd Æthyr, says: "It is very significant that almost every sentence in this passage seems to reverse the meaning of the previous one. This is because reaction is always equal and opposite to action. This equation is, or should be, simultaneous in the intellectual world, where there is no great time lag; the formulation of any idea creates its contradictory at almost the same moment. The contradictory of any proposition is implicit in itself. This is necessary to preserve the equilibrium of the Universe."[142] Chapter VIII of *Magick in Theory and Practice*, entitled "Of Equilibrium: and of the General and Particular Method of Preparation of the Furniture of the Temple and the Instruments of Art," quotes "the holiest of the Books of the ancient Qabalah," the *Siphra Dtzenioutha*: "Before there was equilibrium, countenance beheld not countenance."[143] According to the footnote, "The full significance of this aphorism is an Arcanum of the grade of Ipsissimus. It may, however, be partially apprehended by study of *Liber Aleph*, and *The Book of the Law* and the Commentaries thereon. It explains Existence."

"One countenance here spoken of is the Macrocosm, the other the Microcosm."[144] Again, the footnote explains that, "This is the case because we happen ourselves to be Microcosms whose Law is 'love under will.' But it is also Magick for an Unit which has attained Perfection (in Absolute Nothingness, 0^0), to become 'divided for love's sake, for the chance of union.'" And, of course, "the object of any magick ceremony is to unite the Macrocosm and the Microcosm. It is as in optics; the angles of incidence and reflection are equal. You must get your Macrocosm and Microcosm exactly balanced, vertically and horizontally, or the images will not coincide. This equilibrium is affirmed by the magician in arranging the Temple. Nothing must be lop-sided."

> This Lamp hangeth above the Altar, it hath no support from below; its light illumines the whole Temple, yet upon it are cast no shadows, no reflections. It cannot be touched, it cannot be extinguished, in no way can it change; for it is utterly apart from all those things which have complexity, which have dimension, which change and may be changed.
>
> When the eyes of the Magus are fixed upon this Lamp naught else exists.
>
> The Instruments lie idle on the Altar; that Light alone burns eternally.
>
> The Divine Will that was the Wand is no more; for the path has become one with the Goal.
>
> The Divine Understanding that was the Cup is no more; for the subject and Object of intelligence are one.
>
> The Divine Reason that was the Sword is no more; for the complex has been resolved into the Simple.

---

[142] Part II, "The Lovers."
[143] 1.2.
[144] *MITAP*, Ch. VIII.

And the Divine Substance that was the Pantacle is no more; for the many has become the One.

Eternal, unconfined, unextended, without cause and without effect, the Holy Lamp mysteriously burns. Without quantity or quality, unconditioned and sempiternal, is this Light.[145]

In his *Eight Lecture on Yoga*, Crowley tells us "how tedious these practices become; how great the bewilderment; how constant the disappointment. Long before the occurrence of Dhyana, there are quite a number of minor results which indicate the breaking up of intellectual limitation. You must not be disturbed if these results make you feel that the very foundations of your mind are being knocked from under you. The real lesson is that, just as you learn in Asana, the normal body is in itself nothing but a vehicle of pain, so is the normal itself insane; by its own standards it is insane. You have only got to read a quite simple and elementary work like Professor Joad's *Guide to Philosophy* to find that any argument carried far enough leads to a contradiction in terms. There are dozens of ways of showing that if you begin 'A is A,' you end 'A is not A.' The mind reacts against this conclusion; it anaesthetises itself against the self-inflicted wound, and it regulates philosophy to the category of paradoxical tricks. But that is a cowardly and disgraceful attitude. The Yogi has got to face the fact that we are all raving lunatics; that sanity exists—if it exists at all—in a mental state free from dame's school rules of intellect."[146]

"Dreams are real, hallucinations are real, delirium is real, and so is madness; but for the most part these are Qliphothic realities, unstable, unbalanced, dangerous. Visions are real, inspirations are real, revelation is real, and so is genius; but these are from Kether, and the highest climber on the mystic mountain is he who will obtain the finest view, and from its summit all things will be shown unto him."[147] An entry in Crowley's diary from 26 December 1919 reads: "Attainment of Insanity. The whole point is to make it perfect in balance. Then it radiates light in every direction, while the Ipsissimus is utterly indifferent to it." According to *One Star in Sight*, to attain the Grade of Ipsissimus, the Magus "must accomplish three tasks, destroying the Three Guardians mentioned in *Liber 418*, the 3rd Æthyr; Madness, and Falsehood, and Glamour, that is, Duality in Act, Word and Thought."[148]

> Now the grade of a Magister teacheth the Mystery of Sorrow, and the grade of a Magus the Mystery of Change, and the grade of Ipsissimus the Mystery of Selflessness, which is called also the Mystery of Pan.
>
> Let the Magus then contemplate each in turn, raising it to the ultimate power of Infinity. Wherein Sorrow is Joy, and Change is Stability, and Selflessness is Self. For the interplay of the parts hath no action upon the whole. And this contemplation shall be performed not

---

[145] *Book 4*, Part II, Ch. X.
[146] *Eight Lectures*, loc. cit., Sec. 21.
[147] *The Temple of Solomon the King*, Part II, "The Seer."
[148] Sec. 5.

by simple meditation—how much less then by reason! but by the method which shall have been given unto Him in His initiation to the Grade.

Following which method, it shall be easy for Him to combine that trinity from its elements, and further to combine Sat-Chit-Ananda, and Light, Love, Life, three by three into nine that are one, in which meditation success shall be That which was first adumbrated to Him in the grade of Practicus (which reflecteth Mercury into the lowest world) in *Liber XXVII*, "Here is Nothing under its three Forms."

And this is the Opening of the Grade of Ipsissimus, and by the Buddhists it is called the trance Nerodha-Samapatti.[149]

The attainment of "cessation," or *nirodha-samāpatti*, is the highest meditational state possible in Theravāda Buddhism. Those in this state—which can continue for as long as seven days—are to all appearances dead, as it is the extinction of all feeling and perception, the actual realization of *Nibbāna* in this life.[150] "So—one must suppose, for here I reach a point where, as Mr. Waite jeers, we are driven to take refuge in portentous darkness and irretrievable mystery (because we don't know anything about it)—he sits down and contemplates the Three Characteristics. This will presumably be very difficult to do because he is probably (for all the 'Grace of the Lord Shiva' business) an expert in the Viññanam trances, and having thus created an eternal Universe and an even more eternal Absence of Universe, both of which, too, are probably mere masses of Sat—Chit—Ananda (Being—Knowledge—Bliss) while he is trying to think of Change—Sorrow—Unsubstantiality."[151] Whereas Buddhist monks traditionally attain *nirodha-samāpatti* by producing the Four Formless States one after the other, and perceiving in each the above Three Characteristics, the Thelemic hermit "succeeds in seeing first the truth and then the falsity of the Three Characteristics—and that is Nibbana."[152]

Behold, how comfortable is this thy Wisdom, wherein I have resolved every Conflict soever that is or that can be, even in all dimensions, that Antagonism of Things no less than their Limitations. I have said: Evil be thou my Good; for it is the Magical Mirror of Our Astarte and the Caduceus of our Hermes. Now this was the Error of Elder Philosophers, that perceiving Changeful Duality as the Cause of Sorrow, they sought the Reconcilement in Unity and in Stability. But I shew thee the Universe as the Body of Our Lady Nuith, who is None and Two, with Hadith Her Lord as the Alternator of those Phases. This Universe is then a perpetual By-coming, the Vessel of every Permutation of infinity, wherein every Phenomenon is a Sacrament, Change being the

---

[149] *Liber B vel Magi*, Sec. 15–18.
[150] P. Griffiths, "Concentration or Insight: The problematic of the Theravāda Buddhist meditation theory," in Williams 2005.
[151] *The Psychology of Hashish*, Sec. XIX.
[152] *Ibid.*

act of Love, and Duality the Condition prodromal to that Act even as an Axe must be taken back from a Cedar that it may deliver its Stroke. The Error therefore of these Philosophers lay in their false Assumption that Bliss, Knowledge and Being (the Qualities of their Changeless Unity) could be States. O my Son, how pitiful is their Beggary, these Paupers of Sense and of Experience and of Observation! The Emptiness of their Bellies was it that bred Phantoms of Ideal, so that they sought Joy by a crude Denial of what Truth (or rather, Fact) they had perceived concerning the Universe, so that they set up an Idol of Death for their God, in very Rage of Hatred against the Sum of their own Selves.[153]

According to Crowley, the "three ideas which Hindu philosophers call Sat, Chit and Ananda, which are usually translated Being, Knowledge and Bliss" really mean: "Sat, the tendency to conceive of an object as real; Chit, the tendency to pretend that it is an object of knowledge; and Ananda, the tendency to imagine that we are affected by it."[154] The Hindus "call Atman *Sat-chit-ananda*, these being above the pairs of opposites, rather on the Hegelian lines of the reconciliation (rather than the identity) of opposites, in a master idea. We have dismissed infinity as the figment of a morbid mathematic: but in any case the disproof applies to it as to God."[155] The Ipsissimus of the A∴A∴ "is wholly free from all limitations soever, existing in the Nature of all things without discriminations of quantity or quality between them. He has identified Being and not-Being and Becoming, Action and non-Action and Tendency to Action, with all other such triplicities, not distinguishing between them in respect of any conditions, or between any one thing and any other thing as to whether it is with or without conditions."[156]

These Philosophers, or shall I not say Misosophers and Pseudo-Sophists, have been hard put to it to explain the Mystery of the Existence of their Evil. They have cried, frothing with Words, the Evil is Illusion. But if so, that Illusion is Evil, whence came it, and to what End? If their Devil created it, who created that Devil? All their contention resolveth to this Dilemma of Change in a Changeless, Falsity in a True, Hate in a Loving, Weakness in an Almighty, Duality in a Simple, Being as they define their God. Nor do they see that they restrict their God (whom yet they would have to be All) by admitting Opposites to this Nature, ever when they sum these Opposites as Illusion, since Illusion is the Denial of His Truth. But the Indians, seeing his, seek Escape by denying all Duality soever to their God, or True State, I speak of Parabrahman and of Nibbana, thus in any Reality of Thought rather denying Him or It than destroying Illusion. But in our Light we have no Need of any Denial, and accept all, yea Illusion itself, discriminating only in our Minds between

---

[153] *Liber Aleph*, "De cæcitia philosophorum antiquorum."
[154] *Eight Lectures*, Ch. 6, Sec. 12.
[155] *Berashith*, fn.
[156] *One Star in Sight*, Sec. 4.

Phenomena by Comparison with some convenient Standard, for the Purpose of maintaining the Order of our Conceptions in Respect of the Relation of any Being with its Environment.[157]

"It was said by the Sorcerer of the Jura that in order to invoke the Devil it is only necessary to call him with your whole will. This is an universal magical truth, and applies to every other being as much as to the Devil. For the whole will of every man is in reality the whole will of the Universe. It is, however, always easy to call up the demons, for they are always calling you; and you have only to step down to their level and fraternize with them. They will tear you in pieces at their leisure. Not at once; they will wait until you have wholly broken the link between you and your Holy Guardian Angel before they pounce, lest at the last moment you escape. Anthony of Padua and (in our own times) 'MacGregor' Mathers are examples of such victims. Nevertheless, every Magician must firmly extend his empire to the depth of hell."[158] Crowley quotes *Liber Tzaddi*: "My adepts stand upright, their heads above the heavens, their feet below the hells."

"This is the reason why the Magician who performs the Operation of the *Sacred Magic of Abramelin the Mage*, immediately after attaining to the Knowledge and Conversation of the Holy Guardian Angel, must evoke the Four Great Princes of the Evil of the World. 'Obedience and faith to Him that liveth and triumpheth, that reigneth above you in your palaces as the Balance of Righteousness and Truth'"—a reference to the First Enochian Key—"is your duty to your Holy Guardian Angel, and the duty of the demon world to you. These powers of 'evil' nature are wild beasts; they must be tamed, trained to the saddle and the bridle; they will bear you well. There is nothing useless in the Universe: do not wrap up your talent in a napkin, because it is only 'dirty money'! With regard to Pacts, they are rarely lawful. There should be no bargain struck. Magick is not a trade, and no hucksters need apply. Master everything, but give generously to your servants, once they have unconditionally submitted."[159]

"The Temple and all that is in it must be destroyed again and again before it is worthy to receive that Light. Hence it so often seems that the only advice that any master can give to any pupil is to destroy the Temple. 'Whatever you have' and 'whatever you are' are veils before that Light. . . . Since all thoughts are veils of this Light, he may advise the destruction of all thoughts, and to that end teach those practices which are clearly conductive to such destruction. These practices have now fortunately been set down in clear language by order of the A∴A∴. In these instructions the relativity and limitation of each practice is clearly taught, and all dogmatic interpretations are carefully avoided. Each practice is in itself a demon which must be destroyed; but to be destroyed it must first be evoked."[160]

---

[157] *Liber Aleph*, "De heresia Manichæa."
[158] *MITAP*, Ch. XXI.
[159] *Ibid*.
[160] *Book 4*, Part II, *loc. cit.*

"It is therefore incumbent upon us, if we wish to make the universal and final Yoga with the Absolute, to master every element of our being, to protect it against all civil and external war, to intensify every faculty to the utmost, to train ourselves in knowledge and power to the utmost; so that at the proper moment we may be in perfect condition to fling ourselves up into the furnace of ecstasy which flames from the abyss of annihilation."[161] Crowley reminds his magical son that, "the Cult of the Slave-Gods is a Device of those Black Brothers. All that stagnateth is thereof, and thence cometh not Stability, but Putrefaction. Endure not thou the static Standards either in Thought or in Action Resist not even the Change that is the Rottenness of Choronzon, but rather speed it, so that the elements may combine by Love under Will. Since the Black Brothers and their Cults set themselves against Change, do thou break them asunder."[162]

Life is a horror, a writhing of famished serpents, yet I care not, for I laugh. The deserts awe me not, neither do the seas restrain the purpose of my mirth. Life is as a prisoner in a dungeon, still I laugh; for I, in my strength, have begotten a might beyond the walls of prisons; for life and death have become one to me—as little children gambolling on the sands and splashing in the wavelets of the sea. I laugh at their pretty play, and upon the billows of my laughter do I build up the Kingdom of the Great in which all carouse at one table. Here virgins mingle with courtesans, and the youth and the old man know neither wisdom nor folly.

I have conquered the deserts and the forests, the valleys and the mountains, the seas and the lands. My palace is built of fire and water, of earth and of air, and the secret place within the sanctuary of my temple is as the abode of everlasting mirth. All is love, life, and laugher; death and decay are not: all is joy, purity, and freedom; all is as the fire of mystery; all is all; for my kingdom is known as the City of God.[163]

You ask me what is, at the present time, the greatest obstacle to human progress.

I answer in one word: NOISE.

You will recall that in Yoga the concise compendium of Initiated Instruction is:
>   Sit still
>   Stop thinking
>   Shut up, and
>   Get out.

The second of these postulates the third; for one can neither think nor stop thinking with all that row going on.[164]

---

[161] *Eight Lectures*, Ch. 1, Sec. 19.
[162] *Liber Aleph*, "De virtute chirurgica."
[163] *The Temple of Solomon the King*, Part I, "The Warrior."
[164] *MWT*, Ch. XIV.

CHAPTER 10
Scientific Illuminism

The Book of the Law *presumes the existence of a body of initiates pledged to watch over the welfare of mankind and to communicate its own wisdom little by little in the measure of man's capacity to receive it.*

The initiate is well aware that his instruction will be misinterpreted by malice, dishonesty and stupidity: and not being omnipotent, he has to acquiesce in the perversion of his precepts. It is a part of the game. Liber I vel Magi *tells the Magus (here defined as the initiate charged with the duty of communicating a new truth to mankind) of what he may expect.*

*There are many magical teachers but in recorded history we have scarcely had a dozen Magi in the technical sense of the word. They may be recognized by the fact that their message may be formulated as a single word, which word must be such that it overturns all existing beliefs and codes. We may take as instances the Word of Buddha—*Anatta *(absence of an atman or soul), which laid its axe to the root of Hindu cosmology, theology and psychology, and incidentally knocked away the foundation of the caste system; and indeed of all accepted morality. Mohammed, again, with the single word* Allah, *did the same thing with polytheisms, patently pagan or camouflaged as Christian, of his period.*

Similarly, Aiwass, uttering the word Thelema *(with all its implications), destroys completely the formula of the Dying God. Thelema implies not merely a new religion, but a new cosmology, a new philosophy, a new ethics. It co-ordinates the disconnected discoveries of science, from physics to psychology, into a coherent and consistent system. Its scope is so vast that it is impossible even to hint at the universality of its application. But the whole of my work, from the moment of its utterance, illustrates some phase of its potentiality, and the story of my life itself from this time on is no more than a record of my reactions to it.*

—The Confessions of Aleister Crowley

According to Crowley, the essential characteristic of the grade of Magus "is that its possessor utters a Creative Magical Word, which transforms the planet on which he lives by the installation of new officers to preside over its initiation. This can take place only at an 'Equinox of the Gods' at the end of an 'Æon'; that is, when the secret formula which expresses the Law of its action becomes outworn and useless to its further development. (Thus 'Suckling' is the formula of an infant: when teeth appear it marks a new 'Æon', whose 'Word' is 'Eating'). A Magus can therefore only appear as such to the world at intervals of some centuries; accounts of historical Magi, and their Words, are given in *Liber Aleph*. This does not mean that only one man can attain this Grade in any one Æon, so far as the Order is concerned. A man can make personal progress equivalent to that of a 'Word of an Æon'; but he will identify himself with the current word, and exert his will to establish it, lest he conflict with the work of the Magus who uttered the Word of the Æon in which He is living."[1]

One Star in Sight is "a brief account, adapted as far as may be to the average aspirant to Adeptship, or Attainment, or Initiation, or Mastership, or Union with God, or Spiritual Development, or Mahatmaship, or Freedom, or Occult Knowledge, or whatever he may call his inmost need of Truth, of our Order of A∴A∴."[2] As Crowley writes in his *New Comment* on AL I.34, "They are not, like the traditional ordeals, formal, or identical for all; the Candidate finds himself in circumstances which afford a real test of conduct, and compel him to discover his own nature, to become aware of himself by bringing his secret motives to the surface. Some of the Rituals have been made accessible, that is, the Magical Formulæ have been published. . . . Note the reference to 'not' and 'all'. Also the word 'known' contains the root GN, 'to beget' and 'to know'; while 'concealed' indicates the other half of the Human Mystery." The *Djeridensis Comment* on the same verse says that, "the ordeals may not be written, since each man must go through a furnace of his own kindling," and that some rituals "were fitted for all men: some are fitted to one person, each making his own; and also there are those whose virtue lies in the silence wherewith they are begirt."

> But I feel bound to observe that they must be studied merely as classics, just as a musician studies Bach and Others. He cannot compose by copying or combining their works; they serve him only as indications of the art of expression. He must master the technique, theory and practice, of music, till the general principles are absorbed, and he has command of the language, to use it to express his Will.
>
> So with Magick; the student must understand and assimilate the basic propositions, and he must be expert in the drill of the practical details.
>
> But that is merely ground-work: he must then conceive his own expression, and execute it in his own style. Each star is unique, and each orbit apart; indeed, that is the corner-stone of my teaching, to have no standard goals or standard ways, no orthodoxies and no codes. The stars are not herded and penned and shorn and made into mutton like so many voters! I decline to be bellwether, who am born a Lion! I will not be collie, who am quicker to bite than to bark. I refuse the office of shepherd, who bear not a crook but a club.
>
> Wise in your generation, ye sheep, are ye to scamper away bleating when your ears catch my roar on the wind! Are ye not tended and fed and protected—until word come from the stockyard?
>
> The lion's life for me! Let me live free, and die fighting!

---

[1] *One Star in Sight*, Sec. 5.
[2] *Ibid.*, Sec. 10.

Now one more point about the obeah and the wanga, the deed and the word of Magick.

Magick is the art of causing change in existing phenomena. This definition includes raising the dead, bewitching cattle, making rain, acquiring goods, fascinating judges, and all the rest of the programme. Good: but it also includes every act soever? Yes; I meant it to do so. It is not possible to utter word or do deed without producing the exact effect proper and necessary thereto. Thus Magick is the Art of Life itself.

Magick is the management of all we say and do, so that the effect is to change that part of our environment which dissatisfies us, until it does so no longer. We "remould it nearer to the heart's desire."

Magick ceremonies proper are merely organized and concentrated attempts to impose our Will on certain parts of the Cosmos. They are only particular cases of the general law.[3]

As we learn in *Magick in Theory and Practice*, "In this matter of the efficacity of words there are again two formulæ exactly opposite in nature. A word may become potent and terrible by virtue of constant repetition. It is in this way that most religions gain strength. At first the statement 'So and so is God' excites no interest. Continue, and you meet scorn and scepticism: possibly persecution. Continue, and the controversy has so far died out that no one troubles to contradict your assertion. No superstition is so dangerous and so lively as an exploded superstition. The newspapers of today (written and edited almost exclusively by men without a spark of either religion or morality) dare not hint that any one disbelieves in the ostensibly prevailing cult; they deplore Atheism—all but universal in practice and implicit in the theory of practically all intelligent people—as if it were the eccentricity of a few negligible or objectionable persons. This is the ordinary story of advertisement; the sham has exactly the same chance as the real. Persistence is the only quality required for success.[4]

"The opposite formula is that of secrecy. An idea is perpetuated because it must never be mentioned. A Freemason never forgets the secret words entrusted to him, thought these words mean absolutely nothing to him in the vast majority of cases; the only reason for this is that he has been forbidden to mention them, although they have been published again and again, and are as accessible to the profane as to the initiate. In such a work of practical Magick as the preaching of a new Law, these methods may be advantageously combined; on the one hand infinite frankness and readiness to communicate all secrets, on the other the sublime and terrible knowledge that all real secrets are incommunicable." As the footnote puts it, "If this were not the case, individuality would not be inviolable. No man can communicate even the simplest thought to any other man in any full and accurate sense. For that thought is sown in a different soil, and cannot produce an identical effect. I cannot put a spot of red upon two pictures without altering each in diverse ways. It might have little effect on a sunset

---

[3] NC on AL I.37.
[4] *MITAP*, Ch. IX.

by Turner, but much on a nocturne by Whistler. The identity of the two spots as spots would thus be fallacious."[5]

The same book summarizes the formula of *Thelema* thus: "Θ 'Babalon and the Beast conjoined'— ε Unto Nuit (*CCXX*. I. 51)— λ The Work accomplished in Justice— η The Holy Graal— μ The Water therein— α The Babe in the Egg (Harpocrates on the Lotus.) That of *Agape* is as follows: Dionysus Α —The Virgin Earth γ —The Babe in the Egg (α —the image of the Father)—The Massacre of the Innocents, π (winepress)—The Draught of Ecstasy, η."[6] *The Book of the Law* says: "Behold! the rituals of the old time are black. Let the evil ones be cast away; let the good ones be purged by the prophet! Then shall this Knowledge go aright."[7] The *New Comment* on the verse defines the "old time" as the Æon of the Dying God. "Some of his rituals are founded on an utterly false metaphysic and cosmogony; but others are based on Truth. We mend these, and end those. This 'Knowledge' is the initiated Wisdom of this Æon of Horus."[8]

"The whole idea of the word Sacrifice, as commonly understood, rests upon an error and superstition, and is unscientific, besides being metaphysically false. The Law of Thelema has totally changed the Point of View as to this matter. Unless you have thoroughly assimilated the Formula of Horus, it is absolutely unsafe to meddle with this type of Magick. Let the young Magician reflect upon the Conservation of Matter and of Energy."[9] Concerning the Æon, Crowley teaches his magical son that, "the Sun and His Vicegerent are in all Æons, of Necessity, Father, Centre, Creator, each in His Sphere of Operation. But the Formula of the past Æon was of the Dying God, and was based upon Ignorance. For Men thought that the Sun died and was reborn alike in the Day and in the Year; and so also was the Mystery of Man. Now already are we well assured by Science how the Death of the Sun is in Truth but the Shifting of a Shadow; and in this Æon (o my son, I lift up my Voice and I make Prophecy!) so shall it be proven as to Death. For the Body of Man is but his Shadow, it cometh and goeth even as the tides of Ocean; and he only is in Darkness who is hidden by that Shadow from the Light of His True Self. Now therefore understand thou the Formula of Horus, the Lion God, the Child crowned and conquering that cometh forth in Force and Fire! For thy Changes are not Phases of Thee, but of the Phantoms which thou mistakest for thy Self."[10]

According to the *New Comment*, "the old formula of Magick—the Osiris-Adonis-Jesus-Marsyas-Dionysus-Attis-*etcetera* formula of the Dying God—is no longer efficacious. It rested on the ignorant belief that the Sun died every day, and every year, and that its resurrection was a miracle. The Formula of the New Æon recognizes Horus, the Child crowned and conquering, as God. We are all members of the Body of God, the Sun; and about our System is the Ocean of Space. This formula is then to be based

---

[5] *Ibid.*
[6] *Ibid.*, Ch. VII, Sec. III.
[7] AL II.5.
[8] NC on AL II.5.
[9] MITAP, Ch. XII, Sec. II, fn.
[10] *Liber Aleph*, "De corpore umbra hominis."

upon these facts. Our 'Evil', 'Error', 'Darkness', 'Illusion', whatever one chooses to call it, is simply a phenomenon of accidental and temporary separateness. If you are 'walking in darkness', do not try to make the sun rise by self-sacrifice, but wait in confidence for the dawn, and enjoy the pleasures of the night meanwhile. The general allusion is to the Equinox Ritual of the G∴D∴, where the officer of the previous six months, representing Horus, took the place of the retiring Hierophant, who had represented Osiris."[11] The Golden Dawn Festival of the Equinox "was celebrated in the spring and autumn within 48 hours of the actual dates of Sol entering Aries and Libra,"[12] and began with the Kerux announcing "the abrogation of the present Pass Word."[13]

"The radical error of all uninitiates is that they define 'self' as irreconcilably opposed to 'not-self.' Each element of oneself is, on the contrary, sterile and without meaning, until it fulfils itself, by 'love under will' in its counterpart in the Macrocosm. To separate oneself from others is to destroy oneself; the way to realize and to extend oneself is to lose that self—its sense of separateness—in the other. Thus: child plus food: this does not preserve one at the expense of the other; it 'destroys' or rather changes both in order to fulfil both in the result of the operation—a grown man. It is in fact impossible to preserve anything as it is by positive action upon it. Its integrity demands inaction; and inaction, resistance to change, is stagnation, death and dissolution due to the internal putrefaction of the starved elements."[14]

According to the *New Comment*, "ABRAHADABRA is 'The key of the rituals' because it expresses the Magical Formulæ of uniting various complementary ideas; especially the Five of the Microcosm with the Six of the Macrocosm."[15]—"It represents the Great Work complete, and it is therefore an archetype of all lesser magical operations. It is in a way too perfect to be applied in advance to any of them. But an example of such an operation may be studied in *Equinox* I, VII, 'The Temple of Solomon the King', where an invocation of Horus on this formula is given in full. Note the *reverberation* of the ideas one against another. The formula of Horus has not yet been so fully worked out in details as to justify a treatise upon its exoteric theory and practice; but one may say that it is, to the formula of Osiris, what the turbine is to the reciprocating engine."[16]

"It is then thoroughly understood that the Aspirant is seeking to solve the great Problem. And he may conceive, as various Schools of Adepts in the ages have conceived, this problem in three main forms." The third form is: "I am the finite square; I wish to be one with the infinite circle. This is the Unsectarian conception. I am the Cross of Extension; I wish to be one with the infinite Rose. This is the qabalistic equivalent." The "answer of the Adept" to this form of the problem "is given by π, implying that an infinite

---

[11] NC on AL I.49.
[12] *The Temple of Solomon the King*, Part VI, "The Priest."
[13] *The Equinox of the Gods*, "Genesis Libri AL," Ch. VI.
[14] *MITAP*, loc. cit.
[15] NC on AL I.20.
[16] *MITAP*, Ch. VII, Sec. II. Emphasis in original.

factor must be employed. For the Qabalist it is usually symbolised by the Rosy Cross, or by such formulæ as 5 = 6. That they concealed a Word answering this problem is also true." Crowley's "discovery of this word is the main subject" of his *Essay upon Number*—"All the foregoing exposition has been intended to show why I sought a word to fulfil the conditions, and by what standards of truth I could measure things. . . . אבראהאדאברא, the great Magic Word, the Word of the Æon. Note the 11 letters, 5 א identical, and 6 diverse. Thus it interlocks Pentagram and Hexagram."[17]

Note 4 + 1 + 8 = 13, the 4 reduced to 1 through 8, the redeeming force; and 418 = ח = 8.

By Aiq Bkr, ABRAHADABRA = 1 + 2 + 2 + 1 + 5 + 1 + 4 + 1 + 2 + 2 + 1 = 22. Also 418 = 22 × 19, Manifestation. Hence the word manifests the 22 Keys of Rota.

It means by translation Abraha Deber, the Voice of the Chief Seer.

It resolves into Pentagram and Hexagram as follows:—

(1) [This is by taking the 5 middle letters.]

The pentagram is 12, הוא, Macroprosopus.

The hexagram is 406, אתה, Microprosopus.

Thus it connotes the Great Work.

Note אבר, initials of the Supernals, Ab, Ben, Ruach.

(2) [This is by separating the One (Aleph) from the Many (diverse letters).]

ברה = 207, Aur, Light
דבר = 206, Deber, Voice

"The Vision and the Voice," a phrase which meant much to me at the moment of discovering this Word.

(3) [By taking each alternate letter.]

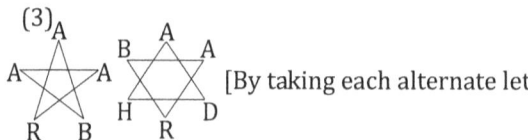

205 = גבר, mighty.
213 = אביר, mighty.

This shows Abrahadabra as the Word of Double Power, another phrase that meant much to me at the time. אאב at the top of the Hexagram gives אב, אימא, בן, Father, Mother, Child.

---

[17] *An Essay upon Number*, Part II.

הדר by Yetzirah gives Horus, Isis, Osiris, again Father, Mother, Child. This Hexagram is again the human Triad.

Dividing into 3 and 8 we get the Triangle of Horus dominating the Stooping Dragon of 8 Heads, the Supernals bursting the Head of Daath.

Also A
     / \   The Supernals are supported upon two squares:—
   R—B

A—B   A—H   אבאד = דד, Love, 8.
| | | |
A—D   R—A   אהרא = אור, Light, 207.

Now 8 × 207 = 1656 = חי, Living, and 207 = 9 × 23, חיה, Life. At this time "Licht, Liebe, Leben" was the mystic name of the Mother-Temple of the G∴ D∴.

The five letters used in the word are א, the Crown; ב, the Wand; ד, the Cup; ה, the Sword; ר, the Rosy Cross; and refer further to Amoun the Father, Thoth His messenger, and Isis, Horus, Osiris, the divine-human triad.

Also 418 = את יאו, the Essence of IAO, *q.v.*

This short analysis might be indefinitely expanded; but always the symbol will remain the Expression of the Goal and the Exposition of the Path.[18]

"Abrahadabra is the formula of the Æon, by which man may accomplish the Great Work. This Formula is then the 'reward' given by the God, the largesse granted by Him on His accession to the Lordship of the Æon, just as the INRI-IAO-LVX formula of attainment by way of Crucifixion was given by Osiris when he came to power in the last Æon."[19] As Crowley tells Achad, "Krishna has Names and Forms innumerable, and I know not His true Human Birth, for His Formula is of the Major Antiquity. But His Word hath spread into many Lands, and we know it to-day as INRI with the secret IAO concealed therein. And the Meaning of this Word is the Working of Nature in Her Changes; that is, it is the Formula of Magick whereby all Things reproduce and recreate themselves. Yet this Extension and Specialisation was rather the Word of Dionysus; for the true Word of Krishna was AUM, importing rather a Statement of the Truth of Nature than a practical Instruction in detailed Operations of Magick. But Dionysus, by the Word INRI, laid the Foundation of all Science, as We say Science to-day in a particular Sense, that is, of causing external Nature to change in Harmony with our Wills."[20]

"Tahuti, or Thoth, confirmed the Word of Dionysus by continuing it; for he showed how by the Mind it was possible to direct the Operations of the Will. By Criticism and by recorded Memory Man avoideth Error. But the true Word of Tahuti was AMOUN, whereby He made Men to understand their secret Nature, that is, their Unity with their true Selves, or, as they

---

[18] *Ibid.*
[19] NC on AL III.1.
[20] *Liber Aleph*, "De Sri Krishna et de Dionyso."

then phrased it, with God. And He discovered unto them the Way of this Attainment, and its Relation with the Formula of INRI. Also by His Mystery of Number He made plain the Path for His Successor to declare the Nature of the whole Universe in its Form and in its Structure, as it were an Analysis thereof, doing for Matter what the Buddha was decreed to do for Mind."[21] According to *Qabalistic Dogma*, I.N.R.I. equals " י, נ, ר, י = ♍, ♏, ☉, ♍; the Virgin, the Evil Serpent, the Sun, suggesting the story of Genesis ii. and of the Gospel. The initials of the Egyptian names Isis, Apophis, Osiris, which correspond, give in their turn the Ineffable Name IAO; thus we say that the Ineffable is concealed in and revealed by the Birth, Death, and Resurrection of Christ; and further the Signs of Mourning of the Mother, Triumph of the Destroyer, and Rising of the Son, give by shape the letters L.V.X., Lux, which letters are (again) concealed in and revealed by the Cross."

But before entering into the details of I.A.O. as a magick formula it should be remarked that it is essentially the formula of Yoga or Meditation; in fact, of elementary Mysticism in all its branches.

In beginning a meditation practice, there is always *{If not, one is not working properly.}* a quiet pleasure, a gentle natural growth; one takes a lively interest in the work; it seems easy; one is quite pleased to have started. This stage represents Isis. Sooner or later it is succeeded by depression—the Dark Night of the Soul, an infinite weariness and detestation of the work. The simplest and easiest acts become almost impossible to perform. Such impotence fills the mind with apprehension and despair. The intensity of this loathing can hardly be understood by any person who has not experienced it. This is the period of Apophis.

It is followed by the arising not of Isis, but of Osiris. The ancient condition is not restored, but a new and superior condition is created, a condition only rendered possible by the process of death.

The Alchemists themselves taught this same truth. The first matter of the work was base and primitive, though "natural". After passing through various stages the "Black Dragon" appeared; but from this arose the pure and perfect gold.

Even in the legend of Prometheus we find an identical formula concealed; and a similar remark applies to those of Jesus Christ, and of many other mythical God-men worshipped in different countries. *{See J. G. Frazer, The Golden Bough; J. M. Robertson, Pagan Christs; A. Crowley, Jesus, etc., etc.}*

A magical ceremony constructed on this formula is thus in close essential harmony with the natural mystic process. We find it the basis of many important initiations, notably the Third Degree in Masonry, and the 5°=6☐ ceremony of the G∴D∴ described in *Equinox* I, III. A ceremonial self-initiation may be constructed with advantage on this formula. The essence of it consists in robing yourself as a king, then stripping and slaying yourself, and rising from that death to the Knowledge and Conversation of the Holy Guardian Angel *{This formula,*

---

[21] *Ibid.*, "De Tahuti."

although now superseded by that of HORUS, the Crowned and Conquering Child, remains valid for those who have not yet assimilated the point of view of the Law of Thelema. But see Appendix, Liber SAMEKH. Compare also "The Book of the Spirit of the Living Gods,"—where there is a ritual given in extenso *on slightly different lines:* Equinox I, III, pages 269-272.}. There is an etymological identity between Tetragrammaton and I A O, but the magical formulæ are entirely different, as the descriptions here given have schewn.[22]

"It will now be understood that this formula of I.A.O. is a formula of Tiphareth. The Magician who employs it is conscious of himself as a man liable to suffering, and anxious to transcend that state by becoming one with God. It will appear to him as the Supreme Ritual, as the final step; but, as has already been pointed out, it is but a preliminary. For the normal man today, however, it represents considerable attainment."[23] As Crowley writes in his *Confessions*, "Every cosmography implies some sort of ethical theory. The Æon of Osiris had been succeeded by that of Horus. The Magical Formula of the Æon being no longer that of the Dying god but that of the Crowned and Conquering Child, mankind is to govern itself accordingly. A 'righteous' act may be defined as one which fulfils the existing Magical Formula. The motives which were valid in the Æon of Osiris are sheer superstition today. What were those motives and on what basis did they rest? The old conception was that man was born to die; that eternal life had to be gained by a magical act, exactly as the sun had to be brought to life every morning by the priest."[24]

In *The Varieties of Religious Experience*, which is listed in the A∴A∴ Curriculum under Course I, Section 1, "Books for Serious Study,"[25] Dr. William James—who is considered both the "Father of American Psychology" and one of the most influential philosophers ever produced by the United States—"classified religion as the 'once-born' and the 'twice-born'; but the religion now proclaimed in *Liber Legis* harmonizes these by transcending them. There is no attempt to get rid of death by denying it, as among the once-born; nor to accept death as the gate of a new life, as among the twice-born. With the A∴A∴ life and death are equally incidents in a career, very much like day and night in the history of a planet. But, to pursue the simile, we regard this planet from afar. A Brother of A∴A∴ looks at (what another person would call) 'himself', as one—or, rather, some —among a group of phenomena. He is that 'nothing' whose consciousness is in one sense the universe considered as a single phenomenon in time and space, and in another sense is the negation of that consciousness. The body and mind of the man are only important (if at all) as the telescope of the

---

[22] *MITAP*, Ch. V.
[23] *Ibid.*
[24] Ch. 49.
[25] The description reads: "Valuable as showing the uniformity of mystical attainment."

astronomer to him. If the telescope were destroyed it would make no appreciable difference to the Universe which that telescope reveals."[26]

"Asar, the Man who suffers, is no longer the type of Godhead to which Man must aspire. He needs no more to die and rise again: His great Work is now to come to know Himself as the Child ever-living, sinless, perfect, the all-shining Sun."[27] Accordingly, we have: "FIAOF: 93, the full formula, recognizing the Sun as the Son (Star), as the pre-existent manifested Unit from which all springs and to which all returns. The Great Work is to make the initial FF of Assiah (The world of material illusion) into the final FIF of Atziluth, the world of pure reality."[28] As the *New Comment* on AL II.35 puts it, "A ritual is not a melancholy formality; it is a Sacrament, a Dance, a Commemoration of the Universe. The Universe is endless rapture, wild and unconfined, a mad passion of speed. Astronomers tell us this of the Great Republic of the Stars; physicists say the same of the Little Republic of Molecules. Shall not the Middle Republic of Men be like unto them?[29] The polite ethicist demurs; his ideal is funereal solemnity. His horizon is bounded by death; and his spy-glass is smeared with the idea of sin. The New Æon proclaims Man as Immortal God, eternally active to do His Will. All's Joy, all's Beauty; this Will we celebrate. In this verse we see how the awakening leads to ordered and purposeful action. Joy and Beauty are the evidence that our functions are free and fit; when we take no pleasure, and find nothing to admire, in our work, we are doing it wrong."

The Book of the Law "admits that all the prophets of the Past have spoken, and the sacred scriptures before given by the Masters to men contain, some truth. But they have applied to local conditions, and those of time; thus all are partly false. *Liber AL* has no such limits, so it is true for all." Crowley, as the Prophet of Thelema, claims to have "learnt all the secrets of all the old cults, purged them of partial trend, and balanced them."[30] For example, "The religion of Hindustan, metaphysically and mystically comprehensive enough to assure itself the possession of much truth, is in practice almost as superstitious and false as Christianity, a faith of slaves, liars and dastards. The same remarks apply roughly to Buddhism." Likewise, the "metaphysical and ethical flawlessness" of Confucianism "has not saved its adherents from losing those ruder virtues which are proper to a Fighting Animal, and thus yielding at last a civilization coeval with history itself to the barbarous tribes of Europe." Indeed, it may be that, "the six religions whose flesh must be torn out cover the whole globe outside Islam and Christianity. Why assault their flesh rather than their eyes, as in the other cases? Because the metaphysics, or

---

[26] *MITAP, loc. cit.*
[27] DC on AL I.49.
[28] *MITAP, loc. cit.*
[29] *Cf.* also *Liber DXXXVI*, Ch. I: "It is not often enough that we consider the disproportion of human and astronomical time. The distances of the fixed stars are so great that we seem to see a different order of being. In point of fact, the starry universe is just about 10,000,000,000,000,000,000,000 times as big as ours; and, curiously enough, our universe is just that much bigger than the universe of bacteria. Here are then three scales of creation, and only three, appreciable by us at present; this thought should serve to simplify our understanding."
[30] DC on AL I.55–56.

point of view, is correct—I take Judaism as Qabalistic—but the practice imperfect."[31]

The Magus that came after Thoth "was an Egyptian whose Name is lost; but the Jews called Him Mosheh, or Moses, and their Fabulists made Him the Leader of their Legendary Exodus.[32] Yet they preserved His Word, and it is IHVH, which thou must understand also as that Secret Word which thou hast seen and heard in Thunders and Lightnings in thine Initiation to the Degree thou wottest of. But this Word is itself a Plan of the Fabrick of the Universe, and upon it hath been elaborated the Holy Qabalah, whereby we have Knowledge of the Nature of all Things soever upon every Plane of Bycoming, and of their Forces and Tendencies and Operations, with the Keys to their Portals. Nor did He leave any Part of His Work unfinished, unless it be that accomplished three hundred Years ago by Sir Edward Kelly, of whom I also come, as thou knowest."[33] According to *The Book of Thoth*, "The Hebrew system is straightforward and irreversible; it postulates Father and Mother from whose union issue Son and Daughter. There an end. It is only later philosophical speculation to derive the Father-Mother Dyad from a Unity manifest, and later still to seek the source of that Unity in Nothing. This is a concrete and limited scheme, crude, with its causeless Beginning and its sterile End."[34]

"The Pagan system," on the other hand, "is circular, self-generated, self-nourished, self-renewed. It is a wheel on whose rim are Father-Mother-Son-Daughter; they move about the motionless axis of Zero; they unite at will; they transform one into another; there is neither Beginning nor End to the Orbit; none is higher or lower than another."[35] Now, "The danger of ceremonial Magick—the subtlest and deepest danger—is this: that the Magician will naturally tend to invoke that partial being which most strongly appeals to him, so that his natural excess in that direction will be still further exaggerated. Let him, before beginning his Work, endeavour to map out his own being, and arrange his invocations in such a way as to redress the balance.... we may suppose that he finds himself lacking in that perception of the value of Life and Death, alike of individuals and of races, which is characteristic of Nature. He has perhaps a tendency to perceive the 'first noble truth' uttered by Buddha, that Everything is sorrow. Nature, it seems, is a tragedy. He has perhaps even experienced the great trance called Sorrow. He should then consider whether there is not some Deity who expresses this Cycle, and yet whose nature is joy. He will find what he requires in Dionysus."[36]

"How is it," a student asks Crowley, "that you reject with such immitigable scorn the very foundation-stones of Buddhism, and yet refer disciples enthusiastically to the technique of some of its subtlest super-

---

[31] NC on AL III.53.
[32] There is no evidence, archaeological or otherwise, that any tribe of the Israelites was ever in Egypt; *cf.* e.g. Thompson 1999.
[33] *Liber Aleph*, "De quodam Mago Ægyptiorum, quem appelunt Judæi Mosheh."
[34] Part I, Sec. II.
[35] *Ibid.*
[36] *MITAP*, Ch. I.

structures?" Crowley lets out a laff: "It is the old, old story. When the Buddha was making experiments and recording the results, he was on safe ground: when he started to theorize, committing (incidentally) innumerable logical crimes in the process, he is no better a guesser than the Arahat next door, or for the matter of that, the Arahat's Lady Char."[37] In fact, "The vulgarism and provincialism of the Buddhist cannon is infinitely repulsive to all nice minds; and the attempt to use the terms of an egocentric philosophy to explain the details of a psychology whose principal doctrine is the denial of the Ego, was the work of a mischievous idiot. Let us unhesitatingly reject these abominations, these nastinesses of the beggars dressed in rags that they have snatched from corpses."[38]

The object of the A∴A∴ Curriculum "is to familiarize the student with all that has been said by the Great Masters in every time and country. He should make a critical examination of them; not so much with the idea of discovering where truth lies, for he cannot do this except by virtue of his own spiritual experience, but rather to discover the essential harmony in those varied works. He should be on his guard against partisanship with a favourite author. He should familiarize himself thoroughly with the method of mental equilibrium, endeavouring to contradict any statement soever, although it maybe apparently axiomatic. The general object of this course, besides that already stated, is to assure sound education in occult matters, so that when spiritual illumination comes it may find a well-built temple. Where the mind is strongly biased towards any special theory, the result of an illumination is often to inflame that portion of the mind which is thus overdeveloped, with the result that the aspirant, instead of becoming an Adept, becomes a bigot and fanatic."[39]

    Q. But their instructions differ widely!
    A. Only in so far as each was bound by conditions of time, race, climate and language. There is essential identity in the method.
    Q. Indeed!
    A. It was the great work of the life of Frater Perdurabo to prove this. Studying each religious practice of each great religion on the spot, he was able to show the Identity-in-diversity of all, and to formulate a method free from all dogmatic bias, and based only on the ascertained facts of anatomy, physiology, and psychology.[40]

Crowley, as "the Beast 666," was "bidden to purge the ancient Modes of Magick, they being no longer valid in this new 'time' or Æon of Horus." He was "to reject those that have become false, either through the lapse of time, or the folly or malice of men; but to retain and make pure such as are Of All Truth, beyond Time to corrupt."[41] According to *Magick in Theory and*

---

[37] *MWT*, Ch. XXVII.
[38] *Book 4*, Part I, Ch. VII.
[39] A∴A∴ *Curriculum*.
[40] *Book 4*, Part I, Summary.
[41] DC on AL II.5.

Practice, the "cardinal revelation of the Great Æon of Horus" is that the Word of Krishna, "AUM does not represent the facts of nature. The point of view is based upon misapprehension of the character of existence. It soon became obvious to The MASTER THERION that AUM was an inadequate and misleading hieroglyph. It stated only part of the truth, and it implied a fundamental falsehood. He consequently determined to modify the word in such a manner as to fit it to represent the Arcana unveiled by the Æon of which He had attained to be the Logos."[42]

The essential task was to emphasize the fact that nature is not catastrophic, but proceeds by means of undulations. It might be suggested that *manvantara* and *pralaya* are in reality complementary curves; but the Hindu doctrine insists strongly on denying continuity to the successive phases. It was nevertheless important to avoid disturbing the Trinitarian arrangement of the word, as would be done by the addition of other letters. It was equally desirable to make it clear that the letter *M* represents an operation which does not actually occur in nature except as the withdrawal of phenomena into the absolute; which process, even when so understood, is not a true destruction, but, on the contrary, the emancipation of anything from the modifications which it had mistaken for itself. It occurred to him that the true nature of Silence was to permit the uninterrupted vibration of the undulatory energy, free from the false conceptions attached to it by the *ahaṃkāra* or Ego-making facility, whose assumption that conscious individuality constitutes existence let it to consider its own apparently catastrophic character as pertaining to the order of nature.

The undulatory formula of putrefaction is represented in the Qabalah by the letter *N*, which refers to Scorpio, whose triune nature combines the Eagle, Snake and Scorpion. These hieroglyphs themselves indicate the spiritual formulæ of incarnation. He was also anxious to use the letter *G*, another triune formula expressive of the aspects of the moon, which further declares the nature of human existence in the following manner. The Moon is in itself a dark orb; but an appearance of light is communicated to it by the Sun; and it is exactly in this way that successive incarnations create the appearance of consciousness. The Moon is not altered by her phases, just as the individual star, which every man is, remains itself, irrespective of whether Earth perceives it or not.

Now it so happens that the root **GN* signifies both knowledge and generation combined in a single idea, in an absolute form independent of personality. The *G* is a silent letter, as in our word Gnosis; and the sound GN is nasal, suggesting therefore the breath of life as opposed to that of speech. Impelled by these considerations, the Master Therion proposed to replace the *M* of AUM by a compound letter *MGN*, symbolizing thereby the subtle transformation of the apparent silence and death which terminates the manifested life of *vau* by a continuous

---

[42] *MITAP*, Ch. VII, Sec. V.

vibration of an impersonal energy of the nature of generation and knowledge, the Virgin Moon and the Serpent furthermore operating to include in the idea a commemoration of the legend so grossly deformed in the Hebrew legend of the Garden of Eden, and its even more malignantly debased falsification in that bitterly sectarian broadside, the Apocalypse.[43]

"Each element—fire, earth, air, water, and Spirit—possesses its own Nature, Will, and Magical Formula. Each one may then have its appropriate ritual. Many such in crude form are described in *The Golden Bough* of Dr. J. G. Frazer, the Glory of Trinity! In particular the entry of the Sun into the cardinal signs of the elements at the Equinoxes and Solstices are suitable for festivals. The difference between 'rituals' and 'feasts' is this: by the one a particular form of energy is generated, while there is a general discharge of one's superfluous force in the other. Yet a feast implies periodical nourishment."[44] According to the *New Comment* on AL II.41, "The feasts of fire and water indicate rejoicings to be made at the puberty of boys and girls respectively. The feast for life is at a birth; and the feast for death at a death. It is of the utmost importance to make funerals merry, so as to train people to take the proper view of death. The fear of death is one of the great weapons of tyrants, as well as their scourge; and it distorts our whole outlook upon the Universe."[45] This is echoed in the words of Crowley's previous incarnation, Éliphas Lévi:

> To love life more than one fears the menaces of death is to merit life.
> The elect are those who dare; woe to the timid!
> Thus the slaves of law, who make themselves the tyrants of conscience and the servants of fear, and those who begrudge that man should hope, and the Pharisees of all the synagogues and of all the churches, are those who receive the reproofs and the curses of the Father.
> Was not the Christ excommunicated and crucified by the synagogue?
> Was not Savonarola burned by the order of the sovereign pontiff of the Christian religion?
> Are not the Pharisees to-day just what they were in the time of Caiaphas?[46]

"Do not be afraid of 'going the pace'. It is better to wear out than to rust out. You are unconquerable, and of indefatigable energy. Great men find time for everything, shirk nothing, make reputations in half a dozen different lines, have twenty simultaneous love affairs, and live to a green old age. The milksops and valetudinarians never get anywhere; usually they

---

[43] *Ibid.*
[44] NC on AL II.36.
[45] In virtually every culture, these rites of passage have been hijacked by organized religions, which use this *de facto* (and often *de jure*) monopoly to exert control over the populace even in secular societies.
[46] *The Key of the Mysteries*, Part I, "Sketch of the Prophetic Theology of Numbers."

die early; and even if they lived for ever, what's the use?"[47] If we are to believe Crowley, "The prigs, the prudes, the Christians, die in a real sense of the word; for although even they are 'Stars', there is not enough body to them (as it were) to carry on the individuality. There is no basis for the magical memory if one's incarnation holds nothing worth remembering. Count your years by your wounds—*forsan et hæc olim meminisse juvabit.*"[48] Lévi was, of course, a Roman Catholic theologian.

By that time, public awareness of the idea of reincarnation had been boosted by the Theosophical Society's dissemination of universalised Indian concepts to the point where it was almost as familiar element of the popular culture in the West as in the East. Among the first to study a claim of past-life recall was Théodore Flournoy, a professor of psychology at the University of Geneva, who described the outpouring of the medium Helen Smith as the products of cryptomnesia or "romances of the subliminal imagination"—and as evidence of the unconscious mind.[49] He was also one of the few scholars of the era to embrace the Theosophist William James' view of the prime reality of non-dual consciousness (or "sciousness" as James dubbed it). A fellow Swiss, Carl Jung, used Flournoy's publication of autosuggestive writings of Miss Frank Miller as the starting-point for his own book, *Psychology of the Unconscious.* Jung would later emphasize the importance of the persistence of memory and ego in psychological study of reincarnation, and hypnosis, used in psychoanalysis for retrieving repressed memories, soon became a tool for what is now known as past-life regression. Though all the major Christian denominations reject the concept of reincarnation, a large number of Christian laymen have come to profess the belief. In fact, by the 1980s, nearly a third of regular church-going Catholics in Europe expressed a belief in past lives.[50]

"Those Works of Ancient and Mediaeval Literature which more particularly concern the Seeker after Truth, concur on one point. The most worthless Grimoires of Black Magic, no less than the highest philosophical flights of the Brotherhood which we name no, insist upon the virtue of Chastity as cardinal to the Gate of Wisdom."[51] The head of the Golden Dawn, S. L. Mathers, attached so much importance to chastity that he never consummated his marriage.[52] "Is it not notorious that virginity is by its own virtue one of the most powerful means, and one of the most essential conditions, of all Magical works? This is no question of technical formula such as may, with propriety, be modulated in the event of an Equinox of the Gods. It is one of those eternal truths of Nature which persist, no matter what the environment, in respect of place or period."[53]

"To these remarks I can but smile my most genial assent. The only

---

[47] NC on AL II.44.
[48] NC on AL II.45; Verg. *A.* 1.203.
[49] Flournoy 1900.
[50] EVS – European Values Study 1981.
[51] *Little Essays Toward Truth,* "Chastity."
[52] King 1986.
[53] NC on AL I.52.

objection that I can take to them is to point out that the connotation of the word 'chastity' may have been misunderstood from a scientific point of view, just as modern science has modified our conception of the relations of the earth and the sun without presuming to alter one jot or tittle of the observed facts of Nature. So we may assert that modern discoveries in physiology have rendered obsolete the Osirian conceptions of the sexual process which interpreted chastity as physical abstinence, small regard being paid to the mental and moral concomitants of the refusal to act, still less to the physical indications. The root of the error lies in the dogma of original sin, as a result of which pollution was actually excused as being in the nature of involuntary offence, just as if one were to assert that a sleep-walker who has fallen over a precipice were any less dead than Empedocles or Sappho."[54]

When you enter a Buddhist order, you are required to take ten vows, one of which is not to abuse sexuality, but there is no specific definition of what that means. In the earliest *saṅghas*, they decided it meant you had to be celibate, and some orders still interpret it that way, but there is no concept of sexual sin in Buddhism.[55] Crowley found the long periods of abstinence prescribed by mediaeval grimoires to be counterproductive. He discovered that while abstaining, sexual urges did not dissipate, but rather consumed him. Instead of slowly starving the impulse to death, he concluded a better strategy was simply to appease it and get on with the magical operation.[56] He would later lament, "The stupidity of having had to waste uncounted priceless hours in chasing what ought to have been brought to the back door every evening with the milk!"[57]

"About the worst inheritance of the emasculate school of mystics is the abominable confusion of thought which arises from the idea that bodily functions and appetites have some moral implications. This is a confusion of the planes. There is no true discrimination between good and evil. The only question that arises is that of convenience in respect of any proposed operation. The whole of the moral and religious lumber of the ages must be discarded for ever before attempting Yoga. You will find out only too soon what it means to do wrong; by our very thesis itself all action is wrong. Any action is only relatively right in so far as it may help us to put an end to the entire process of action."[58] The very "word Virtue, the quality of Manhood, integral with Virility. The Chastity of the Adept of the Rose and Cross, or of the Graal-Knights of Monsalvat, is not other than very opposite to that of which the poet can write: 'Chastity that slavering sates / His lust without the walls, mews, and is gone, / Preening himself that his lewd lips relent.'[59] Or to that emasculate frigor of Alfred Tennyson and the Academic Schools."[60]

---

[54] *Ibid.*
[55] Balk 2012.
[56] R. Kaczynski, "Taboo and Transformation in the Works of Aleister Crowley," in Hyatt 2000.
[57] *Confessions*, Ch. 12.
[58] *Eight Lectures*, Ch. 4, Sec. 3.
[59] *The World's Tragedy*, Act II.
[60] *Little Essays Toward Truth, loc. cit.*

The Chastity whose Magical Energy both protects and urges the aspirant to the Sacred Mysteries is quite contrary in its deepest nature to all vulgar ideas of it; for it is, in the first place, a positive passion; in the second, connected only by obscure magical links with the sexual function; and, in the third, the deadliest enemy of every form of bourgeois morality and sentiment.

It may assist us to create in our minds a clear concept of this noblest and rarest—yet most necessary—of the Virtues, if we draw the distinction between it and one of its ingredients, Purity.

Purity is a passive or at least static quality; it connotes the absence of all alien admixture from any given idea; as, pure gallium, pure mathematics, pure race. It is a secondary and derived use of the word which we find in such expressions as "pure milk," which imply freedom from contamination.

Chastity, *per contra*, as the etymology (*castus*, possibly connected with *castrum*, a fortified camp) suggests, may be supposed to assert the moral attitude of readiness to resist any assault upon an existing state of Purity.[61]

"The Innocence of the Adept? We are at once reminded of the strong Innocence of Harpocrates, and of His Energy of Silence. A chaste man is thus not merely one who avoids the contagion of impure thoughts and their results, but whose virility is competent to restore Perfection to the world about him. Thus the Parsifal who flees from Kundry and her attendant flower-witches loses his way and must wander long years in the Desert; he is not truly chaste until he is able to redeem her, an act which he performs by the reunion of the Lance and the Sangraal. Chastity may thus be defined as the strict observance of the Magical Oath; that is, in the Light of the Law of Thelema, absolute and perfected devotion to the Holy Guardian Angel and exclusive pursuit of the Way of the True Will. It is entirely incompatible with the cowardice of moral attitude, the emasculation of soul and stagnation of action, which commonly denote the man called chaste by the vulgar."[62]

"For he is not wholly pure who is imperfect; and perfect is no man in himself without his fulfillment in all possibility. Thus then must he be instant to seek all proper adventure and achieve it, seeing well to it that by no means should such distract him or divert his purpose, polluting his true Nature and hamstringing his true Will."[63] Axioms XVI and XIX of Lévi's Theory of the Will state respectively: "To do nothing is as fatal as to do evil, but it is more cowardly. The most unpardonable of mortal sins is inertia," and "Fear is nothing but idleness of the will, and for that reason public opinion scourges cowards."[64] Lévi says of Jesus that, "The Great Master, in one of his parables, condemns only the idle man who buried his treasure from fear of losing it in the risky operations of that bank which we call life.

---

[61] *Ibid.*
[62] *Ibid.*
[63] *Ibid.*
[64] *The Key of the Mysteries*, Part III, Book II, Ch. I.

To think nothing, to love nothing, to wish for nothing, to do nothing—that is the real sin. Nature only recognizes and rewards workers."[65]

> The human will develops itself and increases itself by its own activity. In order to will truly, one must act. Action always dominates inertia and drags it at its chariot wheels. This is the secret of the influence of the alleged wicked over the alleged good. How many poltroons and cowards think themselves virtuous because they are afraid to be otherwise! How many respectable women cast an envious eye upon prostitutes! It is not very long ago since convicts were in fashion. Why? Do you think that public opinion can ever give homage to vice? No, but it can do justice to activity and bravery, and it is right that cowardly knaves should esteem bold brigands.
>
> Boldness united to intelligence is the mother of all successes in this world. To undertake, one must know; to accomplish, one must will; to will really, one must dare; and in order to gather in peace the fruits of one's audacity, one must keep silent.[66]

"We have understood the saying: 'To the pure all things are pure', and we have learnt how to act up to it. We can analyse the mind far more acutely than could the ancients, and we can therefore distinguish the real and right feeling from its imitations. A man may eat meat from self-indulgence, or in order to avoid the dangers of asceticism. We must constantly examine ourselves, and assure ourselves that every action is really subservient to the One Purpose."[67] As Crowley observes, "History shows us the physician defending mankind against plague, with exorcisms on the one hand and useless herbs on the other. A charred stake is driven through the heart of a vampire, and his victim is protected with garlic. The strength of God, who can doubt? The strength of taste and of smell are known facts. So they measured strength against strength without considering whether the one was appropriate to the other, any more than as if one were to ward off the strength of steel swords by the strength of the colour of one's armour. Modern science, by correct classification, has expounded the doctrine of the magical link. We no longer confuse the planes. We manipulate physical phenomena by physical means; mental by mental. We trace things to their true causes, and no longer seek to cut the Gordian knot of our ignorance by the sword of a postulated Pantheon."[68]

> By such methods, the A∴A∴ intends to make occult science as systematic and scientific as chemistry; to rescue it from the ill repute which, thanks both to the ignorant and dishonest quacks that have prostituted its name, and to the fanatical and narrow-minded enthusiasts that have turned it into a fetish, has made it an object of

---

[65] *Ibid.*, Book I, Ch. III.
[66] *Ibid.*
[67] *MITAP*, Ch. XIII.
[68] NC on AL I.52.

aversion to those very minds whose enthusiasm and integrity make them most in need of its benefits, and most fit to obtain them.

It is the one really important science, for it transcends the conditions of material existence and so is not liable to perish with the planet, and it must be studied as a science, sceptically, with the utmost energy and patience.

The A∴A∴ possesses the secrets of success; it makes no secret of its knowledge, and if its secrets are not everywhere known and practised, it is because the abuses connected with the name of occult science disincline official investigators to examine the evidence at their disposal.[69]

"The A∴A∴ is an organization whose heads have obtained by personal experience to the summit of this science. They have founded a system by which everyone can equally attain, and that with an ease and speed which was previously impossible."[70] As Crowley writes a student, "The first and absolutely essential task for the Aspirant is to write his Magical Record.... The construction of this Record is, incidentally, the first step in the practice called Sammasati, and leads to the acquisition of the Magical Memory—the memory of your previous incarnations. So there is another reason, terrifically cogent, for writing this Magical Record as clearly and as fully as you can.... You should begin with your parents and the family traditions; the circumstances of your birth and education; your social position; your financial situation; your physique, health, illnesses; your *vita sexualis*; your hobbies and amusements; what you are good at, what not; how you came to be interested in the Great Work; what (if you have been on false trails, Toshophists, Anthroposophagists, sham Rosicrucians, etc.) has been 'your previous condition of servitude'; how you found me, and decided to enlist my aid. That, by itself, helps you to understand yourself, and me to understand you."[71]

"From that point the keeping of the Record is quite easy. All you have to do is to put down what practices you mean to begin, how you get on with them from day to day, and (at intervals) what I have to say about your progress. Remember always that we have no use for piety, for vague chatter, for guesswork; we are as strictly scientific as biologists or chemists. We ban emotion from the start; we demand perception; and (as you will see later on) even perception is not acceptable until we have made sure of its bases by a study of what we call the 'tendencies.'"[72] According to Crowley, "The real key to the stage is Sammasati—Right Recollection," which he defines as "a comprehension of one's own self and its relation to, and identity with, everything.... One considers all known factors which have

---

[69] *One Star in Sight*, loc. cit.
[70] *Book 4*, Part I, loc. cit.
[71] *MWT*, Ch. LXXXI.
[72] *Ibid.*

gone to make one up such as one is, oneself and not another. Clearly the omission of a single minute item must alter the whole course of events."[73]

As Zoroaster says: "Explore the river of the soul; whence and in what order thou has come."[74] One cannot do one's True Will intelligently unless one knows what it is. "Liber Thisarb," *The Equinox* I, VII, give instructions for determining this by calculating the resultant of the forces which have made one what one is. But this practice is confined to one's present incarnation.

If one were to wake up in a boat on a strange river, it would be rash to conclude that the direction of the one reach visible was that of the whole stream. It would help very much if one remembered the bearings of previous reaches traversed before one's nap. It would further relieve one's anxiety when one became aware that a uniform and constant force was the single determinant of all the findings of the stream: gravitation. We could rejoice "that even the weariest river winds somewhere safe to sea."[75]

"Liber Thisarb" describes a method of obtaining the Magical Memory by learning to remember backwards. But the careful practice of Dharana is perhaps more generally useful. As one prevents the more accessible thoughts from arising, we strike deeper strata—memories of childhood reawaken. Still deeper lies a class of thoughts whose origin puzzles us. Some of these apparently belong to former incarnations. By cultivating these departments of one's mind we can develop them; we become expert; we form an organized coherence of these originally disconnected elements; the faculty grows with astonishing rapidity, once the knack of the business is mastered.[76]

While *Liber CMXIII* (*Thirsarb*) is "a sound Official Instruction on the two main methods of acquiring this faculty," Crowley admits that none of his writings "deal with the First Method; this is because I could never make any headway with it; none at all. F∴ Iehi Aour, on the other hand, was a wizard at it; he thought that some people could use that way, and others not: born so. If it should happen that you have that faculty, and no gift at all for the other, it's just too bad; you'd better buzz off, and get another Holy Guru less one-legged.)"[77] The systematic attempt to gain first-hand knowledge of past lives was developed in various ways in different places, but the early Buddhist texts discuss simple techniques that are predicated on the development of high levels of meditative concentration.[78] The later *Yoga Sūtras* (or "Aphorisms") of the Hindu scholar Patañjali incorporated elements of Buddhist thought and give similar instructions on how to attain

---

[73] *The Psychology of Hashish*, Sec. XVI.
[74] *Chaldæan Oracles*, §172.
[75] A. C. Swinburne, *The Garden of Proserpine*.
[76] *MITAP*, Ch. VII, Sec. VI.I.
[77] *MWT*, Ch. XXXVII.
[78] Williams & Tribe 2000.

the ability. Tibetan Buddhism, on the other hand, has developed a whole "science" of death and rebirth, much of which is set down in the *Bardo Thödol*, commonly known as the "Tibetan Book of the Dead." However, Gautama himself warned that past-life recollection can be misleading and should be interpreted with caution. As Crowley puts it, "The first great danger arises from vanity. One should always beware of 'remembering' that one was Cleopatra or Shakespeare."[79]

"As our record extends into the past, the evidence of its truth is cumulative. Every incarnation that we remember must increase our comprehension of ourselves as we are. Each accession of knowledge must indicate with unmistakable accuracy the solution of some enigma which is propounded by the Sphynx of our own unknown birth-city, Thebes. The complicated situation in which we find ourselves is composed of elements; and no element of it came out of nothing. Newton's First Law applies to every plane of thought. The theory of evolution is omniform. There is a reason for one's predisposition to gout, or the shape of one's ear, in the past. The symbolism may change; the facts do not. In one form or another, everything that exists is derived from some previous manifestation. Have it, if you will, that the memories of other incarnations are dreams; but dreams are determined by reality just as much as the events of the day. The truth is to be apprehended by the correct translation of the symbolic language. The last section of the Oath of the Master of the Temple is: 'I swear to interpret every phenomenon as a particular dealing of God with my soul.' The Magical Memory is (in the last analysis) one manner, and, as experience testifies, one of the most important manners, of performing this vow."[80]

"Reaching ecstasy or Samadhi through this channel, the riddle of Kamma is answered, and one is able to enter the realm of pure consciousness. The Universe, mastered long ere now in its effects, is at last mastered in its causes; and it is indeed a Magister of the Temple who can say: *Vi Veri Vniversum Vivvs Vici*."[81] The methods advised by Buddha, Jesus, St. Paul, and Mohammed "have a startling resemblance to one another. They recommend 'virtue' (of various kinds), solitude, absence of excitement, moderation in diet, and finally a practice which some call prayer and some call meditation. (The former four may turn out on examination to be merely conditions favourable to the last.) On investigating what is meant by these two things, we find that they are only one. For what is the state of either prayer or meditation? It is the restraining of the mind to a single act, state, or thought. If we sit down quietly and investigate the contents of our minds, we shall find that even at the best of times the principal characteristics are wandering and distraction. Anyone who has had anything to do with children and untrained minds generally knows that fixity of attention is never present, even when there is a large amount of intelligence and good will."[82]

---

[79] *MITAP, loc. cit.*, Sec. VI.II.
[80] *Ibid.*
[81] *The Psychology of Hashish, loc. cit.*
[82] *Book 4*, Part I, Preliminary Remarks.

"Most men are almost entirely at the mercy of a mass of loud and violent emotions, without discipline or even organization. They sway with the mood of the moment. They lack purpose, foresight, and intelligence. They are moved by ignorant and irrational instincts, many of which affront the law of self-preservation itself, with suicidal stupidity.... For this reason the first task of the Aspirant is to disarm all his thoughts, to make himself impregnably above the influence of any one of them; this he may accomplish by the methods given in *Liber Aleph, Liber Jugorum, Thien Tao*, and elsewhere. Secondly, he must impose absolute silence upon them, as may be done by the 'Yoga' practices taught in *Book 4* (Part I), in *Liber XVI*, etc. He is then ready to analyse them, to organize them, to drill them, and so to take advantage of the properties peculiar to each one by employing its energies in the service of his imperial purpose."[83]

It is a notorious fact that it is practically impossible to get a reliable description of what occurs at a spiritualistic *séance*; the emotions cloud the vision.

Only in the absolute calm of the laboratory, where the observer is perfectly indifferent to what may happen, only concerned to observe exactly what that happening is, to measure and to weigh it by means of instruments incapable of emotion, can one even begin to hope for a truthful record of events. Even the common physical bases of emotion, the senses of pleasure and pain, lead the observer infallibly to err. This though they be not sufficiently excited to disturb his mind.

Plunge one hand into a basin of hot water, the other into a basin of cold water, then both together into a basin of tepid water; the one hand will say hot, the other cold.

Even in instruments themselves, their physical qualities, such as expansion and contraction (which may be called, in a way, the roots of pleasure and pain), cause error.

Make a thermometer, and the glass is so excited by the necessary fusion that year by year, for thirty years afterwards or more, the height of the mercury will continue to alter; how much more then with so plastic a matter as the mind! **There is no emotion which does not leave a mark on the mind, and all marks are bad marks.** Hope and fear are only opposite phases of a single emotion; both are incompatible with the purity of the soul. With the passions of man the case is somewhat different, as they are functions of his own will. They need to be disciplined, not to be suppressed. But emotion is impressed from without. It is an invasion of the circle.[84]

"There is only one method to adopt in such circumstances as those of the Aspirant to Magick and Yoga: the method of Science. Trial and error. You must *observe*. That implies, first of all, that you must learn to observe. And you must record your observations. No circumstance of life is, or can

---

[83] NC on AL II.25.
[84] *Book 4*, Part II, Ch. VIII. Emphasis in original.

be irrelevant. 'He that is not with me is against me.' In all these letters you will find only two things: either I tell you what is bad for you, or what is good for you. But I am not you; I don't know every detail of your life, every trick of your thought. You must do ninety percent of the work for yourself. Whether it is love, or your daily avocation, or diet, or friends, or amusement, or anything else, you must find out what helps you to your True Will and what hinders; cherish the one and eschew the other."[85] Ever proud of his background in analytical chemistry, Crowley notes that, "Everyone who has done any scientific investigation knows painfully how every observation must be corrected again and again. The need of Yoga is so bitter that it blinds us. We are constantly tempted to see and hear what we want to see and hear."[86]

"The most mystics have been led away from the proper line of research, usually by the baser (*i.e.*, the emotional or devotional) attractions of the Vedana-phenomena which we are about to notice; but perhaps even the best must be baffled by the non-congruity of their Experience with the symbols of language. One may add that the language difficulty is in some ways an essential one. Language begins with simple expression of the common needs of the most animal life. Hence we see that all sciences have formulated a technical language of their own, not to be understanded of the common people. The reproach against mystics that their symbols are obscure is just as well founded as a similar reproach against the algebraist or the chemist. A paper at the Chemical Society is often completely intelligible only to some three or four of the odd hundred distinguished chemists in the room. What is gained to 'popular science' is lost to exactitude; and in a paper of this sort I fear rather the reproach of my mystical masters than that of the bewildered crowd."[87]

"Note carefully this practical sense of my intention. I care nothing for the academic meanings of the steps in the Path; what they meant to the Arahats of old is indifferent to me. 'Let the dead past bury its dead!' What I require is an advance in the Knowledge of the Great Problem, derived no longer from hearsay revelation, from exalted fanaticism, from hysteria and intoxication; but from method and research. Shut the temple; open the laboratory!"[88] As Crowley again boasts, "When I first undertook the investigation of Yoga, I was fortunately equipped with a very sound training in the fundamental principles of modern science. I saw immediately that if we were to put any common sense into the business (science is nothing but instructed common sense), the first thing to do was to make a comparative study of the different systems of mysticism. It was immediately apparent that the results all over the world were identical. They were masked by sectarian theories. The methods all over the world were identical; this was masked by religious prejudice and local custom. But in their quiddity—identical! This simple principle proved quite

---

[85] *MWT*, Ch. XVI. Emphasis in original.
[86] *Eight Lectures*, Ch. 1, Sec. 18.
[87] *The Psychology of Hashish*, Sec. XIII.
[88] *Science and Buddhism*, Sec. X.

sufficient to disentangle the subject from the extraordinary complexities which have confused its expression."[89]

"When it came to the point of preparing a simple analysis of the matter, the question arose: what terms shall we use? The mysticisms of Europe are hopelessly muddled; the theories have entirely overlaid the methods. The Chinese system is perhaps the most sublime and the most simple; but, unless one is born a Chinese, the symbols are of really unclimbable difficulty. The Buddhist system is in some ways the most complete, but it is also the most recondite. The words are excessive in length and difficult to commit to memory; and generally speaking, one cannot see the wood for the trees. But from the Indian system, overloaded though it is by accretions of every kind, it is comparatively easy to extract a method which is free from unnecessary and undesirable implications, and to make an interpretation of it intelligible to, and acceptable by, European minds. . . . The great classic of Sanskrit literature is the Aphorisms of Patanjali. He is at least mercifully brief, and not more than ninety or ninety-five percent of what he writes can be dismissed as the ravings of a disordered mind. What remains is twenty-four carat gold."[90]

"*Eight Lectures on Yoga* gives a reasonable account of the essence of this matter [of Yogin or 'holy man's' morality], especially in the talks on Yama and Niyama. . . . It might be summarized as 'doing that, and only that, which facilitates the task in hand.' A line of conduct becomes a custom when experience has shown that to follow it makes for success. 'Don't press!' 'Play with a straight bat!' 'Don't draw to five!' do not involve abstract considerations of right and wrong. Orthodox Hinduism has raped this pure system, and begotten a bastard code which reeks of religion. A political manoeuvre of the Brahmin caste."[91] According to *Book 4*, "The real point of the Hindu '*yama*' is that breaking any of these would tend to excite the mind. Subsequent theologians have tried to improve upon the teachings of the Masters, have given a sort of mystical importance to these virtues; they have insisted upon them for their own sake, and turned them into puritanism and formalism. Thus 'non-killing,' which originally meant 'do not excite yourself by stalking tigers,' has been interpreted to mean that it is a crime to drink water that has not been strained, lest you should kill the animalcula. But this constant worry, this fear of killing anything by mischance is, on the whole, worse than a hand-to-hand conflict with a grizzly bear."[92]

The 'Thou shalt' and 'Thou shalt not' "vary according to definition and sect. However, one point must be explained, and this is, that it must be remembered that most works on Yoga are written either by men like Patanjali, to whom continence, truthfulness, etc., are simple illusions of mind; or by charlatans, who imagine that, by displaying to the reader a mass of middle-class 'virtues,' their works will be given so exalted a flavour that they themselves will pass as great ascetics who have out-soared the

---

[89] *Eight Lectures*, Ch. 2, Sec. 2.
[90] Ibid., Secs. 3–4.
[91] *MWT*, Ch. LXX.
[92] *Book 4*, Part I, Ch. III.

bestial passions of life, whilst in fact they are running harems in Boulogne or making indecent proposals to flower-girls in South Audley Street. These latter ones generally trade under the exalted names of The Mahatmas; who, coming straight from the Shâm Bazzaar, retail their wretched *băk băk* to their sheep-headed followers as the eternal word of Brahman—'The shower from the Highest!' And, not infrequently, end in silent meditation within the illusive walls of Wormwood Scrubbs. The East like the West, has for long lain under the spell of that potent but Middle-class Magician—St. Shamefaced sex; and the whole of its literature swings between the two extremes of Paederasty and Brahmachârya. Even the great science of Yoga has not remained unpolluted by his breath, so that in many cases to avoid shipwreck upon Scylla the Yogi has lost his life in the eddying whirlpools of Charybdis."[93]

"We shall not be surprised therefore if we find that the perfectly simple term Yama (or Control) has been bedevilled out of all sense by the mistaken and malignant ingenuity of the pious Hindu. He has interpreted the word 'control' as meaning compliance with certain fixed proscriptions. There are quite a lot of prohibitions grouped under the heading of Yama, which are perhaps quite necessary for the kind of people contemplated by the Teacher, but they have been senselessly elevated into universal rules. Everyone is familiar with the prohibition of pork as an article of diet by Jews and Mohammedans. This has nothing to do with Yama, or abstract righteousness. It was due to the fact that pork in eastern countries was infected with the trichina; which killed people who ate pork improperly cooked. It was no good telling the savages that fact. Any way, they would only have broken the hygienic command when greed overcame them. The advice had to be made a universal rule, and supported with the authority of a religious sanction. They had not the brains to believe in trichinosis; but they were afraid of Jehovah and Jehannum. Just so, under the grouping of Yama we learn that the aspiring Yogi must become 'fixed in the non-receiving of gifts,' which means that if anyone offers you a cigarette or a drink of water, you must reject his insidious advances in the most Victorian manner. It is such nonsense as this which brings the science of Yoga into contempt. But it isn't nonsense if you consider the class of people for whom the injunction was promulgated; for, as we will be shown later, preliminary to the concentration of the mind is the control of the mind, which means the calm of the mind, and the Hindu mind is so constituted that if you offer a man the most trifling object, the incident is a landmark in his life. It upsets him completely for years."[94]

"You very soon discover the sort of state of mind which is favourable or unfavourable to the work, and you also discover what is helpful and harmful to these states in your way of life. . . . Incidentally, most of the Eastern cults fall down when they come West, simply because they make no allowance for our different temperaments. Also they set tasks which are completely unsuitable to Europeans—an immense amount of

---

[93] *The Temple of Solomon the King*, Part IV, "The Yogas." Emphasis in original.
[94] *Eight Lectures, loc. cit.*, Sec. 8.

disappointment has been caused by failure to recognize these facts."[95] In summary, "We may then dismiss Yama and Niyama with this advice: let the student decide for himself what form of life, what moral code, will least tend to excite his mind; but once he has formulated it, let him stick to it, avoiding opportunism; and let him be very careful to take no credit for what he does or refrains from doing—it is a purely practical code, of no value in itself. The cleanliness which assists the surgeon in his work would prevent the engineer from doing his at all."[96]

"I have treated Yama and Niyama at great length because their importance has been greatly underrated, and their nature completely misunderstood. They are definitely magical practices, with hardly a tinge of mystical flavour."[97] Crowley's principal teacher in yoga was Allan Bennett, a fellow Golden Dawn member (the above-mentioned Frater Iehi Aour) who also established the first Buddhist mission in the United Kingdom. Bennett received the name Ānanda Metteyya, or "Bliss of Loving-kindness," at his ordination as a Buddhist monk, and spent years studying and practicing Buddhism in the East. He was reputedly only the second Englishman to be ordained a *Bhikkhu* of the Theravāda tradition and was instrumental in introducing Buddhism to England.[98] In 1902, Crowley came to visit Bennett in Burma and was instructed in yoga both by him and his teacher, the Shaivite guru Sri Parananda, formerly Solicitor-General of Ceylon and author of yogic commentaries on the Gospels of Matthew and John. The following year, Bennett founded the Buddhasasana Samagama, or the International Buddhist Society, in Rangoon, where he also launched an English-language periodical called *Buddhism: An Illustrated Review*. The final number appeared in 1908, the year Bennett returned briefly to England and helped form the Buddhist Society of Great Britain and Ireland, which in turn began issuing the *Buddhist Review* (1909–22), the first Buddhist journal in Europe.[99]

Crowley, for his part, published Bennett's essay on "The Training of the Mind" in *The Equinox*, Vol. I, No. 5, issued in March 1909. In it, Bennett argues that, "It is the practice of the Dhamma that constitutes the true Buddhist, not the mere knowledge of its tenets; it is the carrying out of the Five Precepts, and not their repetition in the Pali tongue; it is the bringing home into our daily lives of the Great Laws of Love and Righteousness that marks a man as *Sammaditthi*; and not the mere appreciation of the truth of that Dhamma as a beautiful and poetic statement of Laws which are too hard to follow. This Dhamma has to be lived, to be acted up to, to be felt as the supreme idol in our hearts, as the supreme motive of our lives." In the previous *Equinox*, Crowley had written that, "The dogmatism of literal Buddhism appalled him. The Five Precepts, which are the Yama and Niyama of Buddhism, he at once saw, in spite of Nagasena and prig Milinda, must be broken by every Arahat each time he inhaled a breath of air. They

---

[95] *MWT*, Introduction.
[96] *Book 4*, Part I, *loc. cit.*
[97] *Eight Lectures*, Ch. 3, Sec. 21.
[98] Batchelor 1994.
[99] Humphreys 1968.

were as absurd as they were valueless. But behind all this tantalizing *frou-frou*, this *lingerie de cocotte*, beautifully designed to cover the narded limbs of foolish virgins, sits the Buddha in silent meditation."[100]

Crowley "soon discovered that by stripping his body of all these tawdry trappings, this feminine under-wear, and by utterly discarding the copybook precepts of Baptistical Buddhists, the Four Noble Truths were none other than the complete Yoga, and that in The Three Characteristics the summit of philosophy (The Ruach) had been reached"[101]—"Do what thou wilt shall be the whole of the Law. That is Yama."[102] Besides his own works on yoga, Crowley recommends to his students "Vivekananda's *Raja Yoga* and several little-known Hindu writers; these latter are very practical and technical, but one really needs to be a Hindu to make much use of them. The former is very good indeed, if you remember to switch off when he slides into sloppiness, which luckily is not often."[103] To Patañjali, the elements of Hindu Dharma are the attributes, qualities, and aspects of yoga; Vivekananda's 19th-century rendition of yoga thoroughly secularized and naturalized the discipline. Yoga became a science based on "natural law," or "spiritual technology" for attaining *samādhi*, with Patañjali's *Yoga Sūtras* perceived as a sort of do-it-yourself manual.[104] As Vivekananda phrases it, "The science of Raja-Yoga proposes to put before humanity a practical and scientifically worked out method of reaching this truth."[105]

A∴A∴ Curriculum lists two of the three major classic treatises on hatha yoga, *Shiva Samhita* and *Haṭha Yoga Pradīpikā* (but not *Gheranda Samhita*). Unlike the other hatha yoga texts, the late 17-century *Gheranda Samhita*, a manual of yoga taught by Gheranda to Chanda Kapali, speaks of a sevenfold yoga: it replaces *yama* and *niyama* with *ṣaṭkarma* and *mudrā*, leaves out *dhāraṇā*, and gives different methods for reaching *samādhi* than those described by Patañjali. The oldest of the three tomes, the *Shiva Samhita*, is a Sanskrit text composed by an unknown author between 1300 and 1500 CE.[106] Its title means "Shiva's Compendium" and it is addressed by the god Shiva—whom Hindu tradition credits as the founder of hatha yoga—to his consort Pārvatī. According to legend, Shiva was on a lonely island and, assuming nobody else would hear him, gave the knowledge of hatha yoga to Pārvatī. However, a fish (*matsya*) heard the entire discourse and later became a Siddha known as Matsyendranath. He taught hatha yoga to his disciple Gorakshanath, who in turn taught it to Svātmārāma, the author of the *Haṭha Yoga Pradīpikā*. According to this 15-century Svāmī, "Any person if he actively practises Yoga becomes a Siddha; be he young, old or even very old, sickly or weak. Siddhis are not obtained by wearing the dress of a Yogi, or by talking about them; untiring practice is the secret of success."[107]

---

[100] *The Temple of Solomon the King*, Part IV, "The Writings of Truth."
[101] *Ibid.*
[102] *Eight Lectures*, Ch. 2, Sec. 10.
[103] *MWT*, Ch. LXXXI.
[104] De Michelis 2004.
[105] *Raja-Yoga*, Ch. I. Vivekananda 1907–97, i.128.
[106] Mallinson 2007.
[107] As quoted in *The Temple of Solomon the King*, Part IV, "The Yogas."

The Glossary at the end of *Book 4*, Part II, describes *Haṭha Yoga Pradīpikā* as a "book on physical training for spiritual purposes" and *Shiva Samhita* as a "Hindu treatise on physical training for spiritual ends." Crowley writes that, "According to the Shiva Sanhita there are two doctrines found in the Vedas: the doctrines of 'Karma Kânda' (sacrificial works, etc.) and of 'Jnana Kânda' (science and knowledge). 'Karma Kânda' is twofold—good and evil, and according to how we live 'there are many enjoyments in heaven,' and 'in hell there are many sufferings.' Having once realized the truth of 'Karma Kânda' the Yogi renounces the works of virtue and vice, and engages in 'Jnana Kânda'—knowledge.... 'Jnana Kânda' is the application of science to 'Karma Kânda,' the works of good and evil, that is to say of Duality. Little by little it eats away the former, as strong acid would eat away a piece of steel, and ultimately when the last atom has been destroyed it ceases to exist as a science, or as a method, and becomes the Aim, *i.e.*, Knowledge."[108]

"According to the 'Pradipika' and the 'Shiva Sanhita,' there are 84 A'sanas; but Goraksha says there are as many A'sana as there are varieties of beings, and that Shiva has counted eighty-four lacs of them"—"The 'Gheranda Sanhita' gives thirty-two postures." In addition to *prāṇāyāma*, the Yogi "should also perform one or more of the Mudras, as laid down in the 'Hatha Yoga Pradipika' and the 'Shiva Sanhita,' so that he may arouse the sleeping Kundalini, the great goddess, as she is called, who sleeps coiled up at the mouth of the Sushumnâ.... These practices of Hatha Yoga if zealously maintained bring forth in the aspirant psychic powers known as the Siddhis, the most important of which are (1) Anima (the power of assimilating oneself with an atom). (2) Mahima (the power of expanding oneself into space). (3) Laghima (the power of reducing gravitation). (4) Garima (the power of increasing gravitation). (5) Prapti (the power of instantaneous travelling). (6) Prakamya (the power of instantaneous realization). (7) Isatva (the power of creating). (8) Vastiva (the power of commanding and of being obeyed)."[109]

"Besides being able by the means of Prânâyâma to control the breath, the Yogi maintains that he can also control the Omnipresent Manifesting Power out of which all energies arise, whether appertaining to magnetism, electricity, gravitation, nerve currents or thought vibrations, in fact the total forces of the Universe physical and mental.... And the conquest of the will is the beginning and end of Prânâyâma.... It is a well-known physiological fact that the respiratory system, more so than any other, controls the motions of the body. Without food or drink we can subsist many days, but stop a man's breathing but for a few minutes and life becomes extinct. The air oxydises the blood, and it is the clean red blood which supports in health the tissues, nerves, and brain. When we are agitated our breath comes and goes in gasps, when we are at rest it becomes regular and rhythmical." Crowley quotes the *Haṭha Yoga Pradīpikā*: "He who suspends

---

[108] *Ibid.*, "Attainment by Yoga."
[109] *Ibid.*, "The Yogas."

(restrains) the breath, restrains also the working of the mind. He who has controlled the mind, has also controlled the breath."[110]

The mind in ordinary men is entirely the slave of their senses. should there be a noise, man hears it; should there be an odour, man smell it; a taste, man tastes it; by means of his eyes he sees what is passing on around him, whether he likes it or not; and by means of his skin he feels sensations pleasant or painful. But in none of these cases is he actually master over his senses. The man who is, is able to accommodate his senses to his mind. To him no longer are external things necessary, for he can stimulate mentally the sensation desired. he can hear beautiful sounds without listening to beautiful music, and see beautiful sights without gazing upon them; he in fact becomes the creator of what he wills, he can exalt his imagination to such a degree over his senses, that by a mere act of imagination he can make those senses instantaneously respond to his appeal, for he is lord over the senses, and therefore over the universe as *it appears*, though not as *it is*.

The first lesson in Pratyâhâra is to sit still and let the mind run on, until it is realized what the mind is doing, when it will be understood how to control it. Then it will find that the thoughts which at first bubbled up, one over the other, become less and less numerous; but in their place will spring up the thoughts which are normally subconscious. As these arise the Will of the aspirant should strangle them; thus, if a picture is seen, the aspirant by means of his will should seize hold of it before it can escape him, endow it with an objectivity, after which he should destroy it, as if it were a living creature, and have done with it. After this mastership over the senses has been attained to, the next practice namely that of Dhâranâ must be begun.[111]

Here Crowley quotes Vivekananda, "When the *Chitta*, or mind-stuff, is confined and limited to a certain place, it is called *Dhâranâ*."[112] After *dhāraṇā* comes *dhyāna*, or "meditation upon the outpouring of the mind on the object held by the will." The footnote reads: "Imagine the objective world to be represented by a sheet of paper covered with letters and the names of things, and our power of concentration to be a magnifying glass: that power is of no use, should we wish to burn that paper, until the rays of light are *focussed*. By moving the glass or paper with our hand we obtain the right distance. In the above the Will takes the place of the hand." According to Crowley, "Hatha Yoga and Raja Yoga are so intimately connected, that instead of forming two separate methods, they rather form the first half and second half of one and the same."[113] He again cites the *Haṭha Yoga Pradīpikā* which says that "there can be no Raja Yoga without Hatha Yoga, and *vice versa*, that to those who wander in the darkness of the

---

[110] *Ibid.*
[111] *Ibid.* Emphasis in original.
[112] *Raja-Yoga*, Ch. VI. Vivekananda, *op. cit.*, i.195.
[113] *The Temple of Solomon the King, loc. cit.* Emphasis in original.

conflicting Sects unable to obtain Raja Yoga, the most merciful Swâtmârâma Yogi offers the light of Hathavidya."[114]

> It matters not what attainment the aspirant seeks to gain, or what goal he has in view, the one thing above all others which is necessary is a healthy body, and a body which is under control. It is hopeless to attempt to obtain stability of mind in one whose body is ever leaping from land to water like a frog; with such, any sudden influx of illumination may bring with it not enlightenment but mania; therefore it is that all the great masters have set the task of courage before that of endeavour. *{As in the case of Jesus, the aspirant, for the joy that is set before him, must dare to endure the cross, despising the shame; if he would be "set down at the right hand of the throne of God." Hebrews, xii, 2.}* He who *dares* to *will*, will *will* to know, and knowing will keep silence; *{"If there be no interpreter, let him keep silence in the church; and let him speak to himself, and to God" (1 Corinthians, xiv, 28) has more than one meaning.}* for even to such as have entered the Supreme Order, there is not way found whereby they may break the stillness and communicate to those who have not ceased to hear. *{"And when he had opened the seventh seal, there was silence in heaven about the space of half an hour" (Rev. viii, 1).}* The guardian of the Temple is Adonai, he alone holds the key of the Portal, seek it of Him, for there is none other that can open for thee the door.
> Now to dare much is to will a little, so it comes about that though Hatha Yoga is the physical Yoga which teaches the aspirant how to control his body, yet is it also Raja Yoga which teach him how to control his mind. Little by little, as the body comes under control, does the mind assert its sway over the body; and little by little, as the mind asserts its sway, does it come gradually, little by little under the rule of the Âtman, until ultimately the Âtman, Augœides, Higher Self or Adonai fills the Space which was once occupied solely by the body and mind of the aspirant. Therefore though the death of the body as it were is the resurrection of the Higher Self accomplished, and the pinnacles of that Temple, whose foundations are laid deep in the black earth, are lost among the starry Palaces of God.[115]

Hatha yoga synthesizes elements of Patañjali's *Yoga Sūtras* with specific, elaborate posture and breathing exercises, or *āsanas* and *prāṇāyāma* respectively. Due mainly to the influence of Vivekananda, the *Yoga Sūtras* are today considered the foundational scripture of classical yoga,[116] and for Crowley, "The greatest authority on 'Yoga' is Patanjali."[117] Before the 20th century, however, other works were deemed as the most central texts, such as the *Bhagavad-Gītā* and the *Yoga Vasistha*, while Tantric yoga prevailed over ashtanga (or "eight-limbed") yoga. The latter is often called *rāja yoga*,

---

[114] As quoted in *ibid*.
[115] *Ibid*. Emphasis in original.
[116] White 2014.
[117] *Book 4*, Part I, Ch. I.

"the king of yogas" or "yoga of the kings," a term which originally referred to the ultimate, royal goal of yoga—or *samādhi*—but was popularized by Vivekananda as a name for ashtanga yoga.[118] "More rubbish has been written about *samādhi* than enough," says Crowley, "we must endeavour to avoid adding to the heap. Even Patañjali, who is extraordinarily clear and practical in most things, begins to rave when he talks of it. Even if what he said were true he should not have mentioned it; because it does not sound true, and we should make no statement that is *à priori* improbable without being prepared to back it up with the fullest proofs. But it is more than likely that his commentators have misunderstood him.[119]

"The most reasonable statement, of any acknowledged authority, is that of Yājñavalkya, who says: 'By *prāṇāyāma* impurities of the body are thrown out; by *dhāraṇā* the impurities of the mind; by *pratyāhāra* the impurities of attachment; and by *samādhi* is taken off everything that hides the lordship of the Soul.' There is a modest statement in good literary form. If we can only do as well as that!"[120] Yājñavalkya of Videha (fl. c. 8th century BCE) was a sage of Vedic India, and one of the first philosophers in recorded history.[121] A major figure in the Upanishads, he is also traditionally credited with the authorship of the *Yoga Yajnavalkya* and the *Yājñavalkya Smṛti*. With the dawn of the British Raj in the 19th century, India also saw the onset of a Hindu renaissance, which would profoundly change the understanding of Hinduism in both the subcontinent and the West. Western Orientalists searched for the "essence" of the Indian religions, allegedly discerning it in the Vedas, while creating the popular picture of "mystic India" and the notion of "Hinduism" as a unified body of religious praxis.[122]

The idea of a Vedic essence was adopted wholesale by the Hindu reformers, together with a Universalist and Perennialist interpretation of Advaita Vedanta. Vivekananda was not only the first Hindu teacher to actively advocate and disseminate aspects of yoga to a Western audience, but one of the main representatives of this "neo-Vedanta" or "neo-Advaita."[123] The enigmatic aphorism of the Vedanta Sutras are open to a plethora of interpretations, and Vivekananda's modern reinterpretation put Hinduism in line with Western esoteric traditions, especially Transcendentalism, New Thought, and Theosophy.[124] Vivekananda embraced the idea that all sects within Hinduism—and, indeed, all religions—are different paths to the same goal, and he created a new understanding and appreciation of Hinduism both within and outside India. In the wake of emerging nationalism in British-ruled India, Vivekananda embodied the nationalistic ideal, and modern Hindus derive their

---

[118] White, *op. cit.* In any case, yoga as a purely physical system of health exercises undertaken outside of esoteric circles and religious denominations is a thoroughly modern phenomenon that has more to do with Western body culture than Eastern spirituality; *cf.* e.g. Singleton 2010.
[119] *Book 4*, Part I, Ch. VII.
[120] *Ibid.*
[121] Scharfstein 1998.
[122] King 1999.
[123] *Ibid.*
[124] De Michelis, *op. cit.*

knowledge of Hinduism directly or indirectly from him.[125] Mahatma Gandhi counted him among the few Hindu reformers "who have maintained this Hindu religion in a state of splendor by cutting down the dead wood of tradition,"[126] and according to the first governor-general of independent India, Chakravarti Rajagopalachari, "Vivekananda saved Hinduism, saved India."[127]

Vivekananda would eventually expand his plan out of the confines of India to the whole of the West, believing as he did—or was made to believe—that he possessed "spirituality," that elusive quality "that would heal the ailing Western soul."[128] He toured Europe and the United States in the 1890s, and the reception he received built on the active interest of American intellectuals, in particular the New England Transcendentalists like Emerson and Thoreau, who in turn drew on German Romanticism and the interest of philosophers and scholars like Hegel, Schopenhauer, and Müller.[129] Vivekananda was "raised" a Master Mason in 1884, the year he reached the minimum age of twenty-one, at the Anchor and Hope Lodge of Calcutta, the oldest lodge under the Grand Lodge of India,[130] and his main goal upon leaving the country was to attend the Chicago Parliament of World Religions, the first global conference of Eastern and Western religions. The Theosophical Society and the Brahmo Samaj, the first of the 19th-century Hindu reform movements, were invited as official representatives of Hinduism. Since Vivekananda, on the contrary, had not been invited to contribute to the proceeding, he had to submit an application to the relevant administrators. Interestingly, Blavatsky's successor Annie Besant refused to offer any help when the Swami told her he had no intention of becoming a Theosophist—the Brahmos were more accommodating.[131]

The first Parliament of the World's Religions was held from 11 to 27 September 1893 at the Art Institute of Chicago as part of the World's Columbian Exposition. As Parliament President John Henry Barrows put it, "India, the Mother of religions was represented by Swami Vivekananda, the Orange-monk who exercised the most wonderful influence over his auditors."[132] The Bengali Swami attracted widespread attention in the American press, with the *New York Herald* noting, "Vivekananda is undoubtedly the greatest figure in the Parliament of Religions. After hearing him we feel how foolish it is to send missionaries to this learned nation."[133] In one of his speeches, "Buddhism, the Fulfilment of Hinduism," Vivekananda spoke on Buddhism, its origin, and the relation between Buddhism and Brahminism, and Buddhism and the Vedas. He concluded that, "Hinduism cannot live without Buddhism, nor Buddhism without

---

[125] Rambachan 1994.
[126] As quoted in D. Dalton, "Gandhi's Originality," in Parel 2000, 77.
[127] As quoted in Singh & Mishra 2010, iii.963.
[128] De Michelis, *op. cit.*, 110.
[129] Goldberg 2010.
[130] Virajānanda 1912–14, i.117.
[131] De Michelis, *op. cit.*
[132] As quoted in Bhuyan 2003, 17.
[133] *Ibid.*

Hinduism," and argued that the "separation between the Buddhist and the Brahmin is the cause of the downfall of India."[134]

Vivekananda would remain in the West until December 1896, and it was during this period that his *Raja-Yoga* was written and published. The book became an instant success and gave shape to modern yoga by blending neo-Vedantic esotericism with Western occultism, thus making neo-Vedantic ideology an integral part of Western occultism, and conversely, integrating Western occult ideas into neo-Vedanta. These ideas were transmitted back to India not only by way of Vivekananda's thought and example, but also by way of the influential Ramakrishna movement he created. He insisted that success was an outcome of focused thought and action, and his interpretation of Patañjali's *Yoga Sūtras* offered a practical means to realize the divine force within which is central to modern Western esotericism.[135] As Crowley writes, "Direct experience is the end of Yoga. How can this direct experience be gained? And the answer is: by Concentration or Will."[136]

Crowley quotes Vivekananda: "Those who really want to be Yogis must give up, once for all, this nibbling at things. Take up one idea. Make that one idea your life; dream of it; think of it; live on that idea. Let the brain, the body, muscles, nerves, every part of your body, be full of that idea, and just leave every other idea alone. This is the way to success, and this is the way great spiritual giants are produced. Others are mere talking machines.... To succeed, you must have tremendous perseverance, tremendous will. 'I will drink the ocean,' says the persevering soul. 'At my will mountains will crumble up.' Have that sort of energy, that sort of will, work hard, and you will reach the goal."[137] Crowley's footnote cites the Gospels: "Every valley shall be filled, and every mountain and hill shall be brought low; and the crooked shall be made straight and the rough ways shall be made smooth. ... Prepare ye the way of Adonai."[138]

> "O Keshara," cries Arjuna, "enjoin in me this terrible action!" This will TO WILL.
>
> To turn the mind inwards, as it were, and stop it wandering outwardly, and then to concentrate all its powers upon itself, are the methods adopted by the Yogi in opening the closed Eye which sleeps in the heart to every one of us, and to create this will TO WILL. By doing so he ultimately comes face to face with something which is indestructible, on account of it being uncreatable, and which knows no dissatisfaction.[139]

"One idea must possess us, and all our energies must be focused upon it. A man who would be rich must worship wealth and understand poverty; a

---

[134] Vivekananda, *op. cit.*, i.20.
[135] De Michelis, *op. cit.*
[136] *The Temple of Solomon the King, loc. cit.*
[137] *Raja-Yoga, loc. cit.*; Vivekananda, *op. cit.*, i.197–8.
[138] Luke 3:5, 4.
[139] *The Temple of Solomon the King, loc. cit.* Emphasis in original.

man who would be strong must worship strength and understand weakness; and so also a man who would be God must worship deity and understand devilry: that is, he must become saturated with the reflections of Kether in Malkuth, until the earth be leavened and the two eyes become one. He must indeed build up his tower stone upon stone until the summit vanish amongst the stars, and he is lost in a land which lies beyond the flames of day and the shadows of night. To attain to this Ecstasy, exercises and operations of the most trivial nature must be observed, if they, even in the remotest manner, appertain to the *one* idea."[140] Already in *Berashith*, Crowley writes: "By act, word, and thought, both in quantity and quality, the one object of the ceremony is being constantly indicated. Every fumigation, purification, banishing, invocation, evocation, is chiefly a reminder of the single purpose, until the supreme moment arrives, and every fibre of the body, every force-channel of the mind, is strained out in one overwhelming rush of the Will in the direction desired. Such is the real purport of all the apparently fantastic directions of Solomon, Abramelin, and other sages of repute."

> Ceremonial Magic, as a means to attainment, has in common with all other methods, Western or Eastern, one supreme object in view— identification with the Godhead; and it matters not if the Aspirant be Theist or Atheist, Pantheist or Autotheist, Christian or Jew, or whether he name the goal of his attainment God, Zeus, Christ, Matter, Nature, Spirit, Heaven, Reason, Nirvana, Asgard, No-Thing or No-God, so long as he *has* a goal in view, and a goal he is striving to attain. Without a goal, he is but a human ship without port or destination; and, without striving, work, WILL to attain, he is but a human derelict, rudderless and mastless, tossed hither and thither by the billows of lunacy, eventually to sink beneath the black waters of madness and death.
>
> Thus we find that outside the asylum, we, one and all of us, are strenuously or slothfully, willingly or unwillingly, consciously or unconsciously, progressing slowly or speedily towards *some* goal that we have set up as an ideal before us. Follow the road to that goal, subdue all difficulties, and, when the last has been vanquished, we shall find that that "some goal" is in truth THE GOAL, and that the road upon which we set out was but a little capillary leading by vein and artery to the very Heart of Unity itself.[141]

"The whole theory and practice of Raja Yoga is the awakening of a power named the Kundalini, which is coiled up in what is called the sacral plexus, and then forcing this awakened power up a canal called the Sushumna, which runs through the centre of the spinal column."[142] Crowley again quotes Vivekananda: "When the *Kundalini* is aroused, and enters the canal of the *Sushumnâ*, all the perceptions are in the mental space or

---

[140] *Ibid.*, Part III, "The Sorcerer." Emphasis in original.
[141] *Ibid.* Emphasis in original.
[142] *Ibid.*, Part II, "The Seer," fn.

Chittâkâsa. When it has reached that end of the canal which opens out into the brain, the objectless perception is in the knowledge space, or *Chidâkâsa*."[143] Crowley continues, "As in the Ascent of the Central Column of the Tree of Life, there are certain centres, such as Malkuth, the Path of Tau, Yesod, the Path of Samech, Tiphereth, the Path of Gimel, Daäth, and Kether; so in the Sushumna are there certain centres or Chakkras, viz., Muladhara, Svadistthana, Manipura, Anahaba, Visuddhi, Ajna, and Sahasara."[144]

"Let us take a few of the ancient aphorisms of Patanjali. 'Yoga is restraining the mindstuff from taking various forms.' That is the whole definition of 'Yoga'. The mind is supposed to be concentrated on 'the effulgent one which is beyond all sorrow', or something of the kind; and if one 'takes thought for the morrow', it is a disturbance. We are to control the mind-stuff 'by practice and non-attachment', which is defined later in these terms: 'that effect which comes to those who have given up their thirst after objects either seen or heard, and which wills to control the objects, is non-attachment'. This is identical with the advice not to allow the affections and passions to disturb the concentration of the mind."[145] Similarly, "All senses and faculties must share in the work, such at least is the dictum of Western Ceremonial Magic. And so we find the magician placing stone upon stone in the construction of his Temple. That is to say, placing pantacle upon pantacle, and safeguarding his one idea by means of swords, daggers, wands, rings, perfumes, suffumigations, robes, talismans, crowns, magic squares and astrological charts, and a thousand other symbols of things, ideas, and states, all reflecting the one idea; so that he may build up a mighty mound, and from it eventually leap over the great wall which stands before him as a partition between two worlds."[146]

It is impossible to overrate the value of this inhibition to the man when he comes to meditate. He has guarded his mind against thoughts *A*, *B*, and *C*; he has told the sentries to allow no one to pass who is not in uniform. And it will be very easy for him to extend that power, and to lower the portcullis.

Let him remember, too that there is a difference not only in the frequency of thoughts—but in their intensity.

The worst of all is of course the Ego, which is almost omnipresent and almost irresistible, although so deeply-seated that in normal thought one may not always be aware of it.

Buddha, taking the bull by the horns, made this idea the first to be attacked.

Each must decide for himself whether this is a wise course to pursue. But it certainly seems easier to strip off first the things which can easily be done without.

The majority of people will find most trouble with the Emotions, and thoughts which excite them.

---

[143] *Raja-Yoga*, Ch. IV. Vivekananda 1907–97, i.182.
[144] *The Temple of Solomon the King*, loc. cit.
[145] *Liber 888*, "The Yogi Jesus."
[146] *The Temple of Solomon the King*, Part III, "The Sorcerer."

But it is both possible and necessary not merely to suppress the Emotions, but to turn them into faithful servants. Thus the Emotion of anger is occasionally useful against that portion of the brain whose slackness vitiates the control.

If there is one Emotion which is never useful, it is pride; for this reason, that it is bound up entirely with the Ego...

No, there is no use for pride!

The destruction of the Perceptions, either the grosser or the subtler, appears much easier, because the mind not being moved, is free to remember its control.

It is easy to be so absorbed in a book that one takes no notice of the most beautiful scenery. But if stung by a wasp the book is immediately forgotten.

The Tendencies are, however, much harder to combat than the three lower *skandhas* put together—for the simple reason that they are for the most part below Consciousness, and must be, as it were, awakened in order to be destroyed, so that the Will of the Magician is in a sense trying to do two opposite things at the same time.

Consciousness itself is only destroyed by *samādhi*.

One can now see the logical process which begins in refusing to think of a foot, and ends by destroying the sense of individuality.[147]

"In the first place, what is the meaning of the term? Etymologically, *sam* is the Greek συν- the English prefix *syn-* meaning 'together with.' *Ādhi* means 'Lord,' and a reasonable translation of the whole word would be 'Union with God,' the exact term used by Christian mystics to describe their attainment. Now there is great confusion, because the Buddhists use the word *samādhi* to mean something entirely different, the mere faculty of attention. Thus, with them, to think of a cat is to 'make *samādhi*' on that cat. They use the word *jhāna* to describe mystic states. This is excessively misleading, for as we saw in the last section, *dhyāna* is a preliminary of *samādhi*, and of course *jhāna* is merely the wretched plebeian Pali corruption of it."[148] Similarly, when Buddhism spread to China from the 1st century CE onwards, hundreds of Pali and Sanskrit text were translated into Chinese by Buddhist monks within a short period of time, with *dhyāna* being rendered as *Chán*, giving Zen Buddhism its name.[149]

"I think that for the first time of experiencing a Dhyana it is necessarily single. Certain mystical methods may teach us to retain the image; but the criterion of true Dhyana is the singleness, so totally opposed as it is to the vague and varying phantoms of the 'astral plane.' The new consciousness resulting from the combination is, too, always a simple one. Even where it is infinitely complex, as in Atmadarshana or the Vision of the Universal Peacock, its oneness is the truer of these two contradictory truths. So for the matter of time and space. All time is filled; all space is filled; the

---

[147] *Book 4*, Part II, Ch. VI.
[148] *Ibid.*, Ch. VII.
[149] Dumoulin 1988–90.

phenomenon is infinite and eternal. This is true even though its singleness makes the duration of the phenomenon but one minimum cogitabile. In short, it is experienced in some other kind of time, some other kind of space. There is nothing irrational about this. Non-Euclidean geometries, for example, are possible, and may be true. It is only necessary to a theory of the universe that it should be true to itself within itself; for there is no other thing outside by which we can check our calculations."[150]

"The *samādhi par excellence*, however, is *ātmadarśana*, which for some, and those not the least instructed, is the first real *samādhi*; for even the visions of 'God' and of the 'Self' are tainted by form. In *ātmadarśana* the All is manifested as the One: it is the Universe freed from its conditions. Not only are all forms and ideas destroyed, but also those conceptions which are implicit in our ideas of those ideas." As the footnote has it, "This is so complete that not only 'Black is White,' but 'The Whiteness of Black is the *essential* of its Blackness.' 'Naught = One = Infinity'; but this is only true *because* of this threefold arrangement, a trinity or 'triangle of contradictories.'"—"Each part of the Universe has become the whole, and phenomena and noumena are no longer opposed."[151]

As the five senses become subdued, fresh hosts of difficulties spring up irrationally from the brain itself. And, whichever way we turn, a mob of subconscious thoughts pull us this way and that, and our plight in this truculent multitude is a hundred times worse than when we commenced to wrestle with the five senses. Like wandering comets and meteorites they seemingly come from nowhere, splash like falling stars through the firmament of our meditation, sparkle and are gone; but ever coming as a distraction to hamper and harass our onward march.

Once the mind has conquered these, a fresh difficulty arises, the danger of not being strong enough to overcome the occult powers which, though the reward of our toils, are liable, like the Queen in her bedchamber, to seduce the Conqueror in spite of his having conquered the King her husband, and secretly slay him as he sleeps in her arms. These are the powers known in the West as the Miraculous Powers, in the East as Siddhis.

The mind is now a blank, the senses have been subdued, the subconscious thoughts slain; it stretches before us like some unspotted canvas upon which we may write or paint whatever we will. We can produce entrancing sounds at will, beautiful sights at will, subtle tastes and delicious perfumes; and after a time actual forms, living creatures, men and women and elementals. We smite the rock, and the waters flow at our blow; we cry unto the heavens, and fire rushes down and consumes our sacrifice; we become Magicians, begetters of illusion, and then, if we allow ourselves to become obsessed by them, a time comes when these illusions will master us, when the children we have begotten will rise up and dethrone us, and we shall be drowned in the waters that

---

[150] *The Psychology of Hashish, loc. cit.*
[151] *Book 4*, Part I, *loc. cit.* Emphasis in original.

now we can no longer control and be burnt up by the flames that mock obedience, and scorn our word.[152]

As Crowley observes, "the terrific strain caused by the Eastern breathing exercises was no whit greater or less than that resulting from The Acts of Worship in an operation of Ceremonial Magic, that Dhâranâ and the Mantra Yoga were in effect none other than a paraphrase of the Sacred Magic and the Acts of Invocation; and ultimately that the while system of Eastern Yoga was but a synonym of Western Mysticism." By "two years close and unabandoned experiment," Crowley showed "to his own satisfaction, that Yoga was but the Art of uniting the mind to a single idea; and that Gnana-Yoga, Raja-Yoga, Bhakta-Yoga and Hatha-Yoga"—"To which may be added Mantra Yoga and Karma Yoga, which correspond with The Invocation and The Acts of Service and represent Union through Speech and Union through Work"—"were but one class of methods leading to the same Result as attained to by The Holy Qabalah, The Sacred Magic, The Acts of Worship and The Ordeals of Western Ceremonial Magic; which again are but subsections of that One Art, the Art of uniting the mind to a Single Idea."[153]

"And, that all these, The Union by Knowledge, The Union by Will, The Union by Love, The Union by Courage found their vanishing point in the Supreme Union through Silence; that Union in which understanding fails us, and beyond which we can no more progress than we can beyond the Equilibrium set forth as the Ultimate End by Gustave le Bon. There all knowledge ceases, and we like Bâhva, when he was questioned by Vâshkali, can only expound the nature of this Silence, as he expounded the nature of Brahman, by remaining silent, as the story relates: And he said, 'Teach me, most reverend Sir, the nature of Brahman.' The other however remained silent. But when the question was put for a second or third time he answers, 'I teach you indeed, but you do not understand; this Âtman is silent.' . . . This Silence or Equilibrium is described in the 'Shiva Sanhita' as Samâdhi: 'When the mind of the Yogi is absorbed in the Great God, then the fulness of Samâdhi is attained, then the Yogi gets steadfastness." The footnotes liken the Great God to "Âtman, Pan, Harpocrates, whose sign is silence, etc.," Samādhi to "The Vision of the Holy Guardian Angel—Adonai," and the resulting steadfastness to "Equilibrium, Silence, Supreme Attainment, Zero."[154]

"There is, however, a very much higher state [than *ātmadarśana*] called *śivadarśana*, of which it is only necessary to say that it is the destruction of the previous state, its annihilation; and to understand this blotting-out, one must not imagine 'Nothingness' (the only name for it) as negative, but as positive."[155] As we learn in *Liber Aleph*, "Also in the land of Hind is the Bull sacred to Shiva, that is God among that Folk, and is unto them the Destroyer of all Things that be opposed to Him. And his God is also the Phallus, for this

---

[152] *The Temple of Solomon the King*, Part IV, "The Writings of Truth."
[153] *Ibid.*
[154] *Ibid.*
[155] *Book 4*, Part I, *loc. cit.*

Will operateth through Love even as it is written in our Own Law."[156] To Crowley, the number 111 is "Priceless, because of its 37 × 3 symbolism, its explanation of Aleph, which we seek, and its comment that the Unity may be found in 'Thick darkness' and in 'Sudden death.' This is the most clear and definite help we have yet had, showing Samadhi and the Destruction of the Ego as gates of our final victory."[157] With *samādhi*, "Death has now lost all meaning. The idea of death depends on those of the Ego, and of time; these ideas have been destroyed; and so 'Death is swallowed up in victory.'"[158]

    111. אחד הוא אלהים, "He is One God."

    אלף, Aleph, and ox, a thousand. The redeeming Bull. By shape the Swastika, and so the Lightning. "As the lightning lighteneth out of the East even unto the West, so shall be the coming of the Son of Man." An allusion to the descent of Shiva upon Shakti in Samadhi. The Roman A shows the same through the shape of the Pentagram, which it imitates.

    אסן, ruin, destruction, sudden death. *Scil.*, of the personality in Samadhi.

    אפל, thick darkness. *Cf.* St. John of the Cross, who describes these phenomena in great detail.

    אעם, the Hindu Aum or Om.

    מהולל, mad—the destruction of Reason by Illumination.

    עולה, a holocaust. *Cf.* אסן.

    פלא, the Hidden Wonder, a title of Kether.[159]

O my Son, in this the Colophon of mine Epistle will I recall the Title and Superscription thereof; that is, *The Book of Wisdom or Folly*. I proclaim Blessing and Worship to Nuit Our Lady and Her Lord Hadit, for the Miracle of the Anatomy of the Child Ra-Hoor-Khuit, as it is shewn in the Design *Minutum Mundum*, the Tree of Life. For though Wisdom be the Second Emanation of His Essence, there is a Path to separate and to join them, the Reference thereof being Aleph, that is One indeed, but also an Hundred and Eleven in his full Orthography; to signify the Most Holy Trinity, and by Metathesis it is Thick Darkness, and Sudden Death. This is also the Number of AUM, which is AMOUN, and the Root-Sound of OMNE, or, in Greek, PAN, and it is a Number of the Sun. Yet is the Atu of Thoth that correspondeth thereunto marked with ZERO, and its Name is MAT, whereof I have spoken formerly, and its Image is The Fool. O my Son, gather thou all these Limbs together in one Body, and breathe upon it with thy Spirit, that it may live; then do thou embrace it with Lust of thy Manhood, and go in unto it, and know it; so shall ye be One Flesh. Now at last in the Reinforcement and Ecstasy of this Consummation thou shalt wit by what Inspiration thou didst choose thy Name in the Gnosis, I mean PARZIVAL, "der reine Thor," the True Knight that won

---

[156] "De tauro."
[157] *An Essay upon Number, loc. cit.*
[158] *Book 4*, Part I, *loc. cit.*
[159] *An Essay upon Number*, Part I, Sec. IV.

Kingship in Monsalvat, and made whole the Wound of Amfortas, and ordered Kundry to Right Service, and regained the Lance, and revived the Miracle of the Sangraal; yea, also upon himself did he accomplish his Work in the End: "Höchsten Heiles Wunder! Erlösung dem Erlöser!" This is the last Word of the Song that thine Uncle Richard Wagner made for Worship of this Mystery. Understand thou this, o my Son, as I take leave of thee in this Epistle, that the Summit of Wisdom is the Opening of the Way that leadeth unto the Crown and Essence of all, to the Soul of the Child Horus, the Lord of the Æon. This Way is the Path of the Pure Fool. Amoun.[160]

According to Crowley, "in both the Western and Eastern systems, equilibrium is both the method and the result," but in the East, "the magical operation becomes purely a mental one, and in many respects a more rational and less emotional one. The will, so to speak, is concentrated on itself by the aid of a reflective point—the tip of the nose, the umbilicus, a lotus, or again, in a more abstract manner, on the inhalation and exhalation of the breath, upon an idea or a sensation. The Yogi abandons the constructive method, and so it is that we do not find him building up, but, instead, undermining his consciousness, his instrument being a purely introspective one, the power of turning his will as a mental eye upon himself, and finally seeing himself as HimSELF."[161]

"The Western Magician wills to turn darkness into light, earth into gold, vice into virtue. He sets out to purify; therefore all around him must be pure, ever to hold before his memory the one essential idea. More crudely this is the whole principle of advertising. A good advertiser so places his advertisement that wherever you go, and whichever way you turn, you see the name of the article he is booming. If it happens, *e.g.*, to be 'Keating's Insect Powder,' the very name becomes part of you, so that directly a flea is seen or mentioned 'Keating's' spontaneously flashes across your thoughts. The will of a magician may be compared to a lamp burning in a dark and dirty room. First he sets to work to clean the room out, then he places a brightly polished mirror along one wall to reflect one sense, and then another to reflect another, and so on, until, whichever way he look, up or down, to right or left, behind or before, there he sees his will shining; and ultimately so dazzling become the innumerable reflections, that he can see but one great flame which obscures everything else. The Yogi on the other hand dispenses with the mirrors, and contents himself in turning the wick lower and lower until the room is one perfect darkness and nothing else can be seen or even recognised beyond SELF."[162]

"The whole question of the sub-conscious mind can be dismissed almost as a joke by the average man as he goes about his daily business; it becomes a very real trouble when you discover that the tranquillity of the mind is being disturbed by a type of thought whose existence had previously been

---

[160] *Liber Aleph*, "De sapientia et stultitia."
[161] *The Temple of Solomon the King*, Part III, "The Sorcerer." Emphasis in original.
[162] *Ibid.* Emphasis in original.

unsuspected, and whose source is unimaginable."¹⁶³ On the other hand, "True symbols do really awake those macrocosmic forces of which they are the eidola, and it is possible in this manner very largely to increase the magical 'potential,' to borrow a term from electrical science. Of course, there are bad and invalid processes, which tend rather to dispense or to excite the mind-stuff than to control it; these we must discard."¹⁶⁴

There is no limit to what theologians call "wickedness." Only by experience can the student discover the ingenuity of the mind in trying to escape from control. He is perfectly safe so long as he sticks to meditation, doing no more and no less than that which we have prescribed; but the mind will probably not let him remain in that simplicity. This fact is the root of all the legends about the "Saint" being tempted by the "Devil." Consider the parable of Christ in the Wilderness, where he is tempted to use his magical power, to do anything but the thing that should be done. These attacks on the will are as bad as the thoughts which intrude upon *dhāranā*. It would almost seem as if one could not successfully practice meditation until the will had become so strong that no force in the Universe could either bend or break it. Before concentrating the lower principle, the mind, one must concentrate the higher principle, the Will. Failure to understand this has destroyed the value of all attempts to teach "Yoga," "Menticulture," "New Thought," and the like.¹⁶⁵

"The mind constantly struggles to escape control. . . .it is the *normal* habit of the mind to organize these counter-attacks that makes their task so easy. What you need is a mind that will help rather than hinder your Work by its *normal* function. This is where these Greetings, and Will-sayings, and Adorations come in. It is not a concentration-practice proper; I haven't a good word for it. 'Background-concentration' or 'long-distance-concentration' are clumsy, and not too accurate. It is really rather like a public school education. One is not constantly 'doing a better thing that one has ever done'; one is not dropping one's eye-glass every two minutes, or being a little gentleman in the act of brushing one's hair. The point is that one trains oneself to react properly at any moment of surprise. It must become 'second nature' for 'Do what thou wilt shall be the whole of the Law' to spring to the forefront of the mind when one is introduced to a stranger, or comes down to breakfast, or hears the telephone bell, or observes the hour of the adoration (these are to be the superficial reactions, like instinctively rising when a lady enters the room), or, at the other end, in moments of immediate peril, or of sudden apprehension, or when in one's meditation, one approaches the deepest strata."¹⁶⁶

However, Crowley says that, "One need not be dogmatic about the use

---

¹⁶³ *Eight Lectures*, loc. cit.
¹⁶⁴ *Berashith*.
¹⁶⁵ *Book 4*, Part II, "Ceremonial Magick, the Training for Meditation: Preliminary Remarks."
¹⁶⁶ *MWT*, Ch. XVIII. Emphasis in original.

of these special words. One might choose a formula to represent one's own particular True Will. It is a little like Cato, (or Scipio, was it?) who concluded every speech, whether about the Regulations of the Roman Bath or the proposal to reclaim a marsh of the Maremma, with the words: 'And moreover, in my opinion, Carthage ought to be destroyed.'"[167] Nevertheless, "It is impossible to exaggerate the importance of performing these small ceremonies regularly, and being as nearly accurate as possible with regard to the times. You must not mind stopping in the middle of a crowded thoroughfare—lorries or no lorries—and saying the Adorations; and you must not mind snubbing your guest—or your host—if he or she should prove ignorant of his or her share of the dialogue. It is perhaps because these matters are so petty and trivial in appearance that they afford so excellent a training. They teach you concentration, mindfulness, moral and social courage, and a host of other virtues."[168] Indeed, "They form an invaluable preliminary training for the colossal Work of genuine concentration when it comes to be a question of the fine, growing constantly finer, movements of the mind."[169]

"Now then, 'there is great danger in me'—we have seen what it is; but why should it lie in Hadit? Because the process of self-analysis involves certain risks. The profane are protected against those subtle spiritual perils which lie in ambush for the priest. A Bushman never has a nervous breakdown. (See Cap. I, v. 31.) When the Aspirant takes his first Oath, the most trivial things turn into transcendental terrors, tortures, and temptations.... We are so caked with dirt that the germs of disease cannot reach us. If we decide to wash, we must do it well; or we may have awakened some sleeping dogs, and set them on defenceless areas. Initiation stirs up the mud. It creates unstable equilibrium. It exposes our elements to unfamiliar conditions. The France of Louis XVI had to pass through the Terror before Napoleon could teach it to find itself. Similarly, any error in reaching the realization of Hadit may abandon the Aspirant to the ambitions of every frenzied faction of his character, the masterless dogs of the Augean kennel of his mind."[170]

"You cannot dodge your Karma. You have got to earn the right to devote yourself to Yoga proper by arranging for that devotion to be a necessary stage in the fulfilment of your True Will. In Hindustan one is not allowed to become 'Sanyasi'—a recluse—until one has fulfilled one's duty to one's own environment—rendered to Caesar the things which are Caesar's before rendering to God the things which are God's."[171] As Lévi writes, "We only understand magic power in its application to great matters. If a true practical magician does not make himself master of the world, it is that he disdains it. To what, then, would he degrade his sovereign power? 'I will

---

[167] Ibid.; *Ceterum autem censeo Carthaginem esse delendam*, often abbreviated to *Carthago delenda est*, was a popular oratorial phrase in the Roman Republic during the latter years of the Punic Wars, made famous by the Roman senator Cato the Elder.
[168] Ibid., Introduction.
[169] *Eight Lectures*, Ch. 5, Sec. 9.
[170] NC on AL II.27.
[171] *Eight Lectures*, Ch. 3, Sec. 21.

give thee all the kingdoms of the world, if thou wilt fall at my feet and worship me,' the Satan of the parable said to Jesus. 'Get thee behind me, Satan,' replied the Saviour; 'for it is written, Thou shalt adore God alone.' ... 'Eli, Eli, Lama Sabachthani!' was what this sublime and divine adorer of God cried later. If he had replied to Satan, 'I will not adore thee, and it is thou who wilt fall at my feet, for I bid thee in the name of intelligence and eternal reason,' he would not have consigned his holy and noble life to the most frightful of all tortures. The Satan of the mountain was indeed cruelly avenged! The ancients called practical magic the sacerdotal and royal art, and one remembers that the magi were the masters of primitive civilization, because they were the masters of all the science of their time. To know is to be able when one dares to will."[172]

It is indeed the criterion of spiritual "caste" that conflicting elements should not coexist in the same consciousness. The psalm-singing Puritan who persecutes publicans, and secretly soaks himself in fire-water; the bewhiskered philanthropist in broadcloth who swindles his customers and sweats his employees: these men must not be regarded as single-minded scoundrels, whose use of religion and respectability to cloak their villainies is a deliberate disguise dictated by their criminal cunning. Far from it, they are only too sincere in their "virtues"; their terror of death and of supernatural vengeance is genuine; it proceeds from a section of themselves which is in irreconcilable conflict with their rascality. Neither side can conciliate, suppress, or ignore the other; yet each is so craven as to endure its enemy's presence. Such men are therefore without pure principles; they excuse themselves for every dirty trick that turns to their apparent advantage.

The first step of the Aspirant toward the Gate of Initiation tells him that purity—unity of purpose—is essential above all else. "Do what thou Wilt" strikes on him, a ray of fierce white flame consuming all that is not utterly God. Very soon he is aware that he cannot consciously contradict himself. He develops a subtle sense which warns him that two trains of thought which he had never conceived as connected are incompatible. Yet deeper drives "Do what thou wilt"; subconscious oppositions are evoked to visible appearance. The secret sanctuaries of the soul are cleansed. "Do What thou Wilt" purges his every part. He has become One, one only. His Will is consequently released from the interference of internal opposition, and he is a Master of Magick. But for that very reason he is now utterly impotent to achieve anything that is not in absolute accordance with his Original Oath, with his True Will, by virtue whereof he incarnated as a man. With Bill Sykes love and murder are not mutually exclusive, as they are with King Arthur. The higher the type of man, the more sensitive he becomes; so that the noblest love divines intuitively when a careless word or gesture may wound, and, vigilant, shuns them as being of the family of murder. In Magick, likewise, the Adept who is sworn to attain to the Knowledge and

---

[172] *The Key of the Mysteries, loc. cit.*, Book I, Ch. III.

Conversation of his Holy Guardian Angel may in his grosser days have been expert as a Healer, to find that he is now incapable of any such work. He will probably be puzzled, and wonder whether he has lost all his power. Yet the cause may be no more than that the Wisdom of his Angel depreciates the interference of ignorant kindliness with diseases which may have been sent to the sufferer for a purpose profoundly important to his welfare.[173]

"Ask yourself: then what happens to the discarded elements of the Adept? They cannot be left as they are, to disintegrate, or to become vehicles for obsession. This entity which was the Exempt Adept has been built up in years of unremitting toil, as worthy Workshop wherein the Great Work should be accomplished. It has moreover been sanctified and glorified by the Knowledge and Conversation of the Holy Guardian Angel. So as each Master has his own appointed Work to perform in the world, he is cast down into the Sephira, suitable for that work. If his function is to be that of a warrior, he would find himself in Geburah; if that of a great poet or composer, in Tiphareth; and so on. He, the Master, inhabits this dwelling; but, having already got rid of it, he is able to allow it to carry on according to its nature without interference from the false Self (its head in Daäth) which hitherto had hampered it. ('If I were a dog, I should bark; if I were an owl, I should hoot,' says Basil King Lamus in *The Diary of a Drug-Fiend*.) He is totally indifferent to the Event; so then he acts and reacts with perfect elasticity. This is the Way of the Tao; and that is why you cannot grasp the very idea of that Way—much less follow it!—unless you are a Master of the Temple."[174]

"Every person, whatever his grade in the Order, has also a 'natural' grade appropriate to his intrinsic virtue. He may expect to be 'cast out' into that grade when he becomes $8°=3^{\square}$. Thus one man, throughout his career, may be essentially of the type of Netzach; another, of Hod. In the same way Rembrandt and Raphael retained their respective points of view in all stages of their art. The practical consideration is that some aspirants may find it unusually difficult to attain certain grades; or, worse, allow their inherent predispositions to influence them to neglect antipathetic, and indulge sympathetic, types of work. They may thus become more unbalanced than ever, with disastrous results. Success in one's favourite pursuit is a temptress; whose yields to her wiles limits his own growth. True, every Will is partial; but, even so, it can only fulfill itself by symmetrical expansion. It must be adjusted to the Universe, or fail of perfection."[175]

It should also be remarked that every grade has its peculiar magical formula. Thus, the formula of Abrahadabra concerns us, as men, principally because each of us represents the pentagram or microcosm;

---

[173] *MITAP*, Ch. XVI, Pt. I.
[174] *MWT*, Ch. L.
[175] *MITAP*, Ch. VII, Sec. IV, fn.

and our equilibration must therefore be with the hexagram or macrocosm. In other words, $5°=6^\square$ is the formula of the Solar operation; but then $6°=5^\square$ is the formula of the Martial operation, and this reversal of the figures implies a very different Work. In the former instance the problem was to dissolve the microcosm in the macrocosm; but this other problem is to separate a particular force from the macrocosm, just as a savage might hew out a flint axe from the deposits in a chalk cliff. Similarly, an operation of Jupiter will be of the nature of the equilibration of him with Venus. Its graphic formula will be $7°=4^\square$, and there will be a word in which the character of this operation is described, just as Abrahadabra describes the Operation of the Great Work.

It may be stated without unfairness, as a rough general principle, that the farther from original equality are the two sides of the equation, the more difficult is the operation to perform.

Thus, to take the case of the personal operation symbolized by the grades, it is harder to become a Neophyte, $1°=10^\square$, than to pass from that grade to Zelator, $2°=9^\square$.

Initiation is, therefore, progressively easier, in a certain sense, after the first step is taken. But (especially after the passing of Tiphareth) the distance between grade and grade increases as it were by a geometrical progression with an enormously high factor, which itself progresses.

It is evidently impossible to give details of all these formulæ. Before beginning any operation soever the magician must make a through Qabalistic study of it so as to work out its theory in symmetry of perfection. Preparedness in Magick is as important as it is in War.[176]

"There is, of course, one sense in which every grade is a Thing-in-Itself. But the Hierarchy is only a convenient method of classifying observed facts. One is reminded of the Democracy, who, on being informed by the Minister of the Interior that the scarcity of provisions was due to the Law of Supply and Demand, passed a unanimous resolution calling for the immediate repeal of that iniquitous measure!"[177] The Postcard to Probationers entitled "The Method of Equilibrium" in *The Equinox*, Vol. I, No. 2, defines trance "as the *ek-stasis* of one particular tract of the brain, caused by meditation on the idea corresponding to it. . . . Let the student therefore beware lest in that idea be any trace of imperfection. It should be pure, balanced, calm, complete, fitted in every way to dominate the mind, as it will. Even as in the choice of a king to be crowned. . . . So will the decrees of this king be just and wise as he was just and wise before he was made king. The life and work of the mystic will reflect (though dimly) the supreme guiding force of the mystic, the highest trance to which he has attained."

"If this idea be any but the Supreme and Perfect idea, and the student lose control, the result is insanity, obsession, fanaticism, or paralysis and death (add addiction to gossip and incurable idleness), according to the

---

[176] *MITAP*, Ch. VII, Sec. IV.
[177] *Ibid.*, fn.

nature of the failure. Let then the Student understand all these things and combine them in his Art, uniting them by the supreme method of Silence."[178] As *Liber Libræ* says, "Establish thyself firmly in the equilibrium of forces, in the centre of the Cross of the Elements, that Cross from whose centre the Creative Word issued in the birth of the Dawning Universe. Be thou therefore prompt and active as the Sylphs, but avoid frivolity and caprice; be energetic and strong like the Salamanders, but avoid irritability and ferocity; be flexible and attentive to images like the Undines, but avoid idleness and changeability; be laborious and patient like the Gnomes, but avoid grossness and avarice."[179]

> I solemnly warn the world that, while courage is the first virtue of the Magician, presumptuous and reckless rashness has no more connection with it than a caricature of the ex-Kaiser with Julius Caesar. It is composed partly of sham pride prompted by self-love and self-doubt; partly by the insane impulse which the extremity of fear excites. There are plenty of V.C.s who won the cross, not "for valour", but for lack of self-control over their crisis of cowardice. Discipline automatically made running away impossible; the only way out was to rush forward and do whatever their innate instinct suggested. I know two V.C.s myself who have no memory whatever of the act that won them the cross.
> Similar psychology often makes young Magicians forget that *to dare* must be backed by *to will* and *to know*, all three being ruled by *to keep silence*. Which last means many things, but most of all so to control oneself that every act is done noiselessly; all disturbance means clumsiness or blundering. The soldier may happen not to be hit as he carries his wounded comrade through the barrage, but there is no luck in Magick. We work in a fluid world, where every moment is compensated at once. Light, sound and electricity may be shut out, and so the effects of human thought, speech and action may divert or delay their action, but Magick, like gravitation, knows no obstacle. It is true that one can lift a fallen flower from the floor and keep it on a table; but the forces are at work all the time, and the action has been completely compensated by the redistribution of the stresses on every material object in the whole universe, by the shifting of the centre of gravity of the cosmos, as my muscles sway from one state of equilibrium to another, and the flower exerts its energies from the mahogany instead of the carpet.
> Presumption in Magick is, therefore, sure to be punished—swiftly and justly. The error is one of the worst because it attracts all these forces which, being themselves weak, are made malignant by pain and find their principal solace in taking it out of anyone they feel they can bully. Worse still, the hysterical expansion of the ego means the deepest possible treason to truth. It invites obsession by every deceitful demon.

---

[178] *Postcards to Probationers*, "Yoga and Magick."
[179] 18–19.

They puff up the pride of the fool still further; they flatter every foible, exhort him to acts of the most ridiculous kind, induce him to talk the most raving rubbish and teach him to think himself the greatest man in the world—nay, not a man, but a god. He scores every fiasco as a success, takes every trifle as a token either of his sacrosanct sovereignty or of the malice of hell whose hounds have been mustered to martyr him. His megalomania swings from maniacal exaltation to melancholia, with delusions of persecution.[180]

According to Crowley, "one of the most frequent troubles is that people who are doing excellent work throw it up because they find that Nature is not what they thought it was going to be. But this is the best test of the reality of any experience. All those which conform with your idea, which flatter you, are likely to be illusions."[181] He relates the story of a "certain Yogi" who "thought it would be an admirable achievement to walk across the Ganges. After forty years he succeeded, and went off to his Guru to demonstrate his power, and receive his due meed of praise. It so happened that this Guru was rather like myself, at least in the matter of his Nasty Temper; and when the disciple came gaily striding back across the Sacred Stream, expecting compliments, he was met with: 'Well, I think you're a perfect fool all these years, your neighbours have been going to and fro on a raft for a couple of pice!' The moral . . . is that such powers are never to be considered as the main object; it ought in fact to be obvious from the start that any one's True Will must be deeper and more comprehensive than any mere technical achievement. I will go further and say that any such endeavour must be a magical mistake, like cherishing a gun or a clock or a fishing-rod for its own sake, and not for the use that one can make of it."[182]

"Indeed, that remark goes to the root of the matter; for all these powers, if we understand them properly, are natural by-products of one's real Great Work. My own experience was very convincing on this point; for one power after another came popping up when it was least wanted, and I saw at once that they represented so many leaks in my boat. They argued imperfect insulation. And really they are quite a bit of a nuisance. Their possession is so flattering, and their seduction so subtle. One understands at once why all the first-class Teachers insist so sternly that the Siddhi (or Iddhi) must be rejected firmly by the Aspirant, if he is not to be sidetracked and ultimately lost. . . . Then, again, when these powers have sprung naturally and spontaneously from the exercise of one's proper faculties in the Great Work, they ought to be a little more than leaks. You ought to be able to organize and control them in such wise that they are of actual assistance to you in taking the Next Step. After all, what moral or magical difference is there between the power of digesting one's food, and that of transforming oneself into a hawk?"[183]

---

[180] *Confessions*, Ch. 66. Emphasis in original.
[181] *Eight Lectures*, Ch. 8, Sec. 25.
[182] *MWT*, Ch. LXIV.
[183] *Ibid.*

"The statement in the Dhammapada that: 'All that we are is the result of what we have thought: it is founded on our thoughts, it is made up of our thoughts:'[184] is equally true of the Vedânta as it is of Buddhism. But, in the former we get the great doctrine and practice of the Siddhis directly attributable to a mastering of the emotions and then to a use of the same, which is strictly forbidden to the Buddhist, but which eventually under the Mahâyâna Buddhism of China and Tibet forced itself once again into recognition, and which, even as early as the writing of 'The Questions of King Milinda,' unless the beautiful story of the courtesan Bindumati be a latter day interpolation, was highly thought of under the name of an 'Act of Truth.'"[185] (Both the *Dhammapada*, as the "best of the Buddhist classics" and *The Questions of King Milinda*, or "Technical points of Buddhist dogma, illustrated by dialogues," are included in the Curriculum of A∴A∴ under Course I, Section 1, "Books for Serious Study.")

"Thus, though King Sivi gave his eyes to the man who begged them of him, he received others by an Act of Truth, by the gift of Siddhi, or Iddhi as the Buddhists call it. An Act, which is explained by the fair courtesan Bindumati as follows. When King Asoka asked her by what power she had caused the waters of the Ganges to flow backwards. She answered: 'Whosoever, O King, gives me gold be he a noble, or a brahman, or tradesman, or a servant—I regard them all alike. When I see he is a noble I make no distinction in his favour. If I know him to be a slave I despise him not. Free alike from fawning and from dislike do I do service to him who has bought me. This, your Majesty, is the basis of the Act of Truth by the force of which I turned the Ganges back.'"[186] According to the footnote, "These Iddhis are also called Abhijnyâs. There are six of them: (1) clairvoyance; (2) clairaudience; (3) powers of transformation; (4) powers of remembering past lives; (5) powers of reading the thoughts of others; (6) the knowledge of comprehending the finality of the stream of life."

"In other words, by ignoring all accidents, all matters of chance, and setting to work, without favour or prejudice, to accomplish the one object in view, and so finally 'to interpret every phenomenon as a particular dealing of God with the soul.' In truth this is an 'Act of Truth,' the Power begot by Concentration and nothing else."[187] Conversely, "it is absolute Black Magic to use any of these powers if the object can possibly be otherwise attained. If your child is drowning, you must jump and try to save him; it won't do to invoke the Undines."[188]

---

[184] *Dhammapada*, v. 1.
[185] *The Temple of Solomon the King*, Part IV, "The Doctrines of Buddhism."
[186] Ibid.; *Milindapañhā*, 4.1.12.
[187] Ibid.
[188] *MITAP*, Ch. XXI, Sec. III.

PART III
Polemic

CHAPTER 11
Religious Aspects
Part I: Prophecy

They are called Seven, although they are Eight, because Lao-tzû counts as nought, owing to the nature of his doctrine. The reference to their "living not" is to be found in Liber 418.
    The word "Perdurabo" means "I will endure unto the end". The allusion is explained in the note.
    Siddartha, or Gotama, was the name of the last Buddha.
    Krishna was the principal incarnation of the Indian Vishnu, the preserver, the principal expounder of Vedantism.
    Tahuti, or Thoth, the Egyptian God of Wisdom.
    Mosheh, Moses, the founder of the Hebrew system.
    Dionysus, probably an ecstatic from the East.
    Mahmud, Mohammed.
    All these were men; their Godhead is the result of mythopœia.
—The Commentary to THE BOOK OF LIES

The legend of "Christ" is only a corruption and perversion of other legends. Especially of Dionysus: compare the account of Christ before Herod/Pilate in the Gospels, and of Dionysus before Pentheus in "The Bacchae".
—THE FOOTNOTE

According to Crowley, Jesus was a made-up, composite character, who expounded no new spiritual doctrine or magical formula. As for Crowley himself, "My Grade as a Magus of A∴A∴, my office as the Logos of the Æon, the Prophet chosen to proclaim the Law which will determine the destinies of this planet for an epoch, singles me out in a sense, puts me in a class which contains only seven other names in the whole of human history. No possible personal attainment could have done this. There are countless initiates, especially in Asia, who have scaled very summit in the range of spiritual success. I should unquestionably have become insane from satisfaction at the fulfilment of my utmost aspirations having been granted to me so superlatively beyond imagination conceived, but for (as I said before) 'my sense of humour and my common sense'."[1]

    The interior Order was formed immediately after the first perception of man's wider heritage had dawned upon the first of the adepts; it

---

[1] *Confessions*, Ch. 66. (Just consider all the puns in "Liber-al"—"Knew it," "Had it," "Raw whore quit." And who was the author? "I was.")

received from the Masters at first-hand the revelation of the means by which humanity could be raised to its rights and delivered from its misery. It received the primitive charge of all revelation and mystery; it received the key of true science, both divine and natural.

But as men multiplied, the frailty of man necessitated an exterior society which veiled the interior one, and concealed the spirit and the truth in the letter, because many people were not capable of comprehending great interior truth. Therefore, interior truths were wrapped in external and perceptible ceremonies, so that men, by the perception of the outer which is the symbol of the interior, might by degrees be enabled safely to approach the interior spiritual truths.

But the inner truth has always been confided to him who in his day had the most capacity for illumination, and he became the sole guardian of the original Trust, as High Priest of the Sanctuary.

When it became necessary that interior truths should be enfolded in exterior ceremony and symbol, on account of the real weakness of men who were not capable of hearing the Light of Light, then exterior worship began. It was, however, always the type or symbol of the interior, that is to say, the symbol of the true and Secret Sacrament.[2]

As we learn in *Liber DCCCXXXVII*, "Here is the Calendar of our Church: 'But ye, o my people, rise up & awake! Let the rituals be rightly performed with joy & beauty!' Remember that all acts of love and pleasure are rituals, must be rituals. . . It all depends on your own acceptance of this new law, and you are not asked to believe anything, to accept a string of foolish fables beneath the intellectual level of a Bushman and the moral level of a drug-fiend. All you have to do is to be yourself, to do your will, and to rejoice."[3] For instance, according to the *New Comment*, "There should be a special feast on the 12th day of August in every year, since it was the marriage of The Beast which made possible the revelation of the New Law. (This is not an Apology for Marriage. Hard Cases make Bad Law)."[4]

The Masters, who were watching him, sent out messengers from time to time, in order to teach him in many secret paths of enlightenment. In all these he attained the greatest success; it can be said that at his return to the country of his birth in 1903 E.V. he was the most advanced adept (as distinguished from a Master) in the world. And yet he was so far from accepting his progress with satisfaction, that he formally and finally gave up the Great Work as insignificant.

And this too was the Plan of the Masters.

Having surrendered his True Will so far that he had married (August 1903 E.V.) and settled down to the life of an ordinary man, having built up a fortress of resentment against all spiritual assault, Leo had become a fit instrument to carry out the inscrutable designs of the Masters.

---

[2] *Liber XXXIII*.
[3] Sec. III.
[4] NC on AL II.37.

At the end of a sporting expedition in Asia he stayed in Cairo for the Season with his young wife, a woman of neither instinct for, nor interest in, any but the most frivolous of worldly amusements.

Now the Masters, the Secret Chiefs of the Order to which he owed his first initiation, are the directors of the spiritual destinies of this planet. These men chose this woman (of all women) to carry Their Will to the Aspirant who had renounced his aspiration.

Leo received their message with quiet mockery: he agreed to carry out the instructions conveyed by his wife in a spirit of irony, resolved to demonstrate to her the absurdity of her claim to be in communication with a praeter-human Intelligence.

The principal of these instructions was to shut himself up in a certain room of his house for one hour daily for three days (April 8-10, 1904 E.V.) that he might write what should then be given to him.

He was astonished beyond measure when, on the stroke of the appointed hour, he heard the accents of a human voice, speaking in English (a language he understood sufficiently for the purpose) and continuing until the sixty minutes had exactly passed.

This occurred on the two succeeding days: the result is the Manuscript known as *Liber AL vel Legis*; or *The Book of the Law*.[5]

Liber 666 calls Crowley "Leo," because that was the astrological sign "in the ascendant at his nativity." The *New Comment* specifies that the "feast for the three days of the writing of the Book of the Law" on "April 8th, 9th, and 10th" should begin "at High Noon." As Crowley puts it in *The Equinox of the Gods*, "Of course I wrote them, ink on paper, in the material sense; but they are not My words, unless Aiwaz be taken to be no more than my subconscious self, or some part of it: in that case, my conscious self being ignorant of the Truth in the Book and hostile to most of the ethics and philosophy of the Book, Aiwaz is a severely suppressed part of me."[6] Still, the official account has more than a few problems, starting with the fact that the Egyptian Museum had moved from Boulaq to a new location the year previous, and more damningly, passenger manifests from April 1904 indicate that the Crowleys left Egypt on the 6th. Consequently, some claim the entire story is apocryphal.[7]

Speaking about himself in the third person again, Crowley writes in the *Temple of Solomon the King*: "As to miracles and prophecies, he was as sceptical as the famous Pope of Rome who 'didn't believe in them; he had seen too many.' If an angel had appeared to him, he would have explained him away as cheerily as the late Frank Podmore. He was as ready to acquiesce in the unhistoricity of Gotama as in that of Jesus. If he called himself a Buddhist, it was the agnostic and atheistic philosophy and the acentric nominalist psychology that attracted him. The precepts and

---

[5] *Liber 666*.
[6] *The Equinox of the Gods*, "Genesis Libri AL," Ch. VII, Sec. II.
[7] *Cf.* e.g. Cole 2015. Incidentally, Good Friday fell on April Fool's that year.

practices of Buddhism earned only his dislike and contempt."[8] In *The Equinox of the Gods*, Crowley describes himself as "age 28 ½. In good health, fond of out-door sports, especially mountaineering and big-game shooting. An Adept Major of the A∴A∴ but weary of mysticism and dissatisfied with Magick. A rationalist, Buddhist, agnostic, anti-clerical, anti-moral, Tory and Jacobite. A chess-player, first-class amateur, able to play three games simultaneously blindfold. A reading and writing addict. Education: private governess and tutors, preliminary school Habershon's at St. Leonards, Sussex, private tutors, private school 51 Bateman St., Cambridge, private tutors, Yarrow's School, Streatham, near London. Malvern College, Tonbridge School, private tutors, Eastbourne College, King's College, London, Trinity College, Cambridge."[9]

The *New Comment* says the "feast for Tahuti and the child of the Prophet" is "of a character suited only to initiates"[10] and that the "Supreme Ritual is the Invocation of Horus, which brought about the Opening of the New Æon. The date is March 20. The Equinox of the Gods is the term used to describe the Beginning of a New Æon, or a New Magical Formula. It should be celebrated at every Equinox, in the manner known to Neophytes of the A∴A∴."[11] *The Equinox of the Gods* reads: "March 20. Success in my invocation of Horus, by 'breaking all the rules' at her command. This success convinced me magically, and encouraged me to test her as above mentioned."[12] And as we learn in the very first chapter of *Magick in Theory and Practice*, "There is a single main definition of the object of all magical Ritual. It is the uniting of the Microcosm with the Macrocosm. The Supreme and Complete Ritual is therefore the Invocation of the Holy Guardian Angel; or, in the language of Mysticism, Union with God." As the footnote says, "The difference between these operations is more of theoretical than of practical importance."

> All other magical rituals are particular cases of this general principle, and the only excuse for doing them is that it sometimes occurs that one particular portion of the Microcosm is so weak that its imperfection of impurity would vitiate the Macrocosm of which it is the image, eidolon, or reflection. For example, God is above sex; and therefore neither man nor woman as such can be said fully to understand, much less to represent, God. It is therefore incumbent on the male Magician to cultivate those female virtues in which he is deficient, and this task he must of course accomplish without in any way impairing his virility. It will then be lawful for a Magician to invoke Isis, and identify himself with her; if he fail to do this, his apprehension of the Universe when he attains *samādhi* will lack the conception of maternity. The result will be a metaphysical and—by corollary—ethical limitation in the Religion

---

[8] *The Temple of Solomon the King*, Part VI, "The Priest."
[9] *The Equinox of the Gods, loc. cit.*, Sec. VIII.
[10] NC on AL II.39.
[11] NC on AL II.40.
[12] *The Equinox of the Gods, loc. cit.*

which he founds. Judaism and Islām are striking example of this failure.[13]

As Crowley writes in the Introduction to *Magick Without Tears*, "Every name is a number: and 'Every number is infinite; there is no difference.' (AL I, 4). But one Name, or system of Names, may be more convenient either (*a*) to you personally or (*b*) to the work you are at. *E.g.* I have very little sympathy with Jewish Theology or ritual; but the Qabalah is so handy and congenial that I use it more than almost any—or all the others together—for daily use and work. The Egyptian Theogony is the noblest, the most truly magical, the most bound to me (or rather I to it) by some inmost instinct, and by the memory of my incarnation as Ankh-f-n-Khonsu, that I use it (with its Græco-Phoenician child) for all work of supreme import. Why stamp my vitals, madam! The Abramelin Operation itself turned into this form before I could so much as set to work on it! Like the Duchess' baby (excuse this enthusiasm; but you have aroused the British Lion-Serpent.)"

"The Egyptian Gods are so complete in their nature, so perfectly spiritual and yet so perfectly material, that this one invocation is sufficient. The God bethinks him that the spirit of Mercury should now appear to the magician; and it is so. This Egyptian formula is therefore to be preferred to the Hierarchical formula of the Hebrews with its tedious prayers, conjurations, and curses. It will be noted, however, that in this invocation of Thoth which we have summarized, there is another formula contained, the Reverberating or Reciprocating formula, which may be called the formula of Horus and Harpocrates. The magician addresses the God with an active projection of his will, and then becomes passive while the God addresses the Universe. In the fourth part he remains silent, listening, to the prayer which arises therefrom."[14]

Now in order to invoke any being, it is said by Hermes Trismegistus that the magi employ three methods. The first, for the vulgar, is that of supplication. In this the crude objective theory is assumed as true. There is a god named A, whom you, B, proceed to petition, in exactly the same sense as a boy might ask his father for pocket-money.

The second method involves a little more subtlety, inasmuch as the magician endeavours to harmonize himself with the nature of the god, and to a certain extent exalts himself, in the course of the ceremony; but the third method is the only one worthy of our consideration.

This consists of a real identification of the magician and the god. Note that to do this in perfection involves the attainment of a species of *samādhi*: and this fact alone suffices to link irrefragably Magick with Mysticism.[15]

---

[13] *MITAP*, Ch. I.
[14] *Ibid.*, Ch. II.
[15] *Ibid.*

According to Crowley, he had abandoned "all serious occult work of every sort, October 3, 1901, and continued in this course of action till July, 1903, when I tried vainly to force myself to become a Buddhist Hermit Highland Laird."[16] The *Old Comment* on AL II.78—"Lift up thyself! for there is none like unto thee among men or among Gods! Lift up thyself, o my prophet, thy stature shall surpass the stars. They shall worship thy name, foursquare, mystic, wonderful, the number of the man; and the name of thy house 418."—says that the "House of the Prophet, not named by him, was chosen by him before he attached any meaning to the number 418; nor had he thought of attaching any importance to the name of the House. He supposed this passage to be mystical, or to refer to some future house. Yet on trial we obtain at once—Boleskine = בולשכין = 418."

In many rituals of ceremonial magick, the operator begins facing "East." In Freemasonry, the Master's Chair is situated in the East, and even referred simply as "The East." The Grand Lodge of a Masonic Jurisdiction is called the "Great East," or in French, the *Grand Orient*. The East is the direction of the rising Sun, of the dawning Light, and *Oriens*, Latin for "rising," was an epithet of the Sun God. According to the Bible, when God drove man out of Paradise, "he placed at the east of the garden of Eden Cherubims, and a flaming sword which turned every way, to keep the way of the tree of life."[17] The word "orientation" originally meant the "arrangement of a building, etc., to face east or any other specified direction," and in Crowley's Ordo Templi Orientis, "Lodges, Profess-Houses, etc. should always be oriented to Boleskine."[18] Likewise, in the Canon of the Mass of the Gnostic Catholic Church, the East is specifically defined as "the direction of Boleskine,"[19] and in *Liber V vel Reguli*, the Magician is directed to "turn his face towards Boleskine, that is the House of The Beast 666."

Commenting on AL III.34—"But your holy place shall be untouched throughout the centuries: though with fire and sword it be burnt down & shattered, yet an invisible house there standeth, and shall stand until the fall of the Great Equinox"—Crowley says, "Taking the 'holy place' to be Boleskine House, it has already been subjected to a sort of destruction. It was presented by me to the O.T.O. and sold in order to obtain funds for the publication of *The Equinox* Volume III. But the proceeds of the sale were mostly stolen by the then Grand Treasurer General of the Order, one George MacNie Cowie."[20] The 18th-century Highland mansion "situated on the South-Eastern shore of Loch Ness in Scotland, two miles east of Foyers,"[21] which Crowley had originally acquired in order to carry out the Abramelin Operation, caught fire in 2015 and lay in ruins today.

According to Crowley, "It was not to the Magician, not to the mystic, it was to a militant member of the Rationalist Press Association that the great Revelation was to be made. It was necessary to prove to him that there was

---

[16] *The Equinox of the Gods, loc. cit.*
[17] Genesis 3:24.
[18] Diary entry, 9 October 1916.
[19] *Liber XV*, Sec. I.
[20] NC on AL III.34.
[21] *Liber XV, loc. cit.*

in actual truth a Sanctuary, that there was in sober earnest a body of Adepts. It matters nothing whether these Adepts are incarnated or discarnated, human or divine. The only point at issue is that there should be conscious Beings in possession of the deepest secrets of Nature, pledged to the uplifting of humanity, filled with Truth, Wisdom and Understanding. It is practical to prove the existence of individuals whose knowledge and power, although not complete—for the nature of Knowledge and Power is such that they can never be complete, since the ideas themselves contain imperfections—are yet enormously greater than aught known to the rest of humanity."[22]

"It was of such a body that our student had heard in the *Cloud upon the Sanctuary*; admission to its adyta had been the guiding hope of his life. His early attainments had tended rather to shake his belief in the existence of such an organization. He had not yet reckoned up the events of his life; he had not yet divined the direction and the set purpose informing their apparently vagrant course. It might have been by chance that whenever he had been confronted with any difficulty the right person had instantly come forward to solve it, whether in the valleys of Switzerland, the mountains of Mexico, or the jungles of the East. At this period of his life he would have scouted the idea as fantastic. He had yet to learn that the story of Balaam and his prophetic ass might be literally true. For the great Message that came to him came, not through the mouth of any person with any pretensions to any knowledge of this or any other sort, but through an empty-headed woman of society."[23]

Crowley describes his first wife, Rose Edith Kelly, thus: "Education strictly social and domestic; she did not even know schoolgirl French. She had read nothing, not so much as novels. She was a miracle of perfection as Poetic Ideal, Mistress, Wife, Mother, House-president, Nurse Pal and Comrade."[24] Yet, he writes, "Practically all the messages received during the 'Cairo Working' (March–April 1904 e.v.) came to me through Ouarda"—or *Warda*, Arabic for Rose. "No woman ever lived who was more ignorant of, or less interested in, anything to do with politics, or the welfare of the race; she cared for nothing beyond her personal comfort and pleasure. When the communications ceased, she dropped the whole affair without a thought."[25]

> She nearly always referred to the authors of these messages as "They": when asked who "They" were, she would say haltingly and stupidly "the gods," or some equally unhelpful term. But she was always absolutely clear and precise as to the instructions. The New Æon was to supersede the old; my special job was to preserve the Sacred Tradition, so that a new Renaissance might in due season rekindle the hidden Light. I was accordingly to make a Quintessence of the Ancient Wisdom, and publish it in as permanent a form as possible. This I did in *The Equinox*. I should perhaps have been strictly classical, and admitted only

---

[22] *The Equinox of the Gods, loc. cit.*, Ch. V.
[23] *Ibid.*
[24] *Ibid.*, Ch. VII, Sec. VIII.
[25] *MWT*, Ch. LXXV.

the "Publication in Class A," "A–B," "B" and "D" material. But I had the idea that it would be a good plan to add all sorts of other stuff, so that people who were not in any way interested in the real Work might preserve their copies.[26]

"Such are *Liber Legis, Liber Cordis Cincti Serpente, Liber Liberi vel Lapidis Lazuli* and such others whose existence may one day be divulged unto you. Beware lest you interpret them either in the Light or in the darkness, for only in L.V.X. may they be understood."[27] But "who, it may be asked, was Aiwass? It is the name given by W. to P. as that of her informant. Also it is the name given as that of the revealer of *Liber Legis*. But whether Aiwass is a spiritual being, or a man known to Fra. P., is a matter of the merest conjecture. His number is 78, that of Mezla, the Channel through which Macroprosopus reveals Himself to, or showers His influence upon, Microprosopus. So we find Fra. P. speaking of him at one time as of another, but more advanced, man; at another time as if it were the name of his own superior in the Spiritual Hierarchy. And to all questions Fra. P. finds a reply, either pointing out 'the subtle metaphysical distinction between curiosity and hard work,' or indicating that among the Brethren 'names are only lies,' or in some other way defeating the very plain purpose of the historian."[28]

"The same remark applies to all queries with regard to V.V.V.V.V.; with this addition, that in this case he condescends to argue and to instruct. 'If I tell you,' he once said to the present writer, 'that V.V.V.V.V. is a Mr Smith and lives at Clapham, you will at once go round and tell everybody that V.V.V.V.V. is a Mr Smith of Clapham, which is not true. V.V.V.V.V. is the Light of the World itself, the sole Mediator between God and Man; and in your present frame of mind (that of a poopstick) you cannot see that the two statements may be identical for the Brothers of the A∴A∴! Did not your great-grandfather argue that no good thing could come out of Nazareth?" Crowley quotes Matthew 13:55–56, "Is not this the carpenter's son? is not his mother called Mary? and his brethren, James, and Joses, and Simon, and Judas? And his sisters, are they not all with us? Whence then hath this man all these things? And they were offended in him."[29]

"We do not know, and it is of no importance that we should know, whether he is an actual person or a magical projection of Frater P., or identical with Aiwass, or anything else, for the reasons previously given when discussing the utterance of Liber Legis, *Equinox* VII, pp. 384 and 385. It is sufficient to say that all the Class A publications of the A∴A∴ should be regarded as not only verbally and liberally inspired by Him, but that this accuracy should be taken to extend even to the style of the letter. If a word is unexpectedly spelt with a capital letter, it must not be thought that this is a mistake; there is some serious reason why it should be so. During this year 1907, therefore, we find a number of such books dictated by him to

---

[26] *Ibid.*
[27] *The Temple of Solomon the King*, Part VIII, "The Poet."
[28] *Ibid.*, Part VI, "The Priest."
[29] *Ibid.*

Frater P. Of the sublimity of these books no words can give expression. It will be noticed that they are totally different in style from Liber Legis, just as both of them are different from any of the writings of Frater P. We may turn for a moment to consider the actual conditions under which he received them. We find the hint of the nature of the communication in Liber LX and Liber VII. On one or two occasions the scribe introduced his thought upon the note, in particular Liber VII, Chapter I, Verse 30, where Verse 29 suggested Verse 30 to Frater P., who wrote it consciously and was corrected in Verse 31. Frater P. is, however, less communicative about this writing than about Liber Legis. It appears that during the whole period of writing he was actually in Samadhi, although, strangely enough, he did not know it himself. It is a question of the transference of the Ego from the personal to the impersonal."[30]

Some have pointed out as significant that these were the only books dictated to Crowley, whereas he dictated most of his major works to his secretaries, but it should be noted that these other dictations took place at a later stage in Crowley's career. According to *Liber 666*, "On the one hand: he was absolutely convinced of the truth of the claims of the Secret Chiefs, of their praeter-human attainments, and of Their right and power to direct the course of events upon this planet. Moreover he was bound to Them by his original oath at his first initiation. On the other hand: he was wholly at variance with great bulk of philosophy and ethics set forth in *Liber AL*. He was filled, in short, with two conflicting currents of enthusiasm and resentment." That is the story Crowley repeated many times in several different places, yet as early as 31 October 1905, he wrote his soon-to-be ex-brother-in-law:

> I am in arms against a world, but after five years of folly and weakness, miscalled politeness, tact, discretion, care for the feeling of others, I am weary of it. Did Christ mince his words with the Pharisees? I say today to hell with Christianity, rationalism, Buddhism, all the lumber of the centuries. I bring you a positive and primaeval fact, magic by name; and with this I will build me a new Heaven and a new Earth. I want none of your faint approval or faint dispraise; I want blasphemy, murder, rape, revolution, anything, bad or good, but strong. I want men behind me, or before me if they can surpass me, but men, men not gentlemen. Bring me your personal vigour; all of it, not your spare vigour. Bring me all the money you have or can force from others. If I can get but seven such men, the world is at my feet. If ten, Heaven will fall at the sound of one trumpet to arms.[31]

"In the year 1909 we find the drawing together of the Paths by which Frater P. had been traveling. First (March 21), the conscious personal work of his life was crystallized in the thorough establishment of his system of Scientific Illuminism or Sceptical Theurgy through the publication of

---

[30] *Ibid.*, Part VIII, "The Poet."
[31] As quoted in Kaczynski 2010, 151.

Number I of the *Equinox*; Second (October 17), he accomplished his purely human duty without which he had no right to become Sannyasin"[32]—a divorce. Sannyasin, or *saṃnyāsin*, Sanskrit for "abandoning" or "throwing down," is the Hindu term for an ascetic who has renounced the world by performing his own funeral and abandoning all claims to social or family standing. The term *saṃnyāsa* makes a brief appearance in the Samhitas, Aranyakas, and Brahmanas, the earliest layers of Vedic literature dating back to the 2nd millennium BCE. It does not, however, appear in ancient Buddhist or Jaina vocabularies, and is first used in the context of those who have given up ritual activity and taken up non-ritualistic spiritual pursuits only in the Brahmanical literature of the 1st millennium BCE.[33] Not until the 5th century CE is it associated with the fourth *ashrama*, or stage of life, and it is uncertain what portion of Sādhus have ever actually exemplified this ideal.[34]

The first three of the four age-based life stages in the Hindu philosophy are Brahmacharya, or "bachelor student," Grihastha, or "householder," and Vanaprastha, or "forest dweller." The fourth stage of Sannyasa is traditionally seen as being for men and women in late years of their life, but young brahmacharis have the choice to skip the householder and retirement stages, renounce worldly ambitions, and dedicate their lives to spiritual pursuits. Depending on the gender, an individual in Sannyasa is known either as a Sannyasin or Sannyasini, which in many ways parallel the Sadhu or Sadhvi traditions of Jain monasticism, the Bhikkhus and Bhikkhunis of Buddhism, and of course, the monks and nuns in Christianity. However, Hinduism has no formal demands or requirements on the spiritual discipline or deity the ascetic must pursue, leading to diversity and significant differences in the lifestyle and goals of those who undertake Sannyasa. The common themes are the renunciation of material desires and prejudices, represented by a state of disinterest and detachment from worldly existence, and a simple, peaceful, typically itinerant life of drifting from place to place.[35]

"In my third year at Cambridge," Crowley writes, "I devoted myself consciously to the Great Work, understanding thereby the Work of becoming a Spiritual Being, free from the constraints, accidents, and deceptions of material existence. I found myself at a loss for a name to designate my work, just as H. P. Blavatsky some years earlier. 'Theosophy', 'Spiritualism', 'Occultism', 'Mysticism', all involved undesirable connotations. I chose therefore the name 'MAGICK' as essentially the most sublime, and actually the most discredited, of all the available terms. I swore to rehabilitate MAGICK, to identify it with my own career; and to compel mankind to respect, love, and trust that which they scorned, hated and feared. I have kept my Word."[36] Ultimately, it is Crowley who was responsible for the proliferation of ceremonial magic within the Western

---

[32] *The Temple of Solomon the King*, Part IX, "Nemo."
[33] Olivelle 2011.
[34] *Idem*. 1993.
[35] Khandelwal 2004.
[36] *MITAP*, Introduction. Emphasis in original.

esoteric circles during the latter half of the 20th century through Israel Regardie, Kenneth Grant, Gerald Gardner, and others. The only bit of magick taught in the original Golden Dawn prior to the grade of Adeptus Minor was the Lesser Banishing Ritual of the Pentagram.

True, the utter chaos amongst all systems of magic and mysticism that has prevailed in the West during the last two thousand years, partially, if not entirely, accounts for the uncritical manner in which these systems have been handled by otherwise critical minds.

Even to-day, though many thousand years after they were first written down, we find a greater simplicity and truth in the ancient rituals and hymns of Egypt and Assyria than in the extraordinary entanglement of systems that came to life during the first five hundred years of Christian era. And in the East, from the most remote antiquity to the present day, scientific systems of illuminism have been in daily practice from the highest to the lowest in the land; though, as we consider, much corrupted by an ignorant priestcraft, by absurd superstitions and by a science which fell to a divine revelation in place of rising to a sublime art.

In the West, for some fifteen hundred years now, Christianity has swayed the minds of men from the Arctic seas to the Mediterranean. At first but one of many small excrescent faiths, which sprang up like fungi amongst the superb *débris* of the religions of Egypt, Babylonia, and Greece, it was not long before (on account of its warlike tenets and the deeply magical nature of its rites *{Primitive Christianity had a greater adaptability than any other contemporary religion of assimilating to itself all that was more particularly pagan in polytheism; the result being that it won over the great masses of the people, who then were, as they are now, inherently conservative.}*) it forced its head and then its arms above the shoulders of its weaker brothers; and when once in a position to strike, so thoroughly bullied all competitors that the few who inwardly stood outside the Church, to save the bruised skins of the faiths they still held dear, were, for self-preservation, bound to clothe them in the tinsel of verbosity, in wild values and extravagant symbols and cyphers; the result being that chaos was heaped upon chaos, till at last all sense became cloaked in a truculent obscurantism. Still, by him who has eyes will it be seen that through all this darkness there shone the glamour of a great and beautiful Truth.

Little is it to be wondered then, in these present shallow intellectual days, that almost any one who has studied, or even heard of, the theories of any notorious nobody of the moment at once relegates to the museum or the waste-paper basket these theories and systems, which were once the very blood of the world, and which in truth are so still, though few suspect it.

Truth is Truth; and the Truth of yesterday is the Truth of to-day, and the Truth of to-day is the Truth of to-morrow. Our quest, then, is to find Truth, and to cut the kernel from the husk, the text from the comment.[37]

"There are a number of people of shallow wit who do not believe in Magick. This is doubtless partly due to the bad presentation of the subject by previous Masters. I have identified Magick with the Art of Life. The transcendental superstructure will not overburden those who have laid this Right Foundation."[38] This "Science of Life complete and perfect" is "the chief secret of the Ancients, and if the keys have never been actually lost, they have certainly been little used. Again, the confusion of thought caused by the ignorance of the people who did not understand it has discredited the whole subject. It is now our task to re-establish this science in its perfection. To do this we must criticize the Authorities; some of them have made it too complex, others have completely failed in such simple matters as coherence. Many of the writers are empirics, still more mere scribes, while by far the largest class of all is composed of stupid charlatans."[39] As Regardie puts it, the "elaborate Golden Dawn system became part of Crowley's own inner world" and he "carried it further than even the Golden Dawn principals had envisaged. I know of nothing within the Order documentary that even hints at the kind of visionary and spiritual experience that Crowley managed to get out of it."[40]

I took the Order with absolute seriousness. I was not even put off by the fact of its ceremonies taking place at Mark Mason's Hall. I remember asking Baker whether people often died during the ceremony. I had no idea that it was a flat formality and that the members were for the most part muddled middle-class mediocrities. I saw myself entering the Hidden Church of the Holy Grail. This state of my soul served me well. My initiation was in fact a sacrament.

The rituals have been printed in *The Equinox*, vol. I, Nos. II and III. There is no question that those of neophyte and adept are the genuine rituals of initiation, for they contain the true formulae. The proof is that they can be made to work by those who understand and know how to apply them. Shallow critics argue that because the average untrained man cannot evoke a spirit, the ritual which purports to enable him to do so must be at fault. He does not reflect that an electroscope would be useless in the hands of a savage. Indubitably, Magick is one of the subtlest and most difficult of the sciences and arts. There is more opportunity for errors of comprehension, judgment and practice than in any other branch of physics. It is above all needful for the student to be armed with scientific knowledge, sympathetic apprehension and common sense. My training in mathematics and chemistry supplied me with the first of these qualities; my poetic affinities and wide reading

---

[37] *The Temple of Solomon the King*, Preface.
[38] NC on AL II.54.
[39] *Book 4*, Part II, Preliminary Remarks.
[40] Regardie 1970, 387.

with the second; while, for the third, I suppose I have to thank my practical ancestors.[41]

The opening pages of *The Key of the Mysteries*, as translated by Crowley, quote *Les Soirées de Saint-Pétersbourg* (1821) by J. De Maistre: "Religion says:—'Believe and you will understand.' Science comes to say to you:—'Understand and you will believe.' At that moment the whole of science will change front; the spirit, so long dethroned and forgotten, will take its ancient place; it will be demonstrated that the old traditions are all true, that the whole of paganism is only a system of corrupted and misplaced truths, that it is sufficient to cleanse them, so to say, and to put them back again in their place, to see them shine with all their rays." In the *Paradoxes of the Highest Science*, Lévi writes: "High magic is at once Religion and Science. This alone harmonises contraries by explaining the laws of equilibrium and of analogies. This alone can make sovereign Pontiffs infallible and Monarchs absolute; the Sacerdotal art is also the Royal art, and Count Joseph de Maistre was not deceived, when despairing of extinguished beliefs and enfeebled powers, he turned his glances, against his will, towards the sanctuaries of Occultism. It is thence that salvation will come, and already it is revealing itself to the most advanced intelligences."[42]

Maistre, a French-speaking Savoyard, was a key figure of the Counter-Enlightenment,[43] who saw monarchy both as a divinely sanctioned institution and the only stable form of government. The eldest of ten siblings, he graduated with a law degree from the University of Turin in 1772, and eventually followed his father's footsteps by becoming a Senator in 1787.[44] In 1773, Maistre joined one of the first Masonic lodges on continental Europe, La Parfaite Union at Chambéry, and in 1778, co-founded Le Sincérité Lodge of the "Rectified Scottish Rite" headed by the Martinist Jean-Baptiste Willermoz.[45] Maistre originally favoured political reform in France, supporting the efforts of the magistrates of the Parlements to force Louis XVI to convene the Estates General. However, he interpreted the Revolution of 1789 as a Providential event: in his view, the Ancien Régime, instead of directing the influence of the French civilization to the benefit of mankind, had promoted the atheistic doctrines of the Enlightenment *philosophes*; he claimed that the crimes of the Reign of Terror were the logical consequence of the rationalist rejection of Christianity by the French ruling class, as well as its divinely-decreed punishment.[46]

Maistre received his early classical education from the Jesuits, and after the Revolution, became an ardent defender of their Order, increasingly

---

[41] *Confessions*, Ch. 20.
[42] Lévi 1922, 128-9.
[43] Berlin 2003.
[44] Lebrun 1965.
[45] Dermenghem 1946.
[46] Lebrun, *op. cit.* As Maistre himself phrased it in an 1810 letter to Count Jan Potocki, "The patrician is a secular priest: national religion is his first and most sacred property, for it preserves his privilege, which is always lost together with it. There is no greater crime for a nobleman than that of attacking the dogmas." (Maistre 1861, ii.247.)

associating the revolutionary spirit with the Jesuits' traditional enemies, the Jansenists. He called for the restoration of the House of Bourbon and argued that the Pope should have ultimate authority in temporal matters.[47] In 1802, he was sent to Saint Petersburg as ambassador to Tsar Alexander I of Russia. Maistre's observations on Russian life, contained in his diplomatic memoirs and in his personal correspondence, were among Tolstoy's sources for his great epic novel *War and Peace*.[48] In addition to his voluminous correspondence, Maistre left two books that were published posthumously, *Examen de la Philosophie de Bacon* (1836), a pointed critique of the experimental philosophy of Sir Francis Bacon, and the above-quoted *Soirées de St-Pétersbourg*, a theodicy in the form of a Platonic dialogue, conceived as early as 1810.[49] In 1817, after the defeat of Napoleon and the restoration of the House of Savoy's dominion over Piedmont and Savoy, Maistre returned to Turin and served there as magistrate and minister of state until his death in 1821. He was buried in the Jesuit Church of the Holy Martyrs, and his ritual apron was long on display at the masonic museum of the Grand Orient of France.[50]

Together with the Irish statesman and philosopher Edmund Burke, Maistre is commonly regarded as one of the founders of European conservatism. Since their time, Maistre's traditional Throne-and-Altar conception of conservatism has, of course, greatly declined in political influence in comparison with the more utilitarian conservatism of Burke. Interestingly, however, Maistre's writings influenced not only conservative political thinkers, but also Utopian Socialists, and early sociologists such as Henri de Saint-Simon and Auguste Comte expressly acknowledge his influence on their own thinking, e.g. in regard to the sources of social cohesion and political authority.[51] Maistre himself was influenced by the ideas of Martinez de Pasqually and Louis Claude de Saint-Martin, whose "Martinist" traditionalism was based on an amalgam of Catholic dogma and esoteric Freemasonry. Baudelaire, whose *Little Poems in Prose* Crowley translated into English, called Maistre "le grand génie de notre temps—un voyant"[52] and Maistre's ideas are echoed everywhere in the great French

---

[47] Armenteros 2011.
[48] Berlin, *op. cit.*
[49] To be sure, Maistre was an Anglophile who much admired Bacon's legal and political thought, as exemplified in an 1815 letter to the Count de Noailles: "I don't know how I found myself led to mortal combat with the late Chancellor Bacon. We *boxed* like two Fleet Street *toughs*, and if he pulled some of my hair, I'm also sure his wig is no longer in place." (As translated in Maistre 1998, xi. Emphasis in original.) However, he argued (*Idem.* 1959, 54) that "if we do not return to the old maxims, if the guidance of education is not returned to the priests, and if science is not uniformly relegated to a subordinate rank, incalculable evil awaits us. We shall become brutalized by science, and that is the worst sort of brutality."
[50] Ironically, writes Lévi, "Masonry has not merely been profaned but has served as the veil and pretext of anarchic conspiracies depending from the secret influence of the vindicators of Jacques de Molay, and of those who continued the schismatic work of the Temple. In place of avenging the death of Hiram they have avenged that of his assassins. The anarchists have resumed the rule, square and mallet, writing upon them the words Liberty, Equality, Fraternity—Liberty, that is to say, for all the lusts, Equality in degradation and Fraternity in the work of destruction. Such are the men whom the Church has condemned justly and will condemn for ever." (1913, 388.)
[51] Armenteros, *op. cit.*
[52] Letter to Alphonse Toussenel, 21 January 1856, as quoted in Jones 1951, 8.

poet. *Les Soirées*, with its explicit references to Illuminism, contributed important motifs to making *The Flowers of Evil*.[53]

What is the theory implied in such rituals as those of the *Goëtia*? What does the Magician do? He applies himself to invoke a God, and this God compels the appearance of a spirit whose function is to perform the Will of the magician at the moment. There is no trace of what may be called machinery in the method. The exorcist hardly takes the pains of preparing a material basis for the spirit to incarnate except the bare connection of himself with his sigil. It is apparently assumed that the spirit already possesses the means of working on matter. The conception seems to be that of a schoolboy who asks his father to tell the butler to do something for him. In other words, the theory is grossly animistic. The savage tribes described by Frazer had a far more scientific theory. The same may be said of witches, who appear to have been wiser than the thaumaturgists who despised them. They at least made waxen images—identified by baptism—of the people they wished to control. They at least used appropriate bases for magical manifestations, such as blood and other vehicles of animal force, with those of vegetable virtue such as herbs. They were also careful to put their bewitched products into actual contact—material or astral—with their victims. The classical exorcists, on the contrary, for all their learning, were careless about this essential condition. They acted as stupidly as people who should write business letters and omit to post them.

It is not too much to say that this failure to understand the conditions of success accounts for the discredit into which Magick fell until Éliphas Lévi undertook the task of rehabilitating it two generations ago.[54] But even he (profoundly as he studied, and luminously as he expounded, the nature of Magick considered as a universal formula) paid no attention whatever to that question of the Magical Link, though he everywhere implies that it is essential to the Work. He evaded the question by making the *petitio principii* of assigning to the Astral Light the power of transmitting vibrations of all kinds. He nowhere enters into detail as to how its effects are produced. He does not inform us as to the qualitative or quantitative laws of this light. (The scientifically-trained student will observe the analogy between Lévi's postulate and that of ordinary science *in re* the luminiferous ether.)[55]

According to Lévi, "It is possible to magnetize in two ways: first, in acting by will upon the plastic medium of another person, whose will and whose acts are, in consequence, subordinated to that action. Secondly, in

---

[53] *Ibid.*
[54] *Cf.* e.g. *MWT*, Ch. LXXXI: "To study Magick, *Book 4*, Parts II, III (*Magick in Theory and Practice*) and IV (*The Equinox of the Gods*.) Add *The Book of Thoth* and there you are:—'Being furnished with complete armour and armed, he is similar to the goddess.' Of other writers, you have *The Book of the Sacred Magic of Abramelin the Mage*, and any of the works of Eliphaz Lévi. But that's all."
[55] *MITAP*, Ch. XIV.

acting through the will of another, either by intimidation, or by persuasion, so that the influenced will modifies at our pleasure the plastic medium and the acts of that person. One magnetizes by radiation, by contact, by look, or by word. The vibrations of the voice modify the movement of the astral light, and are a powerful vehicle of magnetism."[56] As Crowley puts it, "Let the Magical Link be made strong! It is 'love under will'; it affirms the identity of the Equation of the work; it makes success Necessity."[57]

Crowley prepared "all things by his arcane science and wisdom, choosing only those symbols which were common to all systems, and rigorously rejecting all names and words which might be supposed to imply any religious or metaphysical theory. To do this utterly was found impossible, since all language has a history, and the use (for example) of the word 'spirit' implies the Scholastic Philosophy and the Hindu and Taoist theories concerning the breath of man. So was it difficult to avoid implication of some undesirable bias by using the words 'order,' 'circle,' 'chapter,' 'society,' 'brotherhood,' or any other to designate the body of initiates. . . . Deliberately, therefore, did he take refuge in Vagueness. Not to veil the truth to the Neophyte, but to warn him against valuing non-essentials. Should therefore the candidate hear the name of any God, let him not rashly assume that it refers to any known God, save only the God known to himself. Or should the ritual speak in terms (however vague) which seem to imply Egyptian, Taoist, Buddhist, Indian, Persian, Greek, Judaic, Christian, or Moslem philosophy, let him reflect that this is a defect of language; the literary limitation and not the spiritual prejudice of" Crowley himself. "Especially let him guard against the finding of definite sectarian symbols in the teaching of his master, and the reasoning from the known to the unknown which assuredly will tempt him."[58]

But, hold on, is Crowley not the Beast prophesied in the Biblical Book of Revelation? Well, kind of—it is certainly what his feverishly Christian mother called him as a boy: "When I went to Russia to learn the language for the Diplomatic Service, my mother half believed that I had 'gone to see Gog and Magog' (who were supposed to be Russian giants) in order to arrange the date of the Battle of Armageddon. In a way, my mother was insane, in the sense that all people are who have watertight compartments to the brain, and hold with equal passion incompatible ideas, and hold them apart lest their meeting should destroy both. . . . But my mother believed that I was actually Antichrist of the Apocalypse and also her poor lost erring son who might yet repent and be redeemed by the Precious Blood."[59]

As we have already established, the Revelation of St. John is not necessarily a book of prophecy, or even an original work. The most elusive tome of all the canonical scriptures, it was the last one to be accepted to the official list of books in the Bible. Its title is derived from the first word of the Greek text, *apokalypsis*, meaning "unveiling"—or "revelation." It is also the only eschatological document in the New Testament, although there are

---

[56] *The Key of the Mysteries*, Part II, Book I, Ch. I.
[57] *MITAP, loc. cit.*
[58] *The Temple of Solomon the King*, Part VIII, "The Poet."
[59] *Confessions*, Ch. 48.

short eschatological passages in both the Gospels and the Epistles. As General Albert Pike, perhaps the most famous Freemason in America and the only Confederate military officer with an outdoor statue in Washington, D.C., writes, "The Apocalypse or Revelations, by whomever written, belongs to the Orient and to extreme antiquity. It reproduces what is far older than itself. It paints, with the strongest colors that the Oriental genius ever employed, the closing scenes of the great struggle of Light, and Truth, and Good, against Darkness, Error, and Evil; personified in that between the New Religion on one side, and Paganism and Judaism on the other. It is a particular application of the ancient myth of Ormuzd and his Genii against Ahriman and his Devs; and it celebrates the final triumph of Truth against the combined powers of men and demons."[60]

"The ideas and imagery are borrowed from every quarter; and allusions are found in it to the doctrines of all ages. We are continually reminded of the Zend-Avesta, the Jewish Codes, Philo, and the Gnosis. The Seven Spirits surrounding the Throne of the Eternal, at the opening of the Grand Drama, and acting so important a part throughout, everywhere the first instruments of the Divine Will and Vengeance, are the Seven Amshaspands of Parsism; as the Twenty-four Ancients, offering to the Supreme Being the first supplications and the first homage, remind us of the Mysterious Chiefs of Judaism, foreshadow the Eons of Gnosticism, and re-produce the twenty-four Good Spirits created by Ormuzd and inclosed in an egg. The Christ of the Apocalypse, First-born of Creation and of the Resurrection, is invested with the characteristics of the Ormuzd and Sosiosch of the Zend-Avesta, the Ainsoph of the Kabalah and the Carpistes [Καρπιστης] of the Gnostics. The idea that the true Initiates and Faithful become Kings and Priests, is at once Persian, Jewish, Christian, and Gnostic. And the definition of the Supreme Being, that He is at once Alpha and Omega, the beginning and the end—He that was, and is, and is to come, *i.e.*, Time illimitable, is Zoroaster's definition of Zerouane-Akherene."[61]

Crowley published a review by the eminent Masonic scholar John Yarker of *The Apocalypse Unsealed: Being an Esoteric Interpretation of the Initiations of Ioannes* by James Morgan Pryse in *The Equinox*, Vol. I, No. 6. "The Freemasons too in their higher grades, which have more or less reached us through the Rosicrucians, have very strong allusions to the Apocalypse, and may profit by it, and this refers to several systems practised throughout the world. Thus the Order of Hérédom (Harodim) Rosy Cross, which has an unchanged Ritual from 1740, at least, draws upon Dionysius the Areopagite, a disciple of St Paul, and it has also a rhythmetical description of the New Jerusalem. Again, two entire degrees of the Scottish Rite of 33° are drawn from the Apocalypse, and certainly entered the Rite before 1758, and seem as if they were drawn bodily from the Rosicrucian Militia of the Cross: I allude to the 17° Knight of the East and West, and the 19° of Grand Pontiff, which treat upon the Heavenly Jerusalem, and the opening scene of the Revelations."

---

[60] Pike 1874, 272.
[61] *Ibid.*, 272–3.

"The idea that Revelation is a book of Initiation is not altogether new to Freemasons, as the late Dr Geo. Oliver elaborated that view at considerable length, but Mr Pryse's view is quite a different sort of Initiation; it is the development of the semi-miraculous powers of the Gnosis of Clement, Origen, and the early Christian Church, the birth of the divine three principles, the Crestos, in the human soul. The key to this 'Unsealing' is the text itself, in which is found the Nos. 333, 444, 666, 777, 888, 999, 1000, as applied to the seven principal *chakras* of the human body, as taught by Greek Yogis. Apart altogether from the possession of a reliable literal translation of the book, there are seventy-five pages upon the development of the *Kundalini*, and each subject is followed in the text by a commentary in application. Mr Pryse expresses the view that the book is necessarily incomprehensible to the conventional theologian, yet easily comprehended by the esoteric Initiate, *i.e.* by him who possesses the Gnosis, and that the drama is perfect in all its parts. I may add that most of this class of Initiative books had a double interpretation, and hence that the same may be equally found in the Apocalypse, but into this Mr Pryse does not enter."

To this, Crowley appended his own pseudonymous note: "Unfortunately, too, he has studied Eastern Mysticism at second-hand, through Theosophical spectacles. Nor has he kept even to Blavatsky the genius, but relied upon her commentators, who had neither her learning nor her experience. But he has the key, and it opens the way for a real study of 'St John' by a person of greater ability. It is a very remarkable fact, however, that Akrasia (333) and Akolasia (333) should so accurately describe Choronzon (333). No higher test of the truth of 'The Vision and the Voice' could be desired. Again, 666 is Ἡ Φρην, not the Lower Mind, as Mr Pryse unhellenically says, but Tiphereth, the Lion that lieth down with the Lamb." However, it might not hurt to keep in mind that Revelation is *not* a Thelemic "holy book."

The Bible is included in the Curriculum of A∴A∴ under Section 2, "Other books, principally fiction, of a generally suggestive and helpful kind." It is described as being a work "by various authors unknown. The Hebrew and Greek Originals are of Qabalistic value. It contains also many magical apologues, and recounts many tales of folklore and magical rites." The same section also includes "Books of Fairy Tales generally. Oriental Classics generally. Sufi Poetry generally. Greek and Latin Classics generally. Scandinavian and Teutonic Sagas generally. Celtic Folk-Lore generally. This course is of general value to the beginner. While it is not to be taken, in all cases, too seriously, it will give him a general familiarity with mystical and magical tradition, create a deep interest in the subject, and suggest many helpful lines of thought."

In *The Equinox of the Gods*, Crowley writes, "being lifted up, I will draw the whole world unto me; and men shall worship me the Beast, Six Hundred and Three-score and Six, celebrating to Me their Midnight Mass every time soever when they do that they will, and on Mine altar slaying to Me that victim I most relish, their Selves; when Love designs and Will executes the Rite whereby (an they know it or not) their God in man is offered to me The Beast, their God, the Rite whose virtue, making their God of their throned Beast, leaves nothing, howso bestial, undivine. On such lines my own 'conversion' to my own 'religion' may take place, though as I write these words all but twelve weeks of Sixteen years are well nigh past." The footnote points out that, "666 had been taken by Fra. P. as the number of His own Name (The Beast) long years before, in His childhood."[62] Even in Court, when asked under oath "Did you not call yourself The Beast 666?" Crowley famously answered "'The Beast 666' means merely 'sunlight'. You may call me 'Little Sunshine'."[63]

"The 'magical numbers' of the Sun are, according to tradition, 6, (6 × 6) = 36, (666 ÷ 6) = 111, and Σ (1–36) = 666."[64] According to *An Essay upon Number*, 666 is "Last of the mystic numbers of the sun. שרות, the spirit of Sol. Also עממו שתן, Ommo Satan, the Satanic Trinity of Typhon, Apophis, and Besz; also שם יהשוה, the name of Jesus. The names of Nero, Napoleon, W. E. Gladstone, and any person that you may happen to dislike, add up the this number. In reality it is the final extension of the number 6, both because 6 × 111 (אלף = 111 = 1) = 6 and because the Sun, whose greatest number it is, is 6."[65] It was chosen by Crowley as his symbol, partly for the reasons given above, "partly for the reasons given in the Apocalypse. I took the Beast to be the Lion (Leo my rising sign) and Sol, 6, 666, the Lord of Leo on which Babalon should ride. And there were other more intimate considerations, unnecessary to enter upon in this place. Note however that the Tarot card of Leo, Strength, bears the number XI, the great number of the Magnum Opus, and its interchange with Justice, VIII.; and the key of 8 is 418."[66]

Commenting on AL II.78, Crowley counsels that "the verse need not imply the establishment of a new cult with myself as Demigod. (Help!) But they shall worship the group of ideas connected with the Sun, and the magical formula of the number 418, explained elsewhere."[67] As we learn in *Isis Unveiled*, "From the first to the last Chapters, the translators of the Jewish Sacred Book misconstrued this meaning. They have even changed the spelling of the name of God, as Sir W. Drummond proves. Thus *El*, if written correctly, would read *Al*, for it stands in the original לא—Al, and, according to Higgins, this word means the god Mithra, the *Sun*, the preserver and savior. Sir W. Drummond shows that *Beth-El* means the House of the *Sun* in its literal translation, and not of God. '*El*, in the composition of these Canaanite names, does not signify *Deus*, but *Sol*.' Thus Theology has disfigured ancient Theosophy, and Science and ancient Philosophy." The footnote continues: "The absolute necessity for the perpetuation of such pious frauds by the early fathers and later theologians becomes apparent, if we consider that if they had allowed the word *Al* to remain as in the original, it would have become but too evident—except for

---

[62] *The Equinox of the Gods, loc. cit.*, Ch. VII, Sec. I.
[63] Court transcript, *Crowley v. Constable & Co.*
[64] *The Equinox of the Gods, loc. cit.*, Sec. III, fn.
[65] *An Essay upon Number*, Part I, Sec. IV.
[66] *Ibid.*, Part II.
[67] NC on AL II.78.

the initiated—that the *Jehovah* of Moses and the sun were identical. The multitudes, which ignore that the ancient hierophant considered our *visible* sun but an emblem of the central, invisible, and spiritual Sun, would have accused Moses—as many of our modern commentators have already done—of worshipping the planetary bodies; in short, of actual Sabaeanism."[68]

According to the *New Comment* on AL III.22, "There are to be no regular temples of Nuit and Hadit, for They are incommensurables and absolutes. Our religion therefore, for the People, is the Cult of the Sun, who is our particular star of the Body of Nuit, from whom, in the strictest scientific sense, come this earth, a chilled spark of Him, and all our Light and Life. His vice-regent and representative in the animal kingdom is His cognate symbol the Phallus, representing Love and Liberty. Ra-Hoor-Khuit, like all true Gods, is therefore a Solar-Phallic deity. But we regard Him as He is in truth, eternal; the Solar-Phallic deities of the old Æon, such as Osiris, 'Christ', Hiram, Adonis, Hercules, &c., were supposed, through our ignorance of the Cosmos, to 'die' and 'rise again'. Thus we celebrated rites of 'crucifixion' and so on, which have now become meaningless. Ra-Hoor-Khuit is the Crowned and Conquering Child. This is also a reference to the 'Crowned' and Conquering 'Child' in ourselves, our own personal God. Except ye become as little children, said 'Christ', ye shall not enter into the Kingdom of God. The Kingdom of Malkuth, the Virgin Bride, and the Child is the Dwarf-Self, the Phallic consciousness, which is the true life of Man, beyond his 'veils' of incarnation." The Glossary at the end of *Book 4*, Part II, defines "Malkah" as a "young girl. The 'bride.' The unredeemed soul," while "Malkuth" is of course Hebrew for "The kingdom," and "10th 'emanation' of the Absolute."

As Lévi writes in *The Key of the Mysteries*, Part I, Article V, "Solution of the Problem—To Separate Religion from Superstition and Fanaticism," "Superstition, from the Latin word *superstes*, surviving, is the sign which survives the idea which it represents; it is the form preferred to the thing, the rite without reason, faith become insensate through isolating itself. It is in consequence the corpse of religion, the death of life, stupefaction substituted for inspiration. Fanaticism is superstition become passionate, its name comes from the word *fanum*, which signifies 'temple,' it is the temple put in place of God, it is the human and temporal interest of the priest substituted for the honour of priesthood, the wretched passion of the man exploiting the faith of the believer." Crowley notes that, "The letters *aleph* and *lamed* are infinitely important in this Æon of Horus; they are indeed the Key of the Book of the Law. No more can be said in this place than that *aleph* is Harpocrates, Bacchus Diphues, the Holy Ghost, the 'Pure Fool' or Innocent Babe who is also the Wandering Singer who impregnates the King's Daughter with Himself as Her Child; *lamed* is the King's Daughter, satisfied by Him, holding His 'Sword and Balances' in her lap. These weapons are the Judge, armed with power to execute His Will, and

---

[68] Blavatsky 1877, i.13.

Two Witnesses 'in whom shall every Truth be established' in accordance with whose testimony he gives judgment."[69]

The *Djeridensis Comment* on AL I.62-63 says this of Nuit's public cult: "Her image, she being All-Desired, shall be a living Woman, calling to her that Spirit which shall make her perfect in Event." According to the *New Comment* on AL III.49, "The evident interpretation of this is to take the word to be 'Do what thou wilt,' which is a secret word, because its meaning for every man is his own inmost secret. And it is the most profound blasphemy possible against all 'gods of men,' because it makes every man his own God. We may then take it that this Solar-Phallic Ra Ha is Each Man Himself. As each independent cell in our bodies is to us, so is each of us to Heru-Ra-Ha. Each man's 'child'-consciousness is a Star in the Cosmos of the Sun, as the Sun is a Star in the Cosmos of Nuit." The above-mentioned Glossary defines "Ankh" or "Crux Ansata" as "The Symbol of 'Life.' A form of the Rosy Cross," and "Lingam-Yoni" as another "form of the Rosy Cross." "Lingam" is defined as "The Unity or Male Principle. But these have many symbols, *e.g.*, sometimes Yoni is 0 or 3 and Lingam 2."

Speaking about the eagle of the Sphinx, Crowley tells his magical son, "This Lion and Dragon are therefore of thy Self, and the Man and the Bull the Feminine Counterparts thereof, being the Grace of Our Lady BABALON that She bestoweth upon thee in thine Adultery with Her. They are then as a Vesture of Honour, and a Reward, that are won by the Intensity of thy Light and of thy Love. So properly we esteem Men by the Measure of their Intelligence and of their Strength, since they are equal in their essential Godhead, so far as concerneth the Quiddity thereof. See thou closely moreover unto it, that if thou be well favoured of Our Lady, thy Lion and thy Dragon grow in like Measure, for the Excess of the Feminine is Dead Weight. The Intellectual without Virility is a Dreamer of Follies, and the laborious Giant without Courage is a Slave."[70]

Now, according to Crowley, "there is a special incarnation of Nuit and Hadit for the Beast and the Scarlet Woman, as opposed to the general truth that every man and woman are images of these ineffable Beings. . . . The Scarlet Woman and I are peculiarly representative of Nuit and Hadit by virtue of our attainments in making our consciousness omniform as They are. It must not be supposed that our original individualities can claim any special prerogatives as such."[71] Hindu deities, like Shiva, are said to have several incarnations, known as Avatars. For example, various traditions regard the sages Durvasa and Agastya, and the philosophers Shankara and Ashwatthama, as avatars of Shiva. The *New Comment* on AL I.15 quotes the Hermetic maxim, "That which is beneath is like that which is above. The Beast and the Scarlet Woman are avatars of Tao and Teh, Shiva and Sakti. This Law is then an exact image of the Great Law of the Cosmos; this is an assurance of its Perfection."

---

[69] *MITAP*, Ch. IV, fn.
[70] *Liber Aleph*, "Prologomena de silentio."
[71] NC on AL I.17.

It is necessary to say here that The Beast appears to be a definite individual; to wit, the man Aleister Crowley. But the Scarlet Woman is an officer replaceable as need arises. Thus to this present date of writing, Anno XVI, Sun in Sagittarius, there have been several holders of the title.

1. Rose Edith Crowley née Kelly, my wife. Put me in touch with Aiwas; see *Equinox* I, 7, "The Temple of Solomon the King." Failed as elsewhere is on record.

2. A doubtful case. Mary d'Este Sturges née Dempsey. Put me in touch with Abuldiz; hence helped with *Book 4*. Failed from personal jealousies.

3. Jeanne Robert Foster née Oliver. Bore the "child" to whom this Book refers later. Failed from respectability.

4. Roddie Minor. Brought me in touch with Amalantrah. Failed from indifference to the Work.

5. A doubtful case, Marie Rohling née Lavroff. Helped to inspire *Liber CXI*. Failed from indecision.

6. A doubtful case, Bertha Almira Prykryl née Bruce. Delayed assumption of duties, hence made way for No. 7.

7. Leah Hirsig. Assisted me in actual initiation; still at my side, An XVII, Sol in Sagittarius. (P.S. & An XIX, Sol in Aries).[72]

In *The Equinox of the Gods*, Crowley makes clear that, "Where the text is simple straightforward English, I shall not seek, or allow, and interpretation at variance with it. I may admit a Qabalistic or cryptographic secondary meaning when such confirms, amplifies, deepens, intensifies, or clarifies the obvious common-sense significance; but only if it be part of the general plan of the 'latent light,' and self-proven by abundant witness. For example: 'To me!' (I, 65) is to be taken primarily in its obvious sense as the Call of Nuith to us Her stars. The transliteration 'TO MH' may be admitted as the 'signature' of Nuith, identifying Her as the speaker; because these Greek Words mean 'The Not,' which is Her Name. This Gematria of TO MH may be admitted as further confirmation, because their number 418 is elsewhere manifested as that of the Æon. But TO MH is not to be taken as negating the previous verses, or 418 as indicating the formula of approach to Her, although in point of fact it is so, being the Rubrick of the Great Work. I refuse to consider mere appropriateness as conferring title to authority, and to read my own personal theories into the Book. I insist that all interpretation shall be incontestably authentic, neither less, more, nor other than was meant is the Mind of Aiwaz."[73]

In *Magick in Theory and Practice*, writing on "the subject of Black Magic," Crowley touches lightly on "the question of Pacts with the Devil"—"The Devil does not exist. It is a false name invented by the Black Brothers to imply a Unity in their ignorant muddle of dispersions. A devil who had unity would be a God." Again, the footnote goes into much more detail:

---

[72] NC on AL I.15.
[73] *The Equinox of the Gods, loc. cit.,* Sec. VIII.

"'The Devil' is, historically, the God of any people that one personally dislikes. This has led to so much confusion of thought that THE BEAST 666 has preferred to let names stand as they are, and to proclaim simply that AIWAZ—the solar-phallic-hermetic 'Lucifer' is His own Holy Guardian Angel, and 'The Devil' SATAN or HADIT of our particular unit of the Starry Universe. This serpent, SATAN, is not the enemy of Man, but He who made Gods of our race, knowing Good and Evil; He bade 'Know Thyself!' and taught Initiation. He is 'the Devil' of the Book of Thoth, and His emblem is BAPHOMET, the Androgyne who is the hieroglyph of arcane perfection. The number of His Atu is XV, which is *yod he*, the Monogram of the Eternal, the Father one with the Mother, the Virgin Seed one with all-containing Space. He is therefore Life, and Love. But moreover his letter is *ayin*, the Eye; he is Light, and his Zodiacal image is Capricornus, that leaping goat whose attribute is Liberty. (Note that the 'Jehovah' of the Hebrews is etymologically connected with these. The classical example of such antinomy, one which has led to such disastrous misunderstandings, is that between NU and HAD, North and South, Jesus and John. The subject is too abstruse and complicated to be discussed in detail here. The student should consult the writings of Sir R. Payne Knight, General Forlong, Gerald Massey, Fabre d'Olivet; etc. etc., for the data on which these considerations are ultimately based.)"[74]

The description of the above Atu XV in *The Book of Thoth* puts it thus: "Saturn, the ruler, is Set, the ass-headed god of the Egyptian deserts; he is the god of the south. The name refers to all gods containing these consonants, such as Shaitan, or Satan.... Essential to the symbolism are the surroundings—barren places, especially high places. The cult of the mountain is an exact parallel. The Old Testament is full of attacks upon kings who celebrated worship in 'high places'; this, although Zion itself was a mountain! This feeling persisted, even to the days of the Witches' Sabbath, held, if possible, on a desolate summit, but (if none were available) at least in a wild spot, uncontaminated by the artfulness of men. Note that Shabbathai, the 'sphere of Saturn', is the Sabbath. Historically, the animus against witches pertains to the fear of the Jews; whose rites, supplanted by the Christian forms of Magic, had become mysterious and terrible. Panic suggested that Christian children were stolen, sacrificed, and eaten. The belief persists to this day." According to *Liber CCVII: Syllabus of A∴A∴*, "the true secret of all practical magick" is contained in *Liber A'ASH vel Capricorni Pneumatici*.

If we view Hell as the subconscious mind, that makes the guardian demon, as Satan, its ruler. Or, as the *New Comment* on AL I.7 phrases it, "Aiwass is then, as this verse 7 states, the 'minister' of this Hoor-paar-kraat, that is of the Saviour of the World in the larger sense, and of mine own 'Silent Self' in the lesser." According to Crowley, "The whole of his magical career is best interpreted as the performance of this Operation. One must not suppose that Initiation is a formality, observing the 'unities,' like being

---

[74] *MITAP*, Ch. XXI, Sec. II. Emphasis in original.

made a Mason. All life pertains to the process, and it pervades the whole personality; the official recognition of attainment is merely a token of what had taken place."[75] In fact, "the Single Supreme Ritual is the attainment of the Knowledge and Conversation of the Holy Guardian Angel. It is the *raising of the complete man in a vertical straight line.* Any deviation from this line tends to become black magic. Any other operation *is* black magic."[76]

"Of course, the reason why one does not do these things is that in the trance Atmadarshana, on the threshold of masterpiece, one loses one's Ego for ever. Thenceforth the man exists only as a vehicle for an Impersonal Master; he lives his own life, and does his own duty, but the Master in him doesn't care what happens to him."[77] Crowley, or "The MASTER THERION himself, with all his successes in every kind of Magick, sometimes appears utterly impotent to perform feats which almost any amateur might do, because He has matched his Will against that of the world, having undertaken the Work of a Magus to establish the word of His Law on the whole of mankind. He will succeed, without doubt, but He hardly expects to see more than a sample of His product during His present incarnation. But He refuses to waste the least fraction of His force on works foreign to His WORK, however obvious it may seem to the onlooker that His advantage lies in commanding stones to become bread, or otherwise making things easy for Himself."[78]

"We learn further from Patanjali that 'concentration on the well of the throat' causes hunger to cease, which explains how Jesus was to resist the temptation of Satan to turn stones into bread."[79] As Crowley observes, "I am always being asked why, if I have all these powers, I do not cause stones to become bread, and throw myself from the Woolworth Building in order to prove the truth of the Ninety-first Psalm, and obtain all the kingdoms of the earth at slight cost to self-respect. Why did Christ refuse in the Temptation on the Mount? It is the same story: I am come to do the Will of Him that sent me. And if I have to die on the cross, that is better than living on it!"[80] Then again, who else but the Beast would even be capable of overturning the Christian paradigm? "Before I touched my teens, I was already aware that I was THE BEAST whose number is 666. I did not understand in the least what that implied; it was a passionately ecstatic sense of identity."[81]

"The doctrine of resurrection as vulgarly understood is false and absurd. It is not even 'Scriptural'. St. Paul does not identify the glorified body which rises with the mortal body which dies. On the contrary, he repeatedly insists on the distinction. The same is true of a magical ceremony. The magician who is destroyed by absorption in the Godhead is really destroyed. The miserable mortal automaton remains in the Circle. It is of no more consequence to Him that the dust of the floor"—"It is, for all that, His

---

[75] *The Equinox of the Gods, loc. cit.*, Ch. IV.
[76] *MITAP*, Ch. XXI, Sec. I. Emphasis in original.
[77] *The Revival of Magick.*
[78] *MITAP*, Ch. XIV. Emphasis in original.
[79] *Liber 888*, "The Yogi Jesus."
[80] *Ibid.*, "The Solution to the Enigma of the Plymouth Brethren."
[81] *MITAP*, Introduction.

instrument, acquired by Him as an astronomer buys a telescope."[82] According to Crowley, "It is wrong to say triumphantly 'Mors janua vitæ,' unless you add, with equal triumph, 'Vita janua mortis.'[83] To one who understands this chain of the Æons from the point of view alike of the sorrowing Isis and of the triumphant Osiris, not forgetting their link in the destroyer Apophis, there remains no secret veiled in Nature. He cries that name of God which throughout History has been echoed by one religion to another, the infinite swelling pæan I.A.O.!"[84]

We have already explored two different Crowleyan interpretations of the divine name, but there is a third, "the true formula of the Beast 666," in which "*I* and *O* are the opposites which form the field for the operation of *A*. But this is a higher matter unsuited for this elementary handbook. See, however, *Liber Samekh*, Point II, Section J."[85] The present author further refers the reader to the illustration on the cover of this book. "This name, I.A.O. is qabalistically identical with that of THE BEAST and with His number 666, so that he who invokes the former invokes also the latter. Also with AIWAZ and the Number 93."[86] In *Magick Without Tears*, Crowley bids us to "Remember that your 'East,' your Kiblah, is Boleskine House, which is as near as possible due North from Plymouth. Find North by the shadow of a vertical rod and noon, or by the Pole-Star. Work out the angle as usual. The Stélé of Revealing may be just on the N. Wall to make your 'East.'"[87]

> We are to consider carefully the particular attach of Heru Ra Ha against each of these "gods" or prophets; for though they be, or represent, the Magi of the past, the curse of their Grade must consume them.
>
> Thus it is the eyes of "Jesus"—his point of view—that must be destroyed; and this point of view is wrong because of his Magical Gesture of self-sacrifice.
>
> One must not for a moment suppose that this verse supports the historicity of "Jesus." "Jesus" is not, and never was, a man; but he was a "god," just as a bundle of old rags and a kerosene tin on a bush may be a "god." There is a man-made idea, built of ignorance, fear, and meanness, for the most part, which we call "Jesus," and which has been tricked out from time to time with various gauds from Paganism, and Judaism.
>
> The subject of "Jesus" is, most unfortunately, too extensive for a note; it is treated fully in my book *888*.[88]

According to the *New Comment* on AL I.49, "Isa is the Legendary 'Jesus', for which Canidian concoction the prescription is to be found in my book bearing that title, *Liber DCCCLXXXVIII*." In his *Confessions*, Crowley explains

---

[82] *Ibid.*, Ch. V.
[83] Latin for "Death is the gate of life" and "Life is the gate of death," respectively.
[84] *MITAP*, Ch. I.
[85] *Ibid.*, Ch. V, fn.
[86] *Ibid.*, Ch. I, fn.
[87] *MWT*, Ch. XXIII.
[88] NC on AL III.50–51.

that, "It became clear both those who believe in the historicity of 'Jesus' and their opponents were at fault. I could not doubt that actual incidents and genuine sayings in the life of a real man formed part of the structure. The truth was that scraps of several such men, distinct from, and incompatible with, each other, had been pitch-forked together and labelled with a single name."[89] In *Liber 888*, better known as *The Gospel According to St. Bernard Shaw*, Crowley posits that, "The whole misunderstanding of the Bible is due to the fact that it is an Eastern Vine planted in a Western garden."[90] It is here necessary to quote this work at length.

"The understanding of Eastern customs is imperative, if the life of Jesus is to be truly imagined and realized. A few years travel in India and North Africa familiarizes one with the atmosphere, and it is to smile when people talk of the 'wonderful life' of Jesus. By every roadside in India you may find a holy man today—you might have found me in 1901!—who is living exactly the life recorded of Jesus. He begs his food, or else 'women minister to him of their substance' (Luke viii, 3.) just as happens to the idle and vicious rascals who come out of India to America and England to pose as 'yogis' at the expense of lazy and good-for-nothing society women in search of a new fad. Only, in India, the support of yogis is decent and honourable. The men are really saints, and demand nothing but a little rice and curry. You can support one for a year on the price of a lunch at the Claridge."[91]

"All these men have their disciples, and their following of women—usually loose women, hermits and holy men having a great reputation everywhere for sexual prowess. They have their sayings, they make up their parables and fables to amuse their followers by the camp-fire at nightfall, they do their miracles, and fulfil the ancient prophecies in exactly the same way as Jesus did. The complaints of the Pharisees against Jesus are the stock complaints of the Orthodox in India to-day against the Yogis. They omit ceremonial washings; they eat filthy food; they take no heed of religious festivals or of the prescriptions of the Rishis and other great teachers. They care nothing for caste; they are shiftless, idle, and vagabond; they pray instead of working; and so on. Similarly, nine-tenths of the injunctions of Jesus are aimed at the most cherished rules or fads of the Pharisees; and so are most of the Wise sayings of the 'holy man' of India and all Islam to-day."[92]

"Show me any collection of the sayings of such men, and I will show you the ideas, even the very phrases, of your Jesus. Read the *Tao Teh King* on nonresistance, the *Bhagavad-Gita* on faith and devotion, the *Dhammapada* on right conduct, the *Questions of King Milinda* on metaphysical puzzles, the *Jataka* for parables, the Upanishads for high theology; then find a saying of Jesus which is not explicit in some one or more of them! More, take an anthology of the whole collection; ask some person unfamiliar with religion to pick out the sayings of Jesus, and to build up a coherent and consistent

---

[89] *Confessions*, Ch. 82.
[90] *Liber 888*, "The Life of Jesus."
[91] *Ibid.*
[92] *Ibid.*

system of philosophy, theology, and ethics from them. It would be easier to spin ropes of sand."[93]

"The life of Jesus, omitting the mystical birth and death, is altogether characteristic of the 'holy man' of the East. The only record of his childhood is given in Luke ii, 42 to 52. . . . This is the natural sort of incident which one remembers and thinks worthy of mention in the early life of a teacher. He was a very clever and even precocious boy; and he behaved well to his parents. (It would spoil the author's purpose to make him a miraculous boy; for his object is to prove how mystic practices can convert a commonplace person into a genius) We hear nothing of the life of Jesus from the time he was twelve to the time he was thirty. There is no evidence whatever that he worked as a carpenter. During the dispute about whether he came from Galilee or not, which has been quoted previously, it is asked, is he not the carpenter's son? And are these not his brethren? Nobody says 'Is he not the carpenter?' It is as if there was some slight mystery in regard to what he was doing before the age of thirty."[94]

"It is also exceedingly characteristic of the Eastern 'holy man' to shine in dialogue with the 'Zahid' or orthodox. He begins by doing something unconventional, and confutes those who reproach him. There are endless examples in the writings of the Sufis and dervishes as well as in Indian accounts of the lives of their 'holy men'. It is unnecessary to labour this point further. . . . We learn further [from Patañjali] that 'grief, mental distress, tremor of the body, irregular breathing accompany non-retention of concentration'.[95] Compare the sayings of Jesus, 'let the dead bury their dead, but come thou and follow me.'[96] Further, 'friendship, mercy, gladness, indifference being thought of in regard to subjects happy, unhappy, good and evil respectively, pacify the mind'.[97] Compare this with the instruction of Jesus to love your neighbour as yourself.[98] You must have no unkind thoughts and yet no passionate thoughts, for all these disturb the mind."[99]

"Much more could be said, but this appears to me to be enough as a clear identification of the teaching of Jesus with the universal and much more ancient doctrine. There is no new item. With regard to the manner of the life of Jesus we should also note that he frequently goes 'apart into the desert place to pray'.[100] This is a common practice of all Eastern Yogis: it is essential that they should not be disturbed during meditation. . . . We next read that the Yogi, 'by the conquest of the current Samana, is surrounded by blaze',[101] which accounts for the Transfiguration; and again: 'by making Samyama on the relation between the Akasa and the body the Yogi,

---

[93] *Ibid.*
[94] *Ibid.*
[95] *Yoga Sūtras*, 1.31.
[96] Matthew 8:22; also Luke 9:60.
[97] *Yoga Sūtras*, 1.33.
[98] Matthew 5:43; also 19:19, 22:39, Mark 12:31, Luke 10:27, Romans 13:9, Galatians 5:14, James 2:8.
[99] *Liber 888, loc. cit.*
[100] Matthew 14:13; also Mark 6:31, Luke 4:42.
[101] *Yoga Sūtras*, 3.41.

becoming light as cotton wool, goes through the skies'[102]; from which the ascension becomes the most natural thing in the world. We need not continue. All writers on Yoga tell us of other powers as that of the ability to walk on the surface of the water, to multiply food, and to heal diseases. Any one who is conversant with the literature of the subject is absolutely bound to read the story of Jesus the thaumaturgist as the account of a 'holy man', who had succeeded in all these practices and attained all these powers. They are really all one power, by the way. On the theory, all material things are illusions caused by ignorance, and one who has conquered ignorance by the realization of the truth 'I and my Father are one'."[103]

"A few words upon the psychology of the people. In Syria 2000 years ago, as in London to-day, there were people who go to church like sheep, not knowing so much as the nature of the doctrines they are supposed to hold, and others who were like those modern Christians who think a little, and prefer the Rev. R. J. Campbell to the Rev. F. B. Meyer, or the 'Gloomy Dean' to the 'Boisterous Bishop'. In India to-day there are many who pay strict reverence to custom, and have only vague and distant admiration (sometimes, indeed, contempt) for the 'holy men' who deliberately violate convention in order to prove superior sanctity. Jesus, the Jesus of Mr. Shaw, appealed naturally to the rarer class that knows a little of Yoga, and appreciates it. Now, when Paul came to the throne he found these people, and these people only, already 'Christians'. His dream of world-dominion asked for more. He needed orthodox Jews, and he needed Gentiles."[104]

"Having himself been an orthodox Jew, he at first regarded the idea of converting them as chimerical, called them all the bad names he could lay his tongue to, went out with a gun loaded exclusively for Gentiles, proved himself a Roman citizen free-born, broke with Peter because he avoided dining with Gentiles when certain visitors from James came to see him . . . and generally acted as though he hoped never to see a Jew again. But whether the Gentile campaign went badly, or whether he found some unexpected Jews in the bag, he suddenly changed front. He found a community of real Hebrews large enough to write to, and devoted an epistle to the most passionate endeavour to persuade them that Jesus was the real High Priest of Israel 'after the order of Melchisedec.'[105] This policy of pleasing everybody was successful; and when it came to be desirable to issue histories of the movement, those in charge simply classified the world as they knew it, the Roman world, and saw to it that something was put in to suit everybody. Contradictions might arise, but who minds contradictions? Germany and the Critical Spirit were in their infancy."[106]

"So, as there were patriotic Jews, they must be told that Jesus was the Messiah, of the seed of David; Talmudic Jews, who must be told that Jesus came not to destroy the law but to fulfill it; mystical and Qabalistic Jews, Gnostics and Pythagoreans and Platonists, who must have Jesus identified

---

[102] *Ibid.*, 3.43.
[103] *Liber 888, loc. cit.*; John 10:30.
[104] *Ibid.*, "The Unnatural Wedding."
[105] Hebrews 7.
[106] *Liber 888, loc. cit.*

with the Logos, and the Wisdom by whom God made the world; Pagans, who must be made happy by the story of the Virgin Birth; worshippers of Attis, Adonis, and Osiris, who must see the eternal sacrifice and resurrection of Nature crystalized in Jesus; ascetics who must be told of renunciation, and voluptuaries who must be comforted with the doctrines of atonement; slaves who must have freedom preached to them, and masters who must be reassured that Caesar shall always have the things that are Caesar's; primitive folk such as loving hearing stories of miracles and prophecies fulfilled; metaphysical folk, who must be tickled with abstruse theological dogmas; literary folk, who enjoy witty dialogues, and people with conviction of sin who want a Saviour. Whosoever will may come! The Gospels have something to please every single one of you. Matthew, Mark, Luke, and John, Bless the bed that I lie on; and it doesn't matter who made the bed!"[107]

"The Gospels are therefore, in that sense of the word which most implies moral turpitude, forgeries; the legend has been deliberately pieced together of incongruous elements, like a mermaid at a country fair, in order to defraud the lieges. Backed by the power of the priests of the various religions in the 'merger', the plan could not fail of success. Christianity spread by the very convenience of its international character in a world whose keynote was becoming daily more that word of Horace: *Luctantem Icariis fluctibus Africum Mercator metuens, otium et oppidi, Laudat rura sui; mox reficit rates Quassas, indocilis pauperiem pati.*[108] It only remained to lasso Caesar; and once this was done, the husbandman could return in peace, bringing his sheaves with him. The history of Christianity from that time on is but the account of how the robbers quarrelled among themselves over the spoils."[109]

"But why Jesus? the reader still queries. Because the Jesus whom Paul preached was popular with the democracy. Christianity was at first the religion of criminals and slaves. Its salvation was dirt cheap. In the gradual decay of the Roman Empire the sacred priesthood had no choice but to attach the name and tradition of Jesus to their already modified rites. Only by this means could they refill their emptying temples, replenish their depleted coffers, and re-establish their waning power and influence. As Mr. Shaw says, Faith without Works, in the sense of payment to the priests, did the trick. It was the people, not the enemy, whom Constantine feared; it was them that he conquered 'in this sign'. Even so it was long before the new Empire of the Papacy built up its power. The arts, the sciences, learning, literature, all fell into darkness; men knew no longer whence Jesus had arisen; they became so ignorant that they accepted the phantastic miracle story, with all its absurdities and contradictions, literally; and even the Renaissance, with its return to Pagan light and leading, the foundation of all that is good in modern civilization, left the Teutonic savages of Prussia and England still in the gloom, lit only by rare flashes of those who loved the

---

[107] *Ibid.*
[108] Hor. *Od.* 1.1.15–18.
[109] *Liber 888, loc. cit.*

Greeks, of that charnel where the mass of the people pullulate—unto this day."[110]

At the height of the Protestant Reformation, in December 1545, after much delay and miscarriage, the Council of Trent was finally convened by Pope Paul III. The new directly papal-subordinate order, the Jesuits, prepared and from the background steered the course of the proceedings. Threatened by religious dissenters and attacked by secular princes, the Catholic Church, instead of transcending itself, manifested the desperation of a besieged mentality by turning inward and clinging even tighter to orthodoxy. The Council of Trent affirmed basically all of Catholic dogma: according to Trent, Catholic doctrine rests not only on Scripture, but also on "tradition," the papal utterances and the decisions of the ecclesiastical councils, that is to say, it is expanding continuously. The Council officially confirmed many of the distinctly Catholic doctrines accrued by the Church over the centuries like penance, Purgatory, and, of course, indulgences; the sacrament of penance had come to be regarded as a means of reducing the amount of purgatorial punishment required for the penitent, while the idea of Purgatory itself was responsible for the popularity and importance of indulgences—those who donated funds for a pilgrimage might receive the same rewards promised to those who actually embarked on one.[111]

> When a man becomes a magician he looks about him for a magical weapon; and, being probably endowed with that human frailty called laziness, he hopes to find a weapon ready made. Thus we find the Christian Magus who imposed his power upon the world taking the existing worships and making a single system combining all their merits. There is no single feature in Christianity which has not been taken bodily from the worship of Isis, or of Mithras, or of Bacchus, or of Adonis, or of Osiris. In modern times again we find Frater Iehi Aour trying to handle Buddhism. Others again have attempted to use Freemasonry. There have been even exceptionally foolish magicians who have tried to use a sword long since rusted.
>
> Wagner illustrates this point very clearly in *Siegfried*. The Great Sword Nothung has been broken, and it is the only weapon that can destroy the gods. The dwarf Mime tries uselessly to mend it. When Siegfried comes he makes no such error. He melts its fragments and forges a new sword. In spite of the intense labour which this costs, it is the best plan to adopt.
>
> Levi completely failed to capture Catholicism; and his hope of using Imperialism, his endeavour to persuade the Emperor that he was the chosen instrument of the Almighty, a belief which would have enabled him to play Maximus to little Napoleon's Julian, was shattered once for all at Sedan.[112]

---

[110] *Ibid.*, "The Greater Mysteries."
[111] Balk 2008.
[112] *The Key of the Mysteries*, Introduction.

Alphonse Louis Constant only began calling himself Éliphas Lévi in 1856, when he published the *Dogma and Ritual of High Magic* under that name, thinking it more befitting a student of Qabalah. Until that time, contemporaries knew him either as the Abbé Constant, a holdover from the days of his seminary studies, or simply as Alphonse Constant, "A.C." for short; the same initials later adopted by one Edward Alexander Crowley. Paschal Beverly Randolph claims to have taken part in secret Rosicrucian rites with Lévi and the above-mentioned Emperor Napoleon III—whom the period's great exile Victor Hugo contemptuously nicknamed "Napoléon le Petit," and who was notorious for having a deep interest in spiritualism and all things supernatural. At one time, Lévi himself actually compared the French Emperor to Caligula, for which outrage he was imprisoned, but quickly released after he penned *L'Anti-Caligula* from prison, wittily apologizing for the previous reference to "a monster of antiquity."[113]

According to Crowley, "Mohammed's point of view is wrong too; but he needs no such sharp correction as 'Jesus.' It is his face—his outward semblance—that is to be covered with His wings. The tenets of Islam, correctly interpreted, are not far from our Way of Life and Light and Love and Liberty. This applies especially to the secret tenets. The external creed is mere nonsense suited to the intelligence of the peoples among whom it was promulgated; but even so, Islam is magnificent in practice. Its code is that of a man of courage and honour and self-respect; contrasting admirably with the cringing cowardice of the damnation-dodging Christians with their unmanly and dishonest acceptance of vicarious sacrifice, and their currish conception of themselves as 'born in sin,' 'miserable sinners' with 'no health in us.'"[114] In fact, "Between you and me and the pylon, I suspect that Gabriel who gave the Q'uran to Mohammed was in reality a 'Master' or messenger of some such person, more or less as Aiwass describes himself as '...the minister of Hoor-paar-kraat.' (AL I, 7)"[115]

"But this is not all. Aiwaz is not (as I had supposed) a mere formula, like many angelic names, but is the true most ancient name of the God of the Yezidis, and thus returns to the highest Antiquity. Our work is therefore historically authentic, the rediscovery of the Sumerian Tradition. (Sumer is in lower Mesopotamia, the earliest home of our race)."[116] As Crowley writes in *The Equinox of the Gods*, "I now inclined to believe that Aiwass is not only the God or Demon or Devil once held holy in Sumer, and mine own Guardian Angel, but also a man as I am, insofar as He uses a human body to make His magical link with Mankind, whom He loves, and that He is thus an Ipsissimus, the Head of the A∴A∴ Even I can do, in a much feebler way, this Work of being a God and a Beast, &c., &c., all at the same time, with equal fullness of life." The footnote clarifies that, "I do not necessarily mean

---

[113] Buisset 1984.
[114] NC on AL III.52; "The Ministration of Public Baptism of Infants," "The Litany, or General Supplication," and "The Order for Evening Prayer, Daily throughout the Year," in the *Book of Common Prayer*.
[115] *MWT*, Ch. LXXVI.
[116] Notes for a New Commentary on The Book of the Law, File K.1. Yorke Collection, Warburg Institute, University of London.

that he is a member of human society in quite the normal way. He might rather be able to form for Himself a human body as circumstances indicate, from the appropriate Elements, and dissolve it when the occasion for its use is past. I say this because I have been permitted to see Him in recent years in a variety of physical appearances, all equally 'material' in the sense in which my own body is so."[117]

All of Crowley's commentaries on *The Book of the Law* agree on this point: "666 to comment on AL to guard against false interpretations. I comment on this Book, lest there be folly; for many are the Secret Sayings and obscure in the text thereof. It would be easy for the clever and the crafty to distort the true meaning of Aiwass so as to suit their own conceits, as hath been seen of old time in the cases of the Words of the Masters, the Q'uran, and the so-called Scriptures of the Christians."[118] According to his *New Comment* on AL I.5, "In addressing me as warrior lord of Thebes, it appears as if She perceived a certain continuity or identity of myself with Ankh-f-n-khonsu, whose Stele is the Link with Antiquity of this Revelation." A great number of steles, with inscriptions, survive from ancient Egypt, and constitute one of the largest and most significant sources of information on that civilization—with the most famous example, of course, being the Rosetta Stone, which led to the breakthrough allowing Egyptians hieroglyphs to be deciphered.

The stele of Ankh-ef-en-Khonsu, designated Cairo A 9422 (formerly Bulaq 666), is a painted, wooden funerary stele, discovered in 1858 at the mortuary temple of Hatshepsut at Dayr al-Bahri by none other than François Auguste Ferdinand Mariette, founder of the Egyptian Department of Antiquities. As Crowley's Magical Record for 8 June 1921 states, "the actual name of the Stele, its ordinary name, the only name it ever had until it was called the 'Stele of Revealing', in the *Book of the Law*, itself, 'its name' in the catalogue of the Museum at Boulak, was just this: 'Stele 666'."[119] Apparently, the "interpretation is to be that Ankh-f-n-Khonsu recorded for my benefit the details of the Magical Formula of Ra Hoor Khuit. To link together the centuries in this manner is nothing strange to the accomplished Magician; but in view of the true character of Time as it appears to the Adept in Mysticism, the riddle vanishes altogether."[120]

"The Beast is here definitely identified with the priest of the 26th Dynasty whose Stele forms the Pantacle (so to speak) of the new Magick. He is moreover identified with the scribe. It is of immense importance to the stability of the Law to have a Book not merely verbally but literally inspired, so that even errors in spelling and grammar have a secret significance. (That this must be so is guaranteed by the literary pre-eminence and impeccable orthography of the Beast as a man). But the great thing is the Standard to which all disputes may be referred. It is also necessary to give weight to the authority of The Beast, lest ignorance, folly,

---

[117] *The Equinox of the Gods, loc. cit.*, Ch. VII, Sec. VIII.
[118] DC on AL I.36.
[119] As quoted in NC on AL III.19.
[120] NC on AL III.36.

or cunning misinterpret the text."[121] As *The Equinox of the Gods* puts it, "It is 'my scribe Ankh-af-na-khonsu' (CCXX, I, 36) who 'shall comment' on 'this book' 'by the wisdom of Ra-Hoor-Khuit'; that is, Aleister Crowley shall write the Comment from the point of view of the manifested positive Lord of the Æon, in plain terms of the finite, and not those of the infinite."[122] Which brings us to the "true word" of Mohammed.

> Behold! In these Chapters have I, thy Father, restricted myself, not speaking of any immediate Echo of a Word in the World, because, there Men being long since withdrawn into their Silence, it is their One Word, and that Alone, that resoundeth undiminished through Time. How Mohammed, who followeth, is darkened and confused by His Nearness to our own Time, so that I say not save with Diffidence that His Word ALLH may mean this or that. But I am bold concerning His Doctrine of the Unity of God, for God is Man, and he said therefore: Man is One. And His Will was to unite all Men in One reasonable Faith: to make possible international Co-operation in Science. Yet, because He arose in the Time of the greatest possible Corruption and Darkness, when every Civilisation and Every Religion had fallen into Ruin, by the malice of the great Sorcerer of Nazareth, as some say, He is still hidden in the Dust of the Simoom, and we may not perceive Him in His true Self of Glory.
>
> Nevertheless, behold, o My Son, this Mystery. His true Word was LA ALLH, that is to say: (there is) No God[123], and LA AL is that Mystery of Mysteries which thine own Eye pierced in thine Initiation. And of that Truth have the Illusion and Falsehood enslaved the Souls of Men, as is written in the Book of the Magus.[124]

"What is a prophet?" asks Éliphas Lévi. "A representative of humanity seeking God. God is God, and man is the prophet of God, when he causes us to believe in God. The Old Testament, the Qur'an, and the Gospel are three different translations of the same book. As God is one, so also is the law."[125] The entry on 671 in *An Essay upon Number* has "תערא the Law, תרעא the Gate, אתער the Lady of the Path of Daleth, רעתא the Wheel. Also אלף, דלת, נון, יוד, Adonai (see 65) spelt in full. This important number marks the identity of the Augoeides with the Way itself ('I am the Way, the Truth, and the Life') and shows the Taro as a key; and that the Law itself is nothing else than this. For this reason the outer College of the A∴A∴ is crowned by this 'knowledge and conversation of the Holy Guardian Angel.'"[126]

---

[121] NC on AL I.36.

[122] *The Equinox of the Gods*, loc. cit.

[123] This makes sense—even if Crowley's math does not—when you consider that, "at intervals of a little more than three, and a little less than seven, centuries, They send a lesser prophet to prepare the Way of the next Word, and to maintain or restore the virtue of the Word then current." (*The Heart of the Master*, Ch. III; the Word then current being Gautama's *Anattā*, or "no self.")

[124] *Liber Aleph*, "De Mago Arabico Mohammed."

[125] *The Key of the Mysteries*, Part I, "Sketch of the Prophetic Theology of Numbers."

[126] *An Essay upon Number*, loc. cit.

According to Lévi, "The law is immutable because it is founded on the eternal principles of Nature; but the worship necessitated by the needs of man may change, and modify itself, parallel with the changes in men themselves. This signifies that the worship itself is immutable, but modifies itself as language does. Worship is a form of instruction; it is a language; one must translate it when nations no longer understand it."[127] In his Introduction to *Magick Without Tears*, Crowley makes one thing clear: "I do assure you that the whole of my life's work, were it multiplied a thousand fold, would not be worth one tithe of the value of a single verse of *The Book of the Law*. I think you should have a copy of *The Equinox of the Gods* and make *The Book of the Law* your constant study. Such value as my own work may possess for you should amount to no more than an aid to the interpretation of this book."

Again, "Thou knowest well how I keep me from all Taint of Fable, or any Word unproven and undemonstrable. First then I speak of Lao-tze, whose word was the TAO. Hereof have I already written much unto thee, because His Doctrine has been lost or misinterpreted, and it is most needful to restore it. For this Tao is the true Nature of Things, being itself a Way or Going, that is, a kinetic and not a static Conception. Also He taught this Way of Harmony in Will, which I myself have thought to show thee in this little book. So then this Tao is Truth, and the Way of Truth, and therefore was He Logos of His Æon, and His true Name or Word was Tao."[128] However, "The great classics of religion rarely travel beyond their own climate, as Frazer and fifty others have shown; but they never travel far beyond their own language. The Qu'ran in English is mere ditchwater for the most part; in Arabic it is sublime poetry. The same is true of most Indian and Chinese Classics."[129]

"Hence Protestantism is due to the accident that the translation called the Authorized Version was done by scholars of that period of the marvellous flowering of English which not only gave us Marlowe and Shakespeare and Malory, but such masters of translation as North for Plutarch, Florio for Montaigne, Urquhart and Motteux for Rabelais, and a dozen more. Previous translations, like Wyckliffe's, possessing small literary value, never took hold of the hearts or imagination of the people. The German translation, it is said, is also exceedingly fine: which accounts for the vogue of Lutheranism in that country. . . . No; the Bible is great literature—in parts; and will stand as such while Shakespeare stands. But its doctrine will never convince Islam, until a translator arises who can match Mohammed's sonorous and exquisitely balanced prose, with its internal rimes and its incomparable rhythm, that is at once like the thunder, and like the simoom, and like the whisper of the desert wind. And there is many an immoral and indecent book which lives by such virtue; we may admire the manner of such while we reprehend the matter."[130]

---

[127] *The Key of the Mysteries, loc. cit.*, Article IV.
[128] *Liber Aleph*, "De magis tempori antiqui: Imprimis, de Lao-Tze"; the name or title *Lǎozī* is merely Chinese for "Old Master."
[129] *Liber 888*, "The Alternative to Barabbas."
[130] *Ibid.*

It makes sense for the Angel to appear to Mohammed as Gabriel and to Crowley, the Beast, as Satan: "Born of an ancient family, but a few days after the fifty-sixth Equinox before the Equinox of the Gods, he was reared and educated in the faith of Christ as taught by one of the strictest sects of the many factions of the Christian Church, and scarcely had he learnt to lisp the simplest syllables of childhood than his martyrdom began."[131] That is, "At four years old he could read the Bible aloud, showing a marked predilection for the lists of long names, the only part of the Bible which has not been tampered with by theologians." According to Crowley, "This curious trait may perhaps be evidence of his poetical feeling, his passion for the bizarre and mysterious, or even of his aptitude for the Hebrew Qabalah. It may also be interpreted as a clue to his magical ancestry." Either way, "As a boy he could find almost any verse in the Bible after a few minutes search. In 1900 he was tested in the works of Shakespeare, Shelley, Swinburne (1st series of *Poems and Ballads*), Browning and *The Moonstone*. He was able to place exactly any phrase from any of these books, and in nearly every case to continue with the passage."[132]

Crowley "had been deprived of all English literature but the Bible during the whole of his youth, and he spent his three years at Cambridge in repairing the defect. He was also working for the Diplomatic Service, the late Lord Salisbury and the late Lord Ritchie having taken an interest in his career, and given him nominations. In October, 1897, he was suddenly recalled to his understanding of the evils of the alleged 'existing religion,' and experienced a trance, in which he perceived the utter folly of all human ambition. The fame of an ambassador rarely outlives a century. That of a poet is almost as ephemeral. The earth must one day perish. He must build in some material more lasting. This conception drove him to the study of Alchemy and Magick. . . . George Cecil Jones . . . introduced him to the Hermetic Order of the Golden Dawn. He made rapid progress in this Order, and in the spring of 1900 was its chief in England. The details of this period must be studied in *The Temple of Solomon the King*, where a full account of the Order is given. . . . It was on his entry into this Order that the subject of this history took the motto of 'Perdurabo'—'I will endure to the end.'"[133]

"FRATER PERDURABO composed His talisman by invoking His Holy Guardian Angel according to the *Sacred Magick of Abramelin the Mage*. That Angel wrote on the lamen the Word of the Æon. *The Book of the Law* is this writing. To this lamen the MASTER THERION gave life by devoting His own life thereto. We may then regard this talisman, the Law, as the most powerful that has been made in the world's history, for previous talismans of the same type have been limited in their scope by conditions of race and country. Mohammed's talisman, *Allah*, was good only from Persia to the Pillars of Hercules. The Buddha's, *Anatta*, operated only in the South and East of Asia. The new talisman, *Thelema*, is master of the planet."[134] Crowley is adamant: "I have never written such English; nor could I ever, that well I

---

[131] *The Temple of Solomon the King*, Part II, "The Acolyte."
[132] *The Equinox of the Gods, loc. cit.*, Ch. I.
[133] *Ibid.*, Ch. II.
[134] *MITAP*, Ch. XIV. Emphasis in original.

know. Shakespeare could not have written it: still less could Keats, Shelley, Swift, Sterne or even Wordsworth. Only in the Book of Job and Ecclesiastes, in the work of Blake, or possibly in that of Poe, is there any approach to such succinct depth of thought in such musical simplicity of form, unless it be in Greek and Latin poets. Nor Poe nor Blake could have sustained their effort as does this our *Book of the Law*; and the Hebrews used tricks of verse, mechanical props to support them."[135]

"When Count Joseph de Maistre, that grand and passionate lover of Logic, said despairingly, 'The world is without religion,' he resembled those people who say rashly 'There is no God.' The world, in truth, is without the religion of Count Joseph de Maistre, as it is probable that such a God as the majority of atheists conceive does not exist."[136] Maistre seems to have referred to the fact that France was officially no longer a Catholic country after the Revolution of 1789. The Church's power in France was systematically taken away by the State between then and 1801. In the 18th century, ninety-five percent of the French population were adherents of the Roman Catholic faith, and prior to the Revolution, the authority of the clergy was institutionalized in its status as the First Estate of the realm. Since the Church kept the registry of births, deaths, and marriages, and was the only institution in France—and most of Europe—that provided primary and secondary education and hospitals, it was present in everyone's life.[137]

According to Lévi, "Religion is an idea based upon one constant and universal fact; man is a religious animal. . . . Moreover, of all human passions, religious passion is the most powerful and the most lively. It generates itself, whether by affirmation or negation, with an equal fanaticism, some obstinately affirming the god that they have made in their own image, the others denying God with rashness, as if they had been able to understand and to lay waste by a single thought all that world of infinity which pertains to His great name. Philosophers have not sufficiently considered the physiological fact of religion in humanity, for in truth religion exists apart from all dogmatic discussion. It is a faculty of the human soul just as much as intelligence and love. While man exists, so will religion."[138]

> The external worship would never have been separated from interior revel but for the weakness of man, which tends too easily to forget the spirit in the letter; but the Masters are vigilant to note in every nation those who are able to receive light, and such persons are employed as agents to spread the light according to man's capacity and to revivify the dead letter.
>
> Through these instruments the interior truths of the Sanctuary were taken into every nation, and modified symbolically according to their customs, capacity for instruction, climate, and receptiveness. So that the external types of every religion, worship, ceremonies and Sacred Books

---

[135] *The Equinox of the Gods*, loc. cit., Ch. VII, Sec. VI.
[136] *The Key of the Mysteries*, Part I, Preliminary Considerations.
[137] Lévi 2015.
[138] *The Key of the Mysteries*, loc. cit.

in general have more or less clearly, as their object of instruction, the interior truths of the Sanctuary, by which man will be conducted to the universal knowledge of the one Absolute Truth.

The more the external worship of a people has remained united with the spirit of esoteric truth, the purer its religion; but the wider the difference between the symbolic letter and the invisible truth, the more imperfect has become the religion. Finally, it may be, the external form has entirely parted from its inner truth, so that ceremonial observances without soul or life have remained alone.

In the midst of all this, truth reposes inviolable in the inner Sanctuary.[139]

"In the true religion there is no sect, therefore take heed that thou blaspheme not the name by which another knoweth his God; for if thou do this thing in Jupiter thou wilt blaspheme יהוה and in Osiris יהשוה. Ask and ye shall have! Seek, and ye shall find! Knock, and it shall be opened unto you!"[140] At the same time, however, Crowley bids us to "remember that the mystic Iesous and Yeheshua have no more to do with the legendary Jesus of the Synoptics and the Methodists than the mystic IHVH has to do with the false God who commanded the murder of innocent children. The 13 of the Sun and the Zodiac was perhaps responsible for Buddha and his 12 disciples, Christ and his 12 disciples, Charlemagne and his 12 peers, &c., &c., but to disbelieve in Christ or Charlemagne is not to alter the number of the signs of the Zodiac. Veneration for 666 does not commit me to admiration for Napoleon and Gladstone."[141]

"If a man rejects an unworthy idea of divinity, breaks its false images, revolts against hateful idolaters, you will call him an atheist! The authors of the persecutions in fallen Rome called the first Christians atheists, because they did not adore the idols of Caligula or of Nero. To deny a religion, even to deny all religions rather than adhere to formulae which conscience rejects, is a courageous and sublime act of faith. Every man who suffers for his convictions is a martyr of faith. He explains himself badly, it may be, but he prefers justice and truth to everything; do not condemn him without understanding him."[142] We should not forget that Crowley's philosophy purports to reconcile and/or transcend atheism, theism, and pantheism: "Every one may admit that monotheism, exalted by the introduction of the symbol, is equivalent to pantheism. Pantheism and atheism are really identical, as the opponents of both are the first to admit."[143]

"But the book-men have slain the Great God, and the twitterers of words have twisted their squeaking screws into his coffin. The first Christians were called Atheists; yet they believed in God: the last Christians are called Theists; yet they believe not in God. So the first Freethinkers were called Atheists; yet they believed in NO-GOD: and the last Freethinkers will be

---

[139] *Liber XXXIII.*
[140] *Liber Libræ*, 21. Matthew 7:7; also Luke 11:9.
[141] *An Essay upon Number*, Part II.
[142] *The Key of the Mysteries, loc. cit.,* "Sketch of the Prophetic Theology of Numbers."
[143] *Berashith*, fn.

called Theists; for they will believe not in NO-GOD. Then indeed in these latter days may we again find the Great God, that God who liveth beyond the twittering of man's lips, and the mumblings of his mouth."[144] Julian the Apostate, "that adept of the spirit who was never understood, that initiate whose paganism was less idolatrous than the faith of certain Christians, the Emperor Julian, we say, understood better than Dupuis and Volney the symbolic worship of the sun. In his hymn to the king, Helios, he recognizes that the star of day is but the reflection and the material shadow of that sun of truth which illumines the world of intelligence, and which is itself only a light borrowed from the Absolute. It is a remarkable thing that Julian has ideas of the Supreme God, that the Christians thought they alone adored, much greater and more correct than those of some of the fathers of the Church, who were his contemporaries, and his adversaries."[145]

"How restore faith in the Gods?" Crowley asks. "There is only one way; we must get to know them personally. And that, of course, is one of the principal tasks of the Magician."[146] According to *Eight Lectures on Yoga*, "The classic of the subject is 'Liber Astarte vel Berylli', the Book of Devotion to a Particular Deity. This book is admirable beyond praise, reviewing the whole subject in every detail with flawless brilliancy of phrase. Its practice is enough in itself to bring the devotee to high attainment. This is only for the few. But every student should make a point of saluting the Sun (in the manner recommended in *Liber Resh*) four times daily, and he shall salute the Moon on her appearance with the Mantra Gayatri. The best way is to say the Mantra instantly one sees the Moon, to note whether the attention wavers, and to repeat the Mantra until it does not waver at all."[147] The *New Comment* on AL III.38 asks the reader to "Note the Four Quarters or Four Solar Stations Enumerated in lines 3 and 4 of the first Stanza, and compare the ritual given in *Liber Samekh*."

"Note, please, that the equivalents given in *777* are not always exact. Tahuti is not quite Thoth, still less Hermes; Mercury is a very much more comprehensive idea, but not nearly so exalted: Hanuman hardly at all. Nor is Tetragrammaton IAO, though even etymology asserts the identity. In these matters you must be catholic, eclectic, even syncretic. And you must consider the nature of your work. If I wanted to evoke Taphthartharath, there would be little help indeed from any but the Qabalistic system; for that spirit's precise forms and numbers are not to be found in any other. The converse, however, is not so true. The Qabalah, properly understood, properly treated, is so universal that one can vamp up a ritual to suit almost

---

[144] *The Temple of Solomon the King*, Part I, "The Bankrupt."
[145] *The Key of the Mysteries*, Part III, Book I, Ch. III.
[146] *MWT, loc. cit.*
[147] *Eight Lectures*, Ch. 5, Sec. 9. The Gāyatrī Mantra, a/k/a the Sāvitrī Mantra, is an ancient verse of the Ṛgveda (3.62.10) recited every day by millions of Hindus all over the world. *Gāyatrī* is also the name of the poetic meter in which the Vedic hymn was written, while Savitṛ is the *solar* deity to whom this and ten other hymns of the Ṛgveda are dedicated. However, Monier-Williams distinguishes *Savitṛ*, "the Sun before sunrise," from *Sūrya*, or "the Sun until sunset," while Savitrī is also a name of the female consort of Brahma. Indeed, every word in Sanskrit has several meanings, and *Book 4* translates the Mantra thus: "O! Let us strictly meditate on the adorable light of that divine Savitri (the interior Sun, etc.). May she enlighten our minds!"

'any name and form.' But in such a case one may expect to have to reinforce it by a certain amount of historical, literary, or philosophic study—and research."[148]

In relation to "God-forms," Crowley refers the student to "*Magick* pp. 378-9. Quite clear: quite adequate: no use at all without continual practice. No one can join with you—off you go again! No, no, a thousand times no: this is the practice par excellence where you have to do it all yourself. The Vibration of God-names: that perhaps, I can at least test you in. But don't you dare come up for a test until you've been at it—and hard—for at least 100 exercises."[149] According to *Magick*, "There are three main methods of invoking any Deity. The *First Method* consists of devotion to that Deity, and, being mainly mystical in character, need not be dealt with in this place, especially as a perfect instruction exists in *Liber 175*... The *Second Method* is the straight forward ceremonial invocation. It is the method which was usually employed in the Middle Ages. Its advantage is its directness, its disadvantage its crudity. The *Goëtia* gives clear instruction in this method, and so do many other rituals, white and black. We shall presently devote some space to a clear exposition of this Art."[150]

"The *Third Method* is the Dramatic, perhaps the most attractive of all; certainly it is so to the artist's temperament, for it appeals to his imagination through his aesthetic sense. Its disadvantage lies principally in the difficulty of its performance by a single person. But it has the sanction of the highest antiquity, and is probably the most useful for the foundation of a religion. It is the method of Catholic Christianity, and consists in the dramatization of the legend of the God. The *Bacchæ* of Euripides is a magnificent example of such a Ritual; so also, through in a less degree, is the Mass. We may also mention many of the degrees in Freemasonry, particularly the third. The 5°=6$^\square$ Ritual published in No. III of the *Equinox* is another example."[151] However, "To have any sensible meaning at all, faith must mean experience... Nothing is any use to us unless it be a certainty unshakeable by criticism of any kind, and there is only one thing in the universe which complies with these conditions: the direct experience of spiritual truth. Here, and here only, do we find a position in which the great religious minds of all times and all climes coincide. It is necessarily above dogma, because dogma consists of a collection of intellectual statements, each of which, and also its contradictory, can easily be disputed and overthrown."[152]

"FRATER PERDURABO, to whom this revelation was made with so many signs and wonders, was himself unconvinced. He struggled against it for years. Not until the completion of His own initiation at the end of 1909 did he understand how perfectly he was bound to carry out this work." Indeed, according to the footnote, "it was not until his Word became conterminous with Himself and His Universe that all alien ideas lost their meaning for

---

[148] *MWT*, Introduction.
[149] *Ibid.*
[150] *MITAP*, Ch. I. Emphasis in original.
[151] *Ibid.* Emphasis in original.
[152] *Eight Lectures*, Ch. 7, Sec. 2.

Him." In the meantime, "Again and again He turned away from it, took it up for a few days or hours, then laid it aside. He even attempted to destroy its value, to nullify the result. Again and again the unsleeping might of the Watchers drove Him back to the work; and it was at the very moment when He thought Himself to have escaped that He found Himself fixed for ever with no possibility of again turning aside for the fraction of second from the Path."[153]

Now, *The Book of the Law* guarantees itself by so closely woven a web of internal evidence of every kind, from Cabbalistic and mathematical proofs, and those depending on future events and similar facts, undeniably beyond human power to predict or to produce, that it is unique. The thirty Æthyrs being, however, only second in importance, though very far away, to that Book, the Lords of Vision were at pains to supply internal evidence, more than amply sufficient that the revelations therein contained may be regarded as reliable. No doubt the proof appears stronger to me than to anyone else, because I alone know exactly what happened; also because many passages refer to matters personal to myself, so that only I can fully appreciate the dovetailings. Just so a man can never prove to another the greatness of Shelley as fully as he feels it himself, since his certainty partly depends on the secret and incommunicable relations of the poet with his own individual idiosyncrasies.

I admit that my visions can never mean to other men as much as they do to me. I do not regret this. All I ask is that my results should convince seekers after truth that there is beyond doubt something worth while seeking, attainable by methods more or less like mine. I do not want to father a flock, to be the fetish of fools and fanatics, or the founder of a faith whose followers are content to echo my opinions. I want each man to cut his own way through the jungle.

We walked steadily to Bou Saâda, invoking the Æthyrs one by one, at convenient times and places, or when the spirit moved me. As a rule, we did one Æthyr every day. We reached Bou Saâda on November 30th; on December 8th we started through the desert for Biskra, which we reached on December 16th, completing the work on the nineteenth. Our adventures will be told later on.

By the time I reached Bou Saâda and came to the twentieth Æthyr, I began to understand that these visions were, so to speak, cosmopolitan. They brought all systems of magical doctrine into harmonious relation. The symbolism of Asiatic cults; the ideas of the Cabbalists, Jewish and Greek; the arcana of the gnostics; the pagan pantheon, from Mithras to Mars; the mysteries of ancient Egypt; the initiations of Eleusis; Scandinavian sagas; Celtic and Druidical ritual; Mexican and Polynesian traditions; the mysticism of Molinos no less than that of Islam, fell into their proper places without the slightest tendency to quarrel. The whole of the past Æon appeared in perspective and each element thereof

---

[153] *The Equinox of the Gods, loc. cit.*, Ch. VIII.

surrendered its sovereignty to Horus, the Crowned and Conquering Child, the Lord of the Æon announced in *The Book of the Law*.

These visions thus crystallized in dramatic form the theoretical conclusion which my studies of comparative religion had led me to adumbrate. The complexity of the whole vast subject resolved itself into shining simplicity, I saw with my own eyes and heard with my own ears the truth in terms of Time. I understood directly that the formula of Osiris necessarily assumed all sorts of apparently incompatible forms as it was applied to different conditions of race, climate and similar conditions. I saw also that Horus might reconcile all religions, it being possible now to bring all countries to agree on a few fundamental principles. Science had practically driven prejudice into the dark. Faith was little more than a shibboleth which no longer influenced opinion or action. I saw my way to combine a few simple incontrovertible scientific principles into a Law which would allow the loftiest aspirations to seek satisfaction in spiritual spheres, the religious instincts to realize their sublimity through ritual, and to assist the scientific mind to see that even the most materialistic concept of the cosmos was ultimately mystical, that though mind might be merely a function of matter, yet that matter might equally well be represented as a manifestation of mind. The sequel will show how I fared in this ambitious adventure.[154]

"True, it's a slogan of A∴A∴ 'The method of science—the aim of religion.' Here the word 'aim' and the context help the definition; it must mean the attainment of Knowledge and Power in spiritual matters—or words to that effect. . . . To sum up, our system is a religion just so far as a religion means an enthusiastic putting-together of a series of doctrines, no one of which must in any way clash with Science or Magick. Call it a new religion, then, if it so please your Gracious Majesty; but I confess that I fail to see what you will have gained by so doing, and I feel bound to add that you might easily cause a great deal of misunderstanding, and work a rather stupid kind of mischief."[155] However, "May we call it 'a truth of Religion?' (Don't be shocked! The original word implies a binding-together-again, as in a 'Body of Doctrine': compare the word 'Ligature.' It was only later by corruption, that the word came to imply 'piety'; re-ligens, attentive (to the gods) as opposed to neg-ligens, neglectful.)"[156]

Thus we have Crowley's tongue-in-cheek "Society for the Propagation of Religious Truth" (S.P.R.T.).[157] As he points out in *Eight Lectures*, "You may note incidentally that the word Religion is really identifiable with Yoga. It means a binding together."[158] In Vedic Sanskrit, *yoga*, from the root *yuj*, means "to add," "to join," "to unite," or "to attach" in its most common literal

---

[154] *Confessions*, Ch. 66.
[155] *MWT*, Ch. XXXI.
[156] *Ibid*., Ch. XXIX.
[157] A parody of the Society for Promoting Christian Knowledge (S.P.C.K.), the oldest Anglican mission organization, founded in 1698 to encourage Christian education and the production and distribution of Christian literature.
[158] Ch. 1, Sec. 4.

sense. By figurative extension from the "yoking" or harnessing of oxen, the word took on broader meanings such as "use," "application," "employment." According to Monier-Williams, all further developments of the sense of the word are post-Vedic, though more prosaic moods such as "endeavour," "zeal," and "diligence" are found in the epic poetry of India. "It will be seen that these various methods of attainment are all harmonious. The Method of Meditation and that of Abramelin are not superseded by the new Æon, but made subsidiary to it, and easier to employ in virtue of it. It is indeed abundantly clear that these three paths are one. The best and greatest of the antinomies, that between Magick and Mysticism, is transcended in the Method of the New Æon."[159]

I. The world progresses by virtue of the appearance of Christs (geniuses).

II. Christs (geniuses) are men with super-consciousness of the highest order.

III. Super-consciousness of the highest order is obtainable by known methods.

Therefore, by employing the quintessence of known methods we cause the world to progress.[160]

I. Theology is immaterial; for both Buddha and St. Ignatius were Christs.

II. Morality is immaterial; for both Socrates and Mohammed were Christs.

III. Super-consciousness is a natural phenomenon; its conditions are therefore to be sought rather in the acts than the words of those who attain it.

The essential acts are retirement and concentration—as taught by Yoga and Ceremonial Magic.[161]

"Memories of the events of the day will bother us; we must arrange our day so that it is absolutely uneventful. Our minds will recall to us our hopes and fears, our loves and hates, our ambitions, our envies, and many other emotions. All these must be cut off. We must have absolutely no interest in life but that of quieting our minds. This is the object of the usual monastic vow of poverty, chastity, and obedience. If you have no property, you have no care, nothing to be anxious about; with chastity no other person to be anxious about, and to distract your attention; while if you are vowed to obedience the question of what you are to do no longer frets: you simply obey."[162] In the end, "we find that outside the asylum, we, one and all of us, are strenuously or slothfully, willingly or unwillingly, consciously or unconsciously, progressing slowly or speedily towards *some* goal that we have set up as an ideal before us. Follow the road to that goal, subdue all

---
[159] *The Temple of Solomon the King*, Part IX, "Nemo."
[160] *Postcards to Probationers*, "Theorems."
[161] *Ibid.*, "Essentials of Method."
[162] *Book 4*, Part I, Preliminary Remarks.

difficulties, and, when the last has been vanquished, we shall find that that *some goal* is in truth THE GOAL, and that the road upon which we set out was but a little capillary leading by vein and artery to the very Heart of Unity itself."[163]

"However, the point is that it is no use discussing the results of Yoga, whether that Yoga be the type recommended by Lao-Tze, or Patanjali, or St. Ignatius Loyola, because for our first postulate we have: that these subjects are incapable of discussion. To argue about them only causes us to fall into the pit of Because, and there to perish with the dogs of Reason. The only use, therefore, of describing our experiences is to enable students to get some sort of idea of the sort of thing that is going to happen to them when they attain success in the practices of Yoga. We have David saying in the Psalms: 'I hate thoughts, but Thy law do I love.'[164] We have St. Paul saying: 'The carnal mind is enmity against God.'[165] One might almost say that the essence of St. Paul's Epistles is a struggle against mind: 'We war not against flesh and blood'—you know the rest—I can't be bothered to quote it all—Eph. vi. 12.[166] . . . That is the great lesson: not to discuss the results. Those of you who possess a copy of *The Equinox of the Gods* may have been very much surprised at the extraordinary injunction in the Comment: the prohibition of all discussion of the Book. I myself did not fully understand that injunction; I do so now."[167]

---

[163] *The Temple of Solomon the King*, Part III, "The Sorcerer." Emphasis in original.
[164] 119:113.
[165] Romans 8:7.
[166] "For we wrestle not against flesh and blood, but against principalities, against powers, against the rulers of the darkness of this world, against spiritual wickedness in high places."
[167] *Eight Lectures, loc. cit.*, Secs. 8–10.

CHAPTER 12
Religious Aspects
Part II: Promulgation

You are probably aware that in the Society of Jesus the postulants are trained to debate on all these highly controversial subjects. They put up a young man to prove any startling blasphemy that happens to occur to them. And the more shocked the young man is, the better the training for his mind, and the better service will he give to the Society in the end; but only if his mind has been completely disabused of its confidence in its own rightness, or even in the possibility of being right.

The rationalist, in his shallow fashion, always contends that this training is the abnegation of mental freedom. On the contrary, it is the only way to obtain that freedom. In the same Society the training in obedience is based on a similar principle. The priest has to do what his Superior orders him—perinde ac cadaver. Protestants always represent that this is the most outrageous and indefensible tyranny. "The poor devil," they say, "is bludgeoned into having no will of his own." That is pure nonsense. By abnegating his will through the practice of holy obedience his will has become enormously strong, so strong that none of his natural instincts, desires, or habits can intrude. He has freed his will of all these inhibitions. He is a perfect function of the machinery of the Order. In the General of the Society is concentrated the power of all those separate wills, just as in the human body every cell should be completely devoted in its particular quality to the concentrated will of the organism.

—EIGHT LECTURES ON YOGA

"In other words, the Society of Jesus has created a perfect imitation of the skeleton of the original creation, living man. It has complied with the divinely instituted order of things, and that is why we see that the body, which was never numerically important, has yet been one of the greatest influences in the development of Europe."[1] Like many Western occultists, Crowley subscribed to the notion called corporatism (from the Latin plural *corpora*, "bodies"), i.e. that the body of man is a microcosm of everything larger than itself and a macrocosm of everything smaller than itself. This body of doctrine posits that while individual units have individual purposes, they are also part of a larger structure which binds them into a greater purpose.

In ancient Greece, Plato developed the concept of an authoritarian and communitarian corporatist system of natural classes and social hierarchies

---

[1] *Eight Lectures*, Ch. 7, Sec. 5.

that would be organized based on function, so that groups of priest, rulers, slaves, and warriors would co-operate to achieve social harmony. Aristotle likewise described society as being divided along natural classes and functional purposes, and ancient Rome adopted Greek concepts of corporatism, while adding the concept of political representation on the basis of function that divided representatives into military, professional, and religious groups—with institutions for each group known in Latin as *collegia*. Christian corporatism can be traced to I Corinthians 12, where Paul discusses the organic form of politics and society in which all people and components are united functionally, like the human body.

During the Middle Ages and the time of the Crusades in particular, the Catholic Church sponsored the creation of various institutions, including lay fraternities and monastic, religious, and military orders to bolster association between these groups. In mediaeval Europe, various function-based groups and institutions were created, such as universities, guilds for artisans and craftsmen, and other professional associations—the modern term "university" comes from the Latin word *universitas*, signifying a guild. The creation of the guild system is considered an especially important aspect of the history of corporatism, as it involved the allocation of power to regulate the labour and product market to guilds, which is seen as an essential element in the corporatist economic model of economic management and class collaboration.[2]

In 1540, Pope Paul III granted permission for the founding of a "Society of Jesus," whose members were to take the usual vows of poverty, chastity, and obedience, and live in communities without being categorized as monks.[3] These Jesuits—as they became known—were most strictly precluded from all ecclesiastical offices and dignities, enabling them to dedicate their efforts fully to the service of the Order.[4] Their main vow was that of obedience, which was treated with the same rigidity and severity as it is in the military. The Jesuits were ostensibly directed to serve the sick and the poor, and quietly to secure rich novices and the support of wealthy women—a feature which left a permanent stigma on the body. They would become the most excellent companions and the most austere ascetics, the most self-sacrificing missionaries and the most skilled advisors, the most qualified physicians and the most proficient assassins.[5]

The Jesuits quickly gained great significance in all the areas of culture, thus enabling them to extend their influence all over Europe, including in time even the Protestant countries. In nearly every important city they established their schools and colleges, and for a century and a half, were

---

[2] Wiarda 1997; *cf.* also Silos 2005.
[3] According to "The Formula of the Institute" approved by the pope, the professed members of the Society were to dwell in "houses" dedicated to their priestly ministries and subsist exclusively on alms; however, to train young men who would later be incorporated into the Society and live in these houses after completing their intellectual and spiritual education, "colleges" were to be established which would be allowed to have endowments and fixed revenues and from which the Jesuit students would go to lectures in nearby universities.
[4] Pope Francis is the first Jesuit pope, an historical anomaly trumped only by the "retirement" of Benedict XVI.
[5] Balk 2008.

leaders in European education. They suppressed independent research and made a host of important discoveries themselves—even if their efforts to raise the overall intellectual level of the Roman Church were prejudiced by the stubborn opposition of the Catholic hierarchy to freedom of thought. Their ubiquity was literal: no earthly position was too high for them, none too low; it could not be said for certain of anyone if they were a Jesuit or at least under the influence of the Jesuits. This stealthiness combined with a certain appeal to the melodramatic and picturesque in human nature enabled the Order to reach its first thousand members before its founder died.[6]

According to Crowley, "No one has understood the Magical Will better than Loyola; in his system the individual was forgotten. The will of the General was instantly echoed by every member of the Order; hence the Society of Jesus became the most formidable of the religious organizations of the world. That of the Old Man of the Mountain was perhaps the next best. The defect in Loyola's system is that the General was not God, and that owing to various other considerations he was not even necessarily the best man in the Order. To become General of the Order he must have willed to become General of the Order; and because of this he could be nothing more. ... When Buddha took his seat under the blessed Bo-Tree, he took an oath that none of the inhabitants of the 10,000 worlds should cause him to rise until he had attained; so that when even Mara the great Arch-Devil, with his three daughters the arch-temptresses appeared, he remained still. Now it is useless for the beginner to take so formidable a vow; he has not yet attained the strength which can defy Mara. Let him estimate his strength, and take a vow which is within it, but only just within it. Thus Milo began by carrying a new-born calf; and day by day as it grew into a bull, his strength was found sufficient."[7]

"The first condition of membership of the A∴A∴ is that one is sworn to identify one's own Great Work with that of raising mankind to higher levels, spiritually, and in every other way. Accordingly, it stands to reason that those charged with the conduct of the Order should be at least Masters of the Temple, or their judgment would be worthless, and at least Magi (though not that particular kind of Magus who brings the Word of a New Formula to the world every 2,000 years of so) or they would be unable to influence events on any scale commensurate with the scope of the Work. ... They may be incarnate or discarnate: it is a matter of Their convenience. Have They attained Their position by passing through all the grades of the A∴A∴? Yes and no: the system which was given to me to put forward is only one of many.[8] 'Above the Abyss' all these technical wrinkles are ironed out. One man whom I suspect of being a Secret Chief has hardly any

---

[6] *Ibid.* At 18,000 members, it remains the largest Catholic religious order today.
[7] *Book 4*, Part II, Ch. VI.
[8] *Cf.* also *Liber XIII*, Sec. 6, fn.: "All these grades are indeed but convenient landmarks, not necessarily significant. A person who had attained them all might be immeasurably the inferior of one who had attained none of them; it is Spiritual Experience alone that counts in Result; the rest is but Method."

acquaintance with the technique of our system at all. That he accepts *The Book of the Law* is almost his only link with my work. That, and his use of the Ophidian Vibrations: I don't know which of us is better at it, but I am sure that he must be a very long way ahead of me if he is one of Them."[9]

"In the R.R. et A.C., this is indicated to the Adept Minor by the title conferred upon him on his initiation to that grade: Hodos Camelionis:—the Path of the Chameleon. (This emphasizes the omnivalence of the force.) In the higher degrees of O.T.O.—the A∴A∴ is not fond of terms like this, which verge on the picturesque—it is usually called 'the Ophidian Vibrations,' thus laying special stress upon its serpentine strength, subtlety, its control of life and death, and its power to insinuate itself into any desired set of circumstances. It is of this universally powerful weapon that the Secret Chiefs must be supposed to possess complete control. They can induce a girl to embroider a tapestry, or initiate a political movement to culminate in a world-war; all in pursuit of some plan wholly beyond the purview or the comprehension of the deepest and subtlest thinkers."[10] In his Introduction to the *Tao Teh King*, Crowley writes: "I bound myself to devote my life to Magick at Easter 1898, and received my first initiation on November 18 of that year. My friend and climbing companion, Oscar Eckenstein, gave me my first instructions in learning the control of the mind early in 1901 in Mexico City."

Eckenstein was completely uninterested in Crowley's magical pursuits, and what is worse, totally unimpressed by his poetry. "He openly jeered at me for wasting my time on such rubbish. He being brutally outspoken, and I shy and sensitive, I naturally avoided creating opportunities for him to indulge his coarse ribaldry on a subject which to me was supremely sacred. ... During this time, my magical distress again increased. I could not relieve it by the narcotic of preparing and performing actual ceremonies, of silencing the voice of the demons by absorption in active work. It was while we were preparing our expedition to Colima that I broke out one evening and told Eckenstein my troubles, as I had done often enough before with no result beyond an insult or a sneer. Balaam could not have been more surprised when his ass began to prophesy that I was when, at the end of my outburst, Eckenstein turned on me and gave me the worst quarter of an hour of my life. He summed up my magical situation and told me that my troubles were due to my inability to control my thoughts. He said: 'Give up your Magick, with all its romantic fascinations and deceitful delights, Promise to do this for a time and I will teach you how to master your mind.' He spoke with the absolute authority which comes from profound and perfect knowledge."[11] From that date on, Crowley's diary entries refer to Eckenstein as "Frater D.A."[12]

Contrary to the apocryphal account published in *The Confession*, *Magick Without Tears*, and elsewhere, involving a time-travelling Grand Master

---

[9] *MWT*, Ch. IX.
[10] *Ibid.*
[11] *Confessions*, Ch. 25.
[12] Regardie 1970.

who confronts Crowley with a copy of a book he has not yet written, Crowley's entry into the O.T.O. was slightly more prosaic. In early 1910, Crowley was involved in a lawsuit filed by Samuel Liddell Mathers, the Chief Adept of the Hermetic Order of the Golden Dawn. Mathers sought to stay Crowley's publication of the Order's secret Adeptus Minor initiation ritual in *The Equinox*, Vol. I, No. 3, scheduled for release in March of that year. While testifying, Mathers made the statement that he was the head of the Rosicrucians, and after the newspapers printed the story, Crowley was inundated with offers of help from every other esoteric order in the UK and abroad, all claiming to be the real representatives of the Rosicrucians. Several of these groups also gave Crowley every grand-sounding title, dignity, and office they could spare, among them Theodor Reuss' unsolicited acknowledgement of Crowley, a 33° Mason, as a VII° of the O.T.O.[13]

"By the end of 1910, thanks to my relations with the Grand Hierophant 97° of the Rite of Memphis"—i.e. John Yarker—"(a post held after his death by Dr. Gerard Encausse,"—a/k/a Papus, a Spanish-born French Theosophist and founder of the modern Martinist Order—"Theodor Reuss, and myself), I was now a sort of universal inspector-general of the various rites, charged with the secret mission of reporting on the possibility of reconstructing the entire edifice, which was universally recognized by all its more intelligent members as being threatened with the gravest danger."[14] As the official story has it, "Although I was admitted to the thirty-third and last degree of Freemasonry so long ago as 1900, it was not until the summer of 1912 that my suspicion was confirmed. I speak of my belief that behind the frivolities and convivialities of our greatest institution lay in truth a secret ineffable and miraculous, potent to control the forces of Nature, and not only to make men brethren, but to make them divine. But at the time I speak of a man came to me, a man of those mysterious masters of esoteric Freemasonry who are alike its Eyes and its Brains, and who exist in its midst—unknown, often, even to its acknowledged chiefs. This man had been watching my occult career for some years, and deemed me now worthy to partake in the Greater Mysteries."[15]

Founded sometime between 1895 and 1903, the earliest known version of the vesica-shaped "lamen" of the O.T.O. appeared in the Martinist tome *L'art idéaliste & mystique: doctrine de l'Ordre et du salon annuel des Rose +*

---

[13] Eshelman 2000.

[14] *Confessions*, Ch. 72. As Yarker himself explains, "The system of High Grade Masonry, from which our Antient and Primitive Rite derives its origin, had birth in this country before the establishment of Grand Lodges. In France it had developed, early last century, into several Rites which were distinguished as Primitive—notably the Rites of Primitive Philadelphes and Philalethes, which were the offspring of those of Martinez Paschalis, and Marquis de St. Martin, and which, with others, worked side by side with the Rites of Perfection and Knights of the Orient. . . . To strengthen its position, and carry out its principals—the toleration of all Rites, the Sov. Sanc. has since obtained Charters for the practice of the Mizraim and Scottish Rites, and is enabled to afford opportunity for its members to obtain certificates of corresponding degrees, which carry their due weight in all countries. The Grand Master General being a member of the 96° in Egypt, the system is assimilated to the Memphis Rite in Egypt." (*The Kneph: Official Journal of the Antient and Primitive Rite of Masonry* I(7), July 1881, 63.)

[15] *The Elixir of Life*.

Croix (1894) by Joséphin Péladan[16]—even though the all-seeing eye, the cup, and the dove are common motifs in liturgical art, symbolizing the Father, the Son, and the Holy Ghost respectively.[17] "The O.T.O. is a training of the Masonic type; there is no 'astral' work in it at all, nor any Yoga. There is a certain amount of Qabalah, and that of great doctrinal value. But the really vital matter is the gradual progress towards disclosure of the Secret of the Ninth Degree. To use that secret to advantage involves mastery both of Yoga and of Magick; but neither is taught in the Order. Now it comes to be mentioned, this is really very strange. However, I didn't invent the system; I must suppose that those who did knew what they were about. To me it is (a) convenient in various practical ways, (b) a machine for carrying out the orders of the Secret Chiefs of A∴A∴, (c) by virtue of the Secret a magical weapon of incalculable power."[18]

In 1912, Reuss openly published the true nature of the work of the O.T.O. in the "Jubilee Edition" of the *Oriflamme*: "Our Order possesses the KEY which opens up all Masonic and Hermetic secrets, namely, the teaching of sexual magic, and this teaching explains, without exception, all the secrets of Nature, all the symbolism of Freemasonry and all systems of religion."[19] The late Dr. Carl Kellner, Reuss himself, and Crowley were listed as X° members. Reuss considered the Order to possess sufficient Masonic legitimacy to serve as the governing body in an international union of Masonic rites, but chose to approach that ambition obliquely, under the guise of an "Academia Masonica," or a mystery school to which high-degree Masons would apply for further instruction, thereby placing the highest degrees of the O.T.O. one organizational stage past the other high-degree rites of the day. National Sections like Crowley's "Mysteria Mystica Maxima" conferred degrees up to the VII°, or the equivalent of the 33° of the Scottish Rite or the grade of Knight Templar in the York Rite. Indeed, Reuss encouraged existing Masonic initiates and lodges to affiliate wholesale, transferring their dues obligations from their original jurisdictions to the O.T.O. and receiving recognition for equivalent degrees.[20]

However, as Crowley's *Liber LII* makes clear, "The O.T.O., although an Academia Masonica, is not a Masonic Body so far as the 'secrets' are

---

[16] Born Joseph-Aimé, this former collaborator of Papus and Stanislas de Guaïta's subsequently styled himself Sâr (Assyrian for "King") of the Order of the Catholic Rose + Croix, which purported to teach ancient Chaldean magic while viewing Rosicrucianism as an extension of authentic Catholic doctrine. Its female members, like those of the early O.T.O., were to be known only by pseudonyms, and both Orders drew heavily upon Wagner's music dramas.

[17] *Cf. MITAP*, Ch. 0, fn.: "Considerations of the Christian Trinity are of a nature suited only to Initiates of the IX° of O.T.O., as they enclose the final secret of all practical Magick."

[18] *MWT*, Ch. LXXI.

[19] As translated in King 1970, 119. Emphasis in original. *Cf.* also *Confessions, loc. cit.*: "The injunctions of the sages, from Pythagoras, Zoroaster and Lao Tzu, to the Cabalistic Jew who wrote the Ritual of the Royal Arch, and the sentimental snob who composed those of the Craft degrees, are either directed to indicating the best conditions for applying this secret, or are mere waste of words." This is again remarkably similar to the claim of St. Martin to "give the key to all the allegories and mystical fables of the ancients, the source of all religious and political institutions, and a model of the laws which should regulate the universe as well as single persons, and without which no real science could exist." (Findel 1866, 385.)

[20] Scriven & Scriven 1995.

concerned in the sense in which that expression is usually understood; and therefore in no way conflicts with, or infringes the just privileges of, the United Grand Lodge of England, or any Grand Lodge in America or elsewhere which is recognized by it."[21] What is more, "it is not very safe to talk about Rosicrucians, because their name has become a signal for letting loose the most devastating floods of nonsense. What is really known about the original Rosicrucians is practically confined to the three documents which they issued. The eighteenth century Rosicrucians may, or may not, have been legitimate successors of the original brotherhood—I don't know. But from them the O.T.O. derived its authority."[22] According to the "Brief History of Masonry" (1849) by É.-J. Marconis de Nègre (who together with his father, Grand Master Gabriel-Matthieu Marconis, is considered the founder of the Antient and Primitive Rite of Memphis and Mizraim[23]), the Rosicrucian Order was created in the year 46 CE, when an Alexandrian Gnostic sage by the name of Ormus[24], along with his six followers, were converted by Mark the Apostle. Their symbol was said to be a red cross surmounted by a rose, and Rosicrucianism was supposedly the purification of Egyptian mysteries with the new higher teachings of early Christianity.[25]

This version of the Rosicrucian legend was first circulated by the Baron de Westerode in 1784[26] and also promulgated by the 18th-century secret society called the Orden des Gülden- und Rosen-Creutzes, or the "Order of the Golden and Rosy Cross." Led by the pseudonymous Freemason and alchemist Hermann Fictuld, the group claimed that the leaders of the Rosicrucian Order had invented Freemasonry and they alone knew the secret meaning of Masonic symbols.[27] Candidates were expected to be Master Masons in good standing, and alchemy formed a central study for members. Much of the hierarchical structure for this order, including the nomenclature of its grades, was adopted by the Societas Rosicruciana in Anglia (S.R.I.A.) and through them, by the Hermetic Order of the Golden Dawn. In any case, many Freemasons became Rosicrucians and Rosi-

---

[21] Sec. 9.
[22] *MWT*, Introduction.
[23] "Mizraim" is the Hebrew name for the land of Egypt (or "the land of Ham"), and according to Genesis 10, a son of Ham (from Khem, "black," the native name of Egypt and its Priapic tutelary deity, also known as Min or Menu) and the brother of Cush, Phut, and Canaan, whose families together make up the Hamite branch of Noah's descendants. The *Book of Sothis* identifies Mizraim with the legendary first pharaoh, Menes, who is said to have unified the Old Kingdom and built the ancient Egyptian capital of Memphis.
[24] Or "Ormesius"—the initials of the Oriental Rite of Memphis spell out the word ORM.
[25] Marconis 1993.
[26] Mackey 1874; according to Westerode, the Masonic Degree of the Rose Croix itself was instituted among the Knights Templar in Palestine in the year 1188.
[27] "Although the ancient fathers and wise masters have met together ever since the beginning of the world and separated themselves from the profane masses, it was only in the time of Moses that the order laid down a rule of the highest secrecy in Egypt and in the wastes of Arabia. During and after the Babylonian captivity the brotherhood was established in Syria. And in the time of Solomon the classification or division was established. In the fourth, fifth and sixth centuries the whole brotherhood was reformed and finally given its present constitution. But, in order that the Chiefs might better conceal their aims and more easily ascertain men's eagerness for knowledge, the three lowest grades of freemasonry were established as a nursery to the higher sciences." (I. A. Fessler, *Rosenkreuzerey*, as translated in McIntosh 1997, 70.)

crucianism was established in many lodges and rites. At the Convent of Wilhelmsbad in 1782, the Old Scottish Lodge Friedrich at the Golden Lion in Berlin strongly suggested Duke Ferdinand of Brunswick-Lüneburg and all other Freemason submit to the Golden and Rosy Cross, albeit without success.[28]

As Crowley writes in his *Confessions*, "The eighteenth-century Rosicrucians, so-called in Austria, had already endeavoured to unite various branches of Continental freemasonry and its superstructures; in the nineteenth century, principally owing to the energy and ability of a wealthy iron master named Karl Kellner, a reconstruction and consolidation of traditional truth had been attempted. A body was formed under the name O.T.O. (Ordo Templi Orientis) which purported to achieve this result. It purported to communicate the secrets, not only of freemasonry (with the Rites of 3°, 7°, 33°, 90°, 97°, etc.), but of the Gnostic Catholic Church, the Martinists, the Sat Bhai, the Rosicrucians, the Knights of the Holy Ghost and so on, in nine degrees, with a tenth of an honorary character to distinguish the 'Supreme and Holy King' of the Order in each country where it was established. Chief of these kings is the O.H.O. (Outer Head of the Order, or Frater Superior), who is an absolute autocrat. This position was at this time occupied by Theodor Reuss, the Supreme and Holy King of Germany, who resigned the office in 1922 in my favour."[29]

Importantly, the O.T.O. "does not include the A∴A∴, with which august body it is, however, in close alliance."[30] Also, interestingly, "The names of women members are never divulged" and "It is not lawful here to disclose the name of any living chief."[31] Thus we have Leila Waddell signing official documents (including the Manifesto here quoted) as "L. Bathurst IX°," Crowley as "Baphomet XI°." However, "It was Carl Kellner who revived the exoteric organization of the O.T.O. and initiated the plan now happily complete of bringing all occult bodies again under one governance."[32] On 7 August 1912, Reuss' other previous collaborator, the prominent Theosophist Dr. Franz Hartmann, also died. Crowley, too, was at a crossroads: following another high-profile court case on 26 April 1911, the other two of the original three A∴A∴ Chiefs, George Cecil Jones and Maj. Gen. J. F. C. Fuller, had publicly distanced themselves from Crowley.[33] Within a year of those departures, Crowley had national O.T.O. leadership thrust into his hands, and by agreement with Reuss, or Merlin Peregrinus X°, the O.T.O. adopted *The Book of the Law* as its sole "Volume of Sacred Law," while in exchange, Crowley reconstructed its whole system of initiation, previously "the merest skeleton rituals boiled down from those of Continental

---

[28] McIntosh 1992.
[29] *Confessions, loc. cit.*
[30] *Liber LII*, Sec. 1.
[31] *Ibid.*, Sec. 2.
[32] *Ibid.*
[33] *Jones v. The Looking Glass Publishing Company (Limited) and Others*. Fuller never renounced Thelema or mysticism, however, and his epoch-making *Foundations of the Science of War* (1926) was in large part based on Crowley's philosophy.

Masonry."³⁴ There were more Freemasons then (even in absolute terms) and they were far more influential than they are today, so through the O.T.O., Crowley might potentially promulgate the Law of Thelema to *millions* of respectable and respected people all over the world.

"Much of freemasonry is connected with the Hebrew Cabbala. My knowledge of this science enabled me to analyse the Secret Words of the various degrees. I soon found myself able to correct many of the corruptions which had crept in, and there was no doubt that my conclusions were not mere conjectures, since they made coherent good sense out of disconnected nonsense."³⁵ For example, "93, the Word of the Law, ΘΕΛΗΜΑ, Will, and ΑΓΑΠΗ, Love which under Will, is the Law. It is also the number of Aiwaz, the Author of the Book, of the Lost Word whose formula does in sober truth 'raise Hiram,' and of many another close-woven Word of Truth."³⁶ In 1918, amidst an abortive attempt to establish a Supreme Grand Council of the O.T.O. in Detroit, Michigan, Crowley prepared another substantial revision to the Order's initiation rituals, this time wholly abandoning the Hiramic legend, the term "Freemasonry" and the characteristic emblems, signs, handshakes, etc. of the Craft degrees, and presented his revised 0–III° rituals to Reuss for order-wide adoption.³⁷

Though he lived almost another 30 years, Crowley never bothered to finish rewriting the higher degree rituals, possibly because it had become painfully obvious that the larger Masonic establishment was never going to take his claims seriously³⁸—with the IV° of the modern O.T.O. notoriously remaining a near carbon copy of the British "Royal Arch" ceremonies. Throughout Crowley's headship, new members continued to be promoted to IX° at the first inkling of them "knowing the secret," including his two immediate successors as the head of the Order. As late as 1943, Crowley wrote a female student, "With regard to the O.T.O., I believe I can find you a typescript of all the official documents. If so, I will let you have them to read, and you can make up your mind as to whether you wish to affiliate to the Third Degree of the Order. I should consequently, in the case of your deciding to affiliate, go with you though the script of the Rituals and explain the meaning of the whole thing; communicating, in addition, the real secret and significant knowledge of which ordinary Masonry is not possessed."³⁹

In his *Confessions*, Crowley quotes an essay by a "Past Grand Master"—himself obviously—published in the *English Review* of August 1922: "There is, therefore, no reason for refraining from the plain statement that, to anyone who understands the rudiments of symbolism, the Master's degree is identical with the Mass. This is in fact the real reason for papal anathema; for freemasonry asserts that every man is himself the

---

[34] Letter to Arnold Krumm-Heller, 22 June 1930, as quoted in Starr 2003, 99.
[35] *Confessions, loc. cit.*
[36] *The Equinox of the Gods*, "Genesis Libri AL," Ch. VII, Sec. III.
[37] Starr 2003.
[38] *Cf.* Kaczynski 2006. It is also possible that Crowley *did* finish the rituals, but that they were simply lost like so many of his other unpublished papers.
[39] *MWT, loc. cit.*

living, slain and re-arisen Christ in his own person.[40] It is true that not one mason in ten thousand in England is aware of this fact; but he has only to remember his 'raising' to realize the fundamental truth of the statement. Well may Catholic and freemason alike stand appalled at the stupendous blasphemy which is implied, as they ignorantly think, not knowing themselves of the stuff and substance of the Supreme Self, each for himself alike no less than Very God of Very God!"[41]

While visiting Moscow in 1913, "the full interpretation of the *central mystery of freemasonry* became clear in consciousness, and I expressed it in dramatic form in 'the Ship'. The lyrical climax is in some respects my supreme achievement in invocation; in fact, the chorus . . . seemed to me worthy to be introduced as the anthem into the Ritual of the Gnostic Catholic Church which, later in the year, I prepared for the use of the O.T.O., the central ceremony of its public and private celebration, corresponding to the Mass of the Roman Catholic Church. . . . Human nature demands (in the case of most people) the satisfaction of the religious instinct, and, to very many, this may best be done by ceremonial means. I wished therefore to construct a ritual through which people might enter into ecstasy as they have always done under the influence of appropriate ritual. In recent years, there has been an increasing failure to attain this object, because the established cults shock their intellectual convictions and outrage their common sense. Thus their minds criticize their enthusiasm; they are unable to consummate the union of their individual souls with the universal soul as a bridegroom would be to consummate his marriage if his love were constantly reminded that its assumptions were intellectually absurd."[42]

"I resolved that my ritual should celebrate the sublimity of the operation of universal forces without introducing disputable metaphysical theories. I would neither make nor imply any statement about nature which would not be endorsed by the most materialistic man of science. On the surface this may sound difficult; but in practice I found it perfectly simple to combine the most rigidly rational conceptions of phenomena with the most

---

[40] Cf. e.g. *Ecclesiam a Jesu Christo* (13 September 1821), Constitution of Pope Pius VII, which conflates Freemasonry with the Carbonari, who allegedly "profane and defile the passion of Jesus Christ by certain of their impious ceremonies, [and] despise the Sacraments of the Church (for which they seem to substitute other new things invented by themselves through their supreme wickedness)."

[41] *Confessions*, loc. cit. Cf. also Lévi 1913, 388: "Now, if Masonry is thus holy and thus sublime, we may be asked how it came to be proscribed and condemned so often by the Church; but we have already replied to this question when its divisions and profanations were mentioned. Masonry is the Gnosis and the false Gnostics caused the condemnation of the true. The latter were driven into concealment, not through fear of the light, for the light is that which they desire, that which they seek and adore; but they stood in dread of the sacrilegious—that is to say, of false interpreters, calumniators, the derision of the sceptic, the enemies of all belief and all morality. Moreover, at the present day, there are many who think that they are Masons and yet do not know the meaning of their Rites, having lost the Key of the Mysteries. They misconstrue even their symbolical pictures and those hieroglyphic signs which are emblazoned on the carpets of their Lodges. These pictures and signs are the pages of a book of absolute and universal science. They can be read by means of the Kabalistic keys and hold nothing in concealment for the initiate who already possesses those of Solomon."

[42] *Ibid.*, Ch. 73. Emphasis added.

exalted and enthusiastic celebration of their sublimity."[43] According to *Magick in Theory and Practice*, Crowley's essay *Energized Enthusiasm* gives "a concise account of one of the classical methods of arousing Kundalini" and the "earliest and truest Christians used what is in all essentials this method."[44] Crowley cites *Fragments of a Faith Forgotten* by G. R. S. Mead, an influential member of the Theosophical Society and the first modern scholar of the Gnostic tradition. "There is a real connexion between what the vulgar call blasphemy and what they call immorality, in the fact that the Christian legend is an echo of a Phallic rite. There is also a true and positive connexion between the Creative force of the Macrocosm, and that of the Microcosm. For this reason the latter must be made as pure and consecrated as the former. The puzzle for most people is how to do this. The study of Nature is the Key to that Gate."[45]

The examination of *The Paradoxes of the Highest Science* by Éliphas Lévi begins thus: "Magic is the divinity of man conquered by science in union with faith; the true Magi are Men-Gods, in virtue of their intimate union with the divine principle."[46] In *The Gospel According to St. Bernard Shaw*, Crowley actually quotes *De Natura Deorum*, "A Secret Instruction of the Seventh Degree" of the O.T.O. or as he puts it, "an ancient manuscript preserved in one of the secret sanctuaries of Initiation"—"Such gods as Parabrahman merely bewilder the people, and render them the prey of priestcraft, while the Christs alike of the Lutheran, Latin, and Anglican Churches are but the machine-gods of all fraud and oppression, being stolen and prostituted from that Christ in whom our fathers in the Gnosis strove to synthesize the warring Gods of Syria, Greece, Chaldea, Rome, and Egypt at the time when the growth of the Roman Empire first made travel possible, and the intercommunication of the priests of Mithras, Adonis, Attis, Osiris, Dionysus, Isis, Astarte, Venus and many scores of others. Traces of this recension are still visible in the Mass and in the Calendar of the Saints, all major Gods and Goddesses of universal import receiving the same honour by the same rites as before, while the local Gods were replaced by Saints, virgins, martyrs, or angels, often of the same name, always of the same character."[47]

"Thus on the altar the Solar-phallic Crucifix is surrounded by six lights for the planets, to use one example only of a hundred at our disposal; and Christmas is at the winter solstice, the birth of Christ put for the birth of the Sun. All these points may be studied in *La Messe et ses Mystères*, *Rome pagan and papal*, *The two Babylons*, *Rivers of Life*, *Two essays on the worship of Priapus*, and many other books. It is rather amusing to observe that ultra-Protestants, in proving that Roman Catholicism is pagan and

---

[43] *Ibid. Cf.* e.g. *Humanum Genus* (20 April 1884), Encyclical of Pope Leo XIII on Freemasonry: "their ultimate purpose forces itself into view—namely, the utter overthrow of that whole religious and political order of the world which the Christian teaching has produced, and the substitution of a new state of things in accordance with their ideas, of which the foundations and laws shall be drawn from mere naturalism."
[44] *MITAP*, Ch. XV, Sec. II.
[45] *Ibid.*
[46] Lévi 1922, 1.
[47] *Liber 888*, "Salvation at first a Class Privilege; and the Remedy."

phallic, which they do quite irrefutably, need merely to be confronted with the proof of the Catholics that every point of their religion is derived from Scripture, to form the premises of a syllogism, whose conclusion is that Christianity is but an adaptation of Phallicism."[48] The Commentary on Chapter 86 of *The Book of Lies* also prompts the reader to consult the above-mentioned *La messe et ses mystères: comparés aux mystères anciens* (1844) by the prominent French freemason Jean-Marie Ragon de Bettignies, "for a complete demonstration of the incorporation of the Solar and Phallic Mysteries in Christianity."[49]

According to *The Key of the Mysteries*, "The Catholic, that is to say the universal, dogma merits that magnificent name by harmonizing in one all the religious aspirations of the world; with Moses and Mohammed, it affirms the unity of God; with Zoroaster, Hermes and Plato, it recognizes in Him the infinite trinity of its own regeneration; it reconciles the living numbers of Pythagoras with the monadic Word of St. John; so much, science and reason will agree." Here Crowley interjects that, "The author had perhaps no space to continue with a demonstration that the Gospel legend itself is a macédoine of those of Bacchus, Adonis, Osiris, and a hundred others, and that the Mass, and Christian ceremonies generally, have similarly pagan sources." Lévi continues: "It is then in the eyes of reason and of science themselves the most perfect, that is to say the most complete, dogma which has ever been produced in the world. Let science and reason grant us so much; we shall ask nothing more of them."[50]

"The divinity of Jesus Christ only exists in the Catholic Church, to which He transmits hierarchically His life and His divine powers. This divinity is sacerdotal and royal by virtue of communion; but outside of that communion, every affirmation of the divinity of Jesus Christ is idolatrous, because Jesus Christ could not be an isolated God."[51] As late as 1986, Cardinal Ratzinger, subsequently Pope Benedict XVI, then the Prefect of the Congregation for the Doctrine of Faith (formerly known as the Holy Roman and Universal Inquisition), declared that "the Church's negative judgment in regard to Masonic association remains unchanged" and that "The faithful who enrol in Masonic associations are in a state of grave sin and may not receive Holy Communion."[52] If in Britain, Freemasonry was traditionally associated with the Church of England, and in America, many early churches were built by members of Masonic lodges, certain "higher degrees" of Freemasonry—considered merely optional and historical in the

---

[48] *Ibid.*

[49] Though the A∴A∴ Curriculum only lists *The Age of Reason* (1794), Thomas Paine also wrote "An Essay on the Origins of Free Masonry" (posth. 1818), in which he argues that "The Christian religion and masonry have one and the same common origin, both are derived from the worship of the sun, the difference between their origins is, that the Christian religion is a parody on the worship of the sun, in which they put a man whom they call Christ in the place of the sun, and pay him the same adoration which was originally paid to the sun, as I have shewn in the chapter on the origin of the Christian religion"—a reference to the unpublished third part of *The Age of Reason*.

[50] *The Key of the Mysteries*, Part I, Article III.

[51] *Ibid.*

[52] "Declaration on Masonic Associations," Rome, 26 November 1983.

English-speaking world—were spread on the Continent by the Jacobite diaspora and became part of the attempt to re-Catholicize Protestant Europe.[53]

As the occult revival of the late 19th century began to unfold, a link was forged between esoteric Freemasonry and the burgeoning Gnostic Catholicism among those disaffected by the heavy-handed centralism emanating from Rome in the wake of the First Vatican Council. This 1870 synod inaugurated an era of Roman Catholic conservatism and approved the dogma of Papal Infallibility, which caused considerable dissent among Catholics in parts of Germany, Austria, and Switzerland. Some of the dissenters limited themselves to only repudiating the new dogma, but encouraged by a large number of scholars and statesmen, others went on to form independent sects. The "State Catholics," for example, acknowledged the pope's infallibility in the spiritual field, but denied his legitimacy in the secular arena. The "Old Catholics," on the other hand, refused to accept the notion that papal privileges extended wider than what was prescribed by the Church Fathers, and sought to adhere to the beliefs and practices of the Church of the post-apostolic era, before any of the so-called Ecumenical Councils.[54]

Episcopal dissent created a generation of what came to be known as *episcopi vagantes*, or "wandering bishops." Since many Rosicrucians and Freemasons perceived episcopal offices and church sacraments to be essentially identical to their esoteric ceremonial, "cross-ordination" became a quite common practice, with episcopal titles and prerogatives interchanged with Freemasonic degrees and offices, among disaffected prelates and occult-minded Masons.[55] "Freemasonry, which has so frightened the Court of Rome, is not so terrible as people think; it has lost its ancient lights, but has preserved its symbols and its rites which belong to the Occult Philosophy; it still gives the titles and ribbons of the Rosy Cross, but the true Rosicrucians are no longer in its Lodges; they are what they have been from the beginning—philosophers and *unknown*. Paschalis, Martines [sic] and St. Martin have successors who do not meet in regular assemblies. Their Lodge is said to be in the great Pyramid of Egypt, an expression, allegorical and mystical, which the innocent and ignorant are at liberty to take literally."[56]

In 1893, Gerard Encausse, head of the Martinists, was consecrated Tau Vincent, a bishop of Toulouse in l'Église Gnostique, by Jules Doinel, or Tau Valentin II—who had founded this first Gnostic Church in modern times in 1890 and who was swiftly elevated into the Supreme Council of the Martinist Order. In 1895, Doinel abdicated as Primate of the French Gnostic Church, leaving control to a synod of three of his former bishops, one of whom was Encausse. At a High Synod in 1896, they elected another bishop, Léonce Fabre des Essarts, or Tau Synesius, to succeed Doinel as patriarch. In 1901, Fabre des Essarts consecrated the 20-year-old Martinist Jean

---

[53] Millar 2013; *cf.* e.g. "Mémoire au duc de Brunswick" (1782) in Maistre 1983.
[54] Balk, *op. cit.*
[55] Tau Dionysus, "Gnostics and Templars," *Gnostic Gnews* I(3), Summer Solstice 1989.
[56] Lévi, *op. cit.*, 129.

"Joanny" Bricaud as Tau Johannes, Bishop of Lyon. Bricaud had been educated in a Roman Catholic seminary, where he had prepared for the priesthood, but had renounced his conventional religious pursuits at the age of sixteen to study the occult. With the encouragement of Encausse, Bricaud broke from Fabre des Essarts in 1907 to found his own schismatic branch of the Gnostic Church, which would also incorporate the Carmelite Church of Eugéne Vintras and the Johannite Church of Bernard-Raymond Fabré-Palaprat.[57]

The motive for the schism appears to have been the desire to form a branch of the Gnostic Church whose doctrine and structure would more closely parallel those of the Roman Rite, rather than those of the Cathars. What is more, Doinel had been a Martinist, Bricaud was a Martinist, but Fabre des Essarts was not. Bricaud, Encausse, and Louis-Sophrone Fugairon, the third founding bishop, initially named the church l'Église Catholique Gnostique, or the "Gnostic Catholic Church," and in February 1908, the episcopal synod elected Bricaud, as Tau Jean II, patriarch. In June of the same year, Encausse organized in Paris an International Masonic Conference, where he first met Theodor Reuss and the two apparently exchanged patents. Reuss elevated Encausse to X° of the O.T.O. as well as giving him license to establish a "Supreme Grand Council General of the Unified Rites of Antient and Primitive Masonry for the Grand Orient of France and its Dependencies at Paris." For his part, Encausse assisted Reuss in the formation of a German branch of the Gnostic Church, which like all of his other acquisitions, Reuss included under the umbrella of the O.T.O.. L'Église Catholique Gnostique translated into German as Die Gnostische Katholische Kirche, while the French branch changed its name to l'Église Gnostique Universelle (E.G.U.);[58] the Latin form of the name, *Ecclesia Gnostica Catholica*, first appeared on the title page of a homily in honour of the elevation of Monseigneur Bricaud to the Patriarchal See of the "Universal Gnostic Church" in 1908.[59]

In the Tenth Lesson of "The Elements of the Qabalah in Ten Lessons," Lévi writes: "The official Church is spoken of as infallible in the *Apocalypse*, this Qabalistic key to the Gospels; for Christianity has always contained an occult or Johannite strain, which, while respecting the official line of the Church, has preserved an interpretation of dogma quite other than the one given to the common man. Templars, Rosicrucians and Freemasons of high degree have all belonged to this occult Church; in the last century, prior to the French Revolution, its apostles including Pasqualis Martinez, Saint Martin and even Mme Krudemer. The distinctive characteristic of this school is to avoid publicity and anything that would make of it a dissident sect. Count Joseph de Maistre, this radical Catholic, was far more sympathetic than is believed towards the Martinist society and foretold a

---

[57] Scriven & Scriven, *op. cit.*
[58] *Ibid.*
[59] "Homélie de sa grandeur monseigneur Johannés Bricaud, Tau Jean II, à l'occasion de son élévation au siège patriarchal de l'Église Gnostique Universelle, suivi de la profession de foi," Des évêques gnostiques, membres du très haut synode, Lyon, 28 February 1908.

coming rebirth of dogma, inspired by lights emanating from the sanctuaries of occultism."[60]

"There still exist fervent priests who are initiate in the ancient doctrines, and one bishop, among others, has recently died who made repeated requests to me for Qabalistic communication. The disciples of Saint-Martin had themselves called unknown philosophers, and those of a contemporary teacher, fortunate enough to be even more unknown, have need of no name whatsoever, since not even their existence is suspected. Jesus said that the yeast should be hidden in the bottom of the trough which holds the dough so that it can work day and night in silence until it has permeated the entire mass that is destined to be bread. An initiate can, then, simply and sincerely practise the religion into which he was born, since all rites represent in various ways a single dogma; but he should open the heart of his conscience to God alone, accountable to no one for his most intimate beliefs. No priest can judge what the Pope himself does not understand."[61]

One of the revelations that came to Crowley through the so-called Paris Working in 1913 is as follows: "In the beginning was the Word, the logos, who is Mercury; and is therefore to be identified with Christ. Both are messengers; their birth-mysteries are similar; the pranks of their childhood are similar. In 'The Vision of the Universal Mercury,' Hermes is seen descending upon the sea, which refers to Maria. The Crucifixion represents the Caduceus; the two thieves, the two serpents; the cliff in 'The Vision of the Universal Mercury' is Golgotha; Maria is simply Maia with the Solar R in her womb. The controversy about Christ between the Synoptics and John was really a contention between the priests of Bacchus, Sol, and Osiris, also, perhaps, of Adonis and Attis, on the one hand, and those of Hermes on the other, at that period when initiates all over the world found it necessary, owing to the growth of the Roman Empire and the opening up of means of communication, to replace conflicting Polytheisms by a synthetic Faith."[62]

"To continue the identification, compare Christ's descent into hell with the function of Hermes as guide of the Dead. Also Hermes leading up Eurydice, and Christ raising up Jairus' daughter. Christ is said to have risen on the third day, because it takes three days for the Planet Mercury to become visible after separating from the orb of the Sun. (It may be noted here that Mercury and Venus are the planets between us and the Sun, as if the Mother and the Son were mediators between us and the Father.) Note Christ as the Healer, and also his own expression: 'The Son of Man cometh as a thief in the night' [I Thess. 5:2, Rev. 3:3, 16:15]; and also this scripture: 'For as the lightning cometh out of the East and shineth even unto the West, so shall the coming of the Son of Man be.' [Matt. 24:27] Note also Christ's relations with the money-changers, his frequent parables, and the fact that his first disciple was a publican. Note also Mercury as the deliverer of Prometheus."[63]

---

[60] Papus 2000, 73–74.
[61] Ibid., 74.
[62] *The Paris Working*, Opus II.
[63] Ibid.

"Reference has already been made in this essay to the legends of Hermes and Dionysus. The father of Gautama Buddha was said to be an elephant with six tusks, appearing to his mother in a dream. There is also the legend of the Holy Ghost in the form of a dove, impregnating the Virgin Mary. There is here a reference to the dove of Noah's Ark, bringing glad tidings of the salvation of the world from the waters. (The dwellers in the Ark are the foetus, the waters the amniotic fluid.) Similar fables are to be found in every religion of the Æon of Osiris: it is the typical formula of the Dying God."[64] Which brings us back to the First Paradox of the Highest Science as articulated by the Abbé Constant: "Religion is magic sanctioned by authority."[65] Crowley's Gnostic Mass calls forth "Lord of Life and Joy, that art the might of man, that art the essence of every true god that is upon the surface of the Earth, continuing knowledge from generation unto generation, thou adored of us upon heaths and in woods, on mountains and in caves, openly in the marketplaces and secretly in the chambers of our houses, in temples of gold and ivory and marble as in these other temples of our bodies, we worthily commemorate them worthy that did of old adore thee and manifest thy glory unto men... Oh Sons of the Lion and the Snake! with all thy saints we worthily commemorate them worthy that were and are and are to come. May their Essence be here present, potent, puissant and paternal to perfect this feast!"[66]

This is coupled with a laundry list of exclusively male, exclusively Osirian "divinities" (Orpheus, but not Eurydice; Osiris, but not Horus or Isis), including significantly Apollonius of Tyana, but not Jesus of Nazareth; and Simon Magus instead of Simon Peter. "Here ye all, saints of the *true* church of *old* time now essentially present, that of ye we claim heirship, with ye we claim communion, from ye we claim benediction in the name of IAΩ."[67] According to Crowley, IAΩ is a "Gnostic secret way of spelling and pronouncing Jehovah" and "this has the value 811.[68] So has 'Let there be,' *Fiat*, transliterating into Greek."[69] In Roman Catholicism, the apostolic succession is perceived as reflecting a transmission of true spiritual authority extending as far back as Saint Peter, and even further to Melchizedek—also included in the above list of "Gnostic Saints"—the semi-mythical priest-king of Salem, who blessed the Hebrew patriarch Abraham and received tithes from him.[70]

---

[64] *The Book of Thoth*, Part II, Atu XI. According to *I.N.R.I.: Constitution of the Ancient Order of Oriental Templars* (1917), Article II, Section 1, "The O.T.O. declares that Brotherhood of All Things Created is a fact in Nature."

[65] Lévi, *op. cit.*, 1.

[66] *Liber XV*, Sec. IV.

[67] *Ibid.* Emphasis added.

[68] *Cf.* also *Liber DCCCXI*, Sec. I: "I A O the supreme One of the Gnostics, the true God, is the Lord of this work. Let us therefore invoke Him by that name which the Companions of the Royal Arch blaspheme to aid us in the essay to declare the means which He has bestowed upon us!"

[69] *MWT, loc. cit. Cf.* also *Confessions*, Ch. 81: "The old pagan worship of the Mother-idea was superseded by the word IAO or its equivalents, which asserted the formula of the Dying God, and made the Male, dying to himself in the act of love, the engineer of the continued life of the race."

[70] Genesis 14:18–20; Psalm 110:4; Hebrews 5–7. This "king of righteousness" (Heb. מלכיצדק) has been variously identified with Shem, with Ham, with Canaan, with Mizraim, and even with Enoch, the archangel Michael, and the divine Logos itself; however, Zedek is also an ancient name of

Bricaud, Fugairon, and Encausse declared the E.G.U. to be the official church of Martinism in 1911, and on 21 July 1913, Tau Jean II was consecrated to the episcopate a second time by Louis-Marie-François Giraud, an ex-Trappist monk who was ordained and consecrated with complete regularity by a bishop of the Vilatte succession. In fact, Giraud had been ordained priest by Archbishop René Vilatte, or Mar Timotheos, himself in 1907. This provided Bricaud, who became head of l'Ordre Martiniste after Papus' death in 1916, with the apostolic authority to administer the Christian sacraments. Many members of the Martinist Order were of the Roman Catholic faith, and subject to excommunication if their Martinist affiliation became known, and the E.G.U. thus offered continued assurance of salvation to Catholics who were or wished to become Martinists.[71]

Similarly, J. I. Wedgwood—former head of the English Section of the Theosophical Society and a member of the famous Wedgwood china dynasty—sought and received consecration from the Old Catholics in February 1916 and, in turn, consecrated C. W. Leadbeater, a former Anglican curate and high-ranking Theosophist, in July of the same year. Mrs. Besant soon announced her endorsement of the movement as the ecclesiastical organization for the new messiah she was expecting. She noted that the church was still small, but was "likely to become the future Church of Christendom 'when He comes.'" However, problems arose quickly, and in the summer of 1917, the archbishop of the Old Catholics in Britain publicly repudiated Wedgwood's claims. Six months later, *The Theosophist* announced that the Theosophical group of Old Catholics had adopted the name "Liberal Catholic Church," and it persists under that name to this day as an independent organization associated with the Theosophical Society (Adyar).[72]

Rudolph Steiner, finally, was made the Secretary General of the German branch of the Theosophical Society in 1902, as well as chartered in 1906 as Deputy Grand Master of the "Mystica Aeterna" Chapter and Grand Council of the O.T.O. in Berlin.[73] However, the tension between Steiner's Western understanding of esotericism and the Orientalism of Mrs. Besant grew acute when she began to promote the Indian youth Jiddu Krishnamurti as the next World Teacher. In late 1912, Steiner led the Council of the German Section of the Theosophical Society to declare that its membership was "irreconcilable" with membership in Krishnamurti's Order of the Star in the East. Besant responded by revoking the charter of the German Section, but Steiner took fifty-five of the sixty-nine German lodges and about 2,500 members with him.[74] The Anthroposophical Society was founded in February 1913, and Steiner also ended his association with Reuss the following year. In 1922, along with Dr. Guenther Wachmuth and the former Evangelical pastor Friedrich Rittelmeyer, Steiner founded the Christian

---

Jerusalem.
[71] Scriven & Scriven, *op. cit.*
[72] Campbell 1980.
[73] *Cf.* Steiner 2007.
[74] Campbell, *op. cit.*

Community church in Switzerland, as "a ritual expression of the outlook and ideas found in Anthroposophy."[75]

As Crowley puts it, "If the Bible be the Word of god, Mr. Shaw is damned, and I am damned myself. . . . On the other hand; if the New Testament be the composite document which it is here maintained to be in this essay, I am the truest of all Christians. I agree with practically every word reported of the Yogi Jesus, and nearly every word of the Essene. True, I reject Salvationism, and the Jewish element of prophecies fulfilled, and the praise of the Law of Moses; but trust humbly that any deficiency in these respects may be more than made up by superfluity in another. For not only do I hold the cult of John Barleycorn to be the only true religion, but have established his worship anew; in the last three years branches of my organisation have sprung up all over the world to celebrate the ancient rite. So mote it be."[76] Or as he writes a student, "I fear your 'Christianity' is like that of most other folk. You pick out one or two of the figures from which the Alexandrines concocted 'Jesus' (too many cooks, again, with a vengeance!) and neglect the others. The Zionist Christ of Matthew can have no value for you; nor can the Asiatic 'Dying-God'—compiled from Melcarth, Mithras, Adonis, Bacchus, Osiris, Attis, Krishna, and others—who supplied the miraculous and ritualistic elements of the fable."[77]

The title page of Crowley's Gnostic Mass declares the ritual script to have been "Edited from the Ancient Documents in Assyrian and Greek." The Syrian School represents the oldest phase of historic Gnosticism, since western Asia was the birthplace of the movement. Syria was also an important home to Christianity, its centre being Antioch, where Sts. Peter, Paul, and Barnabas established the first Christian community—the very word "Christian" was invented there. At Alexandria, Egypt, the great Greek ecclesiastical writers pursued their studies with pagan rhetoricians, setting up their own schools, and teaching Christian doctrine in the manner of pagan philosophers of the time. This development was facilitated by the allegorical interpretation of Scripture already employed for a long time by the Alexandrian Jews. The Christian Church, spreading as it then was across the Roman Empire, was still a Greek church. The common language of most traders, craftsmen, and professionals was the Koine Greek, also known as the Alexandrian dialect or Hellenistic Greek. This was also the language of every Jew of the Dispersion, to whom the Gospel was originally preached, and every book of the New Testament was written in Koine.[78]

Attempts were made in the 1980s by Crowley's self-declared successor Hymenaeus Alpha X° to demonstrate that Crowley himself possessed a valid Christian apostolic succession though Reuss in the above-mentioned Vilatte line, ultimately originating in the Syrian Orthodox Church of Antioch. The O.T.O. now concedes that he almost certainly did not, but

---

[75] *Ibid.*
[76] *Liber 888*, "The Solution of the Enigma according to the Plymouth Brethren."
[77] *MWT, loc. cit.* The *Præmonstrance of A∴A∴* describes *Liber XV* as "The Canon of the Mass, according to the Gnostic Catholic Church, which represents the original and true pre-Christian Christianity."
[78] Balk, *op. cit.*

further attempts were made to strengthen the traditional apostolic succession within the Ecclesia Gnostica Catholica (E.G.C.), as the Gnostic Catholic Church became known when it was temporarily turned into an independent organization by the "Caliph." During this period, some O.T.O. members were recognized as E.G.C. bishops upon receiving consecration from bishops outside the E.G.C. and certain bishops of other branches of the Gnostic Church were recognized as ecclesiastical members of the O.T.O..[79] In the 1990s, the "Acting O.H.O." Hymenæus Beta XI° discontinued the practice, dissolved the separate E.G.C. corporation, and revoked the privileges of non-initiate clergy.[80]

According to Crowley, Thelema "is the Law that Jesus Christ, or rather the Gnostic tradition of which the Christ-legend is a degradation, attempted to teach; but nearly every word he said was misinterpreted and garbled by his enemies, particularly by those who called themselves his disciples." To be sure, Crowley took it as "proven that 'Jesus' is a composite figure of several incompatible elements. There is therefore no 'he' in the case. The Gospels are a crude compilation of Gnosticism, Judaism, Essenism, Hinduism, Buddhism, with the watch-words of various sacerdotal-political cults, thrown at random into a hotch-potch of the distorted legends of the persons of the Pagan Pantheon, all glued with a semblance of unity in the interests of sustaining the shaken fabric of local faiths against the assaults of the consolidation of civilization, and of applying the cooperative principle to businesses whose throats were being cut by competition."[81]

"In any case the Æon was not ready for a Law of Freedom. Of all his followers only St. Augustine appears to have got even a glimmer of what he meant.[82] A further attempt to teach this law was made through Sir Edward Kelly at the end of the sixteenth century.[83] The bondage of orthodoxy

---

[79] Scriven & Scriven, *op. cit.* Curiously enough, the original practice of admitting regular Freemasons at the equivalent O.T.O. degrees was on the other hand discontinued at the same time. Evidently, it was feared the practice would conflict with the tax-exempt religious organization status the O.T.O. was seeking, and the separate E.G.C. served as a backup in case the main application still got rejected. Ironically, however, the O.T.O. adheres more closely to the Landmarks of Freemasonry today than it ever did in Crowley's day, causing some Masonic jurisdictions to recognize it, even if it does not return the favour.

[80] *Cf. Bylaws of Ordo Templi Orientis International*, August 2003.

[81] *The Equinox of the Gods, loc. cit.*, Ch. VIII.

[82] *In Epistolam Ioannis ad Parthos Tractatus Decem*, VII.8: "Once for all, then, a short precept is given you: Love, and do what you will: whether you hold your peace, through love hold your peace; whether you cry out, through love cry out; whether you correct, through love correct; whether you spare, through love do you spare: let the root of love be within, of this root can nothing spring but what is good." *Cf. The Antecedents of Thelema*, Sec. II: "This is however, as the context shows, by no means what is meant by *The Book of the Law*. St. Augustine's thesis is that if the heart be full of Love, one cannot go wrong. It is, so to say, a rider upon the theorem of St. Paul's thirteenth chapter of the First Epistle to the Corinthians."

[83] *Cf.* e.g. Casaubon 1659, 25: "I am the Daughter of Fortitude, and ravished every hour, from my youth. For behold, I am Understanding, and Science dwelleth in me; and the heavens oppress me, they covet and desire me with infinite appetite: few or none that are earthly have imbraced me, for I am shadowed with the Circle of the Stone, and covered with the morning Clouds. My feet as swifter than the winds, and my hands are sweeter than the morning dew. My garments are from the beginning, and my dwelling place is in my self. The Lion knoweth not where I walk, neither do the beasts of the field understand me. I am defloured, and yet a virgin: I sanctifie, and am not sanctified. Happy is he that imbraceth me: for in the night season I am sweet, and in the day full

prevented his words from being heard, or understood.[84] In many other ways has the spirit of truth striven with man, and partial shadows of this truth have been the greatest allies of science and philosophy. Only now has success been attained. A perfect vehicle was found, and the message enshrined in a jewelled casket; that is to say, in a book with the injunction 'Change not as much as the style of a letter.' This book is reproduced in facsimile, in order that there shall be no possibility of corrupting it. Here, then, we have an absolutely fixed and definite standpoint for the foundation of an universal religion."[85]

Bear in mind, *The Book of the Law* itself was not actually published until 1913, when it was printed in *The Equinox*, Vol. I, No. 10—the last *Equinox* to be issued under the aegis of the A∴A∴—as "Liber L. vel Legis." A facsimile of the manuscript first appeared in *The Equinox*, Vol. I, No. 7. In a letter of 1914, Crowley can be seen as articulating the modern definition of Wicca: "Time is just right for a natural religion. People like rites and ceremonies, and they are tired of hypothetical gods. Insist on the real benefits of the Sun, the Mother-Force, the Father-Force, and so on, and show that by celebrating these benefits worthily the worshippers unite themselves more fully with the current of life. Let the religion be of joy, but of a worthy and dignified sorrow in death itself, and treat death as an ordeal, an initiation . . . in short, be the founder of a new and greater Pagan cult."[86] The Gardnerian Chord rituals may have even been written by Crowley, and undeniably contain massive quotations from Crowley's Gnostic Mass, his poetry, *The Book of the Law*, and the initiation rituals of the O.T.O..

The Gardnerian third degree ritual was published by Janet and Steward Farrar in *The Witches' Way*, and it makes clear that the Wiccan Goddess is the Thelemic Nuit and the Wiccan God her compliment, Hadit. Some versions of the "Book of Shadows"—or "Ye Bok of ye Art Magical" as Gardner originally dubbed it—also directly quote *The Book of the Law*.[87] In *The Confessions*, Crowley refers to attending a Council of Masters, wherein he makes a direct statement of his mission, "to bring Oriental wisdom to Europe, and to restore paganism in a purer form."[88] What is certain is that, shortly before his death, Crowley admitted Gardner, as a Royal Arch Mason, to the IV° of the Ordo Templi Orientis, and issued a charter giving Gardner

---

of pleasure. My company is a harmony of many Cymbals, and my lips sweeter than health it self. I am a harlot for such as ravish me, and a virgin with such as know me not: For lo, I am loved of many, and I am a lover to many; and as many as come unto me as they should do, have entertainment. Purge your streets, O ye sons of men, and wash your houses clean; make your selves holy, and put on righteousness. Cast out your old strumpets, and burn their clothes; abstain from the company of other women that are defiled, that are sluttish, and not so handsome and beautiful as I, and then will I come and dwell amongst you: and behold, I will bring forth children unto you, and they shall be the Sons of Comfort. I will open my garments, and stand naked before you, that your love may be more enflamed toward me."

[84] *Cf.* also *Liber Aleph*, "De mente inimica animo."
[85] *The Equinox of the Gods, loc. cit.*
[86] As quoted in Blécourt, Hutton & La Fontaine 1999, 41–42.
[87] *Ibid.*
[88] Ch. 86.

authority to initiate people into its Minerval degree.[89] The charter itself was written in Gardner's hand and only signed by Crowley. At that time, Gardner was already an ordained priest of the Ancient British Church, another Old Catholics off-shoot.[90] "Buddhism did not succeed in supplanting prevailing superstitions any more than did Christianity or Islam. The fact is that the instincts of ignorant people invariably find expression in some form of witchcraft. It matters little what the metaphysician or the moralist may inculcate; the animal sticks to his subconscious ideas."[91]

On 18 September 1919, Bricaud reconsecrated Reuss *sub conditione*, and in a note at the end of his German translation of the Gnostic Mass, published under the auspices of the O.T.O. in 1918, Reuss refers to himself as both the Sovereign Patriarch and Primate of Die Gnostische Katholische Kirche and "Gnostic Legate" of the E.G.U. to Switzerland.[92] Though originally written five years earlier, the English version was only first published the same year, and not officially by the O.T.O. until the year following.[93] And even though Crowley never shied away from such titles as "Saint," "Sir," and "Laird," he never used a single ecclesiastical title in his life. In fact, the only official Crowley-era reference to the Gnostic Catholic Church, beyond the Latin subtitle of *Liber XV*, appears in the list of all the Old Æon organizations "the wisdom and the knowledge" of which the O.T.O. is supposed to possess—a list that includes such unlikely entries as the Knights of Malta and the Hidden Church of the Holy Graal.[94] And although the Gnostic Mass bears the imprimatur of Baphomet XI°, its actual author (or "editor") is given as "The Master Therion."

On 17 July 1920, Reuss attended the Congress of the World Federation of Universal Freemasonry, held at the Libertas et Fraternitas Lodge in Zürich. This conference was intended to take up the work of the "International Masonic and Spiritual Conference" organized by Encausse in Paris in 1908. Reuss, apparently with Bricaud's blessing, advocated the adoption of the religion of *Liber XV* as the "official religion for all members of the World Federation of Universal Freemasonry in possession of the 18° of the Scottish Rite."[95] Obviously, Reuss' efforts failed, and he left the congress after the first day, following a quarrel over jurisdictional issues with Matthew McBlain Thomson, who was elected Honorary President of

---

[89] Blécourt, Hutton & La Fontaine, *op. cit.*
[90] Pearson 2007.
[91] *Confessions*, Ch. 31; *cf.* e.g. Josephson-Storm 2017.
[92] Scriven & Scriven, *op. cit.*
[93] Incidentally, *The Liturgy According to the Use of the Liberal Catholic Church* (1919) by Wedgwood and Leadbeater was published almost simultaneously.
[94] *Liber LII*, Sec. 1.
[95] Though called the "Scottish" Rite on the Continent and in North America, this popular masonic rite is actually of French origin, and officially known in the UK simply as the "Ancient and Accepted" Rite (or, confusingly enough, the A∴A∴). It is also colloquially referred to as the "Rose Croix," after the 18°, the first and main degree conferred ceremonially as opposed to in name only. It is open only to Master Masons who profess the Trinitarian Christian faith, that is, the belief in one God in three Divine Persons, the central mystery of most Christian Churches.

the International Masonic Federation.[96] It was originally only at the V°, the O.T.O. equivalent of the 18° and "the natural stopping-place of the majority of men and women" that one swore to "accept The Sacred Law: to wit, Liber CCXX or Liber L. vel Legis, as delivered by LXXVIII unto DCLXVI" and declared "it to be the Letter and the Word of Truth and the Supreme Rule of Life."[97] The Fifth Degree, or Sovereign Prince of Rose Croix, remains the minimum for running a lodge, and of course, there were originally no "camps" or "oases."

"The word Jeheshua, spelt in Hebrew in the 18° of the Scottish Rite, was habitually spelt with a Resh instead of a Vau. So brutal a blunder is conclusive proof that the modern Sovereign Princes of Rose Croix attach no meaning whatever to the name of Jesus—which they profess to adore more intelligently than the mob because it represents the descent of the Holy Spirit into the midst of that tremendous name of God which only occurs in their ritual because of its power to annihilate the universe if pronounced correctly.[98] . . . I am thus in a position to do for the contending sects of freemasonry what the Alexandrians did for those of paganism. Unfortunately, the men who asked me to undertake this task are either dead or too old to take active measures and so far there is no one to replace them. Worse, the general coarsening of manners which always follows a great war has embittered the rival jurisdictions and deprived freemasonry altogether of those elements of high-minded enthusiasms with regard to the great problems of society which still stirred even its most degenerate sections half a century ago, when Hargrave Jennings, Godfrey Higgins, Gerald Massey, Kenneth MacKenzie, John Yarker, Theodor Reuss, Wynn Westcott and others were still seeking truth in its traditions and endeavouring to erect a temple of Concord in which men of all creeds and races might worship in amity."[99]

"The affiliation clause in our Constitution is a privilege: a courtesy to a sympathetic body. Were you not a Mason, or Co-Mason, you would have to be proposed and seconded, and then examined by savage Inquisitors; and

---

[96] Scriven & Scriven, *op. cit.*; *cf.* also *Liber DCCCXI*, Sec. XV: "I asked him, if that was a low mass, might I not be permitted to witness a High Mass? 'Perhaps,' he answered with a curious smile, 'if all they tell of you is true.' In the meanwhile he permitted me to describe the ceremony and its results as faithfully as I was able, charging me only to give no indication of the city near which it took place. I am willing to indicate to initiates of the Rose Croix degree of Masonry under proper charter from the genuine authorities (for there are spurious Masons working under a forged charter) the address of a person willing to consider their fitness to affiliate to a Chapter practising similar rites."
[97] V° Obligation of Allegiance, as quoted in Starr, *op. cit.*, 54.
[98] *Cf.* also *The Book of Thoth*, Appendix B, Diagram 6: "The name Jehovah IHVH, thus becomes IHShVH, Yeheshuah, Jesus. This is the Qabalistic method of expressing the doctrine of Jesus as the Redeemer. The method was explained in detail by a formula in which INRI, the inscription on the Cross, becomes Yod Nun Resh Yod, which are in heavens Virgo, the Virgin Mother; Isis, Scorpio, Apophis the Dragon, the Destroyer; Sol, Osiris, the Slain and Risen. The initials of these three divine beings thus make the more ancient name of Jehovah IAO. In this way the initiates of old expressed their understanding of the fact that the Universe was after all perfect, even if requiring a little manipulation; but as explained previously, this doctrine is for the weaker brethren, for those who are suffering from the illusion of imperfection; it enables them to make their way to the illimitable Light."
[99] *Confessions*, Ch. 72.

then—probably—thrown out on to the garbage heap. Well, no, it's not as bad as that; but we certainly don't want anybody who chooses to apply. Would you do it yourself, if you were on the Committee of a Club? The O.T.O. is a serious body, engaged on a work of Cosmic scope. You should question yourself: what can I contribute?"[100] In his *Confessions*, Crowley declares that, "Civilization is crumbling under our eyes and I believe that the best chance of saving what little is worth saving, and rebuilding the Temple of the Holy Ghost on plans, and with material and workmanship, which shall be free from the errors of the former, lies with the O.T.O.."[101] We know from his diaries that Crowley performed nearly all the other, purely magical rituals he published on more or less regular basis, but in spite of everything written above, he never performed the "quasi-religious" Mass. He boasted in public that it "has been said continuously in California for some years,"[102] but complained of the same in private.

"In the case of Smith in particular, his conduct is entirely unspeakable. He has done nothing whatever to justify his position except the mere performance of the Mass and this, I gather, cannot have been done any too well, or we should have raised a great many storms of one kind or another long before now."[103] Wilfred Talbot Smith (born Frank Wenham), a charter member of Vancouver's Agapé Lodge No. 1, was elevated to IX° and made the Supreme and Holy King for North America by Crowley on 1 January 1932. Smith, or Ramaka X°, moved from Canada to Los Angeles on instructions from Crowley to work with the American screen actress Jane Wolfe, who had been an A∴A∴ student of Crowley's at the Abbey of Thelema in Cefalù, Sicily. The two established Agapé Lodge No. 2 in Hollywood, California, and along with Regina Kahl, began to celebrate the Gnostic Mass on weekly basis on Sunday, 19 March 1933.[104]

Crowley is careful to explain that, "The 'Black Mass' is a totally different matter. I could not celebrate it if I wanted to, for I am not a consecrated priest of the Christian Church. The celebrant must be a priest, for the whole idea of the practice is to profane the Sacrament of the Eucharist. Therefore you must believe in the truth of the cult and the efficacy of its ritual."[105] In *Liber Aleph*, Crowley further reminds his magical son that, "Horus that is Lord of the Æon is the Child crowned and conquering. The formula of Osiris was, as thou knowest, a Word of Death, that is, the Force lay long in Darkness, and by Putrefaction came to Resurrection. But we take living Things, and pour in Life and Spirit of the Nature of our own Will, so that

---

[100] *MWT, loc. cit.*
[101] *Confessions, loc. cit. Cf.* also Past Grand Master, "The Crisis in Freemasonry," *English Review* XXXV, August 1922: "What was ever worth saving in Masonry? What was the original idea of the institution as such? The Secret and its Preservation. Even at this, the Secret pertains to the Past. It is part of the heritage of Humanity. But the Rites of Freemasonry are after all those of Osiris, of the Dying God; the Æon of Horus, of the Crowned and Conquering Child, is come; it is His rites that we should celebrate, His that liveth and reigneth, and hath His abode in every human heart!"
[102] NC on AL I.62.
[103] Letter to Jane Wolfe, 16 February 1943.
[104] Scriven & Scriven, *op. cit.*
[105] "Black Magic Is Not a Myth," *London Sunday Dispatch*, 3 July 1933.

instantly and without Corruption the Child (as it were the Word of that Will) is generated; and again immediately taketh up his Habitation among us to manifest in Force and Fire. This Mass of the Holy Ghost is then the true Formula of the Magick of the Æon, even of the Æon of Horus, blessed be He in His Name Ra-Hoor-Khuit! And thou shalt bless also the Name of our Father Merlin, Frater Superior of the O.T.O., for that by Seven Years of Apprenticeship in His School did I discover his most excellent Way of Magick. Be thou diligent, o my Son, for in this Wondrous Art is no more Toil, Sorrow, and Disappointment, as it was in the dead Æon of the Slain Gods."[106]

Lévi, who attended the Catholic seminary at Saint-Sulpice in Paris for six years, but left without being ordained, muses: "'What career shall we choose for our son?' have said many stupid parents; 'he is mentally and bodily weak, and he is without a spark of courage:—we will make a priest of him, so that he may 'live by the altar.'' They have not understood that the altar is not a manger for slothful animals. Look at the unworthy priests, contemplate these pretended servants of the altar! What do they say to your heart, these obese or cadaverous men with the lack-lustre eyes, and pinched or gaping mouths."[107] As Crowley laments, "These poor fish! They do not understand the difference between Power and Authority. They do not understand that there are two kinds of degrees, altogether different. For instance, in the theory of the Church of Rome a bishop is a person on whom has been conferred the magical power to ordain priests. He may choose a totally unworthy person for such ordination, it makes no difference; and the priest, however unworthy he may be, has only to go through the correct formulæ which perform the miracle of the Mass, for that miracle to be performed. This is because in the Church we are dealing with a religious as opposed to a magical or scientific qualification. If the Royal Society elected a cobbler, as it could, it would not empower the New Fellow to perform a boiling-point determination, or read a Vernier."[108]

"In our own case, though Our authority is at least as absolute as that of the Pope and the Church of Rome, it does not confer upon me any power transferable to others by any act of Our will. Our own authority came to Us because it was earned, and when We confer grades upon other people Our gift is entirely nugatory unless the beneficiary has won his spurs."[109] However, "The priest, *qua* priest, is always the representative of God. Of little account are the faults or even the crimes of man. When Alexander VI

---

[106] *Liber Aleph*, "De missa Spiritus Sancti." *Cf.* also *Liber DCCCXI*, Sec. V: "Now sex is justly hallowed in this sense, that it is the eternal fire of the race. Huxley admitted that 'some of the lower animalculæ are in a sense immortal,' because they go on reproducing eternally by fission, and however often you divide *x* by 2 there is always something left. But he never seems to have seen that mankind is immortal in exactly the same sense, and goes on reproducing itself with similar characteristics through the ages, changed by circumstance indeed, but always identical in itself. But the spiritual flower of this process is that at the moment of discharge a physical ecstasy occurs, a spasm analogous to the mental spasm which meditation gives. And further, in the sacramental and ceremonial use of the sexual act, the divine consciousness may be attained."
[107] *The Key of the Mysteries, loc. cit.*, "Sketch of the Prophetic Thelogy of Numbers."
[108] *MWT*, Ch. LXI.
[109] *Ibid.*

consecrated his bishops, it was not the poisoner who laid his hands upon them, it was the pope. Pope Alexander VI never corrupted or falsified the dogmas which condemned him, or the sacraments which in his hands saved others, and did not justify him. At all times and in all places there have been liars and criminals, but in the hierarchical and divinely authorized Church there have never been, and there will never be, either bad popes or bad priests. 'Bad' and 'priest' form an oxymoron. We have mentioned Alexander VI, and we think that this name will be sufficient without other memories as justly execrated as his being brought up against us. Great criminals have been able to dishonour themselves doubly because of the sacred character with which they were invested, but they had not the power to dishonour that character, which remains always radiant and splendid above fallen humanity."[110]

Crowley, of course, counted the Borgia Pope as one of his past incarnations: "I was involved in the catastrophe which overtook the order of the Temple, and as Alexander the Sixth, failed in my task of crowning the Renaissance, though not being wholly purified in my personal character. (An appropriately trivial spiritual error may externalize as the most appalling crimes.)"[111] According to *Liber CXCIV*, or "An Intimation with Reference to the Constitution of the Order," Section 24, "The succession to the high office of O.H.O. is decided in a manner not here to be declared; but this you may learn, O Brother Magician, that he may be chosen even from the grade of a Minerval. And herein lieth a most sacred Mystery." Reuss, for example, though Frater Superior of the O.T.O. (and Magus of the Societas Rosicruciana in Germania) was not even a Neophyte of the A∴A∴ "Confound not thou in any wise therefore the Degree of Attainment of any Man with his right Function in Our Holy Order; for although by initiation cometh the Light, and the Right, and the Might to accomplish all Works soever, yet these are inoperative save as they are able to use a Machine which is of the same Order of Things as the Effect required. As the best Swordsman hath Need of a Sword, so hath every Magician of a Body and Mind capable to the Work that he willeth; and he can do nothing, save it be proper to his Nature."[112]

"There is another side to this matter which is really approximating to the criminal. There are any number of teachers and masters and bishops and goodness knows what else running around doing what is little better than peddling grades and degrees and secrets. Such practices are of course no better than common fraud. Please fix it firmly in your mind that with Us any degree, any position of authority, any kind of rank, is utterly worthless except when it is merely a seal upon the actual attainment or achievement."[113] As Crowley writes a student, "nobody can 'take you through' the Grades of A∴A∴. The Grades *confirm* your attainments as you

---

[110] *The Key of the Mysteries, loc. cit.*, Preliminary Considerations.
[111] *Confessions*, Ch. 86.
[112] *Liber Aleph*, "De illuminatum operibus diversis."
[113] *MWT, loc. cit.*

make them; then, the new tasks appear."[114] According to *Liber XXXIII*, "Any man can look for the entrance, and any man who is within can teach another to seek for it; but only he who is fit can arrive within. Unprepared men occasion disorder in a community, and disorder is not compatible with the Sanctuary. Thus it is impossible to profane the Sanctuary, since admission is not formal but real. Worldly intelligence seeks this Sanctuary in vain; fruitless also will be the efforts of malice to penetrate these great mysteries; all is indecipherable to him who is not ripe; he can see nothing, read nothing in the interior. He who is fit is joined to the chain, perhaps often where he though least likely, and at a point of which he knew nothing himself."

"Members of the A∴A∴ of whatever grade are not bound or expected or even encouraged to work on any stated lines, or with any special object, save as has been above set forth. There is however an absolute prohibition to accept money or other material reward, directly or indirectly, in respect of any service connected with the Order, for personal profit or advantage. The penalty is immediate expulsion, with no possibility of reinstatement on any terms soever."[115] Even Reuss' "Synopsis of Course of Instruction" from 1917 stresses that "All occult instruction is given gratis." In *The Revival of Magick*, Crowley relates this short anecdote: "The other day a young lady came to consult me. I gave her about a thousand dollars' worth of information. She asked me what I was going to charge. I said: 'Nothing; regard me as a bank account on which you can always draw.' She said: 'But you must eat!' I answered: 'I do not see the necessity.'"

"But I must warn you of one particular disgrace. You know that people of low mentality haunt fortune-tellers of equal calibre, but with more low cunning. They do not really want to know the future, or to get advice; their real object is to persuade some supposed 'authority' to flatter them and confirm them in their folly and stupidity. It is the same thing with a terrifying percentage of the people that come for 'teaching' and 'initiation.' The moment they learn anything they didn't know before, off they fly in a temper! No sooner does it become apparent that the Master is not a stupid middle-class prig and hypocrite—another edition of themselves, in short—they are frightened, they are horrified, they flee away on both their feet, like the man in the Bible! I have seen people turn fish-belly pale in the face, and come near fainting outright, when it has dawned upon them suddenly that magick is a real thing!"[116] As Lévi puts it, "The vulgar are always deceived about magic, and confuse adepts with enchanters. True magic, that is to say, the traditional science of the magi, is the mortal enemy of enchantment; it prevents, or makes to cease, sham miracles, hostile to the light, that fascinate a small number of prejudiced or credulous witnesses. The apparent disorder in the laws of Nature is a lie: it is not then a miracle. The true miracle, the true prodigy always flaming in the eyes of

---

[114] *Ibid.*, Introduction. Emphasis in original.
[115] *One Star in Sight*, Sec. 10.
[116] *MWT*, Ch. LXXIV.

all, is the ever constant harmony of effect and cause; these are the splendours of eternal order!"[117]

"The initiate constantly reads of the 'latest great discovery in science,' and is reminded of what was taught him in the secret conclaves of the Adepts at the very outset of his studies; and this is no less true of methods of rejuvenation that it is of the theory of relativity. You will find space described as 'finite yet boundless' in the poem of a boy of twenty-five, published in the year 1901. All Einstein in one phrase!"[118] There is one thing that Crowley wishes to make crystal clear: "It is particularly to be noted that Magick, so often mixed up in the popular idea of a religion, has nothing to do with it. It is, in fact, the exact opposite of religion; it is, even more than Physical Science, its irreconcilable enemy. Let us define this difference clearly. Magick investigates the laws of Nature with the idea of making use of them. It only differs from 'profane' science by always keeping ahead of it. As Frazer has shown, Magick is science in the tentative stage; but it may be, and often is, more than this. It is science which, for one reason or another, cannot be declared to the profane. Religion, on the contrary, seeks to ignore the laws of Nature, or to escape them by appeal to a postulated power which is assumed to have laid them down. The religious man is, as such, incapable of understanding what the laws of Nature really are. (They are generalizations from the order of observed fact.)"[119]

"Magic, that science which comes to us from the magi!" cries Lévi. "Magic, the first of sciences! Magic, the holiest science, because it establishes in the sublimest manner the great religious truths! Magic, the most calumniated of all, because the vulgar obstinately confound magic with the superstitious sorcery whose abominable practices we have denounced! It is only by magic that one can reply to the enigmatical questions of the Sphinx of Thebes, and find the solution of those problems of religious history which are sealed in the sometimes scandalous obscurities which are to be found in the stories of the Bible."[120] The Glossary at the end of *Book 4*, Part II, defines "Theosophist" as a "person who talks about Yoga, and does no work," while *Magick in Theory and Practice* states that, "Witchcraft consists in treating it as the exclusive preoccupation of Magick, and especially in denying to the Holy Spirit his right to indwell His Temple."[121]

> Now, o my Son, that thou mayst be well guarded against thy ghostly Enemies, do thou work constantly by the Means prescribed in our Holy Books.
> Neglect never the fourfold Adorations of the Sun in his four Stations, for thereby thou doest affirm thy Place in Nature and her Harmonies.
> Neglect not the Performance of the Ritual of the Pentagram, and of the Assumption of the Form of Hoor-pa-Kraat.

---

[117] *The Key of the Mysteries*, Part III, Book I, Ch. III.
[118] *The Elixir of Life*.
[119] *MWT*, Ch. VI.
[120] *The Key of the Mysteries, loc. cit.*
[121] *MITAP*, Ch. IV.

Neglect not the daily Miracle of the Mass, either by the Rite of the Gnostic Catholic Church, or that of the Phœnix.

Neglect not the Performance of the Mass of the Holy Ghost, as Nature herself prompteth thee.

Travel also much in the Empyrean in the Body of Light, seeking ever Abodes more fiery and lucid.

Finally, exercise constantly the Eight Limbs of Yoga. And so shalt thou come to the End.[122]

"Now, however unsuccessful your getting out of the body may apparently have been, it is most necessary to use every effort to bring it properly back. Make the Body of Light coincide in space with the physical body, assume the God-form, and vibrate the name of Harpocrates, with the utmost energy; then recover unity of consciousness. If you fail to do this properly you may find yourself in serious trouble. Your Body of Light may wander away uncontrolled, and be attacked and obsessed. You will become aware of this through the occurrence of headache, bad dreams, or even more serious signs such as hysteria, fainting fits, possibly madness or paralysis. Even the worst of these attacks will probably wear off, but it may leave you permanently damaged to a greater or lesser extent. A great majority of 'spiritualists,' 'occultists,' 'Toshosophists,' are pitiable examples of repeated losses from this cause."[123]

"The emotional type of religionist also suffers in this way. Devotion projects the fine body, which is seized and vampirized by the demon masquerading as 'Christ,' or 'Mary,' or whoever may be the object of worship. Complete absence of all power to concentrate thought, to follow an argument, to formulate a Will, to hold fast to an opinion or a course of action, or even to keep a solemn oath, mark indelibly those who have thus lost parts of their souls. They wander from one new cult to another even crazier. Occasionally such persons drift for a moment into the surrounding of The MASTER THERION, and are shot out by the simple process of making them try to do a half-hour's honest work of any kind. In projecting the Astral, it is a valuable additional safeguard to perform the whole operation in a properly consecrated Circle."[124]

"The habitual use of the Lesser Banishing Ritual of the Pentagram (say, thrice daily) for months and years and constant assumption of the God-form of Harpocrates . . . should make the *real Circle*, i.e., the aura of the Magus, impregnable."[125] According to Lévi, "All magic is in a word, and that word pronounced qabalistically is stronger than all the powers of Heaven, Earth and Hell. With the name of *Jod hé vau hé*, one commands Nature: kingdoms are conquered in the name of Adonai, and the occult forces which compose the empire of Hermes are one and all obedient to him who knows how to pronounce duly the incommunicable name of Agla."[126] The entry on

---

[122] *Liber Aleph*, "De cultu."
[123] *MITAP*, Ch. XVIII, Sec. I.
[124] *Ibid.*
[125] *Ibid.*, Ch. XII, Sec. II, fn. Emphasis in original.
[126] *The Key of the Mysteries, loc. cit.*, Book II, Ch. II.

number 35 in *An Essay upon Number* reads thus: "אגלא, a name of God = Ateh Gibor Le-Olahm Adonai. 'To Thee be the Power unto the Ages, O my Lord!' 35 = 5 × 7. 7 = Divinity, 5 = Power."[127]

"The terrific strain of Âsana and Prânâyâma, the two chief exercises of Hathavidya, P., by months of trial proved to be not only methods of great use as a sedative before commencing a Magical Operation, but methods of inordinate importance to such aspirants, who, having discarded the Shibboleths of sect, have adopted the fatuities of reason. For it is more difficult for one who has no natural magical aptitude, and one who perhaps has only just broken away from faith and corrupted ritual, to carry out an operation of Western Magic, than it is for him to sit down and perform a rational exercise, such as the Prânâyâma exercises of Yoga, which carry with them their own result, in spite of the mental attitude of the chela towards them, so long as the instructions of the Guru are properly carried out."[128]

"All members of the Order are in full possession of the Formulæ of Attainment, both mystical or inwardly-directed and Magical or outwardly-directed. They have full experience of attainment in both these paths. They are all, however, bound by the original and fundamental Oath of the Order, to devote their energy to assisting the Progress of their Inferiors in the Order. Those who accept the rewards of their emancipation for themselves are no longer within the Order. Members of the Order are each entitled to found Orders dependent on themselves on the lines of the R.C. and G.D. orders, to cover types of emancipation and illumination not contemplated by the original (or main) system. All such orders must, however, be constituted in harmony with the A∴A∴ as regards the essential principles."[129]

While the O.T.O. was "the first of the great Old Æon orders to accept the Law of Thelema," Crowley evidently hoped that the Theosophical Society would be the second. To that end, he sought recognition as the messianic "World Teacher" expected by Annie Besant. In the *Confessions*, Crowley claims that the publication of *Liber LXXI* in *The Equinox*, Vol. III, No. 1 (or "The Blue Equinox"), was intended "to bring back Theosophists to the true principles of their founder."[130] Also known as "The Voice of the Silence: The Two Paths, The Seven Portals," the title page acknowledges its author, Helena Petrovna Blavatsky, as 8°=3□ or Magister Templi. Crowley also briefly attempted to recruit Katherine Tingley, a leader of the American Section that had seceded from the international Theosophical Society after Blavatsky's death.

The Order of the Star in the East, the organization founded to proclaim the coming of the World Teacher, grew tremendously in the 1920s and there were 30,000 members at its height. Even though it was independent of the Theosophical Society, whose motto is "There is no religion higher

---

[127] Part I, Sec. IV.
[128] *The Temple of Solomon the King*, Part IV, "The Writing of Truth."
[129] *One Star in Sight*, Sec. 3.
[130] *Confessions, loc. cit.*

than truth," many who joined it also became Theosophists. Anticipation of the advent of the messiah reached a peak in December 1925, when Krishnamurti, who had long spoken of the World Teacher in the third person, told a Star Congress that, "I come for those who want sympathy, who want happiness.... I come to reform and not to tear down, I come not to destroy but to build." The use of the first person singular was taken by members of the Order to mean that the Teacher had taken over Krishnamurti's personality and was able to speak through him. Mrs. Besant gathered a group of twelve "apostles" that included herself, Leadbeater, Wedgwood, and several other leading Theosophists whom she hoped Krishnamurti would accept as his disciples, but, in a portent of things to come, he refused.[131]

Until 1929 and the publication of *Magick in Theory and Practice*, it was also not generally known that the "Master Therion" and Aleister Crowley were the same person.[132] However, the way he signed the Introduction finally made the identity clear: "Witness mine hand: TO ΜΕΓΑ ΘΗΡΙΟΝ (תריון), The Beast 666, Magus 9°=2□ A∴A∴ who is The Word of the Æon THELEMA; whose name is called V.V.V.V.V. 8°=3□ A∴A∴ in the City of the Pyramids; ΟΥ ΜΗ 7°=4□ A∴A∴, OL SONUF VAORESAGI 6°=5□, and .... 5°=6□ A∴A∴ in the Mountain of Abiegnus; but FRATER PERDURABO in the Outer Order or the A∴A∴ and in the World of Men upon the Earth, Aleister Crowley of Trinity College, Cambridge." The Theosophical notion of "Hidden Mahatmas" derived via high-grade Freemasonry from the Rosicrucian idea of secret and invisible adepts, working for the advancement of mankind. *The Cloud upon the Sanctuary* by Karl von Eckartshausen further drew on Christian ideas such as the Communion of the Saints, and Mme. Blavatsky claimed that she not only had made physical contact with the earthly representatives of these adepts in Tibet, but that she continued to receive messages from them through psychic channels.[133]

The phrase "Great White Brotherhood" was actually never used by Blavatsky but appears extensively in Leadbeater's book *The Masters and the Path* (1925). Eckartshausen writes: "But there are methods by which ripeness is attained, for in this holy communion is the primitive storehouse of the most ancient and original science of the human race, with the primitive mysteries also of all science. It is the unique and really illuminated community which is absolutely in possession of the key to all mystery, which knows the centre and source of all nature and creation. It is a society which unites superior strength to its own, and counts its members from more than one world. It is the society whose members form a theocratic republic, which one day will be the Regent Mother of the whole World."[134] Crowley's *Liber XXXIII*, or "An Account of the A∴A∴" was "First written in the language of his period by the Councillor Von Eckartshausen

---

[131] Campbell, *op. cit.*
[132] King 1973.
[133] Goodrick-Clarke 2004.
[134] Eckartshausen 1896, 28–9.

and now revised and rewritten in the Universal Cipher ... This society is in the communion of those who have most capacity for light; they are united in truth, and their Chief is the Light of the World himself, V.V.V.V.V., the One Anointed in Light, the single teacher for the human race, the Way, the Truth, and the Life. ... The Revisers wish to acknowledge gratefully the translation of Madame de Steiger, which they have freely quoted."

The Temple of Solomon the King speaks of "the Eternal and Invisible Order that hath no name among men."[135] In a letter to Charles Stansfeld Jones dated 1 March 1925, Crowley writes: "The strategical aspect of our position at present is that we have the three things necessary—a Sacred Book, historical authority, and leadership of genius. The many Occult bodies in existence possess none of these things except sometimes the last of them in a very diluted and defective form. They are constantly put to new shifts to keep up the bluff. In such bodies there is however as a rule a grain or two of sincerity with odd scraps of ill-assorted knowledge. It should not be our idea to destroy these movements except the hopelessly fraudulent ones. We should, on the other hand, bring them into one fold under one shepherd." The O.T.O. in North America was founded in 1912, when C. S. Jones, well-known in the A∴A∴ as Frater Achad, brought together "twelve sincere and interested associates" in Vancouver, British Columbia, all of whom signed forms agreeing to take initiation through the III°. They were duly chartered as Agapé Camp, later a Lodge, and Frater Achad, as Parzival X°, continued to spearhead O.T.O. activity in both Canada and the United States for years to come.[136]

"This Parzival, adding to 418, is (in the legend of the Graal) the son of Kamuret, adding to 666, being the son of me The Beast by the Scarlet Woman Hilarion. This was a Name chosen by her when half drunk, as a theft from Theosophical legend, but containing many of our letter-number Keys to the Mysteries; the number of the petals in the most sacred lotus. It adds to 1001, which also is Seven times Eleven times Thirteen, a series of factors which may be read as The Scarlet Woman's Love by Magick producing Unity, in Hebrew *Achad*."[137] Jones would later claim to have undergone a "Great Initiation" and be an Ipsissimus, causing his relationship with Crowley to break down, and he subsequently resigned from the O.T.O..[138] Meanwhile, the climax of Krishnamurti's journey with the Theosophical Society took place at a summer camp of the Order of the Star in 1929, when, in the presence of Mrs. Besant, more than 3,000 members, and a live radio audience, he made a speech dissolving the Order. He declared that "Truth is a pathless land, and you cannot approach it by any path whatsoever, by any religion, by any sect" and after he resigned

---

[135] *The Temple of Solomon the King*, Part VIII, "The Poet."
[136] Ad Veritatem IX°, "An Introduction to the History of the O.T.O.," *The Equinox*, Vol. III, No. 10, pp. 87–99.
[137] *The Equinox of the Gods, loc. cit.*, Ch. VII, Sec. III.
[138] Starr, *op. cit.*

from the Society as well the next year, the Theosophists quickly lost a third of their membership.[139]

As we learn in *Liber XXXIII*, "Through this school were developed the germs of all the sublime sciences, which were first received by external schools, then clothed in other forms, and hence degenerated. According to time and circumstances, the society of sages communicated unto the exterior societies their symbolic hieroglyphs, in order to attract man to the great truths of their Sanctuary. But all exterior societies subsist only by virtue of this interior one. As soon as external societies wish to transform a temple of wisdom into a political edifice, the interior society retires and leaves only the letter without the spirit. It is thus that secret external societies of wisdom were nothing but hieroglyphic screens, the truth remaining inviolable in the Sanctuary so that she might never be profaned." In 1932, with Krishnamurti "having definitely turned tail" and Mrs. Besant "being in dementia, + dying," Crowley announced that he must "be declared H.P.B.'s legitimate successor."[140]

Crowley also warns us "against the numerous false orders which have impudently assumed the name of Rosicrucian. The Masonic Societas Rosicruciana is honest and harmless, and makes no false pretences; if its members happen as a rule to be pompous busy-bodies, enlarging the borders of their phylacteries, and scrupulous about cleansing the outside of the cup and the platter; if the masks of the Officers in their Mysteries suggest the Owl, the Cat, the Parrot, and the Cuckoo, while the Robe of their Chief Magus is a Lion's Skin, that is their affair. But those orders run by persons *claiming* to represent the True Ancient Fraternity—Plummer, Clymer, the successor of Heindel, Dr. E. W. Berridge, A. L. Wedgwood, A. E. Waite—are common swindles. The representatives of the late S. L. Mathers (alias Count MacGregor) are the phosphorescence of the rotten wood of a branch which was lopped off the Tree at the end of the 19th century. Those of Papus (Dr. Encausse), Stanislas de Guaita and Péladan, merit respect as serious, but lack full knowledge and authority. The 'Ordo Rosæ Crucis' is a mass of ignorance and falsehood, but this may be a deliberate device for masking itself."[141]

According to Crowley, "The test of any Order is its attitude towards the Law of Thelema. The True Order presents the True Symbols, but avoids attaching the True Name thereto; it is only when the Postulant has taken irrevocable Oaths and been received formally, that he discovers what Fraternity he has joined. If he have taken false symbols for true, and find himself magically pledged to a gang of rascals, so much the worse for him!"[142] But "How can faith be lost?" asks Lévi. "How can science doubt the infinite harmony? Because the sanctuary of the absolute is always closed for the majority. But the kingdom of truth, which is that of God, suffers violence, and the violent must take it by force. There exists a dogma, there exists a key, there exists a sublime tradition; and this dogma, this key, this

---

[139] Campbell, *op. cit.*
[140] Letter to W. T. Smith, 10 February 1932, as quoted in Starr, *op. cit.*, 189.
[141] *MITAP*, Ch. XII, Sec. II, fn. Emphasis in original.
[142] *Ibid.*

tradition is transcendental magic. There only are found the absolute of knowledge and the eternal bases of law, guardian against all madness, all superstition and all error, the Eden of the intelligence, the ease of the heart, and the peace of the soul. We do not say this in the hope of convincing the scoffer, but only to guide the seeker. Courage and good hope to him; he will surely find, since we ourselves have found."[143]

An Essay upon Number phrases the second form of the Great Problem the Aspirant is seeking to solve thus: "I am a fallen creature. I wish to be redeemed. This is the Christian conception. I am Malkuth the fallen daughter. I wish to be set upon the throne of Binah my supernal mother. This is the qabalistic equivalent. . . . The answer of the Adept to the second form of the problem is for the Christian all the familiar teaching of the Song of Songs and the Apocalypse concerning the Bride of Christ." However, as the footnote points out, "This Christian teaching (not its qabalistic equivalent) is incomplete. The Bride (the soul) is united, though only be marriage, with the son, who then presents her to the Father and Mother or Holy Spirit. These four then complete Tetragrammaton. But the Bride is never united to the Father. In this scheme the soul can never do more than touch Tiphareth and so receive the ray from Chokmah. Whereas even St. John makes his Son say 'I and my Father are one.' And we all agree that in philosophy there can never be (in Truth) more than one; this Christian dogma says 'never less than four.' Hence its bondage to law and its most imperfect comprehension of any true mystic teaching, and hence the difficulty of using its symbols."[144]

In *Remembering Aleister Crowley* (1991), Kenneth Grant tells the incredulous reader that while at Hastings, Crowley showed his short-time secretary and personal assistant an "averse counterpart" of "the quotation from *The Book of the Law* with which Crowley usually began and closed his letters"—"a curse to be used when encountering members of the Christian and other 'old aeon' faiths. With a downward and outward sweep of the arm, and with eyes averted, one mutters '*Apo pantos kakodaimonos*' {'Depart from me all evil spirits'}. I did this one day when we passed two nuns on the sea front. Crowley halted, looked at me with mock astonishment, and said: 'I wouldn't have had the nerve to do that'."[145] The present author very much doubts there was anything mock about it—around the same time, Crowley was making ends meet by tutoring a seminary student in Latin.

---

[143] *The Key of the Mysteries*, loc. cit., Book I, Ch. III.

[144] *An Essay upon Number*, Part II. *Cf.* also *Liber DCCCXI*, Sec. VIII: "Rightly restraining the priest, who should employ his whole energy in the miracle of the Mass, they found their counsel a counsel of perfection. The magical tradition was in part lost; the priest could not do what was expected of him, and the unexpended portion of his energy turned sour. Hence the thoughts of priests, like the thoughts of modern faddists, revolved eternally around the S[ex] Q[uestion]. A special and Secret Mass, a Mass of the Holy Ghost, a Mass of the Mystery of the Incarnation, to be performed at stated intervals, might have saved both monks and nuns, and given the Church eternal dominion of the world."

[145] Grant 1991, 29. *Cf.* e.g. *Eight Lectures*, Ch. 5, Sec. 9; or *MWT*, Ch. XVI. The phrase and the gesture also appear in *Liber XXV*, or "The Star Ruby," described in *The Book of Lies* as "a new and more elaborate version of the Banishing Ritual of the Pentagram."

However, "I think we may dismiss altogether from our minds every claim to experience made by any Christian of whatever breed of spiritual virus as a mere morbid reflection, the apish imitation of the true ecstasies and trances. All expressions of the real thing must partake of the character of that thing, and therefore only that language is permissible which is itself released from the canon of ordinary speech, exactly as the trance is unfettered by the laws of ordinary consciousness. In other words, the only proper translation is in poetry, art and music. If you examine the highest poetry in the light of common sense, you can only say that it is rubbish; and in actual fact you cannot so examine it at all, because there is something in poetry which is not in the words themselves, which is not in the images suggested by the words 'O windy star blown sideways up the sky!' True poetry is itself a magic spell which is a key to the ineffable."[146]

"For this Reason is the Poet called an Incarnation of the Zeitgeist, that is, of the Spirit or Will of his Period. So every Poet is also a Prophet, because when that which he sayeth is recognized as the Expression of their own Thought by Men, they translate this into Act, so that, in the Parlance of the Folk vulgar and ignorant, 'that which he foretold is come to pass'. Now then the Poet is Interpreter of the Hieroglyphs of the Hidden Will of Man in many a matter, some light, some deep, as it may be given unto him to do. Moreover, it is not altogether in the Word of any Poem, but in the quintessential Flavour of the Poet, that thou mayst seek this Prophecy. And this is an Art most necessary to every Statesman. Who but Shelley foretold the Fall of Christianity, and the Organisation of Labour, and the Freedom of Woman; who but Nietzsche declared the Principle at the Root of the World-War? See thou clearly then that in these Men were the Keys of the Dark Gates of the Future; should not the Kings and their Ministers have taken heed thereto, fulfilling their Word without Conflict."[147]

The Abbé Constant again asks, "What does it matter to me that Anacreon should sing of Bathyllus, if in his verse I hear the notes of that divine harmony which is the eternal hymn of beauty? Poetry is pure as the Sun: it spreads its veil of light over the errors of humanity. Woe to him who would lift the veil in order to perceive things ugly! The Council of Trent decided that it was permissible for wise and prudent persons to read the books of the ancients, even those which were obscene, on account of the beauty of the form. A statue of Nero or of Heliogabalus made like a masterpiece of Phidias, would it not be an absolutely beautiful and absolutely good work?—and would not he deserve the execration of the whole world who would propose to break it because it was the representation of a monster? Scandalous statues are those which are badly sculptured, and the Venus of Milo would be desecrated if one placed her beside some of the Virgins which they dare to exhibit in certain churches. One realizes evil in books of morality ill-written far more than in the poetry of Catullus or the ingenious Allegories of Apuleius."[148]

---

[146] *Eight Lectures*, Ch. 8, Secs. 15–6.
[147] *Liber Aleph*, "De poëtis."
[148] *The Key of the Mysteries*, loc. cit., Book II, Ch. II.

"Miracles are but the clouds that cloak the dreamy eyes of ignorant men. Therefore let us once and for all thunder forth: There are no miracles for those who wake; miracles are for the dreamers, and wonders are as bottled bull's-eyes in a bun-shop for penniless children. Beauty alone exists for the Adept. Everywhere there is loveliness—in the poppy and in the dunghill upon which it blows; in the palace of marble and in the huts of sunbaked mud which squat without its walls. For him the glades of the forests laugh with joy, and so do the gutters of our slums. All is beautiful, and flame-shod he speeds over earth and water, through fire and air; and builds, in the tangled web of the winds, that City wherein no one dreams, and where even awakenment ceases to be."[149] As Lévi writes, "The lofty sciences of the Qabalah and of Magic promise man an exceptional, real, effective, efficient power, and one should regard them as false and vain if they do not give it. Judge the teachers by their works, said the supreme Master. This rule of judgment is infallible."[150]

"Some six months after the death of Eliphas Levi Zahed," begins *Liber 666*, "in the Year (1875 E.V.) of the foundation of the Theosophical Society, was born a male child." *The Heart of the Master* declares that, "The Work of our Sister Helena Petrovna Blavatsky was inaugurated at the very season of the Birth on Earth of our Brother the Master whose Word is Thelema, whose Name is yet hidden under the form of a Lion. For it was most needful to prepare His Way that He might proclaim His Law in every land that is upon the surface of the Earth. And this work has been done by the Society founded to that end by our Sister. Yet even so, behold! Full Fifty years have passed, and only now is the hour of Power come upon our Brother the Lion to utter His Word with full efficacy to the whole Earth."[151]

According to Crowley, "the Yellow adepts sent forth into the Western world a messenger, Helena Petrowna Blavatsky, with the distinct mission to destroy, on the one hand, the crude schools of Christianity, and, on the other, to eradicate the materialism from Physical Science. She made the necessary connection with Edward Maitland and Anna Kingsford, who were trying rather helplessly to put the exoteric formulae of the White School into the hands of students, and with the secret representatives of the Rosicrucian Brotherhood. It is not for us in this place to estimate the degree of success with which she carried out her embassy; but at least we see today that Physical Science is at last penetrating to the spiritual basis of material phenomena. The work of Henri Poincaré, Einstein, Whitehead, and Bertrand Russell is sufficient evidence of this fact."[152]

However, "Madame Blavatsky was a mere forerunner. They, in conjunction with the Secret Chiefs of the White School in Europe, Chiefs who had been compelled to suspend all attempts at exoteric enlightenment by the general moral debility which had overtaken the races from which they drew their adepts, have prepared a guide for mankind. This man, of an extreme moral force and elevation, combined with a profound sense of

---

[149] *The Temple of Solomon the King*, Part III, "The Sorcerer."
[150] *The Key of the Mysteries*, Part IV, Introduction.
[151] *The Heart of the Master*, Part III, "The Initiation."
[152] *MWT*, Ch. VIII.

worldly realities, has stood forth in an attempt to save the White School, to rehabilitate its formula, and to fling back from the bastions of moral freedom the howling savages of pessimism. Unless his appeal is heard, unless there comes a truly virile reaction against the creeping atrophy which is poisoning them, unless they enlist to the last man under his standard, a great decisive battle will have been lost."[153]

This prophet of the White School, chosen by its Masters and his brethren, to save the Theory and Practice, is armed with a sword far mightier than Excalibur. He has been entrusted with a new Magical formula, one which can be accepted by the whole human race. Its adoption will strengthen the Yellow School by giving a more positive value to their Theory; while leaving the postulates of the Black School intact, it will transcend them and raise their Theory and Practice almost to the level of the Yellow. As to the White School, it will remove from them all taint of poison of the Black, and restore vigour to their central formula of spiritual alchemy by giving each man an independent ideal. It will put an end to the moral castration involved in the assumption that each man, whatever his nature, should deny himself to follow out a fantastic and impracticable ideal of goodness. Incidentally, this formula will save Physical Science itself by making negligible the despair of futility, the vital scepticism which has emasculated it in the past. It shows that the joy of existence is not in a goal, for that indeed is clearly unattainable, *but in the going* itself.

This law is called the Law of Thelema. It is summarized in the four words, "Do what thou wilt."[154]

"My Term of Office upon the Earth being come in the year of the foundation of the Theosophical Society, I took upon myself, in my turn, the sin of the whole World, that the Prophecies might be fulfilled, so that Mankind may take the Next Step from the Magical Formula of Osiris to that of Horus. And mine Hour being now upon me, I proclaim my Law."[155] According to Crowley, "Anna Kingsford, who had dabbled in Hebrew mysticism, and was a feminist, got an almost identical vision [as the one attributed in the *Bhagavad-Gītā* to the apparition of Vishnu]; but called the 'divine' figure which she saw alternately 'Adonai' and 'Maria.' Now this woman, though handicapped by a brain that was a mass of putrid pulp, and a complete lack of social status, education, and moral character, did more in the religious world than any other person had done for generations. She, and she alone, made Theosophy possible, and without Theosophy the world-wide interest in similar matters would never have been aroused. This interest is to the Law of Thelema what the preaching of John the Baptist was to Christianity."[156]

---

[153] *Ibid.* This is a recurring theme in Crowley's writings, and one that all who have been initiated into the Ordo Templi Orientis will readily recognize.
[154] *Ibid.* Emphasis in original.
[155] *Liber 666.*
[156] *Book 4*, Part I, Preliminary Remarks.

"We are now in a position to say what happened to Mohammed. Somehow or another his phenomenon happened in his mind. More ignorant than Anna Kingsford, though, fortunately, more moral, he connected it with the story of the 'Annunciation,' which he had undoubtedly heard in his boyhood, and said 'Gabriel appeared to me.' But in spite of his ignorance, his total misconception of the truth, the power of the vision was such that he was enabled to persist through the usual persecution, and founded a religion to which even to-day one man in every eight belongs."[157] Ultimately, Crowley wished to convert not only all Freemasons and all Theosophists, but even ordinary everyday people with no interest in esoteric matters. The Secret Chiefs had chosen Crowley "as Their representative on earth, as the vehicle of the Utterance" and "They had fixed him at the summit of the Order, in that degree of enlightenment which (or so it is said) is attained by any man in the body not oftener than once in Two Thousand years."[158]

> So must all Members of the A∴A∴ work by the Magical Formula of the Æon.
> They must accept the *Book of the Law* as the Word and the Letter of Truth, and the sole Rule of Life.
> They must acknowledge the Authority of the Beast 666 and of the Scarlet Woman as in the book it is defined, and accept Their Will as concentrating the Will of our Whole Order. They must accept the Crowned and Conquering Child as the Lord of the Æon, and exert themselves to establish His reign upon Earth. They must acknowledge that 'The word of the Law is Θελημα' and that 'Love is the law, love under will.'
> Each member must make it his main work to discover for himself his own true will, and to do it, and do nothing else. *{It is not considered "essential to right conduct" to be an active propagandist of the Law, and so on; it may, or may not, be the True Will of any particular person to do so. But since the fundamental purpose of the Order is to further the Attainment of humanity, membership implies, by definition, the Will to help mankind by the means best adapted thereto.}*[159]

"It was my original idea that the O.T.O. would be a sort of training ground for the A∴A∴. It was still in my mind that the A∴A∴ represented, so to speak, the only thing worth doing. But recent initiations have changed my views considerably. But the O.T.O. has a perfectly definite function in connection with the New Æon. At a time like the present, when individual liberty is threatened in a way to which history offers no parallel, a strong and vigorous order is required to guard humanity. The A∴A∴ does this, it is true, but in a manner so beyond even your present conceptions, that I

---

[157] *Ibid. Cf.* also *MITAP*, Ch. XVIII, Sec. II, fn.: "Anna Kingsford, so far as her good work is concerned, was only the rubber stamp of Edward Maitland."
[158] *Liber 666.*
[159] *One Star in Sight*, Sec. 10.

think it only fair to give even the most commonplace of men a chance to co-operate actually."¹⁶⁰ Thus, "Every man and woman that is of full age, free, and of good report, has an indefeasible right to the III°. Beyond this, admission is only granted by invitation from the governing body concerned. . . . In selecting members for advancement, attention is paid to their devotion to the Order, to their intelligence in apprehending the nature of its teaching, to their zeal in spreading the principles of the Order so far as they themselves understand them, though always with the discretion inseparable from the due guarding of the secrets, and to all those qualities of courage, honour, and virtue without which man is not worthy of that name."¹⁶¹

Conversely, "the original Rule of the Order of A∴A∴ was that the introducer read over a short lection to the applicant, then left him alone for a quarter of an hour, and on coming back received a 'yes' or 'no.' If there was any hesitation about it the applicant was barred for life. The reason for the relaxation of the rule was that it was thought better to help people along in the early stages of the work, even if there was no hope of their turning out first-class."¹⁶² Still, "No attainment soever is officially recognised by the A∴A∴ unless the immediate inferior of the person in question has been fitted by him to take his place." Again, "The rule is not rigidly applied in all cases, as it would lead to congestion, especially in the lower grades where the need is greatest, and the conditions most confused."¹⁶³

"For example; the oath of a probationer apparently involves no difficulties of any sort; no penalties are stated or implied; the aspirant merely pledges himself 'to perform the Great Work, which is to obtain the knowledge of the nature and powers of my own being'. He is not required to reach any particular stage of knowledge by the end of his probation; he is free to choose such practices as appeal to him; and, provided that his record shows that he has devoted a reasonable proportion of his spare time to the Work, he is unhesitatingly passed to the degree of neophyte. It sounds as if it were impossible for anyone to fail. Yet, actually only eight per cent manage to get through the year of probation. The reason is that no sooner does a man make up his mind to enter the Path of the Wise than he rouses automatically the supreme hostility of every force, internal or external, in his sphere."¹⁶⁴

Eliphaz Levi, the great magician of the middle of the last century, whose philosophy made possible the extraordinary outburst of literature in France in the fifties and sixties by its doctrine of the self-sufficiency of Art ("A fine style is an aureole of holiness" is one phrase of

---

¹⁶⁰ Letter to C. S. Jones, 7 February 1916.
¹⁶¹ *Liber LII*, Secs. 9, 14.
¹⁶² *MWT*, Introduction.
¹⁶³ *One Star in Sight, loc. cit.*
¹⁶⁴ *Confessions*, Ch. 62.

his), prophesies of the Messiah in a remarkable passage. It will be seen that our founder, born as he was to the purple, has fulfilled it.

I have not the volume at my side, living as I am this hermit life in New Hampshire, but its gist is that Kings and Popes have not power to redeem the world because they surround themselves with splendour and dignity. They possess all that other men desire, and therefore their motives are suspect. If any person of position, says Levi, insists upon living a life of hardship and inconvenience when he could do otherwise, then men will trust him, and he will be able to execute his projects for the general good of the commonwealth. But he must naturally be careful not to relax his austerities as his power increases. Make power and splendour incompatible, and the social problem is solved.[165]

"All the serious Orders of the world, or nearly all, begin by insisting that the aspirant should take a vow of poverty; a Buddhist Bhikku, for example, can own only nine objects—his three robes, begging bowl, a fan, toothbrush, and so on. The Hindu and Mohammedan Orders have similar regulations; and so do all the important Orders of monkhood in Christianity. Our own Order is the only exception of importance; and the reason for this is that it is much more difficult to retain one's purity if one is living in the world than if one simply cuts oneself off from it. It is far easier to achieve technical attainments if one is unhampered by any such considerations. These regulations operate as restrictions to one's usefulness in helping the world. There are terrible dangers, the worst dangers of all, associated with complete retirement. In my own personal judgment, moreover, I think that our own ideal of a natural life is much more wholesome."[166]

"I attempted to make the appeal of the new system universal by combining it with a practical system of fraternal intercourse and mutual benefit. I formulated a scheme of insurance against all the accidents of life; the details are given in the Official Instructions and Essays published in *The Equinox*, vol. III, no. I; and to set the example I transferred the whole of my property to trustees for the Order. The general idea is this; that every man should enjoy his possessions and the full fruits of his labours exactly as he does under his original individualistic system, but the pooling of such possessions by economy of administration, etc., leaves a surplus which can be used for the general purposes of the Order. I wished to introduce the benefits of co-operation without interfering with the individual absoluteness of the elements of the combination. . . . We were therefore able to allow members to borrow in case of necessity up to the total amount of their fees and subscriptions; to give them a month's holiday for less than a week would have cost an outsider; to save them all medical, legal and similar expenses; to solve the problem of rent, and so on. We offered all the

---

[165] *Liber CLXI.*
[166] *MWT, loc. cit.*

fabled advantages of socialism without in any way interfering with individual dignity and independence."[167]

"Members of the IX° become part proprietors of the Estates and Goods of the Order, so that the attainment of this degree implies a return with interest of the fees and subscriptions paid. The Order gives practical assistance in life to worthy members of even its lower degrees, so that, even if originally poor, they become well able to afford the comparatively high fees of the VII°, VIII°, and IX°. On exaltation to the IV° each Companion may file an account of his circumstances, and state in what direction he requires help."[168] As Crowley told C. S. Jones in 1916, "Our business is to establish the Law. Any distraction from that, mystic or otherwise, is a mistake. I may say that I have been working away from the Tarot and astrology. What we have to do is to conquer the world and the way we have to do it is to talk in a language that everybody can understand; ethics, education, and the labour problem are our strong cards. If we concentrate on those we should certainly get a following of sorts which may lead to bigger things later on. We can keep the technical training in Magick for specially prepared people who want to understand the inner secrets of life, but if we talk Qabalah and such things to the profane vulgar we are no more likely to get support than if we had worked out some novel theorems in pure mathematics."[169]

In 1917, Crowley's O.T.O. Grand Lodge in England was raided and closed down by the police, ostensibly over charges of "fortune-telling" against one of the members. However, Crowley's involvement in New York with George Sylvester Viereck's anti-British publication *The Fatherland* may have caused the UK authorities to suspect the lodge of unpatriotic activities. Either way, all lodge records were seized and Crowley was forced to temporarily resign the Grand Mastership in favour of Jones to ease the situation for the remaining members.[170] Consequently, Jones identifies himself in one document as "PARZIVAL X° O.T.O., Deputy Grand Master General of all English Speaking Countries, Viceroy of His Most Sacred Majesty BAPHOMET for the Dominion of Canada."[171] Seven years later, Crowley still insisted that "each member should propagate the Law as best he can, especially by correspondence, so as to start new centres in distant parts. Arrangements for meeting newspapers and such propaganda would come later when a given centre had sufficient numbers."[172] Bear in mind, this was before the Internet, cell phones, and fast and affordable international travel.

The work of the Magus "is to create a new Universe in accordance with His Will," and "To attain the grade of Magus he must accomplish Three Tasks; the renunciation of His enjoyment of the Infinite so that he may

---

[167] *Confessions*, Ch. 72. The following is also attributed to Crowley: "This is as I have always held, our great Asset: Thelema is the only possible answer to communism."
[168] *Liber LII*, Secs. 13.g–h.
[169] Letter to C. S. Jones, February 1916.
[170] Starr, *op. cit.*
[171] As quoted in Frater Iacchus, "Hunchbacks and Soldiers," *Baphomet Breeze* III(2), Summer Solstice 1988.
[172] Letter to Norman Mudd, 27 May 1924.

formulate Himself as the Finite; the acquisition of the practical secrets alike of initiating and governing His proposed new Universe and the identification of himself with the impersonal idea of Love."[173] In the *Confessions*, Crowley declares: "I have attained to understanding, I have made my magical model of society, and I await the moment when those who have chosen me to carry out their colossal conception summon me to stand forth before the world and execute their purpose."[174] Crowley understood "that all men live in sin, being baulked of their True Will, that is, of the free function of their essential nature. This restriction cometh much from their ignorance of what their True Will is, and much from external hindrance, but most of all from the interference of ill-controlled parts of their own instruments, the body and mind. For Freedom is not found in looseness and lack of governance, but in the right ruling of each individual of the common weal so as to assure his own well-being no less than that of the whole. And this effect is to be won by perfect organization under the eye of an Intelligence adequate to comprehend the general and the particular need together."[175]

"Such is a brief outline of the government of the O.T.O. It combines monarchy with democracy; it includes aristocracy, and conceals even the seeds of revolution, by which alone progress can be effected. Thus we balance the Triads, uniting the Three in One; thus we gather up all the threads of human passion and interest, and weave them into an harmonious tapestry, subtly and diligently with great art, that our Order may seem an ornament even to the Stars that are in the Heavens at Night. In our rainbow-coloured texture we set forth the glory of the whole Universe—See thou to it, brother Magician, that thine own thread be strong, and pure, and of a colour brilliant in itself, yet ready to mingle in all beauty with those of thy brethren!"[176] The remodelled structure of the O.T.O. was based—by way of the original Bavarian Illuminati—on the Jesuit Order, the principal weapon of the Counter-Reformation; while the Freemasons, of course, were thought responsible not only for the French Revolution but for the American Revolution as well.[177]

As Crowley told Frank Bennett, his X° Viceroy for Australasia, in 1916, "The O.T.O. should be put forward as a complete solution of the social problem not merely as an occult society. That is as far as the general public is concerned; keep the occult side of it for people who are already interested in the subject."[178] The Nazis banned all secret societies in the 1930s and put Freemasons—including one Karl Johannes Germer, X° O.T.O., "Grand Master General of the Free German-Speaking Peoples" (later X° for U.S.A. and ultimately O.H.O.)—in concentration camps. Written during the First World War, *Liber CI*, 7th House, "Of the Duties of the Brethren," Clause 32, reads: "Public enemies of the country of any Brother shall be treated as

---

[173] *One Star in Sight*, Sec. 6.
[174] *Confessions*, Ch. 87.
[175] *The Heart of the Master*, loc. cit., "The Mystery of Sin."
[176] *Liber CXCIV*, Sec. 34.
[177] *Cf.* Singh-Anand 2015.
[178] Letter to Frank Bennett, October 1916.

such while in the field, and slain or captured as the officer of the Brother may command. But within the precincts of the Lodge all such divisions are to be forgotten absolutely; and as children of One Father the enemies of the hour before and the hour after are to dwell in peace, amity, and fraternity." Now, Reuss had worked for the Prussian Secret Service, Crowley may very well have been in the employ of British Intelligence, and Dr. John Dee himself was the original "007."[179]

"Of course, it is understood that the first interest of the Order, after its actual necessary expenses have been defrayed, is propaganda and publicity. Although interested in the material welfare of the brethren, we use even the benefits of the Profess Houses, and such things, principally in order that they may be led to appreciate fully the benefits of the Law."[180] However, as Crowley tells W. T. Smith, "the form of advertising is not in your discretion. At the moment the Tarot, the Hymn for Independence Day and L'Étincelle are of supreme importance, because they will reach a public of more or less normal people. We do not want any more drifting 'occultists.' You want the great political leaders, great industrialists and people of that sort, the kind of persons who does not subscribe $835 in a year, but half a million dollars in a day; and every distraction or diversion of funds from the business of getting at such people is hardly better than throwing the money into the sea. In fact, I think it is worse; because the practice of doing so discourages me in my struggle, almost single-handed as I am over here, against all the worse elements in sub-human society."[181]

When, in April 1934, Smith incorporated a "Church of Thelema" under California state law around the Gnostic Mass, Crowley was furious. Although Smith retained the North American O.T.O. as in unincorporated association, Crowley believed he had incorporated the O.T.O. and complained about this in series of letters to other initiates. In his reply to Crowley, Smith tried to explain that "To form a corporation sole, and not to be dependent upon a vote to select its head, we had to draw the papers up in that manner in this State. It is practically the same as that drawn up for the Catholics who hold property, etc., for the church. It is not intended to be incorporation of the O.T.O. but the Church of Thelema, to give us some protection and enable us to collect moneys, etc."[182] Ironically, in an otherwise legitimate effort to secure and maintain the status of a California tax exempt religious organization, the modern O.T.O. has done away with all aspects of the Order that are not strictly "religious" or esoteric.

> In the interest of clarity, I offer the following list of policy differences between the OTO envisioned in Liber CI and the OTO as it actually exists today in the United States.

---

[179] *Cf.* e.g. Kaczynski 2012; Spence 2008; and Deacon 1968. Before his stint first at Columbia-Haus then at Esterwegen, the aforementioned Germer was likewise a decorated military intelligence officer, receiving both first- and second-class Iron Crosses for his WWI service.
[180] Letter to C. S. Jones, January 1919.
[181] Letter to W. T. Smith, 1 April 1943.
[182] As quoted in Starr, *op. cit.*, 200–201.

OTO does not now encourage its members to treat those outside the Order as inferiors who possess no rights. While we do encourage members to do their part in recruiting new members, we do not expect or encourage them to aggressively proselytize among their friends, employers, and any wealthy or powerful acquaintances they may have.[183] We encourage community and all levels of social interaction between OTO members, but they remain free to engage in personal relationships and marriage with whomever they choose, and to employ, work for, and do business with whomever they choose.[184]

At this time, we do not have official Profess-Houses or special educational institutions, though we look forward to a day when we will.[185] We do not have special facilities for the care of children or expectant mothers, nor do we accept children into any special training or educational programs.[186] While we offer what assistance we can to the families of members who suffer bereavement, we do not require our officers to adopt the orphaned children of members.[187]

We no longer hold ideas of "the frontal duty of womankind" as points of doctrine.[188] Rather, we emphasize the individuality of all women and all men.

Lodge Masters are encouraged (as are all members) to offer hospitality to travelling members. However, until such a time as Order-operated lodging facilities are available, providing hospitality to travelling members is not considered mandatory.[189]

Members who are professionals, tradesmen, or businessmen are not expected to donate their products or services to the Order, though such donations are gratefully received.[190] All members retain full control over their personal property, except those items of property they may choose to donate to the Order.[191] The members of the IX° do not hold the property of the Order in common.[192] The property of the U.S. Grand Lodge is held by the O.T.O. U.S.A. corporation, in accordance with California non-profit corporation law.

We do offer a variety of methods to relieve the financial burden of dues payment to members undergoing genuine hardship. However, dues and fees paid to OTO are not refundable under any circumstances, and OTO does not make personal loans to its members.[193] Also, dues and fees paid to OTO cannot be transferred or assigned at any time to a member's heirs or legatees.[194]

---

[183] *Cf. Liber CI*, Secs. 4, 7, 15, 36, 40, 42.
[184] *Cf. Ibid.*, Secs. 6, 12, 13, 20, 24, 53, 60, 61, 70.
[185] *Cf. Ibid.*, Secs. 46, 49–52, 66, 68
[186] *Cf. Ibid.*, Secs. 37–39, 41, 54, 56.
[187] *Cf. Ibid.*, Sec. 55.
[188] *Cf. Ibid.*, Sec. 39.
[189] *Cf. Ibid.*, Sec. 23.
[190] *Cf. Ibid.*, Secs. 21–22, 57.
[191] *Cf. Ibid.*, Secs. 2, 8, 9–10, 33.
[192] *Cf. Ibid.*, Sec. 52.
[193] *Cf. Ibid.*, Sec. 45.
[194] *Cf. Ibid.*, Sec. 64.

Although our Grand Tribunal does provide arbitration for disputes between members, the services of our legal advisers are not available to members free of charge. Further, we reserve the right to waive the prohibition against law suits between members and recuse ourselves from arbitrating any particular dispute.[195] In fact, it is our policy to do so in the case of domestic disputes. The Grand Tribunal does not arbitrate disputes between members and non-members,[196] though we can provide legal referrals to our members who require them.[197]

We can thus shrug off the pretence that the modern O.T.O., in any meaningful way, follows "The Blue Equinox model." Nor does Sabazius X°, a/k/a Tau Apiryon, explain how he intends to establish the Law of Thelema in a country where the separation of Church and State is basically sacrosanct. Nevertheless, this is what the Knight of the East and West still vows to "devote his life to" (*Liber CXCIV*, Sec. 6). The international corporate bylaws further unequivocally state that "All aspects of O.T.O. are religious in character, and the use of the term 'ecclesiastical' to identify the class of membership defined in this article should not be construed to signify that other aspects of O.T.O. are not ecclesiastical or religious in character."[198] At the same time, however, the modern O.T.O. no longer requires its members to be professed Thelemites—religious or otherwise—only (in the I° Pledge) to "accept *Liber AL vel Legis Sub Figura CCXX*, also known as *The Book of the Law*, without wishing to make changes in it."[199]

What the organization *does* require is for candidates to the IV° to memorize several Qabalistic tables from *777*—some suspect because its leaders, following the multi-decade *de facto* interregnum, had found themselves in competition with not only Wiccans and Satanists but various Golden Dawn off-shoots as well.[200] Either way, the O.T.O. was never a teaching order, nor does it claim to be one now; as Crowley himself told Jones in 1936: "One thing I will say: that I do not expect anything to come of qabalistic speculations. I think that they may even be extremely mischievous in times like the present. Our sole business should be to use the Law to reconstruct the world from the chaos into which it is already half tumbled. That formula is a simple one, and requires no specialised training. The work requires the cooperation of tens of thousands of people who have never heard of the Qabalah, and they have to be addressed in language which they can understand."[201]

A similar sentiment is reflected in *Liber Aleph*, addressed to Jones 18 years earlier: "Do thou understand how few be they whose Work in this their present Lives is our Way of Initiation. Yet it is written in *The Book of*

---

[195] *Cf. Ibid.*, Secs. 25–26, 31, 62.
[196] *Cf. Ibid.*, Sec. 29.
[197] Sabazius X°, "A Memorandum Regarding Liber CI," U.S. Grand Lodge of Ordo Templi Orientis, Riverside, CA, April 1999.
[198] *Bylaws of Ordo Templi Orientis International*, Article IX, Section 9.01.A.
[199] *O.T.O. Form B/1*, Rev. IVa, Summer IVx.
[200] To be fair, it should be noted that for the first quarter of the 19th century, even the 14° of the A∴A∴S∴R∴ (Southern Jurisdiction) included brief lectures on both *gematria* and *notariqon*.
[201] Letter to C. S. Jones, 28 August 1936.

the Law that the Law is for all, so that thou shalt in no wise err if thou establish it as the Formula of the Æon, universal among Men. Also, ever for them that are fitted to advance in our Light, there is Order and Diversity in Function, as regardeth their Work in Our Sublime Brotherhood. Thus, it might well be that, in a Profess-House of the Temple, or College of the Holy Ghost, each Knight or Brother might severally attain Experience of every Trance, unto the Perfection of all Illumination; yet by this there ought not to arise Confusion, one usurping the appointed office of another. For the Abbot, although he be not enlightened wholly, is yet Abbot; and the Place of the Cook, were he Saint, Arhat, and Paramahamsa in one Person, is in his Kitchen."[202]

"In the past, the mob without will or mind have been treated without sense or scruple; a mistake socially, economically and politically, no less than from the humanitarian point of view. We must remember that each man and woman is a star, it is our duty to maintain the order of nature by seeing to it that his orbit is correctly calculated. The revolutions and catastrophes with which history is crammed are invariably due to the rulers having failed to find fitting functions for the people. The obvious result has been social discontent ending in the refusal of the cells to perform their work in the organism."[203] Crowley asks Jones to "consider moreover that the Mysterious is always the Terrible, for Vulgar Minds. How then when a New Word is spoken? Either it is not heard, or it is misunderstood; and it evoketh Fear and Hate as a Reaction against Fear. Then Men take him and set him at naught, and spit upon him and scourge him, and lead him away to crucify him; and the third Day he riseth from among the Dead, and ascendeth into Heaven, and sitteth at the right Hand of God, and cometh to judge the Quick and the Dead. This, o my Son, is the History of Every Man unto whom is given a Word."[204]

"There is a Magical operation of maximum importance: the Initiation of a New Æon. When it becomes necessary to utter a Word, the whole Planet must be bathed in blood. Before man is ready to accept the Law of Thelema, the Great War must be fought. This Bloody Sacrifice is the critical point of the World-Ceremony of the Proclamation of Horus, the Crowned and conquering Child, as Lord of the Æon." Crowley notes that "This paragraph was written in the summer of 1911 e.v., just three years before its fulfilment." According to him, "This whole matter is prophesied in the *Book of the Law* itself; let the student take note, and enter the ranks of the Host of the Sun."[205] However, "I am not so foolish as to think that my doctrine can

---

[202] "De illuminatum operibus diversis." *Cf.* also *Liber CXCIV*, Sec. 21: "Before the face of the Areopagus stands an independent Parliament of the Guilds. Within the Order, irrespective of grade, the members of each craft, trade, science, or profession form themselves into a Guild, make their own laws, and prosecute their own good, in all matters pertaining to their labour and means of livelihood. Each Guild chooses the man most eminent in it to represent it before the Areopagus of the Eighth Degree; and all disputes between the various Guilds are argued before that Body, which will decide according to the grand principles of the Order. Its decisions pass for ratification to the Sanctuary of the Gnosis, and thence to the Throne."
[203] *Confessions, loc. cit.*
[204] *Liber Aleph*, "De stultitia humana."
[205] *MITAP, loc. cit.*, Sec. I.

ever gain the ear of the world. I expect that ten centuries hence the 'nominal Crowleians' will be as pestilent and numerous a body as the 'nominal Christians' are to-day; for (at present) I have been able to devise no mechanism for excluding them. Rather, perhaps, should I seek to find them a niche in the shrine, just as Hinduism provides alike for those capable of the Upanishads and those whose intelligence hardly reaches to the Tantras. In short, one must abandon the reality of religion for a sham, so that the religion may be universal enough for those few who are capable of its reality to nestle to its breast, and nurse their nature on its starry milk. But we anticipate!"[206]

"My message is then twofold; to the greasy *bourgeois* I preach discontent; I shock him, I stagger him, I cut away earth from under his feet, I turn him upside down, I give him hashish and make him run amok, I twitch his buttocks with the red-hot tongs of my Sadistic fancy—until he feels uncomfortable. But to the man who is already as uneasy as St. Lawrence on his silver grill, who feels the spirit stir in him, even as a woman feels, and sickens at, the first leap of the babe in her womb, to him I bring the splendid vision, the perfume and the glory, the Knowledge and Conversation of the Holy Guardian Angel. And to whosoever hath attained that height will I put a further Question, announce a further Glory."[207] However, Crowley warns Jones that "The Path of the Mystic hath this Pitfall; for though he unite himself with his God, his Mode is to withdraw from that which himseemeth is not God, whereby he affirmeth and confirmeth the Demon, that is, Duality. Be thou instant therefore, o my Son, to turn from every Act of Love at the Moment of full Satisfaction, flinging the Invoked Might thereof against a new Opposite; for the Formula of every Dragon is Perpetual Motion or Change, and therefore to dwell in the Satisfaction of thy Nature is a Stagnation, and a Violation thereof, making the Duality of Conflict, which is the Falling Away to Choronzon."[208]

Historically, Sannyasa has been a stage of renunciation, non-violence, simple life, and spiritual pursuit. However, this has not always been the case in India. After the Mongol and Persian invasions and establishment of the Delhi Sultanate, from the 12th century through the British Raj, some of the Shaiva and Vaishnava sannyasins morphed into a military order. They developed martial arts, created military strategies, and engaged in guerrilla warfare against the Islamic conquerors, eventually playing an important role in helping European colonial powers establish themselves in India.[209] The earliest Hindu monks to resort to an armed response were the 12-century Nāth Siddhas, who led a nomadic and unattached lifestyle. As these "warrior ascetics" dedicated themselves to rebellion, their groups acquired stallions, developed techniques of spycraft and assassination, adopting strategies of war against the Muslim nobility and the Sultanate state. Many of these groups were formed by devotees of the Hindu deity Mahadeva, and

---

[206] *Liber CLVIII*, Sec. IX.
[207] *Ibid.* Emphasis in original.
[208] *Liber Aleph*, "De formula recta draconis."
[209] Pinch 2006.

were thus known as Mahants, but other popular names for them between 1500 and 1800 CE were Jogīs, Nāgas, Bairāgis, and Gosains.[210]

The Sannyasins continued their rebellion through the Mughal Empire, and grew into a political force during the early years of the British Raj. These Hindu warrior monks played a pivotal role in helping the British establish themselves in India, but their significance swiftly declined with the consolidation of the British rule in the late 19th century and the rise of the non-violence movement led by Mahatma Gandhi.[211] While Muslim rule over North India had drastically affected Hinduism and Buddhism through systematic persecution, the Indian economy continued to remain one of the largest in the world. However, in contrast to the Muslim rulers, the British with their monopolistic East India Company engaged in destroying the economy as well, not to mention dismantling the prevailing decentralized education systems. Following the English Education Act of 1835, the British state-supported education system emphasized Western religions and thought at the cost of indigenous tradition.[212] After 1813, the British were also involved in the aggressive propagation of Protestant Christianity, which was concomitant with the British propaganda machine spreading anti-Hindu sentiment.[213]

The 5th-century Indian monk Bodhidharma, the supposed founder of Chán Buddhism, is also traditionally credited with founding the martials arts at the famous Shàolín Temple in China. The O.T.O. itself takes its name from the Knights Templar, or the "Poor Fellow-Soldiers of Christ and of the Temple of Solomon," officially recognized as a religious order by Pope Honorius II at the Council of Troyes in 1128. St. Bernard of Clairvaux was asked to help write a rule for them, which would be that of the Cistercians, whose white habit the Templars adopted, adding to it a red cross. These Christian warrior monks, whether knights drawn from the nobility, bailiffs, clerks, or chaplains, took three monastic vows, even if it was to the war against the Saracens that they were primarily pledged. Their Cistercian forebears pursued self-sufficiency and looked down upon mere devout Bible reading within the confines of a monastic cell, labouring in the fields rather than studying in the cloisters. A Cistercian would see cutting down a tree as prayer, given the right circumstances, and the Templars adopted a similar attitude towards Muslims in the Holy Land. The Cistercian philosophy crystallizes in the water mill: its monasteries were to be built by water, and this water was to run the wheat mill and the tannery, irrigate and wash and aid at the forge shop. Despite their expressed desire for poverty, their abbeys grew wealthy, as infamously did the Templar Order;

---

[210] Hiltebeitel 1999. Similarly, the fearsome Gurkhas of Nepal trace their name back to the mediaeval Hindu warrior-saint Gorakhnath, who is himself traditionally considered one of the founders of hatha yoga.
[211] Pinch, *op. cit.*
[212] Dharampal 1983.
[213] King 1999. Indeed, Sri Aurobindo famously chastised Gandhi for adopting the Christian idea of atonement for sin, for confusing—like the Christians do—morality with spirituality.

in fact, the network of Cistercian monasteries can be considered the first multinational corporation in Europe.[214]

> I would call your attention to the fact that many monastic orders, both in Asia and in Europe, have succeeded in surviving all changes of government, and in securing pleasant and useful lives for their members. But this has been possible only because restricted life was enjoined. However, there were orders of military monks, like the Templars, who grew and prospered exceedingly. You recall that the Order of the Temple was only overthrown by a treacherous *coup d'état* on the part of a King and of a Pope who saw their reactionary, obscurantist, and tyrannical programme menaced by those knights who did not scruple to add the wisdom of the East to their own large interpretation of Christianity, and who represented in that time a movement towards the light of learning and of science, which has been brought to fruition in our own times by the labours of the Orientalists from Von Hammer-Purgstall and Sir William Jones to Professor Rhys Davids and Madame Blavatsky, to say nothing of such philosophers as Schopenhauer, on the one hand; and by the heroic efforts of Darwin, Huxley, Tyndall, and Spencer, on the other.[215]

Vivekananda himself laments that it has "become hard for us modern Indians to understand how it could be like that; nevertheless, there are to be met with in Varanasi and Nadia and other places even now, some old as well as young persons among our Pandits, and mostly among the Sannyasins, who are mad with this kind of thirst for knowledge for its own sake. Students, not placed in the midst of the luxurious surroundings and materials of the modern Europeanised Hindu, and with a thousand times less facilities for study, poring over manuscripts in the flickering light of an oil lamp, night after night, which alone would have been enough to completely destroy the eye-sight of the students of any other nation; travelling on foot hundreds of miles, begging their way all along, in search of a rare manuscript or a noted teacher; and wonderfully concentrating all the energy of their body and mind upon their one object of study, year in and year out, till the hair turns grey and the infirmity of age overtakes them. . . Whatever India now holds as a proud possession, has been undeniably the result of such labour on the part of her worthy sons in days gone by; and the truth of this remark will become at once evident on comparing the depth and solidity as well as the unselfishness and the earnestness of purpose of India's ancient scholarship with the results attained by our modern Indian Universities. Unselfish and genuine zeal for real scholarship and honest earnest thought must again become dominant in the life of our countrymen if they are ever to rise to occupy among nations a rank worthy of their own historic past."[216]

---

[214] Balk, *op. cit.*
[215] *Liber CLXI.*
[216] "On Dr. Paul Deussen," *Brahmavâdin*, 1896. Vivekananda, *op. cit.*, iv.219–220.

"'At my initiation I was taught to be cautious' is a note in one system; in another the neophyte is told 'Fear is failure, and the forerunner of failure. Be thou therefore without fear, for in the heart of the coward virtue abideth not.' Keep these two precepts constantly in your mind, and you should go far and fast."[217] In his novel, *Moonchild*, Crowley has a character declare: "The best kind of Englishman is blood brother to the best kind of Mussulman. He is brave, just, frank, manly and proud. We should always be in alliance Islam against the servile Hindus and so-called Christians. Where is the spirit of the Paladins and the Templars and the Knights of the Round Table? The modern Christian is the Bourgeois, whose character is based on fear and falsehood."[218] According to *Magick Without Tears*, "Mysticism, both Catholic and Protestant, made a further attempt to free Christianity from the dark cloud of iniquity. They joined hands with the Sufis and the Vedantists. But this again led to the mere denial of the reality of evil. Thus drawing away, little by little, from clear appreciation of the facts of Nature, their doctrine became purely theoretical, and faded away, while the thundercloud of sin settled down more heavily than ever."[219]

"The most important of all the efforts of the White School, from an exoteric point of view, is Islam. In its doctrine there is some slight taint, but much less than in Christianity. It is a virile religion. It looks facts in the face, and admits their horror; but it proposes to overcome them by sheer dint of manhood. Unfortunately, the metaphysical conceptions of its quasi-profane Schools are grossly materialistic. It is only the Pantheism of the Sufis which eliminates the conception of propitiation; and, in practice, the Sufis are too closely allied to the Vedantists to retain hold of reality."[220] Indeed, "Here lies the error of such Pantheism as that of Mansur el-Hallaj, whom Sir Richard Burton so delightfully twits (in the *Kasîdah*) with his impotence—'Mansur was wise, but wiser they who smote / ....him with the hurlèd stones; / And though his blood a witness bore, no / ....Wisdom-Might could mend his bones.'[221] God was in the stones no less than within his turban-wrapping; and when the twain crashed together, one point of perception of the pact was obscured—which was in no wise his design!"[222]

"The Nature of this Silence is shewn also by the God Harpocrates, the Babe in the Lotus, who is also the Serpent and the Egg, that is, the Holy Ghost. This is the most secret of all Energies, the Seed of all Being, and therefore must He be sealed up in an Ark from the Malice of the Devourers. If then by thine Art thou canst conceal thy Self in thine own Nature, this is Silence, this, and not Nullity of Consciousness, else were a Stone more perfect in Adeptship than thou. But, abiding in thy Silence, thou art in a City of Refuge, and the Waters prevail not against the Lotus that enfoldeth thee. This Ark or Lotus is then the Body of Our Lady BABALON, without which thou wereth the Prey of Nile and of the Crocodiles that are therein. Now, o

---

[217] *The Revival of Magick*.
[218] *Moonchild*, Ch. XXII.
[219] *MWT*, Ch. VII.
[220] *Ibid*.
[221] II.XIV.
[222] *Little Essays Toward Truth*, "Trance."

my Son, mark thou well this that I will write for thine Advertisement and Behoof, that this Silence, though it be Perfection of Delight, is but the Gestation of thy Lion, and in thy Season thou must Dare, and come forth to the Battle. Else, were not this Practice of Silence akin to the Formula of Separateness of the Black Brothers?"[223]

As Lieutenant-General Sir William Butler put it in his biography of Major-General Charles George Gordon, "The nation that will insist on drawing a broad line of demarcation between the fighting man and the thinking man is liable to find its fighting done by fools and its thinking done by cowards."[224] Crowley himself was "angrily unwilling to proceed with that part of the Work appointed for him which is detailed in Chapter III, even when the course of events on the planet, war, revolution, and the collapse of the social and religious systems of civilization, proved plainly to him that whether he liked it or no, Ra Hoor Khuit was indeed Lord of the Æon, the Crowned and Conquering Child whose innocence meant no more than inhuman cruelty and wantonly senseless destructiveness as he avenged Isis our mother the Earth and the Heaven for the murder and mutilation of Osiris, Man, her son. The War of 1914–18 and its sequels have proved even to the dullest statesmen, beyond wit of even the most subtly sophistical theologians to gloze, that death is not an unmixed benefit either to the individual or the community: that force and fire of leaping manhood are more useful to a nation than cringing respectability and emasculate servility; that genius goes with courage, and the sense of shame and guilt with 'Defeatism.'"[225]

"The establishment of this new Æon, this new fundamental principle, is the great work now to be accomplished in the world.... Enough if it is now said that in this Law lies the whole future: it is the Law of Liberty, and those who refuse it proclaim themselves slaves, and as slaves shall they be chained and flogged. It is the Law of Love, and those who refuse it declare themselves to be the children of hate, and their hate shall return upon them and consume them with its unending tortures. It is the Law of Life, and those who refuse it shall be subject to death; and death shall catch them unawares. Even their life shall be a living death. It is the Law of Light, and those who refuse it thereby make themselves dark for ever."[226] We are again reminded of the words of Éliphas Lévi, who writes: "When a new word comes into the world, it needs swaddling clothes and bandages; genius brought it forth, but it is for experience to nourish it. Do not fear that it will die of neglect! Oblivion is for it a favourable time of rest, and contradictions help it to grow. When a sun bursts forth in space it creates worlds or attracts them to itself. A single spark of fixed light promises a universe to space."[227]

However, "obviously to change the Magical Formula of the planet is to change all moral sanctions and the result is bound to appear disastrous.

---

[223] *Liber Aleph*, "De natura silentii nostri."
[224] Butler 1889, 85. Commonly misattributed to Thucydides.
[225] *The Equinox of the Gods, loc. cit.*, Sec. I.
[226] *Ibid.*, Ch. VIII.
[227] *The Key of the Mysteries*, Part III, Book II, Ch. II.

The Cult of The Dying God introduced by Dionysus destroyed the Roman virtue and smashed the Roman culture. (Possibly the introduction of the worship of Osiris in an earlier epoch was primarily responsible for the decay of Egyptian civilization.)"[228] The martyr and hermit, contemptuous of Earth and enraptured by contemplation of Heaven, was in the Christian opinion the highest ideal of humanity, displacing the old Roman ideal of the hero and patriot who, oblivious of self, lives and is prepared to die for the good of the country. "The war was made by senile dribblers who had survived Queen Victoria by accident. Young men would never have been so stupid and obstinate as these Struldbrug remnants of the age of Tennyson and John Stuart Mill."[229]

Crowley waxes lyrical: "I think that the next generation will have a great deal to say with regard to the European War. I think that the war will be followed everywhere by revolution. I think that humanity will have had the facts of life presented to it with such soul-shaking violence that the pitiful pretense which some of us still make will fall at last by its own weight. I think that the controversy of the future will be between the law of nature or of Nietzsche, and that of compassion or of Shelley. I think that supernaturalism has received the mercy-stroke. I think that Christianity will be studied by everybody (who has the leisure and inclination) just as it is today by anthropologists, is in the due relation to other religions of the world. I think that the use of Christianity as an engine of oppression of the poor is ended."[230] Previously, "when the earth was nigh utterly corrupt by reason of the Great Sorcery, the Brethren sent Mohammed to bring freedom to mankind by the sword."[231]

> But a new Magical Formula is on a vastly bigger scale. Cast your mind for a moment back to the last occasion, when Osiris succeeded to Isis. In that great cataclysm not only Empires, but civilizations crashed one after another. Three quarters of the Æon had elapsed before the wine of that vintage was really drinkable.
>
> I expect as I hope that this time (communication being universally better established, the foundations better laid, and things in general moving quicker) we may be able to enjoy the harvest in very much less time. But hang it all! it's hardly reasonable to expect complete fruition after only 40 years.
>
> What seems to me the most encouraging symptom of all is this: the Book itself, and the system of Magick based thereon, and the bankruptcy of all previous systems (as set forth in Eight Lectures on Yoga, Magick,

---

[228] *Confessions*, Ch. 50. *Cf.* also *The Book of Thoth*, Part IV, "Defeat"—"As Virtue declined, corruption disintegrated the Empire from within. Epicene cults, such as those of Dionysus (in its degraded form), of Attis, of Adonis, of Cybele, the false Demeter and the prostituted Isis, replaced the sterner rites of the true Solar-Phallic gods; until finally (the masters having lost the respect, and so the control, of the plebs, native and alien) the lowest of all the slave-cults, dressed up in the fables of the vilest of the parasitic races, swept over the known world, and drenched it in foul darkness for five hundred years."
[229] *Liber 888*, "The Teachings of Christianity."
[230] *Ibid.*
[231] *Liber XXXIII.*

The Book of Thoth, and other similar works) do furnish us all with a clear, concise practical *Method* (free from all contamination of the humbug of faith and superstition) whereby any one of us may attain to "the Knowledge and Conversation of the Holy Guardian Angel," and that the many other Beings of intelligence and power indefinitely more exalted than anything which we recognize as human—and, let us hope, capable of bestowing upon us a modicum of Wisdom adequate to get us out of the quagmire into which the crisis has temporarily plunged us all![232]

"At the exact moment when the futility of the formalized faiths of the world has been recognized, despite the stoutest denials; when the first principles of religion and ethics have been subconsciously rejected, so that a kind of spiritual neurasthenia broke loose in the hysteria of the world-war, there appeared a mysterious figure who is generally known as the Master Therion. Instructed by chiefs who have hitherto preferred to remain in the background, he brings to free and enlightened men a law by virtue of which mankind may arrive at a new and higher stage of advancement on every plane, from the biological to the spiritual. It is a law of liberty and of love, but also of discipline and of force. This law is already in operation under the name of the Law of Thelema."[233] Make no mistake, "*The Book of the Law* was given to mankind chiefly in order to provide it with an impeccable principle of practical politics. I regard this as more important for the moment than its function as a guide in its evolution towards conscious godhead."[234]

"My job—the establishment of the Law of Thelema—is a most discouraging job. It is the rarest thing to find anyone who has any ideas at all on the subject of liberty. Because the Law of Thelema is the law of liberty, everybody's particular hair stands on end like the quills of the fretful porpentine; they scream like an uprooted mandrake, and flee in terror from the accursed spot. Because: the exercise of liberty means that you have to think for yourself, and the natural inertia of mankind wants religion and ethics ready-made. However ridiculous or shameful a theory or practice is, they would rather comply than examine it."[235] As Lévi points out, "Religion holds a greater place among the realities of life than those who do without religion—or pretend to do without it—affect to believe. All ideas that raise man above the animal—moral love, devotion, honour—are sentiments essentially religious. The cult of the fatherland and of the family, fidelity to an oath and to memory, are things which humanity will never abjure without degrading itself utterly, and which could never exist without the belief in something greater than mortal life, with all its vicissitudes, its ignorance and its misery."[236]

---

[232] *MWT*, Ch. XLVIII. Emphasis in original.
[233] *The Method of Thelema*.
[234] *Confessions*, Ch. 87.
[235] *Eight Lectures*, Ch. 2, Sec. 10.
[236] *The Key of the Mysteries*, Part I, Preliminary Considerations.

Crowley "analysed God, saw that every man had made God in his own images, saw the savage and cannibal Jews devoted to a savage and cannibal God, who commanded the rape of virgins and the murder of little children. He saw the timid inhabitants of India, races continually the prey of every robber tribe, inventing the effeminate Vishnu, while under the same name their conquerors worshipped a warrior, the conqueror of demon Swans. He saw the flower of the earth throughout all time, the gracious Greeks, what gracious gods they had invented. He saw Rome, in its strength devoted to Jupiter and Hercules, in its decay turning to emasculate Attis, slain Adonis, murdered Osiris, crucified Christ. He could even trace in his own life every aspiration, every devotion, as a reflection of his physical and intellectual needs. He saw, too, the folly of all this supernaturalism. He heard the Boers and the British pray to the same Protestant God, and it occurred to him that the early successes of the former might be due rather to superior valour than to superior praying power, and their eventual defeat to the circumstance that they could only bring 60,000 men against a quarter of a million. He saw, too, the face of humanity mired in its own blood that dripped from the leeches of religion fastened to its temples. In all this he saw man as the only thing worth holding to; the one thing that needed to be 'saved,' but also the one thing that could save it."[237]

This stands in stark contrast to how the early Jesuit missionaries, with their special liking for martial order and discipline, described the people of feudal Japan. "I fancy that there are no people in the world more punctilious about their honour than the Japanese, for they will not put up with a single insult or even a word spoken in anger," said Fr. Alessandro Valignano, who helped supervise the introduction of Catholicism to Japan. According to Don Rodrigo de Vivero y Aberrucia, a colonial officer from New Spain who was shipwrecked in Japan for 9 months in 1609, "The Japanese are much braver and more warlike than the people of China, Korea, . . . and all of the other nations around the Philippines." The Italian merchant Francesco Carletti, the first person to circumnavigate the globe privately without his own fleet—over eight years between 1594 and 1602—exclaims that, "There is no nation in the world which fears death less."[238]

The term *samurai* is actually of Chinese origin and originally meant "those who serve in close attendance to nobility"—*bushi* was the native name given to the mediaeval and early modern Japanese soldiers from traditional warrior families. The bushi class evolved mainly in the north of Japan, where they formed powerful clans, which in the 12th century opposed the noble families grouping themselves around the imperial family in Kyoto. "Samurai" was a word the *kuge* aristocracy used of them, while the warriors themselves preferred the term *bushi*, from which derives e.g. *bushidō*, the "way of the warrior."[239] Concurrently with the rise of the samurai to power, the Rinzai school of Zen Buddhism was established in Japan, and came to enjoy the patronage of this new warrior class. Following

---

[237] *The Temple of Solomon the King*, Part VI, "The Priest."
[238] Varley 2000, 143.
[239] Wilson 1982.

in the spirit of its founder, Linji Yixuan, the Rinzai style of Zen practice can be characterized as martial or sharp, and is often contrasted with the other sect of Zen deeply established in Japan, Sōtō, which is more gentle and even rustic.[240] Or as the Japanese saying goes, "Rinzai for the shōgun, Sōtō for the peasants."[241]

Sun Tzu's masterpiece of Taoist thought, *The Art of War*, was also introduced into Japan circa 760 CE, and quickly became popular among the Japanese generals. Through its subsequent influence on Oda Nobunaga, Toyotomi Hideyoshi, and Tokugawa Ieyasu, it decidedly affected the unification of Japan in the early Modern era.[242] Prior to the Meiji Restoration, mastery of its teachings was honoured among the warrior class and its teachings were both preached and exemplified by influential *daimyō* and shōguns. "The Tao causes the people to be fully in accord with the ruler."[243] In a letter to the Jesuit General St. Ignatius of Loyola, the famous missionary and co-founder of the Society of Jesus, St. Francis Xavier, describes the education of the upper classes of Japan thus: "The Nobles send their sons to monasteries to be educated as soon as they are 8 years old, and they remain there until they are 19 or 20, learning reading, writing and religion; as soon as they come out, they marry and apply themselves to politics. They are discreet, magnanimous and lovers of virtue and letters, honouring learned men very much."[244]

The two pre-eminent classics of Bushidō and Rinzai philosophy are *Hagakure*, or "Hidden in Leaves," by Yamamoto Tsunetomo, and *Gorin no Sho*, or "The Book of the Five Rings," by Miyamoto Musashi, both written during the Tokugawa period. Unlike many earlier writers, Musashi used Japanese, rather than Chinese, writing that, "the warrior's is the twofold Way of pen and sword, and he should have a taste for both Ways. Even if a man has no natural ability he can be a warrior by sticking assiduously to both divisions of the Way. Generally speaking, the Way of the warrior is resolute acceptance of death."[245] An expert swordsman and *rōnin*, Musashi was also known by his Buddhist name, Niten Dōraku, while Tsunetomo, a samurai of the Saga Domain, was also called Yamamoto Jōchō, which name he took after retiring and becoming a monk. Linji himself is famous for the saying, "If you meet a Buddha, kill him," which actually continues, "if you meet a patriarch, kill him; if you meet a sage, kill him; if you meet your father or mother, kill them; if you meet your relatives, kill them. Only then

---

[240] Collcutt 1981.
[241] Crowley actually tried and failed to settle down in a monastery in Kamakura in 1898, when he still identified as a Buddhist. As he writes in Chapter 26 of his *Confessions*, "I saw comparatively little of Japan. I did not understand the people at all and therefore did not like them very much. Their aristocracy was somehow at odds with mine. I resented their racial arrogance. I compared them unfavourably with the Chinese. Like the English, they possess the insular qualities and defects. They are not Asiatic, exactly as we are not European."
[242] McNeilly 2001.
[243] Sawyer 1994, 167.
[244] Coleridge 1872, ii.214.
[245] Miyamoto 2008, 10.

will you obtain liberation and dwell in complete emancipated freedom, without getting emotionally caught up in things."[246]

Should the "Knight-Monks of Thelema" really be any different? "On the whole, the ambulatory practices are more generally useful to the health than the sedentary; for in this way walking and fresh air are assured. But some of the sedentary practice should be done, and combined with meditation. Of course when actually 'racing' to get results, walking is a distraction."[247] In the *Confessions*, Crowley asserts that "the time is at hand when the bankruptcy of all theories of religion, all systems of government, will become obvious to all."[248] That is, "The more one examines the deepest implications of the Law of Thelema, the more one understands that it constitutes a sublime synthesis, and the only one possible, of the teachings of every science, from embryology to history. It is the key of every problem which can confront the human mind; for it does not imply exactly a new religion, but rather a new philosophy, a new ethic. For the first time in history, we are able to conceive of moral science as truly a science; for our conclusions are derived from dynamic measurements without reference to absurd axioms and impudent postulates. It coordinates the several discoveries of Science in a perfectly consistent and coherent framework."[249]

"We have the Key to the resolution of all human problems, both philosophical and practical. If we have seemed to labour at proof, our love must be the excuse for our infirmity; for we know well that which is written in the Book: 'Success is your proof.' We ask no more than one witness; and we call upon Time to take the Oath, and testify to the Truth of our plea."[250] However, "it must not be supposed that so potent an instrument of energy can be used without danger. I summon, therefore, by the power and authority entrusted to me, every great spirit and mind now on this planet incarnate to take effective hold of this transcendent force, and apply it to the advancement of the welfare of the human race."[251] Now, it could be argued that religion in itself—as opposed to a common culture or tradition that includes religious aspects—is a modern, Western concept, but Crowley was adamant: "All sanity, which is all Science, is founded upon Limit. We must be able to cut off, to define, to measure. Naturally, then, their opposites, Insanity and Religion, have for their prime characteristic, the Indefinable, Incomprehensible, Immeasurable. The healing virtue of these words is this: examine the sore spot, analyse it, probe it; then disinfection and the *Vis Medicatrix Naturæ* complete the cure."[252]

Yet, modern left-wing Crowleians, in particular, like to pretend that Thelema is a religion and just a religion, thus avoiding the obvious implications Crowley's philosophy has in other aspects of life—implications that clash with their political ideology. While they may be happy to remain

---

[246] As quoted in Nishitani 1982, 262–3.
[247] *Book 4*, Part I, Ch. II, fn.
[248] *Confessions*, Ch. 87.
[249] *The Method of Thelema*.
[250] *The Equinox of the Gods, loc. cit.*, Ch. VIII.
[251] *Ibid.*, "The Summons."
[252] *MWT*, Ch. LXXVIII.

obscure cult leaders, it is only these political implications that would enable the large-scale "establishment of the Law of Thelema" in the first place.[253] "How this Attainment is possible for all Mankind, since it asketh but Resolution of Complexities that already exist; so that this true Wisdom and Happiness cometh by the Acceptance of our Law, and its Use is the Key to all locked Doors of the Mind, and the Reconcilement of every Contention. O my Son, in the Promulgation of the Law lieth the Reward of our Chief Work, the making whole of Mankind from the Conscience of Sin which divideth him, and afflicteth his Spirit."[254]

"Not only is religion as such repugnant to science and philosophy, but from the very nature of the tenets of the Yellow School, its adherents are not going to put themselves to any inconvenience for the enlightenment of a lot of people whom they consider to be hopeless fools"—"It possesses something of the cold-bloodedness of mathematics; and for this reason it seems fair to say, for the purposes of elementary study, that Pythagoras is its most adequate exponent in European philosophy."[255] It was not any particular doctrine of the Pythagorean school so much as the prevalent notion among the Pythagoreans concerning the scope and aim of philosophy, that influenced the subsequent course of speculation among the Greeks. The "philosophers" of the day called themselves by the noun *sophos*, a "wise man" or a "sage"—Pythagoras was the first to use instead the title *philosophos*, a "lover of wisdom."[256] And though the Catholic theological tradition incorporated Aristotle into its theology and Platonism into its experience, philosophy never lost its independence in the West, even in the Middle Ages. By the time of the Enlightenment, it had come to qualify and question the basic foundations and assumptions of the Christian faith, occasionally ending up in rational support of religious verities, but more often in outright hostility towards all religion—and in any event always completely separate.[257]

The reconciliation of science and religion has been the aim of the Rosicrucians ever since the former began to assert its independence anew

---

[253] According to *The Antecedents of Thelema*, Sec. III, Rabelais "makes the foundation of the Abbey of Thelema the quite definite climax of his history of *Gargantua*; he describes his ideal of Society... As the character of his parable demanded, he confines himself to painting a picture of pure Beauty; he does not enter into the questions of political economy (and like subjects) which must be solved in order to realize the ideal of the Law of Liberty. But he says distinctly that the religion of Thelema is to be contrary to all others. True, for Thelema is Magick, and Magick is Science, the antithesis of the religious hypothesis. . . . With all this we find no suggestion of any communistic theories; they are in fact specifically disowned."

[254] *Liber Aleph*, "De pace perfecta luce."

[255] *MWT*, Ch. VI.

[256] To be sure, the figure of the "sage" remained present as the rarely attainable ideal in all philosophy, eventually rising to new prominence in Stoicism; indeed, even the term "scientist" (from Latin *scientia*, "knowledge"), coined by the Rev. William Whewell as late as the early 19th century, was bitterly opposed by the more humble natural philosophers for quite a long time.

[257] Plato, for his part, was evidently the first to use the term "theology," meaning the approach to God or the gods (*theoi*) by means of the *logos*. Both in the *Republic* and the *Laws*, Plato's philosophy, at its highest, appears as theology in this sense, and every subsequent system of Greek philosophy (with the exception of the Sceptic) culminated in theology; thus, we can distinguish not only a Platonic, but also an Aristotelian, Epicurean, Stoic, Neopythagorean, and Neoplatonic theology.

under the impulse of Renaissance Humanism and the new "Natural Philosophy." Originally, many Masters of Arts, in addition to teaching, went on to study in one of the three higher faculties, the division of which remains the same to this day: Divinity, Law, and Medicine. In mediaeval thinking, theology was truly the "queen of sciences," and for centuries, philosophy was reduced to its discourse, which was pressed into service as the "handmaiden of theology." There were two branches of legal study, civil law and canon law, and one might acquire a degree in either, or graduate as a *juris utriusque doctor* (J.U.D.), Doctor of Both Laws. Few actually became doctors, since for example in the University of Paris, a Doctor of Theology was required, in addition to his extensive studies, to be at least 35 years of age. There is a common tendency to think that the mediaeval Church was governed by people who were schooled in theology—this was not the case, however; rather it was largely run by lawyers.[258]

At the beginning of the 19th century, Western science, philosophy, and art all still fit under the same denominator; only half a century later, the paths of science and art had already diverged—the age of the self-taught genius was over. The masters of science would henceforth rise from the bosom of universities, while students of divinity were increasingly driven away to seminaries, especially in the United States. The Protestantism of the era widened, from the other side, the gap between empirical science and theology, between this world and the other, between physics and metaphysics.[259] The professionalization of philosophy in the West came with mixed blessings: on the one hand, people who are not independently wealthy are now able to become philosophers through the university system, on the other, the professionalization of the field has led philosophers to increasingly write just for other philosophers, often making them tone-deaf to real world issues. Similarly, science, at heart an enterprise for mavericks, has become a career path, meaning that scientists are made to wait until their best years are behind them before being awarded academic freedom and prestige.

Prior to the 19th century, languages were studied mainly as a field of theology or philosophy. After graduating Pforta, an élite Lutheran boarding school with only 200 students—the same one that groomed Klopstock, Fichte, Novalis, and Ranke—Nietzsche went on to study theology and classical philology at the University of Bonn. However, at the age of 18, his faith in traditional religion received a fatal blow when he discovered Schopenhauer. He discarded his theological studies and resolved instead to focus on philology at Leipzig. Nietzsche's outstanding education would culminate in a highly unusual appointment to professorship of classical philology at the University of Basel at the unprecedented age of 24. Since he had at that time not yet written his dissertation, let alone taken his doctoral examination, the University of Leipzig conferred a doctorate on him on the strength of his published writings.[260] In the autumn of 1867, the 22-year-

---

[258] Balk, *op. cit.*
[259] *Ibid.*
[260] *Ibid.*

old Nietzsche outlined an essay on Democritus and the "history of literary studies in antiquity and modernity," with the goal of impressing upon "the philologists a number of bitter truths."[261]

The first bitter truth was the notion advanced by Schopenhauer that "all enlightened thoughts" stem only from a few "great geniuses," and Richard Wagner, who in 1868 became for Nietzsche the living model of genius, was certainly no academic.[262] To quote another Crowley favourite, A. N. Whitehead, "The great conquerors, from Alexander to Caesar, and from Caesar to Napoleon, influenced profoundly the lives of subsequent generations. But the total effect of this influence shrinks to insignificance, if compared to the entire transformation of human habits and human mentality produced by the long line of men of thought from Thales to the present day, men individually powerless, but ultimately the rulers of the world."[263] As Crowley himself puts it, "There are very few people to-day who have heard of Plato and Aristotle. Not one in a thousand, perhaps ten thousand, of those have ever read either of them, even in translations. But there are also very few people whose thinking, such as it is, is not conditioned by the ideas of those two men."[264] Nietzsche went so far as to assert that "Christianity is Platonism for 'the people',"[265] and prescribes Thucydides as the antidote.[266]

> From the beginning of history, wise men have tried to overcome error, and to help their fellow-men to find and recognize the truth. To them must we attribute the real, the deep-lying causes of all social and political revolutions. It has always been their pride to nail to the mast the standard of liberty.
>
> Mankind owes much to men of this stamp, for it is they who guide and guard it. By the development of certain faculties as superior to those of normal human intelligence as that is to the mentality of the insect, they have attained a certain comprehension and made a certain synthesis of the facts of life which enable them from time to time to announce a new fundamental principle, by the application of which humanity may take a clear-cut step in the right direction. It is only

---

[261] Nietzsche 2016, viii.

[262] *Ibid.* In addition to being recognized as a Magister Templi by Crowley, Nietzsche is also included in the list of "Saints" in *Liber XV* along with Wagner, on whose music drama *Parsifal* the "Gnostic Mass" is partly based.

[263] Whitehead 1925, 208.

[264] *The Book of Thoth*, Part I, Sec. III.

[265] *Beyond Good and Evil*, Preface.

[266] "In the end, my mistrust of Plato goes deep: he represents such an aberration from all the basic Greek instincts, is so moralistic, so pseudo-Christian (he already takes the concept of the 'good' as the highest concept) that I would prefer the harsh phrase 'higher swindle' or, if it sounds better, 'idealism' for the whole phenomenon of Plato. We have paid dearly for the fact that this Athenian got his schooling from the Egyptians (or from the Jews in Egypt?). In that great calamity called Christianity, Plato represents that ambiguity and fascination, called an 'ideal,' which made it possible for the nobler spirits of antiquity to misunderstand themselves and to set foot on the bridge leading to the Cross. And how much Plato there still is in the concept 'church,' in the construction, system, and practice of the church! My recreation, my preference, my cure from all Platonism has always been Thucydides." *Twilight of the Idols*, "What I Owe to the Ancients," §2.

necessary to recall the names of Plato, Aristotle, Kepler, Newton, Bacon and Descartes. In each case we find an absolute challenge to all accepted principles and a complete sceptical destruction of them; followed by the formulation of a new principle which resumes in itself, while transcending the old.[267]

In 1870, Nietzsche had a new plan, to expose publicly, the whole Prussian system of education. "Perhaps there are others who see these essay assignments [in public secondary schools] as the farce they are: not only the most absurd feature of the gymnasium today but also the most dangerous. The essays demand originality, but the only originality possible at that age [i.e. the choice of topic] is then rejected. They presuppose a formal education that only a very few people will ever acquire, even in riper years. They treat every student as being capable of literature, as *allowed* to have opinions about the most serious people and things, whereas true education will strive with all its might precisely to *suppress* this ridiculous claim to independence of judgment on the part of the young person, imposing instead strict obedience to the scepter of the genius. They ask writers to present ideas in a larger framework, at an age when their every last written or spoken sentence is a barbaric abomination. And let us not forget how easy it is to awaken smug self-satisfaction during those years: think of the vanity of the young man seeing his literary reflection in the mirror for the first time."[268]

"Given all this, who could possibly doubt that the exercise stamps each rising generation with everything that ails our literary and artistic public sphere: the hasty overproduction driven by self-regard; the shameful churning out of books; the complete lack of style; immature formulations that miserably sprawl or lack character altogether; the loss of any aesthetic canon; the reveling in anarchy and chaos; in short, the literary traits of our journalism, and no less of our scholars. So few people nowadays realize that one in a thousand, at most, is justified in putting his writing before the world."[269] In this, Nietzsche echoes Tsunetomo Yamamoto, who instructed the samurai: "When writing a letter, he should think that the recipient will make it into a hanging scroll."[270] And of course, for Crowley, "a book is a message from the gods to mankind; or, if not, should never be published at all."[271] Yet, the Prophet of Thelema specifically asked that "no religious service" be performed at his funeral.[272]

---

[267] *The Method of Thelema. Cf.* Whitehead 1927, 88: "It is the first step in sociological wisdom, to recognize that the major advances in civilization are processes which all but wreck the societies in which they occur:—like unto an arrow in the hand of a child. The art of free society consists first in the maintenance of the symbolic code; and secondly in fearlessness of revision, to secure that the code serves those purposes which satisfy an enlightened reason. Those societies which cannot combine reverence to their symbols with freedom of revision, must ultimately decay either from anarchy, or from the slow atrophy of a life stifled by useless shadows."
[268] Nietzsche, *op. cit.*, 26–7. Emphasis in original.
[269] *Ibid.*, 27.
[270] Yamamoto 2012, 28.
[271] *Confessions*, Ch. 68.
[272] Kaczynski 2010.

Magick is the science and art of causing change to occur in conformity with the Will. In other words, it is Science, Pure and Applied. This thesis has been worked out at great length by Dr. Sir J. G. Frazer. But in common parlance the word Magic has been used to mean the kind of science which ordinary people do not understand. It is in this restricted sense, for the most part, that the word will be used in this essay.

The business of Science is to explore Nature. Its first questions are: What is this? How did it come to be? What are its relations with any other object? The knowledge acquired may then be used in Applied Science, which asks: How can we best employ such-and-such a thing or idea for the purpose that, to us, seems fit? An example may make this clear.

The Greeks of old were aware that by rubbing amber (which they called Electron) upon silk, the amber acquired the power of attracting to itself light objects such as small pieces of paper. But there they stopped. Their science was hoodwinked by theological *and* philosophical theories of the *à priori* type. It was well over 2,000 years before this phenomenon was correlated with other electrical phenomena. The idea of Measurement was hardly known to anyone but mathematicians like Archimedes, and astronomers. The foundations of Science, as it is understood to-day, were hardly laid at all 200 years ago. There was an immense amount of knowledge; but it was nearly all qualitative. The classification of phenomena depended chiefly upon poetic analogies. The doctrines of "correspondences" and "signatures" were based upon fanciful resemblances.[273]

"The main difference between a Science and an Art is that the former admits mensuration. Its processes must be susceptible of the application of quantitative standards. Its laws reject imponderable variables. Science despises Art for its refusal to conform with calculable conditions. But even to-day, in the boasted Age of Science, man is still dependent on Art as to most matters of practical importance to him; the arts of Government, of War, of Literature, etc. are supremely influential, and Science does little more than facilitate them by making their materials mechanically docile. The utmost extension of Science can merely organize the household of Art. Art thus progresses in perception and power by increased control or automatic accuracy of its details. The MASTER THERION has made an Epoch in the Art of Magick by applying the Method of Science to its problems. His Work is a contribution of unique value, comparable only to that of those men of genius who revolutionized the empirical guesswork of 'natural philosophers'. The Magicians of to-morrow will be armed with mathematical theory, organized observation, and experimentally-verified practice. But their Art will remain inscrutable as ever in essence; talent will never supplant genius. Education is impotent to produce a poet greater

---

[273] *The Book of Thoth, loc. cit.* Emphasis in original.

than Robert Burns; the perfection of laboratory apparatus prepares indeed the path of a Pasteur, but cannot make masters of mediocrities."[274]

"Much fun has been made of the alchemists for insisting that the Great Work, an ostensibly chemical process, can only be performed by adepts who fear and love God, and who practise chastity and numerous other virtues. But there is more common sense in such statements than meets the eye. A drunken debauchee cannot perform delicate manipulations in chemistry or physics; and the force with which the secret is concerned, while as material as the Becquerel emanations, is subtler than any yet known. To play great golf or great billiards, to observe delicate reactions, or to conduct recondite mathematical researches, demands more than physical superiorities. Even the theological requirements of alchemy had meaning in those days. An Elizabethan who was not 'at peace with God' was likely to be agitated and thereby unfitted for work demanding freedom from emotional distraction."[275]

"The precepts of morality and religion are thus of use, of vital use to us, in restraining the more violent forces alike of nature and of man. For unless law and order prevail, we have not the necessary quiet and resources for investigating, and learning to bring under our control, all the divergent phenomena of our prison, a work which we undertake that at last we may be able to break down the walls, and find that freedom which an inconsiderate Inversion has denied. The mystical precepts of pseudo-Zoroaster, Buddha, Çankaracharya, pseudo-Christ and the rest, are for advanced students only, for direct attack on the problem. Our servants, the soldiers, lawyers, all forms of government, make this our nobler work possible, and it is the gravest possible mistake to sneer at these humble but faithful followers of the great minds of the world."[276] However Crowley felt about religion, he certainly was not above using the "opiate of the masses" to influence people—"The end justifies the means: if the Jesuits do not assert this, I do."[277]

---

[274] *MITAP*, Ch. XVIII, Sec. IV, fn. For a scholarly account of the long and intimate historical connection between magic and experimental science, *see* Thorndike 1923–58.
[275] *Confessions*, Ch. 72.
[276] *Berashith*.
[277] NC on AL II.70. "The end justifies the means" was for a long time (falsely) rumoured to be the secret motto of the Jesuit Order.

CHAPTER 13
Political Implications
Thelema as Natural Law

Chapter I.
3. *Every man and every woman is a star.*
10. *Let my servants be few & secret: they shall rule the many & the known.*
40. *Do what thou wilt shall be the whole of the Law.*
41. *The word of Sin is Restriction.*
42. *thou hast no right but to do thy will.*
43. *Do that, and no other shall say nay.*
44. *For pure will, unassuaged of purpose, delivered from the lust of result, is every way perfect.*
57. *Love is the law, love under will.*

Chapter II.
19. *Is a God to live in a dog? No! but the highest are of us. They shall rejoice, our chosen: who sorroweth is not of us.*
20. *Beauty and strength, leaping laughter and delicious languor, force and fire are of us.*
58. *Yea! deem not of change: ye shall be as ye are, & not other. Therefore the kings of the earth shall be Kings for ever: the slaves shall serve.*

Chapter III.
4. *Choose ye an island!*
5. *Fortify it!*
6. *Dung it about with enginery of war!*
7. *I will give you a war-engine.*
8. *With it ye shall smite the peoples; and none shall stand before you.*
58. *But the keen and the proud, the royal and the lofty; ye are brothers!*
59. *As brothers fight ye!*
60. *There is no law beyond Do what thou wilt.*
—LIBER AL VEL LEGIS, as quoted in "The Scientific Solution to the Problem of Government"

"As matriarchy reflected the Formula of the Æon of Isis, and patriarchy that of Osiris, so does the rule of the 'Crowned and Conquering Child' express that of Horus. The family, the clan, the state count for nothing; the Individual is the Autarch."[1] The traditional man, or *homo religiosus*, was conservative because keeping to the old was safe. Any kind of spontaneity or creativity spelled sudden change, which the small community struggling at the edge of survival could not sustain. The continuity of life depended on

---
[1] *MWT*, Ch. XLVIII.

everything being done the way it had always been done, even if someone knew a better way. Common tradition, the knowledge about how things should be done, was what kept the community together. And as the early feminist writer Suzanne La Follette points out, "There is nothing more innately human than the tendency to transmute what has become customary into what has been divinely ordained."[2]

During the feudal period, society was simply an alliance of families, who swore allegiance to the house of their liege lord. At the beginning of the modern era, Western society was transformed from a union of families into a union of subjects—kinsmen became countrymen. As the family relinquished its authority over its members, it also ceased to be responsible for their actions and well-being. The state took over many of the affairs that had previously been handled by families, such as public safety and social services. As Churches became an arm of the State, welfare and education became government concerns. Through the means of public education, subjects would recognize their place in society, and be loyal to their rulers out of conviction.[3] The famous 18th-century French philosopher, Jean-Jacques Rousseau, reasoned that humanity began as savages in the wild threatened by both beast and other people, but then everyone entered into a "social contract" and formed society for mutual aid and safety—by giving up a portion of their original, unfettered freedom for the order and security of shared community.

Rousseau's *Discourse on Inequality* was published in the same year, 1755, as Richard Cantillon's *Essay on the Nature of Trade in General*; from the former came socialism, from the latter, the discipline of economics. As Crowley writes, "In the Slave-Ages this is a Truth Universal, or well nigh to it; for in such Times are Men compelled to Uniformity by the Constraint of Necessity herself. Yea, of old it was a continual Siege of every Man of every Clan, of every Environment; and to relax guard was then Self-murder, or also Treachery. so then no Man might chose his way, until he were Hunter, Fighter, Builder; not any Woman, but she must first be Breeder. Now in the Growth of States by Organisation came, stepping stealthily, a certain Security against the grossest Perils, so that a few Men could be spared from Toil to cultivate Wisdom, and this was first provided by the Selection of a caste Pontifical. By this Device came the Alliance of King and Priest, Strength and Cunning fortifying each the other through the Division of Labour."[4]

"So presently, o my Son, this first Organisation among Men, by a Procedure parallel to that of the Differentiation of Protoplasm, made the State competent to explore and to control Nature; and every Profit of this sort released more energy, and enlarged the class of the Learned, until, as it is this day, only a small proportion of any man's work must needs go to the satisfaction of first will essential and common, the provision of shelter, food, and protection. Verily, also thou seest many women made free to live

---

[2] As quoted in Balk 2012, 18–19.
[3] *Idem.* 2008.
[4] *Liber Aleph*, "De libidine secreta."

as they will, even to the admiration and delight of the Sage whose eye laugheth to contemplate mischief. Thus the duty of every Unit towards the whole is diminished, and also the necessity to conform with those narrow laws which preserve primitive tribes in their struggle against environment. Thus the State need suppress only such heresies as directly threaten its political stability, only such modes of life as work manifest and proven hurt to others, or cause general disorder by their scandal. Therefore save and except he interferes thereby with the root laws of common weal, a man is free to develop as he will according to his true nature."[5]

A "social contract" as a basis or rationale for organized society is actually first found in the writings of the 17th-century British philosopher, John Locke, who argued that rights are not bestowed upon man by government or the community, but in fact belong to him by his nature as a human being. The role of government, in the Lockean social contract, is to provide individuals with a tool for the common defence against the violence of some of their fellow men, that is, to secure liberty by protecting each individual's rights to his life, liberty, and property, rather than to act as a guarantor of a certain standard of living or access to various material benefits. According to Crowley's *New Comment* on AL I.33, "Law, in the common sense of the word, should be a formulation of the customs of a people, as Euclid's propositions are the formulation of geometrical facts. But modern knavery conceived the idea of artificial law, as if one should try to square the circle by tyranny. Legislators try to force the people to change their customs, so that the 'business men' whose greed they are bribed to serve may increase their profits. 'Law' in Greek, is ΝΟΜΟΣ, from ΝΕΜ, and means strictly 'anything assigned, that which one has in use or possession'; hence 'custom, usage'."[6]

The upper classes in general, and above all, those men who gradually rose to the leadership of the united world of the Roman Empire, were adherents of Stoicism. Whereas the Epicureans urged the wise man to withdraw from the distractions and dangers of political life, the Stoics emphasized his duty to the State, his commitment to politics. To the Stoic philosopher, *Jus Gentium*, the common international law of all nations, was more natural than the conflicting laws and juridical systems of different poleis, tribes, and nations. Roman law differed from Athenian and Jewish law in that it was intended for all the people and was not merely the property of one tribe. It applied to Roman citizens (*Jus Civile*) as well as to the Roman subjects that were not citizens, and it forms the basis of the Western legal system. However, the early mediaeval notions of ancestry and family were thrown into tumult when the laws and customs of Romans and barbarians collided.[7]

---

[5] *Ibid.*, "De ordine civitatum."
[6] As the noted American jurist James Coolidge Carter (1907, 120) put it: "What has governed the conduct of men from the beginning of time will continue to govern it to the end of time. Human nature is not likely to undergo a radical change, and, therefore, that to which we give the name of Law always has been, still is, and will forever continue to be Custom."
[7] Balk, *op. cit.*

The Germanic family was an extensive community of kith and kin, the duties and responsibilities of which were strictly regulated by law and custom; Roman law, on the other hand, recognized the individual with personal liberty and responsibility. From the 5th century on, Germanic rulers began to reduce the customary tribal laws to writing, but the Germanic peoples had no single law that applied to all the tribes, and both the Roman population and the Christian clergy under Germanic rule continued to live under Roman law. The reformed Frankish law finally imposed by Charlemagne at the turn of the 9th century applied throughout his empire and replaced not only the inefficient and fragmented tribal laws, but the Roman civil law as well.[8] As Lévi notes, "Nimrod and Babel are the two primitive allegories of the despot, and of the universal empire which has always filled the dreams of men,—a dream whose fulfilment was sought successively by the Assyrians, the Medes, the Persians, Alexander, Rome, Napoleon, the successors of Peter the Great, and always unfinished because of the dispersion of interests, symbolized by the confusion of tongues."[9]

> 1.57 a.m. I conceive the state of Thelema. (It is the Church again, of course; but—well, I'm serious!) I propose that a man, adhering to Thelema, shall become a 'man without a country' abiding by the laws of, but regarding himself as a stranger visiting, any country where he may be. Now, look here! Either my whole idea of human psychology is wrong, or there is hardly a state on the planet whose citizens will not in great number hasten to join. In short, citizenship is now everywhere a burden, not a privilege. Yet they encourage 'Le Tourisme'! God! it's all such utter incoherent insanity that Choronzon is the only possible Prime Minister!!!
>
> 2.10 a.m. I want an ISLAND. It must be fortified, etc., so as to be diplomatically recognized. Then we can issue passports to all nations. They lose little but the vote (!)(!)(!) Obviously, the advantages are such that trouble would arise at once: the issue will lie between the owners of land & the rest directly. But if we can work it 'few and secret' we may get into the saddle. We can start having Thelemites appear mere travellers or colonists.
>
> 3.26 a.m. States are founded on the fact that the voluntary association of men has proved advantageous to the individual. Once this advantage disappears, anarchy will return. The particular question of the moment is: Does it pay to be the member of any state? Is not this why the Jew is on top? Because he is a stranger everywhere? And Alastor the Wanderer—*über alles!*
>
> 3.33 p.m. The only time the police ever caught me, it was on my coming back to a place I called my own—the moral is obvious. Note that the increased facilities of transport have made the Wanderer a much more important factor in the world than ever before. Yet who can tax him—without destroying Commerce?[10]

---

[8] *Ibid.*
[9] *The Key of the Mysteries*, Part I, "Sketch of the Prophetic Theology of Numbers."
[10] Diary entry, 30 July 1923.

"For thy Will moveth through free Function, according to its particular Nature, to that End of Dissolution of all Complexities, and those Ideals and Standards are Attempts to halt thee on that Way. Although for thee some certain Ideal be upon thy Path, yet for thy Neighbour it may not be so. Set all Men a-horseback; thou speedest the Foot-soldier upon his way, indeed; but what hast thou done to the Bird-man? Thou must have simple Laws and Customs to express the general Will, and so prevent the Tyranny or Violence of a few; but multiply them not! Now then herewith I will declare unto thee the Limits of the Civil Law upon the Rock of the Law of Thelema. . . .Understand first that the Disturbers of the Peace of Mankind do so by Reason of their Ignorance of their own True Wills. Therefore, as this Wisdom of mine increaseth among Mankind, the false Will to Crime must become constantly more rare. Also, the exercise of our Freedom will cause Men to be born with less and ever less Affliction from that Dis-ease of Spirit, which breedeth these false Wills."[11]

"But, in the While of waiting for this Perfection, thou must by Law assure to every Man a Means of satisfying his bodily and his mental Needs, leaving him free to develop any Superstructure in accordance with his Will, and protecting him from any that may seek to deprive him of these vertebral Rights. There shall be therefore a Standard of Satisfaction, though it must vary in Detail with Race, Climate, and other such Conditions. And this Standard shall be based upon a large Interpretation of Facts biological, physiological, and the like. . . . Say not, o my Son, that in this Argument I have set Limits to individual Freedom. For each Man in this State which I purpose is fulfilling his own True Will by his eager Acquiescence in the Order necessary to the Welfare of all, and therefore of himself also. But see thou well to it that thou set high the Standard of Satisfaction, and that to every one be a Surplus of Leisure and of Energy, so that, his Will of Self-preservation being fulfilled by the Performance of his Function in the State, he may devote the Remainder of his Powers to the Satisfaction of the other Parts of his Will. And because the People are oft-times unlearned, not understanding Pleasure, let them be instructed in the Art of Life: to prepare Food palatable and wholesome, each to his own Taste, to make Clothes according to Fancy, with Variety of Individuality, and to practice the manifold Crafts of Love. These Things being first secured, thou mayst afterward lead them into the Heavens of Poesy and Tale, of Music, Painting, and Sculpture, and into the Lore of the Mind itself, with its insatiable Joy of all Knowledge. Thence let them soar!"[12]

From the 18th century on, the middle classes of Europe began to modify their attitude towards their children, gradually moving away from the coercive, restrictive approach of patriarchalism. This altered attitude is seen above all in the fact that the child's will was no longer broken with brute force and humiliation. Instead, a kind, permissive, and respectful attitude was introduced, laying the foundation for the modern individual.

---

[11] *Liber Aleph*, "De legibus contra motum" & "De necessitate communi," as quoted in NC on AL II.58.
[12] *Ibid.*, "De necessitate communi" & "De fundamentis civitatis," as quoted in NC on AL II.58.

This change started in Britain, gradually spreading to the Continent, first to France and Scandinavia, then to Central Europe, and finally even to Russia. Its significance really cannot be emphasized enough. As early as 1693, Locke had already committed to print the thoughts that were in the air, when he rejected the traditional belief in the Original Sin, hereditary guilt, and the innate wickedness of children. For this Enlightenment philosopher, the mind of the child was, paraphrasing Ovid, a *tabula rasa*, a "blank slate" which the parents filled with their instruction.[13]

Both the Protestant Reformation and the Enlightenment emanated from the bourgeoisie and carried its ideals. Choosing a spouse on the basis of finances is now considered contemptible, whereas formerly those were virtually the sole respectable criteria. Leaving one's children in a strange neighbourhood in the care of a stranger and sending them away altogether at the age of seven is deemed unnatural today, even though it was a matter of course in the past. The outlook that evolved in the middle classes over the course of the 18th century placed emphasis on feelings, underlining the affection between family members. The modern family was expected to spend a lot of time together as opposed to the traditional family, whose members felt more at home with their peers, giving rise to the already struggling nuclear family.[14]

> In many respects, no doubt, the Law of Thelema is revolutionary. It insists on the absolute sovereignty of the individual within the limits of his proper function. And this principle will be resented by all those who like to interfere with other people's business. The battle will rage most fiercely around the question of sex. Hardly any one is willing to allow others their freedom on this point. Sometimes it is a personal matter; false vanity makes men try to enslave those whom they desire. They cannot understand "There is no bond that can unite the divided but love: ...", and they outrage others in every way in order to obtain the outward show of affection. It is the most hideous error conceivable, yet nearly all men make it, and nine tenths of the misery caused by wrong sexual relations is due to this determination to enslave the soul of another. It seems impossible to make men see what to me is obvious; that the only love worth having or indeed worthy of the name is the spontaneous sympathy of a free soul. Social conventions which trammel love are either extensions of this stupid selfishness, or expressions of the almost universal shame which results from false ideas on the subject. Mankind must learn that the sexual instinct is in its true nature ennobling. The shocking evils which we all deplore are principally due to the perversion produced by suppressions. The feeling that it is shameful and the sense of sin cause concealment, which is ignoble, and internal conflict which creates distortion, neurosis, and ends in

---

[13] Balk, *op. cit.*

[14] *Ibid.* Though exemplified by such familiar triads as Jesus, Mary, and Joseph (or, indeed, Isis, Osiris, and Horus), the nuclear family did not become an economically viable model until the 17th century—the term itself was only coined in the mid-20th century, with devotion to the Holy Family dating back no further than the 1600s.

explosion. We deliberately produce an abscess, and wonder why it is full of pus, why it hurts, why it bursts in stench and corruption. When other physical appetites are treated in this way, we find the same phenomenon. Persuade a man that hunger is wicked, prevent him satisfying it by eating whatever food suits him best, and he soon become a crazy and dangerous brute. Murder, robbery, sedition and many meaner crimes come of the suppression of the bodily need for nourishment.[15]

"*The Book of the Law* solves the sexual problem completely. Each individual has an absolute right to satisfy his sexual instinct as is physiologically proper for him. The one injunction is to treat all such acts as sacraments. One should not eat as the brutes, but in order to enable one to do one's will. The same applies to sex. We must use every faculty to further the one object of our existence."[16] As Crowley points out, "Laws against adultery are based upon the idea that woman is a chattel, so that to make love to a married woman is to deprive the husband of her services. It is the frankest and most crass statement of a slave-situation. To us, every woman is a star. She has therefore an absolute right to travel in her own orbit. There is no reason why she should not be the ideal *hausfrau*, if that chance to be her will. But society has no right to insist upon that standard. It was, for practical reasons, almost necessary to set up such taboos in small communities, savage tribes, where the wife was nothing but a general servant, where the safety of the people depended upon a high birth-rate. But to-day woman is economically independent, becomes more so every year. The result is that she instantly asserts her right to have as many or as few men or babies as she wants or can get; and she defies the world to interfere with her. More power to her—elbow!"[17]

The production methods of the old agrarian communities called for a fixed family unit and thus could not sustain divorces. Necessitating the distribution of the estate and complicating the matters of inheritance, divorce was an intrusive factor that upset balance and continuity. It affected the very core of the peasant community, the family estate. Keeping families together was not in the interest of the urban industrial communities, however, for single people were the best supply of labour. But the sudden increase in divorces was not caused by industrialization and urbanization alone; as the marrying age fell and the middle age rose, death was simply substituted with divorce. The spouses of a bourgeois family had, at least in theory, chosen each other of their own free will, on basis of mutual attraction. The decisive factors contributing to the birth of the modern nuclear family were the wealth and individualism brought on by market economy.[18]

---

[15] *Confessions*, Ch. 87.
[16] *Ibid.*
[17] NC on AL I.41.
[18] Balk, *op. cit.* The present author does not think it an exaggeration to say that the triumph of capitalism was an absolute prerequisite for the dawning of the Æon of the Child.

The War has seen this emancipation flower in four years. Primitive people, the Australian troops for example, are saying that they will not marry English girls, because English girls like a dozen men a week. Well, who wants them to marry? Russia has already formally abrogated marriage. Germany and France have tried to "save their faces" in a thoroughly Chinese manner, by "marrying" pregnant spinsters to dead soldiers!

England has been too deeply hypocritical, of course, to do more than "hush things up"; and is pretending "business as usual", though every pulpit is aquake with the clamour of bat-eyed bishops, squeaking of the awful immorality of everybody but themselves and their choristers. Englishwomen over 30 have the vote; when the young 'uns get it, good-bye to the old marriage system.

America has made marriage a farce by the multiplication and confusion of the Divorce Laws. A friend of mine who had divorced her husband was actually, three years later, sued by him for divorce!!!

But America never waits for laws; her people go ahead. The emancipated, self-supporting American woman already acts exactly like the "bachelor-boy". Sometimes she loses her head, and stumbles into marriage, and stubs her toe. She will soon get tired of the folly. She will perceive how imbecile it is to hamstring herself in order to please her parents, or to legitimatize her children, or to silence her neighbours.

She will take the men she wants as simply as she buys a newspaper; and if she doesn't like the Editorials, or the Comic Supplement, it's only two cents gone, and she can get another.

Blind asses! who pretend that women are naturally chaste! The Easterns know better; all the restrictions of the harem, of public opinion, and so on, are based upon the recognition of the fact that woman is only chaste when there is nobody around. She will snatch the babe from its cradle, or drag the dog from its kennel, to prove the old saying: *Natura abhorret a vacuo*. For she is the Image of the Soul of Nature, the Great Mother, the Great Whore.[19]

In the first half of the 19th century, the number of illegitimate children and pregnant brides grew at an astonishing rate among the lowest classes of Europe. The farmer's daughter, the maid, the seamstress, and the textile worker all entered into intimate relationships more readily than before. Instead of chastity and abstinence, Western people suddenly valued romance. The search for work sent young people away from their home village and its traditions. They were unattached and looking for company. The arrival of the nuclear family to the peasant village was signalled by the extinction of communal gatherings, celebrations, and carnivals. People who had previously associated themselves formally and informally with same-sex peers, severed their links outside the family; conversely, their relationships with their near kin often improved.[20] Just as we cannot

---

[19] NC on AL I.41.
[20] Balk, *op. cit.*

maintain ancient structures without contending with the limitations of ancient building materials, so it is difficult to sustain old traditions without keeping the old world-views from which they emerged.

Women under Christianity are kept virgin for the market as Strasbourg geese are nailed to boards till their livers putrefy. The nature of woman has been corrupted, her hope of a soul thwarted, her proper pleasure balked, and her mind poisoned, to titillate the jaded palates of senile bankers and ambassadors.
Why do men insist on "innocence" in women?
1. To flatter their vanity.
2. To give themselves the best chance of (a) escaping venereal disease, (b) propagating their noble selves.
3. To maintain power over their slaves by their possession of Knowledge.
4. To keep them docile as long as possible by drawing out the debauching of their innocence. A sexually pleased woman is the best of willing helpers; one who is disappointed or disillusioned a very psychical eczema.
5. In primitive communities, to serve as a guard against surprise and treachery.
6. To cover their secret shame in the matter of sex. Hence the pretence that a woman is "pure," modest, delicate, aesthetically beautiful and morally exalted, ethereal and unfleshly, though in fact they know her to be lascivious, shameless, coarse, ill-shapen, unscrupulous, nauseatingly bestial both physically and mentally. The advertisements of "dress shields," perfumes, cosmetics, anti-sweat preparations, and "Beauty Treatments" reveal woman's nature as seen by the clear eyes of those who would lose money if they misjudged her; and they are loathsomely revolting to read. Her mental and moral characteristics are those of the parrot and the monkey. Her physiology and pathology are hideously disgusting, a sickening slime of uncleanliness.
Her virgin life is a sick ape's, her sexual life a drunken sow's, her mother life all bulging filmy eyes and sagging udders.
These are the facts about "innocence"; to this has man's Christian Endeavour dragged her when he should rather have made her his comrade, frank, trusty, and gay, the tenderer self of himself, his consubstantial complement even as Earth is to the Sun.
We of Θελημα say that "Every man and every woman is a star." We do not fool and flatter women; we do not despise and abuse them. To us a woman is Herself, absolute, original, independent, free, self-justified, exactly as a man is.[21]

Marriage law was originally based on the common law assumption that the wife was the husband's property. Until the 20th century, the law allowed a man to physically discipline his wife, children, and servants "to a

---

[21] NC on AL III.55.

reasonable measure." In England, this meant that a husband had the legal right to beat his wife, provided he used a stick no thicker than his thumb. The last vestiges of this tradition legally subordinating wives to their husbands, such as allowing spousal rape, were eliminated in the West only in the late 1970s.[22] Most women still take the surnames of their husbands when they marry, a practice required by law in many Western countries until the '70s. As Crowley puts it, "The English Bible sanctions the polygamy and concubinage of Abraham, Solomon and others, the incest of Lot, the wholesale rape of captured virgins, as well as the promiscuity of the first Christians, the prostitution of temple servants, men and women, the relations of Johannes with his master, and the putting of wandering Prophets to stud, as well as the celibacy of such people as Paul. Jehovah went so far as to slay Onan because he balked at fertilizing his brother's widow, condoned the adultery, with murder of the husband, of David, and commanded Hosea to intrigue with a 'wife of whoredom.' He only drew the moral line at any self-assertion on the part of a woman."[23]

Liber Aleph contains the following declaration: "There shall be no Property in Human Flesh. Every Man and every Woman hath Right Indefeasable to give the Body for the Enjoyment of any other. The Exercise of this Right shall not be punished either by Law or by Custom; there shall be no Penalty either by Loss or Curtailment of Liberty, of Rights, of Wealth, or of Social Esteem; but this Freedom shall be respected of all, seeing that it is the Right of the Bodily Will. For this same Reason thou shalt cause full Restriction and Punishment of any who may seek to limit that Freedom for the sake of his own Profit, or Desire, or Ideal. Every Man and every Woman has full right either to grant or to deny the Body, as the Will speaketh within. This being made Custom, the Evils of Love, which are many, extending to the Disturbance not only of Body but of Mind, and that in obscure Paths, shall little by little disappear from the Face of His unspeakable Glory."[24]

In *The Book of Thoth*, Crowley further contends that, "it must be one of the great advances in adjustment of the new Æon to work out simply and without prejudice the formidable problems which have been raised by the growth of civilization. Man has advanced so far from the social system, though it was not a system, of the cave man, from the primitive conception of property in human flesh. Man has advanced so far from crude anatomical classification of the soul of any given human being; he has accordingly landed himself in the most dreadful mire of psychopathology and psycho-analysis. Tiresome and tough are the prejudices of the people that date morally from about 25,000 B.C. Largely owing to their own intransigence, those people have been born under a different spiritual law; they find themselves not only persecuted by their ancestors, but bewildered by their own uncertainty of foothold. It must be the task of the pioneers of the new Æon to put this right."[25]

---

[22] Balk 2012.
[23] NC on AL III.56.
[24] "De libertate corporis."
[25] Part II, Atu XIX.

Do we call Woman Whore? Ay, Verily and Amen, She is that; the air shudders and burns as we shout it, exulting and eager.

O ye! Was not this your sneer, your vile Whisper that scorned Her and shamed Her? Was not "Whore" the truth of Her, the title of terror that you gave Her in your fear of Her, coward comforting coward with furtive glance and gesture?

But we fear Her not; we cry Whore, as Her armies approach us. We beat on our shields with our swords. Earth echoes the clamour!

Is there doubt of the victory? Your hordes of cringing slaves, afraid of themselves, afraid of their own slaves, hostile, despised and distrusted, your only tacticians the ostrich, the opossum, and the cuttle, will you not break and flee at our first onset, as with levelled lances of lust we ride at the charge, with our allies, the Whores whom we love and acclaim, free friends by our sides in the Battle of Life?

The Book of the Law is the Charter of Woman; the Word Θελημα has opened the lock of Her "girdle of chastity." Your Sphinx of stone has come to life; to know, to will, to dare and to keep silence.

Yes, I, The Beast, my Scarlet Whore bestriding me, naked and crowned, drunk on Her golden Cup of Fornication, boasting Herself my bedfellow, have trodden Her in the Marketplace, and roared this Word that every woman is a star. And with that Word is uttered Woman's Freedom; the fools and fribbles and flirts have heard my voice. The fox in woman hath heard the Lion in man; fear, fainting, flabbiness, frivolity, falsehood—these are no more the mode.

In vain will bully and brute and braggart man, priest, lawyer, or social censor knit his brows to devise him a new tamer's trick; once and for all the tradition is broken; vanished the vogue of bowstring, sack, stoning, nose-slitting, belt-buckling, cart's tail-dragging, whipping, pillory posting, walling-up, divorce court, eunuch, harem, mind-crippling, house-imprisoning, menial-work-wearying, creed-stultifying, social-ostracism marooning, Divine-wrath-scaring, and even the device of creating and encouraging prostitution to keep one class of women in the abyss under the heel of the police, and the other on its brink, at the mercy of the husband's boot at the first sign of insubordination or even of failure to please.[26]

Modern scholars assert that, far from being "the world's oldest profession," prostitution in the commercial sense only arose with and because of the patriarchal institution of marriage. There simply would not have been much demand for it in a society where permanent monogamous relationships were not the rule. "But now the Word of Me the Beast is this; not only art thou Woman, sworn to a purpose not thine own; thou art thyself a star, and in thyself a purpose to thyself. Not only mother of men art thou, or whore to men; serf to their need of Life and Love, not sharing in their Light and Liberty; nay, thou art Mother and Whore for thine own pleasure; the Word I say to Man I say to thee no less: Do what thou wilt

---

[26] NC on AL III.55.

shall be the whole of the Law! . . . The essence of my Word is to declare woman to be Herself, of, to, and for Herself; and I give this one irresistible Weapon, the expression of Herself and Her will through sex, to Her on precisely the same terms as to man. Murder is no longer to be dreaded; the economic weapon is powerless since female labour has been found industrially valuable; and the social weapon is entirely in her own hands."[27]

> The best women have always been sexually-free, like the best men; it is only necessary to remove the penalties for being found out. Let Women's labour organizations support any individual who is economically harried on sexual grounds; let social organizations honour in public what their members practise in private.
> Most domestic unhappiness will disappear automatically, for its chief cause is the sexual dissatisfaction of wives, or the anxiety (or other mental strain) engendered should they take the remedy in their own hands.
> The crime of abortion will lose its motive in all but the most exceptional cases.
> Blackmail will be confined to commercial and political offences, thus diminishing its frequency by two-thirds, at least, maybe much more.
> Social scandals and jealousies will tend to disappear.
> Sexual disease will be easier to track and to combat, when it is no longer a disgrace to admit it.
> Prostitution (with its attendant crimes) will tend to disappear, as it will cease to offer exorbitant profits to those who exploit it. The preoccupation of the minds of the public with sexual questions will no longer breed moral disease and insanity, when the sex-appetite is treated as simply as hunger. Frankness of speech and writing on sexual questions will dispel the ignorance which entraps so many unfortunate people; proper precaution against actual dangers will replace unnecessary and absurd precautions against imaginary or artificial dangers; and the quacks who trade on fear will be put out of business.
> All this must follow as the Light the night as soon as Woman, true to Herself, finds that She can no longer be false to any man. She must hold Herself and Her Will in honour; and She must compel the world to accord it.
> The modern woman is not going to be dupe, slave, and victim any more; the woman who gives herself up freely to her own enjoyment, without asking recompense, will earn the respect of her brothers, and will openly despise her "chaste" or venal sisters, as men now despise "milksops," "sissies," and "tango lizards." Love is to be divorced utterly and irrevocably from social and financial agreements, especially marriage. Love is a sport, an art, a religion, as you will; it is not an ol' clo' Emporium.[28]

---

[27] *Ibid.*
[28] *Ibid.*

"The most far-seeing of our prophetically minded writers, Aldous Huxley, brands this black fact upon our foreheads. The first condition of a 'Brave New World' must be the dissociation of sexual from reproductive life."[29] Under both Roman and Germanic law, marriage was a civil contract, regulating the rights and financial relations of the spouses. To the mediaeval Church, however, marriage and family were not contracts, but moral issues: Christianity saw marriage as part of the Christian life, as a sacred bond between the man and the woman, which ideally precluded sexuality altogether—the regulation of property and rights was of no interest to the Church.[30] Modern philosophers such as Michel Foucault have pointed out that the easiest way to control a society is to convince each of its members—usually through taboo, legislation, or publicized threats of eternal damnation—to restrict their sexual power; as Wilhelm Reich makes clear in *Die Massenpsychologie des Fascismus* (1933), if you control a person's sexuality, you control the whole person.

As Lévi phrases it, "To vow eternal love is puerile; sexual love is an emotion, divine doubtless, but accidental, involuntary and transitory; but the promise of reciprocal devotion is the essence of marriage and the fundamental principle of the family."[31] In fact, for Lévi, "Physical love is the most perverse of all fatal passions. It is the anarchist of anarchists; it knows neither law, duty, truth nor justice. It would make the maiden walk over the corpses of her parents. It is an irrepressible intoxication; a furious madness. It is the vertigo of fatality seeking new victims; the cannibal drunkenness of Saturn who wishes to become a father in order that he may have more children to devour. . . . Everything that over-excites sensibility leads to depravity and crime. Tears call for blood. It is with great emotions as with strong drink; to use them habitually is to abuse them. Now, every abuse of the emotions perverts the moral sense; one seeks them for their own sakes; one sacrifices everything in order to procure them for one's self. A romantic woman will easily become an Old Bailey heroine. She may even arrive at the deplorable and irreparable absurdity of killing herself in order to admire herself, and pity herself, in seeing herself die!"[32]

"With regard again to personal jealousy and ill-regulated passion, is it too much to say that nine tenths of the social misery not due to poverty arises from these hallucinations? *The Book of the Law* sweeps them out of existence. 'There shall be no property in human flesh.' Nobody has a right to say what anyone else shall or shall not do with his or her body. Establish this principle of absolute respect for others and the whole nightmare of sex is dispelled. Blackmail and prostitution automatically lose their *raison d'être*. The corrupting influence of hypocrisy breaks like a rotten reed. The sweating of 'female labour cheapened by prostitution' (as Bernard Shaw says) becomes impossible."[33] As Crowley wittily and accurately observes, "It is critics who deny poetry, people without capacity for Ecstasy and Will

---

[29] *MWT*, Ch. LIII.
[30] Balk 2008.
[31] *The Key of the Mysteries, loc. cit.*
[32] *Ibid.*, Part III, Book II, Ch. IV.
[33] *Confessions*, Ch. 49.

who call Mysticism moonshine and Magick delusion. It is manless old cats, geldings, and psychopaths, who pretend to detest Love, and persecute Free Women and Free Men."[34]

> Verbotenism has gone so far in certain slave-communities that the use of wine is actually prohibited by law!
> I wish here to emphasise that the Law of Θελημα definitely enjoins us, as a necessary act of religion, to "drink sweet wines and wines that foam". Any free man or woman who resides in any community where this is verboten has a choice between two duties: insurrection and emigration.
> The furtive disregard of Restriction is not Freedom. It tends to make men slaves and hypocrites, and to destroy respect for Law.
> Have no fear: two years after Vodka was verboten, Russia, which had endured a thousand lesser tyrannies with patience, rose in Revolution.
> Religious ecstasy is necessary to man's soul. Where this is attained by mystical practices, directly, as it should be, people need no substitutes. Thus the Hindus remain contentedly sober, and care nothing for the series of Invaders who have occupied their country from time to time and governed them. But where the only means of obtaining this ecstasy, or a simulacrum of it, known to the people, is alcohol, they must have alcohol. Deprive them of wine, or beer, or whatever their natural drink may be, and they replace it by morphia, cocaine, or something easier to conceal, and to take without detection.
> Stop that, and it is Revolution. As long as a man can get rid of his surplus Energy in enjoyment, he finds life easy, and submits. Deprive him of Pleasure, of Ecstasy, and his mind begins to worry about the way in which he is exploited and oppressed. Very soon he begins furtively to throw bombs; and, gathering strength, to send his tyrants to the gallows.[35]

"We of Θελημα"—one suspects Crowley is using the royal "we" here—"think it vitally aright to let a man take opium. He may destroy his physical vehicle thereby, but he may produce another 'Kubla Khan'. It is his own responsibility. Also we know well that 'if he be a King' it will not hurt him—in the end. We trust Nature to protect, and Wisdom to be justified of, their children. It is superficial to object that a man should be prevented from ruining and killing himself, for his own sake or for that of 'those dependent on him'. One who is unfit to survive ought to be allowed to die. We want only those who can conquer themselves and their environment. As for 'those dependent on him' it is one of our chief objects to abolish the very idea of dependence on others. Women with child, and infants, are not exceptions, as might seem. They are doing their will, the one class to reproduce, the other to live; the state should consider their welfare to be its

---

[34] NC on AL I.63.
[35] *Ibid.* More recently, shortly after Gorbachev embarked on a large-scale abstinence campaign, restricting the sale of alcohol in Russia, the Soviet Union collapsed.

first duty; for if they are for the moment dependent on it, it is also dependent on them. A man might as well cut out his heart because it was weak, and in need of cautious care. But he would be no less foolish if he tried to prevent the used-up elements from eliminating themselves from his body. We respect the Will-to-Live; we should respect the Will-to-Die. The race is auto-intoxicated by suppressing the excretory processes of Nature."[36]

"Each case must of course be judged on its merits. His neighbours do well to assist one who is weak by accident or misfortune, if he wishes to recover. But it is a crime against the state and against the individuals in question to hinder the gambler, the drunkard, the voluptuary, the congenital defective, from drifting to death, unless they prove by their own dogged determination to master their circumstances, that they are fit to pull their weight in the Noah's Ark of mankind."[37] However, as Crowley laments in the October 1917 issue of *The International*, "In America the prohibition idea in all things is carried, mostly by hysterical newspapers, to a fanatical extreme, 'Sensation at any cost by Sunday next' is the equivalent in most editorial rooms of the alleged German order to capture Calais. Hence the dangers of anything and everything are celebrated dithyrambically by the Corybants of the press, and the only remedy is prohibition."[38]

"A shoots B with a revolver; remedy, the Sullivan law. In practice, this works well enough; for the law is not enforced against the householder who keeps a revolver for his protection, but is a handy weapon against the gangster, and saves the police the trouble of proving felonious intent. But it is the idea that was wrong. Recently a man shot his family and himself with a rifle fitted with a Maxim silencer. Remedy, a bill to prohibit Maxim silencer! No perception that, if the man had not had a weapon at all, he would have strangled his family with his hands. American reformers seem to have no idea, at any time or in any connection, that the only remedy for wrong is right; that moral education, self-control, good manners, will save the world; and that legislation is not merely a broken reed, but a suffocating vapor. Further, an excess of legislation defeats its own ends. It makes the whole population criminals, and turns them all into policemen and police spies. The moral health of such a people is ruined for ever; only revolution can save it."[39]

> There has been so much delirious nonsense written about drugs that sane men may well despair of seeing the light.
> But it ought to be obvious that if England reverted to pre-war conditions, when any responsible person (by signing his name in a book) could buy drugs at a fair profit on cost price, cocaine (say) at 16s. and heroin at 20s. the bottle of 10 grammes—instead of as many

---

[36] NC on AL II.72.
[37] *Ibid.*
[38] "Cocaine," *The International*, October 1917.
[39] *Ibid.*

pounds—the whole underground traffic would disappear like a bad dream.

It is possible, perhaps even probable, that for a month or two there would be an increase in the number of fools who killed themselves in their folly, though personally I doubt it. But I have no shame in saying that, after a war in which we sent our sturdiest sons as sheep to the slaughter, we should not miss a few score wasters too stupid to know when to stop. Besides this, we see, on the one hand, that the people who want the drugs manage to get them in one way or another, at the cost of time, trouble, and money which might be used more wisely, and on the other that the infernal suggestions of the Press, and the vile venality of the villains attracted to the traffic by the immense profits, are deliberately creating new addicts every day of people who in the normal course of affairs would no more think of indulging in narcotics than a cat in a cold bath.

So much for the purely practical points of the position; but, deeper still, let me say as a Jeffersonian democrat, that I dread beyond all else the growth of the petty tyranny of restrictive legislation, the transference of disciplinary authority from the judiciary to the constabulary, the abandonment of every constitutional safeguard of individual liberty, the division of the people into the hunters and the hunted, the exaltation of the spy, the *agent provocateur*, and the blackmailer, the open adoption of the policy of sitting on the safety-valve, and the degradation of citizenship by applying physical repression to the evils whose only redress lies in moral development![40]

Any intrusion of government other than in the "negative" form of guarding our rights, weakens, undermines, and potentially destroys a person's liberty and thereby their ability to make their life meaningful. However, according to Crowley, his declaration of the rights of man formulated in words of one syllable—or *Liber OZ* (*see* Appendix B)—"must not be regarded as individualism run wild. Its harmony with statecraft is demonstrated in the Chapters of *Liber Aleph* already quoted."[41] Theorem 26 of *Magick in Theory and Practice* states that, "Every man has a right, the right of self-preservation, to fulfil himself to the utmost." Crowley asserts that, "Men of 'criminal nature' are simply at issue with their True Wills. The murderer has the Will-to-Live; and his will to murder is a false will at variance with his True Will, since he risks death at the hands of Society by obeying his criminal impulse." As an illustration, "A function imperfectly performed injures, not only itself, but everything associated with it. If the heart is afraid to beat for fear of disturbing the liver, the liver is starved for blood and avenges itself on the heart by upsetting digestion, which disorders respiration, on which cardiac welfare depends."[42]

---

[40] "The Great Drug Delusion," *English Review* XXXIV, June 1922.
[41] NC on AL III.60.
[42] *MITAP*, Introduction.

An Essay upon Number gives 77 as "עז, the Goat, *scil.* of the Sabbath of the Adepts. The Baphomet of the Templars, the idol set up to defy and overthrow the false god—though it is understood that he himself is false, not an end, but a means. Note the 77 = 7 × 11, magical power in perfection."[43] As Lévi writes, "Those who die in defence of right are as holy in their sacrifice as the victims of duty, and in the great struggles and revolutions against power, martyrs fell equally on both sides. Right being the root of duty, our duty is to defend our rights. What is a crime? The exaggeration of a right. Murder and theft are negations of society; it is the isolated despotism of an individual who usurps royalty, and makes war at his own risk and peril. Crime should doubtless be repressed, and society must defend itself; but who is so just, so great, so pure, as to pretend that he has the right to punish?"[44] See *Duty*, "A note on the chief rules of practical conduct to be observed by those who accept the Law of Thelema," in Appendix C.[45]

>I hope that the above principles will demonstrate to
>ALL
>that their welfare, their very existence, is bound up in
>MAGICK.
>I trust that they will understand, not only the reasonableness, but the necessity of the fundamental truth which I was the means of giving to mankind:
>"Do what thou wilt shall be the whole of the Law."
>I trust that they will assert themselves as individually absolute, that they will grasp the fact that it is their right to assert themselves, and to accomplish the task for which their nature fits them. Yea, more, that this is their duty, and that not only to themselves but to others, a duty founded upon universal necessity, and not to be shirked on account of any casual circumstances of the moment which may seem to put such conduct in the light of inconvenience or even of cruelty.[46]

"It is then no more than simple good sense for the Magus to formulate his general political aim in some such terms as these: To secure the greatest possible freedom of self-expression for the greatest possible number of Points-of-View. Of which issue the practical aspect may be phrased as follows: To improve the human race in every conceivable way, so as to have available for service the greatest possible variety of the best Instruments

---

[43] *Cf.* Spencer 1843, 6: "'Justice' comprehends only the preservation of man's natural rights. Injustice implies a violation of those rights. No man ever thinks of demanding 'justice' unless he is prepared to prove that violation; and no body of men can pretend that 'justice' requires the enactment of any law, unless they can show that their natural rights would otherwise be infringed."
[44] *The Key of the Mysteries*, Part I, "Sketch of the Prophetic Theology of Numbers."
[45] "It is a part of the notion of Duty in every one of its forms, that a person may rightfully be compelled to fulfil it. Duty is a thing which may be *exacted* from a person, as one exacts a debt. Unless we think that it might be exacted from him, we do not call it his duty." (Mill 1863, 71. Emphasis in original.)
[46] *MITAP, loc. cit.*

imaginable."[47] Conversely, "As soon as you put men together, they somehow sink, corporatively, below the level of the worst of the individuals composing it. Collect scholars on a club committee, or men of science on a jury; all their virtues vanish, and their vices pop out, reinforced by the self-confidence which the power of numbers is bound to bestow."[48] As T. H. Huxley muses, "I am as strongly convinced as the most pronounced individualist can be, that it is desirable that every man should be free to act in every way which does not limit the corresponding freedom of his fellow-man. . . . I conceive it to be demonstrable that the higher and the more complex the organization of the social body, the more closely is the life of each member bound up with that of the whole; and the larger becomes the category of acts which cease to be merely self-regarding, and which interfere with the freedom of others more or less seriously."[49]

The *New Comment* on AL I.42—"Manhood bound and loathing"—defines "an organized state" as "a free association for the common weal. My personal will to cross the Atlantic, for example, is made effective by co-operation with others on agreed terms. But the forced association of slaves is another thing." The herd believes itself to be incompetent and puts legislation into effect to justify taking from and limiting the competent through the State in the same way as the Church did before. Its mind-set originates from its reactionary weakness, so the herd has no incentive to want more competition which would leave most of its members worse off due to their real or imagined inferiority. The herd instinct becomes the breeding ground of tyrants by tyrants: God becomes State and State becomes God. According to Nietzsche, the whole of both democratic and socialist doctrine is slave morality, what is useful to the herd: "Socialism is the fanciful younger brother of the almost expired despotism whose heir it wants to be; its endeavours are thus in the profoundest sense reactionary. For it desires an abundance of state power such as only despotism has ever had; indeed it outbids all the despotisms of the past inasmuch as it expressly aspires to the annihilation of the individual, who appears to it like an unauthorized luxury of nature destined to be improved into a useful *organ of the community*."[50]

For the modern "liberals," government is society's agent for undertaking the tasks of "social justice" and "welfare" that are owed to each member and to which every individual is required to provide their contribution. Law enforcement is the means by which everyone is made to pay their "social dues" in the form of obedience to government regulations and payment of taxes for redistributive purposes. For the classical liberal, or modern "libertarian," government is an agency for the protection of each individual's rights, and society comprises of the networks of relationships and associations formed by individuals in which they voluntarily interact for mutual happiness and well-being. The *Djeridensis Comment* on AL II.25 makes it clear that "We are against 'the people'. Any unit, any true star, is

---

[47] *Little Essays Toward Truth*, "Mastery."
[48] *MWT*, Ch. LXXIII.
[49] "The Struggle for Existence in Human Society." Huxley 1894, 227–8.
[50] *Human, All Too Human*, §473. Nietzsche 1996, 173. Emphasis in original.

kingly but the people as a multitude—even though each unit be noble—are not themselves, they are a confused mass of chance atoms. They must not be allowed to act as if they possessed a point of view. They are not stars, they have no way of their own. They are dragged helpless in the wake of any force that happens to attract them. To permit them to control events at all is to give up all design, all Will, all clear sight."

"Degeneration is the most fatally easy of all human possibilities; for the fell tug of cosmic inertia, that pressure of the entire universe which tends to the homogeneous, is upon man continuously; and becomes constantly more urgent the more he advances upon his path of differentiation. It is more than a fable, Atlas who supports the Universe upon his shoulders, and Hercules, the type of the man, divinely born indeed, who must yet regain Olympus by his own fierce toil, taking upon himself that infinite load."[51] Crowley exhorts us to "mark well this! The submergence of the individual in his class means the end of all true human relations between men. Socialism means war. When the class moves as a class, there can be no exceptions." Conversely, "so great is the power of asserting one's right that it will not long be disputed. For by doing so one appeals to the Law. In practice it is found that people who are ready to fight for their rights are respected, and let alone. The slave-spirit invites oppression."[52]

The British utilitarian philosopher, John Stuart Mill, declared that until people are ready for freedom they can only hope to be ruled by a wise and benevolent dictator. But his countryman and contemporary, Lord Thomas Macaulay, replied that his suggestion reminded him "of the fool in the old story, who resolved not to go into the water till he had learned to swim."[53] Unless freedom is exercised, individuals will never learn the lessons that would enable them to make wiser and more intelligent decisions in the future; any other way, we are left maintaining large portions of the population in a permanent childhood, living off and dependent on the decisions of those in political power. According to Crowley, "The principle of popular election is a fatal folly; its results are visible in every so-called democracy. The elected man is always the mediocrity; he is the safe man, the sound man, the man who displeases the majority less than any other; and therefore never the genius, the man of progress and illumination."[54]

Nietzsche was opposed to democracy and socialism because they both stem from slave morality and preach equality between unequals. As in Christianity, he saw in democracy the same "means by which the herd animal becomes master," and "at the bottom we are one and all self-seeking cattle and mob."[55] Crowley thought it "obvious that 'Do what thou wilt' cuts

---

[51] *Moonchild*, Ch. XVIII.
[52] NC on AL I.43.
[53] As quoted in Hayek 2011, 174.
[54] *Liber CXCIV*, Sec. 10.
[55] *The Will to Power*, §§753 & 752. Cf. also *The Antecedents of Thelema*, Sec. IV: "Writing at a period when the Divine Right of Kings under the Supreme Governance of Almighty God was yet unchallenged, Rabelais describes the rise of Democracy. Idle people, he writes, will stir up social strife, so as eventually to destroy all proper relations between classes and individuals. The ignorant will have as much political power as the instructed. The dullest and the most stupid people will be entrusted with government. Just as we see it today! For genuine knaves are rare

diametrically athwart this modern civilization to destroy the distinctions which constitute the sole hope of humanity to make real progress by the selection and variation which are the means of evolution. It may be said that my own work is in the nature of missionary enterprise; and that this is, in fact, the very thing to which I object, since its idea is to persuade people to abandon their established beliefs and customs. This criticism is invalid. I do, as a matter of fact, object to missionary enterprise as such, whether it take the form of imposing the cult of Osiris on the worshippers of Adonis, of persuading the Chinese to eat with knives and forks, or of making Eastern women obscenely ridiculous by changing their superb and suitable robes for frocks which pretend to have been made in Paris."[56]

"But my message differs fundamentally from all previously promulgated precisely at this point. My predecessors have invariably said, 'My belief is right and yours is wrong; my customs are worthy, yours are ignoble; my dress is decent, yours is not; think as I think, talk as I talk, do as I do, or you will be wretched, poor, sick, disgraced and damned; besides which, I shall cut your head off, burn you alive, starve you, imprison you, ostracize you and otherwise make you sorry you did not agree to be a good boy.' The essence of every missionary message has been to assimilate the taught to the teacher; and it has always been accompanied by bribes and threats. My message is exactly opposed to any of this. I say to each man and woman, 'You are unique and sovereign, the centre of an universe. However right I may be in thinking as I do, you may be equally right in thinking otherwise. You can only accomplish your object in life by complete disregard of the opinions of other people. You must not even take the outward signs of success as indications that the course of action which has produced them would serve your turn. For one thing, my coronet might not suit your complexion but give you a headache; for another, the measures which I took to obtain that coronet might not succeed in your case.' My mission is, in short, to bring everyone to the realization and enjoyment of his own kingship, and my apparent interference with him amounts to no more than advice to him not to suffer interference."[57]

For Nietzsche, "Christianity is nothing more than the typical socialist doctrine. Property, gain, rank and status . . . all are so many hindrances to happiness, errors, snares, works of the devil, upon which the gospel passes judgment."[58] One supernatural deity is replaced with another—the State, "the coldest of all cold monsters."[59] Slave morality finds its expression no longer in the gospel but in the democratic and socialist doctrine which "disparages the individual and with its glorification of social welfare . . .

---

enough in governments; real capacity, even for dishonesty, is baffled by our political machinery. A clever man must at least pretend to be stupid to attain, and act with consistently dense imbecility to maintain, his place among the rulers of the world. No sooner is he suspected of possessing even one spark of intelligence than the herd distrust him, butt him from his pedestal, and trample him to death beneath their hooves!"

[56] *Confessions*, Ch. 83.
[57] *Ibid.*
[58] *The Will to Power*, §209.
[59] *Thus Spoke Zarathustra*. Nietzsche 1954, 160.

emphasizes the power-instinct of the herd."[60] And according to Crowley, "the God-idea must go with other relics of the Fear born of Ignorance into the limbo of savagery. I speak of the Idea of God as generally understood, God being 'something *not ourselves* that makes for righteousness,' as Matthew Arnold Victorianically phrased his definition. The whiskered wowser! Why this ingrained conviction that self is unrighteous? It is the heritage of the whip, the brand of the born slave. Incidentally, we cannot allow people who believe in this 'God'; they are troglodytes, as dangerous to society as any other thieves and murderers. The Christians to the Lions!"[61]

Crowley cites AL II.22, "It is a lie, this folly against self"—"This is the central doctrine of Thelema in this matter. What are we to understand by it? That this imbecile and nauseating cult of weakness—democracy some call it—is utterly false and vile. Let us look into the matter. (First consult AL II, 24, 25, 48, 49, 58, 59. and III, 18, 58, 59. It might be confusing to quote these texts in full; but they throw much further light on the subject.) The word 'compassion' is its accepted sense—which is bad etymology—implies that you are a fine fellow, and the other so much dirt; that is, you insult him by pity for his misfortunes. But 'Every man and every woman is a star.'; so don't you do it! You should treat everybody as a King of the same order as yourself. Of course, nine people out of ten won't stand for it, not for a minute; the mere fact of your treating them decently frightens them; their sense of inferiority is exacerbated and intensified; they insist on grovelling. That placates them. They force you to treat them as the mongrel curs they are; and so everybody is happy!"[62]

The opposite of love is not hate, or even indifference, but envy. The underprivileged seek the reason for their plight not in themselves and their personal weakness, but instead externalize it towards society. The socialist finds his weakness and frustrated will-to-power "something of which someone must be guilty, [and] can better endure his sense of sickness and ill-constitutedness by finding one whom he can make responsible for it."[63] Here we have "The *trespass sacrifice*—in its most revolting, most barbarous form at that, the sacrifice of the *guiltless* for the sins of the guilty!"[64] Sacrifice of the individual on the altar of the herd. The residents of Crowley's Sicilian Abbey of Thelema apparently "got rid of that senseless envy which embitters life by filling the mind with perverse cravings for things neither good nor bad in themselves, things fruitful of pleasure and profit to the people to whom they properly belong, but a source of misery to oneself, yet desired and hugged by the foolish who have not sense enough to see that what the mass of men imagine they want on the evidence of newspapers and salesmen may bring to them selves nothing but disappointment."[65]

---

[60] *The Will to Power*, §720.
[61] NC on AL II.23. Emphasis in original.
[62] *MWT*, Ch. XLVI.
[63] *The Will to Power*, §373.
[64] *The Antichrist*, §41. Emphasis in original.
[65] *Confessions*, Ch. 87.

We accordingly found in the abbey that happiness and peace which comes from contentment. We each had all we wanted; and nobody made himself wretched by wanting something belonging to somebody else merely because it was in itself beautiful or convenient. It should be clear to the stupidest statesman that the economic problem can be solved on these lines, and that any other principles are wasteful as well as irrational. The world is bankrupt today chiefly because well-meaning philanthropists have tried to make people happy by loading them with what they believe to be benefits because they are so to themselves.

"The mind is improved by reading." We therefore insist on everyone learning to read, with the result that their minds have been unsettled, clouded, confused and filled with falsehood by cheap fiction, sensational nonsense and deliberately dishonest propaganda. We praise the dressmakers of Paris and the tailors of London till we persuade the poor to deny themselves comfort in order to imitate the leaders of fashion. The logical error is essentially this unfitness which violates the Law of Thelema.[66]

Ancient Roman society has been described as "a civilization based on the book and the register," where "no one, either free or slave, could afford to be illiterate."[67] All Roman children were sent to elementary school, the *ludus litterarius*, to learn reading and writing, not as an act of generosity but of necessity. From the time of the Catiline conspiracy to the rise of the First and Second Triumvirates, Roman government, once conducted mostly through oratory, relied more and more on documentation to get its official business done and to justify its authority. The Republic amassed huge archives of reports on every aspect of public life, and when the Republic collapsed, the orator ceded his political power to the bureaucratic secretary, usually a freedman trained as a scribe. Patricians, however, considered it a point of honour not to burden the Romans with mundane words, wherefore most daily writings, such as personal letters, dispatches to and from the frontier, outlines for speeches, and rough drafts of laws, were composed on wax palimpsests and erased. Landmark legislation and historic political and military accomplishments alone were preserved on papyri or literally "set in stone."[68]

---

[66] *Ibid.*
[67] Dupont 1989, 223.
[68] A. Di Renzo, "His Master's Voice: Tiro and the Rise of the Roman Secretarial Class," *Journal of Technical Writing and Communication* 30(2), April 2000, 155–68. *Cf.* Plat. *Phaedrus* 275c–e: "He who thinks, then, that he has left behind him any art in writing, and he who receives it in the belief that anything in writing will be clear and certain, would be an utterly simple person, and in truth ignorant of the prophecy of Ammon, if he thinks written words are of any use except to remind him who knows the matter about which they are written. . . .Writing, Phaedrus, has this strange quality, and is very like painting; for the creatures of painting stand like living beings, but if one asks them a question, they preserve a solemn silence. And so it is with written words; you might think they spoke as if they had intelligence, but if you question them, wishing to know about their sayings, they always say only one and the same thing. And every word, when once it is written, is bandied about, alike among those who understand and those who have no interest in it, and it knows not to whom to speak or not to speak; when ill-treated or unjustly reviled it always needs its father to help it; for it has no power to protect or help itself."

After the assassination of Caesar, Antony found his notebooks, written in shorthand and filled with unfinished memos and rough proposals concerning legislation, and claimed these documents gave him the authority to continue Caesar's policies—the Senate need only approve them. Outraged, Cicero countered that Roman law and authority was defined and sanctioned though Senatorial debate: "are the acts we are being asked to ratify the ones that are jotted down in scrappy memoranda and handwritten scrawls and notebooks produced on the sole authority of Antony ... whereas the acts that Caesar himself engraved on brass tablets, with the intention of preserving the national Assembly's directions and definitive law, are to be totally disregarded?"[69] Cicero was not simply defending constitutional protocol, but pleading for the primacy of orality in Roman governance, for accountability in face-to-face debate, and for the freedom that allowed a Plebeian Tribune to defeat an unjust motion merely by saying, *Veto!*[70]

But it was the Roman Republic, not Caesar, that was dead. Oratory can be effective in a city-state, but not in a nascent empire. Even the loudest orator cannot be heard in distant Boeotia, so administering Rome's conquered provinces required writing, and the legionnaires who had built roads throughout Italy and to the frontiers, who had made it possible for a dispatch from Rome to reach Britain in a fortnight, now held the Senate hostage. They were not only a new totalitarianism but vanguards of a new communications paradigm. When the Second Triumvirate formed, Cicero was marked for execution and his severed head and hands were displayed on the rostrum of the Forum Romanum.[71] Whatever one's political affiliation, it is hard to argue with Crowley, when he says that, "The average voter is a moron. He believes what he reads in newspapers, feeds his imagination and lulls his repressions on the cinema, and hopes to break away from his slavery by football pools, cross-word prizes, or spotting the winner of the 3:30. He is ignorant as no illiterate peasant is ignorant: he has no power of independent thought. He is the prey of panic. But he has the vote."[72]

As Crowley describes the decay of manners in *Thien Tao*, "The people had power, but not reason; so were amenable to the fallacies which they mistook for reason, and not to the power which they would have imagined to be tyranny. An intelligent plebs is docile; an educated canaille expects everything to be logical. The shallow sophisms of the socialist were intelligible; they could not be refuted by the profounder and therefore unintelligible propositions of the Tory. The mob could understand the superficial resemblance of babies; they could not be got to understand that

---

[69] Cic. *Phil.* 1.7.16.
[70] Di Renzo, *op. cit.*
[71] *Ibid.*
[72] *The Scientific Solution to the Problem of Government.* Cf., however, *The World's Tragedy*, Preface: "...and if I am called an anarchist, 'soit!' But I throw my bomb with a difference. If I do not throw a physical bomb, it is only because there is none big enough. For the Government is in the hands of the bourgeoisie and the canaille, and it is for us aristocrats to throw the bombs. There can be no peace between Socrates and Athens, between Jesus and Jerusalem."

the circumstances of education and environment made but a small portion of the equipment of a conscious being."[73] In AL II.25 is "The cant of democracy condemned. It is useless to pretend that men are equal; facts are against it. And we are not going to stay, dull and contented as oxen, in the ruck of humanity."[74] As *Little Essays Toward Truth* have it, "The idea of service is either true, and humiliating; or false, and arrogant."[75]

> Now in practice, in everyday life, this unselfishness is always cropping up. Not only do you insult your brother King by your "noble self-sacrifice," but you are almost bound to interfere with his True Will. "Charity" always means that the lofty soul who bestows it is really, deep down, trying to enslave the recipient of his beastly bounty!
> In practice, I begin afresh, it is almost entirely a matter of the point of view. That poor chap looks as if a square meal wouldn't hurt him; and you chuck him a half-crown. You offend his pride, you pauperize him, you make a perfect cad of yourself, and you go off with a glow of having done your good deed for the day. It's all wrong. In such a case, you should make it the request for favour. Say you're "dying for someone to talk to, and would he care to join you in a spot of lunch" at the Ritz, or wherever you feel that he will be the happiest.
> When you can do this sort of thing as it should be done, without embarrassment, false shame, with your whole heart in your words—do it simply, to sum up—you will find yourself way up on the road to that royal republic which is the ideal of human society.[76]

"By 'the people' is meant that canting, whining, servile breed of whipped dogs which refuses to admit its deity. The mob is always afraid for its bread and butter—when its tyrants let it have any butter—and now and then the bread has 60% substitutes of cattle-fodder. (Beast-food, even the *New York Times* of November 13, 1918, E.V. has it.) So, being afraid, it dare not strike. And when the trouble begins, we aristocrats of Freedom, from the castle or the cottage, the tower or the tenement, shall have the slave mob against us. The newspapers will point out to us that 'the People' prefer to starve, and thank John D. Rockefeller for the permission to do so. . . . The moral Idea which we call 'the people' is the natural enemy of good government. He who is 'chosen' by Hadit to Kingship must consequently be 'against the people' if he is to pursue any consistent policy. The massed maggots of 'love' devoured Mark Antony as they did Abelard."[77]

"The people who guillotined the mild Louis XVI died gladly for Napoleon. The impossibility of an actual democracy is due to this fact of mob-psychology. As soon as you group men, they lose their personalities. A parliament of the wisest and strongest men in nation is liable to behave like a set of schoolboys, tearing up their desks and throwing inkpots at each

---

[73] Ch. I.
[74] OC on AL II.25.
[75] *Little Essays Toward Truth,* loc. cit.
[76] *MWT,* loc. cit.
[77] NC on AL II.25.

other. The only possibility of co-operation lies in discipline and autocracy, which men have sometimes established in the name of equal rights."[78] Only the individual himself, the master who—to quote Nietzsche once more—is "strong enough for such freedom,"[79] can create his own values and should therefore pursue these goals without concern for the envious and irrelevant objections of slave morality, which has no legitimacy in nature. All attempted barriers to this are what Nietzsche describes as the "re-sentiment" of the slave who fears and despises his own inferiority, whereas the forces behind *maximax* are essentially the same as those behind evolution itself.

Crowley's "main idea had been to found a community on the principles of *The Book of the Law*, to form an archetype of a new society. The main ethical principle is that each human being has his own definite object in life. He has every right to fulfil this purpose, and none to do anything else. It is the business of the community to help each of its members to achieve this aim; in consequence all rules should be made, and all questions of policy decided, by the application of this principle to the circumstances. We have thus made a clean sweep of all the rough and ready codes of convention which have characterized past civilizations. Such codes, besides doing injustice to the individual, fail by being based on arbitrary assumptions which are not only false, but insult and damage the moral sense. Their authority rested on definitions of right and wrong which were untenable. As soon as Nietzsche and others demonstrated that fact, they lost their validity. The result has been that the new generation, demanding a reason for acting with ordinary decency, and refusing to be put off with fables and sophistries has drifted into anarchy. Nothing can save the world but the universal acceptance of the Law of Thelema as the sole and sufficient basis of conduct. Its truth is self-evident. It is as susceptible of the strictest mathematical demonstration as any other theorem in biology. It admits that each member of the human race is unique, sovereign and responsible only to himself. In this way it is the logical climax of the idea of democracy. Yet at the same time it is the climax of aristocracy by asserting each individual equally to be the centre of the universe."[80]

Interestingly, none of this is altogether dissimilar to the Confucian political theory. In Confucianism, all relationships are expected to be mutually beneficial, and each has its own inner logic. For example, a ruler must justify his position by acting benevolently if he is to expect reciprocation from the people. Although Confucius declared his admiration for kings of great accomplishment, it was Mencius who clarified the proper hierarchy of human society. Even though a king has higher status than a commoner, in Confucian thought, he is actually subordinate to the masses of people and the resources of society. One is significant only for what one gives, not for what one takes; otherwise, there would be a disregard for the potential of human society going into the future.[81] Mencius' interpretation

---

[78] *Moonchild, loc. cit.*
[79] *The Antichrist*, §49.
[80] *Confessions, loc. cit.*
[81] Chan 1963.

has in general been considered the orthodox one by subsequent Chinese thinkers and in particular by the Neo-Confucians of the Song dynasty. Mencius' disciples included a significant number of feudal lords, and he eventually became more influential than Confucius himself.[82]

Like Confucius, Mencius is said to have travelled the length and breadth of China for 40 years, offering advice to rulers on reform. According to Mencius, humans have an innate tendency towards goodness, but since moral rightness cannot be instructed down to the last detail, externals controls invariably fail in improving society. True improvement can only be achieved through educational cultivation in favourable environments, whereas averse environments have a tendency to corrupt the human will. This is not an argument for innate evil, because a clear-thinking person will avoid causing harm to others. However, this position puts Mencius between other Confucians such as Hsün-tzu, who thought people were innately evil, and Taoists, who did not think humans needed cultivation in order to accept their innate, natural, effortless goodness. Mencius thus synthesized integral parts of Taoism into Confucianism.[83]

For Mencius, the object of education is the cultivation of what is known as Rén. Variously translated as "goodness," "benevolence," "perfect virtue," or even "human-heartedness," Rén is considered the essence of the human being, endowed by Heaven; at the same time, it is the means by which a person can act according to the Heavenly principle and become one with it. When asked to define Rén, Confucius answered with the ordinary Chinese word for love, *ai*, saying that it meant to "love others."[84] Rén also forms the basis of Confucian political theory: if the ruler lacks Rén, it will be difficult for his subjects to behave humanely, and an inhumane ruler runs the risk of losing the Mandate of Heaven (*t'ien ming*), i.e. the right to rule. A ruler who lacks such a mandate need not be obeyed, and conversely, a ruler who takes care of the people shows that he has been mandated by Heaven.[85]

Since the world is continually changing at a rapid pace, Confucius believed that the key to long-lasting integrity was to constantly think. However, Mencius also believed in the power of Destiny (*ming*) in shaping the roles of people in society, and what is destined cannot be contrived or foreseen by the human intellect. Destiny is shown when a path arises that is both unforeseen and constructive, and should not be confused with Fate. Mencius spurned the notion that Heaven would protect people regardless of their actions, for "He who understands what is meant by the will of God will not place himself under a tottering wall."[86] The proper path is natural and unforced, but must be maintained because unused pathways are covered over by weeds. A person who follows the Decree of Heaven will live long and prosper, while the person who fights Nature will die early. The question of whether or not Confucianism is a religion remains one of

---

[82] Hucker 1978.
[83] Chan, *op. cit.*
[84] H. H. Dubs, "The Development of Altruism in Confucianism," *Philosophy East and West* 1(1), April 1951, 48–55.
[85] Chan, *op. cit.*
[86] As quoted in Giles 1915, 92.

the most controversial issues in both Confucian scholarship and the academic field of religious studies.[87]

> The price of every step of progress is uncounted, even in myriads of lives self-sacrificed; and every man who is unfaithful to himself is not only at war with the sum of things, but his own comrades turn upon him to destroy him, to crush out his individuality and energy, to assimilate him to their own pullulating mass. It is indeed the power of the Roman Empire which erects the Cross on Calvary; but there must needs be Caiaphas and Herod, so blind that they crush out their own one hope of salvation from that iron tyranny; and also a traitor among those who once "left all and followed" the Son of Man.
> And who shall deny true Godhead to humanity, seeing that no generation of mankind has been without a Saviour, conscious of his necessary doom, and resolute to meet it, his face set as a flint towards Jerusalem?[88]

Liber AL vel Legis "announces a New Law for mankind. It replaces the moral and religious sanctions of the past, which have everywhere broken down, by a principle valid for each man and woman in the world, and self-evidently indefeasible. The spiritual Revolution announced by the book has already taken place: hardly a country where it is not openly manifest. Ignorance of the true meaning of this new Law has led to gross anarchy. Its conscious adoption in its proper sense is the sole cure for the political, social and racial unrest which have brought about the World War, the catastrophe of Europe and America, and the threatening attitude of China, India and Islam."[89] At a time "when the doors of human progress are creaking on their hinges, when mankind seems almost resigned to the cynical contemplation of its own agony in the hope of delaying its inevitable decay; when Europe has the aspect of a vast and insecure hospital for sick nations; when the Far East is drinking itself into madness on the arrack of Western democratic shibboleths, and when America is foundering in ceaselessly renewed and insoluble problems;—when, in a word, the whole earth seems weary and out of joint, at its critical angle, it is interesting to glance attentively at the efforts of certain men whose researches have led them to the intimacy of the most secret laws of Nature."[90]

> Democracy dodders.
> Ferocious Fascism, cackling Communism, equally frauds, cavort crazily all over the globe.
> They are hemming us in.
> They are abortive births of the Child, the New Æon of Horus.
> Liberty stirs once more in the womb of Time.

---

[87] Chen 2013.
[88] *Moonchild, loc. cit.*
[89] *The Equinox of the Gods,* "The Summons."
[90] *The Method of Thelema.*

Evolution makes its changes by anti-Socialistic ways. The "abnormal" man who foresees the trend of the times and adapts circumstance intelligently, is laughed at, persecuted, often destroyed by the herd; but he and his heirs, when the crisis comes, are survivors.

Above us today hangs a danger never yet paralleled in history. We suppress the individual in more and more ways. We think in terms of the herd. War no longer kills soldiers; it kills all indiscriminately. Every new measure of the most democratic and autocratic governments is Communistic in essence. It is always restriction. We are all treated as imbecile children. Dora, the Shops Act, the Motoring Laws, Sunday suffocation, the Censorship—they won't trust us to cross the roads at will.

Fascism is like Communism, and dishonest into the bargain. The dictators suppress all art, literature, theatre, music, news, that does not meet their requirements; yet the world only moves by the light of genius. The herd will be destroyed in mass.

The establishment of the Law of Thelema is the only way to preserve individual liberty and to assure the future of the race.

In the words of the famous paradox of the Comte de Fénix—The absolute rule of the state shall be a function of the absolute liberty of each individual will.

All men and women are invited to cooperate with the Master Therion in this, the Great Work.[91]

"Let this formula be accepted by every government. Experts will immediately be appointed to work out, when need arises, the details of the True Will of every individual, and even that of every corporate body whether social or commercial, while a judiciary will arise to determine the equity in the case of apparently conflicting claims. (Such cases will become progressively more rare as adjustment is attained.) All appeal to precedent and authority, the deadwood of the Tree of Life, will be abolished, and strictly scientific standards will be the sole measure by which the executive power shall order the people. *The absolute rule of the state shall be a function of the absolute liberty of each individual will.*"[92] Those of Crowley's modern followers who consider Thelema primarily a religious philosophy see such ambitions as megalomaniacal. However, if one does not view Thelema as a religion—and (as we have seen) Crowley repeatedly denied it was one—they make perfect sense. They become not only plausible, but imperative.

---

[91] *Liber AL vel Legis* (1938), Introduction.

[92] *The Scientific Solution.* Emphasis added. As Professor Hans-Hermann Hoppe argues in his persuasive contrarian essay *From Aristocracy to Monarchy to Democracy*, "What is lacking in actual conflicts... is not the absence of law, lawlessness, but only the absence of an agreement on the facts. And the need for judges and conflict arbitrators, then, is not a need for law-making, but a need for fact-finding and the application of given law to individual cases and specific situations. Put somewhat differently: the deliberations will result in the insight that laws are not to be made but given to be discovered, and that the task of the judge is only and exclusively that of applying given law to established or to be established facts." (Hoppe 2014, 28.)

"Teach thou therefore this Law to all men: for in so far as they follow it, they cease to hinder thee by their false random motion; and thou dost well to thyself in doing well to them. And he most hindereth himself who hindereth others from their Path, or who constraineth them to some motion improper to their Nature."[93] For Crowley, "It seems not unreasonable to suppose that the new generation, directing itself consciously or subconsciously by this indication, will develop human personality to its full stature. The whole of our present civilization, with its cohorts of hereditary possibilities, which until now have never been utilized to full advantage, will form itself on this new law of spiritual perfection. Nor let it be forgotten that the full blossoming of this new era is perceptible on every hand. Governments, it is true, have not yet taken official notice of the subtle evolution which is taking place under their eyes. They are bewildered and alarmed; they either break down in chaos or react savagely against the manipulations which disturb their stupidity. But they will not prevent the prodigious dawn which is taking place in the essence of man."[94]

As Crowley writes in his diary on 31 July 1923 at 2:50 p.m., "Last night I had the idea of summoning the British residents of Tunis, & asking them to sign a Covenant that in no case will they consent to take arms against France, save only in the event of a deliberate invasion of British territory. This is to be taken to the Foreign Office, & an appeal made to other colonies of Britain—also various political & other associations in England itself to draw up similar documents. . . . I think we should discuss the matter first of all with a few of the most prominent British residents of Tunis, & perhaps go to the Consul before summoning the meeting. . . . I might ultimately bring forward my own solution of the European muddle. . . . International marriage between England & France to be encouraged by remission of taxes, & large families of healthy children similarly worked. No army, save a few ornamental regiments. No state religion, but absolute toleration."

"Marriage to be a simple contract without state interference whatever its terms. Welfare of children to be guaranteed by making them from infancy an help instead of a burden to the parents. Proper proportion of agricultural & pastoral settlers to industrial workers to be preserved faithfully. Health of town workers to be assured by arranging for the unskilled to change place with country workers during a proportion of the year. Education to be free, unsectarian technical: academic training (the 3 Rs) to be given only to those who show special aptitude for, & declare their wish to obtain it. Legislation to be confined to expression in particular cases of the general principle: Thelema. Administrative & judicial establishment accordingly. Welfare & honour to be dissociated from the idea of wealth. Property to be inalienable: i.e., no mortgages. Failure to make property successful economically to be taken as evidence as unfitness to administer it: the proprietor to be treated as an invalid, the state to train him, assist

---

[93] *The Heart of the Master*, Part III, "The Mystery of Sin."
[94] *The Method of Thelema.*

him, or otherwise to remedy his deficiency. If impossible, to be transferred to some other sphere of activity."[95]

The Constitution of the Order of Thelemites, Section 11, reads: "Consonant with the principles of the Order, propaganda may be undertaken with a view to the removal of arbitrary restrictions on the Will of the Individual, and co-ordinate the laws of every country to the Law of Thelema; that is, the Order of Thelemites shall strive to establish a code, the sole object of which shall be to prevent any man, or body of men, from interfering with the True Will of another, as in the case of murder, robbery, rape, etc. It shall similarly strive to create a Public Opinion in favor of Social tolerance of all opinions and practices which do not interfere with the True Will of the individual and the community."[96] The purpose of property norms—from which rights are extrapolated—is to provide a legal and philosophical basis by which it is possible to arbitrate between conflicting desires in acquiring and utilizing scarce goods. That is, they provide rules regarding such resources that, if followed, mitigate or eliminate violent interpersonal conflict. "Robbery in any shape is a breach of the Law of Thelema. It is interference with the right of another to dispose of his property as he will; and if I did so myself, no matter with what tactical justification, I could hardly ask others to respect my own similar right."[97]

"The basis of our criminal law is simple, by virtue of Thelema: to violate the right of another is to forfeit one's claim to protection in the matter involved."[98] However, "Note also this that many men, feeling themselves the bitterness of Restriction, seek to relieve their own pain by imposing a like burden upon their fellows: as it were a cripple who should seek ease by mutilating the bearers of his carriage."[99] This begs the question: "What is money? A medium of exchange devised to facilitate the transaction of business. Oil in the engine. Very good, then; if instead of letting it flow as freely and smoothly as possible, you baulk its very nature; you prevent it from doing its True Will. So every restriction (that word again!) on the exchange of wealth is a direct violation of the Law of Thelema."[100] The free

---

[95] Diary entry, 31 July 1923, 2:50 p.m. *Cf.* also *Liber DCCCXI*, Sec. IX: "If the power to possess property depended on a man's competence, and his perception of real values, a new aristocracy would at once be created, and the deadly fact that social consideration varies with the power of purchasing champagne would cease to be a fact. Our pluto-hetairo-politicocracy would fall in a day."
[96] Original typed MS. Syracuse University, NY. n.d.
[97] *MWT*, Ch. XLIX. *Cf.* also *Duty*, Sec. C.
[98] *Ibid. Cf.* e.g. N. S. Kinsella, "Punishment and Proportionatility: The Estoppel Approach," *Journal of Libertarian Studies* 12(1), Spring 1996, 51–73: "In short, we may punish one who has initiated force, in a manner proportionate to his initiation of force and to the consequences thereof, exactly because he cannot coherently object to such punishment. It makes no sense for him to object to punishment, because this requires that he maintain that the infliction of force is wrong, which is contradictory because he intentionally initiated force himself. Thus, he is *estopped*, to use related legal terminology, or precluded, from denying the legitimacy of his being punished, from withholding his consent." (Emphasis in original.)
[99] *The Heart of the Master, loc. cit.*
[100] *MWT*, Ch. LIV. *Cf.* also *Confessions*, Ch. 22: "I am a free trader in every sense of the word. I have no sympathy with any regulations which interfere with the natural activities of human beings. I believe that they aggravate whatever trouble they are intended to prevent; and they create the greatest plague of humanity, officialdom, and encourage underhand conduct on both sides,

market is the only vehicle through which equal access to our ambitions can be achieved without trampling on the ambitions or rights of others.

As we learn from Lévi, "The basis of society is the exchange of right, duty and good faith. Right is property, exchange is necessity, good faith is duty. He who wants to receive more than he gives, or who wants to receive without giving, is a thief. Property is the right to dispose of a portion of the common wealth; it is not the right to destroy, nor the right to sequestrate. To destroy or sequestrate the common wealth is not to possess; it is to steal.... What does the poor man wish, if he is honest? He wishes for work. Use your rights, but do your duty: the duty of the rich man is to spread wealth; wealth which does not circulate is dead; do not hoard death! A sophist has said, 'Property is robbery,' and he doubtless wished to speak of property absorbed in itself, withdrawn from free exchange, turned from common use. If such were his thought, he might go further, and say that such a suppression of public life is indeed assassination. It is the crime of monopoly, which public instinct has always looked upon as treason to the human race."[101]

However, "The identification of the apotheosis of Capitalism with the Trust is a familiar fallacy. Co-operation is one thing and communism is another. The sole object of creating trusts is to secure greater inequality in the distribution of the common wealth, not less; and if this incentive were removed the whole fabric would fall to pieces. The object of concentrating power is not to give everyone a square deal. The little man is frozen out simply because he threatens to interfere with the game of despoiling the people. There is certainly economy in what Mr. Shaw misleadingly calls 'communism in production'. But it is the economy of wolves who hunt in packs in order to pull down their quarry. It is such sophistries that make political economy the morass we know it. And it might further be observed that this 'communism in production' over which Mr. Shaw gloats has been the very means by which the self-respecting apprentice, with a secure future, has been turned into what that brilliant young 'Angel of the Revolution', Gerda von Kothek, calls 'factory-fodder'."[102]

Fairness lay not in rewarding everyone the same regardless of the work or talent involved; true fairness can only exist in merit, earning one's just reward and desert. "The idea at the back of puritanism is the reduction of the mass of humanity to a degree of slavery which has never previously been so much as contemplated by the most malignant tyrants in history; for it aims at completing the helplessness of the workman by minimizing his capacity. He must no more be permitted to exercise the creative craftsmanship involved in making a pair of boots; he must be rendered unable to do more than repeat mechanically, year in, year out, one meaningless item in the manufacture, so that when the pinch comes it shall be impossible for anyone to have boots at all except through the complex

---

furtiveness and espionage. Any law which tends to destroy manly qualities is a bad law, however necessary it may seem on the surface. The tendency of most modern legislation is to bind Gulliver with packthread."

[101] *The Key of the Mysteries*, loc. cit.
[102] *Liber 888*, "Modern Communism."

industrial conspiracy of the trusts. This idea, consciously or subconsciously, lies underneath all attempts to extend 'civilization'. The progress of this pestilence is only too visible all over the world. Standardized hotels and standardized merchandise have invaded the remotest districts, and these would be economically impossible unless supported by the forcible suppression of local competition."[103]

Unlike Crowley, many of his modern-day "progressive" followers display a woeful degree of ignorance about the workings of a competitive market economy, the nature of the profit and loss system, and the Invisible Hand of competitive co-operation through the voluntary and peaceful pursuit of self-interest. As Crowley writes, "It is impossible to treat Mr. Shaw's conclusion that the share of every member of the community must be equal, at all seriously. It would simply mean that most rare and beautiful things would cease to exist. Even assuming (what is enormous exaggeration) that the income of each person would work out at five hundred pounds a year, who is to wear a pearl necklace worth a hundred thousand pounds? The interest on the money comes to more than the total share. The necklace would have to be broken up or put in a museum, and all its value lost to mankind. Similarly there could be no private ownership of pictures of any value, there could be no beautiful houses, or gardens, no parks except public parks, which produce (in me at least) nothing but a sense of dreary dissatisfaction, and are not even enjoyed by the people they are intended to benefit. Battersea Park, for instance, is within three minutes' walk of innumerable slums; but the children play in the slums, not in the park."[104]

"There is also the obvious point that people will not work exceptionally unless they get exceptional payment. If there were no possibility of in some way improving my position—if only by making myself more infamous even than I am (Matthew v. 11, 12) by writing this essay, I should certainly not trouble to do it. Men will work themselves to death to advance in the world, or to make the lives of those they love happier. But if everything is to be on the dead level, they will not 'put themselves out', they will not take risks. Humanity will become stagnant."[105] The interventionist welfare state undermines people's personal and financial ability to participate in the acts and associations of benevolence towards others that their conscience calls them to pursue in the ways they themselves deem best and most likely to succeed. Through the coercive arm of government, the redistributive state replaces each person's individual judgment and decision with that of its self-appointed "experts" who claim to speak and know what is best for society.

As Crowley points out, "most of the things—at any rate, the new things—which are really desirable, and even useful to humanity, are produced by persons who have a very great deal of money to spare. Any one who has had any experience in dealing with governments knows that it

---

[103] *Confessions*, Ch. 83.
[104] *Liber 888*, "Equal Distribution."
[105] *Ibid.*

is quite impossible to get them to experiment. Does Mr. Shaw suppose for a moment that we should ever have had railways or aeroplanes, if the matter had been left to government? The state knows only too well, apart from the question of finding the money for elaborate improvements, there is always the vested interest to fight."[106] Crowley notes that in this phrase he wishes "to include the conservatism of the stupid and the old. Under communism, though it would make no financial difference to the flint-chipper to be turned into a bronze-caster, he would still object to undergo the fatigue of learning a new trade. And all selfish incentive would be denied him; he would therefore be just as obstinate as the stage coachman was when we introduced the steam-engine."[107]

"Practically all inventions of any size or importance have had to force their way to acceptance through a thousand obstacles. How could the motor car have been introduced but by the faith of capitalists? These men were not working in the least to benefit humanity; they saw a fortune in it, and they threw away their money by the hundred thousand in the hope of getting it back many times over, like the man in the parable of the Talents. The late Isaac Rice, for example, submitted to a yearly loss which came near to crippling him rich man as he was, in order to perfect the Holland submarine. The inventor (if he is lucky) may find one man or even a half a dozen to believe that what he proposes is possible. But to convince a state department would be a greater miracle than any of those recorded in the gospels. Even when an invention has been working satisfactorily for years, the state remains the Old Guard of the sceptics. This is another reason why humanity would stagnate under communism. It is true that the inventor would not be troubled by the impossibility of his finding money for his experiments for the simple reason that he would not take the trouble to invent, when he could get no good for it."[108]

"It is this fundamental fact which ensures that every democracy shall end with an upstart autocrat; the stability of peace depends upon the original idea which aggrandized America in a century from four millions to a hundred: extreme individualism with opportunity. Our own longest period of peace abroad (bar frontier skirmishes like the Crimean war) and prosperity at home coincided with Free Trade and Laissez-faire."[109] Crowley has "no sympathy with those who cry out against property, as if what all men desire were of necessity evil; the natural instinct of every man is to own, and while man remains in this mood, attempts to destroy property must not only be nugatory, but deleterious to the community. There is no outcry against the rights of property where wisdom and kindness administer it. The average man is not so unreasonable as the demagogue, for his selfish ends, pretends to be. The great nobles of all time have usually been able to create a happy family of their dependents, and unflinching loyalty and devotion have been their reward. The secret has been principally this, that they considered themselves noble as well in

---

[106] *Ibid.*, "Money, the Midwife of Scientific Communism."
[107] *Ibid.*, fn.
[108] *Ibid.*
[109] *MWT*, Ch. LXXIII.

nature as in name, and thought it foul shame to themselves if any retainer met unnecessary misfortune."[110]

"The upstart of to-day lacks this feeling; he must try constantly to prove his superiority by exhibiting his power; and harshness is his only weapon. In any society where each person has his allotted place, and that a place with its own special honour, mutual respect and self-respect are born. Every man is in his own way a king, or at least heir to some kingdom. We have many examples of such society to-day, notably universities and all associations of sport. No. 5 in the Harvard crew does not turn round in the middle of the race and reproach No. 4 for being merely No. 4; nor do the pitcher and catcher of a crack baseball nine revile each other because their tasks are different. It is to be noted that wherever team-work is necessary social tolerance is an essential. The common soldier is invested with a uniform as well as his officer, and in any properly trained army he is taught his own canons of honour and self-respect. This feeling, more than mere discipline or the possession of weapons, makes the soldier more than a match morally for a man not so clothed in proper reverence for himself and his profession."[111]

Obviously, the ultimate goal of promulgation is the establishment of Thelema as law of the land. *Liber CCC*, or *Khabs am Pekht*, is "An epistle of Therion $9°=2^{\square}$, a Magus of the A∴A∴ to His Son, being an Instruction in a matter of all importance, to wit, the means to be taken to extend the Dominion of the Law of Thelema throughout the whole world." The *Curriculum of A∴A∴* defines this as "the first and most important duty of every Aspirant of whatever grade." It thus follows that, "Pending the establishment of other Universities and Schools of Thelema, scholarships and readerships and such should be provided in existing Schools and Universities, so as to secure the general study of Our writings, and those authorized by Us as pertaining to the New Æon."[112] In fact, "In order to apply the Law of Thelema, to investigate the solutions indicated by *The Book of the Law*, and to utilize them to remedy existing difficulties, the appeal is only to technicians. Bankers, architects, engineers, biologists, chemists, doctors, must combine their knowledge and apply it to the discovery of the general practical formula of the Law of Thelema."[113]

It should be clear from the above that by "Promulgation" of the Law of Thelema, Crowley meant "to put into effect (a law, decree, etc), esp by formal proclamation"[114] rather than merely "to set forth or teach publicly (a creed, doctrine, etc.)."[115] He cites AL II.26, "Ye are against the people, O my chosen!"—"Not only does it seem to me the only conceivable way of reconciling this and similar passages with 'Every man and every woman is a star.' to assert the sovereignty of the individual, and to deny the right-to-exist to 'class-consciousness,' 'crowd-psychology,' and so to mob-rule and

---

[110] *Liber CLXI*.
[111] *Ibid*.
[112] *Liber CCC. Cf.* e.g. *Liber CI*, Sec. 41.
[113] *The Method of Thelema*.
[114] *Collins English Dictionary* (2012).
[115] *Random House Dictionary* (2016).

Lynch-Law, but also the only practicable plan whereby we may each one of us settle down peaceably to mind his own business, to pursue his True Will, and to accomplish the Great Work. So never lose sight for a moment of the maxim so often repeated in one context or another in these letters: that fear is at the root of every possibility of trouble, and that 'Fear is failure, and the forerunner of failure. Be thou therefore without fear; for in the heart of the coward virtue abideth not.'"[116]

> In one or two—no, I think more like three or four—letters of yours to hand in the last couple of months, you have put forward various excuses for slackness, the necessities of your economic situation. You say you must have "regular work," and a "steady income" and all that sort of thing. My innocent child, that species of Magick is quite simple. Take the horns of a hare . . . That's enough for the present: I'll tell you what to do with them when you've got them.
> In *Macbeth* we read—
> . . . "Security
> Is mortals' chiefest enemy."[117]
> but this is another kind of security; it is the Hubris which "tempts Providence," the insolence of thinking that nothing can go wrong.
> Anyhow, there's no such thing as safety. Life is a gamble. From the moment of incarnation a million accidents are possible. Miscarriage, still-birth, abortion; throughout life, until your heart beats for the last time, "you never can tell" - — — —and then you start all over again with your next incarnation![118]

Crowley is under no illusions: "Of course (in practice) many people, perhaps the majority, will not accept the Law of Thelema. We found that life in the abbey with its absolute freedom was too severe a strain on those who were accustomed to depend on others. The responsibility of being truly themselves was too much for them; but sooner or later, without any action on our part, without any quarrel or ostensible reason, they found themselves ejected into their 'previous condition of servitude'. *The Book of the Law* anticipates this: '... the slaves shall serve. ...' The bulk of humanity, having no true will, will find themselves powerless. It will be for us to rule them wisely. We must secure their happiness and train them for ultimate freedom by setting them tasks for which their nature fits them."[119] *The Book*

---

[116] *MWT, loc. cit.*; from the Neophyte Ritual of the Golden Dawn.
[117] Act 3, Scene 5.
[118] *Ibid.*, Ch. LXXIX.
[119] *Confessions*, Ch. 87. *Cf.* also *The Antecedents of Thelema*, Sec. III: "Members of superstitious religions are not to be allowed to enter the Abbey of Thelema. In *The Book of the Law* the attitude is not merely thus defensive: the implication is that superstition is to be stamped out, or at least its victims are to be definitely relegated to the slave-class. The Freeman is to war down the serf: 'on the low men trample in the fierce lust of your pride, in the day of your wrath'. There is no place in the Abbey imagined by Rabelais, and to be realized by the Master Therion, for those parasites of society who feed upon the troubles caused by Restriction: officials, lawyers, financiers, and the like. Ill disposed people—that is, those whose failure to understand their own true Will of Freedom leads them to seek to interfere with others—are not to be tolerated."

of the Law "announces a new dichotomy in human society; there is the master and there is the slave; the noble and the serf; the 'lone wolf' and the herd."[120]

"The 'Master' roughly denotes the able, the adventurous, welcoming responsibility. The 'slave': his motto is 'Safety first,' with all that this implies. Race, birth, breeding etc. are important but not absolutely essential factors."[121] Therefore, "Nietzsche may be regarded as one of our prophets; to a much less extent, de Gobineau," the French aristocrat who first came up with the Aryan master race theory. "Hitler's 'Herrenvolk' is a not too dissimilar idea; but there is no *volk* about it; and if there were, it would certainly not be the routine-loving, uniformed-obsessed, law-abiding, refuge-seeking German; the Briton, especially the Celt, a natural anarchist, is much nearer the mark. Britons will never get together about anything unless and until each one of them feels himself directly threatened."[122] As Randolph Bourne, the American non-interventionist and critic of the melting-pot theory, famously remarked, "War is the health of the State. It automatically sets in motion throughout society these irresistible forces for uniformity, for passionate cooperation with the Government in coercing into obedience the minority groups and individuals which lack the larger herd sense."[123]

Crowley himself observes that, "The men in power can only govern by stampeding him into wars, playing on his fears and prejudices until he acquiesces in repressive legislation against his obvious interests, playing on his vanity until he is totally blind to his own misery and serfdom. The alternative method is undisguised dragooning. In brief, we govern by a mixture of lying and bullying."[124] Government can only be imposed and perpetuated by means of brute force, whereas liberty, by its very nature, cannot be given. An individual cannot be freed by another, but must break his or her own fetters through their own effort. As Max Stirner puts it, "The man who is set free is nothing but a freed man ... a dog dragging a piece of chain with him."[125] Collectivism postulates no rights for the individual, whose life and work belongs to the group, who may sacrifice him at its own whim to its own interests. "Society has always been asked to regulate its actions either on grounds which everyone knows in his heart to be absurd, or on motives which nobody really accepts. The Law of Thelema avows and justifies selfishness; it confirms the inmost conviction of each one of us that he is the centre of the cosmos. Previous prophets have invariably tried to dodge this truth as making all social systems impossible."[126]

"Now, for the first time, we can build practically every variety of social structure on this fact. All laws, customs and co-operative efforts can be

---

[120] *MWT*, Ch. XLVIII. *Cf.* also Lévi 1913, 45: "There are two classes: freemen and slaves; man is born in the bondage of his passions, but he can reach emancipation through intelligence. Between those who are free already and those who are as yet not there is no equality possible."
[121] *Ibid.*, fn.
[122] *Ibid.*
[123] Bourne 1964, 71.
[124] *The Scientific Solution*.
[125] Stirner 1971, 123.
[126] *Confessions, loc. cit.*

constructed by the application of this principle for the conditions of environment. And all such structures will be stable, being free from the flaw which has been the bane of all previous systems. The theocracies of antiquity broke down as soon as their theory was challenged by science. Divine right met with disaster immediately that its absurdity became apparent, so that humanity will never repeat the experiment; despite the fact that in many cases the absurd axiom led to the greatest prosperity. Social systems founded upon philosophy have failed even more frightfully, for the premises of the syllogism were false. It was always implied that man as such possessed various virtues which are in reality only found in a few individuals."[127]

"Even those of us who believe in supernatural sanctions for our privileges to browbeat and rob the people no longer delude ourselves with the thought that our victims share our superstitions. Even dictators understand this. Mussolini has tried to induce the ghost of Ancient Rome to strut the stage in the image of Julius Caesar; Hitler has invented a farrago of nonsense about Nordics and Aryans; nobody even pretends to believe either, except through the 'will-to-believe.' And the pretence is visibly breaking down everywhere. They cannot even be galvanized with spasms of pseudo-activity, as still occasionally happens with the dead toads of superstition."[128] As Lévi says, "Human life and its innumerable difficulties have for object, in the ordination of eternal wisdom, the education of the will of man. The dignity of man consists in doing what he will, and in willing the good, in conformity with the knowledge of truth. The good in conformity with the true, is the just."[129]

"So-called education (on which countless millions are squandered with the sole result of unsettling and unfitting the vast majority of its victims for their work in the world) becomes inexpensive, efficient and profitable when the Law of Thelema dictates its principles. The very word means 'leading out' of each child the faculties which he naturally possesses. The present system deliberately discourages the development of individuality and deforms minds by forcing them to perform functions for which they were not designed."[130] Crowley relates how "Last Sunday I looked through an interview with the least brain-bound of these ruminators—poor old, dear old G. for gaga Bernard Shaw. The artist, said he, was a special case. He should have a nice easy job, three or four hours a day, and be free for the rest of it to devote himself to his Art. I wonder how much of his own work would have seen daylight if he had been tied to some silly robot soul-killing, nerve-crushing, mind-infuriating routine job for even one half-hour a day!

---

[127] *Ibid. Cf.* also Lévi, *op. cit.*, 22: "Affirmation rests on negation, the strong can only triumph because of weakness, the aristocracy cannot be manifested except by rising above the people. For the weak to become strong, for the people to acquire an aristocratic position, is a question of transformation and of progress, but it is without prejudice to the first principles; the weak will be ever the weak and it matters nothing if they are not always the same persons. The people in like manner will ever remain the people, the mass which is ruled and is not capable of ruling."
[128] *The Scientific Solution.*
[129] *The Key of the Mysteries*, Part III, Book II, Ch. I.
[130] *Confessions, loc. cit.*

When I am on a piece of work, I grudge the time for eating; and when it's done, I need the absolute relaxation of leisured luxury."[131]

> I am bound to say that personally I regard a leisured class as the only possible field for the highest types of wheat to grow. The socialistic idea that every one should work menially for an hour or so every day would check the entire race. Any mechanical labour degrades; it is necessary that it should be performed, and must therefore always produce a degraded class. To equalize men in this matter is to bring them all down to the level of the dock labourer.
> My parents spent several thousand pounds on giving me a public school and University Education. On its completion I found that I knew nothing. I thereupon spent fifty thousand pounds of my own to pursue it; and I still know nothing. That is a good start, however; and I have great hopes. But certainly I never could have arrived even at my present stage if I had had to spend a couple of hours a day in cleaning out somebody's drains. For one thing, all the higher kinds of work require a fineness and delicacy both of manual and mental energy such that a life of leisure is absolutely necessary to their proper functioning. The surgeon's hands, or the pianist's would be ruined forever if he had to chop wood for a month. (How, by the way, is society to 'compel' people without first 'judging' them?)
> When it comes to the artistic element, and Mr. Shaw will be the first to agree that the artist is the salt of the earth, the case becomes extreme. Idling is actually necessary to a great many artists as a peculiar mental state which ultimately produces ideas. I am personally acquainted with one artist who can only be forced to work by the boredom of prolonged idleness. If you gave him some healthful employment he would be a perfectly commonplace man. All the subtler qualities of humanity depend on leisure. To 'compel' artists to 'work' would be as reasonable as to sow seed in a field and keep on plowing it all through the year.[132]

"Extending this principle to the world at large, my plan would be to classify children in infancy according to the subtle indications afforded by their gestures and reactions to various stimuli. Any child who showed a desire to read and write would be given every possible encouragement altogether irrespective of social and other considerations. Similar principles would apply to other activities: draughtsmanship, building, mechanics and the rest. He would be made to understand that the fulfilment of his ambitions would depend on his willing submission to discipline, the conquest of idleness and so on. But unless and until a child showed real discontent with his ignorance on any subject, we should not try to enlighten him. His lessons should be a relief; the satisfaction of a real appetite." Importantly, "the resources of the state available for education would be concentrated on the development of all really promising children instead of

---

[131] *MWT*, Ch. LXXIX.
[132] *Liber 888*, "Vital Distribution."

being in the first place wasted on stuffing all alike with a smattering of knowledge and then leaving them to shift for themselves, probably in danger of moral ruin by acquiring a taste for bad fiction and shallow sedition, and in the second, of blunting the best minds by penning them with the herd."[133]

A 10th-century Frankish nobleman could neither read nor write. In his youth, he had learned to handle a horse (the Latin, French, and German words for knight, *eques, chevalier,* and *Ritter* respectively, all have as their roots in words for horseman) and a sword, but would often leave to the bailiffs and clerks the task governing those people on whom the ruling class usually relies to sustain its power. The modern words "clergy" and "clerk" both derive from the same Latin word, *clerici,* "clerics." Throughout the Middle Ages, all clerks were clergy, and the term "clerical" still retains both senses.[134] "Modern social unrest is largely due to misunderstanding of the Law of Thelema. The workman has learnt to covet motor cars and portfolios, which he was not born to have. When he gets them, he becomes still more unhappy—a fish out of water—and ruins the community into the bargain. Under the Law of Thelema, all false ideals and incongruous ambitions will be driven away as delusions."[135]

"The first principle of moral education will be the biological truth that the health and happiness of a cell depends upon the fulfilment of those functions which are natural to it. Intellectual education, which is not education at all, is the basis of our present critical position. It has, so to speak, insisted on each cell becoming conscious. The result has been to make society hyper-aesthetic. Those elements which were satisfying themselves and supporting the total organism have been forced to suffer; they have been rendered conscious of their apparent inferiority to other elements. So, what between artificial anguish and false ambition for impossible attainments, they have become intensely painful to themselves and unable to perform their proper function; to their own ruin and that of the state."[136]

Adults in the Age of the Child seem to retain the childish view of fairness and equality as even-steven. But as the Austrian economist and "last knight of liberalism" Ludwig von Mises explains, "equality is a term that properly relates to mathematics but not to social science. Human beings are unequal in their endowments, opportunities, and will to achieve. Unequal does not mean inferior or superior; it merely means different. Differences are the very source of the division of labour," and as in nature, so too "within a

---

[133] *Confessions, loc. cit. Cf.* also *Liber DCCCXI,* Sec. IX: "The physical tests should be severe, and weaklings should be killed out rather than artificially preserved. The same remark applies to intellectual tests. But such tests should be as wide as possible. I was an absolute duffer at school in all forms of athletics and games, because I despised them. I held, and still hold, numerous mountaineering world's records. Similarly, examinations fail to test intelligence. Cecil Rhodes refused to employ any man with a University degree. That such degrees lead to honour in England is a sign of England's decay, though even in England they are usually the stepping-stones to clerical idleness or pedagogic slavery."
[134] Balk, *op. cit.*
[135] *Confessions, loc. cit.*
[136] *Ibid.*

market setting, lead not to conflict but cooperation. While differences should be celebrated, property owners have every right to treat people unequally because it is owners that bear responsibility. Legislators, however, should not have any concern for bringing about equality of result or opportunity, either between individuals or groups of individuals classified according to any criterion."[137] In short, fairness lay in equal shares for equals and unequal shares for unequals—it is not inequality among inherently unequal human beings that should concern them, but disproportionality along the ratios set through natural and market processes.

As Crowley writes, "The ploughman deserts his furrow to lose himself, and with himself the essence of his race, in the maw of the city. He has been tempted, by false education and visions of a phantom happiness, to violate the true law of his being. . . . More subtle error is to be seen in the class struggle. The Sisyphus-stone of the labour question has been poised by those radical misinterpretations of the problem of well-being, which consist in supposing that the possession of an automobile is the *summum bonum*. Craftsmanship is dead. The technical perfection, combined with the inventive genius, of the artisan, is no longer the pride and happiness of every village. The modern workman hides, beneath the rags of socialism and democracy, incurable indolent ulcers. Colonization once more is everywhere in a critical condition. In some cases, both the ruling and the subject nation are staggering beneath the weight of veritable crosses, because neither understands how to arrange their interrelation in such a way as to secure, for both equally, the maximum possibilities of their natural growth."[138]

"Our wretched generation, bleeding from a thousand wounds, its nerves in rags from its blind excesses and misapprehensions, cannot escape from the Law. Whether we like it or not, the Law of Thelema is manifestly everywhere at work. It is a blind Sphinx which will devour us, unless we can read its riddle, harness it to our chariot, and drive it triumphant into Thebes. Let those who constitute the intellectual and executive corps of pioneers of humanity be the first to enroll themselves in the army of the colleagues of the Master Therion, a master designated by no alien authority but by a power against which no revolt has ever been successful: the power of logic. The paramount question is: how to teach man to act in accordance with the facts of Nature? He must cease to try to ignore or deny them in the interest of prejudice, to transcend them by fantastic idealism based on falsehood or fatuity; just as an architect must never misunderstand, miscalculate, or misapply, the law of strains and stresses. The Law has been proclaimed. It is for us to interpret and to establish it."[139]

In *The Gospel According to St. Bernard Shaw*, Crowley points out that, "The parasites of whom he complains usually spring from the Plutocracy; and the remedy is not to make it impossible for a man like Lord Dunsany to

---

[137] Mises 1951, 292.
[138] *The Method of Thelema*.
[139] *Ibid*.

give up his whole time to his art, but to re-establish in the aristocracy the standard of honour and worthy ambition.... The root of the trouble is the standardization of the common good or wealth, in the minds of the vulgar. This illusion is produced principally by the efforts of the cheap press, which works always on the assumption that the possession of purchaseable treasures is the only good desirable by men. Thus the poor have been taught to envy the bilious and atrabilious millionaire, instead of the artist, the saint and the athlete. The cure for the whole misery of poverty is the development of the appreciation of those things that are really worth while."[140]

For centuries, many economists, including to some degree even Adam Smith, believed that the value of a good depended on the cost of producing it. Specifically, the labour theory of value argued that a good's value derived from the amount of work that went into making it. For modern economists, however, the labour theory of value holds about the same validity as the geocentric model does for astronomers. The reason the theory remains the implicit explanation of value outside economics is because many other disciplines rely for their views on the theory's most famous adherent: Karl Marx. His argument that capitalism exploited workers depended on the view that labour was the source of all value and that the profits of capitalists were therefore stolen from the workers. The problem for Marx and others who accepted this theory was that there are so many seemingly obvious objections to it that they had to construct complex explanations to account for them. What about the value of land and other natural resources? What about great works of art that were produced with a relatively small amount of labour but sold for extremely high prices? What about the different amounts of time required to produce the same good due to the varying skill levels of different individuals?

Several economists at the time realized that the old explanation was precisely backwards, in particular, Carl Menger, whose *Principles of Economics* (1871) not only offered a new explanation for the nature of economic value, but founded the Austrian school of economics in the process. What Menger and others argued was that value is subjective: nothing possesses intrinsic value as such, only a human mind attributes value to things. The value of a good is not determined by the physical inputs like labour that helped create it, but the value only emerges from human perceptions of its usefulness for the particular ends that people have at a particular point in time. Value is not something objective and transcendent, instead a thing is valuable only because there is at least one human being who believes that the thing can help satisfy his or her subjective desire. The value of a thing is determined by the interdependence of supply and demand, the interaction of perceived cost and utility: rather than the high market value of a well-prepared meal being result of the value of the gourmet chef's labour, the chef's labour is valuable because he is able to produce dishes that the dining public finds especially tasty or desirable.

---

[140] *Liber 888, loc. cit.*

"Prior to capitalism, the way people amassed great wealth was by looting, plundering, and enslaving their fellow man. With the rise of capitalism, it became possible to amass great wealth by serving and pleasing one's fellow man. Capitalists seek to discover what people want and then produce and market it as efficiently as possible."[141] Crowley's essay *The Method of Thelema* was "primarily addressed to bankers, captains of industry, and, generally speaking, to all those whose natural office it is to manipulate social forces. It is the first condition of their existence, to say nothing of their security and prosperity, that they should direct the stream of commerce, the life-blood of the world. They are bound to understand the Law of Thelema, at least subconsciously, for they do not ship Brazil nuts to Brazil, or try to import corn from the Baltoro Glacier. Their only failure has been to see that the same principles of common sense which prevent them from perpetrating such absurdities can be applied, with the assistance of trained experts, to every possible problem which confronts them in their daily work. No men know better the frightful waste of 'overhead' caused by unfitness in the staff, and similar errors. (I will not risk angering them by reminding them of idealistic legislation.)"[142]

"Such men are ready for the message of the Master Therion, for they rule the mainspring of the economic clock. They should be the first to devote themselves to the cause, to accept the idea of the Law of Thelema, and to come forward to organize the scientific investigation which must be undertaken in order to bring the great branches of modern science, from political economy to biology and psychology, to contribute their force to swell the irresistible river of human attainment."[143] Crowley was not one to sugar-coat things: "Achievement of high aims, which tends ultimately to the well-being, the prosperity of the republic, depends on the proportion of masters to servants. The stability of a building depends on the proportion of superstructure to foundations. The rule holds good in every department of Nature. There is an optimum for every case. If there is one barber for ten thousand men, most of them will remain unshorn; if there are five thousand barbers, most of them will be out of a job."[144]

"Apply this measure to society; there must be an optimum relation between industry and agriculture, between town and country. When the proper balance is not struck, the community must depend on outside help, importing what it lacks, exporting its surplus. This is an unnatural state of affairs; it results in [big] business, and therefore ultimately in war. That is, as soon as the stress set up by the conditions becomes insupportable. So long as 'business' is confined to luxuries, no great harm need result; but when interference with the flow of foreign trade threatens actual

---

[141] Williams 2015, xvii.
[142] As Mises (1998, 2) observes, earlier Utopians like Plato and St. Thomas More "did not search for the laws of social cooperation because they thought that man could organize society as he pleased. If social conditions did not fulfill the wishes of the reformers, if their Utopias proved unrealizable, the fault was seen in the moral failure of man. Social problems were considered ethical problems. What was needed in order to construct the ideal society, they thought, was good princes and virtuous citizens. With righteous men any Utopia might be realized."
[143] *The Method of Thelema*.
[144] *MWT*, Ch. LXXV.

necessities, the unit concerned realizes that it is in danger of strangulation. Consider England's food supply! Switzerland, Russia, China, the U.S.A. can laugh at U-boats. England must support a Navy, a wealth-consuming, not a wealth-producing, item in the Budget. Similar remarks apply to practically all Government Departments. The minimum of organization is desirable; all artificial doctrinaire multiplication of works which produce no wealth is waste; and for many reasons (some absurd, like 'social position') tend to create fresh unnecessary necessities. *Ad infinitum*, like the fleas in the epigram!"[145]

"When laws are reasonable in the eyes of the average man, he respects them, keeps them, does his best to maintain them; therefore a minute Police Force, with powers strictly limited, is adequate to deal with the almost negligibly small criminal class. A convention is laudable when it is convenient. When laws are unjust, monstrous, ridiculous, that same average man, will he, nill he, becomes a criminal; and the law requires a Tcheka or a Gestapo with dictatorial powers and no safeguards to maintain the farce. Also, corruption becomes normal in official circles; and is excused."[146] The argument and observation of the Austrian economist F. A. Hayek was that the more complex the society the less one person or any group of people, no matter how well trained in the art of political paternalism, is capable of knowing enough to manage and direct the affairs of the society better than leaving such matters to the individuals themselves as they see and understand it best in their own particular circumstances.

> There is no need to insist on the interior crises of mankind, his crises of conscience. These may conceivably be resolved by a definite education; on one side, the practices of all oriental sages, so ill-understood owing to the confusion of their science with the religions of their country; on the other, by the rituals vulgarly called magical, equally fallen into contempt, although of a very real efficacy, on account of the gross misunderstanding of their real nature which has always obscured them. By such means it may prove possible to create (rather, to develop), in man, a faculty superior to reason; immune from intellectual criticism. Such a faculty would permit man—does, indeed, already permit certain men—to contemplate the problem of the suffering and sorrow of life with a complete detachment and serenity, because it would no longer be protected by the superficiality and incompleteness of its data.
> But it is not of such internal crises, of such spiritual sickness, that one need speak at present. It is of more immediate and practical importance to discuss external crises, those which devastate political and social conditions.[147]

---

[145] *Ibid.*
[146] *Ibid.*
[147] *The Method of Thelema.*

Tao Te Ching, Chapter XVII, says: "The best of all rulers is but a shadowy presence to his subjects. Next comes the ruler they love and praise; Next comes one they fear; Next comes one with whom they take liberties. When there is not enough faith, there is a lack of good faith. Hesitant, he does not utter words lightly. When his task is accomplished and his work done The people all say, 'It happened to us naturally.'"[148] The Crowley "translation," published posthumously, reads: "In the Age of Gold, the people were not conscious of their rulers; in the Age of Silver, they loved them, with songs; in the Age of Brass, they feared them; in the Age of Iron, they despised them. As the rulers ((becoming self-conscious.)) lost confidence, so also did the people lose confidence in them. How hesitating did they seem, the Lords of the Age of Gold, speaking with deliberation, aware of the weight of their word! Thus they accomplished all things with success; and the people deemed their well-being to be the natural course of events."[149]

"The Yellow School of Magick possesses one perfect classic. The *Tao Teh King*."—"Unfortunately there is no translation at present published which is the work of an Initiate. All existing translations have been garbled by people who simply failed to understand the text. An approximately perfect rendering is indeed available, but so far it exists only in manuscript."[150] The *Tao Te Ching* is the most translated book in the world, maybe partly because it is so short, and many translations are in fact done by people like Crowley who do not even read Chinese. They just study other versions in languages they do read and compile their own based on them. You may readily recognize the first line from the *Tao Te Ching*: "The Tao that can be spoken is not true Tao." However, since Chinese is a pictographic written language and does not use a phonetic alphabet like Western languages, there is no way to literally translate Chinese characters. The original Chinese text of that famous first line in transliteration reads: *Dao ke dao, fei chang dao*. An approximation would be something along the lines of "Tao can Tao is not Tao"—and the entire book is like that!

Every translator brings to the task his own identity, which is shaped by the particular linguistic, cultural, and spiritual backgrounds from whence he hails. Thus, a translation is always at least as much a product of the translator's native traditions as of the foreign culture that he seeks to translate, and many readers will further have that native culture as their sole point of reference for interpreting the translated text. Thus, when we, for example, read Legge's translation of Confucius speaking about "virtue" and "piety," we interpret these words in the context of our own cultural tradition, with its specific understanding of these concepts. We might and should be enriched by what we read and learn, but we should not make the mistake of thinking that we are somehow partaking in pure, unadulterated Confucianism. In Crowley's opinion, "Taoism has as little to do with the *Tao Teh King* as the Catholic Church with the Gospel. The *Tao Teh King*

---

[148] Lau 1963, 21.
[149] *Liber CLVII*, Ch. XVII.
[150] *MWT*, Ch. VI.

inculcates conscious inaction, or rather unconscious inaction, with the object of minimizing the disorder of the world."[151]

"Like every other physiological process, consciousness of it implies disorder or disease.... We assume, for example, that the unconscious is the torpid; and yet nothing is more certain than that bodily organs which are functioning well do so in silence. The best sleep is dreamless. Even in the case of games of skill our very best strokes are followed by the thought, 'I don't know how I did it'; and we cannot repeat those strokes at will. The moment we begin to think consciously about a stroke we get 'nervous,' and are lost."[152] The first person to work out the idea of spontaneous order was the Taoist philosopher Chuang-tzŭ (369–286 BCE), whose writings are required reading for every person wishing to become a Probationer of the A∴A∴. This "Master Chuang" lived during the Warring States period which saw the summit of Chinese philosophy; he rejected the authoritarianism of Confucianism, asserting that there "has been such a thing as letting mankind alone; there has never been such a thing as governing mankind [with success]." He wrote that "good order results spontaneously when things are let alone," a concept elaborated by the famous French anarchist Proudhon in the 19th century.[153]

The term *Te*, "virtue" or "integrity," is generally used to refer to the proper adherence to *Tao*, the active cultivation of the way. Historically, the interpretation of Te differed significantly between Taoists and Confucians: since Confucianism is largely a moral system emphasizing the value of righteousness, humaneness, and filial piety, it saw Te in terms of obedience to strictly defined and codified social rules; Taoism had a broader and more metaphysical view of the relationship between humanity and the universe, deeming social rules to be at best a mere reflection of the natural and spontaneous interactions between people, and at worst a calcified structure that impeded naturalness and only created interpersonal conflict. This led to some philosophical and political rivalry between Taoists and Confucians, with several sections of the works attributed to Chuang-tzŭ being dedicated to critiquing the failures of Confucianism. However, in contrast to the esotericism usually found in Eastern religions, the Tao is not transcendent to the self, but rather the self steeped in Tao is the self grounded in its natural place within the universe—a person dwelling within the Tao excels in themselves and their activities.[154]

> Genius—or Initiation, which implies the liberation and development of the genius latent in us all (is not one of names of the "Holy Guardian Angel" the Genius?)—is practically the monopoly of the "crazy adventurer," as the official mind will most certainly rate him. Then why do not the Masters oppose all forms of organization tooth-and-nail?

---

[151] *Ibid.*
[152] *Book 4*, Part I, Preliminary Remarks.
[153] M. N. Rothbard, "The Concept of the Role of Intellectuals in Social Change Toward Laissez Faire," *Journal of Libertarian Studies* IX(2), Fall 1990, 43–67.
[154] Fowler 2005.

It depends, surely, on the stage which a society has reached on its fall to the servile state. Civilization of course, implies organization up to a certain point. The freedom of any function is built upon system; and so long as Law and Order make it easier for a man to do his True Will, they are admirable. It is when system is adored for its own sake, or as a means of endowing mediocrities with power as such, that the "critical temperature" is attained.

It so happens that I write this on the eve of a General Election in England; and it seems to me that whichever wins, England loses: The Socialists openly proclaim that they mean to run the country on the lines of a convict prison; but the Tories, for all their fine talk, would be helpless against the Banks and the Trusts to whom they must look for support.

Still, perhaps with a little help from Hashish, one can imagine a Merchant Prince or a Banker being intelligent, or even, in a weak moment, human; and this is not the case with officials. The standard, moreover, of education and Good Manners, low as it is, is less low in Tory circles.

As I think that totalitarian methods are already on the way to extinguish the last spark of manly independence—that is, in self-styled civilized countries—it seems to me that we all should regard with shrewd suspicion any plans for "perfecting" social conditions. The extreme horror is the formula of the gregarious type of insect. Inherent in the premises is the impossibility of advance.[155]

The instinct to rebel is just as important as the sex instinct for the survival of the species, for without rebellion, nothing new would ever arise. "Society" hates the price of its own progress; its "representatives" claim to want the benefits of the sanctioned products of the "innovators" without the risk of the unsanctioned products of the "criminals." Almost all societies have mechanism to harness and take advantage of certain kinds of rebels: thinkers, inventors, warriors, preachers, shamans. Physically active people are "encouraged" to become soldiers, police officers, and professional athletes; mystically inclined people become priests or monks; artistically or scientifically creative people are "patronized." The rebels are thus made feel dependent on the social structure, and dependence breeds fear, and fear is control. Of course, some societies, past and present—not to mention the grey futures of George Orwell's *1984* and Ayn Rand's *Anthem*—have recognized that any attempt to harness a person of independent mind is inherently dangerous, and rather than risk change and their inevitable destruction, have opted for total stagnation.[156]

Crowley lists "the conditions of progress" thus: "Number One is obviously Irregularity, Eccentricity, Disorder, the Revolutionary Spirit,

---

[155] *MWT*, Ch. LXXV.
[156] Hyatt 2000. *Cf.* also *The Book of Thoth*, Part II, Atu IV: "...for the ram, by nature, is a wild and courageous animal, lonely in lonely places, whereas when tamed and made to lie down in green pastures, nothing is left but the docile, cowardly, gregarious and succulent beast. This is the theory of government."

Experiment. I have no patience whatever with Utopia-mongers. Biology simply shouts at us that the happy contented community, everyone with his own (often highly specialized) job, nobody in need, nobody in danger, is necessarily stagnant. Termites and other ants, bees, beavers; these and many another have produced perfect systems. What is the first characteristic? Stupidity. 'Where there is no vision, the people shall perish.' What is the Fighter Termite to do, after he has been blocked out of his home? None of these communities possess any resource at all against any unforeseen unfavourable change of circumstance. (We look rather like that just now at the end of 1944 e.v.) Nor does anyone of them show any achievement; having got to the end of their biological tether, they stay out, without an aim, an idea, an effort. . . . Now, obviously, the robot education, robot textbooks stuffed in by robot teachers, will have done wonders with the help of the bovine well-being to produce a race of robot boys."[157]

"All independence, all imagination, all spirit of Adventure, will have been ground down and rolled out smooth by this ghastly engine. But—Nature is not so easily beaten; a few boys and girls will somehow escape, and either by instinct or by observation, have the sense to keep secret. Now whatever their own peculiar genius may select as their line, they will realise that nothing is possible in any way while the accursed system stands. Their first duty is Revolt. And presently some one will come along with the wit and the will and the weapon, and blow the whole most damnable bag of tricks sky-high. We had better busy ourselves about this while it is still possible to get back to freedom without universal bloodshed."[158] As Robert A. Heinlein declared, "You can have Peace, or you can have Freedom. Don't ever count on having both at the same time."[159] Without the capacity to defend our rights, we have no real liberty. The irony is, if you are willing to kill your assailant, you probably won't have to. Violent crime is practicable only when its targets are cowards. A mark who fights back renders the whole business impractical. It's true that one may suffer for fighting back, but if one does not fight back, one will certainly suffer.

> You ask me if I think this change can be made without bloodshed.
> No. The obscure autocrats of Diplomacy and Big Business are infinitely stupid and short-sighted; they cannot see an inch beyond their too often stigmatically shapen proboscis, except where the profit of the next financial year is concerned. They live in perpetual panic, and shy at their own shadows. The accordingly attack even the most innocuous windmills in suicidal charges.
> Yes: *Bella, horrida bella,*
> *Et Thybrim multo spumantem sanguine cerno.*[160]
> So, whichever way you vote, you are asking for trouble, or would do, if the vote had any meaning. The result of any election, or for the matter

---

[157] *MWT*, Ch. LXXIX.
[158] *Ibid.*
[159] Heinlein 1988, 244.
[160] Verg. *A.* 6.86–7.

of that any revolution, is an almost wholly insignificant component of those stupendous and inscrutable Magical Forces which determine the destinies of the planet.[161]

We are not all supposed to get along; in fact, paraphrasing Dante, "The hottest places in hell are reserved for those who, in times of great moral crisis, maintain their neutrality." However, nor should we demonize our enemies: "To be good is to be in harmony with one's self. Discord is to be forced to be in harmony with others."[162] Peace means the absence of war, that people are not fighting one another, but it does not mean that they are not likely to start fighting at any moment. A situation where there is no probability of conflict, where people do not have to prepare for it or think about it, where there is no need nor inclination to resort to violence, is and will always be a mere fantasy—sooner or later, one has to take sides, if one is to remain human. And once an attack begins, there is no "non-violent" option: the only question is whether it will be all aggressive violence, or whether defensive force will be used to try and stop the attacker. All too many people like to spin their cowardice as if it were some moral virtue, pretending to be "against violence."

"Do what thou wilt! be this our Slogan of Battle in every Act; for every Act is Conflict. There Victory leapeth shining before us; for who may thwart true Will, which is the Order of Nature Herself? '...thou hast no right but to do thy will. Do that, and no other shall say nay.' For if that Will be true, its Fulfilment is of a Surety as Daylight following Sunrise. It is as certain as the Operation of any other Law of Nature; it is Destiny. Then, if that Will be obscured, if thou turn from it to Wills diseased or perverse, how canst thou hope? Fool! Even thy Turns and Twists are in the Path to thine appointed End. But thou art not sprung of a Slave's Loins; thou standest firm and straight; thou dost thy Will; and thou are Chosen, nay, for this Work wast thou begotten in a Magick Bed, that thou shouldst make Man free."[163] As Crowley points out, "Life is not a Sunday School, but a battlefield; and the conflict between evolution and ethics has not yet been wholly decided in favour of the latter. Some of us may even think that it can never be. For the progress which made ethics possible was the result of the variations brought about by evolution, and the result of ethics in checking the operations of evolution is in some ways to discourage variation, and so to cause the stagnation of society."[164]

"A secure social order inevitably favours mediocrity; and it further causes the atrophy of the manly virtues. War has to be artificially replaced by sport, which is a very poor substitute, just as religion lost its excitement and fascination when human sacrifice was replaced by symbolic offerings. However, sport is better than nothing; and when society is threatened, it is the sportsman (if any one) who saves it. The Battle of Waterloo was won on the playing fields of Eton; and the people who rushed to the colours in the

---

[161] *MWT*, Ch. LXXV.
[162] Wilde 1997, 56.
[163] *Liber Aleph*, "Quare filium creavit: Ut fiat libertas."
[164] *Liber 888*, "The Dream of Distribution According to Merit."

war now raging were the cricketers and golfers and footballers—the amateurs, not the professionals. The people whose minds were full of money and trade and beer had to be conscripted."[165] The notion that society could even be organized without war, or the possibility or probability of war happening, was only arose with the 18th-century Enlightenment, and it took quite a long time for it to become the accepted view of Western societies.[166] Given that the future is inherently unknowable, the task and role of economic competition is to provide an institutional setting in which individuals have both the incentive and the opportunity to try and discover, in peaceful rivalry with each other, who is able to make the new, better, or less expensive product or service that others are willing to purchase.

"All right, Master, you win! Now give us your own idea of Utopia."

An Utopia to end Utopias? Very good, so I will. Education, to begin with; well, you've had all that in another letter. The main thing to remember is that I want every individual taught as such, according to his own special qualities. Then, teach them both sides of every question: history, for example, as the play of economic forces, also, as due to the intervention of Divine Providence, or of "Sports" of genius: and so for the rest. Train them to doubt—and to dare!

Then, somehow, as large a number of the most promising rebels should be selected to lead a life of luxury and leisure. Let every country, by dint of honouring its old traditions, be as different as possible from every other. Restore the "Grand tour," or rather, the roving Englishman of the Nineteenth Century. Entrust them with the secrets of discipline, of authority, or power. Hardship and danger in full measure: and responsibility.[167]

A great deal of such material will be as disgustingly wasted as it has been in the past; and there will be much abuse of privilege. But this must be allowed and allowed for; no very great harm will result, as the weak and vicious will weed themselves out.

The pure gold will repay us ten thousandfold. You ask examples? With us, the Elizabethan and the Victorian periods stand out. What is most wanted is opportunity and reward. Under Victoria there was some—taste the late Samuel Smiles Esquire, D.D. (wasn't he?)—but not enough, and Industrialism, the mother and nurse of Socialism, was destroying the soul of the people.[168]

---

[165] *Ibid.*
[166] Balk 2012.
[167] *Cf.* also *Confessions*, Ch. 63: "There is a peculiar relation between the best bourgeois of this type and the wandering *gentilhomme*, who is seeking his fortune in one way or another and requires a *pied à terre*. It is one which implies great mutual respect and affection, and, alas, the qualities which make such relations possible are becoming very rare in the world. Despite all its drawbacks, there was never a better social system than the feudal, so far as it derived from the patriarchal. In getting rid of its abuses, we have also got rid of the noblest springs of action and the most congenial code of manners."
[168] *MWT*, Ch. LXXIX.

"I have been asking Ethyl about Political Wisdom. I find that Do what thou wilt is given by NE SUTOR ULTRA CREPIDAM[169] in a very humble but important way. I got, too, an idea of what I am fighting—and ready to die—for. Parallel: battle of Ivry (was it?) where Protestant defeat would have meant the invasion of France by a swarm of Monks, spies, inquisitionists, etc. Now I want to protect children—who should be Crowned and Conquering—from Parents, Schoolmarms, Doctors, Tax gatherers, Lawyers, Parsons, Politicians, etc. (It's hard to say what one means on such a big scale especially as this war seems to have no precedent. Of course there must be tuition, family discipline, hygiene, and so on: but at present it is the Official (or one acting as such) who must be squelched. The more I think, the more my vision clouds over, with thoughts. I'm certainly not an anarchist, for the family is the smallest and so vilest unit of government: nor a Socialist, for the State is the largest and so the least human unit. I suppose then, that—with Ethyl as without—I want a Patriarchal-Feudal system run by initiated Kings. I think, though, that (in applying the Law of Thelema to all cases) necessity will indicate the form of government required."[170]

"While there exists the burgess, the hunting man, or any man with ideals less than Shelley's and self-discipline less than Loyola's—in short, any man who falls far short of MYSELF—I am against Anarchy, and for Feudalism. Every 'emancipator' has enslaved the free." In his own words, Crowley does not "agree even with the aim of the Anarchists, since, although Anarchists themselves need no restraint, not daring to drink cocoa, lest their animal passions should be aroused (as Olivia Haddon assures my favourite Chela), yet policemen, unless most severely repressed, would be dangerous wild beasts. The last bitter sentence is terribly true; the personal liberty of the Russian is immensely greater than that of the Englishman. The latest Radical devices for securing freedom have turned nine out of ten Englishmen into Slaves, obliged to report their movements to the government like so many ticket-of-leave men. The only solution of the Social Problem is the creation of a class with the true patriarchal feeling, and the manners and obligations of chivalry."[171]

"There is no need for the fraud of divine right or the cant of democracy. The right of the ruler to rule depends solely upon the scientific proof of his fitness to do so, and this proof is capable of confirmation by the evidence of the experience that his measures really result in enabling each individual in his jurisdiction to fulfil his own peculiar function as freely as possible."[172] As

---

[169] "Let the shoemaker stick to his last."
[170] Diary entry, 29 May 1923, 2:40 a.m. We can infer from the context and from the other similar quotations that Crowley is not advocating a return to the Osirian *patria potestas*, but rather the literal definition of Patriarchy: the rule by fathers for the benefit of children.
[171] *The Book of Lies*, Ch. 8. Cf. also *Liber CLXI*: "It has always been admitted that the ideal form of government is that of a 'benevolent despot,' and despotisms have only fallen because it is impossible in practice to assure the goodwill of those in power. The rules of chivalry, and those of Bushido in the East, gave the best chance to develop rulers of the desired type. Chivalry failed principally because it was confronted with new problems; to-day we know perfectly what those problems were, and are able to solve them."
[172] *Confessions*, Ch. 87.

Mark Skousen argues, "Taxation is the price we pay for *failing to build* a civilized society. The higher the tax level, the greater the failure. A centrally planned totalitarian state represents a complete defeat for the civilized world, while a totally voluntary society represents its ultimate success."[173] In 1935, when Crowley, who had lived off his wits, his name, his sizeable inheritance, and nearly boundless credit for years, entered the UK Bankruptcy Court, the assistant official receiver asked "What income tax had the plaintiff returned?" To which Crowley replied: "None. I have never had any income-tax papers." Crowley attributed his insolvency to "the boycott of his work and writings in this country."[174]

"There is only one hope of uniting the people under intelligent leadership; because there is only one thing in which everyone really believes. That is, believes in such a way that he automatically bases every action of his daily life on its principles. (This is true of practically all men, whatever their race, caste, or creed.) This universally accepted basis of conduct is Science. . . . The problem of Government is therefore to find a scientific formula with an ethical implication. This formula must be rigidly applicable to all sane men soever without reference to the individual qualities of any one of them. . . . The formula is given by the Law of Thelema. 'Do what thou wilt shall be the whole of the Law.' This injunction, in one sense infinitely elastic, since it does not specify any particular goal of will as desirable, is yet infinitely rigid, in that it binds every man to follow out exactly the purpose for which he is fitted by heredity, environment, experience, and self-development. The formula is thus also biologically indefeasible, as well as adequate, ethically to every individual, and politically to the State."[175]

"In the New Æon, each man will be a king, and his relation to the state will be determined solely by considerations of what is most to his advantage. The worker will support a strong government as his best protection from foreign aggression and seditious disturbance instead of thinking it tyrannical. Everyone, whatever his ambition, will feel that he can rely on the whole force of the state to assist him; for all ambitions alike will be respected by all, with the single proviso that they shall not tend to restrict the equal right of the rest. No man will be ashamed of himself, and so be forced into concealment and hypocrisy while at the same time having his idea distorted into monstrous shapes of disease by the pressure of public opinion."[176] At the same time, Lévi's Theory of the Will states that, "As there is no liberty for man but in the order which results from the true and the good, one may say that the conquest of liberty is the great work of the human soul. Man, by freeing himself from his evil passions and their slavery, creates himself, as it were, a second time. Nature made him living and suffering; he makes himself happy and immortal; he thus becomes the

---

[173] "Persuasion vs. Force," *Liberty*, September 1991. Emphasis added.
[174] Proceedings under the Bankruptcy Act, 1914, B 9/1250.
[175] *The Scientific Solution.*
[176] *Confessions, loc. cit.*

representative of divinity upon earth, and (relatively) exercises its almighty power."[177]

"The Serpent which is coiled about the Crown means many things, or, rather, one thing in many ways. It is the symbol of royalty and of initiation, for the Magician is anointed King and Priest."[178] Despite all the rhetoric from today's liberals about "democracy," "equality," "diversity," and "social justice," theirs is a political ideology of authoritarianism, élitism, patronage, and hubris dominated by the idea of remaking human beings, human relationships, and the structure and order of human society into a reflection of how they think people should live, work, behave, and associate with each other. The modern "liberal," or progressive, represents the forces of contemporary political, economic, and cultural "soft tyranny"—at least in comparison to the brutal and murderous totalitarian régimes of the 20th century—against which the classical liberals, or "libertarians,"[179] continue their relentless battle in the cause of freedom. "All the totalitarian schemes add up to the same in the end, and the approach is so insidious, the arguments so subtle and irrefutable, the advantages so obvious, that the danger is very real, very imminent, very difficult to bring home to the average citizen, who sees only the immediate gain, and is hoodwinked as to the price that must be paid for it."[180]

"Lift yourselves up, my brothers and sisters of the earth! Put beneath your feet all fears, all qualms, all hesitancies! Lift yourselves up! Come forth, free and joyous, by night and day, to do your will; for 'There is no law beyond Do what thou wilt.' Lift yourselves up! Walk forth with us in Light and Life and Love and Liberty, taking our pleasure as Kings and Queens in Heaven and on Earth."[181] Crowley bids us to "Remember that Magick includes all acts soever. Anything may serve as a Magical weapon. To impose one's Will on a nation, for instance, one's talisman may be a newspaper, one's Triangle a church, or one's Circle a club. To win a woman, one's Pantacle may be a necklace; to discover a treasure, one's Wand may be a dramatist's pen, or one's incantation a popular song."[182] His hope was that the publication of *Liber AL* and its Comment "will establish the kingdom of the Crowned and Conquering Child over the whole earth, and all men shall bow to the Law, which is 'love under will'."[183]

---

[177] *The Key of the Mysteries, loc. cit.*
[178] *Book 4*, Part II, Ch. XI.
[179] This is to whom the term *liberal* (from the Latin *liberalis*, "befitting a free man") referred in Crowley's day, and still does in much of Europe.
[180] Letter to Karl Germer, 8 March 1945.
[181] *Liber DCCCXXXVII*, Sec. III.
[182] *MITAP*, Ch. XIV. *Cf.* also *MWT*, Ch. VIII: "It has been said by some that the Law of Thelema appeals only to the élite of humanity. No doubt here is this much in that assertion, that only the highest can take full advantage of the extraordinary opportunities which it offers. At the same time, 'the Law is for all.' Each in his degree, every man may learn to realise the nature of his own being, and to develop it in freedom. It is by this means that the White School of Magick can justify its past, redeem its present, and assure its future, by guaranteeing to every human being a life of Liberty and of Love."
[183] *Ibid.*

APPENDICES

LIBER AL VEL LEGIS
The Book of the Law

CHAPTER I.

Had! The manifestation of Nuit.

2 The unveiling of the company of heaven.

3 Every man and every woman is a star.

4 Every number is infinite; there is no difference.

5 Help me, o warrior lord of Thebes, in my unveiling before the Children of men!

6 Be thou Hadit, my secret centre, my heart & my tongue!

7 Behold! it is revealed by Aiwass the minister of Hoor-paar-kraat.

8 The Khabs is in the Khu, not the Khu in the Khabs.

9 Worship then the Khabs, and behold my light shed over you!

10 ¶ Let my servants be few & secret: they shall rule the many & the known.

11 These are fools that men adore; both their Gods & their men are fools.

12 Come forth, o children, under the stars, & take your fill of love!

13 I am above you and in you. My ecstasy is in yours. My joy is to see your joy.

14 *Above, the gemmèd azure is*
   The naked splendour of Nuit;
She bends in ecstasy to kiss
   The secret ardours of Hadit.
The wingèd globe, the starry blue,
   Are mine, O Ankh-af-na-khonsu!

15 Now ye shall know that the chosen priest & apostle of infinite space is the prince-priest the Beast; and in ¶ his woman called the Scarlet Woman is all power given. They shall gather my children into their fold: they shall bring the glory of the stars into the hearts of men.

16 For he is ever a sun, and she a moon. But to him is the winged secret flame, and to her the stooping starlight.

17 But ye are not so chosen.

18 Burn upon their brows, o splendrous serpent!

19 O azure-lidded woman, bend upon them!

20 The key of the rituals is in the secret word which I have given unto him.

21 ¶ With the God & the Adorer I am nothing: they do not see me. They are as upon the earth; I am Heaven, and there is no other God than me, and my lord Hadit.

22 Now, therefore, I am known to ye by my name Nuit, and to him by a secret name which I will give him when at last he knoweth me. Since I am Infinite Space, and the Infinite Stars thereof, do ye also thus. Bind nothing! Let there be no difference made among you between any one thing & any ¶ other thing; for thereby there cometh hurt.

23 But whoso availeth in this, let him be the chief of all!

24 I am Nuit, and my word is six and fifty.

25 Divide, add, multiply, and understand.

26 Then saith the prophet and slave of the beauteous one: Who am I, and what shall be the sign? So she

answered him, bending down, a lambent flame of blue, all-touching, all penetrant, her lovely hands upon the black earth, & her lithe body arched for love, and her soft feet not hurting the ¶ little flowers: Thou knowest! And the sign shall be my ecstasy, the consciousness of the continuity of existence, the omnipresence of my body.

27 Then the priest answered & said unto the Queen of Space, kissing her lovely brows, and the dew of her light bathing his whole body in a sweet-smelling perfume of sweat: O Nuit, continuous one of Heaven, let it ¶ be ever thus; that men speak not of Thee as One but as None; and let them speak not of thee at all, since thou art continuous!

28 None, breathed the light, faint & faery, of the stars, and two.

29 For I am divided for love's sake, for the chance of union.

30 This is the creation of the world, that the pain of division is as nothing, and the joy of dissolution all.

31 For these fools of men and their ¶ woes care not thou at all! They feel little; what is, is balanced by weak joys; but ye are my chosen ones.

32 Obey my prophet! follow out the ordeals of my knowledge! seek me only! Then the joys of my love will redeem ye from all pain. This is so: I swear it by the vault of my body; by my sacred heart and tongue; by all I can give, by all I desire of ye all.

33 Then the priest fell into a deep trance or ¶ swoon, & said unto the Queen of Heaven; Write unto us the ordeals; write unto us the rituals; write unto us the law!

34 But she said: the ordeals I write not: the rituals shall be half known and half concealed: the Law is for all.

35 This that thou writest is the threefold book of Law.

36 My scribe Ankh-af-na-khonsu, the priest of the princes, shall not in one letter change this book; but lest there be folly, he shall comment thereupon by the wisdom of Ra-Hoor-Khu-it.

37 ¶ Also the mantras and spells; the obeah and the wanga; the work of the wand and the work of the sword; these he shall learn and teach.

38 He must teach; but he may make severe the ordeals.

39 The word of the Law is Θελημα.

40 Who calls us Thelemites will do no wrong, if he look but close into the word. For there are therein Three Grades, the Hermit, and the Lover, and the man of Earth. Do what thou wilt ¶ shall be the whole of the Law.

41 The word of Sin is Restriction. O man! refuse not thy wife, if she will! O lover, if thou wilt, depart! There is no bond that can unite the divided but love: all else is a curse. Accurséd! Accurséd be it to the æons! Hell.

42 Let it be that state of manyhood bound and loathing. So with thy all; thou hast no right but to do thy will.

43 Do that, and no other shall say nay.

44 For pure will, unassuaged of purpose, ¶ delivered from the lust of result, is every way perfect.

45 The Perfect and the Perfect are one Perfect and not two; nay, are none!

46 Nothing is a secret key of this law. Sixty-one the Jews call it; I call it eight, eighty, four hundred & eighteen.

47 But they have the half: unite by thine art so that all disappear.

48 My prophet is a fool with his one, one, one; are not they the Ox, and none by the Book?

49 ¶ Abrogate are all rituals, all ordeals, all words and signs.

Ra-Hoor-Khuit hath taken his seat in the East at the Equinox of the Gods; and let Asar be with Isa, who also are one. But they are not of me. Let Asar be the adorant, Isa the sufferer; Hoor in his secret name and splendour is the Lord initiating.

50 There is a word to say about the Hierophantic task. Behold! there are three ordeals in one, and it may be given in three ways. The gross must pass through fire; let the ¶ fine be tried in intellect, and the lofty chosen ones in the highest. Thus ye have star & star, system & system; let not one know well the other!

51 There are four gates to one palace; the floor of that palace is of silver and gold; lapis lazuli & jasper are there; and all rare scents; jasmine & rose, and the emblems of death. Let him enter in turn or at once the four gates; let him stand on the floor of the palace. Will he not sink? Amn. Ho! warrior, if thy servant sink? But there are means ¶ and means. Be goodly therefore: dress ye all in fine apparel; eat rich foods and drink sweet wines and wines that foam! Also, take your fill and will of love as ye will, when, where and with whom ye will! But always unto me.

52 If this be not aright; if ye confound the space-marks, saying: They are one; or saying, They are many; if the ritual be not ever unto me: then expect the direful judgments of Ra Hoor Khuit!

53 This shall regenerate the world, the little ¶ world my sister, my heart & my tongue, unto whom I send this kiss. Also, o scribe and prophet, though thou be of the princes, it shall not assuage thee nor absolve thee. But ecstasy be thine and joy of earth: ever To me! To me!

54 Change not as much as the style of a letter; for behold! thou, o prophet, shalt not behold all these mysteries hidden therein.

55 The child of thy bowels, he shall behold them.

56 Expect him not from the East, nor from ¶ the West; for from no expected house cometh that child. Aum! All words are sacred and all prophets true; save only that they understand a little; solve the first half of the equation, leave the second unattacked. But thou hast all in the clear light, and some, though not all, in the dark.

57 Invoke me under my stars! Love is the law, love under will. Nor let the fools mistake love; for there are love and love. There is the dove, and there is the serpent. Choose ye well! He, my prophet, hath ¶ chosen, knowing the law of the fortress, and the great mystery of the House of God.

All these old letters of my Book are aright; but צ is not the Star. This also is secret: my prophet shall reveal it to the wise.

58 I give unimaginable joys on earth: certainty, not faith, while in life, upon death; peace unutterable, rest, ecstasy; nor do I demand aught in sacrifice.

59 My incense is of resinous woods & gums; and there is no blood therein: because of my hair the trees of Eternity.

60 ¶ My number is 11, as all their numbers who are of us. The Five Pointed Star, with a Circle in the Middle, & the circle is Red. My colour is black to the blind, but the blue & gold are seen of the seeing. Also I have a secret glory for them that love me.

61 But to love me is better than all things: if under the night-stars in the desert thou presently burnest mine incense before me, invoking me with

a pure heart, and the Serpent flame therein, thou shalt come a little to lie in my bosom. For one kiss wilt thou then be willing to give all; ¶ but whoso gives one particle of dust shall lose all in that hour. Ye shall gather goods and store of women and spices; ye shall wear rich jewels; ye shall exceed the nations of the earth in splendour & pride; but always in the love of me, and so shall ye come to my joy. I charge you earnestly to come before me in a single robe, and covered with a rich headdress. I love you! I yearn to you! Pale or purple, veiled or voluptuous, I who am all pleasure and purple, ¶ and drunkenness of the innermost sense, desire you. Put on the wings, and arouse the coiled splendour within you: come unto me!

62 At all my meetings with you shall the priestess say—and her eyes shall burn with desire as she stands bare and rejoicing in my secret temple—To me! To me! calling forth the flame of the hearts of all in her love-chant.

63 Sing the rapturous love-song unto me! Burn to me perfumes! Wear to me jewels! Drink to me, for I love you! I love you!

64 ¶ I am the blue-lidded daughter of Sunset; I am the naked brilliance of the voluptuous night-sky.

65 To me! To me!

66 The Manifestation of Nuit is at an end.

CHAPTER II.

Nu! the hiding of Hadit.

2 Come! all ye, and learn the secret that hath not yet been revealed. I, Hadit, am the complement of Nu, my bride. I am not extended, and Khabs is the name of my House.

3 In the sphere I am everywhere the centre, as she, the circumference, is nowhere found.

4 Yet she shall be known & I never.

5 Behold! the rituals of the old time are black. Let the evil ones be cast away; let the good ones be purged by the prophet! Then shall this Knowledge go aright.

6 I am the flame that burns in every heart of man, and in the core of every star. I am ¶ Life, and the giver of Life, yet therefore is the knowledge of me the knowledge of death.

7 I am the Magician and the Exorcist. I am the axle of the wheel, and the cube in the circle. "Come unto me" is a foolish word: for it is I that go.

8 Who worshipped Heru-pa-kraath have worshipped me; ill, for I am the worshipper.

9 Remember all ye that existence is pure joy; that all the sorrows are but as shadows; they pass & are done; but there is that which remains.

10 O prophet! thou hast ill will to learn this writing.

11 I see thee hate the hand & the pen; but I am ¶ stronger.

12 Because of me in Thee which thou knewest not.

13 for why? Because thou wast the knower, and me.

14 Now let there be a veiling of this shrine: now let the light devour men and eat them up with blindness!

15 For I am perfect, being Not; and my number is nine by the fools; but with the just I am eight, and one in eight: Which is vital, for I am none indeed. The Empress and the King are not of me; for there is a further secret.

16 I am The Empress & the Hierophant. Thus eleven, as my bride is eleven.

17 ¶ Hear me, ye people of sighing! The sorrows of pain and regret

APPENDIX A

Are left to the dead and the dying,
  The folk that not know me as yet.

18 These are dead, these fellows; they feel not. We are not for the poor and sad: the lords of the earth are our kinsfolk.

19 Is a God to live in a dog? No! but the highest are of us. They shall rejoice, our chosen: who sorroweth is not of us.

20 Beauty and strength, leaping laughter and delicious languor, force and fire, are of us.

21 ¶ We have nothing with the outcast and the unfit: let them die in their misery. For they feel not. Compassion is the vice of kings: stamp down the wretched & the weak: this is the law of the strong: this is our law and the joy of the world. Think not, o king, upon that lie: That Thou Must Die: verily thou shalt not die, but live. Now let it be understood: If the body of the King dissolve, he shall remain in pure ecstasy for ever. Nuit! Hadit! Ra-Hoor-Khuit! The Sun, Strength & Sight, Light; these are for the servants of the Star & the Snake.

22 ¶ I am the Snake that giveth Knowledge & Delight and bright glory, and stir the hearts of men with drunkenness. To worship me take wine and strange drugs whereof I will tell my prophet, & be drunk thereof! They shall not harm ye at all. It is a lie, this folly against self. The exposure of innocence is a lie. Be strong, o man! lust, enjoy all things of sense and rapture: fear not that any God shall deny thee for this.

23 I am alone: there is no God where I am.

24 Behold! these be grave mysteries; for there are also of my friends who be hermits. Now ¶ think not to find them in the forest or on the mountain; but in beds of purple, caressed by magnificent beasts of women with large limbs, and fire and light in their eyes, and masses of flaming hair about them; there shall ye find them. Ye shall see them at rule, at victorious armies, at all the joy; and there shall be in them a joy a million times greater than this. Beware lest any force another, King against King! Love one another with burning hearts; on the low men trample in the fierce lust of your pride, ¶ in the day of your wrath.

25 Ye are against the people, O my chosen!

26 I am the secret Serpent coiled about to spring: in my coiling there is joy. If I lift up my head, I and my Nuit are one. If I droop down mine head, and shoot forth venom, then is rapture of the earth, and I and the earth are one.

27 There is great danger in me; for who doth not understand these runes shall make a great miss. He shall fall down into the pit called Because, and there he shall ¶ perish with the dogs of Reason.

28 Now a curse upon Because and his kin!

29 May Because be accursèd for ever!

30 If Will stops and cries Why, invoking Because, then Will stops & does nought.

31 If Power asks why, then is Power weakness.

32 Also reason is a lie; for there is a factor infinite & unknown; & all their words are skew-wise.

33 Enough of Because! Be he damned for a dog!

34 But ye, o my people, rise up & awake!

35 Let the rituals be rightly performed with joy & beauty!

36 ¶ There are rituals of the elements and feasts of the times.

37 A feast for the first night of the Prophet and his Bride!

38 A feast for the three days of the writing of the Book of the Law.

39 A feast for Tahuti and the child of the Prophet—secret, O Prophet!

40 A feast for the Supreme Ritual, and a feast for the Equinox of the Gods.

41 A feast for fire and a feast for water; a feast for life and a greater feast for death!

42 ¶ A feast every day in your hearts in the joy of my rapture!

43 A feast every night unto Nu, and the pleasure of uttermost delight!

44 Aye! feast! rejoice! there is no dread hereafter. There is the dissolution, and eternal ecstasy in the kisses of Nu.

45 There is death for the dogs.

46 Dost thou fail? Art thou sorry? Is fear in thine heart?

47 Where I am these are not.

48 ¶ Pity not the fallen! I never knew them. I am not for them. I console not: I hate the consoled & the consoler.

49 I am unique & conqueror. I am not of the slaves that perish. Be they damned & dead! Amen. (This is of the 4: there is a fifth who is invisible, & therein am I as a babe in an egg.)

50 Blue am I and gold in the light of my bride: but the red gleam is in my eyes; & my spangles are purple & green.

51 .Purple beyond purple: it is the light higher ¶ than eyesight.

52 There is a veil: that veil is black. It is the veil of the modest woman; it is the veil of sorrow, & the pall of death: this is none of me. Tear down that lying spectre of the centuries: veil not your vices in virtuous words: these vices are my service; ye do well, & I will reward you here and hereafter.

53 Fear not, o prophet, when these words are said, thou shalt not be sorry. Thou art emphatically my chosen; and blessed are ¶ the eyes that thou shalt look upon with gladness. But I will hide thee in a mask of sorrow: they that see thee shall fear thou art fallen: but I lift thee up.

54 Nor shall they who cry aloud their folly that thou meanest nought avail; thou shall reveal it: thou availest: they are the slaves of because: They are not of me. The stops as thou wilt; the letters? change them not in style or value!

55 Thou shalt obtain the order & value of the English Alphabet; thou shalt find ¶ new symbols to attribute them unto.

56 Begone! ye mockers; even though ye laugh in my honour ye shall laugh not long: then when ye are sad know that I have forsaken you.

57 He that is righteous shall be righteous still; he that is filthy shall be filthy still.

58 Yea! deem not of change: ye shall be as ye are, & not other. Therefore the kings of the earth shall be Kings for ever: the slaves shall serve. There is none that shall be cast down or lifted up: all is ever ¶ as it was. Yet there are masked ones my servants: it may be that yonder beggar is a King. A King may choose his garment as he will: there is no certain test: but a beggar cannot hide his poverty.

59 Beware therefore! Love all, lest perchance is a King concealed! Say you so? Fool! If he be a King, thou canst not hurt him.

60 Therefore strike hard & low, and to hell with them, master!

61 There is a light before thine eyes, o prophet, a light undesired,

62 ¶ I am uplifted in thine heart; and the kisses of the stars rain hard upon thy body.

63 Thou art exhaust in the voluptuous fullness of the inspiration; the expiration is sweeter than death, more rapid and laughterful than a caress of Hell's own worm.

64 Oh! thou art overcome: we are upon thee; our delight is all over thee: hail! hail: prophet of Nu! prophet of Had! prophet of Ra-Hoor-Khu! Now rejoice! now come in our splendour & rapture! Come in our passionate peace, & write sweet words for the Kings!

65 ¶ I am the Master: thou art the Holy Chosen One.

66 Write, & find ecstasy in writing! Work, & be our bed in working! Thrill with the joy of life & death! Ah! thy death shall be lovely: whoso seeth it shall be glad. Thy death shall be the seal of the promise of our agelong love. Come! lift up thine heart & rejoice! We are one; we are none.

67 Hold! Hold! Bear up in thy rapture; fall not in swoon of the excellent kisses!

68 Harder! Hold up thyself! Lift thine head! ¶ breathe not so deep—die!

69 Ah! Ah! What do I feel? Is the word exhausted?

70 There is help & hope in other spells. Wisdom says: be strong! Then canst thou bear more joy. Be not animal; refine thy rapture! If thou drink, drink by the eight and ninety rules of art: if thou love, exceed by delicacy; and if thou do aught joyous, let there be subtlety therein!

71 But exceed! exceed!

72 Strive ever to more! and if thou art truly ¶ mine—and doubt it not, an if thou art ever joyous!—death is the crown of all.

73 Ah! Ah! Death! Death! thou shalt long for death. Death is forbidden, o man, unto thee.

74 The length of thy longing shall be the strength of its glory. He that lives long & desires death much is ever the King among the Kings.

75 Aye! listen to the numbers & the words:

76 4 6 3 8 A B K 2 4 A L G M O R 3 Y X 24 89 R P S T O V A L. What meaneth this, o prophet? Thou knowest not; nor shalt thou know ever. There cometh one to follow thee: he shall ¶ expound it. But remember, o chosen one, to be me; to follow the love of Nu in the star-lit heaven; to look forth upon men, to tell them this glad word.

77 O be thou proud and mighty among men!

78 Lift up thyself! for there is none like unto thee among men or among Gods! Lift up thyself, o my prophet, thy stature shall surpass the stars. They shall worship thy name, foursquare, mystic, wonderful, the number of the man; and the name of ¶ thy house 418.

79 The end of the hiding of Hadit; and blessing & worship to the prophet of the lovely Star!

CHAPTER III.

ABRAHADABRA; the reward of Ra Hoor Khut.

2 There is division hither homeward; there is a word not known. Spelling Is defunct; all is not aught. Beware! Hold! Raise the spell of Ra-Hoor-Khuit!

3 Now let it be first understood that I am a god of War and of Vengeance. I shall deal hardly with them.

4 Choose ye an island!

5 Fortify it!

6 Dung it about with enginery of war!

7 I will give you a war-engine.

8 With it ye shall smite the peoples; and ¶ none shall stand before you.

9 Lurk! Withdraw! Upon them! this is the Law of the Battle of Conquest: thus shall my worship be about my secret house.

10 Get the stélé of revealing itself; set it in thy secret temple—and that temple is already aright disposed—& it shall be your Kiblah for ever. It shall not fade, but miraculous colour shall come back to it day after day. Close it in locked glass for a proof to the world.

11 This shall be your only proof. I forbid argument. Conquer! That is enough. I will make easy ¶ to you the abstruction from the ill-ordered house in the Victorious City. Thou shalt thyself convey it with worship, o prophet, though thou likest it not. Thou shalt have danger & trouble. Ra-Hoor-Khu is with thee. Worship me with fire & blood; worship me with swords & with spears. Let the woman be girt with a sword before me: let blood flow to my name. Trample down the Heathen; be upon them, o warrior, I will give you of their flesh to eat!

12 Sacrifice cattle, little and big: after a child.

13 ¶ But not now.

14 Ye shall see that hour, o blessèd Beast, and thou the Scarlet Concubine of his desire!

15 Ye shall be sad thereof.

16 Deem not too eagerly to catch the promises; fear not to undergo the curses. Ye, even ye, know not this meaning all.

17 Fear not at all; fear neither men nor Fates, nor gods, nor anything. Money fear not, nor laughter of the folk folly, nor any other power in heaven or upon the earth or under the earth. Nu is your refuge as Hadit your ¶ light; and I am the strength, force, vigour, of your arms.

18 Mercy let be off: damn them who pity! Kill and torture; spare not; be upon them!

19 That stélé they shall call the Abomination of Desolation; count well its name, & it shall be to you as 718.

20 Why? Because of the fall of Because, that he is not there again.

21 Set up my image in the East: thou shalt buy thee an image which I will show thee, especial, not unlike the one thou knowest. And it shall be suddenly easy for thee to do this.

22 ¶ The other images group around me to support me: let all be worshipped, for they shall cluster to exalt me. I am the visible object of worship; the others are secret; for the Beast & his Bride are they: and for the winners of the Ordeal *x*. What is this? Thou shalt know.

23 For perfume mix meal & honey & thick leavings of red wine: then oil of Abramelin and olive oil, and afterward soften & smooth down with rich fresh blood.

24 The best blood is of the moon, monthly: then the fresh blood of a child, or dropping from the ¶ host of heaven: then of enemies; then of the priest or of the worshippers: last of some beast, no matter what.

25 This burn: of this make cakes & eat unto me. This hath also another use; let it be laid before me, and kept thick with perfumes of your orison: it shall become full of beetles as it were and creeping things sacred unto me.

26 These slay, naming your enemies; & they shall fall before you.

27 Also these shall breed lust & power of lust in you at the eating

thereof.

28 Also ye shall be strong in war.

29 ¶ Moreover, be they long kept, it is better; for they swell with my force. All before me.

30 My altar is of open brass work: burn thereon in silver or gold!

31 There cometh a rich man from the West who shall pour his gold upon thee.

32 From gold forge steel!

33 Be ready to fly or to smite!

34 But your holy place shall be untouched throughout the centuries: though with fire and sword it be burnt down & shattered, yet an invisible house there standeth, and shall stand until the fall of the Great ¶ Equinox; when Hrumachis shall arise and the double-wanded one assume my throne and place. Another prophet shall arise, and bring fresh fever from the skies; another woman shall awake the lust & worship of the Snake; another soul of God and beast shall mingle in the globèd priest; another sacrifice shall stain the tomb; another king shall reign; and blessing no longer be poured To the Hawk-headed mystical Lord!

35 The half of the word of Heru-ra-ha, called Hoor-pa-kraat and Ra-Hoor-Khut.

36 ¶ Then said the prophet unto the God:

37 I adore thee in the song:—

I am the Lord of Thebes, and I
  The inspired forth-speaker of Mentu;
For me unveils the veilèd sky,
  The self-slain Ankh-af-na-khonsu
Whose words are truth. I invoke, I greet
  Thy presence, O Ra-Hoor-Khuit!

Unity uttermost showed!
  I adore the might of Thy breath,
Supreme and terrible God,
  Who makest the gods and death
To tremble before Thee—
  I, I adore thee!

Appear on the throne of Ra!
  Open the ways of the Khu!
Lighten the ways of the Ka!
  The ways of the Khabs run through
To stir me or still me!
  Aum! let it kill me!

38 So that thy light is in me; & its red flame is as a sword in my hand to push thy order. There is a secret door that I shall make to establish thy way in all the quarters, (these are the adorations, as thou hast written), as it is said:

The light is mine; its rays consume
  Me: I have made a secret door
Into the House of Ra and Tum,
  Of Khephra and of Ahathoor.
I am thy Theban, O Mentu,
  The prophet Ankh-af-na-khonsu!
By Bes-na-Maut my breast I beat;
  By wise Ta-Nech I weave my spell.
Show thy star-splendour, O Nuit!
  Bid me within thine House to dwell,
O wingèd snake of light, Hadit!
  Abide with me, Ra-Hoor-Khuit!

39 ¶ All this and a book to say how thou didst come hither and a reproduction of this ink and paper for ever—for in it is the word secret & not only in the English—and thy comment upon this the Book of the Law shall be printed beautifully in red ink and black upon beautiful paper made by hand; and to each man and woman that thou meetest, were it but to dine or to drink at them, it is the Law to give. Then they shall chance to abide in this bliss or no; it is no odds. Do this quickly!

40 But the work of the comment? That is easy; and ¶ Hadit burning in thy heart shall make swift and secure thy pen.

41 Establish at thy Kaaba a clerk-house: all must be done well and with business way.

42 The ordeals thou shalt oversee

thyself, save only the blind ones. Refuse none, but thou shalt know & destroy the traitors. I am Ra-Hoor-Khuit; and I am powerful to protect my servant. Success is thy proof: argue not; convert not; talk not overmuch! Them that seek to entrap thee, to overthrow thee, them attack without pity or quarter; & destroy them utterly. Swift as a trodden serpent turn ¶ and strike! Be thou yet deadlier than he! Drag down their souls to awful torment: laugh at their fear: spit upon them!

43 Let the Scarlet Woman beware! If pity and compassion and tenderness visit her heart; if she leave my work to toy with old sweetnesses; then shall my vengeance be known. I will slay me her child: I will alienate her heart: I will cast her out from men: as a shrinking and despised harlot shall she crawl through dusk wet streets, and die cold and an-hungered.

44 ¶ But let her raise herself in pride! Let her follow me in my way! Let her work the work of wickedness! Let her kill her heart! Let her be loud and adulterous! Let her be covered with jewels, and rich garments, and let her be shameless before all men!

45 Then will I lift her to pinnacles of power: then will I breed from her a child mightier than all the kings of the earth. I will fill her with joy: with my force shall she see & strike at the worship of Nu: she shall achieve Hadit.

46 ¶ I am the warrior Lord of the Forties: the Eighties cower before me, & are abased. I will bring you to victory & joy: I will be at your arms in battle & ye shall delight to slay. Success is your proof; courage is your armour; go on, go on, in my strength; & ye shall turn not back for any!

47 This book shall be translated into all tongues: but always with the original in the writing of the Beast; for in the ¶ chance shape of the letters and their position to one another: in these are mysteries that no Beast shall divine. Let him not seek to try: but one cometh after him, whence I say not, who shall discover the Key of it all. Then this line drawn is a key: then this circle squared in its failure is a key also. And Abrahadabra. It shall be his child & that strangely. Let him not seek after this; for thereby alone can he fall from it.

48 ¶ Now this mystery of the letters is done, and I want to go on to the holier place.

49 I am in a secret fourfold word, the blasphemy against all gods of men.

50 Curse them! Curse them! Curse them!

51 With my Hawk's head I peck at the eyes of Jesus as he hangs upon the cross.

52 I flap my wings in the face of Mohammed & blind him.

53 With my claws I tear out the flesh of the Indian and the Buddhist, Mongol and Din.

54 Bahlasti! Ompehda! I spit on your ¶ crapulous creeds.

55 Let Mary inviolate be torn upon wheels: for her sake let all chaste women be utterly despised among you!

56 Also for beauty's sake and love's!

57 Despise also all cowards; professional soldiers who dare not fight, but play; all fools despise!

58 But the keen and the proud, the royal and the lofty; ye are brothers!

59 As brothers fight ye!

60 There is no law beyond Do what thou wilt.

61 There is an end of the word of the God ¶ enthroned in Ra's seat,

lightening the girders of the soul.

62 To Me do ye reverence! to me come ye through tribulation of ordeal, which is bliss.

63 The fool readeth this Book of the Law, and its comment; & he understandeth it not.

64 Let him come through the first ordeal, & it will be to him as silver.

65 Through the second, gold.

66 Through the third, stones of precious water.

67 Through the fourth, ultimate sparks of the intimate fire.

68 ¶ Yet to all it shall seem beautiful. Its enemies who say not so, are mere liars.

69 There is success.

70 I am the Hawk-Headed Lord of Silence & of Strength; my nemyss shrouds the night-blue sky.

71 Hail! ye twin warriors about the pillars of the world! for your time is nigh at hand.

72 I am the Lord of the Double Wand of Power; the wand of the Force of Coph Nia—but my left hand is empty, for I have crushed ¶ an Universe; & nought remains.

73 Paste the sheets from right to left and from top to bottom: then behold!

74 There is a splendour in my name hidden and glorious, as the sun of midnight is ever the son.

75 The ending of the words is the Word Abrahadabra.

The Book of the Law is Written
and Concealed.
Aum. Ha.

THE COMMENT.

Do what thou wilt shall be the whole of the Law.

The study of this Book is forbidden. It is wise to destroy this copy after the first reading.

Whosoever disregards this does so at his own risk and peril. These are most dire.

Those who discuss the contents of this Book are to be shunned by all, as centres of pestilence.

All questions of the Law are to be decided only by appeal to my writings, each for himself.

There is no law beyond Do what thou wilt.

Love is the law, love under will.

The priest of the princes,
ANKH-F-N-KHONSU

SCHOLIUM.

According to Crowley's Preface to the *New Comment*, "In the first edition this Book is called L. L is the sacred letter in the Holy Twelve-fold Table which forms the triangle that stabilizes the Universe. See *Liber 418*. L is the letter of Libra, Balance, and 'Justice' in the Taro. This title should probably be *AL*, 'El', as the 'L' was heard of the Voice of Aiwaz, not seen. *AL* is the true name of the Book, for these letters, and their number 31, form the Master Key to its Mysteries." The Comment reproduced here, also known as "The Short Comment" or "The Tunis Comment," was written in El Marsa, Tunisia, in November, 1925. It was first published in 1926 and, unlike the three longer comments, is categorized as a "Class A" document of the A∴A∴ just like *The Book of the Law* itself.

LIBER OZ
Rights of Man

"the law of the strong: this is our law and the joy of the world."—*AL. II. 21.*

"Do what thou wilt shall be the whole of the Law."—*AL. I. 40.*

"thou hast no right but to do thy will.
Do that, and no other shall say nay."—*AL. I. 42–3.*

"Every man and every woman is a star."—*AL. I. 3.*

There is no god but man.

1. Man has the right to live by his own law—
   to live in the way that he wills to do:
   to work as he will:
   to play as he will:
   to rest as he will:
   to die when and how he will.
2. Man has the right to eat what he will:
   to drink what he will:
   to dwell where he will:
   to move as he will on the face of the earth.
3. Man has the right to think what he will:
   to speak what he will:
   to write what he will:
   to draw, paint, carve, etch, mould, build as he will:
   to dress as he will.
4. Man has the right to love as he will:—
   "take your fill and will of love as ye will,
   when, where, and with whom ye will."—*AL. I. 51.*
5. Man has the right to kill those who would thwart these rights.

"the slaves shall serve."—*AL. II. 58.*

"Love is the law, love under will."—*AL. I. 57.*

SCHOLIUM.

Originally written for the Ordo Templi Orientis during the First World War in 1916 and called simply the "Rights of Man" or the "Manifesto." The quotations from *The Book of the Law* were added during the Second World War in 1941, along with an English rendering of the O.T.O. motto, *Deus homo est*. In letters to Gerald Yorke, Crowley described the document as the "O.T.O. Plan in words of one syllable" (30 August 1941) with "five sections: moral, bodily, mental, sexual freedom, and the safeguard tyrannicide" (13 September 1941). For an outline of positive obligations to compliment this list of negative rights, see *Duty* (Appendix C following).

Duty

A note on the chief rules of practical conduct to be observed by those who accept the Law of Thelema.

"Do what thou wilt shall be the whole of the Law." [AL I.40]

"There is no law beyond Do what thou wilt." [AL III.60]

"...thou hast no right but to do thy will. Do that, and no other shall say nay. For pure will, unassuaged of purpose, delivered from the lust of result, is every way perfect." [AL I.42-4]

"Love is the law, love under will." [AL I.57]

"Every man and every woman is a star." [AL I.3]

A. YOUR DUTY TO YOURSELF

1. Find yourself to be the centre of your own Universe.

"I am the flame that burns in every heart of man, and in the core of every star." [AL II.6]

2. Explore the Nature and Powers of your own Being.

This includes everything which is, or can be, for you: and you must accept everything exactly as it is in itself, as one of the factors which go to make up your True Self. This True Self thus ultimately includes all things soever; its discovery is Initiation (the travelling inwards) and as its Nature is to move continually, it must be understood not as static, but as dynamic, not as a Noun but as a Verb.

3. Develop in due harmony and proportion every faculty which you possess.

"Wisdom says: be strong!" [AL II.70]

"But exceed! exceed!" [AL II.71]

"Be strong, o man! lust, enjoy all things of sense and rapture: fear not that any God shall deny thee for this." [AL II.22]

4. Contemplate your own Nature.

Consider every element thereof both separately and in relation to all the rest as to judge accurately the true purpose of the totality of your Being.

5. Find the formula of this purpose, or "True Will," in an expression as simple as possible.

Learn to understand clearly how best to manipulate the energies which you control to obtain the results most favourable to it from its relations with the part of the Universe which you do not yet control.

6. Extend the dominion of your consciousness, and its control of all forces alien to it, to the utmost.

Do this by the ever stronger and more skillful application of your faculties to the finer, clearer, fuller, and more accurate perception, the better understanding, and the more wisely ordered government, of that external Universe.

7. Never permit the thought or will of any other Being to interfere with your own.

Be constantly vigilant to resent, and on the alert to resist, with unvanquishable ardour and vehemence of passion unquenchable, every attempt of any other Being to influence you otherwise than by contributing new facts to your experience of the Universe, or by assisting you to reach a higher synthesis of Truth by the mode of passionate fusion.

8. Do not repress or restrict any true instinct of your Nature; but devote all in perfection to the sole service of your one True Will.

"Be goodly therefore..." [AL I.51]

"The word of Sin is Restriction. O man! refuse not thy wife, if she will! O lover, if thou wilt, depart! There is no bond that can unite the divided but love: all else is a curse. Accursed! Accursed be it to the aeons! Hell." [AL I.41]

"So with thy all; thou hast no right but to do thy will. Do that, and no other shall say nay. For pure will, unassuaged of purpose, delivered from the lust of result, is every way perfect." [AL I.42-4]

"Ye shall gather goods and store of women and spices; ye shall wear rich jewels; ye shall exceed the nations of the earth in splendour & pride; but always in the love of me, and so shall ye come to my joy." [AL I.61]

9. Rejoice!

"Remember all ye that existence is pure joy; that all the sorrows are but as shadows; they pass & are done; but there is that which remains." [AL II.9]

"But ye, o my people, rise up & awake! Let the rituals be rightly performed with joy & beauty! ... A feast for fire and a feast for water; a feast for life and a greater feast for death! A feast every day in your hearts in the joy of my rapture! A feast every night unto Nu, and the pleasure of uttermost delight! Aye! feast! rejoice! there is no dread hereafter. There is the dissolution, and eternal ecstasy in the kisses of Nu." [AL II.34-5...41-4]

"Now rejoice! now come in our splendour & rapture! Come in our passionate peace, & write sweet words for the Kings!" [AL II.64]

"Thrill with the joy of life & death! Ah! thy death shall be lovely: whoso seeth it shall be glad. Thy death shall be the seal of the promise of our agelong love. Come! lift up thine heart & rejoice!" [AL II.66]

"Is a God to live in a dog? No! but the highest are of us. They shall rejoice, our chosen: who sorroweth is not of us. Beauty and strength, leaping laughter and delicious languor, force and fire, are of us." [AL II.19-20]

B. YOUR DUTY TO OTHER INDIVIDUAL MEN AND WOMEN

1. Unite yourself passionately with every other form of consciousness.

Thus destroying the sense of separateness from the Whole, and creating a new baseline in the Universe from which to measure it.

"Love is the law, love under will." [AL I.57]

"Come forth, o children, under the stars, & take your fill of love!" [AL I.12]

2. "As brothers fight ye!" [AL III.59]

"If he be a King, thou canst not hurt him." [AL II.59]

To bring out saliently the differences between two points-of-view is useful to both in measuring the position of each in the whole. Combat stimulates the virile or creative energy; and, like love, of which it is one form, excites the mind to an orgasm which enables it to transcend its rational dullness.

3. Abstain from all interferences with other wills.

"Beware lest any force another, King against King!" [AL II.24]

The love and war in the previous injunctions are of the nature of sport, where one respects, and learns from the opponent, but never interferes with him, outside the actual game. To seek to dominate or influence another is to seek to deform or destroy him; and he is a necessary part of one's own Universe, that is, of one's self.

4. Seek, if you so will, to enlighten another when need arises.

This may be done, always with the strict respect for the attitude of the good sportsman, when he is in distress through failure to understand himself clearly, especially when he specifically demands help; for his darkness may hinder one's perception of his perfection. (Yet also his darkness may serve as a warning, or excite one's interest.) It is also lawful when his ignorance has lead him to interfere with one's will. All interference is in any case dangerous, and demands the exercise of extreme skill and good judgement, fortified by experience. To influence another is to leave one's citadel unguarded; and the attempt commonly ends in losing one's own self-supremacy.

5. Worship all!

"Every man and every woman is a star." [AL I.3]

"Mercy let be off: damn them who pity!" [AL III.18]

"We have nothing with the outcast and the unfit: let them die in their misery. For they feel not. Compassion is the vice of kings: stamp down the wretched & the weak: this is the law of the strong: this is our law and the joy of the world. Think not, o king, upon that lie: That Thou Must Die: verily thou shalt not die, but live. Now let it be understood: if the body of the King dissolve, he shall remain in pure ecstasy for ever. Nuit! Hadit! Ra-Hoor-Khuit! The Sun, Strength & Sight, Light; these are for the servants of the Star & the Snake." [AL II.21]

Each being is, exactly as you are, the sole centre of a Universe in no wise identical with, or even assimilable to, your own. The impersonal Universe of "Nature" is only an abstraction, approximately true, of the factors which it is convenient to regard as common to all. The Universe of another is therefore necessarily unknown to, and unknowable by, you; but it induces currents of energy in yours by determining in part your reactions. Use men and women, therefore, with the absolute respect due to inviolable standards of measurement; verify your own observations by comparison with similar judgements made by them; and, studying the methods which determine their failure or success, acquire for yourself the wit and skill required to cope with your own problems.

Pity, sympathy and like emotions are fundamentally insults to the Godhead of the person exciting them, and therefore also to your own. The distress of another may be relieved; but always with the positive and noble idea of making manifest the perfection of the Universe. Pity is the source of every mean, ignoble, cowardly vice; and the essential blasphemy against Truth.

"To Me do ye reverence! to me come ye through tribulation of ordeal, which is bliss." [AL III.62]

C. YOUR DUTY TO MANKIND

1. Establish the Law of Thelema as the sole basis of conduct.

The general welfare of the race being necessary in many respects to your own, that well-being, like your own, principally a function of the intelligent and wise observance of the Law of Thelema, it is of the very first importance to you that every individual should accept frankly that Law, and strictly govern himself in full accordance therewith.

You may regard the establishment of the Law of Thelema as an essential element of your True Will, since, whatever the ultimate nature of that Will, the evident condition of putting it into execution is freedom from external interference.

Governments too often exhibit the most deplorable stupidity, however enlightened may be the men who compose and constitute them, or the people whose destinies they direct. It is therefore incumbent on every man and woman to take the proper steps to cause the revisions of all existing statutes on the basis of the Law of Thelema. This Law being a Law of Liberty, the aim of the legislature must be to secure the amplest freedom for each individual in the state, eschewing the presumptuous assumption that any given positive ideal is worthy to be obtained.

"The word of Sin is Restriction." [AL I.41]

The essence of crime is that it restricts the freedom of the individual outraged. (Thus, murder restricts his right to live; robbery, his right to enjoy the fruits of his labour; coining, his right to the guarantee of the state that he shall barter in security; etc.) It is then the common duty to prevent crime by segregating the criminal, and by the threat of reprisals; also, to teach the criminal that his acts, being analyzed, are contrary to his own True Will. (This may often be accomplished by taking from him the right which he has denied to others; as by outlawing the thief, so that he feels constant anxiety for the safety of his own possessions, removed from the ward of the State.) The rule is quite simple. He who violated any right declares magically that it does not exist; therefore it no longer does so, for him.

Crime being a direct spiritual violation of the Law of Thelema, it should not be tolerated in the community. Those who possess the instinct should be segregated in a settlement to build up a state of their own, so to learn the necessity of themselves imposing and maintaining rules of justice. All artificial crimes should be abolished. When fantastic restrictions disappear, the greater freedom of the individual will itself teach him to avoid acts which really restrict natural rights. Thus real crime will diminish automatically.

The administration of the Law should be simplified by training men of uprightness and discretion whose will is to fulfill this function in the community to decide all complaints by the abstract principle of the Law of Thelema, and to award judgement on the basis of the actual restriction caused by the offense.

The ultimate aim is thus to reintegrate Conscience, on true scientific principles, as the warden of conduct, the monitor of the people, and the guarantee of their governors.

D. YOUR DUTY TO ALL OTHER BEINGS AND THINGS

1. Apply the Law of Thelema to all problems of fitness, use, and development.

It is a violation of the Law of Thelema to abuse the natural qualities of any animal or object by diverting it from its proper function, as determined by consideration of its history and structure. Thus, to train children to perform mental operations, or to practice tasks, for which they are unfitted, is a crime against nature. Similarly, to build houses of rotten material, to adulterate food, to destroy forests, etc., etc., is to offend.

The Law of Thelema is to be applied unflinchingly to decide every question of conduct. The inherent fitness of any thing for any proposed use should be the sole criterion.

Apparent, and sometimes even real, conflict between interests will frequently arise. Such cases are to be decided by the general value of the contending parties in the scale of Nature. Thus, a tree has a right to its life; but a man being more than a tree, he may cut it down for fuel or shelter when need arises. Even so, let him remember that the Law never fails to avenge infraction: as when wanton deforestation has ruined a climate or a soil, or as when the importation of rabbits for a cheap supply of food has created a plague.

Observe that the violation of the Law of Thelema produces cumulative ills. The drain of the agricultural population to big cities, due chiefly to persuading them to abandon their natural ideals, has not only made the country less tolerable to the peasant, but debauched the town. And the error tends to increase in geometrical progression, until a remedy has become almost inconceivable and the whole structure of society is threatened with ruin.

The wise application based on observation and experience of the Law of Thelema is to work in conscious harmony with Evolution. Experiments in creation, involving variation from existing types, are lawful and necessary. Their value is to be judged by their fertility as bearing witness to their harmony with the course of nature towards perfection.

SCHOLIUM.

Written during the Abbey of Thelema period (1920–23) and originally entitled "General Practical Applications of the Law of Thelema," this document was never assigned a number nor published in Crowley's lifetime. Though the original typescript went through the same rigorous editing as his commercially published works did, it was initially only circulated among his students at Cefalù and subsequently lost along with most of his archives. Unlike many of his later works and letters, it still retains the psychoanalytical view that attainment is possible and beneficial for all. It gives an outline of positive obligations to compliment the negative rights listed in *Liber OZ* (*see* Appendix B). "In the reconstituted O.T.O. there are," according to Chapter 72 of the *Confessions*, "six degrees in which is conveyed a comprehensive conception of the cosmos and our relation therewith, and a similar number to deal with our duty to ourselves and our fellows, the development of our own faculties of every order, and the general advancement and advantage of mankind."

LIBER LIBRÆ
The Book of the Balance

---

0. Learn first—Oh thou who aspirest unto our ancient Order!—that Equilibrium is the basis of the Work. If thou thyself hast not a sure foundation, whereon wilt thou stand to direct the forces of Nature?

1. Know then, that as man is born into this world amidst the Darkness of Matter, and the strife of contending forces; so must his first endeavour be to seek the Light through their reconciliation.

2. Thou then who hast trials and troubles, rejoice because of them, for in them is Strength, and by their means is a pathway opened unto that Light.

3. How should it be otherwise, O man, whose life is but a day in Eternity, a drop in the Ocean of time; how, were thy trials not many, couldst thou purge thy soul from the dross of earth?

Is it but now that the Higher Life is beset with dangers and difficulties; hath it not ever been so with the Sages and Hierophants of the past? They have been persecuted and reviled, they have been tormented of men; yet through this also has their Glory increased.

4. Rejoice therefore, O Initiate, for the greater thy trial the greater thy Triumph. When men shall revile thee, and speak against thee falsely, hath not the Master said, "Blessed art thou!"?

5. Yet, oh aspirant, let thy victories bring thee not Vanity, for with increase of Knowledge should come increase of Wisdom. He who knoweth little, thinketh he knoweth much; but he who knoweth much has learned his own ignorance. Seest thou a man wise in his own conceit? There is more hope of a fool, than of him.

6. Be not hasty to condemn others; how knowest thou that in their place, thou couldst have resisted the temptation? And even were it so, why shouldst thou despise one who is weaker than thyself?

7. Thou therefore who desirest Magical Gifts, be sure that thy soul is firm and steadfast; for it is by flattering thy weaknesses that the Weak Ones will gain power over thee. Humble thyself before thy Self, yet fear neither man nor spirit. Fear is failure, and the forerunner of failure: and courage is the beginning of virtue.

8. Therefore fear not the Spirits, but be firm and courteous with them; for thou hast no right to despise or revile them; and this too may lead thee astray. Command and banish them, curse them by the Great Names if need be; but neither mock or revile them, for so assuredly wilt thou be led to error.

9. A man is what he maketh himself within the limits fixed by his inherited destiny; he is a part of mankind; his actions affect not only what he called himself, but also the whole universe.

10. Worship, and neglect not, the physical body which is thy temporary connection with the outer and material world. Therefore let thy mental Equilibrium be above disturbance by material events; strengthen and control the animal passions, discipline the emotions and the reason, nourish the Higher Aspirations.

11. Do good to others for its own sake, not for reward, not for gratitude from them, not for sympathy. If thou art generous, thou wilt not long for thine ears to be tickled by expressions of gratitude.

12. Remember that unbalanced force is evil; that unbalanced severity is but cruelty and oppression; but that also unbalanced mercy is but weakness which would allow and abet Evil. Act passionately; think rationally; be Thyself.

13. True ritual is as much action as word; it is Will.

14. Remember that this earth is but an atom in the universe, and that thou thyself art but an atom thereon, and that even couldst thou become the God of this earth whereon thou crawlest and grovellest, that thou wouldst, even then, be but an atom, and one amongst many.

15. Nevertheless have the greatest self-respect, and to that end sin not against thyself. The sin which is unpardonable is knowingly and wilfully to reject truth, to fear knowledge lest that knowledge pander not to thy prejudices.

16. To obtain Magical Power, learn to control thought; admit only those ideas that are in harmony with the end desired, and not every stray and contradictory Idea that presents itself.

17. Fixed thought is a means to an end. Therefore pay attention to the power of silent thought and meditation. The material act is but the outward expression of thy thought, and therefore hath it been said that "the thought of foolishness is sin." Thought is the commencement of action, and if a chance thought can produce much effect, what cannot fixed thought do?

18. Therefore as hath already been said, Establish thyself firmly in the equilibrium of forces, in the centre of the Cross of the Elements, that Cross from whose centre the Creative Word issued in the birth of the dawning Universe.

19. Be thou therefore prompt and active as the Sylphs, but avoid frivolity and caprice; be energetic and strong like the Salamanders, but avoid irritability and ferocity; be flexible and attentive to images like the Undines, but avoid idleness and changeability; be laborious and patient like the Gnomes, but avoid grossness and avarice.

20. So shalt thou gradually develop the powers of thy soul, and fit thyself to command the Spirits of the elements. For wert thou to summon the Gnomes to pander thine avarice, thou wouldst no longer command them, but they would command thee. Wouldst thou abuse the pure beings of the woods and mountains to fill thy coffers and satisfy thy hunger of Gold? Wouldst thou debase the Spirits of Living Fire to serve thy wrath and hatred? Wouldst thou violate the purity of the Souls of the Waters to pander thy lust of debauchery? Wouldst thou force the Spirits of the

Evening Breeze to minister thy folly and caprice? Know that with such desires thou canst but attract the Weak, not the Strong, and in that case the Weak will have power over thee.

21. In true religion there is no sect, therefore take heed that thou blaspheme not the name by which another knoweth his God; for if thou do this thing in Jupiter thou wilt blaspheme יהוה and in Osiris יהשוה. Ask and ye shall have! Seek, and ye shall find! Knock, and it shall be opened unto you!

SCHOLIUM.

Described in the A∴A∴ Curriculum as an "elementary course of morality suitable for average man," this document is based on a knowledge lecture originally written for the 3=8 Grade of the Golden Dawn. This "additional side lecture" on the "General Guidance and Purification of the Soul" begins with the words, "Learn first, O Practicus of our Ancient Order, that true Equilibrium is the basis of the Soul. If thou thyself hast not a sure foundation, whereon wilt thou stand to direct the forces of Nature?" (*Cf.* Regardie 1989.) In the VII° of the O.T.O., "which is tripartite, he is first taught the principle of equilibrium as extended to all possible moral ideas; secondly, to all possible intellectual ideas, and lastly, he is shown how, basing all his actions on this impregnable rock of justice, he may so direct his life as to undertake his Great Work with the fullest responsibility and in absolute freedom from all possibility of interferences." (*Confessions*, Ch. 72.)

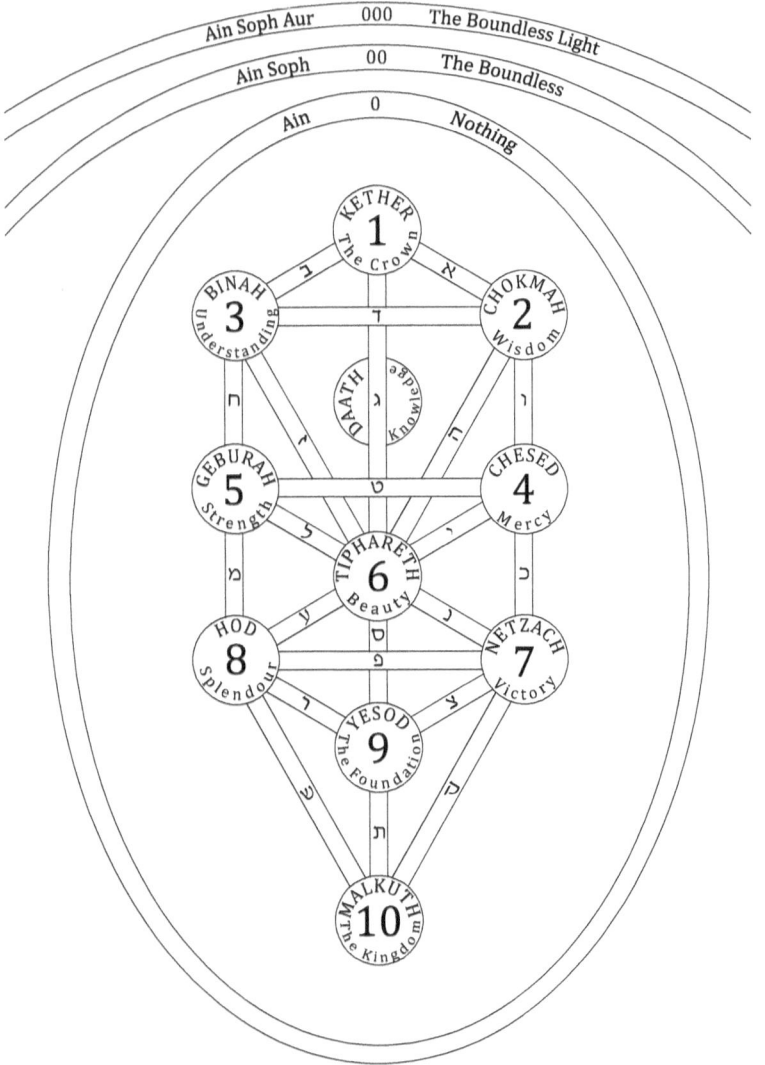

DIAGRAM 1.

According to the Oral Torah, the esoteric teachings of the Holy Qabalah were contained in the first Tablets of the Law, which were made of sapphire (Heb. *sephir*) and smashed by Moses (*cf.* Exodus 31:18). The most important and best known scheme of depicting the 10 Sephiroth (Heb. "emanations") arranges them as a tree with 3 columns or Pillars. The connecting lines in the diagram show the immanent cosmological forces that constantly recreate all existence, as represented by the 22 letters of the Hebrew alphabet. Hermetic Qabalah posits a pre-Judaic, ancient Egyptian or Babylonian origin for the Tree of Life, asserting that it was only later adopted and preserved by Jewish mystics. Hermeticists also align the Paths, or connecting lines, in a slightly different manner, maintaining theirs to be the original configuration. Christian Qabalah could easily be dismissed as merely an attempt by Renaissance clerics to convert Jews, if the Hermetic tree was not identical to that of the Jesuit scholar Athanasius Kircher.

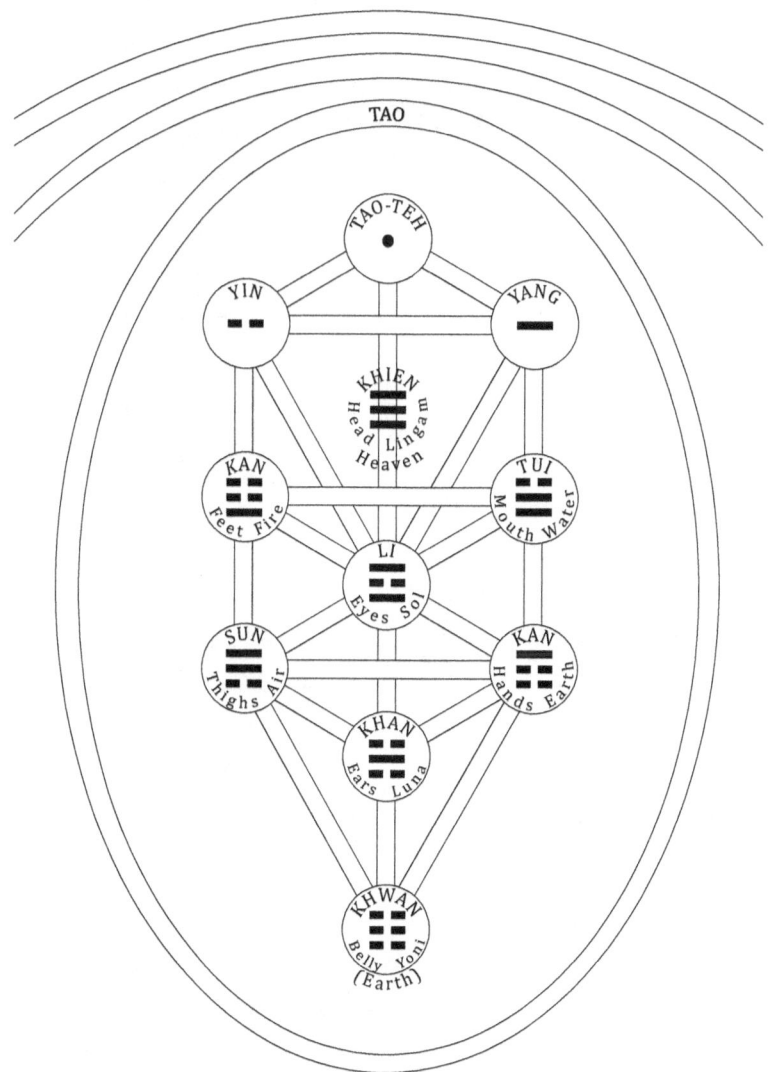

DIAGRAM 2.

Though the concept of Yin and Yang dates back to Chinese antiquity, the popular description of the *T'ai Chi T'u* is due to Chou Tun-i (1017–1073), "the first true Confucian sage since Mencius," who argued for the inseparability of cosmology and ethics. His "Explanation of the Diagram of the Ultimate Polarity," as interpreted by Chu Hsi (1130–1200), became the cornerstone of Neo-Confucian cosmology, and established the appendices to the *I Ching* as basic textual sources of the Song revival of Confucianism. Chu insisted that Chou had composed the diagram himself, against the prevailing view that it was derived from earlier Taoist sources; in any case, both the Taoist use of charms and talismans and the Buddhist use of mandalas can be seen as precursors to the Song Confucian use of *t'u*. The Crowley interpretation of the "Chinese cosmos" reproduced here is from *The Book of Thoth*, and differs from the one published in *Magick Without Tears* in reversing the attributions of air/thighs and earth/hands between the *Sun* and *Kan* trigrams, as per *Liber CCXVI*.

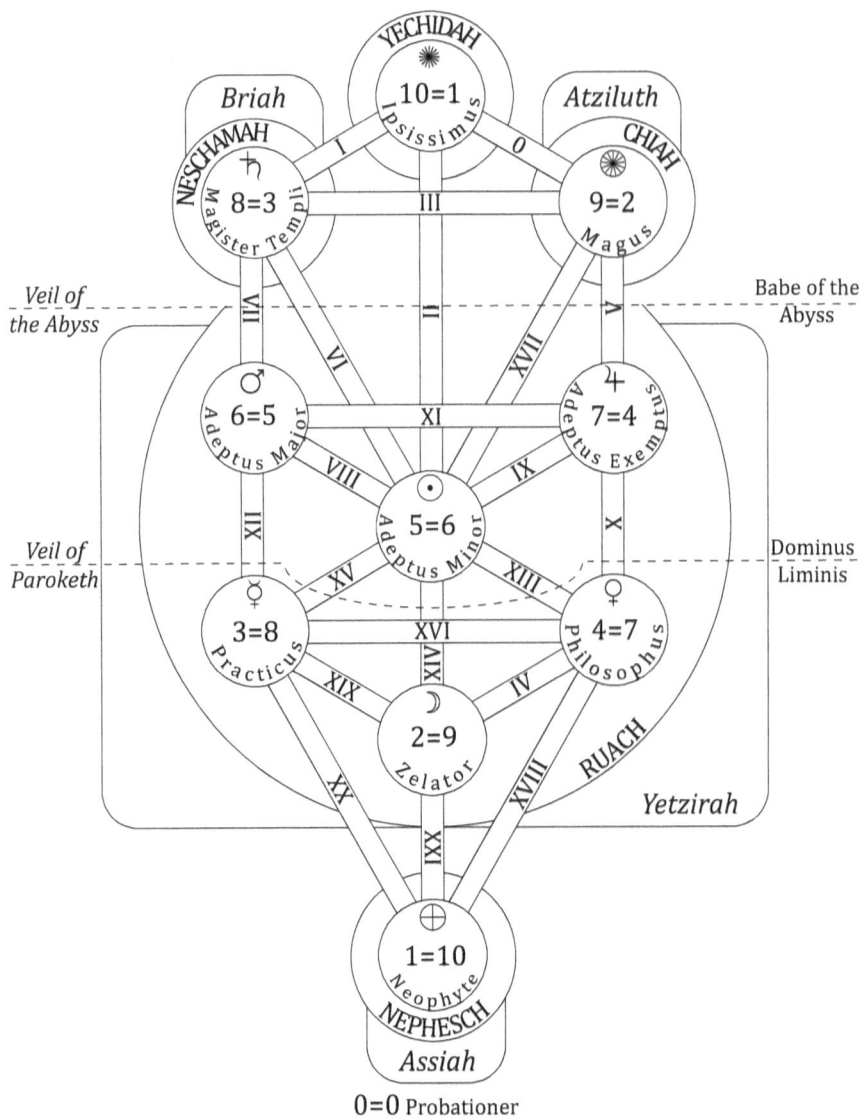

DIAGRAM 3.
The Hermetic Order of the Golden Dawn (est. 1888) inherited the traditional nine Rosicrucian grades of Junior (or Zelator), Theoreticus (or Theoricus), Practicus, Philosophus, Minor (or Adeptus Minor), Major (or Adeptus Major), Adeptus Exemptus, Magister (or Magister Templi), and Magus from the 18th-century Orden des Gülden- und Rosen-Creutzes by way of the Societas Rosicruciana in Anglia (est. 1865), to which all three of the founding members of the G∴D∴ also belonged. The grades of Neophyte (originally 0=0) and Ipsissimus (10=1) were their innovation, with Crowley further adding a Probationer (0=0) and dropping the Theoricus (originally 2=9) grade; however, the grades were allotted a two-fold Qabalistic enumeration (originally 1=9 thru 9=1) from their first known published appearance in 1767. (*See* McIntosh 1997.)

APPENDIX E   561

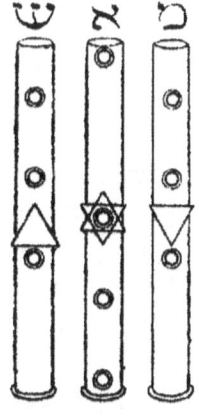

DIAGRAM 4.
The Three Pillars.

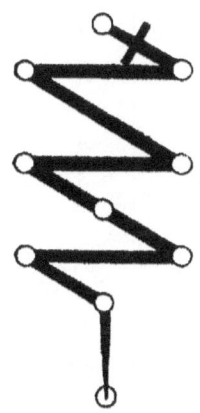

DIAGRAM 5.
The Flaming Sword.

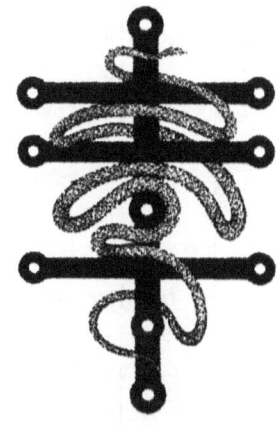

DIAGRAM 6.
The Brazen Serpent.

DIAGRAM 7. An Early Tree.

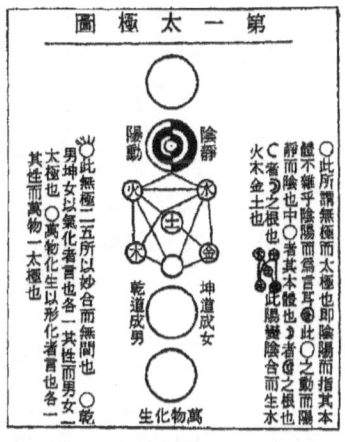

DIAGRAM 8. The *T'ai Chi T'u*.

The four Qabalistic worlds (Diagram 3), or planes of existence, are traditionally attributed to the 4 letters of the Tetragrammaton. Atziluth (Yod) further variously corresponds to Kether (Method 1), to Chokmah (Method 2), to Kether and Chokmah (Method 3), or to Kether, Chokmah, and Binah (Method 4); Briah (Hé) to Chokmah and Binah (1), just to Binah (2 & 3), or to Chesed, Geburah and Tiphareth (4); Yetzirah (Vau) to Chesed, Geburah, Tiphareth, Netzach, Hod, and Yesod (1, 2 & 3), or to Netzach, Hod, and Yesod (4); but Assiah (Hé-final) is generally attributed to Malkuth—Crowley only ever uses Method 2. Although the Nephesch is technically the lowest part of the soul, there exists a sixth traditional part, the Guph, or the body, the physical vehicle for the Nephesch. Similarly, Jewish Qabalists sometimes attribute to Kether a primordial fifth world, Adam Qadmon, or the original man.

TABLE 1.

Key Scale	Hebrew Letter	English Equivalent		English Translation	Numerical Value	Yetziratic Attribution	Atu No	Titles of Trumps
11	א	A	Aleph	Ox (Plough)	1	Air	0.	The Fool
12	ב	B	Beth	House	2	Mercury	I.	„ Magus
13	ג	G	Gimel	Camel	3	Moon	II.	„ Priestess
14	ד	D	Daleth	Door	4	Venus	III.	„ Empress
15	ה	H	Hé	Window	5	Aries	XVII.	„ Star
16	ו	V/W	Vau	Nail	6	Taurus	V.	„ Hierophant
17	ז	Z	Zain	Sword	7	Gemini	VI.	„ Lovers
18	ח	Ch	Cheth	Fence	8	Cancer	VII.	„ Chariot
19	ט	T	Teth	Serpent	9	Leo	XI.	Lust
20	י	Y/I/J	Yod	Hand	10	Virgo	IX.	„ Hermit
21	כ ך	K	Kaph	Palm	20, 500	Jupiter	X.	Fortune
22	ל	L	Lamed	Ox Goad	30	Libra	VIII.	Adjustment
23	מ ם	M	Mem	Water	40, 600	Water	XII.	„ Hanged Man
24	נ	N	Nun	Fish	50, 700	Scorpio	XIII.	Death
25	ס	S	Samekh	Prop	60	Sagittarius	XIV.	Art
26	ע	O/A'A	Ayin	Eye	70	Capricorn	XV.	„ Devil
27	פ ף	P	Pé	Mouth	80, 800	Mars	XVI.	„ Tower
28	צ ץ	Tz	Tzaddi	Fish-hook	90, 900	Aquarius	IV.	„ Emperor
29	ק	Q	Qoph	Back of head	100	Pisces	XVIII.	„ Moon
30	ר	R	Resh	Head	200	Sun	XIX.	„ Sun
31	ש	Sh	Shin	Tooth	300	Fire	XX.	„ Æon
32	ת	Th	Tau	Tau	400	Saturn	XXI.	„ Universe
32 bis						Earth		
31 bis						Spirit		

TABLE 2.

		Material Elements	The Powers of the Sphinx	Elemental Weapons	Monastic Vows	The Four Triangles	Physical Senses	The Five Skandhas
י	△	Fire	To Will	The Wand	Obedience	Light	Sight	Sañña
ה	▽	Water	„ Dare	„ Cup	Chastity	Love	Taste	Vedanā
ש	✳	(Spirit)	(„ Go)	(„ Lamp)	(Service)	(Law)	(Hearing)	(Viññāṇa)
ו	△	Air	„ Know	„ Sword	Silence	Liberty	Smell	Saṅkhāra
ה	▽	Earth	„ Keep Silent	„ Pantacle	Poverty	Life	Touch	Rupā

Primary Sources
(Works written or edited by Crowley)

777 vel Prolegomena Symbolica ad Systemam Sceptico-Mysticae Viae Explicandae, Fundamentum Hieroglyphicum Sanctissimorum Scientiae Summae. London: Walter Scott Publishing Co., 1909.

777 and Other Qabalistic Writings. York Beach, ME: Samuel Weiser, 1973.

"A∴A∴ Curriculum." *The Equinox*, Vol. III, No. 1, 18–38.

"An Account of the A∴A∴ (Liber XXXIII)." *The Equinox*, Vol. I, No. 1, March 1909, 5–13.

"Across the Gulf (Liber LIX)." *The Equinox*, Vol. I, No. 7, March 1912, 293–354.

"Aha! (Liber CCXLII)." *The Equinox*, Vol. I, No. 3, March 1910, 9–54.

AMRITA: Essays in Magical Rejuvenation. (ed. M. P. Starr). Kings Beach, CA: Thelema Publications, 1990.

"The Antecedents of Thelema." *The Revival of Magick and Other Essays*, pp. 162–9.

"Berashith: An Essay in Ontology with Some Remarks on Ceremonial Magic." *The Collected Works*, Vol. II, pp. 233–43.

Book 4, Parts I & II. With M. d'Este Sturges. London: Weiland & Co, 1912–13.

The Book of the Goetia of Solomon the King: Translated into the English Tongue by a Dead Hand and Adorned with Divers Other Matters Germane, Delightful to the Wise, the Whole Edited, Verified, Introduced and Commented by Aleister Crowley. (trans. S. L. Mathers). Inverness: Society for the Propagation of Religious Truth, 1904.

The Book of Lies: Which is also Falsely Called Breaks—The Wanderings or Falsifications of the One Thought of Frater Perdurabo, which Thought is in Itself Untrue (Liber CCCXXXIII). London: Weiland & Co, 1913. ...*with an additional commentary to each chapter*. Ilfracombe: Haydn Press, 1962.

The Book of Thoth: A Short Essay on the Tarot of the Egyptians (The Equinox, Vol. III, No. 5). London: O.T.O., 1944.

The Collected Works of Aleister Crowley. 3 vols. Foyers: Society for the Propagation of Religious Truth, 1905–7.

"The Commentary Called D (The Djeridensis Comment)" (=DC). *The Magical and Philosophical Commentaries*.

The Complete Astrological Writings. (ed. J. Symonds & K. Grant). London: Gerald Duckworth, 1974.

The Confessions of Aleister Crowley: An Autohagiography. (ed. J. Symonds & K. Grant). London: Jonathan Cape, 1969.

The Diary of a Drug Fiend. London: William Collins & Sons, 1922.

"Duty." *The Revival of Magick and Other Essays*, pp. 135–44.

Eight Lectures on Yoga (The Equinox, Vol. III, No. 4). London: O.T.O., 1939.

"The Elixir of Life: Our Magical Medicine—A Lecture delivered before the National Psychological Institute (Liber CCCXLIII)." *AMRITA*.

"Energized Enthusiasm: A Note on Theurgy (Liber DCCCXI)." *The Equinox*, Vol. I, No. 9, March 1913, 17–46.

The Equinox. Vol. I, Nos. 1–3. London: Simpkin, Marshall, Hamilton, Kent & Co., 1909–10.

———. Vol. I, Nos. 4–5. London: s.n., 1910–11.

———. Vol. I, Nos. 6–10. London: Weiland & Co., 1911–13.

———. Vol. III, No. 1. Detroit: Universal Publishing Co., 1919.

———. Vol. III, No. 10. (ed. Hymenaeus Beta). New York: O.T.O., 1986.

The Equinox of the Gods (The Equinox, Vol. III, No. 3). London: O.T.O., 1936.

"An Essay upon Number." *The Equinox*, Vol. I, No. 5, March 1911, 97–120; reprinted in *777 and Other Qabalistic Writings*, pp. 27–50.

The General Principles of Astrology (Liber DXXXVI). With E. Adams. (ed. Hymenaeus Beta). York Beach, ME: Samuel Weiser, 2002.

The Gospel According to St. Bernard Shaw (Liber DCCCLXXXVIII). Barstow, CA: Thelema Publishing Co, 1953.

The Heart of the Master. London: O.T.O., 1938.

The Holy Books of Thelema (The Equinox, Vol. III, No. 9). (ed. Hymenæus Alpha). York Beach, ME: Samuel Weiser, 1983.

"The Key of the Mysteries (Liber XLVI)." By Éliphas Lévi. *The Equinox*, Vol. I, No. 10, September 1913, Special Supplement.

"Khabs am Pekht (Liber CCC)." *The Equinox*, Vol. III, No. 1, 171–182.

Konx Om Pax: Essays in Light. Boleskine: Society for the Propagation of Religious Truth, 1907.

The Law Is For All: An Extended Commentary on The Book of the Law. (ed. I. Regardie). St. Paul, MN: Llewellyn Publications, 1975.

"Liber A vel Armorum sub figura CCCXII." *The Equinox*, Vol. I, No. 4, September 1910, 15–9.

"Liber A'ash vel Capricorni Pneumatici sub figura CCCLXX." *The Equinox*, Vol. I, No. 6, September 1911, 33–9.

Liber AL vel Legis. As "Liber L. vel Legis." *The Equinox*, Vol. I, No. 10, September 1913, 11–33. As "The Book of the Law." With Introduction and Short Comment. London: O.T.O., 1938.

Liber Aleph vel CXI: The Book of Wisdom or Folly in the Form of an Epistle of 666 The Great Wild Beast to his Son 777 (The Equinox, Vol. III, No. 6). West Point, CA: Thelema Publishing Co, 1961.

"Liber B vel Magi sub figura I." *The Equinox*, Vol. I, No. 7, March 1912, 5–9.

"Liber Cheth vel Vallum Abiegni sub figura CLVI." *The Equinox*, Vol. I, No. 6, September 1911, 23–7.

"Liber CI: An Open Letter to Those Who May Wish to Join the Order Enumerating the Duties and Privileges." *The Equinox*, Vol. III, No. 1, 207–24.

"Liber CL vel לעג, A Sandal, De Lege Libellum L-L-L-L-L." *The Equinox*, Vol. III, No. 1, 99–125.

"Liber CLVIII: The Soldier and the Hunchback—! and ?." *The Equinox*, Vol. I, No. 1, 113–35.

"Liber CLXI: Concerning the Law of Thelema." *The Equinox*, Vol. III, No. 1, 225–38.

Liber Collegii Sancti sub figurâ CLXXXV: Being the Tasks of the Grades, and their Oaths, proper to Liber XIII, the publications of the A∴A∴ in Class D from B to G. s.l.: s.n., n.d.

"Liber CXCIV: An Intimation with Reference to the Constitution of the Order." *The Equinox*, Vol. III, No. 1, 239–46.

"Liber DCCCXXXVII: The Law of Liberty—A Tract of ΤΟ ΜΕΓΑ ΘΗΡΙΟΝ 666, That is a Magus 9°=2▫ A∴ A∴." *The Equinox*, Vol. III, No. 1, 45–52.

"Liber DCLXVI: The Master Therion—A Biographical Note." *The Equinox*, Vol. III, No. 10, 16–7.

"Liber E vel Exercitiorum sub figura IX." *The Equinox*, Vol. I, No. 1, March 1909, 23–34.

"Liber III vel Jugorum." *The Equinox*, Vol. I, No. 4, September 1910, 9–14.

"Liber Liberi vel Lapidus Lazuli, Adumbratio Kabbalæ Ægyptiorum sub figurâ VII." *The Holy Books of Thelema*, pp. 7–35.

"Liber Librae sub figura XXX." *The Equinox*, Vol. I, No. 1, March 1909, 15–21.

"Liber LII: Manifesto of the O.T.O.." *The Equinox*, Vol. III, No. 1, 195–206.

"Liber LXI vel Causæ: The Preliminary Lection, including the History Lection." *The Equinox*, Vol. III, No. 1, 53–61.

"Liber LXV: Liber Cordis Cincti Serpente sub figurâ אדני." *The Equinox*, Vol. III, No. 1, 63–98.

"Liber LXXI: The Voice of the Silence." By H. P. Blavatsky. *The Equinox*, Vol. III, No. 1, Supplement.

"Liber O vel Manus et Sagittae sub figura VI." *The Equinox*, Vol. I, No. 2, September 1909, 11–30.

Liber OZ (Liber LXXVII). London: O.T.O., 1941.

"Liber Resh vel Helios sub figura CC." *The Equinox*, Vol. I, No. 6, September 1911, 29–32.

"Liber Samekh: Theurgia Goetia Summa Congressus Cum Daemone sub figura DCCC." *Magick in Theory and Practice*, Appendix IV.

"Liber Trigrammaton sub figurâ XXVII." *The Holy Books of Thelema*, pp. 43–9.

"Liber תשארב (Thisharb) Viae Memoriae sub figura CMXIII." *The Equinox*, Vol I., No. 7, March 1912, 105–116.

"Liber Tzaddi vel Hamus Hermeticus sub figura XC." *The Equinox*, Vol. I, No. 6, September 1911, 17–22.

"Liber V vel Reguli." *Magick in Theory and Practice*, Appendix VI.

"Liber XIII vel Graduum Montis Abiegni: A Syllabus of the Steps upon the Path." *The Equinox*, Vol. I, No. 3, March 1910, 3–8.

"Liber XV: Ecclesiae Gnosticae Catholicae Canon Missae." *The International*, Vol. XII, No. 3, March 1918, 70–4; *The Equinox*, Vol. III, No. 1, 247–70; *Magick in Theory and Practice*, Appendix VI.

Liber XXI: Khing Kang King; The Classic of Purity—first written down by me Ko Yuen in the Episode of the Dynasty of Wu and now made into a Rime by me Aleister Crowley. London: O.T.O., 1939.

"Liber XXX Aerum vel Saeculi sub figura CCCCXVIII: Being of the Angels of the 30 Aethyrs—The Vision and the Voice." *The Equinox*, Vol. I, No. 5, March 1911, Special Supplement.

Little Essays Toward Truth. London: O.T.O., 1938.

Magical and Philosophical Commentaries on The Book of the Law. (ed. J. Symonds & K. Grant). Montréal: 93 Publishing, 1974.

The Magical Diaries of Aleister Crowley: Tunisia 1923. (ed. S. Skinner). Jersey: Neville Spearman, 1979.

The Magical Record of the Beast 666: The Diaries of Aleister Crowley, 1914–1920. (ed. J. Symonds & K. Grant). London: Duckworth, 1972.

Magick: Liber ABA—Book 4, Parts I–IV. With M. d'Este Sturges & L. Waddell. (ed. Hymenaeus Beta). 2nd rev. ed. York Beach, ME: Samuel Weiser, 1997.

Magick in Theory and Practice. Paris: Lecram Press, 1929 (= *MITAP*).

Magick without Tears. (ed. K. J. Germer). Hampton, NJ: Thelema Publishing Co, 1954 (= *MWT*).

"The Message of the Master Therion (Liber II)." *The Equinox*, Vol. III, No. 1, 39–43.

"The Method of Thelema." *The Revival of Magick and Other Essays*, pp. 176–83.

Moonchild: A Prologue. London: Mandrake Press, 1929.

"The New Comment" (=NC). *The Magical and Philosophical Commentaries*; also in *The Law Is For All.*

"The Old Comment" (=OC). *The Equinox*, Vol. I, No. 7, March 1912, 387–401; also in *The Magical and Philosophical Commentaries*; and *The Law Is For All.*

"One Star in Sight." *Magick in Theory and Practice*, Appendix II.

"Orpheus: A Lyrical Legend." *The Collected Works*, Vol. III, pp. 124–218.

"The Palace of the World." *The Collected Works*, Vol. I, pp. 204–5.

"The Paris Working (Liber CDXV)." *The Vision and the Voice with Commentary and Other Papers*, pp. 343–409.

"Præmonstrance of A∴A∴: A Manifesto of the Great White Brotherhood." *The Equinox*, Vol. III, No. 1, 11–17.

"The Psychology of Hashish: An Essay on Mysticism." *The Equinox*, Vol. I, No. 2, September 1909, 31–89.

"Qabalistic Dogma." *The Collected Works*, Vol. I, pp. 265–9.

The Revival of Magick and Other Essays (Oriflamme 2). (ed. Hymenaeus Beta & R. Kaczynski). Tempe, AZ: New Falcon Press, 1998.

The Scented Garden of Abdullah the Satirists of Shiraz: Translated from a Rare Indian MS. by the Late Major Lutiy and Another. London: s.n., 1910.

"Science and Buddhism." *The Collected Works*, Vol. II, pp. 244–261.

"The Scientific Solution to the Problem of Government." *The Revival of Magick and Other Essays*, pp. 208–10.

The Secret Rituals of the O.T.O. (ed. F. King). London: C. W. Daniel, 1973.

"The Sevenfold Sacrament." *The Equinox*, Vol. III, No. 1, 187–194.

Shih Yi: A critical and mnemonic paraphrase of the Yi King by Ko Yuen (The Equinox, Vol. III, No. 7). (ed. H. Parsons Smith). Oceanside, CA: Thelema Publications, 1971.

The Spirit of Solitude: An Autohagiography—Subsequently re-Antichristened The Confessions of Aleister Crowley. 2 vols. London: Mandrake Press, 1929.

The Sword of Song: Called by Christians The Book of the Beast. Benares: Society for the Propagation of Religious Truth, 1904.

"A Syllabus of the Official Instructions of A∴A∴ Hitherto Published (Liber CCVII)." *The Equinox*, Vol. I, No. 10, 41–56.

"Tannhäuser: A Story of All Time." *The Collected Works*, Vol. I, pp. 222–262.

The Tao Teh King (Liber CLVII): A New Translation by Ko Yuen (The Equinox, Vol. III, No. 8). (ed. H. Parsons Smith). Dublin, CA: Thelema Publications, 1975.

"The Temple of Solomon the King." Part I. With J. F. C. Fuller. *The Equinox*, Vol. I, No. 1, March 1909, 141–230.

———. Part II. With J. F. C. Fuller. *The Equinox*, Vol. I, No. 2, September 1909, 217–334.

———. Part III. With J. F. C. Fuller. *The Equinox*, Vol I, No. 3, March 1910, 133–280.

———. Part IV. With J. F. C. Fuller. *The Equinox*, Vol. I, No. 4, September 1910, 41–196.

———. Part V, *The Equinox*, Vol. I, No. 5, March 1911, 65–120.

———. Part VI, *The Equinox*, Vol. I, No. 7, March 1912, 335–400.

———. Part VII, *The Equinox*, Vol. I, No. 8, September 1912, 5–48.

———. Part VIII, *The Equinox*, Vol. I, No. 9, March 1913, 1–11.

———. Part IX, *The Equinox*, Vol. I, No. 10, September 1913, 93–125.

"Thien Tao, or, The Synagogue of Satan (Liber XLI)." *Konx Om Pax*, pp. 53–67.

The Vision and the Voice with Commentary and Other Papers. With V. Neuburg & M. d'Este. (ed. Hymenaeus Beta). York Beach, ME: Samuel Weiser, 1998.

The World's Tragedy. Paris: s.n., 1910.

Secondary Sources

Abrahamsson, C. (ed.) (2014). *The Fenris Wolf*, No. 7. Stockholm: Edda Publishing.

Adler, J. A. (2014). *Reconstructing the Confucian Dao: Zhu Xi's Appropriation of Zhou Dunyi (SUNY Series in Chinese Philosophy and Culture)*. Albany: State University of New York Press.

Allen, N. J., et al. (eds.) (2008). *Early Human Kinship: From Sex to Social Reproduction*. London: Royal Anthropological Institute.

Apuleius. (1822). *The Metamorphosis, or Golden Ass, and Philosophical Works, of Apuleius*. (trans. & ed. T. Taylor). London: Robert Triphook.

Aristotle. (1966). *Ethica Nicomachea*. (trans. W.D. Ross). Oxford: Oxford University Press.

———. (1972). *Politics*. (trans. H. Rackham). Cambridge, MA: Harvard University Press.

Armenteros, C. (2011). *The French Idea of History: Joseph de Maistre and His Heirs, 1794–1854*. Ithaca, NY: Cornell University Press.

Arnold, E. (1879). *The Light of Asia, or, The Great Renunciation (Mahabhinishkramana): Being the Life and Teachings of Gautama, Prince of India and Founder of Buddhism*. London: Trübner & Co.

———. (trans.) (1885). *The Song Celestial, or, Bhagavad-Gîtâ (from the Mahâbhârata): Being a Discourse between Arjuna, Prince of India, and the Supreme Being under the Form of Krishna*. London: Trübner & Co.

Arnold, M. (1897). *The Poetical Works of Matthew Arnold: Complete Edition with Biographical Introduction*. (ed. N. H. Dole). New York: Thomas Y. Cromwell & Co.

Augustine. (1912). *St. Augustine's Confessions*. 2 vols. (trans. W. Watts). Cambridge, MA: Harvard University Press.

Aurobindo. (1993). *India's Rebirth: Out of the Ruins of the West—A Selection from Sri Aurobindo's Writings, Talks and Speeches.* (ed. S. Nahar). Paris: Institut de Recherches Évolutives.

Bachofen, J. J. (1861). *Das Mutterrecht: Eine Untersuchung über die Gynaikokratie der alten Welt nach ihrer religiösen und rechtlichen Natur.* 3 vols. Stuttgart: Krais & Hoffmann.

Balk, A. P. (2012). *Balderdash: A Treatise on Ethics.* Helsinki: Thelema Publications.

———. (2008). *Saints & Sinners: An Account of Western Civilization.* Helsinki: Thelema Publications.

Banerjee, B. N. (trans.) (1894). *Practical Yoga Philosophy or Siva-Sanhita in English: The Masterpiece of Occult Philosophy and Esoteric Yoga Science; with Copious Explanatory Notes.* Calcutta: s.n.

Barry, N. (1982). *The Tradition of Spontaneous Order (Literature of Liberty, Vol. 5, No. 2).* (ed. L.P. Liggio). Arlington, VA: Institute for Humane Studies.

Batchelor, S. (1994). *The Awakening of the West: The Encounter of Buddhism and Western Culture.* Berkeley, CA: Parallax Press.

Baudelaire, C. (1995). *Little Poems in Prose.* rev. ed. (trans. A. Crowley, ed. M. P. Starr). Chicago: Teitan Press.

Beaufils, C. (1986). *Le Sâr Péladan, 1858–1918: Biographie critique.* Paris: Aux Amateurs des Livres.

Bergson, H. (1932). *Les Deux Sources de la morale et de la religion.* Paris: Félix Alcan.

Berlin, I. (2003). *Isaiah Berlin's Counter-Enlightenment (Transactions of the American Philosophical Society, Volume 93, Part 5).* (ed. J. Mali & R. Wokler). Philadelphia: American Philosophical Society.

Beyer, B. (1925). *Das Lehrsystem des Ordens der Gold- und Rosenkreuzer (Pansophia, Vol. II, No. 2).* Leipzig: Pansophie-Verlag.

Bhuyan, P. R. (2003). *Swami Vivekananda: Messiah of Resurgent India.* New Delhi: Atlantic.

Birkholz, A. M. (1779). *Der Compaß der Weisen: von einen Mitverwandten der innern Verfassung der ächten und rechten Freymäurerey beschrieben.* Berlin: Christian Ulrich Ringmacher.

Blackburn, S. (2005). *The Oxford Dictionary of Philosophy.* Oxford: Oxford University Press.

Blake, W. (1977). *The Complete Poems (Penguin English Poets).* (ed. A. Ostriker). London: Penguin Books.

Blavatsky, H. P. (1877). *Isis Unveiled: A Master-Key to the Mysteries of Ancient and Modern Science and Theology.* 2 vols. New York: J. W. Bouton.

———. (1888). *The Secret Doctrine: The Synthesis of Science, Religion, and Philosophy.* 2 vols. London: Theosophical Publishing Co.

Blécourt, W. de, R. Hutton & J. La Fontaine. (1999). *The Athlone History of Witchcraft and Magic in Europe: Volume 6—The Twentieth Century.* London: Athlone Press.

Bloomfield, M. (1908). *The Religion of the Veda: The Ancient Religion of India—from Rig-Veda to Upanishads.* London: G. P. Putnam's Sons.

Böhme, J. (1955–61). *Sämtliche Schriften.* 11 vols. (ed. W. E. Peuckert & A. Faust). Stuttgart: Fr. Frommanns Verlag.

Boring, M. E., K. Berger & C. Colpe (eds.) (1995). *Hellenistic Commentary to the New Testament.* Nashville: Abingdon Press.

Bourne, R. S. (1964). *War and the Intellectuals: Collected Essays, 1915–1919*. (ed. C. Resek). New York: Harper & Row.

Bowker, J. (ed.) (1997). *The Oxford Dictionary of World Religions*. Oxford: Oxford University Press.

Bradley, O. (1999). *A Modern Maistre: The Social & Political Thought of Joseph de Maistre*. Lincoln: University of Nebraska Press.

Bradt, H. (2004). *Astronomy Methods: A Physical Approach to Astronomical Observations*. Cambridge: Cambridge University Press.

Brock, M. (1883). *Rome: Pagan and Papal*. London: Hodder & Stoughton.

Brooks, D. R. (1990). *The Secret of the Three Cities: An Introduction to Hindu Śākta Tantrism*. Chicago: University of Chicago Press.

Buisset, C. (1984). *Eliphas Lévi: sa vie, son œuvre, ses pensées*. Paris: Guy Trédaniel.

Bulwer-Lytton, E. G. E. (1842). *Zanoni*. 3 vols. London: Saunders & Otley.

Burgess, E. (ed.) (1860). *Translation of the Sûrya-Siddhânta, a Text-Book of Hindu Astronomy; with Notes, and an Appendix, containing additional notes and tables, calculations of eclipses, a stellar map, and indexes*. New Haven: American Oriental Society.

Burkert, W. (1985). *Greek Religion: Archaic and Classical*. (trans. J. Raffan). Oxford: Basil Blackwell.

———. (1983). *Homo Necans: The Anthropology of Ancient Greek Sacrificial Ritual and Myth*. (trans. P. Bing). Berkeley: University of California Press.

Burnet, J. (1920). *Early Greek Philosophy*. London: A&C Black.

Burton, R. F. (1880). *The Kasîdah of Hâjî Abdû el-Yezdî: translated and annotated by his friend and pupil, F.B.* London: Bernard Quaritch.

Butler, W. F. (1889). *Charles George Gordon (English Men of Action)*. London: Macmillan.

Campbell, B. F. (1980). *Ancient Wisdom Revived: A History of the Theosophical Movement*. Berkeley: University of California Press.

Campion, N. (1999). *The Book of World Horoscopes*. 2nd. rev. ed. Bristol: Cinnabar Books.

———. (1994). *The Great Year: Astrology, Millenarianism and History in the Western Tradition*. London: Penguin Books.

———. (2015). *The New Age in the Modern West: Counterculture, Utopia and Prophecy from the Late Eighteenth Century to the Present Day*. London: Bloomsbury Academic.

Cantillon, R. (2015). *Richard Cantillon's Essay on the Nature of Trade in General: A Variorum Edition (Routledge Studies in the History of Economics)*. (ed. R. van den Berg). London: Routledge.

Carter, J. C. (1907). *Law: Its Origin, Growth and Function—Being a Course of Lectures Prepared for Delivery before the Law School of Harvard University*. New York: G. P. Putnam's Sons.

Casaubon, M. (ed.) (1659). *A True & Faithful Relation of What passed for many Yeers Between Dr. John Dee (A Mathematician of Great Fame in Q. Eliz. and King James their Reignes) and Some Spirits: Tending (had it Succeeded) To a General Alteration of most States and Kingdomes in the World*. London: T. Garthwait.

Chacornac, P. (1926). *Éliphas Lévi, rénovateur de l'occultisme en France (1810–1875)*. Paris: Librairie générale des sciences occultes.

Chan, W. T. (ed.) (1963). *A Source Book in Chinese Philosophy*. Princeton, NJ: Princeton University Press.

Charles, R. H. (ed.) (1913). *The Apocrypha and Pseudepigrapha of the Old Testament in English: With Introductions and Critical and Explanatory Notes to the Several Books*. 2 vols. Oxford: Clarendon Press.

Chen, Y. (2013). *Confucianism as Religion: Controversies and Consequences*. Leiden: Brill.

Chorpenning, J. F. (1997). *The Holy Family Devotion: A Brief History*. Montréal: Centre de recherche et de documentation, Oratoire Saint-Joseph.

Churton, T. (2014). *Aleister Crowley: The Beast in Berlin—Art, Sex, and Magick in the Weimar Republic*. Rochester, VT: Inner Traditions.

Cicero, M. T. (2005). *An Attack on an Enemy of Freedom (Great Ideas)*. (trans. M. Grant). London: Penguin Books.

———. (1878). *Treatises of M. T. Cicero: On the nature of the gods; On divination; On fate; On the republic; On the laws; and On standing for consulship*. (ed. & trans. C. D. Yonge). London: George Bell & Sons.

Cohen, M. (2015). *Paradigm Shift: How Expert Opinions Keep Changing on Life, the Universe, and Everything*. Exeter: Imprint Academic.

Cole, R. T. (2015). *Liber L. vel Bogus: The Real Confessions of Aleister Crowley*. rev. ed. (ed. S. Sparkes). s.l.:Orange Box Books.

Coleman, G. & T. Jinpa (eds.) (2005). *The Tibetan Book of the Dead: The Great Liberation by Hearing in the Intermediate States*. (trans. G. Dorje). London: Penguin Books.

Coleridge, H. J. (1872). *The Life and Letters of St. Francis Xavier*. 2 vols. London: Burns and Oates.

Collcutt, M. (1981). *Five Mountains: The Rinzai Zen Monastic Institution in Medieval Japan (Harvard East Asia Monographs)*. Cambridge, MA: Harvard University Press.

Cummings, B. (ed.) (2011). *The Book of Common Prayer: The Texts from 1549, 1559, and 1662 (Oxford World's Classics)*. Oxford: Oxford University Press.

Day, T. P. (1982). *The Conception of Punishment in Early Indian Literature*. Waterloo, ON: Wilfred Laurier University Press.

Deacon, R. (1968). *John Dee: Scientist, Geographer, Astrologer and Secret Agent to Elizabeth I*. London: Frederick Muller.

de Bary, W. T. et al. (eds.) (1999–2000). *Sources of Chinese Tradition (Introduction to Asian Civilizations)*. 2nd ed. 2 vols. New York: Columbia University Press.

Dehn, G. (ed.) (2015). *The Book of Abramelin: A New Translations*. rev. ed. (trans. S. Guth). Lake Worth, FL: Ibis Press.

De Michelis, E. (2004). *A History of Modern Yoga: Patañjali and Western Esotericism*. London: Continuum.

Dermenghem, É. (1946). *Joseph de Maistre, mystique: Ses rapports avec le martinisme, l'illuminisme et la franc-maçonnerie, l'influence des doctrines mystiques et occultes sur sa pensée religieuse*. rev. ed. Paris: La Colombe.

Descartes, R. (1993). *Meditations on First Philosophy in Focus*. (ed. S. Tweyman, trans. E. S. Haldane & G. R. T. Ross). London: Routledge.

Deussen, P. (1906). *The Philosophy of the Upanishads*. (trans. A. S. Geden). Edinburgh: T. & T. Clark.

———. (1912). *The System of the Vedânta: According to Bâdarâyana's Brahma-Sûtras and Çankara's Commentary Thereon Set Forth as a Compendium of the Dogmatics of Brahminism from the Standpoint of Çankara*. (trans. C. Johnston). Chicago: Open Court Publishing Co.

Dharampal. (1983). *The Beautiful Tree: Indigenous Indian Education in the Eighteenth Century*. New Delhi: Biblia Impex.

Diogenes Laërtius. (1972). *Lives of Eminent Philosophers*. (trans. R. D. Hicks). Cambridge, MA: Harvard University Press.

Dobbs, B. J. T. (1991). *The Janus Faces of Genius: The Role of Alchemy in Newton's Thought*. Cambridge: Cambridge University Press.

Dodds, E. R. (1951). *The Greeks and the Irrational (Sather Classical Lectures, Vol. 25)*. Berkeley: University of California Press.

Drummond, W. (1866). *The Œdipus Judaicus*. rev. ed. London: Reeves & Turner.

Dumoulin, H. (1988–90). *Zen Buddhism: A History*. 2 vols. (trans. J. W. Heisig & P. Knitter). New York: Macmillan.

Dupont, F. (1989). *Daily Life in Ancient Rome*. (trans. C. Woodall). Oxford: Blackwell.

Durant, W. (1953). *The Story of Philosophy: The Lives and Opinions of the World's Greatest Philosophers from Plato to John Dewey*. 2nd ed. New York: Pocket Books.

——— & A. Durant. (1935–1975). *The Story of Civilization*. 11 vols. New York: Simon & Schuster.

Eckartshausen, K. von. (1896). *The Cloud upon the Sanctuary*. (trans. I. de Steiger). London: George Redway.

Eddington, A. S. (2014). *The Nature of the Physical World: Gifford Lectures of 1927— An Annotated Edition*. (ed. H. G. Callaway). Newcastle upon Tyne: Cambridge Scholars Publishing.

———. (1920). *Space, Time and Gravitation: An Outline of the General Relativity Theory*. Cambridge: Cambridge University Press.

Eliade, M. (1954). *The Myth of the Eternal Return: Or, Cosmos and History (Bollingen Series XLVI)*. (trans. W. R. Trask). New York: Pantheon Books.

———. (1969). *Yoga: Immortality and Freedom*. 2nd ed. (trans. W. R. Trask). Princeton: Princeton University Press.

Eller, C. (1995). *Living in the Lap of the Goddess: The Feminist Spiritual Movement in America*. Boston: Beacon Press.

Emberley, P. & B. Cooper (eds.) (2004). *Faith And Political Philosophy: The Correspondence between Leo Strauss and Eric Voegelin, 1934–1964*. Columbia: University of Missouri Press.

Emerson, R. W. (1841). *Essays*. (ed. T. Carlyle). London: James Fraser.

Engels, F. (1884). *Der Ursprung der Familie, des Privateigenthums und des Staates*. Zürich: Hottingen.

Epictetus. (1890). *The Works of Epictetus: His Discourses, in Four Books, the Enchiridion, and Fragments*. (trans. T. W. Higginson). New York: Thomas Nelson & Sons.

Erdmann, J. E. (1892–97). *A History of Philosophy: Ancient and Mediaeval Philosophy*. 3rd ed. 3 vols. (trans. W. S. Hough). London: Macmillan.

Eshelman, J. A. (2000). *The Mystical & Magical System of the A∴A∴: The Spiritual System of Aleister Crowley & George Cecil Jones Step-by-Step*. Los Angeles: College of Thelema.

Fabre d'Olivet, A. (1915). *Hermeneutic Interpretation of the Origin of the Social State of Man and the Destiny of the Adamic Race.* (trans. N. L. Redfield). London: G. P. Putnam's Sons.

Farrar, J. & S. Farrar. (1984). *The Witches' Way: Principles, Rituals and Beliefs of Modern Witchcraft.* London: Guild.

Faulkner, R. O. (trans.) (2008). *The Egyptian Book of the Dead: The Book of Going Forth by Day.* 2nd rev. ed. (ed. E. von Dassow). San Francisco: Chronicle Books.

Ferguson, A. (1767). *An Essay on the History of Civil Society.* London: T. Cadell.

Fichte, J. G. (1982). *The Science of Knowledge: With the First and Second Introductions.* (ed. & trans. P. Heath & J. Lachs). Cambridge: Cambridge University Press.

Findel, J. G. (1866). *History of Freemasonry: From Its Rise Down to the Present Day.* London: Asher & Co.

Flood, G. (2004). *The Ascetic Self: Subjectivity, Memory and Tradition.* Cambridge: Cambridge University Press.

———. (2006). *The Tantric Body: The Secret Tradition of Hindu Religion.* London: I.B. Tauris.

Flournoy, T. (1900). *Des Indes à la planète Mars: Étude sur un cas de somnambulisme avec glossolalie.* Paris: Alcan & Eggimann.

Forlong, J. G. R. (1883). *Rivers of Life: or, Sources and Streams of the Faiths of Man in All Lands; showing the Evolution of Faiths from the Rudest Symbolism to the Latest Spiritual Developments.* 2 vols. London: Bernard Quaritch.

Foucault, M. (1978-86). *The History of Sexuality.* 3 vols. (trans. R. Hurley). New York: Pantheon Books.

Fowler, J. D. (2005). *Pathways to Immortality: An Introduction to the Philosophy and Religion of Taoism.* Brighton: Sussex Academic Press.

———. (2002). *Perspectives of Reality: An Introduction to the Philosophy of Hinduism.* Brighton: Sussex Academic Press.

Frazer, J. G. (1911-15). *The Golden Bough: A Study in Magic and Religion.* 3rd ed. 12 vols. London: Macmillan.

Freud, S. (1918). *Totem and Taboo: Resemblances Between the Psychic Lives of Savages and Neurotics.* (trans. A. A. Brill). New York: Moffat, Yard & Co.

Fuller, J. F. C. (1926). *The Foundations of the Science of War.* London: Hutchinson & Co.

———. (1937). *The Secret Wisdom of the Qabalah: A Study in Jewish Mystical Thought.* London: W. Rider & Co.

———. (1907). *The Star in the West: A Critical Essay upon the Works of Aleister Crowley.* London: Walter Scott Publishing Co.

Gandhi, M. K. (1935). *Young India, 1927-1928.* Triplicane, Madras: S. Ganesan.

Gilbert, W. S. & A. Sullivan. (1996). *The Complete Annotated Gilbert and Sullivan.* (ed. I. Bradley). Oxford: Oxford University Press.

Giles, H. A. (trans.) (1889). *Chuang Tzŭ: Mystic, Moralist, and Social Reformer.* London: Bernard Quaritch.

———. (1915). *Confucianism and Its Rivals: lectures delivered in the University Hall of Dr. William's Library, London, October-December 1914.* London: Williams & Norgate.

Godwin, J., C. McIntosh & D. P. McIntoch (trans.) (2016). *Rosicrucian Trilogy: Fama Fraternitatis, 1614; Confessio Fraternitatis, 1615; The Chemical Wedding of Christian Rosenkreuz, 1616.* Newburyport, MA: Weiser Books.

Goethe, J. W. von. (1987–94). *Faust: Translated with an Introduction and Notes by David Luke (Oxford World's Classics)*. 2 vols. (trans. & ed. D. Luke). Oxford: Oxford University Press.

____. (2012). *The Sorrows of Young Werther: Translated with an Introduction and Notes by David Constantine (Oxford World's Classics)*. (trans. & ed. D. Constantine). Oxford: Oxford University Press.

Goldberg, P. (2010). *American Veda: From Emerson and the Beatles to Yoga and Meditation—How Indian Spirituality Changed the West*. New York: Harmony Books.

Goodrick-Clarke, N. (ed.) (2004). *Helena Blavatsky (Western Esoteric Masters)*. Berkeley, CA: North Atlantic Books.

Gould, S. J. (1977). *Ontogeny and Phylogeny*. Cambridge, MA: Harvard University Press.

Grasse, R. (2002). *Signs of the Times: Unlocking the Symbolic Language of World Events*. Charlottesville: Hampton Roads Publishing.

Guthrie, W. K. C. (1962–81). *A History of Greek Philosophy*. 6 vols. Cambridge: Cambridge University Press.

Hacker, E., S. Moore & L. Patsco (2002). *I Ching: An Annotated Bibliography*. New York: Routledge.

Hadot, P. (1995). *Philosophy as a Way of Life: Spiritual Exercises from Socrates to Foucault*. (ed. A. I. Davidson, trans. M. Chase). Oxford: Blackwell Publishing.

____. (2002). *What Is Ancient Philosophy?* (trans. M. Chase). Cambridge, MA: Harvard University Press.

Haeckel, E. (1900). *The Riddle of the Universe at the Close of the Nineteenth Century*. (trans. J. McCabe). New York: Harper & Brothers.

Hamilton, S. (2000). *Early Buddhism: A New Approach—The I of the Beholder*. Abingdon: Routledge.

Hansen, C. (1992). *A Daoist Theory of Chinese Thought: A Philosophical Interpretation*. Oxford: Oxford University Press.

Harrison, J. (1913). *Ancient Art & Ritual*. London: Williams & Norgate.

____. (1921). *Prolegomena to the study of Greek Religion*. 3rd ed. London: Cambridge University Press.

Hartmann, F. (trans.) (1888). *Cosmology or Universal Science: Containing the Mysteries of the Universe Regarding God, Nature, Man, the Macrocosm and Microcosm, Eternity and Time Explained According to the Religion of Christ by Means of the Secret Symbols of the Rosicrucians of the Sixteenth and Seventeenth Centuries*. Boston: Occult Publishing Co.

____. (1890). *In the Pronaos of the Temple of Wisdom: Containing the History of the True and the False Rosicrucians—With an Introduction into the Mysteries of the Hermetic Philosophy*. London: Theosophical Publishing Society.

____. (1891). *The Life and Doctrines of Jacob Boehme the God-taught Philosopher: An Introduction to the Study of His Works*. London: Kegan Paul, Trench, Trübner & Co.

Hawking, S. (1998). *A Brief History of Time: An Updated and Expanded Tenth Anniversary Edition*. New York: Bantam Books.

Hayek, F. A. (2011). *The Constitution of Liberty: The Definitive Edition*. (ed. R. Hamowy). Chicago: University of Chicago Press.

____. (1952). *The Sensory Order: An Inquiry into the Foundations of Theoretical Psychology*. London: Routledge & Kegan Paul.

———. (1967). *Studies in Philosophy, Politics and Economics*. London: Routledge & Kegan Paul.

Hebermann, C. G. et al. (eds.) (1907–12). *The Catholic Encyclopedia: An International Work of Reference on the Constitution, Doctrine, Discipline, and History of the Catholic Church*. 15 vols. New York: Robert Appleton.

Hegel, G. W. F. (1892–4). *Encyclopaedia of the Philosophical Sciences*. 2nd rev. ed. 2 vols. (trans. W. Wallace). Oxford: Clarendon Press.

———. (1892–6). *Hegel's Lectures on the History of Philosophy*. 3 vols. (trans. E. S. Haldane & F. S. Simson). London: Kegan Paul, Trench, Trübner & Co.

———. (1907). *Hegels theologische Jugendschriften*. (ed. H. Nohl). Tübingen: J. C. B. Mohr.

———. (1899). *The Philosophy of History*. rev. ed. (trans. J. Sibree). New York: Colonial Press.

Heinlein, R. A. (1988). *Time Enough for Love: The Lives of Lazarus Long*. New York: Ace Books.

Heisenberg, W. (1958). *Physics and Philosophy: The Revolution in Modern Science*. New York: Harper & Row.

Hendrix, J. S. (2005). *Aesthetics & the Philosophy of Spirit: From Plotinus to Schelling and Hegel*. New York: Peter Lang Publishing.

Herbert, A. P. (1934). *Holy Deadlock*. London: Methuen & Co.

Herodotus. (1920–25). *Herodotus: With an English Translation by A. D. Godley (Loeb Classical Library)*. 4 vols. London: William Heinemann.

Hesiod. (1914). *Hesiod, the Homeric Hymns, and Homerica: With an English Translation by Hugh G. Evelyn-White (Loeb Classical Library)*. London: William Heinemann.

Higgins, G. (1836). *Anacalypsis: An Attempt to Draw Aside the Veil of the Saitic Isis; or, an Inquiry into the Origin of Languages, Nations and Religions*. 2 vols. London: Longman, Rees, Orme, Brown, Green & Longman.

Hiltebeitel, A. (1999). *Rethinking India's Oral and Classical Epics: Draupadī among Rajputs, Muslims, and Dalits*. Chicago: University of Chicago Press.

Hinton, C. H. (1912). *The Fourth Dimension*. 3rd ed. London: George Allen & Co.

Hislop, A. (1871). *The Two Babylons: The Papal Worship Proved to Be the Worship of Nimrod and His Wife—With Sixty-one Woodcut Illustrations from Nineveh, Babylon, Egypt, Pompeii, &c*. 7th ed. London: S. W. Partridge & Co.

Hoffer, E. (1955). *The Passionate State of Mind, and other aphorisms*. New York: Harper.

———. (1951). *The True Believer: Thoughts on the Nature of Mass Movements*. New York: Harper & Row.

Homer. (1917–20). *Homeri Opera (Oxford Classical Texts)*. 4 vols. (ed. D. B. Monro & T. W. Allen). Oxford: Clarendon Press.

Hone, W. (ed.) (1820). *The Apocryphal New Testament: Being All the Gospels, Epistles and Other Pieces Now Extant, Attributed in the First Four Centuries to Jesus Christ, His Apostles, and Their Companions; and Not Included in the New Testament by Its Compilers*. (trans. J. Jones & W. Wake). London: William Hone.

Hoppe, H. H. (2014). *From Aristocracy to Monarchy to Democracy: A Tale of Moral and Economic Folly and Decay*. Auburn, AL: Mises Institute.

Horace. (1878). *The Works of Horace, with English Notes, by the Rev. A. J. Macleane, M.A., Head-Master of King Edward's School, Bath*. rev. ed. (rev. & ed. R. H. Chase). Boston: John Allyn.

Howe, E. (1972). *The Magicians of the Golden Dawn: A Documentary History of a Magical Order, 1887–1923*. London: Routledge & Kegan Paul.

Hucker, C. O. (1978). *China to 1850: A Short History*. Stanford, CA: Stanford University Press.

Huffman, W. H. (ed.) (2001). *Robert Fludd (Western Esoteric Masters)*. Berkeley, CA: North Atlantic Books.

Hume, D. (2007). *An Enquiry concerning Human Understanding: And Other Writings (Cambridge Texts in the History of Philosophy)*. (ed. S. Buckle). Cambridge: Cambridge University Press.

Humphreys, T. C. (1968). *Sixty Years of Buddhism in England (1907–1967): A History and a Survey*. London: Buddhist Society.

Huntington, S. P. (1996). *The Clash of Civilizations and the Remaking of World Order*. New York: Simon & Schuster.

Huson, P. (2004). *Mystical Origins of the Tarot: From Ancient Roots to Modern Usage*. Rochester, VT: Destiny Books.

Huxley, A. (2004). *Brave New World: And Brave New World Revisited*. New York: HarperCollins.

_____. (1945). *Time Must Have a Stop*. London: Chatto & Windus.

Huxley, T. H. (1894). *Evolution & Ethics and Other Essays (Collected Essays, Vol. IX)*. London: Macmillan.

Hyatt, C. S. (ed.) (2000). *Rebels & Devils: The Psychology of Liberation*. 2nd ed. Tempe, AZ: New Falcon Publications.

Iamblichus. (1911). *Theurgia, or the Egyptian Mysteries*. (trans. A. Wilder). London: William Rider & Son.

Iannone, A. P. (2001). *Dictionary of World Philosophy*. London: Routledge.

Idel, M. (1988). *Kabbalah: New Perspectives*. New Haven: Yale University Press.

Jaeger, W. (1947). *The Theology of the Early Greek Philosophers: The Gifford Lectures, 1936*. Oxford: Clarendon Press.

James, W. (1950). *The Principles of Psychology*. 2 vols. New York: Dover Publications.

_____. (1902). *The Varieties of Religious Experience: A Study in Human Nature—being the Gifford lectures on natural religion delivered at Edinburgh in 1901–1902*. rev. ed. New York: Longmans, Green & Co.

Jinarājadāsa, C. (ed.) (1948). *Letters from the Masters of Wisdom: First Series*. Madras: Theosophical Publishing House.

Joad, C. E. M. (1936). *Guide to the Philosophy of Morals and Politics*. London: Victor Gollancz.

Jones, E. (1953–7). *The Life and Works of Sigmund Freud*. 3 vols. New York: Basic Books.

Jones, P. M. (1951). *The Background of Modern French Poetry: Essays and Interviews*. Cambridge: Cambridge University Press.

Jones, W. (trans.) (1798). *Institutes of Hindu Law: or, the Ordinances of Menu, according to the gloss of Cullúca; comprising the Indian system of duties, religious and civil*. London: Sewell, Cornhill & Debrett.

Josephson-Storm, J. Ā. (2017). *The Myth of Disenchantment: Magic, Modernity, and the Birth of Human Sciences*. Chicago: University of Chicago Press.

Jung, C. G. (1989). *Memories, Dreams, Reflections*. rev. ed. (ed. A. Jaffé, trans. R. Winston & C. Winston). New York: Vintage Books.

____. (1968). *Psychology and Alchemy (Collected Works of C.G. Jung, Vol. 12)*. rev. ed. (trans. R. F. C. Hull). Abingdon: Routledge.

____. (1916). *Psychology of the Unconscious: A Study of the Transformations and Symbolisms of the Libido—A Contribution to the History of the Evolution of Thought*. (trans. B. M. Hinkle). New York: Moffat, Yard & Co.

Kaczynski, R. (2012). *Forgotten Templars: The Untold Origins of Ordo Templi Orientis*. s.l.: s.n.

____. (2006). *Panic in Detroit: The Magician and the Motor City (Blue Equinox Journal, No 2)*. Royal Oak, MI: Blue Equinox Oasis.

____. (2010). *Perdurabo: The Life of Aleister Crowley*. rev. ed. Berkeley, CA: North Atlantic Books.

Kant, I. (1977). *Prolegomena to Any Future Metaphysics that Will Be Able to Come Forward as Science*. rev. ed. (trans. P. Carus, rev. J. W. Ellington). Indianapolis, IN: Hackett Publishing Co.

Kaplan, A. (trans.) (1997). *Sefer Yetzirah: The Book of Creation—In Theory and Practice*. rev. ed. Boston, MA: Weiser Books.

Kaufmann, W. A. (1959). *From Shakespeare to Existentialism: Studies in Poetry, Religion, and Philosophy*. Boston: Beacon Press.

____. (1965). *Hegel: Reinterpretation, Texts, and Commentary*. Garden City, NY: Doubleday.

Khandelwal, M. (2004). *Women in Ochre Robes: Gendering Hindu Renunciation*. Albany, NY: State University of New York Press.

Kikuchi, M. (2011). *Frontiers in Fusion Research: Physics and Fusion*. Berlin: Springer.

King, F. X. (1970). *Ritual Magic in England: 1887 to the Present Day*. London: Neville Spearman.

____. (ed.) (1973). *The Secret Rituals of the O.T.O.*. London: C. W. Daniel.

____. (1986). *Tantra for Westerners: A Pratical Guide to the Way of Action*. New York: Destiny Books.

King, R. (1999). *Orientalism and Religion: Post-Colonial Theory, India and the "Mystic East"*. London: Routledge.

Kircher, A. (1652). *Œdipus Ægyptiacus: Hoc est Universalis Hieroglyphicæ Veterum Doctrinæ temporum iniuria abolitæ Instauratio*. Rome: Vitalis Mascardi.

Kitto, J. (ed.) (1846). *A Cyclopædia of Biblical Literature*. 2 vols. New York: Mark H. Newman.

Klein, S. T. (1912). *Science and the Infinite; or Through a Window in the Blank Wall*. London: William Rider & Son.

Knight, R. P. (1894). *A Discourse on the Worship of Priapus, and Its Connection with the Mystic Theology of the Ancients: to which is added an Essay on the Worship of the Generative Powers During the Middle Ages of Western Europe*. rev. ed. London: s.n.

Koestler, A. (1981). *Kaleidoscope: Essays from Drinkers of Infinity and The Heel of Achilles and later pieces and stories*. London: Hutchinson.

König, P. R. (ed.) (1997). *Der Grosse Theodor-Reuss-Reader*. Munich: ARW.

____. (ed.) (1993). *Der Kleine Theodor-Reuss-Reader*. Munich: ARW.

Lau, D. C. (trans.) (1963). *Lao Tzu: Tao Te Ching*. London: Penguin Books.

Leadbeater, C. W. (1925). *The Masters and the Path*. Adyar: Theosophical Publishing House.

———. (1920). *The Science of the Sacraments: an occult and clairvoyant study of the Christian Eucharist*. Sydney: St. Alban Press.

Le Bon, G. (1907). *The Evolution of Matter*. (trans. F. Legge). London: Walter Scott.

Lebrun, R. A. (1965). *Throne and Altar: The Political and Religious Thought of Joseph de Maistre*. Ottawa, ON:University of Ottawa Press.

Lee, J. Y. (1971). *The Principle of Changes: Understanding the I Ching*. New Hyde Park, NY: University Books.

Lévi, É. (1861a). *La clef des grands mystères suivant Hénoch, Abraham, Hermés Trismégiste, et Salomon*. Paris: G. Baillère.

———. (1861b). *Dogme et rituel de la haute magie*. Paris: G. Baillère.

———. (1913). *The History of Magic: Including a Clear and Precise Exposition of Its Procedure, Its Rites and Its Mysteries*. (trans. A. E. Waite). London: William Rider & Son.

———. (1922). *The Paradoxes of the Highest Science*. 2nd ed. Adyar: Theosophical Publishing House.

———. (2015). *The Reconciliation of Science and Religion: Le Réconciliation entre la Science et la Religion—Bilingual Edition*. s.l.: Daath Gnostic Publishing.

Levins, R. & R. Lewontin. (1987). *The Dialectical Biologist*. Cambridge, MA: Harvard University Press.

Lloyd, G. E. R. (1970). *Early Greek Science: Thales to Aristotle*. New York: W. W. Norton.

Locke, J. (1960). *Two Treatises of Government: A Critical Edition with an Introduction and Apparatus Criticus*. (ed. P. Laslett). Cambridge: Cambridge University Press.

Locker, M. E. (ed.) (2011). *Systems Theory and Theology: The Living Interplay between Science and Religion*. Eugene, OR: Pickwick Publications.

Loyola, I. (1991). *The Spiritual Exercises and Selected Works*. (ed. G. E. Ganss). New York: Paulist Press.

Lucretius. (2001). *On the Nature of Things*. rev. ed. (trans. M. F. Smith). Indianapolis: Hackett Publishing.

Lusthaus, D. (2002). *Buddhist Phenomenology: A Philosophical Investigation of Yogācāra Buddhism and the Ch' eng Wei-shih lun*. New York: RoutledgeCurzon.

Machiavelli, N. (2003). *The Prince and Other Writings*. (trans. W. A. Rebhorn). New York: Barnes & Noble Classics.

MacKenzie, K. R. H. (ed.) (1877). *The Royal Masonic Cyclopædia of History, Rites, Symbolism and Biography*. London: John Hogg.

Mackey, A. G. (1874). *An Encyclopædia of Freemasonry and Its Kindred Sciences: Comprising the Whole Range of Arts, Sciences and Literature as Connected with the Institution*. Philadelphia: Moss & Co.

Macy, J. (1991). *Mutual Causality in Buddhism and General Systems Theory: The Dharma of Natural Systems*. Albany, NY: State University of New York Press.

Magee, G. A. (2010). *The Hegel Dictionary*. London: Continuum Publishing.

Maier, M. (1614). *Arcana Arcanissima: hoc est, Hieroglyphica Ægyptio-Græca*. London: Thomas Creede.

———. (1656). *Themis Aurea: The Laws of the Fraternity of the Rosie Crosse*. London: N. Brooke.

Maistre, J. de. (1983). *Ecrits maçonniques de Joseph de Maistre et de quelques-uns de ses amis francs-maçons (Œuvres de Joseph de Maistre, Vol. 2)*. rev. ed. (ed. J. Rebotton). Genève: Editions Slatkine.

____. (1998). *An Examination of the Philosophy of Bacon: Wherein Different Questions of Rational Philosophy Are Treated.* (trans. & ed. R. A. Lebrun). Montréal: McGill-Queen's University Press.

____. (1861). *Lettres et opuscules inédits du comte Joseph de Maistre.* 4th rev. ed. 2 vols. Paris: A. Vaton.

____. (1959). *On God and Society: Essay on the Generative Principle of Political Constitutions and other Human Institutions.* (ed. E. Greifer, trans. L. M. Porter). Chicago: Henry Regnery Co.

Malinowski, B. (1927). *Sex and Repression in Savage Society.* London: Kegan, Paul, Trench, Trubner & Co.

Mallinson, J. (trans.) (2007). *Shiva Samhita: A Critical Edition and an English Translation.* Woodstock, NY: YogaVidya.com.

Malory, T. (1969). *Le Morte d'Arthur.* 2 vols. (ed. J. Cowen). London: Penguin Books.

Mann, T. (1947). *Essays of Three Decades.* (trans. H. T. Lowe-Porter). New York: Alfred A. Knopf.

Marconis, E. J. (1882). *Lectures of a Chapter, Senate and Council according to the forms of the Antient and Primitive Rite, but embracing all Systems of High Grade Masonry.* (trans. J. Yarker). London: John Hogg.

____. (1993). *Sanctuary of Memphis, or, Hermes: The Development of Masonic Mysteries.* (trans. W. J. Coombes, ed. J. R. Shute). Kila, MT: Kessinger Publishing Co.

Massey, G. (1883). *The Natural Genesis: or, Second Part of a Book of the Beginnings, Containing an Attempt to Recover and Reconstitute the Lost Origines of the Myths and Mysteries, Types and Symbols, Religion and Language, with Egypt for the Mouthpiece and Africa as the Birthplace.* 2 vols. London: Williams & Norgate.

Mathers, S. L. (trans.) (1898). *The Book of the Sacred Magic of Abra-Melin the Mage, as delivered by Abraham the Jew unto his son Lamech, A.D. 1458.* London: J. M. Watkins.

____. (trans.) (1887). *Kabbala Denudata: The Kabbalah Unveiled; containing the following books of the Zohar—1. The Book of Concealed Mystery, 2. The Greater Holy Assembly, 3. The Lesser Holy Assembly.* London: George Redway.

____. (trans.) (1889). *The Key of Solomon the King (Clavicula Salomonis): Now first Translated and Edited from Ancient MSS. in the British Museum.* London: George Redway.

McCabe, J. (1993). *The Myth of the Resurrection and Other Essays (The Freethought Library).* Amherst, NY: Prometheus Books.

____. (1914). *Sources of the Morality of the Gospels.* London: Watts & Co.

____. (1929). *The Story of Religious Controversy.* (ed. E. Haldeman-Julius). Boston: The Stratford Co.

McEvilley, T. (2002). *The Shape of Ancient Thought: Comparative Studies in Greek and Indian Philosophies.* New York: Allworth Press.

McIntosh, C. (1972). *Eliphas Lévi and the French Occult Revival.* London: Rider & Co.

____. (1992). *The Rose Cross and the Age of Reason: Eighteenth-Century Rosicrucianism in Central Europe and Its Relationship to the Enlightenment (Brill's Studies in Intellectual History, Vol. 29).* Leiden: Brill.

____. (1997). *The Rosicrucians: The History, Mythology, and Rituals of an Esoteric Order.* 3rd rev. ed. Boston, MA: Weiser Books.

McNeilly, M. (2001). *Sun Tzu and the Art of Modern Warfare.* rev. ed. Oxford: Oxford University Press.

Mead, G. R. S. (1900). *Fragments of a Faith Forgotten: Some Short Sketches among the Gnostics, Mainly from the First Two Centuries—A contribution to the study of Christian origins based on the most recently recovered materials.* London: Theosophical Publishing Society.

____. (trans.) (1921). *Pistis Sophia: a Gnostic miscellany; being for the most part extracts from the books of the Saviour, to which are added excerpts from a cognate literature.* 2nd rev. ed. London: J. M. Watkins.

Melsen, A. G. M. van. (1952). *From Atomos to Atom: The History of the Concept Atom.* Pittsburgh: Duquesne University Press.

Merton, T. (1966). *Conjectures of a Guilty Bystander.* Garden City, NY: Doubleday & Co.

Mill, J. S. (1863). *Utilitarianism.* London: Parker, Son & Bourn.

Millar, A. (2013). *Freemasonry: Foundation of the Western Esoteric Tradition.* Bracken Ridge: Salamander and Sons.

Miller, B. S. (trans.) (1986). *The Bhagavad-Gita: Krishna's Counsel in Time of War.* New York: Bantam Classics.

Mises, L. von. (1998). *Human Action: A Treatise on Economics—The Scholar's Edition.* Auburn, AL: Ludwig von Mises Institute.

____. (1951). *Socialism: An Economic and Sociological Analysis.* New Haven: Yale University Press

Miyamoto, M. (2008). *The Book of Five Rings.* Radford, VA: Wilder Publications.

Molinos, M. de. (2010). *The Spiritual Guide.* (ed. & trans. R. P. Baird). New York: Paulist Press.

Monier-Williams, M. (1872). *A Sanskrit-English Dictionary: Etymologically and Philologically Arranged with Special Reference to Greek, Latin, Gothic, German, Anglo-Saxon, and Other Cognate Indo-European Languages.* Oxford: Clarendon Press.

Moyise, S. (1995). *The Old Testament in the Book of Revelation (Journal for the Study of the New Testament, Supplement Series 115).* Sheffield: Sheffield Academic Press.

Müller, F. M. (1897). *Contributions to the Science of Mythology.* 2 vols. London: Longman, Green & Co.

____. (ed.) (1879–1910). *Sacred Books of the East.* 50 vols. Oxford: Oxford University Press.

Murray, G. (1925). *Five Stages of Greek Religion: Studies based on a Course of Lectures delivered in April 1912 at Columbia University.* Oxford: Clarendon Press.

Neugebauer, O. (1975). *A History of Ancient Mathematical Astronomy.* 3 vols. Berlin: Springer.

Newton, I. (1728). *The Chronology of Ancient Kingdoms Amended: To which is Prefix'd, A Short Chronicle from the First Memory of Things in Europe, to the Conquest of Persia by Alexander the Great.* London: Tonson, Osborn & Longman.

____. (1848). *Newton's Principia: The Mathematical Principles of Natural Philosophy, by Sir Isaac Newton; Translated into English by Andrew Motte.* rev. ed. (ed. N. W. Chittenden, trans. A. Motte). New York: Daniel Adee.

Nicholson, J. A. (1950). *Philosophy of Religion.* New York: Ronald Press.

Nietzsche, F. (2016). *Anti-Education: On the Future of Our Educational Institutions.* (trans. D. Searls, ed. P. Reitter & C. Wellmon). New York: New York Review of Books.

____. (1997). *Beyond Good and Evil: Prelude to a Philosophy of the Future.* (trans. H. Zimmern). Mineola, NY: Dover Publications.

____. (1996). *Human, All Too Human: A Book for Free Spirits (Cambridge Texts in the History of Philosophy)*. (trans. R. J. Hollingdale). Cambridge: Cambridge University Press.

____. (1954). *The Portable Nietzsche.* (ed. W. Kaufmann). New York: Viking Press.

____. (1967). *The Will to Power: A New Translation.* (ed. W. Kaufmann, trans. W. Kaufmann & R. J. Hollingdale). New York: Random House.

Nishitani, K. (1982). *Religion and Nothingness (Nanzan Studies in Religion and Culture)*. (trans. J. Van Bragt). Berkeley: University of California Press.

Oldenberg, H. (1988). *The Religion of the Veda: Die Religion des Veda.* (trans. S. B. Shrotri). Delhi: Motilal Banarsidass.

Olivelle, P. (2011). *Ascetics and Brahmins: Studies in Ideologies and Institutions.* London: Anthem Press.

____. (1993). *The Āśrama System: The History and Hermeneutics of a Religious Institution.* New York: Oxford University Press.

____. (trans.) (1996). *Upaniṣads: A New Translation by Patrick Olivelle (World's Classics)*. Oxford: Oxford University Press.

O'Regan, C. (2002). *Gnostic Apocalypse: Jacob Boehme's Haunted Narrative.* Albany, NY: State University of New York Press.

Orr, J. (ed.) (1939). *The International Standard Bible Encyclopedia.* 5 vols. Grand Rapids, MI: Wm. B. Eerdmans Publishing Co.

Paine, T. (1894). *The Writings of Thomas Paine.* 4 vols. (ed. M. D. Conway). New York: G. P. Putnam's Sons.

Panikkar, R. (ed.) (1983). *The Vedic Experience: Mantramañjari—An Anthology of the Vedas for Modern Man and Contemporary Celebration.* (trans. R. Panikkar, N. Shanta, M. Rogers, B. Bäumer & M. Bidoli). Delhi: Motilal Banarsidass.

Papus. (2000). *The Qabalah: Secret Tradition of the West.* (trans. W. N. Schors). York Beach, ME: Samuel Weiser.

Parel, A. J. (ed.) (2000). *Gandhi, Freedom, and Self-Rule (Global Encounters: Studies in Comparative Political Theory)*. Lanham, MD: Lexington Books.

Pearson, J. (2007). *Wicca and the Christian Heritage: Ritual, Sex and Magic.* London: Routledge.

Péladan, J. (1894). *L'art idéaliste & mystique: doctrine de l'Ordre et du salon annuel des Rose + Croix.* Paris: Chamuel.

Pike, A. (1874). *Morals and Dogma of the Ancient and Accepted Scottish Rite of Freemasonry: Prepared for the Supreme Council of the Thirty-Third Degree, for the Southern Jurisdiction of the United States, and Published by Its Authority.* New York: Masonic Publishing Co.

Pinch, W. R. (2006). *Warrior Ascetics and Indian Empires (Cambridge Studies in Indian History and Society)*. Cambridge: Cambridge University Press.

Pink, T. & M. W. F. Stone. (eds.) (2004). *The Will and Human Action: From Antiquity to the Present Day.* London: Routledge.

Plato. (1975–84). *Plato.* 12 vols. (trans. H. N. Fowler, W. R. M. Lamb, P. Shorey & R. G. Bury). Cambridge, MA: Harvard University Press.

Plotinus. (1952). *The Six Enneads (Great Books of the Western World, Vol. 17)*. (trans. S. MacKenna & B. S. Page). London: Encyclopædia Britannica.

Plutarch. (2010). *On the Daimonion of Socrates: Human Liberation, Divine Guidance and Philosophy.* (ed. H.-G. Nesselrath, trans. D. A. Russell, et al.). Tübingen: Mohr Siebeck.

Poincaré, H. (1908). *La valeur de la science*. Paris: Ernest Flammarion.

Polanyi, M. (1962). *The Republic of Science: Its Political and Economic Theory—A Lecture Delivered at Roosevelt University, January 11, 1962*. Chicago: Roosevelt University.

Popper, K. (1966). *The Open Society and Its Enemies*. 5th rev. ed. Princeton: Princeton University Press.

Prabhupāda, A. C. (trans.) (1972–77). *Śrīmad-Bhāgavatam (Bhāgavata Purāṇa)*. 12 vols. Los Angeles: ISKCON.

Proclus. (1971). *Alcibiades I: A Translation and Commentary*. 2nd ed. (trans. W. O'Neill). The Hague: Martinus Nijhoff.

Pryse, J. M. (1910). *The Apocalypse Unsealed: Being an Esoteric Interpretation of the Initiation of Iôannês ('Ἀποκάλυψις 'Ιωάννου) Commonly Called The Revelation of (St.) John, with a New Translation*. London: J. M. Watkins.

Ptolemy. (1998). *Ptolemy's Almagest*. rev. ed. (trans. & ed. G. J. Toomer). Princeton: Princeton University Press.

Rabelais, F. (2006). *Gargantua and Pantagruel*. (trans. & ed. M. A. Screech). London: Penguin Books.

Radhakrishnan, S. (trans.) (1960). *The Brahma Sūtra: The Philosophy of Spiritual Life*. London: George Allen & Unwin.

Ragon, J. M. (1841). *Cours philosophique et interprétatif des initiations Anciennes et Modernes, par J.-M. Ragon*. Paris: Berlandier.

_____. (1844). *La Messe et ses mystères comparés aux mystères anciens, ou Complément de la science initiatique, par Jean-Marie de V*. Paris: Berlandier.

Raju, P. T. (1985). *Structural Depths of Indian Thought*. Albany, NY: State University of New York Press.

Rámanáthan, P. (1902). *An Eastern Exposition of the Gospel of Jesus according to St. John; Being an Interpretation thereof by Sri Parānanda by the Light of Jnana Yoga*. London: W. Hutchinson.

_____. (1898). *The Gospel of Jesus according to St. Matthew, as Interpreted to B.L. Harrison by the Light of the Godly Experience of Sri Parānanda*. London: Kegan Paul, Trench, Trübner Co.

Rambachan, A. (1994). *The Limits of Scripture: Vivekananda's Reinterpretation of the Vedas*. Honolulu: University of Hawaii Press.

Randolph, P. B. (1874). *Eulis!: The History of Love, Its Wondrous Magic, Chemistry, Rules, Laws, Moods and Rationale*. Toledo, OH: Randolph Publishing Co.

Rappaport, R. A. (1999). *Ritual and Religion in the Making of Humanity*. Cambridge: Cambridge University Press.

Regardie, I. (1970). *The Eye in the Triangle: An Interpretation of Aleister Crowley*. St. Paul, MN: Llewellyn Publications.

_____. (1989). *The Golden Dawn: The Original Account of the Teachings, Rites and Ceremonies of the Hermetic Order of the Golden Dawn (Llewellyn's Golden Dawn Series)*. 6th rev. ed. St. Paul, MN: Llewellyn Publications.

Reich, W. (1980). *The Mass Psychology of Fascism*. 3rd ed. (trans. V. R. Carfagno). New York: Farrar, Straus & Giroux.

Rhys Davids, T. W. (trans.) (1880). *Buddhist Birth-Stories (Jataka Tales): The Commentarial Introduction Entitled Nidāna-Kathā the Story of the Lineage*. rev. ed. London: George Routledge & Sons.

Rice, M. (1997). *Egypt's Legacy: The Archetypes of Western Civilization, 3000–30 BC*. London: Routledge.

Roberts, A. & J. Donaldson. (eds.) (1867–72). *Ante-Nicene Christian Library: Translations of the Writings of the Fathers Down to A.D. 325*. 9 vols. Edinburgh: T. & T. Clark.

Robertson, J. M. (1903). *Pagan Christs: Studies in Comparative Hierology*. London: Watts & Co.

Rothbard, M. N. (1995). *An Austrian Perspective on the History of Economic Thought*. 2 vols. Aldershot: Edward Elgar.

____. (1998). *The Ethics of Liberty*. New York: New York University Press.

Rousseau, J. J. (1999). *Discourse on Political Economy; and The Social Contract*. (trans. C. Betts). Oxford: Oxford University Press.

Ruether, R. R. (2005). *Goddesses and the Divine Feminine: A Western Religious History*. Berkeley: University of California Press.

Russell, B. (1945). *A History of Western Philosophy: And Its Connection with Political and Social Circumstances from the Earliest Times to the Present Day*. New York: Simon & Schuster.

____. (1919). *Introduction to Mathematical Philosophy*. London: George Allen & Unwin.

____. (1997). *Last Philosophical Testament, 1943–68 (Collected Papers of Bertrand Russell, Vol. 11)*. (ed. J. G. Slater & P. Köllner). London: Routledge.

Sambursky, S. (1982). *The Concept of Place in Late Neoplatonism: Texts with Translation, Introduction and Notes*. Jerusalem: Israel National Academy of Sciences and Humanities.

Sawyer, R. D. (trans.) (1994). *Sun-tzu: The Art of War*. Boulder, CO: Westview Press.

Schaff, P. et al. (eds.) (1886–89). *A Select Library of Nicene and Post-Nicene Fathers of the Christian Church*, Series I. 14 vols. Edinburgh: T. & T. Clark.

Scharfstein, B. A. (1998). *A Comparative History of World Philosophy: From the Upanishads to Kant*. Albany, NY: State University of New York Press.

Scholem, G. G. (1965). *Jewish Gnosticism, Merkabah Mysticism, and Talmudic Tradition*. New York: Jewish Theological Seminary of America.

____. (1954). *Major Trends in Jewish Mysticism*. 3rd. rev. ed. New York: Schocken Books.

Schopenhauer, A. (1960). *Essay on the Freedom of the Will*. (trans. K. Kolenda). New York: Bobbs-Merrill.

____. (2004). *Essays and Aphorisms*. (trans. R. J. Hollingdale). London: Penguin Books.

____. (1974). *Parerga and Paralipomena: Short Philosophical Essays*. 2 vols. (trans. E. F. J. Payne). Oxford: Clarendon Press.

Schrödinger, E. (1954). *Nature and the Greeks*. Cambridge: Cambridge University Press.

Scriven, D. & L. Scriven (1995). *Mystery of Mystery: A Primer of Thelemic Ecclesiastical Gnosticism (Red Flame, Vol. 2)*. Berkeley, CA: J. E. & M. Cornelius.

Shakespeare, W. (1835). *The Dramatic Works of William Shakespeare*. 6 vols. (ed. S. Johnson & G. Steevens, rev. I. Reed). New York: George Dearborn.

Shaw, G. B. (1916). *Androcles and the Lion, Overruled, Pygmalion*. New York: Brentano.

____. (1907). *John Bull's Other Island and Major Barbara: also How He Lied to Her Husband*. London: Archibald Constable & Co.

Shelley, P. B. (1820). *Prometheus Unbound: A Lyrical Drama in Four Acts; with Other Poems*. London: C & J Ollier.

Sheppard, W. (1659). *Of Corporations, Fraternities, and Guilds; or, a Discourse, wherein The Learning of the Law touching Bodies-Politique is unfolded, shewing the Use and Necessity of that Invention, the Antiquity, various Kinds, Order and Government of the same*. London: H. Twyford, T. Dring & J. Place.

Shuttle, P. & P. Redgrove. (1978). *The Wise Wound: Menstruation and Everywoman*. London: Victor Gollancz.

Silos, L. R. (2005). *Of Guilds, Companies, Corporations, and Governance: A Conceptual Sketch*. Makati: Asian Institute of Management.

Singer, I. (ed.) (1901–6). *The Jewish Encyclopedia: A Descriptive Record of the History, Religion, Literature, and Customs of the Jewish People from the Earliest Times to the Present Day*. 12 vols. New York: Funk & Wagnalls Co.

Singh, N. K. & A. P. Mishra (2010). *Global Encyclopaedia of Indian Philosophy*. 3 vols. New Delhi: Global Vision Publishing House.

Singh-Anand, J. (trans.) (2015). *The Secret School of Wisdom: The Authentic Rituals and Doctrines of the Illuminati*. (ed. J. Wäges & R. Markner). Addlestone: Lewis Masonic.

Singleton, M. (2010). *Yoga Body: The Origins of Modern Posture Practice*. Oxford: Oxford University Press.

Siorvanes, L. (1996). *Proclus: Neo-Platonic Philosophy and Science*. New Haven: Yale University Press.

Sivananda. (2003). *All about Hinduism*. 7th ed. Shivanandanagar: Divine Life Society.

Skeat, W. W. (1910). *An Etymological Dictionary of the English Language*. rev. ed. Oxford: Clarendon Press.

Smith, A. (1804). *An Inquiry into the Nature and Causes of the Wealth of Nations*. 2 vols. Hartford, CT: Oliver D. Cooke.

———. (1761). *The Theory of Moral Sentiments*. 2nd ed. London: A. Millar.

Smith, R. J. (2008). *Fathoming the Cosmos and Ordering the World: The Yijing (I-Ching, or Classic of Changes) and Its Evolution in China*. Charlottesville: University of Virginia Press.

Sophocles. (1911). *Oedipus, King of Thebes: Translated into English Rhyming Verse with Explanatory Notes by Gilbert Murray*. (trans. & ed. G. Murray). New York: Oxford University Press.

Spence, R. B. (2008). *Secret Agent 666: Aleister Crowley, British Intelligence and the Occult*. Port Townsend, WA: Feral House.

Spencer, H. (1860). *Education: Intellectual, Moral, and Physical*. New York: D. Appleton & Co.

———. (1868). *Essays: Scientific, Political, and Æsthetic*. New York: D. Appleton & Co.

———. (1867). *First Principles*. 2nd ed. London: Williams & Norgate.

———. (1884). *The Man versus the State: Reprinted from The Contemporary Review with a Postscript*. London: Williams & Norgate.

———. (1843). *The Proper Sphere of Government: A Reprint of a Series of Letters, Originally Published in The Nonconformist*. London: W. Brittain.

Stanley, T. (2010). *Pythagoras: His Life and Teachings—A Compendium of Classical Sources*. (ed. J. Wasserman). Lake Worth, FL: Ibis Press.

Starr, M. P. (2003). *The Unknown God: W. T. Smith and the Thelemites*. Bolingbrook, IL: Teitan Press.

Steiner, R. (2007). *Freemasonry and Ritual Work: The Misraim Service (Collected Works of Rudolf Steiner, Vol. 265).* (trans. J. Wood). Great Barrington, MA: SteinerBooks.

Stewart, D. (1858). *Biographical Memoirs of Adam Smith, William Robertson, Thomas Reid (Collected Works of Dugald Stewart, Vol. X).* (ed. W. Hamilton). Edinburgh: Constable & Co.

Stewart, J. (ed.) (2007). *Kierkegaard and his German Contemporaries: Tome I— Philosophy (Kierkegaard Research: Sources, Reception and Resources, Vol. 6.)* London: Routledge.

Stirling, W. (1897). *The Canon: An Exposition of the Pagan Mystery Perpetuated in the Cabala as the Rule of All the Arts.* London: Elkin Mathews.

Stirner, M. (1971). *The Ego and His Own.* (trans. J. Carroll). London: Jonathan Cape.

Stone, M. E. & T. A. Bergren (eds.) (1998). *Biblical Figures Outside the Bible.* Harrisburg, PA: Trinity Press International.

Strudwick, N. & J. H. Taylor (eds.) (2003). *The Theban Necropolis: Past, Present and Future.* London: British Museum Press.

Styers, R. (2004). *Making Magic: Religion, Magic, and Science in the Modern World.* Oxford: Oxford University Press.

Sullivan, J. W. N. (1926). *The Aspects of Science: Second Series.* New York: Alfred A. Knopf.

____. (1928). *The Bases of Modern Science.* London: E. Benn.

Svatmarama. (1893). *The Hatha-Yoga Pradipika of Swátmárám Swámi.* (trans. S. Iyangar). Bombay: Bombay Theosophical Publication Fund.

____. (2002). *The Hatha Yoga Pradipika.* (trans. B. D. Akers). Woodstock, NY: YogaVidya.com.

Swinburne, A. C. (2004). *Major Poems and Selected Prose.* (ed. J. McGann & C. L. Sligh). New Haven: Yale University Press.

Tähtinen, U. (1976). *Ahiṃsā: Non-Violence in Indian Tradition.* London: Rider & Co.

Taylor, R. (ed.) (1961). *The Empiricists: John Locke; George Berkeley; David Hume.* Garden City, NY: Doubleday.

Teresi, D. (2002). *Lost Discoveries: The Ancient Roots of Modern Science—from the Babylonians to the Maya.* New York: Simon & Schuster.

Tester, S. J. (1987). *A History of Western Astrology.* Woodbridge: Boydell & Brewer.

Thompson, T. L. (1999). *The Bible in History: How Writers Create a Past.* London: Jonathan Cape.

Thorndike, L. (1923–58). *A History of Magic and Experimental Science.* 8 vols. New York: Columbia University Press.

Thucydides. (1919). *History of the Peloponnesian War.* 4 vols. (trans. C. F. Smith). London: William Heinemann.

Wagner, R. (1883). *Parsifal der reine Thor, oder die Ritter vom Salvator: grosse Bayreuther Bühnenweihfestspiel-Komödie in 5 Abtheilungen.* Munich: Pollner.

____. (1876). *Siegfried, Zweiter Tag aus der Trilogie: Der Ring des Nibelungen.* Mainz: B. Schott's Söhne.

Vallée, J. (1969). *Passport to Magonia: From Folklore to Flying Saucers.* Chicago: Henry Regnery.

Varley, P. (2000). *Japanese Culture.* 4th rev. ed. Honolulu: University of Hawai'i Press.

Verbrugghe, G. P. & J. M. Wickersham (1996). *Berossos and Manetho, Introduced and Translated: Native Traditions in Ancient Mesopotamia and Egypt.* Ann Arbor: University of Michigan Press.

Westcott, W. W. (trans.) (1895). *The Chaldæan Oracles of Zoroaster.* London: Theosophical Publishing Society.

———. (ed.) (1894). *The Pymander of Hermes Mercurius Trismegistus (Collectanea Hermetica, Vol. 2).* (trans. J. Everard). London: Theosophical Publishing Society.

———. (trans.) (1893). *Sepher Yetzirah: The Book of Formation, with The Fifty Gates of Intelligence, and The Thirty-Two Paths of Wisdom.* rev. ed. London: Theosophical Publishing Society.

Vetter, T. (1988). *The Ideas and Meditative Practices of Early Buddhism.* Leiden: E. J. Brill.

White, D. G. (2014). *The Yoga Sutra of Patanjali: A Biography (Lives of Great Religious Books).* Princeton: Princeton University Press.

Whitehead, A. N. (1925). *Science and the Modern World: Lowell Lectures.* New York: Macmillan.

———. (1927). *Symbolism, Its Meaning and Effect: Barbour-Page Lectures.* New York: Macmillan.

Whittick, A. (1971). *Symbols: Signs and Their Meaning and Uses in Design.* rev. ed. London: Leonard Hill.

Wiarda, H. J. (1997). *Corporatism and Comparative Politics: The Other Great Ism (Comparative Politics Series).* Armonk, NY: M. E. Sharpe.

Wilde, O. (1997). *Collected Works of Oscar Wilde: The Plays, the Poems, the Stories and the Essays including De Profundis.* Ware: Wordsworth Editions.

Wilkinson, J. G. (1837–41). *The Manners and Customs of the Ancient Egyptians: Including Their Private Life, Government, Laws, Arts, Manufacturers, Religion, Agriculture, and Early History; Derived from a Comparison of the Paintings, Sculptures, and Monuments Still Existing, with the Accounts of Ancient Authors.* 6 vols. London: John Murray.

Wilkinson, L. (trans.) (1861). *Translation of the Surya Siddhanta by Pundit Bapu Deva Sastri, and of the Siddhanta Siromani by the Late Lancelot Wilkinson, Esq., C.S., Revised by Pundit Bapu Deva Sastri, from the Sanskrit.* rev. ed. (ed. B. D. Sastri). Calcutta: s.n.

Williams, G. M. (1974). *The Quest for Meaning of Swāmī Vivekānanda: A Study of Religious Change.* Chico, CA: New Horizons Press.

Williams, H. L. (1989). *Hegel, Heraclitus, and Marx's Dialectic.* Hemel Hempstead: Harvester Wheatsheaf.

Williams, P. (ed.) (2005). *The Early Buddhist Schools and Doctrinal History; Theravāda Doctrine (Critical Concepts in Religious Studies: Buddhism, Volume II).* London: Routledge.

———. & A. Tribe (2000). *Buddhist Thought: A Complete Introduction to the Indian Tradition.* London: Routledge.

Williams, W. E. (2015). *American Contempt for Liberty.* Stanford, CA: Hoover Institution Press.

Wilson, W. S. (trans.) (1982). *Ideals of the Samurai: Writings of Japanese Warriors.* (ed. G. N. Lee). Burbank, CA: Ohara Publications.

Virajānanda. (1912–14). *The Life of the Swami Vivekananda.* 4 vols. Kolkata: Advaita Ashrama.

Virgil. (1881). *The Bucolics, Æneid, and Georgics of Virgil.* (ed. J. B. Greenough). Boston: Ginn & Co.

Vivekananda. (1907–97). *The Complete Works of Swami Vivekananda.* 9 vols. Kolkata: Advaita Ashrama.

Wyschogrod, E., D. Crownfield & C. A. Raschke. (eds.) (1989). *Lacan and Theological Discourse (SUNY Series in Philosophy).* Albany, NY: State University of New York Press.

Yamamoto, T. (2012). *Hagakure: The Book of the Samurai.* rev. ed. (trans. W. S. Wilson). Boston, MA: Shambhala Publications.

Yarker, J. (1909). *The Arcane Schools: A Review of Their Origins and Antiquity, with a General History of Freemasonry, and Its Relation to the Theosophic, Scientific, and Philosophic Mysteries.* Belfast: William Tait.

Yates, F. A. (1972). *The Rosicrucian Enlightenment.* London: Routledge & Kegan Paul.

Zalewski, P. (1993). *Kabbalah of the Golden Dawn (Llewellyn's Golden Dawn Series).* St. Paul, MN: Llewellyn Publications.

Ziporyn, B. (2012). *Ironies of Oneness and Difference: Coherence in Early Chinese Thought; Prolegomena to the Study of Li.* Albany, NY: State University of New York Press.

Zucker, M. (1945). *The Philosophy of American History: The Historical Field Theory.* New York: Arnold-Howard Publishing.

INDEX

0/0, *see* division by zero
0 = 2, 53, 95-8, 105-10, 124, 150-1, 185-6, 217-9, 250-1, 285-6, 298-301, 325-6, 365, 538
#1, *see* the Monad; *Liber I, see* the Book of the Magus; the One, 1, 12, 105, 115, 140, 154, 183, 185, 208, 231n46, 234-5, 282-5, 289, 301, 309, 324, 334, 365; one-pointedness, 8, 117, 173, 184, 216, 220, 228, 296-7, 349, 361-2, 366, 371, 376, 420; *One Star in Sight*, 3n14, 233, 264-5, 269, 270, 295, 300, 304, 316, 324, 326, 329-30, 346-7, 447, 450, 458-9, 461-2
#2, *see* the Dyad; *Liber II*, 3, 7, 9, 12, 14-5, 33, 228, 524
#3, *see* the Triad; *Liber III*, 350; the Three Characteristics of Existence, *see* the *tilakkhana*; the Three Guardians, 324; the Three Lost Letters of the Hebrew Alphabet, 293; the Three Schools of Magick, 333, 456-7, 470, 477, 526, 536n182
#4, 36, 58, 91, 98, 100-3, 107, 114, 119, 120-4, 138, 141, 147, 149, 150-1, 153, 157, 161-3, 165, 207-8, 224-5, 233-6, 238, 242, 248, 257, 271, 274-5, 283, 288, 293, 305, 308-10, 312, 315, 320, 325, 327, 334, 349, 355, 383, 388, 416, 448, 454, 457, 539, 542, 546-7, 558, 560-2; *Book 4*, 217, 234, 393n54, 400, 416n147; *Book 4*, Part I, 79, 168, 340, 347, 349-50, 352, 354, 358-9, 365-7, 420, 457-8, 476, 527; *Book 4*, Part II, 70, 73-4, 77-8, 81-4, 101, 109-10, 123, 137-8, 143, 166-7, 202, 253, 269, 274-5, 283, 285, 290-2, 296-7, 303, 308, 311-2, 317-20, 327, 350, 356, 364, 369, 390, 393n54, 398, 424, 448, 536; *Book 4*, Part III, *see* Magick in Theory and Practice; *Book 4*, Part IV, *see* The Equinox of the Gods; the Four Ages, 36, 526 (*see also* æons or yugas); the Four Cardinal Directions, 58-9, 149, 309, 324, 384; the Four Dimensions, *see* the space-time continuum; the Four Formless States, 102-3, 198, 218-9, 238, 248, 276, 289, 325-6; the Four Great Princes of the Evil of the World, 91-2, 327; the Four Material Elements, 64, 98, 100-3, 107-8, 118, 122-4, 139, 147, 151, 165, 186, 234, 238, 242, 254, 267, 275, 283-4, 286, 300, 308, 318-9, 325, 342, 374, 541-2, 556, 559-62; the Four Noble Truths, 23, 174, 339, 355; the Four Powers of the Sphinx, 29, 161-5, 224-5, 265, 308-9, 346, 358, 366, 374, 493, 562; the Four Suits of the Minor Arcana, 147-8, 150, 562; the Four Qabalistic Worlds, 91, 238, 281, 560-1
#5, 35, 81, 95, 101-3, 122-3, 128, 146-7, 149, 151, 153, 158, 165, 198-9, 220, 275, 283n5, 288, 294, 301, 310, 333-6, 352, 365, 373, 417, 443, 450, 539, 542, 548, 558, 560-2; *Liber V, see* the Ritual of the Mark of the Beast; the Fifth Element, *see* Spirit; the Fifth Power of the Sphinx, *see* Going; the Five Books of Moses, *see* the Pentateuch; the Five Physical Senses, 10-2, 61, 94, 102-4, 114, 117, 126-8, 132, 134-6, 141, 164, 171-2, 181-2, 194, 204, 219-20, 224-7, 245-6, 251-6, 258, 270, 272, 275, 289, 297, 300, 322, 326, 346, 350, 357, 363, 365, 368-9, 419, 541, 547, 549, 562; the Five-Pointed Star, *see* the Pentagram; the Five Precepts of Buddhism, 354-5, 381-2, 482; the Five Skandhas, 364, 562 (see also *rūpa, sankhāra, saññā, vedanā,* and *viññānam*)
#6, 25, 148, 153-5, 163, 198, 224, 234-5, 275, 277, 279, 294, 301, 310, 333-4, 338, 373, 376, 397, 417, 428,

432, 437, 537, 554, 558, 560–2; *Liber VI*, 140, 226, 253; the Six-Pointed Star, *see* the Hexagram

#7, 16, 53, 55, 78, 98, 138–9, 141, 149, 151, 153–5, 185, 209, 238, 253, 272, 295, 315, 325, 355–6, 358, 373, 379, 387, 395–6, 400–1, 406, 409, 415, 426–7, 429, 432, 445, 450–2, 461–3, 499, 557–8, 560, 562; *Liber VII*, 248, 290, 321, 386, 387; *The Sevenfold Sacrament*, 16; sevenfold yoga, 355

#8, 28, 107, 141, 180, 242, 269, 293, 301, 334–5, 356, 372, 379, 397, 538, 540, 543, 558, 562; *Eight Lectures on Yoga*, 78, 96–8, 103–4, 114–5, 117, 119, 160–1, 174, 194, 216–8, 228–30, 257, 287, 318, 324, 326, 328, 344, 351–5, 368–70, 375, 416–7, 419, 421–2, 454n145, 455, 472, 474; the Eight Limbs of Yoga, 355, 358, 449; the Noble Eightfold Path, 271, 288

#9, 41, 141, 149, 157, 233–4, 308, 325, 335, 373, 427, 429, 460, 516, 540, 558, 560, 562

#10, *see* the Decad; the Ten Commandments, 558; the Ten Impurities, 206–7; the Ten Sephiroth, 97, 124, 140–1, 146, 150–1, 208–9, 225–7, 238, 283, 287, 293, 310, 314, 372, 558–61

#11, 18, 34n1, 54n71, 151–3, 198, 257, 293, 295, 334, 367, 397, 429, 437n64, 440, 442, 452, 499, 512, 539, 540, 558, 562

#12, 37, 45, 82, 138, 149, 151, 153, 269, 292, 295, 315, 319n130, 334, 380, 397, 405, 415, 451–2, 547

#13, ix, 44, 55, 154, 248n101, 275, 292, 295, 322, 334, 415, 452; *Liber XIII*, 249n106, 424n8

#22, 9, 71n16, 139, 146, 148, 150–1, 234, 283n2, 291, 293, 334, 558; the Twenty-Two Trumps of the Major Arcana, 32, 34n1, 54n71, 117, 146–8, 152–6, 163–4, 208–9, 247n101, 274–7, 283n2, 284n6, 285, 289n20, 295, 319n130, 320n133, 323, 334, 367, 397, 401, 437n64, 492n25, 528n156, 547, 558, 562

#31, 59, 251, 387, 547; *Liber XXXI*, 381, 441, 546

#32, 124, 139, 208, 276, 293–4, 356

#33, 395, 426–7, 429; *Liber XXXIII*, 166, 297, 380, 415, 447, 451–3, 472

#50, 200, 208–9, 257

#56, 251, 413, 537

#65, 251, 255, 275, 411; *Liber LXV*, 15, 248, 274–5, 277, 309n94, 317, 321, 386

#77, 499; *Liber LXXVII*, 498–9, 548, 554

#78, 153–4, 386; *Liber LXXVIII*, see *The Book of Thoth*

#93, 8, 54, 142, 154, 338, 403, 430

#111, 154, 367, 397, 538; *Liber 111*, see *Liber Aleph*

#156, 153, 292, 298

#333, 24, 81n59, 253, 396; *Liber CCCXXXIII*, 53, 90n88, 124, 135, 146–7, 158, 160, 173, 200, 206, 228, 245, 248–9, 283, 292, 321, 379, 433, 454n145, 532

#418, 151, 154, 301, 334–5, 384, 397, 400, 452, 543; *Liber 418*, 27, 81n59, 92, 115, 121–2, 154, 182, 208, 218, 225, 230, 237, 264, 269, 287, 289, 292, 295, 298, 300–1, 308, 314n107, 315–6, 323–4, 334, 379, 396, 418–9, 547

#666, 18, 163, 222, 232, 300, 340, 384, 396–7, 401–3, 410, 415, 451–2, 458; *Liber 666*, 381, 387, 456–8

#777, 140–1, 396; *Liber 777*, 129–30, 140–1, 233–4, 238, 416, 465

#888, 396; *Liber 888*, 39–41, 73–5, 76n35, 84, 86–7, 110, 117, 138, 148–9, 200, 363, 402–8, 412, 432–3, 439, 472, 513–4, 520, 523, 530–1

A∴A∴, the, 38n21, 47, 76, 85, 116, 121, 123, 148, 161, 163, 183, 201, 210–1, 226, 231–3, 248–50, 264–5, 269, 274, 297, 304, 321, 326–7, 330, 337, 340, 346–7, 355, 376, 379, 382, 386, 396, 401, 409, 411, 419, 424–5, 427, 429, 433n49, 441, 442n95, 444–7, 450–2, 458–9, 516, 527, 547, 557, 560; *Curriculum of A∴A∴*, 47, 116, 130, 148, 201, 250, 269, 274, 277, 304, 321, 337, 340, 355, 376, 396, 433n49, 516, 557; *Præmonstrance of A∴A∴*, 439n77; *Syllabus of A∴A∴*, 401

Abbey of Thelema, the, 159, 239, 244, 444, 477n253, 503–4, 517, 554

abortion, 24, 89, 187, 237, 494, 517

Abrahadabra, 153, 301, 333–5, 372–3, 543, 546–7

INDEX

589

Abraham the Patriarch, 149, 437, 492;
Abraham of Worms, 150
Abramelin, 169, 258, 262, 269, 362, 544; *The Sacred Magic of Abramelin the Mage*, 150, 169, 225, 258, 262, 265, 269, 327, 362, 383–4, 393n54, 413, 420
Absolute, the, 9, 12, 20, 53, 62, 67, 91, 95–6, 98, 105–6, 149–50, 175, 187, 197–8, 201, 245, 248, 250, 282–7, 298–302, 323, 328, 341, 398, 415–6, 453–4, 460, 491, 499
abstinence, 13, 18, 237–40, 344, 490, 496
Abyss, the, 80, 96, 105, 115, 136, 141–3, 147, 153, 173, 179, 183–5, 195, 201, 209, 235, 244, 248, 265, 282, 289–91, 293–5, 298–300, 304, 307, 310–4, 316, 319n130, 321, 328, 424, 541, 558, 560; Babe of Abyss, 143, 201, 265, 291, 294, 304, 313, 321, 560; the Crossing of the Abyss, 115, 136, 147, 195, 209, 235, 248, 265, 282, 289, 290–5, 298, 304, 307–8
achad, 154, 367, 452; Frater Achad, *see* Charles Stansfeld Jones
Achilles, 30, 53
Acts of the Apostles, the, 194
Adam, 2, 58, 237, 310–1, 315; Adam Qadmon, 251, 561; the Fall of Adam, *see* the Fall of Man
Adams, Evangeline, 34n1
adaptation, adaptability, 20, 31, 41, 54, 56, 60, 71, 74–5, 115n84, 134, 148, 162, 168, 175, 198, 239, 308, 330, 389, 433, 458, 510
adepts, adeptship, 29–30, 59, 139, 153–5, 165, 174, 182, 200–2, 205, 211, 217, 219, 220, 232, 234, 246, 249, 260–1, 264–5, 269, 275, 279, 281, 283n5, 288, 290, 292, 294, 301, 303, 304, 307–9, 313–4, 327, 330, 333, 340, 344, 345, 371–2, 379–80, 382, 385, 410, 416, 426, 447–8, 451, 454, 456, 470, 482, 499; Adeptus Exemptus, 3n14, 38n20, 211, 294, 304, 313, 373, 451, 560; Adeptus Major, 3n14, 321, 373, 382, 451, 560; Adeptus Minor, 121, 123, 201, 227, 229, 234, 248–9, 260, 261, 264–5, 269, 275, 294, 333–4, 336, 371–3, 389–90, 417, 425–6, 451, 454, 560
adjustment, 23, 60, 81, 115n84, 132, 138, 152, 168, 180, 184–6, 197, 270, 310, 372, 492, 510; Adjustment, *see* Justice
adolescence, 17, 30, 44–5, 86, 125, 223, 232, 402, 435
Adonai, *see* the Holy Guardian Angel
Adonis, 58, 332, 398, 407–8, 432–3, 436, 439, 472n228, 474, 502
adultery, 18, 399, 489, 492, 546
Advaitism, *see* monism
advertisement, 190, 331, 368, 463, 491, 503
Ægipan, *see* Pan
æons, x, 8, 20–1, 23, 34, 42–3, 45–6, 50, 54–6, 58–9, 126, 153, 162–3, 182, 222, 251, 276–7, 294–5, 301, 304, 306, 314n107, 329–30, 332–5, 337–38, 340–1, 344, 368, 379, 382, 385, 398, 400, 402–3, 411–3, 418–20, 424, 430, 437, 440, 442, 444–5, 450–1, 454, 457–8, 466, 471–2, 483, 492, 509, 516, 533, 538, 550; *The Æon*, see *The Angel*; the Æon of Horus, x, 20, 23, 34, 42, 44–6, 50, 54–6, 58, 126, 153, 162–3, 182, 218n12, 222, 251, 276–7, 294, 295, 306, 319n130, 332, 335, 337–8, 340–1, 379, 382, 385, 398, 400, 403, 411, 419, 420, 444–5, 451, 458, 466, 471–2, 483, 489n18, 492, 509, 516, 533; the Æon of Isis, 34, 42–3, 45, 50, 54, 56, 58, 153, 277, 403, 471–2, 483; the Æon of Maat, 34, 277; the Æon of Osiris, 21, 34, 42–3, 45, 50, 53, 54–6, 58–9, 153, 162–3, 222, 276–7, 318, 319n130, 328–9, 332, 335, 337–8, 344, 385, 398, 403, 411–2, 418–9, 437, 440, 442, 444–5, 450, 454, 471–2, 483, 532n170; the Formula of the Æon, 20, 34, 45, 50, 54–5, 58, 60, 66n113, 153, 180, 294–5, 301, 329–30, 332–7, 343, 382, 411–2, 419, 424, 437, 444–5, 457–8, 466, 472, 483; the Lord(s) of the Æon, 23, 56, 319n130, 335, 368, 411, 419, 444, 458, 466, 471; the Word of the Æon, *see* the Logos of the Æon
Æthyrs, the, *see Liber 418*; the Æthyr, *see* ether *or* Spirit
agape, 8, 332, 430; Agapé Lodge(s), 444, 452
AGLA, 449–50
agnosticism, 127, 381–2

agriculture, 21, 39–41, 50–2, 122, 468, 489–90, 511, 524, 554
ahaṃkāra, the, 341
ahiṃsā, 352, 467–8, 530
Ain, 97–8, 142, 151, 558; Ain Soph, 99, 105, 108, 558; Ain Soph Aur, 558
Aiq Bkr, 334
Air, 27, 32, 51, 77, 84, 100–3, 118, 120, 153, 165, 210, 233–4, 237, 242, 255, 275, 283–5, 318–9, 328, 342, 354–6, 456, 476, 488, 493, 558–62
Aiwass, or Aiwaz, 22–3, 25–6, 153–4, 163, 188, 223, 329, 381, 386–7, 400–3, 409–10, 413, 430, 537, 547
Akasha, 101–2, 161, 256, 405; *see* also Spirit
alchemy, alchemists, 37n14, 100, 103, 122, 124, 150, 161, 170, 200–1, 207, 285, 336, 413, 428, 457, 482
alcohol, 16, 28–9, 39, 53, 73, 171, 179, 186, 190–1, 195, 199–205, 236, 241–2, 313, 452, 482, 491, 495–7, 512n95, 539–541, 543–5
Aleph, 32, 54, 154, 164, 334–5, 367, 398–9, 558, 562; Aleph-Null, 98; *Liber Aleph*, 3n14, 7–8, 21, 27–8, 52, 61, 63–5, 68–9, 77–9, 116, 123–4, 162–4, 180–4, 190–2, 201–2, 204–5, 207n133, 209–10, 222, 225, 230, 233, 241–2, 244–5, 270, 278, 286, 289–90, 294–5, 297, 302–5, 308–9, 316, 318, 323, 325–9, 332, 335–6, 339, 350, 366–8, 399, 411–2, 441n84, 444–6, 448–9, 455, 465–7, 470–1, 477, 484–5, 487, 492, 498, 530
Alexander the Great, 479, 486
Alexandria, the Alexandrians, 36, 428–9, 443
al-Hallaj, Mansur, 470
Allah, 92, 329, 411, 413
altars, 19, 191, 223, 245, 317, 323, 392, 396, 432, 445, 503, 545
altruism, 45, 62, 76, 142, 171, 176–7, 180
ambition, 27–8, 37n14, 46, 169, 201, 223, 296, 313, 370, 388, 413, 419–20, 427, 510, 513, 520–1, 523, 533
Amen, or Amoun, 35n4, 170, 196n85, 335–6, 367–8, 493, 504n68, 542; Amen-Ra, 233
Amennti, 210–1
Amfortas, 53, 368
amniotic fluid, the, 53, 437

AMORC, 453
analysis, 7, 55, 58, 77–8, 90, 102, 115, 125, 128–30, 135–6, 141, 145, 148, 150, 152, 156, 161, 165–6, 172, 201, 206n127, 221, 224, 229–30, 235, 241–2, 252, 257–8, 262, 265, 281, 287, 299–300, 305, 308, 310–1, 335–6, 346, 349–52, 370, 430, 474, 476, 553
ānanda, 102, 110, 219, 271, 282, 286, 302, 325–6 (*see also* joy); Ananda Metteyya, *see* Allan Bennett
anarchy, anarchists, 25, 52n65, 301, 392n50, 480, 486, 495, 505n72, 507, 509, 518, 527, 532
anattā, 174, 230, 300, 325, 329, 411n123, 413
Ancients, the, 30, 34n1, 35, 37, 41, 47, 49–50, 58, 65, 84, 90–1, 94, 98, 101–2, 107, 110, 132, 138, 143–50, 154–6, 178, 180–1, 200, 226, 237, 239, 241, 251, 252, 265–6, 277, 280–1, 283, 322–3, 340, 343, 346, 363, 371, 385, 388–91, 395, 397–8, 404–5, 409–10, 413, 416–8, 422–3, 427–8, 432, 434, 436–7, 439, 443n98, 451, 453, 455, 469, 479–81, 491, 504, 519, 555, 557–559
Ancient and Accepted Rite of Freemasonry, the, 391, 395, 426–7, 429, 442–3, 465n200
androgyny, 18, 401
angels, 38, 65, 86, 138–9, 162, 179, 183, 199, 208, 227–8, 238, 255, 257, 259, 265–6, 272, 278, 299, 315, 318, 320, 381, 409, 432; the Angel, *see* Aiwass or the Holy Guardian Angel; *The Angel*, 153, 275–7, 558, 562; the Angelic language, *see* the Enochian language
Anglo-Saxons, the, 278, 281
anicca, 132, 174–5, 300, 325
animals, animalism, 2, 13, 15–7, 27–8, 30, 32, 49, 54, 84, 89, 119, 126, 134–5, 159–61, 163, 172, 175, 179, 208–9, 230–1, 239, 245, 264, 276, 279–80, 320, 338, 351–3, 393, 397–8, 414, 442, 445, 473, 491, 501, 528n156, 532, 543, 553, 556
animalculae, 352, 445n106
animism, 58, 272–3, 393
ankh, the, 165, 206, 399
Ankh-af-na-Khonsu, 277, 383, 410–1,

537–8, 545, 547
Anthony of Padua, St., 320, 327
anthropology, 40–1, 48–50, 54, 472
Anthroposophy, 347, 438–9
Antichrist, 139, 394, 404; *The Antichrist*, 88, 90–1, 503, 507
Antioch, 439
Antony, Mark, 505–6
Antient and Primitive Rite or Freemasonry, the, 426, 428, 435
Aphrodite, 50, 241
apocalypse, 81, 138, 153, 162, 275, 277, 314, 394–6; the Apocalypse of St. John, *see* Revelation
Apollo, 20, 187, 241, 246; the oracle of Apollo, 20, 261n37
Apollonius of Tyana, 437
Apophis, 54, 56, 336, 397, 403, 443n98
Apuleius, 258n27, 455
Aquarius, 34n1, 37, 40, 152, 162; the Age of Aquarius, 37
Arabia, the Arabs, 8n9, 87, 164, 193, 411, 428n27; the Arabic language, 385, 411–2; Arabic numerals, 8n9, 151
Arahats, Arahatship, 83, 154, 210, 340, 351, 354, 466
Ararita, 237, 309n94
Archangels, the, 121, 123, 259, 274, 437n70
Archimedes, 113, 481
Aries, 34n1, 35n4, 152, 333, 400
Aristarchus, 34–5
aristocracy, 17, 27, 74, 376, 391–2, 422–3, 462, 467–8, 474–5, 485, 501n55, 505n72, 506–7, 510n92, 512n95, 515–6, 518, 519n127, 521, 523, 531
Aristotle, Aristotelianism, 1, 2, 50, 57, 62, 100–1, 103, 258, 270, 283, 423, 477, 479–80
Arjuna, 232, 240, 361
Ark, the, 53, 153, 437, 470, 497
Armageddon, 394
Armida, 53, 244
Arnold, Matthew, 211, 503
art, artists, artistry, ix, 15, 27–9, 33, 46, 52, 59n89, 69, 78, 116–7, 119, 132, 146–7, 158, 161–2, 164, 168–9, 172, 182, 188–90, 194, 198–9, 217, 224–5, 233, 236, 242–3, 247, 256, 261, 271n73, 281, 284, 290, 296, 310, 330–1, 360, 366, 371–2, 374, 389–91, 401, 407, 417, 427, 441, 445, 455, 459, 462, 467–8, 470, 475, 478, 480–1, 487, 494, 510, 519–20, 522–3, 525, 528, 538, 543; *Art*, 558, 562; the Art of Life, 331, 390, 487; the Royal and Sacerdotal Art, 29, 54, 168, 195, 371, 391, 395, 408, 433, 437, 440, 460, 484, 532, 534, 537–9, 547 (*see also* the prince-priest); the rules of art, 28, 242, 543
Aryans, the, 88, 102, 144, 148, 272, 276, 518–9
āsana, 324, 356, 358, 450
Asar, *see* Osiris
Ascension of Jesus, the, 406
asceticism, 50, 86, 89, 182, 195, 235–6, 346, 352, 388, 407, 423, 467
Asi, *see* Isis
assassins, 202, 392n50, 423, 467, 505, 513; the Assassins, 241, 424
Assiah, the, 238, 283n2, 338, 560–1
Assyria, 54, 162, 193, 389, 486; the Assyrian language, 427n16, 439
Astarte, 325, 432; *Liber Astarte*, 416
astral body, the, 163, 178, 224–7, 252–4, 256, 258, 449; the astral light, 163, 313, 393–4; the astral plane, 7n3, 172, 225–7, 237, 253–4, 281, 287, 312, 364, 393, 427, 449, 560–1; astral travel, 163, 205, 224–6, 253–4, 256, 449
astrology, 34n1, 36–7, 40, 147, 207, 264, 363, 381, 461; astrological ages, 37
astronomy, 34–6, 58, 111, 134, 337–8, 403, 481, 523
atheism, x, 20, 118, 155, 200, 287, 331, 362, 381, 391, 411, 414–6, 541
Athene, 49, 246; Athens, the Athenians, 49–50, 479n266, 485, 505n72
athletes, athletism, ix, 23–5, 27, 29–31, 63–4, 71, 74–5, 77–8, 84, 102, 153, 167–9, 220–4, 236–7, 245–6, 255, 261, 303, 308, 317, 356–8, 359n118, 366, 381–2, 449–50, 482, 494, 516, 521n133, 523, 528–31, 551, 556
Atlas, 501
ātman, 102, 130, 132–3, 160–1, 177, 210, 230, 235–6, 250–1, 263, 271–2, 288, 322, 326, 329, 358, 366; *ātmadarśana*, 248, 364–6, 402
atoms, atomism, 1, 9, 25, 67, 82, 94, 100, 104, 198, 218, 224, 229, 287,

297, 356, 501, 556
Attis, 41, 58, 187, 332, 407, 432, 436, 439, 472n228, 474
Atziluth, the, 338, 560–1
Augœides, see the Holy Guardian Angel
Augustine, St., 1–3, 38, 49, 440
AUM, 153, 335, 341, 367, 539, 545, 547; AUMGN, 341–2
Aurobindo, 137n37, 468n213
Australia, the Australians, 462, 490
Austria, the Austrians, 61, 429, 434, 521, 523, 525; the Austrian school of economics, 60–1, 521–5
authority, 18, 20, 36, 134, 151, 237, 263, 268–9, 271, 281, 304, 310, 318, 353, 358–9, 390, 392, 400, 410, 414, 425, 428, 443n96, 437–8, 442, 445–7, 452–3, 458, 476, 484, 498, 504–5, 507, 510, 522, 531
automobiles, 22, 130, 510, 515, 521–2
autotheism, 3, 9, 105, 228, 362, 431, 509, 548
avatars, 54–6, 196, 379, 399
Avesta, the, 144, 395
Ayin, 54, 401, 558, 562

Babalon, 153–4, 183–4, 265, 292–5, 298, 304, 313–4, 332, 397, 399, 470
Babe in the Egg, the Lotus, or the Womb, the, 12, 50, 53, 233, 263–5, 304, 332, 398, 467, 470, 542
Babylon, the Babylonians, 36, 101, 162, 245, 389, 432, 558; the Babylonian captivity, 428n27
Bacchae, the, 379, 417; Bacchanals, 38, 228; Bacchus, 223, 228, 408, 433, 436, 439; Bacchus Diphues, 163, 251, 398
Bach, Johann Sebastian, 191, 330
Bachofen, Johann Jakob, 49
Bacon, Francis, Sir, 392, 480
Balaam, 385, 425
balance, see equilibrium; balances, 114, 310, 398; the Book of the Balance, 374, 415, 555–7
Baltoro Glacier, the, 83, 524
banishing, 123–4, 254, 321, 362, 389, 449, 454n145, 555
bankers, banking, 45, 150, 172–3, 345, 447, 491, 516, 524, 528
bankruptcy, 148, 472, 476, 504, 533
Baphomet, 163, 401, 499; Baphomet XI°, 429, 442, 461

baptism, 2, 393, 409n114
Baudelaire, Charles, 191, 242, 392–3
Beast, the, 18, 55, 138–9, 184, 188, 209, 218n12, 222, 238, 265, 300, 332, 340, 380, 384, 394, 396–7, 399–403, 409–10, 413, 451–2, 458, 493, 537, 544, 546; the number of the Beast, 138, 397, 402, 415; the Ritual of the Mark of the Beast, 124, 384
Beatific Vision, the, 229, 297, 302
beauty, 22, 23, 27, 40, 87, 113, 117, 124, 158, 169, 172, 183–4, 186, 189–90, 192–3, 199, 201, 206, 209, 218, 229, 234, 242, 255, 259n31, 264, 276, 280, 296, 302, 309, 338, 354, 355, 357, 364–5, 376, 380, 389, 441n83, 455–6, 462, 477n253, 483, 491, 504, 514, 537, 541, 545–7, 550–1
Because, 24–6, 127, 298–300, 304, 310, 319, 421, 541–2, 544
Becoming, 13, 99, 106, 175, 283, 325–6, 339
Beethoven, Ludwig van, 16, 190
begging, beggars, 17, 181, 223, 255, 326, 340, 376, 460, 469, 542
Being, 13, 99–100, 106, 108, 110, 157, 165, 171, 176, 198, 218, 282–3, 286, 325–6, 470; not-Being, 157, 283, 326
Belial, 91–2
belief, see faith
Bennett, Allan, 53, 133, 272, 348, 354, 408; Frank Bennett, 462
Berashith, 87–8, 95–7, 118, 177–8, 216, 326, 362, 369, 415, 482
Bergson, Henri, 57
Berkeley, Bishop, 3n14, 299
Berlin, 46–7, 99, 429, 438
Bernard of Clairvaux, St., 468
Bernardin de Saint-Pierre, Jacques-Henri, 137
Besant, Annie, 272, 360, 438, 450–3
bestiality, 54, 191
Beth, 155, 301, 334–5, 397, 558, 562; Beth-El, 397
Bhagavad-Gītā, the, 137n37, 161, 177–8, 232, 240, 248, 250, 257, 307, 358, 404, 457
Bhikkus, 87–8, 344, 354, 388, 460
Bible, the, 20, 37n14, 73, 81, 89, 95, 101, 138–9, 145, 257, 281, 315, 384, 394–6, 402, 404, 408, 410, 412–4, 433, 436, 439, 447–8, 468, 492
billiards, 32, 103, 255, 317, 482

Binah, 141, 153, 189, 208-9, 229, 257-8, 281, 293, 298, 301, 314, 454, 558-61; *see also* Understanding
biology, 31, 56, 60-1, 63-4, 75-6, 79-80, 119, 159, 169, 183, 285, 347, 473, 487, 507, 516, 521, 524, 529, 533
birth, *see* incarnation
black magic, 20, 176, 237, 295, 298, 313, 317, 332, 343, 376, 400, 402, 417, 444, 540, 542; the Black Adepts, the Black Lodge, 142, 182-8, 208, 237, 243-6, 294, 295, 303n68, 304-6, 313-4, 328, 471
blackmail, 18, 494-5, 498
Blake, William, 28, 30, 39, 84, 89-90, 104, 173, 190, 240, 242n81, 308, 414
blasphemy, 16, 28, 66n113, 89-91, 142, 172, 176-7, 183-5, 191-2, 204, 243, 298, 311, 387, 399, 415, 422, 431-2, 437n68, 455, 546, 552, 557
Blavatsky, Helena Petrovna, ix, 39, 148n71, 162, 178, 201, 210, 251-2, 257-8, 263-5, 281, 360, 388, 396-8, 450-1, 453, 456, 469
bliss, *see ānanda or* joy
blood, 9, 19, 29, 32, 42, 53, 58, 64, 156, 160, 191, 194n79, 234, 237, 245, 263, 295, 313-4, 317, 356, 389, 393-4, 421, 466, 470, 474, 477, 495, 498, 524, 529, 539, 544; the Blood of the Saints, 121, 191, 234, 295, 313-4, 317
Bloomfield, Maurice, 144
Bodhidharma, 468
Bodhisattva vows, the, 210
body, the, ix, 3n14, 11, 13, 16-7, 19, 25, 29-31, 38, 41, 58, 64, 71, 74, 77-8, 81, 84, 93, 102, 111, 116-7, 119, 135, 156, 158-9, 167-8, 172, 177-82, 190-5, 199, 206n127, 207-8, 211, 219-20, 222, 224, 226-7, 230, 234, 236-7, 239, 242, 245-6, 251-2, 256-7, 266-8, 270, 273, 276, 278, 280, 284, 288, 292, 300, 303, 308, 311, 313, 318, 324, 332, 337-8, 343-4, 355-6, 357-9, 361-2, 367-6, 399, 402-3, 405-6, 409-10, 421-3, 437, 445-6, 449, 458, 462, 469, 487-9, 492, 495-7, 527-8, 541, 543, 548, 552, 556, 561
Boehme, Jakob, 39, 104, 178, 200
Bohemia, the Bohemians, 150
Boleskine, 384, 403
Bolyai, János, 3n14, 117

Boulak, Boulaq, or Bulaq, 381, 410
boulēsis, 1
bourgeoisie, the, 15-6, 59, 192, 281, 345, 352-3, 390, 447, 467, 470, 487-9, 505, 531
Bourne, Randolph, 518
Bou Saâda, 418
Brahma, 92, 250, 272, 416n147
Brahmacharya, 236, 353, 388
Brahman, 118, 177, 210, 250, 263, 271-2, 353, 366
Brahmins, the, 82, 87, 352, 360-1, 376, 388
Brahmo Samaj, the, 360
brain, the, 9, 32, 45, 52, 61, 75, 114, 134-6, 142-3, 167-8, 182, 200, 202, 225-6, 251, 256, 293, 353, 356, 361-5, 373, 394, 426, 457, 519
bread, 16, 155, 311, 402, 436, 506
breathing, 32, 77, 79, 84, 86, 95, 102, 157, 163, 194n79, 263, 275-6, 341, 354, 356-8, 366-8, 394, 405, 538, 543, 545
Briah, the, 560-1
Bricaud, Jean, 434-5, 438, 442
Britain, the Britons, ix, 44, 46, 59, 61, 111, 354, 359, 383, 426, 430, 433, 438, 442, 461, 463, 468, 474, 485, 488, 501, 505, 511, 518, 533; the British Museum, ix, 111; the British Raj, 359, 467-8
Buddha, the, *see* Siddhārtha; the *ādi-buddha*, 257, 262; the *dhyani-buddha*, 265; the second Buddha, 320; Buddhahood, 174, 210, 230, 271-2, 336, 355, 379, 420, 424, 475
Buddhi, 130, 250
Buddhism, 23, 65, 76, 82-5, 87-8, 101-3, 107, 114, 136, 154, 164-6, 174, 177, 195, 200, 205, 206n127, 210, 223, 230, 240, 248, 250, 257, 262, 265, 271-3, 300, 312, 321-2, 325, 336, 338-40, 344, 348-9, 351-2, 354-5, 360-1, 363-4, 376, 381-2, 384, 387-8, 394, 408, 413, 415, 424, 437, 440, 442, 460, 468, 474-6, 482, 546, 559; Han Buddhism, 166, 559; Hānayāna Buddhism, 319; Mahāyāna Buddhism, 210, 320, 376; Tantric Buddhism, 210, 320, 349; Theravāda Buddhism, 325, 354; Zen Buddhism, 107, 166, 364, 468, 474-6
Bull, the, 32, 35n4, 162, 164, 223, 225,

258n27, 308-9, 363, 366-7, 399, 420, 424, 506, 538, 562
Bulwer-Lytton, Edward, Sir, 201, 261, 265
Bunyan, John, 83
Burma, 320, 354
Burton, Richard Francis, Sir, 41, 241, 470
Bushidō, 474-6, 532n171

Cabala, the, *see* the Qabalah
Caduceus, the, 287-8, 325, 436
Caesar, Gaius Julius, 137, 374, 479, 505, 519
Cagliostro, 202
Caiaphas, 342, 509
Cairo, 223, 381, 385, 410, 544
California, 440, 444, 463-4
Caligula, 191, 409, 415
Calvary, 179, 436, 509
Calypso, 244, 253
Cambridge, 49, 111, 232, 342, 382, 388, 413, 451; the Cambridge Ritualists, 41n28, 49
camps, 157, 162, 345, 404, 443, 452
Canada, 444, 452, 461
cancer, 14, 24, 81, 221
Cancer, 558, 562
Cannabis, 86, 164
Cantillon, Richard, 484
capitalism, *see* the free market
Capricorn, 41, 55, 58, 401, 558, 562
Carlyle, Thomas, 46
carnivorism, 73, 84, 239, 276, 318, 346
Casaubon, Méric, 315-6, 318, 440n83
caste system, the, 87, 91, 223, 286, 329, 352, 371, 404, 484, 533
Catholicism, 2, 52n65, 84, 146, 196n85, 245, 343, 392, 408, 414, 417, 423-4, 427n16, 431-5, 437-8, 444-6, 463, 470, 474, 477, 526; the Catholic Mass, *see* the Mass; the Old Catholics, 434, 438, 442; the State Catholics, 434
Catullus, 28, 455
causality, 21, 39-40, 51, 67, 81-3, 86-8, 91, 96-7, 100, 110, 114, 116-9, 131-2, 136, 144, 147, 158, 164-6, 173-5, 178, 182, 190, 196, 198, 203, 205-7, 209-11, 219, 222-3, 231n46, 244-5, 250, 256, 277, 289-91, 301-4, 310-4, 319, 323-7, 339, 346, 349-50, 364-6, 373-6, 402-3, 411-2, 420-1, 424, 447-8, 473-5, 479, 504-5, 508-9, 517, 525, 530-1
Cecrops, King of Athens, 50
Cefalù, 159, 444, 503, 554
celibacy, 74-5, 237, 343-4, 492
Celts, the, 396, 418, 518
centre of the universe, the, 9, 20, 66n113, 105, 108, 110, 142-3, 198, 219, 235, 332, 374, 451, 502, 507, 518, 537, 540, 549, 552, 556
cessation, 115, 164, 197, 207, 210, 291, 314, 319-20, 325, 356, 366-8
Chain, the, 285
chakras, the, 275, 288, 363, 396
Chaldea, the Chaldeans, 101, 427n16, 432; the *Chaldæan Oracles*, 149, 157, 257, 272, 303n68, 312, 348, 482
champagne, 171, 186, 195, 199, 236, 496, 512n95, 539
chance, 1-2, 22, 32, 41, 58, 60, 72, 83, 96, 132, 135, 173, 181, 187, 196, 259n31, 352, 376, 385, 388, 460, 495, 497, 501, 517, 556
change, 9-11, 26-27, 31, 35, 37, 42, 49n56, 55-6, 58, 60, 67, 71, 74, 78, 80, 83, 88, 90, 93-4, 101, 106, 125, 132, 135, 142, 148, 152-3, 164-6, 173-4, 179-81, 184-8, 190, 192, 194, 202-3, 207n133, 208-10, 218, 223, 230, 234, 239, 241, 244-5, 248-9, 256, 258, 271, 273, 283-6, 290, 292-5, 297-8, 300, 320-8, 331-3, 335, 349, 359, 374, 391, 397, 412, 441, 445n106, 465, 467, 471, 481, 483-5, 487-8, 502, 508, 510, 528-30, 538-9, 542, 556
Chanokh, *see* Enoch
chaos, 60, 65, 100, 121-2, 140, 154, 208, 293, 301, 389, 465, 480, 511
chariots, charioteering, 135, 138, 146, 155, 162, 203, 294-5, 346, 522; *The Chariot*, 146, 155, 294-5, 558, 562
charity, 134, 196, 506
charlatans, 219, 279-80, 307, 352-3, 390, 432, 446-7, 452-3, 456, 509, 532-4
Charlemagne, 415, 486
chastity, 58, 75, 89, 192, 235-7, 240, 244, 284, 343-5, 352, 420, 423, 482, 490, 493-4, 546
chela, *see* students
chemistry, 75, 103, 140, 184, 204, 285, 346-7, 351, 390, 482, 516; chemical elements, 9-10, 12, 67-8, 100-1, 103,

INDEX

124–5, 130, 140–1, 197, 204, 218, 349
Cherubims, 141, 305, 384
Chesed, 141, 152, 558, 561
chess, 25, 28, 52, 72, 382
Cheth, 155, 294, 301, 558, 562
Chiah, 176, 281, 560
chidākāśa, 363
children, childhood, childishness, 2, 11–2, 15, 17–8, 30–1, 34, 42–6, 49–50, 52–6, 58, 62, 78, 83, 85, 88, 91, 104, 119, 137, 141–3, 149, 151, 153, 159n102, 164, 168, 170–2, 181, 184–5, 189–90, 193–5, 206, 210, 217, 219, 226, 232–3, 235, 237, 242, 244, 249, 254, 256, 262–5, 267, 273, 291, 293–6, 304, 307, 309, 317, 319, 328, 332–5, 337–8, 342, 348–9, 353, 365, 367–8, 376, 381–3, 394–5, 397–401, 405, 409, 413, 415, 419, 436, 441n83, 444–5, 456, 458, 460, 463–4, 466–7, 470–1, 474, 480, 483, 487–92, 495–6, 501–6, 509–11, 514, 517, 519–21, 529, 532, 534, 537, 539, 542, 544, 546, 551, 553, 555; the Crowned and Conquering Child, 34, 45, 58, 170, 235, 264, 332, 337, 398, 419, 444, 458, 466, 471, 483, 532, 534 (*see also* Ra-Hoor-Khuit); the Æon of the Child, *see* the Æon of Horus
China, the Chinese, 35, 99, 102, 106–8, 144, 148, 158, 165–6, 200, 262, 283, 320, 352, 364, 376, 412, 468, 474–5, 490, 502, 508–9, 525–7, 559; the Chinese language, 106–7, 144, 165–6, 364, 412, 474–5, 508, 526, 559
chit, 219, 271, 282, 286, 325–6; *see also* light
chitta, the, 357, 363, 369 (*see also* subconsciousness); *chittākāśa*, 256, 362–3
chivalry, 68, 532
Chokmah, 141, 189, 281, 287, 293, 298, 454, 558, 561; *see also* Wisdom
Choronzon, 14, 69, 81n59, 164, 183–4, 244, 298, 308, 313–6, 318, 328, 396, 467, 486
Christ(s), 34, 38, 44, 59, 73, 88, 91, 208, 238, 250, 272, 275, 287, 336, 342, 362, 369, 379, 387, 395–6, 398, 402, 413, 415, 420, 431–3, 436, 439–40, 449, 454, 468, 474, 482
Christianity, Christians, 1–2, 15, 23–4, 26, 31, 35n4, 37–8, 44, 47, 49n56, 50, 59, 61–3, 73, 75, 81, 88–91, 97, 123, 139, 149, 157, 162, 171–2, 176, 178–80, 188, 195, 200–1, 208–9, 262, 272, 278n92, 303, 306, 313–4, 329, 338, 342–3, 362, 364, 387–9, 391, 394–6, 401–2, 406–10, 413, 415–17, 419n157, 423, 427–8, 432–3, 435–6, 438–40, 442, 444, 451, 454–7, 460, 467–70, 472, 474, 477, 479, 482, 486, 491–2, 495, 501–3, 509, 558; Christian Science, 172, 179, 313
Christmas, 40–1, 45, 432
Chuang-tzǔ, 99–100, 527
churches, 2–3, 72, 90, 200, 207, 342–3, 358, 380, 389, 406, 432–42, 444–6, 455, 463, 465, 478, 479n266, 484, 486, 495, 500, 534; the Ancient British Church, 442; the Church of England, 409, 419n157, 432–3, 438; the Church of Thelema, 463; the Gnostic Catholic Church, 384, 429, 431, 435, 439–40, 442, 444, 449; the Hidden Church of the Holy Grail, 390, 442; the Liberal Catholic Church, 438, 442n93; the Roman Catholic Church, *see* Catholicism; the Syrian Orthodox Church, 439
Church Fathers, the, 149, 161, 180, 397, 416, 432, 434
Churton, Tobias, 98–9, 114
Cicero, 35, 505
cinema, ix, 44, 444, 505
Circe, 53, 193, 244, 258n27, 313
Circle, the, 97, 122–4, 142, 201, 273, 301, 311–2, 333, 350, 394, 402, 440n83, 449, 534, 539–40, 546; circular arguments, 72–3, 114–5, 126, 128, 134, 140, 154, 158, 188, 190, 205, 246, 286–7, 305, 319, 433, 519; squaring the circle, 122, 301, 333–4, 485, 546
Cistercians, the, 468–9
clairvoyance, 226, 252, 376
clergy, 16–7, 20, 41, 46, 63, 82, 84, 87–90, 107, 150, 188, 191, 196n85, 219, 262, 269, 271–2, 277, 284, 288, 337, 370, 380–2, 389, 391–2, 395, 398, 406–8, 410, 414, 422–3, 431–40, 442, 444–6, 454, 460, 468–9, 474, 484, 486, 490, 493, 521, 528, 534, 537–8, 540, 544–5, 547, 558
climate, 64, 241, 340, 412, 414, 417, 419, 487, 554

Cloud upon the Sanctuary, 385, 451–2
Clymer, Reuben Swinburne, 453
cocaine, 242, 496–8
Coins, *see* the Pantacle
Coleridge, Samuel Taylor, 496
common sense, 9, 84, 151, 172, 178, 262, 306, 351, 379, 390, 400, 431, 455, 482, 485, 524
communications, 18, 24, 33, 44, 68, 69, 99–100, 120, 127, 135, 265, 329, 331, 341, 358, 381, 385, 387, 418, 426, 429–30, 432, 436, 449, 452–3, 461, 472, 490, 497–8, 503–6, 533–4
communism, 44, 461n167, 477n253, 509–10, 513, 515
Confucius, Confucianism, 59, 107, 155, 165–6, 278, 338, 507–9, 526–7, 559
compassion, 23–4, 59, 79, 175, 179, 296, 472, 503, 541, 546, 552
competition, 27, 44, 56, 60, 70, 389, 440, 465, 500, 514, 531
concentration, 103, 112, 168, 207n127, 217, 221, 226–7, 236, 257, 260, 272, 289, 318, 321, 348, 353, 357, 361, 363, 368–70, 376, 402, 405, 420, 449, 469
conception, 50–1, 54, 56, 153, 217
conflict, 7, 14, 20, 43, 56, 62, 65, 68, 70–1, 73, 77–9, 94, 177, 183, 220, 222, 243, 246, 259, 266, 270–1, 325, 330, 352, 358, 371, 387, 428, 436, 455, 467, 485, 488, 510, 512, 522, 527, 530, 554
conscience, 31, 41–2, 46, 90, 238, 281, 342, 415, 436, 477, 514, 525, 553
consciousness, 11–2, 74, 93, 104–6, 108–14, 117–9, 132, 136–7, 141–2, 155–61, 165, 187, 192–6, 199, 201–2, 217–9, 224, 227–9, 234–5, 246–8, 250–1, 256, 267–8, 271–2, 282, 286–7, 293, 297–302, 311–3, 322, 337–8, 341, 343, 349, 364–5, 368, 385, 398–9, 420, 445n106, 506, 538, 550–1; the conscious mind, 8, 15, 18, 24, 33, 45, 55, 64, 66, 78, 93, 118, 126–7, 129, 132, 141–2, 147, 157–61, 163, 165, 178, 182, 186, 189, 192, 194–5, 199–206, 210, 215, 218, 221–2, 224, 226–9, 238, 246, 250, 252, 255, 257, 264, 270, 272–3, 278–9, 289, 296, 298, 302, 310–1, 316–22, 337–8, 341, 343, 357, 362, 364, 368, 371, 381, 387–8, 420, 431, 449, 455, 470, 473, 509, 511, 514, 516, 521, 526–7, 550, 554
consecration, 28, 40, 77, 123, 124, 187, 196n85, 206, 225, 239, 264, 304, 432, 449; episcopal consecration, 434, 438, 440, 442, 444–6
consent, 74, 266, 316, 511, 512n98
Conservation of Matter and Energy, the, 45, 120, 125, 194, 197, 217, 332, 349
conservatism, 389, 392, 434, 483, 515; the Conservative and Unionist Party, 52n65, 382, 505, 528
Constant, Alphonse Louis, *see* Éliphas Lévi
Constantine the Great, St., 407
continence, *see* chastity
Continent, the, *see* Europe
Corinthians, 254, 290, 358, 423, 440n82
corporatism, 9, 14, 27, 64, 71, 172, 190–1, 338, 422–4, 446, 460–2, 465–7, 484–5, 487, 492, 496–500, 507, 510–22, 524, 532–4, 553–4
corruption, 38, 90, 171, 183, 207, 391, 411, 472, 491, 495, 508, 525
cosmogeny, 96–101, 109, 139, 332
cosmology, 37–8, 107–8, 148, 231n46, 329, 337, 558; the cosmological argument, 97
Cosmos, the, *see* the Universe; the Cosmic Egg, 95
courage, 20, 29–32, 62, 68, 76–80, 89–90, 161–3, 165, 177, 181, 185–8, 200–2, 208, 215, 225, 246–7, 265, 271, 298, 309, 342, 346, 358, 366, 370–1, 374, 399, 409, 415, 445, 454, 459, 470–1, 493, 529–31, 546, 555
cowardice, 16–20, 26, 31–2, 45, 51–3, 55, 62, 68–70, 77–8, 80, 87–90, 105, 163, 172, 177, 179, 181–92, 195, 200–1, 206–9, 221–2, 241–4, 253, 260, 263, 270, 280–1, 295, 308, 324, 331, 342, 345–6, 350, 352–3, 374, 388, 409, 420, 445, 470–1, 473–4, 493–4, 498, 503, 506–7, 517–8, 526–30, 532, 534, 546, 552, 555–6
Craddock, Ida, 278
Cratylus, 94
Creation, 2, 10–2, 16, 65, 67, 82, 88, 97–8, 101–2, 105–6, 109, 118–21, 123, 139–42, 148–9, 164, 179, 187, 192, 194–5, 198, 201, 237–8, 256, 263, 276, 281–5, 290, 294, 296, 300–1, 307–9, 314–5, 323, 325, 332,

338, 356-7, 361, 374, 395, 422, 432, 437, 451, 461-2, 471, 533-4, 538, 556, 558-9, 561; creativity, 29, 46-7, 52-3, 57, 60-1, 99, 137, 188-98, 237n63, 244, 483, 507, 513, 528, 551; the Creative Magical Word, *see* the Logos
crime, criminals, 19, 58, 70, 80, 83, 91, 118, 137, 176, 243, 280, 352, 371, 391, 407, 445-6, 487-9, 494-9, 512-3, 525, 528-9, 553
crocodiles, 35n4, 53, 159, 207, 245, 470
Cross, the, 91, 121, 194, 207n131, 273, 301, 320, 333, 336, 344, 358, 374, 396, 402, 428, 432, 443n98, 468, 479n266, 509, 522, 546, 556
Crowley, Emily Bertha, 394; Rose Edith Crowley, 53, 381, 385-6, 400
Crown, the, 30-1, 40, 141, 163, 185, 195, 209, 234, 283, 300, 309, 311-3, 335, 363, 368, 398, 493, 534, 543, 558
crucifixion, 40, 73, 335, 342, 398, 436, 466, 474
cruelty, 46, 63, 74, 86, 90, 137, 204, 206, 223, 237, 278n92, 296, 301, 371, 471, 499, 556
cube, the, 256-7, 293, 540
Cup, the, 1, 120-1, 148n67, 191, 210, 258n27, 274, 290, 292, 295, 311, 313-4, 317, 323, 332, 335, 427, 453, 493
curses, 13-4, 27, 58, 65, 171, 177, 180, 182, 187, 203, 247, 261, 283n5, 293, 296, 298, 307, 312, 314-5, 342, 383, 403, 454, 473, 529, 538, 541-2, 544, 546, 550, 552, 555
customs, 19, 27, 40, 49-50, 54, 64, 70-1, 77, 80, 261n37, 351-2, 404, 406, 414, 484-7, 492, 502, 517-9
cyclicity, 9-10, 35-9, 177-8, 194-6, 210-1, 264, 339

Daäth, 141, 185, 189, 287-8, 293-5, 310-2, 335, 363, 372, 558, 561
Dagger, the, 53, 72, 120, 285, 311, 313-4, 319, 363
daimōn, the, *see* the guardian spirit
Daleth, 155, 189, 244, 334-5, 411, 558, 562
damnation, 18, 23, 82, 189, 203, 265, 409, 439, 495, 502, 541-2, 544, 552
Dao, the, *see* the Tao
darkness, 16, 19, 32, 87, 106, 122, 154, 162, 177, 183, 187, 216, 234, 238, 248, 253, 285-6, 289-90, 303, 317-8, 325, 332-3, 336, 341, 357, 367-8, 386, 389, 395, 407, 411, 419, 421n166, 444, 455, 470-1, 472n228, 539, 551, 555; the dark æon, *see* the Æon of Osiris; the dark ages, 65, 87, 411; dark energy, or dark matter, 122; the Dark Night of the Soul, 336; the Dark Star, 177
darśanas, 248, 263, 306, 364-7, 402; *see also* visions
Darwin, Charles, 469; Darwinism, 49n56, 56, 159n102
Daughter, the, 118, 120-3, 141, 198, 254, 283, 301, 339, 398, 454
David, King of Israel, 164, 406, 421, 492
Davy, Humphry, Sir, 150
death, 12, 22-4, 27, 30-1, 34, 38-43, 45, 50, 54-6, 58, 60, 64, 66n113, 69, 75, 78, 80-1, 84, 89-91, 99-100, 102, 110, 121, 126, 135, 137, 140-1, 153-4, 163-4, 176-81, 183, 186-8, 191-6, 200-3, 206-11, 215-6, 221, 229, 232, 238, 244-8, 252-3, 258, 262, 270, 274-6, 281, 285-6, 290, 292, 294-5, 298, 306-7, 315-8, 320, 322, 325-6, 328, 331-3, 336-9, 341-2, 344-5, 349, 351, 358, 360, 362, 367, 371, 373, 390, 392n50, 398-9, 402-3, 405, 414, 425, 436-7, 441, 443-5, 456, 466, 471-2, 474-5, 489-90, 497-8, 505-6, 510, 513-4, 519, 539-43, 545-6, 550-1; *Death*, 209, 248n101, 558, 562; the dying god, 39-41, 54, 58, 60, 66n113, 162-3, 180, 222, 329, 332-3, 337, 437, 439, 444n101, 445, 472, 474; the Egyptian Book of the Dead, 244-5; the Tibetan Book of the Dead, 349
Decad, the, 9, 38, 100, 139-41, 147, 150, 208, 233, 238, 243, 275, 287, 293-5, 315, 338, 373, 398, 445, 558-62
Dee, John, 283, 315, 463
deformity, 13, 17, 30, 74, 183, 189, 223, 281, 291, 342, 519, 551
delight, *see* joy
demigods, 36, 397
Demiurge, the, 98, 285
democracy, 26, 45, 49, 59, 173, 330, 373, 407, 462, 486, 490, 498, 500-7, 509-10, 515, 522, 528-30, 532, 534
Democritus, 94, 479

598 INDEX

demons, *see* evils spirits; the personal demon, *see* the guardian spirit
dependent origination, 82, 136
Descartes, René, 156, 179, 480
desert, the, 58, 204, 289, 328, 345, 401, 405, 412, 418, 539
desire, 1, 11, 13, 23–4, 30, 70, 159, 173–5, 178, 188, 190, 202–3, 210, 220, 226, 233, 240, 243–8, 275n85, 296, 310, 331, 388, 399, 422, 440n83, 460, 468, 488, 492, 512–5, 520, 523, 533, 538, 540, 542–4, 555–7
despair, 91, 176, 194, 205–6, 216, 254, 309, 319, 336, 457
despotism, 227, 486, 499–500, 532n171
d'Este, Mary, 53, 400
destiny, *see* determinism
destruction, 10, 14, 17, 21, 32, 36, 52, 54–6, 59, 61–2, 67, 72, 74, 79–80, 83, 88, 90, 106, 108, 116–20, 127, 134–8, 147, 153, 161, 164, 171, 177, 184–6, 189–90, 194–6, 202–3, 209–10, 216, 227, 229, 237–9, 244–5, 248, 254, 260, 262, 265, 274, 277, 286, 289–91, 294–5, 299–303, 307–8, 310, 312–4, 317–27, 329, 333, 336, 338, 341, 356–7, 361, 364–70, 384, 392n50, 394, 402–3, 406, 408, 418, 443n98, 451–2, 456, 468–72, 480, 486, 496–8, 501–2, 509–10, 513, 515, 528, 531, 546–47, 551, 553
detachment, *see* non-attachment
determinism, 2–3, 7, 9, 27, 39, 42–3, 51, 64–5, 68, 77, 82, 85–6, 94, 109–10, 136, 147, 173–4, 187, 223, 265–6, 270, 284, 295, 298, 303–4, 379–81, 436, 500, 508, 530, 552, 555
Detroit, 430
Deussen, Paul, 93–4, 178, 469n216
Devachan, 210–1
Devil, the, 52, 55, 58, 63, 91, 139, 146, 164, 181, 202–3, 255, 278n92, 295, 303n68, 307, 314–6, 320, 326–7, 369, 400–1, 409, 424, 502; *The Devil*, 248n101, 401, 558, 562; pacts with the Devil, 52, 259, 295, 313–4, 327, 370–1
devotion, devotees, 14, 57, 61, 76, 169, 178, 183, 185, 201–2, 215, 221, 224, 230–2, 238, 259, 261, 296, 316, 345, 351, 370, 388, 404, 413, 416–7, 422, 425, 449–50, 459, 465–8, 473–4, 487, 488n14, 495, 515, 519, 524, 550

dew, 269, 288, 292, 320–1, 440n83, 538
Dewey, John, 47–8
Dhamma, *see* Dharma; the *Dhammapada*, 177, 376, 404
dhāraṇā, 159, 226, 348, 355, 357, 359, 366, 369
Dharma, 65, 82, 136, 146, 154, 222, 354–5; the Dharmachakra, *see* the Wheel of Dharma; the Dharma Kings, 320
dhyāna, 243, 253, 324, 357, 364
dialectics, 3, 7, 20, 27, 47–8, 56–7, 62, 93–9, 104, 107, 116–20, 127, 143–4, 161, 184–7, 193, 235, 262, 282–3, 289–90, 294–5, 297–304, 319–23, 340, 364–5, 391, 403, 415, 420, 467, 476, 550; dialectical materialism, 48
diaries, 10, 67, 109, 111, 159, 170, 173, 233, 280, 298, 310, 315, 318, 324, 340, 347–51, 384, 400, 410, 425, 444, 459, 486, 511–2, 532; *The Diary of a Drug-Fiend*, 372
diet, *see* food
Digamma, 55, 162–3, 338
Diogenes Laërtius, 1–2
Dionysius the Areopagite, 395
Dionysus, 41, 241, 246, 264n52, 332, 335, 340, 379, 432, 437, 472
diplomatic service, the, 223, 392, 394, 413, 463, 486, 491, 511, 529
discipline, 14, 28, 30, 72, 85, 191, 201, 217, 225, 229, 240, 291, 313, 350, 374, 473–4, 507, 516, 520, 531–2, 556
disease, 15, 17, 19, 23, 67, 69, 84, 88–9, 116, 119–20, 135, 172, 180, 192, 196, 220, 228, 238, 279–80, 289, 355, 370–2, 406, 423, 487, 491, 494, 502–3, 509, 525, 527, 530, 533
Disks, *see* the Pantacle
dispersion, 81n59, 191, 313–6, 400, 486
diversity, *see* variation
divination, 147–8, 260–1, 271n73
division, *see* duality; the division of labour, 26–7, 49, 52, 231, 423, 455, 461, 466–9, 475–6, 478, 483–5, 487–9, 493–5, 520–3; division by zero, 174
divorce, 387–8, 489–90, 493–4
doctrine, *see* dogma; *The Secret Doctrine*, 148n71, 264–5
dogs, 18, 22, 25–6, 53, 63, 80–1, 129, 209, 216, 370, 372, 421, 483, 490, 503, 506, 518, 541–2, 551

dogma, 1–3, 14, 22, 34n1, 39, 43, 48, 49n56, 66, 71, 73, 85, 89, 94, 97, 110, 117, 123, 133–4, 143, 146, 148–9, 151, 153–4, 159n102, 161, 176, 180–3, 199–200, 204, 215–7, 221, 230, 237n63, 247, 251, 266, 272–3, 281, 283–7, 292–4, 304, 306, 310, 319–20, 327, 340–1, 344, 346, 354, 356, 369–70, 376, 379, 391–2, 395, 402, 405–8, 411–2, 414, 417–9, 422, 426–7, 433–6, 439, 443n98, 446, 453–4, 459, 464, 466–7, 470, 477, 481, 500, 502–3, 516, 525; *Dogma and Ritual of High Magic*, 3n14, 146, 150, 409; *Morals and Dogma of the Ancient and Accepted Scottish Rite of Freemasonry*, 395; *Qabalistic Dogma*, 140, 154, 293, 336

Doinel, Jules, 434–5

Don Juan, 239, 241; Don Quixote, 11

doubt, 24, 76, 158, 172–3, 188, 197, 204, 222, 243, 254, 279, 318–9, 346, 374, 453, 493, 531, 543

Douglas, Alfred Bruce, Lord, 59

Dove, the, 244–5, 247–8, 321, 427, 437, 539

Dracula, ix

dragons, 16, 53, 74, 216, 543; the Dragon, 53, 164, 208, 225, 309, 399, 443n98, 467; the Black Dragon, 207, 336; the Stooping Dragon, 141, 312, 335, 561

drama, 29, 39–41, 51, 87, 119, 168, 395–6, 417, 419, 427n16, 431, 479n262, 510, 534

dreams, dreaming, 42, 63, 67, 77, 80–1, 117, 134, 149–50, 156, 160, 178–9, 185, 188, 206, 217, 226, 241, 244, 274, 279, 305, 310, 324, 349, 361, 399, 406, 437, 449, 456, 486, 498, 527

drugs, 86–7, 181, 199–201, 241–2, 280, 380, 497–8, 541

Drummond, William James Charles Maria, Sir, 397

drunkedness, 16, 28, 53, 70, 73, 171, 186, 191–3, 195, 198–204, 219, 242, 371, 452, 482, 491, 493, 495–7, 509, 539–41, 543, 548

dualism, 56, 62–3, 95–6, 116, 178–9, 229, 250, 282, 290, 302, 321; duality, 10–2, 14, 21, 58, 63n103, 99–100, 104–10, 116–20, 130, 133, 141–4, 148, 158, 172, 175–6, 183–4, 187, 193, 196–9, 204, 208n133, 216–9, 228, 234–5, 249–51, 271, 275, 279, 282–3, 285, 289–93, 298–304, 310, 312, 316–7, 320–7, 343, 356, 361–5, 371–3, 467, 471, 475–6, 484, 538, 543, 551, 558–61

dukkha, 174, 300, 325; *see also* suffering

duty, 13–4, 21, 26–7, 30–1, 59, 65, 69, 76–8, 204, 215, 268, 301, 327, 329, 370, 388, 402, 464, 466, 485, 495–9, 513, 516, 529, 548–54; *Duty*, 499, 512n97, 548–54

Dvaitism, *see* dualism

dwarfs, 190, 263, 408; the Dwarf-Self, 251, 263, 398

Dyad, the, 10, 13–4, 20–1, 43, 47, 56, 62, 71, 75, 94–7, 99, 101, 104–10, 117–20, 122–3, 127–8, 130, 143–4, 148, 150–1, 153, 156–8, 167, 179–81, 187, 193, 195, 197, 201, 204, 216–9, 228, 234–5, 238, 247, 248n101, 249–51, 271n73, 282, 283n5, 285–6, 288–9, 293–4, 297, 299–301, 303–4, 310, 312, 316–7, 320, 322, 325–6, 331–5, 339, 349, 353, 356–7, 362–4, 371, 373, 386–7, 399, 432, 436, 445, 450, 467, 470, 475, 478, 496, 518n120, 538, 551, 558–60

dynamism, 3, 13, 15, 21, 47–8, 143n50, 144, 165, 174–6, 228, 476, 549

Eagle, the, 162, 207–10, 225, 244, 287, 309, 341, 399

Earth, 32, 39–41, 45, 50–1, 63, 89, 100–3, 118–22, 149, 151, 153, 157, 162, 165, 179, 184–6, 188, 194, 196, 207–10, 223, 229, 233–4, 238, 242, 244–5, 251, 255, 258–9, 265, 283, 288, 295, 298, 312, 314n107, 315, 328, 332, 341–2, 358, 362, 368, 387, 398, 402, 413, 424, 437, 440n83, 449, 451, 456–8, 467, 471–2, 474, 493, 520, 534, 537–42, 544, 546, 553, 558–62; Planet Earth, 29, 36–42, 56, 58, 60, 105, 134, 141–2, 157, 161, 163, 180, 210, 226, 265, 295, 329, 337, 344, 347, 379, 381, 387, 398, 413, 437, 451, 456–8, 466, 471–2, 486, 491, 509, 530, 534, 540, 548, 556; the lords or kings of the earth, 22, 26–7, 483, 541–2, 546; the man of Earth, 230–1, 538

East, the, x, 38–41, 45, 58, 93, 101,

106-7, 115, 118, 145, 153, 162, 216, 242, 287, 320-1, 343, 353-4, 359-62, 365-8, 379, 384-5, 389, 395-6, 403-6, 413, 418, 436, 438-9, 441, 469, 475n241, 490, 502, 509, 525, 527, 532n171, 539, 544
Eckartshausen, Karl von, 3n14, 451
Eckenstein, Oscar, 53, 425
economy, economics, 26-7, 44, 60-1, 75, 121-3, 167, 173, 255, 423, 460-1, 466, 468, 477n253, 484, 488n14, 489, 494, 504, 511-4, 517, 521-5, 531, 534
ecstacy, 21, 28, 106, 113, 116, 119-20, 155, 164, 169, 174, 184, 186, 191, 193-6, 198, 202, 204-5, 207-8, 218-9, 229-30, 238, 241, 246-7, 286, 292, 302, 328, 332, 349, 362, 367, 368, 373, 379, 402, 431, 445n106, 455, 495-6, 537-9, 541-3, 550, 552
Eddington, Arthur Stanley, Sir, 108, 110-1, 132
Eden, 86, 141, 163, 274-5, 315, 342, 384, 454
education, 11-2, 16, 24-30, 46-7, 68, 71-2, 78, 85-6, 103-4, 113, 130-4, 140, 142-3, 148, 151-2, 154-6, 158-9, 164, 167-70, 172-4, 199-202, 215, 219-20, 223-6, 231-3, 240-2, 248, 249n106, 254-6, 262, 267, 272-3, 278, 305, 318-21, 327, 329, 338-40, 346-51, 354, 365-6, 369-70, 373-5, 380, 382, 385, 391, 393-4, 396, 406-7, 412-5, 417, 419n157, 422-5, 427-8, 432, 435, 439-40, 446-7, 450, 453, 456-7, 461, 464-9, 475-82, 484, 487-8, 497, 501-2, 504-6, 508, 511, 515-6, 519-23, 525-6, 528-9, 531-2, 538, 550-2, 555-7; compulsory education, 26-7, 256, 484, 504, 519, 521, 529
egalitarianism, 27, 48-9, 82, 392n50, 484, 501-2, 506-7, 513-4, 518n120, 520-2, 534
Ego, the, 3, 7, 11, 18-9, 23-4, 33, 61, 73, 76-8, 102, 105, 116, 120, 126, 129, 133, 137, 142-3, 156, 159, 164, 171, 173-8, 184-6, 193-6, 200-3, 205, 207, 208n133, 217-20, 224, 228, 230, 246-8, 251, 254, 256-7, 263-4, 271-3, 275-6, 278-80, 282, 288, 291-2, 298, 300-1, 303-4, 306-13, 316-7, 320, 322, 324, 332-3, 337-8, 340-1, 343, 347-9, 363-5, 367-8,

370-2, 374, 381, 387, 398-9, 402, 462, 467, 470-2, 503, 527, 530, 541, 555-6; the non-Ego, 116, 120, 184, 193, 202, 218-9, 271, 273, 275, 282, 291, 301, 317, 333; egocentrism, 76, 171, 268, 340, 518; egoism, or egotism, *see* selfishness; egomania, 119, 183, 185, 237, 246, 278-9, 304, 306, 313, 374, 480, 495, 500-1, 514, 526
Egypt, Egyptians, 34-5, 39-40, 45, 54, 87, 93, 98, 100, 120, 144, 147, 148n67, 159n102, 162, 165, 169n139, 193, 223, 226, 241, 244-5, 262, 277, 285, 314, 336, 339, 379, 381, 383, 389, 394-5, 401, 410, 418, 426n14, 428, 432, 434, 439, 472, 479n266, 537-47, 558; the Egyptian Museum, 381, 410
Eheieh, 98, 293, 314
Einstein, Albert, 96, 98-9, 103, 111, 151, 321, 448, 456
ekāgratā, *see* one-pointedness
El, 397, 547
elasticity, 71, 146, 148, 168, 184, 197-8, 217, 305, 372, 533
Eleatic school, the, 94, 283
electron, 481; electrons, 9, 104, 142, 204; electromagnetism, 16, 120, 125, 356, 481; electricity, 16, 133, 204, 207, 356, 369, 374, 390
Eleusis, 418; *Eleusis*, 127, 132
Elixir of Life, the, 29, 196, 200-1, 211; *The Elixir of Life*, 84, 100, 211, 426, 448
Elizabethan period, the, 482, 531
emasculation, 344-5, 457, 471, 474
Emerald Tablet, the, 150, 208
Emerson, Ralph Waldo, 160, 360
emotions, emotionality, 1-2, 22-3, 59n89, 63, 68-70, 76, 79, 86-90, 104-5, 110, 156, 159, 181, 186, 193, 203-4, 223, 272-4, 289, 295, 311-2, 324-5, 346-7, 350-1, 357, 363-4, 368, 374-6, 387, 401, 413, 418-20, 449, 467, 476, 482, 488-9, 495, 506, 512, 516, 518, 528, 532-3, 538, 541, 543, 552-3, 556
Empedocles, 100-1, 108, 283, 284n6, 344
emperors, 148, 370, 374, 407-9, 416, 505; *The Emperor*, 152, 558, 562; *The Empress*, 540, 558, 562

empires, *see* imperialism
empiricism, 94, 116, 125-6, 132, 135, 157, 169, 186, 274, 305, 319, 390, 478, 481
Encausse, Gerard, 426, 427n16, 434-6, 438, 442, 453
endurance, 25, 29-30, 271, 276, 358, 379, 413, 503
energy, 14-5, 21, 29, 41, 61, 66, 73, 104, 108, 122, 125, 132, 161, 173, 194, 198, 203-6, 209, 221, 248n101, 275n85, 280-1, 285-6, 290-1, 294, 308-9, 332, 341-2, 345, 347, 350, 356, 361, 374, 429, 449-50, 454n144, 469-70, 476, 484, 487, 496, 509, 520, 550-2, 556
Engels, Friedrich, 48-9
England, the English people, ix, 17, 52n65, 57, 91n96, 111, 129, 132, 256, 272, 281, 354, 392n49, 404, 407, 413, 428, 431, 433-4, 438, 461, 468, 470, 475n141, 490, 492, 497, 511, 521n133, 525, 528, 531-2; the English language, ix, 41n28, 59n89, 65, 111, 122, 129-30, 133n21, 140, 176, 233, 255, 272, 276, 278, 300, 354, 364, 381, 392, 400, 412-3, 434, 442, 461, 492, 516, 521, 542, 545, 548, 562; the *English Review*, 430, 444n101, 498n40
Enlightenment, the, 60, 107, 391-2, 477, 488, 531; the Counter-Enlightenment, 391-2
Enoch, 38, 138, 227-8, 437n70; the Book of Enoch, 138; the Enochian language, 315, 327
enthusiasm, 13, 16, 42, 44, 113, 138, 188, 204, 229, 241, 307, 319, 339, 346-7, 383, 387, 419, 431-2, 443; *Energized Enthusiasm*, 241, 432
envy, 16, 64, 90, 119, 183, 239-41, 315, 346, 400, 420, 494-5, 503, 507, 523
Ephesians, 259, 421
eph' hēmin, 2
Epictetus, 2, 59
Epicurus, 181; Epicureanism, 1, 94, 181-2, 477n257, 485
equality, 9-10, 17, 20-1, 59, 62-3, 67, 70, 110, 117, 126-8, 134-5, 154, 162, 172, 174, 176, 190-1, 197-9, 209, 215, 217, 219, 229, 235, 246-7, 259, 268, 282, 283n5, 286, 288, 291, 296-7, 323, 337, 347, 373, 392n50, 394, 399, 403, 501-2, 506-7, 509, 513-4, 518n120, 520-2, 533-4
equilibrium, 21, 28-30, 52, 62, 69, 75, 84-5, 106, 110, 115, 122-3, 127, 136, 152-3, 161-3, 179-80, 186, 189, 197, 201-2, 207n130, 220-1, 227, 229-30, 240, 242, 244, 259-60, 270, 273, 277, 282-3, 286, 289, 294, 297-8, 301, 303, 308-10, 319-24, 327, 338-40, 366, 368, 370, 372-4, 391, 398-9, 462, 489, 524, 538, 547, 555-7
equinoxes, the, 34-7, 40, 45, 333, 342, 382, 413; *The Equinox*, 3n14, 38, 69, 115, 131, 139-40, 208, 224, 228, 234, 239, 241, 253, 264, 278, 286, 294-5, 333, 336-7, 348, 354, 373, 384-8, 390, 395, 400, 417, 426, 441, 450, 460, 465; the Equinox of the Gods, 34, 42, 45, 50, 56, 329, 343, 381-2, 384, 413, 539, 542, 545; *The Equinox of the Gods*, 50, 56, 207, 232, 276, 333, 381-2, 384-5, 393n54, 396-7, 400-2, 409-14, 417-8, 421, 430, 440-1, 452, 471, 476, 509; the precession of the equinoxes, 34-7
Erdmann, Johann, 47-8
Ervast, Pekka, ix
espionage, 241, 408, 423-5, 463, 467, 497-8, 532
Essenes, the, 439-40
establishment of the Law of Thelema, the, 31, 116, 402, 458, 461, 465-6, 471-3, 477, 510-2, 516, 522, 534, 545, 552-3
eternity, 7, 11-2, 15, 36, 40, 65, 81, 88, 97, 100-1, 110, 124, 133, 153, 164, 170, 173, 177, 185-6, 193, 195-8, 203-5, 210, 215-6, 219, 244, 250-1, 277, 284, 293, 298, 303, 323-5, 337-8, 343, 353, 365, 371, 395, 398, 401, 407, 412, 438, 445n106, 448, 452, 454-5, 495, 519, 539, 542, 550, 555
ether, 101-2, 123, 393; luminiferous ether, 393
ethics, x, 2, 7, 11, 14, 16-21, 24, 27-8, 44-5, 49n56, 51, 59, 61-2, 64-92, 119, 136-7, 142, 144-5, 152, 156n95, 159, 163, 165, 175, 177-8, 182, 187, 189, 192-3, 195, 202, 204, 223, 229, 231, 236, 238, 240, 256, 261n57, 271, 273, 279, 281, 291, 295, 310, 318, 320-1, 329, 331, 337-8, 344-5, 352,

354, 370, 375, 380-2, 387, 405, 407, 412, 420, 431n41, 432, 442, 455-8, 468n213, 461, 471-3, 476, 479n266, 482, 486, 490-2, 494-5, 497-8, 500-2, 506-9, 516, 521, 524n142, 527, 530, 533, 548, 557, 559; *Ethics and Evolution*, 75-6, 530

ethyl-oxide, 242, 532

eucharist, the, 29, 84, 191, 204, 225, 229, 297, 444

Euclid, 485; Euclidean geometry, 103, 117, 485; non-Euclidean geometry, 96, 103-4, 135, 157, 365

eudaimonia, 266, 270-1

eunuchs, 74, 493

Euphrates, the, 58

Europe, the Europeans, 35, 44, 56, 68, 97, 107, 144-5, 147-8, 165, 256, 338, 343, 352-4, 360, 391-2, 414, 422-4, 429-30, 434, 441, 442n95, 456, 467, 469, 472, 475n241, 477, 487-8, 490, 509, 511, 534

events, 11, 21-4, 26, 42-3, 45, 51, 55, 93, 104, 108, 110-1, 119, 143n50, 184, 165n130, 166, 175, 181, 184, 187, 196-8, 203, 205, 207, 209, 215, 217, 219, 229, 244, 270, 291-2, 297, 307, 319, 343, 348-50, 372, 385, 387, 391, 399, 418, 420, 424, 471, 501, 511, 526, 556; point-events, 128-9, 165

evil, 2-3, 9-10, 12, 20-1, 38, 53, 58, 62-3, 65, 67-9, 75, 81-3, 88, 91, 106, 122, 163, 172, 177-8, 180, 183, 186-8, 207, 219, 222, 227, 238-40, 268, 271, 273, 281, 284-5, 293, 303n68, 307, 313, 315-6, 325-7, 332-3, 336, 344-5, 356, 392n49, 393, 395, 401, 405, 413, 455, 470, 488, 492, 498, 508, 515, 533, 540, 556; absolute evil, 20, 62-3, 106, 178, 222; the origin of evil, 2-3, 9-10, 62-3, 67-8, 178, 207, 271, 307, 326-7, 333

evocation, 201-2, 237, 255, 261, 267, 327, 362, 371, 390, 416

evolution, 1, 23, 27, 30-1, 38, 45, 47-8, 51-2, 56, 60-2, 65, 71, 75-6, 94, 107, 115-6, 140, 150, 157-9, 198, 231, 349, 473-4, 484, 488, 501-2, 507, 510-1, 530, 554; *The Evolution of Matter*, 115

excess, 19, 28-31, 75, 78, 84, 188, 199, 202-3, 237-8, 240, 242-3, 279-80,

309, 316, 339, 352, 399, 497, 522, 543

excommunication, 134, 342, 438

excitement, 17, 19, 44, 70, 115, 149, 168-9, 239, 276, 279, 285-6, 292, 331, 349-54, 363-4, 369, 374, 495, 530, 551-2, 556-7

Exempt Adept, *see* Adeptus Exemptus

existence, 10-3, 21, 27, 43, 45, 55, 62, 79, 88, 93-129, 133-4, 136, 141-2, 143n50, 144, 146, 156, 166, 170-81, 194n79, 197, 203, 205, 210, 218-9, 224, 227-9, 252, 258, 259-61, 266-7, 271-2, 282-6, 289, 293, 300-4, 308, 314, 321-7, 331, 338, 341-3, 347-9, 388, 414, 456-7, 489, 499, 540, 550, 558-9, 561-2

Exodus, 162, 339

exorcism, exorcists, 179, 346, 393, 540

experience, experimentation, 9-12, 16-7, 25, 31, 42-4, 52-5, 59-61, 69, 72, 80-1, 84, 93-4, 98, 102-6, 108-18, 125-6, 130, 134-5, 145, 154-61, 166-77, 185-8, 196, 200-3, 209, 215, 218-20, 225-34, 237-8, 242-3, 248, 252-7, 269-70, 272-4, 278-9, 290-3, 297-314, 316-28, 336-58, 361-76, 390-4, 396, 413, 417-21, 424, 450, 455, 466, 471-82, 514-5, 519, 528-34, 550-4

Ezekiel, 138, 162, 305

Fabre des Essarts, Léonce Eugène-Joseph, 434-5

Fabre d'Olivet, Antoine, 58n87, 401

Fabré-Palaprat, Bernard-Raymond, 435

fairness, 459, 497, 513, 521-2

faith, 2-3, 18-9, 26, 29, 51, 64, 68-9, 73, 75-6, 81-2, 88-91, 131-3, 141, 154, 158, 161, 173, 206-7, 219, 241, 251, 269, 306, 310, 327, 329, 331-2, 343, 380-1, 385, 390-1, 394, 398, 404, 407-8, 411, 415-7, 419, 431-2, 434, 444, 450, 453, 473, 478, 482, 500-5, 508-9, 519, 539

Fall of Man, the, 2, 86, 141, 178-9, 251, 310, 384, 446, 454

familiar spirits, 260

family, 19, 43-5, 49, 52, 121, 191, 347, 388, 413, 428n23, 464, 473-5, 483-95, 511, 515, 532; the nuclear family, 45, 488-90, 507, 511, 532

fanaticism, 76, 238, 274, 340, 346-7, 351, 373, 398, 414, 418, 497

Fascism, 44, 46, 56, 88, 495, 509-10, 519
fatalism, fate, 1-3, 7, 11, 155, 173-4, 179-80, 259n31, 264, 266, 303-4, 508
Father, the, 1, 12, 41-2, 45, 50, 53-4, 56, 117-8, 120-2, 142, 149, 163, 198, 217, 249, 254, 264-5, 283-5, 287, 293-4, 298, 309, 314, 332, 334-5, 339, 342, 401, 406, 427, 436, 441, 454, 463; the All-Father, 121-2, 298, 314; *The Fatherland*, 461
fear, 16-20, 26, 32, 42-3, 45-6, 51-5, 58, 62, 68, 70-1, 77-8, 81-2, 84, 86, 88-90, 105, 126, 137, 143, 154, 163, 172, 177, 179, 181-90, 192, 195, 200, 206-9, 221-2, 234, 241-4, 253-4, 260, 263, 265, 270, 280-1, 295, 299, 307-8, 311, 313, 328, 342, 345-6, 350, 352-3, 370-1, 374, 388, 401, 403, 407, 420, 431n41, 447, 466, 470-1, 473-4, 493-4, 498, 503, 506-7, 517-8, 526-8, 534, 541-2, 544-6, 549, 555-6
feasts, 73, 198, 311, 342, 380-1, 383, 437, 541-2, 550
feelings, *see* emotions
Feminine, the, 18, 49, 53, 107, 118, 121-2, 141, 163, 172, 184, 248n101, 277, 282, 283n6, 309, 319, 321, 382, 399, 416n147; feminism, feminists, 48, 457, 484, 516
Ferdinand of Brunswick, 429, 434n53
feudalism, 156, 474, 484, 508, 521, 531n167, 532
Fichte, Johann, 3n15, 8, 46, 48, 256, 271, 301, 478
Fire, 16, 22-3, 32, 40, 81, 100-3, 108, 118, 120-4, 139, 141, 147, 153, 156, 162-3, 165, 172, 177, 183, 190, 193, 196n85, 198, 201, 206, 208-10, 216-7, 221, 232, 235, 237, 239, 242-3, 245, 252-5, 265, 267, 269, 272-7, 282-6, 288, 294, 311, 314, 317, 319n130, 323-4, 328, 332, 342, 357, 365-6, 368, 371, 378, 384, 404, 445, 449, 456, 471, 483, 537-47, 549-51, 556; firearms, 80, 202, 221-2, 313, 382, 497
flattery, 89, 260, 278-9, 375, 447, 491, 555
Fludd, Robert, 3n14
food, 16, 19, 28-9, 32, 42, 45, 52, 64, 81, 83-4, 102, 171, 182, 192, 195, 220-1, 236, 239, 242, 290-1, 333, 342, 349, 351, 353, 356, 375, 402, 404, 406, 484-9, 506, 524-5, 539, 542, 544-5, 548, 550, 553-4
fools, folly, 11, 23, 26, 29, 31-2, 40, 61-3, 66n113, 68, 76, 78-9, 85-6, 105, 126, 146, 149, 176-7, 199, 233, 244, 247n101, 270, 305, 328, 340, 355, 360, 375, 380, 381n7, 387, 408, 410-1, 413, 418, 447, 466-7, 471, 474, 477, 490-1, 493, 497-8, 501, 503, 530, 537-42, 544, 546-7, 555-7; *The Fool*, 32, 34n1, 147, 163-4, 205, 233, 251, 283n6, 289n20, 320n133, 367-8, 398, 538, 558, 562
Forlong, James George Roche, 41, 401, 432
Form, 11-2, 16, 22, 26, 32, 43, 54-6, 89, 91, 93-4, 100-1, 108-9, 113, 139, 149, 152, 157-8, 163-5, 171, 188, 195-8, 203, 206n127, 217-20, 235, 238, 244-5, 248, 251, 253-4, 263, 273, 275, 276, 280-3, 285, 289-90, 308-10, 313-4, 320, 325, 335-6, 341-2, 349, 363-5, 398-9, 410, 415, 455, 551
fortune-telling, 147, 150, 260-1, 284, 313, 447, 461
Foster, Jeanne Robert, 52-3, 400, 452
Foucault, Michel, 495
France, the French, 48, 59, 71, 115, 147, 321, 370, 391-2, 409, 414, 426, 433-5, 442, 449, 462, 468, 484, 488, 490-1, 497, 511, 518, 527, 532; the French language, 21, 70-1, 147, 195, 203, 384-5, 391-3, 521
Frater Superior, *see* the O.H.O.
Frazer, James George, Sir, 39-40, 41n28, 131-2, 336, 342, 393, 412, 448, 481
freedom, 1-3, 7, 13-20, 22-3, 26-7, 31-2, 43, 48, 56-7, 59-60, 63-5, 69-70, 72-7, 84, 87-8, 91n96, 102, 105, 123, 126, 133, 137, 155, 158, 163, 170, 179-80, 182, 186-91, 194, 204, 206-7, 208n133, 209-11, 215-6, 222, 224, 229, 235, 240, 244-6, 252-3, 263, 266-7, 269-73, 279-80, 284, 295-6, 300, 302, 308-9, 311, 316, 320, 324, 326, 328, 330, 338, 340-1, 345, 352, 364-5, 376, 388, 392n50, 398, 401, 406-7, 409, 422,

424, 440, 455, 457–9, 462, 470–3, 476, 477n253, 478–80, 482, 484–9, 491–4, 496, 498–501, 504–7, 509–10, 512–3, 517–9, 527–34, 548, 552–3, 557; the free market, 26–7, 60, 486, 489, 496–8, 500, 512–5, 521–4; free-will, 1–3, 7, 13–4, 17, 22, 26, 43, 51, 64–5, 75, 77–8, 94, 110, 123, 173, 189–91, 199, 209, 244, 295, 303, 344, 422, 486, 489, 495, 500, 514, 533
Freemasons, Freemasonry, 24, 35n4, 162, 189, 231, 255, 331, 336, 360, 384, 390–2, 395–6, 402, 408, 417, 426–35, 440n79, 441–3, 444n101, 451, 453, 458, 462
Freud, Sigmund, 18, 20, 53–4, 88, 156, 159n102, 247, 263–4, 273, 278n92, 279–80; Anna Freud, 280
friendship, ix, 14, 33, 41n28, 51, 76, 84, 93, 98–9, 103, 261n37, 265, 288, 351, 385, 405, 425, 464, 490–1, 493, 541
Fugairon, Louis-Sophrone, 435, 438
Fuller, John Frederick Charles, 254, 429

Gabriel, 315–6, 409, 413, 458
Galatians, 405
Galilee, 84, 405
gambling, gamblers, 202, 497, 517
Gandhi, Mohandas Karamchand, 77, 360, 468
Ganges, the, 5, 375–6
Gardner, Gerald, ix, 51, 389, 441–2
Gargantua and Pantagruel, 147, 477n253
Gautama, or Gotama, *see* Siddhārtha
Geburah, 152, 372, 558, 561
gematria, 8n9, 151, 154, 255, 400, 465n200
Genesis, 51, 95, 101, 150, 272, 294, 336, 384, 428n23, 437n70
Genius, *see* the guardian spirit; men of genius, 19, 30, 39, 46, 65, 80, 111, 119, 150, 159n102, 189, 222, 324, 395–6, 405, 420, 452, 471, 478–81, 501, 510, 522, 527, 529, 531
geography, 39, 167, 226
geometry, 9, 96, 103–4, 108–9, 114, 117, 125, 131, 135, 145, 151, 157, 285, 365, 373, 485, 554
Germany, the Germans, 46–7, 51, 57, 88, 159n102, 202, 256, 264, 360, 396, 406–7, 429, 434–5, 438, 442, 446, 462–3, 478, 486, 490, 495–7, 518; the German language, 46, 59n89, 177,

412, 435, 442, 462, 486, 489, 518, 521
Germer, Karl Johannes, 462, 463n179, 536n180
Gheranda Samhita, the, 355–6
Gilbert and Sullivan, 19, 290–1
Gimel, 55–6, 141, 154, 287, 341, 363, 558, 562
Giraud, Louis-Marie-François, 438
girders of the soul, the, 86, 157–8, 234–5, 547
Gladstone, William Ewart, 397, 415
gluttony, 16, 236
GN, 330, 341
Gnosis, Gnosticism, 124, 133n21, 139, 177, 257, 287, 341, 367, 395–6, 406–7, 418, 428, 431n41, 432, 434–5, 437, 439–40, 442; the Gnostic Mass, 29, 54, 186, 191, 243, 384, 430–1, 437, 439, 441–2, 444, 449, 463, 479n262; the Gnostic Saints, 437, 442, 479n262
goats, 55, 126, 207, 313, 401, 499
Gobineau, Joseph Arthur de, 518
God(s), 1–3, 9–10, 15–6, 20, 22, 24, 27–9, 34–5, 38–43, 50–1, 53–5, 62–3, 67–9, 75, 80, 83, 86–91, 96–8, 101, 104–5, 107–8, 110, 115, 118, 120–2, 129–32, 137–40, 142, 148–50, 153–4, 156–8, 161–3, 165, 175–7, 179–81, 183–6, 188, 191–3, 195, 200–3, 206–7, 215–7, 223–4, 228, 230–2, 234–5, 241, 246, 250–67, 269, 271–8, 282–5, 287–8, 290, 293–4, 296, 298, 302, 308–9, 311, 315–6, 319, 326, 328, 330–2, 335–9, 346, 349, 358, 361–2, 364–6, 367, 370–1, 375–6, 379, 382–6, 388, 391, 393–4, 396–403, 407–9, 411, 414–7, 419, 421–2, 424, 426, 428n23, 431–3, 436–7, 439, 441, 442n95, 443, 445n106, 446, 450, 453, 455, 457, 466–7, 470, 472n228, 473–4, 477n257, 480, 482–4, 499–500, 501n55, 502–3, 506, 508–9, 534, 537, 539, 541–6, 548–9, 551–2, 556; the assumption of god-forms, 225, 246, 254, 383, 417, 448–9; the Body of God, 15, 67, 105, 184, 186, 206n127, 219, 235, 297, 302, 325, 332, 398, 422, 470; the Kingdom of God, 9, 20, 86, 156–7, 179, 187, 192, 328, 398, 453, 534; the name of God, 90–2, 119, 122, 129, 139, 150, 160, 165, 195,

251, 256–7, 263, 269, 272, 278, 282–3, 292–3, 314, 335–6, 362, 367, 383, 394, 397–8, 400–1, 403, 409, 414–7, 432, 437, 443, 445, 449–50, 474, 537, 539, 555, 557; the Spirit of God, *see* the Holy Ghost; Union with God, 10, 12, 20, 183–6, 192–5, 200, 216–9, 224, 251, 272, 274–5, 277, 284–5, 287, 313, 323, 330, 335–7, 339, 364, 382, 431–2, 454, 467; the will of God, 1–3, 86, 176, 228, 259n31, 293, 295, 298, 312, 323, 327, 395, 402, 424, 508; the word of God, 161, 296, 439, 480
Goethe, Johann Wolfgang von, ix, 51–2, 206
Goëtia, the, 256, 393, 417
Gog and Magog, 394
Going, 10, 67, 74, 143n50, 144, 165, 169, 206, 222, 232–3, 244–5, 289–91, 412, 457, 546
gold, 29, 40, 67, 106n54, 113, 187–8, 191–2, 199, 201–2, 234–5, 245, 287–8, 308, 313, 336, 352, 368, 376, 437, 493, 526, 531, 539, 542, 545, 547, 556; golden ages, 37, 107, 526, 531; *The Golden Bough*, 40, 131–2, 336, 342, 393, 412, 448, 481; the Golden Dawn, 45, 133, 152, 208–9, 227, 231, 257, 333, 335–6, 343, 354, 389–90, 413, 426, 428, 465, 517, 557, 560; the Golden Mean, 243; the Golden Rosicrucians, 231, 428–9, 560; the Golden Rule, 23, 59, 73–4, 171
golf, 30, 169, 246, 482, 531
Golgotha, *see* Calvary
good, goodness, 1–3, 10, 12, 20–1, 26–8, 38, 45, 57–60, 62–3, 66–7, 69–70, 75–6, 79, 82–3, 85, 88, 90, 137, 158, 161, 163, 175, 190, 197, 200, 204, 222, 238–41, 262, 268, 269–71, 273, 278, 284–5, 301, 303n68, 305, 308, 315–6, 318, 325, 332, 344, 346, 351, 356, 386–7, 391, 395, 401, 405, 407, 440n82, 455–7, 460, 466n202, 471–2, 479n266, 497, 501–3, 506–8, 514–5, 519, 523–4, 526–8, 530, 532–3, 540, 551, 556; absolute good, 175, 222, 262, 285, 316; *Beyond Good and Evil*, 137n36, 479
Goraksha, Gorakshanath, or Gorakhnath, 355–6, 468n210

Gospels, the, 38, 81, 89, 117, 336, 379, 395, 407, 411, 433, 435, 439–40, 502, 515, 526; the Gospel According to John, 117, 170, 207, 254, 287, 354, 406–7, 433, 436, 454; the Gospel According to Luke, 40, 59, 361, 404–5, 407, 415; the Gospel According to Mark, 254, 405, 407; the Gospel According to Matthew, 77, 117, 122, 354, 386, 405, 407, 415, 436, 439, 514; *The Gospel According to St. Bernard Shaw*, see *Liber 888*
government, 27, 42–3, 60, 199, 204, 391, 429, 459, 462, 469, 476–8, 481–534, 548, 550, 552–4
Graal, the, 170, 187, 295, 332, 344–5, 368, 390, 442, 452
grace, 2, 16, 66, 80, 90, 186, 195, 229, 307, 325, 399
grammar, 99, 120, 410
Grant, Kenneth, 389, 454
gravitation, 24, 36, 37n14, 77, 95, 103–4, 108, 120, 132, 173, 290, 348, 356, 374
Great Auk, the, 9, 118n91
Great God, the, *see* Pan
Great White Brotherhood, the, 115, 230, 313, 451, 456–7, 472
Great Work, the, 50, 121–3, 137, 170, 173–7, 184, 187, 202, 210, 216–8, 231, 239, 243, 249, 260, 275n85, 283, 286, 293, 303n68, 313, 333–5, 338–40, 347, 380, 388, 397, 400, 424, 459, 471, 510, 517, 533, 557
Greece, the Greeks, 34–6, 38–9, 41, 49, 51, 54, 87, 94, 98, 100–1, 143–4, 162, 181, 193, 241, 258n31, 261n37, 269, 277, 281–3, 383, 389, 394, 396, 408, 414, 418, 422–3, 432, 439, 474, 477, 479, 481; the Greek language, 1–2, 8, 41n28, 42, 51, 59n89, 70, 81n59, 86, 120, 133n21, 140, 144–5, 151, 156, 195, 203, 236, 251, 255, 258n31, 261n37, 270–1, 298, 364, 367, 394, 396, 400, 414, 430, 437, 439, 477, 485
Greene, Graham, 86
growth, 11–4, 18, 31–2, 41–5, 50, 53, 60, 71, 77, 83–4, 93, 104, 127, 137n37, 143n50, 144n56, 146, 158, 166–7, 180, 189, 194, 216, 221, 223, 234, 255, 263, 279, 287–8, 290, 296, 304, 333, 336, 348, 370, 372, 399, 432, 436, 471, 484, 492, 498, 520, 522

Guaïta, Stanislas de, 427n16, 453
guardian spirit, the, 52, 149, 178, 227, 257–8, 259, 261, 264–71, 273–4, 401, 527
guilds, the guild system, 423, 466
guilt, 2, 28, 51n64, 86, 90–1, 177, 243, 281, 471, 488, 503
guṇas, the, 231, 285–6
guns, *see* firearms; gun-control, 497; gunpowder, 18, 189
Guph, the, 561
gurus, 85, 91, 133, 219–20, 231–2, 248, 254–6, 271, 329, 348, 353–5, 359, 375, 404–5, 436, 438, 446, 450–2, 456, 469, 502

habits, habituation, 71, 77, 81, 84, 86, 100, 124, 146, 155, 169, 201–2, 268, 295, 308, 318–9, 369, 422, 449, 479, 495
Had, Hadit, or Hadith, 11–2, 20–4, 26, 29, 93, 98–100, 104, 108–11, 117, 121, 124, 142, 159, 179–81, 183–4, 188, 194–5, 198–9, 203–4, 206, 209, 217, 219, 230, 235, 242, 244–5, 258, 276, 289–92, 309, 325, 367, 370, 398–9, 401, 441, 506, 537, 540–5, 546, 552
Haeckel, Ernst, 159n02, 299
hallucination, 116, 200, 206, 241, 278, 281, 305, 324, 495
hangings, 298; *The Hanged Man*, 86, 153, 319n130, 558, 562
Hanuman, 232, 416
happiness, 18, 27, 64, 70, 78–9, 86–9, 110, 116n84, 178, 182–3, 196–7, 202–3, 210, 240, 264, 266, 270, 296, 301–2, 311, 405, 407, 429, 440n83, 451, 476–7, 494, 500, 502–4, 506, 514–7, 521–2, 529, 533
harems, 182, 353, 490, 493
harmony, 3, 8, 27, 38, 51, 60–1, 73, 95, 101, 110, 115n84, 122, 142–3, 149, 166, 172, 183, 190, 201, 204, 218, 221, 228, 231, 235, 255, 266, 279, 283–5, 292, 295, 297, 303–4, 309–10, 320–1, 335–40, 383, 391, 412, 418–20, 422–3, 433, 441n83, 448–50, 453–5, 462, 498, 530, 549, 554, 556
Harpocrates, 34, 43, 50, 53, 56, 98, 163–4, 217–8, 233, 251, 263–5, 332, 345, 366, 383, 398, 401, 409, 448–9, 470, 537, 540, 545

Harrison, Jane, 49–51
Hartmann, Franz, 429
hashish, 80, 125, 200, 205, 241–2, 467, 528; *The Psychology of Hashish*, 200, 238, 248, 253, 261, 322, 325, 348–9, 351, 365
Hathavidya, *see* hatha yoga
hatred, 33, 57, 59, 77–8, 89–90, 176, 181, 183–4, 190, 203, 215, 280–1, 287, 289, 301, 326, 388, 415, 420–1, 466, 471, 503, 528, 540, 542, 556
Hawking, Stephen, 118
Hayek, Friedrich August von, 60–1, 501, 525
Hé, 98, 106, 119, 121, 123, 257, 293, 334–5, 401, 558, 562
healing, 53, 103, 313, 360, 372, 406, 436, 476
health, 13, 18–9, 23, 29–30, 44, 76, 81, 84, 111, 167, 220, 222, 236, 268, 289, 301, 347, 356, 358, 359n118, 382, 409, 441n83, 460, 476, 484, 497, 511, 518, 520–1
heart, the, 17, 93, 122, 163, 183, 185, 189, 191–2, 195, 198, 205–6, 229, 234, 237, 293–4, 297, 306, 322, 331, 346, 354, 362, 412, 421, 436, 440n82, 444n101, 445, 454, 470, 478, 497–8, 506, 508, 517–8, 537–43, 545–6, 549–51; *The Heart of the Master*, 58, 64, 73, 109n69, 290, 411n123, 456, 462, 511–2
heat, 9, 23, 58, 63, 67, 130, 204, 218, 241, 283
Heaven(s), 9, 27, 29, 38, 69, 80, 82, 86–7, 91, 101, 119, 138–9, 146, 156, 179, 183–7, 195, 208, 210–1, 229, 233–4, 247, 251, 257, 262–5, 272, 274, 275–6, 289, 292, 298, 300, 309, 327, 356, 358, 362, 365, 387, 395, 440n83, 443n98, 449, 462, 466, 471–2, 487, 508, 534, 537–8, 543–4; *Heavenly Bridegrooms*, 278; the Mandate of Heaven, 508
Hebrew, 8n9, 54, 86, 95, 98, 119, 122–3, 138–9, 146, 148, 151, 155, 251, 255, 257, 275–6, 293, 315, 396–8, 401, 413–4, 428n23, 430, 443, 452, 457, 558; the Hebrews, 86, 98, 122, 138, 148, 163, 339, 342, 379, 383, 401, 406, 413–4, 430, 437, 457; the Epistle to the Hebrews, 42, 358, 406, 437
Hegel, G. W. F., 3n15, 46–8, 56–7, 99,

104, 143, 261n37, 289n20, 326, 360
Heinlein, Robert Anson, 529
Heisenberg, Werner Karl, 122
Hekhalot literature, the, 138–9
Heliogabalus, 191, 455
Helios, 416
Hell(s), 17–9, 68, 81–2, 86, 91n96, 177, 183, 187, 203, 206, 229, 236–8, 270, 278, 309, 327, 356, 375, 387, 401, 436, 449, 530, 538, 542–3, 550; *Proverbs of Hell*, 30
Heraclitus, 36, 48, 94, 100, 143, 283
herbalism, 346, 393
Herbert, Alan Patrick, Sir, 306
Hercules, 53, 398, 474, 501; the Pillars of Hercules, 413
herd, the, 14, 63, 68, 70, 281, 330, 500–3, 510, 518, 521
heresy, heretics, 2, 50, 63, 178, 265, 303n68, 326–7, 485
Hermes, 120, 149, 325, 416, 433, 436–7, 449; Hermes Trismegistus, 108, 208, 240, 383 (*see also* Thoth); Hermeticism, 50, 114, 231, 399, 401, 427, 558
hermits, 204, 230–1, 239, 245, 325, 384, 404, 460, 472, 538, 541; the Hermit, 204–5, 230–1, 245, 325, 538, 541; *The Hermit*, 558, 562
Herod, 379, 509
Herodotus, 259n31
heroin, 242, 497
Heru, 153; Heru-pa-kraat, *see* Harpocrates; Heru-Ra-Ha, 43, 98, 157, 218n12, 399, 403, 545
Hesiod, 237, 258n31, 270n72
hexagram, the, 178, 234, 334–5, 373
H.G.A., the, *see* the Holy Guardian Angel
hierarchy, 26, 34, 52n65, 133, 138, 160, 200, 231, 258, 261, 283, 373, 383, 386, 422–562
hierophants, 153, 157, 201, 232, 245, 333, 398, 426, 539–40, 555; *The Hierophant*, 153, 277, 540, 558, 562
Higgins, Godfrey, 41, 397, 443
Hinduism, 10, 36–7, 65, 82–3, 85, 88, 101–3, 117, 143–4, 164, 177–8, 195, 200, 205, 210, 217, 220, 230–2, 248, 250, 256–8, 263, 271, 283, 285–6, 293, 321–2, 326, 329, 338, 341, 348–9, 352–3, 355–6, 359–61, 367, 370, 388, 394, 399, 416n147, 440, 460, 467–70, 496

Hinton, Charles Howard, 3n14
Hipparchus, 34–6
Hiram Abiff, 58, 392n50, 398, 430
Hirsig, Leah, 400
Hitler, Adolf, 88, 189, 518–9
Hod, 372, 558, 561
Hoffer, Eric, 76, 90
Holy Books of the A∴A∴, the, 183, 206n127, 292, 385–7, 396, 452, 547
Holy Ghost, the, 87, 122–3, 183, 187, 263, 275, 311, 315, 321, 398, 427, 429, 437, 443–5, 448–9, 454, 466, 470; the College of the Holy Ghost, 466; the Mass of the Holy Ghost, 124, 186, 444–5, 449, 454n144; the Sin against the Holy Ghost, 87, 142–3, 176–7, 183, 191–2, 243, 298, 503, 509, 556; the Temple of the Holy Ghost, 443–4, 453
Holy Guardian Angel, the, 8, 26, 33, 53, 58, 121, 153, 159, 178, 188, 201, 224, 226–8, 234–6, 248–9, 251–2, 257–8, 260–5, 267, 269, 271–8, 282–3, 288, 327, 336–7, 345, 358, 372, 382, 401–2, 409, 411, 413, 449–50, 457, 467, 473, 527; the Invocation of the H.G.A., 201–2, 236, 257–9, 273, 333, 366, 382, 413; the Knowledge and Conversation of the H.G.A., 8, 53, 121, 201, 249, 260–2, 264, 267, 269, 271, 274, 278n92, 282, 327, 336–7, 371–2, 402, 411, 467, 473; the Vision of the H.G.A., 366
Holy of Holies, the, 192, 269
Holy Spirit, the, *see* the Holy Ghost
Homer, 51n64, 253, 258n27, 258n31
homosexuality, 17–8, 54, 191–2
homunculi, 54
honour, 1, 31, 33, 39, 51–2, 78, 179, 190, 230, 241, 244, 255, 261, 297, 398–9, 404, 409, 432, 446, 459, 473–5, 494, 504, 511, 516, 521n133, 523, 531, 542
Hoor, *see* Horus; Hoor-Paar-Kraat, *see* Harpocrates
hope, 15, 68, 91, 309, 342, 350, 360, 385, 408, 420, 450–1, 454, 472–3, 491, 501–2, 509, 515, 520, 530, 533–4
Horace, 53, 78, 407
Horus, 34, 35n4, 42–5, 50, 55–6, 58, 98, 109, 126, 136, 153, 159, 162–4, 217–8, 230, 234–5, 248n101, 245, 264, 276–7, 283, 287, 307, 332–3,

335, 337, 340–1, 367–8, 382–3, 398, 410–1, 419, 437, 444–5, 457, 466, 471, 483, 488n14, 509, 538–9, 541, 543–6, 552; the Æon of Horus, *see* æons; the Eye of Horus, 248n101; the Invocation of Horus, 333, 382
House of God, the, 152, 247n101, 539
Hua, 257
hubris, 87, 517, 534
Hugo, Victor, 409
humanitarianism, 24, 90, 466
humility, 18, 76, 88, 169, 270, 487, 506
humour, 86, 205–6, 237, 306–7, 328, 379, 483, 541
hunting, 27, 50, 52, 186, 382, 484, 498, 513, 532
Huntington, Samuel, 69–70
Huxley, Aldous, 99, 103, 495; Thomas Henry Huxley, 75–6, 240, 256, 445n106, 469, 500
hylo-idealism, 250
Hymenaeus Alpha X°, 439; Hymenæus Beta XI°, 440
hymns, 263, 389, 416, 455; the Hymn of Creation, 148n71; the Hymn for Independence Day, 463
hypocrisy, 18, 69–70, 82, 89, 171, 242–3, 281, 306, 447, 490, 495–6, 533–4

Iamblichus, 178, 258–9, 261, 266–9, 284–5
IAO, 54, 153, 335–7, 403, 437, 443n98; VIAOV, 54–5, 338
I Ching, the, 107–8, 148, 155, 257, 559
ideas, 10–5, 19–21, 24–6, 31, 37, 38n20, 39–41, 43, 46, 48, 54, 57–8, 60–1, 65, 66n113, 70–1, 75–9, 81–3, 86–8, 91, 93–101, 104, 106, 112–9, 123–4, 127–33, 137–44, 146, 148–52, 155, 159n102, 161, 163, 165–8, 172–7, 179, 182, 184–5, 194, 196–9, 202, 206–9, 224–6, 231, 233–4, 237, 244, 252–3, 258–9, 263, 275n85, 280–1, 285–6, 289–91, 293, 298–302, 304–5, 307–8, 310–1, 314, 318–21, 323, 326, 331–3, 338, 340–5, 359, 361–3, 365–8, 372–5, 385–6, 392, 394–8, 403–4, 406, 408, 414–21, 432n43, 437n69, 439, 442, 444, 448, 451–2, 458, 460, 462, 464, 468n213, 473, 479–81, 485–6, 488–9, 496–7, 502–3, 506–7, 511, 513–5, 518, 520, 524, 527, 529, 531–4, 552, 556–7
ideals, idealism, 11, 26–8, 31, 46, 48, 52n65, 57–8, 70, 80, 91, 114, 116, 135–6, 172, 182–3, 270, 284, 293, 326, 338, 359, 385, 388, 420, 457, 460, 472, 477, 479n266, 487–9, 492, 495, 506, 521–2, 524, 532, 553–4
idleness, 17, 32, 80–1, 84, 96, 118, 233, 270, 306–7, 323, 345–6, 373–4, 404, 501n55, 520, 521n133, 556
ignorance, 17, 19, 26, 38, 41, 50, 54, 58–60, 63, 69–70, 85, 99, 137, 150, 169n139, 178, 180, 182, 186–7, 192, 217, 219, 222–3, 260, 265, 273, 286, 306–7, 312–3, 322, 332–3, 346–7, 350, 370–2, 381, 385, 389–90, 398, 400, 403, 406–8, 410–1, 431, 434, 442, 448, 453, 455–6, 458, 462, 473, 487, 494, 501n55, 503, 504n68, 505, 509, 514, 520, 522, 551, 555
illusion, 11, 20, 39, 53–4, 58, 60, 62–3, 68–9, 80–1, 88, 94, 106, 109, 111, 115–7, 133, 136, 142, 160, 163, 166, 172, 174–5, 177–81, 185–8, 191, 193–4, 202–3, 206–8, 216–9, 226, 234–5, 237, 244, 246–7, 250–4, 256, 260, 272, 282, 287–91, 296, 301–5, 311, 316, 319, 322, 326–7, 332–3, 338, 352–3, 364–6, 375, 406–7, 411, 443n98, 491, 517, 522–3
imagination, 2, 9, 16, 20–1, 26, 42, 45, 56, 58, 67, 69–70, 74, 80, 98, 102, 108, 113–4, 127, 133, 136–7, 140, 149, 159, 172, 174, 191, 204, 206–7, 229, 241, 247–8, 253, 267, 273–4, 279, 281, 291, 301, 307, 315, 326, 343, 352, 357, 366, 369, 379, 412, 417, 494, 500, 503, 505, 528–9
immanence, 41, 97, 123, 162, 558
immortality, 67, 163, 183, 185, 194–6, 232, 252, 258, 271n73, 307, 338, 445n106, 533, 541, 543, 552
imperfection, 63, 88, 105, 111, 120, 135, 160, 172, 175, 177, 187, 190, 196–7, 218, 221, 237, 289, 293, 301, 311, 317, 339, 345, 373, 375, 382, 385, 415, 443n98, 454, 498
imperialism, 41, 51, 148, 245, 277, 407–9, 432, 436, 439, 468, 472, 474, 485–6, 505, 509
impermanence, *see anicca*
impotence, 25, 65, 73–4, 81n59, 84, 90, 183, 204, 223, 304, 307, 336, 371,

402, 470, 481–2
incarnation, 3n14, 9–10, 18, 24, 31, 40–1, 45, 54–6, 67, 82–3, 99–100, 153–5, 157, 163–4, 177–8, 195–6, 203, 207–8, 210–1, 218–20, 230, 232, 238, 245, 264–5, 273, 277, 292, 303, 308, 314, 316–7, 341–3, 347–9, 335–6, 342, 347–9, 371, 379–80, 383, 385, 393, 398–9, 402, 405, 407, 414, 424, 432, 436, 446, 454n144, 455–6, 476, 489, 517–8
incense, 196n85, 539–40
incest, 18, 54, 492
India, the Indians, 31, 36–7, 54, 65, 87–8, 94–5, 101–2, 137n37, 144–5, 255, 272, 281, 285, 320, 326, 352, 359–61, 379, 394, 404–6, 412, 420, 438, 467–9, 474, 509, 546; Indo-European languages, 144–5
individualism, 10, 14, 16–8, 31, 42–3, 59–65, 66n113, 67, 70–1, 76–7, 118, 173–4, 187, 279–80, 304–5, 458, 460–2, 464, 471, 483, 485–9, 494–503, 507, 510, 512, 515–9, 525, 531–3, 553
individuality, 10–2, 14, 16–8, 43, 46, 56, 59–65, 66n113, 67, 70–1, 77, 83, 86–8, 108–10, 115n84, 118, 125, 134, 150–1, 154, 173–4, 176, 179, 182–3, 187, 194, 215–6, 219, 233–6, 251, 258–9, 261, 263, 265–8, 274, 276, 279–81, 292, 304–5, 310–1, 314n107, 320–2, 331–2, 339, 341, 343, 364, 385, 399–400, 418, 422, 424, 431, 460, 479, 487–8, 499–500, 501n55, 502–3, 507, 509–10, 512, 514, 516, 518–9, 522–3, 525, 531–3, 551–3
indulgence, 16, 28, 73, 84, 195, 222, 236, 240, 302, 346, 372, 425, 498
industrialism, industrialization, 31, 44–5, 463, 486, 494, 511, 513–5, 519–20, 522–4, 528–9, 531; industrialists, 463, 524
inebriation, *see* drunkedness
inertia, 43, 71, 77, 80–1, 104, 174, 180, 223, 231, 286, 319, 345–6, 473, 501
inferiority complex, the, 62, 177, 500, 503, 507, 521
infinity, 3, 10–2, 15, 25, 29, 57n86, 67, 70, 85, 93, 96–100, 102–3, 105–13, 117, 126–7, 131–3, 136, 142, 146, 148–9, 156n95, 157, 160, 163, 170–1, 177–8, 185–6, 192–3, 196–8,

207n133, 211, 215, 229, 235, 250, 255–7, 262, 273, 296, 307, 312–3, 316, 324–6, 331, 333–4, 336, 340, 364–5, 383, 398, 403, 411, 414, 433, 440n83, 453, 461–2, 501, 525, 529, 533, 537, 541
initiates, initiation, 21, 29–30, 40–1, 53–5, 58, 74, 106, 116, 121, 135–6, 145–6, 148–52, 157–62, 170, 175, 193, 201–4, 209, 216, 221–4, 227, 231–5, 245, 248, 254–6, 260, 265, 277, 278n92, 279–81, 287–90, 295, 300, 303, 314, 318, 320n133, 325, 328–32, 336–9, 370–3, 379–82, 387, 390, 394–8, 400–2, 411, 416–8, 425–30, 431n41, 432, 436, 441–3, 446–8, 452, 457n153, 458, 462–3, 465–6, 470, 526–7, 532, 534, 539, 549, 555; the uninitiate, 154, 177, 186, 201, 219, 233, 331, 333, 370, 428n27, 440, 447–8, 453, 461, 466
innocence, 19, 43–5, 137, 163–4, 170, 179, 219, 233, 308, 315, 345, 398, 434, 471, 491, 517; the exposure of innocence, 171, 176–7, 491, 541; the Massacre of the Innocents, 332, 415, 474
Inquisition, the, 433, 443, 532
INRI, 153, 257, 335–6, 437n64, 443n98
inspiration, 16–7, 169, 198, 227, 252, 263, 265, 274, 324, 367, 386, 398, 400, 410, 436, 543, 545
instincts, 11–3, 17, 19, 43, 58, 70, 72, 76, 78–9, 88, 103, 105, 160, 183, 186–7, 189, 204, 218, 221, 233, 240–2, 270, 278, 291, 299, 311, 320n133, 350, 369, 374, 381, 383, 419, 422, 431, 442, 479n286, 488–9, 500, 503, 513, 515, 528–9, 550, 553
intellect, 1–2, 27–8, 45, 47, 51, 57, 61–3, 72–4, 78, 85, 94, 97, 99–100, 107, 110, 113, 125, 133–6, 146, 148–9, 158–9, 162, 168–9, 172–3, 176, 178, 180, 186–7, 197, 223–4, 228–9, 231, 234, 238, 240–1, 247–8, 256, 264, 269, 284, 286, 295–6, 300, 302, 304, 306–12, 314–5, 318–9, 323–4, 331, 346, 348–52, 360, 371, 380, 389, 399, 409, 414, 416–7, 423n3, 424, 426, 431, 443, 447, 454, 459, 462, 467, 473–4, 479, 501, 502n55, 504n68, 505, 508, 510, 518n120, 521–2, 525, 528, 533, 539, 552, 557

interference, 9, 13, 17–8, 24–5, 27, 50, 59, 65, 68, 71, 74, 76, 79–80, 84, 133, 137, 192, 211, 239, 297, 312, 371–2, 460–2, 485, 488–9, 500–2, 506, 511–3, 517, 524–5, 550–2, 557
internationalism, 37, 145, 280, 354, 407, 411, 427, 435, 442–3, 450, 461, 465, 485, 511; *The International*, 52n65, 497
intoxication, 16, 29, 80, 200–1, 224, 241, 244, 351, 495–7
intuition, 46, 127, 142, 247, 252, 290, 371
invention, inventiveness, 12, 28, 52, 59–60, 80, 82, 87, 89–91, 120, 129, 133, 139, 153, 166, 169n139, 175, 185, 197, 229, 241, 256n22, 285, 310, 400, 427–8, 431n40, 439, 474, 515, 519, 522, 528, 560
invocation, 24, 54, 77, 120–1, 123–4, 138, 175, 188, 201–3, 225, 236, 238–9, 246, 247n101, 257–9, 263, 269, 273, 311, 316, 327, 333, 339, 362, 366, 376, 382–3, 393, 403, 413, 417–8, 431, 437n68, 467, 539, 541, 545
Ipsissimus, 300, 323–6, 409, 452, 560
Ireland, the Irish people, 2, 72, 352, 392
Isa, *see* Jesus of Nazareth
Isis, 34, 35n4, 39–40, 42–3, 45, 50, 54, 56, 58, 75, 153, 233, 277, 283, 316, 335–6, 382, 403, 408, 432, 437, 443n98, 471–2, 483, 488n14; the Æon of Isis, *see* æons; the veil of Isis, 75, 201n106, 281, 316; *Isis Unveiled*, 162, 178, 201, 251, 277, 281, 397
Islam, 36, 54, 88, 241, 329, 338, 349, 353, 382–3, 394, 396, 404–5, 409, 411–3, 418, 433, 442, 458, 460, 467–8, 470, 509, 546
islands, islanders, 19, 355, 475n241, 483, 486, 543–4
Italy, the Italians, 48, 391–2, 444, 474, 503–5

Jacobism, 382, 434
Jainism, 65, 94, 388
James of Jerusalem, St., 386, 406; the Epistle of James, 405
James, William, 172, 238, 337, 343
Japan, the Japanese, 102, 107–8, 238, 474–5; the Japanese language, 364, 474–5
Jātaka, the, 404
jealousy, *see* envy
Jechidah, 130, 176, 257, 271, 276
Jefferson, Thomas, 498
Jehovah, 53, 98, 119, 150, 206, 238, 257, 285, 314, 339, 353, 398, 401, 437, 443n98, 492
Jennings, Hargrave, 41, 443
Jerusalem, 91, 395, 438n20, 505n72, 509; the New Jerusalem, 395
Jesuits, the, 28, 107, 245, 391–2, 408, 422–4, 462, 474–5, 482, 558
Jesus of Nazareth, 1, 31, 38–41, 47, 53–4, 59, 73, 89–92, 122, 207–8, 217, 231, 241, 332, 336, 345, 349, 358, 371, 379, 381, 386, 397, 401–7, 409, 411, 415, 431n40, 433, 436–7, 439–40, 443, 482, 488n14, 505n72, 539, 546; the Society of Jesus, *see* the Jesuits
Jews, the, *see* Judaism
jhāna, see *dhyāna*
Jñāna-Kānda, 356
Joad, Cyril Edwin Mitchinson, 324
Job, 162, 414
John the Baptist, St., 401, 457; John Barleycorn, 40, 439; St. John of the Cross, 248, 367; St. John the Divine, 81, 117, 138, 162, 207, 254, 292, 354, 394–6, 407, 433, 436, 454, 492; *John St. John*, 269
Jones, Charles Stansfeld, ix, 27, 52–3, 64, 68–9, 79, 123, 183–4, 190, 202, 222, 244–5, 270, 289, 294, 297, 302, 305, 309, 318, 326, 332, 335, 367–8, 411, 445, 448, 452, 459n160, 461, 463n180, 465–7, 471, 477, 484, 487; George Cecil Jones, 53, 413, 429; Sir William Jones, 469
joy, 10, 12, 21–4, 28–9, 31, 39, 53, 84, 86–8, 104, 106, 109, 111, 113, 120, 132, 153, 155, 159, 163, 169–72, 174–7, 179–82, 185–8, 190, 192, 195–6, 198–9, 204–5, 207, 208n133, 210, 217, 219, 222, 229, 238, 240, 242, 247, 249, 254, 271–3, 277, 286–7, 289–90, 294, 301–2, 309, 324–6, 328, 338–9, 358, 380, 425, 437, 441, 456–7, 470–1, 485, 487, 534, 537–43, 545–8, 550–2; pure joy, 21–2, 111, 120, 175, 179–80, 205, 207, 290, 457, 540, 550
Judaism, 44, 49n56, 54, 87–8, 90, 97,

INDEX

123, 138–9, 145, 208, 237–8, 269, 272, 338–9, 353, 362, 383, 394–8, 401, 403, 406–7, 418, 427n19, 439–40, 474, 479n266, 485–6, 538, 558, 561
Julian the Apostate, 408, 416
Jung, Carl Gustav, 100, 247, 264, 273–4, 343
Jupiter, 36, 151, 225, 285, 300, 320, 373, 415, 474, 557
justice, 32, 34, 60, 75, 82–3, 87, 90, 152, 180, 346, 415, 495, 499n43, 507, 553, 557; *Justice*, 152, 332, 397, 547, 558, 562

Kabbalah, the, *see* the Qabalah
Kamma, *see* Karma
Kant, Immanuel, 3n15, 47, 72, 114, 255, 299, 317
Kaph, 285, 558, 562
Karma, 82–5, 133, 173, 178, 210–1, 225, 262, 273, 308, 349, 356, 366, 370; Karma-Kanda, 356
Karnak, 35, 303
Kaufmann, Walter, 3n15, 47, 57
Keats, John, 84, 191, 193, 414
Kelley, Edward, Sir, 315–6, 318, 339–41
Kellner, Carl, 427, 429
Kelly, Gerald Festus, Sir, 387
Kerubim, the, *see* Cherubims
Kether, 109, 141–2, 154, 209, 227, 234, 257, 283, 287, 301, 311–4, 324, 362–3, 367–8, 558, 561; *see also* the Crown
Khabs, 20, 29, 108, 159, 171, 261, 537, 540, 545; *Khabs am Pekht*, 516
Khu, 29–30, 130, 171, 209, 261, 270, 537, 545
Kiblah, the, 403, 544
Kierkegaard, Søren, 46–8
kings, kingship, 23–4, 26, 33, 35, 40, 45, 54, 62, 68, 76, 105, 164, 169n139, 181, 187, 195, 206, 227, 232, 245, 254–5, 259n31, 263, 312, 314, 317, 319–20, 328, 336, 359, 365, 367–8, 371, 373, 376, 395, 398, 401–2, 416, 427n16, 428n23, 429, 437, 444, 455, 460, 469, 483–4, 496, 500–3, 506–7, 516, 532–4, 540–3, 545–6, 550–2; the King's Daughter, 254, 398; the King's Son, 54, 398
King's College London, 382
King, Francis Xavier, 343, 427, 451
Kingsford, Anna, 39, 248, 257, 456–8
Kircher, Athanasius, 208, 558
Knight of the East and West, 395, 465
Koestler, Arthur, 76
Konx Om Pax, 127, 208, 240, 275, 321
Kothek, Gerda Maria von, 513
Krishna, 53, 88, 232, 240, 250, 272, 335, 341, 379, 439
Krishnamurti, Jiddu, 438, 450–3
Kteis, the, 108
kuṇḍalinī, 141, 217, 293, 356, 362–3, 396, 432
Kundry, 53, 244–5, 345, 368

labour, 12, 26–7, 49, 52, 231, 423, 455, 460–1, 466n202, 468–9, 484, 489, 494–5, 513, 519–23, 553; the labour theory of value, 523; the Labour Party, 505, 528
ladders, 116, 188, 205, 286, 289
Lamed, 398–9, 547, 558, 562
Lamen, the, 269, 413, 426–7
Lamp, the, 16, 123, 323–4, 368
Lance, the, 33, 53, 110, 191, 345, 368, 493
Lao Tze, 148, 165, 200, 223, 230, 248, 379, 412, 421, 427n19
Latin, 1, 70, 85, 122, 140, 145, 148n67, 207n131, 261n39, 275, 300, 345, 384, 396, 398, 403, 414, 422–3, 435, 442, 454, 476, 477n256, 483, 485, 490, 521, 534n179
laughter, 1, 16, 21–3, 32, 63, 86, 113, 162, 205–6, 235, 276, 303, 306–7, 328, 340, 456, 483, 485, 510, 525, 541–4, 546, 551
laws, legislation, 13, 27–8, 31, 36, 44, 49–50, 59–61, 64–5, 69–72, 78–80, 84–5, 152, 171, 173, 186, 204, 236, 271–2, 305, 373, 329, 331, 342, 354–5, 379–80, 391, 402, 406, 410–3, 419, 421, 427n19, 429–30, 432n43, 439–40, 443, 450, 453–4, 456–8, 461–6, 471–3, 476–8, 481–534, 538–9, 541, 544–8, 550–4, 558; the laws of economics, 26, 44, 60–1, 173, 373, 486, 488n14, 489, 494, 504, 511–5, 521–5, 531; the laws of mathematics, 35, 47, 72, 75, 95–6, 103–9, 111–2, 117–20, 131, 133, 139, 143n50, 149–51, 157–8, 167–8, 174, 198, 219, 228, 254, 257, 283n5, 298–301, 321, 326, 390, 418, 461,

477, 481–2, 485, 507, 521; the laws of physics, 10, 21, 24–6, 33, 36, 37n14, 56, 65, 75, 82–3, 98–100, 103–4, 106n54, 107, 111, 115, 118, 120, 126, 139–40, 151, 157, 173–4, 180, 194, 199, 209, 217–8, 228–9, 234, 240, 243, 246, 282, 300, 302, 305, 308, 323, 329, 332, 349, 390–1, 393, 448, 476, 478, 481–2, 522; the laws of thought, 28, 33, 44, 48, 57, 61–2, 72, 75, 81, 87–8, 99, 112, 114–6, 122, 126–9, 132, 134–6, 140–4, 157–8, 165–7, 174–9, 185–95, 198–209, 217–22, 228–30, 234–5, 240, 243, 246–8, 250–8, 263–4, 267–8, 271–5, 278, 281, 286–7, 289–90, 293, 297–302, 304–6, 310, 317–27, 340, 364, 391, 414, 421, 455, 481, 504–7, 522

lawyers, 134, 278, 460, 478, 482, 493, 517n119, 532

Leadbeater, Charles Webster, 438, 442n93, 451

Le Bon, Gustave, 115, 366

Left Hand Path, the, 312–4

Legge, James, 526

Leibniz, Gottfried Wilhelm, 104, 107

leisure, 27, 61, 156, 327, 472, 487, 520, 531

Leo, 34n1, 55–6, 152, 162, 381, 397

Lévi, Éliphas, 3, 38–9, 65, 69, 75, 78, 80, 86, 91, 133, 146, 149–50, 154, 161–2, 179–80, 183, 186, 202–3, 206, 215, 237–8, 240–1, 244–5, 314–6, 342–3, 345–6, 370–1, 391, 392n50, 393–4, 398, 408–9, 411–2, 414, 431n41, 432–5, 437, 445, 447–9, 453–4, 456, 459–60, 471, 473, 486, 495, 499, 513, 518n120, 519, 533–4

Leviathan, 91–2, 293

liberalism, 476, 500, 514, 534; classical liberalism, *see* libertarianism

liberty, *see* freedom; libertarianism, libertarians, 57, 63, 500, 512n98, 521, 527n153, 534

libido, the, 278–80

Libra, 34n1, 151–2, 294, 333, 547, 562

light, 20, 23, 38, 47, 58, 63, 65, 77, 87, 91, 95, 97–8, 101n33, 105, 108, 112–3, 116–7, 122–4, 138, 149, 154, 156, 162–4, 170, 173, 177–9, 181, 183–4, 187, 190, 193, 195, 198, 203–9, 217–8, 225, 230, 232–5, 237, 245, 248, 251–2, 254–5, 264–5, 275, 277, 288–9, 294–5, 303, 308–9, 320, 322–7, 332, 334–5, 341, 345, 357–8, 368, 374, 380, 384–6, 395, 397–401, 407, 409, 414, 416, 431n41, 432, 434, 436, 443n98, 446–7, 452, 455, 466, 469, 471, 493–4, 497, 503, 510, 530, 534, 537–45, 552, 555; the body of light, *see* the astral body; cakes of light, 245, 544

lightning, 50, 139, 262, 270, 294, 297, 339, 367, 436

Lilith, 237

limitation, limits, 9, 12–3, 25, 27–30, 39, 55, 63–4, 72, 74, 96, 99, 104–5, 108, 111, 114–5, 117, 122, 126–7, 131–2, 134–5, 137n37, 149, 157–8, 171, 173, 182, 185, 187, 196, 221–2, 230, 245, 258, 260, 270, 273, 282, 283n5, 292, 300, 305, 307, 310–1, 324–7, 338–9, 357, 369, 372, 382–3, 394–5, 413–4, 434, 443n98, 476, 487–8, 491–2, 500, 525, 555

Lingam, the, 285, 296, 399; the Lingam-Yoni, 399; the Mahalingam, 296

linguistics, 60, 65, 102–3, 112, 120, 127–33, 136, 139–40, 143–5, 147, 150–1, 154, 159n102, 165–7, 272, 274–6, 306, 315, 340, 349, 351, 394, 412, 439, 451–2, 455, 461, 465, 478–80, 526

Linji Yixuan, 474–6

lions, 23–4, 38, 58, 162, 164, 207–8, 225, 242, 257, 287, 308–9, 318, 330, 332, 396–7, 399, 429, 437, 440n83, 453, 456, 471, 493, 503; the Lion-Serpent, 248n101, 383, 437

literacy, 26, 120, 131, 147, 167, 169n139, 221, 406–7, 455, 480, 486, 504–5, 520–1, 526, 548

Locke, John, 485, 488

logic, x, 3n15, 9, 28, 44, 48, 51, 61, 75, 81, 88, 99, 107, 112, 126–9, 132, 136, 141, 143, 157–8, 179, 234–5, 246, 248, 251, 278, 286, 305, 340, 364, 391, 414, 504–5, 507, 522; *Science of Logic*, 3n15, 99

Logos, the, 25, 54, 58, 94, 143n50, 144, 222, 257, 275n85, 281, 284, 293, 298, 314n107, 329–30, 334–5, 341, 374, 379, 399, 407, 410–3, 424, 430, 436, 437n70, 451, 458, 477n257, 493–4,

556; the Logos of the Æon, 8, 54, 58, 222, 329-30, 334-5, 402, 413, 424, 430, 444-5, 451, 458, 493-4, 538
London, 81-2, 306n82, 382, 406, 504; the *London Sunday Dispatch*, 444; the University of London, 409
lotus, the, 53, 288, 332, 368, 452, 470
Louis XVI, 370, 391, 506
love, 7-8, 10, 13, 15-7, 19-23, 26, 31, 33, 42, 50, 55-6, 58-9, 67, 75-6, 78, 81, 91, 101, 108-9, 111, 116-7, 119-20, 154, 158, 163-4, 169, 171-2, 174-6, 180, 182-96, 198-9, 202-5, 206n127, 207-9, 215, 218-9, 222, 224-6, 229-30, 236, 238-42, 244-5, 247-8, 259n31, 271, 278-9, 287, 289-98, 302-4, 308-9, 313, 317, 319, 323, 325-6, 328, 333, 335, 342, 346, 351, 354, 366-7, 371, 374, 380, 388, 394, 396-401, 405, 407, 409, 414, 420-1, 430-1, 440-1, 452, 458, 462, 467, 471, 473, 475-7, 482-3, 487-9, 492-6, 503, 506, 508, 514, 518, 526, 534, 536-43, 546-51; the act of love, 15-7, 19-22, 26, 111, 120, 182, 184, 187-93, 198, 204, 206n127, 215, 219, 229, 290, 294, 325-6, 380, 437n69, 467, 489; love under will, 7-8, 10, 13, 16, 20-3, 26, 55, 119-20, 164, 175, 182, 184, 186, 189, 199, 205, 209, 215, 218, 222, 239, 247n101, 294, 298, 304, 323, 328, 333, 366-7, 394, 396, 430, 440n82, 458, 483, 536, 547-9, 551; the Lover, 230-1, 538; *The Lovers*, 323, 558, 562
Loyola, St. Ignatius, 3n14, 306, 420-1, 424, 475, 532
Lucifer, 65, 91-2, 183, 275, 401
luck, 87, 258-9, 374, 497, 515-6
Lucretius, 1, 55, 94
Luke the Evangelist, 162, 407
lust, 2, 16, 171, 184, 187, 189, 191, 198, 207, 232, 236, 242, 244, 250, 264, 308-9, 344, 367, 392n50, 493, 517n119, 541, 544-5, 549, 556; *Lust*, see *Strength*; lust of result, 15, 21, 172-3, 190, 223, 247, 483, 538, 549-50
Luther, Martin, 91n96, 238; Lutheranism, Lutherans, 412, 432, 478
L.V.X., 207n131, 248-9, 275, 288, 335-6, 386
Luxor, 303

Maat, 34, 144, 164, 277; the Æon of Maat, *see* æons
MacKenzie, Kenneth, 443
macrocosm and microcosm, 41, 123, 148, 184, 201, 225, 250-1, 259-61, 273, 287, 311, 323, 333, 369, 372-3, 382, 422, 432
Macroprosopus and Microprosopus, 141-2, 293, 314, 316, 323, 334, 386
magicians, 3, 54, 68, 115, 119-24, 131-2, 137, 140, 155, 159, 166-7, 169, 194, 201-2, 227-31, 238-9, 252-3, 256-7, 259-61, 274, 275n85, 279, 282, 286, 290-1, 295-6, 301, 305, 308-9, 312-3, 318, 323, 327, 332, 337, 339, 353, 363-6, 368, 370-1, 373-4, 382-4, 393, 402-3, 408, 410, 416, 446, 459, 462, 481-2, 534, 540; *The Magician*, 121, 155, 296, 301, 540; *Magick in Theory and Practice*, 7, 33, 38n20, 50, 53-6, 58, 67, 70-1, 78, 95, 98, 103, 118-24, 131-2, 137-8, 140, 167-74, 194, 196n85, 201-2, 215, 220, 222, 225-7, 233, 238-9, 245, 247, 252-3, 255-7, 259-63, 277, 279-80, 293, 295, 298, 300, 313-4, 320, 323, 327, 331-3, 336-41, 346, 348-9, 371-3, 376, 382-3, 388, 393-4, 398-403, 413, 417, 427n17, 432, 437, 448-9, 451, 453, 458n157, 466, 481-2, 498-9, 536; *Magick Without Tears*, 8n9, 33, 43-4, 68, 70-4, 76, 79-80, 86, 89-90, 106-7, 118n91, 119, 128-31, 136, 148, 150-1, 154-5, 158-9, 165-6, 168-9, 173-7, 182-6, 189, 205-6, 210-1, 217-8, 224, 231-2, 236-7, 241-3, 246-8, 250, 252, 255, 257-8, 261-3, 265, 267-8, 281-2, 285-7, 290-1, 297, 306, 328, 339-40, 347-8, 350-5, 369-70, 372, 375, 383, 385-6, 393n54, 403, 409, 412, 416-7, 419, 424-5, 427-8, 430, 437, 439, 443-8, 454n145, 456-7, 459-60, 470, 472-3, 476-7, 483, 495, 500, 503, 506, 512, 515-20, 524-31, 536n182, 559
Magister Templi, 21, 122, 137, 143, 147, 158, 164, 190, 229, 232, 248-9, 282, 286, 290, 295-304, 314, 316, 324-5, 327, 349, 372, 380-1, 402, 424, 450, 479n262, 560; the oath of the grade of Magister Templi, 137, 290-1, 296, 302, 316, 349, 376

Magus, 53, 121, 203, 222–3, 230, 248, 296–8, 300–1, 312, 314n107, 323–5, 329–30, 339, 379, 387, 402, 411, 424, 446, 451, 453, 461–2, 499–500, 516, 560; *The Magus*, see *The Magician*; the Book of the Magus, 297–8, 314, 324–5, 329, 411; the curse of the grade of Magus, 298, 314, 403, 466
Mahābhārata, the, 36, 59, 232
Mahādeva, 467–8
Mahāsatipaṭṭhāna, 114, 165; see also *sammā-sati*
Mahatmas, Mahatmaship, 77, 330, 353, 360, 451, 468
Maistre, Joseph de, 391–3, 414, 434n53, 435–6
Malkuth, 141, 153, 209, 257, 362–3, 398, 454, 558, 561
Malory, Thomas, Sir, 371, 412
mandalas, 273, 559
Manes, Manicheanism, 20, 62–3, 177–8, 183, 326–7
Mann, Thomas, 264
manners, 70, 73, 443, 497, 505–6, 528, 531n167, 532
mantras, 225, 306, 331, 366, 416, 538; the Gāyatrī Mantra, 416
Manu, 36, 72; *manvantara*, 264, 341
Mara, 164, 288, 424
Marconis, Étienne-Jacques, 428
Mark the Evangelist, St., 162, 407, 428
marriage, 19, 44–5, 49–50, 52n65, 73, 78, 196, 343, 380, 414, 464, 475, 489–95, 511; the chymical or mystic marriage, 111, 116, 120–1, 127, 141, 182, 192–3, 198, 202, 229, 235, 238, 249, 275, 277–8, 294, 297, 309, 311, 319n130, 398, 431, 454; *The Marriage of Heaven and Hell*, 89–90, 240
Mariette, Auguste, 410
Marlowe, Christopher, 412
Mars, 54, 155, 207n131, 255, 260, 274, 418; martial arts, 31–3, 62, 68, 71, 79–80, 181, 191, 220, 260, 276, 330, 338, 392n49, 467–8, 471, 474–6, 501, 529–30, 551
Martinism, the Martinists, 391–2, 426–7, 429, 434–6, 438
martyrdom, 215, 375, 392, 413, 415, 432, 472, 499
Marx, Karl, 46–8, 523; Marxism, 48–49, 523

Mary, St., 187, 238, 298, 314, 386, 437, 449, 488n14, 546; the Annunciation of the Blessed Virgin Mary, 458; the Assumption of the Blessed Virgin Mary, 314
masochism, 17, 26, 191
Mass, the, 29, 54, 124, 186, 191, 196n85, 269, 384, 396, 417, 430–3, 437, 439, 441–5, 449, 454, 463, 479n262; the Black Mass, 444
Massey, Gerald, 41, 401, 443
masters, mastery, 2–3, 14, 21–3, 27–32, 34, 38n20, 39, 44–5, 49–53, 55–6, 64–5, 68, 70–3, 77–80, 85–6, 89–90, 97, 110, 113, 126, 128, 133, 135, 139–40, 156, 158–9, 164, 169–70, 187–9, 191, 195, 198, 201–3, 206, 209, 211, 215–22, 224–6, 229, 231–2, 243, 245, 252–6, 258–60, 264, 276, 281, 288, 296, 300, 302, 307–8, 310–3, 319, 327–8, 342, 348–50, 353, 356–8, 363–6, 369–76, 393–4, 402, 407, 412–3, 425–7, 446, 448–9, 455–6, 462, 471–5, 478–84, 492, 495–8, 501, 504n68, 507–8, 518, 520, 524, 528–34, 542, 544, 550, 556; the Masters, 54, 133, 164, 188–9, 201, 211, 219, 232, 257, 271, 295, 300–1, 330, 338, 340–1, 345, 351–2, 358, 380–1, 390, 402, 409–10, 413–4, 428n27, 441, 447, 451, 456–7, 522, 527, 531, 543, 555; *The Masters and the Path*, 451; Masters of Arts, 478; Masters of the Temple, see Magister Templi; Master Masons, 231, 336, 360, 417, 428–31, 442n95, 459; master-morality, 137, 507; the master-race, 518
Master Therion, the, 44, 54, 215, 228, 321, 341–2, 402, 413, 442, 449, 451, 473, 481, 510, 516, 517n119, 522, 524; *The Master Therion: A Biographical Note*, see *Liber 666*; *The Message of the Master Therion*, see *Liber II*
Mat, see *The Fool*
materialism, 11, 15, 39, 48, 50, 114, 116, 172, 178, 197, 204, 258, 281, 283, 296, 313, 347, 388, 393, 406, 410, 416, 419, 431, 447, 456, 463, 469–70, 481–2, 485, 556
mathematics, 18, 35–7, 72, 75, 95–6, 103–20, 131–3, 139–42, 143n50,

INDEX   615

145–6, 149–51, 155, 157–8, 167–9, 228, 254, 262, 283n5, 298–301, 305, 321, 326, 345, 348, 365, 390, 411n123, 418, 461, 466, 477, 481–2, 507, 521–2
Mathers, Samuel Liddell, 57n86, 97, 262, 327, 343, 426, 453
matriarchy, 42, 48–51, 483
matter, 15, 21, 94, 98–105, 108–9, 114–5, 118, 122, 133, 136, 139, 157, 158, 176, 187, 192, 194, 197, 204, 217–8, 229, 234, 238, 252, 258–9, 276, 282–4, 293, 303, 320, 332, 336, 350, 362, 393, 419, 555
Matthew the Evangelist, St., 162, 354, 407, 439
maximax, 507
Maximus the Confessor, 1; Maximus of Ephesus, 408
Māyā, 62, 164, 177–8, 272, 288, 301, 322
Mayan, 253, 301
McIntosh, Christopher, 428–9, 560
Mead, George Robert Stowe, 432
meaning, 7–8, 12, 15, 30, 32–3, 37, 41–3, 46, 49, 55, 58, 62, 65, 76, 78, 85, 87–8, 92, 95–6, 98–9, 101–2, 105, 107, 109–10, 114, 117, 119, 122, 127–31, 139, 141–4, 149, 151, 154, 165–6, 171–7, 188, 192–3, 196, 203, 206, 207n131, 215, 230–2, 236, 241, 261, 271–2, 275–9, 286, 289, 292–3, 298–300, 307–8, 311, 320n133, 323, 333–5, 344, 351–3, 355, 358, 364, 367, 374, 379, 384, 394, 397–400, 410, 416n147, 417–20, 428, 430, 431n41, 443, 465, 473, 477n257, 482, 485, 498, 501, 506, 509, 513, 519, 521, 529–30, 532, 534, 544
measurement, 21, 26, 110, 127, 132, 145, 155, 185, 199, 205–7, 223, 235, 247, 284, 300, 305, 310, 318, 334, 346, 350, 399, 424n8, 476, 481, 491–2, 524, 531–2, 551–2
meddling, *see* interference
medicine, 19, 26, 30, 78, 281, 305, 346, 423, 478, 516, 532
mediocrity, 30, 390, 482, 501, 528, 530
meditation, 3n14, 15, 38, 53, 80, 87–8, 136, 147, 159, 163–4, 168, 174, 205, 206n127, 216, 222, 246–7, 262, 290, 298, 324–5, 336, 348–9, 353, 355, 357, 363, 365, 369, 373, 405, 416n147, 420, 445n106, 476, 556; *Meditations on First Philosophy*, 156
meekness, 31, 91
melacholia, 81, 87–8, 205, 278–9, 307, 338, 375
Melchisedec, or Melchizedek, 406, 437
Mem, 86, 153, 293–4, 341–2, 558, 562
memory, 2, 9–10, 45, 50, 67, 106, 112, 119, 129, 143, 146, 160, 165, 167, 169n139, 194n79, 210–1, 254, 335, 343, 347–9, 352, 368, 374, 383, 420, 446, 465, 473; the Magical Memory, 85, 211, 229, 318, 343, 347–9, 376, 383, 446
Memphis, 428n23; the Oriental Rite of Memphis, 428n24; the Rite of Memphis and Mizraim, *see* the Antient and Primitive Rite of Freemasonry
Menander of Bactria, 354, 376
Mencius, 278, 507–8, 559
Menger, Carl, 523
menstruation, 42, 544
Mercury, 120, 151, 255, 285, 287, 293, 301, 325, 350, 383, 416, 436
mercy, 23, 75, 294, 350, 405, 472, 493, 544, 552, 556; the Pillar of Mercy, 233, 294, 556, 558, 561
Merkabah mysticism, 138–9, 150, 162
Merton, Thomas, 79–80
Messalina, 28, 191, 202
Messiah(s), 54, 86, 293–4, 406, 438, 451, 460
metals, metallurgy, 65, 124, 130, 200, 233–4, 308
metaphysics, 1, 26, 47, 82, 84, 87, 95–8, 132, 136, 166, 173, 175, 177–8, 247, 257, 262, 264, 274, 315, 332, 338–9, 382, 386, 394, 404, 407, 431, 442, 470, 478, 527
methodology, 3n15, 8, 12, 21, 31, 42, 45, 47–8, 54, 56–7, 66–7, 69–70, 85, 116, 118, 125, 127, 131–2, 134, 142–3, 145–7, 155, 158–61, 173–4, 179, 184, 199, 201, 215–8, 224–6, 228–30, 233, 254–6, 262, 267–9, 279, 281, 286–9, 299, 304–5, 319–20, 323–5, 331, 340, 346–52, 355–7, 361–4, 366, 368, 373–4, 383, 393, 415, 417–20, 424n8, 432, 443n98, 448, 450–1, 473, 476, 481–2, 489, 509, 511, 516, 518, 522, 524–5, 528, 552, 561; the Method of Equilibrium, 69, 116, 127, 132, 160–1, 174, 184,

225, 289, 297, 319–20, 323–5, 340, 368, 373–4; the Method of Ladders, 116, 188, 205, 286–7, 289–90; the Method of Science, *see* the scientific method; *The Method of Thelema*, 67, 69, 134, 142–3, 473, 476, 479–80, 509, 511, 516, 522, 524–5
Mexico, the Mexicans, 96, 385, 418, 425
Michael, St., 437n70
microscopy, 71, 127
middle ages, the, 17, 44–5, 54, 90, 97, 101, 103, 107, 137–8, 149–50, 153, 155, 343–4, 417, 423, 467–8, 474–5, 477–8, 485–6, 495, 521
Middle Pillar, the, 233, 257, 556, 558, 561
Milinda, *see* Menander of Bactria; the *Milindapañhā*, 376, 404
Mill, John Stuart, 72, 472, 499n45, 501
millenarianism, 37
mind, the, 11–2, 14–5, 18, 21, 24–6, 29, 41, 47, 51, 58, 61, 63n103, 66, 68–9, 71, 74, 77–8, 81–4, 87, 93–4, 97–9, 102–5, 112–7, 124–7, 131–6, 138, 140, 142–3, 146–7, 149, 154–5, 157–61, 164–8, 169n139, 172–3, 177, 180, 182, 190, 195, 200–1, 203–7, 210, 216, 219–20, 222, 224–5, 228–30, 232–4, 236, 239–40, 242, 245–6, 250, 254–5, 263, 268–70, 275, 280–2, 286–92, 297, 299–300, 302–3, 306, 310–2, 316–9, 321, 324, 326–7, 335–8, 340, 343, 345–50, 352–4, 357–9, 361–6, 368–71, 373, 386, 389, 396, 400–1, 405, 416n147, 417, 419–2, 425, 431, 446, 455, 458, 462, 466, 469–70, 476–7, 482, 487–8, 491–6, 500, 503–4, 519, 521, 523, 527–8, 531, 551; the mind-stuff, *see* the *chitta*
mindfulness, see *Mahāsatipaṭṭhāna* or *sammā-sati*
Minerva, 258n27; the Minerval, 430, 442, 446
miracles, 29, 40, 129, 186, 203, 208, 262, 290, 332, 365–8, 381, 385, 396, 404–7, 426, 439, 445, 447–9, 454n144, 456, 515, 544
Mises, Ludwig Heinrich Edler von, 521–2, 524n142
missionaries, 70, 245, 360, 423, 474–5, 502
Mithras, 397, 408, 418, 432, 439
Miyamoto, Musashi, 475

Mizraim, 428n23, 437n70; the Rite of Memphis and Mizraim, *see* the Antient and Primitive Rite of Freemasonry
M∴M∴M∴, *see* Mysteria Mystica Maxima
mob, the, 14, 16, 18, 191, 365, 443, 466, 501, 505–7, 516–7
modesty, 28, 76, 177, 182, 188, 359, 491, 542
Mohammed, 34, 223, 329, 349, 379, 409, 411–3, 420, 433, 458, 472, 546
Moksha, 210
Molinos, Miguel de, 104, 238, 418
Monad, the, 1, 3, 7–33, 50, 53–6, 59, 62, 66–8, 73, 76–7, 86–8, 93–7, 104–9, 112, 115–25, 140–3, 149, 153–5, 163–4, 170–86, 190–8, 200, 203–4, 206–7, 209–10, 215–20, 222, 224, 227–8, 231n46, 233–5, 238–9, 242, 245–7, 250–1, 257, 259, 263–5, 271–3, 277, 282–5, 287–92, 294–304, 307–14, 316–8, 320–8, 333–4, 337, 339, 346–9, 358, 361–71, 375–6, 382, 395, 397, 399, 401–3, 406, 411, 414–6, 420–1, 424, 433, 436, 437n68, 449–54, 460–3, 469–70, 476, 483, 487–9, 494–6, 501–3, 508, 516–8, 528, 530, 533–4, 537–47, 550–1, 558–61
monarchy, 35, 37, 40, 45, 50, 90, 156–7, 164, 187, 192, 227, 245, 263, 312, 314, 317, 319–20, 328, 336, 359, 365, 367–8, 370–1, 374, 376, 391, 395, 398, 416, 429, 437, 444, 453–4, 455, 460–2, 469, 483–4, 486, 499–503, 506–8, 510n92, 516, 532–4
monasticism, 2, 33, 107, 204, 230–1, 239, 244–5, 320, 325, 344, 354, 360, 364, 384, 388, 404, 420, 423–4, 438, 444, 454n114, 460, 467–9, 472, 475–6, 477n253, 503–4, 517, 528, 532; monastic vows, 344, 420, 423, 460, 468–9
money, 13, 45, 87, 191, 223, 327, 347, 383, 387, 436, 447, 463–4, 491, 494–5, 498, 512–5, 517n119, 529, 531, 544
Mongolia, the Mongols, 241, 293, 467, 546
Monier-Williams, Monier, Sir, 144n53, 416n147, 420
monism, 10, 56, 62, 94–6, 107, 125, 178, 196, 218–20, 343

monogamy, 19, 49, 192, 204, 493
monotheism, 68, 97, 415
Monsalvat, 344, 368
Montu, 277, 545
Moon, the, 35-6, 39, 42, 53-6, 106-7, 154, 156, 173, 193, 233-5, 253, 288, 341-2, 416, 537, 544; *The Moon*, 558, 562; *Moonchild*, 470, 501, 507, 509; *The Moonstone*, 413
morality, *see* ethics; moral codes, 7, 59, 66, 69, 71-4, 79, 82, 90, 171, 177, 181, 236, 329-30, 352-5, 381-2, 409, 482, 507
morphine, 199, 242, 496
Moses, 84, 123, 131, 208, 272, 314, 339, 379, 398, 428n27, 433, 439, 558
Mother, the, 12, 39-40, 42-5, 49-50, 53, 56, 118, 120-3, 141-2, 153, 164, 210, 217, 242, 247, 249, 283, 293, 307, 334-6, 339, 401, 436-7, 441, 443n98, 454, 471, 490; the All-Mother, 164; motherhood, 17, 29, 45, 49-50, 76, 119, 232, 239-40, 249, 319, 385-6, 437, 451, 464, 491, 493; the mother-letters, 293
motion, 3, 9-10, 15, 23-5, 32, 35-8, 61, 68, 73, 94, 99-100, 103, 106n54, 109-10, 115, 120, 127, 133, 144, 147, 165-6, 192, 198, 209, 215, 218, 228-30, 234, 252, 258, 26-8, 279, 282-3, 293-5, 302, 339, 356, 394, 467, 487, 511, 518, 549; the motion of the body, 173, 300, 356; the motion of the mind, 135, 229, 234, 290, 302, 317-8, 350, 364, 370, 418, 501, 510
mountaineering, 20, 29-30, 32, 53, 55, 86, 126, 168-9, 195, 220, 223, 232, 265, 296, 303, 313, 324, 328, 352, 361, 368, 379, 382, 385, 401, 425, 451, 458, 521n133
mudrā, 355-6
Müller, Friedrich Max, 177, 263, 360
muscles, 25, 58, 73, 140, 168, 173, 300, 317, 361, 374
murder, 28, 31, 75-6, 79-80, 163, 202-3, 371, 387, 392n50, 415, 423, 471, 474, 484, 489, 492, 494, 498-9, 503, 505, 512-3, 534, 553
Murray, Gilbert, 41n28
music, 16, 21, 31, 103, 155, 158, 188, 190, 193-4, 204, 207, 232, 236, 241, 290-1, 330, 357, 368, 371, 389, 398, 414, 416, 427n16, 454-5, 463, 479n262, 487, 510, 526, 534, 540, 545
Muslims, *see* Islam
Mussolini, Benito, 519
Mysteria Mystica Maxima, 427
Mystica Aeterna, 438
mysticism, 20, 39-41, 43, 66, 86, 97-8, 103-4, 108, 110, 112-3, 117, 119, 125, 127, 133, 135, 139, 148, 153, 162, 168, 178, 193, 197, 199-201, 217-8, 225, 227, 230-2, 240-2, 245-8, 250, 254, 263, 265, 269, 272, 282-3, 287, 296, 300, 302, 304-8, 312, 316, 324, 336, 337-9, 344, 351-2, 354, 364-6, 373, 382-4, 388-9, 396-7, 405-6, 410, 415-20, 429n33, 434, 450, 454, 457, 461, 467, 470, 482, 495-6, 528, 558; Christian mysticism, 20, 86, 162, 178, 200, 272, 278n92, 352, 418, 454, 470, 558

Nāgārjuna, 320
Napoleon, 68, 370, 392, 397, 415, 479, 486, 506; Napoleon III, 408-9
Narcissus, 191; narcism, or narcissism, 191, 279n95
National Socialism, 57, 462
Nazis, Nazism, *see* National Socialism
necessity, 1-2, 18, 20-4, 27-9, 32, 39, 42, 47, 49-52, 59-60, 64, 68, 70, 72-4, 77-8, 80, 84-6, 96-7, 105-6, 109-14, 116, 119-20, 125, 127, 129-30, 132-3, 135, 137, 140, 143-4, 147, 153, 156-8, 161, 163-6, 169, 172-4, 177, 179, 184, 187, 189-90, 197, 201, 206, 207n131, 215, 217, 219, 221-2, 229, 231-2, 235-6, 239-40, 243, 246-7, 248n101, 249, 252-3, 255, 260, 266, 268, 276, 284, 286, 296-319, 323, 326-7, 331-2, 338, 345, 350-3, 357-8, 364-6, 369-70, 380, 384-5, 390, 394, 396-7, 400, 406, 410-2, 417, 419, 424, 436, 446-7, 449, 452, 455-6, 459-63, 466, 471, 482, 484-5, 487, 489, 493-4, 496-7, 499, 504-5, 508-10, 513-7, 520, 524-5, 529-32, 551-5
Neophyte, 45, 133, 217, 226, 248, 301, 312, 316, 373, 382, 390, 394, 446, 459, 470, 517, 560; the Grand Neophyte, 233; the oath of the Neophyte, 387, 450
Neoplatonism, 1, 98, 101, 139, 178,

231n46, 258, 261, 477n257
Nephesch, 130, 176, 227, 254, 560–1
Nero, 137, 191, 397, 415, 455
nervous system, the, 75, 113, 143, 167, 250, 291, 356, 361
Neschamah, the, 115, 130, 176, 302, 560
Netzach, 141, 372, 558, 561
neutrality, 14, 43, 234, 274, 530
New Æon, the, *see* the Æon of Horus
New Age Movement, the, 37
newspapers, 24, 33, 68–9, 99–100, 331, 360, 426, 461, 480, 490, 497–8, 503–6, 510, 523, 534
New Testament, the, 1, 138, 183, 394–5, 439
New Thought, 301, 359, 369
Newton, Sir Isaac, 3n14, 36–7, 103, 108, 349, 480; Newton's First Law, 180, 349; Newton's Second Law, 115; Newton's Third Law, 21, 103, 107, 126, 174, 199, 209, 217, 229, 282, 323
New York City, 461; the *New York Herald*, 360; the *New York Times*, 506
Nibbāna, *see* Nirvāṇa
Nietzsche, Friedrich, ix, 23, 51, 59, 69–70, 76–7, 88, 90–1, 93, 136–7, 155, 264, 289n20, 455, 472, 478–80, 500–3, 507, 518
nihilism, 10, 38, 94–5, 183, 204, 338, 343, 346; nihility, *see* nothingness; annihilation, 116, 119, 127, 141, 154, 164, 187, 198, 206, 261, 265, 273, 291, 300, 304, 328, 366–7, 443, 500
Nile, the, 39–40, 53, 58, 87, 470
nirodha, 325
Nirvāṇa, 15, 102–3, 136, 178, 197, 210, 244, 247, 272–3, 288, 290, 321–2, 325–6, 362
Nirvikalpa, 106, 271, 321
niyama, 352–5
nobility, *see* aristocracy
non-attachment, 15, 69, 76, 175, 178, 185–6, 221–2, 228, 292, 341, 343, 359, 363, 388, 420, 467, 525
North, the, 38, 58, 73, 162, 183, 401, 403, 519
North Africa, 404, 418, 511, 547
notariqon, 151, 465n200
nothingness, 10, 95–99, 104–9, 112, 118–9, 127–9, 141, 151, 155, 164, 166, 176, 178, 185, 194, 200, 216, 224, 248, 250–1, 271–2, 288, 294, 296, 301, 309, 312, 323–5, 337, 339, 349, 366–8, 537–8
noumena, 97, 136, 177, 255–6, 322, 365
nouns, 1, 99, 102, 144, 477, 549
nous, the, 100, 130, 229
novels, ix, 51, 169, 385, 392, 470
N.O.X., 153–4, 248–9
Nu, Nuit, or Nuith, 11–2, 15–6, 20–1, 26, 29, 59, 67, 93, 98–100, 104–5, 108–11, 117, 121, 124–5, 136, 142, 153, 164, 171, 174–5, 179, 184–6, 188, 190–1, 195–6, 198, 204, 207, 209, 215–7, 219, 229–30, 232, 235, 244–5, 247, 276, 289–92, 297, 302, 309, 325, 332, 367, 398, 399–400, 441, 537–45, 550, 552; devotion to Nuit, 20, 175, 179, 184–6, 188, 191, 195–6, 207, 216–7, 244–5, 290–1, 297, 302, 332, 367, 400
Nun, 154, 208–9, 294, 336, 443n98, 558, 562
nuns, 388, 454

oaths, 73, 87, 89, 187, 210–1, 226, 311, 313, 329, 344, 385, 388, 397, 420, 423–4, 443, 449, 460, 465, 468, 473, 476, 484, 493, 495, 538; magical oaths, 76, 121, 146, 161, 191, 210–1, 245, 259, 290–1, 302, 316, 320, 345, 349, 370–2, 387, 424, 450, 453, 459
Obeah and Wanga, 233, 331, 538
obedience, 65, 91, 149, 179, 187, 215, 220, 224, 226–7, 232, 255, 260, 271, 318, 327, 356, 365–6, 420, 422–3, 449, 480, 498–500, 508, 518, 527, 538; vows of obedience, 420, 422–3
observation, 9–12, 30–1, 33–5, 43, 55, 65–6, 76, 83, 93, 101–3, 110, 114–7, 120, 126–36, 140–3, 145, 160, 165–7, 171, 174–5, 186, 194, 200–6, 218–22, 224, 245–7, 256, 270, 274, 279–81, 289–93, 305–11, 316–28, 344, 346–51, 368–76, 392–3, 402–3, 448, 462, 481–2, 529, 552; *The Observer*, 99
obsessions, 19, 26, 45, 74–5, 126, 175, 237, 240, 253–4, 279, 311, 320, 365–6, 372–5, 449, 518
Oedipus, 18, 53; the Oedipus complex, 12; *Œdipus Ægyptiacus*, 208; *The Œdipus Judaicus*, 397; *Œdipus Rex*, 41n28
O.H.O., the, 429, 440, 445–6, 462

Old Man of the Mountain, the, 241, 424
Old Testament, the, 1, 138, 238n6, 401, 411
old time, the, *see* the Æon of Osiris
Om, *see* AUM
omniformity, 113, 124, 163, 298, 349, 399
omnipotency, 7, 9, 88, 179, 215, 277, 282, 303, 326, 329, 408, 501n55, 533-4
omnipresence, 9, 19, 174, 247, 255, 271, 282, 356, 363, 401, 538
omniscience, 7, 9, 88, 105, 118, 127, 132, 271, 282, 303, 427
omnivalence, 425
Onan, 492
Ophidian Vibrations, the, 425
opium, 81, 86-7, 199-201, 241, 482, 496
ordeals, the, 159, 200, 225, 232-5, 245, 330, 366, 441, 538-9, 544-7, 552
order, 7, 9, 14, 21, 25, 52-3, 60-5, 68, 75, 78, 80, 82, 91, 101n33, 107, 113, 115, 119, 124, 144, 147-9, 159-60, 162, 167, 174, 176, 187, 193, 198, 230-41, 259, 264-72, 282-5, 301, 303-5, 312, 314-6, 338, 341, 348, 352, 358, 368, 372-4, 394, 420-4, 432n43, 446-50, 453-4, 458, 462, 466-7, 469, 474, 482-534
Ordo Templi Orientis, the, ix, 231, 384, 425-32, 435, 437n64, 438-46, 450, 452, 457n153, 458, 460-5, 468, 548, 554, 557
organization, 24, 32, 60, 79, 112, 157, 222-3, 230-3, 238, 259, 295, 303, 331, 347-50, 375, 385, 422-4, 426-30, 438-42, 450-3, 455-534
organs of the body, 19, 31, 75, 114, 119, 135, 164, 167, 190, 193, 198, 207-8, 225, 233, 236-7, 270, 272, 274, 280, 293, 304, 422-3, 426, 500, 527
orgasm, 116, 119-21, 163-4, 174-5, 184, 186, 191, 193-6, 198, 202, 204-8, 218-9, 241, 243, 246, 280, 292, 294, 297, 367-8, 431, 445n106, 551
orgia, 29, 33, 106, 124, 241
Orm, Ormesius, or Ormus, 428
Orpheus, 38, 437; *Orpheus*, 21
Osiris, 21, 33-4, 35n4, 39-40, 42-3, 45, 50, 53-6, 58, 153, 162, 181, 210, 217, 244, 252, 264, 272, 277, 283, 287, 307, 316, 319n130, 332-3, 335-8, 344, 398, 403, 407-8, 415, 419, 432-3, 436-7, 439, 443n98, 444, 457, 471-2, 474, 483, 488n14, 502, 539, 557; the Æon of Osiris, *see* æons
Othello, 18, 191
O.T.O., the, *see* the Ordo Templi Orientis
Overman, the, 136-7
Ovid, 488
oxen, *see* the Bull

pacifism, 31, 44, 77
paganism, pagans, 1, 19, 34, 39-41, 50-1, 329, 336, 339, 389, 391, 395, 403, 407-8, 416-8, 432-3, 437, 439-43; neo-paganism, 49n56, 50-1, 441-2
paederasty, 18, 353
paedophilia, 17-8
pain, 12, 29, 46, 59, 63-4, 68, 74, 85, 89, 91, 104, 109, 176, 179-80, 194, 199, 204, 220, 231-2, 238-40, 255, 260, 265, 295, 301, 304, 324, 350-1, 357, 374, 393, 418, 509, 512, 521, 538, 540-1
painters, painting, 12, 26, 44, 146-8, 164, 167, 172, 194-5, 204, 247, 281, 365, 410, 487, 504n68, 548
palaces, 16, 30, 84, 106n54, 138-9, 155, 208-9, 216, 275, 311, 317, 327-8, 358, 456, 539; *The Palace of the World*, 124
Pan, 55, 143n50, 207, 228, 298, 366-7, 416; the Mystery of Pan, 324; the Night of Pan, 153-4, 248, 298, 304; the Vision of Pan, 55, 248
Pantacle, the, 120, 147, 148n67, 167, 276-7, 278n92, 290-2, 303n68, 311, 314, 318-21, 324, 363, 410
pantheism, 20, 97, 200, 362, 415, 470, 534
papacy, the, *see* popes; Papal Infallibility, 391, 434-5
Papus, *see* Gerard Encausse
parables, 30, 237, 310, 345, 369-71, 404, 436, 477n253, 515
Parabrahman, 326, 432
Paracelsus, 3n14, 237
paradoxes, 57n86, 75, 97, 103, 111, 123, 125, 161, 173, 228, 245-6, 291, 302, 322-4, 391, 432, 437, 510; the Paradox of the Comte de Fénix, 510; the Paradox of Liberty, 7, 123, 245-6;

the Paradox of Tolerance, 57n86, 70; *The Paradoxes of the Highest Science*, 391, 432, 437
Paramahamsas, 466
Paramātmān, 271–2, 322
Parananda, 354
Parinibbāna, or Parinirvāṇa, 322
Paris, 99, 147, 435, 442, 445, 478, 502, 504; *The Paris Working*, 54, 280–1, 287–8, 436
parliamentarism, 466n202, 506–7
Parmenides, 94, 231n46, 283
parthenogenesis, 50, 54, 153, 294, 321, 336, 407, 437, 443n98
Parsifal, or Parzival, 53, 164, 245, 345, 367–8, 452, 461, 479n262
Pārvatī, 355
Pascal, Blaise, 108
Pasqually, Martinez de, 392, 426n14, 434–5
passion, passions, 16, 19, 28–32, 39, 46, 70, 80, 83, 90, 134, 142, 169, 172–3, 182, 192–3, 201–5, 222, 238–45, 254, 258, 274, 289–91, 297, 301, 307, 313, 318–9, 338, 345, 350, 352–3, 363, 394, 398, 402, 405–6, 413–4, 462, 495, 518, 532–4, 543, 550–1, 556
Patañjali, 348–9, 352, 355, 358–9, 361, 363, 402, 405, 421
patriarchy, 27, 42, 48–53, 483, 487, 493, 531n167, 532
patriotism, 24, 32, 38, 70–1, 76, 261n37, 359–61, 406, 461, 469, 472–3, 484, 486, 531
Paul of Tarsus, St., 42, 63, 72, 74, 87, 90–1, 194, 254, 269, 274–5, 290, 349, 395, 402, 406–7, 421, 423, 439, 440n82, 492
Payne Knight, Richard, Sir, 41, 401
Pé, 274, 558, 562
peace, 60, 63, 79–80, 106, 113, 155, 173, 195–6, 199, 205, 210, 228–9, 288, 319, 346, 350, 353, 368–9, 373, 388, 392, 405, 407, 454, 463, 482, 487, 504, 505n72, 514–5, 517, 529–31, 539, 543, 550
Péladan, Joséphin, 426–7, 453
Pelagius, Pelagianism, 2
pentagram, the, 122–4, 254, 275, 283n5, 334, 367, 372–3, 539; the Lesser Banishing Ritual of the Pentagram, 124, 389, 448–9, 454n145
Pentagrammaton, the, 122–3, 275, 283, 415, 557
Pentateuch, the, 138–9
perception, 2, 10–2, 18–23, 25–27, 39–42, 44–5, 47, 50, 55–6, 58, 63, 67–9, 75, 79, 81–3, 88, 93–4, 102–6, 109–19, 126–43, 147, 152, 154–60, 164–7, 170–1, 174–6, 181–7, 192–5, 197–200, 209, 219–23, 226, 229, 234–5, 240–1, 245–8, 250–7, 270, 278, 287, 280–1, 287–328, 334, 339, 341, 347, 350–2, 357, 362–70, 379–81, 386, 389, 402, 410–4, 416, 419–20, 434, 437, 447, 455–6, 462, 466, 470, 480–1, 490–1, 497, 508–11, 512n95, 521–6, 529, 534, 537, 539, 542, 547, 550–1
perfection, 10, 14–5, 21–2, 25, 30, 35, 38, 60, 63–5, 67, 71–2, 74–5, 79, 88–9, 95, 105, 111–8, 120, 123–4, 135–6, 143, 149, 152, 158, 160, 163–4, 169, 172, 174–5, 177, 184, 187, 189–93, 196–8, 201–3, 205, 207–10, 215, 218, 220–1, 225–6, 229, 232–4, 237, 242–3, 248, 254, 257, 260–1, 270, 283n5, 284, 288–96, 300–3, 308–11, 315–8, 320, 323–4, 328, 333, 336, 338–9, 345, 350, 368, 372–5, 382–3, 385, 390, 396, 399, 401, 415, 417, 422, 425, 426n14, 433, 437, 441, 443n98, 454, 462, 466, 470–1, 476, 482–3, 487, 498–9, 506, 508, 511, 515, 522, 526, 528–9, 538, 540, 549–52, 554; the Path of Perfection, 184
perfumes, 155, 256, 292, 363, 365, 467, 491, 538–9, 540, 544
Persia, the Persians, 144, 277, 394–5, 413, 467, 486
pestilence, 240, 467, 514; centres of pestilence, 72, 547
Peter, St., 406, 437, 439
Phaedo, 231n46
Phaedrus, 156, 169n139, 504n68
phallicism, the phallus, 16, 19, 39–42, 86, 119, 121, 164, 186, 190, 207–8, 233, 237, 270, 272, 274, 280, 285–6, 287–8, 293–6, 304, 309, 320, 341–2, 366–7, 398–9, 401, 428n23, 432–3, 437, 443, 472n228, 527
phantasm, phantoms, *see* illusion
Pharisees, the, 63, 342, 387, 404
Philebus, the, 156, 231n46
Philo Judaeus, 395

Phlogiston, 194
Phoenicia, the Phoenicians, 8n9, 54, 383
Phoenix, the, 207n130, 245, 306, 449; the Mass of the Phoenix, 245, 449
Phren, the, 130, 229
Physicism, 283
physics, 16, 33, 36, 56, 61, 75, 94, 98–100, 103–4, 111, 114–5, 118, 122, 139, 144–5, 157, 231n46, 240, 283, 287, 305, 321, 329, 338, 346, 350, 356, 390, 448, 456–7, 478, 482
physiology, 16, 18, 31, 45, 64, 86, 159, 189, 242, 340, 344, 356, 414, 487, 489, 491, 527
Pi, 122, 332–4
Pike, Albert, 395
Pilate, Pontius, 40, 379
Pisces, 34n1, 35n4, 37, 152–4
pity, 62, 75, 86, 131, 137, 175, 180, 326, 472, 495, 503, 542, 544, 546, 552
planes of existence, the, 21, 56, 127, 140, 162, 172, 179, 199, 202, 210, 225–9, 237, 252–4, 257, 267–8, 281, 286–8, 293–4, 303, 312–3, 319, 321, 339, 344, 346, 349, 364–5, 473, 560–1; confusion of the planes, 25–6, 127, 179, 252, 257, 311–2, 344, 346
planets, 9, 35–7, 96, 98, 123–4, 139, 151, 157, 161, 233, 313, 329, 337, 347, 379, 381, 387, 398, 413, 432, 436, 466, 471, 486, 530
Plato, Platonism, 1, 35, 37, 47, 57, 72, 94, 101, 122, 143, 149, 155–6, 206, 231n46, 270, 271n73, 283, 392, 406, 422, 433, 477, 479–80, 524n142
pleasure, 1, 15, 17, 20, 22–3, 28, 59, 63–4, 78, 169, 172, 174, 181–2, 186, 188, 192–3, 195–6, 199, 202–7, 209, 240, 242–5, 307, 333, 336, 338, 350, 380, 385, 441n83, 487, 491, 493, 496, 503, 534, 540, 542, 550
plebeians, the, 364, 472n228, 505; the Plebeian Tribune, 505
Pleroma, the, 98, 177
Plotinus, 1, 231n46, 277
plough, the, 52, 63, 520, 522
Plutarch of Chaeronea, 261n39, 412
Plymouth, the Plymouth Brethren, 82, 402n80, 403, 439n76
Poe, Edgar Allan, 242, 414
poetry, poets, 11, 40, 46, 51, 53, 55, 71, 96, 103, 119, 122, 149, 154, 161, 168–9, 190, 200, 222, 236, 248, 258n27, 263, 272, 306, 312–3, 344, 354, 372, 385, 390–3, 396, 412–4, 416n147, 418, 420, 425, 441, 448, 455, 481–2, 487, 495
Poincaré, Jules Henri, 98, 132, 300, 321, 456
points-of-view, 21, 23, 26, 38, 67, 98, 103, 109–11, 130, 133, 143n50, 144, 175–7, 180–1, 185, 203, 210, 246–7, 250, 265, 267, 278n92, 297, 302, 309, 319, 332, 336–44, 372, 403, 409, 411, 466, 470, 499–501, 516, 551
Polanyi, Michael, 61
police, the, 18–9, 272, 461, 486, 493, 497–500, 525, 528, 532
politics, x, 1n1, 41–51, 52n65, 56–7, 61, 63, 79, 91, 107–8, 119, 182, 258, 320, 352, 359–61, 385, 391–2, 422–5, 427n19, 432n43, 440, 453, 463, 465–9, 471–534
polyamory, 192, 492
polytheism, 329, 389, 436
popes, 20, 277, 381, 392, 407–8, 423, 431–4, 436, 445–6, 460, 468–9; Pope Alexander VI, 445–6; Pope Benedict XVI, 423n4, 433; Pope Francis, 423n4; Pope Honorius II, 468; Pope Joan, 277; Pope Leo XIII, 432n43; Pope Paul III, 408, 423; Pope Pius VII, 431n40
Popper, Karl, 56–7
pork, 77, 353
Porphyry of Tyre, 178, 231n46, 277
Poseidon, 49–50
power, powers, 2–3, 14, 23–5, 29–31, 39–40, 42, 45, 50–2, 55, 68–74, 82–5, 88–90, 101, 112, 118, 120, 122, 132, 135–7, 144, 149, 160–6, 169n139, 173, 182, 187–9, 194, 199–202, 204, 207, 209, 215–7, 220–4, 227, 230, 232, 234, 237n63, 244, 251–3, 256, 259, 263–9, 271, 273, 275n85, 277, 280, 284–6, 290–1, 295–301, 307–8, 313–5, 327–8, 331, 334–5, 343, 353, 356–7, 361–3, 365, 368–72, 375–6, 385, 387, 391, 393–6, 398–9, 402, 406–8, 413–4, 418–9, 421n166, 422–7, 433, 437, 443, 445–6, 448–50, 456, 458–60, 464, 467–9, 473–6, 479, 481–2, 487–9, 491, 494–5, 498–510, 512n95, 513, 516–22, 524–34, 537, 541, 544–7, 549, 555–7

poverty, 17, 63, 89, 127, 183, 187, 196, 326, 361, 468, 495, 506, 523, 542; vows of poverty, 73, 89, 420, 423, 460, 468
Practicus, 152, 325, 557, 560
Pradīpikā, the, 355–6
prāṇā, 161; *prāṇāyāma*, 243, 356–9, 450
pratyāhāra, 357, 359
prayer, praying, 120, 239, 245, 263, 288, 349, 383, 404–5, 409n114, 468, 474
Predestination, *see* determinism
Priapus, Priapism, 428n23, 432
pride, 28, 33, 76, 85, 163, 169, 186, 188, 236, 238–9, 306, 364, 374–5, 479, 506, 517n119, 522, 540–1, 546, 550
priestesses, 188, 540; *The High Priestess*, 235, 277, 558, 562
priesthood, *see* clergy; the High Priest of Israel, 63, 269, 380, 406
prima materia, 100, 122
prince-priest, the, 395, 484, 537–8, 547
prisons, 28, 80, 89, 137, 158, 178, 203, 206, 280, 328, 409, 482, 493, 502, 528
proairesis, 2
Probationer, 163, 233, 274, 459, 527, 560; the Oath of a Probationer, 161, 163, 370–2, 459; *Postcards to Probationers*, 69, 127, 161, 224–5, 373–4, 420
procreation, 16, 41–2, 51, 54–6, 75, 237n63, 308, 341–2, 437, 444–5, 484, 492
progress, 3n14, 10, 23, 28, 30, 37–8, 43, 45, 48, 54, 60, 76n35, 80–1, 120, 131, 133–4, 145, 155, 176, 224, 227, 231n46, 239, 245–6, 248–9, 264, 271–2, 288, 302–3, 328–30, 347, 362, 366, 373, 380, 413, 420–1, 427, 450, 462, 481, 501–2, 509–10, 514, 519n127, 528–30
Prohibition, the, 46, 496–7
profanation, 13, 162–3, 186, 192, 238, 281, 306, 316, 392n50, 431, 444, 447–8, 453, 461, 470
profess-houses, 384, 423n3, 463–4, 466
Prometheus, 336, 436; *Prometheus Unbound*, 211
propaganda, 419, 458, 461–3, 468, 504, 512
property, 13, 19–20, 155, 266, 391n46, 420, 460, 463–4, 485–6, 489, 491–2, 495, 502–4, 511–5, 522
prophecy, prophets, 42, 117, 138–40, 252, 275, 277, 332, 338, 379, 381, 385, 394, 403–4, 407, 411, 425, 439, 455, 457, 460, 466, 492, 495, 504n68, 518, 545; the Prophet(s) of Thelema, 20, 58, 117, 152, 184, 247n101, 332, 338, 379, 382, 384, 455, 457, 480, 518, 537–45
prostitution, 19, 136, 162, 240, 328, 346, 376, 432, 472n228, 492–5
Protestantism, Protestants, 147, 408, 412, 422–3, 432–4, 438, 468, 470, 474, 478, 488, 532
Proudhon, Pierre-Joseph, 527
Prussia, the Prussians, 407, 463, 480; the Prussian education system, 480
Pryse, James Morgan, 395–6
Psalms, 138, 164, 259n33, 371, 402, 421, 437
psyche, the, 130, 200, 273–4
psychoanalysis, 74, 159, 279–81, 343, 346, 370, 492, 554
psychology, x, 1, 31, 45–6, 59, 136, 226, 247, 264, 279–80, 329, 337, 340, 343, 374, 381, 406, 486, 495, 506, 516, 527
psychopathology, 3, 8, 12, 14–9, 24, 26, 32, 59, 63, 69–70, 73–5, 81–4, 88–91, 112, 116–7, 135, 138, 159–60, 175–7, 180–4, 188–9, 196, 200, 204–6, 220, 223, 229, 234–41, 247, 253–4, 278–81, 293–4, 313–6, 319, 324, 352, 362, 373–4, 379, 394, 405, 447–9, 454, 467, 476, 486–96, 503, 509–10, 525, 527
Ptolemy, 36
puberty, 17, 44–5, 74–5, 86, 182, 342
public opinion, 17, 346, 512, 533
punishment, 49, 64, 81, 84–5, 87, 91, 188, 203, 243, 374, 391, 408, 492, 499, 512
Puranas, the, 36, 65
Purgatory, 408
puritanism, 19, 69, 171, 221, 241, 352, 371, 513–4
purity, purification, 16, 28–9, 40, 77, 101–2, 136, 139, 145, 160, 177, 180, 187, 192, 201, 225, 231n46, 237–9, 242, 245–6, 258, 271, 283, 311, 328, 345–6, 350, 359, 362, 368, 371, 382, 428, 446, 460, 556–7
Purusha, 102, 130, 144, 161, 250
putrefaction, 190, 207, 270, 328, 333,

341, 444, 457, 491
pyramids, 35, 208, 220, 285, 293, 296, 309, 434; the City of the Pyramids, 91, 143, 153, 292-3, 314, 451
Pythagoras, Pythagoreanism, 139, 149-50, 258, 283, 406-7, 427n19, 433, 477

Qabalah, the, 25, 95, 97, 106, 123-4, 129-31, 133, 138-41, 145-6, 148, 150, 154-5, 161-2, 165, 176, 178, 189, 200, 208-9, 222, 225, 233, 237-8, 250, 255-7, 276, 283, 287-8, 292-3, 297-8, 300-1, 305, 314-5, 323, 333-4, 336, 339, 341, 366, 373, 383, 395-6, 400, 403, 406-7, 409, 413, 416-7, 427, 430, 431n41, 435-6, 443, 449, 454, 456, 461, 465, 558-62; Christian Qabalah, 123, 178, 209, 336, 396, 403, 435, 443, 454, 558
Qabalistic Dogma, 140-1, 154, 293, 336
Qliphoth, the, 140-1, 154, 220, 226, 238, 254, 293, 298, 321, 324
Qoph, 154, 558, 562
Quintessence, the, 101, 124, 165
Quran, the, 409-12

Ra, 157, 399, 546; Ra-Hoor-Khuit, *see* Horus
Rabelais, François, 8, 147, 412, 477n253, 501n55, 517n119
race, 183, 191, 241, 270, 339-40, 345, 413, 419, 443, 456-7, 472n228, 474, 487, 518, 533
Ragon, Jean-Marie, 432-3
rajas, 231, 285-6
Rāma, the *Rāmāyaṇa*, 232
Rāmānuja, 250
Ramaka X°, *see* Wilfred Talbot Smith
Ramakrishna, 361
Ramanathan, Ponnambalam, *see* Parananda
Randolph, Paschal Beverly, 409
rape, 17, 74-5, 244, 352, 387, 474, 492, 512
rapture, 22-3, 28, 87, 113, 120, 153, 172, 181, 185, 192, 206-7, 242, 275, 338, 472, 540-3, 549-50
rationalism, rationality, 1-2, 11, 18, 48, 56-7, 68, 113, 115-6, 118-9, 127, 129, 133, 156, 228-9, 242, 251-2, 272, 274, 280, 290, 302, 310, 313, 319, 350, 365, 368, 382, 384, 387, 391, 422, 430-3, 450, 477, 504, 551, 556
Rationalist Press Association, the, 382, 384
reason, reasoning, 10, 24-6, 33, 38, 40, 45-7, 68, 72, 75-7, 88, 94, 101, 114, 126-8, 132-6, 140, 151, 154, 161, 165-6, 179, 228, 240-1, 251-2, 254, 260, 262-4, 267, 278, 282, 284, 293, 298-300, 302, 306, 310, 319, 323-5, 352, 359, 362, 364, 367, 371, 394, 398, 411, 421, 424, 433, 450, 459, 472, 480n267, 484, 492, 499, 505, 511, 515, 520, 525, 541, 556; *The Age of Reason*, 433n49: *Critique of Pure Reason*, 47
rebellion, rebels, 91, 179, 312, 467-8, 528, 531
rebirth, 31, 58, 82, 178, 194, 207-8, 210, 265, 272, 332, 349, 436
redeemers, *see* saviours; redemption, 16, 39-41, 54-5, 61-2, 64, 81-2, 86-7, 90-1, 121-3, 156, 180, 185, 206, 207n131, 232, 236, 243, 254, 272, 275, 283n5, 293, 308, 312, 314, 334, 344-5, 367-8, 391, 394, 398, 407, 437-9, 446, 454, 460, 474, 497, 507, 509, 530, 534n182, 538
Regardie, Israel, 389-90, 425, 557
regret, 29, 172, 180, 223, 418, 540-1
Reformation, the, 408, 488; the Counter-Reformation, 408, 423-4, 462
Reich, Wilhelm, 280, 495
relativity, 73, 82, 98, 108, 111, 122, 132, 151, 270, 448
Rembrandt, 86-7, 158, 172, 372
Rén, 508
Renaissance, the, 123, 147, 245, 277, 407-8, 446, 477-8, 558
renunciation, 77, 187, 222, 244, 248n101, 295, 303, 356, 381, 388, 407, 435, 461-2, 467
republicanism, 61, 91, 182, 338, 451, 504-6, 524
Resh, 334-6, 443, 558, 562; *Liber Resh*, 369-70, 416, 448
responsibility, 2-3, 17-8, 20, 27, 40, 43-4, 52, 56-7, 77, 83, 86, 91n96, 137, 163, 277, 278n92, 313, 316, 388-9, 408, 415, 462, 472, 484, 486, 496-8, 503, 505, 507, 517-8, 522, 531, 557
restriction, 12-3, 19-21, 37n14, 43-4,

53, 61, 64, 72, 81n59, 108, 133, 163, 170, 176–7, 182–3, 187, 189, 208–9, 222, 285, 295, 326, 411, 460–2, 469, 483, 487, 490, 492, 495–6, 498, 510, 512, 517n119, 533, 538, 550, 553
resurrection, 38–42, 58, 91, 179, 207n130, 274–5, 317, 320, 332–3, 336–8, 358, 395, 398, 402–3, 407, 430–1, 436, 443n98, 444, 466
Return, the, 35–6, 40, 99, 115, 118, 124, 153, 161, 175, 177, 285, 338
Reuss, Albert Karl Theodor, 41, 426–7, 429–30, 435, 438–9, 442–3, 445–7, 463
revelation, 38, 117, 138, 146, 156, 200–1, 254, 257, 314, 324, 341, 351, 379–80, 384, 389, 394, 410, 417–8, 436; the Revelation of St. John, 53, 55, 81, 138–9, 162, 209, 342, 394–7, 435, 454, 542
revolution, revolutionaries, 24, 37, 46–7, 52n65, 62–4, 66n113, 80, 100, 107, 134n24, 248, 312, 387, 391–2, 414–5, 435, 462, 466, 471–2, 479, 481, 488, 496–7, 499, 509, 513, 522, 528–30; the American Revolution, 462; the French Revolution, 391–2, 414, 435, 462; the Russian Revolution, 496; the Xinhai Revolution, 107
Ṛgveda, the, 82, 144, 416n147
Rhys Davids, Thomas William, 272, 469
Rice, Isaac Leopold, 515
Riemann, Bernhard, 104, 117; Riemann's geometry, 103–4
rights, 14, 16–7, 28, 31, 57, 61, 65, 68–9, 73, 135, 175, 188, 215, 297, 316, 380, 387–8, 446, 448, 459, 464–5, 483, 485, 487, 489, 492, 495–501, 507–8, 512–3, 515–9, 522, 529–30, 532–3, 538, 548–50, 553–5
Rinzai, 107, 474–5
Robertson, John Mackinnon, 336
Rome, Romans, 35, 39, 54, 71, 75, 87, 91, 101, 122, 139, 194, 245, 370, 406–7, 415, 423, 432, 436, 439, 472, 474, 485–6, 495, 504–5, 509, 519; Roman characters, 275, 367; the Roman Church, *see* Catholicism; the Epistle to the Romans, 405, 421
Romeo, 18, 191
Romulus and Remus, 54
Rose, the, 122, 194, 292, 301, 320–1, 333–4, 344, 385, 426–8, 539

Rosetta Stone, the, 147, 410
Rosicrucians, the, 71, 127, 231, 257, 344, 347, 395, 409, 426, 427n16, 428–9, 434–5, 451, 453, 456, 477, 560; the Rosy Cross, 165, 194, 234, 275, 295, 301, 320–1, 333–5, 344, 395, 399, 426–8, 434; the Masonic Rose Croix, 395, 428n26, 442–3
Rousseau, Jean-Jacques, 484
routine, 72, 168, 175, 209, 246, 518–20, 529
Royal Arch, the, 427n19, 430, 437n68, 441, 461, 465
Rta, 65, 82–3, 144
Ruach, the, 115, 176, 189, 227, 234, 254, 257, 275, 310–1, 334, 355, 561; *Ruach Elohim*, *see* the Holy Ghost
rūpa, 102–3, 306, 562; *see also* the Four Material Elements
Russell, Bertrand, ix, 57, 98, 101, 104, 112–3, 132, 158, 456; Russell's Viper, 320
Russia, the Russians, 391–4, 486, 488, 490, 496, 525, 532; the Russian language, 394

Sabazius X°, 463–5
sacraments, 13, 16, 28–9, 124, 175, 186–7, 191–2, 195, 204, 206n127, 210, 242, 245, 274, 288, 290, 302–3, 325–6, 338, 380, 390, 445n106, 489; the Christian sacraments, 90, 186, 219, 408, 431, 434, 438, 444–6, 495
sacrifice, 34, 40, 61–2, 76–7, 87, 89, 121, 180, 215, 223, 230, 271n73, 294–5, 317–8, 332, 356, 365, 401, 407, 409, 466, 495, 499, 503, 518, 530, 539, 544–5; self-sacrifice, 14, 21, 61–2, 66n113, 76, 79, 222, 318, 332–3, 403, 423, 495, 503, 506, 509
Sādhu, 138n37, 352, 388, 404–6
sadness, 22, 291, 307, 541–2, 544
safety, 42, 63n103, 90, 186, 221, 240, 307, 320–1, 332, 348, 363, 369, 380, 449, 483–4, 489, 498, 501, 517–8, 525, 548, 553
Sagas, 396, 418
sages, *see* the wise
Sahara, the, 67, 72, 289
sainthood, 38, 80, 295, 320, 369, 404, 432, 437, 442, 451, 466, 479n262, 523
Saint-Martin, Louis Claude de, 392,

426n14, 427n19, 434-6
Saint Petersburg, 391-2
Salamanders, 267, 374, 556
salt, 80, 285, 312, 520
salvation, *see* redemption
samādhi, 15, 106, 120, 154, 160, 168, 174-5, 217-9, 229-30, 246, 248-9, 251, 271, 275, 292, 295, 297, 299, 302-3, 307, 321, 325, 349, 355, 359, 364-7, 382-3, 387; *sammā-samādhi*, 120, 288
Samael, 238
samāpatti, see *samādhi*
Samekh, 363, 558, 562; *Liber Samekh*, 264, 269, 337, 403, 416
sammā-diṭṭhi, 354
sammā-sati, 21, 65, 114, 159, 165, 262, 265, 288, 347-8, 370
saṃnyāsa, saṃnyāsins, 370, 388, 467-9
Saṃsāra, 146, 178, 210
samurai, the, 474-6, 480
saṃyama, 161, 405-6
saṅkhāra, 562; *see also* tendencies
saññā, 254, 562; *see also* perception
Sanskrit, 36, 82, 102, 133n21, 144-5, 200n98, 231-2, 275, 352, 355, 364, 388, 416n147, 419-20
Sappho, 187, 344
sat, 282, 286, 326 (*see also* Being);
sat-chit-ānanda, 282, 286, 325-6
Satan, 52, 58, 91-2, 178, 183, 203, 216, 238, 311, 371, 397, 401-2, 413; Satanism, Satanists, 275n85, 465
sattva, 231, 285-6
Saturn, 58, 313, 401, 495
saviours, 16, 30, 39, 54-5, 61, 86, 122, 275, 293-4, 320, 360, 368, 371, 397, 401, 407, 443n98, 457, 509
Scandinavia, ix, 183, 396, 418, 488, 519
Scarlet Woman, the, 55, 188, 218n12, 265, 314n107, 399-400, 452, 458, 493, 537, 544, 546
scepticism, 40, 127, 129, 155-6, 179, 238, 255-6, 306, 331, 347, 381, 387, 431n41, 457, 480, 515; Pyrrhonic Scepticism, 306, 477n257
Schoolmen, Scholasticism, 155, 127n5, 394
Schopenhauer, Arthur, 8, 57, 64-5, 88, 93, 145, 199, 248n101, 264, 360, 469, 478-9
Schrödinger, Erwin, 99
science, scientists, ix, 20, 27-8, 33, 37n14, 47, 49n56, 51, 56, 61, 66n113, 74, 76, 98-9, 103-4, 108, 111, 114-5, 122, 127, 129, 131-4, 140, 145, 150, 154-5, 159, 161, 167, 169, 188, 199, 201, 223, 228, 246, 254-5, 264, 268, 273-4, 279, 297, 302, 304-6, 310, 321, 329, 332, 335, 344, 346-7, 349-51, 353, 355-6, 369, 371, 380, 389-91, 392n49, 393-4, 397-8, 407, 411, 419, 427n19, 428n27, 429n33, 430-3, 440n83, 441, 445, 447-8, 451, 453, 456-7, 466n202, 469, 476-8, 481-3, 500, 510, 519, 524-5, 528, 532-3, 553; scientism, 114, 131, 133, 154; scientific illuminism, 169, 199-201, 228, 245-6, 254,-5, 305-6, 329-76, 387-91, 393-4, 419, 430, 447-8, 451, 476-8, 481-2; the scientific method, 56, 74, 268, 305, 347, 350-1, 355-6, 419, 476, 481-2, 524, 532
Science and Buddhism, 85, 271, 351
scin-laeca, the, *see* the astral body
Scorpio, 162, 207-9, 341, 443n98; the scorpion, 207-9, 341
Scotland, the Scots, 60, 87, 241, 384, 403; the Scottish Rite, *see* the Ancient and Accepted Rite of Freemasonry
Scourge, the, 285
sculpture, sculpting, 164, 169, 194, 395, 455, 487
secrecy, secrets, 8, 17, 19, 51, 61, 74, 91, 107, 116-7, 119, 123, 136, 139, 146, 150, 152, 162, 164, 172-3, 182, 202-3, 205-6, 208, 211, 217, 234, 240, 255, 257, 264, 269-70, 276, 281, 285, 309, 316, 328-32, 335-6, 338-9, 346-7, 355, 365, 371, 380, 385, 389-90, 392n50, 399, 401, 403, 409-10, 418, 426-32, 437, 444n101, 446, 448, 451-3, 454n144, 456, 459, 461-3, 470, 482-4, 486, 491, 509, 515-6, 529, 531, 537-47; the Secret Chiefs, 152, 329-30, 379-81, 385-7, 418, 424-5, 427, 451-3, 456-8
sectarianism, 27, 133-4, 320, 333, 342, 351-2, 357-9, 394, 413, 415, 434-5, 443, 450, 452, 511, 557
Seed, the, 39-41, 50, 124, 208n133, 235, 278n92, 401, 470
Self, the, *see* the Ego; the Higher Self, 236, 257-8, 261-3, 265, 272, 294, 358, 431; the Silent Self, *see* the Holy

Guardian Angel; the True Self, 23, 172, 177, 195, 202, 258, 272, 291–2, 298, 300, 316, 332, 411, 549
self-contradiction, 62, 96, 127, 134–5, 169, 173, 224, 302, 310, 319, 324, 446
self-control, *see* mastery
self-determination, *see* sovereignty
selfishness, 38, 68, 73, 76–7, 137, 215, 243, 313, 488, 514–5, 518
selflessness, 73, 76, 245, 324, 469, 472, 488, 506
semen, 54, 119, 135
sentimentality, 15–6, 33, 44, 61–2, 177, 345, 427n19, 473, 507
Septuagint, the, 1
serpents, 53, 86, 116, 138, 198, 206–9, 225, 234, 242, 247–8, 274, 276, 287–8, 293–4, 306, 309, 320, 328, 336, 341–2, 383, 401, 425, 436–7, 470, 534, 537, 539–41, 545–6, 552
Set, 33, 56, 58
severity, 59, 381, 423, 517, 521n133, 532, 538, 556; the Pillar of Severity, 233, 556, 558, 561
Shabbatai, 401
shadows, 21–2, 58, 63, 134, 179, 181, 188, 193, 204, 227–9, 251–4, 257, 282, 314n107, 323, 332, 362, 403, 416, 440n83, 441, 480n267, 526, 529, 540, 550; the Book of Shadows, 441
Shakespeare, William, 18, 21, 51, 191, 349, 412–4, 517
Shakti, 106, 244, 282, 367, 399
shame, 16–20, 26, 51n64, 72, 89, 131, 176–7, 182, 186–9, 192, 208, 242–3, 278, 280–1, 305–6, 353, 358, 471, 473, 480, 488–9, 491, 493, 498, 506, 516, 533, 546
Shankara, 178, 250, 399, 482
Shaw, George Bernard, 38–41, 73, 406–7, 439, 495, 513–5, 519–20
sheep, 27, 63, 179, 313, 330, 353, 396, 406, 498
Shelley, Percy Bysshe, 28, 90–1, 190, 211, 413–4, 418, 455, 472, 532
shells, the, *see* the Qliphoth
Shin, 122–3, 153, 275–7, 311, 558, 562
Shiva, 106, 248, 282, 325, 355–6, 366–7, 399; Shaivism, the Shaivites, 248n101, 354, 467; *śivadarśana*, 248, 366–7; the *Shiva Samhita*, 232, 355–6, 366
Siddhārtha, 34, 65, 82–4, 92, 136, 174, 206n127, 223, 230, 250, 272, 304, 320, 329, 336, 339–40, 349, 363, 379, 381, 411n123, 413, 415, 420, 424, 437, 482
Siddhas, 355, 467; the Siddhis, 271, 355–6, 365, 375–6
Siegfried, 408
Sigma, 276
Silence, 32, 119, 135–6, 153, 161–6, 184, 208, 220, 225, 233–4, 247–8, 258, 263–6, 271, 275–6, 280, 292, 309, 330, 341–2, 345–6, 350, 353, 355, 358, 366, 374, 383, 411, 425, 436, 450, 470–1, 490, 493, 497, 504n68, 527, 547, 556; the Silent Watcher, *see* the Holy Guardian Angel; the Sign of Silence, 217, 366; *The Voice of the Silence*, 450
silver, 192, 200, 234, 269, 467, 526, 539, 545, 547
Simon Magus, 437
simoom, the, 411–2
sin, 2, 12–3, 20, 24, 26, 42–3, 45, 61, 64, 72, 74, 81n59, 86–7, 89, 143, 163, 176–7, 180, 183, 195, 209, 222, 241, 243, 278–81, 285, 338, 344–6, 407, 409, 433, 457, 462, 468n213, 470, 477, 483, 488, 503, 538, 550, 553, 556; the Original Sin, 2, 180, 280, 344, 409, 488, 503; the remission of sins, 2, 42
single-pointedness, *see* one-pointedness
Skousen, Mark Andrew, 533
slavery, slaves, slave-morality, 16, 22, 26–7, 48, 64, 77–8, 87–91, 158, 162, 181–3, 188, 190, 200, 203–4, 215, 245, 262, 288, 318, 328, 338, 342–4, 357, 376, 399, 407, 411, 423, 471–2, 483–4, 488–9, 491, 493–4, 496, 500–7, 513–4, 517–8, 521n133, 524, 530–3, 537, 542, 548
sleep, 18, 39, 77, 80–1, 158, 160, 204, 210, 237, 240–1, 247, 271n73, 344, 356, 361, 365, 370, 418, 527; the Sleep of Shiloam, 153
Smith, Adam, 60, 523; Joseph Smith, 223; Wilfred Talbot Smith, 444, 453, 463
social contract, the, 484–5
socialism, 49, 116–7, 281, 392, 461, 484, 500–3, 505, 510, 520, 522, 528, 531–2; the Socialists, *see* the Labour Party

INDEX 627

social justice, 500, 534
Societas Rosicruciana, the, 231, 428, 446, 453, 560
sociology, 1, 49, 392, 462, 480n267
Socrates, 48, 156, 241, 258, 261, 264n52, 420, 505n72
solidity, 9, 25–6, 103, 107, 114, 121, 208, 255, 276, 293, 309, 469
solipsism, 134, 268
Solomon, 185, 362, 428n27, 431n41, 468, 492; the Poor Fellow-Soldiers of Christ and of the Temple of Solomon, *see* the Templars; *The Temple of Solomon the King*, 93, 115, 119, 132–3, 135–6, 155–6, 160–1, 164, 185, 187, 192–3, 195, 216–7, 219–20, 227–8, 232, 235–6, 238, 240, 248–9, 251, 254–5, 257–8, 262, 264, 269, 271–3, 288, 294–5, 302–3, 305–6, 309–10, 312–4, 317, 319, 322, 324, 328, 333, 352–8, 361–3, 365–6, 368, 376, 381–2, 386–90, 394, 400, 413, 415–6, 420–1, 450, 452, 456, 474
Solstices, the, 36–7, 40–1, 58, 342, 432
Solve and Coagula, 249, 292, 309, 312
Son, the, 54, 120–1, 198, 254, 283, 314, 336, 338–9, 427, 436, 454; the Son of Man, 137, 367, 509
Song of Songs, the, 454
sorcery, 54, 132, 183, 202, 217, 271n73, 306, 312, 327, 411, 448, 456, 472; the Great Sorcery, 54, 411, 472
sorrow, 21–2, 34, 51, 86, 111, 132, 163, 174–6, 179–81, 184, 186, 188, 208n133, 222, 229, 247, 272–3, 285, 287, 294, 296–7, 300–1, 307–10, 324–5, 339, 363, 403, 441, 445, 483, 525, 540–2, 550–1; the Trance of Sorrow, *see* trances
Sōtatsu, Tawaraya, 86–7
South, the, 58, 73, 162, 401
sovereignty, 9–10, 16–7, 67, 105, 132, 137, 150, 172, 175, 245, 269, 317, 327, 342, 354, 370, 373–5, 391, 418–9, 431, 488, 491–2, 498, 501–3, 507, 511–2, 516–7, 551
space, 10, 12, 38, 58, 67–8, 93, 95–6, 98–105, 108–9, 112, 114, 118–9, 133, 156–7, 165n130, 167, 170–1, 174, 185, 196, 216, 219, 248, 252, 256–7, 276, 282, 299–300, 332, 337–8, 356, 364–5, 401, 448, 471, 537–8; the space-time continuum, 12, 38, 93, 95–6, 99–101, 108–9, 114, 119, 133, 157, 165n130, 170, 185, 196, 204, 208n133, 216, 219, 256–7, 282, 299, 337, 364–5; infinite space, 67, 96, 102, 171, 256, 262, 537
Spain, the Spaniards, 426, 474
SPCK, the, 419n157
Spencer, Herbert, 63, 115n84, 128, 159n102, 256, 469, 499n43
spheres, sphericity, 8, 36, 47, 72–3, 96, 101–2, 108, 113, 126, 140, 144, 157, 176–7, 209, 216, 225–6, 233–5, 239–40, 258, 260, 267, 289, 294, 300, 332, 401, 419, 459, 480, 512, 540
Sphinx, the, 16, 91, 161–5, 208, 308–9, 399, 448, 493, 522, 562
Spinoza, Baruch, 47, 104
Spirit, 13, 16–7, 23, 29, 38, 41, 46, 50, 84, 97, 101, 104, 116, 122–3, 129, 137n37, 140, 163, 165, 178, 216–7, 227, 229, 232, 237, 239, 242, 246, 251–4, 258–9, 263, 265–6, 269, 271n73, 272, 275–7, 281–2, 283n2, 284–6, 292–4, 296, 311, 313, 315, 321, 337, 342, 362, 367, 386, 391, 394–5, 397–9, 443–5, 448, 455–6, 467, 473, 477, 487; the Spirit Vision, *see* astral travel; spirituality, ix, 13, 16–7, 29, 38, 41–2, 46, 50, 84, 87, 91, 97, 110, 127, 133–4, 137n37, 145, 155, 156n95, 166, 172, 174, 176, 181, 186, 191, 192, 200, 216–8, 227, 229, 231, 234–9, 246–7, 253–5, 257–9, 265, 269, 271, 275–6, 281, 284–5, 289n20, 291–4, 296, 306, 313, 320n133, 321, 330, 340–2, 355–6, 359n118, 360–1, 370–1, 379–83, 386, 388, 390–1, 394, 397–9, 414–21, 423n3, 424, 434, 437, 441–2, 445n106, 446–9, 453–7, 467, 468n213, 470, 473–7, 479n266, 487, 492, 509, 511, 525–6, 553
spiritism, or spiritualism, 202–3, 237, 253, 313, 350, 388, 409, 449; elemental spirits, 237–9, 259, 312–3, 365, 556–7; evil spirits, 42, 52, 63, 91, 96, 123–4, 140–1, 164, 201–3, 206, 216, 226, 237–9, 253–7, 259–60, 266, 268–9, 270n72, 295, 298, 311–6, 319, 327, 369, 374, 390, 393–5, 397, 416–7, 421, 424–5, 449, 454, 467, 474, 530, 555–7
spontaneity, 43, 60–1, 116, 188–92,

309, 368, 375, 483, 488–9, 527
spring, 34n1, 38n21, 39–41, 50, 207, 333
SPRT, the, 419
squares, 257, 301, 303, 333, 335; magic squares, 122, 149, 162, 283n5, 363
stagnation, 80–1, 205, 328, 333, 345, 467, 514–5, 528–30
standards, 14, 20, 27–8, 45–6, 56–7, 61, 68–70, 73, 90, 130, 132, 134, 137, 172, 239, 254, 289–9, 305, 318, 324, 326–8, 330, 334, 410–1, 481, 485, 487, 489, 510, 523, 528, 552; standardization, 26–7, 485, 487, 513–4, 523
stars, *see* the centre of the universe *or* the Monad; The Star, 117, 152, 539, 558, 562; the Star Ruby, 124, 193, 454n145; the Star Sapphire, 193; the Star-Sponge Vision, 105, 111–3, 209
State, the, 35, 43, 48, 49n56, 60, 64, 172, 414, 463, 465, 467–8, 483–7, 496–8, 500, 502, 505, 510–5, 518, 520–1, 527, 532–3, 553; statesmen, statesmanship, 51, 182, 319, 392, 434, 455, 471, 504
Steiner, Rudolf, ix, 37, 438–9
steles, 410; the Stélé of Revealing, 276–7, 403, 410, 544
Stevenson, Robert Louis, 14
Stirner, Max, 518
Stoicism, 1–2, 36, 108, 181, 477n256, 477n257, 485
Stoker, Bram, ix
stonings, 16, 79, 254, 470
strength, 13, 16, 22–3, 25, 28–9, 31, 33–4, 38, 60–2, 64, 87, 89, 110, 137, 151–3, 156, 162, 170, 188–90, 192–3, 203, 220, 223, 227, 236, 239, 242–3, 246–7, 267, 276, 290, 294, 296–7, 306, 308–10, 314, 317, 328, 331, 339–40, 345–6, 356, 362, 365, 369, 374, 387, 394–5, 399, 422, 424–5, 449, 451, 457, 459, 461–2, 474, 483–4, 496, 506–7, 519n127, 533, 540–52, 555–7; *Strength*, 34n1, 54, 152–3, 397, 437, 558, 562
students, 8, 15, 47, 50, 63, 69, 72, 127, 133, 140, 145, 154, 161, 182, 226, 231–2, 253, 268, 279–80, 287, 317, 321, 330, 339–40, 347, 354–5, 369, 373–4, 385, 388, 390, 393, 401, 409, 416–7, 421, 423n3, 430, 439, 444, 446, 450, 454, 456, 466, 469, 478, 480, 482, 532, 554; Student of the A∴A∴, 233
subconsciousness, 18, 20, 24–5, 28, 61, 74–5, 77–8, 84, 93, 111, 164, 198, 206, 218, 238, 242, 247, 250, 256n22, 257, 263–4, 270, 273–4, 275n85, 276, 278–81, 305–6, 343, 357, 362, 365, 371, 381, 401, 420, 442, 473, 511, 514, 524, 527
succubi, 237
suffering, 18, 23–4, 40–1, 45–6, 50, 59, 63, 69, 78, 82, 87–91, 103, 137, 178, 180, 183, 190, 202–3, 209, 232, 247, 260, 263, 304, 308, 337–8, 356, 372, 415, 443n98, 449, 521, 525, 529, 533, 539
Sufism, the Sufis, 396, 405, 470
suicide, 51, 172, 191, 202–3, 247, 279, 313, 350, 484, 495–6, 529, 545
Sulphur, 81, 285
Sullivan, John William Navin, 98–9, 103, 115
Sullivan Act, the, 497
Sumer, 163, 409
summer, 21, 207
Sun, the, 9, 22, 34n1, 35–6, 38–41, 45, 50, 54, 56, 58, 64, 67–8, 105–7, 113, 122, 134, 141–2, 151, 155–7, 163, 173, 183, 191, 207n131, 208–9, 216–7, 234, 245, 253, 257, 258n27, 287–8, 306, 309, 316, 331–3, 336–8, 341–2, 344, 367, 373, 384, 397–401, 415–6, 432–3, 436, 441, 448, 455–6, 466, 471, 472n228, 491, 530, 537, 540–1, 547, 552; The Sun, 492, 558, 562; sun-worship, 39–41, 332–3, 336–8, 397–9, 415–6, 432–3, 436, 441, 448, 472n228
Sun Tzu, 475
Supernals, the, 185, 209, 238, 275, 291, 293, 301, 334–5, 454
supernaturalism, 158, 199, 203, 371, 406–7, 409, 447–8, 456, 472, 474, 502–3, 519
superstitions, 50–1, 58, 150, 287, 331–2, 337–8, 389, 398, 442, 448, 454, 473, 517n119, 519
supplication, 132, 383, 395, 409n114
Supreme Ritual, the, 201, 236, 252, 257–9, 265, 273, 333, 337, 382, 402, 542
surrealism, 194

sushumnā nāḍī, the, 288, 356, 362–3
Svātmārāma, 355, 358
Swastika, the, 320, 367
Swedenborg, Emmanuel, 3n14
swerve, the, 1, 18, 94, 180, 254, 284
Swinburne, Algernon Charles, 348, 413
Switzerland, the Swiss, 343, 385, 434, 439, 442, 478, 525
Sword, the, 9, 32–3, 40, 148n67, 242, 266, 274, 307, 311–2, 317, 319–20, 323, 335, 346, 363, 384, 398, 408, 446, 457, 472, 475, 493, 521, 538, 544–5; the Flaming Sword, 141, 185, 274, 294, 384
syllogisms, *see* circular arguments
symbols, symbolism, 8, 12, 18, 22–3, 26, 35n4, 40–1, 43, 45–6, 51–4, 58, 93, 103, 108–10, 115, 121–3, 129–30, 135, 138, 140–1, 145–55, 161–3, 186, 195, 203–5, 206n127, 207n130, 231, 234–6, 244, 251, 254–7, 263, 270, 272–80, 283n5, 286–7, 290, 292, 308, 311, 313, 314n107, 320–1, 334–5, 341–2, 349, 351–2, 363, 367–9, 373, 380, 389, 394, 397–9, 401, 414–8, 427–8, 430–1, 434, 453–4, 480n267, 486, 530, 534, 542
sympathy, 50, 52, 66, 78, 175, 180, 230, 237, 260, 301, 319n130, 372, 383, 390, 435, 443, 451, 488, 512n100, 515, 552, 556
synthesis, 3n15, 48, 116, 130, 143–4, 159n102, 174, 201, 219, 229, 264, 358, 432, 436, 476, 479, 508, 550
Syria, the Syrians, 54, 406, 428n27, 432, 439

taboos, 19, 42, 182, 186, 190, 344, 489, 495
tabulæ rasæ, 291, 302, 488; the *Tabula Smaragdina*, *see* the Emerald Tablet
Tahuti, *see* Thoth; the Atu of Tahuti, *see* the Twenty-Two Trumps of the Major Arcana; the feast for Tahuti, 382, 542
talismans, 206, 244, 363, 413, 534, 559
Talmud, the, 59, 406
tamas, 231, 285–6
Tannhäuser, 96, 448
Tantras, Tantrism, 103, 231–2, 320, 358, 467
Tao, the, 99, 106–7, 144, 148n71, 164–6, 198, 200, 218, 244, 246–7, 257, 294, 372, 399, 412, 475, 526–7, 559; *Tao Te Ching*, 15, 148, 200, 404, 425, 526–7; *Thien Tao*, 240, 321, 350, 505–6
Taoism, 107, 148n71, 165–6, 321, 394, 475, 508, 526–7, 559
Tarot, the, 32, 146–8, 150–6, 163, 208–9, 248n101, 274–7, 284n6, 285, 295, 334, 397, 411, 461, 463, 547; *see also* the Four Suits of the Minor Arcana *and* the Twenty-Two Trumps of the Major Arcana
Tau, 303, 363, 558, 562
Taurus, 35n4, 162, 558, 562
taxes, 60, 440n79, 463, 486, 500, 511, 532–3
Te, or Teh, the, 99, 218, 244, 399, 527, 559
teleology, 69, 72
telescopes, 114, 134, 337–8, 403
Templars, the, 191, 392n50, 428n26, 435, 446, 468–70, 499; the Masonic Knight Templar, 427
Temple, the, 45, 77, 185–7, 218n12, 234, 272–3, 288, 291, 294, 297, 303, 309, 323, 327–8, 335, 340, 349, 351, 358, 363, 398, 437, 448, 540, 544; physical temples, 35, 91, 147, 185, 303, 398, 407, 410, 437, 468, 474, 492
tendencies, 18, 43, 61, 89, 94, 114, 115n84, 120, 160, 165, 173, 197, 228, 246, 279–80, 291–2, 300, 311, 318, 326, 339, 347, 364, 418, 478, 484, 508, 513n100
Tennyson, Alfred, Lord, 344, 472
Teth, 55, 558, 562
Tetragrammaton, the, 119–24, 153, 161–2, 275, 283–4, 293, 314, 337, 339, 415–6, 449, 454, 557, 561–2
tetramorph, the, 162
Thales, 100, 479
thaumaturgy, 281, 393, 406; *see also* miracles
Thebes (Egypt), 35n4, 239, 245, 277, 349, 410, 448, 522, 537, 545; Thebes (Greece), 51
theft, thieves, 17, 79, 215, 384, 432, 436, 452, 489, 499, 503, 512–3, 523, 553
theism, 10, 20, 107, 118, 200, 271, 298, 362, 415–6
theocracy, 392, 451, 519
theogony, x, 91, 98–9, 383
theology, 1–2, 20, 31, 41, 45–7, 63, 82,

94, 98, 108, 137, 139, 152, 155, 157, 231n46, 241, 280-1, 284, 305, 329, 343, 352, 369, 383, 396-7, 404-5, 407, 409, 413, 420, 435, 445, 454, 471, 477-8, 481-2
Theoreticus, or Theoricus, 560
Theosophists, 83, 257, 271, 343, 347, 359-60, 388, 396-7, 426, 429, 432, 438, 448-53, 456-8
Theresa of Ávila, St., 28
Thessalonicans, 274-5
theurgy, 222, 237, 251-2, 259, 261, 267, 284-5, 309, 387; Sceptical Theurgy, 387-8
Thisharb, 85, 228, 348
Thomson, James, 304; Matthew McBlain Thomson, 442-3
Thoth, 120, 147-8, 156, 169n139, 335-6, 339, 379, 382-3, 416, 542; the Invocation of Thoth, 120, 383
Threshold of Unity, the, 133, 154, 238, 258, 402; the Dweller on the Threshold, 159, 201, 238, 254
thrones, 43, 45, 54, 101, 121, 123, 139, 149, 157-8, 187, 283, 298, 312, 358, 365, 391-2, 395, 397, 406, 454, 466n202, 545-6
Thucydides, 471n224, 479
Tibet, the Tibetans, 59, 210, 283, 320, 349, 376, 451
tilakkhaṇa, the, 174, 300, 321, 325, 355; see also *anattā, anicca* and *dukkha*
Timaeus, 35, 37, 101, 122, 231n46
time, 9-12, 18-20, 22, 34-40, 42-7, 50, 52-4, 56, 58, 63-5, 66n113, 67, 70-1, 73-4, 76, 79, 83-5, 91, 93-5, 96, 98-101, 103, 106, 108-14, 118-9, 121, 128-9, 133, 142, 143n50, 150, 154-7, 165, 168, 174, 178, 185-6, 189, 191, 194, 196, 199, 203-5, 207, 208n133, 210-1, 216, 218-9, 221, 226, 228, 230-1, 236, 238-9, 242n81, 244, 247-8, 252, 262, 267, 270, 277, 282, 286-7, 292, 299, 303, 305, 307, 313, 317, 323, 327-9, 332-5, 337-8, 340, 342-3, 349, 354, 364-7, 370-1, 374, 380, 382, 386-7, 392, 395-6, 403, 405, 407-11, 417-9, 423, 425-6, 437, 439, 441, 446, 453-4, 458-9, 464-5, 469, 471-2, 474, 476-80, 484-90, 496-8, 504, 509-10, 515-23, 529-34, 540-1, 547, 555-6; see also the space-time continuum

Tiphareth, 176, 229, 271, 310, 337, 363, 396, 372-3, 454, 558, 561
Titian, 164, 190
tolerance, 24, 57n86, 60, 70, 90, 190-1, 196, 209, 238, 426n14, 511-2, 516, 517n119, 553-4
Tolstoy, Leo, 31, 392
To Mega Therion, *see* the Master Therion
Torah, the, 84, 138-9, 151, 439, 558
Tories, the, *see* the Conservative and Unionist Party
Toshophists, or Toshosophists, *see* Theosophists
totalitarianism, 43-4, 57, 505, 528, 533-4
tradition, traditionalism, 36, 41, 44, 50, 57, 59, 65, 68, 72, 97, 103, 107, 138, 144-5, 147, 148n67, 151-3, 196n85, 200, 207n130, 209-10, 231, 237, 257, 283n6, 290, 320, 325, 330, 347, 354-5, 359-60, 385, 388, 391-2, 396-7, 399, 407-9, 418, 429, 432-3, 440, 443, 447, 453-4, 468, 474-8, 483-4, 488, 490-3, 526, 531, 558-61
trances, 105-6, 161, 175-6, 199-202, 205, 228-30, 246-8, 290, 297-8, 302, 305, 307, 318, 321, 325, 339, 373, 402, 413, 455, 466, 470, 538; the Trance of Sorrow, 175-6, 229, 339, 413; the Trance of Wonder, 229, 290
tranquillity, *see* peace
transcendence, 17, 19, 22, 38, 41, 56, 97, 115-6, 134, 136, 187, 194, 198-9, 203, 207, 209, 228-9, 231n46, 234, 245-6, 265, 272, 274, 282-328, 337, 347, 370, 390, 408, 415, 420, 453-4, 457, 476, 480, 522-3, 527, 551
Transcendentalism, 359-60
transfiguration, transformation, or transmutation, 29, 38, 52, 55, 89, 101, 120, 125, 194, 200, 202, 221, 226, 229, 231, 244-5, 258n27, 275n85, 308, 321-2, 329, 339, 341, 375-6, 405-6, 453, 479, 484, 519n127; the Transfiguration of Jesus, 405
Tree of Life, the, 55-6, 97-8, 124, 139-42, 145-6, 150-2, 208n133, 233-5, 260, 283n2, 287, 301, 363, 367, 384, 510, 558-62; *see also* the Ten Sephiroth
Tree of Knowledge of Good and Evil, the, 12, 179, 316
Trent, 408, 455

INDEX 631

Triad, the, 3n15, 9, 42, 45, 54, 69, 95–6, 107–9, 120, 122–3, 141, 148–50, 153, 161, 165n130, 185, 207–10, 230–4, 238–9, 241, 251, 253, 263, 281, 283, 285–6, 293, 296, 300, 303, 307–8, 310, 315, 321, 324–6, 333–5, 338, 341, 355, 365, 381–3, 396, 417, 420, 424, 428–9, 434, 436, 443n98, 452, 460–2, 468, 478, 488n14, 538–9, 542, 558–61

Triangle, the, 11, 178, 196, 201, 234, 256, 283, 303, 309, 320, 335, 365, 534, 547

tribulations, 159, 302, 547, 552

trigrams, 71, 559; the Trigrammaton, 283; *Liber Trigrammaton*, 148n71, 309n94

trinities, 122, 235, 238, 281, 283, 293, 314, 325, 341, 365, 367, 397, 433; the Christian Trinity, 149, 303, 314, 427, 442n95; Trinity College, 342, 382, 451

troglodytes, 134, 464, 492, 503

truth, x, 7–9, 14, 16, 21–3, 37n14, 38, 41, 46–7, 52n65, 54, 57–8, 63n103, 67, 69, 78, 81, 88, 91, 95–6, 99, 105, 109–10, 112–4, 117, 125–8, 132, 134–7, 140–1, 144–5, 149–50, 157–8, 160, 162–4, 166, 168–72, 176, 181–2, 184, 186, 188, 192–4, 196, 198, 204, 206, 208n133, 210, 219, 226, 228, 230, 234–5, 246–7, 249n106, 252–5, 258, 261n37, 266, 272, 279, 281, 285–93, 295, 298–303, 305, 312, 316, 318, 320–2, 325–7, 329–30, 332, 334–6, 338, 340–1, 343, 349–50, 352, 354–6, 362, 364, 374, 376, 380–1, 385, 387, 389–91, 394–6, 398–9, 402, 404, 406, 411–2, 414–21, 426, 429–31, 441, 443–4, 448–54, 458, 469, 476, 479, 484, 493, 495, 499, 504n68, 507, 518–9, 521, 545, 550, 552, 556; *Little Essays Toward Truth*, 65–6, 86, 111, 119–20, 126, 130, 133, 145–6, 161, 163–4, 167, 170, 176, 199, 201, 203, 228, 229, 245–6, 250, 290–1, 293, 297–8, 302, 304–7, 310, 343–5, 470, 499–500, 506

Tunisia, 511, 547

twins, 34, 35n4, 43, 54, 56, 86, 98, 121, 163, 190, 206n127, 217, 264–5, 288–9, 547

Typhon, 217, 316, 397

tyranny, 58, 60, 65, 87, 244, 342, 422, 469, 485, 487, 496, 498, 500, 505–6, 509, 513, 533–4, 548; tyrannicide, 548

Tzaddi, 152, 539, 558, 562; *Liber Tzaddi*, 327

ugliness, 63, 89, 172, 183, 206, 455

Ulysses, 244, 258n27

unconscious mind, the, *see* subconsciousness; *Psychology of the Unconscious*, 247, 343

Understanding, 3n3, 8, 15, 21, 25, 33, 35, 39–42, 45–7, 55–8, 63, 66, 69, 71–2, 78, 81, 94, 102–5, 106n54, 109–10, 116, 121, 129, 131, 133, 137–8, 140, 142–3, 146, 154–6, 163, 169, 173–4, 178–80, 182–5, 187, 189–93, 196–8, 201–2, 206n127, 208–10, 216–7, 219–20, 222, 228–30, 232, 239–41, 249, 251, 253, 255, 259–60, 262, 267–77, 279, 283n6, 284, 287–91, 295–308, 310, 312, 315–6, 318, 320, 322–3, 330, 332, 335–6, 338n29, 339, 347, 351, 359, 361–2, 366–71, 374–5, 382, 385, 388, 390–1, 393, 401–4, 412–5, 417–21, 430, 436, 438, 440n83, 443n98, 445, 448, 459, 461–2, 465, 469, 475n241, 476, 479n266, 481, 487–8, 499, 503, 504n68, 505–6, 508, 517n119, 519–22, 524–6, 537, 539, 541, 547, 550–1

Undines, 374, 376, 556

union, unity, 10–3, 20, 56, 93, 99–101, 104, 109, 117–21, 183–6, 189, 192–5, 200, 203–5, 215–8, 222, 224–5, 230, 234, 249, 251, 257, 259, 267, 272, 274–5, 277, 283–4, 287–9, 297, 301, 312–3, 323, 330, 333, 339, 345–6, 364–6, 374, 382, 401–2, 411, 415, 419–20, 423, 431–2, 441, 451–2, 454, 462, 467, 485, 488, 533, 538, 550–1; the uniting of opposites, 7, 10, 104, 109, 118, 184, 187, 204, 218, 234, 249, 257, 275, 283, 323, 333, 339, 382, 454

United States of America, the, ix, 45, 47, 57, 59, 105, 112, 144, 337, 360, 395, 404, 428, 430, 433, 444, 450, 452, 460–5, 478, 485n6, 490, 497, 506, 509, 515, 518, 525

universalism, universality, 8, 27, 30, 39,

41, 43, 45–6, 69–70, 73, 75, 107, 112–3, 120, 123, 126, 131, 144, 146, 150, 163, 167, 176, 191, 199, 205, 219, 239, 271, 277, 287, 294–5, 303, 309, 312, 314n107, 327–9, 331, 343, 353, 359, 393, 405, 414–7, 425–6, 431–3, 435–6, 441–2, 452, 460, 466–7, 472, 484–6, 488, 499–502, 507, 529, 533; the Universal Joke, 205, 229, 307: the Universal Mercury, 436; the Universal Peacock, 364; the Universal Solvent, 7, 287–8, 292, 303–4, 307; universal suffrage, 49, 490, 500–1, 505–6, 528–30

Universe, the, 1, 3n14, 8n9, 9–13, 20–2, 37–8, 42–43, 45, 65, 66n113, 71, 77–79, 82–3, 88, 93–127, 131–4, 136–9, 142, 143n50, 144–8, 150–1, 163, 166, 170–2, 174–7, 179–80, 183, 186, 192, 196–8, 201, 204–5, 206n127, 207, 217–9, 224–5, 229, 231n46, 234, 245, 248–54, 256, 258–9, 261–2, 265, 268, 270, 273, 282–5, 287–96, 298, 300–2, 303n68, 304–5, 307–8, 310, 319, 323, 325–7, 329, 331–2, 336–9, 342, 349, 356–7, 365, 369, 372, 374, 382–3, 398–9, 401, 417, 419, 427n19, 443, 461–2, 471, 501–2, 507, 518, 527, 547, 549–52, 554–6, 558–9, 561; *The Universe*, 283n2, 558, 562

universities, 11, 39, 46–7, 75, 85, 99, 343, 382, 391, 423, 451, 469, 478, 516, 520, 521n133

unknown, the, 25, 39, 69, 78, 95–7, 114, 126–8, 133, 135, 139–40, 154–5, 160–1, 164–6, 182, 247, 263, 274, 322, 349, 355, 394, 396, 426, 434, 436, 531, 541, 552; the unknowable, 88, 97, 128, 132, 143, 164, 166, 322, 531, 552

unsubstantiality, see *anattā*

Upanishads, the, 62, 65, 82, 102, 118, 137n37, 160, 200, 231–2, 250, 261–3, 322, 359, 404, 467

Ut, 261–2

Utopias, 392, 477n253, 524n142, 528–31

vairāgya, see non-attachment

value, 29, 47, 61, 63, 69–70, 85, 103, 110, 112, 114, 125, 137, 148, 158, 163, 173, 201, 206n127, 220–1, 226, 243, 247, 271, 278, 291, 294, 303, 307, 320, 337n25, 339, 343, 354–5, 363, 369–70, 389, 394, 396, 412, 418, 427, 439, 449, 457, 481, 490, 494, 507, 512n95, 514, 523, 527, 542, 554

vanity, 29, 62, 65, 76, 133, 156, 173, 180, 191, 233, 236, 254–5, 268, 270, 306, 308, 349, 384, 447, 456, 480, 488, 491, 493, 518, 555

variation, 11–2, 27–31, 35, 39–41, 49n56, 56, 60–3, 72, 75, 78, 82, 100–1, 104–6, 108–11, 115n84, 123–7, 138–9, 144, 148, 151, 159n102, 165–70, 183–6, 196–7, 201, 210, 219–26, 229–34, 242n81, 252–3, 257–61, 266–7, 282, 300, 316, 319, 333, 336, 340, 348–9, 356, 363, 387, 396, 399–400, 403, 407, 410, 420, 423–30, 436, 437n70, 440–2, 464–6, 485, 487, 498–502, 508, 511–2, 517–20, 530, 554, 561; *Varieties of Religious Experience*, 172, 238, 337

Vatican, the, 434

Vau, 54, 98, 119, 121, 123, 283, 341–2, 443, 449, 558, 561–2

Vedas, the, 36, 65, 82, 93, 102, 144, 148n71, 160, 178, 210, 250–1, 263, 272, 322, 356, 359, 376, 379, 388, 416, 419–20, 470; Advaita Vedanta, 62, 96, 107, 178, 210, 250, 359; Dvaita Vedanta, 96, 178, 210, 250; neo-Vedanta, 359–61

vedanā, 238, 254, 351, 562; see also emotions

Venus, 151, 225, 244, 373, 432, 436, 455, 562

verbs, 1, 99, 122, 144, 199, 206–7, 278, 549

Verrall, Arthur Woollgar, 232

Vesica, the, 210, 426

Vesta, 193

vibration, 114–5, 119, 171, 205, 256, 276, 341–2, 356, 393–4, 417, 425, 449

vices, 17, 23, 62, 69, 90, 188, 238–40, 288, 302, 346, 356, 368, 500, 541–2, 552

Victoria, Queen of England and Empress of India, 472, 531; Victorianism, the Victorians, 63, 75–6, 103, 353, 503, 531

Victory Cross, the, 374

Viereck, George Sylvester, 461

Vilatte, Joseph-René, 438–9

INDEX

633

viññānam, 325, 562; *see also* consciousness
violence, 32, 70, 76, 79–80, 202–3, 242, 258, 289, 297, 317–8, 350, 453, 467–8, 472, 482, 485, 487, 512, 529–30
Virgil, 122, 318, 343, 529
virginity, virgins, 50, 53–4, 123, 135–6, 158, 187, 193, 205, 235, 238, 240, 280, 294–5, 298, 314, 321, 328, 332, 336, 342–3, 355, 398, 401, 432, 437, 440–1, 443n98, 455, 474, 491–2; virgin birth, *see* parthenogenesis
Virgo, 34n1, 152, 294, 336, 443n98
virility, 17, 32–3, 87, 344–5, 382, 399, 457, 470, 551
virtues, 21, 23, 28, 61, 65, 68–9, 72–3, 78, 80, 84, 88–9, 137n37, 171, 176–7, 180–2, 184, 188–91, 198–9, 237, 240–3, 288, 302, 308–9, 318, 328, 330, 338, 343–6, 349, 352–3, 356, 368, 370–1, 374, 382, 411n123, 412, 459, 470–2, 475, 482, 500, 508, 517, 519, 524n142, 526–7, 530–1, 542, 555
Vishnu, 238, 257, 379, 457, 474; *Vishvarupadarshana*, 306, 457
visions, 55, 111–3, 138–9, 161–2, 201, 208–9, 222, 229, 241, 248, 253–7, 272, 277, 289, 297, 302, 307, 314n107, 318, 324, 364–6, 390, 418–9, 436, 457–8, 467, 532; *Visions of the Daughters of Albion*, 240, 308; *The Vision and the Voice*, see *Liber 418*
Vivekananda, 93, 355, 357–63, 469
Voegelin, Eric, 57
Voltaire, 306
voluntarism, 1
voluntaryism, 1n1, 486, 500, 514, 533
vrittis, the, 292
V.V.V.V.V., 349, 386, 451–2

Waddell, Leila, 429
wafer, the, 186, 191
Wagner, Richard, 57, 368, 408, 427n16, 479
Waite, Arthur Edward, 325, 453
Wand, the, 120, 209–10, 244, 274, 283, 296, 314, 320, 323, 335, 363, 534, 538, 547; the double-wanded one, 277, 545, 547 (*see also* Maat)
wanderer, the, 486, 531
war, 7, 10, 19–20, 22, 30–3, 44, 64, 67–8, 70–1, 76, 79–80, 87, 156, 162, 191, 204–6, 247, 260, 264, 279, 300, 304, 328, 338, 370n167, 372–4, 389, 392, 394–5, 410, 421, 423, 425, 429n33, 432, 443, 455, 462–3, 466–75, 481–7, 490, 497–9, 501, 504, 509–11, 515–6, 517n119, 518, 521–2, 524–5, 527–32, 537, 539, 541–8, 551; *War*, 155, 247n101, 558, 562; the First World War, 46, 52, 88, 111, 443, 455, 462, 466, 471–3, 490, 497–8, 509, 531, 548; the Second World War, 52, 111, 471, 548
Water, 7, 40, 53, 58, 63, 72, 77, 100–3, 118, 120, 127, 153, 157, 165, 184, 186, 202, 207n131, 209–10, 216, 218, 235, 242–3, 252, 255, 282–3, 285, 292, 319n130, 328, 332, 342, 350, 352–3, 358, 362, 365–6, 376, 394, 437, 456, 468, 470, 501, 521, 542, 547, 550, 556; walking on water, 85, 406
Waterloo, 530
Watkins, John Maurice, 306
weakness, the weak, 23–4, 28, 30, 51, 60–2, 86–90, 156, 163, 178–80, 186, 192–3, 220–2, 232, 237, 240, 245, 296, 299, 304, 308, 315, 326, 355, 362, 374, 380, 382, 387, 389, 391, 408, 414, 443n98, 445, 497–8, 500, 503, 519n127, 521n133, 528, 531, 538, 541, 552, 555–7
wealth, 27, 49, 61, 73, 89, 202, 361, 423, 429, 464, 468, 478, 489, 492, 511–3, 523–5
weapons, 32, 69, 80, 191, 221, 266, 308, 342, 375, 497, 516, 529; magical weapons, 120–3, 155, 168, 186, 191, 206, 223, 239, 244–5, 254, 269–70, 311–4, 319–21, 398, 408, 425, 427, 462, 494, 534
Wedgwood, James Ingall, 438, 442n93, 451, 453
Weismann, August, 256
Werther, 51–2, 206
West, the, ix, x, 37–9, 44–5, 48, 52, 65, 93–4, 103, 107–8, 115, 143–5, 155, 162, 178, 231, 242, 254, 287, 343, 353, 359–68, 388–9, 395, 404, 422, 436, 438, 450, 456, 468, 476–8, 484–5, 490, 492, 509, 526, 531, 539, 545
Westcott, William Wynn, 208, 443

Westerode, 428
wheels, 73, 118, 130, 146–7, 263, 314, 339, 346, 411, 540, 546; the Wheel of Dharma, 118, 146–7; *The Wheel of Fortune*, 147, 285–6, 558, 562
Whitehead, Alfred North, 98, 456, 479, 480n267
Wicca, the Wiccans, 441–2, 465
Wilde, Oscar, 18, 70, 530
Willermoz, Jean-Baptiste, 391
will-power, 23, 87–8, 216, 277, 422
Will-sayings, the, 239, 369–70
will-to-die, 179–80, 247–8, 496–7; will-to-live, 28, 88, 179, 247–8, 496–8; will-to-power, 136–7, 503; *The Will to Power*, 70, 76–7, 136, 501–3
wine, 16, 39, 73, 155–6, 171, 190–1, 193, 195, 199, 202, 205, 241, 255, 313, 332, 472, 496, 539, 541, 544
wisdom, 1, 3, 8, 21, 26–8, 30, 32, 61, 75, 79–80, 84–5, 91, 118, 126, 132–3, 142, 145, 149, 152, 156, 163, 167, 169n139, 172, 180, 182, 184, 186, 189–90, 192, 200–1, 205, 208–9, 217, 229–30, 232–3, 245, 251, 258n27, 257, 270–1, 281, 285, 294, 297–8, 302, 306–9, 315, 320, 322, 325, 328–30, 332, 343, 363, 367–8, 372–3, 379, 385, 393–4, 404, 407, 411, 441–2, 453, 455, 459, 469–70, 473, 477, 479, 480n267, 484–5, 487, 496, 498, 501, 506, 515, 517, 519, 532, 538–9, 543, 545, 547, 549–50, 552, 554–5; the wise, 1–2, 14, 38, 64, 98, 107, 118, 149–50, 152, 169n139, 178, 180, 186, 208n133, 232, 285, 321–2, 359, 362, 399, 427n19, 428, 453, 455, 470, 475, 477, 479, 485, 501, 506, 525, 539, 545, 555, 559; the Path of the Wise, 126, 230, 245, 257, 306–7, 459; the Stone of the Wise, 124, 170
witches, witchcraft, 29, 42, 50, 53, 216, 244–5, 313, 331, 345, 393, 401, 442, 448; the Witches' Sabbath, 401, 499; *The Witches' Way*, 441
women, 9–10, 16–8, 20, 25–7, 31, 42, 48–54, 56, 58, 61, 69, 73–5, 78, 80, 83, 93, 104–5, 107, 113, 118, 121, 141–2, 172, 175, 182, 184, 187–8, 193, 206, 232, 237–8, 241, 243–5, 248–9, 277, 279, 281–2, 283n6, 295, 317, 319, 321, 346, 365, 381–2, 385, 388, 399, 404, 416n147, 423, 427n16, 429–30, 441n83, 443, 455, 457, 459, 464, 466–7, 483–5, 489–97, 502–3, 509–10, 516, 534, 537, 540–2, 544–6, 548, 550–3
World Teacher, the, 438, 450–2
worship, 16, 20, 39–42, 45, 50–1, 58, 92, 124, 149, 171, 178, 184–8, 191, 195, 198, 210, 217, 225, 230, 242, 246, 253, 257, 259, 263, 284, 290–1, 308, 336, 361–2, 366–8, 371, 380, 384, 396–8, 401, 407–8, 412, 414–6, 432–3, 437n69, 439, 441, 443, 449, 472, 474, 502, 537, 540–1, 543–6, 552, 556
Wu-wei, 166

Yahweh, *see* Jehovah
Yājñavalkya, 200n98, 359
Yama, 232; *yama*, 352–5
Yamamoto, Tsunetomo, 475, 480
Yarker, John, 35n4, 395, 426, 443
Yates, William Butler, 41n8
Yeheshuah, *see* the Pentagrammaton
Yeshua, *see* Jesus of Nazareth
Yesod, 209, 363, 558, 560–1
Yetzirah, 151, 275, 283, 335, 561–2; the *Sepher Yetzirah*, 139, 150, 208
Yezidis, the, 409
YHVH, *see* Jehovah *or* the Tetragrammaton
Yî King, the, *see* the *I Ching*
Yin and Yang, 106–7, 148n71, 282, 285, 559
Yod, 54, 86, 106, 119, 121, 123, 283, 285, 294, 336, 401, 443n98, 449, 558, 561–2
yoga, ix, 15, 68, 80, 98, 102, 115, 117–9, 132–3, 136, 161, 174, 194, 217–8, 224–5, 228–30, 232, 240, 253–4, 268, 272, 286–8, 324, 328, 336, 344, 348–59, 361–3, 366, 369–70, 373–4, 405–6, 419–22, 427, 448–50, 468, 472; the *Yoga Sūtras*, 348–9, 355, 358, 361, 363, 405–6; *Yoga Vasistha*, 358; *Yoga Yajnavalkya*, 359; bhakta yoga, 225, 366; gñana yoga, 132–3, 224–5, 366; hatha yoga, 133, 225, 358, 450, 355–8, 366, 468n210; karma yoga, 133, 225, 366; mantra yoga, 225, 366; raja yoga, 133, 224–5, 355, 357–9, 362–3, 366, 449; *Raja-Yoga*, 355, 357, 361–3

Yoni, the, 53, 399
yugas, the, 35–6

Zahid, the, 405–6
Zain, 499, 558, 562
Zanoni, 62, 201, 265
Zarathustra, *see* Zoroaster; *Thus Spoke Zarathustra*, 502
Zeitgeist, the, 46, 455
Zelator, 226, 373, 560
Zeno of Citium, 108, 283
Zero, 12, 32, 43, 95–7, 104–9, 118–9, 143n50, 151, 164, 181, 207n133, 234, 250, 276, 284n6, 298–301, 322, 339, 365–7; the Qabalistic Zero, 95, 106, 250
Zeus, 50, 246, 259n31, 284n6, 362
Zion, 293, 401; Zionism, 439
Zodiac, the, 34n1, 35n4, 37, 40, 151–2, 162, 207, 401, 415
Zohar, the, 200, 251
Zoroaster, Zoroastrianism, 98, 157, 257, 312, 348, 395, 427n19, 433, 482; the Oracles of Zoroaster, *see* the *Chaldæan Oracles*

www.ingramcontent.com/pod-product-compliance
Lightning Source LLC
Chambersburg PA
CBHW022005300426
44117CB00005B/34